Guide to Reference Books
for
School Media Centers

Guide to Reference Books
for
School Media Centers

Fourth Edition

MARGARET IRBY NICHOLS

1992
LIBRARIES UNLIMITED, INC.
Englewood, Colorado

This work is dedicated to my reference students and workshop attendees of more than 30 years and to my beloved children, Nina, Nick, and Thommy, all of whom have enriched my life in their own special ways.

LIBRARIES UNLIMITED, INC.
P.O. Box 6633
Englewood, CO 80155-6633

Library of Congress Cataloging-in-Publication Data

Nichols, Margaret Irby.
   Guide to reference books for school media centers / Margaret Irby
Nichols. -- 4th ed.
     xiv, 463 p. 19x26 cm.
     Rev. ed. of: Guide to reference books for school media centers /
Christine Gehrt Wynar.
     Includes bibliographical references and index.
     ISBN 0-87287-833-3
     1. Children's reference books--Bibliography. 2. Bibliography-
-Best books--Children's literature. 3. Bibliography--Best books-
-Reference books. 4. School libraries--Book lists. 5. Media
programs (Education)   I. Wynar, Christine Gehrt, 1933-
II. Title.
Z1037.1.W95   1992
[PN1009.A1]
011'.02--dc20   91-45242
                                                      CIP

Contents

Introduction........................xi

Publications Cited..................xiv

Part I
MEDIA SOURCES

MEDIA SOURCES.....................1
  General..........................1
    Review Journals..................1
    Publishers' Directories...........4
  Audiovisual.......................4
    Review Indexes..................4
    General Catalogs................5
    Films and Video.................5
    Producers and Distributors........8
    Sound Recordings...............8
    Talking Books and Braille.........9
  Books...........................10
    Review Journals................10
    Trade Bibliographies............12
    Core Collections................14
    Children's Lists.................15
    High/Low Lists................19
    Young Adult Lists..............20
  Computer Software.................21
    Review Journals................21
    Reviews.......................22
    Review Indexes/Digests..........23
    Trade Bibliographies............23
    Selection Aids..................23
  Government Publications...........24
  Pamphlets and Free Materials........26
  Periodicals.......................26

Part II
GENERAL REFERENCE

GENERAL REFERENCE...............29
  Guides.........................29
  Almanacs and Fact Books...........31
  Chronologies....................35

  Dictionaries.....................35
    General.......................35
    Abbreviations and Acronyms......35
    Allusions......................35
    Cultural Literacy...............36
  Directories......................36
  Electronic Services.................38
  Encyclopedias....................39
    Guides........................39
    Desk Size.....................39
    Adult and Juvenile Sets..........41
  Handbooks......................46
  Indexes........................47

Part III
SOCIAL SCIENCES

ANTHROPOLOGY....................51

ARCHAEOLOGY.....................52

BIOGRAPHY.........................53
  General Works....................53
  Bibliographies and Indexes..........53
  Living Persons...................54
  Living and Deceased Persons........55
  Deceased Persons.................56
  Nicknames and Pseudonyms.........60

BUSINESS AND ECONOMICS.........62
  Almanacs and Handbooks..........62
  Dictionaries and Encyclopedias.......63
  Directories......................65
  Biography......................65
  Small Business...................65

CAREERS...........................67
  Bibliographies...................67
  Dictionaries, Encyclopedias, and
    Handbooks...................68
  Directories......................71
  Self-Employment.................71

CONSUMER EDUCATION............72
   Consumer Education...............72
   Personal Finance................73
   Social Security....................73

EDUCATION.........................73
   Bibliographies......................73
   Dictionaries and Encyclopedias.......74
   Directories.........................74
   Handbooks, Almanacs, and
      Yearbooks.....................77
   Indexes...........................79
   Biography.........................80
   College Handbooks.................80
   College Planning....................84
   Gifted............................86
   Instructional Technology............87
      General.......................87
      Audiovisual....................87
      Videodiscs....................88
   Learning Disabled.................88
   Study Abroad.....................90
   Tests............................91
      General.......................91
      ACT, GED, and SAT...........91

ETHNIC MINORITIES.................92
   General Works.....................92
   Atlases...........................93
   Encyclopedias, Handbooks, Bibliog-
      raphies, and Directories............93
   African-Americans..................94
   Asian-Americans 97
   Hispanic-Americans.................97
   Jews.............................99
   Native-Americans.................101

ETIQUETTE 104

GENEALOGY AND PERSONAL
NAMES..............................105
   Flags.............................105
   Genealogy 105
   Personal Names..................106

GEOGRAPHY........................106
   Bibliographies.....................106
   Atlases...........................107
      General.......................107
      Electronic 113
   Encyclopedias and Handbooks.......114
   Gazetteers.......................117
   Exploration......................118
   Travel...........................119

HANDICAPPED......................121
   Handbooks and Guides.............121
   Hearing Impaired.................122
   Visually Impaired.................123

HISTORY 123
   Atlases 123
   Bibliographies.....................125
   Chronologies.....................126
   Dictionaries and Encyclopedias.......126
   Middle Ages and Renaissance.........128
   Modern History...................129
   World Conflicts...................129
   Asia 132
   Canada..........................133
   China 133
   Germany 133
   Italy 133
   Latin America....................134
   Russia and the USSR..............134
   Spain 134
   United Kingdom and the Republic
      of Ireland.....................135
   United States.....................135
      Bibliographies.................135
      Atlases.......................137
      Chronologies.................138
      Dictionaries and Encyclopedias...139
      Source Material................141
      Biography 142
      Historic Places................143

HOBBIES AND GAMES................143
   Amusements 143
   Card Games and Board Games.......144
   Clubs and Elections...............145
   Collecting 145
   Outdoor Recreation................148
   Summer Camps...................148
   Trivia 149
   Word Games.....................149

HOLIDAYS AND SPECIAL DAYS......150

LAW 152
   Dictionaries and Encyclopedias.......152
   Handbooks.......................153
   Crime...........................154
   Human Rights...................156

LIBRARY SCIENCE..................157
   Bibliographies.....................157
   Dictionaries, Encyclopedias, and
      Yearbooks....................157

Handbooks 158
Book Repair 158
Cataloging 158
Censorship 162
Collection Development 162
Computers 163
Management 166
Media Skills 169
Planning Facilities 171
Publicity 172

MILITARY SCIENCE 173

OCCULT 175

POLITICAL SCIENCE 176
Dictionaries and Encyclopedias 176
Handbooks and Almanacs 177
Biography 179
International Relations 180
Federal Government 181
General Works 181
Congress 182
The First Ladies 184
The Presidency 184
The Vice-Presidency 187
State Government 187
Local Government 188

SOCIAL STUDIES 188
Bibliographies 188
Current Events and Issues 188
Global Studies 191
African Studies 194
Asian Studies 194
Australian Studies 195
Canadian Studies 195
European and Soviet Studies 195
Japanese Studies 196
Latin American Studies 196
Middle East Studies 197
New Zealand Studies 197

SPORTS 198
Chronologies 198
Dictionaries and Handbooks 199
Biography 201
Baseball 201
Basketball 203
Cheerleading 204
Football 204
Golf 205
Gymnastics 205
Hockey 205

Horsemanship 206
Olympic Games 206
Rodeo 207
Soccer 207
Wrestling 207

STATISTICS 207
United States 207
The World 209

WOMEN'S STUDIES 210
Atlases 210
Bibliographies 210
Encyclopedias and Handbooks 211
Indexes 212
Biography 212

Part IV
HUMANITIES

CHILDREN'S LITERATURE 215
General Works 215
Bibliographies About 216
Bibliographies Of 217
Dictionaries and Encyclopedias 220
Indexes 221
Biography 221
Awards 225
Plot Outlines 227
Plays 228
Poetry 228
Storytelling and Activities 230

COMMUNICATION 234
General Works 234
Calligraphy 234
Copyright 234
Forensics 234
Journalism 235
Publishing 236
Radio 237
Television and Video 237
Writing and Reports 238

DECORATIVE ARTS 241
Arts and Crafts 241
Fashion and Costume 241
Furniture and Interior Design 242
Sewing and Needlework 243
Textiles 244

FILM STUDY............................244
    Dictionaries and Encyclopedias.......244
    Filmographies.....................246
    Handbooks........................247

FINE ARTS..............................248
    Catalogs..........................248
    Dictionaries and Encyclopedias.......248
    Directories.........................250
    Bibliographies.....................251
    Handbooks........................251
    Indexes...........................251
    Biography.........................252
    Architecture.......................253
    Photography.......................254

LANGUAGE............................256
    General Works.....................256
    English as a Second Language.......256
    Unabridged Dictionaries............257
    Desk Dictionaries..................258
    Juvenile Dictionaries...............260
    Picture Dictionaries................263
    Americanisms and Slang............264
    Eponyms.........................266
    Etymology........................266
    Foreign Phrases...................267
    Rhymes..........................268
    Spelling and Pronunciation.........268
    Synonyms........................269
    Usage and Grammar...............271
    Chinese Dictionaries...............272
    French Dictionaries................273
    German Dictionaries...............274
    Japanese Dictionaries..............274
    Latin Dictionaries.................274
    Russian Dictionaries...............274
    Spanish Dictionaries...............275

LITERATURE..........................276
    Bibliographies.....................276
    Dictionaries and Encyclopedias.......276
    Digests and Surveys...............279
    Biography.........................280
    Criticism.........................282
    Drama...........................284
    Genre............................285
    Poetry...........................288
    Short Stories......................289
    Reading Guidance.................290
    American Literature................290
        Bibliographies..................290
        Dictionaries and Encyclopedias...291
        Digests and Surveys.............292
        Biography.....................292
        Criticism.....................294

    English Literature..................294
        Bibliographies..................294
        Dictionaries and Encyclopedias...294
        Biography.....................295
        Criticism.....................295
        Shakespeare...................296
    Australian Literature...............297
    Canadian Literature................297
    Classical Literature................297
    French Literature..................298
    German Literature.................298
    Hispanic Literature................298
    Scandinavian Literature............299
    Slavic Literature..................299

MUSIC.................................300
    Chronologies.....................300
    Dictionaries and Encyclopedias.......300
    Biography.........................302
    Bands............................303
    Choral...........................304
    Classical..........................304
    Instruments.......................305
    Opera............................305
    Popular..........................306
        General.......................306
        Country.......................306
        Jazz..........................307
        Musicals......................307
        Rock.........................308
    Songs............................308

MYTHOLOGY AND FOLKLORE.......310
    General Works.....................310
    Dictionaries and Encyclopedias.......310
    Handbooks........................313
    Indexes...........................314

PHILOSOPHY..........................315

QUOTATIONS.........................315

RELIGION..............................319
    Bibliographies.....................319
    Atlases...........................319
    Dictionaries and Encyclopedias.......319
    Handbooks........................321
    Bible Studies......................322
    Biography.........................324
    Customs.........................325
    Saints............................325

CONTENTS □ ix

THEATER AND DANCE............326
  Theater........................326
    Dictionaries and Encyclopedias...326
    Handbooks..................327
    Indexes....................328
    Biography..................328
  Dance........................329

Part V
SCIENCE AND TECHNOLOGY

ASTRONOMY......................331
  General Works..................331
  Atlases........................331
  Dictionaries and Encyclopedias......332
  Field Guides and Handbooks........333
  Indexes........................334
  Planetology....................334

BIOLOGY........................334

BOTANY........................335
  Dictionaries, Encyclopedias, and
    Handbooks..................335
  Flowering Plants................336
  Nonflowering Plants............338
  Trees and Shrubs..............338
  Activities......................339

CHEMISTRY......................340

COMPUTERS AND ELECTRONICS.....341
  Dictionaries and Encyclopedias......341
  Directories....................343
  Handbooks....................343
  Biography......................345
  Activities......................345

EARTH SCIENCES..................345
  Atlases........................345
  Dictionaries and Encyclopedias......345
  Handbooks....................346
  Climate and Weather............347
  Fossils and Prehistoric Life..........347
  Mineralogy and Gemstones..........349
  Oceanography..................350

FOOD AND NUTRITION............351

HEALTH AND FAMILY..............355
  Aging........................355
  Alternative Health Care............355
  Child Abuse....................356
  Death and Dying................356
  Drugs and Substance Abuse.........357
  Family........................359
  Homosexuality..................361
  The Human Body................361
  Medicine......................362
  Mental Health..................366
  Self-Help......................368

HORTICULTURE....................369

MATHEMATICS....................370
  Bibliographies..................370
  Dictionaries and Encyclopedias......371
  Handbooks....................372
  Activities......................372

NATURAL RESOURCE SCIENCES.....373
  Conservation..................373
  Energy........................373
  Environment..................374
    Atlases....................374
    Bibliographies..............375
    Dictionaries................375
    Directories................375
    Handbooks................375
    Yearbooks................377
  Natural History................377

PETS...........................380
  General......................380
  Aquariums....................380
  Cage Birds....................381
  Cats.........................381
  Dogs........................382
  Snakes......................383

PHYSICS........................383

SCIENCE IN GENERAL..............384
  Bibliographies..................384
  Chronologies..................385
  Dictionaries and Encyclopedias......386
  Handbooks and Yearbooks..........389
  Indexes.......................390
  Resource Material..............391
  Biography.....................391
  Activities......................392

TECHNOLOGY IN GENERAL.........393
    Bibliographies.....................393
    Dictionaries, Encyclopedias, and
       Handbooks......................393
    Biography........................396
    Automotive.......................396
    Bicycles..........................397
    Building and Fix-It.................397
    Electricity........................398
    Metal Work.......................398

TRANSPORTATION...................399
    General Works....................399
    Automobiles and Motorcycles.......399
    Aviation and Space Flight...........400
    Railroads and Urban Systems........404
    Ships............................404

ZOOLOGY...........................405
    Atlases...........................405
    Dictionaries and Encyclopedias.......405
    Field Guides and Handbooks.........407
    Birds............................407
    Fishes...........................410
    Insects and Spiders.................411
    Invertebrates......................411
    Mammals.........................412
    Reptiles and Amphibians............414

Author/Title Index.................417

Subject Index.....................451

Introduction

The completely updated *Guide to Reference Books for School Media Centers*, as did its predecessors, addresses the reference needs of students from kindergarten through high school and the librarians and teachers who work with them. When the first edition appeared in 1973, guidance for the reference book selector was restricted to a few lists produced by state agencies, local school districts, and a small number of reference works cited in basic catalogs and other selection aids. Reference guides designed to meet the needs of academic and public libraries provided limited assistance. The major juvenile review media focused on reading materials with little attention given to reference works. Carolyn Sue Peterson's *Reference Books for Elementary and Junior High School Libraries*, which first appeared in 1970 (Scarecrow), attempted to fill the void, but was limited in scope, with only 370 entries. The initial volume of *Guide to Reference Books*, by contrast, had 2,575 entries. It offered extensive coverage of general and specific reference tools, selection aids, and professional sources for school library media specialists. Favorably received by major reviewing media, the first edition and its successors (1981 and 1986) became standard selection tools for school library media centers and public libraries that served the assignment needs of K-12 students.

Christine Gehrt Wynar authored the first edition of *Guide to Reference Books for School Media Centers* in 1973, updated it with the *1974-75 Supplement* (1976), and introduced a number of changes and improvements in the subsequent second (1981) and third (1986) editions.

Initially, few reference books were designed specifically for children and young adults, but in the 1980s publishers began to give more attention to the needs of these age groups. As a consequence, more reviews of juvenile reference materials now appear in the media. Each spring *School Library Journal* publishes the "Reference Roundup" of significant titles for school library media centers, and other review journals, such as *The Book Report*, offer sections that focus on reference materials.

Today, school boards, administrators, teachers, and the nation are working to promote academic achievement and to develop critical thinking skills. Library media specialists are striving to respond to changes in curriculum and teaching methods and to integrate library skills into the general education curriculum. Students and teachers are demanding quality reference materials of all types from a broad spectrum of subjects. This 4th edition has been thoroughly revised and updated to help librarians and teachers meet these demands.

SCOPE AND PURPOSE

Intended as a comprehensive survey of current reference materials suitable for elementary, middle, and high schools, this work focuses on the needs of students, teachers, school media specialists, and educators in library schools, children's and young adult literature, and education. The reference materials included cover all curricular areas as well as the extracurricular interests of children and young adults. They vary in reading level, style of presentation, depth of coverage, and cost.

The list of reference sources is extensive, with 2,280 entries, and the annotations provide assistance in identifying basic sources suitable for a core collection. Some sets and specialized sources are beyond the means of most school library media centers, but their high costs may be met at the school district level or through cooperative arrangements in which their use can be shared. Librarians and teachers also need to be aware of more comprehensive sources in order to refer students to them at larger libraries.

The needs of school library media specialists in the selection of all types of media and the administration of the library media center receive special attention. Selection and acquisition aids, including general and specialized review journals, children's and young adult literature sources, and library management and media skills materials, are each covered in separate sections, such as "Media Sources," "Children's Literature," and "Library Science." The needs of teachers are emphasized in the "Education" section and in subject chapters relevant to their specialties.

Limitations of the *Guide to Reference Books* should also be noted. Entries are restricted to currently available materials, making it necessary to omit a number of excellent sources now out of print. Titles focus on materials that have been reviewed and recommended in major review journals. Omissions may include some reference books published within the time span of the guide that have not been evaluated by the review media. Most works have been published and are distributed in the United States, but some Canadian publications have been included.

SELECTION

Entries have been selected from some 8,500 reference titles published from 1985 through the early part of 1991 and reviewed in *American Reference Books Annual, Recommended Reference Books for Small and Medium-sized Libraries and Media Centers, The Book Report, Booklist and Reference Books Bulletin, Kliatt Young Adult Paperback Book Guide, Library Journal, School Library Journal, Science Books and Films, Voice of Youth Advocates, Wilson Library Bulletin,* or other professional sources. New editions of some titles included in the 3d edition have been listed, as have other significant older titles, if no comparable later works have appeared.

Although published reviews provide evaluation of most selections, the materials themselves have been examined whenever possible. Criteria for selection include appropriateness in meeting curricular/ teaching needs and interests of elementary and secondary students; reading and interest level; currency and accuracy of material; treatment, accessibility, and format of information; and comparison to similar sources on the same topic.

The accepted definition of a reference work has been applied: a book or other source that is designed to be consulted for information rather than read consecutively and in its entirety. Most reference tools, such as encyclopedias, dictionaries, and handbooks, contain information that is arranged for easy access. Others, such as indexes and bibliographies, serve as bridges to information. The majority of entries meet these conventional requirements of a reference tool and are intended for quick reference (e.g., *World Almanac, New York Public Library Desk Reference*) or for general usage (e.g., *World Book, Concise Dictionary of American History*). Others included may not meet all requirements of the term *reference book* because traditional reference sources for the topic do not exist. Some sets, series, and collections of source material, especially in the sciences, social studies, and history, fall into this latter category. These types of materials may be placed in the circulating or reference collection, depending on the needs of the students and faculty.

Some titles listed are designed specifically for children and young adults, while many others that were intended for a broad general audience or adult readers have also been judged to be appropriate for students (usually middle or high school level). Titles designed for professional use appear in several sections. The suggested age/grade level for each title is included in the annotation or with a symbol that indicates level (see below). Annotations note a book's professional focus, if such is not obvious from the title or from the section in which it is included.

Titles listed in the 1991 *Books in Print Plus* or in their publisher's most current catalog are considered to be in print; conversely, titles not listed are assumed to be out of print. A few out-of-print titles are mentioned in annotations with their status so noted.

CHANGES IN THE FOURTH EDITION

The arrangement of the current *Guide to Reference Books* differs somewhat from that of the 3d edition. The 54 subject categories are divided into 5 sections: "Media Sources," "General Reference," "Social Sciences," "Humanities," and "Science and Technology." The last three divisions are arranged by subject category. All chapters are divided by form or topic. "Energy Sources" and "Environmental Sciences" have been combined under "Natural Resource Sciences." The chapter title for the disabled has been changed to "Handicapped," and a new chapter, "Etiquette," has been added.

HOW TO USE

Arrangement: The section entitled "Media Sources" is divided by type of material (e.g., audiovisual, books); "General Reference" is arranged by form of publication (e.g., guides, almanacs and fact books). Subject chapters within the remaining three sections are arranged by form (e.g., general works, bibliographies, dictionaries) and then by topic.

Cross-references: When appropriate, cross-references to related sections are provided at the beginning of the chapter or at the beginning of the subsection. Titles appropriate to more than one section are included as a main entry in the primary chapter and cross-referenced from others following this symbol ■.

Entries: Consecutively numbered entries include full bibliographic data, price as listed in *Books in Print Plus* or by the publisher, ISBN, ISSN, and LC card number (when available). Entries for government publications include stock number (S/N). Technological requirements are given for electronic materials. Addresses are provided for materials available from publishers not listed in standard sources.

Grade level codes: Codes, printed above the entry, indicate estimated level of usefulness for the item. "E" denotes K-5; "E+" means K-5 and up. The suggested audience levels are indicated in the annotation for other entries: middle school (grades 6-8) or high school (grades 9-12). The term *secondary level* is used in the annotation when a reviewer has used the term to indicate level.

Annotations: Most annotations describe the work's content, organization, and special features, but some include critical comments, usually indicating limitations or cautions. All works cited are recommended with the terms *recommended* and *highly recommended* denoting publications of exceptional merit.

Citations to reviews: These are listed at the end of the annotations. A list of reviewing sources and their abbreviations is given on page xiv.

Index: All materials cited appear in the author/title and the subject indexes.

Publications Cited

FORM OF CITATION	PUBLICATION TITLE
ARBA	American Reference Books Annual
BL	Booklist
BR	Book Report
CLJ	Canadian Library Journal
EL	Emergency Librarian
JOYS	Journal of Youth Services in Libraries
Kliatt	Kliatt Young Adult Paperback Book Guide
LJ	Library Journal
RBB	Reference Books Bulletin
SBF	Science Books & Films
SLJ	School Library Journal
SLMQ	School Library Media Quarterly
VOYA	Voice of Youth Advocates
WLB	Wilson Library Bulletin

☐ _____ **Media Sources** _____ ☐

GENERAL

Review Journals

See also **Books** and **Computer Software** in
Media Sources for print and nonprint media.

1   **The Book Report: The Journal for Junior and Senior High School Librarian.** Worthington, Ohio: Linworth Publishing, 1982- . 5 issues/yr. (Sept.-May). $39.00/yr. (5701 N. High St., Suite 1, Worthington, OH 43985).
   Level: Junior high and high school, ages 12-17.
   Focus: Each issue is devoted to a theme (e.g., making and using audiovisuals, teaching library skills, reading motivation, public relations, microcomputers) containing some 20 pages of feature articles; emphasis is on alternative solutions to problems.
   Reviews: School librarians evaluate new titles and give their recommendations on books, audiovisual material, and computer software. Reviews of some 100 items, 125-175 words in length, give standard bibliographic data, ISBN, LC card number, reading level, and hardware specifications for computer software.
   Print: Fiction and nonfiction trade books, some professional books.
   Nonprint: Films, filmstrips, videocassettes, software.
   Features: Computer applications in the library, profiles of authors who write for teenagers, trade paperbacks.

2   **Booklist: Includes *Reference Books Bulletin*.** Chicago: American Library Association, 1905- . twice monthly Sept.-June, monthly July and Aug. $56.00/yr. (50 E. Huron St., Chicago, IL 60611).
   Level: Preschool through high school, adults.
   Focus: Print, nonprint, and software materials suggested for school library media centers and small to medium-sized public libraries.
   Booklist reviews: Evaluative reviews written and signed by staff members; some 12,000 to 13,000 reviews per year, 125-200 words in length; starred reviews indicate exceptional quality; full bibliographic/order information, DDC number, LC subject headings, and LC card number.
   Reference Books Bulletin reviews: Evaluative reviews by members of RBB editorial board for encyclopedias, dictionaries, atlases, and other reference books; news and comments about reference materials; reviews range from 175-200 words to 800-1,000 words; general encyclopedias, atlases, dictionaries, and other works which use a continuous revision policy are reviewed again about every five years; reviews of best reference books for a given topic (e.g., religion, sports, genealogy) appear frequently; reviews for the period of September through August of the following year are compiled and published in *Reference Books Bulletin*.
   Print: Fiction and nonfiction trade books; reference books.
   Nonprint: Video, computer software.
   Features: Advance book reviews, news from libraries, publicity, foreign language books, small press books, lists of books on contemporary issues, high/low books, paperback reprints, magazines, occasional lists on special topics.
   Index: Monthly author/title index; semiannual cumulative indexes.

3   **CM: A Reviewing Journal of Canadian Material for Young People.** Ottawa: Canadian Library Association, 1971- . bimonthly. $42.00. (200 Elgin St., Suite 602, Ottawa, Ont., Canada K1P 1L5).
   Level: Preschool through young adult.

Focus: Reviews professional books and material for school and public libraries serving young people; feature articles concerning books and other professional interests.

Reviews: Evaluative reviews, 175-250 words in length, of Canadian books and videos for young people; arranged by grade level (K-6, 7-9, 10 and up); reviews written and signed by librarians and other professionals.

Print Fiction and nonfiction trade and reference books.

Nonprint: Videos.

Features: Biobibliographic essays; interviews with well-known authors and illustrators; articles on such topics as library programs, censorship, and literacy; lists of paperback reprints.

Index: Index each issue and annual cumulations.

E +

4 **Curriculum Review**. Janine Wood, ed. Chicago: Curriculum Review Co., 1960- . monthly except June-Aug. $59.00/yr. (407 S. Dearborn St., Suite 1360, Chicago, IL 60605).

Level: K-12.

Focus: Articles on educational trends, teaching methods, innovative programs, and other topics related to curriculum; reviews of curriculum materials of all types (textbooks, supplementary materials, media, and software).

Reviews: Some 200 reviews each year, averaging three-fourths of a page each, arranged by subject; bibliographic/order information.

Print: Textbooks, supplementary materials, professional books.

Nonprint: Microcomputer software, videocassettes, film and filmstrips.

Features: "What's Working" reports strategies that administration and faculty are using in their schools; editorials on curricular changes.

E

5 **Library Talk: The Magazine for Elementary School Librarians**. Carolyn Hamilton, ed., Worthington, Ohio: Linworth Publishing, 1988- . 5 issues/yr. $35.00/yr. (5701 N. High St., Suite 1, Worthington, OH 43085).

Level: Elementary school (ages 6-11).

Focus: Feature articles on a special theme by librarians who work with children (e.g., library supervision, book fairs, public relations, audiovisuals, evaluation of the library and the librarian).

Reviews: Experienced librarians evaluate new books in areas of easy readers, fiction for grades 3-4, fiction for grades 5 and up, nonfiction, mysteries and fantasies, books in Spanish, traditional stories, reference series, audiovisuals, and software.

Print: Fiction and nonfiction trade books, some professional books.

Nonprint: Films, filmstrips, videocassettes, software.

Features: Practical ideas, paraprofessionals and part-time workers, news from publishers, free and inexpensive material, annual review of new holiday books.

E +

6 **Media & Methods**. Andrea Epstein, ed. Philadelphia: North American Publishing, 1964- . 5 issues/ yr. $29.00/yr. (1429 Walnut St., Philadelphia, PA 19102).

Level: Elementary and secondary.

Focus: Practical application of instructional technology and media management; innovative projects; reviews and previews of instructional media products and equipment.

Reviews: Descriptive and evaluative, 125-200 words; signed, usually by a staff member; system needs and hardware requirements, price, and grade level.

Print: Some trade books, textbooks.

Nonprint: Films, video, filmstrips, software, databases, recordings and cassettes, equipment.

Features: Videodisc update, news and events, announcements on new software and audiovisual products, annual buyers' guide.

7 **School Library Journal: The Magazine of Children's, Young Adult, and School Librarians**. Lillian N. Gerhardt, ed. New Providence, N.J.: R. R. Bowker, 1954- . 10 issues/yr. (none June and July). $63.00/yr. (P.O. Box 1978, Marion, OH 43305-1978). *Star Track: Supplement to School Library Journal*, 2/yr. free.

Level: Preschool through young adult.

Focus: Articles on trends, programs, books, authors, and a wide variety of other topics of interest to school and public librarians; professional news; review of youth materials.

Reviews: Some 3,000 reviews annually, with an aim toward reviewing all materials submitted; 100-250 words in length, evaluative, with recommendations; written and signed by librarians, contributing editors, and staff members; outstanding materials starred; bibliographic/order information and LC card number; reviews of professional books.

Print: Trade books, fiction, nonfiction. At intervals during year are reviews of Spanish books for children and YA, holiday books, and books back in print. *Star Track* features the best among all the books for young readers reviewed over the six-month period; indexed by author/illustrator and title.

Nonprint: Filmstrips, films and videocassettes, recordings, slides, software for computer-aided instruction, professional software.

Features: Annual survey of school library media center expenditures; spring roundup of outstanding reference books; checklists of pamphlets, posters, free material, and other items of interest; special buyer's guide; audiovisual software buyer's guide.

Index: Monthly index; annual author/title book review index, and audiovisual index.

E+

8 **Science Books & Films**. Washington, D.C.: American Association for the Advancement of Science, 1965- . 9 issues/yr. (none Jan., July, and Aug.). $35.00/yr. (P.O. Box 3000, Dept. SBF, Denville, NJ 07834).

Level: Preschool-grade 12, college, professional, general audience.

Focus: Critical evaluations by librarians and subject specialists; covers all scientific fields, mathematics, computer science, and some social sciences; some professional books; articles on topics related to use of science materials with children, young adults, and college students.

Reviews: 1,300-1,400 reviews per year, arranged by broad subject (DDC); separate sections for adults, junior high and young adults, and children's books; written and signed by librarians and scientists; bibliographic/order information; evaluative reviews include ratings—highly recommended (**), recommended (*), acceptable (AC), or not recommended (NR); codes for 10 user levels; reviews are slow in appearing, sometimes long after book is published.

Print: Trade books, some textbooks.

Nonprint: Films, videos, filmstrips, software.

Features: Annual lists of notable books and films; articles on science education, science books in specific areas, and other topics of interest to teachers and parents.

Index: Annual.

■ *Star Track*. *See School Library Journal* (entry 7).

9 **Voice of Youth Advocates**. Dorothy M. Broderick, ed. Metuchen, N.J.: Scarecrow Press, Dept. VOYA, 1978- . bimonthly (Apr.-Feb.). $32.50/yr.

Level: Young adults.

Focus: Youth services in public and school libraries; reviews of books for teenagers and professionals; news of interest to youth librarians.

Reviews: 250-300 each issue; descriptive with evaluative comments; written and signed by school and public librarians; arranged by format, subdivided by genre and subject; 100-200 words in length; give bibliographic/order information, grade level (M, J, S), and a coded evaluation (1Q-5Q for quality, 1P-5P for popularity).

Print: Fiction and nonfiction trade books, paperbacks and reprints, professional books.

Nonprint: Films, videotapes, recordings.

Features: Bibliographic essays on special topics; suggestions for programming; notes concerning pamphlets, booklists, and other products of interest to youth librarians.

Index: Titles and authors in each issue.

10 **Wilson Library Bulletin**. Mary Jo Godwin, ed. Bronx, N.Y.: H. W. Wilson, 1914- . 10 issues/yr. (none July and Aug.). $50.00/yr.

Level: Public, college, and school libraries.

Focus: Wide variety of topics of professional interest including library education, new technologies, library conferences, and public relations; columns on management, technology, media; reviews of books, reference books, and other materials.

Reviews: 600-700 trade books and some 250 reference books each year; style and length vary from one section to another; bibliographic/order information.

Print: Picture books, middle school and young adult, adult; university press; science fiction, mystery, and other topics; current reference books.

Nonprint: Software, CD-ROM/online, reference on discs, recordings, video, other audiovisual.

Features: Regular columns; "Marketplace" highlights products, services, and resources; articles on issues and trends.

Publishers' Directories

See also **Communications**.

E+
11 Alternative Press Publishers of Children's Books: A Directory. 3d ed. Kathleen T. Horning, ed. Madison, Wis.: Cooperative Children's Books Center, 1988. 89p. $12.00pa. ISBN 0-931641-02-4. (P.O. Box 5288, Madison, WI 53705-0288).

This directory focuses on independent publishers (identified as those not affiliated with national or multinational corporations) whose major function is to publish books for children and YAs. Of the 139 listed, 55 are new to this edition. Entries, arranged alphabetically by name, give address, telephone number, a description of publications, ISBN prefix, contact person, founding year, information about catalogs, discounts, billing, and names of distributors. Indexed by bilingual publishers, distributors, geography, and subject. [R: ARBA 90; BL, 1 Jan 89]

E+
12 AV Market Place. New Providence, N.J.: R. R. Bowker. annual. $99.95pa.

AV Market Place, 1991, identifies 6,300 companies that create, supply, or distribute an extraordinary range of audiovisual equipment and services. An index of 1,300 products and services is cross-referenced to companies in the main body. The products, services, and company index identifies all firms geographically under audio, audiovisual, computer systems, film, video, programming, and miscellaneous sections. Companies are also indexed by name. Updated annually.

E+
13 Children's Media Market Place. 3d ed. Delores Blythe Jones, ed. New York: Neal-Schuman, 1988. 397p. $45.00. ISBN 1-55570-007-1. LC 88-60792.

This directory of sources for children's materials (mainly grades K-8) addresses books, software, television and radio programs, audiovisuals, and periodicals. It is arranged in two parts: a directory of children's media sources, and a names and numbers index to children's media sources. The directory is divided into 24 areas that include publishers, wholesalers, audiovisual producers and distributors, software producers and distributors, state school media officers, and a bibliography of selection tools. The index gives names, addresses, and telephone numbers for all entries in the first part. Questionnaires and telephone interviews generated the information. This is a convenient and useful directory for those who purchase materials for elementary and junior high schools. [R: ARBA 90]

14 Publishers, Distributors, and Wholesalers of the United States. New Providence, N.J.: R. R. Bowker. annual. $124.95.

More than 50,000 publishers, wholesalers, distributors, software firms, museum and association imprints, and other trade organizations are listed in this directory, the most comprehensive of its kind. Access is provided by name; imprints, subsidiaries, and divisions; state; firms with toll-free numbers; ISBN prefix; and publisher's field of activity. Additional information includes discount schedules and lists of inactive and defunct publishers. Updated annually. [R: ARBA 92]

AUDIOVISUAL

Review Indexes

See **General** in **Media Sources** for **Review Journals**.

15 Media Review Digest. Ann Arbor, Mich.: Pierian Press. annual. $245.00/yr. ISSN 0363-7778.

MRD provides annual indexing for reviews of nonbook media included in some 130 periodicals. Reviews focus on videocassettes and videodiscs; filmstrips; educational spoken-word records, tapes, and compact discs; slides, transparencies, kits, maps, globes, charts, games, and other such items; and educational and feature films.

Each volume is divided into four sections: film and video, filmstrips, audio, and miscellaneous. These sections are followed by a list of film awards and prizes (Academy Awards, American Film Festival Awards, Columbus International Film Festival Awards, CINE Awards, and Houston

International Film Festival Awards); mediagraphics or summaries of media-related articles that are more complex than reviews; indexes by subject, categories, reviewer, geographical region, and video; and a directory of major producers and distributors.

Covering more than 75,000 media sources and a quarter million reviews, awards, and prizes, *MRD* is the most comprehensive guide to reviews of educational nonprint media.

General Catalogs

See also **Films and Video**, **Sound Recordings**, and **Talking Books and Braille** under **Audiovisual** in **Media Sources**.

16 **Media Resource Catalog**. Capitol Heights, Md.: National Archives and Records Administration, National Audiovisual Center. annual. free. (8700 Edgeworth Dr., Capitol Heights, MD 20743-3701).

Media Resource Catalog, published annually, contains more than 600 programs produced by federal agencies and designed for classrooms, training programs, library collections, and home use. Programs are available in a wide range of media including 16mm film, ¾-inch and VHS video, filmstrips, slide sets, and multimedia kits. The catalog is divided into 28 subject areas (e.g., biology, civics and governments, computer science, fine arts, health, history, physical sciences) and over 100 subsections.

Each entry provides title, format, color or black-and-white, running time, producing agency, description of content, and prices for various formats. Some programs are available for rental at the rate of $40.00 for 3 days, and some may be previewed. Indexed by title.

Films and Video

See also **General Catalogs** and **Filmography** in **Film Study**.

■ *AIT Catalog of Instructional Materials*. See entry 428.

E+
17 **Bowker's Complete Video Directory, 1990**. New Providence, N.J.: Bowker, 1990. 2v. with free mid-year supplement to subscribers. $169.00. ISBN 0-8352-2891-6.

Detailed listings for over 120,000 programs on 75,000 videos comprise this new video reference work, which merges Bowker's Education/Special Interest video database and *Variety's Complete Home Video Directory*. It provides order information for virtually all programs available in any format (e.g., VHS, Beta, 8mm, laserdisc). Volume 1 covers entertainment, and volume 2 treats educational special interest. Indexed by title, genre, cast, and director.

18 **Catalog of Free-Loan Videos/16mm Films and Teaching Materials**. St. Petersburg, Fla.: Modern Talking Picture Service. annual with fall supplement. free. (5000 Park St. North, St. Petersburg, FL 33709).

This catalog lists programs available on a free-loan basis in 16mm and videocassette format. Among subject areas covered are art, business, energy/ecology, health/safety, social studies, and sports. Each title includes a short description, running time, available formats, title number, accompanying materials (if any), suggested audience level, sponsor, and other pertinent ordering information. Programs appropriate for more than one subject area are described under the first listing and cross-referenced from others. Many titles are accompanied by education kits that consist of teacher's guides, posters/wall charts, reproducible masters, worksheets, and other teaching materials.

E+
19 **Educational Film & Video Locator of the Consortium of College and University Media Centers and R. R. Bowker**. 4th ed. New Providence, N.J.: R. R. Bowker, 1990. 2v. $175.00/set. ISBN 0-8352-2624-0. LC 86-71233.

The *Film Locator* is a union list of some 52,000 films and videos, over 9,400 of which are new to this edition. All are available for rental from the 46-member Consortium of University Film Centers (CUFC). The broad selection of films (e.g., scientific, feature, vocational, documentary) covers subjects from ability testing to zoology. Annotations give running time, video film format, color, production date, former title, series notation, subjects, audience levels, and rental sources. Separate indexes of subject (621 headings), title, and audience level are provided. The work also gives complete contact information and lending terms for all media centers nationwide. Updated triennially. [R: ARBA 91; RBB, 1 Oct 90; VOYA, July 90]

E+
20 **Educators Guide to Free Audio and Video Materials**. Randolph, Wis.: Educators Progress Service. annual. $24.25.

21 **Educators Guide to Free Films**. Randolph, Wis.: Educators Progress Service. annual. $27.95.

22 **Educators Guide to Free Filmstrips and Slides**. Randolph, Wis.: Educators Progress Service. annual. $23.95. (214 Center St., Randolph, WI 53956).
    These guides, updated annually, annotate titles available for free loan from a variety of sponsors and agencies. Material is screened for availability and educational value. The arrangement is under curriculum-related subject areas, and indexing is by title, subject, and source.
    Audio Guide covers audiotapes, videotapes, and records. *Film Guide* and *Filmstrip Guide* cover free films, filmstrips, and slides. All are bound volumes.

E+
23 **Film & Video Finder**. 3d ed. Medford, N.J.: National Information Center for Educational Media, 1991. 3v. $295.00/set.

24 **Index to AV Producers & Distributors**. Medford, N.J.: National Information Center for Educational Media, 1991. $75.00pa. (available from Plexus Publishing Co., 143 Old Marlton Pike, Medford, NJ 08055-8750).
    The *Film & Video Finder* gives information about 92,000 films and videos, making it the most comprehensive guide to educational audiovisual materials. Entries include description of content, audience level, format, running time, date of release, purchase/rental cost, and source.
    Volume 1, which contains the indexes and locators, includes a subject heading outline, an index to subject headings, a subject section, and producers and distributors directories by code and by full name. Volumes 2 and 3 list every film and video alphabetically by title, with complete descriptions and order information. Bowker's *Educational Film & Video Locator* contains similar information but includes more detailed annotations. *Audiocassette Finder* (2d ed., 1991, $95.00) and *Filmstrip & Slide Set Finder* (1991, $225.00) are also available.
    Index to AV Producers & Distributors is a directory of 25,000 producers and distributors of audiovisual materials of all kinds. In addition to supplying addresses and telephone numbers, the directory gives the type of media produced or distributed.
    NICEM is based at the offices of Access Innovations, Inc. (P.O. Box 40130, Albuquerque, NM 87196). All publications of NICEM are available online from Dialog as A-V Online (File 46) and on CD-ROM from SilverPlatter. [R: ARBA 91]

E+
25 Gallant, Jennifer J. **Best Videos for Children and Young Adults: A Core Collection for Libraries**. Santa Barbara, Calif.: ABC-Clio, 1990. 185p. $36.75. ISBN 0-87436-561-9.
    Over 250 highly recommended videos for children and young adults (K-12) are listed alphabetically by title. Entries include audience level, usage (recreation, discussion, or classroom), release date (most since the mid-1970s), description (color, sound, and running time), price, credits, and a critical annotation. The entries, all on VHS ½-inch, complement every subject in the curriculum. Indexed by subject/title and audience/usage. Recommended for all levels. [R: ARBA 92; JOYS, Spring 91; RBB, 15 Sept 91; SLJ, Feb 91]

E+
26 **The Great Plains National Instructional Television Library (GPN) Catalog**. Lincoln, Nebr.: Great Plains National Instructional Television Library. annual. free. (P.O. Box 80669, Lincoln, NE 68501).
    GPN, a self-supporting service agency of the University of Nebraska, makes quality videotaped instructional courses, slides, and videodiscs available to educational institutions and agencies. Their annual catalog describes products available to public broadcasting stations and to schools (K-12 and college level). Delivery systems cover the technological gamut—open circuit VHF and UHF broadcasting facilities, 2,500 MHz(ITFS) systems, closed circuit, and community/educational cable

operations. GPN also engages in the preparation of new and original materials for educational media users.

The catalog describes the products (arranged alphabetically by title), giving a lengthy description, number of videocassettes, running time, price, guides (student and teacher), and appropriate audience. The free *GPN Newsletter* (4/yr.) discusses new programs and services.

E +

27 Notable Children's Films and Videos, Filmstrips, and Recordings, 1973-1986. By the Association of Library Services to Children. Chicago: American Library Association, 1987. 118p. $8.95pa. ISBN 0-8389-3342-4.

This guide is a compilation of the annual recommendations of the Association of Library Services to Children's "notable" films, videos, filmstrips, and recordings, 1973-1986. Entries are listed alphabetically within each media category and provide title, producer, distributor, release date, format, length, grade level, and purchase/lease price. Items no longer available are so noted. Indexed by subject, author, illustrator, and producer.

E +

28 Variety's Video Directory Plus. New Providence, N.J.: R. R. Bowker. $395.00/yr., MS-DOS or Apple Macintosh version.

Video Plus includes 62,000 videos (34,000 educational and 28,000 entertainment) that are searchable by combining any or all of 20 search criteria to find the exact title needed. In addition to indexing (via nine access points) and obtaining contact information/discount schedule/return policies for manufacturers and distributors, searchers may display and print out over 2,500 full-text, critical reviews from *Variety*.

E +

29 Video Rating Guide for Libraries. Beth Blenz-Clucas, ed. Santa Barbara, Calif.: ABC-Clio, 1990- . quarterly. $89.50/yr. ISSN 1045-3393.

Every quarterly issue of *Video Rating Guide for Libraries* reviews some 450 newly-released videos. Each review, written by a librarian with expertise in a specific subject area, gives a coded rating that ranges from one to five stars. Complete bibliographic, ordering, and cataloging information is given for each video. Indexed by subject, title, price, audience, and the best videos of the issue.

30 Video Rating Guide for Libraries. Santa Barbara, Calif.: ABC-Clio, 1990- . 4th quarterly issue. ISSN 1045-3393.

The fourth quarterly issue cumulates the index and gives the user fast access to the year's video releases.

31 Recommended Videos for Schools, 1990. Santa Barbara, Calif.: ABC-Clio, 1991. 300p. $50.00. ISBN 0-87436-644-5.

Recommended Videos for Schools compiles the reviews of those educational videos which are specifically for high school students and have been awarded a four- or five-star rating during the previous year. Cataloging, indexing, and ordering information is included with each review.

32 The Video Source Book. David J. Weiner, ed. Detroit: Gale. annual. $220.00/set.

This is the most comprehensive guide to video available. Over 64,000 entries describe 125,000 currently available programs in entertainment, education, culture, medicine, and business. Each entry, arranged alphabetically by title, gives up to 20 points of information, such as date of release, running time, major plot, theme, Motion Picture Association of America ratings for major films, closed captions or signing for hearing impaired, and availability.

Listings are identified according to eight main subject areas, with the largest being general interest/ education, movie/entertainment, and health/science. More than 43,000 titles are available for use in schools. The directory of distributors lists 1,450 outlets. [R: ARBA 92]

33 The Whole Video Catalog, 1991-92, K-6. Bohemia, N.Y.: Charles Clark Co., 1991. 102p. free.

34 The Whole Video Catalog, 1991-92, 7-12. Bohemia, N.Y.: Charles Clark Co., 1991. 182p. free. (170 Keyland Court, Bohemia, NY 11716).

These catalogs each list 1,500 quality educational videocassettes. Entries include a descriptive annotation, DDC number, grade level, running time, format (all products are available in VHS only), and price. The catalogs are arranged by curriculum category, American history through world history, and include such topics as Indians, astronomy, and sex education.

Two types of videocassettes are included: full motion (live action), and filmstrips enhanced to videocassettes, using pans, scans, dissolves, and rotation to suggest motion. Each entry is clearly coded as to which type it is.

Producers and Distributors

35   Pemberton, J. Michael. **Policies of Audiovisual Producers and Distributors: A Handbook for Acquisition Personnel**. 2d ed. Metuchen, N.J.: Scarecrow, 1989. 381p. $35.00pa. ISBN 0-8108-2264-4. LC 89-10950.

This handbook examines the policies of nonprint producers and distributors whose educational products require electronic enhancement. The main body of the manual gives information on each organization (arranged alphabetically by name); ordering address; policies on discounts, previewing, duplication, returns, and closed-circuit transmission; and other data. The relational index provides current, former, and popular names of the organizations. The index lists organizations alphabetically by state. [R: ARBA 91]

Sound Recordings

E +
36   Jarnow, Jill. **All Ears: How to Use and Choose Recorded Music for Children**. New York: Viking, 1991. 206p. $17.95; $9.95pa. ISBN 0-670-82313-9; 0-14-011254-5pa.

This selection guide to children's recordings opens with an introduction explaining the importance of music and family listening habits. The main body describes recordings by over 75 artists, including Peter Seeger, Ellen Jenkins, and Sally Rogers. Since children's recordings usually remain available for a long time, this annotated discography should have lasting value. [R: LJ, 1 Feb 91]

See also **General Catalogs** under **Audiovisual** in
Media Sources.

37   **The New Penguin Guide to Compact Discs and Cassettes: Yearbook, 1989**. By Edward Greenfield and others. New York: Viking Penguin, 1989. 494p. $13.95pa. ISBN 0-14-012377-6.

This volume supplements *The New Penguin Guide to Compact Discs and Cassettes* (Viking, 1988) which evaluates recordings available in 1988. The *Yearbook* appraises material released in 1989. Each book can stand alone. The reviews affirm that the musical and sonic quality of each recording is of exceptionally high quality. The reviewers make a special effort to recommend good buys. [R: ARBA 91; RBB, 15 Mar 90]

38   **Opus: America's Guide to Classical Music**. Chatsworth, Calif.: Schwann, 1990- . 4 issues/yr. $20.00/yr.

39   **Spectrum: Your Guide to Today's Music**. Chatsworth, Calif.: Schwann, 1990- . 4 issues/yr. $16.50/yr. (21625 Prairie St., Chatsworth, CA 91311).

Opus and *Spectrum* are companion publications that replace *Schwann Quarterly*. *Opus* covers classical and electronic music, and *Spectrum* includes rock, pop, jazz, gospel, Christmas and religious music, children's recordings, and spoken recordings. Both cover musicals, soundtracks, and New Age music. Each is organized by category. [R: ARBA 91; RBB, 15 Mar 90]

40   **Words on Cassette**. New Providence, N.J., R. R. Bowker. annual. $124.95.

To develop this new title, R. R. Bowker has merged its own *On Cassette* with *Words on Tape*, which was purchased from Meckler. To be published annually, *Words on Cassette* lists spoken-word audiocassettes in many and varied subject areas (e.g., art, biography, business, drama, education, foreign language instruction, health and fitness, literature, religion). Information on each includes reader's name, author, title, playing time, number of cassettes, purchase/rental price, order number, and publisher. Many titles have an annotation. Indexing is by title, subject, author, producer/distributor, and reader. Contact information on more than 900 producers and distributors is provided.

Talking Books and Braille

See also **Handicapped** and **Learning Disabled** in
Education.

E +
41 **Braille Book Review**. Washington, D.C.: National Library Service for the Blind and Physically Handicapped, 1933- . bimonthly. free. (1291 NW Taylor St., Washington, DC 20542).

Braille Book Review is distributed free to blind and physically handicapped persons who participate in the Library of Congress free reading program. The large-print catalog lists braille magazines and books available through a network of cooperating libraries. The bimonthly issues of *BBR* annotate titles recently added to the national collection, which contains thousands of fiction and nonfiction titles — classics, biographies, gothics, mysteries, how-to books, and self-help guides.

Books in press or handcopied braille are listed for children and adults. Handcopied braille from other agencies, such as the Jewish Braille Institute of America and the Lutheran Library for the Blind, are listed separately with instructions for obtaining them. Some 40 braille magazines in the Library of Congress program, available on free subscription to participants, are cited.

Each entry gives title, order code, author, number of volumes, annotation, and date of original print edition. Indexed monthly and annually.

■ *Discoveries: Fiction for Elementary Readers*. *See* entry 79.

■ *Discoveries: Fiction for Intermediate School Years*. *See* entry 80.

■ *Discoveries: Fiction for Young Teens*. *See* entry 81.

E +
42 **Library Resources for the Blind and Physically Handicapped**. Washington, D.C.: National Library Services for the Blind and Physically Handicapped, 1990. free. (1291 NW Taylor St., Washington, DC 20542).

This directory lists network libraries and machine-lending agencies that participate in the free service program to blind and physically handicapped children and adults. Arranged alphabetically by state, regional libraries appear first, followed by subregional libraries listed alphabetically by city. For each facility there is complete directory information, including fax number, hours of service, formats of materials in the collection, special collections, services, assistance devices, and publications (e.g., newsletters, catalogs). Tables of readership and circulation by state, and other statistical data, complete the directory.

43 **Recording for the Blind. Catalog of Recorded Books**. Princeton, N.J.: Recording for the Blind, 1960- . irregular. $14.00. (20 Roszel Rd., Princeton, NJ 08540).

Recordings for the Blind catalog, which lists free taped educational books for the visually handicapped, provides some 60,000 titles of textbooks available in cassette format.

E +
44 **Talking Books Topics**. Washington, D.C.: National Library Services for the Blind and Physically Handicapped, 1935- . bimonthly. free. (1291 NW Taylor St., Washington, DC 20542).

Talking Books Topics, published bimonthly in large-print, cassette, and disc formats and distributed free to blind and physically handicapped persons who participate in the Library of Congress free reading program, is similar to *Braille Book Review*. It lists recorded books and magazines available through a national network of cooperating libraries. Each issue is limited to descriptive listings of titles recently added to the national collection, which contains thousands of items.

Sections cover news briefs; books for adults and books for children, subdivided by disc/cassette and fiction/nonfiction; foreign language books, divided by language (Spanish, French, Italian, and Polish); and talking book magazines. Indexed by disc and cassette. All book entries are annotated.

BOOKS

Review Journals

See also **Review Journals** under **General** in **Media Sources**.

45 Appraisal: Children's Science Books. Diane Holzeimer, ed. in chief. Boston: Children's Science Book Review Committee, Boston University School of Education, 1967- . quarterly. $34.00/yr. (605 Commonwealth Ave., Boston, MA 02215).
   Level: Preschool through high school.
   Focus: Reviews almost all science and math books published each year that are written for children and young adults.
   Reviews: Some 70 trade books and series are reviewed in each quarterly issue; two signed reviews, 100-200 words each, by two reviewers, a librarian and a subject specialist; complete bibliographic and order information and grade level; five rating codes (unsatisfactory to excellent).
   Print: Trade books in science and mathematics.
   Nonprint: None.
   Features: Articles on science books and teaching science.
   Index: Index each issue, cumulated annually.

E
46 Book Links: Connecting Books, Libraries, and Classrooms. Chicago: American Library Association, 1991- . 6 issues/yr. $18.00/yr.
   Level: Elementary schools.
   Focus: Began as an insert in *Booklist* and became an independent magazine in September 1991; designed to help teachers select the best books for literature-based programs, to help librarians integrate the best children's literature into the curriculum, and to help parents ensure that kids make the best use of free time.
   Reviews: Old and new books included in several sections: "Book Strategies" critiques books about a specific theme or topic; "Classroom Connections" analyzes a group of books with similar themes; "Visual Links" evaluates illustrations in a picture book and reviews seven or eight titles; "The Inside Story" focuses on one work, such as an award book, with a review of it, comments by the author, and suggestions for using it as a basis for research; and "Poetry" contains interviews with children's poets. All have bibliographic and order information for titles treated and for those listed as additional suggested titles.
   Print: Books.
   Nonprint: None.

■ *The Book Report*. *See* entry 1.

■ *Booklist*. *See* entry 2.

47 Bulletin of the Center for Children's Books. Betsy Hearne, ed. Chicago: University of Chicago Press, 1945- . monthly (except Aug.). $27.00/yr. (P.O. Box 37005, Chicago, IL 60637).
   Level: Preschool through grade 10.
   Focus: Reviews books of exceptional value in writing and usefulness, but warns against others that are poor in quality.
   Reviews: Some 800 each year; 100-150 words in length; written by the editor; reviews describe content, characters, and theme, and indicate developmental values or curricular uses; nine codes, such as * (special distinction) and NR (not recommended), are used for evaluation; gives grade or age (for preschool) level.
   Print: Mostly trade fiction, some nonfiction.
   Nonprint: None.
   Features: "Bulletin Blue Ribbon Books" published each January for outstanding books of previous year—arranged by picture books, fiction, poetry, and nonfiction; reviews are cumulated every five years as *The Best in Children's Books*.
   Index: Author-title index for each volume.

48   Emergency Librarian. Ken Haycock, ed. Seattle, Wash.: Dyad Services, 1962- . 5 issues/yr. (bimonthly, none July/Aug). $45.00/yr. (Box C34069, Dept. 284, Washington, DC 98124-1069).
   Level: Children and YA.
   Focus: Features articles mainly on youth library services and children's literature; reviews of professional reading and books, software, and recordings.
   Reviews: Sections on professional reading, outstanding new books K-12, AV materials, paperbacks for children and YAs, software reviews, children's recordings, and Canadian and Australian books. Reviews vary from 175-200 words in some sections to 50-100 in others.
   Print: Professional reading, books K-12, paperbacks for children and YAs.
   Nonprint: Films, videos, sound recordings, software.
   Features: Best Canadian and Australian books; best picture books, children's books, and YA novels of the year.

E +
49   The Horn Book Guide to Children's and Young Adult Books. Volume 1, Number 1. Ann Flowers, ed. Boston: Horn Book, 1990. 176p. $25.00pa., $50.00/yr. ISBN 0-87675-036-6. ISSN 1044-405X.
   This is the inaugural issue of a semiannual, critical survey of new U.S. trade books intended for children and young adult audiences. It provides brief reviews of over 1,600 recommended titles published in 1989.
   Nonfiction is arranged alphabetically by DDC headings, fiction by level (younger, intermediate, older) or genre. Books are then rated on a scale of 1 (the best) to 6 (the worst). Other features include full bibliographic data; citations to previous reviews in *Horn Book*; a few black-and-white illustrations; indexing by author/illustrator, title, subject, and series; and the "Horn Book Fanfare 1990" (books selected by *Horn Book* as the best of 1989). Recommended for elementary and middle schools. [R: ARBA 91; EL, Nov-Dec 90; JOYS, Fall 90; RBB, July 90]

50   The Horn Book Magazine. Anita Silvey, ed. Boston: The Horn Book, 1924- . 6 issues/yr. $38.00/yr. (14 Beacon St., Boston, MA 02108).
   Level: Preschool through YA.
   Focus: Reviews of books that meet the editor's high standard of quality and literary merit; directed toward parents but useful to librarians and others interested in children's literature.
   Reviews: Evaluative; 150-250 words in length; 250-300 each year; starred titles judged outstanding; reviews give bibliographic/order data, size, age level (younger, age 6-8; intermediate age 9-12; and older, 12-YA), summary of content, characterizations, themes, and comments on writing and illustrating; categories are picture books, fiction, poetry, and nonfiction; recommended paperbacks; new editions and reissues; books in Spanish; books in the classroom.
   Print: Trade books.
   Nonprint: None.
   Features: Articles about authors and illustrators, writing and publishing; annual lists of best books; column about books in the classroom; column highlighting out-of-print books on a topic or genre that may be found in the library.
   Index: By author and title in each issue; cumulated annual index.

51   Jim Kobak's Kirkus Reviews. Anne Larsen, ed. Joanna Rudge Long, YA and Children's ed. New York: The Kirkus Service, 1933- . semimonthly. looseleaf. $325.00/yr. ($75.00/yr. for libraries with budgets of $5,000 or less). (200 Park Ave. South, New York, NY 10003).
   Level: Adult and juvenile.
   Focus: Prepublication reviews of trade books; directed toward booksellers and libraries.
   Reviews: Descriptions/evaluations written by staff members; some 4,000 reviews each year, 100-250 words in length; entries give bibliographic/order information, paging, and the month and day book will be released; juvenile books also give type of book and grade level.
   Print: Trade books, juvenile and adult, with emphasis on latter.
   Nonprint: None.
   Features: Looseleaf; separate juvenile section, arranged by author; symbol indicates books of unusual merit or appeal.
   Index: Author index in each issue; cumulated at three- and six-month intervals.

52   Kliatt Young Adult Paperback Book Guide. Doris Hiatt and Claire Rosser, eds. Newton, Mass.: Kliatt Paperback Book Guide, 1967- . 8 issues/yr. (Jan.-Feb., Apr.-June, Sept.-Nov.). $33.00/yr. (425 Watertown St., Newton, MA 02158).

Level: Ages 12-19.

Focus: Paperback books useful in classrooms and libraries.

Reviews: Either by editorial staff and unsigned or by outside reviewers and signed (initials, with guide in back of some issues). Sections for such areas as fiction, science fiction and fantasy, literature and language arts, poetry, biography and personal narratives, education and guidance, consumer education, health and sex education, nature and ecology, and sports. Audio book reviews divided by fiction and nonfiction. Reviews of 124-200 words include guidance codes such as A (advanced students-intellectually demanding) and E (low reading ability). Exceptional quality highlighted.

Print: Reprints, reissues, and original paperbacks.

Nonprint: None.

Features: Essays on special topics.

Index: Title index.

53 **Library Journal**. John N. Berry, III, ed. in chief. Nora Rawlinson, ed. New Providence, N.J.: R. R. Bowker, 1976- . 20 issues/yr. (twice monthly, monthly Jan., July, Aug., Dec.). $74.00/yr. (order from P.O. Box 1977, Marion, OH 43306-2077).

Level: Adult, general audience.

Focus: Articles and news items on topics of professional interest to public, college, and special librarians; reviews of print and nonprint media.

Reviews: Some 250 reviews each issue; 150-175 words in length; signed reviews by practitioners, academics, or staff members; most descriptive, but some give recommendations and audience; entries, arranged by broad categories, give bibliographic/order information; starred reviews indicate outstanding quality or popular appeal; reference reviews, arranged alphabetically, introduce review section.

Print: Adult fiction and nonfiction trade books, reference books, magazines, professional reading.

Nonprint: Videocassettes, films, audiocassettes.

Features: Management and online database columns; prepublication alert; topical lists of bestsellers; "Word of Mouth," a reader's advisory column. Special spring and fall announcement issues, buyers' guide to hardware and equipment issue; best reference books of year; lists of outstanding books in science, technology, and medicine.

Index: Monthly author index to book reviews, classic returns, and professional reading; six-month cumulative index in July; annual cumulative index.

■ *Book Review Digest*. *See* entry 215.

■ *Book Review Index*. *See* entry 216.

■ *Children's Book Review Index*. *See* entry 218.

■ *Media & Methods*. *See* entry 6.

■ *Olderr's Young Adult Fiction Index*. *See* entry 1171.

■ *School Library Journal*. *See* entry 7.

■ *Science Books & Films*. See entry 8.

■ *Voice of Youth Advocates*. See entry 9.

■ *Wilson Library Bulletin*. *See* entry 10.

Trade Bibliographies

54 **American Book Publishing Record**. New Providence, N.J.: R. R. Bowker, 1960- . monthly. $129.95/yr. ISSN 0002-7707.

55 **American Book Publishing Record Cumulative**. New Providence, N.J.: R. R. Bowker. annual. $174.95.

ABPR is a monthly compilation of the titles cataloged by the Library of Congress which were previously recorded in *Weekly Record* (ceased publication 1991). The arrangement is by the DDC number, with special sections for fiction, juvenile fiction, and mass-market paperbacks. Information includes full cataloging data, LC and DDC numbers, subject headings, and price. Indexed by author, title, and subject.

E+
56 **Books in Print**. New Providence, N.J.: R. R. Bowker. annual. $374.95/set.

57 **Subject Guide to Books in Print**. New Providence, N.J.: R. R. Bowker. annual. $239.95/set.

58 **Books in Print Supplement**. New Providence, N.J.: R. R. Bowker. 2 issues/yr. $185.00/set.

59 **Forthcoming Books**. New Providence, N.J.: R. R. Bowker. bimonthly. $199.00/yr. ISSN 0015-8119.

60 **Books Out-of-Print 1984-1988**. New Providence, N.J.: R. R. Bowker, 1989. 3v. $110.00/set. ISBN 0-8352-2506-2.
   Books in Print (BIP) provides bibliographic and order information for works published and distributed in the United States. The 1991-1992 annual lists over 860,000 books of all kinds—adult, juvenile, popular, scholarly, and reprint—entered under authors (3 v.) and titles (3 v.). Volume 7 includes some 110,000 titles declared out-of-print or out-of-stock indefinitely from August 1990 through July 1991. Volume 8, an index of publishers, is a directory to more than 32,000 firms. Textbooks are excluded, since they are listed in *El-Hi Textbooks and Serials in Print*.
   Subject Guide to Books in Print indexes almost 700,000 nonfiction titles from *BIP* under some 65,000 LC subject headings. New since the 1990-1991 annual is a volume entitled *Subject Thesaurus*, which cites and cross-references all subject headings from the *Subject Guide*, along with subject-heading numbers for online and CD-ROM uses.
   The *Supplement*, issued in March, updates all data contained in *BIP*, including listings for new publications. The bimonthly *Forthcoming Books* includes titles published since the previous *BIP* and those scheduled for publication during the next five months.
   Books Out-of-Print 1984-1988 lists 280,000 backlist titles declared by their publishers to be out-of-print or out-of-stock indefinitely. The work also provides a directory of over 3,000 remainder dealers, out-of-print retailers, search services, and on-demand publishers.
   Books in Print Plus (MS-DOS version or Apple Macintosh version, $995.00/yr.) applies Boolean and key word searching capabilities to the entire *BIP* database. *Books in Print Online* is available from Dialog, File #470, at a search rate of $60.00/hr. search time, plus nominal charges for display, and from BRS, File Name BBIP, at a search time royalty of $40.00/hr., plus variable subscription access rates.
   Books in print 1990-91 on Microfiche (quarterly: Jan., Apr., July, Oct., 148 × 105 mm/42: 1/170 fiche per issue, $735.00/yr.) completely updates *BIP* and *Forthcoming Books*. *Subject Guide to Books in Print 1990-91 on Microfiche* (quarterly: Jan., Apr., July, Oct., 148 × 105 mm/42: 110 fiche per issue, $525.00/yr.) includes all nonfiction books in *BIP* and forthcoming titles. [R: ARBA 91]

E+
61 **Children's Books in Print**. New Providence, N.J.: R. R. Bowker. annual. $124.95.

62 **Subject Guide to Children's Books in Print**. New Providence, N.J.: R. R. Bowker. annual. $124.95.
   These two volumes, similar in format to the *Books in Print* family, provide bibliographic and order information for all levels of juvenile books. The 1991-1992 *CBIP* covers more than 60,000 titles by author, illustrator (where appropriate), and title. The *Subject Guide* for 1991-1992 provides access to the same titles under Sears subject headings, supplemented by LC headings. Both volumes exclude textbooks. Recommended for elementary schools.
   Children's Reference Plus (MS-DOS version, $595.00/yr.), a CD-ROM version of *CBIP* and the *Subject Guide*, also lists children's serials from *Ulrich's International Periodicals Directory*, children's audiocassettes from *Words on Cassette*, and children's videos from *Bowker's Complete Video Directory*. *CR Plus* also provides full-text critical reviews of juvenile and young adult materials from 10 periodicals (e.g., *School Library Journal, Booklist*); contents of bibliographies such as *A to Zoo* and *Best Books for Children*; and activity books such as *Juniorplots 3* and *Primaryplots*.

63 **The Complete Directory of Large Print Books and Serials**. New Providence, N.J.: R. R. Bowker. annual. $119.95pa.

Order information for some 6,500 large-print titles (950 new to this edition) are entered by subject, author, and title. Subject headings include mystery and suspense, sports and games, crossword puzzles, humor, historical fiction, and children's books. The serials index lists some 65 large-print periodicals and newspapers.

E+

64 **El-Hi Textbooks and Serials in Print**. New Providence, N.J.: R. R. Bowker. annual. $109.95.

Compiled from textbook publisher's catalogs, this bibliography aims at completeness rather than selectivity. It lists some 35,000 textbooks (K-12), periodicals, maps, teaching aids, and other classroom materials, all arranged under 21 broad headings. The work also includes sections on books and serials for professional educators.

Entries provide bibliographic and order information, grade and reading level, author, title, and series indexing. A directory of publishers supports the listings.

Reviewers have criticized this work for its inclusion of out-of-print materials not yet purged from the database; nonetheless, it does contain the most complete list of these types of materials. [R: ARBA 92]

65 **University Press Books for Public and Secondary School Libraries**. New York: Association of American University Presses, 1991. 114p. free pa. ISSN 1055-4173.

Formerly issued as *University Press Books for Public Libraries* and *University Press Books for Secondary Libraries*, this newly combined annotated bibliography of more than 500 titles has been designed for collection development in both public and secondary school libraries. The titles which have been arranged by the DDC system have complete bibliographic information, a short annotation, coding to indicate reading level, and expected appeal (general, regional, or special interest). A directory of contributing publishers and author and title indexes complete the volume. Schools offering honors or advanced programs will find this guide particularly useful.

Core Collections

E

66 **Children's Catalog**. 16th ed. Bronx, N.Y.: H. W. Wilson, 1991. 1298p. $90.00 (includes 4 supplements). ISBN 0-8242-0743-2. LC 86-15751.

This is a selection tool for libraries serving children preschool through grade 6. The main volume contains more than 6,500 recommended fiction and nonfiction titles; each of the annual supplements lists approximately 550 additional titles. A panel of librarians from throughout the United States has selected the books cited. Audiovisual materials are not included.

The arrangement is the same as that followed in other volumes of the Wilson Standard Catalog series. The "Classified Catalog," the main section, lists books by *Abridged Dewey Decimal Classification*, with separate sections for fiction, story collections, and easy books. Entries provide complete bibliographic and order information, recommended grade level, subject headings, and descriptive/ critical annotations. Information on paperback and variant editions is provided. The analytical index is a single-alphabet listing of authors, subjects, titles, and analytical references to composite works. A directory of publishers and distributors constitutes the final section. [R: ARBA 87]

E

67 **The Elementary School Library Collection: A Guide to Books and Other Media. Phases 1-2-3**. 17th ed. Lois Winkel, ed. Greensboro, N.C.: Brodart, 1990. 1149p. $99.95. ISBN 0-87272-094-2. LC 89-22382.

This standard work recommends quality books and media that meet high educational standards for grades K-6, either published or available between April 15, 1988 and April 15, 1990. Arranged by the abridged version of the DDC system, it is supported by author, title, and subject indexes. "Phases 1-2-3" refers to the suggested order of selecting the books contained in each section.

While *ESLC* has a heavy overlap with *Children's Catalog*, its closest competitor, there are several differences. *ESLC* has almost twice as many entries and includes media, reference, professional materials, and periodicals, which *CC* does not. *CC*'s annotations tend to be critical and include excerpts from reviews, while *ESLC*'s annotations are primarily descriptive. Finally, *ESLC*, revised annually, is more current, while *CC* is revised at five-year intervals with annual supplements. Since the publishers emphasize fiction and easy books, both lists are biased toward literature, making it necessary for librarians to seek selection assistance from other tools that focus on nonfiction.

Despite its cost — $99.95, as compared to $90.00 for the basic volume of *CC* and its four supplements — *ESLC* is highly recommended for the new library building a start-up collection, and for the older library concerned with collection development. [R: ARBA 91; EL, Sept/Oct 90]

68   **Fiction Catalog**. 12th ed. Bronx, N.Y.: H. W. Wilson, 1991. 951p. $98.00. ISBN 0-8242-0804-8. LC 85-32298.

The latest edition of this work, a standard since its appearance in 1908, is an annotated list of over 5,200 of the best in-print and out-of-print fiction titles, ranging from popular contemporary works to literary classics. Designed to aid librarians in developing and maintaining their collections, it is a companion to *Public Library Catalog*, which includes only nonfiction.

The arrangement is alphabetical by author, with title and subject indexes. Large-print books are in a separate section. The entries provide complete bibliographic data, price, and an outline of the plot (or a list of contents for story collections). The extensive subject indexing provides access by literary theme or genre, geographical setting, events, historical period, people, occupations, and nationalities.

A subscription to *Fiction Catalog* includes the initial volume and four supplements, each citing some 600 additional titles. Since *Senior High School Catalog* contains only a limited number of fiction titles, this work supplements it and, therefore, serves as an important source for building high school library collections. [R: ARBA 92]

69   **Junior High School Library Catalog**. 6th ed. Juliette Yaakov, ed. Bronx, N.Y.: H. W. Wilson, 1990. 850p. $80.00 (includes 4 supplements). ISBN 0-8242-0799-8. LC 90-44498.

This guide, a member of the Wilson Standard Catalog series, is an annotated list of fiction and nonfiction titles recommended for grades 7 through 9. Librarians from all sections of the United States have selected the books cited. The basic volume includes 3,219 titles; the 4 annual supplements (1991-1994) will each add more than 500 newly published works.

The main section of the catalog arranges books by *Abridged Dewey Decimal Classification* with separate sections for fiction and story collections. Entries give complete bibliographic and order information (including paperback and variant editions information), suggested Sears subject headings, and descriptive/critical annotations; quotations from a review are often provided. Author, title, subject, and analytical (references to composite works) indexing and a directory of publishers and distributors complete the volume. An essential holding for junior high school libraries, but many school media specialists report that the catalog has not kept abreast of the research-based teaching needs of today's schools. [R: ARBA 91]

70   **Senior High School Catalog**. 13th ed. Bronx, N.Y.: H. W. Wilson, 1987. 1324p. $96.00 (includes 4 supplements). ISBN 0-8242-0755-6. LC 87-7377.

The *Senior High School Catalog* has been a standard work for more than 60 years in collection development and maintenance, selection and purchasing, cataloging and classification, general reference, and readers' advisory work. The initial volume lists almost 5,000 books; the four annual supplements (1988-1991) each cite some 500 additional titles. A panel of librarians from across the United States has chosen the books cited. An effort is made to include works that reflect the interests and concerns of young adults (e.g., data processing, marriage and family, college preparation, alcoholism, teenage suicide).

The catalog is arranged by DDC, with separate sections for fiction and story collections. Entries offer bibliographic and order information (including paperback and variant editions), Sears subject headings, and descriptive/critical annotations. Author, title, subject and analytical (references to composite works) indexing, and a directory of publishers and distributors complete the volume, an essential holding for high school libraries. [R: ARBA 88]

Children's Lists

See also **Children's Literature**.

E
71   **Adventuring with Books: A Booklist for Pre-K-Grade 6**. 9th ed. Mary Jett-Simpson, ed., and the Committee on the Elementary School Booklist of the National Council of Teachers of English. Urbana, Ill.: National Council of Teachers of English, 1989. 549p. $16.50pa. ISBN 0-8141-0078-3. ISSN 1045-7488. LC 89-12906.

This selective bibliography includes 1,800 children's books published between 1985 and 1988 and chosen for their literary or artistic merit, accuracy of presentation, and appeal to children preschool through sixth grade. Entries, arranged in 20 major categories and then subdivided to more specific areas, include bibliographic data, age and grade level, and annotations. Indexing is by author, title, subject, and illustrator.

The selection committee notes the increase in material being published for very young children (babies and toddlers) and the trend toward beautiful books that are works of art. This selection aid is an essential choice for elementary school libraries. [R: ARBA 90]

E
72 Barstow, Barbara, and Judith Riggle. **Beyond Picture Books: A Guide to First Readers**. New Providence, N.J.: R. R. Bowker, 1989. 354p. $39.95. ISBN 0-8352-2515-1. LC 89-30798.

First readers are defined as books having simple vocabularies, short sentences, many illustrations, and large print. Those selected for this list were also judged on their attractiveness, quality of writing, accuracy, and interest to first- and second-grade students. An "Outstanding First Readers" list includes 200 of those regarded as being of superior quality. The main body of the work includes 1,600 titles; fiction and nonfiction, in-print and out-of-print. Entries—arranged alphabetically by author—include bibliographic information, reading level, subject, and an annotation. Indexed by title, illustrator, series, and readability level. [R: ARBA 90; RBB, 1 Oct 89]

E
73 Baskin, Barbara H., and Karen H. Harris. **Books for the Gifted Child**. New Providence, N.J.: R. R. Bowker, 1980. 267p. $34.95. ISBN 0-8352-1164-4. LC 79-27431.

74 Hauser, Paula, and Gail A. Nelson. **Books for the Gifted Child. Volume 2**. New Providence, N.J.: R. R. Bowker, 1988. 244p. $39.95. ISBN 0-8352-2467-8. LC 79-27431.

Introductory chapters identify the gifted and describe various types of literature that usually interest them. The suggested titles were chosen because of their potential challenge to gifted children ages 3 to 12. Picture books, biographies, stories, poetry, science, math, and game books are all arranged alphabetically by author. The authors provide lengthy annotations, complete bibliographic information, and reading level and evaluate the plot, characters, and style. These are useful guides for professionals and others who work with gifted children. It should be noted that the books listed in volume 2 were published between 1981 and 1987. [R: ARBA 89]

E+
75 **The Best in Children's Books: The University of Chicago Guide to Children's Literature, 1979-1984**. Zena Sutherland, ed. Chicago: University of Chicago Press, 1986. $35.00. ISBN 0-226-78060-0. LC 85-31820.

The editor has selected 1,400 reviews of children's books (preschool through grade 10) contained in the highly regarded *Bulletin of the Center for Children's Books*, 1979 through 1984. All of the titles listed have received a "Recommended" rating (except for a few coded "Additional" or "Special Reader"). An asterisk indicates books of distinction. Two similar collections of "best books" cover 1966-1972 (1973) and 1973-1978 (1980).

The concise evaluations (75-100 words) provide critical comments on style and a description of the plot and theme. Entries include full bibliographic data and suggested age level. The reviews are supported by six indexes: title, developmental values (e.g., mother-daughter relationships), curricular use (e.g., reading aloud, science), reading level, subject, and type of literature (e.g., folk, biography). Recommended. [R: ARBA 87; RBB, 1 Dec 86]

E+
76 **Canadian Books for Young People. Livres Canadiens pour la Jeunesse**. 4th ed. Andre Gagnon and Ann Gagnon, eds. Toronto and Buffalo, N.Y.: University of Toronto, 1988. 186p. $14.95pa. ISBN 0-8020-6662-3.

Librarians who wish to build a collection of Canadian books for preschool through high school levels will welcome this update of the 1980 edition. It contains over 2,500 English and French titles and includes bibliographic and order information, plus a brief annotation of each title in the language of publication. Each language section is arranged by subject with divisions for professional materials, award books, and periodicals. Separate indexes by author, title, and illustrator integrate both languages. [R: ARBA 89]

E+
77 **Children's Books of the Year**. New York: Child Study Children's Book Committee, Bank Street College. annual. $4.00pa. (610 W. 112th St., New York, NY 10025).

The Child Study Children's Book Committee, composed of librarians, authors, illustrators, and professionals in education, psychology, and related fields, selects an annual list of high-quality books for children up to age 14. Criteria for fiction include age suitability, realistic treatment, accuracy in portraying ethnic and religious differences, and the absence of stereotypes. Nonfiction titles are judged on clarity, accuracy, readability, and differentiation of facts from theory.

Entries provide complete bibliographic data, one-sentence annotations, and symbols noting titles of outstanding merit. Titles are either divided by age group (five and under, five to nine, nine and up) or by nonfiction categories and poetry. Indexed by author/illustrator. This is a worthwhile, inexpensive annual. [R: ARBA 91]

E+
78 Cianciolo, Patricia J. **Picture Books for Children**. 3d ed. Chicago: American Library Association, 1990. 230p. $25.00pa. ISBN 0-8389-0527-7. LC 89-29718.

This work provides guidance for teachers, librarians, and others responsible for the selection of well-written and imaginatively illustrated books for children from preschool through junior high levels. Cianciolo has chosen 464 books (most published between 1985 and 1989 and new to this edition) judged to be excellent in literary and artistic quality.

The annotated entries are arranged in four broad categories: "Me and My Family," "Other People," "The World I Live In," and "The Imaginative World," with works of fiction, nonfiction, and poetry in each section. Information for titles, arranged by author in each group, includes illustrator, publisher and date, intended age group, and translator or adapter (if applicable).

Annotations, which vary from 50 to 200 words, include a concise summary of the story and a description of the illustrations. Indexed by author, title, and illustrator. Recommended for elementary and junior high school libraries. [R: ARBA 91; RBB, 15 Dec 90]

E
79 **Discoveries: Fiction for Elementary School Readers**. Washington, D.C.: National Library Service for the Blind and Physically Handicapped, 1986. 93p. free. ISBN 0-8444-0530-2. LC 86-600075.

E+
80 **Discoveries: Fiction for Intermediate School Years**. Washington, D.C.: National Library Service for the Blind and Physically Handicapped, 1986. 90p. free. ISBN 0-8444-1531-0. LC 86-600076.

E+
81 **Discoveries: Fiction for Young Teens**. Washington, D.C.: National Library Service for the Blind and Physically Handicapped, 1986. 108p. free. ISBN 0-8444-0532-9. LC 86-600078.

The National Library Service for the Blind and Physically Handicapped provides free disks, cassettes, and braille versions of books to persons through network libraries, usually state libraries. These bibliographies list fiction available for children: *Elementary School Readers*, grades kindergarten-6; *Intermediate*, 4-7; and *Young Teens*, 4-9 and senior high school. Each entry includes a suggested grade level. [R: ARBA 88]

E+
82 Gillespie, John T., and Corinne J. Naden. **Best Books for Children: Preschool through Grade 6**. 4th ed. New Providence, N.J.: R. R. Bowker, 1990. 950p. $44.95. ISBN 0-8352-2668-9. LC 89-29625.

This edition of a standard work, last revised in 1985, maintains its original aims: to cite quality recreational reading and to provide a bibliography of worthwhile curriculum-related books for children from preschool through grade 6. Half of the 12,382 titles are new to this edition. Reference tools, professional books, and mass-media series (e.g., Nancy Drew) are not included. Titles selected were favorably reviewed by at least two recognized sources, such as *Children's Catalog*, *Elementary School Library Collection*, and *Horn Book Magazine*.

The arrangement is by broad subject/curricular areas and author within each section. (An alphabetical list of subject headings follows the table of contents.) Information includes bibliographic/order information and citations to reviews. Indexing is by author, illustrator, title, and subject/grade level. Highly recommended for elementary schools.

The Best in Children's Books: The University of Chicago Guide to Children's Literature, 1979-1984, edited by Zena Sutherland, another "best books" guide, is not as useful, since it covers an earlier time period. The 1,400 titles listed received "Recommended" ratings in the highly regarded *Bulletin of the Center for Children's Books*. [R: ARBA 91; LJ, 15 Dec 90; RBB, 15 Dec 90]

E+
83   Schon, Isabel. **Basic Collection of Children's Books in Spanish**. Metuchen, N.J.: Scarecrow, 1986. 230p. $17.50. ISBN 0-8108-1904-X. LC 86-13911.

This work identifies high-quality children's books in Spanish for school or public libraries in the United States or in any Spanish-speaking country. The more than 500 titles, for preschool through grade 6, are arranged as follows: reference; nonfiction, classified according to the 11th abridged edition of Dewey; publishers' series, arranged alphabetically by series title; fiction; easy books; and professional books. A directory of dealers of books in Spanish (from the United States, Spain, and 11 Latin American countries) follows. Indexed by author, title (in Spanish only), and subject.

Entries include author, title in Spanish and English, illustrator, translator, publisher and date, number of pages, ISBN, price, and suggested grade level. Most books, in print in 1986, were published in the United States, Spain, Mexico, and Argentina. Descriptive annotations provide brief plot summaries or commentaries on nonfiction, note titles containing materials of particular interest to the Hispanic world, and indicate negative features (e.g., "poor binding," "insipid illustrations").

There is a great deal of overlap between this work and Schon's *Books in Spanish for Children and Young Adults*, but this is a useful bibliography for libraries serving Spanish-speaking children or developing collections to support programs in Spanish as a second language. [R: ARBA 87; BL, 1 Mar 87]

E+
84   Schon, Isabel. **Books in Spanish for Children and Young Adults: An Annotated Guide, Series V**. Metuchen, N.J.: Scarecrow, 1989. 180p. $20.00. ISBN 0-8108-2238-5. LC 89-10526.

85   Schon, Isabel. **Books in Spanish for Children and Young Adults: An Annotated Guide, Series IV**. Metuchen, N.J.: Scarecrow, 1987. 301p. $29.50. ISBN 0-8108-2004-8. LC 87-9785.

86   Schon, Isabel. **Books in Spanish for Children and Young Adults: An Annotated Guide, Series III**. Metuchen, N.J.: Scarecrow, 1985. 208p. $16.50. ISBN 0-8108-1807-8. LC 85-2196.

87   Schon, Isabel. **Books in Spanish for Children and Young Adults: An Annotated Guide, Series II**. Metuchen, N.J.: Scarecrow, 1983. 162p. $15.00. ISBN 0-8108-1620-2. LC 83-3315.

88   Schon, Isabel. **Books In Spanish for Children and Young Adults: An Annotated Guide, Series I**. Metuchen, N.J.: Scarecrow, 1978. 165p. $15.00. ISBN 0-8108-1176-6. LC 78-10299.

The five volumes in this series are critical guides to books written in Spanish for children in preschool through high school. Included are fiction and nonfiction, plus bilingual books and translations. The arrangement is by country of origin (e.g., South and Central American countries), subdivided by broad categories (e.g., fiction, folklore). Books are described and rated as outstanding, marginal, not recommended, or *caveat emptor*. A suggested grade level is also given. Indexed by author/title and supported by a list of U.S. book dealers who specialize in Spanish books. This series is a useful selection tool for librarians who need to build their collection of Spanish-language materials. [R: ARBA 90]

E
89   Winkel, Lois, and S. Kimmel. **Mother Goose Comes First: An Annotated Guide to the Best Books and Recordings for Your Preschool Child**. New York: Henry Holt, 1990. 194p. $14.95pa. ISBN 0-8050-1001-7. LC 89-26833.

Winkel, a former editor of *The Elementary School Library Collection*, and Kimmel identify over 700 titles they believe are especially worthwhile for the very young child (infancy to age five). Entries for in-print books are divided into 10 broad subject categories such as folktales and contemporary classics. They include title, illustrator, publisher, date, pagination, illustrations, availability of hardcover or paperback, and a brief description. If a recorded version or a read-along kit is available, it is noted. Indexed by author/illustrator/performer and title. This guide is intended for parents, but it is equally useful to those who work with young children. [R: ARBA 92]

High/Low Lists

E +
90   **Choices: A Core Collection for Young Reluctant Readers. Volume 2.** Julie Cummins and Blair Cummins, eds. Evanston, Ill.: John Gordon Burke, 1990. 544p. $45.00. ISBN 0-934272-22-0. (P.O. Box 1492, Evanston, IL 60204-1492).

This compilation supplements volume 1 (John Gordon Burke, 1983) and describes 275 titles published between 1983 and 1988 that are recommended for reluctant readers grades 1-6. The first section, arranged by author, gives bibliographic data and an annotation of 70-300 words that covers the plot, strengths, weaknesses, interest, reading level, and subject headings. The main section repeats the entries as described but arranges the books by subject, using genre and Sears subject headings. A separate section lists 25 bestsellers.

The book's caveats include the unnecessary repetition of complete entries in part 2 and its small, dim type. Recommended for elementary and junior high school libraries. [R: ARBA 92; JOYS, Winter 91]

91   LiBretto, Ellen V. **High/Low Handbook: Encouraging Literacy in the 1990s.** 3d ed. New Providence, N.J.: R. R. Bowker, 1990. 290p. $39.95. ISBN 0-8352-2804-5. LC 90-53823.

This guide addresses the needs of disabled (reading at lower than a fourth-grade level) or reluctant-to-read junior and senior high school students. It is divided into three parts. The first, "Serving the High/Low Reader," contains essays on literacy efforts, writing for reluctant readers, reading with closed-caption television, and the California Reading Initiative. Part 2, on selecting and evaluating high/low material, includes four essays, two only slightly revised from the last edition, that cover computers, readability factors, magazines for reluctant readers, and using audiovisuals.

The heart of the book, part 3, annotates 312 titles recommended for independent reading. Books, on a first- to fifth-grade reading level, are primarily fiction. The author has attempted to select titles about adolescent American experiences as well as those of interest to diverse ethnic groups. Entries, arranged by author, include bibliographic and order information, subject headings (new to this edition), a brief plot description, an analysis of the theme, and citations to similar titles. About one-fifth of the titles are new to this edition.

Two appendixes list about 100 books that have been used successfully with students who read on a fourth- to eighth-grade level, and cite bibliographies and sources of current reviews, covering professional tools. Indexing is by title, subject, reading level, and interest level. Recommended for junior and senior high schools. [R: ARBA 91; RBB, 1 Nov 90]

92   McBride, William G., ed. **High Interest Easy Reading: A Booklist for Junior and Senior High School Students.** 6th ed. Urbana, Ill.: National Council of Teachers of English, 1990. 133p. $7.95pa. ISBN 0-8141-2097-0. LC 90-6657.

Teenagers who are reluctant readers present a problem and a challenge to teachers, librarians, and parents. This bibliography, now in its 6th edition, cites books with special appeal, exciting stories with "suspenseful action and likeable characters," and others that address the everyday concerns of today's youth.

The more than 400 fiction and nonfiction titles are arranged under broad subject headings, such as fantasy and science fiction, love and friendships, ghosts and the supernatural, and humor. Citations include bibliographic and order information; annotations contain a brief summary of the story (or subject content) and always indicate the age of leading characters. Highly recommended. [R: ARBA 91]

E +
93   Pilla, Marianne Laino. **The Best: High/Low Books for Reluctant Readers.** Englewood, Colo.: Libraries Unlimited, 1990. $12.50. ISBN 0-87287-532-6. LC 90-5756.

This list of high interest-low vocabulary books for grades 3-12, selected for their literary quality, assists school media specialists in collection development and making recommendations to reluctant readers. For each of the carefully selected titles, it provides complete bibliographic data, a brief annotation, suggested subject headings, and reading/interest levels. Indexed by reading level and subject. Recommended.

The disk version, which may be customized to fit the library's collection and used to produce printed reading lists by subject or reading level, is available in three formats: Apple for AppleWorks ($16.00), Mac for Microsoft Works ($17.00), and IBM-ASCII comma delimited files ($16.50). [R: ARBA 91]

94   Ryder, Randall J., and others. **Easy Reading: Book Series and Periodicals for Less Able Readers**. 2d ed. Newark, Del.: International Reading Association, 1989. 90p. $24.95pa. ISBN 0-87207-234-7. LC 89-7642.
    This excellent bibliography critically reviews 44 book series and 15 periodicals that it recommends for the less able reader. Critiques include order information; reading/interest level; an overall annotation of the series or periodical, with descriptions of a representative book or article, including its length, number of words, and illustrations; availability of related cassettes, filmstrips, and so forth; a critical review that indicates the series/periodical's strengths and weaknesses; and a list of individual titles in the series, teacher's guides, and workbooks. Indexed by genre, ethnicity (Asian, Hispanic, Native American, and Caucasian), and reading/interest level. Recommended. [R: ARBA 91]

Young Adult Lists

See also **Reading Guidance** in **Literature**.

95   Biagini, Mary K. **A Handbook of Contemporary Fiction for Public Libraries and School Libraries**. Metuchen, N.J.: Scarecrow, 1989. 247p. $25.00. ISBN 0-8108-2275-X.
    This guide, designed to assist public and school librarians in selection and in advising readers, identifies fiction by authors who have gained prominence since World War II, plus a few older writers whose popularity has extended into contemporary times. Part 1 covers fiction by genre, such as spy stories and science fiction. Part 2 lists contemporary fiction writers by country of origin. An essay about the genre opens each section, followed by a bibliography of reference sources, the authors, and their books. A typical entry includes the author's name and dates, pseudonyms, and titles with their dates. Generous cross-referencing and indexing provide excellent access to the information.
    This work is similar to *Genreflecting* by Rosenberg and is recommended for high school libraries. [R: ARBA 91; RBB, 15 May 90]

96   **Books for the Teen Age**. New York: New York Public Library. annual. $6.00pa. (Office of Branch Libraries, 455 Fifth Ave., New York, NY 10016).
    Since 1929, the New York Public Library's Office of Branch Libraries has prepared this annual list of books for teenagers. The 1991 list consists of 1,250 titles, 350 of which are new and replace an equal number that have been deleted. The books are arranged under almost 50 headings, many of which address current concerns (e.g., AIDS, planet Earth, looking good, love and sex). Most of the books listed receive only brief notice, but a few important titles earn paragraph-long excerpts from reviews. This well-balanced list, useful in any library serving teenagers, is indexed by title. [R: ARBA 91; SLJ, June 91]

97   **Books for You: A Booklist for Senior High Students**. 10th ed. Richard F. Abrahamson and B. Carter, eds. Urbana, Ill.: National Council of Teachers of English, 1988. 507p. $13.95. ISBN 0-8141-0364-2. LC 88-25367.
    This work lists 1,200 titles, published between 1985 and 1987, that range in reading level from preteen to advanced. Titles are those that teenagers have enjoyed reading. Arranged by 35 subject categories related to teenage interests, the books also can be accessed by author and title indexes. Annotations, contributed by teenagers themselves, offer readable descriptions and indicate books written for mature readers and those that have language and scenes that could be offensive to some students. [R: ARBA 87; VOYA 89; WLB, Mar 86]

98   Carter, Betty, and R. F. Abrahamson. **Nonfiction for Young Adults: From Delight to Wisdom**. Phoenix, Ariz.: Oryx Press, 1990. 233p. $32.50pa. ISBN 0-89774-555-8. LC 90-7046.
    Nonfiction works "characterized by beautifully written prose, definable themes, unifying structure, and stimulating topics" constitute the focus of this work. Chapters on such topics as the reading interests of teenagers and using informational books to promote recreational reading alternate with those that explore ways to use nonfiction books effectively or that contain interviews with prominent authors (Milton Meltzer, James Cross Giblin, and Daniel and Susan Chen). Each chapter suggests many recommended titles, and those about authors end with bibliographies of their writings. Indexed. This excellent work is recommended for middle and high schools.

99   Estell, Doug, and others. **Reading Lists for College-Bound Students**. New York: Arco/Prentice Hall, 1990. 255p. $8.95pa. ISBN 0-13-635251-0. LC 90-293.

For the convenience of high school students who wish to get an early start on reading required by their chosen college, the compilers of this work have collected and reprinted the lists of books recommended by 103 colleges. These vary from a single title (the Bible) to "read whatever you wish." For students whose college plans are indefinite or whose choice is not included, a composite list of the 100 most often recommended works, annotated by the compilers, is included. [R: ARBA 91]

100   Kies, Cosette. **Supernatural Fiction for Teens: More Than 1300 Good Paperbacks to Read for Wonderment, Fear, and Fun**. 2d ed. Englewood, Colo.: Libraries Unlimited, 1992. 200p. $24.95pa. ISBN 0-87287-940-2.

Compiled for teenagers and those who work with them, the first edition of this bibliography presented 500 selected books of supernatural fiction. The 2d edition covers over 1,300 books. Criteria for inclusion are suitability for the age group and availability in paperback. Other requirements pertain to subject matter: the books are required to be either tales and legends with strong magical or occult elements, or to concern horror, parapsychology, or psychic phenomena. Fantasy and science fiction stories are excluded unless they have mystic/occult themes or concern lost worlds, time travel, or science gone awry.

Alphabetically arranged by author, entries include bibliographic information, a brief annotation, a code indicating reading level (young teens, teens, adults, or classic), notes on movie versions, and classification of book (e.g., ghosts, voodoo). Indexed by subject fields such as abominable snowman or Arthurian legend. Recommended for secondary libraries.

101   Walker, Elinor, comp. **Book Bait: Detailed Notes on Adult Books Popular with Young Adults**. 4th ed. Chicago: American Library Association, 1988. 166p. $10.95pa. ISBN 0-8389-0491-2. LC 88-987.

Fifteen teenagers in grades 7 through 9 have selected 96 works of fiction, biography, and nonfiction highlighted in this excellent guide. For each book the compiler discusses notable qualities, suggests passages for use in book talks, and briefly annotates additional genre titles. Some selections are carried over from the previous edition, but most are new recommendations. A subject index refers only to main entries, but a title index includes all books. This work is useful as a selection aid and guide to book talks for adolescents. [R: ARBA 89; BL, 1 Oct 88; VOYA, Feb 89]

E+
102   **Your Reading: A Booklist for Junior High and Middle School Students**. 8th ed. Edited by Alleen Pace Nilson and Committee on the Junior High and Middle School Booklist of the NCTE. Urbana, Ill.: National Council of Teachers of English, 1991. 494p. $16.95pa. ISBN 0-8141-5940-0. LC 91-23533.

Many new categories have been added to this edition of a standard list that is designed to encourage students to read. Among the new areas covered are abuse, Black experiences, computers, ecology, and picture books for older readers. The guide annotates some 3,000 fiction and nonfiction titles that represent a broad spectrum of interests and reading levels. The work continues to be an excellent reference for grades 5 through 9. [R: ARBA 92]

COMPUTER SOFTWARE

Review Journals

■ *The Book Report*. *See* entry 1.

■ *Booklist*. *See* entry 2.

E+
103   **Computing Teacher: Journal of the International Society for Technology in Education**. Eugene, Oreg.: ISTE, 1979- . 8 issues/yr. $28.50/yr. w/membership. (1787 Agate St., Eugene, OR 97403-1923).

Level: Elementary through high school.

Focus: The use of computers for instructional use; articles about computers in education, classroom-tested projects; reviews of computer programs designed for instruction.

Reviews: Long, signed reviews provide descriptions and evaluations of software; give producer, age group, subject, system and hardware requirements, cost, strengths and weaknesses, and user comments.

Print: None.

Nonprint: Software.

Features: Articles and columns on particular subject areas, such as language arts, LOGO, science, mathematics, telecommunications, equity, and international connections.

Note: Members also receive *ISTE Update* (8 times/yr.), which contains articles by a broad range of leaders in the field of technology in education, and *Journal of Research on Computing in Education* (4 times/yr.), offering articles on research and development systems and project evaluations.

■ *Curriculum Review*. *See* entry 4.

104 **Electronic Learning**. Jonathan Goodspeed, ed. New York: Scholastic, 1981- . 8 times/yr. (monthly Sept. through Apr., bimonthly Nov./Dec. and May/June). $23.95/yr. (P.O. Box 2041, Mahopac, NY 10541).

Level: Elementary and secondary schools.

Focus: Nontechnical articles of general interest to teachers who are not computer specialists, ideas that work, special reports, industry news, software reviews.

Reviews: A buyer's guide for learning-disabled elementary children that reviews software for science, mathematics, and other areas; reviews of software for elementary, middle, and high school classrooms, each section addressing from two to six programs and including order information; "Spotlight On" covers one or more software packages that can be used at several levels; "Software At-a-Glance," contains shorter reviews of three or four programs for various levels.

Print: Reviews one or more books on electronic learning.

Features: Industry news, research, special reports.

■ *Media & Methods*. *See* entry 6.

■ *School Library Journal*. *See* entry 7.

■ *Science Books & Films*. *See* entry 8.

105 **Technology & Learning** (formerly *Classroom Computer Learning*). Holly Brady, ed. Dayton, Ohio: Peter Li, Inc., 1980- . 8 issues/yr. monthly except June-Aug., and Dec. $24.00/yr. (2451 E. River Rd., Dayton, OH 45439).

Level: Elementary and secondary schools.

Focus: Articles on use of technology in schools to restructure education; the merger of the computer with video and other technologies; software reviews; new hardware, software, peripherals, and publications.

Reviews: Four or five signed software and multimedia reviews per issue; 750-1,000 word reviews give hardware requirements, emphasis, grade level, and publisher with address and telephone number; description of software manuals and guides; overall rating; detailed description, strengths, weaknesses, comments, and name of evaluator.

Print: None.

Nonprint: Microcomputer software, multimedia.

Features: "What's New" is a description of newest educational materials; "Reader Inquiry" provides free information on the newest products; "Industry News"; "Newsline."

Reviews

106 Nicholls, Paul T. **CD-ROM Collection Builder's Toolkit: The Complete Handbook of Tools for Evaluating CD-ROMs**. Weston, Conn.: Pemberton Press, 1990. 180p. $29.95pa. ISBN 0-910965-01-3. (11 Tannery Lane, Weston, CT 06883).

This handbook evaluates CD-ROM products and provides guidelines for evaluation and selection. The main section profiles 67 CD-ROM products designed for reference and research in different types of libraries, including those in schools. Profiles give publisher, hardware requirements, software, frequency of update, price, order information, an evaluative description, a one- to four-star rating, and citations of other reviews. Some profiles also include a sample screen. Other features include a survey of CD-ROM products and their library applications; a list of directories and catalogs; a list of journals, newsletters, and selection tools; and an extensive bibliography.

107   **Software Reviews on File**. New York: Facts on File. monthly. $195.00/yr. includes binder.
This monthly file reviews over 600 software programs per year—educational, word processing, computer graphics, recreational, business, personal, and more—designed for all major microcomputer systems and languages. Each 64-page issue condenses reviews of 50 new software programs published in 125 journals. Each monthly issue contains cumulative indexing by subject and computer (e.g., IBM, Apple, Macintosh). The entries for each program include publisher, address, and price; a lengthy publisher's description; and a 100-word condensation of reviews, citing journal, date, page, and name of reviewer. [R: ARBA 86; WLB, June 85]

Review Indexes/Digests

E+
108   **Digest of Software Reviews: Education**. Ann Lathrop, ed. Fresno, Calif.: School and Home Courseware, 1983- . monthly. $147.50 looseleaf. (3999 N. Chestnut, Suite 333, Fresno, CA 93726-4797).
Each year the *Digest* reviews some 300 instructional software programs designed for students in grades K-12. Each entry is printed on a single looseleaf page labeled with its curricular area for easy filing. Uniform descriptions give title, author, producer and address, copyright, price, system requirements, contents, publisher's suggested grade level and group size, instructional mode, DDC number, and Sears subject headings. A lengthy publisher's description follows, along with 50- to 100-word excerpts from published reviews (a minimum of two required for inclusion).
"Editor's Choice" items are considered unique, innovative, or of outstanding quality. Each issue also includes guest editorials by educators in the field of instructional computing. Subject, microcomputer, title, and publisher indexes cumulate with each issue. Recommended.

Trade Bibliographies

■ *Microcomputer Software Sources*. *See* entry 116.

109   **Scholastic Software Catalog, K-12, 1990-91**. Jefferson City, Mo.: Scholastic Inc., 1991. 126p. free. (P.O. Box 7502, Jefferson City, MO 65102).
This catalog describes software programs recommended by the Scholastic National Advisor Board for grades K-12 and that are available through Scholastic Inc. Descriptions are arranged by curricular areas (e.g., Language Arts, Science, Social Sciences) and by skills (e.g., critical thinking, computer literacy). In each section, a chart lists products by curricular topic, developmental skills, and hardware (Apple, Macintosh, MD-DOS, and Commodore). Each entry gives description, grade level, price, and producer. Indexed by title and subject.

110   **The Software Encyclopedia**. New Providence, N.J.: R. R. Bowker. annual. $189.95/set.
This bibliography is to software as *Books in Print* is to books. The 1990 edition provides annotated listings for 21,192 software programs (3,448 new and 6,129 updated) indexed by title and by compatible system and application. Among those for new products are 201 publishing-related programs, 179 word processing and related programs, 87 database programs, and 94 spreadsheet programs. This annually updated work is considered the most comprehensive and current list available.
Microcomputer Software Guide Online is available through Dialog, File #278, $60.00 per connect hour, plus minimal charge for display. [R: VOYA, Apr 90]

Selection Aids

See also **Computers and Electronics**.

111   **Guide to Free Computer Materials**. Randolph, Wis.: Educators Progress Service. annual. $36.95pa. (214 Center St., Randolph, WI 53956).
Some 250 free computer brochures, programs, booklets, demonstration software, and catalogs are listed in each annual. The materials, classified according to type or field (e.g., hardware, software, systems, business, communications), are nonevaluative. Indexed by title, subject, and source. [R: ARBA 90]

E+

112   Neill, Shirley Boes, and George W. Neill. **Only the Best 1985-89: The Cumulative Guide to Highest-Rated Educational Software, Preschool-Grade 12**. New Providence, N.J.: R. R. Bowker, 1989. 313p. $49.95. ISBN 0-8352-2851-7.

113   Neill, Shirley Boes, and George W. Neill. **Only the Best: The Annual Guide to Highest-Rated Educational Software, Preschool-Grade 12**. New Providence, N.J.: R. R. Bowker. annual. $29.95pa.
       These excellent selection guides identify the best educational software indicated by 37 highly authoritative sources (e.g., the U.S. Department of Education, state educational agencies, the Educational Software Evaluation Consortium's "Preview Guide"). The first volume (1985-1989) recommends and describes the best 500 programs on the market. The 1991 annual adds some 200 programs (from among over 8,000 evaluated). Each entry provides a brief description that notes system compatibility, subject areas, grade level recommendation, order information, annotation, and citations of reviews. *Only the Best* purchasers receive a twice-yearly ALERT service, which highlights promising programs. [R: ARBA 90]

114   **Software Information! for Apple II Computers**. Pittsburgh, Pa.: Black Box, 1990. 829p. $19.95pa. ISBN 0-942821-18-1.
       This directory lists 12,000 programs for Apple II computers arranged in eight categories: productivity, education, industries, personal activities, entertainment, science, professions, and systems (e.g., programming language, operating systems). For each listing it gives name, address, system information, disk medium, RAM requirements, a brief description, ISPN (International Standard Program Number), and price. A list of publishers with addresses and telephone numbers concludes the volume.
       The directory is also available online through Dialog and Applelink and is promised on CD-ROM. Recommended. [R: ARBA 91]

E+

115   **T.E.S.S.: The Educational Software Selector**. Hampton Bay, N.Y.: EPIE Institute. annual. $49.95. (103-3 W. Montauk Highway, Hampton Bay, NY 11946).
       The 1991-1992 edition of T.E.S.S. lists some 3,000 currently available educational software, plus a group of 530 "classics," programs that have been particularly popular with reviewers and educators. There also are 79 entries for administrative software. T.E.S.S. provides descriptions in terms of educational philosophy, subject and grade levels, instruction methods, and hardware requirements. This is a useful quick reference to educational courseware. It is available through CompuServe and updated bimonthly. [R: ARBA 85; LJ, 15 Apr 84; SLJ, Sept 84]

E+

116   Truett, Carol. **Microcomputer Software Sources: A Guide for Buyers, Librarians, Programmers, Businesspeople, and Educators**. Englewood, Colo.: Libraries Unlimited, 1990. 176p. $28.50pa. ISBN 0-87287-560-1. LC 90-6240.
       Microcomputer Software Sources is divided into eight sections. The first two focus on the software industry and its sources—journals, newsletters, books, indexes, and abstracting services. Sections 3 through 5 cover business, education, and library applications and include general guides and specific subject resources for each area.
       Guides to machine-specific software (e.g., Apple II, Atari, DEC, IBM and compatibles) comprise section 6. Section 7 lists guides to inexpensive and free software. The final section cites directories, handbooks, journals, and newsletters for those who wish to market their own software. Appendixes include a number of evaluation worksheets and checklists to use before purchasing software packages. An index concludes the volume. [R: ARBA 91; LJ, 1 Oct 90]

GOVERNMENT PUBLICATIONS

E+

117   Bailey, William G. **Guide to Popular U.S. Government Publications**. 2d ed. Englewood, Colo.: Libraries Unlimited, 1990. 314p. $35.00. ISBN 0-87287-796-5. LC 90-5726.
       LeRoy Schwarzkopf's initial edition of this guide identified and described informative and useful government publications that appeared between June 1978 and June 1985. The 2d edition continues the same tradition and includes some 2,500 publications published between June 1985 and the end of June 1989. All are available from the Government Printing Office, various issuing agencies, or the Consumer

Information Center. Noteworthy titles published prior to 1985 (but no earlier than 1980) that are still available are also listed.

Entries are alphabetically arranged by title under topics such as aging and problems of the elderly, careers and occupations, and energy. Each entry provides bibliographic information (title, issuing agency, and date), illustrative material, stock number, price, and SuDocs classification number. Additional features are instructions for acquiring government publications, an explanation of the role of depository libraries, a guide to common government abbreviations and initialisms, and a list of selected agency publication catalogs. Recommended for all levels. [R: ARBA 91; BL, 1 Nov 90; VOYA, Dec 90; WLB, Oct 90]

118   Ekhaml, Leticia T., and Alice J. Wittig. **U.S. Government Publications for the School Library Media Center**. 2d ed. Englewood, Colo.: Libraries Unlimited, 1991. 156p. $22.50. ISBN 0-87287-822-8.

This 2d edition of a popular quick reference guide identifies 500 government publications that are potentially useful in school libraries and classrooms. Part 1 provides a brief history of government printing, explains the SuDocs Classification and depository systems, and suggests basic reference tools that provide access to government documents.

The annotated bibliography of selected publications in part 2, arranged by subject (accidents to zoos), includes books, posters, sound recordings, microfiche, pamphlets, coloring books, decals, and mobiles. Each entry includes grade level suitability and bibliographic/order information. Appendixes list GPO bookstores, agencies distributing publications not sold by GPO, suggestions for using government publications, and GPO bestsellers. Indexed by title and subject. [R: ARBA 92]

119   **Monthly Catalog of United States Government Publications**. Superintendent of Documents, U.S. Government Printing Office. Washington, D.C.: Government Printing Office, 1895- . monthly. $185.00/yr. LC 4-18088.

This catalog lists and indexes current publications of the major branches, departments, and bureaus of the U.S. government. The format has changed over the years, but at the present time it is arranged according to the SuDocs classification system. A Library of Congress catalog-card format uses Anglo-American Cataloging Rules (AACR2) and LC subject headings, supplemented by depository and order information. Only those documents with stock numbers (S/N) are sold by SuDocs. Separate indexes in each issue, cumulated annually, give access to authors, titles, subjects, and series numbers. A serial supplement is issued each spring. Each issue also gives locations of government bookstores and over 1,400 depository libraries. *Monthly Catalog* is also available online through Dialog and BRS.

120   **New Books: Publications for Sale by the Government Printing Office**. Superintendent of Documents, U.S. Government Printing Office. Washington, D.C.: Government Printing Office, 1982- . quarterly. free. (Government Printing Office, Washington, DC 20402).

New Books lists GPO publications under 17 subject headings—agriculture through transportation—and then alphabetically by title within each category. Information given includes title, issuing agency and date, paging, SuDocs number, stock number, and price. The quarterly lacks annotations and an index. A "Best Sellers" list of 10 to 12 titles and an order form conclude the small paperback.

121   Schwarzkopf, LeRoy C., comp. **Government Reference Books 88/89: A Biennial Guide to U.S. Government Publications**. Englewood, Colo.: Libraries Unlimited, 1990. 368p. $55.00. ISBN 0-87287-849-X. ISSN 0072-5188. LC 76-146307.

Since its start in 1970, this biennial has listed and described hundreds of documents in each of its 11 volumes. Reference publications, from pamphlets and folders to multivolume sets, are arranged in four sections: general library reference, social sciences, science and technology, and humanities. All cite atlases, bibliographies, catalogs, compendiums, dictionaries, directories, guides, handbooks, indexes, and other reference tools. Serials, except those of a monographic nature, such as *Yearbook of Agriculture*, are now listed in a separate work, *Government Reference Serials* (Libraries Unlimited, 1988).

Annotated entries include detailed bibliographic citations, LC card numbers, ISBNs and ISSNs, OCLC numbers, *Monthly Catalog* numbers, GPO stock numbers, current price as of date of publication, and SuDocs classification numbers. School districts should hold this guide for the use of their school media centers. [R: ARBA 91]

122   **Subject Bibliography Index**. Superintendent of Documents, U.S. Government Printing Office. Washington, D.C.: Government Printing Office. free. (Government Printing Office, Washington, DC 20402).

This free index lists more than 250 subject bibliographies (also free) that give titles of selected publications on popular topics such as smoking, drugs, and aging. The index is designed as an order form for requesting the bibliographies.

123 **U.S. Government Books**. Superintendent of Documents, U.S. Government Printing Office. Washington, D.C.: Government Printing Office, 1982- . quarterly. free. (Government Printing Office, Washington, DC 20402).

This free catalog cites and annotates about 1,000 government publications, arranged topically (e.g., agriculture, business and industry, careers, consumer aids). It also gives order information, including stock number and SuDocs classification number. Each issue begins with a "Recent Releases" section. Dates of other publications vary. An order form with instructions concludes each issue.

PAMPHLETS AND FREE MATERIALS

E+

124 **Educators Guide to Free Teaching Aids**. Randolph, Wis.: Educators Progress Service. annual. $43.95.

125 **Educators Index to Free Materials**. Randolph, Wis.: Educators Progress Service. annual. $45.75.

E+

126 **Elementary Teachers Guide to Free Curricular Materials**. Randolph, Wis.: Educators Progress Service. annual. $23.75. (214 Center St., Randolph, WI 53956).

These annual guides list free teaching aids sponsored by trade and professional organizations, companies, foreign countries, and associations. They cover a wide range of curricular areas and cite and annotate materials under broad subject headings. Each item is checked for availability and educational value.

Free Teaching Aids is a looseleaf book covering pamphlets, pictures, and charts for all grade levels. *Free Mateirals*, also looseleaf, covers the same type of aids for high schools and colleges. *Elementary Teachers*, a bound volume, lists materials for elementary and middle school levels. Other EPS guides cover curricular areas, such as science and social sciences, and formats such as film, filmstrips and slides, and audio and video materials.

127 **Vertical File Index: A Subject and Title Index to Selected Pamphlet Material**. Bronx, N.Y.: H. W. Wilson, 1932- . monthly (except Aug.). $45.00/yr. Available Dec. 1985- online.

Pamphlet materials are an essential part of most library collections, since they often provide the most current information on many topics for the least expense. *Vertical File Index* focuses on free and inexpensive publications (e.g., pamphlets, maps, charts, posters) on occupations, hobbies, nutrition, health, consumer issues, tourist guides, and similar topics. It includes many government publications.

The index is arranged alphabetically by subject and supported by a title index. It provides order information and short descriptions for most items. The reader should be aware, however, that inclusion does not assure quality or usefulness.

PERIODICALS

128 Katz, Bill, and Linda Sternberg Katz. **Magazines for Libraries**. 6th ed. New Providence, N.J.: R. R. Bowker, 1989. 1159p. $124.95. ISBN 0-8352-2632-8.

Magazines for Young People should meet the needs of most school libraries, but when a special need arises, librarians should turn to *Magazines for Libraries*. This work, last revised in 1982, provides descriptions of 6,521 magazines and periodicals listed under 139 subject headings. Some 2,000 titles are new to this edition; older entries have been updated to reflect current editorial policy, content, and relevancy to today's needs. Entries give full bibliographic data; frequency; cost; size of circulation; where indexed; type of intended audience; and availability of microform, microfiche, or online. [R: ARBA 90; LJ, 15 Oct 89; RBB, 15 Nov 89]

E+

129 Katz, Bill, and Linda Sternberg Katz. **Magazines for Young People: A Children's Magazine Guide Companion Volume**. 2d ed. New Providence, N.J.: R. R. Bowker, 1991. 250p. $49.95. ISBN 0-8352-3009-0.

Formerly *Magazines for School Libraries*, this guide evaluates over 1,100 magazines appropriate for preschool through high school levels. The titles include curriculum-related periodicals, others of general interest, and professional journals directed toward educators.

An introduction and core list of titles preface each of the 60 subject areas. Entries contain the beginning year of publication; frequency; cost; address; presence of illustrations, advertising, and an index; circulation; availability in other formats; indexing elsewhere; inclusion of book reviews; and suggested library level. The evaluations indicate strengths, weaknesses, and political bias. This work is the most current magazine selection aid available. [R: RBB, 15 Sept 91]

E+

130   Richardson, Selma K. **Magazines for Children: A Guide for Parents, Teachers, and Librarians**. 2d ed. Chicago: American Library Association, 1991. 139p. $19.95. ISBN 0-8389-0552-8. LC 90-45152.

Some 90 magazines for children, preschool through eighth grade, are described in this useful guide, first published in 1983. About one-third of the titles are new (e.g., *Sports Illustrated for Kids, Ladybug*); they replace roughly the same number of magazines that have ceased publication. Long entries (up to three pages) give a detailed profile of a recent issue, indicate whether the title is indexed in *Children's Magazine Index*, and give appropriate age or grade level. Appendixes include magazines listed by when they began, circulation size, and age/grade level; magazines from religious publishing houses; and titles available for the visually impaired. Indexed by subject.

Magazines for Libraries lists more than 1,000 periodicals for preschool through high school. The work's annotations are briefer but more critical than those found in Richardson's work. Both are recommended, the latter for elementary and junior high schools only. [R: ARBA 92; JOYS, Summer 91; RBB, 1 Mar 91]

131   **Standard Periodical Directory**. 14th ed. Matthew Manning, ed. New York: Oxbridge Communications; distr., Detroit: Gale, 1991. 1822p. $325.00. ISBN 0-917460-30-8. LC 64-7598.

This is a directory of 70,000 United States and Canadian periodicals arranged under 230 subject headings. It covers newspapers, consumer magazines, trade journals, newsletters, government serials, house organs, directories, and other regularly issued (at least every two years) publications. It provides complete bibliographic and order information for each periodical. An exhaustive title index and cross-index to subjects provide access to the periodicals.

Ulrich's International Periodical Directory (R. R. Bowker, 1990-1991) is far more extensive (and, of course, international in coverage), listing nearly 120,000 regularly and irregularly issued serials.

General Reference

GUIDES

132 American Reference Books Annual. Bohdan S. Wynar, ed. in chief. Anna Grace Patterson, ed. Englewood, Colo.: Libraries Unlimited. annual. $85.00. ISSN 0065-9959. LC 75-120328.

133 Index to American Reference Books Annual, 1985-1989: A Cumulative Index to Subjects, Authors, and Titles. By Anna Grace Patterson. Englewood, Colo.: Libraries Unlimited, 1989. 275p. $55.00. ISBN 0-87287-793-0. LC 75-120328.

Published annually since 1970, *ARBA* is considered the most comprehensive review source for reference materials published in North America. The 1991 edition consists of 1,833 reviews, arranged by subject, of reference books published or distributed in the United States or Canada.

The signed reviews, contributed by over 350 scholars, librarians, and practitioners, give complete bibliographic and order information, a descriptive and critical evaluation, and citations to reviews in major journals. Author/title and subject indexes support each volume.

Cumulative indexes covering various intervals, such as that for 1985-1989, are available for all annuals since 1970. *Recommended Reference Books for Small and Medium-sized Libraries and Media Centers* is an abridged version of *ARBA*. *Best Reference Books, 1986-1990* identifies sources of lasting value. [R: BL, 1 June 83]

134 Best Reference Books, 1986-1990: Titles of Lasting Value Selected from *American Reference Books Annual*. G. Kim Dority, comp. Bohdan S. Wynar, ed. Englewood, Colo.: Libraries Unlimited, 1992. 550p. $58.00. ISBN 0-87287-936-4.

Some 1,000 titles of outstanding and enduring value have been selected from *ARBA* 1987-1991, covering imprints of 1986-1990. The reviews appearing in the annual volumes have been updated and, in some instances, rewritten in order to cover the expanded content of new editions. Additional citations and price changes have also been added. *Best Reference Books, 1981-1985* (Libraries Unlimited, 1986) includes titles of lasting value from the earlier period.

135 General Reference Books for Adults: Authoritative Evaluations of Encyclopedias, Atlases, and Dictionaries. Marion Sader, ed. New Providence, N.J.: R. R. Bowker, 1988. 614p. $69.95. ISBN 0-8352-2393-0. LC 88-10054.

This work evaluates more than 200 U.S. general reference sources (print materials, online and CD-ROM products) for adults. It applies accepted standards and criteria to general encyclopedias, world atlases, dictionaries and word books, and large-print reference books. Reviews vary from one or two pages to eight pages and cite additional review sources. This guide, a valuable selection tool for high school libraries, is revised triennially. [R: ARBA 89; LJ, Dec 88; RBB, 15 Jan 89; SLJ, May 89; WLB, Nov 88]

136 Hede, Agnes Ann. Reference Readiness: A Manual for Librarians and Students. 4th ed. Hamden, Conn.: Library Professional Publications/Shoe String Press, 1990. 206p. $29.50; $21.00pa. ISBN 0-208-02228-7; 0-208-02229-5pa. LC 90-30394.

Last revised in 1977, this work lists basic reference sources and explains the usefulness of each type. Similar to traditional guides of this genre, the volume is arranged by category (e.g., dictionaries, encyclopedias, handbooks). Each begins with an explanation of the functions of the type of source, followed by a number of examples. For each suggested reference work, full bibliographic data and a detailed description are provided.

New to this edition are several chapters about electronic sources available to small libraries, such as online search services and CD-ROMs. As practical exercises, each chapter contains search questions.

This is a valuable guide for any high school's library support staff, persons with limited reference experience, or those who wish to review basic reference tools. [R: ARBA 91; RBB, Aug 90]

137   Katz, William A. **Introduction to Reference Work**. 5th ed. New York: McGraw-Hill, 1987. 2v. $39.95/v. ISBN 0-07-033537-0(v.1); 0-07-033538-9(v.2).

This standard textbook, divided into two volumes, *Basic Information Sources* and *Reference Services and Reference Processes*, covers all aspects of reference sources and services. The first volume is a guide to basic reference books, grouped by type, and computer-assisted reference services. The second volume concerns the principles and practices of reference service.

138   **Recommended Reference Books for Small and Medium-sized Libraries and Media Centers**. Bohdan S. Wynar, ed. Englewood, Colo.: Libraries Unlimited. annual. $38.50. ISSN 0277-5948. LC 81-12394.

This valuable guide to reference sources addresses the needs of small and medium-sized libraries of all types. It includes reviews of 550 titles published or distributed in the United States during 1990. The reviews, written by over 200 librarians, subject specialists, and library educators, are selected from the most recent edition of *American Reference Books Annual*.

Clearly written analytical reviews that consist of several paragraphs are arranged in four major groups—general works, social sciences, humanities, and science and technology—and then by specific subject. Symbols indicate suitability for college, public, or school libraries. Indexing is by author/title and subject.

139   **Reference Books Bulletin, 1989-90: A Compilation of Evaluations Appearing in Reference Books Bulletin, September 1, 1989-August 1990**. Sandy Whiteley, ed. Penny Spokes, comp. Chicago: American Library Association, 1990. 227p. $22.50pa. ISBN 0-8389-3392-0. LC 73-159565.

This compilation of reviews of reference sources found in *Reference Books Bulletin* [the journal], from September 1, 1989 through August 1990, continues a series that began in 1969. Each compilation contains unsigned reviews (a group effort of the Reference Bulletin Editorial Board), ranging from a paragraph to a page and providing detailed analysis and criticism. Omnibus articles, which have appeared in recent compilations, cover several topics and provide succinct annotations for the sources listed. Among the topics included in 1989-1990 are reference books for young children; reference books on the Bible, genealogy, and antiques; and an update on encyclopedias. Indexing provides access by subject, type of material, and title. This convenient compilation of reviews in *RBB* is an indispensable tool for developing reference collections. [R: ARBA 92]

E+

140   **Reference Books for Children's Collections**. Compiled by the Children's Reference Committee, the New York Public Library. Dolores Vogliano, ed. New York: Office of Children's Services of the New York Public Library, 1988. 79p. (455 Fifth Ave., New York, NY 10016).

The 362 titles in this guide are reference books of the highest quality "that will be of use in the widest variety of children's rooms." The source is intended for use by parents, teachers, librarians, and others involved in meeting the reference needs of children. Most titles were in print at the time of publication; those few that are out of print are so labeled.

The slim volume contains nine sections that begin with general reference and religion, and end with sports and recreation and literature. These broad units, in turn, are subdivided into specific areas. Information for each entry includes basic bibliographic data, cost, and a brief annotation. Indexed by author/title. Highly recommended.

141   **Spanish-Language Reference Books: An Annotated Bibliography**. Compiled by Bibliotecas para la Gente Reference Committee. Berkeley, Calif.: Chicano Studies Library Publication Unit, 1988. 45p. (Chicano Studies Library Publications Series, no.15). $10.00pa. ISBN 0-918520-15-0. (3404 Dwinelle Hall, University of California at Berkeley, Berkeley, CA 74720).

Librarians requiring reference sources for Spanish-speaking patrons will find this bibliography useful. The 117 annotated listings—arranged by broad subject and indexed by title—include a wide range of sources. Each source's strengths and weaknesses are indicated. However, the list is limited to titles held by the California libraries of the compilers. The user also should be cautioned that some works are out of print, while others do not meet accepted standards for English-language tools or are poorly bound. This bibliography is unique. [R: BL, 1 Apr 89]

E+
142 Swidan, Eleanor. **Reference Sources: A Brief Guide**. 9th ed. Baltimore, Md.: Enoch Pratt Free Library, 1988. 175p. $7.95pa. ISBN 0-910556-26-1.

The latest update of this reference guide, first published in 1938, has changed its title to include *Reference Sources* instead of *Reference Books*, due to the addition of computerized databases and resources in microform. The guide is intended for the user who is bewildered "by the staggering array of reference works that confront him on the shelves of the library," and is meant to be suggestive rather than complete. It covers general reference books, the humanities, sciences, and social sciences. Materials in genealogy, medicine, and law are excluded. This guide continues to help librarians identify significant reference sources. [R: BL, 15 Nov 88; WLB, Nov 88]

ALMANACS AND FACT BOOKS

E+
143 Anthony, Susan C. **Facts Plus: An Almanac of Essential Information**. Anchorage, Alaska: Instructional Resources Company, 1991. 250p. $15.95pa. ISBN 1-879478-00-5. (1013 E. Diamond Blvd., #188, Anchorage, AK 99515).

Designed for children in grades 4 through 8, this almanac focuses on curricular needs. Among the topics covered are time zones, calendars, notables, countries of the world, inventions, and Indian tribes. There also are timelines of history and maps. These lists would be helpful in choosing report subjects. [R: BL, 1 June 91]

144 **Canadian Almanac and Directory**. Toronto: Canadian Almanac and Directory Publications; distr., Detroit: Gale. annual. $102.00.

This standard work provides an extensive list of business-directory information. The 1991 edition includes 9,000 provincial and national associations, giving postal codes; telephone, telex and fax numbers; and electronic mail addresses. Also listed are provincial government information; municipalities, listed by province; exhibition and show planners; and Canadian law firms. Conventional and topical tables of contents, an alphabetical listing, a "Frequently Used Information" index, and a keyword index all give access to the text.

145 **The Canadian World Almanac and Book of Facts 1991**. John Wilion, ed. Agincourt, Ont.: Global Press, 1990, 725p., $14.95pa. ISBN 0-7715-3975-4. ISSN 0833-532X.

Libraries requiring statistics, political and geographical data, and other facts about Canada will find this almanac useful. As the title states, it also provides international coverage for history, current events, sports, and other topics. World coverage largely duplicates that of other almanacs, however, making its Canadian material the featured attraction for U.S. libraries. The reasonably priced and well-organized work is extensively indexed.

E+
146 **Charts on File**. By the Diagram Group. New York: Facts on File, 1988. $145.00 looseleaf w/binder. ISBN 0-8160-1727-1. LC 87-36423.

Like others in the On File series, this looseleaf work is designed so that its contents can be reproduced for educational purposes. More than 300 black-and-white charts are arranged in 8 categories: physical science; earth science; life science; numbers; humanities; home economics and health; geography, geology, paleontology, and space; and general. *Charts on File* resembles both an almanac and an encyclopedia. Examples of almanac-type materials are a perpetual calendar, lists of birthstones, and conversion tables for units of measure. Encyclopedia-like data includes illustrations of how tides work, a musical conductor's hand movements, anatomical drawings, and the seals of the 50 states. The charts are indexed by subject. [R: BL, Aug 88; WLB, Sept 88]

147 **Chronicle of the Year, 1989**. New York: Simon & Schuster, 1990. 128p. $7.95pa. ISBN 0-13-133430-1.

A double-page spread for each week of the year summarizes major events and prints obituaries of notables, with an accompanying photograph on most pages. A separate section lists nations of the world, with a small map, flag, statistics, and an item of current interest. The abstracts and photographs should attract even the most reluctant readers. Highly recommended for secondary schools. [R: BR, Sept/Oct 90]

E+

148   **Current News on File**. New York: Facts on File, Sept. 1990- . biweekly (every 3 weeks in July and Aug.). $225.00/yr. w/binder.

This is a junior high school version of *Facts on File World News Digest*. It was started at the request of librarians who believed that the parent work was too sophisticated for young students who needed a news digest. The biweekly issues are written at a sixth- to seventh-grade reading level. Designed also to appeal to young readers, it contains illustrative materials, such as photographs, charts, political cartoons, graphs, and tables, and uses a large typeface. Similar to the *World News Digest*, it summarizes reports drawn from a variety of newspapers and magazines. The publisher supplies a toll-free number for customer support. Recommended for middle and junior high schools. [R: BL, 1 Apr 90]

E+

149   Elwood, Ann, and C. O. Madigan. **The Macmillan Book of Fascinating Facts: An Almanac for Kids**. New York: Macmillan, 1989. 436p. $16.95. ISBN 0-02-733461-9. LC 88-22844.

Begun in 1981 as *Almanac for Kids*, this work became *Macmillan Illustrated Almanac for Kids* in 1984. Its latest title is a fitting one, for it does indeed contain "fascinating facts" for students in grades 4 through 7. Topics range from the everyday concerns and interests of children (e.g., drug and alcohol abuse, ways to help people and animals in distress, starting a club, making a video) to trivia lists and interesting facts. This compendium not only serves as a good introduction to almanacs but also as a quick-reference tool. [R: ARBA 90; VOYA, Aug 89]

150   **Facts on File News Digest CD-ROM, 1980-1990**. New York: Facts on File, 1989. CD-ROM disk, software, and 64p. manual. $695.00/Facts on File subscribers. $795.00/nonsubscribers. System requirements: IBM/MS-DOS-based system—IBM PC, XT, AT, or compatible, or IBM PS/2, 640K, MS-DOS levels 3.1, 3.2, 3.3, or 4.0, hard disk, monitor with graphics capability, CD-ROM drive, microsoft extension (version 2.0 minimum), mouse, printer (optional). Macintosh system—Mac II, SE, or Plus; 1 MB memory; CD-ROM drive with SCSI interface; printer (optional).

The system contains 11 years of *Facts on File World News Digest*, over 500 detailed maps, and the cumulative index. Features include a tutorial, help screens, searching by key word (with Boolean logic), browsing the index, date-limited searching, *see also* cross-references, audit trail of searches, placemarking, full-text and map printouts, and customized printout setting. The service is updated annually with a new disk incorporating the last year of news.

151   **Facts on File World News Digest**. New York: Facts on File, 1940- . weekly. looseleaf w/annual volumes. $605.00/yr.

Facts on File, a weekly digest of news, draws its information from 75 of the most important newspapers and magazines from throughout the world. The arrangement is by broad areas, such as world affairs, national affairs, and U.S. affairs. A miscellaneous section reports on such things as sports, people, and deaths. Looseleaf, full-page political/physical maps in color are a part of the service. Indexes are published twice monthly and cumulated throughout the year.

The *Facts on File Yearbook* ($95.00/yr.) is a compilation of the 52 weekly digests and the annual index. *Facts on File* is available online through Dialog and as *Facts on File News Digest CD-ROM*. This is a basic, quick-reference source for high schools. A junior high school version, *Current News on File*, started in September 1990.

E+

152   Feldman, David. **Why Do Dogs Have Wet Noses? and Other Imponderables of Everyday Life**. New York: HarperPerennial/HarperCollins, 1990. 249p. $17.95. ISBN 0-06-016293-7.

This work is not a reference book in the true sense, but it will occasionally answer questions asked by curious children and young adults. As in Feldman's earlier work, *Imponderables: The Solution to the Mysteries of Everyday Life* (William Morrow, 1986), he uses questions and answers arranged in no predictable sequence to explain how rainfall is measured, why the cold water knob is on the right, and many other phenomena. Unlike his first work, this one is indexed, which helps to overcome its unorthodox arrangement. [R: RBB, 15 Sept 90]

153   **Great Disasters**. By the editors of *Reader's Digest*. New York: Reader's Digest, 1989. 320p. $28.95. ISBN 0-89577-321-X.

Essays on some 80 disasters that occurred from prehistoric times to 1988 are arranged by date in four sections. Included are earthquakes, tornadoes, hurricanes, volcanic eruptions, droughts, famines, and plagues. Each two- to four-page entry is enhanced by quotations and anecdotes. Illustrations include drawings and color photographs. A final chapter presents a retrospect and commentary. [R: BL, 15 Sept 89; LJ, 1 Oct 89; VOYA, Apr 90]

154   **The Guinness Book of Answers: The Complete Reference Handbook**. 8th ed. Enfield, England: Guinness; distr., New York: Sterling Publishing, 1991. 596p. $17.95. ISBN 0-85112-334-1.

This compendium contains useful information for junior and senior high school students at a reasonable price, but it is not an essential purchase. Its British origin is reflected in spelling variations and the amount of space devoted to the United Kingdom (80 pages) as compared to the United States (9 pages).

The *Book of Answers* focuses on 31 areas of knowledge, such as astronomy, plants and animals, the arts, sports, computers, and nations. An index provides easy access to the entries. Except for its British emphasis, it compares favorably with *The New York Public Library Desk Reference*, which it resembles, and offers accurate, easy-to-find, quick-reference information. [R: ARBA 90; BL, 1 Apr 90; BR, May/June 90; SLJ, May 90; WLB, Jan 91]

E +
155   **Guinness Book of Records**. New York: Facts on File. annual. $12.95. LC 65-24391.

A well-known guide to superlatives, this annual brings together new world records and feats of nature, human endurance, scientific achievement, entertainment, business, and sports. All are arranged under 12 broad headings and indexed by subject. Many of the records are useful for reference purposes, but some will interest only the browser. Needless to say, currency is important, and the work must be replaced annually. This is an essential holding for school libraries. [R: ARBA 90]

E +
156   **Information Please Almanac: The New Universe of Information**. Boston: Houghton Mifflin. annual. $17.95; $6.95pa. LC 47-845.

This well-known almanac, a spinoff of a popular radio show of the 1940s, covers a broad range of factual and statistical information, articles and listings on popular topics, and what could be termed "for the curious." Examples include information on AIDS, drugs (e.g., crack, cocaine), the 24 most influential scientific theories and discoveries, a list of banned books, a crossword puzzle guide, a guide to correct English, and a career-planning guide. These extras are unique features for almanacs. Much of the other statistical and factual material duplicates that available in *World Almanac*, its closest competitor. [R: ARBA 90]

E +
157   Kane, Joseph Nathan. **Famous First Facts**. 4th ed. Bronx, N.Y.: H. W. Wilson, 1981. 1350p. $80.00. ISBN 0-8242-0661-4. LC 81-3395.

This unusual work focuses on "firsts" on the North American continent (1,007 to date) that concern a wide range of subjects (e.g., events, inventions, discoveries) – 9,000 in all. Arrangement is by subject with appropriate cross-references and concise explanations for each entry. Indexing is by year and month/date of occurrence, names of persons directly and indirectly involved, and location of the event.

E +
158   **The New York Public Library Desk Reference**. New York: Webster's New World; distr., New York: Prentice Hall Press, 1989. 836p. $32.95. ISBN 0-13-620444-9.

An amazing collection of ready-reference information, this work is designed to answer the most frequently asked questions in general libraries. It is filled with facts, dates, terms, symbols, and information about people, events, movements, and discoveries. Arranged in 26 broad categories (e.g., weights and measures, the animal world), it offers graphs, boxed charts, sidebars, tables, and lists. Additional sources of information that follow each category include organizations, services, and a bibliography. Indexed.

Reviewers have noted errors of omission and commission, but the first edition of a work of this type always suffers from lacunae. *Desk Reference* is a reasonably priced and remarkable first effort that all libraries should hold. It is also fun to browse. [R: ARBA 91; BL, 1 Nov 89; Choice, Jan 90; SLJ, May 90]

159   **The Old Farmer's Almanack**. Dublin, N.H.: Yankee Publishing. annual. $2.50pa. (Main St., Dublin, NH 03444).

The oldest continuously published almanac in the United States, this popular work provides U.S. and regional weather forecasts based on a variety of techniques using astronomical and astrological data. Other sections provide a calendar of dates, feasts, and other phenomena; tide tables; eclipse schedules; star information; mathematical puzzles; and much more.

160   Robbins, Michael. **Top 10: The Best of Everything According to the Numbers**. New York: Workman. annual. $5.95pa. LC 90-50370.

This new annual, scheduled to go to press each February, is a compendium of superlatives (biggest, best, or most popular) on scores of topics from sports to entertainment and governments to demographics. The statistics are gathered and cited from the most authoritative sources in each field, making it valuable to the small library unable to afford such a variety of material. Indexing is by company, person, and field. [R: LJ, 15 June 91]

161   Slavens, Thomas. **Number One in the U.S.A.: Records and Wins in Sports, Entertainment, Business, and Science, with Sources Cited**. 2d ed. Metuchen, N.J.: Scarecrow, 1990. 175p. $22.50. ISBN 0-8108-2350-0. LC 90-42090.

This compilation of records and other accomplishments consists of four sections—sports, entertainment, business, and science—each arranged alphabetically by topic. Each entry includes a brief description of the record or event, followed by a full citation to its source. The information has been gleaned from a variety of magazines and newspapers, most of which were published during 1989. Much of the material, especially sports records and Academy Award winners, can be found in other library holdings. Nonetheless, this compilation is convenient for reference purposes and useful for browsing. The first edition was published in 1988. [R: BL, 1 Mar 89; VOYA, Apr 89]

E+
162   **The Universal Almanac**. John W. Wright, ed. Kansas City, Mo.: Andrews & McMeel. annual. $19.95; $9.95pa.

This new almanac, which began in 1990, includes some topics not found in the *World Almanac*, such as AIDS, the homeless, the Fortune 500, the Strategic Defense Initiative budget, foreign military aid, and the 50 largest toxic waste sites. The *World Almanac*, however, contains much information not found here. *Universal* deserves an accolade for its readability and good index. School libraries at all levels should hold it to supplement other standard almanacs. [R: ARBA 92; BL, 1 Mar 90; LJ, 1 Feb 90; SLJ, May 90]

163   **Whitaker's Almanac**. London: J. Whitaker; distr., Detroit: Gale. annual. $65.00.

Issued annually since 1869, this British counterpart of *World Almanac* emphasizes Great Britain, Commonwealth countries, and dependent territories. Here one finds extensive government information and statistics on such topics as housing, agriculture, employment, and shipping. There also are obituaries of notables, a directory of British royalty and peerage, literary and other types of prizes and awards, and much more. There is little duplication of material contained in American almanacs. Extensively indexed.

E+
164   **World Almanac and Book of Facts**. New York: World Almanac/Pharos Books; distr., New York: St. Martin's Press. annual. $14.95; $6.95pa. LC 4-3781.

Published since 1868, this best-known and most useful American almanac offers factual and statistical data on almost every area of human activity (e.g., agriculture, military affairs, sports, politics, manufacturing, nations of the world, education). It is worldwide in scope but strongest on topics related to the United States.

Among its many useful sections are a chronology of the previous year's events, consumer information (e.g., business directory, who owns what, mortgage payment tables), major actions of Congress and decisions of the Supreme Court for the previous year, obituaries of deceased notables, and tax information. Other regular features include color reproductions of the flags of 160 nations and a chronology of world history. Highly recommended for all levels. [R: Kliatt, Jan 90]

CHRONOLOGIES

E+
165 Wetterau, Bruce. **The New York Public Library Book of Chronologies: The Ultimate One-Volume Collection of Dates, Events, People, and Pastimes**. New York: Prentice Hall Press, 1990. 634p. $29.95. ISBN 0-13-620451-1. LC 90-46768.

This book provides over 233 chronologies divided into 13 categories (e.g., explorers and exploration, nations and empires). It also includes a unique section: "Necessities to Notoriety." Each entry briefly describes the topic, and a detailed index gives access to the text. There are some inconsistencies and omissions, but overall this is a worthwhile general source. Recommended for all levels. [R: ARBA 91; LJ, Jan 91; RBB, 15 Dec 90; SLJ, May 91]

DICTIONARIES

General

166 **The Harper Dictionary of Modern Thought**. 2d ed. Alan Bullock and Stephen Trombley, eds. New York: Harper & Row, 1988. 904p. $29.95. ISBN 0-06-015869-7. LC 87-45604.

The current edition constitutes a substantial revision of the original work, which appeared in 1977. Designed for the layperson, it treats key terms across the spectrum of human thought (e.g., economics, politics, philosophy, psychology, physical sciences, the arts). Among the 1,000-plus new entries reflecting current history are genetic engineering, *glasnost*, and Reaganism.

The present edition retains more than three-quarters of the original 4,000 articles but deletes notables in modern thought in order to include them in a planned companion volume. Reading lists appended to most entries have been updated. This unique reference tool is recommended for high school libraries. [R: ARBA 89; RBB, 1 Sept 88]

Abbreviations and Acronyms

167 De Sola, Ralph. **Abbreviations Dictionary**. 7th ed. New York: Elsevier Science Publishing, 1985. 1184p. $58.75. ISBN 0-444-00807-1. LC 81-179.

Long a standard work, DeSola's dictionary lists 46,000 abbreviations, acronyms, contractions, slang, signs and symbols, and other short forms. It also includes numerous lists, such as constellations, stars and symbols, bell codes, and diacritical and punctuation marks. However, DeSola's coverage cannot compare to the 500,000 listings identified in *Acronyms, Initialisms & Abbreviations Dictionary*, 15th ed. (Gale, 1990). Volume 1 identifies the listings; volume 2 is a supplementary update between biennial revisions; and volume 3 lists organizations, terms, and so forth, giving their abbreviations, acronyms, and initialisms.

E+
168 Miller, Stuart W. **Concise Dictionary of Acronyms and Initialisms**. New York: Facts on File, 1988. 192p. $22.95. ISBN 0-8160-1577-5. LC 87-9140.

Miller's dictionary, which covers only the 3,000 most commonly used acronyms and initialisms, is more practical for the school library than *Abbreviations Dictionary*. Abbreviations are identified and often annotated (e.g., "GMC—General Motors Corporation [used like a brand name for its trucks]").

Terms are drawn from many areas, such as government agencies, companies, organizations, airports, politics, and international relations. They are often used in newspapers, magazines, and other popular reading materials. [R: ARBA 89; LJ, July 88; RBB, 1 Oct 88]

Allusions

169 **Facts on File Dictionary of 20th Century Allusions: From Abbott and Costello to Ziegfield Girls**. By Sylvia Cole and Abraham H. Lass. New York: Facts on File, 1991. 292p. $24.95. ISBN 0-8160-1915-0. LC 90-41796.

This work focuses on modern allusions based on people (e.g., Darth Vader, John Wayne), places (e.g., Haight-Ashbury), events, phrases, and literary works. The alphabetically arranged allusions are defined and contain explanations of their backgrounds. Entry length varies but most are a paragraph or more. Cross-references and an index support the volume. [R: ARBA 92; Choice, June 91; RBB, 15 Feb 91; SLJ, May 91]

170 Webber, Elizabeth, and M. Feinsilber. **Grand Allusions: A Lively Guide to Those Expressions, Terms, and References You Ought to Know but Might Not**. Washington, D.C.: Farragut, 1990. 389p. $21.95; $12.95pa. ISBN 0-918535-09-3; 0-918535-03-Xpa. LC 90-34023.
    The subtitle says it all. Those who do not understand allusions to Colonel Blimp, the Final Solution, Horatio Alger, Type A, or Major-domo will find entertaining anecdotes about them in this inexpensive volume. Recommended for secondary school reference collections. [R: ARBA 91; BL, July 90; Kliatt, Sept 90]

Cultural Literacy

171 **The Dictionary of Cultural Literacy**. E. D. Hirsch, Jr., and others. Boston: Houghton Mifflin, 1988. 586p. $19.95. ISBN 0-395-43748-2. LC 88-9363.

E
172 **A First Dictionary of Cultural Literacy: What Our Children Need to Know**. E. D. Hirsch, Jr., ed. Boston: Houghton Mifflin, 1989. 271p. $14.95. ISBN 0-395-51040-6. LC 89-33776.
    Hirsch's works stem from the premise that there is a body of knowledge that members of modern society should share in order to communicate intelligently. *The Dictionary of Cultural Literacy* addresses subjects "widely recognized for more than fifteen years," or that seem "likely to be recognized by a majority of the people fifteen years from now." The 23 categories range from the Bible to technology. Some minor errors are noted, but this is a fascinating collection of data. The work, however, is of more interest for browsing than as a reference tool.
    While Hirsche's original work defines what adults should know, *A First Dictionary of Cultural Literacy* indicates what children should know by the end of sixth grade, according to a survey of several hundred teachers and parents. Its 21 categories are arranged alphabetically by specific entry. The brief, clear definitions identify a body of knowledge rather than define specific terms. Readers who wish to know more about a subject are encouraged to use the annotated bibliography keyed to the topical sections. An index to the entire contents provides subject access. Due to interest in the Hirsch premise, purchase is warranted, but this is not an essential acquisition. [R: ARBA 90; BL, 15 Jan 90; SLJ, Mar 89; WLB, Jan 90]

DIRECTORIES

E
173 Bergstrom, Joan M., and Craig Bergstrom. **All the Best Contests for Kids**. Berkeley, Calif.: Ten Speed Press. biennial. $6.95pa. (P.O. Box 7123, Berkeley, CA 94707).
    This work is designed to help children ages 6 to 12 and the adults who work with them to identify appropriate contests. For each, the directory provides an address and cites useful comments from former contestants. The 1990-1991 edition of this biennial includes photography contests, horse shows, the National Rotten Sneaker Championship, and competition for a cover design for the 1992-1993 edition. [R: SBF, May/June 89]

E+
174 **Contests for Students**. Mary Ellen Snodgrass, ed. Detroit: Gale, 1990. 350p. $29.95. ISBN 0-8103-7731-4. LC 91-100616.
    Educators seeking ways to recognize students' talents and to encourage their interests will welcome this guide. It lists 600 regional, national, and international contests that promote creativity and excellence for students from elementary grades through high school.
    Arranged by subject (art, music, speech, vocational fields, and writing), entries provide name, purpose, eligibility, description, awards, judging, registration deadline, notification, former winners, frequency, years established, contact person, and sponsoring organization with directory information. A special section on how to enter and win a contest gives good advice to prospective contestants. Five

comprehensive indexes provide access by contest name, sponsoring organizations, types and value of prizes, types of activities, and age/grade. This work and *All the Best Contests for Kids*, which includes some unique entries, provide a vast amount of information on the topic. [R: LJ, 1 Feb 91; RBB, 1 Mar 91; WLB, Mar 91]

175   **Encyclopedia of Associations, 1991: A Guide to Over 30,000 National and International Organizations.... Volume 1: National Organizations of the U.S.** Deborah M. Burck and others, eds. Detroit: Gale, 1990. 3 pts. $305.00/set. ISBN 0-8103-7419-6. ISSN 0071-0202. LC 76-46129.

The first two parts of this three-part volume provide names and addresses for some 23,000 U.S. associations, organizations, and other nonprofit groups. All areas of business, public administration, education, social welfare, sports, fraternities, and fan clubs are covered. Part 3 consists of a name and keyword index to the organizations listed in the first two parts. Entries, arranged by broad category, include directory information, officers, publications, and meetings. This annual is available online through Dialog and on CD-ROM.

The other volumes in the series are *Geographic and Executive Indexes*, *New Associations and Projects*, and *Update Service*.

176   Erickson, Judith B. **Directory of American Youth Organizations, 1990-91.** Minneapolis, Minn.: Free Spirit, 1989. 168p. $16.95pa. ISBN 0-915793-16-4. LC 88-295.

This directory cites over 400 national clubs, groups, lodges, societies, and other organizations for children and young adults. National headquarters, address, telephone number, and a brief description are given for each. Clubs are classified according to purpose, such as patriotism, conservation, career interest, sport, school subject, and hobby. The 1992-1993 edition is expected to be published in December 1991. [R: ARBA 91; BL, 15 Feb 90; LJ, 1 Feb 90]

177   Gilbert, Sara. **Lend a Hand: The How, Where, and Why of Volunteering.** New York: William Morrow, 1988. 162p. $11.95. ISBN 0-688-07247-4. LC 87-32077.

Lend a Hand focuses on voluntary organizations that offer a wide variety of services and that "welcome the assistance of young people." Letter/questionnaires were sent to 250 nonprofit groups selected from the *Encyclopedia of Associations*. Chapter 3, arranged by broad subject categories, lists over 100 that give positive responses.

The work's three sections—"Why Volunteer?" "Where to Volunteer," and "How to Volunteer"—contain information for guidance counselors and others working with young people. An alphabetical list of organizations and a subject index conclude the volume. Recommended for junior high and high school libraries. [R: ARBA 89]

178   **National Five-Digit ZIP Code and Post Office Directory.** U.S. Postal Service. Washington, D.C.: Government Printing Office. annual. $15.00pa.

This annual provides a comprehensive list of zip code information for all post offices and street addresses in the United States, plus APOs and FPOs. The arrangement is by state, town, and city; the latter is broken down by street address. Mailing information and current postal regulations are also included. The directory may be acquired from the U.S. Government Printing Office or any U.S. post office.

E
179   Osborn, Susan. **Free Things for Teachers.** rev. ed. New York: Perigee Books/Putnam, 1987. 127p. $6.95pa. ISBN 0-399-51334-5. LC 87-2409.

Supplementary materials such as pamphlets, coloring books, and other free or almost free publications of interest to primary teachers are listed in this directory. Some 250 items are arranged by 16 categories (e.g., arts and crafts, health and safety, games and hobbies).

180   **World of Winners: A Current and Historical Perspective on Awards and Their Winners.** Gita Siegman, ed. Detroit: Gale, 1991. 1000p. $75.00. ISBN 0-8103-6981-8.

Winners of awards, honors, and prizes in contemporary culture are the focus of this volume. Coverage includes 2,000 awards and the 75,000 persons who have received them over the years. The awards are arranged in 12 subject categories: arts and letters; business, management, and marketing; design and architecture; health and medicine; humanities, education, and library science; lifestyles; live performance; mass media; music; public affairs; science, engineering, and technology; and sports and hobbies. Members of various Halls of Fame, persons designated as the Time Magazine Man of the Year, and winners of the America's Cup and the Boston Marathon are among those named.

Details on the awards and the organizations that give them are followed by all past winners' names. Indexing is by award name, sponsoring organization, and winners' names.

ELECTRONIC SERVICES

181 **BRS/Search Service**. McLean, Va.: BRS Information Technologies. (8000 Westpark Dr., McLean, VA 22102. 1-800-955-0906).

BRS Information Technologies offers several product lines, but they are best known for BRS Search Service and BRS After Dark. Databases cover business, education, life sciences, medicine/pharmacology, physical/applied sciences, social sciences, and humanities. Among the more popular databases they provide are *Books in Print*, Magazine ASAP III, Magazine Index, National Newspaper Index, Popular Magazine Review Online, and Readers' Guide Abstracts.

BRS/Search Service, the company's principal product, is similar to most standard online services and functions with Boolean and proximity operators to connect search terms. BRS After Dark, a menu-driven system, is available at cheaper rates during evenings and on weekends.

182 **CompuServe**. Columbus, Ohio: CompuServe Information Service. (5000 Arlington Centre Blvd., P.O. Box 20212, Columbus, OH 43220. 1-800-848-8199).

CompuServe is an online, interactive medium that connects personal computer users to more than 1,400 information and communication databases. Included are *Academic American Encyclopedia* and Peterson's College Database, the online version of their four- and two-year college guides. Supersite provides demographic information for the entire United States and every state, county, SMSA, ADI, DMA, census tract, and zip code. General demographic, income, housing, education, and employment information is given.

Microsearch provides microcomputer information—software, hardware, services, accessories, and manufacturers—and is updated each month. Disclosure II compiles financial statements, business descriptions, and other information from SEC filings. PaperChase, a user-friendly version of MEDLINE, the National Library of Medicine's database of references on biomedical literature, contains the latest information published on medical topics. Other databases included cover news, sports, business, investments, and entertainment.

183 **DIALOG**. Palo Alto, Calif.: Dialog Information Services. (3460 Hillview Ave., Palo Alto, CA 94304. 1-800-3-DIALOG).

Dialog Information Services, the most extensive of its kind, provides search services to over 380 databases from a broad array of disciplines. Subject coverage includes science, business, technology, law, medicine, engineering, social sciences, business, economics, and current events. Among the more popular databases accessible through Dialog are Magazine Index, National Newspaper Index, Book Review Index, *Books in Print*, ERIC, Marquis Who's Who, *Academic American Encyclopedia*, A-V Online, and Magazine ASAP.

The most extensive searches on DIALOG use a variety of commands. In addition to searching subject words and dozens of other access points, there are proximity search capabilities and cross-file techniques. More than 220 databases are searchable, however, via easy menu, requiring no training or prior search experience.

Knowledge Index, Dialog's simplified search service which provides access to more than 85 databases in the evenings and on weekends, may be searched using either a command language or a menu option.

Vu/text, owned by Dialog Information Services and located in Philadelphia (325 Chestnut St., Suite 1300, Philadelphia, PA 19106), is the largest U.S. newspaper database, offering full-text of over 70 regional newspapers. Vu/text also provides access to more than 200 business journals and numerous wire services.

Dialog offers instructional programs designed to introduce informational retrieval to students at a reasonable cost. CLASSMATE, which can be used from elementary level up, offers access to over 80 popular databases. DIALOG Cip (Classroom Instruction Program) introduces students to over 300 databases in a wide assortment of subject areas. DIALOG Business Cip covers many areas in the business field.

184 **WILSONLINE Information System**. Bronx, N.Y.: H. W. Wilson. (212-588-8400).

WILSONLINE Information System provides several services for libraries, including WILSON-DISC CD-ROM Retrieval System and the WILSONLINE Online Retrieval System. Both services give access to the 18 indexes in the Wilson family of printed indexes, such as *Readers' Guide to Periodical Literature, Readers' Guide Abstracts, General Science Index, Book Review Digest,* and *Essay and General Literature Index.*

WILSONDISC offers each of the indexes on a separate compact disc, which is updated and cumulated quarterly. Subscribers also have access to the most current data via unlimited online search time in the database. WILSONDISC offers three search modes: BROWSE, WILSEARCH, and WILSONLINE. BROWSE provides the same easy-to-use subject access available with the Wilson printed indexes, which includes subject headings and *see also* references. WILSEARCH, for those with little or no online experience, allows the user to respond to menu options in making a search. WILSONLINE, a more complex system, permits the searcher to use **Boolean** logic and proximity commands to retrieve bibliographic information. WILSONLINE is also available as a stand-alone service.

The most sophisticated service, WILSONLINE offers up to 43 access points to bibliographic records and allows the searcher to transform a reference query into a search strategy that pinpoints the information needed. Among the access capabilities are **Boolean** logic, proximity searching, free text and controlled searching, and truncation. WILSONLINE searching requires training, generally acquired through tutorials, institutes, and other such arrangements.

ENCYCLOPEDIAS

Guides

E+
185 Kister, Kenneth F. **Kister's Concise Guide to Best Encyclopedias**. Phoenix, Ariz.: Oryx, 1988. 108p. $16.50pa. ISBN 0-89774-484-5. LC 88-24044.

Kister, an authority on encyclopedias, has prepared this guide for laypersons who wish to buy an encyclopedia, but it also provides guidance for librarians. The *Concise Guide* – an update of his larger work, *Best Encyclopedias* (Oryx, 1986) – contains in-depth reviews and comparisons of 32 juvenile and adult sets, shorter reviews of 187 specialized encyclopedias, and brief reviews of 17 discontinued general encyclopedias. [R: ARBA 89; RBB, 15 Dec 88; VOYA, Apr 89]

E+
186 **Purchasing an Encyclopedia: 12 Points to Consider**. 3d ed. By the Editorial Board of *Reference Books Bulletin*. Chicago: American Library Association, 1990. 40p. $4.95pa. ISBN 0-8389-7375-2.

The editors have addressed this authoritative guide to parents searching for a good encyclopedia for their children, but small libraries with limited access to selection tools will find it useful. Each of the "12 points to consider" (e.g., age level, authority, objectivity) receives a one- or two-page exposition. Also provided is information on yearbooks and CD-ROM formats. Reviews of the 11 major multivolume encyclopedias are reprinted from the October 15, 1989, *Reference Books Bulletin* section of *Booklist. Best Encyclopedias* by Kenneth Kister (Oryx, 1986) reviews a larger number of general encyclopedias (52) and 187 subject encyclopedias. Moreover, Kister's reviews are more detailed. [R: ARBA 91]

Desk Size

187 **Barron's Student's Concise Encyclopedia**. Compiled by the editors of Barron's Educational Series, Inc. Hauppauge, N.Y.: Barron's Educational Series, 1988. 1200p. $19.95. ISBN 0-8120-5937-9. LC 87-22976.

This one-volume work is recommended for high school students requiring brief information on basic topics in history, art, literature, computers, biology, chemistry, and other fields. The book is arranged alphabetically by 23 subject areas and then alphabetically, chronologically, or in some other appropriate arrangement according to the field. Most biographical entries cover deceased notables, but some treat living persons who continue to influence contemporary society and culture.

Entries, which range from one line to several pages, are supported by drawings, graphs, photographs and maps (most in black-and-white), and a detailed index. Place-names on maps are, unfortunately, not indexed. [R: ARBA 89; WLB, Sept 88]

E+
188 **The Cambridge Encyclopedia**. David Crystal, ed. New York: Cambridge University, 1990. 1489p. $49.50. ISBN 0-521-39528-3.

The Cambridge Encyclopedia, a British work, is used in libraries primarily as a quick reference tool. For that purpose, it is a valuable addition to all levels of school libraries. It provides international coverage of world knowledge in concise entries, most of them fewer than 250 words long—15,000 topical, 5,500 biographical, and 4,000 geographical. Entry terms are given in British and American spellings, linked by cross-references; alphabetically arranged entries are also well cross-referenced.

A ready-reference section at the end includes 7,000 additional entries; tables of nations and their leaders, weights and measures, forms of address, and other almanac-type data that is common to many other reference sources. The work is more comprehensive than any other desk-size encyclopedia. [R: ARBA 92; LJ, 15 Apr 91; WLB, Jan 91]

189   **The Concise Columbia Encyclopedia**. 2d ed. New York: Columbia University Press, 1989. 944p. $39.95. ISBN 0-231-06938-3.

Concise Columbia, designed to meet basic factual needs, is an excellent compendium of information about persons, geographic features, and topics of current interest. The 2d edition (1st ed., 1983) contains some 15,000 entries; 500 are new to this edition, and more than a third of the older ones have been updated or revised. Tables and charts (e.g., rulers of various countries, elements), full-color and black-and-white maps, and line drawings scattered throughout the text all enhance the work's usefulness. There is no index, but the alphabetical arrangement and extensive cross-referencing make the information readily accessible. [R: ARBA 90; BL, 1 Jan 90; WLB, Dec 89]

E+
190   Dupre, Jean-Paul. **Barron's Junior Fact Finder**. Barron's Educational Series, 1989. 304p. $19.95. ISBN 0-8120-6072-5. LC 89-6454.

This attractively illustrated work, an English-language adaptation of a French encyclopedia, provides an overview of subjects of interest to elementary and middle school students. The eight subject areas (history, geography, language, mathematics, physical science, natural science, English grammar, and arithmetic) are subdivided into specific topics. Full-color illustrations appear on every page. The arrangement hinders quick reference, and the brief index provides only superficial access. However, students will enjoy browsing through it. [R: ARBA 90; BL, 1 Mar 90]

E
191   **Picture Encyclopedia for Children**. John Paton, ed. New York: Grosset & Dunlap/Putnam, 1987. 380p. $19.95. ISBN 0-448-18999-2. LC 86-817788.

This single-volume encyclopedia in no way competes with the standard multivolume sets, but it will appeal to children in grades 3 to 6. It contains some 750 alphabetically arranged articles that focus on pcoplc, animals, placcs, scicncc, technology, and history. Well-written articles, each averaging two pages, often include references to other entries; an index containing over 2,700 entries gives access to the articles.

Although there are a few inconsistencies (e.g., some major cities are covered in separate articles, but others are not; some countries are included, but others are omitted), the volume provides accurate information and offers an opportunity for younger students to look things up alphabetically and use cross-references and an index. Families not wishing to buy a multivolume encyclopedia will find this reasonably priced book an excellent home-reference work. Elementary libraries will also find it to be a worthwhile acquisition. [R: ARBA 89; SLJ, May 88]

E+
192   **The Random House Encyclopedia**. 3d ed. James Mitchell and Jess Stein, eds. New York: Random House, 1990. 2781p. $129.95. ISBN 0-394-58450-3. LC 90-38567.

This edition maintains the same features and arrangement as its predecessors (1977 and 1983). Its main sections are "Colorpedia," a time chart, "Alphapedia," and an atlas. More than half of the text is contained in the Colorpedia, which addresses seven broad themes (e.g., the universe, life on Earth, history and culture). Topics in each area are treated in double-page spreads, about one-third text and two-thirds photographs, diagrams, and other illustrations, most in color. A separate column, "Connections," refers the reader to related articles in the same section.

The time chart lists significant events in all fields from earliest times through early 1990. The Alphapedia contains some 25,000 topical entries, the majority of which cover people and events, with 35,000 cross-references to entries in other sections. Each page includes three black-and-white illustrations.

There is a bibliography of some 1,500 items arranged to correspond to the seven themes. The atlas section, 80 pages of color maps produced by Rand McNally (it has its own index/gazetteer) completes the work. There is no index, however, for the entire work.

This is an attractive volume, but it is useful primarily for browsing. Those seeking information on specific topics in a one-volume format would be better served by *The Cambridge Encyclopedia* or *The Concise Columbia Encyclopedia*. [R: ARBA 91; LJ, 15 Nov 90]

193 **Troll Student Encyclopedia**. By Michael Dempsey and Keith Lye. Mahwah, N.J.: Troll Associates, 1991. 128p. $14.95; $9.95pa. ISBN 0-8167-2257-9; 0-8167-2258-7pa.

This children's encyclopedia provides articles ranging from 2 to 20 lines on 1,500 to 2,000 topics that include people, places, things, events, and ideas. At least one colored drawing, photograph, or chart is on each page, with up to two-thirds of a page being used for illustrations. Birth and death dates are given for people as current as the mid-1990s. Few Blacks and women were found; political and military leaders, explorers, and folk heroes prevail. There are no cross-references.

Troll has at least twice as many entries as *Picture Encyclopedia for Children*. Of *Troll*'s entries, 60 percent are not duplicated in *Picture Encyclopedia*, 36 percent are in both, and fewer than 3 percent are in *Picture Encyclopedia* only. *Troll* seems to be accurate and offers a cross between a language dictionary — without pronunciation or etymology — and a geographical dictionary for upper elementary students.

Adult and Juvenile Sets

194 **Academic American Encyclopedia**. K. Anne Ranson, ed. in chief. Danbury, Conn.: Grolier, 1990. 21v. $800.00/set; $660.00/set (schools). LC 87-17594.

195 **The New Grolier Electronic Encyclopedia**. CD-ROM. Danbury, Conn.: Grolier. $395.00 (Teacher's manual, $49.00). Macintosh and IBM-compatible versions and network version available.

Academic American, created in 1980, is the youngest of the major encyclopedias. Designed for high school and college students, its primary purpose is to provide short, factual data rather than lengthy analytical material, which makes it especially useful when searching for basic information. It is a current, accurate, well-written set that, according to its editors, devotes almost equal space to the humanities, sciences, and social sciences. As the name implies, it attempts to reflect the current curricula of American schools and colleges. Due to its recent origin, *Academic American* is not burdened with outdated language that reflects ethnic and gender biases. A concerted effort is made to present all topics impartially and to give equal space to contrasting points of view.

Pronunciation guides are included for about half of the subject headings, and more than one-third of the entries have appended bibliographies. When technical jargon must be used, it is either explained in the text or included in an attached glossary. The set is heavily illustrated, containing almost 17,000 photographs, drawings, reproductions of art works, maps, and graphs — most in color — that occupy about one-third of the total page space. The index provides detailed and broad subject access to the set, including illustrations, maps, and bibliographies.

Due to the brevity of the articles and concentration on essential information, *Academic American* can be used by students younger than its primary audience. It is highly recommended for high schools but can serve as a supplementary set for upper elementary and middle schools. In addition to the CD-ROM version that follows, it is available online and in laser and videodisc versions.

The New Grolier Electronic Encyclopedia is similar to the earlier version, *New Electronic Encyclopedia*, with the incorporation of visual materials. The IBM version of this CD-ROM set requires a microcomputer with 512K RAM that runs under DOS version 3.0 or higher. A VGA graphic capability is required to view the illustrations, and a color monitor is preferred. The Macintosh version requires a Macintosh Plus, SE or SE/30, or Macintosh II with IBM RAM and 1 MB. Installation is easy, and even a novice can run the set's menu-driven program.

The contents are that of the *Academic American* plus additional materials. All articles, fact boxes, bibliographies, and other such items included in the print version, along with 1,300 illustrations selected from over 16,000 in the parent set, are searchable on the CD-ROM. "Browse Titles" mode permits the reader to peruse the table of contents; "Browse Word Index" is the equivalent of the printed index. "Word Search" mode enables the reader to perform Boolean (and, or, not) searches for terms within articles. Illustrations can be retrieved through the "Picture Index," available at any time during the search, or for any article with a "Picture" notation at the bottom of the screen. It should be observed, however, that the illustrations available on screen in no way compare with the great number available in the printed version, and maps are not reproduced for the CD-ROM version.

The New Grolier is the only electronic encyclopedia available in a Macintosh version and is the least expensive of the current products, facts which may influence the selection decision of some school libraries. It should be noted that *Compton's MultiMedia Encyclopedia* includes 15,000 illustrations, 60 minutes of audio, and a dictionary, but it is directed toward ages 9 through high school. *The New Grolier* is more appropriate for upper high school and college levels and serves only as a supplementary set for younger students. [R: ARBA 90; BL, 15 Dec 90]

E
196 Childcraft: The How and Why Library. 15v. Chicago: World Book, 1989. $170.00/set. ISBN 0-7166-0189-3. LC 89-50463.

Childcraft is not an encyclopedia per se but a 15-volume "resource library" designed for children preschool through primary grades. Volumes 1-3 are anthologies of quality literature, 4-7 focus on science (e.g., "About Animals," "The Green Kingdom"), 7 explains the workings of over 500 simple machines and devices, and 8-10 cover the social sciences (e.g., workers and their products, holidays, famous places around the world). Chapter 11 includes 700 creative activities, while 12 discusses visual communication. Chapter 13 introduces mathematics through stories, puzzles, and games; 14 focuses on children and is illustrated with over 400 photographs; and 15 provides an index and a guide for parents and teachers. Information volumes (4-10, 13) include bibliographies, with a list for 5- to 8-year-olds and another for 9- to 12-year-olds.

Childcraft, usually regarded as a family set, contains accurate articles written within the understanding of young children. It should be considered for elementary libraries serving preschool and primary grades. [R: ARBA 90; BL, 15 Jan 90, 1 June 90]

E +
197 Children's Britannica. 1991 ed. Chicago: Encyclopaedia Britannica, 1991. 20v. $375.00. ISBN 0-85229-226-0. LC 87-81078.

Designed for students in grades 3 through 8, this set introduces a wide range of subject areas in over 4,000 alphabetically arranged entries, supported by over 6,000 illustrations and photographs. It is especially strong in science, geography, and biography. Articles on every country in the world include fact boxes that contain short statistical profiles. An atlas section at the end of volume 19 provides full-color maps of the world, U.S. states, and Canadian provinces.

The titles of the first and last entry in the volume appear on each spine, and headings on every page identify the reader's current position in the alphabetical sequence. Most articles direct the reader to related entries, and all major essays end with a study guide listing supportive entries on the topic.

Volume 20, the index volume, gives the volume and page number for more than 30,000 topics. Most entries contain a brief descriptive phrase. The index, moreover, has about 6,000 capsule entries, averaging 6 lines each, that give basic information about the topic. Recommended for elementary and middle schools. [R: RBB, 1 Oct 91]

198 Collier's Encyclopedia: With Bibliography and Index. Bernard Johnston, ed. in chief. New York: Macmillan, 1990. 24v. $1,399.50/set; $899.00/set (schools and libraries). LC 87-61118.

Collier's began as a 24-volume set in 1949-1951 but evolved from a single-volume compendium that appeared in 1882. The set is a prestigious, accurate, and readable work, popular with its intended audience (high school/college students and adults). It favors a broad topic approach but contains many short articles among its 25,000 entries. Almost all articles are signed by the contributors, who are recognized authorities in their fields.

Collier's has a number of outstanding features, such as its comprehensive index of 400,000 entries that provides access to articles, bibliographies, illustrations, and geographic information on maps. Illustrations are numerous, taking up about one-fifth of the page space, but only a small percentage of the work's 17,600 photographs, drawings, and graphs are in color. A number of color transparencies and color and black-and-white maps are placed with relevant articles rather than in a separate section. A 200-page classified bibliography that contains 11,500 items appears in volume 24 rather than being distributed among the articles.

This excellent set is recommended as a first choice for high schools; middle schools with accelerated programs should also consider it. [R: ARBA 92; RBB, 1 Oct 91]

E +
199 Compton's Encyclopedia and Fact Index. Philip W. Goetz, ed. in chief. Chicago: Encyclopaedia Britannica, 1990. 26v. $699.00/set; $539.00/set (schools and libraries). LC 87-73073.

E +
200 Compton's MultiMedia Encyclopedia. CD-ROM. Chicago: Britannica Software, 1990. $845.00; $795.00 (schools and libraries). ISBN 1-55730-125-5.

Compton's, a pioneer in developing encyclopedias for readers from age 9 through high school, was first published in 1922. It claims to be the first "pictured encyclopedia" and over the years has become known for its "Fact-Index," which contains capsule articles that give basic information for many topics not included in the main set (about 26,000 in recent sets). Although the editors maintain a policy of continuous revision, they thoroughly revised the set in the early 1980s.

A broad subject approach (about 5,200 entries) is followed; most long articles are accompanied by study guides, fact summaries, and bibliographies that are divided by level—younger readers, advanced students, and teachers. Only articles of three or more pages are signed.

Compton's uses a controlled vocabulary appropriate to its audience. Objective, well-written, and well-illustrated articles cover all areas of knowledge. Most are curriculum-oriented, although non-curricular subjects are also treated. Long essays are written in pyramid style, beginning with the most basic material and progressively becoming more complex and detailed. An index in each volume covers that volume and related articles in others; the last volume is a compilation of all of the "Fact-Indexes." "Exploring Volumes- " is a special feature in which questions are asked that can be answered in that specific volume. The set is profusely illustrated with pictures and photographs of superior quality; maps are by Hammond.

Over the years, *Compton's* has been faulted for its failure to include controversial subjects, a criticism that in recent years it has made a concerted effort to remedy, but it continues to omit some topics of interest to young adults.

Still this attractive encyclopedia has made a valiant effort to overcome valid criticisms. It now ranks as one of the best sets on the market and deserves a place in most school libraries with *World Book* and *Merit*. Recommended for all levels.

Compton's MultiMedia Encyclopedia, the CD-ROM version of *Compton's*, integrates sound, pictures, animation, and text, introducing an exciting new concept in encyclopedias. It duplicates the 5,200 articles and 26,000 "Fact-Index" entries in the latest edition of *Compton's Encyclopedia*; the product will be updated annually. It is designed for use with an IBM-compatible computer that has at least a 20 MB hard disk drive, 640K RAM, and Microsoft extensions. The system requires a mouse, a VGA monitor display card, and a VGA or multisync monitor.

The CD-ROM has several unique features. The 65,000-word *Merriam-Webster Intermediate Dictionary*, which is loaded on the same disc, enables the user to display words found in the text with their definitions and pronunciations. Some 15,000 illustrations (5,000 in color), 60 minutes of sound, and an audio glossary of 1,500 terms are also accessible.

A variety of entry paths may be used in locating information. The "Title Finder" accesses the articles under their alphabetically arranged headings, which the user may scroll through to locate. The "Idea Search" enables the searcher to enter a phrase or question; the computer seeks the answer under the keywords it contains. The "Topic Tree" classifies articles by broad heading and subtopics. The "U.S. History Timeline," which summarizes important events, can be accessed a number of ways and is more complex to use. The "Picture Explorer" can be accessed by typing a description of the item, chosen from a list of captions or from a portion termed "some of the best pictures in the encyclopedia." The "World Map," accessed by typing in a place-name or choosing one from an alphabetical list, permits the user to zoom in to see an area more closely or to zoom out to see a larger area. The "Science Feature Articles," one of the most exciting features, uses text, animation, and an audio glossary.

This set is more innovative than two other CD-ROM sets, *New Grolier Electronic Encyclopedia*, and World Book's *Information Finder*. By allowing the user to learn through different sensory modes, this encyclopedia will appeal to many. It is highly recommended for school media centers. [R: ARBA 90; BL, Oct 89]

E +
201 The Doubleday Children's Encyclopedia. John Paton, ed. New York: Doubleday, 1989. 4v. $69.95/set. ISBN 0-385-41210-X. LC 89-77208.

This attractive encyclopedia is well worth its relatively small cost. Over 1,300 entries on topics of interest to elementary and middle school students and teachers are illustated by over 2,000 color photographs and drawings. The text, in large type, consists of brief entries (100-125 words) with a few longer articles on such topics as birds and the United States.

Special features include fact panels giving historical data/statistics and "nuggets" of strange facts—these are located in the margins—and small maps of continents, countries, and U.S. states. One or more of sixteen subject symbols heads each main entry, which helps children organize information by broad category (e.g., animals, plants, food). Volume 4 includes an index to the set. This work does not compete in usefulness and quality with *New Book of Knowledge* or *Children's Britannica*, but it is appealing. Recommended. [R: ARBA 91; RBB, 15 Dec 90]

202 **Enciclopedia Hispanica**. Chicago: Encyclopaedia Britannica, n.d. 18v. $899.00/set. ISBN 0-85229-532-4.

Enciclopedia Hispanica, which replaces *Enciclopedia Barsa de Consulta Facil*, provides Spanish-language coverage of the world from a Hispanic viewpoint. The arrangement, similar to that of the *New Encyclopaedia Britannica*, is in four parts: *Micropedia*, 2 volumes containing 30,000 short entries and an index; *Macropedia*, 14 volumes consisting of 6,000 long articles on a wide variety of subjects; *Datapedia*, a single volume with a world atlas and a compilation of world statistics; and *Temapedia*, a volume that offers a series of subject essays and a thematic index to the set. The well-illustrated, authoritative set, appropriate for high school and college levels, is supplemented by *Libro del Ano*, which focuses on the people, events, and trends of a given year.

203 **The Encyclopedia Americana**. international ed. David T. Holland, ed. in chief. Danbury, Conn.: Grolier, 1989. 30v. $1,200.00/set; $995.00/set (schools). LC 88-16397.

The first important encyclopedia produced in the United State, *Americana* has been published continuously since 1829, and by Grolier since 1945. Intended for high school/college students and the general public, its goal is to serve "as a bridge between the world of the specialist and the general reader." It is essentially topic-specific in approach (52,000 entries averaging 600 words each) but has many long articles up to 200 pages in length. *Americana* is still best known for its coverage of United States and Canadian history, geography, and biography, but this emphasis has been reduced in the last few years. The articles on scientific and technical topics are strong, and the surveys of each century are a unique feature not found in any other set.

Since 1936, *Americana* has followed the industry's practice of annual, continuous revision, which involves updating and deleting entries as needed, targeting some subjects for major revision, and adding new material and articles. The set has been commended for its recent efforts to make the text more current.

The set uses *see* and *see also* references sparingly in its main body but provides excellent, accurate access through its 353,000-entry index, which subdivides broad subjects into narrow topics. Long articles, written by well-known subject experts, are signed and supported by current bibliographies for further reading. The numerous illustrations (some 23,000) indicate that the editors have made a commendable effort to update them and add color. *Americana*, a reliable and balanced set, is a first choice for high schools and suitable for many middle schools. [R: ARBA 90]

204 **Merit Student Encyclopedia**. Bernard Johnston, ed. in chief. New York: Macmillan, 1990. 20v. $1,399.50/set; $579.00/set (schools and libraries). LC 87-61604.

First published in 1967, this set, designed for grades 5 through high school, is curriculum-oriented, as are its closest competitors, *World Book* and *Compton's*. *Merit* maintains a good subject balance in its 22,000 entries, which are revised annually on a continuous basis. Major entries begin with simple information for young children and progress to complex data for older readers.

Special features consist of some 200,000 illustrations, about half in color, including plates and overlays; 1,570 maps in color and black-and-white; student guides that indicate the scope and major headings in long articles and suggest related entries; frequent use of *see* and *see also* references; and a 140,000-entry index.

The list of contributors who wrote most of the articles (some are by the editorial staff) is impressive, and the articles are accurate, objective, and clearly written. The balanced treatment of controversial topics is commendable. Caveats include lack of currency in bibliographies and some material, and the omission of some topics of current interest. Overall, however, the set receives a rating of excellent. Recommended for middle and high schools. [R: ARBA 92; RBB, 1 Oct 91]

E+
205 **New Book of Knowledge**. Jean E. Reynolds, ed. in chief. Danbury, Conn.: Grolier, 1990. 21v. $750.00/set; $625.00/set (schools). LC 88-16408.

The alphabetically arranged *New Book of Knowledge* (*NBK*) is the 1966 descendant of the topically arranged *Book of Knowledge*, published since 1910. The set is designed to meet the curricular needs of children in grades 3 through 6, but it may be used by young children with adult guidance and junior high students unable to handle more sophisticated information. Prepared by educators and subject specialists, this highly regarded set is commended for its reliability, accessibility, currentness, and attractiveness.

NBK has several special features. Articles about authors include excerpts from their books, and those about illustrators show examples of their works. There are numerous how-to-do-it essays on sports, hobbies, crafts, and school assignments (e.g., book reports). Brief entries, called "Dictionary Index" articles, appear in the index section of each volume. Glossaries accompany many articles, such as those for cooking and computers. Fact boxes, tables, and "wonder questions" (e.g., Why don't most clowns speak?) are scattered throughout the set. *Home and School Reading and Study Guide*, a separate paperbound volume, includes lists of books for children at reading levels from kindergarten through grade 9; it suggests ways in which *NBK* can be used to stimulate learning and help children become involved in hobbies and other leisure activities.

The set is well illustrated, with about one-third of the page space devoted to pictures and photographs. Some 1,000 maps depict continents, countries, U.S. states, Canadian provinces, and a few cities; historical and other thematic maps are also numerous. A first choice for elementary schools, *NBK* should also be considered as a supplementary set for middle schools. [R: ARBA 90; RBB, 1 Oct 90]

206 **The New Encyclopaedia Britannica**. 15th ed. Philip W. Goetz, ed. in chief. Chicago: Encyclopaedia Britannica, 1990. 32v. $1,399.00/set; $1,069.00/set (schools and libraries). LC 86-82929.

207 **Britannica World Data, 1989**. Chicago: Encyclopaedia Britannica, 1990. priced as part of the set w/*Britannica Book of the Year*.

Britannica (or *Britannica 3*, as it is sometimes called), the largest and most famous English-language encyclopedia, began in Scotland in 1768 but moved to this country in 1901. In 1974, the work appeared in a unique three-part arrangement that has evoked criticism from those who think the new organization makes the encyclopedia more difficult to use. Critics generally agree, however, that it is an authoritative set, providing more depth of coverage on more subjects than any other encyclopedia in English.

The 12-volume *Micropaedia* contains 66,000 short articles that range in length from a few sentences to 3,000 words. The 17-volume *Macropaedia* contains comprehensive essays on 580 broad subjects, ranging from 20 to 200 pages. The *Propaedia*, a single-volume outline of knowledge designed to show relationships among ideas, persons, and events, serves as a synoptic table of contents to the *Micropaedia* and *Macropaedia*. The final two volumes are a comprehensive index to the entire set.

The *Micropaedia*, termed the quick-reference section, covers topics not treated in the *Macropaedia* or summarizes longer articles found in that section. It contains some 15,000 illustrations, usually small but clear and colorful. The *Macropaedia* provides "knowledge-in-depth" coverage that features the following aids: an introduction; an outline showing the main sections; marginal notes highlighting special aspects of the topics; and extensive, briefly annotated bibliographies. Over 8,000 black-and-white and color illustrations and full-color maps, 162 color plates, and 12 transparency overlays support the text. Articles are signed by the contributors, authorities in their fields. The *Propaedia*, intended as a study guide, provides an introductory essay for the 10 major fields of knowledge and suggests specific articles and biographies in the set that relate to the outlines. The index contains 419,436 entries, including references and cross-references.

The annual *Britannica World Data*, a work that can stand alone, is an important component of the set and has been bound with the *Britannica Book of the Year* since 1985. It is given to first-time purchasers of the set. Designed to update information found within the main set, it offers current geographic, demographic, economic, and financial data for 220 countries and dependencies. The set's index also refers to its content.

The lack of currency of the material, a common criticism, has been systematically addressed by the editors, with the result that many articles, especially those in the *Macropaedia*, have been rewritten and many new articles added to the *Micropaedia*. Despite the arrangement, which many users consider cumbersome, *Britannica 3* is the most comprehensive English-language encyclopedia and is recommended for high schools. [R: ARBA 92; RBB, 1 Oct 91]

E
208 **The New Grolier Student Encyclopedia**. Terry Borton, ed. in chief. Danbury, Conn.: Grolier, 1989. 24v. $235.00/set (schools). ISBN 0-7172-9029-8. [also available from Field Publications, Middleton, Conn. as *Young Students Encyclopedia* ($19.98/v.)].

This was first published in 1972 as *Young Students Encyclopedia*. For the next five years, separate editions appeared, one by Xerox Educational Publications and the other by Funk and Wagnalls, that were sold in supermarkets until 1977 and thereafter to schools and libraries. The present Grolier edition and the *Young Students* edition are identical.

Some 3,000 entries, aimed at meeting the curricula needs and outside interests of elementary school children, begin with simple information that becomes more detailed as the article progresses. The most important points, or "Nuggets," are presented in a capsule, printed in boldface type in the margin. Other features include a "Learn By Doing" section on activities, an atlas with maps by Rand McNally (continents, important countries, U.S. states, and Canadian provinces), and a dictionary that contains 34,000 entries. The set is well illustrated, and an index provides references to 22,000 topics. Recommended as a supplementary set for elementary schools. [R: ARBA 90]

E+

209   **World Book Encyclopedia**. Robert O. Zeleny, ed. in chief. Chicago: World Book, 1991. 22v. $559.00/set (schools and libraries). ISBN 0-7166-0090-0. LC 89-51290.

210   **Information Finder**. CD-ROM. Chicago: World Book. $549.00; $795.00 w/set of *World Book Encyclopedias*; network version available for a licensing fee. ISBN 0-7166-8009-2.

This outstanding set, now in its 74th year, continues to justify its reputation as a current, accurate, authoritative, and objective set written in a clear and lively style. Over the past decade it has placed even greater emphasis on color illustrations, extensive annual revision, and the addition of excellent new articles designed to meet the needs and interests of students from grade 4 through high school.

World Book uses a specific-entry approach, treating most topics in short articles. However, there are many survey essays that are 25 pages or more in length and divided by section headings and subheadings. Most articles, contributed or authenticated by over 3,000 subject specialists, are signed. The set's 17,800 entries, arranged alphabetically (word by word), address the age group most likely to read them. The readability and information level of each article is based on curriculum analysis and classroom research, a successful practice used by its editors for many years. Cross-referencing (within and at the end of articles) is used extensively to support the 150,000-entry index.

About one-third of *World Book*'s space is devoted to 29,000 well-captioned illustrations, more than 80 percent of which are in color. Illustrations are frequently revised. All of the set's 2,300 maps are in color; they cover the states of the United States and all countries of the world, plus many of the world's largest cities. This outstanding set is highly recommended for all school libraries.

A recorded cassette format designed for the visually handicapped is available from American Printing House for the Blind (P.O. Box 6085, Louisville, KY 40206-6085).

Information Finder, the CD-ROM version of *World Book*, contains the set's 17,800 articles and 1,600 reading lists but lacks the illustrations. The CD-ROM also includes the *World Book Dictionary* (139,000 definitions). It runs on IBM or IBM-compatible microcomputers with 640k of memory, 2 megabytes of free space on the hard disk drive, DOS 3.1 or higher, version 2.0 or higher of MS-DOS CD-ROM Extension, and CD-ROM drive. A color monitor is desirable for viewing overlays and color used in highlighting search terms, but it is not essential; a printer is optional. Installation is clearly described in the manual and simple to execute.

Information Finder permits several functions that the printed version does not. It is searchable by topic and keyword. Topic searching is similar to using the printed index. Keyword mode, a more thorough system, searches keywords contained in the articles. If a keyword is not found, the program searches the *World Book Dictionary* and displays a definition of the keyword, if found. Keyword concepts also can be combined using Boolean operators (and, or, not), and proximity commands can be selected. When articles are displayed, the screen shows an outline on the left and the text on the right.

The CD-ROM provides numerous other conveniences, such as highlighted cross-references within the text area and downloading and printing capabilities. A decided disadvantage, however, is the lack of illustrations, which constitutes about one-third of the printed version of *World Book*. Both *Compton's MultiMedia Encyclopedia* and *The New Grolier Electronic Encyclopedia* offer graphic images; *Compton's*, moreover, includes sound. In all other areas, *Information Finder* is competitive and, of course, carries the strength of its parent set, an undisputed leader in the field. [R: RBB, 1 June 90]

HANDBOOKS

211   Blocksma, Mary. **Reading the Numbers: A Survival Guide to the Measurement, Numbers, and Sizes Encountered in Everyday Life**. New York: Viking, 1989. 256p. $18.95; $7.95pa. ISBN 0-670-82682-0; 0-14-010654-5pa. LC 88-23219.

This practical work focuses on numerical concepts such as roman numerals, radio frequency, time, prime rate, calendars, money, lumber, nails, and age. Arranged alphabetically by subject, the explanations are clear, concise, and nontechnical. A comprehensive index provides access. Recommended for secondary schools. [R: ARBA 91; Kliatt, May 89; LJ, 1 Apr 89]

INDEXES

E+
212 Appel, Marsha C. **Illustration Index**. 4th ed. Metuchen, N.J.: Scarecrow, 1980. 568p. $34.00. ISBN 0-8108-1273-8. LC 79-26091.

213 Appel, Marsha C. **Illustration Index V: 1977-1981**. Metuchen, N.J.: Scarecrow, 1984. 421p. $34.00. ISBN 0-8108-1656-3. LC 83-15201.

214 Appel, Marsha C. **Illustration Index VI: 1982-1986**. Metuchen, N.J.: Scarecrow, 1988. 541p. $42.50. ISBN 0-8108-2146-4. LC 88-18207.
The Appel indexes identify useful illustrations printed in a small group of popular magazines: *American Heritage, Ebony, Life, National Geographic, National Wildlife, Natural History, Smithsonian, Sports Illustrated*, and *Travel/Holiday*. The 4th edition, covering the years 1972 to 1976, and volume 5, spanning 1977 to 1981, each lists some 25,000 illustrations under 12,000 subject headings. The latest index, 1982 to 1986, includes some 35,000 entries under 17,000 subject headings. Among the entries are persons (if they have a separate entry in *World Book Encyclopedia*) and countries of the world.
Typical citations include title of magazine, volume number, and pagination; type of illustration, if other than a photograph (e.g., drawing, painting); color or black-and-white; size; and date of publication. [R: ARBA 90; RBB, 1 June 89]

215 **Book Review Digest**. Bronx, N.Y.: H. W. Wilson, 1905- . 10 issues/yr. w/cumulations in May, Aug., and Oct., and annual cumulation. sold on service basis. LC 6-24490. (available online, CD-ROM, and tape from January 1983. CD-ROM $1,095/yr.).
BRD provides excerpts from, and citations to, reviews of adult and juvenile fiction and nonfiction, trade books, and reference books. It currently covers reviews of almost 7,000 English-language publications each year that appear in 95 (26 recent additions) American, British, and Canadian periodicals in the humanities, social sciences, and general sciences, plus library review media.
Entries, arranged alphabetically by author or title (as appropriate), give author, title, paging, price, publisher and year, ISBN, a descriptive introduction to the book, age or grade level (for juvenile works), suggested Sears subject headings, and LC card number. Reviewing information includes citations of reviews, name of reviewers, approximate length of each review, and up to four review excerpts chosen to provide a balance of opinion.
Only works that receive a minimum number of reviews (e.g., four for adult fiction) are included, but all reviews in *Reference Books Bulletin* are indexed. This is an essential reference and selection tool for secondary schools. [R: ARBA 92]

216 **Book Review Index**. Detroit: Gale, 1965- . bimonthly. $185.00/yr. w/annual cumulations. LC 65-9908.
This comprehensive index cites all reviews appearing in more than 500 popular and professional periodicals. Included are adult and juvenile fiction, nonfiction, and reference books—some 132,000 review citations for about 74,000 new books each year. Arranged alphabetically by author, *BRI* gives only author, title, and the review. There is a title index. No descriptive summaries or excerpts from reviews, such as those found in *Book Review Digest*, are offered; nor is any subject access provided. *BRI* also may be accessed online through Dialog, File 137. [R: ARBA 92]

217 **Canadian Periodical Index**. Ottawa: Canadian Library Association, 1938- . monthly w/annual cumulations. (200 Elgin St., Suite 602, Ottawa, Ont., Canada K1P 1L5).
CPI indexes 384 English and French periodicals (including 17 U.S. titles) chosen for their usefulness in Canadian libraries. A single alphabetical arrangement includes authors and both English and French subject headings. Article citations are under English headings only; French subject headings are cross-referenced to their English equivalents. Access is also provided by form—reviews (book, drama,

computer hardware and software), poems, and short stories. The index makes generous use of *see* and *see also* references. [R: ARBA 92]

E+
218 **Children's Book Review Index**. Detroit: Gale, 1975- . annual. $95.00. LC 75-27408.

219 **Children's Book Review Index: Master Cumulation, 1965-1984**. Detroit: Gale, 1985. 5v. $375.00/ set. LC 75-27408.

Each annual cites more than 17,700 reviews of more than 10,000 children's books, preschool through grade 10. The same citations also appear in *Book Review Index*, of which this is a spinoff. Reviews cited can be found in the 470 periodicals indexed in *BRI*. It is arranged in a single alphabet by author.

The 1965-1984 cumulation provides over 200,000 citations to reviews of children's books. The set also includes a complete title index for the 20-year period.

E
220 **Children's Magazine Guide**. New Providence, N.J.: R. R. Bowker. 9 issues/yr. $35.00/yr.

Formerly *Subject Index to Children's Magazines*, *CMG* is the only periodical guide compiled especially for children and the professionals who serve them. It indexes over 35 magazines, such as *SuperScience Blue*, *SuperScience Red*, *Cricket*, *Highlights for Children*, *Ranger Rick*, *Junior Scholastic*, *1-2-3 Contact*, and *Jack and Jill*, as well as professional journals such as *Learning* and *School Library Journal*. Indexing is by subject only.

Filmstrip Kit: How to Use Children's Magazine Guide (R. R. Bowker) is a full-color filmstrip and audiocassette combination in which Mickey Magazine presents basic periodical reference skills. *Reference Skills Unit: How to Use Children's Magazine Guide* (R. R. Bowker) explains periodical index usage for children age eight and older.

221 **The Cover Story Index, 1960-1989**. Robert Skapura, ed. Fort Atkinson, Wis.: Highsmith, 1990. 381p. $42.00. ISBN 0-917846-02-8.

This work is a 30-year subject index and chronology to the cover stories published in *Newsweek*, *Time*, and *U.S. News & World Report*. Part 1 cites 6,829 stories, giving story title, magazine, date, and page. These are arranged by Sears subject headings and listed in reverse chronological order (the latest first). Part 2 lists the cover stories for each of the magazines in chronological order, side by side on the page to enable the reader to compare topics covered for a given week. This one-volume index provides more convenient access to these standard news magazines than does the *Readers' Guide to Periodical Literature*. Recommended for high school libraries. [R: ARBA 91; LJ, 1 Oct 90; RBB, 1 Nov 90; WLB, Oct 90]

222 **Essay and General Literature Index**. New York: H. W. Wilson, 1934- . 2 issues/yr. w/annual and 5-year cumulations. $95.00/yr. LC 34-14581. (also available online, CD-ROM, and tape from January 1985. CD-ROM $695.00/yr.).

This subject-author index provides access to essays and articles in collections and anthologies published in English. It emphasizes the humanities and social sciences but analyzes some collections in science and other areas. Literature receives special attention, making this an excellent source for criticism of authors around the world.

The annual subscription includes a paperbound issue in June that covers January to June, a bound issue in December for the entire year, and monthly buying guides that preview books to be indexed.

Since the first cumulation for 1900-1933 appeared in 1934, 10 supplementary volumes, each covering 5-year intervals, have kept it current. The latest cumulation, *Essay and General Literature Index, 1985-1989*, indexes 19,579 essays from 1,593 collections. [R: ARBA 91]

223 **Magazine Index**. Los Altos, Calif.: Information Access, 1976- . monthly. microfilm. (362 Lakeside Dr., Foster City, CA 94404; 1-800-227-8431).

Each month's microfilm, which cumulates the previous five years, indexes 435 popular magazines. After five years, citations are dropped. The alphabetical section has two groups of data: names of persons in the news and authors, and subject headings, titles of reviewed materials, and product names. The most recently published materials appear first.

Two printed looseleaf services are included with the subscription: *Hot Topics*, which lists recent articles on subjects of current interest, and *Product Evaluations*, which cites recent product reviews. *Magazine Index* is available online through Dialog.

224 The New York Times Index. New York: The New York Times; distr., Ann Arbor, Mich.: University Microfilms, 1913- . semimonthly w/3 quarterly cumulations and annual. $475.00/yr. ISSN 0147-538X. (UMI-Newspapers, 300 N. Zeeb Rd., Ann Arbor, MI 48106).

The New York Times provides excellent coverage of all major events, national and international, and is an important source of information. The *Index*, issued twice each month, with three cumulations on microfilm and an annual bound volume, has provided coverage since 1851. It is currently in a dictionary arrangement with cross-references to names and related topics. Entries, chronologically arranged within topics, include brief abstracts of the news stories, which often can be used instead of the actual newspaper accounts. Book and theater reviews are grouped in a separate section.

Selected *New York Times* articles on microfiche are available as *New York Times File: Current Events Edition*.

225 Popular Periodical Index. Roslyn, Pa.: Popular Periodical Index, 1973- . quarterly. $40.00/yr. ISSN 0092-9727.

Formerly published twice a year but now published quarterly with an annual cumulation, this tool indexes periodicals not currently in *Readers' Guide to Periodical Literature*. Included are regional periodicals (e.g., *Philadelphia Magazine*, *Texas Monthly*, *Ohio Magazine*, *New Jersey Monthly*) and magazines that focus on computers (*PC World*), photography (*Modern Photography*), recordings and audio equipment (*Audio American Record Guide*), and many other areas. High school libraries may wish to consider this supplement to *Readers' Guide*. [R: LJ, 15 Feb 90]

226 Readers' Guide to Periodical Literature. Bronx, N.Y.: H. W. Wilson, 1900- . 18 issues/yr., w/quarterly and annual cumulations. $160.00/yr. LC 6-8232.

227 Abridged Readers' Guide to Periodical Literature. Bronx, N.Y.: H. W. Wilson, 1960- . 9 issues/yr. (none in June, July, and Aug.), w/quarterly and annual cumulations. $80.00/yr. LC 38-34737.

228 Readers' Guide Abstracts. Bronx, N.Y.: H. W. Wilson, 1988- . 10/yr. $249.00/yr. to subscribers of *Readers' Guide* or *Abridged Readers' Guide*; $199.00/yr. to *Readers' Guide* subscribers; $229.00/yr. to *Abridged Readers' Guide* subscribers.

229 WILSONDISC: Readers' Guide Abstracts. Bronx, N.Y.: H. W. Wilson, 1990. system requirements: IBM-PC, minimum 640K RAM, hard disk, CD-ROM drive. $1,495.00/yr. for elementary and secondary schools. cumulated quarterly. free online access for more recent data.

Readers' Guide, the best known and most basic periodical index, offers easy-to-use access to a broad range of popular magazines that concern such topics as news and current events, business, the arts, computers, health, fashion, politics, crafts, food and cooking, education, photography, science, sports, history, and home improvement. It currently indexes 186 magazines to which many school libraries commonly subscribe. Title/subject entries are in a single alphabet, and a wealth of cross-referencing aids in expanding and narrowing the scope of the search. The abridged version of *RG*, which may be a better choice for smaller libraries holding a limited periodical collection, indexes 65 of the most popular general-interest magazines, following the same format as the basic set.

Readers' Guide Abstracts, which abstracts the articles indexed in *RG*, started on microform in 1984 and began in-print format in September 1988. The 10 issues per year are cumulated semiannually. The abstracts are substantive, current, and relevant to the interests of high school and college students. Some 25,000 articles, arranged by subject, are condensed each year.

The CD-ROM version of *RGA* includes indexing and abstracts for the past five years. The first of three search levels is "Browse," in which the user enters a subject term and receives a display of terms and subject headings with the number of citations for each. With a function key, the user retrieves the article citations (listed in reverse chronological order), including bibliographic data and 6- to 10-line abstracts. The user also can search by subject, author, title words, journal, and organization, and by using Boolean operators. This is an excellent product with relatively few inconveniences.

RGA also is available on microfiche (8 cumulative issues per year. Call the H. W. Wilson toll-free number for price information, 1-800-462-6060; in Canada, call collect 1-212-588-8400. [R: ARBA 92]

Part III
Social Sciences

☐ ——————————————— **Anthropology** ——————————————— ☐

See also **Native Americans** under **Ethnic Minorities** for American Indians.

230 Brace, C. Loring, and others. **Atlas of Human Evolution**. 2d ed. New York: Holt, Rinehart and Winston, 1979. 178p. $19.95pa. ISBN 0-03-045021-7. LC 78-27723.

The main body of this excellent work provides chronologically arranged evidence of human evolution. Drawings of human and primate skulls, jaws, and teeth are supported by commentaries that identify the site and date of the discovery, any additional finds at the site, and the name of the discoverer. Also discussed are any controversies related to the discovery and how it is viewed within the field of anthropology. Citations to sources follow. The introduction explains geological time, anatomical features, and general theories concerning evolution. Several possible family trees conclude the volume.

231 Driver, Harold E. **Indians of North America**. 2d ed. Chicago: University of Chicago, 1969. 632p. $24.95pa. ISBN 0-226-16467-5. LC 79-76207.

Indian tribes from the Arctic to Panama comprise the focus of this work. Chapters cover such topics as historical and cultural changes, government controls, and Indian-Caucasian relations. For each tribe, the work provides a summary of such data as traditional clothing, everyday life (e.g., food, housing), and language group. Maps and a bibliography support the text. Appropriate for secondary level.

232 **The Illustrated Encyclopedia of Mankind**. Richard Carlisle and others, eds. New York: Marshall Cavendish, c1989, 1990. 22v. $449.95/set. ISBN 1-85435-032-3. LC 88-22903.

This outstanding set, a revision of the 1984 edition, offers a "description of the subsistence patterns, historical backgrounds, and cultural orientations of over 500 different people and cultures." Introducing the work are 38 pages of maps depicting population, climate, vegetation, and language groups. The remainder of volume 1 and volumes 2-15 contain alphabetically arranged entries (2 to 8 pages) covering nationalities (e.g., Irish, Korean), specific cultures (e.g., Aborigines, Lapps), tribes (e.g., American Indians), and religious groups (e.g., Amish). Content varies, but most entries treat history, language, religion, dress, and customs.

Articles in volumes 16-21 cover general themes and show how they differ among cultures (e.g., religious beliefs, costumes, social structure). Volume 22 contains general/thematic/geographic indexes, population charts, a bibliography, and a glossary of terms.

Articles are readable and well illustrated. There are more than 3,000 photographs, most in color, and numerous maps and charts. The work, however, suffers from several lacunae: the omission of many cultural and linguistic groups, inadequate coverage of others, and poor cross-referencing. Nonetheless, this excellent set should be considered by high school libraries. Those holding the 1984 edition need not purchase the 1989 set, because the revision is limited. [R: ARBA 91; RBB, 1 Feb 90]

Archaeology

□   □

233   Coe, Michael, and others. **Atlas of Ancient America**. New York: Facts on File, 1986. 240p. $45.00. ISBN 0-8160-1199-0. LC 84-25999.

This outstanding work summarizes current thought about ancient American archaeology. Part 1, on the New World, gives a survey of European discoveries and early theories about the origin of native people; part 2, on the First Americans, gives a concise summary of movements into the New World. Part 3 on North America, part 4 on Mesoamerica, and part 5 on South America constitute the main body of the volume and focus on archaeological findings in these areas. Part 6, "The Living Heritage," covers present-day cultures. Different points of view are presented, but the interpretations of the authors, well-qualified archaeologists, are clearly stated. Illustrations—black-and-white drawings, photographs, and detailed color maps—are wonderful. Highly recommended for high schools.

Other atlases in the series, also recommended, are *Atlas of Ancient Egypt* by John Baines and Jaromir Malek (Facts on File, 1980); *Atlas of the Greek World* by Peter Levi (Facts on File, 1980); and *Atlas of the Roman World* by Tim Cornell and John Matthews (Facts on File, 1982). [R: ARBA 87; BL, 1 Jan 87; LJ, 15 Apr 87; SLJ, Mar 87]

234   **The Facts on File Dictionary of Archaeology**. rev. ed. Ruth C. Whitehouse, ed. New York: Facts on File, c1983, 1988. 597p. $35.00; $16.95pa. ISBN 0-87196-048-6; 0-8160-1893-6. LC 83-16396.

This attractive volume, published in 1984 and reprinted in paperback in 1988, is written in a clear, direct style. It provides worldwide coverage of sites and cultures from the Paleolithic Era through the Middle Ages in Europe; the Islamic period in North Africa and Asia; and the early Colonial period in the Americas, Africa, and Australia. Also included are articles on techniques used in field work and biographies of prominent archaeologists.

Some of the brief entries (a few run to one or more pages) may prove taxing to the general reader due to their technical nature, but most can be readily understood. About 200 line drawings and a subject index support the text. Recommended for high schools. [R: ARBA 89]

235   **Hammond Past Worlds: The Times Atlas of Archaeology**. Maplewood, N.J.: Hammond, 1988. 319p. $85.00. ISBN 0-7230-0306-8. LC 88-675201.

This beautiful atlas draws on all the resources of modern archaeology to depict the evolution of mankind. The 750 original maps, photographs, illustrations, and site reconstructions, all in color, reveal how our ancestors lived during the 2.5 million years of their existence.

The work examines not only the well-documented classical civilizations—Greece, Rome, Persia, India, and China—but also the lesser-known ones, such as the tattooed nomads of the Steppes, the Mayas of the Yucatan rain forest, and the Incas of the Andes.

Among the spectacular site reconstructions (some of which appear to be three-dimensional) are Chinese Tonglushan copper mines from the Bronze Age and Roman water mills in fourth-century (A.D.) France. A 10-page comparative chronology, a comprehensive technical and historical glossary, an extensive bibliography, and a 6,000-entry index (by place-name and subject) all support the atlas. Highly recommended for high schools. [R: BL, 15 Jan 89; BR, Mar/Apr 89; SLJ, Feb 89; SLJ, May 89; WLB, Jan 89]

236   **Historical Dictionary of North American Archaeology**. Edward B. Jelks and Juliet C. Jelks, eds. Westport, Conn.: Greenwood Press, 1988. 795p. $95.00. ISBN 0-313-24307-7.

This extensive work lists 1,800 archaeological sites, periods, artifact types, and cultures. The 151 contributors to this authoritative work give sources for each entry, making the bibliography a list of major titles that cover the archaeology of the United States and Canada. Cross-references and an appended list of sites by states and provinces further enhance the work. The dictionary is more extensive than most high schools require, but it is recommended for those with strong demands for the subject. [R: ARBA 89; LJ, 15 Apr 89; RBB, 15 Sept 88]

237   **The World Atlas of Archaeology**. Michael Wood, ed. New York: Crown, 1988. 423p. $29.95. ISBN 0-517-66876-9.

The term *atlas* is used here in a broad sense for this volume of plates that systematically illustrate the subject. More than 1,000 color illustrations support and explain the text of this outstanding work.

Arranged geographically and chronologically, the atlas provides extensive social, economic, and cultural information. Sections treat prehistoric Europe, the classical world, the Middle Ages, Byzantium, Islam, the modern period, and 12 major geographic areas. A glossary, bibliography, and subject index enhance the volume. Recommended for high schools requiring in-depth coverage of the field. [R: ARBA 86; BL, 15 May 86; LJ, 1 Dec 85; WLB, Feb 86]

□ Biography □

GENERAL WORKS

See specific subject areas (e.g., **Literature, Women's Studies**) for related biographical works.

238 **Portraits: Focusing on Biography and Autobiography in the Secondary Schools**. Margaret Fleming and Jo McGinnis, eds. Urbana, Ill.: National Council of Teachers of English, 1985. $8.95.

Using models such as *I Know Why the Caged Bird Sings* by Maya Angelou and *Abe Lincoln Grows Up* by Carl Sandburg, this work provides detailed explanations for nine approaches to teaching biographies and autobiographies. A bibliography that lists additional suggested titles concludes the volume.

BIBLIOGRAPHIES AND INDEXES

239 **Almanac of Famous People: A Comprehensive Reference Guide to More Than 25,000 Famous and Infamous Newsmakers from Biblical Times to the Present**. 4th ed. Susan L. Statler, ed. Detroit: Gale, 1989. 3v. $95.00/set. ISBN 0-8103-2784-8. ISSN 1040-127X.

Almanac of Famous People, formerly *Biography Almanac*, provides citations to biographical information for over 25,000 past and present notables in sports, politics, business, science, and a wide range of other activities. Despite the claim to being a biographical dictionary, its information is limited to pseudonym, real name, or nickname; nationality; occupation; and birth and death dates and places. The book's primary purpose is to cite biographical sketches and articles that appear in over 300 biographical sources.

Volumes 1 and 2 contain citations. Volume 3, the indexes, provides a chronological list by birth and death dates; a geographical index for birth and death locations by city, state, and nation; and an occupational index. High school students will welcome this set, which refers to sources within the library and elsewhere. [R: ARBA 90; BL, 15 Dec 89; WLB, Apr 89]

240 **Biographical Books, 1950-1980**. Gertrude Jemmings, ed. in chief. New Providence, N.J.: R. R. Bowker, 1980. 1577p. $135.00. ISBN 0-8352-1315-3. LC 80-149017.

A bibliography of in-print and out-of-print biographies and autobiographies, this work lists 42,152 titles distributed in the United States. Arranged alphabetically by biographee, entries give full bibliographic data, LC subject headings, and DDC and LC numbers. Separate name (including persons in collective biographies), author, title, vocational, and imprint indexes support the listings. A similar volume, *Biographical Books, 1876-1949* (R. R. Bowker, 1983), covers the earlier period.

241 **Biography Index: A Cumulative Index to Biographical Material in Books and Magazines**. Bronx, N.Y.: H. W. Wilson, 1946- . quarterly (Aug. issue is a cumulation). $110.00/yr. LC 47-6532.

This important index cites biographical information for famous persons throughout the world, from ancient times to the present, who represent almost every area of specialization. It lists a variety of sources: biographical data in more than 2,600 periodicals; current English-language books dealing with individual and collective biography (some 1,000 annually); fiction (biographical novels), drama, and poetry; pictorial works; juvenile literature; and biographical information from otherwise nonbiographical works.

It is divided into two sections: a name index and an index to professions and occupations. The first provides birth and death dates, nationality, and bibliographic citations. The second lists the names of biographees covered in that issue by profession and occupation. The index is also available through WILSONLINE and on CD-ROM ($1,095/yr.). *Biography Index* is recommended for high schools and other libraries needing extensive biographical materials.

E +
242 Breen, Karen. **Index to Collective Biographies for Young Readers**. 4th ed. New Providence, N.J.: R. R. Bowker, 1988. 494p. $44.95. ISBN 0-8352-2348-5. LC 88-19410.

This index identifies short biographical material about historic and contemporary notables that is suitable for elementary and junior high school reading levels. The latest edition indexes the contents of 1,129 collective biographies covering 9,773 people. Most titles indexed in the first three editions (1970, 1975, and 1979) have been retained; works now out-of-print are noted. The 4th edition adds 187 volumes that contain 2,528 biographies.

The index is inclusive rather than selective. Titles have been chosen from the following sources: the holdings of large public libraries in the New York City area, ordering guides of the New York City Board of Education, *The Elementary School Library Collection*, *Books in Print*, and publisher's catalogs.

An alphabetical list of biographees provides basic data (birth and death dates, nationality, and field of endeavor), followed by symbols that indicate books that include the person. The subject list of biographies cites biographees by fields of activity and nationality. The collective biographies are also indexed by title. [R: ARBA 89; BL, 1 Mar 89; LJ, 15 Mar 89]

243 **Research Guide to American Historical Biography**. Robert Maccigrosso, ed. Washington, D.C.: Beacham, 1988. 3v. $189.00. ISBN 0-933833-09-1. LC 88-19316.

This set has three objectives: to help college and secondary students prepare term papers, to aid college teachers and graduate students in doing research in fields outside their specialities, and to serve librarians as a ready-reference guide and selection tool. It is a guide to sources of biographical information about popular notables in politics, business, education, labor, journalism, religion, and the military. Excluded are literary notables since they are covered in an earlier companion volume, *Research Guide to Biography and Criticism* (Beacham, 1985).

For each of the 282 individuals (several in joint entries), there is a chronology of the subject's life, coverage of activities of historical significance, and a survey of biographical sources. Principal sources are critically annotated and coded: "A" for academic, "G" for general, and "Y" for young audiences. Another section describes novels, films, plays, and other creative works in which the person is portrayed.

An appendix in each volume groups subjects by era, and the last volume contains an index of major sources cited. This work is similar to *Great Lives from History: American Series*. Recommended for high school libraries. [R: BL, 15 May 89; LJ, 15 Mar 89; WLB, Apr 89]

LIVING PERSONS

E +
244 **Current Biography Yearbook**. Bronx, N.Y.: H. W. Wilson. annual. $52.00. ISSN 0084-9499. LC 40-27432.

245 **Current Biography**. Bronx, N.Y.: H. W. Wilson, 1940- . 11 issues/yr. (Jan.-Nov.). $52.00/yr.

246 **Current Biography Cumulated Index, 1940-1990**. Bronx, N.Y.: H. W. Wilson, 1991. 133p. $25.00. ISBN 0-8242-0722-X. LC 40-27432.

Current Biography, focusing on "today's newsmakers" and "tomorrow's history makers," appears in two forms: a monthly periodical and a yearbook in which the year's profiles are accumulated. Libraries may subscribe to both formats, but if one is chosen, the *Yearbook* is preferable.

More than 175 profiles (15-18 each month) appear each year on artists, politicians, scientists, writers, motion picture and television personalities, journalists, and other notables. The biographical articles, which range from one to seven pages, are vivid, informative, and accurate. Essays recount the subject's career, and frequent quotations reveal the biographee's opinions and personality. A recent photograph, an address, and references to additional sources are provided. Biographies included in past issues are often rewritten and updated if the subject continues to be newsworthy.

The monthly issues and annuals contain death notices for those who have appeared in the past. Each issue provides a cumulative index for the current year, and each annual contains an index for several previous years. The *Cumulative Index* for 1940-1990 gives access to almost 20,000 biographies; entries include career identification and cross-references for name variants and pseudonyms. Recommended for upper middle school through high school. [R: ARBA 92]

247 **Newsmakers**. Peter M. Gareffa, ed. Detroit: Gale, 1985- . quarterly w/annual cumulation. $85.00/yr.

248 **Newsmakers: The People behind Today's Headlines. 1991 Cumulation**. Louise Mooney, ed. Detroit: Gale, 1991. $85.00. ISBN 0-8103-5452-7. ISSN 0899-0417.
        Formerly *Contemporary Newsmakers*, the title was changed in 1988 to *Newsmakers*. Similar in format to *Current Biography*, each quarterly issue contains some 50 biographical profiles and concise obituaries of people in the news. The two- to three-page essays include photographs. Each issue is indexed by name, nationality, occupation, and subject.
        People who have up-to-date sketches in *Current Biography* do not receive full treatment in *Newsmakers*. Due to the lack of duplication, *Newsmakers* is recommended as a supplement to *Current Biography*. [R: ARBA 90; BR, Sept/Oct 89]

249 **Who's Who in America 1989-1991: Junior & Senior High School Version**. Wilmette, Ill.: Marquis Who's Who, 1989. 4v. $79.00pa./set. ISBN 0-8379-1250-4. LC 04-16934.
        Designed especially for junior and senior high school students, this work is a paperback spinoff of *Who's Who in America*. The editors have selected 6,000 persons from 77,000 in the parent set whom they believe will interest the intended audience. Each of the four volumes covers a subject area: science and technology, politics and government, sports, and entertainment. Biographical information is identical to that contained in the parent volumes. Entries, however, contain no abbreviations and are set in a larger typeface, which makes them easier to read.
        Coverage, appropriate for the audience, includes all members of Congress, important foreign leaders (taken from *Who's Who in the World*), actors, musicians, composers, authors, artists, professional sports figures, and other notables. At less than half the cost of the parent set, school libraries should consider it a bargain. Recommended. [R: ARBA 91; RBB, 1 Jan 90]

250 **Who's Who in America: Junior & Senior High School Version**. [Volume 5-Volume 8]. Wilmette, Ill.: Marquis Who's Who, 1991. 4v. $87.00pa./set. ISBN 0-8379-1251-2. LC 04-16934.
        The first four volumes in the series provided nearly 6,000 entries about subjects from the fields of science and technology, politics, sports, and entertainment. The new volumes add 5,000 more entries from business and industry, literary and visual arts, and world leaders. Data for each includes vital statistics, parents, marital status, career patterns, and achievements, creative works, civic and political activities, military record, awards and fellowships, and more. This companion volume of worthwhile information will be useful to students.

251 **Who's Who in America 1990-91**. 46th ed. Wilmette, Ill.: Marquis Who's Who, 1990. 2v. $375.00. ISBN 0-8379-0146-4. LC 4-16934.
        Some high schools may require the full version of *Who's Who in America* rather than the *Junior & Senior High School Version*. It is, of course, a basic, current biographical directory of prominent Americans and others who identify with American life and interests.
        Most of the information for each entry is generated by a questionnaire sent to the biographee. Selection of the 77,000 persons listed is based on rigorous criteria, especially activities of reference value. Names are often deleted due to retirement or death. New editions are issued biennially. *Who's Who in America Index*, a separate publication, arranges names by geographic and professional areas. Marquis Who's Who also issues regional biographical directories: *Who's Who in the West*, *Who's Who in the Midwest*, *Who's Who in the South and Southwest*, and *Who's Who in the East*. [R: ARBA 91]

LIVING AND DECEASED PERSONS

252 **Contemporary Heroes and Heroines: A Biographical Guide**. Detroit: Gale, 1990. 451p. $49.95. ISBN 0-8103-4860-8.
        The editors have selected 103 twentieth-century heroes and heroines for inclusion in this volume, which is useful at junior and senior high school levels. The subjects represent many fields of endeavor: peace activists (e.g., Desmond Tutu), political figures (e.g., Eleanor Roosevelt), civil rights advocates

(e.g., Medgar Evers), news commentators (e.g., Walter Cronkite), foreign leaders (e.g., Lech Walesa), and entertainers (e.g., Bill Cosby).

Entries begin with a small portrait, a significant quotation by or about the person, birth (and death) date, and current address (if any). A two- to four-page essay that describes the person's background and accomplishments is followed by a short (current) bibliography. Those included are notables most frequently asked about in libraries. [R: ARBA 91; RBB, 1 May 90; WLB, May 90]

E
253 **People to Know.** Chicago: World Book, 1989. 256p. $15.95. ISBN 0-7166-0689-5. LC 65-25105.

A supplement to *Childcraft*, *People to Know* relates the stories of 30 famous men and women, living and deceased, written for children in the elementary grades. The articles, averaging seven pages each, consist of a picture, a short biographical profile, and an account of an incident in the person's life. An information box that highlights the subject's accomplishments concludes the entry. Among those included are Rosa Parks, Mother Theresa, Clara Barton, Sequoyah, and Sally Ride. Indexed. [R: ARBA 91; RBB, 15 Feb 90]

E+
254 **The World Almanac Biographical Dictionary.** By the editors of the *World Almanac*. New York: World Almanac/St. Martin's Press, 1990. 390p. $19.95. ISBN 0-88687-564-1. LC 90-45309.

This compact volume, designed to replace the publisher's *World Almanac Book of Who* (1980), provides brief biographies of 8,000 historical and contemporary notables. All are grouped in 15 broad categories (e.g., actors, composers, ballet, and opera; philosophy and religion) and then alphabetically within each group. Writers and entertainers comprise more than one-third of this quick-reference volume. [R: RBB, 15 Jan 91]

DECEASED PERSONS

255 **American Reformers.** Alden Whitman, ed. Bronx, N.Y.: H. W. Wilson, 1985. 944p. $83.00. ISBN 0-8242-0705-X. LC 85-636.

This outstanding work offers concise biographies of 508 notable American reformers from the seventeenth century to the present (e.g., Thomas Paine, Harriet Tubman, Clarence Darrow, Margaret Sanger, Malcolm X, Louis Brandeis). Persons covered represent contrasting political and ideological viewpoints on religious tolerance, freedom of speech, racial and sexual equality, prison reform, temperance, and many other areas. The one- to two-page profiles, written by historians and subject specialists, include bibliographies by and about the reformer; most also have a portrait. A list of biographees by category supports this excellent volume. Recommended for high school libraries. [R: ARBA 86; BL, 15 June 86; WLB, Dec 85]

256 **Cambridge Biographical Dictionary.** Magnus Magnusson, ed. New York: Cambridge University Press, 1990. 1604p. $34.00. ISBN 0-521-39518-6.

Chambers Biographical Dictionary, a standard source for many decades, has changed its title to *Cambridge Biographical Dictionary*. The latest edition has also expanded its coverage by almost one-third to cover 19,000 international personalities, both living and deceased. Due to its British origin, coverage of European notables predominate, but important Americans are profiled. Despite their brevity, the well-written articles contain much information. Its editor also has made a special effort to include perceptive assessments of each biographee's personality and achievements. The best single-volume work that provides worldwide coverage for all time periods, it is recommended for secondary schools. [R: ARBA 92; LJ, Jan 91; RBB, 1 Feb 91]

257 **Concise Dictionary of American Biography.** 4th ed. Scribner's, 1990. 1536p. $150.00. ISBN 0-684-19188-1. LC 90-8951.

This condensed version of *Dictionary of American Biography* retains all of the 18,110 persons covered in the original set and first eight supplements (these extends the coverage to persons deceased prior to 1971). Some entries give only basic data—dates and places of birth and death, field of endeavor, family, education, and achievements—but articles about more important persons contain evaluative comments and information on character and influence. An occupational index, including *see also* references, has been added to this edition. Highly recommended for middle and high schools, especially those that do not have *DAB*. [R: ARBA 92; LJ, 1 Apr 91; RBB 15 Mar 91]

258 **Dictionary of American Biography**. Prepared under the auspices of the American Council of Learned Societies. Allen Johnson and Dumas Malone, eds. New York: Scribner's, 1928-1988. 10v. and 8 suppl. $1,499/set. ISBN 0-684-19075-3. LC 44-41895.

259 **Dictionary of American Biography Comprehensive Index: Complete through Supplement Eight**. New York: Scribner's, 1990. 1100p. $85.00. ISBN 0-684-19114-8.

This classic set, usually cited as *DAB*, contains evaluative articles about noteworthy deceased persons who resided in what is now the United States. For the early period, British officers who served in America after the colonies declared independence are excluded. The original set appeared between 1928 and 1937; supplements have been added at 8- to 10-year intervals. The current reprint incorporates the original set and first four supplements. The remaining supplements are separate volumes, which can be purchased individually or as part of the set.

The long, analytical articles, written and signed by subject experts, are supported by bibliographies of primary sources and secondary accounts. The main set and supplements now include 18,120 essays that range from 500 to over 16,000 words. There are separate indexes for names, contributors, birthplaces, occupations, schools and colleges, and topics.

Supplement 8, the newest addition to the set, adds 454 notables who died between 1966 and 1970 (e.g., Dwight D. Eisenhower, Martin Luther King, Jr., Robert Kennedy). The *Comprehensive Index* provides access to the basic set and all supplements.

DAB is highly recommended to high school libraries. Those unable to afford it should hold the concise version. [R: ARBA 91; BL, 15 May 90; WLB, June 90]

260 **Dictionary of Canadian Biography (Dictionnaire Biographique du Canada)**. Marc La Terreur, ed. English ed., Toronto: University of Toronto Press; French ed., Quebec: Les Presses de l'Universite' Laval, 1966-1990. 12v. $75.00-$150.00/v.

261 **Dictionary of Canadian Biography. Index to Volumes I-XII**. 1991. 557p. $85.00. ISBN 0-8020-3464-0.

High school students involved in Canadian studies will require this work. The Canadian counterpart of *Dictionary of American Biography*, it contains critical essays about persons who played important roles in that country's history, Canadians as well as persons from England, France, America, and other countries. Arranged in chronological order by death date and then alphabetically by name, the set is complete for the earliest period of Canadian history through 1900.

The first three volumes cover the period through 1770; subsequent volumes cover 20 to 30 years each. Volume 12 completes the first part of the series.

The format is not uniform, but most volumes contain a survey of the period and an alphabetical list of persons included. Biographies for 500 or more persons follow. The volume concludes with a general bibliography of frequently cited sources; a list of contributors; and indexes by category and occupation, geographical area, and name. The cumulative index replaces the index to volumes 1-4 and indexing in each volume. [R: ARBA 92]

262 **The Dictionary of National Biography**. Leslie Stephen and Sidney Lee, eds. London and New York: Oxford University Press, 1882-1953. 22v. [includes first supplement]. $1,250.00. ISBN 0-19-865101-5.

263 **The Dictionary of National Biography. Supplement: January 1901-December 1911**. London and New York: Oxford University Press, c1912, 1963. 3v. in 1. $125.00. ISBN 0-19-865201-1.

264 **The Dictionary of National Biography: 1912-1921**. H. W. C. Davis, ed. London and New York: Oxford University Press, 1927. 623p. $105.00. ISBN 0-19-865202-X.

265 **The Dictionary of National Biography: 1922-1930**. J. R. H. Weaver, ed. London and New York: Oxford University Press, 1937. 962p. $110.00. ISBN 0-19-865203-8.

266 **The Dictionary of National Biography: 1931-1940**. L. G. Wickham Legg, ed. London and New York: Oxford University Press, 1949. 968p. $110.00. ISBN 0-19-865204-6.

267 **The Dictionary of National Biography: 1941-1950**. L. G. Wickham Legg and E. T. Williams, eds. London and New York: Oxford University Press, 1959. 1031p. $98.00. ISBN 0-19-865205-4.

268   The Dictionary of National Biography: 1951-1960. E. T. Williams and Helen M. Parker, eds. London and New York: Oxford University Press, 1971. 1150p. $89.00. ISBN 0-19-865206-2.

269   The Dictionary of National Biography: 1961-1970. E. T. Williams and Helen M. Parker, eds. London and New York: Oxford University Press, 1981. 1178p. $110.00. ISBN 0-19-865207-0.

270   The Dictionary of National Biography: 1971-1980. Robert Blake and Christine S. Nicholls, eds. London and New York: Oxford University Press, 1986. 1184p. $89.00. ISBN 0-19-865208-9.

271   The Dictionary of National Biography: 1981-1985. Robert Blake and C. S. Nicholls, eds. New York: Oxford University press, 1990. 518p. $78.00. ISBN 0-19-865210-0. LC 89-39766.

This preeminent dictionary, which set a high standard for other national biographical works when it first appeared in 1885, contains long, analytical essays on prominent deceased British subjects "who have achieved any reasonable measure of distinction in any walk of life." A few legendary heroes, such as King Arthur and Robin Hood, are also included.

The original set spans the period from earliest times to the end of 1900; the supplements, each covering a decade, include persons who died between 1901-1985, bringing the total coverage to over 32,000. Articles vary from long entries for the most prominent persons (over 60 pages for Shakespeare) to brief essays on minor figures. Each entry, written and signed by an expert, is supported by a bibliography of primary sources and secondary accounts. A cumulative index ends each supplement and indexes all previous supplements. Beginning with the 1981-1985 volume, supplements will be issued at five-year intervals.

The Concise Dictionary of National Biography, containing condensed versions of the original articles, was produced in two parts: *From the Beginning to 1900* (Oxford University Press, repr. 1906, 1953) and *1901-1970* (Oxford University Press, 1982). [R: ARBA 91]

E +
272   The Doubleday Book of Famous Americans. By Suzanne Levert. New York: Doubleday, 1989. 305p. $15.95. ISBN 0-385-23699-9. LC 87-26215.

Profiles of some 100 noted Americans from the seventeenth through the twentieth centuries comprise this volume, which is suitable for grades 5 and up. Using quotations and anecdotes, essays of about 550 words relate the major events and accomplishments for each notable. Black-and-white photographs of biographees illustrate the volume. Indexed. [R: BR, Nov/Dec 89; SLJ, Dec 89]

E +
273   Downs, Robert B., John T. Flanagan, and Harold W. Scott. More Memorable Americans 1750-1950. Englewood, Colo.: Libraries Unlimited, 1985. 397p. $30.00. ISBN 0-87287-421-4. LC 84-27780.

This work supplements *Memorable Americans 1750-1950* (Libraries Unlimited, o.p.), which included 150 individuals who were "memorable" for their contributions in politics, the arts, entertainment, journalism, medicine, education, science, the military, and other areas. The supplement adds 151 persons of achievement for the same period. One- to six-page sketches recount basic biographical facts and achievements. Appendixes list biographees by date of birth and by careers. Most of those listed are also included in *Dictionary of American Biography*; nonetheless, this highly readable work is recommended for students in upper elementary through high school. [R: ARBA 86; BL, 15 Jan 86; VOYA, Dec 85; WLB, June 85]

E +
274   Fradin, Dennis Brindell. Remarkable Children: Twenty Who Made History. Boston: Little, Brown, 1987. 207p. $14.95. ISBN 0-316-29126-9. LC 87-3820.

Some of the profiles included in this collection will help students with assignments, but all will evoke inspiration. The work treats 20 living and deceased prodigies who performed, created, or made a discovery at an early age. Some are well-known personalities (e.g., Pablo Picasso, Hellen Keller) while others are relatively unknown (e.g., Hilda Conkling, a young poet). Fradin interviewed several of the subjects or others who knew them. [R: ARBA 89; BL, 1 Dec 87; SLJ, Dec 87]

E+
275 Great Lives. Simon Boughton, comp. New York: Doubleday, 1988. 208p. $19.95. ISBN 0-385-24283-2. LC 87-22147.

Over 1,000 persons worldwide "who have shaped history" are described—politicians, entertainers, scientists, philosophers, athletes, writers, and many others. Alphabetically arranged entries range from 50 to 200 words, but major world leaders receive 2-page coverage.

A table of contents places the biographees in chronological order and cites the pages on which they appear. A subject index lists the biographees according to such things as the historical event in which each participated, titles of books or other creative accomplishments, and countries. Most of the notables can be found in other sources, but this is a convenient compilation of biographical data designed for upper elementary level through high school. [R: BR, Nov/Dec 88; SLJ, May 89]

E+
276 Great Lives from History: American Series. Frank N. Magill, ed. Pasadena, Calif.: Salem Press, 1987. 5v. $325.00/set. ISBN 0-89356-529-6. LC 86-31561.

This set on American notables initiates a biographical series on outstanding men and women who have played prominent roles throughout history. Other sets in the series, such as *Great Lives from History: Renaissance to 1900 Series*, cover different eras and geographical areas.

Essays, which range from 5 to 7 pages, cover 456 persons who have made contributions in many fields, such as politics, science, the arts, entertainment, and sports. All biographies follow the same format, and each includes birth and death dates, speciality and contributions, early life, career, place in history, and annotated bibliography. The signed articles, contributed by scholars, are indexed by name and "Area of Achievement." [R: ARBA 88; LJ, June 87; RBB, 15 Oct 87, WLB, Sept 87]

277 Great Lives from History: Renaissance to 1900 Series. Frank N. Magill, ed. Pasadena, Calif.: Salem Press, 1989. 5v. $350.00/set. ISBN 0-89356-551-2. LC 89-24039.

Similar in format and scope to *Great Lives from History: American Series*, this set contains readable articles on 495 notables from the non-English-speaking world. The emphasis is on Europeans, and among those covered are Martin Luther, Karl Marx, Galileo, and Rembrandt. The signed essays, which average five pages, were contributed by scholars. Each article covers the subject's early life, work, and place in history, and lists an annotated bibliography. Indexing is by name and area of achievement. The set is designed for high school and college level but can be used by younger students. [R: ARBA 91; WLB, Mar 90]

278 McGraw-Hill Encyclopedia of World Biography. David I. Eggenberger, ed. in chief. New York: McGraw-Hill, 1975. 12v. $550.00/set. ISBN 0-07-079635-5. LC 70-37402.

279 Encyclopedia of World Biography. 20th Century Supplement. Palatine, Ill.: Jack Heraty Associates, 1987. 4v. $229.00/set. ISBN 0-910081-02-6. LC 86-63173.

This work is designed to support the curricular needs of students from junior high through college. The original set covers some 5,000 decreased world leaders from throughout history in signed articles that vary from 500 to 3,500 words. Portraits, maps, other illustrations, and bibliographies all support the text. The last volume consists of a study guide and analytical index that contains entries for people, places, events, inventions, and categories of biographees (e.g., child prodigies, handicapped, immigrants).

The *20th Century Supplement* adds notables, both living and deceased, such as Yasser Arafat, Henry Cisneros, and Anne Frank. Women and persons from the Third World and Middle East are emphasized. Entries, which average one page, are followed by references for further reading. The last volume contains a study guide and analytical index patterned after those included in the basic set. Highly recommended. [R: ARBA 74, 88, 89]

280 Nobel Prize Winners: An H. W. Wilson Biographical Dictionary. Tyler Wasson, ed. Bronx, N.Y.: H. W. Wilson, 1987. 1165p. $90.00. ISBN 0-8242-0756-4. LC 87-16468.

Biographical profiles of 566 people and institutions that have received the Nobel Prize between 1901 and 1986 comprise this dictionary. It is arranged alphabetically by prize winner and indexed by a chronological list divided into categories. Each entry contains a 1,200- to 1,500-word essay that includes a survey of the person's life and career, a description of the work for which the prize was awarded, an evaluation of the laureate's contribution to the field, a photograph, and a bibliography of works by and about the subject. Supplements are promised every five years, beginning in 1992. A valuable source for secondary libraries. [R: ARBA 88; BL, 15 Apr 88; BR, May/June 88; SLJ, May 88; WLB, Mar 88]

281   Oxbury, Harold. **Great Britons: Twentieth Century Lives**. New York: Oxford University Press, 1985. 370p. $35.00. ISBN 0-19-211599-5. LC 84-27214.

All of the 645 famous personalities of modern Britain selected for this work died between 1915 and 1980. Oxbury, the principal editor of the *Concise Dictionary of National Biography*, has made an excellent selection of persons who represent a wide range of fields. He includes both native-born and naturalized British subjects. Over 200 photographs and illustrations accompany the short, informative biographies. An occupation/interest index gives access to the volume. This affordable work is highly recommended for secondary schools. [R: ARBA 87; LJ, 15 Feb 86; RBB, 1 May 86]

282   Schlessinger, Bernard S., and June H. Schlessinger, eds. **The Who's Who of Nobel Prize Winners 1901-1990**. 2d ed. Phoenix, Ariz.: Oryx Press, 1991. 234p. $39.50. ISBN 0-89774-599-X. LC 90-23882.

This edition of the Schlessingers' guide to Nobel prize winners includes a foreword discussing the background of the prizes and 593 entries for winners in chemistry, economics, literature, medicine and physiology, peace, and physics from 1901 to 1990. Entries for those winners included in the previous edition have been revised. The book is arranged first by subject category of the prize, then chronologically. Each entry includes the full name of the winner; category of prize and year awarded; dates of birth and death; names of the winner's parents, spouse, and children; nationality or citizenship; religion; education; career; other awards; selected publications; biographical sources; and commentary. Name, education, nationality, and religion indexes simplify access to the information provided. Recommended as a useful reference source for high school libraries.

283   Vernoff, Edward, and Rima Shore. **The International Dictionary of 20th Century Biography**. New York: New American Library/Dutton, 1987. 736p. $24.95; $12.95pa. ISBN 0-452-00529-2; 0-452-00952-9pa. LC 88-21885.

Articles of 100 to 250 words cover 5,600 twentieth-century notables, living and deceased, throughout the world. Each alphabetically arranged entry provides dates and education, identifies contributions and important events in the person's life, and cites book-length biographies of the subject. Indexing classifies persons by broad fields of endeavor (e.g., literature, art science, politics, sports) broken down by nationality. Students assigned to report on a prominent individual in a given field will welcome this feature. Appropriate for middle and high school libraries. [R: ARBA 88; SLJ, May 88]

E+
284   **Webster's American Biographies**. Charles Van Doren, ed. Springfield, Mass.: Merriam-Webster, c1974, 1979. 1248p. $18.95. ISBN 0-87779-253-4. LC 74-6341.

This work focuses on well-known Americans, living and deceased, who are prominent in a variety of fields. The 3,082 entries, which range from a few sentences to a paragraph, give dates, field of endeavor, career highlights, and significant contributions. A geographic index to biographees by states and territories and a career/professional index support the volume. This is a standard work for all school library media centers. [R: ARBA 81]

E+
285   **Webster's New Biographical Dictionary**. Springfield, Mass.: Merriam-Webster, 1988. 1130p. $21.95. ISBN 0-87779-543-6. LC 87-28302.

The new edition of this standard ready-reference source, the first complete revision in 40 years, contains brief entries for some 30,000 "important, celebrated, or notorious figures." These individuals come from all countries, but emphasis is on British and American notables. Other nationalities, however, are well represented. The basic difference between the old version and the new is the absence of living persons.

The arrangement is alphabetical by family name, with cross-references for titles of nobility, pseudonyms, nicknames, and variant spellings. Entries vary from a few sentences to a page and provide pronunciation, dates, nationality, occupation, and details about the subject's place in history. This is an indispensable reference tool for all levels of school media centers. [R: ARBA 90]

NICKNAMES AND PSEUDONYMS

286   Atkinson, Frank. **Dictionary of Literary Pseudonyms: A Selection of Modern Popular Writers in English**. 4th ed. Chicago: American Library Association, 1987. 304p. $20.00. ISBN 0-8389-2045-4. LC 86-28775.

This update of a 1977 work adds 2,000 new pseudonyms, bringing the total to 11,500 English-language writers who lived in the twentieth century. The dictionary focuses on British authors, but many Americans and some Latin Americans receive attention. It is a useful source for high school libraries. [R: ARBA 88; WLB, Sept 87]

287 **Pseudonyms and Nicknames Dictionary**. 3d ed. Jennifer Mossman, ed. Detroit: Gale, 1986. 2v. 2207p. $235.00/set. ISBN 0-8103-0541-0.

288 **New Pseudonyms and Nicknames**. Jennifer Mossman, ed. Detroit: Gale, 1988. 306p. $120.00pa. ISBN 0-8103-0548-8.
The 80,000 pseudonyms and nicknames used by over 55,000 persons in the third edition, and the 9,000 names in the supplement, cover historical and contemporary notables chosen from a variety of fields (e.g., entertainers, sports figures). Entries furnish original and assumed names, dates, nationality, occupation, and codes that refer to additional sources of information. Cross-references take the reader from the assumed name to the main entry, which gives the original name. [R: ARBA 88]

E+
289 Room, Adrian. **A Dictionary of Pseudonyms and Their Origins: With Stories of Name Changes**. Jefferson, N.C.: McFarland, 1989. 342p. $35.00. ISBN 0-89950-450-7. LC 89-42750.
This is a revised and enlarged edition of *Naming Names* (McFarland, 1981). The first section contains a group of essays that address the significance of names, the reasons for name changes, and the problem of names in general. The main portion contains an alphabetical list of around 4,000 pseudonyms and changed or adopted names, including many drawn from literature, entertainment, and the world in general.
Stories behind name changes are a special feature. There are no cross-references from the original name, but this omission causes no problem, since the reader is seeking the real name of such well-known persons as Joyce Brothers, Mike Nichols, or Pope John XXIII. The book is far less extensive than Sharp's *Handbook of Pseudonyms and Personal Nicknames*; nonetheless, this entertaining and informative volume is recommended for all levels. [R: ARBA 90; BL, 1 May 90; WLB, Mar 90]

290 Sharp, Harold S., comp. **Handbook of Pseudonyms and Personal Nicknames**. Metuchen, N.J.: Scarecrow, 1972. 2v. $59.50/set. ISBN 0-8108-0460-3. LC 71-189886. *First Supplement*, 1975. 2v. $69.50/set. ISBN 0-8108-0807-2. *Second Supplement*, 1982. 295p. $27.50. ISBN 0-8108-1539-7.
The 50,000-plus nicknames and pseudonyms identified in this work and its supplements cover over 30,000 persons worldwide from all time periods. Entries provide real names, dates, brief identifiers, and pseudonyms; there are cross-references from nicknames, pseudonyms, and variant spellings to the real name. The extensive coverage provided by these volumes makes them an excellent choice for secondary schools. [R: ARBA 83]

291 **Twentieth Century American Nicknames**. Laurence Urdang, ed. Bronx, N.Y.: H. W. Wilson, 1979. 398p. $35.00. ISBN 0-8242-0642-8. LC 79-23390.
Some 4,000 nicknames—mainly for persons, but some of places, events, and animals—for twentieth-century America are identified in this work, which complements *American Nicknames* by George Earlie Shankle (2d ed., H. W. Wilson, 1955). Nicknames and proper names are arranged alphabetically with identifying information under the proper name. Entries for people list legal name and dates with all relevant nicknames; events and other entries are similarly covered. Nickname entries refer the reader to the proper name. Included are the famous and the notorious in all fields of endeavor. [R: ARBA 81; LJ, 1 Mar 80; SLJ, Dec 80; WLB, May 80]

Business and Economics

ALMANACS AND HANDBOOKS

See also **Consumer Education** for personal finance.
See **Careers** for occupations and summer jobs.

292 **Business One-Irwin Business & Investment Almanac**. Homewood, Ill.: Business One-Irwin. annual. $49.95. LC 82-643830.

This annual provides ready-reference material on all aspects of business, including statistical data; articles on new laws, regulations, taxation, and current events; information on the stock market; and economic activities. Other sections explain how to read financial statements, give comparative living costs in U.S. metropolitan areas, and show how to calculate equivalency figures. This excellent compilation of current data is highly recommended for high schools. [R: ARBA 91]

■ *Career Opportunities in Advertising and Public Relations*. *See* entry 332.

■ *Clothiers*. *See* entry 337.

293 DeVries, Mary A. **The Office Sourcebook**. Englewood Cliffs, N.J.: Prentice-Hall, 1989. 393p. $12.95pa. ISBN 0-13-798430-8. LC 89-31209.

A paperback version of DeVries's *Secretary's Almanac and Fact Book* (Prentice-Hall, 1985) with minor updating, this work provides quick-reference facts on such topics as postal regulations, foreign exchange, government agencies (p.o., passport, tax), copyright, and a wide variety of office practices and procedures. Indexed. An inexpensive compilation for secretaries and other office personnel, it is a good choice for high school libraries. [R: ARBA 90]

294 Downes, John, and Jordan E. Goodman. **Barron's Finance and Investment Handbook**. 3d ed. Hauppauge, N.Y.: Barron's Educational Series, 1990. 1152p. $24.95. ISBN 0-8120-6188-8. LC 86-10906.

This outstanding handbook provides investors with the necessary background for making sound investments. Part 1 covers all types of investments from annuities to zero-coupon securities, including when to buy, sell, and hold options. It also explains the risk, tax, and economic considerations of each. Part 2 tells how to read annual reports; part 3 explains how to interpret newspaper financial pages and ticker tapes, including stock options, futures, corporate bonds, and government securities. The final section is a dictionary of concisely defined terms. Highly recommended for high schools.

E+
295 Elliot, Charles. **Atlas of Economic Issues**. New York: Facts on File, 1991. 64p. $16.95. ISBN 0-8160-2481-2.

This atlas gives students from upper elementary grades through junior high school an introduction to basic economic concepts and terms. Among the subject areas covered are the social frameworks within which economic systems function; economic problems (poverty, unemployment, and inflation); the forces of production (e.g., manufacturing industries, the role of unions); economic consumption; and the organization of economic systems. The work contains color graphics on every page. Recommended.

296 Folbre, Nancy. **A Field Guide to the U.S. Economy**. New York: Pantheon Books/Random House, 1987. 1v. (various paging). $10.95pa. ISBN 0-394-75047-0. LC 86-42974.

Brief entries that explain how the U.S. economy works comprise the text of this small book, usually one topic to a double-page spread. The delightful essays include graphs, charts, statistical tables, and cartoons. Ten chapters, covering such topics as farmers, government spending, and macroeconomics, cite general sources for each chapter and data sources for each page. A section entitled "Toolkit" that explains various techniques (e.g., how to read and create graphs) and a glossary complete the volume. Recommended for secondary schools. [R: ARBA 88; BR, May 88; Kliatt, Apr 88; WLB, Apr 88]

297 Hoover's Handbook: Profiles of Over 500 Major Corporations. Austin, Tex.: Reference Press; distr., Emeryville, Calif.: Publishers Group West, 1990. 646p. $19.95pa. ISBN 1-878753-00-2.

Over 500 public and private companies, mostly from the United States, are profiled in full-page summaries. Alphabetically arranged entries give the nature of the business, a brief history, financial worth, officers, address with telephone and fax numbers, products, and competitors. A section in the front arranges companies by metropolitan area and product. This reasonably priced work contains a gold mine of information about major corporations. Highly recommended for high schools. [R: ARBA 92; BR, May/June 91; LJ, 1 Mar 91; LJ, 15 Apr 91; RBB, 1 Mar 91]

■ *Occupational Outlook Handbook*. *See* entry 342.

298 Post, Elizabeth L. **Emily Post on Business Etiquette**. New York: HarperCollins, 1990. 176p. $4.50pa. ISBN 0-06-081036-X.

Using a question-and-answer format, topical chapters address such topics as interviews, meetings, working with retail customers, and relationships with coworkers. Indexed. Most of this information can be found in books on office procedures, but this is a convenient, up-to-date, inexpensive volume most high schools will welcome.

299 Webster's Guide to Business Correspondence. Springfield, Mass.: Merriam-Webster, 1988. 400p. $12.95. ISBN 0-87779-031-0. LC 87-31333.

This guide covers a variety of topics concerning business correspondence (e.g., forms of address, style, grammar, punctuation) and provides some 40 samples for virtually every type of letter. Line drawings, facsimiles, tables for stationery and envelope sizes, and stylings for letterheads and envelopes enhance the volume's usefulness. Indexing is by subject and sample letter. Much of the same information is covered in *Webster's Secretarial Handbook*, but this is a useful tool for high schools. [R: ARBA 89; LJ, July 88]

300 Webster's New World Secretarial Handbook. 4th ed. By In Plain English, Inc. Englewood Cliffs, N.J.: Prentice-Hall, 1989. 560p. $15.95; $9.95pa. ISBN 0-13-949256-9; 0-13-949249-6pa. LC 89-5698.

Webster's New World, useful as a basic reference tool, has been revised (3d ed., 1981) to reflect new technologies in office automation, including laptop computers and laser printers. Nine chapters cover such areas as correspondence, accounting and finance, legal principles, and special functions (e.g., travel arrangements and organizing conferences).

The text also addresses the professional secretary in different settings (e.g., medical, law, and technical), provides ready-reference information (e.g., signs and symbols, U.S. holidays, weights and measures), and offers domestic and foreign travel information (e.g., distances, time zones, dialing codes, foreign currency). A 33,000-word spelling and syllabification list is a special feature. Highly recommended for high schools. [R: ARBA 90; RBB, 1 Nov 89]

301 Webster's Secretarial Handbook. 2d ed. Springfield, Mass.: Merriam-Webster, 1984. 592p. $10.95. ISBN 0-87779-136-8. LC 83-1036.

This standard work includes basic information on all aspects of writing (e.g., punctuation, style). As well, there is data on automated equipment, records management, bookkeeping, meeting and conference planning, composing and typing letters, and use of the telephone. There are abundant "how to do it" suggestions on other phases of secretarial functions. Over 2,000 illustrations, including charts, diagrams, and letter facsimiles, support the text. Indexed. Recommended for high schools.

DICTIONARIES AND ENCYCLOPEDIAS

302 Ammer, Christine. **The A to Z of Investing**. New York: New American Library, 1987. 320p. $4.50pa. ISBN 0-451-62751-2.

Over 1,000 terms used by brokers who deal with options, pension plans, life insurance, mutual funds, and other investment plans are defined in this excellent volume. Appendixes provide addresses of major stock and commodity exchanges, sources of financial information, and an exposition of leading stock indexes and averages. Suggested for high schools. [R: ARBA 88]

303 Downes, John, and Jordan E. Goodman. **Dictionary of Finance and Investment Terms**. 3d ed. Hauppauge, N.Y.: Barron's Educational Series, 1991. 500p. $9.95pa. ISBN 0-8120-4631-5.

This dictionary, a revision of the 1985 edition, covers the jargon and traditional vocabulary of finance and investment. Definitions are clear, concise, and easy to understand. Business acronyms are listed and defined in the back of the volume. The book is well designed with good typography and helpful use of boldface type, but its small size may be a deterrent to its selection as a library reference tool. Its content, however, is excellent. [R: ARBA 92]

304 **Encyclopedia of American Business History and Biography: The Automobile Industry, 1896-1920**. George S. May, ed. New York: Facts on File, 1990. 485p. $75.00. ISBN 0-8160-2084-1. LC 89-11672.

305 **Encyclopedia of American Business History and Biography: The Automobile Industry, 1920-1980**. George S. May, ed. New York: Facts on File, 1989. 520p. $75.00. ISBN 0-8160-2083-3. LC 89-11671.
Each volume in this encyclopedia is designed to stand alone. These books cover people, events, and accomplishments in the formative years of the automotive industry through 1980. The volume for the period 1896 to 1920 contains 157 entries that include biographies of pioneers in the field, corporations, associations, and automotive technology. Henry Leland, the Packard, and the Pierce-Arrow are among its entries.
The volume for 1920-1980 consists of 105 articles. Long essays treat Henry Ford, Charles F. Kettering, and Alfred P. Sloane, Jr., while shorter entries cover such notables as Edsel Ford, Lee Iacocca, and Leonard F. Woodcock. Major and minor U.S. companies (e.g., Ford, Chrysler, Jeep, Rickenbacker) and major foreign manufacturers that export thousands of cars to this country (e.g., Volkswagen, Toyota, Renault, Rolls-Royce) also receive coverage. Both volumes are illustrated with black-and-white photographs. [R: ARBA 90, 91; BL, May 90]

306 **Encyclopedia of American Business History and Biography: The Iron and Steel Industry in the Nineteenth Century**. Paul Paskoff, ed. New York: Facts on File, 1989. $75.00. ISBN 0-8160-1890-1.
This detailed survey of the early days of the iron and steel industry in the United States covers the moguls (e.g., Henry Clay Frick, Andrew Carnegie, James Laughlin) and profiles large and small companies (e.g., Allentown Rolling Mills, Lackawanna Iron & Steel Company). The alphabetically arranged entries, which vary in length from a half page to 20 pages, include descriptions of iron and steel-making techniques and accounts of such issues as the Bessemer-Kelly litigation over the right to steel-making processes.
Some 200 black-and-white photographs illustrate the volume. Indexed by names, corporations, organizations, laws, and technologies. Recommended for high schools. A companion volume, *Iron and Steel in the 20th Century*, is scheduled for publication. [R: ARBA 90; BR, Sept/Oct 89; LJ, Aug 89]

307 Friedman, Jack P. **Dictionary of Business Terms**. Hauppauge, N.Y.: Barron's Educational Series, 1987. 500p. $9.95pa. ISBN 0-8120-3775-8.
Lucid, current definitions of over 6,000 business terms, supported by generous cross-references, make this a useful work. Appendixes include a list of abbreviations and acronyms, compound interest factors, and economic indicators. Recommended for high schools. [R: ARBA 88]

308 **Professional Secretary's Encyclopedic Dictionary**. 4th ed. Mary A. DeVries and the Prentice-Hall Editorial Staff. Englewood Cliffs, N.J.: Prentice-Hall, 1988. 608p. $24.95. ISBN 0-13-725417-2.
The 17 chapters of this dictionary are divided into 6 sections: office procedures and practices, written communications, business law and organization, accounting and finance, real estate and insurance, and references. The 1,100 entries, alphabetically arranged in each chapter, provide definitions and are supported by pertinent forms, techniques, procedures, examples, charts, and other illustrations. This outstanding work is recommended for its value as a basic reference tool and its excellent coverage of secretarial functions. [R: ARBA 90]

309 **The Random House Handbook of Business Terms**. By Jay N. Nisberg. New York: Random House, 1988. 352p. $14.95. ISBN 0-394-53047-0.
Terms applicable to all areas of business make up this dictionary (e.g., finance, accounting, economics, automation). The 3,500 brief definitions are written in nontechnical language. *See* and *see also* references are used to direct the reader to related terms. *Dictionary for Business & Finance* is a similar work, but there is surprisingly little overlap. Most high school library media centers should hold both. [R: ARBA 90]

310   Terry, John V. **Dictionary for Business & Finance**. rev. ed. Fayetteville, Ark.: University of Arkansas Press, 1990. 450p. $22.95; $12.95pa. ISBN 1-55728-169-6; 1-55728-170-Xpa.

This work provides concise definitions of terms for all areas of business and finance, including legal terms that apply to the field. Except for the latter, it is similar to *The Random House Handbook of Business Terms*. Appendixes contain real estate and financial abbreviations, a table analyzing different types of investments, sources of investment information, and a description and analysis of the 1986 Tax Reform Act.

DIRECTORIES

311   **Editor and Publisher Market Guide**. New York: Editor and Publisher. annual. $70.00.

This work, published annually since 1924, supplies useful reference data on United States and Canadian cities and metropolitan areas. Each guide offers data on the market areas for some 1,600 daily newspapers (e.g., population, personal income, department stores and other retail outlets).

312   **Manufacturing USA: Industry Analyses, Statistics, and Leading Companies, 1990**. Arsen J. Darnay, ed. Detroit: Gale, 1991. 1500p. $159.00.

Manufacturing USA gives statistics for 448 U.S. manufacturing industries, including information about companies within each. All are analyzed by state, region, and topic. The top 50 companies of each industry are listed. This valuable reference tool is recommended for high schools requiring this kind of treatment of American industry.

313   **Thomas Register of American Manufacturers and Thomas Register Catalog File**. New York: Thomas Publishing. annual. $240.00.

Thomas Register, the best source for determining the manufacturer of a product, tracing a brand name, or identifying the products of a manufacturer, is available in many public libraries for student use. The directory devotes the first 16 volumes to products and services, listed alphabetically by product with names of manufacturers. Volumes 17-18 provide company profiles, giving addresses, telephone numbers, branch offices, assets, and names of key personnel. Volumes 19-25, sometimes called "Tom Cat," reprint the catalogs of the companies in the first 18 volumes, arranging them alphabetically and cross-referencing them to volumes 1-18. In all, the set covers some 100,000 manufacturers, over 50,000 product categories, and over 100,000 trade names. The *Register* is also available online from Dialog.

BIOGRAPHY

314   Ingham, John N., and Lynne B. Feldman. **Contemporary American Business Leaders: A Biographical Dictionary**. Westport, Conn.: Greenwood Press, 1990. 788p. $99.50. ISBN 0-313-25743-4. LC 89-11866.

Ingram's previous four-volume set, *Biographical Dictionary of American Business Leaders* (Greenwood, 1983), contains 835 entries describing 1,100 notables in American industry and commerce. None are reproduced in this work, which includes 150 important persons in 116 biographical entries. Persons who are "historically significant" are treated in entries several pages in length. Each profile ends with a bibliography of articles in popular media and books by and about the biographee. The appendix provides lists of the subjects by industry, company, place of business, and place of birth. Indexed by name, company, and product name. [R: ARBA 91; LJ, 1 Apr 90; RBB, 15 May 90; WLB, Sept 90]

SMALL BUSINESS

315   Bond, Robert E., and Christopher E. Bond. **The Source Book of Franchise Opportunities**. 1990-91 ed. Homewood, Ill.: Business One-Irwin, 1991. 501p. $27.95pa. ISBN 1-55623-331-0.

The Source Book profiles more than 2,500 franchises, grouped into various categories (e.g., rental services, travel, lawn and garden) giving the history, financial requirements, and training/support for each. Entries also indicate where franchises are registered, the contract period, and whether the business has membership in the International Franchise Association.

Although it should be noted that many of the profiles are the same as entries in *Franchise Opportunities Handbook*, some have not appeared in that government publication. Recommended for high schools.

316   Foster, Dennis L. **The Encyclopedia of Franchises and Franchising**. New York: Facts on File, 1989. 465p. $65.00. ISBN 0-8160-2081-7. LC 89-11774.

This outstanding encyclopedia covers basic concepts and terms pertinent to franchising. The main section contains a general discussion of the subject and provides information, arranged alphabetically, on virtually every franchise available in the United States. Other sections give investment data, statistics on the number of outlets, and additional useful information. Over 100 illustrations support the text. Indexed. Highly recommended for high schools. [R: ARBA 90; BL, 1 Jan 90]

317   Foster, Dennis L. **The Rating Guide to Franchises**. rev. ed. New York: Facts on File, 1991. 236p. $40.00. ISBN 0-8160-2517-7. LC 88-3740.

Critical evaluations of some 210 franchises comprise this volume, which is organized in 12 sections (e.g., automotive franchises, business services). Each franchise is rated on six counts: industry experience, financial strength, fees and royalties, franchising experience, training and service, and satisfied franchisees. Additional sections give projected earnings, franchise services, and contract highlights. An introduction discusses recent trends in franchising and explains the steps to follow in evaluating them. A name index and an index by category complete the volume.

Due to the limited number of franchises covered, this work should serve as a supplement to more extensive guides, such as *Source Book of Franchise Opportunities* and *Franchise Opportunities Handbook*.

318   **Franchise Opportunities Handbook**. 21st ed. U.S. Department of Commerce, Bureau of Industrial Economics and the Minority Business Development Agency. Washington, D.C.: Government Printing Office, 1988. 303p. $18.00. S/N 003-009-00528-1.

Some 1,500 franchise opportunities are listed under 46 subject headings. A brief citation gives the address, a description of the business, the number of franchises, how long the company has been in business, estimated capital needed, whether financing and training are provided, and other useful facts. Articles cover such topics as risks involved and how to investigate franchises. A four-page bibliography of sources concludes the handbook.

An almost verbatim paperbound reprint of this government publication, *Franchise Opportunities*, is offered by Sterling Publishing for only $10.95. *The Source Book of Franchise Opportunities* by Robert E. Bond and Christopher E. Bond also reprints many of the entries.

319   Harrington, Kevin, and Mark N. Cohen. **The 100 Best Spare-Time Business Opportunities Today**. New York: John Wiley, 1990. 235p. $27.95; $12.95pa. ISBN 0-471-61134-4; 0-471-61133-6pa. LC 89-22765.

From the thousands of companies that offer part-time franchises or licensing opportunities that provide products or services, the authors have selected the 100 they consider the best, based on income, potential, stability, ease of entry into the market, and fun. Among those included are miniature golf, popcorn vending machines, maid services, and repairing bad credit. The two-page entries analyze each franchise, but they do not give financial data on the companies covered, cost, training offered, or comments from investors, all of which would be helpful. [R: ARBA 91]

320   **The Macmillan Small Business Handbook**. By Mark Stevens. New York: Macmillan, 1988. 408p. $35.00. ISBN 0-02-614490-5. LC 88-13329.

This excellent guide focuses on the essential information required to succeed in the small business world. Its straightforward, nontechnical, practical approach makes it a worthwhile desk reference/ instructional manual for anyone comtemplating opening a business. Stevens offers tips on cutting costs and taxes, handling competition, and many other areas. Indexed by subject. Highly recommended for high school reference and circulating collections. [R: ARBA 90; LJ, 15 Feb 89]

Careers

BIBLIOGRAPHIES

E
321   Baldauf, Gretchen S., comp. **Career Index: A Selective Bibliography for Elementary Schools**. Westport, Conn.: Greenwood Press, 1990. 212p. (Bibliographies and Indexes in Education, no.7). $35.00. ISBN 0-313-24832-X. LC 89-28611.

The *Career Index*, designed for teachers, counselors, and librarians, focuses on career education for children in kindergarten through grade 6. The bibliography cites a variety of materials published in the last 20 years. The 1,066 annotated entries, print and nonprint, cover fiction, nonfiction, biography, and poetry in many fields. Due to the amount of information available, sports are excluded.

The guide is arranged by 20 broad categories (e.g., animal care, the arts, business) subdivided by specific careers (e.g., dance). It is indexed by subject, author, and biographee. [R: ARBA 91; RBB, 15 May 90; WLB, May 90]

322   **Educators Guide to Free Guidance Materials**. Randolph, Wis.: Educators Progress Service. annual. $25.95. (214 Center St., Randolph, WI 53956).

This annually updated bibliography lists and annotates career-planning materials, print and nonprint, available free or on loan from many sources. The arrangement is by media and subdivided by broad topical headings. Indexed by title, subject, and source.

323   **Job Hunting Sourcebook: Where to Find Employment Leads and Other Job Search Resources**. Michelle LeCompte, ed. Detroit: Gale, 1991. 1106p. $44.95. ISBN 0-8103-7717-9.

This comprehensive guide to finding employment cites information sources for job opportunities in 155 professions and occupations. Alphabetically arranged entries list help wanted advertisements, placement services, employment directories, networking lists, handbooks, manuals, and employment agencies. [R: LJ, 1 Mar 91]

324   **Professional Careers Sourcebook: An Information Guide to Career Planning**. Kathleen M. Savage and Charity Anne Dorgan, eds. Detroit: Gale, 1990. 1094p. $69.95. ISBN 0-8103-4901-9. ISSN 1045-9863.

This handbook focuses on career planning for college graduates in executive, managerial, professional, and technical fields that require high levels of education and skill. Entries provide information on 111 jobs excerpted from *Occupational Outlook Handbook* but supplement this data with additional information. Included are career guides, professional associations, accreditation and licensing agencies, test study guides, scholarships and grants, internships and special training programs, professional and trade publications, reference sources used by the field (e.g., directories), and dates and locations of professional meetings and conferences. This sourcebook does not compete with other career guides, but it does bring together a wide range of data not found in other works on the topic. [R: ARBA 91; LJ, 1 Apr 90; RBB, 1 Apr 90; SLJ, Sept 90; WLB, May 90]

325   Smith, Devon Cottrell, and James LaVecks, eds. **Great Careers: The Fourth of July Guide to Careers, Internships, and Volunteer Opportunities in the Nonprofit Sector**. 2d ed. Garrett Park, Md.: Garrett Park Press, 1990. 605p. $35.00pa. ISBN 0-912048-74-3. LC 90-30546.

This revision replaces *Fourth of July Resource Guide for the Promotion of Careers in Public, Community and International Service* (1987). Similar to its predecessor, it is a directory of source material for job opportunities in the nonprofit sector, including work with the homeless, animal rights, women's issues, and other fields often overlooked in career planning manuals.

Each of the 28 chapters, written by career planning and placement specialists, contains a survey of the field followed by annotated citations to books, directories, organizations (professional and non-profit), periodicals, and job listings. Indexed by title/organization name. [R: ARBA 91]

326   **Where to Start Career Planning: Essential Resource Guide for Career Planning and Job Hunting**. 8th ed. Carolyn Lloyd Lindquist and Diane June Miller, eds. Ithaca, N.Y.: Cornell University Career Center; distr., Princeton, N.J.: Peterson's Guides, 1991. 302p. $17.95pa. ISBN 1-56079-056-3.

This bibliography is divided into two major parts: career fields, which covers specific areas such as biological sciences and fine/performing arts, and extended topics, which covers such things as career planning, financial aid, minorities, and study abroad. Items listed in both sections are annotated. Appendixes cite audiovisual resources and periodicals that list jobs. Indexed by book title.

DICTIONARIES, ENCYCLOPEDIAS, AND HANDBOOKS

327   Basta, Nicholas. **Top Professions: The 100 Most Popular, Dynamic, and Profitable Careers in America Today**. Princeton, N.J.: Peterson's Guides, 1989. 200p. $10.95pa. ISBN 0-87866-866-7. LC 89-22898.

Designed for high school and college students seeking to continue their education, Basta has selected the "top professions" on the basis of size, growth rate, appeal, and "their importance over the last five to ten years." Despite the title, all chosen are not the best-paying jobs, since some, such as social work, are popular due to the personal satisfaction they offer.

The volume offers only basic information—education, licensing requirements, and potential earnings—and refers the user to professional associations for further information. *Occupational Outlook Handbook*, which Basta highly recommends, was heavily used in making these projections. [R: ARBA 91]

328   Block, Deborah Perlmutter. **How to Write a Winning Resume**. Skokie, Ill.: National Textbook/ VGM, 1989. $7.95pa. ISBN 0-8442-6639-6. LC 88-60901.

329   Block, Deborah Perlmutter. **How to Get and Get Ahead in Your First Job**. Skokie, Ill.: National Textbook/VGM, 1988. $6.95pa. ISBN 0-8442-6691-4. LC 87-83717.

These are excellent guides for job seekers. *How to Write* offers advice on gathering and organizing information, recording personal data, writing an impressive description of work experience, and compiling other information. Also included, are sample resumes and cover letters in different styles. The appendix lists sources for finding jobs, a bibliography, and sample job descriptions.

How to Get covers skills needed to get a job, traditional steps in finding employment, traits of a good employer, and how to succeed on the job. Sample application forms, resumes, and letters are also included. Both publications are recommended for high schools. [R: BR, Mar/Apr 90]

330   Bolles, Richard Nelson. **The 1992 What Color Is Your Parachute**. Berkeley, Calif.: Ten Speed Press, 1991. 448p. $18.95; $11.95pa. ISBN 0-89815-440-5; 0-89815-439-1pa.

Since its appearance 20 years ago, this "practical manual for job hunters and career changers" has been very popular. According to the publisher, the book has now reached the five-million mark in sales. Revisions not only reflect changes in the employment world but also provide guidance in identifying one's own strengths and weaknesses, researching a career, and finding a job. Although this guide is directed toward adults, high school students will find it helpful.

E+
331   **Career Discovery Encyclopedia**. E. Russell Primm, ed. Chicago: J. G. Ferguson Publishing, 1990. 4v. $99.95/set. ISBN 0-89434-106-5. LC 89-26000.

The publisher of the standard four-volume *Encyclopedia of Careers and Vocational Guidance*, which is intended for high school students and adults, has produced this set for use in elementary and junior high schools. The work consists of two-page profiles of 504 alphabetically arranged careers. For each occupation, an entry explains the nature of the work, education and training required, earnings and employment outlook, and sources of additional information. Photographs that show people performing their duties accompany each entry. All volumes contain a glossary of occupational terminology and indexes to the set. The language can be understood by most fourth graders but will also appeal to reluctant readers at the high school level. Highly recommended. [R: ARBA 91; BL, 15 Mar 90; BR, Sept/Oct 90; WLB, Apr 90]

332   **Career Opportunities in Advertising and Public Relations**. By Shelly Field. New York: Facts on File, 1990. 340p. $27.50; $14.95pa. ISBN 0-8160-2080-9; 0-8160-2348-4pa.

333   **Career Opportunities in Art**. By Susan H. Haubenstock. New York: Facts on File, 1988. 192p. $27.50; $12.95pa. ISBN 0-8160-1398-5; 0-8160-1982-7pa.

334 Career Opportunities in Sports. By Shelly Field. New York: Facts on File, 1990. 272p. $27.50. ISBN 0-8160-2241-0.

These works provide detailed job descriptions and career paths for their respective areas. *Advertising and Public Relations* addresses 85 occupations within the fields, such as those in radio and television, sports and entertainment, hospitality and touring, and consulting. *Art* covers museums, galleries, advertising, art journalism, art-related businesses, publishing, and others. *Sports* treats scholastic, collegiate, and professional sports, as well as officiating, training, journalism, communication, education, recreation, sports medicine, and therapy. For each field, the work gives a clear picture of its positive and negative aspects, education, experience requirements, salary ranges, and career paths. Other career books from Facts on File cover television, cable, and video; the music industry; and writing. [R: BL, 1 Mar 90; BR, Feb 89; BR, Feb 91; BR, 1 Sept 90; SLJ, Mar 90]

335 Dictionary of Occupational Titles. 4th ed. U.S. Employment Service. Washington, D.C.: Government Printing Office, 1977; repr., 1988. 1412p. $32.00pa. S/N 029-013-00079-9. *Supplement*, 1986. 115p. $5.50. S/N 029-014-00238-1.

Often referred to as *DOT*, this work provides occupational titles, descriptions, and codes (9-digit numbers) for 40,000 job titles in 20,000 occupations. The supplement contains 761 job titles, codes, and definitions for positions that have emerged since 1977, and for 79 older occupations that were inadvertently omitted from the 1977 publication.

In addition to instructions on how to use the guide, a glossary section and an alphabetical index of occupational titles arranged by industry designation are provided. *Selected Characteristics of Occupations Defined in the Dictionary of Occupational Titles* and *Occupational Outlook Handbook* are companion volumes and essential tools for counselors and high school reference collections.

336 The Encyclopedia of Careers and Vocational Guidance. 8th ed. William E. Hopke, ed. in chief. Chicago: J. G. Ferguson, 1990. 4v. $129.95/set. ISBN 0-89434-117-0. LC 90-3743.

A comprehensive guide to career and vocational guidance, this set defines and describes more than 1,000 occupations, each identified by *Dictionary of Occupational Titles* code number. Volume 1, "Industrial Profiles," evaluates 26 major industries. The treatment differs from that of earlier editions by the inclusion of more data on industry histories, structure, career paths, and outlook.

Volumes 2-4, covering professional, general and special, and technical careers, provide detailed information on the work, social and psychological qualifications required, education and training requirements, working conditions, and earnings and advancement. A prospectus for the future of each profession and occupation, addresses for obtaining additional information, and black-and-white illustrations are also provided for all fields. Indexing in each volume covers the entire set. Highly recommended.

This work is more comprehensive than *VGM's Careers Encyclopedia* and others of its kind. *The Encyclopedia of Careers and Vocational Guidance* and *Occupational Outlook Handbook*, with its companion volumes, are first choices for high schools. [R: ARBA 91]

E+
337 Franck, Irene M., and David M. Brownstone. Work Throughout History Series. New York: Facts on File, 1986-1988. 15v. $17.95/v.; $199.00/set. ISBN 0-8160-2119-8.

This series, directed toward young readers from age 10 upward, is highly recommended. Every volume treats a number of related occupations, chronicling the evolution of each from its beginning to the present. Topics include specific tasks performed while on the job, how society has viewed the occupation over its history, and how technology and social changes have affected it. Volumes, written in clear, colorful language, include illustrations, indexing, and a suggested reading list.

Volumes in the series include *Artists and Artisans, Builders, Clothiers, Communicators, Financiers and Traders, Harvesters, Healers, Helpers and Aides, Leaders and Lawyers, Manufacturers and Miners, Performers and Players, Restauranteurs and Innkeepers, Scholars and Priests, Scientists and Technologists*, and *Warriors and Adventurers*.

338 Krantz, Les. The Jobs Rated Almanac. New York: World Almanac, 1988. 349p. $14.95pa. ISBN 0-88687-307-X.

This paperback volume rates 250 jobs (accountant to zoologist) based on salary, stress, work environment, physical demands, security, outlook, perks, and travel opportunities. Jobs range from those that require only an apprenticeship or on-the-job training to those that demand a college or professional education. Overall, actuary ranks first and migrant farm worker last. Secondary schools should hold this inexpensive work. [R: LJ, 1 Nov 88]

339   Mitchell, Joyce Slayton. **The College Board Guide to Jobs and Career Planning**. New York: College Board, 1990. 306p. $12.95pa. ISBN 0-87447-354-3. LC 90-082324.

The major part of this work is adapted from the 1990-1991 *Occupational Outlook Handbook*. Within broad categories the guide provides information on job opportunities, outlook, characteristics, and requirements. The remainder of the work makes suggestions on career planning, recounts career stories from magazines and newspapers, and treats such topics as student jobs. The book's direct and optimistic approach will appeal to high school and college students. [R: ARBA 91]

340   **Occu-Facts: Information on 565 Careers in Outline Form**. 1989-90 ed. Elizabeth Handville, ed. Largo, Fla.: Careers, 1989. 1v. (various paging). $38.00pa. ISBN 0-9623657-0-X. (P.O. Box 135, Largo, FL 34649-0135).

The 1989-1990 edition of *Occu-Facts* summarizes information for 565 white- and blue-collar occupations. Careers are arranged according to the U.S. Department of Commerce's Standard Occupation Classification (SOC) codes.

An outline summarizes information for each career: general duties, working conditions, physical surroundings, physical demands, general aptitudes, desirable temperaments, and educational requirements. Moreover, it gives employment outlook, salary levels, and sources for additional information. The U.S. Department of Labor's *Occupational Outlook Handbook* offers more detailed information of the same type, but *Occu-Facts* is more useful to those with limited reading ability. [R: ARBA 91; RBB, 1 Apr 90; WLB, Feb 90]

341   **Occupational Briefs**. Moravia, N.Y.: Chronicle Guidance. (66 Aurora St., P.O. Box 1190, Moravia, NY 13118-1190).

Available by subscription, in sets or by individual publication, *Occupational Briefs* covers over 2,000 occupations. Each of the 600 briefs follows a standard outline that matches criteria of the Career Information Review Service of the National Career Development Association. The outline covers work performed, working conditions, hours and earnings, education and training, licenses and certificates, personal qualifications, social and psychological factors, where employed, employment outlook, entry methods, advancement, and related occupations. There is also a referral section for further information. The briefs are coded to the *Dictionary of Occupational Titles* and other classification standards.

The briefs cover specific careers from academic deans to zoologists and include all types of occupations. Unusual ones, such as beekeepers, bill collectors, circus performers, farriers, greeting card writers, nannies, signwriters, and production planners, appear along with more conventional occupations.

342   **Occupational Outlook Handbook, 1990-91**. Compiled by the U.S. Department of Labor. Washington, D.C.: Government Printing Office, 1990. 502p. $22.00; $17.00pa. S/N 029-001-03021-5; 029-001-03022-3pa.

This standard work, published biennially since 1941, provides authoritative information on over 250 professions and occupations, from architect to welder. Information in the job section covers duties, working conditions, education and training requirements, earnings and advancement possibilities, and job forecasts. Also included are sources of additional information and other occupations that require similar aptitudes, interest, and training. Jobs requiring extensive training or education receive more in-depth coverage. This section is arranged by broad occupational field, which clusters related jobs.

The jobs-by-industry section focuses on 35 industries, projecting the future job market and the effects of the economy on employment. Indexing is alphabetical and by *Dictionary of Occupational Titles* code numbers. This handbook is updated by *Occupational Outlook Quarterly*, which includes articles on emerging fields, new technologies affecting jobs, and other trends.

343   **Selected Characteristics of Occupations Defined in the Dictionary of Occupational Titles**. By U.S. Employment Service. Washington, D.C.: Government Printing Office, 1987. $24.00. S/N 029-014-00202-0.

The physical demands, environmental conditions, and training time required for jobs named and described in *Dictionary of Occupational Titles* constitute the focus of this volume, a reprint of the 1981 edition. Occupations involving the same general type of work and requiring similar abilities are grouped in clusters in part 1. Part 2 indexes occupations according to the 9-digit DOT code.

344   **VGM's Careers Encyclopedia**. 2d ed. Craig T. Norback, ed. Skokie, Ill.: VGM/National Textbook, 1988. 484p. $29.95. ISBN 0-8442-6132-7. LC 87-62404.

This volume provides information for 180 alphabetically arranged careers, giving a description of the work, the workplace, working conditions, education and training, qualifications, income, advancement, and additional sources of information. The entries are briefer than those contained in *The Encyclopedia of Careers and Vocational Guidance* and *Occupational Outlook Handbook*, but the volume is inexpensive and accurate. There are no illustrations, but there is an index. Recommended for high schools. [R: ARBA 89; BR, May/June 88; RBB, 15 Apr 88]

DIRECTORIES

345 **Federal Career Directory: The U.S. Government, Career America**. Washington, D.C.: Government Printing Office. annual. $31.00 looseleaf w/binder.
This colorful, well-designed directory was started several years ago to attract more qualified people to positions in the federal government. The looseleaf service, divided by agency, provides descriptions of job possibilities for each and gives an address for obtaining further information. The directory also explains the Civil Service rating system, its pay scale, and the register that announces jobs. It is indexed by major field. Highly recommended for high schools.

346 Feingold, S. Norma, and G. A. Hansard-Winkler. **Where the Jobs Are: A Comprehensive Directory of 1200 Journals Listing Career Opportunities**. Garrett Park, Md.: Garrett Park Press, 1989. 126p. $15.00. ISBN 0-912048-67-0.
This guide cites over 1,200 periodicals that contain job advertisements. A separate list provides access by occupation to relevant journal titles. Instructions on reading classified advertisements, responding to them, and writing one, plus tips on filling out application forms, are features of this small work. [R: Kliatt, Jan 90]

347 **Finding a Job in the Nonprofit Sector, 1991**. William Wade, ed. Rockville, Md.: Taft Group, 1991. 696p. $95.00pa. ISBN 0-914756-93-1.
Those seeking employment in the nonprofit or public-interest sector will welcome this volume. Over 4,000 alphabetically arranged entries provide the organization's name, address, type of activity, and annual income. About half of the entries add a paragraph that gives the number of employees, representative job titles, preferred college majors, and other information. Indexed by activity and geographical location.

SELF-EMPLOYMENT

E+
348 Belliston, Larry, and Kurt Hanks. **Extra Cash for Kids**. Brentwood, Tenn.: Wolgemuth & Hyatt, 1989. $9.95pa. ISBN 0-943497-70-1. (1749 Mallory Lane, Suite 110, Brentwood, TN 37027).
Extra Cash supplies children from grades 4 through 8 with well-known and novel ways of making money in their spare time.
The Teenage Entrepreneur's Guide, 2d ed. by Sarah L. Riehm (Surrey Books, 1990) provides general information on how to set up a business and gives advice about appropriate enterprises for teenagers. [R: LJ, 1 Apr 91]

Consumer Education

☐ ☐

CONSUMER EDUCATION

349 Automobile Book, 1992: The Complete New Car Buying Guide. By the editors of Consumer Guide. New York: E. P. Dutton, 1991. 240p. $9.99. ISBN 0-451-82229-3.

Those seeking help in selecting a new car will welcome this guide, which rates automobiles on the basis of quality, comfort, convenience, reliability, economy, and other characteristics. It then makes comparisons with competing models and sizes.

Consumer Reports Books publishes the similar *New Car Buying Guide* (1991). *Complete Guide to Used Cars* (New American Library/Signet, 1991) rates over 200 foreign and domestic cars, giving service history, recall record, fuel economy, and other information. [R: Kliatt, Apr 89]

350 Buying Guide Issue. Mt. Vernon, N.Y.: Consumer Reports Books. annual. $7.95pa. ISSN 0010-7174.

This guide is the December issue of *Consumer Reports*, but it may be purchased separately. It summarizes product evaluations published over the last several years and cites the magazine issue in which the full appraisal appeared.

For evaluation purposes, an agent of the magazine buys a product from a retail store without the manufacturer's knowledge; experts then test it to determine its characteristics, such as quality, performance, convenience, and safety. Products range from household items, such as food and laundry detergent, to major appliances and automobiles. Brands or models are ranked in order of their estimated overall quality.

An annual feature of the *Buying Guide* is the frequency-of-repair records of automobile models over the last five years. Highly recommended. [R: ARBA 90]

351 The Complete Car Cost Guide. 1990 ed. Steve Gross, ed. San Jose, Calif.: IntelliChoice, 1990. $39.00pa. ISBN 0-941443-09-4.

Unlike other guides to the purchase of automobiles, this work is a "guide to the economics of buying and owning" one. It compares the cost-per-year of owning 500 new makes and models, including light trucks, vans, and station wagons. The alphabetical arrangement in this edition differs from that in previous editions, which listed cars by size.

The ratings, which use data gathered from a number of sources, are based on computer modeling using a sophisticated program devised by Gross. Highly recommended for high schools. [R: ARBA 88; ARBA 89; BL, 15 Nov 87; LJ, Aug 88; WLB, Oct 87]

352 Consumer Information Catalog. Pueblo, Colo.: Consumer Information Center, 1970- . quarterly. free. (P.O. Box 100, Pueblo, CO 81002).

Each quarterly catalog lists and describes some 100 free and inexpensive consumer-information pamphlets and more extensive publications available from the Center. Topics include personal finance, food, health and physical fitness, drugs, housing, and household products. Librarians and educators may receive batches of 25 catalogs on request.

353 The Kids' Catalog Collection: A Selective Guide to More Than 500 Catalogs.... By Jane Smolik. Chester, Conn.: Globe Pequot Press, 1990. 276p. $11.95pa. ISBN 0-87106-433-2. LC 90-42796.

This selective guide for children's merchandise presents catalogs from over 500 companies. Smolik indicates that she received and read each of the catalogs. Chapters are organized into 24 major categories that cover more than 135 different areas of interest. In each category, company-by-company listings, arranged alphabetically, describe each company's typical offerings, prices, and shipping policies. Most entries include the catalog's mailing address, telephone number, and cost. Many catalogs are free on request.

In addition to the bonanza of resources, there are many unexpected items and a host of imaginative ideas (e.g., left-handed products, pinatas, a build-your-own erupting volcano). Since catalog offerings and mail-order companies are subject to periodic change, it is possible that some of the products may not be available. Separate indexes by company name and area of interest make the book easy to use.

PERSONAL FINANCE

E+
354   Kyte, Kathy S. **The Kid's Complete Guide to Money**. New York: Alfred A. Knopf, 1984. 96p. $10.99; $4.95pa. ISBN 0-394-96672-4; 0-394-86672-Xpa. LC 84-3962.

Designed for young readers from fifth through eighth grade, this slim volume offers advice on money matters (e.g., shopping, budgeting, saving) and provides instruction on making complaints about products.

SOCIAL SECURITY

355   **Social Security Handbook**. 10th ed. Washington, D.C.: Government Printing Office, 1988. $13.00. S/N 017-070-00437-7.

The official handbook of the Social Security Administration, this periodically revised work covers all retirement and survivors benefits, supplemental income programs, and health insurance. Chapters concerning broad areas are divided into specific topics. The work is supported by an extensive index, making the publication easy to use.

Since federal publications are not copyrighted, this handbook is often reprinted by commercial publishers under other titles, with or without reorganization and new material, and often at exorbitant prices.

□ ─────────── **Education** ─────────── □

BIBLIOGRAPHIES

See **Language** for **English as a Second Language**.
See **Media Sources** for lists of instructional media.

356   Buttlar, Lois J. **Education: A Guide to Reference and Information Sources**. Englewood, Colo.: Libraries Unlimited, 1989. 258p. (Reference Sources in the Social Sciences Series, no.2). $35.00. ISBN 0-87287-619-5. LC 89-2651.

This guide to reference materials for education and related fields cites and annotates 59 major periodical titles and 900 bibliographies, indexes, abstracts, encyclopedias, dictionaries, and online databases. Most reference books were published after 1980 and are still in print. An earlier work, *A Guide to Sources of Educational Information* by Marda Woodbury (2d ed., Information Resources Press, 1982), is similar, but Buttlar's guide includes many works published after 1982. [R: ARBA 90; LJ, 15 Oct 89; WLB, Nov 89]

357   **Core List of Books and Journals in Education**. By Nancy Patricia O'Brien and Emily Fabiano. Phoenix, Ariz.: Oryx Press, 1991. 160p. $39.95. ISBN 0-89774-559-4.

School districts should have access to this selection tool, which describes almost 1,000 recent books and journals essential to educators, scholars, and researchers. The annotated bibliography is divided into major subject areas (e.g., guidance, mathematics, vocational education) and supported by author, subject, and title indexes. [R: ARBA 92; VOYA, June 91]

■ *El-Hi Textbooks and Serials in Print*. *See* entry 64.

■ *Free Things for Teachers*. *See* entry 179.

E+
358   Kruse, Janice. **Resources for Teaching Thinking: A Catalog**. Philadelphia, Pa.: Research for Better Schools, 1989. 1v. (unpaged). $29.95pa.

This catalog identifies materials on how to teach thinking skills to students K-12. More than 500 sources are listed, giving title, author, kind of material, purpose, description, and order information.

Each entry is coded by subject and cross-referenced or indexed by the type of skill emphasized. Recommended for all levels. [R: ARBA 91; LJ, Dec 89]

DICTIONARIES AND ENCYCLOPEDIAS

359 Dejnozka, Edward L., and others. **American Educator's Encyclopedia**. rev. ed. Westport, Conn.: Greenwood Press, 1991. $96.00. ISBN 0-313-25269-6. LC 81-6664.
This revision of a useful single-volume encyclopedia gives brief information on some 2,000 topics related to all levels and areas of education, important educators, organizations, and many other topics. Entries cite references for further study. Since the aging 10-volume work *Encyclopedia of Education* (Free Press/Macmillan, 1971) is now out of print, this is an important source for the field.

360 **Encyclopedia of Educational Research**. 5th ed. Harold E. Mitzel, ed. New York: Free Press/Macmillan, 1982. 4v. $315.00/set. ISBN 0-02-900450-0. LC 82-2332.
Sponsored by the American Educational Research Association and revised about every 10 years, this work is designed to provide a critical analysis and interpretation of educational research on all levels of education. The 256 signed articles, written by experts in language suitable for the nonprofessional, discuss traditional topics as well as trends and developments. Extensive bibliographies follow. Numerous charts and tables, cross-references, and an index support the text. [R: ARBA 84; BL, 1 Oct 83; LJ, 1 Jan 83; LJ, 15 May 83; WLB, Jan 83]

E +
361 **Encyclopedia of School Administration and Supervision**. Richard A. Gorton and others, eds. Phoenix, Ariz.: Oryx Press, 1988. 352p. $74.50. ISBN 0-89774-232-X. LC 87-34959.
Today's society expects school administrators to be experts in such things as personnel management, community relations, discipline, counseling, and business. This comprehensive work, which focuses on around 300 important topics and issues of concern to administrators and supervisors, is perceptive and informative. Each of the well-written, succinct articles is followed by a bibliography of suggested readings that emphasize important research on a specific subject. A guide to related topics highlights information subsumed in essays, covering broad categories. Some 200 distinguished education specialists have contributed the entries. Highly recommended for professional collections. [R: ARBA 89; BL, 15 Dec 88; WLB, Sept 88]

E +
362 **The Facts on File Dictionary of Education**. By Jay Shafritz and others. New York: Facts on File, 1988. 512p. $40.00. ISBN 0-8160-1636-4. LC 88-24554.
This dictionary defines some 5,000 terms for all areas of primary and secondary education. It serves as an update for *Dictionary of Education* by Carter V. Good (McGraw-Hill, 1973), the standard for many years. It cites legislation, court cases, organizations, tests, government agencies, periodicals, and individuals. Entries present concise definitions, many supported by bibliographies for further reading. [R: ARBA 90; BL, 1 Feb 89; BR, May/June 89; WLB, Jan 91]

DIRECTORIES

See also **College Handbooks** under **Education**.
See **Hobbies and Games** for **Summer Camps**.

■ *American Art Directory*. *See* entry 1346.

363 Cheatham, Annie. **Directory of School Mediation and Conflict Resolution Programs**. Amherst, Mass.: National Association for Mediation in Education, 1988. 169p. $12.50/spiralbound.
The system of conflict resolution was begun by the Quakers in 1972 and was supported by the Carter administration in the late 1970s through neighborhood justice centers. This work refers to programs that train leaders while trying to mediate disputes among students and providing them a place to work together to solve their problems. The five points in the mediation process are: state what happened and how you feel about it without blaming anyone, listen to the other person(s) involved, express what you want from the other person, think together about possible solutions, and mutually agree on a solution. This directory of local school mediation programs, arranged alphabetically by state, gives a brief history of the program, its training, and successes. Indexed. [R: ARBA 90]

364 The College Board Guide to High Schools. Princeton, N.J.: College Board, 1990. 2490p. $89.95pa. ISBN 0-87447-357-8. LC 90-081604.

This large work, based on information provided by the schools in March 1990, replaces the multi-volume *Guide to Secondary Schools*. Entries for the 25,000 public and private secondary schools, arranged by state and then alphabetically by the school's name, vary in length, depending on how fully schools responded to the questionnaire. Only about half of those listed gave complete data.

Entries, if complete, include address; type of school (e.g., public, suburban, urban); regional accreditation; enrollment by grade; percentage of minority students; course offerings; program offerings (e.g., special education, gifted and talented, cooperative education); SAT/ACT scores; and percentage of graduates who go to college, the military, and the work force. Indexing is by country, specialty, schools with advanced placement courses, and name. *Patterson's American Education* is more complete but gives less information. [R: ARBA 91; BL, 1 Nov 90; WLB, Nov 90]

365 Directory of Student Science Training Programs for High Ability Precollege Students. 1991 ed. Washington, D.C.: Science Service, 1991. 1v. $3.00 (free to schools). (1719 N St. NW, Washington, DC 40036).

This directory, published by *Science News*, lists 626 science, math, and engineering programs for talented high school students. Location, program type, dates, grade level, cost, scholarship information, and application deadlines are provided. [R: RBB, 1 Mar 91]

366 The Handbook of Private Schools. Boston: Porter Sargent. annual. $60.00. ISSN 0072-9884. LC 15-12869.

This guide provides reliable information for about 1,765 of the leading private schools (day and boarding) in the United States. Entries, arranged regionally by states and alphabetically by city, begin with basic data such as enrollment, size of faculty, number of admissions each year, grades offered, costs, and name of admissions officer.

A section in each profile contains information about the last graduating class: the total number, how many continued to college, the six colleges preferred by those graduating. Curricular descriptions (e.g., college preparatory, general academic) and accelerated or advanced course information follow. A paragraph focuses on a description of the school, its history, and academic extracurricular programs. Those that pay a fee are grouped in a section containing more detailed information. Summer academic programs and camps are listed in a separate section.

Private Independent Schools (Bunting and Lyon, annual) includes similar information, but the amount of data varies; schools paying the top rate receive 2-page write-ups, instead of a standard 12-line entry. [R: ARBA 90]

367 The Independent Study Catalog: NUCEA's Guide to Independent Study Through Correspondence Instruction. 4th ed. John H. Wells and Barbara C. Ready, eds. Princeton, N.J.: Peterson's Guides, 1989. 121p. $11.95pa. ISBN 0-87866-757-1. ISSN 0733-6020.

The Independent Study Catalog identifies correspondence courses designed for students working toward the completion of a high school diploma or college degree, and for those who wish to meet certificate or vocational requirements through study at home. The introductory material provides extensive information about correspondence study, special programs, and external degrees. The main body of the volume identifies over 10,000 courses offered by over 70 institutions in the United States and Canada, most of which are accredited by the National University Continuing Education Association (NUCEA).

Five levels of courses are listed: elementary, high school, undergraduate, graduate, and noncredit. Information on courses includes number, unit credit, level of instruction, special features, and supplemental technology (e.g., videocassette, computer-aided instruction). However, the course content is not described. *The Macmillan Guide to Correspondence Study* gives a narrative description of the courses. [R: ARBA 90]

368 Levin, Shirley. Summer on Campus: College Experiences for High School Students. New York: College Board, 1989. 394p. $9.95pa. ISBN 0-87447-322-5. LC 88-062770.

This volume, designed for high school students seeking an early exposure to college, is an expanded and updated version of the 1985 edition. The 258 summer programs on 150 campuses, arranged alphabetically by the host institution, provide program name, address, contact person, dates, entrance requirements, cost, financial aid, a description of the area, housing, courses, college credit (if offered), admission procedures, and notes. Indexed by host school, program name, geographical location, financial aid, and courses.

Programs and locations are surprisingly diverse. High schools should consider this unique volume. [R: ARBA 90; Kliatt, Apr 89; LJ, 15 Apr 89; SLJ, Oct 87]

369 **The Macmillan Guide to Correspondence Study**. 3d ed. Compiled and edited by Modoc Press, Inc. New York: Macmillan, 1988. 676p. $85.00. ISBN 0-02-921641-9. LC 88-8603.

This guide to correspondence study is designed to assist interested persons in locating institutions that offer programs and courses to those who wish to study at home. It is arranged in four parts: colleges and universities; proprietary schools; private, nonprofit, and government institutions; and computer-based programs. Schools are listed alphabetically within each section and then by subject; course descriptions follow. While its closest competitor, *The Independent Study Catalog*, merely cites courses, *The Macmillan Guide* provides narrative descriptions of each course, including prerequisites, name of faculty members, material required, library services, and accreditation information. [R: ARBA 90]

370 **NCEA/Ganley's Catholic Schools in America 1989**. 17th ed. Mary Mahar, ed. Montrose, Colo.: Fisher Publishing, 1989. 315p. $36.00pa. ISBN 0-686-29255-3.

Catholic schools are arranged by states and territories and then subdivided by diocese, giving names and addresses of administrators. Directory information for each school follows. Arranged alphabetically by name, the entry for each school gives grades, principal's name, enrollment, teacher/ pupil ratio, and staffing. The regional distribution of institutions is also provided. The appendix contains historical statistics for 1985 through 1989. [R: ARBA 90]

371 **Patterson's American Education. Volume LXXXVI**. 1990 ed. Douglas Moody, ed. Mount Prospect, Ill.: Educational Directories, 1989. 755p. $60.00. ISBN 0-910536-46-5. ISSN 0079-0230. LC 4-12953.

372 **Patterson's Elementary Education. Volume II**. 1990 ed. Douglas Moody, ed. Mount Prospect, Ill.: Educational Directories, 1990. 728p. $60.00. ISBN 0-910536-47-3. ISSN 1044-1417.

Together, these two directories list all schools in the United States—public, private, parochial, vocational, technical, and trade, and kindergarten to postgraduate. *Elementary Education* covers kindergarten through middle school; *American Education* ranges from middle school through high school, with 6,400 postsecondary schools and over 400 educational associations. Provided are directory information, the superintendents of and addresses for school districts and private and parochial schools, the principals of and addresses for public schools, and top administrators for other institutions. Both directories list state education officials. [R: ARBA 91]

373 **Private Schools of the United States: Council for American Private Education (CAPE) Schools**. Shelton, Conn.: Market Data Retrieval. annual. $44.95pa./set. ISSN 0885-1603.

This annual directory lists some 15,000 schools (preschool through high school) that belong to at least 1 of the 13 national associations that comprise the Council for American Private Education. Volume 1 cites schools, arranged by state and then by name. For each school, entries provide directory information, chief officials, founding date, grade span and enrollment, faculty composition, tuition, programs, percentage of graduates entering higher education, and association membership. Volume 2 provides indexing by associations, grade level, and school name. Most of the listings are for church-affiliated schools.

This is the most comprehensive list of private schools available, but it includes only basic data. Other guides, such as *Handbook of Private Schools* and *Patterson's American Education*, provide more information. [R: ARBA 90; BL, 15 May 86; WLB, Feb 89]

374 Townsend, Kiliaen V. R. **The Boarding School Guide**. Athens, Ga.: Agee, 1989. 282p. $16.50. ISBN 0-9352-6518-X. LC 89-84769. (P.O. Box 526, Athens, GA 30603).

The author prepared this guide to assist parents and students in making "intelligent preliminary choices" about boarding schools. Included are facts about 231 U.S. schools (144 coed, 35 for girls, 52 for boys) with more than 60 boarders. A one-page entry for each school provides founding date, closest airport, student enrollment (by sex, grade level, states, and counties represented), cost, admission deadline, financial aid, advanced placement areas, class size, student-teacher ratio, SAT scores, facilities (numbers of rooms, library volumes, and acres of campus and its value), locale, and other facts of interest.

The work also includes 30 charts of comparative data (e.g., size, endowment, average SAT scores). Information was gathered from questionnaires and school catalogs. The guide is comparable to other directories, except that it includes only boarding schools instead of private schools in general. [R: ARBA 90; BL, 15 Jan 90; WLB, Feb 90]

HANDBOOKS, ALMANACS, AND YEARBOOKS

E+
375   Clark, Gilbert A., and Enid D. Zimmerman. **Resources for Educating Artistically Talented Students**. Syracuse, N.Y.: Syracuse University Press, 1987. 176p. $22.00. ISBN 0-8156-2401-8. LC 86-23183.
    Educators who teach artistically talented students will find this guide helpful. Chapters explain federal, state, and local policies and programs; procedures for establishing programs; and instruments useful in identifying those with artistic talent. The work also evaluates a wide range of instructional materials designed for programs at all levels. [R: ARBA 88; LJ, 1 Apr 87]

376   **Community, Technical, and Junior College Statistical Yearbook**. Jim Mahoney, ed. Washington, D.C.: American Association of Community and Junior Colleges. annual. $35.00pa.
    This accurate and authoritative guide, also known as *AACJC Statistical Yearbook*, is arranged in two parts. The first offers data on individual colleges, giving credit and noncredit enrollment, number of full-time and part-time faculty, professional staff and administration, tuition, and other fees. The second part presents state-by-state surveys—number of colleges and faculty, and credit-class and minority enrollment. [R: ARBA 91]

377   DeRouche, Edward F. **The Newspaper: A Reference Book for Teachers and Librarians**. Santa Barbara, Calif., ABC-Clio, 1991. 216p. index. $32.50. ISBN 0-87436-584-8. LC 91-633.
    This work focuses on instructional strategies and resources for teachers and librarians. It includes summaries of research studies, sample lesson and unit plans, suggestions for incorporating newspapers into content areas (e.g., health, science), and an annotated bibliography of journal articles and ERIC documents published between 1980 and 1989. Of special interest is the alphabetical directory of 500 U.S. and foreign newspapers that have NIE programs.
    The Newspaper can assist teachers in helping students to "understand and appreciate the newspaper as a source of information, entertainment, and service" and help librarians "to deepen and broaden classroom and library instruction." It will be particularly useful in secondary and adult basic education classrooms.

378   **Digest of Educational Statistics**. By National Center for Educational Statistics. Washington, D.C.: Government Printing Office. annual. $24.00.

379   **Projections of Educational Statistics to 2001: An Update**. By National Center for Educational Statistics. Washington, D.C.: Government Printing Office, 1990. 208p. $9.50. S/N 065-000-00440-2.

380   **The Condition of Education: Statistical Report**. By National Center for Educational Statistics. Washington, D.C.: Government Printing Office. annual. $9.50/v.
    Digest of Educational Statistics provides annual information on all levels of U.S. education, preschool through graduate, gathered from government and private sources. Among the topics covered are the number of schools, colleges, teachers, and graduates; enrollment and educational attainment figures; funding at local, state, and federal levels; libraries; and international education.
    Projections of Educational Statistics, published biennially, gives projections for several years on enrollment, expenditures, teachers, students, and graduates for elementary, secondary, and higher education.
    The Condition of Education, issued annually, provides indicators of student progress and performance, participation in various curricula, size and growth of schools, student and fiscal characteristics, school climate, and other information. Volume 1 covers elementary and secondary schools; volume 2 covers the postsecondary level.

E+
381   Freed, Melvyn N., and others. **The Educator's Desk Reference (EDR): A Sourcebook of Educational Information and Research**. New York: American Council of Education/Macmillan, 1989. 536p. $49.95. ISBN 0-02-910740-7. LC 88-9249.

This work directs the student or professional to authoritative source materials in the field of education. The six major sections supply a guide to reference materials, information on publishing (how to submit articles to journals and manuscripts to book publishers), microcomputer software for educational research, standardized tests, research processes (e.g., research designs, statistical procedures, sampling techniques), and a list of national and regional educational organizations. A useful source for educators at all levels. [R: ARBA 90; BL, 15 Nov 89; LJ, 15 Nov 89]

E+
382   Froschl, Merle, and Barbara Sprung. **Resources for Educational Equity: A Guide for Grades Pre-Kindergarten-12.** Hamden, Conn.: Garland, 1988. 266p. $47.00. ISBN 0-8240-0443-4. LC 88-16445.

There is no other work comparable to this one, which claims to be the most comprehensive and up-to-date compilation of resources to help teachers locate materials that focus on equity in the classroom. The volume lists curriculum guides, teacher packets, student texts and workbooks, audiovisual materials, and periodicals that address sex equity, stereotyping, and bias due to race and disability.

The thematic arrangement includes 11 sections on such topics as early childhood, guidance counseling, computers, and sports, each by a different subject authority. Each chapter begins with an essay on the given topic, followed by an annotated bibliography of 50 to 60 titles arranged by subject under broad categories (e.g., teacher resources, classroom materials). Indexed by author and subject. Highly recommended for professional collections. [R: ARBA 90; BL, 1 June 89; LJ, 15 June 89]

383   Haley, Beverly A. **Focus on School: A Reference Handbook.** Santa Barbara, Calif.: ABC-Clio, 1990. 217p. $35.00. ISBN 0-87436-099-4. LC 89-18637.

This handbook, a part of the Teenage Perspectives series, focuses on the educational process and gives practical advice on such matters as how to make the most of school, how to get along with teachers, how to take tests, how to grow outside of school, how to get help, and how to make judicious choices after graduation. Each of the chapters presents a 15- to 20-page essay on the issue it addresses, followed by an annotated bibliography of fiction and nonfiction titles, nonprint sources, organizations, and hotlines for further information. Chapters are well written, and the tone is impartial. [R: ARBA 91; BL, 1 Dec 90]

384   Heller, Dawn Hansen, with Ann Montgomery. **Winning Ideas from Winning Schools: Recognizing Excellence.** Santa Barbara, Calif.: ABC-Clio, 1989. 195p. $27.59pa. ISBN 0-87436-527-9. LC 89-15179.

The U.S. Department of Education's Secondary School Recognition Program, established in 1982, recognizes schools that have demonstrated their effectiveness. The book's coauthors have examined the 271 schools honored during the first 5 years, searching for ideas that are readily transferable to any school situation. The winning ideas have been divided into 19 chapters that cover such topics as goals and objectives, the teaching of writing, study skills, discipline, and drug use. Each chapter, written in a simple and straightforward style, explains the issue and offers an assortment of practical ideas. Each principal's name, address, and telephone number are listed in the appendix. [R: BR, May/June 90; SLJ, Feb 90]

385   **Peterson's Guide to Certificate Programs at American Colleges and Universities.** George L. Lopos and others, eds. Princeton, N.J.: Peterson's Guides, 1988. 343p. $35.95pa. ISBN 0-87866-741-5. LC 88-43018.

Developed in cooperation with the National University Continuing Education Association, this guide describes over 1,000 certificate programs in 225 categories at some 300 U.S. colleges and universities. A few programs are in the liberal arts, but most are in such areas as business, computer science, and health and social services, or in specializations such as fire prevention, horticulture, and precision metal work.

For each program, the guide gives descriptions of the content, prerequisites, methods of student evaluation, cost, student services, and directory information. Arranged by state and institution, the text is supported by an index of schools and programs. The work claims to list only programs with high academic standards. [R: ARBA 89; RBB, 1 Apr 89; WLB, Jan 89]

E+
386   Ramsey, Patricia G., and others. **Multicultural Education: A Source Book.** Hamden, Conn.: Garland, 1989. 192p. $27.00. ISBN 0-8240-8558-2. LC 88-31061.

Essays and annotated bibliographies are arranged into five chapters: the evolution of multicultural education; ethnic diversity and children's learning; multicultural programs, curricula, and strategies;

multicultural teacher education; and the future of multicultural education. The 189 annotated books and journal articles were published from 1976 to 1988. Indexed by subject and name. This is an appropriate selection for professional collections that serve elementary and secondary levels. [R: ARBA 90]

E+

387 Requirements for Certification of Teachers, Counselors, Librarians, Administrators for Elementary Schools, Secondary Schools, Junior Colleges. Chicago: University of Chicago Press. annual. price varies. ISSN 0080-1429.

This annual lists certification requirements (regular, temporary, and emergency) for each type of position (e.g., counselor, librarian). The directory, arranged by state, also cites reciprocal arrangements.

388 Wells, Shirley E. **At-Risk Youth: Identification, Programs, and Recommendations**. Englewood, Colo.: Teacher Ideas Press/Libraries Unlimited, 1990. 158p. $28.50. ISBN 0-87287-812-0. LC 90-31098.

The author presents a study of youth at risk of dropping out of school, based on her own research and contacts with over 100 school districts and state departments of education. She provides concise information on the characteristics of these students, identification systems, and recommendations to school districts about early intervention and special programs. Particular attention is given to at-risk Hispanic students and the programs to which they are most responsive. Other features include samples of identification checklists, individual program descriptions, and a bibliography. Indexing is by grade level, location, and subject. [R: ARBA 91]

INDEXES

389 **Education Index**. Bronx, N.Y.: H. W. Wilson, 1932- . monthly (except July and Aug.); cumulates quarterly and annually. sold on service basis.

Educators, administrators, librarians, and others involved with education will require this index to current information drawn from 337 English-language periodicals, yearbooks, and monographic series. Included are materials in all areas of education: audiovisual and educational technology; classroom computers; comparative, vocational, multicultural/ethnic, special, and religious education; psychology; student counseling; and education on different levels and in specific subject fields. Subject/author indexing in a single alphabet is provided. A separate section indexes current book reviews. *Education Index* is also available from 1983 to date online (WILSONLINE) and on CD-ROM ($1,295.00/yr.).

390 **ERIC Database**. Bethesda, Md.: National Institute of Education and Educational Resource Information Center. available through various vendors, including Dialog and BRS, and on CD-ROM from several companies.

The ERIC Database is a collection of over half a million citation records produced by the Educational Resource Information Center (ERIC) of the National Institute of Education. It consists of two subfiles: the machine-readable version of *Resources in Education* (*RIE*), an indexing and abstracting journal of "fugitive" (mainly noncopyrighted reports and other materials) publications on education, and *Current Index to Journals in Education* (*CIJE*), an index to more than 700 serial publications important to education. Both *RIE* and *CIJE* are also available in hardcopy.

ERIC covers 16 broad subject areas, such as adult, career, and vocational education; counseling and personnel services; early childhood education; handicapped and gifted children; reading and communication skills; and urban education. These areas correspond to 16 decentralized clearinghouses that share the responsibility for finding, collecting, indexing, and abstracting documents falling within their subject areas, and producing bibliographic records representing the document.

The documents cited by ERIC Database that are indexed in *RIE* are available at a reasonable cost from the Educational Resource Information Center in Maryland. The Center also produces the documents on microfiche and places them in some 750 library collections, mainly college and university libraries, throughout the United States. *A Directory of ERIC Information Providers* is available from the Center.

The articles contained in educational journals that are indexed in *CIJE* are not available in microfiche format in these depository locations. Those seeking copies of items cited must either find them in hardcopy at a library or request copies on interlibrary loan.

When searching the ERIC Database through Dialog or other vendors, one may either use a controlled vocabulary of subject headings (as outlined in the *Thesaurus of ERIC Descriptors*), free text, or natural language. Additionally, there are a variety of other approaches.

391 Exceptional Child Education Abstract. quarterly. Reston, Va.: Council for Exceptional Children, 1969- . $20.00/yr. ISSN 0160-4309.

This reference tool abstracts a broad spectrum of material pertinent to special education: trade, academic, and professional books; unpublished conference papers and proceedings; state and federal documents; curriculum-related materials produced by school districts and other agencies; dissertations; and articles selected from over 200 journals in education and related fields. Each quarterly issue contains some 800 citations indexed by author, title, and subject.

Since the Council for Exceptional Children serves as one of the ERIC clearinghouses, ECEA is similar to *Current Index to Journals in Education* and *Resources in Education*, using the same thesaurus and format (major and minor descriptors and identifiers, indication of ERIC document reproduction and availability). Only about half of the references, however, are duplicated in *CIJE* and *RIE*. ECEA is also available for online searching. This abstracting service is essential for professional libraries serving special education practitioners.

392 Thesaurus of ERIC Descriptors. 12th ed. James E. Houston, ed. Phoenix, Ariz.: Oryx Press, 1990. 672p. $69.00. ISBN 0-89774-561-2. ISSN 1051-2993. LC 87-647380.

The thesaurus of search terms for the ERIC Database and its printed components, *Resources in Education* (*RIE*) and *Current Index to Journals in Education* (*CIJE*), is updated triennially. The 12th edition lists almost 10,000 descriptors and nonindexable terms (USE references, defunct descriptors, and invalid terms). Over 280 descriptors are new to this edition.

The introduction explains the ERIC indexing and searching system. The main section, the alphabetical descriptor display, also includes the number of postings for each term in *CIJE* and *RIE*; a group code; scope notes; and lists of narrower, broader, and related terms. A keyword index to all descriptors and reference terms, a two-way hierarchical term display (familiar or generic trees for each descriptor), and a descriptor group display (in 9 categories and 41 subgroups) conclude the volume. All schools with access to the ERIC database will need this thesaurus. [R: ARBA 91]

BIOGRAPHY

393 Biographical Dictionary of American Educators. John F. Ohlers, ed. Westport, Conn.: Greenwood Press, 1978. 3v. $175.00/set. ISBN 0-8371-9893-3.

Similar in format and inclusion criteria to *Dictionary of American Biography*, this authoritative source provides 1,665 sketches for outstanding educators from colonial times to 1976, including educational leaders, reformers, teachers, and administrators.

COLLEGE HANDBOOKS

394 American Universities and Colleges. 13th ed. New York: Walter de Gruyter, 1987. 2024p. $119.50. ISBN 0-89925-179-X. ISSN 0066-0922.

This unique guide, published since 1928, provides information that the reader requires to form practical conclusions about the nature and purpose of a particular college. The usual descriptions of student life and academic excellence (or lack thereof) are absent. Some examples of this work's unusual contents are a breakdown of faculty by sex and academic rank, the number of faculty in each rank in each department, the number of degrees conferred by discipline and type, library holdings, and age distribution of the student body. The arrangement is by state. Other sections address foreign students in the United States and the structure and financing of higher education. Appendixes list accredited professional programs, the number of graduate degrees awarded annually since 1861, and academic regalia. Indexed by institution. This guide is expensive and its information is often dated; several less costly guides are more current. [R: ARBA 89; WLB, May 88]

395 Barron's Profiles of American Colleges: Descriptions of the Colleges. 17th ed. Compiled and edited by the College Division of Barron's Educational Series. Hauppauge, N.Y.: Barron's Educational Series, 1990. 1472p. $16.95pa. ISBN 0-8120-4351-0. LC 84-9319.

Barron's Profiles surveys accredited U.S. colleges and universities, giving enrollment, costs, environment, student life, programs, admissions, and financial aid data. Moreover, it includes guidelines for choosing a college; a description of entrance examinations; and charts that compare colleges by cost, enrollment, test scores of the freshman class, and admission selectivity.

This biennial is similar in content to *Peterson's Guide to Four-Year Colleges* but includes some additional information such as faculty salaries, computer facilities, handicapped services, and placement programs. However, it lacks Peterson's directory of majors and the two-page, illustrated descriptions of many schools. Since each work contains unique information and is available at a reasonable cost, most libraries should purchase both.

396 Barron's 300 Best Buys in College Education. By Lucia Solorzano. Hauppauge, N.Y.: Barron's Educational Series, 1990. 658p. $12.95pa. ISBN 0-8120-4260-3. LC 90-40060.

Designed for high school seniors seeking an affordable education, this guide provides profiles of 300 colleges, giving for each the setting, enrollment, student/faculty ratio, cost, financial aid, facilities, special programs, and application/financial aid deadlines. One section is devoted to costs not always considered in figuring college expenses—textbooks, travel costs home, and incidental expenses. Highly recommended. [R: ARBA 91; LJ, 1 Nov 90]

397 Cass, James, and Max Birnbaum. Comparative Guide to American Colleges for Students, Parents and Counselors. 14th ed. New York: Harper & Row, 1989. 838p. $35.00; $17.95pa. ISBN 0-06-271513-5; 0-06-461013-6pa. ISSN 0893-1216. LC 89-648772.

Highly regarded and freqquently revised, this standard work provides general, comparative, and analytical information about 1,000-plus accredited 4-year American colleges. Data for each school includes admission requirements; curriculum; degrees offered; academic, social, and cultural atmosphere; student-faculty ratio; church affiliation; costs and tuition; and special programs.

Each profile, prefaced by a statistical summary statement, includes an admissions selectivity rating, information on athletic programs and NCAA status, out-of-state acceptance rate and enrollment (for public institutions), percentage of graduates who enter professional schools, and changes in graduation requirements. Indexed by state, selectivity level, religious orientation, and institutions conferring the largest number of degrees in selected fields. Highly recommended. [R: ARBA 89]

398 College Admissions Data Handbook. Rebecca A. Basch and Linnea Meyer, eds. Concord, Mass.: Orchard House. annual. $150.00pa./set; $165.00pa./looseleaf.

This annual handbook, a companion to *College Admissions Index of Majors & Sports*, provides detailed information about 1,550-plus 4-year and upper-division colleges and universities from the United States, Canada, Mexico, and Western Europe. Admission requirements, costs, academic programs, extracurricular activities, living accommodations, and so forth, are given. Each volume covers a specific geographic area (Midwest, West, Northeast, or Southeast) and contains a regional index listing colleges alphabetically by state. Profiles are designed to facilitate the comparison of institutions, but no evaluations are given. Information is well arranged and current; the set compares favorably with similar multivolume publications. [R: ARBA 90]

399 The College Blue Book. 22d ed. New York: Macmillan, 1989. 5v. $200.00/set. ISBN 0-02-695969-0. LC 79-66191.

This standard work, revised biennially, provides extensive information about over 3,000 United States and Canadian colleges and universities, 2-year colleges, and specialized schools. The set is valuable as a whole, but each volume can stand alone and be purchased separately.

Narrative Descriptions gives basic directory, statistical, and profile data on each institution. *Degrees Offered by Colleges and Subject* consists of two indexes: by colleges with majors and by majors. *Tabular Data* repeats statistical data found in *Narrative Descriptions*, plus the number of credit hours required for degrees and administrators' names. *Scholarships, Fellowships, Grants, and Loans* lists some 1,800 sources of financial aid (most from the private sector), arranged by fields of study. *Occupational Education* lists some 9,000 U.S. business, trade, and technical schools.

Occupational Education is less likely to duplicate information found in other guides and is a first purchase. *Fellowships, Grants, and Loans* is an excellent source, but other, less expensive directories may meet the needs of many libraries. Information in the remaining volumes is similar to that covered in *Peterson's Guide to Four-Year Colleges* and *Peterson's Guide to Two-Year Colleges* at far less cost; nonetheless, the set is recommended for its comprehensiveness.

400   **College Explorer**. New York: College Board, 1990. $49.95.

401   **College Planner**. New York: College Board, 1990. $29.95.

402   **College Cost Explorer**. New York: College Board, 1990. $49.95. System requirements: IBM-PC or compatible; Apple IIe, IIc, IIc plus, or IIGS. Available on 3½-inch or 5¼-inch disks.

The *College Explorer* provides over 600 data elements for 1,800 colleges and universities. For each institution, the basic screen contains four boxes that give general information, costs, admissions and test requirements, and a menu for finding data on other topics (e.g., associate degree programs, majors offered, student life). A special feature enables the user to create a personal profile that, when matched to the college profiles, produces two lists: schools with all the chosen features and others with preferred features (e.g., setting, location). A "What Doesn't Match" command reveals why a specific institution does not match the user's profile.

The *College Planner* rates a specific college on various academic and campus features; provides customized letters for requesting catalogs, forms, and interviews; and gives a calendar for 1990 to 1994 with admission deadlines and other dates. *College Cost Explorer* gives financial information on 2,800 institutions, including payment plans, financial aid history, and other fee information. [R: WLB, Nov 90]

403   **The College Handbook**. New York: College Board. annual. $17.95pa. LC 41-12971.

Information for this important guide, gathered and verified annually, now covers over 3,000 2- and 4-year institutions. Profiles include description, major/academic programs, academic regulations, admissions, student life, athletics, annual expenses, financial aid, and address and telephone number. Information is current and accurate. The introductory section surveys admission practices and offers advice on selecting a college and financing an education. Indexing provides numerous access points. Highly recommended. [R: ARBA 91]

404   DelVecchio, Valentine. **Cadet Gray: Your Guide to Military Schools, Military Colleges, and Cadet Programs**. Morro Bay, Calif.: Reference Desk Books, 1990. 212p. $11.95pa. ISBN 0-96257490-2. (655 Morro Bay Blvd., Suite 146, Morro Bay, CA 93442).

Cadet Gray is arranged by type of school: U.S. service academies, four-year military colleges, universities with cadet corps, state maritime colleges, two-year military colleges with prep schools, and military secondary schools or civilian schools with cadet programs. Entries of four to six pages, listed alphabetically within each section, provide the history and philosophy of each school plus academic requirements, cost, and student life (e.g., plebe system, demerit system, daily schedule). The work is illustrated with black-and-white pictures. Four indexes provide access alphabetically, geographically, by cost, and by grade level. This guide complements other standard guides. [R: BL, 15 Dec 90]

405   Fiske, Edward B., and others. **The Fiske Guide to Colleges 1991**. New York: Times Books/ Random House, 1990. 761p. $12.95. ISBN 0-8129-1862-2. LC 89-645313.

Colleges and universities judged by Fiske, educational columnist of the *New York Times*, to be the "best and most interesting" constitute the focus of this volume. The 300-plus institutions profiled in informative and well-written essays are located in 44 states and the District of Columbia.

Each entry includes a chart containing enrollment, costs, academic rating, test-score ranges, and more, followed by an essay about housing, social life, extracurricular activities, and academics. Each also contains information about admission and financial aid. Indexes (in the front of the volume) are by state and school and by cost (ranging from least expensive to most expensive). [R: ARBA 90; BR, Jan/Feb 91; SLJ, Mar 91]

406   Goldberg, Lee, and Lana Goldberg. **The Jewish Student's Guide to American Colleges**. New York: Shapolsky, 1989. 221p. $14.95pa. ISBN 0-933503-32-6.

Over 100 public and private colleges and universities in all areas of the United States are included in this unique guide. Institutions are selective, popular, secular colleges that have a reasonable percentage of Jews enrolled and to which Jewish students are likely to apply.

Entries, arranged alphabetically by name, include a campus photograph, the number and percentage of Jewish students, availability of religious services and kosher food, and a subjective rating of Jewish campus life (extensive, good, moderate, or limited). Known anti-Semitic campus incidents are mentioned.

Appendixes include several summary lists, such as student bodies that are at least 20 percent Jewish, colleges serving kosher meals, and steps in the application process. This is a valuable source for students desiring to maintain a Jewish lifestyle at college. [R: ARBA 91]

407 Lovejoy's College Guide: A Complete Reference Book to Some 2,500 American Colleges and Universities.... 19th ed. Charles T. Straughn, II, and Barbarasue Lovejoy Straughn, eds. New York: Simon & Schuster, 1989. 1024p. $34.95; $18.95pa. ISBN 0-671-68756-5; 0-671-68757-3pa. LC 89-27089.

This frequently revised work provides compact comparative and descriptive data for some 2,500 2-and 4-year colleges, accredited and nonaccredited. It also offers information about application procedures, career areas, special academic programs, sports programs, and scholarships. Services to the handicapped are covered in *Lovejoy's College Guide for the Learning Disabled*.

Despite this work's utility, other guides such as *Peterson's Guide to Four-Year Colleges* and *Barron's Profiles of American Colleges* provide more data. [R: ARBA 91]

408 Peterson's Competitive Colleges, 1991-1992. 10th ed. Princeton, N.J.: Peterson's Guides, 1991. 382p. $12.95pa. ISBN 1-56079-041-5. ISSN 0887-0152.

This work defines "competitive" as admission based primarily on two main factors: SAT or ACT scores and class rank. The volume includes some 300 4-year colleges and universities judged to be competitive. A few music and art schools that use less traditional admission policies are listed in a separate section.

For each school cited, a one-page entry provides a profile of the student body, with the percentages of women, Blacks, and students who complete degrees; data on test scores and rank for the freshman class; and majors, athletic programs, financial aid, costs, and application information. Unlike most college guides, this one provides no information on student life, the campus, or location. Students wishing to identify schools with high academic admission policies will find this volume useful, but they will need to turn to standard guides for complete information on their schools of interest.

■ *Peterson's Drug and Alcohol Programs and Policies at Four-Year Colleges*. See entry 1957.

409 Peterson's Guide to Four-Year Colleges. Princeton, N.J.: Peterson's Guides. annual. $33.95; $17.95pa.

This standard guide to undergraduate schools provides concise information on United States and Canadian institutions. Over 1,800 accredited schools offering the baccalaureate degree constitute the focus of this annual. "The College Adviser" offers suggestions on choosing a college and a major and on obtaining financial aid. The main section profiles each college, giving enrollment, cost, admission requirements, financial aid, majors, campus life, and more. About 800 of those included have contributed 2-page "Special Announcements" that provide more details about the college; many have campus photographs.

Indexes designed to assist the student in selecting colleges group schools under several headings: entrance difficulty, costs, majors, and test scores. This guide, a first choice for most libraries, provides a vast amount of information in an easy-to-use format and at a reasonable cost. Its closest competitor is *Barron's Profiles of American Colleges*.

410 Peterson's Guide to Two-Year Colleges. Princeton, N.J.: Peterson's Guides. annual. $29.95; $13.95pa.

Similar to other college guides published by Peterson's, this annual provides concise information on two-year schools. The "College Adviser" section contains information about financial aid, standardized tests, majors, and careers. The "College Finder" is divided into two parts. The first is a list of schools arranged by state with data on enrollment, application requirements, types of financial aid available, sports, and majors offered. The second is an alphabetical list of majors with names of two- and four-year colleges that offer associate degrees in the field.

The main section, "College Profiles and Special Announcements," provides descriptions of some 1,400 colleges, giving background, enrollment, faculty size, admission and graduation requirements, costs, financial aid, special programs, placement service, sports, majors, and contact person. Messages from the colleges, written by college officials, give additional information on programs, student life, policies, and so forth. The volume is indexed. [R: ARBA 91]

411 The Right College, 1991. By College Research Group of Concord, Massachusetts. New York: Arco/Prentice Hall Press, 1990. 1441p. $18.95pa. ISBN 0-13-781212-4.

Descriptions of some 1,500 colleges give information on costs, enrollment, faculty size, selectivity, student body, programs, student life, athletics, admissions, financial aid, student employment, computer facilities, graduate career data, and prominent alumni. Indexed by majors; intercollegiate sports; and comparative data on certain selectivity factors, SAT/ACT scores, costs, and enrollment. Special features include essays on job outlook, racial tension on campuses, costs, and financing an education. [R: ARBA 91]

412 **300 Most Selective Colleges**. By College Research Group of Concord, Massachusetts. New York: Arco/Prentice Hall Press, 1989. 499p. $12.95pa. ISBN 0-13-602913-2. LC 88-645975.

This guide to America's 300 most selective colleges and universities gives a profile of each institution (e.g., programs of study, student life, athletics), its graduate and professional school placement rate, a selectivity rating, and general information about such things as cost and enrollment. Essays that are especially useful include the areas that colleges and universities usually emphasize in evaluating applicants, financial aid criteria, required scores on standardized tests, and questions designed to help the applicant appraise personal qualifications. Highly recommended. [R: ARBA 91]

COLLEGE PLANNING

413 **Barron's Profiles of American Colleges: Index to College Majors**. 16th ed. Compiled and edited by the College Division of Barron's Educational Series. Hauppauge, N.Y.: Barron's Educational Series, 1988. 381p. $29.95; $11.95pa. ISBN 0-8120-5907-7; 0-8120-3983-1pa. LC 87-640099.

Designed to supplement *Barron's Profiles of American Colleges: Descriptions of the Colleges*, this index enables the student to identify institutions offering majors in specific fields and to determine the type of careers to which each program leads. The directory rates hundreds of colleges according to difficulty of admission and percentage of applicants admitted. It also indicates men's and women's colleges, those with religious affiliations or a large international enrollment, those offering ROTC, and those that have only upper-level programs. For additional information on institutions covered, the user must turn to the companion volume or another directory.

Dollars for Scholars by Marguerite J. Dennis (Barron's Educational Series, 1989) focuses on the types of financial aid available for a college education and how to obtain them. [R: ARBA 90]

414 Blum, Laurie. **Free Money for College**. New York: Facts on File, 1990. 272p. $24.95. ISBN 0-8160-2313-1. LC 90-2921.

Some 1,000 grants and scholarships for a college education are arranged by state or area of study. The guide also lists financial aid for women, ethnic minorities, and the handicapped. Each entry provides directory information, dollar amount, and restrictions. Unfortunately, there is no index. Other sources provide far more coverage, but this guide does list some sources of funding not found in others. [R: ARBA 91; BL, 1 Jan 91]

415 Cassidy, Daniel J., and Michael J. Alves. **The Scholarship Book: The Complete Guide to Private-Sector Scholarships, Grants and Loans for Undergraduates**. 3d ed. Englewood Cliffs, N.J.: Prentice-Hall, 1990. 400p. $29.95; $19.95pa. ISBN 0-13-792052-0; 0-13-792060-1pa. LC 90-30898.

This guide identifies over 1,753 scholarships, grants, loans, internships, and contest prizes available from the private sector—corporations, unions, trust funds, religious and fraternal organizations, and philanthropists. The data are provided by the National Scholarship Research Service, from which students may acquire even more current information for a fee.

Arranged by field of study, entries include award name, address, telephone number, amount of money, deadline, requirements, and number of awards given each year. Indexed by major field of study, award name, state of residence, state of intended study, family ancestry, and physical handicap. This modestly priced source contains valuable information and many helpful tips for those seeking financial assistance. Highly recommended.

Chronicle Student Aid Annual (Chronicle Guidance, 1989) is a similar guide to scholarships, loans, and other financial assistance programs. *The Student Loan Handbook* by Lana J. Chandler and Michael D. Boggs (2d ed. Betterway Publications, 1991), an inexpensive work, focuses on guaranteed student loan programs, Pell Grants, Supplementary Education Opportunity Grants, work study, military support, and ethnic/minority aid. [R: ARBA 91; BL, 15 Sept 90; LJ, Aug 90]

416 **College Admissions Index of Majors & Sports**. Concord, Mass.: Orchard House. annual. $25.00pa.

This guide to majors and sports at 1,558 4-year and upper-division colleges and universities in the United States, Canada, Mexico, and Western Europe is a companion volume to *College Admissions Data Handbook*; both are revised annually. Some 6,000 majors, arranged in 300 categories, are also grouped into 19 general areas designed to assist those undecided about a major. Around 460 sports are arranged under 38 headings. Athletic scholarships and each college's NCAA division are also cited.

Both sections are arranged alphabetically by state and institution under each category. The work includes indexes for religious affiliation and tuition range ($4,000-$6,999, $7,000-$9,999, and $10,000-up).

The index and its companion volume are similar in content to *College Blue Book*, which also includes graduate level and two-year/vocational education. [R: ARBA 90]

417 **The College Cost Book, 1991.** 11th ed. New York: College Board, 1990. 295p. $13.95pa. ISBN 0-87447-375-6. LC 80-648095.

This work, which provides an accurate profile of college costs and financial aid processes, begins with a survey of college expenses, major types of aid, and application forms and procedures. The work also includes a bibliography of sources for further information, a glossary of terms, and other helpful materials for the prospective college student.

The main body of the work, arranged by state and institution, provides an estimate of costs (for commuters and residents), lists financial aid options with deadlines and required documents, and gives the percentage of applicants who receive aid. Profiles are offered for 3,100 2- and 4-year colleges and universities. This inexpensive guide is a worthwhile purchase for secondary schools. [R: ARBA 91]

418 Fiske, Edward, and others. **How to Get into the Right College: Secrets of College Admission Officers.** New York: Times Books/Random House, 1988. 193p. $8.95pa. ISBN 0-8129-1686-7. LC 87-40598.

The authors surveyed over 150 college and university admission officers to obtain the practical information in this inexpensive volume. The 27 humorous chapters attempt to prepare the student for the application process and rejection (if that is the result). Among its topics are SAT/ACT testing, college visits, completing application forms, seeking financial aid, writing the application essay, and letters of recommendation. One chapter provides a timeline for the student's junior and senior years in high school, and another summarizes the College Board's guidelines on fair admission practice. [R: BR, May/June 89; LJ, 1 Nov 88; VOYA, June 89]

419 **Index to Majors.** New York: College Board. annual. $14.95pa. LC 80-648202.

This annual contains current information on over 500 major fields of study offered at the undergraduate and graduate levels that lead to a certificate, associate, bachelor's, master's, doctoral, or other professional degree. The programs listed are for the 3,000 institutions described in *The College Handbook*, a companion volume.

In order to help a prospective student identify an institution offering a specific major or academic program in the desired geographical area, the index is arranged alphabetically by major and then by state. The guide employs the classification system developed by the Center of Instruction Programs (CIP).

A special feature is the inclusion of 17 special academic programs such as double majors, combined bachelors/graduate degrees, honors programs, and weekend college opportunities. [R: ARBA 91]

420 Lederman, Ellen. **College Majors: A Complete Guide from Accounting to Zoology.** Jefferson, N.C.: McFarland, 1990. 122p. $18.95. ISBN 0-89950-462-0. LC 89-29540.

The *Occupational Outlook Handbook* (*OOH*) provides much of the same information, but this directory lists many more technical occupations, making it a worthwhile supplement to *OOH*. The work is designed to help college or college-bound students select a major. For each of the 399 fields of study included, it gives a definition of the major, level of degrees offered (from associate through doctoral), typical courses, related or complimentary majors, needed abilities, and career possibilities. Colleges offering degrees in a particular major are not cited, but readers are referred to the *College Blue Book* and the *Index to Majors*.

Appendixes list majors by broad disciplines, provide cross-references among majors, and correlate occupations and majors. This information is compiled from college catalogs, NCES Classification of Instructional Programs, and HEGIS Taxonomy. [R: ARBA 91]

421 Peterson's College Money Handbook 1991: The Only Complete Guide to Scholarships, Costs, and Financial Aid at U.S. Colleges. 8th ed. Princeton, N.J.: Peterson's Guides, 1991. 585p. $35.95; $19.95pa. ISBN 1-56079-001-6; 1-56079-000-8pa.

For each of the schools listed, this guide gives typical expenses and financial aid available, a description of the school's aid program, and the name of the school's financial officer. It also provides introductory material on the financial aid process and an index to the types of aid given by each institution. Despite its subtitle, neither this guide, nor similar works, are definitive, but this is a practical and inexpensive source of information. [R: Kliatt, Apr 91]

422 Schlachter, Gail Ann, with Sandra E. Goldstein. Directory of Financial Aids for Minorities 1989-1990: A List of Scholarships, Fellowships, Loans, Grants, Awards, and Internships.... San Carlos, Calif.: Reference Service Press, 1989. 514p. $45.00. ISBN 0-918276-08-X. ISSN 0736-4122. LC 85-25068.

This biennial describes over 2,250 sources of financial assistance for minority students: scholarships, fellowships, grants, loans, internships, and state benefits. Each entry provides directory information, purpose, eligibility, amount of award or stipend, number of annual awards, deadlines, and other useful data. The guide is indexed by program title, sponsoring organization, geographic location, subject, and deadline date. This excellent directory is the most current source available on the topic. [R: ARBA 90; LJ, Aug 89; VOYA, June 89]

423 Schlachter, Gail Ann, with Sandra E. Goldstein. Directory of Financial Aids for Women 1991-1992. San Carlos, Calif.: Reference Service Press, 1991. $45.00. ISBN 0-918276-06-3. LC 84-24582.

This biennial lists essential data concerning some 1,900 scholarships, fellowships, loans, grants, awards, internships, and state benefits for women. The information is useful to students entering college and teachers who are seeking graduate and professional programs. Indexed by program, title, sponsoring organization, geography, and subject.

■ *The Winning Edge. See* entry 1056.

GIFTED

424 Colangelo, Nicholas, and Gary A. Davis, eds. Handbook of Gifted Education. Needham, Mass.: Allyn and Bacon, 1991. 463p. index. $44.95. ISBN 0-205-12652-9. LC 90-36623.

This publication surfaces as the first truly comprehensive handbook in the field of the gifted. As such, it is a "must-have" book for anyone seriously interested in the topic.

A handbook that purports to represent any field should meet at least two criteria: it should contain information about virtually every aspect of the field; and the theory, research, and applications represented should come from the leaders of the field. This meets both criteria superbly. First, it is comprehensive. Chapters examine such diverse issues and topics as identification of gifted students; instructional models and practices; creativity and thinking skills; psychological and counseling needs of the gifted and talented; preschool gifted students; and ethnic, minority, culturally different, and gifted-handicapped youths. Past, present, and future perspectives relative to gifted and talented education are also included. Second, the author list is a virtual who's who of names from the areas of gifted education and intelligence definition. Salient and cogent writing abounds.

425 Greenlaw, Jean, and M. E. McIntosh. Educating the Gifted: A Sourcebook. Chicago: American Library Association, 1988. 512p. $45.00. ISBN 0-8389-0483-1.

Teachers, counselors, administrators, and parents will find this sourcebook informative and useful. Chapters cover all areas of educating the gifted student: historical background, defining and identifying the gifted, counseling, programming, curricular needs, education of teachers, and parenting. An extensive bibliography supports each chapter. Other features include state involvement in gifted programs, evaluation of curricular materials, and a comprehensive index. [R: VOYA, Feb 89]

INSTRUCTIONAL TECHNOLOGY

General

See also **Media Sources** and **Library Science**.

426 **Educational Media and Technology Yearbook**. Brenda Branyan-Broadbent and R. Kent Wood, eds. Englewood, Colo.: Libraries Unlimited, published in cooperation with the Association for Educational Communications and Technology. annual. $50.00. ISSN 8755-2094.

Published annually since 1973, this yearbook focuses on current trends in educational media and technology and related fields. Each volume contains several essays written especially for the yearbook. Other sections include a survey of the field, a directory of organizations and associations, a technology update, profiles of notables, a list of relevant graduate programs, a directory of foundations and other funding agencies, bibliographies of print and nonprint material published during the preceding year, and directories of media publishers and distributors. [R: ARBA 91; VOYA, Apr 89]

■ *Nonprint Production for Students, Teachers, and Media Specialists*. *See* entry 825.

E+
427 Rosenberg, Kenyon C., and John J. Elsbree. **Dictionary of Library and Educational Technology**. 3d ed. Englewood, Colo.: Libraries Unlimited, 1989. 196p. $32.50. ISBN 0-87287-623-3. LC 89-7987.

The dictionary, a revised and enlarged version of the 1982 edition, defines 1,000 terms related to audiovisual equipment, reprography, computer software and hardware, telecommunication, micrographics, photography, CD-ROM, and videodiscs. The first section discusses criteria for equipment selection for library and school use and includes an evaluation checklist for each type of equipment; the second section defines or identifies terms, acronyms, professional organizations, and other topics related to the technologies. [R: ARBA 90; BR, Jan/Feb 90]

Audiovisual

E+
428 **AIT Catalog of Instructional Materials: Audiovisual: Video, Laserdisc, Print, Software**. Bloomington, Ind.: Agency for Instructional Technology, 1991. (P.O. Box A, Bloomington, IN 47402-0120).

The Agency for Instructional Technology annual catalog lists products designed to enhance learning and classroom instruction. AIT, founded in 1960, holds an inventory of some 2,500 videocassette titles representing all core-curriculum subjects, career guidance, mental health, vocational education, staff development, and early childhood care, addressing audiences from preschool through high school. The collection comprises United States and Canadian (states and provinces) consortium, co-produced, and acquired material which can be purchased or rented.

The main section, covering video series arranged alphabetically by subject area (Arts to Vocational Education), is followed by a section listing interactive videodisc/instructional software. Entries include grade level, subject area, cost, producer and date of production, awards (if any), closed-captioned information, a description, and length. New programs appear in bold type. A grade level index and a subject index conclude the catalog.

429 **The Equipment Directory of Audio-Visual, Computer and Video Products**. Fairfax, Va.: NAVA/The International Communications Industries Association. annual. $45.00pa. LC 53-35264. (3150 Spring St., Fairfax, VA 22031).

This annual publication lists and illustrates some 3,000 audiovisual, computer, and video products and furniture from over 400 manufacturers. Additional sections list trade names, a directory of ICIA members, and a glossary of terms.

430 Schroeder, Don, and Gary Lare. **Audiovisual Equipment & Materials. Volume II**. Metuchen, N.J.: Scarecrow, 1989. 133p. $20.00pa. ISBN 0-8108-2265-2. LC 79-384.

Librarians with a lot of audiovisual equipment but limited troubleshooting experience will welcome this illustrated manual. The volume covers television, video, and computer equipment; videocassettes; compact discs; and videodiscs. Two chapters on equipment/materials and maintenance/repair will be especially useful. The nontechnical instructions are illustrated by black-and-white photographs.

Appendixes describe tools, cables, and connectors and provide instructions on soldering. [R: BR, Sept/Oct 90]

See also **Computers and Electronics** and **Library Science** for microcomputer software.

■ *Guide to Free Computer Materials*. *See* entry 111.

Videodiscs

431   Schwartz, Ed. **The Educators' Handbook to Interactive Videodiscs**. 2d ed. Washington, D.C.: Association for Educational Communications and Technology, 1987. 151p. $22.95pa. ISBN 0-89240-049-8.

This handbook provides descriptions of interactive videodiscs, laser videodisc players, video monitors and projectors, and software for developing instructional units for videodiscs. Its primary purpose, however, is to list available videodiscs of interest to educators, on subjects that range from aeronautics to telemarketing. For each, it gives a brief description of the program, system requirements, publisher, and price. [R: ARBA 89]

LEARNING DISABLED

See also **Handicapped**.

E +
432   **Concise Encyclopedia of Special Education**. rev. ed. Cecil R. Reynolds and Elaine Fletcher-Janzen, eds. New York: John Wiley, 1990. 1215p. $99.95. ISBN 0-471-51527-2. LC 90-12684.

An abridged version of the three-volume *Encyclopedia of Special Education* (1987), this encyclopedia includes entries for terms specific to the field, general concepts from a special education viewpoint, deceased leaders in the field, organizations, schools, legal cases, learning theory, publications, special education worldwide, testing and assessment, physiology, disabilities and disorders, and teaching methodologies. About 90 percent of the original articles have been condensed to give "basic facts and ideas." Libraries unable to afford the parent set should consider this work for professionals working with special education students. [R: ARBA 92; RBB, 1 May 91]

E +
433   Davis, William E. **Resource Guide to Special Education: Terms, Laws, Assessment Procedures, Organizations**. 2d ed. Newton, Mass.: Allyn and Bacon, 1986. 317p. $40.00pa. ISBN 0-205-08546-6. LC 85-18647.

An updated and expanded version of a work that appeared in 1981, this guide is arranged in five parts. Section 1, the largest, defines terms found in special education and includes a new division that lists roots, stems prefixes, and suffixes often used in the field's terminology.

Section 2 identifies relevant abbreviations and acronyms. Section 3 covers assessment instruments (e.g., tests, scales, surveys). For each, a brief description, age range, purpose and use, date of publication, and publisher is given. Section 4 examines federal laws and litigation concerning the handicapped. Section 5 consists of a directory of agencies and organizations engaged in helping the handicapped. This is a tool for all levels. [R: ARBA 87]

E +
434   **The Directory for Exceptional Children 1990-91: A Listing of Educational and Training Facilities**. 12th ed. Boston: Porter Sargent, 1990. 1362p. $50.00. ISBN 0-87558-124-2. ISSN 0070-5012. LC 54-4975.

This directory, revised approximately every three years, lists schools and training facilities for handicapped children and adolescents. It indicates which are publicly supported, private, or residential, or that have daycare programs.

Training centers are classified according to the disability treated: learning disabled, emotionally disturbed, autistic, orthopedically impaired, mentally retarded, visually impaired, learning impaired, and speech handicapped. Each section, arranged by state and city, lists facilities and their enrollment, staff size, type of therapy, and fees. A concise description of the program and services is also supplied.

A directory of associations and government agencies concerned with the handicapped concludes the volume. [R: ARBA 91]

435 Directory of College Facilities and Services for People with Disabilities. 3d ed. Carol H. Thomas and James L. Thomas, eds. Phoenix, Ariz.: Oryx Press, 1991. 361p. $115.00. ISBN 0-89774-604-X.

The 3d edition of this work includes over 2,000 institutions of higher learning in the United States and Canada—technical and vocational schools, junior and community colleges, and 4-year colleges and universities—that provide services for the disabled. Entries, arranged alphabetically by state and then city, provide name, address, telephone number, contact person, fax number, total student enrollment, disabled student enrollment, and degrees or certificates offered.

Other information includes number of specially equipped dormitory rooms, specific facilities accessible to those whose mobility or vision is impaired, itemized specialized services (e.g., tutoring, financial aid, physical therapy, adaptive P.E., career counseling), and indication of special fees charged. Indexing is alphabetical by institution and disability served.

This is the most complete and up-to-date directory on college facilities and services available for the disabled. Highly recommended. [R: ARBA 92; CLJ, June 91; RBB, 1 May 91]

436 Encyclopedia of Special Education: A Reference for the Education of the Handicapped and Other Exceptional Children and Adults. Cecil R. Reynolds and Lester Mann, eds. New York: John Wiley, 1987. 3v. $285.00/set. ISBN 0-471-82858-0. LC 86-33975.

Professional libraries should hold this set, which provides extensive coverage of special education and related fields. More than 2,000 signed articles contributed by 400 subject specialists cover biography, educational and psychological testing, disabling conditions, legal problems, professional associations, information sources, curricula, programs, special education abroad, and many other topics. The historical and critical essays require background knowledge and understanding of technical language. [R: ARBA 88; LJ, 15 Apr 88; SLB, Oct 89]

■ *Exceptional Child Education Abstracts*. *See* entry 391.

437 Lindsey, Mary P. Dictionary of Mental Handicap. New York: Routledge, Chapman & Hall, 1989. 345p. $55.00. ISBN 0-415-02810-8.

This work focuses on mental retardation—its causes, manifestations, diagnosis, symptoms, prevention, treatment, education, and training. Over 2,400 entries provide legislation, associations concerned about the condition, and concise definitions that often cite references for further information. The work is British, which is evident in citations to laws and organizations, but the definitions are sound, so the work is useful to students and professionals in the United States. [R: ARBA 91; RBB, 1 Feb 90]

438 Lipkin, Midge. The School Search Guide to Private Schools for Students with Learning Disabilities. Belmont, Mass.: Schoolsearch Press, 1989. 334p. $29.95pa. ISBN 0-9620326-1-1. LC 89-091087.

This guide is designed for parents and others searching for private schools with programs designed for a specific learning disability. The first section focuses on schools that accept severely handicapped persons, followed by a section on schools that offer programs for children with moderate learning disabilities by supplementing their regular curriculum. The last section describes schools that have tutorial services for students with minimal impairment or whose disability was detected after enrollment. For the 305 facilities covered, this guide gives historical and general information, admission requirements, a faculty profile, costs, the progress-reporting system, and any unique features the school may have. [R: ARBA 91; BL, 15 Dec 89]

439 Peterson's Guide to Colleges with Programs for Learning-Disabled Students. 2d ed. Charles T. Mangrum, II, and Stephen S. Strichart, eds. Princeton, N.J.: Peterson's Guides, 1988. 398p. $19.95pa. ISBN 0-87866-689-3. LC 88-25954.

This updated volume greatly expands the original edition (1985), which cited only those four-year schools that had fully developed programs for the learning disabled. Prepared by two recognized specialists in the field, it includes detailed information on 928 junior and senior colleges, most with services available to learning-disabled students, and some with complete programs for them. The guide also contains chapters on learning disabilities and selecting and gaining admission to a college of choice. *Lovejoy's College Guide for the Learning Disabled* (2d ed. Monarch Press/Simon & Schuster, 1988) provides similar information for about 400 colleges and universities. [R: ARBA 90; Kliatt, Jan 89]

E+
440   White, James P. **Materials and Strategies for the Education of Trainable Mentally Retarded Learners**. Hamden, Conn.: Garland, 1990. 368p. (Reference Library of Social Sciences, v.476). $40.00. ISBN 0-8240-6345-7.

This selective, annotated bibliography of materials published from 1970 to 1988 is intended for teachers of trainable mentally retarded students, preschool to adult. Two major areas are covered: programming and strategies for teaching. Appendixes provide listings of resource agencies, suppliers, publishers, and computer resources. [R: ARBA 91; LJ, 15 Nov 90]

STUDY ABROAD

441   Cassidy, Daniel J. **The International Scholarship Book: The Complete Guide to Financial Aid for Study Abroad**. 2d ed. Englewood Cliffs, N.J.: Prentice-Hall, 1990. 333p. $29.95pa. ISBN 0-13-477589-0.

For the student seeking an international education, this is the best source of information. It reveals that the private sector provides over seven billion dollars in scholarships for students studying overseas. The "Quick Find" index indicates awards available only to the physically handicapped, to certain racial/ethnic groups, or to students interested in study in a specific country (e.g., Albania, Zimbabwe). The field of study index focuses on scholarships, broken down into undergraduate and graduate areas, for students who wish to study in a particular field. Eligibility requirements, deadline dates, and sources of additional information are cited for each award. Indexed. [R: BL, 15 Sept 90]

442   **ISS Directory of Overseas Schools, 1990-91**. 10th ed. Mea Johnston, ed. Princeton, N.J.: Peterson's Guides, 1990. $29.95. ISBN 0-913663-07-7.

English-speaking schools for all levels of students in all parts of the world are listed in this directory. Each geographical section begins with brief information about the region. The school listings that follow give directory information, such as name of school, grades, address, telephone number, and name of director. Additional information includes staff size, teacher/student ratio, enrollment, fees, admission requirements, curriculum, campus, facilities, and school calendar.

443   **Scholarships, Fellowships & Grants for Programs Abroad: A Handbook of Awards for U.S. Nationals for Study or Research Abroad**. Houston, Tex.: American Collegiate Service, 1989. 299p. $29.75pa. ISBN 0-940937-02-6. LC 89-084074.

Students who wish to study in a foreign country will welcome this small volume. The introduction addresses the subject of foreign study in general terms. Part 1, the main part, lists 374 granting agencies, giving directory information, names and numbers of awards, award duration, fields of study, requirements, eligibility, application procedure, and amount of award (only those for $500.00 or more are included). The final section profiles 120 countries, with basic data on area, population, religion, language spoken, linguistic skills required, and contact person. Indexed. [R: ARBA 91; LJ, 15 Apr 90; RBB, 15 Feb 90]

444   **Study Abroad, 1992-1994**. 27th ed. Paris, Unesco; distr., Lanham, Md.: UNIPUB, 1990. 1150p. $24.00pa. ISBN 92-3-002715-4.

International study programs at the postsecondary level offered in over 100 countries are listed. Subjects offered, admission requirements, length of program, cost, and application procedures are provided. Another section gives information about scholarships, assistantships, travel grants, courses, and seminars.

445   **The Teenager's Guide to Study, Travel, and Adventure Abroad, 1989-90**. By Council on International Educational Exchange. New York: St. Martin's Press, 1988. 293p. $9.95pa. ISBN 0-312-02296-4.

High school students seeking interesting activities abroad will value this handbook. It lists over 150 organized programs with information on sponsors, housing, supervision, costs, and comments by past participants. Indexed by topic. [R: Kliatt, Apr 89; RBB, 1 Apr 89; SLJ, Apr 89]

See **Media Skills** in **Library Science** for study skills.

TESTS

General

. E+
446 The ETS Test Collection Catalog. Volume 2: Vocational Tests and Measurement Devices. Compiled by Test Collection, Educational Testing Service. Phoenix, Ariz.: Oryx Press, 1988. 168p. $43.00pa. ISBN 0-89774-439-X.

E+
447 The ETS Test Collection Catalog. Volume 3: Tests for Special Populations. Compiled by Test Collection, Educational Testing Service. Phoenix, Ariz.: Oryx Press, 1989. 208p. $55.00pa. ISBN 0-89774-477-2. LC 86-678.

E+
448 The ETS Test Collection Catalog. Volume 4: Cognitive Aptitude and Intelligence Test. Compiled by Test Collection, Educational Testing Service. Phoenix, Ariz.: Oryx Press, 1990. 158p. $45.00pa. ISBN 0-89774-558-2. LC 86-678.

Vocational Tests lists some 1,400 tests and measurements that will help counselors and others advise persons of all ages in planning careers. Some of the devices are standardized tests, but others are research instruments more difficult to acquire.

Tests for Special Populations describes 1,700 tests for persons who are mentally, physically, emotionally, linguistically, visually, or aurally handicapped; gifted; bilingual; older; and members of various ethnic groups. Included are tests for the development of the at-risk child.

Cognitive Aptitude and Intelligence Tests offers listings for 1,300 tests for cognitive style and ability, concept formation, creative and divergent thinking, aptitudes, intelligence, memory and recall, abstract thinking, and spatial ability.

Each entry provides a full citation of the test or questionnaire, information about its availability, and a brief description. Indexed by author, title, and subject. [R: ARBA 90; ARBA 91]

449 Mental Measurements Yearbook. Lincoln, Nebr.: Buros Institute of Mental Measurement, University of Nebraska; distr., Lincoln, Nebr.: University of Nebraska Press, 1938- .

The *Yearbook* is designed to assist test users in choosing appropriate instruments in the areas of education, psychology, and industry. The annual provides a critical review and complete bibliographic information for all new or revised tests published separately in the English-speaking world, some 1,200 in all. Indexed by acronym, subject, and name. A publisher's directory is also provided.

450 Tests: A Comprehensive Reference for Assessments in Psychology, Education, and Business. 3d ed. Richard Sweetland and Daniel Keyser, eds. Austin, Tex.: Pro-Ed, 1990. 1251p. $69.00; $44.00pa. ISBN 0-89079-255-0; 0-89079-256-9pa. (8700 Shoal Creek Blvd., Austin, TX 78758-6897).

Tests is a quick-reference dictionary to some 2,300 English-language tests arranged in three categories: psychology, education, and business and industry. Each section is divided into some 60 subsections in which tests are grouped by academic subject or usage in educational institutions.

Entries give title and author, circumstances of administration, time required, age level (child, teen, or adult), grade, purpose, description, scoring, cost, and publisher. No evaluations or data on validity are given.

ACT, GED, and SAT

451 The College Board Achievement Tests. rev. ed. New York: College Board, 1990. 1v. $12.95pa. ISBN 0-87447-394-2.

This work describes the content of achievement tests in English composition, literature, American history and social studies, European history and world cultures, mathematics, French, German, Hebrew, Latin, Spanish, biology, chemistry, and physics. The guide also explains why the tests are given, when they should be taken, how to prepare for them, and how they are scored.

452 How to Prepare for the American College Test (ACT). Hauppauge, N.Y.: Barron's Educational Series, 1989. 576p. $9.95pa. ISBN 0-8120-4184-4.

453 How to Prepare for the Preliminary Scholastic Aptitude Test/National Merit Scholarship Qualifying Test – PSAT/NMSQT. 7th ed. Hauppauge, N.Y.: Barron's Educational Series, 1989. $9.95pa. ISBN 0-8120-4191-7.

454 How to Prepare for the Scholastic Aptitude Test (SAT). 15th ed. Hauppauge, N.Y.: Barron's Educational Series, 1989. 768p. $9.95pa. ISBN 0-8120-4185-2.

Advice on preparing and taking each type of test, and practice exercises similar to those used in the actual exams comprise these guides. Also included are reviews for each test area, vocabulary lists and exercises, and other useful preparation tools. Disk versions for Apple, Macintosh, and IBM-PC computers are available.

455 How to Prepare for the New High School Equivalency Examination (GED). 7th ed. Hauppauge, N.Y.: Barron's Educational Series, 1988. 912p. $31.50; $9.95pa. ISBN 0-8120-5787-2; 0-8120-3888-6pa.

456 Como Prepararse Para el Examen de Equivalencia de Escuela Superior en Espanol. Hauppauge, N.Y.: Barron's Educational Series, 1979. 256p. $8.95pa. ISBN 0-8120-0488-4.

Instructions in all five areas of the GED exam (writing skills, social studies, science, reading skills, and mathematics) are provided in these guides. They include information on preparing for the examination, explanations of test scores, diagnostic examinations patterned after GED tests, and instructional lessons. Separate study guides for each of the five subject areas are also available.

457 10 SATs: Scholastic Aptitude Tests of the College Board. 4th ed. New York: College Board, 1990. $11.95pa. ISBN 0-87447-366-7.

This book gives descriptions of the SAT tests, describes each type of question, gives alternative ways to arrive at correct answers, suggests how to prepare for the SAT, and explains how the tests are scored and what the scores mean.

☐ ──────── # Ethnic Minorities ──────── ☐

GENERAL WORKS

E+
458 America's Ethnic Heritage Series. David M. Brownstone and Irene M. Franck, eds. New York: Facts on File. $16.95/v.

Each of the volumes in this series presents a portrait of an American ethnic group. One of the best, *The Chinese-American Heritage* (1988), contains a wealth of well-written information that ranges from the arrival of the first immigrants to California in the nineteenth century to the present. Over 40 black-and-white photographs illustrate the work. Other volumes in the series, all published in 1988, include *The German-American Heritage*, *The Irish-American Heritage*, *The Jewish-American Heritage*, and *The Scandinavian-American Heritage*. [R: ARBA 89; BL, 1 Mar 89; BR, Sept 89; VOYA, June 89]

459 Moss, Joyce, and George Wilson. Peoples of the World: North Americans: The Culture, Geographical Setting, and Historical Background of 37 North American Peoples. Detroit, Gale, 1991. 441p. $39.95. ISBN 0-8103-7768-3.

This work follows the "salad bowl" concept by profiling separate cultures and their contributions to the whole society. The authors believe that to truly understand events, one must know the individuals behind them and learn about various ethnic upbringings and peoples' experiences on the continent. Therefore, the entries focus on the human dimension in historical and current events. Before the immigrants from Europe arrived, a great mix of natives occupied the continent. All told, 3 lost cultures and 34 current ones are profiled. Maps show the greatest concentrations of these peoples, and their histories are described, from their immigration reasons to their statuses today.

This volume would be an excellent resource as a reference for school and public libraries from junior high level because it collects information regarding population, location, and language. Geographical setting and culture are examined in detail. Drawings and photographs enhance the information and make it more understandable.

ATLASES

460   Allen, James, and Eugene Turner. **We the People: An Atlas of America's Ethnic Diversity**. New York: Macmillan, 1988. 315p. $125.00. ISBN 0-02-901420-4. LC 87-28194.

This outstanding atlas is the first to focus exclusively on American ethnicity. Using data gathered in the 1980 census and other sources, Allen and Turner have produced a remarkable amount of information on immigration and ethnic settlement. Bright color-coded maps, 111 in all, show the distribution and density of 67 ethnic and racial groups for all 3,100 U.S. counties or equivalents. All obvious groups (e.g., Blacks, Jews, Chinese) are included, as well as smaller ones with at least 20,000 members counted in the census such as Thais, Basques, and Albanians.

One of the book's 13 chapters focuses on Native Americans, while others describe ethnic ancestry geographically, arranged by place of origin. The last chapter discusses general patterns of ethnic diversity.

Explanatory essays and tables describe immigration history and settlement patterns. Accompanying the full-page maps, which reflect the 1980 census figures, are smaller ones showing similar data for the 1920 census. The appendixes contain tables of ethnic and racial populations by state and county, and four regional maps identify all U.S. counties. Indexing is by ethnic group and geographical location. This handsome reference work is recommended for high school libraries. [R: ARBA 89; LJ, 15 Apr 89]

ENCYCLOPEDIAS HANDBOOKS, BIBLIOGRAPHIES, AND DIRECTORIES

■ *America's Architectural Roots*. *See* entry 1363.

461   **Dictionary of American Immigration History**. Francesco Cordasco, ed. Metuchen, N.J.: Scarecrow, 1990. 784p. $97.50. ISBN 0-8108-2241-5. LC 89-37041.

This volume contains a broad spectrum of data on immigration history: essays on almost all ethnic groups; profiles of leaders and others involved in colonization movements; brief entries on organizations; and abstracts of books, articles, and dissertations on the subject. There are more than 2,500 entries in all. The work achieves its stated goal of providing "a reference compendium on most aspects of American immigration history." Suggested for high schools. [R: ARBA 91; LJ, July 90; RBB, 1 June 90]

462   **Harvard Encyclopedia of American Ethnic Groups**. Stephan Thernstrom, ed. Cambridge, Mass.: Harvard University Press, 1980. 1102p. $95.00. ISBN 0-674-37512-2. LC 80-17756.

The *Harvard Encyclopedia*, the most comprehensive reference work of its kind, contains authoritative articles about 106 ethnic minority, religious, and regional groups. The essays, some quite long (up to 60 pages), treat historical, cultural, social, economic, and religious aspects of each group. There are also 29 substantial articles on topics related to ethnicity (e.g., migration, assimilation), statistical tables, and 87 black-and-white maps. Cross-referencing is limited; there is no subject or name index, and some groups are covered inadequately or not at all. Nonetheless, this is a basic reference tool on ethnicity. Recommended for high school libraries. [R: ARBA 82]

463   Weinberg, Meyer, comp. **Racism in the United States: A Comprehensive Classified Bibliography**. Westport, Conn.: Greenwood Press, 1990. 682p. (Bibliographies and Indexes in Ethnic Studies, no.2). $75.00. ISBN 0-313-27390-1. LC 89-78118.

This comprehensive bibliography addresses not only racism but also sexism and anti-Semitism. It includes thousands of references to books, chapters, articles, documents, and more. The entries are arranged alphabetically by author under 87 subject headings, such as affirmative action and Blacks and Jews. No other bibliographies on racism are as current or as broad in coverage. Advanced students will find this useful.

464   **World Directory of Minorities**. By Minority Rights Group. Chicago: St. James Press, 1990. 427p. $85.00. ISBN 0-55862-016-8.

Historical and cultural experiences of ethnic minorities worldwide comprise this volume, which is based on the investigation of the Minority Rights Group and material provided by other research organizations. Sections cover groups arranged in 11 geographical areas. For each minority there is a heading that gives alternative names, location, numbers, percentage of the population, religion, language, and a history of the region, with emphasis on the political and cultural developments that affect the group. Entries, ranging from 200 to 5,000 words, are cross-referenced to related groups. Maps show locations, and black-and-white photographs illustrate the volume. This is an important source for high schools. [R: ARBA 91; RBB, 1 June 90]

AFRICAN-AMERICANS

E+
465   Altman, Susan. **Extraordinary Black Americans from Colonial to Contemporary Times**. Chicago: Children's Press, 1989. 240p. $30.60. ISBN 0-516-00581-2. LC 89-11977.

This volume addresses 85 men and women who have faced adversity in their quest for recognition and achievement. Among those treated are such notables as Jesse Jackson and Martin Luther King, Jr., but the book covers many lesser known persons who have made contributions to American history and society. Most of the two-page articles include a photograph or portrait of the subject. Also provided are 15 brief essays on historical events and a bibliography. The volume is an excellent source for upper elementary and junior high school students. [R: BL, 15 June 89; SLJ, Mar, June 89]

466   **Black Adolescence: Current Issues and Annotated Bibliography**. By Consortium for Research on Black Adolescence, with Velma McBride Murry and Georgie Winter. Boston: G. K. Hall, 1990. $29.95. ISBN 0-8161-9080-1. LC 89-26995.

Students and professionals interested in African-American studies will welcome this work. Topical chapters cover developmental issues, psychological and physical health, academic performance, educational and occupational choice, employment, family relationships, sexuality, and teen parenting. Each chapter, contributed by an expert in the area, begins with a survey of the subject or problem. An outstanding contribution to the study of black adolescence, this book is highly recommended for middle and high schools. [R: ARBA 91]

■ *Black American Women in Literature*. *See* entry 1577.

■ *Black American Women Novelists*. *See* entry 1578.

■ *Black Americans in Congress, 1870-1989*. *See* entry 962.

467   **Black Americans Information Directory, 1990-91**. Darren L. Smith, ed. Detroit: Gale, 1990. 424p. $69.50. ISBN 0-8103-7443-9. ISSN 1045-8050. LC 90-648616.

Some 4,700 entries give directory information for and about Black Americans. The 17 chapters cover such areas as nonprofit, private, public, religious, educational, and governmental organizations/ agencies; important library collections, research centers, awards, and educational programs; and publishers, periodicals, and radio and television stations. Indexed by organization/publication name and key word. [R: LJ, 1 Mar 90; RBB 15 Jan 90; WLB, Apr 90]

E+
468   **The Black Experience in Children's Books, 1989**. By the Black Experience in Children's Books Committee, New York Public Library. New York: New York Public Library, 1989. 64p. $5.00pa.

This bibliography describes 450 books on Black culture suitable for children of all ages. It is arranged geographically, with sections for the United States, Africa, South and Central America, the Caribbean, and England. Information provided for each citation (picture books, stories, folktales, and biographies) includes an annotation, illustrator, bibliographic data, and price. This list, an update of the 1984 edition, is useful to teachers and librarians. [R: ARBA 90]

469   **Black Leaders of the Nineteenth Century**. Leon Litwack and August Meier, eds. Champaign, Ill.: University of Illinois Press, 1988. 344p. $29.95. ISBN 0-252-01506-1. LC 87-19439.

Subject experts contributed each of the 16 chapters on selected Black American leaders of the nineteenth century. The editors chose the subjects for their significance but make no claim that they were the only notable Blacks of the period. Each essay begins with a picture of the leader and provides an extensive narrative and evaluation of the subject's contributions. This scholarly work is highly recommended for high schools.

Earlier works also provide lengthy erudite biographies of major Black leaders: *Black Leaders of the Twentieth Century*, edited by John Hope Franklin and August Meier (University of Illinois Press, 1982), and *Southern Black Leaders of the Reconstruction Era*, edited by Howard N. Rabinowitz (University of Illinois Press, 1982). [R: ARBA 89; LJ, 15 May 88]

■ *Black Music Biography*. See entry 1640.

470 **The Black Resource Guide**. 1990-91 ed. Washington, D.C.: Black Resource Guide, 1990. 316p. $50.00. ISBN 0-9608374-7-7. LC 85-91077.

This annually revised directory, which began in 1981, has added new topics that enhance its utility. Listings, which give address, telephone number, and director or contact person, include businesses of many types; associations; organizations (e.g., civil rights, fraternal, health); book publishers, bookstores, and other media; adoption services; higher education institutions; churches; and many other groups and services of interest to Blacks.

Directory information for Black public administrators, politicians, and members of the judiciary is also provide. A statistical section on Black economic and social issues concludes the volume. Information is compiled from annual questionnaires sent to each listee. [R: ARBA 91]

■ *Black Union Soldiers in the Civil War*. See entry 721.

■ *Blacks in American Film and Television*. See entry 1311.

■ *The Dictionary of Afro-American Slavery*. See entry 713.

471 **Dictionary of American Negro Biography**. Rayford W. Logan and Michael R. Winston, eds. New York: W. W. Norton, 1983. 680p. $50.00. ISBN 0-393-01513-0.

Lucid articles, based on scholarly research, cover some 800 historically significant Black Americans who died prior to 1970. Those included had a "major influence in their region or local community." Their stories demonstrate the broad participation of Blacks in the development of the United States. The signed essays by 280 specialists range from a column to several pages. Each concludes with a bibliography of primary sources and secondary accounts. There is no index. This work, which complements *Dictionary of American Biography* and *Notable American Women*, is recommended for high schools. [R: ARBA 84]

E +
472 **Ebony Pictorial History of Black Americans**. Chicago: Johnson Publishing, 1971-1973. 4v. $38.90/set. ISBN 0-87485-073-8.

More than 1,000 pictures with text depict Black culture and the contribution of African-Americans to American life through the early 1970s. The chronologically arranged volumes each cover a broad time span: volume 1, from African roots through the Civil War; volume 2, Reconstruction through the Supreme Court decision of Brown vs. Topeka, Kansas Board of Education (1954); volume 3, the civil rights movement to the end of the 1960s; and volume 4 (reprint of the *1973 Yearbook*), changes through 1972. Suitable for grades 5 through 12.

473 **Encyclopedia of Black America**. W. Augustus Low, ed. New York: McGraw-Hill, 1981. 921p. $112.00; $35.00pa. ISBN 0-07-038834-2; 0-306-80221-Xpa.

Recommended for all middle and high schools, this comprehensive work is widely recognized as an accurate and reliable one-volume encyclopedia that covers the contributions of Blacks in nearly all fields. Black organizations, colleges, religions/churches, and culture are also discussed. Signed entries, arranged alphabetically, include 325 articles and more than 1,000 biographies. These vary in length but are usually a page or less. A few major essays cover such topics as Black American literature, dance, athletics, religion, and science.

Black-and-white photographs, bibliographies for each entry, numerous cross-references, and an annotated list of references are special features. A 45-page index concludes the volume. Prospective purchasers should note that the paperback edition was released in 1984 by Da Capo Press, but the text has not been updated.

■ *Harlem Renaissance and Beyond*. See entry 1594.

E +
474 Hughes, Langston, and others. **A Pictorial History of Black Americans**. 5th ed. New York: Crown, 1983. 400p. $29.95. ISBN 0-517-55072-5. LC 83-7742.

Students from elementary school through high school will welcome this pictorial history of Black Americans. Over 1,200 black-and-white illustrations with brief text document Black history from the sixteenth century to the present. The latest edition of this periodically revised work concludes with 1983. [R: BL, 1 June 84; SLJ, May 85]

■ *An Illustrated Bio-Bibliography of Black Photographers, 1940-1988*. *See* entry 1377.

475   **Images of Blacks in American Culture: A Reference Guide to Information Sources**. Jessie C. Smith, ed. Westport, Conn.: Greenwood Press, 1988. 390p. $49.95. ISBN 0-313-24844-3. LC 87-24964.

Well-written and informative chapters on Black stereotyping cover film and television, musical theater, games, children's books, and dolls. A bibliography concludes each chapter, and filmographies are included for movies and television. Despite the implication of the title, these are the only references to "information sources." Appropriate for high schools. [R: ARBA 89; BL, 1 Dec 88]

476   Lee, George L. **Interesting People: Black American History Makers**. Jefferson, N.C.: McFarland, 1989. 210p. $15.95. ISBN 0-89950-403-5. LC 88-43542.

This work contains over 200 short biographies of prominent Black Americans, chronologically arranged and accompanied by the author's pen-and-ink drawings of each subject. Included are political leaders, musicians, sports figures, scientists, writers, and soldiers, ranging from the famous to the obscure. The volume highlights the contributions of the subjects to U.S. history. Highly recommended for junior and senior high schools.

Two sets of prints by Lee with 100- to 175-word biographies are available from the publisher. *Interesting People Prints, Set I* includes 12 black-and-white art prints, 11" × 15", of such notables as James Baldwin, George Washington Carver, Coretta Scott King, and Toni Morrison. *Interesting People Prints, Set II* includes a similar set of 12 lesser-known men and women, including Daniel James, Jr., the first Black four-star general in the Air Force; Sadie Tanner Alexander, the first Black woman to receive a Ph.D.; and Richard Hunt, an accomplished sculptor.

477   **The Negro Almanac: A Reference Work on African Americans**. 5th ed. Harry A. Ploski and James Williams, comps. and eds. Detroit: Gale, 1989. 1622p. $110.00. ISBN 0-8103-7706-3. LC 86-72654.

Long considered the most comprehensive ready-reference source on Black culture in America, this updated work justifies its reputation. It appeared in 1967, and John Wiley published the first four editions; it was last revised in 1983.

Arranged in 33 chapters, it includes historical and statistical data, documents, biographies, and articles on broad topics, with emphasis on the current status of Black culture in the United States. A 100-page chronology covers Black history through 1989. Many chapters remain relatively unchanged from the previous edition, except for updating at the end. Some lists, however, need revision.

An extensive bibliography (25 pages) focuses on materials published since 1983. This outstanding work is highly recommended for secondary school libraries. Those holding the 1983 edition must judge whether updating from mid-1982 through spring 1989 warrants replacing it with this edition. [R: ARBA 90]

478   **Statistical Record of Black America**. Carrell P. Horton and Jessie Carney Smith, eds. Detroit: Gale, 1990. 1000p. $89.50. ISBN 0-8103-7724-1.

Comprehensive statistics on Black Americans, presented in nearly 1,000 graphs, tables, and charts drawn from published and unpublished commercial and governmental sources, make up this biennial compilation. The arrangement is by broad topic, such as population, social services, professions, military affairs, religion, and the arts. High school students writing reports and research papers will welcome this compilation of data.

479   **Who's Who among Black Americans 1990/91**. 6th ed. Iris Cloyd, ed. Detroit: Gale, 1990. 1539p. $110.00. ISBN 0-8103-2243-9. ISSN 0362-5653.

This biographical directory, published since 1976 and now a biennial, provides the most comprehensive coverage available for contemporary Blacks who have made significant contributions to American life. Individuals are executives, government officials, doctors, lawyers, athletes, performers and technical artists, journalists, scientists, and educators, among others.

Information contained in the 5th edition (1987) has been updated and the content expanded by nearly 5,000 biographees, to some 17,000. The entries are based on questionnaires and provide occupation, personal and career information, education, honors and special achievements, military service, and address. Biographical and occupational indexes and an obituary section for those who have died since 1987 complete this standard work. This is an important tool, since relatively few African-Americans are listed in *Who's Who in America*. [R: ARBA 91; LJ, 15 May 90; RBB, July 90]

ASIAN-AMERICANS

■ *Chinese-American Heritage*. *See* entry 458.

480 **Dictionary of Asian American History**. Hyung-Chan Kim, ed. Westport, Conn.: Greenwood Press, 1986. 627p. $75.00. ISBN 0-313-23760-3.

The main body of this work contains 800 alphabetically arranged entries on the major persons, places, events, and concepts of the Asian-American experience. The dictionary also includes 15 essays on particular groups in America and general topics. The best ready-reference tool on the subject, it is recommended for secondary schools. [R: BL, 15 May 87]

481 Haseltine, Patricia. **East and Southeast Asia Material Culture in North America: Collections, Historical Sites, and Festivals**. Westport, Conn.: Greenwood Press, 1989. 163p. $39.95. ISBN 0-313-25343-9.

The 191 entries, arranged alphabetically by state and Canadian province, describe library and archival collections, significant historical sites, and Asian festivals in North America. The work is incomplete, especially in its coverage of collections, but it is valuable for its unique data.

E

482 Jenkins, Esther C., and Mary C. Austin. **Literature for Children about Asians and Asian Americans: Analysis and Annotated Bibliography, with Additional Readings for Adults**. Westport, Conn.: Greenwood Press, 1987. 303p. $45.95. ISBN 0-313-25970-4. LC 87-23627.

Librarians, teachers, and others who recommend literature for children and young adults about Asians and Asian-Americans will find this bibliography indispensable. Each of the four major groupings—Chinese, Japanese, Koreans, and South-East Asians—begins with an overview of the literature, subdivided by folk literature, contemporary literature, and books about the ethnic group in America. An annotated bibliography that indicates suitable grade level follows the introduction. The third section consists of a bibliography of background reading for adults. Separate indexes for author, title, and subject support the volume. Highly recommended. [R: BL, 15 May 88]

483 Li, Marjorie H., and Peter Li, comps. and eds. **Understanding Asian Americans: A Curriculum Resource Guide**. New York: Neal-Schuman, 1990. 186p. $29.95pa. ISBN 1-55570-047-0.

This guide, which promotes cultural understanding, focuses on Asians and Asian-Americans. Part 1 reports the results of a survey on the perception of Asian-Americans by non-Asians and by Asian-Americans. The second part describes 25 classroom activities designed to promote interracial and inter-cultural understanding, and the third part suggests ways to implement programs as a part of the school's curricula. The final section, a selective bibliography with brief annotations, is arranged by reading level. Highly recommended for secondary schools. [R: ARBA 91]

German-Americans. *See German-American Heritage*, entry 458.

HISPANIC-AMERICANS

■ *Biographical Dictionary of Hispanic Literature in the United States*. *See* entry 1590.

■ *Chicano Literature*. *See* entry 1591.

484 Graham, Joe S., comp. **Hispanic-American Material Culture: An Annotated Directory of Collections, Sites, Archives, and Festivals in the United States**. Westport, Conn.: Greenwood Press, 1989. 257p. (Material Culture Directories, no.2). $42.95. ISBN 0-313-24789-7.

This guide gives access to the artifacts, activities, and culture of Hispanic-Americans in the United States and Puerto Rico. Directory information, hours of service, usage rules, a description, and other data are included for museum collections (private and public), national register sites (mostly buildings), and folklore archives. Also listed are festivals and their sponsors, dates, activities, size, and admission. Indexed by subject. [R: ARBA 90; BL, July 90]

485   **Hispanic Americans Information Directory, 1990-91**. Darren L. Smith and Donna L. Weyd, eds. Detroit: Gale, 1990. 395p. $69.50. ISBN 0-8103-7444-7. ISSN 1046-3933.
     A directory about Hispanic-American life and culture, this work gives access to information about 4,500 organizations, agencies, programs, and publications. Included are national, state, and local Hispanic associations; print and broadcast media; bilingual education programs and Hispanic studies; and federal, state, and local government agencies of interest to Hispanic Americans. Indexed by organization/publication name and key word.
     This directory overlaps Schorr's *Hispanic Resource Directory*, which provides more information on each organization or group, but this work gives more extensive coverage. [R: ARBA 91; LJ, 15 May 90; RBB, 15 Jan 90]

■ *Hispanic Writers. See* entry 1619.

486   Meier, Matt S., and Feliciano Rivera. **Dictionary of Mexican American History**. Westport, Conn.: Greenwood Press, 1981. 498p. $49.95. ISBN 0-313-21203-1. LC 80-24750.

487   Meier, Matt S. **Mexican American Biographies: A Historical Dictionary, 1836-1987**. Westport, Conn.: Greenwood Press, 1988. 300p. $49.95. ISBN 0-313-24521-5. LC 87-12025.
     Dictionary of Mexican American History contains some 1,000 entries that deal with topics related to Mexican-American history since the Texas Revolution (1835-1836). Articles focus on events and notables (e.g., politicians, civil rights leaders, entertainers, sports figures). The appendix includes a bibliography, a chronology of Mexican-American history, texts of documents such as the Treaty of Guadalupe Hidalgo (Spanish and English), a glossary of terms, and statistics on population and other topics.
     In *Mexican American Biographies*, Meier expands the biographical entries contained in the earlier work and adds new ones for nineteenth- and twentieth-century notables. He begins with the Texas Revolution and covers persons in many fields. Some personal information, such as marriage and family, is omitted; the readable profiles emphasize the principal activities for which the subject is noted, include birth/death dates, and cite a few sources. The appendix lists biographees by field of activity and then by state. A subject index concludes the volume. Both works are highly recommended. [R: BL, 15 May 88; LJ, 15 Apr 89; VOYA, Sept 88]

488   Schick, Frank, and Renee Schick. **Statistical Handbook of U.S. Hispanics**. Phoenix, Ariz.: Oryx Press, 1991. 255p. $49.50. ISBN 0-89774-554-X. LC 90-48167.
     This work consists of reprints of statistical charts, tables, and graphs drawn mainly from post-1985 government sources. The 298 tables, on a broad spectrum of subjects, are arranged topically under demographics, immigration, education, politics, employment, economic status, health, and social characteristics. To make comparisons, many tables include data about other minority groups. This is a very useful source for high school students researching papers and reports. [R: ARBA 92; RBB, 1 May 91; WLB, May 91]

489   Schon, Isabel. **A Hispanic Heritage: A Guide to Juvenile Books about Hispanic People and Cultures**. Metuchen, N.J.: Scarecrow, 1980. 178p. $20.00. ISBN 0-8108-1290-8. LC 80-10935.

490   Schon, Isabel. **A Hispanic Heritage: A Guide to Juvenile Books about Hispanic People and Cultures. Series II**. Metuchen, N.J.: Scarecrow, 1985. 164p. $20.00. ISBN 0-8108-1727-6. LC 84-13964.

491   Schon, Isabel. **A Hispanic Heritage: A Guide to Juvenile Books about Hispanic People and Cultures. Series III**. Metuchen, N.J.: Scarecrow, 1988. 158p. $17.50. ISBN 0-8108-2133-8. LC 88-18094.
     These annotated bibliographies not only recommend works in English about Hispanic people and cultures but also cite caveats about others that are poorly written or organized, simplistic, awkwardly translated, or somehow flawed. Listings, primarily nonfiction, drama, poetry, and folklore, are about Latin Americans, Spaniards, and Hispanics in the United States.

Titles are grouped alphabetically by the country they concern and then alphabetically by author. Each title is critically annotated, and grade levels (mostly for 9 and up) are assigned; noteworthy titles are starred. Indexed by author, title, and subject. Series 3 includes some 200 works published between 1984 and 1987. [R: ARBA 86; ARBA 89; BL, 1 Apr 89; BR, Mar/Apr 89]

See also lists in **Media Sources**.

492   Schorr, Alan. **Hispanic Resource Directory**. Juneau, Alaska: Denali Press, 1988. 347p. $37.50pa. ISBN 0-938737-15-5.
This directory identifies 951 Hispanic organizations, such as Chicano studies programs, chambers of commerce, political action groups devoted to the overthrow of Fidel Castro, and legal service agencies for farm workers. Each entry, organized by state and city, provides address, telephone number, contact person, founding date, number of members, budget, statement of purpose, publications, and category (e.g., professional association, health services, political organization). Appendixes include lists of publishers, book distributors, colleges, bilingual programs, and more. Indexed by categories.
Hispanic Americans Information Directory is far more extensive in coverage, but the detailed information in this work makes it a worthwhile selection. [R: ARBA 89; BL, 15 May 89; LJ, 15 Apr 89; WLB, Mar 89]

493   **Who's Who among Hispanic Americans**. Amy L. Unterburger, ed. Detroit: Gale, 1991. 550p. $89.95. ISBN 0-8103-7451-X.
Brief information about 6,000 notable, contemporary Hispanic Americans who trace their lineage to Mexico, Puerto Rico, Cuba, Spain, or other Spanish-speaking countries of Central and South America, is the focus of this biographical source. Those included represent a wide range of professions and occupations (e.g., medicine, social issues, labor, sports, entertainment). Indexed by occupation, geographic location, and nation of descent. [R: ARBA 92; RBB, July 90]

Irish-Americans. *See The Irish-American Heritage*, entry 458.

JEWS

See also **Religion**.

494   **American Jewish Year Book 1990**. By the American Jewish Committee. New York: American Jewish Committee, 1990. 600p. $30.00; $28.50pa. ISBN 0-8276-0359-2; 0-8276-0351-7pa.
This basic reference tool, broad in scope, covers current issues of concern to Jews. "Review of the Year," a major section, includes demographic and population statistics for the United States and selected foreign countries. One section provides directory information and brief descriptions of Jewish organizations. Others contain obituaries of notable Jewish residents of the United States who died during the preceding year (and an index to those in previous volumes); a summary of the Jewish calendar for the next several years; and a brief list of recent articles of interest. Two long essays on American Jewish life and recent trends in American Judaism are special features.

E+
495   Ben-Asher, Naomi, and Hayim Leaf. **Junior Jewish Encyclopedia**. 10th ed. New York: Shengold, 1984. 352p. $19.95. ISBN 0-88400-110-5. LC 84-51583.
Junior Jewish Encyclopedia is a comprehensive work covering Jewish history worldwide. Entries, which vary from a short paragraph to essays of three or more columns, include religious ceremonies, events, and people who played significant roles in Jewish history and culture. Noted for its clarity and judicious treatment, this encyclopedia is recommended for grades 6 and up.

496   **The Blackwell Companion to Jewish Culture: From the Eighteenth Century to the Present**. Glenda Abramson, ed. Cambridge, Mass.: Basil Blackwell, 1989. 512p. $50.00. ISBN 0-631-15111-7. LC 89-1008.
This outstanding work provides an encyclopedic guide to the role played by Jews in the arts, social and natural sciences, and media for the past two centuries. Over 1,100 alphabetically arranged entries,

written by a group of international scholars, focus on the Ashkenazic (East European) Jews, whether they live in the United States, South Africa, Australia, or Europe.

The work includes three types of articles: biographies containing factual data and an evaluation of the subject's work; essays on topics relevant to Jewish culture; and survey articles, which often cover controversial issues. Biographical entries are limited to creators, not performers; thus, Woody Allen is included, but not Itzhak Perlman. The length of essays ranges from one paragraph to several pages. Highly recommended for secondary schools. [R: BL, 15 Feb 90; LJ, Jan 90]

497   De Lange, Nicholas. **Atlas of the Jewish World**. New York: Facts on File, 1984. 240p. $45.00. ISBN 0-87196-043-5.

Text and maps cover and illustrate Jewish culture and history. Among the topics included are population distribution and migration; languages; location of archaeological discoveries; problems of Jewish identity and assimilation; relationship with other religions; geographical surveys; and a country-by-country review of Jewish life today, especially in cities such as Jerusalem, New York, and Paris, which have large Jewish populations. There are 175 color and 145 black-and-white photographs, 45 maps, a glossary, a gazetteer, and an index. This handsome volume, part of the Cultural Atlas series, should be a welcome addition to any high school collection. [R: BL, Jan 85; BR, Oct 85; SLJ, May 86]

498   **Encyclopedia of Jewish History: Events and Eras of the Jewish People**. Ilana Shamir and others, eds. New York: Facts on File, 1986. 287p. $35.00. ISBN 0-8160-1220-2.

Contributed by subject specialists, concise articles (averaging 800 words) on events and leaders from earliest times to the present constitute this volume. Over 500 excellent maps, photographs, and diagrams illustrate the work. *See also* references, called "connections," on each pair of pages direct the reader to related articles.

Twelve appendixes cover culture and ethnography (including articles on Hebrew script, manuscripts, costumes, and art) and provide a chronology of Jewish and world history from 500 B.C. to A.D. 1984. A glossary of terms and an index to text and illustrations conclude this outstanding work. Appropriate for high schools. [R: BL, Apr 86; BR, June 87]

■ *The Encyclopedia of Judaism*. See entry 1743.

499   Friesel, Evyatar. **Atlas of Modern Jewish History**. New York: Oxford University Press, 1990. 159p. $49.95. ISBN 0-19-505393-1. LC 88-765689.

Jewish history from the seventeenth century to the mid-1980s is the focus of this excellent reference work, which contains maps, charts, graphs, and illustrations that portray major historical events and demographic changes in modern times. The maps contain far more detail than those offered by general atlases. A revised and updated version of the Hebrew edition (Carta, 1983), this book is recommended for high schools requiring the historical and geographical depth this atlas provides. [R: BL, 1 Sept 90; LJ, Jan 91; WLB, Sept 90]

500   **The Illustrated Atlas of Jewish Civilization: 4000 Years of Jewish History**. Martin Gilbert, ed. New York: Macmillan, 1990. $35.00. ISBN 0-02-543415-2. LC 90-675150.

This beautifully illustrated, well-written atlas covers 4,000 years of Jewish life, emphasizing the historical, religious, and cultural contributions of Jews. The maps are especially notable. This work supersedes Gilbert's earlier work, *Jewish Historical Atlas* (Macmillan, 1976). Highly recommended for secondary schools. [R: LJ, 1 Mar 91; LJ, 15 Apr 91]

■ *The Jewish Primer*. See entry 1752.

501   Karkhanis, Sharad. **Jewish Heritage in America: An Annotated Bibliography**. Hamden, Conn.: Garland, 1989. 456p. (Garland Reference Library of Social Sciences, v.467). $59.00. ISBN 0-8240-7538-2.

Popular journal articles and monographs on Jews and Judaism comprise this bibliography. Each item, selected for the general reader, is briefly annotated. Many of the entries can be located through the *Readers' Guide to Periodical Literature*, but this is a convenient bibliography of materials on the subject. The age of the bibliography should be taken into consideration. [R: ARBA 90; LJ, 1 Feb 89; RBB, 1 June 89]

E+
502 Shamir, Ilana, and Shlomo Shavit. **The Young Reader's Encyclopedia of Jewish History**. New York: Viking, 1987. 125p. $15.95. ISBN 0-670-81738-4. LC 87-10599.

An excellent, attractive, and easy-to-use work, this survey of Jewish history contains concise information about almost every name and place of importance from around 5,000 B.C. to the present. A timeline places Jewish history within the context of general world history. Maps, diagrams, and other graphic materials support the text. [R: BL, 15 Mar 88; BR, May 88; SLJ, Feb 88]

NATIVE-AMERICANS

■ *American Indian Literature*. *See* entry 1586.

503 Bancroft-Hunt, Norma. **The Indians of the Great Plains**. New York: Peter Bedrick Books; distr., Emeryville, Calif.: Publishers Group West, 1989. 128p. $24.95. ISBN 0-87226-198-0.

This volume, part of the *Echoes of the Ancient World* series, focuses on the culture of the Great Plains Indians. The excellent color photographs by Werner Forman complement the portrait of the Indians' lifestyle and beliefs. This worthwhile work is appropriate for middle and high school levels. [R: BR, Mar 90; VOYA, Apr 90]

E
504 **Books without Bias: Through Indian Eyes**. 2d ed. Beverly Slapin and Doris Seale, eds. Berkeley, Calif.: Oyate, 1988. 462p. $25.00 spiralbound. ISBN 0-9625175-0-X.

Books without Bias opens with essays on stereotypes and errors that often appear in children's books about Indians, showing positive and negative examples from books on the market. The main body of the work provides three- to four-page entries, each consisting of a large picture of the cover, a description of the book, and a critical evaluation. A briefly annotated list of additional, recommended titles concludes the volume. [R: ARBA 90]

505 **The Chelsea House Series on Indians of North America**. New York: Chelsea House, 1987-1988. 53v. $17.95/v. $951.35/set. ISBN 1-55546-685-0.

The 53 volumes in this series on Indians of North America for young adult audiences includes well-known groups (e.g., Apache, Navajo, Sioux) and obscure ones (e.g., Lambee, Quapaw, Tunica-Biloxi).

Every volume begins with a historical introduction, but the major part of each work covers contemporary problems and cultural issues, such as relations between the tribe and the federal government or economic problems. Black-and-white and color photographs, line drawings, maps, a glossary, and a short bibliography support the text. A subject expert is responsible for each accurate and cogent volume. Suggested for secondary schools. [R: ARBA 89; BR, Jan 90; BR, Sept 90]

506 Klein, Barry T. **Reference Encyclopedia of the American Indian**. 5th ed. West Nyack, N.Y.: Todd; distr., Santa Barbara, Calif.: ABC-Clio, 1990. 1078p. $125.00. ISBN 0-915-34416-5. LC 90-070527.

This work, a directory of organizations, persons, and print/nonprint materials about native Americans in the United States and Canada, condenses two previous volumes (1986) into one massive work. Section 1, arranged alphabetically by state, provides names and addresses for reservations, tribal councils, government agencies, associations, crafts centers, health facilities, Indian schools, colleges that offer courses in Native American history and culture, and information centers. Section 2 gives the same type of directory information for Canada.

Section 3, a bibliography of in-print books, contains some 3,500 entries arranged alphabetically by title and indexed by subject. Section 4, once a separate volume, is a "who's who" of over 2,400 contemporary Indians and others active in Indian affairs. The biographical data, compiled primarily from questionnaires, focuses on professional achievements.

Caveats include omission of many important books and well-known Native American facilities, incomplete data on some college course offerings, a few inaccuracies, and a number of typos. Nonetheless, high school libraries not holding the earlier edition may wish to consider this volume, which brings together a wealth of useful information. [R: ARBA 91; BR, Mar/Apr 91]

507 Kuipers, Barbara J. **American Indian Reference Books for Children and Young Adults**. Englewood, Colo.: Libraries Unlimited, 1991. 176p. (Libraries Unlimited Data Book). $32.50. ISBN 0-87287-745-0. LC 91-6880.

Kuipers's work has two parts: a discussion about selecting books of reference value for American Indian children and youth, including an evaluative checklist to aid librarians and teachers in making decisions; and an annotated bibliography of approximately 200 titles meant to serve as a basic collection on the topic. The discussion chapters, while occasionally repetitious, offer valuable advice on avoiding materials that are inaccurate and perpetuate stereotypes. Kuipers includes lists of sources consulted in preparing her checklist and provides an interesting overview of related studies. Not reference books in the strict sense of the word, these basic works about Indians in categories such as social sciences, history, and biography have been selected by using the Fry reading level test and reviews by Indian authors or organizations. Only recent, mainly nonfiction items are included. Arrangement is alphabetical by author within Dewey classification areas. Author/title and subject indexes are provided as well as a list of publishers.

E+

508   Leitch, Barbara A. **A Concise Dictionary of Indian Tribes of North America**. Algonac, Mich.: Reference Publications, 1979. 646p. $59.95. ISBN 0-917256-48-4.

Concise articles on 281 past and present American Indian tribes comprise this dictionary, suitable for grades 5 and up. Each essay surveys the tribe's history, location, culture, religion, and current status. Special features consist of black-and-white photographs, maps, a glossary, and an extensive index. [R: ARBA 81; LJ, 1 Apr 80; SLJ, May 81; WLB, June 80]

■ *Native American Architecture*. See entry 1368.

509   **Native American Voluntary Organizations**. Armand S. La Potin, ed. Westport, Conn.: Greenwood Press, 1987. 204p. (Ethnic American Voluntary Organizations Series). $45.00. ISBN 0-313-23633-X. LC 86-25764.

Brief essays (a paragraph to several pages) on 121 historically significant, voluntary American Indian organizations of the nineteenth and twentieth centuries are the focus of this directory. Entries for the organizations, most of which were founded by non-Indian groups, include a brief history, discuss persons and events associated with them, and list sources for further investigation. It should be noted that some organizations are now defunct.

The appendix lists organizations classified under one of four headings: political-reformist, cultural-educational, social-fraternal, or professional. Organizations are also listed in chronological order, with dates and key events. Indexed. Suggested for high schools. [R: ARBA 88; BL, 15 Nov 87]

510   Prucha, Francis Paul. **Atlas of American Indian Affairs**. Lincoln, Nebr.: University of Nebraska Press, 1990. 191p. $47.50. ISBN 0-8032-3689-1. LC 90-675000.

Maps contained in the main section of this atlas, based on U.S. census data from the nineteenth century to the present, show American Indian populations by counties, urban areas, local cessions, reservations, agencies, schools, and hospitals. Due to their unique Native American populations, Oklahoma and Alaska receive separate treatment. There also are maps showing military posts and battles with various tribes in the latter half of the nineteenth century. "Notes and References" provides statistics and sources for the maps. *Atlas of the North American Indians* remains the most important work of this type, but Prucha's atlas is a good supplement. [R: ARBA 92; BL, 15 Apr 91; SLJ, Oct 91]

511   Stuart, Paul. **Nations within a Nation: Historical Statistics of American Indians**. Westport, Conn.: Greenwood Press, 1987. 251p. $45.00. ISBN 0-313-23813-8.

The historical statistics and interpretations reported in this volume confirm that Native Americans have not fared well over the centuries since Europeans settled North America. Stuart provides many indicators of the past and present status of American Indians in chapters on land and climate, population, relocation and urbanization, vital statistics and health, government activities, health care and education, employment and earnings, and economic development. For each table, the author provides sources, most published by the federal government during the past century. The index distinguishes between citations to text and tables. [R: ARBA 89; BL, 1 Jan 89; WLB, Mar 88]

512   Verrall, Catherine, and Patricia McDowell. **Resource Reading List, 1990: Annotated Bibliography of Resources by and about Native People**. Toronto: Canadian Alliance in Solidarity with the Native people, 1990. 157p. $15.00pa. (P.O. Box 574, Station P, Toronto, Ontario, Canada M5S 2T1).

This annotated bibliography of materials by and about Canadian native peoples includes Indians, Inuit (Eskimos), and Metis (French-Indian ancestry). The editors have designed this work for several audiences. The 1,800 books and audiovisual materials listed, most from the 1980s, are divided into four sections: children and elementary schools, teaching resources, youth and adults, and directories/ indexes. Annotations tend to be evaluative and usually are coded to indicate a specific level or type of author. A final section lists periodicals and publishers/sources/distributors, followed by indexes to authors, book titles, and audiovisual titles. [R: ARBA 91; CLJ, Oct 90; RBB, Aug 90]

513 Waldman, Carl. **Atlas of the North American Indians**. New York: Facts on File, 1985. 288p. $29.95; $16.95pa. ISBN 0-87196-850-9; 0-8160-2136-8pa. LC 83-9020.

Waldman illustrates Native American history with 120 well-drawn 2-color maps on varying subjects (e.g., Indian prehistory, contact with Europeans, military conflicts, cultural patterns) and 75 photographs. An extensive text places the maps and illustrations within the context of North American history.

The appendixes contain a chronology of historical events, Indian place names in the United States and Canada, current tribal reservations and locations, and a directory of museums and historical societies. A bibliography and index complete the volume, which is highly recommended for high school libraries. [R: ARBA 86]

514 Waldman, Carl. **Encyclopedia of Native American Tribes**. New York: Facts on File, 1988. 293p. $35.00. ISBN 0-8160-1421-3. LC 86-29066.

This authoritative work provides concise cultural and historical information about 150 Native American tribes of the United States, Canada, and Mexico. Arranged alphabetically by tribal name (Abnaki to Zuni), the volume also includes entries under cultural names (e.g., Mound Dwellers, Cliff Dwellers), civilizations (e.g., Aztec, Maya), and language families (e.g., Algonquin, Iroquois). Two- or three-page articles give a brief historical survey and basic information about housing, clothing, outstanding features, and major conflicts. This unique reference tool is recommended for high schools. [R: BR, Sept/Oct 88; SBF, Jan 89; SBF, Mar/Apr 89; SLJ, May 88]

515 Waldman, Carl. **Who Was Who in Native American History: Indians and Non-Indians from Early Contacts through 1900**. New York: Facts on File, 1990. 416p. $45.00. ISBN 0-8160-1797-2.

This volume focuses on persons who influenced American-Indian history before the twentieth century. Some 1,000 entries provide concise biographies of tribal leaders, warriors, soldiers, explorers, army scouts, traders, artists, government officials, reformers, and scholars.

The subject's name is followed by tribe, dates, summary of role in Native American history, and other biographical data. The factual, noncritical entries do not evaluate the subject's contributions or historical significance. Some 50 black-and-white pictures accompany the text. Appendixes list Indians by tribe and non-Indians by their most relevant role. [R: ARBA 90; LJ, Apr 90; SLJ, Nov 90; RBB, 15 Sept 90; WLB, Oct 90]

E+
516 Wolfson, Evelyn. **From Abenaki to Zuni: A Dictionary of Native American Tribes**. New York: Walker, 1988. 215p. $18.95. ISBN 0-8027-6790-7.

Short descriptions of 68 Native American tribes in the United States (excluding Alaska) comprise this volume, intended for children in grades 5 to 8. Each tribe is covered in a two- to four-page historical/ethnological essay that gives tribal name, pronunciation, and meaning; cultural area; geographical location; dwelling type; clothing material; mode of transportation; and staple food. Each entry concludes with a paragraph about current conditions. Some 250 black-and-white photographs illustrate the text. This dictionary, which is similar to but less erudite than *Encyclopedia of Native American Tribes*, is recommended for elementary and middle schools. [R: ARBA 89; BR, Nov/Dec 88; VOYA, June 88]

Scandinavian Americans. *See The Scandinavian-American Heritage*, entry 458.

☐ # **Etiquette** ☐

517 Baldrige, Letitia. **Letitia Baldrige's Complete Guide to the New Manners for the '90s**. New York: Rawson Associates, 1990. 646p. $24.95. ISBN 0-89256-320-6. LC 89-43052.

Rapid social changes have generated more questions of etiquette than most persons can answer. Written in a lively style, this work, by a recognized authority, attempts to answer questions about everyday life, including those generated by the use of new technologies, such as answering machines and voice mail, and those created by special occasions, such as rites of passage, gift giving, entertaining, and correspondence. Indexed. This timely work is recommended for secondary schools. [R: ARBA 91; BL, 15 Nov 89; LJ, Jan 90]

E

518 Brainard, Beth, and Sheila Behr. **Soup Should Be Seen, Not Heard**. New York: Dell, 1990. 152p. $9.95pa. ISBN 0-440-50333-7.

A mother and a grandmother have collaborated to present "dos" and "don'ts" for children ages 4 to 12 about how to behave in everyday situations. Ten chapters explain in simple, readable text why good manners are necessary and treat such topics as table manners, dress and grooming, party behavior, telephone etiquette, and other situations at home and away. Behr's pen-and-ink drawings illustrate the volume. [R: WLB, Feb 91]

519 Ford, Charlotte. **Etiquette: Charlotte Ford's Guide to Modern Manners**. New York: Clarkson N. Potter; distr., New York: Crown, 1988. 524p. $19.95. ISBN 0-517-56823-3. LC 87-32893.

A special section in this well-known work deals with topics of concern to teenagers, such as dating, proms, and job interviews. Most of the volume, however, addresses adult behavior and contemporary situations, such as safe sex, visiting a friend with AIDS, birth announcements for unmarried parents, and intoxicated or drugged guests. Traditional topics (e.g., weddings, correspondence, travel) do receive attention. This comprehensive, well-written work is recommended for secondary school libraries. [R: ARBA 89; LJ, Oct 88]

520 Martin, Judith. **Miss Manners' Guide for the Turn-of-the-Millennium**. New York: Pharos Books/ St. Martin's Press, 1989. 742p. $24.95; $15.95pa. ISBN 0-88687-551-X; 0-671-72228-Xpa.

Miss Manners, the pseudonym assumed by Judith Martin, answers her "Gentle Readers'" questions about the proper handling of social situations and "refuses to allow society to seek its own level." This collection of her responses, published in her syndicated newspaper column, supplements such standard guides as *Emily Post's Etiquette*. Miss Manners's advice, written in a witty style, is at once didactic and entertaining. An excellent index gives easy access to the 10 topical chapters. Recommended for secondary schools. [R: BL, Aug 89; WLB, Mar 90]

521 Post, Elizabeth L. **Emily Post on Invitations and Letters**. New York: HarperCollins, 1990. 148p. $4.50pa. ISBN 0-06-081037-8.

This small book is a part of a series on etiquette that includes *Emily Post on Entertaining*, *Emily Post on Weddings*, *Emily Post on Business Etiquette*, and *Emily Post on Etiquette* (Perennial, 1990). All are arranged in topical chapters and use a question-and-answer format. *Invitations and Letters*, in four sections, covers personal and business correspondence and social and wedding invitations. These are useful, inexpensive volumes. Recommended for high schools.

522 Post, Elizabeth L. **Emily Post's Etiquette**. 14th ed. New York: HarperCollins, 1984. 1018p. $27.50. ISBN 0-06-181683-3. LC 83-48375.

This standard work is a current guide to correct social behavior. Arranged in six parts, the volume provides answers to questions about traditional rites (e.g., weddings, funerals), correspondence, table manners, and many other topics. "Your Professional Life," a new section, focuses on the business world and discusses resumes, hiring and firing, dress, two-income families, and so forth. Amusing excerpts from the first edition (published in 1922) are a special feature. The volume provides easy-to-find information about what is considered proper behavior. [R: ARBA 86]

Genealogy and Personal Names

FLAGS

E+
523   Haban, Rita D. **How Proudly They Wave: Flags of the Fifty States**. Minneapolis, Minn.: Lerner, 1989. 111p. $17.95. ISBN 0-8225-1799-X. LC 89-2302.

Each of the 50 state flags is pictured in color and described in a double-page spread. The text, arranged alphabetically by state, gives a brief history of the state and explains the evolution of the flag. The outstanding illustrations and lucid style make this an excellent choice for upper elementary through high school levels. [R: SLJ, Mar 90]

E+
524   **Our Flag**. By U.S. Congress Joint Committee on Printing. Washington, D.C.: Government Printing Office, 1989. 52p. $2.00. S/N 052-071-00873-0.

Out of print since 1979, this inexpensive, attractive work has been revised. A guide to the history and display of the American flag, it explains flag laws, regulations, and care, and it depicts flags of the states and territories and flag stamps. Many color illustrations and a bibliography support the text. Highly recommended for all levels. [R: LJ, 15 May 91]

GENEALOGY

525   Doane, Gilbert Harry, and James B. Bell. **Searching for Your Ancestors: The How and Why of Genealogy**. 5th ed. Minneapolis, Minn.: University of Minnesota Press, 1980. 270p. $15.95. ISBN 0-8166-0934-9. LC 79-27474.

This guides provides a comprehensive introduction for the beginning genealogical researcher. Part 1 discusses locating and using family papers and town, cemetery, and church records. Part 2 covers international research and discusses the availability of documents in foreign countries. The appendix contains a bibliography, state vital records offices with addresses and dates of records, National Archives locations and the areas each serves, and census records. Indexed. [R: BL, 15 Apr 90]

526   Greenwood, Val D. **The Researcher's Guide to American Genealogy**. 2d ed. Baltimore, Md.: Genealogical Publishing, 1990. 609p. $24.95. ISBN 0-8063-1267-X. LC 89-81464.

Considered the definitive genealogical reference guide, this work has been updated to reflect developments since the first edition appeared in 1973. The first part explains the basic principles of genealogical research. The second part examines records in depth and explains their use and value. There are separate chapters on legal documents and census, church, burial, cemetery, and military records. Chapters have been added on genealogical evidence, personal computers and genealogy software, and family history. Indexed. [R: ARBA 91; LJ, 1 Apr 90; RBB, 15 Apr 90]

527   Lawson, Sandra M. **Generations Past: A Selected List of Sources for Afro-American Genealogical Research**. By Library of Congress. Washington, D.C.: Government Printing Office, 1988. 101p. $4.50pa. S/N 030-001-00129-6.

This excellent guide to African-American genealogical research contains state-by-state lists of family histories, reference works, useful newspapers, organizations, periodicals, and other materials. Indexed by author/title.

Black Genesis by James Rose and Alice Eichholz (Gale, 1978) is the standard guide to African-American genealogical research. *Generations Past* serves as a useful supplement to it. Guides to other specific areas include *From Generation to Generation: How to Trace Your Jewish Genealogy and Personal History* by Arthur Kurzweil (Schocken Books, 1982) and *Ethnic Genealogy* edited by Jessie Carney Smith (Greenwood Press, 1983). [R: LJ, 15 May 90]

528   Neagles, James C. **The Library of Congress: A Guide to Genealogical and Historical Research**. Salt Lake City, Utah: Ancestry Publishing, 1990. 381p. $35.95. ISBN 0-916489-48-5.

A companion volume to *Guide to Genealogical Research in the National Archives* (National Archives, 1985), this work is divided into three parts: the history and arrangement of the library and how to find material, sources covering individuals and families, and resources on U.S. locales. Selective bibliographies accompany each section. [R: ARBA 91; LJ, 15 May 90; RBB, 15 Apr 90]

529 **The Source: A Guidebook of American Genealogy**. Arlene Eakle and Johni Cerny, eds. Salt Lake City, Utah: Ancestry Publishing, 1984. 786p. $39.95. ISBN 0-916489-00-0. LC 81-70206.

The Source is a comprehensive guide to U.S. genealogical records. Part 1 covers major sources such as census, cemetery, legal, and church records; part 2 identifies indexes, newspapers, biographies, and other published sources; and part 3 focuses on ethnic sources. Other features include sample records, tables, a glossary of terms, a bibliography, and a subject index. [R: ARBA 85; BL, 1 Sept 84]

PERSONAL NAMES

E +
530 Coghlan, Ronan, and others. **Book of Irish Names: First, Family & Place Names**. New York: Sterling Publishing, 1989. 128p. $22.95. ISBN 0-8069-6944-X. LC 89-32660.

This brief guide provides the history and meaning of Irish proper and place-names and gives a short chronology of Irish history, Irish root words, and a pronunciation guide. It has been compiled and edited from three pocket guides published in Belfast. Book 1 gives the derivation and meaning of Irish first names; Book 2 focuses on 80 Irish family names; and Book 3 gives over 600 Irish place-names in anglicized form, followed by the Irish form and its meaning. [R: ARBA 90; BL, 1 Dec 89; LJ, Dec 89]

531 Dunkling, Leslie, and William Gosling. **Facts on File Dictionary of First Names**. New York: Facts on File, 1984. 320p. $24.95. ISBN 0-87196-274-8. LC 84-4175.

Dunkling's work, the most extensive on first names for the English-speaking world, has some 4,500 entries that often mention dimunitives, related names, and variations. In all, some 10,000 forms of first names appear.

Information for each name includes gender, linguistic origin (if known), exact or possible meaning, literary uses, and popularity. The latter is based on surveys and other cited sources. Recommended for middle and high school. [R: BR, Nov/Dec 85]

532 Hanks, Patrick, and Flavia Hodges. **A Dictionary of Surnames**. New York: Oxford University Press, 1988. 826p. $75.00. ISBN 0-19-211592-8. LC 88-21882.

This volume focuses on surnames with a European heritage. Most are common names, but some are unusual. The work is organized by last-name group and supported by a 230-page index that refers the user from variations to the surname group.

Entries include country of origin, etymology in original language, variations of the name, and earliest occurrences (where available). The compilers designed this scholarly work for historians, genealogists, and other professionals, but high school students can use it. Highly recommended. [R: ARBA 90; BL, July 89; LJ, 1 Jan 89; LJ, 15 Apr 89]

☐ _____ **Geography** _____ ☐

BIBLIOGRAPHIES

See also **Social Studies**.

E +
533 **The Map Catalog**. 2d ed. Joel Makower, ed. New York: Random House, 1990. 364p. $27.50; $16.95pa. ISBN 0-394-58326-4; 0-679-72767-1pa. LC 89-43158.

This outstanding work, first published in 1986, provides comprehensive information on how to obtain map-related products, software, and other materials. More than 112 pages have been added to this edition, which includes hundreds of new sources and sections on geographical education materials, map copyright laws, and atlases. It addresses more than 50 categories of maps, such as historical, weather, military, travel, bicycle, wildlife, and globes. This is the definitive source for obtaining cartographic products. [R: BR, Sept/Oct 90]

ATLASES

General

534   The Atlas of Central America and the Caribbean. By the Diagram Group. New York: Macmillan, 1985. 250p. $60.00. ISBN 0-02-908020-7. LC 85-675575.
This small volume, which is more a fact book than an atlas, surveys the Central American and Caribbean areas (e.g., geography, climate, history, population, land use, politics) in text, maps, illustrations, graphs, and tables. A section on each country includes a fact box; an essay; and an outline map showing principal cities, roads, mountains, and rivers. Graphs indicate statistics such as the percentage, by country, of people in different population groups. An appropriate selection for high school level. [R: BL, 1 Oct 86]

535   The Atlas of China. Skokie, Ill.: Rand McNally, 1990. 48p. $8.95pa. ISBN 0-528-83385-5. LC 89-43157.
Secondary schools requiring more coverage of China than general atlases provide should acquire this inexpensive, oversized paperback. Double-page maps present the world, Asia, China as a whole, and China's regions; four single-page maps detail areas surrounding major cities. The text and picture captions summarize information about the nation's history, economy, land, and people. An index containing 11,000 entries gives locations for cities and geographic features. Its use of coordinates by degrees may confuse younger readers accustomed to map references by letters and numbers. [R: ARBA 91; RBB, 15 Apr 90]

536   Atlas of the People's Republic of China. Foreign Language Press; distr., San Francisco, Calif.: China Books & Periodicals, c1989, 1990. 1v. (various paging). $49.95. ISBN 0-8351-2319-7.
The first English-language atlas to be published in China since 1949, this work is based on a 1983 pinyin edition. It consists of colorful two-page spreads that contain excellent maps of each province, including Taiwan, autonomous regions, and municipalities directly under the central government. Also given are four maps of geographic areas, such as South China Sea islands.
Each map is prefaced by a title page that gives its name, scale, and location in the People's Republic of China. Following each map is a textual description that provides population, nationalities, land features, climate, altitude, products, neighboring areas, and more. Next is a series of one-page topographical maps. A comprehensive index of place-names, a brief pronunciation guide, and a list of basic geographical terms in pinyin (translated into English) complete the volume. This atlas provides excellent coverage of China. [R: BL, 1 Nov 90]

537   Atlas of the United States. Jilly Glassborow and Gilliam Freedman, eds. New York: Macmillan, 1986. 127p. $50.00. ISBN 0-02-922830-1. LC 85-675603.
A thematic atlas of the United States, this work covers population trends, climate, geology, land use, crime, agriculture, literacy, and other topics. Part 1 uses national maps for its comparison of states and regions; part 2 employs world maps to compare the United States with other regions of the world. Unfortunately, there is no index, and the maps, in general, are unattractive. Since the more extensive *National Atlas of the United States* (U.S. Geological Survey) is out of print, this atlas and the more recent *Contemporary Atlas of the United States* can serve as replacements for it. [R: ARBA 87; BL, 15 Feb 87; LJ, 1 Feb 87; WLB, Jan 87]

E
538   Courage Children's Illustrated World Atlas. Brian Dicks, ed. Philadelphia: Running Press, c1981, 1989. 128p. $12.98. ISBN 0-89471-703-0. LC 88-43388.
Prepared in Great Britain for the upper elementary grades, this atlas begins with a section written for American children, focusing on their immediate world—classroom, neighborhood, country, and continent. The maps, which comprise most of the work, consist of two-page spreads of continents and individual countries or groups of nations, varying in scale. Color photographs, drawings, fact boxes, and activities for children are scattered throughout the work. Thematic maps treat weather, vegetation, geology, and the seas.

This atlas compares favorably with other standard works, such as *The Facts on File Children's Atlas* and *Doubleday Children's Atlas*, and is recommended for elementary level. [R: ARBA 91; RBB, 1 Mar 90]

E
539 The Doubleday Atlas of the United States of America. By Josephine Bacon. New York: Doubleday, 1990. 125p. $15.95. ISBN 0-385-26395-3. LC 89-675329.
Intended to stimulate a child's interest in geography, this colorful and readable atlas focuses on the United States. Each state, alphabetically arranged within each region, is depicted in a two-page spread; a relief map showing geographical features; and several paragraphs about its demographics, agriculture, and other resources. For each state, there are photographs of scenery, a statistical fact box that includes famous residents, and drawings of state symbols (e.g., birds, trees, flowers). Indexed. This handsome volume is recommended for grades 3 through 6. [R: ARBA 91; BL, 15 Oct 90; SLJ, Sept 90]

E
540 Doubleday Children's Atlas. Jane Oliver, ed. Garden City, N.Y.: Doubleday, 1987. 93p. $12.95. ISBN 0-385-23760-X. LC 86-67523.

E
541 The Doubleday Picture Atlas. Wendy Roebuck, ed. Garden City, N.Y.: Doubleday, c1988, 1989. 61p. $10.95. ISBN 0-385-26253-1. LC 88-675244.
Children's Atlas, a colorful introduction to this type of reference work, includes photographs, political and relief maps, and easy-to-read charts of facts and figures. The first section explains how to use maps and is followed by two-page spreads on the nations of the world and a political map of the continents. A section on maps and map making makes clear why distortions occur when the Earth is projected onto a flat surface.
Maps and information are arranged by groups of nations, except for large countries such as the United States (divided into regions), the Soviet Union, and China. Each section includes political and relief maps and charts containing area, population, capital, official language, currency, and major products. The maps, which are clear and uncluttered, have been designed especially for children. Recommended for elementary schools.
Picture Atlas, similar in purpose, is useful for grades 3 through 6. It has an excellent introduction on how maps are developed and used. Each double-page spread bears a simple, uncluttered map with a paragraph of general information. Other features include captioned photographs and drawings. Recommended. [R: ARBA 91; RBB, Jan 90]

542 Earth Book: World Atlas. Boulder, Colo.: Graphic Learning International, 1987. 327p. $65.00. ISBN 0-87746-100-7. LC 86-072452. (1123 Spruce St., Boulder, CO 80802).
Produced by the Esselte Map Service of Stockholm, Sweden, this beautiful atlas begins with a section entitled "Encyclopedia of the Earth" (96 pages), arranged under the ancient philosopher's elements: air, water, earth, and fire. Topics such as the earth's wind patterns, deserts, erosion, urbanization, and volcanoes are treated in two-page spreads and illustrated by 240 colorful photographs.
The "World in Maps" section, organized by continent, includes 185 full-color environmental maps. Topical maps for each continent show political boundaries, population, organic and inorganic products, ocean depths and land heights, rainfall, temperature, and soil. Satellite imagery is used to produce the relief maps and show topographical features, which are enhanced by overlays that provide names, political boundaries, and highways. The section concludes with 13 pages of world thematic maps for such topics as animal plankton and calorie consumption. An index locating 57,000 names by page and grid is found in the third section.
This atlas has fewer index entries than most other world atlases, but it excels in the physical beauty of its maps, the effective use of relief, and color. Recommended for elementary and secondary schools. *Concise Earth Book: World Atlas* (Earthbooks, 1990) includes 70 color maps and a statistical section arranged by country. [R: ARBA 88; BL, 1 Oct 87; LJ, 1 Mar 88; LJ, 1 Dec 90; WLB, Nov 87]

543 The Facts on File Children's Atlas. By David Wright and Jill Wright. New York: Facts on File, 1991. 96p. $14.95. ISBN 0-8160-2703-X. LC 91-13725.
This revised edition shows its British parentage in several ways—in the Philip Ltd. maps (which are generally very good, with pleasing color combinations and a depiction of relief); in the relatively low percentage of maps devoted to the North American continent (about 13 percent, which is commensurate with the percentage of the Earth's land surface that North America occupies, but is less than most

U.S.-produced atlases devote to it); and in some of the text, which reflects a British point of view. Unfortunately, the world maps at the beginning of the volume give an incorrect idea of the relative sizes of such areas as Greenland. While scale and legend are given for the regional maps, projection is not. Text and photographs take up about two-thirds of the volume; combined with the maps, these do give a feeling for the "differentness" of various places on the Earth's surface. The text occasionally has odd statements, such as the one on page 11 that defines rich countries as those where persons usually have enough to eat. Intended age group is nowhere indicated; it is probably for grades 3 through 6.

544 Hammond Gold Medallion World Atlas. Maplewood, N.J.: Hammond, 1990. 668p. $85.00. ISBN 0-8437-1247-3. LC 85-675147.

545 Hammond Ambassador World Atlas. Maplewood, N.J.: Hammond, 1990. 522p. $49.95. ISBN 0-8437-1244-9. LC 87-675319.

Libraries do not need both the *Medallion* and the *Ambassador*, since maps in the two are the same. There are some 400 full-color, physical maps (24 pages); U.S. maps (128 pages); and foreign, continent, and world maps (192 pages). Small physical maps and others that show land use support the political maps. The *Medallion* also offers sections on world and U.S. history. Libraries holding other historical atlases should consider the less expensive *Ambassador*. Hammond uses a dual-indexing system; there is a separate index for each map and a 100,000-entry comprehensive index to all maps (except the *Medallion*'s history sections). Both are thumb-indexed. Recommended for secondary schools. *Citation World Atlas* is a concise version of the above atlases, containing maps of continents and countries with 25,000 entries in the index. [R: BL, 1 Dec 90]

E +
546 Hammond Large Type World Atlas. Boston: G. K. Hall, 1989. 144p. $28.95. ISBN 0-8161-4701-9. LC 88-657480.

Designed to serve visually handicapped students in grades 4 through 9, this atlas includes 100 pages of simple, 4-color, double-page maps of countries and regions of the world, with emphasis on the United States. The use of large type results in less detail than is usually contained in regular maps; nonetheless, this atlas shows bodies of water, political boundaries, main cities, elevations, and latitudes and longitudes. A gazetteer identifies continents, countries, states, and other major geographical areas. Alphanumeric coordinates are given in an index of some 2,000 locations.

The effort to produce a large-type atlas is commendable, but names are often ill-placed, running through boundary lines, rivers, or other features. Since this is the only such atlas available, it is recommended for all libraries serving visually handicapped students. [R: ARBA 90]

■ *Illustrated Atlas of Jerusalem*. *See* entry 1740.

E +
547 Maps on File. Lester A. Sobel, ed. New York: Facts on File, 1981-1985. 2v. $165.00/set. looseleaf w/binder and annual updates. $35.00/yr. ISBN 0-8160-2638-6. ISSN 0275-8083.

This looseleaf collection of some 400 maps and a comprehensive index of 5,000 entries is designed for photocopying. The two binders, divided into more than a dozen geographic sections, include maps for every country in the world, every U.S. state and Canadian province, and all oceans and continents. Some maps depict major economic and political issues.

Each annual update generates 25 to 49 new or replacement maps, with a totally new, consolidated index that includes every city, county, state, and geographic feature on the maps. Recommended for all levels. [R: ARBA 82]

548 Mattson, Catherine, and Mart T. Mattson. **Contemporary Atlas of the United States**. New York: Macmillan, 1990. 118p. $90.00. ISBN 0-02-897281-3. LC 90-675182.

The quality maps, tables, and graphs contained in this atlas present a contemporary portrait of the United States. The seven sections cover the land, the past, the people, the economy, transportation and communication, the government, and the environment. Each section is divided into more specific topics. Among the many subjects covered, usually displayed on facing pages, are unemployment on Indian reservations, state appropriations for the arts, and ratio of students per teacher for each state. Through the use of color, symbols, and numbers, a single map may supply information on three or four topics. A subject index provides access to maps and other representations, and an annotated bibliography completes the volume. Recommended for high schools. [R: ARBA 92; BL, 15 June 91]

549 National Geographic Atlas of North America: Space Age Portrait of a Continent. Wilbur Garrett and others, eds. Washington, D.C.: National Geographic Society, c1985, 1988. 264p. $49.95; $39.95 flexicover. ISBN 0-318-32993-X; 0-318-32992-1 flexicover.

This superb atlas intersperses traditional physical and political maps with those using space-age technology. Produced in a large format, this work emphasizes the United States, with lesser coverage for Canada, Mexico, Central America, and the Caribbean area. It is heavily illustrated with photographs taken from satellites, spacecraft, and aircraft using infrared radiation.

The atlas begins with continental thematic maps that treat such topics as mineral resources, climate, and population. The remainder of the volume, divided into geographic areas (11 sections for the United States; 1 on Canada; and 1 on Central America, Mexico, and the Caribbean), begins with a political map, followed by remote-sensing photographs and a section on tourist information (e.g., state parks, historic sites, addresses to write for information). The work concludes with maps of major metropolitan areas and national parks and an index of place-names. Recommended for secondary schools as a reference tool and for browsing.

550 National Geographic Atlas of the World. 6th ed. Washington, D.C.: National Geographic Society, 1990. 1v. (various paging). $74.95; $59.95pa. ISBN 0-87044-399-2; 0-87044-398-4pa. LC 90-675129.

National Geographic Atlas, noted for its excellent, large maps and updated to reflect the world as it existed at the end of August 1990, features satellite images of continents and detailed political maps of countries, regions, and urban areas. It also provides maps of the ocean floors and thematic maps depicting climate, resources, industry, language, and land use. Other features include illustrations, charts, tables, and a 150,000-entry place-name index.

Throughout its six-edition history, *National Geographic* has offered maps of exceptional quality and legibility, similar to those of the *National Geographic Magazine*. Publication of this edition was postponed so that recent changes in Europe could be indicated on its maps. [R: ARBA 92; WLB, May 91]

551 NBC News Rand McNally World News Atlas. Skokie, Ill.: Rand McNally. annual. $9.95pa. LC 89-43152.

This inexpensive work, a new annual, does not replace standard atlases, but it does "contribute to worldwide news and geographical literacy" by providing information on selected international issues and maps of the pertinent locations.

The first two sections, furnished by NBC News, focus on important news topics of the preceding year (disarmament, the environment, drugs, terrorism, and air safety in the 1990 annual) and discuss the countries and regions involved. Chronologies of events, key persons and organizations, and a survey of the issues are found in subsections.

The remaining sections contain world maps taken from the Rand McNally's *New International Atlas* and world information tables. The latter provide English and local names; area; population; population density; and the political situation in each nation and political subdivision of the United States, Soviet Union, Australia, the United Kingdom, and China. The index cites some 11,000 place-names and the location of each on the maps. [R: ARBA 91; RBB, 1 Apr 90]

552 Nelson Canadian Atlas. By Geoffrey J. Matthew. Scarborough, Ont.: Nelson Canada, 1988. 96p. $11.95pa. ISBN 0-17-602672-X.

This attractive atlas of Canada, designed for school use, contains a good introduction to map skills that is followed by double-page thematic maps and photographs that indicate major physical, economic, and cultural patterns for the country as a whole. Next, detailed maps depict provinces, territories, and major cities illustrated by Landsat color images. Some basic data, a glossary, and an index conclude the volume. [R: ARBA 90]

553 New Cosmopolitan World Atlas. Skokie, Ill.: Rand McNally, 1991. 304p. $60.00. ISBN 0-528-83442-8. LC 91-14589.

The *New Cosmopolitan World Atlas* contains colorful maps, an index of place-names, and a section on U.S. and world statistics and other tables and charts of international political information. This edition includes a section of thematic maps and charts that show population trends, languages, climate, and other data. A feature on the fragile Earth introduces the atlas. This edition shows the renamed Soviet city of St. Petersburg, which appears along with its former designation of Leningrad. The independent Baltic States are featured as well. The atlas seems accurate and easy to use. Recommended for secondary schools.

Rand McNally World Atlas (1992) is a smaller atlas that contains excellent quality political maps, newly-designed maps, a section on world environmental issues, and the 1990 U.S. census data. *Rand McNally Concise World Atlas* (1987), which is even smaller, serves basic needs in secondary schools.

554 New International Atlas. anniversary ed. Skokie, Ill.: Rand McNally, 1991. 1v. (various paging). $125.00. ISBN 0-528-83413-4. LC 90-53098.

Now in its twentieth year, *New International* is a comprehensive worldwide atlas of excellent quality. It contains 255 pages of full-color maps and charts, providing balanced coverage for all nations and regions of the world. It also depicts continents, oceans, and some 60 world metropolitan areas. Special maps show surface features, climate and temperature, transportation, minerals, and energy resources. Native place-names with an English translation are used; the text is written in five languages.

Appendixes include a glossary, tables of areas and political data, and population figures for cities. The index contains 168,000 place-names with location keys by geographical coordinates. Maps in *Britannica Atlas* (Encyclopaedia Britannica, 1990) are identical to those in *New International*. Recommended for high schools. [R: ARBA 92; WLB, Feb 91]

555 New York Times Atlas of the World. rev. ed. New York: Random House, 1987. 288p. $49.95. ISBN 0-8129-1626-3.

This is a condensed version of *Times Atlas of the World* (8th ed. Random House, 1990), the most comprehensive one-volume atlas available. Like its parent edition, *New York Times Atlas of the World* is compiled by Bartholomew & Sons and *The Times* of London. Introductory material, including world maps, world thematic maps, and star charts, is followed by 147 pages of full-color maps and an index to some 100,000 place-names. This excellent medium-priced atlas is recommended for high schools. [R: BL, 1 Dec 90]

556 Peters Atlas of the World. New York: Harper & Row, 1990. 230p. $50.00. ISBN 0-06-016540-5.

This atlas attempts to overcome the disadvantages found in most others: disproportionate coverage of the world, inconsistencies in scale, and distorted projections. The effort makes this work a worthy competitor in a field dominated by a few publishers. Based on the concept of "equal status of all the peoples of the Earth," Peters presents 43 double-page physical maps and 246 thematic maps that depict the world's demography and resources. There is also an index to 18,000 place-names.

This format allows for comparison of size and area, but it also results in countries being displayed on more than one page. The thematic maps are grouped under 45 subjects (e.g., life expectancy, energy, status of women, land usage). The colorful and readable maps are produced by Kummerly & Frey, a Swiss firm, and Oxford Cartographers in England. The atlas will not replace traditional atlases but will serve as a unique complement to them. [R: ARBA 91; RBB, 1 Dec 90; LJ, Jan 91]

E +

557 Rand McNally Children's Atlas of the United States. Skokie, Ill.: Rand McNally, 1989. 109p. $12.95. ISBN 0-528-83362-6. LC 89-42815.

A double-page spread is devoted to each of the alphabetically arranged states, showing topography, rivers, and cities. The left side includes several paragraphs of text about the state's history and geography, a box with statistical data (e.g., population, size), the state's emblem, and illustrations. The right side contains a state map with relief and political features and a U.S. map that highlights the state. The maps are indexed. This attractive atlas is recommended for elementary and middle school students. [R: ARBA 90; BL, 15 Jan 90]

558 Rand McNally Children's World Atlas. Skokie, Ill.: Rand McNally, 1989. 93p. $12.95. ISBN 0-528-83348-0. LC 88-061950.

This atlas, an upgraded version of *Children's Atlas of the World* (1985), is designed for junior high school students. It contains a colorful series of conventionally arranged maps, photographs, and illustrations and an index to most places shown on the maps. Maps of economic activities and characteristic animal species for each continent are a special feature. Recommended. [R: ARBA 90; RBB 15 Dec 89]

E +

559 Rand McNally Goode's World Atlas. 18th ed. Edward B. Espenshade, Jr., ed. Skokie, Ill.: Rand McNally, 1990. 367p. $24.95. ISBN 0-528-83128-3. LC 89-40419.

Goode's, in a class by itself, is designed to serve the needs of students from an early age through high school. It has been a leader among school atlases for almost 70 years.

Introductory materials focus on mapmaking and discuss such things as scale, projections, and the use of new technologies in cartography. Each of the seven sections (the world and six continents) includes a brief introduction, followed by clear, usually uncluttered political/physical and thematic maps on such topics as natural resources, population centers, energy, annual precipitation, language groups, and specific crops. North America receives the most attention, followed by world thematic maps and Europe. Antarctica is grouped with Africa.

The atlas also contains 62 maps for cities throughout the world. The index, which includes all places named on the maps (34,000 in all), provides page locations, latitude and longitude, and phonetic spellings for hard-to-pronounce names. For many important cities, the index gives local names and English translations. This is a first choice for all levels of school libraries. [R: ARBA 91; RBB, 15 June 90, 1 Dec 90]

E+
560   **Rand McNally Photographic World Atlas**. Skokie, Ill.: Rand McNally, 1989. 192p. $34.95. ISBN 0-528-83363-4. LC 89-42683.

The maps in this atlas are secondary to 175 beautiful color photographs of landscapes, people, cities, and industries. The 34 full-color physical/political maps are arranged by continent, with emphasis on the United States and Europe. It should be noted, however, that the maps of the United States do not include North Dakota, South Dakota, and Oklahoma, ostensibly due to space limitations.

Each section begins with a survey of the continent's size, climate, landscape, history, and economy, followed by the maps, which alternate with captioned photographs. Some 23,000 sites are indexed. This attractive work is recommended for all levels as a supplement to standard atlases. [R: ARBA 90; BL, 15 Jan 90; BL, 1 Dec 90; WLB, Dec 89]

561   **Rand McNally Picture Atlas of the World**. Skokie, Ill.: Rand McNally, 1991. 80p. $19.95. ISBN 0-528-83437-1. LC 90-27485.

This slim atlas for children is engagingly illustrated with pictorial maps by British artist Brian Delf. After some 10 pages of text and maps on worldwide matters (e.g., climate), there are about 60 pages of maps and a 4-page index. Each map is accompanied by brief text with facts and figures. The text is clearly written without being patronizing; the colors used are pleasant. Maps are generally of continents with some regional and country maps; the atlas is aimed toward a U.S. audience. It seems to be for students from grades 3 through 6. [R: ARBA 92]

562   **Rand McNally Road Atlas: United States, Canada, Mexico**. Skokie, Ill.: Rand McNally. annual. $7.95pa.

Updated annually, this work's claim that it is "America's most up-to-date, useful road atlas" appears to be justified. Detailed maps of the 50 states, Canadian provinces, and Mexico identify principal highways (e.g., free or toll-limited access, four-lane, double-lane), paved and unpaved roads, and scenic routes. Mileage between major cities, rest areas, camp grounds, airports, dams, national parks and forests, points of interest, mountain peaks, major colleges and universities, and ferries are all indicated. A new edition is published every October. [R: ARBA 90]

563   **Reader's Digest Atlas of the World**. Pleasantville, N.Y.: Reader's Digest; distr., Skokie, Ill.: Rand McNally, 1987. 240p. $39.95. ISBN 0-89577-264-7. LC 87-675016.

The collaborative effort of the Reader's Digest Association and Rand McNally produced this attractive atlas, a revision of the 1979 volume. This updated work includes 63 pages of physical/cultural maps (geology, ocean floor, climate, anthropology, history, and finance) and 128 pages of world and regional maps. Many of the latter were extracted from Rand McNally's flagship publication, the *New International Atlas*. The index contains some 40,000 entries. This large-format, reasonably priced atlas will meet the needs of most high school students. [R: ARBA 88; BL, 1 Dec 90]

564   **State Maps on File Collection**. New York: Facts on File, 1989. 7v. $375.00/set; $75.00/v. ISBN 0-8160-0116-1. LC 84-657108.

Copyright-free and designed for reproduction, each volume of this set of outline maps (e.g., Mid-Atlantic, New England) contains an average of 20 maps for each state, geared to that state's curriculum (e.g., maps for New Mexico show the Spanish explorers' routes). Seven types of maps are provided for each state: political, historical, geographical, environmental, cultural, economic, and natural resources. An index of place-names accompanies each set.

Maps have a directional marker, distance bar scale, and legend, but no map scale. The clearly drawn maps have more information and less clutter than the state maps in *Maps on File*. Physical and historical maps have been criticized, however, for their oversimplification, which has resulted in occasional misrepresentations and errors. Recommended. [R: ARBA 86; BL, 1 Apr 85; LJ, 15 Mar 85; WLB, Mar 85]

565   United States, Canada, [and] Mexico Road Atlas. San Jose, Calif.: H. M. Gousha; distr., New York: Prentice Hall Press, 1990. 80p. $3.95pa. ISBN 0-13-622390-7.

This road atlas is a convenient size although its smaller dimensions mean that detail and large-scale maps are not included. The atlas, with maps for Mexico and each of the provinces of Canada, is arranged in alphabetical order by state. State maps include a partial location index to cities and towns and census figures. There are larger scale maps of 35 U.S. cities. Additional information includes U.S. weather maps; a mileage chart; the location and length of principal toll roads; and tourist regulations for Canada and Mexico.

566   The United States Today: An Atlas of Reproducible Pages. Wellesley, Mass.: World Eagle, 1990. 182p. $36.95; $26.50pa.; $26.50 looseleaf. ISBN 0-930141-29-6; 0-930141-27-Xpa.; 0-930141-28-8 looseleaf.

These reproducible pages, depicting demographics and other topics concerning the United States, are designed for use in junior and senior high school social studies classes. Outline maps of the United States are superimposed against similar maps for India, Indonesia, South America, and Australia. Other maps, graphs, and tables provide information about such topics as agriculture and manufacturing, gleaned from various government publications, newspapers, and similar sources. The looseleaf format is most convenient for reproduction. [R: ARBA 91]

E +
567   World Book Atlas. rev. ed. Chicago: World Book, 1990. 432p. $69.00. ISBN 0-7166-3184-4. LC 89-50794.

This atlas, designed as a companion to *World Book Encyclopedia*, is a joint product of World Book and Rand McNally. The editors have drawn maps from atlases that include *Cosmopolitan World Atlas*, *Rand McNally Goode's World Atlas*, and the *Atlas of the United States*.

The maps cover the world but emphasize the United States and Canada (each state and province appears on a single-page map). Drawn on a variety of scales, the maps are supported by continental profiles, statistics, and an index of 70,000 entries. This atlas meets the needs of upper-elementary and high school students. [R: RBB, 1 Dec 90]

E +
568   Wurman, Richard Saul. USAtlas. New York: ACCESS Press; distr., New York: Prentice Hall Press, 1990. 156p. $9.95pa. ISBN 0-13-946831-5.

USAtlas is a good choice for libraries requiring a road atlas. Unlike other atlases, which provide one map for each state (or parts thereof), this work divides the country into 70 areas, each 250 × 250 miles. The adjacent regions of Canada and Mexico are shown, but not the entire countries. All maps use the same scale and are arranged along an axis extending from the Pacific Northwest to southern Florida. Maps are clear and types of roads are identified.

Additional materials include metropolitan and downtown centers, an index map, a map of the United States that shows east-west and north-south interstate highways, an index to 10,000 place-names, and a mileage chart. Limited tourist information—downtown hotels for major cities, museums, amusement parks, weather extremes, and a calendar of events—is also provided.

The *Rand McNally Road Atlas*, a standard for many years, is arranged alphabetically by state, uses a variety of scales, and covers all of Mexico and Canada. Choice between it and *USAtlas* is a matter of personal preference.

Electronic

569   Electromap World Atlas. Version 1.1. Fayetteville, Ark.: Electromap, 1989. Hardware requirements: IBM-PC or compatible, 525K RAM, DOS 3.1 or higher, microsoft CD-ROM Extensions, CD-ROM Player, and EGA or VGA graphic adapter with color monitor; mouse is optional. $129.00. (P.O. Box 1153, Fayetteville, AR 72702-1153).

This CD-ROM application brings together 235 color maps and a database that provides information on specific nations and areas. A world map enables the user to interface topics selected from a menu of such data as population density, literacy rate, and life expectancy. The user can focus on geography, communications, economy, and government for over 200 countries and regions. Other capabilities enable the user to send text and maps to a printer or a disk file and create black-and-white shaded maps using an Epson-compatible dot matrix printer. However, map printing is a slow process, taking up to 15 minutes per map. [R: BL, 1 Dec 90]

570 **PC Globe 4.0**. Tempe, Ariz.: P.C. Globe, 1990. $69.95. System requirements: IBM PC/XT/AT/ PS2 or compatible; 512K RAM; DOS 2.2 or higher; Hercules monochrome, CGA, EGA, or VGA display. (4700 S. McClintock, Suite 150, Tempe, AZ 85282-9692).

Middle and high school students will enjoy using this computerized atlas, which provides profiles of 190 countries in clear maps and charts. Maps can be printed, and other data is transferable to many software packages. Special features include time zones, currency conversion, major world organizations, and visa requirements. Purchasers receive upgraded information. [R: BL, 1 Dec 90]

E +

571 **PC USA**. Tempe, Ariz.: PC World, 1989. 3 disks + guide. System requirements: IBM-PC or compatible, 512K RAM. $69.95.

Similar to *PC Globe 4.0* this useful reference tool consists of an electronic atlas and database that provide details on U.S. geography – the country as a whole, regions, states, and cities. The menu allows students to obtain political-demographic information on a region; to display a small-scale map and gain access to 19 categories of geographic, demographic, and economic information; to compare data with that of other states; and to look up data on 683 cities. Recommended for grades 5 and up. [R: BL, 1 Dec 90]

572 **USA Geography**. St. Paul, Minn.: Minnesota Educational Computing Corp., 1989. 2 microfloppy disks, user guide, classroom guide, 2 quick reference cards. System requirements: Apple IIGS computer, 768K RAM, RGB monitor (color recommended), mouse.

This unique geographic reference tool combines a database with on-screen maps. The four map views include an overview map of the Northern Hemisphere and part of the Southern Hemisphere, the 50 states, a regional map, and a map showing close-ups of one or more states or territories. "Data Cards" provide 105 categories of information on states and territories and can be displayed in atlas form. There also are color-coded "Theme Maps," which compare data on 24 topics (e.g., temperature, population), and "Comparison Maps," which rank demographic and other information by states. Maps, data cards, and data tables can be printed, but the process is slow. This program should enhance the study of geography on junior high and high school levels. [R: SLJ, Apr 90]

ENCYCLOPEDIAS AND HANDBOOKS

573 Carpenter, Allen. **The Encyclopedia of the Central West**. New York: Facts on File, 1990. 488p. $35.00. ISBN 0-8160-1661-5.

574 Carpenter, Allen. **The Encyclopedia of the Far West**. New York: Facts on File, 1990. 544p. $35.00. ISBN 0-8160-1662-3.

575 Carpenter, Allen. **The Encyclopedia of the Midwest**. New York: Facts on File, 1989. 544p. $35.00. ISBN 0-8160-1660-7.

576 O'Brien, Robert. **The Encyclopedia of New England**. New York: Facts on File, 1985. 400p. $29.95. ISBN 0-87196-759-6.

Each volume covers a cluster of states and provides an extensive article on each state that surveys history, statistics, and other data. Shorter essays address a variety of topics: biographies of notables; historic, economic, cultural, and political events; cities, parks, museums, and landmarks; Indian tribes; schools; products; and more. Other features include a map of each state, a few black-and-white photographs, reproductions of paintings depicting the area, an index, and a subject bibliography. The editing is uneven, but overall the set is worthy of consideration. General encyclopedias either neglect the subjects these volumes cover, or treat them in less detail. Appropriate for high school libraries. [R: ARBA 90]

577   Clay, James, and others. **Land of the South**. Birmingham, Ala.: Oxmoor House, 1988. 320p. $29.95. ISBN 0-8487-0547-5.

Land of the South complements the broader-based *Encyclopedia of Southern Culture*. This work combines prose, photographs, and maps to show how the land influenced the social and economic development of the area. Each of the 17 chapters covers a specific region, explaining how the geology, landforms, and ecology affected the farm-based economy, the institution of slavery, and cultural developments. An extensive bibliography and index conclude the volume. Recommended for high schools. [R: WLB, Nov 89]

E +
578   Dickson, Paul. **What Do You Call a Person from ...? A Dictionary of Residential Terms**. New York: Facts on File, 1990. 161p. $19.95. ISBN 0-8160-1983-5.

Many of the names for persons from a certain place (e.g., country, city, state) can be found in a good general dictionary, but this is a convenient compilation of over 1,000 such terms. Entries for places and terms, arranged in one alphabet, often provide historical background for the name, which is especially helpful when people are called by a country's former name. Derogatory, religious, and racial epithets are excluded. An extensive bibliography cites sources. [R: ARBA 91; BR, Sept/Oct 90; LJ, Jan 90; WLB, Feb 90]

579   **Encyclopedia of Southern Culture**. Charles Reagan Wilson and William Ferris, eds. Chapel Hill, N.C.: University of North Carolina Press, 1989. 1634p. $59.95. ISBN 0-8078-1823-2. LC 88-17084.

Sponsored by the Center for the Study of Southern Culture at the University of Mississippi, this distinguished work identifies the American South as "a geographical entity, a historical fact, a place of the imagination, and the homeland of an array of Americans who consider themselves southerners." The focus is on the 11 states that comprised the Confederacy (Alabama, Arkansas, Florida, Georgia, Louisiana, Mississippi, North Carolina, South Carolina, Tennessee, Texas, and Virginia), with some information about the border states that did not secede (Kentucky, Maryland, and Missouri), and others considered a part of the "census South" (Delaware, West Virginia, Oklahoma, and the District of Columbia).

Arranged in 24 alphabetical sections, from agriculture and arts and architecture to violence and women's life, the volume examines every aspect of southern culture. Each section begins with a survey essay, followed by alphabetically arranged thematic articles contributed and signed by over 700 scholars. There are outstanding essays on literature, music, Black life, folk life, social life, and history and manners. Biographies profile 250 living and deceased persons as diverse as Willie Nelson, Jesse Helms, Paul "Bear" Bryant, and Davy Crockett. Over 300 black-and-white, current and historical photographs and a few maps are scattered throughout the volume, which concludes with a 33-page index. Highly recommended for high schools. [R: ARBA 90; BR, Nov/Dec 89; LJ, July 89]

E +
580   **Exploring Your World: The Adventure of Geography**. Washington, D.C.: National Geographic Society, 1989. 608p. $39.95. ISBN 0-87044-726-2. LC 89-13099.

This volume provides 334 entries, varying from a paragraph to 15 pages, on a wide range of geographic topics, such as rivers, mountains, countries, states, bays, lagoons, climate, and agriculture. Articles are supported by over 1,000 full-color photographs, maps, plates, charts, and diagrams. An index and bibliography conclude the volume. While most of the information is available elsewhere, this attractive work will enhance the study of geography. Highly recommended for elementary and middle school levels. [R: ARBA 91; BL, 1 May 90; SLJ, May 90]

581   **Facts about the States: A Compendium of Information about the Fifty States, Puerto Rico and Washington, D.C.** Joseph Nathan Kane and others, comps. Bronx, N.Y.: H. W. Wilson, 1989. 556p. $55.00. ISBN 0-8242-0407-7. LC 89-14829.

Part 1 contains a chapter for each state, Puerto Rico, and the District of Columbia. Information, drawn from a wide range of sources, includes general data (e.g., date of admission to statehood, origin of name), geography and climate, a chronology of the state's history, statistics (e.g., population, ethnic and religious groups), finance (e.g., revenue sources, general expenditures), employment and production statistics for major industries, and an annotated list of important fiction and nonfiction works that reflect the state's history and culture. Historical sites, parks, government, politics, culture, education, and transportation also receive attention.

Part 2 consists of comparative tables that rank states by population, average temperature and rainfall, literacy (highest and lowest levels), personal wealth, and many other areas. This convenient compendium brings together thousands of facts about each state. Recommended for secondary schools. [R: ARBA 90; BL, 15 Feb 90; BR, May/June 90; LJ, Dec 89; SLJ, May 90; WLB, Jan 90]

E+
582   Hauck, Eldon. **American Capitols: An Encyclopedia of the State, National and Territorial Capitol Edifices of the United States**. Jefferson, N.C.: McFarland, 1991. 310p. $39.95. ISBN 0-89950-551-1. LC 90-53609.

Four- or five-page profiles provide detailed histories of the 50 U.S. state capitol buildings; the federal capitol in Washington; and those of American Samoa, Guam, the Northern Mariana Islands, Puerto Rico, and the Virgin Islands. The alphabetically arranged entries are interesting and informative. For upper elementary grades through high school. [R: ARBA 92; LJ, 15 June 91; RBB, 15 Sept 91]

583   Hill, A. David, and Regina McCormick. **Geography: A Resource Book for Secondary Schools**. Santa Barbara, Calif.: ABC-Clio, 1989. 387p. (Social Studies Resources for Secondary School Librarians, Teachers, and Students). $39.00. ISBN 0-87436-519-8. LC 88-33354.

A combination textbook on geography and lengthy bibliography of sources, this work is divided into six sections. The first two are textual sections that provide a survey of how geography examines the world and the history and nature of the discipline. The third section explains how geographers communicate through maps, charts, diagrams, and other formats. A directory of organizations, associations, and geographic agencies makes up the fourth section, while the latter two sections consist of bibliographies of reference works and classroom materials. This is an excellent selection for any secondary school library media center that wishes to strengthen its geographic collection. [R: ARBA 90; BR, Sept/Oct 89]

E
584   Jennings, Terry. **Exploring Our World Series**. North Bellmore, N.Y.: Marshall Cavendish, 1987. 6v. $89.95/set. ISBN 0-86307-818-4.

Each volume in this series about the geographical features of our world contains a number of brief articles supported by several full-color photographs, drawings, or diagrams. Each volume also features an index and some 10 pages of suggested projects, activities, experiments, places to visit, and recommended readings. Volumes cover deserts, mountains, polar regions, rivers, temperate forests, and tropical forests. For primary level. [R: SLJ, May 88]

E
585   Knowlton, Jack. **Geography from A to Z: A Picture Glossary**. New York: Thomas Y. Crowell; distr., New York: Harper & Row, 1988. 47p. $12.89. ISBN 0-690-04618-9. LC 86-4594.

This delightful glossary of geographic terms contains 63 entries, each with brief (but adequate) text and bright, imaginative illustrations. Of course, basic terms such as *river* or *lake* are defined, but lessknown phenomena such as *palisade*, *seamount*, and *badlands* are included as well. This colorful book is highly recommended for the elementary grades. [R: ARBA 90; BL, 1 Nov 88; SLJ, Nov 88]

E+
586   Ross, Wilma S. **Fabulous Facts about the Fifty States**. rev. ed. New York: Scholastic, 1986. 224p. $2.50pa. ISBN 0-590-33958-3.

This inexpensive work, updated about every five years, devotes four pages to each state and includes a black-and-white map with several political and relief features; a U.S. map with the state highlighted; statistical data and state flower, tree, bird, and so forth; a "fabulous fact" section; a short description; sights to see; and a list of principal products. The format is unattractive, but this is a solid work, well worth adding to the reference collection in elementary and middle schools. [R: SLJ, Feb 87]

587   Small, John, and Michael Witherick. **A Modern Dictionary of Geography**. 2d ed. New York: Edward Arnold; distr., New York: Routledge, Chapman & Hall, 1989. 247p. $45.00; $17.95pa. ISBN 0-340-49317-8; 0-340-49318-6pa.

Advanced high school students may require this dictionary, which includes physical and cultural geographical terms. It contains precise definitions presented clearly and accurately. The need for such a dictionary has become necessary due to the separation of the discipline into two distinct fields (physical and cultural), each with its own terminology. Special features include good cross-referencing and some 125 illustrations. [R: ARBA 90]

588 **The World and Its People**. North Bellmore, N.Y.: Marshall Cavendish, 1986. 19v. $409.95/set. ISBN 0-86307-571-1.

The World and Its People covers all areas of geography—physical, economic, social, and theoretical—in over 1,300 alphabetically arranged articles. Each volume includes a table of contents and an average of 75 articles. Longer articles, such as the one on Africa, are divided into major subdivisions covering such topics as the land, climate, and wildlife.

More than 1,800 colorful photographs and maps (thematic, topographical, and political) illustrate the volume. The last volume contains an index of over 20,000 entries and a thematic index that cites major articles arranged under 31 areas of study. The work complements *Illustrated Encyclopedia of Mankind*.

E +
589 **Worldmark Encyclopedia of the States**. 2d ed. Moshe Y. Sachs and others, eds. New York: Worldmark Press; distr., New York: John Wiley, 1986. 690p. $120.00. ISBN 0-471-83213-8. LC 85-26455.

Worldmark offers demographic, economic, political, and social information on the 50 states, Puerto Rico, the District of Columbia, and the U.S. Caribbean and Pacific dependencies. For each state/territory, chapters provide basic information, such as name origin and nickname, and a picture of the state seal and flag. This is followed by descriptions of climate, population, educational and judicial systems, taxation, arts, press, and famous citizens. Each section concludes with a bibliography.

Over 100 maps depict political divisions, elevations, metropolitan areas, and places of interest. This is a worthwhile purchase for school libraries at all levels. [R: ARBA 87; BL, 1 Sept 86]

GAZETTEERS

590 **Cambridge World Gazetteer: A Geographical Dictionary**. David Munro, ed. New York: Cambridge University Press, c1988, 1990. 880p. $39.50. ISBN 0-521-39438-4.

Originally published in 1988 as *Chambers World Gazetteer*, this international directory of place-names reflects a British bias, but its entries contain more information than those found in *Webster's New Geographical Dictionary*, its American counterpart. *Cambridge* includes political units (e.g., countries, states, cities) and physical features (e.g., rivers, mountains). In entries for cities and nations, *Webster's* locates sites and identifies chief physical features and industries. *Cambridge* gives the same kind of information, but describes the setting in greater detail.

Cambridge contains fewer than half of the entries offered by *Webster's* (20,000 to 47,000), but black-and-white maps that show political and administrative divisions support 150 national entries. It also includes a 120-page, full-color atlas by Bartholomew, the distinguished Scottish cartographer. Recommended for secondary schools.

591 ***Reader's Digest* Guide to Places of the World**. Pleasantville, N.Y.: Reader's Digest Association; distr., New York: Random House, 1987. 735p. $29.95. ISBN 0-276-39826-2. LC 87-670034.

This work, which is both gazetteer and dictionary, covers more than 7,000 cities, states, regions, natural and man-made features, terms, and other geographical phenomena worldwide. Two-hundred-fifty color photographs, one-hundred-fifty-eight color relief maps, and a number of feature articles enhance the value of this volume. "A Day in the Life of ..." essays describe people (e.g., a Cypriot shopkeeper, a Leningrad shipyard worker) and discuss physical features (e.g., oceans, volcanoes). The book concludes with a section illustrating the flags of the world and a list of international organizations.

Standard gazetteers, such as *Webster's New Geographical Dictionary*, are more comprehensive, but this attractive work is worthy of consideration by secondary schools. [R: ARBA 88]

592 **The Statesman's Year-Book World Gazetteer**. 4th ed. John Paxton, comp. New York: St. Martin's Press, 1991. 693p. $49.95. ISBN 0-312-85597-8. LC 85-26263.

A supplement to *Statesman's Year-Book*, this gazetteer includes 8,000 place-names, giving location, population, industries, and relevant historical information. A dictionary of some 700 geographical terms is appended. For high school libraries. [R: ARBA 92]

E +
593 **Webster's New Geographical Dictionary**. rev. ed. Springfield, Mass.: Merriam-Webster, 1984. 1376p. $19.95. ISBN 0-87779-446-4. LC 83-22019.

More than 47,000 entries describe and locate towns, cities, countries, states, provinces, rivers, lakes, mountains, and other geographical features. Some 15,000 cross-references from variant spellings, name changes, and similar relationships provide easy access to the text, which is illustrated by 218 maps. Entries for places include pronunciations, population (1980 census for United States), and foreign terms translated into English. This gazetteer is a standard work and a first choice for all school libraries. [R: ARBA 86]

EXPLORATION

594   Brown, Julie, and Robert Brown. **Exploring the World**. Milwaukee, Wis.: Gareth Stevens, 1990. 64p. (My First Reference Library). $12.95. ISBN 0-8368-0032-X. LC 89-11285.

In 10 colorful chapters, the Browns introduce exploration of various parts of the world throughout history. Notable journeys and the activities of important explorers are covered in two-page spreads, most of which include photographs, drawings, explanatory insets, and maps of exploration routes. Young readers, grades 2 and 3, will be attracted to this book because of its format, which includes large print and adequate white space. A useful glossary and index are included. However, there are no pronunciation guides in the text or the glossary, and users may need help in relating areas shown on the maps to the world as a whole and to the United States. [R: ARBA 92; SBF, Mar 91, p. 53]

595   Lomask, Milton. **Great Lives: Exploration**. New York: Scribner's, 1988. 258p. $22.95. ISBN 0-684-18511-3. LC 88-15744.

This work presents the lives and discoveries of 15 famous explorers, ranging from the well-known Marco Polo, Christopher Columbus, and Robert Peary to the most obscure individuals, such as Hoei-shin, a Chinese monk who is believed to have explored North America in the fifth century. The essays, intended for middle school children, are well written and interesting and should stimulate further reading about these notables. A chronology of significant exploration dates is a special feature. [R: ARBA 90; BR, May/June 89]

596   **The Marshall Cavendish Illustrated Encyclopedia of Discovery and Exploration**. North Bellmore, N.Y.: Marshall Cavendish, 1990. 17v. $449.95/set. ISBN 1-85435-114-1. LC 89-15723.

Chronologically arranged, the encyclopedia begins with prehistory and ends with the space shuttle. The volumes are written for readers at the high school level although adults will find them pleasant and quick reading. Each volume is individually authored and covers a specific historical period or topic. Ranging from explorations in the ancient and medieval worlds, Christopher Columbus, Vasco da Gama, establishment of the Spanish empire, to polar, deep-sea, mountain, and space exploration from their beginnings to the present, this encyclopedia seems to cover almost every important geographical discovery in the history of mankind.

Each volume contains a narrative account with beautiful prints, paintings, and photographs. Color maps frequently complement the text. Most volumes provide a glossary of terms, a short biographical dictionary on explorers that lists those individuals alphabetically by name, describes their accomplishments, and sometimes supplies a small black-and-white map of their explorations.

The factual contents of the volumes are generally reliable; some maps in the set become a little crowded when they try to show the routes of too many explorers at the same time. Readers will find this a source of enjoyable reading. [R: ARBA 92]

E +
597   **National Geographic Index, 1888-1988**. Wilbur E. Garrett, ed. Washington, D.C.: National Geographic Society, 1989. 1215p. $24.95. ISBN 0-87044-764-5. LC 88-33086.

This work indexes 100 years of *National Geographic* articles and supersedes the 1947-1974 and 1947-1983 indexes. Some 7,000 articles are listed chronologically under subject headings. Indexing is provided for authors, photographers, and article titles, as well as for maps that accompanied magazine issues, books, television specials, and videos produced by the Society. [R: ARBA 91]

E +
598   **Quick Reference Guide to National Geographic: 1955-Mid 1990**. Los Angeles, Calif.: Geoimages, 1990. $8.00pa. ISBN 0-9623093-0-3. LC 89-84482. (P.O. Box 45677, Los Angeles, CA 90045).

This simplfied index to the last 35 years of *National Geographic* is adequate to meet the needs of most school libraries but will not replace *National Geographic Index, 1888-1988*, which covers 100 years of the magazine and provides access to subjects, titles, authors, and photographers. This index classifies articles under general headings (e.g., places, environment, underwater study), and gives the topic of the article and month and year of the issue, but not article titles. The maps included with the magazine over the same time span are indexed in a separate section. Recommended for all levels. [R: ARBA 92; BL, 1 Jan 91]

599   Tinling, Marion. **Women into the Unknown: A Sourcebook on Women Explorers and Travelers**. Westport, Conn.: Greenwood Press, 1989. 356p. $65.00. ISBN 0-313-25328-5. LC 88-18677.

Forty-two women explorers who "went into unknown territory, sought new information, and brought back fresh ideas" are profiled in articles five to six pages in length. A few travelers are well known (e.g., Margaret Bourke-White, Elspeth Huxley), but others are obscure. Most wrote books about their experiences, which are quoted in the sketches herein. Each entry concludes with a bibliography of works by and about the traveler. The volume ends with a subject index and a lengthy bibliography on exploration and travel by women. Appropriate for high school libraries. [R: ARBA 90; RBB, 15 June 89]

TRAVEL

■   *Access America. See* entry 613.

600   Brownstone, David M., and Irene M. Franck. **Natural Wonders of America**. New York: Antheneum, 1989. 64p. $14.95; $7.95pa. ISBN 0-689-31430-2; 0-689-71229-4pa.

This book consists of easy-to-read articles about 43 natural wonders, including Pikes Peak, Lake Louise, Niagara Falls, and Acadia National Park. Each entry provides short descriptions and one or more pictures. This small volume is appropriate for upper elementary and middle school media centers. [R: BL, July 89; SLJ, Sept 89; VOYA, Dec 89]

601   **The International Youth Hostel Handbook 1991-92. Volume 1: Europe and the Mediterranean**. New York: HarperPerennial/HarperCollins, 1991. 336p. maps. $10.95pa. ISBN 0-06-273076-2. LC 90-5590.

602   **The International Youth Hostel Handbook 1991-92. Volume 2: Africa, America, Asia and Australasia**. New York: HarperPerennial/HarperCollins, 1991. 254p. $10.95pa. ISBN 0-06-273077-0. LC 90-5590.

This valuable directory, in English, French, German, and Spanish, focuses on budget accommodation mainly for young members of the International Youth Hostel Federation. There are currently over 5,500 hostels around the world, each offering low-cost accommodation with assured standards to members. The introduction in both volumes offers such general information as age limits, membership, advance booking, insurance, vaccinations, time zones, and monthly average temperatures. This section also contains addresses of embassies and of travel sections of national organizations that provide a wide range of inexpensive holidays. The main body of both volumes is devoted to listings of hostels by countries. For each listing there is information on address, location (frequently with a sketch map), transportation, fees, facilities, opening hours, number of beds, method of payment, and more. The hostel listings for each country are followed by a section entitled "Concessions" that contains information about various financial privileges accorded to members such as fee discounts (or free entrance) to museums, use of transportation, sport facilities, and shopping. Each volume has an excellent map with names in the local language. The directories are factually and linguistically correct. [R: ARBA 92]

E+
603   Matthews, Rupert. **The Atlas of Natural Wonders**. New York: Facts on File, 1988. 240p. $35.00. ISBN 0-8160-1993-2. LC 88-16387.

This guide describes more than 50 of the world's geographic phenomena, such as Mount Everest, Victoria Falls, the Grand Canyon, the Dead Sea, the Great Barrier Reef, and the Namib Desert. Each is generously illustrated with photographs and maps, over 200 in all. A glossary, gazetteer, bibliography, and index support this work, which is appropriate for upper-elementary grades through high school. [R: ARBA 89; BL, 15 Nov 88; BR, Mar/Apr 89; SLJ, May 89]

E+
604   **National Geographic's Guide to the National Parks of the United States**. Elizabeth L. Newhouse, ed. Washington, D.C.: National Geographic Society, 1989. 432p. $29.95pa. ISBN 0-87044-808-8.

This compact guide portrays 50 national parks in beautifully illustrated articles, giving the political and natural history of each. There are also travel suggestions—how to get there; the best time of the year to visit; half- and full-day excursions within the park; park policies; lists of nearby lodgings; and information on other trips in the area (within 250 miles) to national forests, wildlife refuges, rivers, and monuments. A detailed color map of each park supports the text. Recommended for all levels. [R: WLB, May 90]

E +
605   **Our National Parks: America's Spectacular Wilderness Heritage**. Pleasantville, N.Y.: Reader's Digest Association; distr., New York: Random House, 1989. 352p. $26.95. ISBN 0-89577-336-8. LC 89-33561.

Articles on 41 parks, from Acadia in Maine to Zion in Utah, are lavishly illustrated with color photographs. The alphabetically arranged essays profile each park, giving its history and highlighting the wonders of each. A map of the park accompanies every article.

E +
606   *Reader's Digest* **America's Historic Places: An Illustrated Guide to Our Country's Past**. Pleasantville, N.Y.: Reader's Digest Association, 1988. 352p. $26.95. ISBN 0-89577-265-5. LC 87-4757.

Listed under 5 regional headings are 500 historic sites arranged alphabetically by state within each area—famous American homes, museum villages, forts, battlefields, government buildings, historic districts, churches, ghost towns, and engineering wonders. Natural wonders, such as the Grand Canyon and Niagara Falls, are excluded. Each site is briefly described and located on a regional map. The volume is profusely illustrated with color photographs for almost every site. [R: ARBA 89; BL, 15 May 89]

E +
607   Scott, David L., and Kay W. Scott. **Guide to the National Park Areas: Eastern States**. 2d ed. Chestern, Conn.: Globe Pequot Press, 1987. 251p. $12.95pa. ISBN 0-87106-838-9. LC 87-8692.

608   Scott, David L., and Kay W. Scott. **Guide to the National Park Areas: Western States**. 2d ed. Chester, Conn.: Globe Pequot Press, 1987. 346p. $13.95pa. ISBN 0-87106-840-0. LC 87-8403.

National parks, seashores, monuments, memorials, historic sites, recreation areas, battlefield sites, and rivers all appear in these two volumes, which are revisions of a 1979 work. The concise information covers the facilities, services, and programs of each site. Arranged alphabetically by state, each entry provides well-written historical, geographical, and archaeological data, describes nature trails and other programs, and gives directory information. The work includes detailed (but crude) maps—160 in *Eastern States* and 120 in *Western States*—plus many full-page black-and-white photographs. [R: ARBA 88]

609   **The Sierra Club Guide to the Natural Areas of New England**. By John Perry and Jane Greverus Perry. San Francisco, Calif.: Sierra Club; distr., New York: Random House, 1990. 379p. $12.95pa. ISBN 0-87156-744-X. LC 89-5736.

This volume covers natural areas within six New England states. Each chapter is prefaced by an exposition of the flora, fauna, climate, recreational opportunities, private and public lands, state agencies, and more. The natural areas of the state are listed alphabetically and grouped according to the zones in which they are located (South, Coastal, or North). The main entries cover 350 areas, including state and national parks, forest and wildlife preserves, and lands in the public domain. Physical features, publications available, and hazards are given for each. No information is provided about campgrounds or rules and regulations of interest to the traveler. [R: ARBA 91]

E +
610   Smallwood, Carol. **An Educational Guide to the National Park System**. Metuchen, N.J.: Scarecrow, 1989. 387p. $39.50. ISBN 0-8108-2137-0. LC 88-21639.

This volume includes all 328 sites in the national park system, many of which are little known, arranged by 47 major theme areas (e.g., architecture, literature, World War II). For each park the guide provides directory information; size; location relative to major highways; a description of its purpose, trails, guided tours, and accommodations; and printed matjerials and audiovisuals with costs, if any. Indexing is by state and name. [R: ARBA 90; RBB, 1 Oct 89; VOYA, Oct 89]

611 *The Washington Post* **Guide to Washington**. 2d ed. Robert L. Price, comp. and ed. New York: McGraw-Hill, 1989. 430p. $12.95pa. ISBN 0-07-068394-8. LC 88-26728.

Written by the staff of the *Washington Post* and notables such as David Broder and Art Buchwald, this outstanding guide covers cultural life, monuments and museums, neighborhoods and suburbs, and architecture of the nation's capital. The usual travel guide information on hotels and restaurants also appears. The 30 chapters include in-depth descriptions of the capitol, museums and art galleries, public rooms of the White House, and other landmarks. The quality of the writing is better than that usually found in travel guides. [R: ARBA 90; BL, July 89]

Handicapped

HANDBOOKS AND GUIDES

See **Education** for **Learning Disabled**.

612 Abrams, A. Jay, and Margaret Ann Abrams. **The First Whole Rehab Catalog: A Comprehensive Guide to Products and Services for the Physically Disadvantaged**. Whitehall, Va.: Betterway, 1990. 240p. $16.95pa. ISBN 1-55870-131-1. LC 89-29934.

This catalog describes products that will help physically handicapped persons live more independent lives. Product entries, arranged by use (e.g., access, transportation, home management, health and fitness, personal care, recreational aids), have a description, price range, and manufacturer with address. Many products related to sports/recreastion or to telephones and other electronic devices are pictured. The appendix lists information centers, databases, and advocacy organizations. [R: ARBA 91; RBB, 15 Sept 90]

E+

613 **Access America: An Atlas and Guide to the National Parks for Visitors with Disabilities**. Burlington, Vt.: Northern Cartographers, 1988. 444p. $89.95 spiralbound. ISBN 0-944187-00-5. LC 87-72038. (P.O. Box 133, Burlington, VT 05402).

Each of the 37 chapters of this guide covers a national park, giving addresses and telephone numbers of the office responsible for accessibility; a history of the park; and a description of its flora, fauna, and unique attractions. The volume also details medical and support services, relevant publications, availability of interpreters and TDD devices, self-guided programs, accessibility of the park to specific impairments, and other relevant data. This unique work is recommended for all levels. [R: ARBA 89]

614 Karolides, Nicholas J. **Focus on Physical Impairments: A Reference Handbook**. Santa Barbara, Calif.: ABC-Clio, 1990. 332p. $35.00. ISBN 0-87436-428-0. LC 90-47032.

This volume will help those without a physical impairment to better understand those who have such problems (e.g., visual and hearing disabilities, speech/language impairment, cerebral palsy, neuromuscular diseases). Concise essays cover the impairments' causes, address the emotional and social aspects involved, describe education and employment available to the disabled, and explain how to interact with disabled persons. Recommended for secondary schools. [R: ARBA 92]

■ *Meeting the Needs of People with Disabilities. See* entry 885.

E+

615 Moore, Cory. **A Reader's Guide for Parents of Children with Mental, Physical, or Emotional Disabilities**. 3d ed. Rockville, Md.: Woodbine House, 1990. 248p. $14.95pa. ISBN 0-933149-27-1. LC 89-40590.

Designed for parents of disabled children, this publication can also be useful to professionals. The guide contains annotated citations to public and private agencies that serve disabled children, publications about specific disabilities (autism to visual impairment), and information about the care of disabled children. One section lists books that will help young children live with their disabilities. Newsletters, journals, and directories are cited by subject. Indexed by organization, author, title, and subject. A valuable source. [R: ARBA 91; LJ, 1 Sept 90; RBB, 1 Sept 90]

616   Paciorek, Michael J., and Jeffrey A. Jones. **Sports and Recreation for the Disabled: A Resource Handbook**. Indianapolis, Ind.: Benchmark Press, 1989. 396p. $25.95pa. ISBN 0-936157-31-3. LC 88-42866.

Fifty-three major sports and recreational activities for the disabled constitute the focus of this handbook. Each chapter treats one sport, from all-terrain vehicles through wilderness experiences. For each are given rules and instructions, organization sponsoring the event, rationale for offering the sport to the disabled, adapted equipment and supplies, sources for additional information, and a bibliography. Drawings and photographs illustrate the volume. Appendixes list manufacturers of equipment and lightweight wheelchairs, sports organizations, national handicapped sports and recreation chapters, and Special Olympics chapters and directors. [R: ARBA 91]

HEARING IMPAIRED

E +
617   Butterworth, Rod R. **The Perigee Visual Dictionary of Signing: An A to Z Guide to Over 1,200 Signs of American Sign Language**. New York: Putnam, 1983. 450p. $9.95pa. ISBN 0-399-50863-5. LC 83-9728.

The Perigee Dictionary provides 1,200 alphabetically arranged signs in American Sign Language. Each clearly drawn sign is accompanied by a written description, memory aid, and sentence using the word. A main entry and synonym index refers the reader to the appropriate sign. Introductory material illustrates basic hand movements, the manual alphabet, and numbers.

This dictionary is not as comprehensive as Sternberg's *American Sign Language*, but it is a solid addition to the literature of sign language. *The Pocket Dictionary of Signing* is a shorter version of Butterworth's guide. [R: ARBA 85]

E +
618   Butterworth, Rod R., and Mickey Flodin. **The Pocket Dictionary of Signing**. New York: Perigee/Putnam, 1987. 190p. $4.95pa. ISBN 0-399-51347-7. LC 86-25596.

E +
619   Lane, Leonard G. **The Gallaudet Survival Guide to Signing**. Washington, D.C.: Gallaudet University Press, 1990. 194p. $4.95pa. ISBN 0-930323-67-X. LC 89-25686.

Neither of these small guides is comprehensive, but each supplies the basic words and concepts expressed in American Sign Language (ASL), the most widely used signing system. Either volume should serve general reference needs in school libraries at all levels. The handshapes and movements for each line drawing are clear, and each sign is accompanied by a brief description of hand movements/positions and a memory aid. The guides also contain charts of the basic handshapes, the ASL alphabet, and signs for numbers. *The Pocket Dictionary* is based on Butterworth's *Perigee Visual Dictionary of Signing*, a more detailed work. [R: ARBA 92]

620   **The Comprehensive Signed English Dictionary**. Harry Bornstein, Karen L. Saulnier, and Lilliam B. Hamilton, eds. Washington, D.C.: Gallaudet University Press, 1983. 456p. $28.95. ISBN 0-913580-81-3. LC 82-82830.

This dictionary contains 3,100 sign words for Signed English, providing extensive coverage of the language and including slang common to children. Written descriptions accompany each illustrated sign. Gallaudet University Press publishes other books on Signed English, such as the more compact *Gallaudet Survival Guide to Signing*. [R: ARBA 85]

E +
621   Sternberg, Martin L. A. **American Sign Language: A Comprehensive Dictionary**. New York: Harper & Row, 1981. 1132p. $43.95. ISBN 0-06-014097-6.

This important work provides extensive coverage of American Sign Language, with 5,430 word entries and cross-references and some 8,000 drawings. Each entry includes a pronunciation guide, part of speech, description of the sign, and at least one illustration to aid in signing. An extensive index, subject index, and appendixes of English word equivalents for seven foreign languages conclude the volume.

This work is also available in abridged format as *American Sign Language Dictionary* by Martin Sternberg (Harper & Row, 1981). Both are recommended. [R: ARBA 82]

VISUALLY IMPAIRED

■ *Access to Art*. *See* entry 1349.

■ *Hammond Large Type World Atlas*. *See* entry 546.

See also **Talking Books and Braille** under **Audio-visuals** in **Media Sources.**

622   **Living with Low Vision: A Resource Guide for People with Sight Loss**. 2d ed. Lexington, Mass.: Resources for Rehabilitation, 1990. 151p. $35.00pa. ISBN 0-929718-04-6. (33 Belford St., Suite 19A, Lexington, MA 02173).

623   **Rehabilitation Resource Manual: Vision**. 3d ed. Lexington, Mass.: Resources for Rehabilitation, 1990. 151p. $39.95pa. ISBN 0-929718-05-4.
      Living with Low Vision, a large-print publication, is intended for the visually impaired person; *Rehabilitation Resource Manual*, a similar publication, is designed for the professional. Both provide information about services, publications, and visual aids.
      The first publication begins with an explanation of the rehabilitation agency's role in assisting the disabled. It then lists different types of agencies and resources to aid the visually impaired. Among those cited are national organizations and their publications, sources for large-print and recorded books/periodicals, sources for technical devices that aid in daily living, services for special groups (e.g., the elderly, adolescents), and services and products for specific eye diseases. Appendixes list United States and Canadian state/province agencies for the visually impaired.
      The second publication is similar in content to the first; it, too, addresses self-help groups and gives information on specific eye diseases, vocational rehabilitation programs, and agencies/products for special populations. Both are useful publications. [R: ARBA 91; BL, 15 Sept 90; BL, 15 Nov 90]

624   Sardegna, Jill, and T. Otis Paul. **The Encyclopedia of Blindness and Visual Impairment**. New York: Facts on File, 1991. 329p. $45.00. ISBN 0-8160-2153-8. LC 90-3374.
      An ophthamological encyclopedia directed toward laypersons and professionals, this work provides over 500 lengthy articles on eye conditions and diseases, medical terminology, types and methods of surgery, medications, and economic and social aspects of blindness. Appendixes list referral, federal, and state agencies; schools and institutions; national organizations; and rehabilitation services. This concise, clearly written reference work is highly recommended for professional libraries. [R: LJ, 1 Feb 91]

History

ATLASES

See also **Archaeology**.

625   **Atlas of Classical History**. Richard J. A. Talbert, ed. New York: Macmillan, 1985. 217p. $50.00; $18.50pa. ISBN 0-02-933110-2; 0-415-03463-9pa. LC 85-675113.
      Epochs of classical antiquity from the Bronze Age to the fall of Rome in the fifth century are arranged chronologically. The 132 black-and-white maps, with accompanying text, illustrate such topics as political entities, towns, military campaigns, and trade routes. An extensive gazetteer/index provides access. Recommended for high schools with classical studies programs. [R: ARBA 86]

626   **The Atlas of the Crusades**. Jonathan Riley-Smith, ed. New York: Facts on File, 1990. 192p. $40.00. ISBN 0-8160-2186-4. LC 90-33846.
      Spanning the years 1095 to 1798, this atlas traces the rise, development, and decline of the Crusades. Over 150 excellent maps supported by narrative text, quotations from participants, and color illustrations, depict Christendom's Holy Wars. Among the many topics treated are the Roman Catholic

and Greek Orthodox churches, various Moslem empires, the persecution of Jews, and the battles of each Crusade. A chronology, index, glossary, and bibliography complete the volume. Highly recommended for high schools. [R: ARBA 92; BR, May/June 91]

E+
627   **Cultural Atlases for Young People Series.** New York: Facts on File, 1989-1990. 4v. $17.95/v.
    These volumes, on ancient Rome, ancient Egypt, ancient Greece, and the Middle Ages, begin with a table of dates, a chronology of history, art, and literature. The remainder of each work covers different topics in double-page spreads. The books are designed for upper-elementary through ninth grade levels.
    Part 1 of *Ancient Rome* covers important events in Roman history, such as the wars with Carthage. Part 2 focuses on regions and subsections such as the Roman town and town and city life. There are a number of physical/political maps in both sections.
    Part 1 of *Ancient Egypt* discusses history; geography; and standard topics such as food, shelter, religion, and burial customs. Part 2 is a voyage down the Nile from Nubia to the Mediterranean, heavily illustrated with maps and photographs of surviving monumunts, pyramids, statues, and tombs.
    The Middle Ages covers European civilization from the decline of the Roman Empire to the beginning of the sixteenth century. Maps and texts cover political and cultural events (e.g., the Crusades, the Byzantine Empire, the growth of urban society) and provide portraits of everyday life, region by region. Part 1 consists of a chronology; part 2 examines the countries and places of medieval Europe.
    Part 1 of *Ancient Greece* covers the Minoan/Mycenaean period through the Alexandrian Empire, interspersed with articles on popular topics, such as Greek coinage. Part 2 deals with mythology, art, and architecture. Numerous maps support the text.
    These works are well illustrated with color photographs and drawings and are supported by glossaries, gazetteers (citing grid locations on major maps), and indexes. Their arrangement will inspire browsing more than reference work, but they are worthwhile additions to any library serving the age groups. [R: ARBA 91; RBB, 1 Apr 90; SLJ, Feb 90. Aug 90]

628   **The Harper Atlas of World History.** Pierre Vidal-Naquet, ed. New York: Harper & Row, 1987. 340p. $35.00. ISBN 0-06-181884-4. LC 87-675015.
    Harper is a colorful, medium-sized atlas that resembles a lavishly illustrated text. It traces the history of mankind from the appearance of prehistoric man to the explosion of the space shuttle Challenger. Each double-page spread focuses on a particular event and includes maps, text, a chronology, and illustrations. This more inclusive approach (in comparison to other historical atlases, which emphasize maps) results in smaller maps but additional illustrative materials and text.
    In addition to its small maps, *Harper's* other weaknesses include the lack of a table of contents and a topical index that does not highlight references to maps. The work, however, will meet many basic needs for high school students. [R: ARBA 89; BL, 15 Feb 88; LJ, 1 Feb 88; WLB, Feb 88]

629   **Historical Maps on File.** New York: Facts on File, 1984. 1v. (various paging). $145.00 looseleaf w/binder. ISBN 0-87196-708-1. LC 82-675379.
    The 332 political, military, and economic outline maps in this set are grouped in nine categories: ancient civilization, Europe to 1500, Europe 1500-1815, Europe 1815 to the present, the United States, the Western Hemisphere (Canada and Latin America), Africa and the Middle East, Asia, and Australia. Themes include wars and battles, trade routes, colonial empires, the Crusades, revolution, the voyages of discovery, demography, and religion. Each map is captioned and gives essential place-names, distance bar scale, and legend, but omit latitude and longitude. A 3,800-entry place-name index supports the maps.
    All maps, as with others in the series, are printed in black-and-white to produce clear photocopies; all are free of copyright restrictions. The set was produced in consultation with high school teachers to establish curricular needs. [R: ARBA 85]

630   Nebenzahl, Kenneth. **Atlas of Columbus and the Great Discoveries.** Skokie, Ill.: Rand McNally, 1990. 168p. $75.00. ISBN 0-528-83407-X. LC 90-52620.
    This handsome atlas commemorates Columbus's discoveries and contains 50 beautiful reproductions of color plates dating from the fifteenth and sixteenth centuries. Part 1 focuses on maps that may have encouraged Columbus to undertake his first voyage. Here one finds the world map of Claudius Ptolemy, the Greek astronomer and geographer who made his observations in Alexandria, Egypt, around A.D. 150.

Part 2 contains maps prepared by Columbus's contemporaries, and those in part 3 include a series showing the voyages of discovery of the sixteenth century. Part 4 includes Geradus Mercator's famous projection of the world (1569) and Batista Boazio's charts of Sir Francis Drake's activities in the Spanish West Indies.

The text is written by Nebenzahl, himself a distinguished map historian. A bibliography of works cited and an index conclude this specialized atlas, which brings alive the world of Columbus. Recommended for high school level. [R: ARBA 91; LJ, Dec 90; WLB, Dec 90]

631   **Rand McNally Atlas of World History.** rev. ed. R. I. Moore, ed. Skokie, Ill.: Rand McNally, 1987. 191p. $18.95pa. ISBN 0-528-83288-3. LC 81-51409.

Libraries holding earlier editions (1981 and 1983) need not invest in this "revision," which is almost identical to its predecessors. The work is divided into two sections: a world historical section, with 87 maps and text originally published by Hamlyn Publishing Group of Great Britain; and a U.S. historical section, produced by Rand McNally and containing 8 maps.

Emphasis is on the major economic, social, cultural, and political developments of Western civilization, but the emergence of African, Asian, and Middle Eastern cultures also receives attention. Excellent maps focus on specific events or periods; they have sufficient size to be useful and enough detail to be informative. The text is scholary and well written. Recommended for high school level. [R: ARBA 89; BL, 15 June 88]

E +
632   **Rand McNally Children's Atlas of World History.** Skokie, Ill.: Rand McNally, 1988. 93p. $12.95. ISBN 0-528-83349-9. LC 88-61951.

This atlas, intended for ages 8 to 12, surveys major developments in world history from earliest times to the mid-1980s. The five chronologically arranged sections cover the ancient world, the Middle Ages, the age of discovery, the age of revolution, and the modern world.

Two-page spreads deal with periods, regions, and continents and include an informative text supported by excellent illustrations and maps in color. Thematic maps cover world climate, population, and economy, and physical-political maps outline national boundaries and geographical features. This attractive work is recommended for elementary and middle schools. [R: ARBA 90; BL, 15 Dec 89]

633   **The Times Atlas of World History.** 3d ed. Norman Stone, ed. Maplewood, N.J.: Hammond, 1989. 358p. $85.00. ISBN 0-7230-0304-1. LC 89-675246.

This attractive atlas, published in 1978 and completely revised in 1984, has become a standard reference source that has been translated into 13 languages. It graphically presents a global view of history, whereas most world atlases have a European focus. The 3d edition contains 600 full-color maps, a 300,000-word text, a glossary of terms, and a detailed index with over 7,500 entries.

Most maps have not been changed, but there are revisions and additions throughout the volume. There are new maps for the Mesoamerican period, major trading routes in Eurasia between 3500 B.C. and 1500 B.C., early agriculture in China, revolutionary France, and major stages of World War II. The analytical text has been substantially revised. The last chapter displays the world of the 1980s, replete with maps on population growth, foreign-aid recipients, and migrant workers. The updated text covers events in early 1989.

Since the atlas is expensive, high school libraries holding the 1984 edition may not wish to replace it. Those without the 1984 edition should consider buying this superb atlas. [R: ARBA 91; BL, 1 Mar 90; WLB, Feb 90]

BIBLIOGRAPHIES

E +
634   Adamson, Lynda G. **A Reference Guide to Historical Fiction for Children and Young Adults.** Westport, Conn.: Greenwood Press, 1987. 401p. $65.00. ISBN 0-313-25002-2. LC 87-7533.

A valuable source for teachers and librarians who wish to identify good historical fiction, this comprehensive guide describes works published since 1940 by 80 award-winning authors. The arrangement is in one alphabet, with entries for authors, titles, protagonists, historical persons, places, and terms found in historical fiction.

Each author's entry, two or more pages in length, includes a bibliography of that person's historical fiction, a brief biographical sketch, a list of honors, a summary of the author's general themes and style, and an annotation for each title. Appendixes list titles by period, locale, and reading level;

provide a bibliography of works about each author; and cite works by them that discuss historical fiction.

This guide covers titles more thoroughly than *Literature for Today's Young Adults* by Alleen P. Nilsen and Kenneth L. Donelson (2d ed. Scott, Foresman, 1985) or the *Wilson* standard catalogs. Recommended for high school libraries. [R: ARBA 89; BL, 15 Feb 88]

CHRONOLOGIES

E+

635 **Chronicle of the World**. Jerome Burne, ed. Mount Kisco, N.Y.: ECAM; distr., New York: Prentice Hall Press, 1989. 1296p. $49.95. ISBN 0-13-133463-8.

A companion to *Chronicle of America*, this volume describes historical events in a newspaper-story format with large headlines and colorful illustrations. Several thousand years per two-page spread are covered in early times (starting with 3,500,000 B.C.). From the end of the eighteenth century on, each year is covered individually. Stories include artistic and cultural events, political problems, and other happenings. This work will not replace traditional chronologies, but it will attract the interest of students in elementary and middle school. Recommended. [R: ARBA 91; BR, Nov/Dec 90; SLJ, Aug 90]

636 DeFord, Miriam, and Joan S. Jackson. **Who Was When: A Dictionary of Contemporaries**. 3d ed. Bronx, New York: H. W. Wilson, 1976. 184p. $50.00. ISBN 0-8242-0532-4. LC 76-2404.

This chronology lists and indexes 10,000 eminent individuals by birth and death dates for the period 500 B.C. to A.D. 1974. Each is categorized according to one of 10 broad fields of activity, enabling the user to identify leaders in the cultural, political, and religious life of any given era. Despite its publication date, this work continues to be useful.

637 Steinberg, S. H. **Historical Tables: 58 BC-AD 1985**. 11th ed. Updated by John Paxton. Hamden, Conn.: Garland, 1986. 277p. $27.50. ISBN 0-8240-8951-0. LC 86-18326.

Its lack of an index is a disadvantage, but *Historical Tables* remains a standard, well-organized chronology that enables the user to scan important events in the evolution of civilizations around the world. Each two-page spread, divided into six (sometimes four) columns and covering a decade or more, indicates occurrences in specific geographical areas. Since each new edition adds only a few pages of updated material with limited revision elsewhere in the volume, libraries may not need to hold the latest edition. [R: ARBA 88]

■ *This Day in American History*. See entry 708.

638 **Time Lines on File**. Edited by the Diagram Group. New York: Facts on File, 1989. 300p. $145.00 looseleaf w/binder. ISBN 0-8160-1897-9. LC 88-26050.

In this work, timelines and "life lines" are used to show major historical events and lifespans of notables. As with other On File publications, the use of heavy paper and a looseleaf format facilitates photocopying.

Three hundred illustrated plates are divided into seven chapters on world history, American history, European history, religion and ideas, the arts, science and technology, and Canadian history. As an example of content, the world history chapter includes charts on general world history, the classical world, life lines of leaders, and charts of major empires. Chapters on the history of specific areas are similar. The chapter on religion and ideas has charts on Christianity, the Jewish Diaspora, Islam, Buddhism, Hinduism, Sikhism, Greek philosophers, Roman thinkers, and movements such as the Renaissance and the Enlightenment.

A two-page table of contents in chart form describes timelines by period and date. Access is also provided by a 28-page personal name index, which refers to appropriate chapters and pages. This is a useful resource for high school students. [R: BL, 15 June 89; LJ, 1 May 89; WLB, May 89]

DICTIONARIES AND ENCYCLOPEDIAS

639 Brownstone, David M., and Irene M. Franck. **Dictionary of 20th Century History**. New York: Prentice Hall Press, 1990. 444p. $24.95. ISBN 0-13-209883-0.

Although universal in coverage, this dictionary places emphasis on the United States and includes major people, events, and concepts of this century. However, it does list some notables from the past who had an impact on contemporary times. The entries, ranging from a few sentences to more than a page, emphasize political, military, economic, scientific, religions, and medical topics. Cross-referencing is used, but there is no index. Nonetheless, high school libraries will find this a worthwhile reference source. [R: ARBA 91; BL, 15 Nov 90; LJ, Aug 90]

640 Canby, Courtlandt. **Encyclopedia of Historic Places.** New York: Facts on File, 1984. 2v. $175.00/set. ISBN 0-87196-126-1. LC 80-25121.
Some 100,000 worldwide historic sites are identified and located (e.g., countries, kingdoms, regions, rivers and lakes, battle sites and forts, archaeological digs). Each entry gives current and former names of places and locations and the sites' historical significance. Over 200 black-and-white photographs, line drawings, and maps illustrate the set. This work serves as an excellent supplement to *Webster's New Geographical Dictionary*. [R: ARBA 85]

641 Cook, Chris, **Dictionary of Historical Terms.** 2d ed. New York: Peter Bedrick Books; distr., Emeryville, Calif.: Publishers Group West, 1990. 350p. $34.95. ISBN 0-87226-331-2. LC 89-14934.
This work contains a wealth of valuable information on "every epoch of modern world history." Alphabetically arranged entries for political, religious, and social terms range from a brief sentence to an essay of 500 words or more. People and events are excluded. Origins and translations of foreign terms appear in parentheses following the entry. The 2d edition is a substantial revision of the previous one. For high school level.

642 Kohn, George C. **Dictionary of Historic Documents.** New York: Facts on File, 1991. 400p. $40.00. ISBN 0-8160-1978-9. LC 90-42305.
This unique work provides short entries on over 2,200 significant documents throughout human history, from about 1700 B.C. to date. Such topics as the substance of United Nations Resolution 242, the Vatican bull that proclaimed the dogma of Papal infallibility, and the important clauses of the Magna Carta are covered in articles that focus on the who, what, when, and why of each document. The volume uses abundant cross-references, and each entry defines foreign words or concepts when necessary. A bibliography and index support this authoritative work. Recommended for high schools. [R: ARBA 92; LJ, 1 May 91; RBB, 1 June 91; WLB, Sept 91]

643 Langer, William L., comp. and ed. **An Encyclopedia of World History: Ancient, Medieval, and Modern, Chronologically Arranged.** 5th ed. Boston: Houghton Mifflin, 1972. 1567p. $32.00. ISBN 0-395-13592-3. LC 68-14147.
This standard work, arranged by broad periods and subdivided by region and nation, is a historical chronology that covers the rise and fall of civilizations and empires from prehistoric times to 1970. Entries present concise information on political, military, diplomatic, and cultural history. Also included are genealogical charts of ruling families; lists of popes, prime ministers, and other notable political figures; and some 60 outline maps. The volume is extensively indexed.

644 McEvedy, Colin. **The Macmillan World History Factfinder.** New York: Macmillan, c1985, 1989. 208p. $15.98pa. ISBN 0-8317-9557-3. LC 85-4774.
This lively presentation of world history is arranged in eight major sections that begin with "The Ancient World" and end with "The Triumph of Technology." For each section there are historical tables, maps, essays, and well-selected illustrations. The index provides complete references to subjects and individuals in the text and tables. For middle and high school levels.

E+
645 **Oxford Illustrated Encyclopedia, Volume 3: World History from the Earliest Times to 1800.** Harry Judge, ed. New York: Oxford University Press, 1988. 391p. $45.00. ISBN 0-19-869135-1. LC 85-4876.

646 **Oxford Illustrated Encyclopedia, Volume 4: World History from 1800 to the Present Day.** Robert Blake, ed. New York: Oxford University Press, 1988. 391p. $45.00. ISBN 0-19-869136-X.
Volumes 1 and 2 of the proposed nine-volume *Oxford Illustrated Encyclopedia* covers the physical and natural world, and volume 5 focuses on the arts. Volumes 3 and 4 span world history from the earliest records to the present, with 1800 as the dividing date for the two volumes. Persons and events overlapping the century mark are included in both, enabling each volume to stand alone. Some important people, however, are omitted, since their contributions fit more appropriately with the themes of other volumes.

Entries averaging 200 words are alphabetically arranged and illustrated by some 800 maps, drawings, paintings, charts, and tables. Time charts are included on the endpapers. Information, which is concise and focused on sharply defined topics, is similar to that found in *Encyclopedia of World History*. Since that work is chronologically arranged, the volumes complement each other. The *Oxford Illustrated Encyclopedia* has the advantage of currency. [R: BL, 1 Apr 89; LJ, 1 Feb 89; SLJ, Aug 89]

647   Ritter, Harry. **Dictionary of Concepts in History**. Westport, Conn.: Greenwood Press, 1986. 490p. $65.00. ISBN 0-313-22700-4. LC 85-27305.
This work focuses on historical concepts (e.g., antiquarianism). Essays on some 100 terms provide concise definitions, the origin and evolution of the meaning, illustrative quotations, and an annotated bibliography of reference materials. Indexing is by subject, author, and title of works cited. The work is intended for college and graduate students, but advanced high school students can use it with profit. [R: ARBA 87; WLB, Feb 87]

648   Sifakis, Carl. **Encyclopedia of Assassinations**. New York: Facts on File, 1991. 228p. $35.00. ISBN 0-8160-1935-5. LC 90-3435.
Assassinations and attempted assassinations that made history constitute the focus of this work. Biographies of some 350 victims, arranged alphabetically and followed by short bibliographies, summarize the subject's career, briefly describe the circumstances and murder, and relate the fate of the perpetrator. The time period covered is from Roman times to the present. Some 50 black-and-white photographs, a bibliography, and an index support the volume. [R: ARBA 92; LJ, 15 May 91; RBB, 1 June 91; SLJ, May 91; WLB, May 91]

649   **Travel and Trade Routes Series**. Adapted by Irene M. Franck and David M. Brownstone. New York: Facts on File, 1990. 8v. $115.00/set; $17.95/v. ISBN 0-8160-2676-9. LC 89-11694.
These attractive books were adapted from the adult book, *To the Ends of the Earth: The Great Travel and Trade Routes of Human History* (Facts on File, 1984). The individual volumes are *Across Africa and Arabia*, *Across Asia by Land*, *The American Way West*, *Around Africa and Asia by Sea*, *The European Overland Routes*, *From Gibraltar to the Ganges*, *The Northern World*, and *The Southern World*. Each volume focuses on a particular geographic region and provides in words and pictures a history of its trade and travel routes, showing how they evolved and contributed to the area's social and economic development. Among the well-known routes covered are the Northwest Passage, the Spice Route, the Cape Horn Route, and the California Mission Trail.
Volumes are illustrated by 40 to 50 black-and-white drawings, photographs, and maps; bibliographies conclude each chapter. Indexed. These volumes provide a unique and stimulating approach to the study of world history. Appropriate for secondary schools. [R: SLJ, Oct 90]

MIDDLE AGES AND RENAISSANCE

650   Matthew, Donald. **Atlas of Medieval Europe**. New York: Facts on File, 1983. 240p. $45.00. ISBN 0-87196-133-4. LC 82-675303.
This atlas/history is arranged chronologically in four sections: the breakup of the ancient world and emergence of northern Europe; the growth of Christianity and towns; the development of trade, industry, travel, education, and the arts; and the rise of European kingdoms. Maps depict trade routes and commerce, political affairs, architectural styles, and so forth, and essays treat such topics as daily life and commerce. Appendixes include a glossary, a gazetteer, and an index. This is an excellent work for middle and high school levels. [R: ARBA 84; SLJ, May 85]

651   **The Middle Ages: A Concise Encyclopedia**. H. R. Loyn, ed. London: Thames and Hudson; distr., New York: W. W. Norton, 1989. 352p. $39.95. ISBN 0-500-25103-7. LC 88-50254.
Nearly 1,000 entries for the period 400 to 1500 cover people, places, customs, and concepts, from Scandinavia to the Middle East. The majority of the alphabetically arranged entries are short, but some on broad topics (e.g., medicine, climate, Jews) are two pages in length; most conclude with one or two references. Well-written and easy-to-understand articles provide a panorama of the era. Some 250 black-and-white illustrations, several maps, and a few genealogical charts enhance the text. For high school level. [R: ARBA 90; LJ, 1 Sept 89; RBB, 15 Sept 89]

MODERN HISTORY

652   Day by Day: The Forties. By Thomas M. Leonard. New York: Facts on File, 1977. 2v. $125.00/set. ISBN 0-87196-375-2. LC 77-13251.

653   Day by Day: The Fifties. By Jeffrey Merrit. New York: Facts on File, 1979. 2v. $125.00/set. ISBN 0-87196-383-3. LC 79-19952.

654   Day by Day: The Sixties. By Thomas Parker and Douglas Nelson. New York: Facts on File, 1983. 2v. $195.00/set. ISBN 0-87196-684-4. LC 80-22432.

655   Day by Day: The Seventies. By Thomas Leonard, Cynthia Crippen, and Marc Aronson. New York: Facts on File, 1988. 2v. $195.00/set. ISBN 0-8160-1020-X. LC 83-11520.
   This series, now complete through December 31, 1979, chronicles each of the decades in diary format. A summary of events and several pages of photographs introduce each year, which is followed by 2-page spreads capsuling each day's events in 10 columns. Five columns cover world politics, Europe, Africa and the Middle East, the Americas, and Asia and the Pacific. Three columns cover U.S. social, political, and economic/environmental issues, and two columns deal with science/technology and culture. An index provides access to specific topics. [R: BL, 1 Jan 89; SLJ, Nov 88; SLJ, May 89; WLB, Oct 88]

656   The Longman Handbook of Modern European History 1763-1985. By Chris Cook and John Stevenson. White Plains, N.Y.: 1987. 672p. $36.95; $19.95pa. ISBN 0-582-48585-1; 0-582-48584-3pa. LC 86-18618.
   This is an excellent handbook of modern European history. The seven major sections bring together chronological, statistical, biographical, and tabular information useful to high school students.
   The chronology, arranged by topic and then by year, gives brief descriptions of events. Statistics cover such diverse topics as the production of crude oil and number of children in school. The biography section includes short biographies of more than 150 notables. This work also contains a bibliography of books, documents, and journal articles; several black-and-white maps; and a comprehensive index. [R: ARBA 89]

657   Time Navigator. St. Paul, Minn.: Minnesota Educational Computing Corp., 1989. 3 disks plus guide. System requirements: Apple II family computer. $59.00.
   This time machine program, which permits the user to travel backward in time to the year 1900, should motivate students to use a variety of reference sources to answer questions and sharpen their research skills. A knowledge of historical events and their dates, at two levels of difficulty, is required to move from one stop to the next. Teachers may set categories of questions, number of years jumped between stops, specific years for stops, and level of difficulty. This computer program is useful for junior high and high school levels. [R: SLJ, Apr 90]

WORLD CONFLICTS

See also **Military Science**.

658   Cargas, Harry James. The Holocaust: An Annotated Bibliography. 2d ed. Chicago: American Library Association, 1986. 196p. $27.50. ISBN 0-8389-0433-5. LC 85-20069.
   Cargas is a recognized authority and scholar in the field of the Holocaust. This bibliography is a useful tool for advanced high school students. Some 500 books in English, published in the United States, are divided into 15 topical chapters (e.g., biography, memoirs, histories, fiction, drama, poetry, collections, oral history). Annotations averaging 100 words are descriptive as well as critical. A final chapter, which addresses the beginning researcher, includes a list of research centers on the Holocaust in the United States. Indexing is by nation and concentration camp. [R: ARBA 87]

659   Chandler, David G. Battles and Battlescenes of World War Two. New York: Macmillan, 1989. 160p. $19.95. ISBN 0-02-897175-2. LC 89-12122.
   This volume covers 52 major battles of World War II in Europe, Asia, and North Africa. Alphabetically arranged entries provide basic facts—date, location, object, opposing sides, forces

engaged, casualties, and outcome—and suggested titles for further reading. A two- to three-page narrative describing each battle is illustrated with black-and-white maps and photographs. A chronology at the end of the book lists the battles and pertinent information about them. For high school libraries. [R: ARBA 90; BL, 1 Mar 90; SLJ, May 90]

660   Dictionary of the Vietnam War. James Olson, ed. Westport, Conn.: Greenwood Press, 1988. 585p. $65.00; $16.95pa. ISBN 0-313-24943-1; 0-87226-238-3pa. LC 87-12023.

The Vietnam War and related issues—the fundamental causes of the war, the antiwar movement on the homefront, the conflict itself, and its consequences—are the focus of this excellent volume. Novels and films that have attempted to interpret the war and U.S. involvement are also covered. Numerous cross-references and an index help to pull many topics together, and brief bibliographies of additional sources support most of the alphabetically arranged entries. The appendix contains a topical bibliography, a chronology, census table for South Vietnam, a glossary of slang terms and acronyms, and maps of military regions. The paperback version is distributed by Publishers Group West. Suggested for high school libraries. [R: ARBA 89]

661   Encyclopedia of the Holocaust. Israel Gutman, ed. New York: Macmillan, 1990. 4v. $285.00/set. ISBN 0-02-896090-4. LC 89-13466.

This set provides an objective treatment of the happenings of 1939-1945, allowing the events to speak for themselves. Major scholars from around the world contributed the 950 signed articles, which average 1 or 2 pages.

Entries fall into four broad categories: the Nazi machine and its instruments of destruction (e.g., antisemetic and racist laws and policies, cultural or social institutions); the world of European Jewry (e.g., Jewish life in towns and cities before, during, and after the Nazi rise to power); America, the world, and the Holocaust (e.g., the world response to Nazi persecution, actions of Roosevelt); and the Holocaust in today's world (e.g., war criminal trials, the impact on survivors and their children).

Articles are followed by a list of 3 to 5 suggested readings and enhanced by photographs, maps, tables, charts, and other illustrations. An alphabetical list of entries at the beginning of the set and a detailed index make the content accessible. Recommended for high schools requiring a comprehensive treatment of the topic. [R: ARBA 91; BL, 1 Mar 90; LJ, 15 Apr 90; SLJ, May 90; WLB, Apr 90]

662   Enser, A. G. S. A Subject Bibliography of the Second World War, and Aftermath: Books in English 1976-1987. Brookfield, Vt.: Gower, 1990. 287p. $59.95. ISBN 0-566-05736-0.

This volume continues two earlier compilations. The current edition focuses on books about World War II published after 1974, the date the British government made classified documents on the war available to the public. Items listed, all nonfiction, are arranged by subject. Indexing is by author and subject. Highly recommended for high school level. [R: ARBA 91]

663   Gray, Randal, with Christopher Argyle. Chronicle of the First World War. Volume 1: 1914-1916. New York: Facts on File, 1990. 352p. $40.00. ISBN 0-8160-2139-2. LC 90-31333.

The two-volume chronology will encompass the period July 1914 to August 1921, with this, the initial volume, ending in 1916. Information is presented in nine vertical columns, each one representing a geographic area or category of activity. This format allows the reader to pursue information across columns in a timeline perspective or vertically down the various categories.

Supplementing the main chronology is a variety of other helpful features. A succinct essay covers the war fronts with an annual focus. All major campaigns are treated in the map section. Tables furnish overall war statistics and figures for military operations, forces engaged, and losses incurred. Guns and prisoners lost are highlighted. A glossary alphabetically lists wartime terminology and abbreviations, with entries furnishing the strengths and weaponry of military formations and units. Sources used for the compilation are noted. A thorough index, keyed to dates, rounds out the volume. Recommended.

664   Laska, Vera. Nazism Resistance & Holocaust in World War II: A Bibliography. Metuchen, N.J.: Scarecrow, 1985. 183p. $15.00. ISBN 0-8108-1771-3. LC 84-23586.

An excellent survey of the Holocaust and the Resistance Movement prefaces this subject bibliography and enhances its value. It cites some 2,000 books, most of which are in English and published in the United States or Great Britain. The items are arranged in 13 subject categories, such as Jews and Anti-Semitism, Nazism, and the Resistance. Indexing is by author only. [R: ARBA 86]

665   The Marshall Cavendish Illustrated Encyclopedia of World War I. Peter Young, ed. North Bellmore, N.Y.: Marshall Cavendish, 1984. 12v. $409.95/set. ISBN 0-87307-181-3. LC 83-20879.

This set contains balanced treatments of all aspects of World War I, from its beginning in 1914 through the Versailles Treaty Conference in 1919. Well-written articles, many by participants in the war and recognized military historians, deal with military, political, economic, and social topics on the battlefield and the home front. The set is heavily illustrated with photographs, drawings, and maps and has a chronology, several indexes (generals, commanders, statesmen, ships, and illustrations), and a list of major battles. Recommended for high schools. [R: ARBA 85; BL, 15 June 85]

666   **The Marshall Cavendish Illustrated Encyclopedia of World War II**. rev. ed. Peter Young, ed. North Bellmore, N.Y.: Marshall Cavendish, 1985. 12v. $409.95/set. ISBN 0-85685-948-6.

A companion to the *Marshall Cavendish Illustrated Encyclopedia of World War I*, this chronologically arranged set begins with the rise of the Nazis in the 1930s and ends with their defeat in 1945. Lavishly illustrated articles cover all phases of the war, military operations, land and sea battles, weaponry, and the home front. Boxed entries scattered throughout the text profile major figures of the war, and maps in color depict major campaigns. The final volume includes a chronology and general and thematic indexes.

667   Messenger, Charles. **The Chronological Atlas of World War Two**. New York: Macmillan, 1989. 255p. $32.50. ISBN 0-02-584391-5. LC 89-2567.

This chronologically arranged atlas contains 200 well-drawn maps that provide coverage of the world's longest and bloodiest conflict. Two pages are allotted to each time period and major battle. Other features include an excellent chronology, an index, and a one-page bibliography. This work does not compare with *The Times Atlas of the Second World War*, which is far more extensive, but it is likely to meet most of the needs of high school social studies classes. [R: ARBA 90; BL, 1 Nov 89; WLB, Dec 89]

668   Perrett, Bryan, and Ian Hogg. **Encyclopedia of the Second World War**. Novato, Calif.: Presidio Press, 1989. 447p. $40.00. ISBN 0-89141-362-6. LC 89-8533.

Articles, which range from a few lines to several paragraphs, cover people, places, events, weapons, and code names of World War II. The work concentrates on the military aspects of the war and is generously illustrated with portraits, black-and-white photographs of battle scenes and weapons, drawings of ships, and maps of battles. Suggested for high schools. [R: ARBA 90; WLB, Jan 90]

669   **The Pictorial History of the Holocaust**. Yitzhak Arad, ed. New York: Macmillan, 1990. 396p. $85.00. ISBN 0-02-897011-X. LC 90-8044.

This work provides an exceptional look at the horror of the Holocaust. The pictorial history is divided into four chronological periods, beginning with the first persecution by the Nazis and ending with the efforts of surviving Jews to reach Palestine, 1945-1948. A comprehensive narrative accompanies the more than 400 photographs (many published for the first time) contributed by the Yad Vashem Holocaust Martyrs' and Heroes' Remembrance Authority in Jerusalem. The work lacks an index, but its organization and frequent use of headings make the material readily accessible. Recommended for high schools. [R: SLJ, May 91]

670   Pitt, Barrie, and Frances Pitt. **The Month-by-Month Atlas of World War II**. New York: Summit Books/Simon & Schuster, 1989. 178p. $35.00. ISBN 0-671-68880-4. LC 89-675257.

Each month of World War II receives a two-page spread that contains full-color maps (over 300) and a narrative of events. Some important battles and campaigns, such as D-Day, also get two-page treatment. This well-designed atlas is helpful in keeping track of what was occurring simultaneously on different fronts. Appropriate for high school level. [R: ARBA 91; RBB, 1 May 90]

671   Summers, Harry G. **Korean War Almanac**. New York: Facts on File, 1990. 288p. $24.95; $14.95pa. ISBN 0-8160-1737-9; 0-8160-2463-4pa. LC 89-33560.

672   Summers, Harry G. **Vietnam War Almanac**. New York: Facts on File, 1987. 288p. $27.95; $14.95pa. ISBN 0-8160-1017-X; 0-8160-1813-8pa. LC 83-14054.

Summers, an infantry colonel and combat veteran of Korea and Vietnam and a military analyst, has compiled useful handbooks of these conflicts. The arrangement of the two volumes is the same: a history of the war's origin; a chronology of the events of each conflict; and an alphabetical section (the main body) that includes entries for key leaders/officers, battles, strategies and tactics, weapons, political factors, and the effects of the war on the countries involved. Entries range from a paragraph to a page, and numerous maps and black-and-white photographs illustrate the text.

Each volume contains many cross-references, suggestions for further reading, and a detailed index. High schools requiring more information about these wars than general sources provide should consider their purchase. [R: ARBA 92; BL, 1 Apr 90; BR, Nov/Dec 90]

673   The Times Atlas of the Second World War. John Keegan, ed. New York: HarperCollins, 1989. 256p. $50.00. ISBN 0-06-016178-7. LC 89-45070.

This magnificent atlas contains 450 full-color maps, 150 photographs and illustrations, a 14-page month-by-month chronology, and an extensive narrative. Maps are arranged chronologically and regionally, covering major battles of the war, intelligence (security and counterintelligence substations), special forces missions, and concentrations camps. There also are maps that focus on Stalingrad, site of the worst battle of the war; the bombardment of Japan in 1945; the travels of Adolf Hitler; and the sites of war conferences. One unique feature is the skewing of some maps to reflect different viewpoints (e.g., the invasion of Poland in September, 1939, from the German viewpoint).

Numerous charts compare the wartime economies of Great Britain, the United States, and Japan, and show military and civilian casualties (around 25 million men, women, and children). A key to the symbols used on the map is produced on a page of the atlas and on a convenient loose card. The outstanding work is highly recommended for high schools. [R: BL, 15 Feb 90; WLB, Jan 90]

674   War in Peace: The Marshall Cavendish Illustrated Encyclopedia of Postwar Conflict. Ashley Brown and Mark Dartford, eds. North Bellmore, N.Y.: Marshall Cavendish, 1984. 13v. $499.00/set. ISBN 0-86307-293-3. LC 84-19386.

War in Peace extends Marshall Cavendish's encyclopedias of World War I and World War II by providing coverage of wars and other conflicts from 1945 to 1984. The chronologically arranged volumes contain 450 articles that give the political/historical background, military action, and outcome of each conflict. They are heavily illustrated with 1,800 color pictures and maps and 2,500 black-and-white photographs. Each volume is accessed by its own index. The final volume contains a table of contents and a comprehensive index for the set, a classified list of articles, a chronology by year and region, and a bibliography. Recommended for high schools.

675   Wheal, Elizabeth-Anne, and others. A Dictionary of the Second World War. New York: Peter Bedrick Books; distr., Emeryville, Calif.: Publishers Group West, 1990. 541p. $39.95. ISBN 0-87226-337-1. LC 90-312.

This excellent volume contains a wealth of information about World War II. Some 1,600 alphabetically arranged articles, varying from a sentence to several pages, cover people, events, weapons, battles, and other aspects of the war and its era. Special features include chronologies for each of the 7 major military theaters and 37 campaign maps. Useful for browsing and quick reference. Highly recommended for grades 8 through 12. [R: ARBA 91; BL, 1 Nov 90; BR, Jan/Feb 91; LJ, 15 Sept 90; WLB, Nov 90]

676   The World at Arms: *The Reader's Digest* Illustrated History of World War II. Pleasantville, N.Y.: Reader's Digest Association; distr., New York: Random House, 1989. 480p. $29.95. ISBN 0-89577-333-3.

The text gives a detailed history of World War II illustrated by over 800 maps, drawings, and other pictures. Other features include short biographies of military leaders, a chronology, a glossary of terms, and an index. Highly recommended for junior high and high schools. [R: BR, Jan/Feb 90; VOYA, Apr 90]

ASIA

677   Encyclopedia of Asian History. Ainslie T. Embree, ed. New York: Scribner's, 1988. 4v. $360.00/set. ISBN 0-684-18619-5. LC 87-9891.

Advanced high school students will find this an excellent source. It covers most of Asia, including various past and present countries, but emphasizes the last 300 years. Entries describe historical events, people, places, literature, religious and cultural concepts, music, and social developments. Maps, thorough indexing, and short reading lists support the text. [R: ARBA 89; LJ, 15 Apr 89]

CANADA

See also **Social Studies**.

678   **The Collins Dictionary of Canadian History: 1867 to the Present**. By David J. Bercuson and J. L. Granatstein. Don Mills, Ont.: Collins, 1988. 270p. $34.95. ISBN 0-00-217758-7.

The history and culture of Canada since Confederation is the focus of this work. The volume presents 1,600 alphabetically arranged articles that cover geography; economics; history; foreign policy; biographies of notables in government, the arts, business, and sports; and scientific achievements. Cross-references; black-and-white illustrations; timelines; lists of governors general, prime ministers, and provincial premiers; election results, and other demographic data all support the text. For middle and high school levels. [R: ARBA 89]

CHINA

See also **Social Sciences**.

679   O'Neill, Hugh B. **Companion to Chinese History**. New York: Facts on File, 1987. 397p. $27.50; $14.95pa. ISBN 0-87196-841-X; 0-8160-1825-1pa. LC 83-11685.

Those requiring concise information on Chinese history and culture from the earliest times to 1985 will welcome this volume, which contains nearly 1,000 entries that range from a sentence to several pages. Articles focus on important historical events, movements, philosophies, religions, and notables (e.g., explorers, emperors, military leaders).

Special features include copious cross-references, 14 pages of maps, a chronology from 1506 to 1985, and tables that list dynasties from 2205 B.C. to A.D. 1911. This is an excellent ready-reference source for secondary schools. [R: ARBA 88]

GERMANY

680   **The Encyclopedia of the Third Reich**. By Christian Zentner and Friedemann Bedurftig. New York: Macmillan, 1991. 2v. $185.00/set. ISBN 0-02-897500-6. LC 90-49885.

This translation of *Das Grosse Lexikon des Dritten Reiches* (Munich: Sudwest Verlag, 1985) covers the Third Reich from the rise of the National Socialist Party through the end of World War II and the Nuremberg trials. Articles summarize the careers and activities of military and political figures, events, ideology, laws, organizations, and other aspects of the period. Numerous captioned black-and-white photographs enhance the text. Most articles are entered under their English names; the index provides references from German names used. Appropriate for high schools. [R: ARBA 92; LJ, 15 Apr 91; RBB, 1 June 91; WLB, May 91]

681   Taylor, James, and Warren Shaw. **The Third Reich Almanac**. New York: World Almanac; distr., New York: Pharos Books/St. Martin's Press, c1987, 1988. 400p. $24.95. ISBN 0-88687-363-0.

The book opens with a chronology of major events during the period 1933-1945. The main body of the work consists of alphabetically arranged entries for people, places, events, concepts, legal terms, and other matters related to Nazism, from the rise of Hitler through the post-war period. Entries range from a few words to eight-page essays.

Appendixes contain chronologies of various military campaigns, a list of quotations from Hitler and others, a short bibliography, and a few maps. *Encyclopedia of the Third Reich* provides more extensive coverage, but this is a good work. [R: BL, 1 Apr 89]

ITALY

682   **Dictionary of Modern Italian History**. Frank J. Coppa, ed. Westport, Conn.: Greenwood Press, 1985. 496p. $59.95. ISBN 0-313-22983-X. LC 84-6704.

This work focuses on the major events, personalities, institutions, systems, and problems of Italian history from the eighteeenth century to the 1980s. In alphabetically arranged entries that range from 100 to 900 words, the volume covers important subjects such as the pontificates of Popes Pius IX and XXIII, foreign relations, movements, and cultural history. Signed articles are supported by bibliographies. An index and appendixes of chronologies of events, ministries, presidents, kings, and popes conclude this excellent and authoritative work. Appropriate for high school level. [R: BL, 1 Apr 86]

LATIN AMERICA

See also **Social Sciences**.

683   **The Cambridge History of Latin America**. New York: Cambridge University Press, 1985- . price varies/v.

The volumes published in this series so far, cover colonial Latin America, independence to 1870, 1870-1930, and 1930-on. As in other Cambridge historical sets, subject specialists around the world have contributed outstanding essays. This is the most authoritative work available on the subject and should be useful to high school students. [R: LJ, 15 Apr 86]

RUSSIA AND THE USSR

684   Paxton, John. **Companion to Russian History**. New York: Facts on File, 1983. 503p. $27.50; $9.95pa. ISBN 0-87196-771-5; 0-8160-5192-3pa. LC 82-5192.

Some 2,500 alphabetically arranged entries cover the basic facts of Russian and Soviet history and culture over the last thousand years. Ballet and architecture receive as much attention as politics and Russian revolutionaries. Bibliographies, a chronology, and maps (historical and current) support the text. This is a useful ready-reference tool on the events and personalities of Russian history. [R: ARBA 84]

685   Shaw, Warren, and David Pryce. **The World Almanac of the Soviet Union: From 1905 to the Present**. New York: World Almanac/St. Martin's Press, 1990. 360p. $24.95. ISBN 0-88687-565-X. LC 90-46041.

Eighty-five years of Russian/Soviet history (1905-1990) are condensed in this work, which focuses on internal politics and economic development and their impact on the world. The concise, clearly written entries are divided into three parts—topics, biographies, and a chronology—followed by a gazetteer, a lengthy bibliography, maps, and an index. Topics and biographies are arranged alphabetically in entries that range from a line or two of identification to detailed essays. This excellent quick-reference source is recommended for junior and senior high schools. [R: ARBA 91; BL, 15 Feb 91]

686   **The Soviet Union**. 3d ed. Daniel D. Diller, ed. Washington, D.C.: Congressional Quarterly, 1990. 352p. $22.95pa. ISBN 0-87187-574-8. LC 90-35821.

This handbook recounts the contemporary history of the Soviet Union through 1989 only but does not ignore important events of earlier periods. Brief essays cover Imperial Russia, current notables, geography, the problems of reforming the system, ethnicity, the military, foreign policy, Soviet-American relations, and much more. [R: ARBA 91]

SPAIN

687   **Historical Dictionary of Modern Spain, 1700-1988**. Robert W. Kern and Meredith D. Dodge, eds. Westport, Conn.: Greenwood Press, 1990. 697p. $95.00. ISBN 0-313-25971-2. LC 89-7471.

Almost 300 years of Spanish history are recounted in this excellent volume, which covers people, events, politics, and international relations. The alphabetically arranged articles, ranging from 1 to 15 or more pages, are well written and informative. Entries, which are written by scholars, include brief bibliographies and numerous cross-references. A list of abbreviations, several maps, a detailed chronology, a selective bibliography, and an extensive index conclude the volume. Recommended for high schools. [R: ARBA 91; BL, 15 June 90; LJ, 15 Feb 90; WLB, June 90]

UNITED KINGDOM AND THE REPUBLIC OF IRELAND

688   **The Cambridge Historical Encyclopedia of Great Britain and Ireland**. Christopher Haigh, ed. New York: Cambridge University Press, 1985. 392p. $44.50; $16.95pa. ISBN 0-521-25559-7; 0-521-39552-6pa. LC 85-47568.

This comprehensive work surveys British and Irish history from 100 B.C. to A.D. 1975. Some 60 scholars compiled the 7 chronological chapters with thematic subsections on England, Scotland, Wales, and Ireland. Marginal notes serve as fact guides, which are useful for ready-reference. A who's who section provides essential data on notables. Numerous excellent illustrations make this an attractive volume. Recommended for high schools. [R: BL, 15 Apr 86; SLJ, May 86]

689   **The Cambridge Illustrated Dictionary of British Heritage**. Alan Isaacs and Jennifer Monk, eds. New York: Cambridge University Press, 1986. 484p. $24.95. ISBN 0-521-30214-5. LC 86-13708.

This informative, authoritative, well-written volume contains 1,500 unsigned articles on British life and history. Alphabetically arranged entries on topics that range from popular culture to history are supported by generous cross-references, maps, genealogies, charts, and black-and-white photographs. An excellent addition to any secondary school library. [R: ARBA 87]

690   Delderfield, Eric R. **Kings & Queens of England & Great Britain**. New York: Facts on File, 1990. 192p. $24.95. ISBN 0-8160-2433-2. LC 89-25905.

In this work readers will find entries for more than 60 British kings and queens, from the first Anglo-Saxon rulers to Elizabeth II. Chronologically arranged essays include birth, reign, and death dates; places of birth, death, and burial; marriages; children; and how the monarch shaped the times. The entries are supplemented by genealogical charts, longevity statistics, illustrations, and maps. Some errors mar this attractive work, but overall it is a competently written and well-illustrated volume. Suggested as a supplementary purchase for high schools. [R: ARBA 91]

691   Ross, Stewart. **Monarchs of Scotland**. New York: Facts on File, 1990. 192p. $27.95. ISBN 0-8160-2479-0.

Concise biographies cover all Scottish rulers, from the early wars between Celts and Anglo-Saxons in the ninth century A.D. to the 1707 Act of Union with England. Since little is known about the earliest kings, these entries are brief. Some 80 color and black-and-white illustrations; maps of boundaries, strategic strongholds, major settlements and towns, and important battles; and a detailed family tree all support the text. An index and brief chronology conclude the volume. Suggested for high schools. [R: ARBA 91]

692   **Victorian Britain: An Encyclopedia**. Sally Mitchell, ed. Hamden, Conn.: Garland, 1988. 986p. (Garland Reference Library of Social Sciences, v.438). $125.00. ISBN 0-8240-1513-4. LC 87-29947.

Queen Victoria's reign, 1837 to 1901, is the focus of this definitive work. Over 330 international scholars contributed some 900 signed articles, covering historical events, prominent persons, groups, institutions, and culture. A brief chronology of people and events introduces the main text, which consists of concise, factual articles that average about a page in length. Short bibliographies of major and recent secondary works are appended to each entry; an additional bibliography appears at the end of the volume. Illustrations consist of black-and-white pictures, many of which appeared in contemporary periodicals such as the *Illustrated London News*. A 75-page index concludes this excellent work. Recommended for high schools. [R: ARBA 90; BL, 15 May 89; BR, May/June 89; LJ, 15 Mar 89; WLB, Mar 89]

UNITED STATES

Bibliographies

693   Gerhardstein, Virginia Brokaw. **Dickinson's American Historical Fiction**. 5th ed. Metuchen, N.J.: Scarecrow, 1986. 352p. $32.50. ISBN 0-8108-1867-1. LC 85-27656.

This standard bibliography is designed for teachers who wish to use fiction to bring American history to life for their students. The annotated listings classify 3,048 novels, published from 1917 to 1984, into 11 chronological periods, colonial times through the turbulent 1960s and 1970s. Historical novels are defined as those that provide identifiable time and place and "social, political, or economic phenomena characteristic of a period." Recommended for high schools. [R: ARBA 87]

694   Giese, James R., and Laurel R. Singleton. **U.S. History: A Resource Book for Secondary Schools. Volume 1: 1450-1865**. Santa Barbara, Calif.: ABC-Clio, 1989. 347p. $32.95. ISBN 0-87436-505-8. LC 88-38952.

695   Giese, James R., and Laurel R. Singleton. **U.S. History: A Resource Book for Secondary Schools. Volume 2: 1865-Present**. Santa Barbara, Calif.: ABC-Clio, 1989. 340p. $32.95. ISBN 0-87436-506-6. LC 88-38952.

These two volumes in the Social Studies Resources for Secondary School Libraries, Teachers, and Students series can stand alone, since both treat sources that overlap the time period that divides them. They list and annotate all types of reference works useful to students in the study of American history (e.g., atlases, dictionaries, encyclopedias, biographical sources, chronologies, indexes, online databases). Audiovisual materials, textbooks, and supplementary materials all provide additional coverage.

Each volume contains a chronology for the time period it covers and concise biographies of a number of prominent historians. Volume 1 includes samples of various types of primary sources, and volume 2 prints excerpts from documents, such as diaries, letters, and census data, showing how historians use them. An essay in volume 1 that explains the value of history and how historians work is especially valuable. Recommended for all secondary schools. [R: ARBA 90]

696   **Harvard Guide to American History**. Frank Freidel and Richard K. Showman, eds. Cambridge, Mass.: Harvard University Press, 1974. 1212p. $20.00pa. ISBN 0-674-37555-6. LC 72-81272.

The two-volume hardcover edition of this classic work is out of print; only the massive one-volume paperback is available. The first part (formerly volume 1) covers research methods, biography, comprehensive and regional histories, and works on special subjects; the second part (formerly volume 2) is arranged by chronological periods from 1789 to the mid-1970s. This standard bibliographic guide on American history is, of course, severely hampered because of the date.

697   Howard, Elizabeth F. **America as Story: Historical Fiction for Secondary Schools**. Chicago: American Library Association, 1988. 137p. $17.50pa. ISBN 0-8389-0492-0. LC 88-3453.

Those who teach history and social studies in secondary schools will welcome this bibliography, which is a compilation of recommended historical fiction. The guide lists some 150 adult and young adult titles (the production of 126 authors), dividing them into seven chronological chapters that range from the colonial period to the present. The greatest number of selections concern westward expansion and the Civil War. Entries average a page and provide title, author, date, number of pages, a synopsis of the book, comments on its ideas, suggested reports and activities, and recommended grade levels.

Titles were drawn from standard sources, such as *School Library Journal*, *Horn Book Magazine*, lists from the National Council for the Social Studies, and other bibliographies. A number of social studies teachers and history professors were also consulted. [R: ARBA 89; BL, 15 Nov 88; VOYA, Feb 89]

■ *Research Guide to American Historical Biography*. *See* entry 243.

E+
698   VanMeter, Vandelia. **American History for Children and Young Adults: An Annotated Bibliographic Index**. Englewood, Colo.: Libraries Unlimited, 1990. 324p. $32.50. ISBN 0-87287-731-0. LC 90-5815.

This outstanding bibliography of American history, a volume in the Libraries Unlimited Data Book series, is highly recommended for all levels. Titles listed were selected from books reviewed in standard journals between 1980 and 1988, including *Booklist*, *Library Journal*, and *Voice of Youth Advocates*. Also included are in-print titles listed in *American History in Juvenile Books* by Seymour Metzner (H. W. Wilson, 1966).

Each of the 2,901 entries is placed in its historical period and then listed under a Sears subject heading. Information includes title, author/editor, series, publisher/distributor, publication date, cost, physical description, grade level, and brief annotation. Indexed by grade level.

This guide is also available on computer disks: Apple for AppleWorks (microfloppy diskettes only) ($25.00); Mac for Microsoft Works ($26.00); and IBM-ASCII comma delimited files ($25.50). The disk format permits the user to tailor the index to the library's collection and to program a search using various descriptors. [R: ARBA 91; BL, 1 Sept 90; BR, Nov/Dec 90

Atlases

699 **Atlas of American History**. 2d ed. New York: Scribner's, 1984. 306p. $55.00. ISBN 0-684-18411-7. LC 84-675413.

This work, regarded as the standard atlas of American history, was published in 1943 as a supplement to the *Dictionary of American History* and revised in 1978. The 2d edition adds only 12 pages of topical maps (e.g., nuclear power plants, hazardous waste sites, intercontinental ballistic missile bases) and provides some revision for others.

The volume consists of 200 black-and-white maps that represent events from exploration and colonization to the early 1980s. Meticulously drawn maps convey information concisely and clearly, and use of signs and symbols is skillful; these are the hallmarks of this classic work.

An index of some 5,000 entries lists populated places, natural features, and historical events keyed to appropriate maps. Highly recommended, but libraries holding the 1978 edition may want to wait for the next edition before purchasing, since revision is slight.

An older classic atlas is still available: *Atlas of Early American History: The Revolutionary Era, 1761-1790*, edited by Lester Cappon (1976). It is available from either Chicago Newberry Library, or Princeton University Press. [R: ARBA 86]

700 Beck, Warren A., and Ynez D. Haase. **Historical Atlas of the American West**. Norman, Okla.: University of Oklahoma Press, 1989. 1v. (unpaged). $29.95. ISBN 0-8061-2193-9. LC 88-40540.

The American West, as covered by this atlas, encompasses the area that lies west of the meridian running from North Dakota through Texas. Seventy-eight black-and-white maps, located on the left-hand pages, depict such topics as early expedition routes, territorial annexation, livestock and crop distribution, and Indian wars/conflicts. The explanatory text appears on the right-hand pages. A bibliography and index conclude the volume. Recommended for high schools. [R: ARBA 90; BL, 1 Oct 89; WLB, Oct 89]

701 Ferrell, Robert H., and Richard Natkiel. **Atlas of American History**. New York: Facts on File, 1987. 192p. $27.95; $19.95pa. ISBN 0-8160-1028-5; 0-8160-2544-4pa. LC 87-675628.

This atlas focuses on American military history. Almost two-thirds of its two hundred two-tone maps and nine four-tone maps are devoted to wars, from the campaigns and battles of the American Revolution through the invasion of Grenada. American activities in the two world wars, Korea, and Vietnam are well represented. The Mercator projections, drawn to various scales. are easy to use. An essay by historian Ferrell, which attempts to give a survey of the period covered, introduces each of the six sections. Some 140 prints and photographs illustrate the volume.

When compared to Scribner's *Atlas of American History*, this work provides better coverage for the period after the Civil War, especially more recent times, but is not as thorough for the earlier years. The major fault of the Ferrell-Natkiel work is its inadequate index. Despite this criticism, it is a good work. Recommended for high schools. [R: ARBA 89; BR, May/June 88; LJ, Jan 88; RBB, 1 Mar 88; WLB, Jan 88]

702 **Historical Atlas of the United States**. Centennial ed. Wilbur E. Garrett and others, eds. Washington, D.C.: National Geographic Society, 1988. 289p. $59.95. ISBN 0-87044-747-5. LC 88-675398.

In honor of its 100th anniversary, the National Geographic Society donated 35,000 copies of this beautiful atlas to U.S. high schools. The 187 oversized pages contain 300 maps and 450 photographs, plus numerous timelines, graphs, and historical charts.

Six thematic chapters on the land, peoples, boundaries, economy, networks, and communications, and five chronological chapters that highlight changes from 1400 to 1980 make up the volume. The interweaving of thematic and chronological chapters is sometimes confusing. A bibliography that contains notes on all maps, photographs, and other illustrative materials lists sources and consultants for each section. The index to maps and text is essential, since some topics are covered in several sections. The atlas comes with a magnifying glass and an overlay depicting the United States from the perspective of the four scales used in the volume.

This work does not replace other standard atlases, such as Scribner's *Atlas of American History*, but it should be held by most high school libraries. [R: ARBA 90; BL, 1 May 89; LJ, 15 Apr 89]

703 McEvedy, Colin. **The Penguin Atlas of North American History**. New York: Viking Penguin, 1988. 112p. $6.95pa. ISBN 0-14-051128-8.

North American history from 20,000 B.C. to A.D. 1870 is the focus of this small atlas. The continental United States is emphasized, but some coverage for Mexico and the Caribbean is provided.

The 48 full-page maps, in blue, black, white, and gray, and 9 inset maps are clear and uncluttered. The text, printed on the lefthand page, explains boundary changes shown in the map on the right. The maps are not indexed, but the text is. This work does not replace more extensive atlases, but it does provide the basic information high school students require for the time period covered. [R: ARBA 89; BL, 1 Feb 89]

Chronologies

704   Carruth, Gorton. **The Encyclopedia of American Facts & Dates**. 8th ed. New York: Harper & Row, 1987. 1006p. $35.00. ISBN 0-06-181143-2. LC 86-45645.

705   Carruth, Gorton. **What Happened When: A Chronology of Life and Events in America**. New York: Harper & Row, 1989. 499p. $13.95pa. ISBN 0-06-096318-2. LC 88-45550.
   Events and other information contained in the chronologically arranged *Encyclopedia* are presented in four parallel columns: politics and government, war, disasters, and vital statistics; books, paintings, drama, architecture, and sculpture; science, industry, economics, education, religion, and philosophy; and sports, fashion, popular entertainment, folklore, and society. The 8th edition extends coverage to July 4, 1986, and expands facts in many sections. Extensively indexed. Recommended for junior and senior high school libraries.
   What Happened When, the abridged version of the *Encyclopedia*, uses the same four-column format and covers the same topical areas, but it focuses on the most significant historical and cultural events. It, too, is extensively indexed. It is useful for secondary libraries not requiring the detail of the parent volume. [R: ARBA 88]

E+
706   **Chronicle of America**. John W. Kirshon, ed. Mount Kisco, N.Y.: ECAM; distr., New York: Prentice Hall Press, 1989. 956p. $49.95. ISBN 0-13-133745-9.
   This heavily illustrated chronology, which presents events in an easy-to-read newspaper-story style with large headlines, has proven attractive to middle and high school students. Two to five pictures on each page consist of paintings, etchings, photographs, political cartoons, and magazine covers. Each era is prefaced by a survey of the period and a list of important events that occurred at the time. Extensively indexed.
   This work will not replace traditional chronologies, but it deserves a place beside them. The pictures alone are worth the price. It is highly recommended for grades 6 through 12. *Chronicle of the World* is a companion volume. [R: ARBA 91; BL, 15 June 90; BL, 1 Sept 90; VOYA, Mar/Apr 90]

707   Dickson, Paul. **Timelines**. Reading, Mass.: Addison-Wesley Publishing, 1990. 357p. $18.95. ISBN 0-201-17277-1. LC 90-31597.
   For each year from 1945 to 1989, Dickson has compiled a monthly timeline that covers U.S. political, social, cultural, and economic events. Additionally, each year's fads and trends, famous faces, bumper stickers, and words and phrases have special sections. Another section highlights yearly statistical information. The attractive format will appeal to students from junior high level to adult level. Blank lines have been left on each page so readers may record personal and family history. The extensive index allows the reader to trace persons or movements across the years.

708   Gross, Ernie. **This Day in American History**. New York: Neal-Schuman, 1990. 477p. $39.95. ISBN 1-55570-046-2.
   This chronology lists 11,000 significant events and people in American history from precolonial times to the present, with succinct commentary. *The Encyclopedia of American Facts & Dates* contains more information about each event, but *This Day* is current and cheaper. Gross also cites more events in sports and entertainment. Indexed by name and event. [R: ARBA 91; LJ, 15 Sept 90; RBB, 15 Nov 90; WLB, Oct 90]

709   Murphy, Paul C. **Since 1776: A Year-by-Year Timeline of American History**. Los Angeles, Calif.: Price Stern Sloan, 1988. 1v. (unpaged). $6.95pa. ISBN 0-8431-2276-5.
   Libraries from middle school upward will welcome this volume. One page per year, 1776 to 1987, records events in four columns: politics, science and technology, religion, and art/culture. The lack of an index is a handicap in using the work as a reference tool, but its clear and concise language and attractive format make it a worthwhile purchase. However, *Encyclopedia of American Facts & Dates* gives more detailed coverage. [R: ARBA 90; BL, 15 Feb 89]

Dictionaries and Encyclopedias

E+
710   **American Heritage Illustrated History of the United States.** By Robert G. Athearn. Englewood Cliffs, N.J.: Silver Burdett Press, 1989. 19v. $399.00/set. ISBN 0-382-09878-1. LC 89-50419.

This attractive set, which first appeared in 1963, has been reissued with additional material covering the last 25 years. Each volume focuses on an important movement or period in American history and includes two or three chapters of text; two sections of pictures; an essay by a well-known scholar; and an encyclopedic section with entries for people, places, and events related to the theme. The last volume contains an index and bibliography. The books are easy to read, well illustrated (2,500 pictures in all), and informative. The set should appeal to students from upper elementary through lower high school levels. [R: ARBA 90; BL, 1 Dec 89]

711   **Battle Chronicles of the Civil War.** James M. McPherson, ed. New York: Macmillan, 1989. 6v. $299.00/set. ISBN 0-02-920661-8. LC 89-8316.

This history of the Civil War contains 100 essays, by some 40 distinguished historians, reprinted from the periodical *Civil War Times Illustrated*. The essays focus on military campaigns and individual battles, but some cover other aspects of the war.

Each of the first five volumes covers one year of the war, beginning with 1861 and ending with 1865. The final volume contains essays on the leading figures of the war (e.g., Robert E. Lee, Ulysses S. Grant, William T. Sherman, Abraham Lincoln, Jefferson Davis, Stonewall Jackson), a list of recommended readings, and an index. Illustrations throughout the set include black-and-white and sepia photographs, drawings, and maps.

Those purchasing the set also receive a 35-minute videotape, narrated by Edwin Newman, that uses archival photographs and current shots taken at battlefield parks. Secondary schools will find this a valuable source on this tragic period of our country's history. [R: ARBA 91; LJ, 15 Mar 90; RBB, 15 May 90]

712   **The Civil War Battlefield Guide.** Frances H. Kennedy, ed. Boston: Houghton Mifflin, 1990. 317p. $29.95; $16.95pa. ISBN 0-395-52282-X. LC 89-29619.

Issued by the nonprofit Conservation Fund, this concise guide to 65 Civil War battlefields and campaigns of the National Park System was prepared by a distinguished group of historians and politicians. Each essay, illustrated by photographs and a map showing movements of the armies and contemporary/period landmarks, discusses strategy, significant military leaders, casualties, current status of land ownership, and preservation. Additional essays cover the role of Black soldiers and map-making. Special features include a list of battles, combat strengths and casualties, war statistics, a glossary, and an index. For middle and high school levels. [R: ARBA 91]

713   **The Dictionary of Afro-American Slavery.** Randall M. Miller and John David Smith, eds. Westport, Conn.: Greenwood Press, 1988. 866p. $95.00. ISBN 0-313-23814-6. LC 87-37543.

Signed articles by 200 subject specialists explain the terms of slavery (e.g., octaroons, fugitive slaves, hiring out) and related topics such as the culture, daily life, and trading practices pertaining to slavery. This work also contains biographical entries for important persons and statistics on the slave population. Entries that range from one to eight pages in length are supported by brief bibliographies, extensive internal cross-references, and a subject index. [R: ARBA 90; BL, 15 Apr 89; LJ, 1 Apr 89; WLB, Apr 89]

714   **Dictionary of American History.** rev. ed. New York: Scribner's, 1976. 8v. $625.00/set. ISBN 0-684-13856-5.

715   **Concise Dictionary of American History.** New York: Scribner's, 1983. 1140p. $95.00. ISBN 0-684-17321-3. LC 82-42731.

Dictionary of American History, a standard set originally edited by the distinguished historian James Truslow Adams, is the most comprehensive work of its type. The 6,200 articles, which vary from a paragraph to several pages, address all aspects of American history. There are no biographies, however, since historical figures are ably covered in *Dictionary of American Biography*. The signed entries, contributed by over 1,800 scholars, include references for further reading.

The one-volume *Concise* contains abridged versions of all entries contained in the eight-volume set, with updated materials for many entries and new articles that bring coverage to 1982. The alphabetically arranged entries cover a wide range of topics: politics, law, economics, culture, society, science, medicine, and international affairs, from the pre-Columbian period to 1982. This version is highly recommended for secondary schools. [R: ARBA 84]

716   **The Encyclopedia of Colonial and Revolutionary America**. John Mack Faragher, ed. New York: Facts on File, 1990. 484p. $50.00. ISBN 0-8160-1744-1. LC 88-26049.

This work contains a wealth of information about the colonial period and the Revolutionary War. The 1,500 entries cover notables and social, economic, cultural, and military/political topics (e.g., diseases, Indian tribes, religion, each of the original British colonies). Biographical entries (almost half of the total) include all major colonial and Revolutionary figures and many minor figures. Some articles include bibliographies. The volume is supported by 150 black-and-white illustrations, maps, topical guides, and an index.

This reference work includes far more information on the period than other historical dictionaries; nonetheless, it suffers from several sins of omission. Virtually ignored are British West Florida, Spanish rule in Louisiana and Florida, and French participation in the American Revolution. Recommended for high school level. [R: ARBA 91; BL, 1 Feb 90; BR, May/June 90]

■ *Encyclopedia of Southern Culture*. See entry 579.

717   **The Encyclopedia of Southern History**. David C. Roller and Robert W. Twyman, eds. Baton Rouge, La.: Louisiana State University, 1979. 1421p. $95.00. ISBN 0-8071-0575-9. LC 79-12666.

This massive volume covers the history, culture, politics, religions, and other topics concerning the 16 states (and the District of Columbia) where slavery was legal. Some 2,900 signed articles include biography, geography, political and social conditions, agriculture, economics, industry, the arts, and literature. For high schools. [R: ARBA 81]

718   **Franklin D. Roosevelt: His Life and Times**. Otis L. Graham, Jr. and Meghan Robinson Wander, eds. Boston: G. K. Hall, 1985. 472p. $42.00; $22.50pa. ISBN 0-8161-8667-7; 0-306-80410-7pa. LC 84-25149.

This volume in the Presidential Encyclopedia series is far more than a biographical work, since its focus is on the historical period between 1933 and 1945. The 321 readable entries cover notables, events, and concepts of the period. Each is supported by a bibliography, often annotated, and illustrations. There are several in-depth articles on complex topics, such as the elections in which Roosevelt was a candidate. The work, suggested for high school level, is an excellent reference tool for the years of the Roosevelt presidency. The paperback edition is available from Da Capo Press. [R: ARBA 86]

719   Garraty, John A. **1,001 Things Everyone Should Know about American History**. New York: Doubleday, 1989. 207p. $19.95. ISBN 0-385-24432-0. LC 88-14446.

Interesting facts about American history are found in this volume, which is arranged in eight thematic areas. The 1,001 entries concern people, places, music, books, songs, events, and much more. Numerous illustrations and an index finish the volume. History teachers and students in junior and senior high schools will enjoy this volume. [R: ARBA 90; LJ, 1 Apr 89]

720   **Great Battles of the Civil War**. Woodstock, N.Y.: Beekman House; distr., Lincolnwood, Ill.: Publications International, 1989. 96p. $19.95. ISBN 0-517-68765-8. LC 89-63242.

Beginning with background information and a year-by-year account of major campaigns, this work focuses on 36 of the most important battles of the Civil War. Narratives are illustrated by full-color reproductions of Louis Kurz and Alexander Allison's chromolithographs of the 1880s and 1890s, which depict a somewhat romanticized view of the bloodiest war in American history. Sidebars highlight notables and events of the war. This authoritative work is recommended for high schools. [R: ARBA 91]

721   Hargrove, Hondon B. **Black Union Soldiers in the Civil War**. Jefferson, N.C.: McFarland, 1988. 250p. $22.95. ISBN 0-89950-337-3. LC 88-42511.

High school students writing reports will welcome this volume, which discusses the participation of Blacks in the Union Army during the Civil War. The chronologically arranged narrative covers Black soldiers in each battle. Special features include an extensive bibliography and nine appendixes that reprint documents and include rosters and statistics. [R: VOYA, June 89]

722   **The Harry S. Truman Encyclopedia**. Richard S. Kirkendall, ed. Boston: G. K. Hall, 1989. 404p. $60.00. ISBN 0-8161-8915-3. LC 89-38738.

Virtually every event, issue, and notable person from the Truman presidency is included in this volume. Well-written, factual entries that vary from 200 words to several pages are followed by short bibliographies of important works on the topic. Cross-references, an extensive index, and a list of articles inside the front and back covers are also included. This attractive work is suggested for high schools. [R: ARBA 91; BL, 15 Feb 90; VOYA, July 90; WLB, Apr 90]

723 Neely, Mark E., Jr. **The Abraham Lincoln Encyclopedia**. New York: Da Capo Press, c1982, 1984. 368p. $18.95pa. ISBN 0-306-80209-0. LC 81-7296.

Articles about all aspects of Lincoln and his life and the people, places, events, and issues surrounding him are found in this excellent volume. Some 200 photographs, prints, and cartoons of the times are included. Highly recommended for high schools. [R: ARBA 83]

724 Olson, James S. **Historical Dictionary of the 1920s: From World War I to the New Deal, 1919-1933**. Westport, Conn.: Greenwood Press, 1988. 420p. $55.00. ISBN 0-313-25683-7. LC 87-29987.

This volume focuses on prominent persons and events in U.S. history during the 1920s, or from the 1919 Treaty of Versailles to the inauguration of President Franklin D. Roosevelt in 1933. Politicans, sports figures, radicals, writers, and filmmakers; landmark legal cases, legislation, and social issues; and popular culture (e.g., radio shows, games, fads) are covered. Over 700 alphabetically arranged entries are followed by suggestions for further reading. Other features are copious cross-references, a 12-page chronology, and a 43-page topical bibliography. Indexing is primarily by proper name. Appropriate for high school libraries. [R: ARBA 89; BL, 15 Nov 88; WLB, Oct 88]

725 **The Reader's Companion to American History**. Eric Foner and John A. Garraty, eds. Boston: Houghton Mifflin, 1991. 226p. $35.00. ISBN 0-395-51372-3. LC 91-19508.

Similar in scope to the *Concise Dictionary of American History*, this more current and less expensive volume consists of alphabetically arranged entries that range from brief identifications to multipage essays. The work provides signed entries on historical figures, events, movements, issues, sociological topics (e.g., abortion, divorce), and popular culture and personalities. Some 400 subject experts have contributed to this book. The editors have made generous use of *see also* references throughout the well-written, often entertaining text. Recommended for high school libraries. [R: ARBA 92; LJ, 1 Nov 91]

726 Sifakis, Stewart. **Who Was Who in the Civil War**. New York: Facts on File, 1988. 766p. $60.00. ISBN 0-8160-1055-2. LC 84-1596.

This volume contains biographies of some 2,500 individuals, from both the military and civilian life, who were part of the Civil War era (e.g., abolitionists, journalists, politicians, scouts). Wartime accomplishments are emphasized, but briefer information is given for prewar and postwar activities. Short bibliographies follow many entries, and there are some 250 black-and-white illustrations. The appendixes include a chronology of important Civil War events and battles.

Mark Mayo Bowman's *The Civil War Dictionary* (rev. ed. McKay, 1988) and its earlier edition (1959) have fewer (and briefer) biographical entries, but they also describe campaigns, battles, and skirmishes. *Who Was Who in the Civil War* is highly recommended for high school libraries. [R: BL, 1 Oct 88; LJ, July 88]

Source Material

727 **Album of American History**. rev. ed. James T. Adams, ed. New York: Macmillan, c1969, 1981. 3v. $290.00/set. ISBN 0-684-16848-0. LC 74-91746.

728 **Album of American History. Supplement, 1968 to 1982**. New York: Scribner's, 1985. 267p. $65.00. ISBN 0-684-17440-5. LC 82-42761.

The basic 3-volume set presents 3,300 reproductions of photographs and paintings that chronicle American history and life from 1783 to 1968. The supplement adds 300 photographs organized in 10 chapters, covering topical areas such as the presidency, Vietnam, ecology, architecture, and daily life. Captions accompany the black-and-white pictures. Suggested for high schools. [R: ARBA 86]

729 **The Civil War**. Carter Smith, ed. New York: Facts on File, 1989. 1v. (various paging). $125.00 looseleaf w/binder. ISBN 0-8160-1609-7. LC 86-32751.

A part of the American Images on File series, this volume of reproducible illustrations about the Civil War contains over 200 photographs, engravings, lithographs, paintings, and other visual representations. The set includes portraits of many well-known persons of the time (e.g., John Brown, Stephen Douglas, Jefferson Davis, Robert E. Lee, Daniel Webster), pictures of events (e.g., sinking of the *Cumberland*), and maps (e.g., the Underground Railroad).

The volume is divided into seven sections, one for the prelude to the war, one for each of the five war years, and one for Reconstruction. A biographical sketch or description of the event accompanies each picture. Indexed by subject. This set is an excellent source for research papers written by junior and senior high school students.

Other sets in the series include *The Black Experience, Colonial and Revolutionary America, Key Issues in Constitutional History*, and *The Native American Experience* by Lelia Wardwell. *The Faces of America* and *The Faces of America II* are also a part of the series. [R: ARBA 90]

730 **Documents of American History. Volume 1: To 1898**. 10th ed. By Henry S. Commager and others. Englewood Cliffs, N.J.: Prentice-Hall, 1988. $41.00. ISBN 0-13-217274-7.

The first volume of this renowned collection of documents on American history, which appeared in 1974, has been revised. (Volume 2, in preparation, is currently available only in the 1974 edition.) The set includes treaties, letters, speeches, acts, legal decisions, and other documents from 1492 to 1898. Selections are prefaced by brief notes on their historical significance, with some additional references to the topic.

Other collections of documents on American history include *Sources and Documents Illustrating the American Revolution, 1764-1788 and the Formation of the Federal Constitution*, edited by Samuel E. Morrison (2d ed. Oxford University Press, c1929, 1965); *Basic Documents in American History*, edited by Richard B. Morris (Krieger, c1960, 1980); and *Fifty Basic Civil War Documents*, edited by Henry S. Commager (Krieger, c1965, 1982).

See also **Biography** and **Women's Studies**.

E+

731 **The Faces of America**. New York: Facts on File, 1988. $145.00 looseleaf. ISBN 0-8160-1608-9. LC 87-6707.

732 **The Faces of America II**. New York: Facts on File, 1990. 288p. $145.00 looseleaf. ISBN 0-8160-2225-9.

Using the familiar Facts on File format that is intended for reproduction, *Faces of America* contains 300 portraits, each on a single page, of famous Americans. The companion volume, *Faces of America II*, places emphasis on statesmen, reformers, political figures, artists, musicians, and sports personalities. The black-and-white portraits are chronologically arranged and indexed by name and subject. Each sheet also includes a brief biography of the person plus margin notes that identify the process used in creating the original picture and its source. [R: WLB, Apr 89]

733 Wakelyn, Jon L. **Biographical Dictionary of the Confederacy**. Westport, Conn.: Greenwood Press, 1977. 601p. $65.00. ISBN 0-8371-6124-X. LC 72-13870.

The 651 biographies of Confederate leaders include not only generals but also office-holders on national and state levels, businesspeople, farmers, scientists, industrialists, and others who made a significant contribution to the war effort. Sketches of between 200 and 300 words provide basic biographical data, war and postwar activities, and one or two sources for further reading. The appendixes list biographies by geographical area, occupation, religion, education, and political party. [R: ARBA 78]

Biography

734 Wright, Robert K., and Morris J. MacGregor, Jr. **Soldier-Statesmen of the Constitution**. Washington, D.C.: Government Printing Office, 1987. 298p. $25.00; $22.00pa. S/N 008-029-00153-5; S/N 008-029-00159-4pa. LC 87-1353.

The 23 Revolutionary War veterans who were among the creators and signers of the U.S. Constitution are the focus of this beautifully illustrated book. The work includes brief biographies that summarize the careers of each of the soldier-statesmen, with color portraits. Biographies and pictures of other signers and copies of some 25 historical documents are also included. Recommended for high schools.

Historic Places

See also **Geography**.

E+

735 Brownstone, David M., and Irene M. Franck. **Historic Places of Early America**. New York: Macmillan, 1989. 64p. $14.95; $7.95pa. ISBN 0-689-31439-6; 0-689-71234-0pa. LC 88-27521.

Easy-to-read articles about historic places (e.g., Bunker Hill, Mount Vernon, Independence Hall) indicate historical significance and provide at least one photograph. This slim volume is suggested for upper elementary and middle school levels. [R: VOYA, Dec 89]

736 Stevens, Joseph E. **America's National Battlefield Parks: A Guide**. Norman, Okla.: University of Oklahoma Press, 1990. 337p. $29.95. ISBN 0-8061-2268-4. LC 89-40739.

The 38 major national battlefield parks are covered in this excellent volume. Detailed narratives of the events commemorated provide background, strategy, tactics, and consequences. Arranged by region (east to west), entries also give directions for reaching the site, describe facilities and activities available, and assess handicap access. Illustrations include paintings that depict the battle and contemporary photographs. Maps show the battle lines, present-day roads, and numbered stations for auto tours. [R: ARBA 92; WLB, Mar 91]

□ Hobbies and Games □

AMUSEMENTS

See also **Sports**.

■ *All the Best Contests for Kids*. *See* entry 173.

737 Botermans, Jack, and others. **The World of Games: Their Origins and History, How to Play Them, and How to Make Them**. New York: Facts on File, 1989. 240p. $29.95. ISBN 0-8160-2184-8. LC 89-31359.

This volume focuses on 150 games played in every society from ancient to modern times. It is arranged in five broad categories: board, dice, card, dominoes, and activity games. Entries, one-half page to a page in length for each game, begin with a brief historical and geographical survey, followed by a discussion of the objectives, rules, and strategies.

Black-and-white illustrations show some aspects of the game (e.g., playing pieces, the board, hands in a game). Some games are omitted or covered briefly, such as chess and bridge (because entire books focus on them) and Monopoly and Scrabble (because persons interested in these games know about them). Some unexpected inclusions are instructions for making kites, blowing soap bubbles, and playing with tops and yo-yos. Access to the games is via the table of contents only; there is no index.

The volume concludes with a bibliography of 100 classic books on games. The work's chief value consists of its historical coverage of cross-cultural information. High school libraries may wish to consider it. [R: ARBA 90; BL, 1 Feb 90; BR, June 90; LJ, 1 Oct 89]

■ *Contests for Students*. *See* entry 174.

E

738 Delamar, Gloria T. **Children's Counting-Out Rhymes, Fingerplays, Jump-Rope and Bounce-Ball Chants and Other Rhythms: A Comprehensive English-Language Reference**. Jefferson, N.C.: McFarland, 1983. 224p. $19.95. ISBN 0-89950-064-1. LC 82-24904.

Hundreds of favorite rhymes of childhood are listed in this engaging volume. In addition to the types of chants mentioned in the title, there are tongue twisters, repeater tales, and narrative verses for all ages. Instructions are provided where needed. Indexed in one alphabet by title, first line, author, and subject. [R: BL, 1 Oct 83]

739 Dewey, Patrick R. **Interactive Fiction and Adventure Games for Microcomputers 1988: An Annotated Directory**. Westport, Conn.: Meckler, 1988. 189p. $39.50. ISBN 0-88736-170-6. LC 87-16473.

The best known of the interactive computer programs is *Zork*, which may require a week or longer to solve. The author lists and describes interactive and adventure games with which he is familiar and reviews their strengths and weaknesses. For games he does not know, he paraphrases the information printed on the game boxes. Coverage extends to the end of 1987. General information includes name, producer, cost, hardware, level of difficulty, type, and a description. Educators building collections of interactive fiction games for their students will find this guide useful. [R: ARBA 89; BL, 15 Sept 88; WLB, Feb 88]

740 Harbin, E. O., and Bob Sessoms. **The New Fun Encyclopedia**. Nashville, Tenn.: Abingdon Press, 1983-1985. 5v. $47.50/set. ISBN 0-687-27759-0. LC 83-2818.

This standard game book (Cokesbury, 1940) by a youth director for the Methodist church has been revised by Sessoms to reflect language and objects of the 1980s. Other than volumes on home and family fun and sports and outdoor fun, which are sold separately, the set includes *Games*, volume 1, which contains mixers, games for small groups, and other activities suitable for a variety of ages. Volume 2 covers parties and banquets, and volume 4, on skits, plays, and music, also includes magic and puppetry. [R: ARBA 86]

741 Hay, Henry. **The Amateur Magician's Handbook**. 4th ed. New York: E. P. Dutton, 1983. 414p. $5.99pa. ISBN 0-451-15502-5. LC 80-7878.

A standard manual on magic and illusion, this work covers tricks, performing for specific audiences and under varying conditions, and many other topics useful to the amateur magician. The appendix includes biographies of noted magicians, a bibliography, and a list of tricks and illusions. Recommended for middle and high school levels. *Encyclopedia of Card Tricks* by Jean Hugard (Dover, c1937, 1974), another recommended work, gives directions for performing over 600 card tricks.

742 Waters, T. A. **The Encyclopedia of Magic and Magicians**. New York: Facts on File, 1988. 384p. $35.00; $19.95pa. ISBN 0-8160-1349-7; 0-8160-1981-9pa.

This comprehensive guide covers the great magicians, magic techniques and illusions, and views toward the art through the ages. Over 2,000 entries provide readers with a clear understanding of magic. There are more than 100 illustrations. This unique work is recommended for secondary schools. [R: BR, Dec 88; WLB, Apr 89]

Birding. *See* **Birds** in **Zoology**.

CARD GAMES AND BOARD GAMES

743 Arnold, Peter. **The Book of Card Games**. London: Christopher Helm; distr., New York: Hippocrene Books, 1988. 279p. $14.95pa. ISBN 0-87052-730-4.

Entries for 77 card games and their variations include a brief introduction, number of players, dealing, action, and strategy. Entries range from short (e.g., old maid) to more than 20 pages (e.g., bridge). Illustrations include sample hands, melds, and trick-taking. The index lists games for a given number of players (one to five or more), gambling games, and games for children; the table of contents cites games alphabetically. Since books on card games are limited, this one has value, despite its limited information about each game. [R: ARBA 90; RBB, Aug 89]

744 Hooper, David, and Kenneth Whyld. **The Oxford Companion to Chess**. New York: Oxford University Press, 1984. 407p. $29.95; $13.95pa. ISBN 0-19-217540-8; 0-19-281986-0pa. LC 83-23733.

Almost 2,000 alphabetically arranged entries provide information on chess players, games, openings, variations, terms, strategies, and history. Illustrations include photographs of masters, pieces, and board layouts.

Appendixes classify openings (with variations) and tabulate moves and cross-reference them to entries in the text. Also included is a glossary of chess terms in six languages. This outstanding compendium supplants former standard tools such as *Encyclopedia of Chess* by Anne Sunnucks (St. Martin's Press, 1976). [R: ARBA 86]

E +
745   **Hoyle's Rules of Games**. 2d ed. Albert M. Horehead and Geoffrey Mott-Smith, eds. New York: Doubleday, 1983. 408p. $8.95pa. ISBN 0-452-26049-3. LC 83-13297.

The expression "according to Hoyle," which means according to the highest authority, is derived from this work, which has long been considered the authoritative source for the rules of classic games. The 250 games listed include old maid, gin rummy, children's games, chess, cribbage, bridge, poker, and versions of solitaire. There are charts, illustrations, and a glossary of game terms.

746   Keene, Raymond. **The Simon & Schuster Pocket Book of Chess**. New York: Simon & Schuster, 1989. 192p. $12.95; $7.95pa. ISBN 0-671-67923-6; 0-671-67924-4pa. LC 88-30555.

Keene, a British chess champion and international grand master since 1976, has written widely on the game. This work emphasizes chess strategy and tactics and covers rules, algebraic notation, popular openings, the middle game, and the end game. Also included are profiles of world champions and grand masters, a commentary on computer chess, and tournament tips. Some 200 full-color diagrams illustrate the text, and review quizzes conclude each chapter. Highly recommended for beginners and those who wish to review their knowledge of the game. [R: BR, 1 June 89; BR, Nov/Dec 89; Kliatt, Sept 89]

747   Scarne, John. **Scarne's Encyclopedia of Games**. New York: Harper & Row, c1973, 1983. 448p. $13.95pa. ISBN 0-06-091052-6. LC 83-47571.

Instructions for over 1,000 games are found in this authoritative and comprehensive work, a standard for many years. Twenty-eight chapters give the rules for bridge, poker, chess, checkers, and children's and parlor games, as well as variations of solitaire, rummy, pinochle, and hearts. A glossary and index complete the volume.

CLUBS AND ELECTIONS

■ *Directory of American Youth Organizations, 1990-91*. See entry 176.

E +
748   Dunnahoo, Terry. **How to Win a School Election**. New York: Franklin Watts, 1990. 92p. $12.40. ISBN 0-531-10695-0.

Students in grades 5 through 8 who plan to run for a school office will need this volume. Dunnahoo discusses the school election process, the decision to run, offices to seek and what they involve, the nomination and election process, and campaign strategies. Black-and-white drawings, a brief bibliography, and an index are provided. [R: BR, Nov/Dec 89; SLJ, July 89; VOYA, Oct 89]

E +
749   Powers, David Guy, and Mark K. Harmon. **How to Run a Meeting**. rev. ed. New York: Franklin Watts, 1985. 72p. $10.40. ISBN 0-531-04641-9. LC 84-23441.

This slim volume will help students in grades 5 through 8 learn how to conduct a meeting and how to be good club members. The book introduces parliamentary procedure, committee structure, elections, and constitutions and bylaws. This is an excellent introduction to the topic. [R: BL, 15 Apr 85; SLJ, Oct 85]

COLLECTING

750   **Baseball Card Price Guide**. Jeff Kurowski, ed. Iola, Wis.: Krause Publications. annual. $13.95. LC 87-080033.

Baseball card collecting, once a hobby for children, has attracted more and more adults over the last two decades. The increase in interest and value has resulted in the publication of more and more guides. This annual price guide, one of the best, is a catalog of some 75,000 cards issued over the past century. The entries, arranged by the set's best known names and then grouped by years, provide a description of the cards, the price for each in three grade categories, and a reproduction of a sample card. Each player's rookie card is italicized in the citation. This catalog is published under the auspices of *Sports Collectors Digest*.

751   Breen, Walter. **Walter Breen's Complete Encyclopedia of U.S. and Colonial Coins**. New York: Doubleday, 1988. 754p. $100.00. ISBN 0-385-14207-2. LC 79-6855.

Considered to be the definitive encyclopedia of U.S. specie, this volume describes in detail 8,035 coins, using over 4,000 black-and-white illustrations to depict the obverse and reverse of common pieces. Almost every major and minor coin, from the first brass Bermuda shillings (1616) to current sandwich mintage, is included in the 49 topical and chronological chapters.

Each chapter begins with background information. For almost every coin, data includes historical circumstances of issue, physical characteristics, designer, engraver, mint of issue, quantity issued, and rarity. Since the work is an encyclopedia designed for continual use, price information is not given. Highly recommended. [R: ARBA 89; LJ, 1 Sept 88]

752   **Coin World Almanac: A Handbook for Coin Collectors**. 6th ed. Compiled by the staff of *Coin World*. Sidney, Ohio: Amos Press; distr., New York: World Almanac/St. Martin's Press, 1990. 743p. $29.95; $15.95pa. ISBN 0-88687-462-9; 0-88687-460-2pa.

A wealth of information is contained in this compendium, produced by the staff of *Coin World*, a weekly newspaper for the coin trade. The almanac provides information about all areas of numismatics: coins, paper money, coins as an investment, auction records, renowned collections, errors, books and periodicals, organizations, museums, grading, grading services, and bullion issues. Despite this work's advanced nature, it is recommended for secondary schools serving serious collectors. [R: ARBA 91; Kliatt, Jan 91]

753   Cribb, Joe, and others. **The Coin Atlas: The World of Coinage from Its Origins to the Present Day**. New York: Facts on File, 1990. 337p. $40.00. ISBN 0-8160-2097-3. LC 89-1353.

This work, an authoritative and attractive volume, is neither an in-depth study of coinage nor a catalog of every coin. It does, however, provide highlights of the almost 3,000-year history and evolution of coins in 200 modern nations. The authors, curators at the British Museum, describe selected coins and discuss political and other events that have influenced each country's currency. Wonderful graphics and color photographs illustrate the volume. An excellent choice for high schools. [R: ARBA 91; BR, Nov/Dec 90; LJ, July 90]

E +
754   **The Guinness Book of Stamps: Facts & Feats**. By James MacKay. Enfield, England: Guinness; distr., New York: Sterling Publishing, 1982. 225p. $17.95. ISBN 0-85112-241-8. LC 82-241731.

Similar to other Guinness books, this one emphasizes the unusual and superlatives in the history of postage stamps, the postal service, postmarks, kinds of stamps, and other philatelic subjects. Sixteen pages of color illustrations show individual stamps, cancellations, equipment, and more. Indexing is by personal name and place. This interesting work will appeal to stamp collectors of all ages. [R: ARBA 84; BL, July 83; LJ, 15 Apr 83]

E +
755   Hegenberger, John. **Collector's Guide to Comic Books**. Radnor, Pa.: Chilton Book, 1990. 224p. $12.95pa. ISBN 0-87069-548-7.

The author provides a history of comic books and discusses starting a collection, buying comic books, and caring for them. He then indicates sources for purchasing new and used books. This excellent guide is recommended for all levels.

E +
756   Hobson, Burton. **Coin Collecting as a Hobby**. New York: Sterling Publishing, 1982. 192p. $7.95. ISBN 0-8069-6018-3. LC 67-27759.

E +
757   Hobson, Burton. **Stamp Collecting as a Hobby**. New York: Sterling Publishing, 1982. 192p. $13.29. ISBN 0-8069-4795-0.

Beginning coin and stamp collectors in grades 5 and up will enjoy these clearly written guides, which discuss all aspects of their topics, from selecting a hobby and getting started to developing a specialized collection. The coin guide explains how coins are made, coin identification, mint marks, and many other subjects. The stamp guide discusses similar information for stamps and includes over 700 photographs of regular and special issue stamps. These practical guides are highly recommended for young collectors at all levels. [R: ARBA 83; SLJ, Mar 83]

758 Martin-Smith's Official 1948-1989/90 Baseball Card Alphabetical Cross-Reference Guide. By John F. Remark and Nathan M. Bisk. Tampa, Fla.: Martin-Smith, 1989. 623p. $15.95pa. ISBN 0-88128-368-1.

This reference guide to baseball cards lists players alphabetically by name and year, with the card numbers of the various sets (e.g., Fleer) in which they appear. This arrangement differs from most guides, which are classified by the popular name of each set. Rookie cards are listed alphabetically and by year in a separate section. Collectors who wish to identify all cards depicting particular players will need this guide. [R: ARBA 91; LJ, June 89]

759 Reinfeld, Fred, and Burton Hobson. **Catalogue of the World's Most Popular Coins**. 12th ed. New York: Sterling Publishing, 1988. 576p. $6.95pa. ISBN 0-8069-4740-3. LC 83-606.

This frequently revised catalog of coins lists and values over 10,000 of the most interesting, valuable, and popular coins of all ages from more than 350 countries. Countries are listed alphabetically, with coins for each arranged chronologically. Each new edition updates prices and adds new coins.

760 Scott Standard Postage Stamp Catalogue. Sidney, Ohio: Scott Publishing. annual. $49.95/v.; $26.00pa./v.

761 Scott Specialized Catalogue of United States Stamps, 1991. Sidney, Ohio: Scott Publishing, 1990. $39.95; $26.00pa. ISBN 0-89487-151-X; 0-89487-146-3pa.

Considered the most comprehensive stamp catalog available, *Scott Standard* has been published for almost seven decades. It covers the world, with the exception of North Vietnam, North Korea, and Libya. Volume 1 includes stamps issued by English-speaking countries; the remaining three volumes cover all other nations, arranged alphabetically. Each volume has an introduction and explanation of the price/value system. Beginning with the 1989 edition, stamp values have reflected the average retail price; formerly, the price-value structure was significantly higher than the retail price. Each volume has a brief index and an identifier that sorts out seemingly identical issues.

Scott Specialized is exhaustive in its detail of American stamps, well beyond that found in volume 1 of the four-volume set. [R: BL, 1 Nov 90; LJ, 1 Feb 91]

762 Sugar, Bert Randolph, comp. and ed. **The Sports Collector's Bible**. 4th ed. Indianapolis, Ind.: Bobbs-Merrill, 1983. 578p. $12.95pa. ISBN 0-672-52605-0.

Most of this book focuses on baseball trading cards, but sections also cover other baseball collectibles (e.g., programs and scorecards, autographs, books and yearbooks, pins, pennants). The work is valuable only as a checklist of collector's items. Indexed. [R: ARBA 85]

763 Yeoman, R. S. **A Guide Book of United States Coins**. Racine, Wis.: Western Publishing. annual. $7.95.

764 Yeoman, R. S. **Handbook of United States Coins**. Racine, Wis.: Western Publishing. annual. $3.95pa.

A Guide Book of United States Coins, known as the "Red Book," is an outstanding reference on U.S. coins designed for use in identifying and grading coins. All issues from 1616 to the present are covered. The guide provides historical data, statistics, values, and detailed photographs for each coin. Additional sections deal with specialties such as Civil War and Hard Times tokens, misstruck coins, and uncirculated and proof sets. Prices provided are based on dealer averages.

Handbook of United States Coins, the "Blue Book," is a complementary work that gives the standard wholesale price list for U.S. coins from colonial times to the present. Photographs are provided for each coin.

Crafts. *See* **Arts and Crafts** in **Decorative Art** for crafts.

OUTDOOR RECREATION

See **Natural Resource Science** for nature study.

765 Blandford, Percy W. **Maps and Compasses**. 2d ed. Blue Ridge Summit, Pa.: TAB Books, 1991. $22.95; $14.95pa. ISBN 0-8306-2141-5; 0-8306-2140-7pa. LC 83-24218.

Maps and compass skills explained in this volume are useful for indoor and outdoor purposes. Blandford presents clear instructions on such things as map reading, the use of different types of maps, and mapmaking. A directory of map sources, a glossary, and index complete the volume. Recommended for middle and high schools.

Suggested for the same audience is *Land Navigation Handbook* by W. S. Kals (Sierra Club Books, 1983), which is a map and compass primer for anyone who needs to chart a course in the wilderness.

E+
766 **Boy Scouts of America. Fieldbook**. 3d ed. Bellwood, Ill.: Boys Scouts of America, c1985, 1989. 640p. $7.95pa. ISBN 0-8395-3200-8. LC 84-72053.

The *Fieldbook* is a worthwhile guide for those involved in outdoor activities as well as Boy Scouts. The volume addresses hiking, camping, mountaineering, horseback riding, cross-country skiing, swimming, orienteering, canoeing, fitness conditioning, first aid, and outdoor safety. The concise text is supplemented by clear black-and-white and color photographs. Recommended for grades 5 and up.

767 Elman, Robert, with Clair Rees. **The Hiker's Bible**. rev. ed. New York: Doubleday, 1982. 148p. $4.95pa. ISBN 0-385-17505-1. LC 81-43776.

Designed for the beginning hiker, this slim book covers the basics: shoes, clothing, canteens, and other supplies; safety; foot care; using compasses; walking while carrying a pack; and other important topics. Additional information includes a state-by-state list of trails; major trail systems; a directory of hiking organizations; Canadian hiking information; and suggestions for bike-hikes, canoe and horseback trips, and mountaineering.

Walking Softly in the Wilderness by John Hart (rev. ed. Sierra Club Books, 1984) provides basic information on gear and supplies, camping, safety, and other topics. *The Complete Walker III* by Fletcher Colin (3d ed. Alfred A. Knopf, 1984), the definitive guide on the subject, is appropriate for the more experienced hiker and backpacker.

768 Olsen, Larry Dean. **Outdoor Survival Skills**. 5th ed. Chicago: Chicago Review Press, 1990. 240p. $11.95pa. ISBN 1-55652-084-0. LC 89-49670.

Olsen is a highly regarded survival skills instructor. The basic and special survival skills that he covers are written in simple language and illustrated by examples of conditions one might encounter in the wild. Photographs, including plates of basic plants and other foods found in the wild, enhance the volume.

SUMMER CAMPS

769 **Guide to Summer Camps and Summer Schools 1990/91**. 26th ed. Boston: Porter Sargent, 1990. 488p. $26.00; $21.00pa. ISBN 0-87558-123-4; 0-87558-125-0pa. LC 37-4715.

This standard directory of youth camps and summer schools is updated biennially from questionnaires sent to United States and Canadian directors. It gives detailed information on student body (e.g., boys, girls) age, grade level, number accepted, fees, day or boarding, and special activities for some 1,100 programs. Indexed geographically and by name. A classified index gives access to special offerings, such as remedial and tutorial programs, dance, computers, and mountain climbing. [R: ARBA 92]

E+
770 **Peterson's Summer Opportunities for Kids and Teenagers, 1991**. 8th ed. Terry Schneider and John Wells, eds. Princeton, N.J.: Peterson's Guides, 1990. 591p. $33.95; $17.95pa. ISBN 0-87866-971-X; 0-87866-972-8pa. ISSN 0894-9417.

Some 1,300 summer developmental programs for elementary through high school students are arranged geographically in chart format. Program types include traditional camps, summer schools, workshops, college-sponsored programs, travel groups, and special programs. Codes and symbols indicate gender, age, grade levels, lodging availability, and activities emphasized. A program profile section supplies cost, length, focus, year established, and contact person (with address and telephone number). Some programs are given in-depth treatment. The guide also provides sections on programs with religious affiliations, programs that offer financial assistance, and special programs designed for handicapped or emotionally disturbed children. The directory is also useful to teenagers seeking summer employment as counselors. Recommended for all levels.

TRIVIA

E
771   Sobol, Donald J. **Encyclopedia Brown's Third Record Book of Weird & Wonderful Facts.** New York: William Morrow, 1985. 134p. $11.95. ISBN 0-688-05705-5. LC 85-11613.

Encyclopedia Brown's provides trivia fun with some 300 illustrated entries for children in grades 3 through 6. While these odd facts are entertaining, there are more serious collections of factual data, also interesting, such as *Macmillan Illustrated Almanac for Kids* and *Universal Almanac*. [R: SLJ, Dec 85]

■ *Summer on Campus. See* entry 368.

WORD GAMES

772   Moore, Thurston. **The Original Word Game Dictionary.** Chelsea, Minn.: Scarborough House, 1983. $16.95; $8.95pa. ISBN 0-8128-2926-3; 0-8128-6191-4pa. LC 83-42631.

The dictionary introduces beginners to 40 word games (e.g., Scrabble, Lexicon, Boggle) and provides a list of 27,000 words of 9 characters or less to use in playing them. Each game is briefly described with a chart showing manufacturer, number of players, and age level. Also included are nine parlor games that require no special equipment. The dictionary section gives simple definitions, and a supplement addresses word game skills and offers advice on using the games to increase vocabulary. [R: ARBA 85; BL, 15 Jan 84]

773   **Oxford Guide to Word Games.** By Tony Augarde. New York: Oxford University Press, 1984. 250p. $14.95; $7.95pa. ISBN 0-19-214144-9; 0-19-282005-2pa. LC 83-25140.

The *Oxford Guide* provides background information on classic word games such as crossword puzzles, rebuses, riddles, puns, and Scrabble, each in a separate chapter. For each, the work supplies the game's origin, explains how it is played, illustrates it, and notes variations. The detailed information makes this a basic source on the best-known word games of all times. [R: BL, 1 June 85]

774   **The Random House Crossword Puzzle Dictionary.** New York: Random House, 1989. 1093p. $19.95. ISBN 0-394-53513-8. LC 88-32554.

This work is a boon to crossword puzzle fans who do not view "looking it up" as an unethical practice. Its content is based on the *Random House Dictionary* and thesaurus files. Terms are listed alphabetically and then by the number of letters in the synonym (numbered), arranged in descending order. Where it seems appropriate, other information is given; for example, the names of horses belonging to famous riders are listed under the entry word *horse*. Thus, this dictionary is useful for purposes other than solving crossword puzzles and browsing. *The New York Times Crossword Puzzle Dictionary* by Thomas Pulliam and Clare Grundman (2d ed. Warner Books, c1984, 1989) is another comprehensive work that arranges terms first by number of letters and then alphabetically. [R: ARBA 90; WLB, Oct 89]

☐ # **Holidays and Special Days** ☐

See **Religion** for religious customs.
See **History** for historical chronologies.
See **Earth Sciences** for geological chronologies.

E
775   Bauer, Caroline Feller. **Celebrations: Read-Aloud Holidays and Theme Book Programs**. Bronx, N.Y.: H. W. Wilson, 1985. 301p. $42.00. ISBN 0-8242-0708-4. LC 85-714.

This work consists of 16 read-aloud children's book programs based on holidays, events, and other phenomena. *Celebrations* brings to life such notable "holidays" as National Nothing Day, Gone Fishin', and Pigmania (a paper-cutting story of the Three Little Pigs), and traditional holidays such as Christmas, Valentine's Day, and Halloween. Each celebration features prose selections, poetry, bulletin board displays, snacks (easy recipes), and activities. Highly recommended.

E+
776   **Chase's Annual Events: Special Days, Weeks & Months**. Chicago: Contemporary Books. annual. $27.95. ISSN 0740-5286. LC 57-14540.

The current volume of this standard work, published annually since 1958, identifies some 9,000 events, many new to this edition. Arranged in a calendar format and illustrated with small woodcuts, the book identifies each special occurrence anywhere in the world: holidays; holy, national, and ethnic days; seasons; astronomical phenomena; festivals; fairs; anniversaries; birthdays; special events; and traditional observances of all kinds. Addresses are given for sponsors for further information.

Also provided are tables for phases of natural phenomena, time zones, hurricane names, anniversary gift lists, lists of major awards, and facts about each state. Indexes by name of the event, location, and broad subject give access to this unique work, which is recommended for all levels. [R: ARBA 91; BL, 15 Dec 90]

E+
777   Dunkling, Leslie. **A Dictionary of Days**. New York: Facts on File, 1988. 176p. $22.95; $10.95pa. ISBN 0-8160-1416-9; 0-8160-2138-4pa. LC 88-3825.

Dunkling's delightful and informative work, a compendium of named days, contains over 800 entries that focus on the real and the imaginary. Real days include all kinds of events in the English-speaking world—national, regional, historical, ethnic, sporting, military, religious, and business. Days celebrated in literature include those mentioned in the works of Shakespeare, Boswell, and others, and in titles of books, such as *Day of the Jackal*.

In an A-to-Z arrangement (Acadia Day to Yule Day), Dunkling explains the day's significance, gives its fixed or movable date, and notes its place of celebration. He also cites reference works used in collecting the information, such as *Oxford English Dictionary* and *Brewer's Dictionary of Phrase and Fable*.

This work is more selective than Gregory's *Anniversaries and Holidays*, but it provides more information about the day's significance. Recommended as a browsing and ready-reference tool. [R: ARBA 89; BL, Aug 88; LJ, 15 Apr 88; WLB, May 88]

■ *Folklore of American Holidays*. See entry 1708.

E+
778   Gregory, Ruth W. **Anniversaries and Holidays**. 4th ed. Chicago: American Library Association, 1983. 262p. $27.00. ISBN 0-8389-0389-4. LC 83-3784.

This standard guide to some 4,000 events is divided into three parts: a calendar of fixed days (the largest section), which offers day-to-day anniversaries and holidays with background information about each; a calendar of movable days, subdivided according to the Christian, Islamic, Eastern, and Western worlds; and an annotated bibliography about anniversaries and holidays. Useful at all levels. [R: ARBA 85]

E+
779   Haglund, Elaine J., and Marcia L. Harris. **On This Day: A Collection of Everyday Learning Events and Activities for the Media Center, Library, and Classroom**. Englewood, Colo.: Libraries Unlimited, 1983. 470p. $21.50. ISBN 0-87287-502-4.

This calendar of "learning events" is arranged in five parts: "Events and Activities," a chronological list of events for every day of each month; "Extra-Know-How," techniques for using the information in the first section and addresses for obtaining more information; "Task Cards" of suggested activities; "Reproducibles," with worksheets and diagrams; and "Sample Packet," which has directions and worksheets for individual contract-based programs. Appendixes list famous persons included in the calendar who represent special groups (e.g., Black, Native American, women) by month. A bibliography and index conclude the volume. Appropriate for all levels. [R: ARBA 84; BL, 1 June 83; SBF, Sept/Oct 83]

E+
780   Hatch, Jane M., comp. and ed. **American Book of Days**. 3d ed. Bronx, N.Y.: H. W. Wilson, 1978. 1214p. $50.00. ISBN 0-8242-0593-6. LC 78-16239.

More than 700 articles explore our nation's history through birthdays of celebrities; anniversaries of great events; religious and secular holidays; and celebrations connected with sports, commerce, and local customs. The arrangement, January through December, is supported by a detailed index that provides access to topic, name, and event. The appendix contains information on the calendar, days of the week, the zodiac, and other topics. [R: ARBA 80]

E
781   **Holidays**. Santa Barbara, Calif.: ABC-Clio, 1990. 300p. $21.95pa. ISBN 0-87436-592-9.

In this work, over 200 ideas for displays, programs, and library promotions that celebrate the major secular and religious holidays (including festivities such as Children's Book Week) are described. Suggestions range from a brief paragraph to complete lesson plans for media programs. Ideas were gleaned from issues of *School Library Media Activities Monthly* published over a five-year period. Recommended for elementary schools.

782   **Holidays and Anniversaries of the World: A Comprehensive Catalogue Containing Detailed Information on Every Month and Day of the Year....** 2d ed. Jennifer Mossman, ed. Detroit: Gale, 1990. 1080p. $85.00. ISBN 0-8103-4870-5. ISSN 1045-2621. LC 85-10350.

For each day of the year, this work cites and briefly describes holidays, saint's days, birthdays of the famous, and world historical events. At the beginning of each month, an introduction lists movable holidays, special religious days, and special events. This work includes 23,000 holidays and anniversaries, more events than other books of its kind, but the entries are briefer than those found in such standard works as Gregory's *Anniversaries and Holidays*. [R: ARBA 91; LJ, 1 Mar 90]

E
783   Hughes, Paul. **The Days of the Week: Stories, Songs, Traditions, Festivals, and Surprising Facts about the Days of the Week from All Over the World**. Ada, Okla.: Garrett Educational Corp., 1989. 63p. $15.95. ISBN 0-944483-32-1. LC 89-11758.

784   Hughes, Paul. **The Months of the Year: Stories, Songs, Traditions, Festivals, and Surprising Facts about the Months of the Year from All Over the World**. Ada, Okla.: Garrett Educational Corp., 1989. 63p. $15.95. ISBN 0-944483-33-X.

Days of the Week gives a brief history of the name of each day, lists its name in 17 languages, and describes a perpetual calendar. *Months of the Year* lists the months in 13 languages; discusses the lunar and solar year; supplies the Moslem, Jewish, Hindu, and Chinese calendars; and indicates the flower and gemstone of each month. For each day of the week and month of the year, Hughes provides folk beliefs, sayings, and superstitious associations. These two small books bring together enjoyable information for children in grades 3 to 6. [R: SLJ, June 90]

E+
785   Limburg, Peter R. **Weird! The Complete Book of Halloween Words**. New York: Bradbury Press/Macmillan, 1989. 122p. $12.95. ISBN 0-02-759050-X. LC 88-38678.

Written in a conversational style, this slim volume presents etymologies of terms and words related to Halloween and traces them to their present day use within the context of the holiday. "Do You Know," which addresses several related words, follows several of the definitions. A table of contents and an index give structure to the randomly arranged entries. The book is profusely and humorously illustrated with pen-and-ink drawings. A worthwhile addition to the holiday collection. [R: ARBA 91; BL, 1 Sept 89; SLJ, Sept 89]

■ *This Day in American History*. See entry 708.

Law

DICTIONARIES AND ENCYCLOPEDIAS

786   **Academic Freedom**. Haig A. Bosmajian, ed. New York: Neal-Schuman, 1988. 176p. $35.00. ISBN 1-55570-004-7.

787   **Freedom of Expression**. Haig A. Bosmajian, ed. New York: Neal-Schuman, 1988. 117p. $35.00. ISBN 1-55570-003-9.

788   **The Freedom of Religion**. Haig A. Bosmajian, ed. New York: Neal-Schuman, 1987. 163p. $35.00. ISBN 1-55570-002-0. LC 86-33317.

789   **The Freedom to Publish**. Haig A. Bosmajian, ed. New York: Neal-Schuman, 1989. 230p. $35.00. ISBN 1-55570-005-5.

790   **The Freedom to Read: Books, Films, and Plays**. Haig A. Bosmajian, ed. New York: Neal-Schuman, 1987. 205p. $35.00. ISBN 1-55570-001-2.
These five volumes in the First Amendment in the Classroom series begin with a foreword by a First Amendment advocate and an introduction by Bosmajian. The main body of each volume explains how important cases (chronologically arranged) have tested these rights over the past 30 years. Indexed by specific topic and case. Professional libraries should hold this important set. The five books are available as a set for $150.00. [R: ARBA 91; SLJ, Apr 89]

791   **Black's Law Dictionary: Definitions of the Terms and Phrases of American and English Jurisprudence, Ancient and Modern, with Guide to Pronunciation**. 6th ed. By Henry Campbell Black and others. St. Paul, Minn.: West Publishing, 1990. 1657p. $24.95. ISBN 0-314-76271-X. LC 90-36225.
First published in 1891, *Black's* is a standard tool in most general libraries. It includes legal words, terms, and maxims in all areas of law. Terms affected by legislation or court decisions are indicated with appropriate citations. *Ballantine's Law Dictionary with Pronunciations* by William S. Andrews (3d ed. Lawyers Co-operative, 1969) is another widely used work. [R: ARBA 92]

792   Fay, John J. **The Police Dictionary and Encyclopedia**. Springfield, Ill.: Charles C. Thomas, 1988. 370p. $32.75. ISBN 0-398-05494-0. LC 88-10133.
Some 5,000 terms, phrases, and concepts from law enforcement, police slang, and street slang are clearly defined. Important Supreme Court cases that affected law enforcement are summarized. The appendixes include definitions of felony and capital offenses, sentences for various types of crimes, methods of execution, and other useful information. This work is designed for law enforcement professionals, but its subject matter and clear language make it useful for a broad clientele. [R: ARBA 90]

793   Gifis, Steven H. **Law Dictionary**. 3d ed. Hauppauge, N.Y.: Barron's Educational Series, 1991. 638p. $11.95pa. ISBN 0-8120-4628-5. LC 90-28288.
Definitions in this work, some 3,000 in all, are abridged to meet the quick-reference needs of law students and lawyers. The scope of the 2d edition has been expanded to include corporate, securities, and tax law terms. Clearly written definitions contain documented citations. A key to using the dictionary explains its letter-by-letter arrangement and cross-referencing system. This is a good basic source for high school libraries. [R: ARBA 92]

794   The Guide to American Law: Everyone's Legal Encyclopedia. St. Paul, Minn.: West Publishing, 1985. 12v. $900.00/set. ISBN 0-314-73224-1. LC 83-1134.

This comprehensive work, the first of its kind, provides encyclopedic coverage of American law in nontechnical language. Some 4,600 entries, including 420 major articles, deal with legal principles and concepts, landmark documents, historic events, legal organizations, famous legal practitioners, government departments and regulatory agencies, and more.

Each volume begins with a topical table of contents and ends with a detailed name and subject index. Entries, varying from a brief identification to 20 or more pages, are illustrated with photographs, portraits, and cartoons. An appendix in each volume supplies a table of cited cases and popular name acts. The last volume gives the text of important legal documents; sample legal forms; and separate indexes to the set for quotations by speaker and topic, illustrations, names, and subjects. [R: ARBA 86; BL, July 84; LJ, 15 Sept 85]

795   Kurian, George Thomas. World Encyclopedia of Police Forces and Penal Systems. New York: Facts on File, 1988. 582p. $95.00. ISBN 0-8160-1019-6. LC 88-3553.

This work, the first of its kind, surveys the police forces of 183 nations. For each country the encyclopedia gives a history of the force; its current structure, recruitment, and training practices; and a description of its penal system. Appendixes include directories for Interpol and world police forces. For high schools. [R: ARBA 90; BL, 15 Sept 89; LJ, May 89; WLB, May 89]

796   Leonard, Robin D., and Stephen R. Elias. Family Law Dictionary. Berkeley, Calif., Nolo Press, 1990. 181p. $13.95pa. ISBN 0-87337-129-1. LC 88-60701.

As it stands, *Family Law* covers a wide range of topics within the family law category: adoption, alimony, battered women's syndrome, custody, divorce, marriage, surrogate mother, summaries of important cases, and major legislation such as the Uniform Marriage and Divorce Act (UMDA).

Geared to general audiences, the definitions are written in plain English. The authors also use illustrative examples to clarify certain legal usages. Tables within the text expand on particular definitions and usually show how a point of law is handled in each state, such as factors for setting or terminating alimony, defenses to custodial interference, fault considerations in distributing marital property, and grounds for divorce. *See also* notations are appended to most entries, with cross-references indicated in boldface type within the main text.

This dictionary fills an important niche in the area of popular legal references. The book's easy-to-understand definitions, appealing format, and low cost make it suitable for high school.

797   The Oxford Companion to Law. By David M. Walker. New York: Oxford University Press, 1980. 1366p. $65.00. ISBN 0-19-866110-X. LC 79-40846.

Concise entries provide definitions for legal institutions, courts, judges, jurists, systems, branches of law, legal ideas and concepts, doctrines, and principles. The work has broad coverage of Western legal systems, with long survey articles on each country, but British law is emphasized. However, the United States is well covered. [R: ARBA 81; WLB, Oct 80]

HANDBOOKS

798   Congressional Quarterly's Guide to the U.S. Supreme Court. 2d ed. By Elder Witt. Washington, D.C.: Congressional Quarterly, 1989. 1060p. $149.00. ISBN 0-87187-502-0. LC 89-22262.

An update of the 1979 edition, this revision retains the same broad topic arrangement as the first (e.g., origins and developments, the Court and the individual, the Court and the federal system). It offers an informative, encyclopedic look at the Court's history, procedures, members, and significant rulings and events through the 1988-1989 term. Indexed by name/subject and cases. *A Reference Guide to the United States Supreme Court*, edited by Stephen P. Elliot (Facts on File, 1986), also provides comprehensive coverage of the Court's origin, history, structure, function, activities, decisions, and influence. Both works are highly recommended. [R: ARBA 91]

799   Guggenheim, Martin, and Alan Sussman. The Rights of Young People. 2d ed. New York: Bantam Books, 1985. 312p. $4.95pa. ISBN 0-553-24818-9.

This American Civil Liberties Union handbook focuses on the rights and legal status of young people, infants through age 18. The question-and-answer format covers three major areas: juvenile delinquency, child abuse and neglect, and adolescents' rights to medical treatment. Extensive endnotes cite legal cases in each area. The appendixes list such things as legal organizations concerned with the rights of young people, state-by-state summaries of ages of majority and consent, compulsory school attendance age, and alcohol/tobacco legal buying age. This handbook is recommended for high schools. [R: ARBA 86; BL, 1 Feb 85; Kliatt, Fall 85]

800   Hay, Peter. **The Book of Legal Anecdotes**. New York: Facts on File, 1989. 314p. $24.95. ISBN 0-8160-1523-6. LC 88-19925.
    Hundreds of serious and humorous anecdotes about lawmakers, jurists, lawyers, and others involved with the legal profession will be found in this entertaining and informative volume. The stories, ranging from a few sentences to several pages, are topically arranged (e.g., personalities, sentencing, courtroom boredom). All eras are covered, and stories about many famous individuals, such as Daniel Webster, Abraham Lincoln, and Oliver Windell Holmes, are included. For high schools. [R: BR, Sept/Oct 87; LJ, Aug 89]

■ *Leaders and Lawyers. See* entry 337.

801   Lindop, Edmund. **The Bill of Rights and Landmark Cases**. New York: Franklin Watts, 1989. 144p. $12.90. ISBN 0-531-10790-6. LC 89-8960.
    This work provides an informative and readable description of the Bill of Rights, fundamental freedoms, legal protection, and individual rights. It also explains how personal and civil liberties are involved. Issues such as flag burning, the death penalty, and abortion are examined, as are landmark decisions that the courts have made concerning the Bill of Rights. [R: BL, 1 Jan 90; BR, Jan/Feb 90; SLJ, Nov 89; VOYA, Feb 90]

802   Marwick, Christine M. **Your Right to Government Information**. 2d ed. Carbondale, Ill.: Southern Illinois University Press, 1985. 352p. $4.95pa. ISBN 0-8093-9960-1.
    The rights of individuals to information in government files, equal protection, due process, and privacy are discussed in question-and-answer format similar to that of other American Civil Liberties Union handbooks. The clearly written guide also explains how to obtain information contained in federal files, a process created by the Privacy Act of 1974. Recommended for high schools. [R: BL, 15 Feb 85; Kliatt, Fall 85]

803   Sack, Steven Mitchell. **The Employee Rights Handbook: Answers to Legal Questions—From Interview to Pink Slip**. New York: Facts on File, 1991. 240p. $24.95. ISBN 0-8160-2064-7.
    The Employee Rights Handbook is a guide to getting, holding, and leaving a job. It includes practical advice, such as steps to take when resigning or getting fired; what one should do in the face of discrimination because of race, age, religion, or handicap; and how to protect oneself from on-the-job sexual harassment. It also contains copies of employment contracts, releases, personnel manuals, and similar documents. Other features include charts of legal issues on a state-by-state basis, decisions in recent court cases concerning employment, and a glossary of terms. Recommended for high schools.

804   **The Supreme Court at Work**. Carolyn Goldinger, ed. Washington, D.C.: Congressional Quarterly, 1990. 351p. $15.95pa. ISBN 0-87187-540-3. LC 89-71226.
    This work provides an account of the procedure and decisions of the Supreme Court over the past 200 years. Part 1 surveys its history, from the first session in New York City in 1790 to its present status as the most powerful court in the world. Part 2 explains how it works: setting the schedule, workload, procedure, opinions, reporting, precedents, and more. Biographies of the Court's members constitute part 3, and part 4 reviews its major decisions from 1790 through 1989. This work contains historical, theoretical, and anecdotal material that high school social studies teachers and students will find useful. [R: ARBA 91; LJ, July 90; Kliatt, Sept 90]

CRIME

805   De Sola, Ralph. **Crime Dictionary**. rev. ed. New York: Facts on File, 1988. 222p. $27.95. ISBN 0-8160-1872-3. LC 87-20133.
    An enlarged and updated version of a 1982 work, this dictionary defines more than 10,000 terms about all aspects of crime (e.g., acronyms and abbreviations, legal terminology for various offenses, slang or argot words, nicknames, foreign phrases). It is a worthwhile addition to any library requiring a ready-reference source on crime. [R: ARBA 89; BL, Aug 88; BR, Dec 88]

806　**Encyclopedia of Crime and Justice**. Sanford H. Kadish, ed. New York: Free Press/Macmillan, 1983. 4v. $375.00/set. ISBN 0-02-918110-0. LC 83-7156.

The nature and causes of criminal behavior, the laws that define it, and the punishment and treatment of offenders constitute the focus of this authoritative work. It has been prepared by experts in criminal justice, law, sociology, and related fields. The 186 broad topic articles, varying from 1,000 to 10,000 words, explain basic concepts, with their history and landmark legal decisions. The set emphasizes the United States but often makes comparisons with other nations.

Special features include a guide to legal citations and documents, an extensive glossary, tables of cases, and legal and general indexes. The work is directed toward professionals and students in fields related to criminal justice, but it is also useful for general audiences at the high school level. [R: ARBA 84; BL, 1 Oct 84; WLB, Feb 84]

807　**The Encyclopedia of Police Science**. William G. Bailey, ed. Hamden, Conn.: Garland, 1989. 718p. (Garland Reference Library of Social Science, v.413). $85.00. ISBN 0-8240-6627-8. LC 88-11455.

Intended as an introduction to the subject, the 143 entries in this volume survey all aspects of police work—administrative issues, types of crime, psychological factors, social issues, famous individuals, and histories of various police departments. Also provided are step-by-step procedures for different kinds of investigations, statistical tables, and important legal cases. Bibliographies conclude most articles, and in addition there are a lengthy bibliography of police history and a bibliography of bibliographies. Indexes include a general one and another by legal cases cited. [R: ARBA 90; LJ, 15 Apr 89; RBB, July 89; WLB, May 89]

808　Nash, Jay Robert. **Encyclopedia of World Crime: Criminal Justice Criminology, and Law Enforcement**. 6v. Wilmette, Ill.: CrimeBooks; distr., North Bellmore, N.Y.: Marshall Cavendish, 1990. $500.00/set. ISBN 0-923582-00-2. LC 88-92729.

World Crime is written in a popular tone, making the set an excellent acquisition for high school library media centers. Articles on persons and places from early times to the present, selected on the basis of historical prominence, are based on a wide range of material provided by correctional and criminal facilities, criminal investigation agencies, public media, historical societies, and worldwide police departments. The biographical, historical, and literary articles in volumes 1-4 are supported by bibliographies that include film and works of fiction. Volume 5, a dictionary of crime terms, covers individuals, events, and literature; volume 6 consists of an index and documentation for the set. [R: ARBA 92; BL, 1 Oct 90; LJ, Aug 90; SLJ, May 91]

809　Sander, Daryl. **Focus on Teens in Trouble: A Reference Handbook**. Santa Barbara, Calif.: ABC-Clio, 1991. 182p. (Teenage Perspectives). $35.00. ISBN 0-87436-207-5. LC 90-24777.

This reference handbook defines, offers commentary on, and references fiction, nonfiction, and nonprint materials related to youth gangs and violence, teenage substance abuse, crime, and teenage runaways. The work is well organized; individual chapters relate to each of the topics and include information such as hotline resources and organizations dealing with legal services for children. One chapter addresses statistics about teens in trouble.

The inclusion of an extensive index and resource lists (with brief descriptors) of 16mm film and videotape resources dated mostly from the mid-1970s to the late 1980s enhance this title. This relatively simple work is appropriate for a youthful readership and teachers or counselors at the junior high or high school level.

810　Sifakis, Carl. **The Encyclopedia of American Crime**. New York: Facts on File, 1982. 816p. $49.95. ISBN 0-87196-620-4. LC 81-600.

811　Sifakis, Carl. **The Mafia Encyclopedia**. New York: Facts on File, 1988. 367p. $40.00; $17.95pa. ISBN 0-8160-1172-9; 0-8160-1856-1pa. LC 84-21220.

American Crime deals with crime, scams and hoaxes, victims of crime, gangs, criminal justice and law terminology, persons whose careers relate to crime, and well-known criminals from the seventeenth century to the 1980s. Over 200 photographs, drawings, and charts illustrate the volume. Indexed by type of crime and geographical location.

Mafia Encyclopedia, a similar work, provides over 400 entries about the Mafia and organized crime during the past century. Major syndicate criminals are covered (e.g., Al Capone, John Gotti, Meyer Lansky, Longy Zwillman), as are crime techniques, myths and lore, and locations associated with organized crime in America.

812 Stark, James, and Howard Goldstein. **The Rights of Crime Victims**. New York: Boston, 1985. 347p. $4.95pa. ISBN 0-8093-9952-0.

In a question-and-answer format similar to that of other American Civil Liberties Union handbooks, this volume explains the rights of crime victims to restitution, actual and punitive damages, and additional compensations. Victims of rape, domestic violence, and other crimes are discussed. The appendix provides a state-by-state analysis of victim compensation laws. [R: BL, 15 Feb 85]

HUMAN RIGHTS

813 **Amnesty International Report**. London: Amnesty International; distr., New York: Dodd, Mead. annual. $10.00pa.

This annual contains Amnesty International's assessment of the status of human rights abuses in over 100 countries. Nations are arranged alphabetically within regional groups. The appendix reprints human rights resolutions and documents.

814 **Basic Documents on Human Rights**. 3d ed. Ian Brownlie, ed. New York: Oxford University Press, 1981. 505p. $89.00; $38.00pa. ISBN 0-19-825683-3; 0-19-825712-0pa. LC 79-27225.

This collection of representative international documents related to human rights is arranged in 10 categories, each with an introductory survey and bibliographic references. Sections include such areas as concepts of equality; fundamental rights in national legal systems; and conventions sponsored by the United Nations, the International Labor Office, and Unesco.

815 Fenton, Thomas P., and Mary J. Heffron, comps. and eds. **Human Rights: A Directory of Resources**. Maryknoll, N.Y.: Orbis Books, 1989. 156p. $9.95pa. ISBN 0-88344-534-4. LC 89-9295.

This book, a part of the Third World Resources Directory series, uses the term *human rights* to include economic issues as well as individual freedom and security. The work is divided into five chapters that cover organizations, books, periodicals, pamphlets and articles, and audiovisual material. The selection focuses on human rights in the Third World but includes material from elsewhere. The appendix lists Amnesty International national sections in 41 countries. Subject indexes give access to organizations, individuals, titles, notations, and subjects. [R: ARBA 90]

816 Jacobs, William Jay. **Great Lives: Human Rights**. New York: Scribner's, 1990. 278p. $22.95. ISBN 0-684-19036-2. LC 89-37211.

Jacobs presents the lives of some 30 men and women known principally for their defense of individual freedoms. Arranged in four sections that roughly cover chronological periods of American history, the work presents well-written biographies that portray the courageous struggles for freedom and justice each biographee endured. The lives of some of the 30 are fairly well known to young people (e.g., Benjamin Franklin, Martin Luther King, Jr., Eleanor Roosevelt) while others (e.g., John Peter Zenger, Sojourner Truth, Emma Goldman) are less familiar. All are portrayed not only as courageous and heroic but also as people with ordinary human frailties.

This work provides information that is not easily found elsewhere. Those working with young people should find this volume a welcome addition to their biography collection.

817 **North American Human Rights Directory**. 3d ed. Laurie S. Wiseberg and Hazel Sirett, eds. Washington, D.C.: Human Rights Internet, 1984. 264p. $30.00pa. ISBN 0-939338-02-5. (semiannual update, $10.00/yr.).

Human Rights Internet, a communications network and clearinghouse for human rights information, cites all organizations in the United States and Canada that champion the security and integrity of individuals while defending their civil and political rights. Omitted are groups with an exclusively domestic focus. [R: ARBA 85; BL, 1 Nov 84]

818 Whalen, Lucille. **Human Rights: A Reference Book**. Santa Barbara, Calif.: ABC-Clio, 1989. 218p. $39.50. ISBN 0-87436-093-5. LC 89-15039.

A brief prologue, a chronology of major human rights events from 1941 to 1988, and biographical sketches of leaders throughout the world introduce this volume. A directory of organizations and an annotated list of print and nonprint sources on human rights follow. The largest section reprints the text of human rights documents, such as the United Nation's Universal Declaration of Human Rights. This volume, a part of the Contemporary World Issues series, is indexed by author, title, organization, document, and subject. Recommended for high schools. [R: ARBA 90; SLJ, May 90]

Library Science

BIBLIOGRAPHIES

E+
819   Rudin, Claire. **The School Librarian's Sourcebook**. New Providence, N.J.: R. R. Bowker, 1990. 504p. $34.95. ISBN 0-8352-2711-1. LC 89-25274.

This annotated bibliography should assist school media specialists in "their own independent learning." It identifies and describes the best books (most published since 1980) in such diverse areas as automation, public relations, booktalking, and serving special learners. The five sections are administration, collections, services, user education, and technology. Each section is subdivided into specific topics.

Lengthy annotations, often more than a page, cover purpose, contents, utility, and the authority of the author. Chapters conclude with briefly annotated bibliographies of additional works. Appendixes include directories of professional periodicals and publishers. Author, title, and subject indexes provide access. Recommended for all levels. [R: ARBA 91; BL, 15 Apr 90; VOYA, Aug 90]

DICTIONARIES, ENCYCLOPEDIAS, AND YEARBOOKS

E+
820   **The ALA Glossary of Library and Information Science**. Heartsill Young, ed. Chicago: American Library Association, 1983. 245p. $50.00. ISBN 0-8389-0371-1. LC 82-18512.

The 4,700 terms defined in this glossary concern library and information science, publishing, printing, educational technology, computer science, graphic arts, and other related fields. The concise definitions were contributed by well-known librarians and library educators. This is a basic reference tool for the professional librarian and information scientist. [R: ARBA 84]

E+
821   **The Bowker Annual Library and Book Trade Almanac**. New Providence, N.J.: R. R. Bowker. annual. $129.95. ISSN 0068-0540. LC 55-12434.

Published annually for over 50 years, this work contains library and book trade highlights for the past year and statistical information on book prices, number of books published, and library expenditures. Sections include reports from the field; legislation, funding, and grants; library/information science education, placement and salaries; research and statistics; reference information; and directory of information. Due to feature variation, librarians should retain the last five volumes. [R: ARBA 91]

822   **Libraries and Information Services Today: The Yearly Chronicle**. June Lester, ed. Chicago: American Library Association. annual. $36.00pa. ISSN 1055-3665.

The successor to the *ALA Yearbook of Library and Information Services* (1974-1990), this new annual focuses on activities, events, personalities, and issues in American librarianship. The three sections are current affairs, reports from the field, and biographies. A final section contains reports for ALA, International Federation of Library Associations, and Canadian and United Kingdom library activities.

Among the issues covered in the 1991 edition are funding for NEA and library school closings. The current affairs section, arranged alphabetically, reports on topics such as collection management, preservation, and types of libraries. Black-and-white photographs illustrate the volume, which is indexed by subjects and names.

823   **School Library Media Annual**. Jane Bandy Smith and J. Gordon Coleman, eds. Englewood, Colo.: Libraries Unlimited. annual. $34.50. ISSN 0739-7712.

This annual, which began in 1984, is designed to keep practitioners abreast of new developments in the school media area. It is an essential source for school media specialists.

Part 1 contains articles of current interest. The 1991 volume includes essays on prekindergarten students in the library media center, unlocking the easy collection, distance education and school library media specialists, collection development in the school environment, multicultural books in schools, and the need for African-American literature in the world of children's books. Part 2 has reports from professional organizations and governing bodies; a list of institutions that offer degree programs in library and information science, school library media services, and educational media; and award recipients. The final part lists the best books and software and award-winning books for the previous year. [R: ARBA 92]

824 Soper, Mary Ellen, and others. **The Librarian's Thesaurus**. Chicago: American Library Association, 1990. 164p. $18.00. ISBN 0-8389-0530-7. LC 90-147.

Intended for library school students and others who need explanations for library terminology, this guide provides lengthy commentaries. The three parts—general concepts, procedures and processes, and technology—are divided into several subsections. Some terms common to school media centers are omitted, but others are retained. The generous use of cross-references and a thorough subject index provide ready accessibility. [R: ARBA 91; LJ, Dec 90; WLB, Dec 90]

HANDBOOKS

E+
825 Thomas, James L. **Nonprint Production for Students, Teachers, and Media Specialists: A Step-by-Step Guide**. 2d ed. Englewood, Colo.: Libraries Unlimited, 1988. 140p. $23.50. ISBN 0-87287-591-1. LC 88-26727.

This how-to book provides step-by-step instructions for nonprint production, using video slides and filmstrips with sound tapes, computer graphics, and overhead transparencies. Topics covered include storyboarding and scripting, different types of equipment and their uses, transparency lifts and lamination, animation, and single-camera television programs. Highly recommended. [R: BR, May/June 89; VOYA, Apr 89]

BOOK REPAIR

E+
826 Greenfield, Jane. **Books: Their Care and Repair**. Bronx, N.Y.: H. W. Wilson, 1984. 204p. $38.00. ISBN 0-8242-0695-9. LC 83-25926.

A useful how-to manual on repairing books, pamphlets, maps, documents, and other printed matter, this is an informative and reliable handbook by an expert on book conservation. The entire range of repair topics is covered, from causes of deterioriation to repair and mending techniques.

E+
827 Morrow, Carolyn Clark, and Carole Dyal. **Conservation Treatment Procedures: A Manual of Step-by-Step Procedures for the Maintenance and Repair of Library Materials**. 2d ed. Englewood, Colo.: Libraries Unlimited, 1986. 225p. $32.00pa. ISBN 0-87287-437-0.

This comprehensive manual describes and illustrates procedures for basic book repair, maintenance, and protection, recommending a variety of procedures. Appended are a decision-making checklist for repair, a directory of equipment and supply sources, a dexterity text, a glossary, and a bibliography. The 2d edition incorporates improvements and changes in techniques and expands the decision-making section. [R: ARBA 83]

CATALOGING

828 **ALA Filing Rules**. By the RTSD Filing Committee. Chicago: American Library Association, 1980. 50p. $10.00pa. ISBN 0-8389-3255-X. LC 80-22186.

829 Seely, Pauline A. **ALA Rules for Filing Catalog Cards. second edition, abridged**. Chicago: American Library Association, 1968. $10.00pa. ISBN 0-8389-0001-1.

The rules set forth in *ALA Filing Rules*, which apply to the arrangement of bibliographic records of library materials in card, book, or online format, are based on the "file-as-is" principle. The *ALA Rules for Filing Catalog Cards, second edition abridged*, consists of the basic rules and selected examples that are especially useful to school media centers and small public libraries.

Library of Congress Filing Rules, prepared by John C. Rather and Susan C. Biebel (Cataloging Distribution Service, Library of Congress, 1980), generally follows the "file-as-is" principle but retains the "person, place, thing, title" hierarchical arrangement. [R: ARBA 82]

830 Byrne, Deborah J. **MARC Manual: Understanding and Using MARC Records**. Englewood, Colo.: Libraries Unlimited, 1990. 260p. $29.50. ISBN 0-87287-813-9.

This concise, easy-to-use manual is designed for the librarians new to MARC as well as for those accustomed to the system. The manual explains the three types of records—bibliographic, authority, and holdings—and gives specifications for MARC database processing, MARC products, and online systems. Libraries planning to automate their catalogs, or already involved in the process, will want this volume.

831 **C. A. Cutter's Three-Figure Author Table**. Swanson-Swift revision. distr., Englewood, Colo.: Libraries Unlimited, 1969. 29p. $17.00. ISBN 0-87287-209-2.

832 **C. A. Cutter's Two-Figure Author Table**. Swanson-Swift revision. distr., Englewood, Colo.: Libraries Unlimited, 1969. 4p. $11.00. ISBN 0-87287-208-4.

833 **Cutter-Sanborn Three-Figure Author Table**. Swanson-Swift revision. distr., Englewood, Colo.: Libraries Unlimited, 1969. 34p. $18.00. ISBN 0-87287-210-6.

The two-figure table is used by small libraries; larger libraries use one of the three-figure forms. The Cutter-Sanborn table has a different number-figure pattern and is not compatible with the other two tables.

E
834 **Cataloging Correctly for Kids: An Introduction to the Tools**. rev. ed. Sharon Zuiderveld, ed. Chicago: American Library Association, 1991. 78p. $12.50pa. ISBN 0-8389-3395-5.

Focusing on such questions as the annotated card program, cataloging nonbook materials, and vendors of cataloging for children's materials, this slim work is an invaluable source for the elementary level. The editor has compiled articles that recognize that users of children's materials have unique characteristics and requirements. The contributors, all catalogers for the level, have based their theories on the "Guidelines for Standardized Cataloging of Children's Material," prepared in 1982 and revised in 1986. Their insights also highlight various tools available to help librarians maintain cataloging standards.

835 Chan, Lois Mai. **Immroth's Guide to the Library of Congress Classification**. 4th ed. Englewood, Colo.: Libraries Unlimited, 1990. 436p. $38.50; $28.50pa. ISBN 0-87287-604-7; 0-87287-763-9pa.

This thorough update of the 3d edition (1980) reflects the recently revised LC classification schedules and provides a basic understanding of the system. Completely new examples are included in separate chapters that cover the classes, A through Z. The volume concludes with a revised bibliography, appendixes that have tables of general applications and individual schedules, and an extensive index. This excellent work offers clear and understandable explanations of the LC classification system. [R: LJ, 15 Feb 91]

836 **Dewey Decimal Classification and Relative Index**. 20th ed. By Melvil Dewey. John P. Comaromi and others, eds. Albany, N.Y.: Forest Press/OCLC Online Computer Library Center, 1989. 4v. $200.00/set. ISBN 0-910608-37-7. LC 88-24629.

E+
837 **Abridged Dewey Decimal Classification and Relative Index**. 12th ed. John P. Comaromi and others, eds. Albany, N.Y.: Forest Press, 1990. 857p. $75.00. ISBN 0-910608-42-3. LC 90-31428.

The *Dewey Decimal Classification*, 20th edition (*DDC 20*), in four volumes, is used by medium and large libraries. Most small school and public libraries with collections of less than 50,000 items use the *Abridged Dewey Classification* (*ADDC*).

DDC 20, the first update in 10 years, includes revisions for Data Processing and Computer Science and the Social Sciences (300-307) and presents a complete revision of the Music schedule. The first volume provides tables; the second and third have schedules; and the fourth contains an index and a greatly improved classifier's manual, which offers extensive notes on the use of some numbers. Any school library that does a significant amount of original cataloging should buy the revision.

ADDC offers changes and improvements in numbers throughout the schedules. Number building is easier due to clearer internal notes. There is better guidance for the use of some numbers, and all instructions are more readable. Nonautomated libraries may not need to purchase the revision, but those that rely on CIP data and automated transfer of library records into local systems will require it. [R: ARBA 90; ARBA 91]

838   Frost, Carolyn. **Media Access and Organization: A Cataloging and Reference Sources Guide for Nonbook Materials**. Englewood, Colo.: Libraries Unlimited, 1989. 265p. $31.50. ISBN 0-87287-583-0. LC 88-27302.
This work focuses on the AACR2 rules for nonbook materials. Different types of nonprint materials and the problems each presents are treated in detail, with citations to relevant AACR2 rules. Descriptive cataloging examples are given, and MARC coding and tagging in OCLC format are provided. Each chapter includes a bibliography. This excellent source is recommended to all school library media centers that catalog nonbook materials. [R: BR, Jan/Feb 90; VOYA, Dec 89]

839   Gorman, Michael. **The Concise AACR2, 1988 Revision**. Chicago: American Library Association, 1989. 161p. $17.00pa. ISBN 0-8389-3362-9. LC 89-15110.

840   Maxwell, Margaret F. **Handbook for AACR2 1988 Revision: Explaining and Illustrating the Anglo-American Cataloging Rules**. Chicago: American Library Association, 1989. 436p. $30.00pa. ISBN 0-8389-0505-6. LC 88-36703.
In the abridged version of *Anglo-American Cataloging Rules, Second Edition* (*AACR2R*), Gorman has written a lucid and succinct text that explains the rules catalogers in small libraries frequently face. It draws examples from materials commonly cataloged in libraries. Users are referred to the full text for information about problems not covered in the concise version or for fuller explanations. Appendixes include sections on capitalization, a glossary, and a table that correlates rules in the concise edition to their equivalent in the full text. Indexed.
The *Handbook* is designed to assist catalogers in the application of the most common rules for description, choices of access points, and forms of headings. This edition, which updates the 1980 *Handbook*, has added chapters on computer files and analysis and on Library of Congress rule interpretations issued since the previous edition. [R: ARBA 90]

E+
841   Intner, Sheila S., and Jean Weihs. **Standard Cataloging for School and Public Libraries**. Englewood, Colo.: Libraries Unlimited, 1990. 208p. $26.50. ISBN 0-87287-737-X.
This is a good, basic text that addresses the cataloging needs of school and other small libraries in a clear, nontechnical manner. It offers the beginning cataloger a solid foundation in theory and principles while providing instruction on all aspects of cataloging procedures. The authors cover description, access, classification, subject headings, bibliographic utility, automated cataloging networks, local systems, MARC format, and standard tools (Library of Congress and Dewey Decimal classification and *Sears List of Subject Headings*). Over 100 examples illustrate card style entries in LC, MARC, and CANMARC formats. [R: ARBA 91]

842   **Library of Congress Subject Headings**. By Subject Cataloging Division, Library of Congress. Washington, D.C.: Cataloging Distribution Service, Library of Congress. annual. $150.00/set.
LCSH, updated annually, is used in all but the smallest libraries. The 12th edition continues the policy of hierarchical subject listings established in the 10th edition. The structure, like that used in many technical thesauri, uses BT (broader terms), NT (narrower terms), and similar labels in place of the older *see* and *see also* terminology. The practice of indirect/direct subdivisions has been simplified by the use of "May Subd Geog" or "Not Subd Geog." Each of the annual updates includes a list of cancelled and replaced headings. Users of *LCSH* will also need the *Subject Cataloging Manual*, since the annuals do not have an explanatory section.
The "Annotated Card Program" (AC subject headings) is of limited value to school libraries that have children's collections, since the AC list is incomplete, citing only headings that differ from those used in the main list. School libraries downloading cataloging data from MARC records would be better served by the inclusion of a complete list of all subject headings used on AC cards. [R: ARBA 90]

843   Osborn, Jeanne. **Dewey Decimal Classification, 20th Edition: A Study Manual**. rev. and ed. by John Phillip Comaromi. Englewood, Colo.: Libraries Unlimited, 1991. 303p. $45.00. ISBN 0-87287-870-8.

Comaromi, editor of *Dewey Decimal 20*, has revised and updated Jeanne Osborn's 1982 detailed analysis of the 19th edition of the DDC system. Following an introductory survey of the DDC system and its current modernization of schedules, notations, and terminology, the work deals with specific changes in the new edition, with comparisons between the 19th and 20th editions. Special features include exercises in number analysis and synthesis at the end of each chapter and examples of LC classification for the purpose of illustration. The final two chapters cover the 12th abridged edition and special treatment of such matters as classification of nonprint materials, reasons for using the Dewey system, and Dewey numbers on LC bibliographic records. Indexed by author/title/subject.

844 Rogers, JoAnn V., with Jerry D. Saye. **Nonprint Cataloging for Multimedia Collections**. 2d ed. Englewood, Colo.: Libraries Unlimited, 1987. 294p. $29.50. ISBN 0-87287-523-7.
This cataloging tool for nonprint materials, which follows the mnemonic structure of AACR2, provides clearly written explanations and many examples to clarify basic cataloging rules. It incorporates changes in AACR2 and the MARC format, includes current rule interpretation of LC cataloging procedures, and describes the use of online bibliographic utilities for cataloging nonprint materials. The manual includes a chapter on cataloging computer software. [R: BL, 1 Apr 88; WLB, Jan 88]

845 **Sears List of Subject Headings**. 14th ed. Bronx, N.Y.: H. W. Wilson, 1991. 731p. $42.00. ISBN 0-8242-0803-X. LC 91-10290.
Sears, now fully revised, updated, and expanded, focuses on the needs of the small- to medium-sized library. The editors have reevaluated each heading from the previous edition and added many new ones in subject areas of current interest, such as drugs, environment, genetics, instructional materials, and popular culture. Older headings have been revised to reflect current terminology. The editors have increased the number of scope notes and instructional references; they also follow ALA Filing Rules without modification.
Sears List of Subject Headings: Canadian Companion, compiled by Ken Haycock and Lynne Lighthall (3d ed. H. W. Wilson, 1987), supplements the 13th edition of *Sears*, thus facilitating its use in Canadian libraries. *Sears Lista de Encabezamientos de Materia*, translated by Carmen Rovira (H. W. Wilson, 1984), is a Spanish translation of the 12th edition of the *Sears List*.
The 13th edition of the *Sears List* is also available on WILSONTAPE, WILSONDISC, and WILSONLINE. [R: ARBA 92]

846 Taylor, Arlene G., with Rosanna M. O'Neill. **Cataloging with Copy: A Decision-Maker's Handbook**. 2d ed. Englewood, Colo.: Libraries Unlimited, 1988. 354p. $36.00. ISBN 0-87287-575-X. LC 88-13840.
This work emphasizes the importance of relating the catalog to the needs of its users. The guide takes the cataloger through every component of the library retrieval system: document description; choice and form of name; title and subject access headings; classification; and the problems of author, title, and issue notation. Chapters also deal with sources of cataloging information and the impact of electronic databases on the cataloging process. The decision-making process is emphasized throughout, and specific examples of catalog cards and MARC records illustrate alternatives that can be considered. [R: ARBA 88; BR, Sept/Oct 89; LJ, 1 May 89]

847 Wynar, Bohdan S. **Introduction to Cataloging and Classification**. 8th ed., by Arlene G. Taylor. Englewood, Colo.: Libraries Unlimited, 1991. 633p. $45.00; $32.50pa. ISBN 0-87287-811-2; 0-87287-967-4pa. LC 91-24851.
The 8th edition of this standard introductory textbook for cataloging and classification has changes in almost all areas of bibliographic control. AACR2R has been implemented; new editions and supplements of LCSH, LC classification, DDC, and Sears are now in use. Networking and online catalogs are part of a librarian's way of life. Many chapters are entirely new or have been fully revised to show the continuity in development of cataloging rules. This new edition has resulted in a state-of-the-art professional text. Cataloging professionals will certainly appreciate this latest edition.

CENSORSHIP

848   Green, Jonathan. **The Encyclopedia of Censorship**. New York: Facts on File, 1990. 388p. $45.00. ISBN 0-8160-1594-5. LC 89-1210.
Some 1,000 articles cover individuals (censors and the censored), works censored, organizations (advocates and the opposition), important legal decisions, and other topics related to the history and current status of censorship throughout the world. The United States and United Kingdom receive extensive coverage, but shorter articles discuss the issue in other European nations, China, the Third World, and elsewhere. This authoritative and comprehensive work holds a vast amount of information on an important subject. Recommended for high schools. [R: ARBA 91; BL, 15 Mar 90; BR, Sept/Oct 90; WLB, Mar 90]

849   Hoffmann, Frank. **Intellectual Freedom and Censorship: An Annotated Bibliography**. Metuchen, N.J.: Scarecrow, 1989. 244p. $27.50. ISBN 0-8108-2145-1. LC 88-18811.
This annotated bibliography, which includes books, articles, and legal material, is divided into five parts: theoretical foundations of intellectual freedom and censorship, key court cases, professional concerns, procensorship/anticensorship stances of individuals and groups, and cases in the mass media. Critical annotations and a subject index conclude the volume. The average high school collection is likely to contain many of the items cited here. [R: ARBA 90; BL, Aug 89]

E +
850   **Intellectual Freedom Manual**. 3d ed. Compiled by the Office for Intellectual Freedom and Intellectual Freedom Committee. Chicago: American Library Association, 1989. 230p. $20.00. ISBN 0-8389-3368-8. LC 88-39674.
This handbook is at once a guide to resisting censorship of library materials and a "compilation of documents, policies, and statements of professional principles and ideas developed by the American Library Association." "ALA and Intellectual Freedom," the first section, surveys the Association's concepts and explains such documents as the Library Bill of Rights and the Freedom to Read Policy. This edition, which updates the 1983 manual, has added sections that contain policy statements about access in school media programs, circulation of motion pictures, the use of libraries by persons with physical or mental impairments, and legal developments in school library censorship. One section, "Before the Censor Comes: Essential Preparation," should be required reading for all librarians.

851   Reichman, Henry. **Censorship and Selection: Issues and Answers for Schools**. Chicago: American Library Association, 1988. 141p. $15.00. ISBN 0-8389-3350-5. LC 88-16815.
This succinct volume provides school administrators, teachers, and librarians with the knowledge and skills necessary to combat censorship pressures and develop a selection policy. Reichman addresses the difference between censorship and selection and attempts to explain why self-appointed censors challenge books or other materials. In so doing, he stresses the need for a selection policy and suggests the proper procedure for defending challenged works. [R: BR, May/June 89; VOYA, Feb 90]

852   West, Mark. **Trust Your Children: Voices Against Censorship in Children's Literature**. New York: Neal-Schuman, 1988. 178p. $19.95pa. ISBN 1-55570-021-7. LC 87-31452.
Eighteen author interviews discuss the reasons why would-be censors have objected to certain books for children and adolescents. The authors explain how they felt when their books were targeted, and some relate instances in which they were forced to make changes in their writings in order to appease editors. This practical volume contains information useful for high school reports and research papers on censorship. [R: BR, Sept/Oct 89; LJ, 1 Nov 88; WLB, Mar 89]

COLLECTION DEVELOPMENT

E +
853   Doll, Carol A., and Pamela Petrick Barron. **Collection Analysis in the School Library Media Center: A Practical Approach**. Chicago: American Library Association, 1991. 73p. $10.00pa. ISBN 0-8389-3390-4. LC 90-40208.
This slim volume provides guidance in gathering data about library collections in order to evaluate the collection and consistently meet the library's objectives. Chapters, giving step-by-step instructions for each phase of the analysis, cover such topics as quantitative and qualitative methods of appraisal,

estimating the cost of updating the collection, working to achieve set goals, weeding, communicating with teachers, and preparing a collection for automation. Sample forms and reports support the text. [R: SLJ, June 91]

E+
854 Guide for Written Collection Policy Statements. By the Subcommittee on Guidelines for Collection Development, Collection Management and Development Committee, Resource Section, Resources and Technical Services (now ALCTS). Chicago: American Library Association, 1989. 32p. $6.00. ISBN 0-8389-3371-8. LC 89-145.

Designed for libraries of all types and sizes, this booklet is an update of *Guidelines for the Formation of Collection Development Policies* (1979). The introduction expounds the arguments for a written policy, followed by principles governing formulation, the application of collection policies, and elements of a collection policy statement. Appendixes contain a glossary; a bibliography of monographs, articles, reports, manuals, newsletters, and SPEC kits; worksheets for developing a policy; and references to published collection policies.

855 School Library and Media Center Acquisition Policies and Procedures. 2d ed. Betty Kemp, ed. Phoenix, Ariz.: Oryx Press, 1986. 280p. $33.00. ISBN 0-89774-160-9.

This guide to designing a selection policy is based on questionnaires and existing policies of a number of school libraries. The main body of the work consists of reprints of 15 representative policies and excerpts from 41 additional ones that address specific issues for school libraries, such as philosophy, selection criteria, ordering procedures, interlibrary loan, and weeding. [R: BL, 1 Apr 87; VOYA, June 87; WLB, Apr 87]

856 Sitter, Clara L. The Vertical File and Its Alternatives: A Handbook. Englewood, Colo.: Libraries Unlimited, 1991. 275p. $28.00. ISBN 0-87287-910-0. LC 79-12773.

This guide is a complete revision and update of *The Vertical File and Its Satellites* by Shirley Miller (2d ed. Libraries Unlimited, 1977). It provides step-by-step instructions on how to develop and use vertical files. Sitter gives tips on locating resources, processing and circulating materials, organizing special collections (e.g., careers, local history), handling special materials (e.g., maps, pictures, newspaper clippings), weeding, and more. Special features include a glossary and a directory of vendors.

857 Slote, Stanley J. Weeding Library Collection: Library Weeding Methods. 3d ed. Englewood, Colo.: Libraries Unlimited, 1989. 284p. $29.50. ISBN 0-87287-633-0.

Slote's work, a classic that focuses on an essential, if unpopular, professional activity, is recommended for all types of libraries. He discusses traditional approaches to weeding as well as newer concepts, such as computer applications to the task. Examples of the approach used by over 40 libraries of all kinds are especially useful. He also provides a complete analysis of the literature. Highly recommended. [R: BL, 1 Apr 90; LJ, 1 May 90; SLJ, Apr 90]

858 Van Orden, Phyllis J. The Collection Program in Schools: Concepts, Practices, and Information Sources. Englewood, Colo.: Libraries Unlimited, 1988. 347p. $27.50. ISBN 0-87287-572-5. LC 84-28872.

The author designed this text for use in library education programs, but the practicing school media specialist can use it as a basic tool. The introduction examines the factors that influence collection development, and succeeding chapters survey selection criteria and selection tools. The third section addresses the functions of acquiring and maintaining materials and evaluating the collection. Appendixes list associations and agencies, bibliographic and selection tools, and reprint documents pertinent to intellectual freedom and the right to read. [R: BL, July 88; BR, Sept/Oct 88]

COMPUTERS

See also **Computers and Electronics** and **Instructional Technology** in **Education.**

See **Selection Aids** under **Computer Software** in **Media Sources** for software.

859 Aversa, Elizabeth S., and J. C. Mancall. Management of Online Search Services in Schools. Santa Barbara, Calif.: ABC-Clio, 1989. 175p. $32.50. ISBN 0-87436-513-9. LC 88-25903.

School media specialists who are already online and others planning to offer the service will welcome this easy-to-follow guide. It provides expert advice on initiating a search service, hardware and communication linkage, formulation of policies, selecting a vendor and CD-ROMs, costs, record-keeping, and other pertinent issues. The first part of the volume is textual, but the second consists of reproducible checklists, logs, worksheets, and other useful material. Highly recommended. [R: BR, Sept/Oct 89; WLB, May 89]

860   Aversa, Elizabeth S., and others. **Online Information Services for Secondary School Students**. 2d ed. Chicago: American Library Association, 1989. 83p. $11.95pa. ISBN 0-8389-0524-2. LC 89-17910.
Four chapters address the role of online searching in secondary schools and offer suggestions for planning and implementing services. Among the topics covered are the advantages and goals of online searching in student research; a 1988 survey of online users, systems, and funding in secondary schools; and the "online environment." The final chapter is an annotated bibliography of guides, texts, articles, and relevant journals through 1989. A directory of selected documents delivery services concludes the work. [R: BL, 1 Apr 90; BR, Sept/Oct 90; VOYA, June 90]

E +
861   **Computers and the School Library**. Santa Barbara, Calif.: ABC-Clio, 1990. 130p. $24.95pa. ISBN 0-87436-607-0.
This book has ideas contributed by experienced school librarians and gleaned from eight years of "The Computing Librarian" column of *The Book Report*. Hundreds of valuable uses of computers take into consideration such factors as cost, accessibility of hardware and software, budget, school politics, and public relations.

862   Corbin, John. **Directory of Automated Library Systems**. 2d ed. New York: Neal-Schuman, 1989. 305p. $55.00. ISBN 1-55570-050-0. LC 89-12750.
This volume addresses the comparative feastures of 24 selected automated library systems, ranging from high-capacity systems suitable for large university libraries to circulating systems for small libraries. Charts indicate features of each system by noting whether specific functions are present or absent. A directory of installations lists the type of user that has adopted each system. While the directory is better suited to large libraries, it includes information useful to the school library media specialist who is evaluating and comparing automated library systems. [R: ARBA 91; BL, 1 Apr 90; BR, May/June 90; CLJ, June 90]

E +
863   Dewey, Patrick R. **101 Microcomputer Projects to Do in Your Library: Putting Your Micro to Work**. Chicago: American Library Association, 1990. 151p. $25.00pa. ISBN 0-8389-0518-8. LC 89-6957.
Dewey collected the ideas reported in this volume through a survey, a search of the literature, and personal contact. The microcomputer projects, which cover several areas of library operations, are arranged by application—acquisition, compiling of bibliographies, budgeting and accounting, bulletin boards, circulation, and miscellaneous.
Information on each project includes name, library location, contact person with address and telephone number, library profile, hardware requirements, software used, project description, problems encountered, references to literature, project date, cost, and self-rating. This work supplies excellent ideas for automation projects. Highly recommended. [R: ARBA 91; BR, Sept/Oct 90]

864   Epler, Doris. **Online Searching Goes to School**. Phoenix, Ariz.: Oryx press, 1989. 160p. $29.95pa. ISBN 0-89774-546-9. LC 88-13927.
Online searching, a common service offered by college and university libraries, is moving into school library media centers where it is likely to become an equally valuable function. This how-to book surveys the available services and explains how they can enhance learning and instruction in schools. Fifteen schools using online services are profiled, and expenditures are outlined. The appendix provides a bibliography and a selective list of databases appropriate for online service in schools. Any library planning to offer these services should hold this guide. [R: BR, May/June 90; WLB, Mar 89]

865   Franklin, Carl, and Susan Kinnell. **Hypertext/Hypermedia in Schools: A Resource Book**. Santa Barbara, Calif.: ABC-Clio, 1990. 274p. $35.00pa. ISBN 0-87436-563-5. LC 90-1167.
This guide to two of the newest and most powerful educational technologies, hypertext and hypermedia, is divided into two parts. The first describes the hardware and software involved, defines terms,

and explains the theoretical foundations of hypertext and hypermedia. The second part focuses on sources. Successful school programs using the media are listed and described, with directory information and a contact person for each. Hypertext/hypermedia software, organized according to hardware requirements, is reviewed. The final section, a bibliography of articles, books, and proceedings through early 1990, is organized by type of publication and then subject. A glossary and index conclude this practical handbook. [R: BR, Sept/Oct 91]

866   Lathrop, Ann, comp. **Online and CD-ROM Databases in School Libraries: Readings**. Englewood, Colo.: Libraries Unlimited, 1989. 372p. $32.50. ISBN 0-87287-756-6. LC 89-8143.

School library media specialists who provide online and CD-ROM services share their experiences in this volume. The essays address managing the services, the techniques involved in searching, and the critical thinking skills enhanced by using the technologies. District and state projects underway are also covered. A bibliography of databases of special interest to schools and a glossary complete the volume. Highly recommended for librarians who wish to implement these services. [R: BL, 1 Jan 90; BR, May/June 90; VOYA, Apr 90]

867   Lee, Joann H. **Online Searching: The Basics, Settings, and Management**. 2d ed. Englewood, Colo.: Libraries Unlimited, 1989. 130p. $33.00pa. ISBN 0-87287-738-8.

Essays by librarians experienced in online searching in various types of libraries (including schools) make up this small volume. Contents cover training, search strategies, evaluating searches, establishing policy, and setting up and managing services. Not all essays apply to school settings, but those that do make this a worthwhile guide for school library media specialists. A general index and an annotated bibliography of books, articles, serial titles, journal columns, and annuals conclude the volume. Recommended. [R: BR, Jan/Feb 90]

E+
868   Pagel, Mary I. **Computer Tutor 1.0: Your Complete Guide to Self-Computer Training**. Fort Collins, Colo.: Computer Tutor, 1989. 171p. $14.95pa. ISBN 0-9621823-0-3.

This manual, designed for the beginner facing the computer for the first time, uses simple, concise language in instructional chapters, which include definitions and illustrations. The first three chapters describe the parts of the computer and how they work. The middle three chapters address DOS commands and explain how they are used to manage files and organize a hard disk. The last three are how-to chapters on applications: learning software, purchasing a computer, and choosing a training program.

869   Palmer, Roger C. **Online Reference and Information Retrieval**. 2d ed. Englewood, Colo.: Libraries Unlimited, 1987. 189p. $26.50. ISBN 0-87287-536-9.

This is an excellent introduction to online retrieval systems with information on the techniques of searching and commercial online bibliographic systems (e.g., BRS, DIALOG, WILSONLINE). Numeric databases, home information utility, microcomputer software and hardware, vocabulary control, and management concerns are all covered. The textbook also contains exercises, search problems, and illustrations. [R: BL, July 88; SLJ, Sept 89]

870   Parisi, Lynn S., and Virginia L. Jones. **Directory of Online Databases and CD-ROM Resources for High Schools**. Santa Barbara, Calif.: ABC-Clio, 1988. 136p. $32.50. ISBN 0-87436-515-5. LC 88-18717.

This directory is designed to assist high school teachers, librarians, and students in selecting the online databases and CD-ROM resources that are the most useful for social studies, science, and English. Databases for each discipline are described in separate sections; a fourth section addresses general databases useful in many curricular areas. Within each section, entries for databases, listed alphabetically, provide a general description, type of material covered, dates of coverage and frequency of updating, applicability to high school research needs, and availability. Recommended. [R: ARBA 90; BR, Sept 89; WLB, Mar 89]

871   Wright, Kieth C. **Workstations and Local Area Networks for Libraries**. Chicago: American Library Association, 1990. 156p. $27.00pa. ISBN 0-8389-0538-2. LC 90-489.

Libraries of all types are moving rapidly toward the use of computer workstations and local area networks (LANs). This worthwhile handbook is designed for librarians who seek basic information about the use of these technologies and why they are needed in libraries, their applications to library operations, the equipment and software required, and the management problems they generate. Each chapter is supported by drawings, tables, and a bibliography for further reading. Appendixes include directories of workstation producers and LAN manufacturers, and a general bibliography. Indexed. [R: BL, 1 Jan 91; LJ, 15 Nov 90]

MANAGEMENT

872   Adams, Helen R. **School Media Policy Development: A Practical Process for Small Districts**. Englewood, Colo.: Libraries Unlimited, 1986. 174p. $23.50. ISBN 0-87287-450-8.

The processes involved in developing, using, and reviewing media center policies constitute the focus of this work. Adams discusses policies concerning all management responsibilities (e.g., supervising staff, selecting materials and equipment, cooperating internally and externally) and emphasizes involving all interested groups in their development, tailoring policies to the local situation, and making them flexible enough to allow for decision-making initiative. Case studies and sample policies are included. [R: VOYA, Feb 87; WLB, Mar 87]

E +
873   **Case Studies in Managing School Library Media Centers**. Daniel Callison and Jacqueline Morris, eds. Phoenix, Ariz.: Oryx Press, 1989. 208p. $26.95pa. ISBN 0-89774-441-1. LC 89-3360.

This volume contains 32 situational problems typical of those encountered by school library media specialists. Examples include flexible scheduling, school and public library cooperation, censorship, video copyright, and unneeded or unwanted donations. Experienced school librarians cogently debate these case studies, suggesting to professionals, students, and administrators alternative courses of action. Bibliographies are included for each case. Recommended for all levels. [R: BL, 1 Oct 89]

E +
874   Eaglen, Audrey. **Buying Books: A How-To-Do-It Manual for Librarians**. New York: Neal-Schuman, 1989. 166p. $35.00pa. ISBN 1-55570-013-6.

This work instructs librarians about the publishing industry so that they can locate and purchase books at reasonable prices. The author discusses the profit motive, book prices, discount practices, distribution, vendors, and much more. Recommended. [R: BR, Jan/Feb 90; SLJ, Dec 89]

E +
875   Gillespie, John T., and Diana L. Spirt. **Administering the School Library Media Center**. 3d ed. New Providence, N.J.: R. R. Bowker, 1991. 400p. $39.95. ISBN 0-8352-3092-9.

This worthwhile work begins with a brief history of media centers; the authors then address program development, instructional objectives for media skills, and administrative responsibilities. The revised edition covers AALS's *Information Power* and updates all sections.

876   Haycock. Ken. **School Library Program in the Curriculum**. Englewood, Colo.: Libraries Unlimited, 1990. 170p. $19.50pa. ISBN 0-87287-776-0.

This work consists of selected articles from *Emergency Librarian*—which Haycock edits—that concern the integration of the library program into the total school curriculum. The essays are organized to show various aspects of the subject (e.g., the role of the teacher-librarian, specific curricular applications, online searching, teaching information skills). Articles, which date from 1977, have implications for applying the recommendations of *Information Power*. [R: VOYA, Apr 91]

E +
877   **Information Power: Guidelines for School Library Media Programs**. By American Association of School Librarians and Association for Educational Communication and Technology. Chicago: American Library Association, 1988. 171p. $14.00pa. ISBN 0-8389-3352-1.

This comprehensive guide, prepared by ALA and AECT, sets forth guidelines to assist library media professionals in meeting the needs of students, teachers, and parents in the twenty-first century. *Informational Power* does not provide quantitative standards but offers guidelines based on high service programs identified by the Center for Educational Statistics, U.S. Department of Education. *The School Librarian's Sourcebook* states that these guidelines provide "a rational, needs-based imperative for change and the suggested means by which it may be accomplished—leadership, planning, and example." Highly recommended. [R: BR, Nov 88; VOYA, Dec 88]

878 Loertscher, David V. **Taxonomies of the School Library Media Program**. Englewood, Colo.: Libraries Unlimited, 1988. 336p. $26.50. ISBN 0-87287-662-4. LC 87-35367.

The author suggests models for building exemplary library media programs. The three basic components, according to Loertscher, are warehousing (the facility, equipment, materials), direct services to students and teachers, and resource-based teaching (use of multiple resources in a variety of formats to achieve curricular objectives). Vertical program features are added according to interests, talents, and school needs, and may include such things as library skills, reading motivation, and cultural literacy.

Two specific models are analyzed—"Services of School Resource Centers" by Haycock, and *Helping Teachers Teach* by Turner. The work concludes with a chapter on evaluation of programs and services. The appendixes critique and reproduce several evaluative instruments, including the Purdue Self-Evaluation System (PSES). A bibliography concludes the volume. Recommended. [R: BL, July 88; SLJ, Oct 88; VOYA, Oct 88]

E+
879 **Measures of Excellence for School Library Media Centers**. David V. Loertscher, ed. Englewood, Colo.: Libraries Unlimited, 1988. 148p. $18.50. ISBN 0-87287-652-7. LC 87-29802.

The evaluation process, an important function of school media specialists, is the subject of this collection of essays, which first appeared in the November 1986 issue of the *Drexel Library Quarterly*. The articles, contributed by practitioners and academicians, suggest a variety of measures for use in evaluating programs and services. Among the various approaches are mapping techniques for assessing the collection's support of the curriculum, a survey designed to evaluate an audiovisual program, and data collected to measure the quality of research services to students. These and other studies will benefit school media specialists in secondary schools. [R: BL, 1 Oct 88; VOYA, June 88; WLB, Sept 88]

880 Merrill-Oldham, Jan, and Paul Parisi. **Guide to the Library Binding Institute Standards for Library Binding**. Chicago: American Library Association, 1990. 60p. $20.00. ISBN 0-8389-3391-2.

This guide is designed to clarify the 8th edition (1986) of the *Library Binding Institute Standards for Library Binding* (*LBI Standards*) and "to improve communication between librarians and binders." The three sections—introduction, technical specifications, and material specifications—employ a numbering system used in the parent work to explain each standard. The work does not address the problem of options in a particular binding situation. Appendixes provide three sample decision trees; describe how to inspect a bound volume; examine nonstandard methods of binding; address products and services of binderies; outline the key elements of a bindery agreement; and give a sample customer profile. There is no index.

881 Scholtz, James C. **Developing and Maintaining Video Collections in Libraries**. Santa Barbara, Calif.: ABC-Clio, 1989. 196p. $40.95. ISBN 0-87436-497-3. LC 88-16871.

Those who are starting a video collection or expanding one will welcome this guide. Eight chapters survey the evolution of the video phenomenon and cover such areas as collecting goals, components of a collection development policy, selecting and maintaining equipment, and copyright law. Special features include tables; illustrations; and a copy of the document "Freedom to View," adopted by the Intellectual Freedom Committee of the American Library Association. [R: BR, May/June 89; LJ, 1 Mar 89; WLB, Mar 89]

E+
882 **School Library Media File: Folders of Ideas for Library Excellence. No. 1**. David V. Loertscher and others, eds. Englewood, Colo.: Libraries Unlimited, 1989. 288p. $27.50 looseleaf. ISBN 0-87287-685-3. ISSN 1042-4245.

This "personal vertical file" consists of practical ideas, source material, and documents related to school library media centers. Each idea, on a single or double page, is labeled according to grade level and placed in the appropriate section: collection development, curriculum, management, public relations, or technology. The content includes ideas for integrating the library program into classroom instruction, producing newsletters, publicizing School Library Media Month, and much more. Materials are reproduced from a variety of sources, such as *ERIC Digest* and publications of the American Library Association and the Foundation Center. Highly recommended. [R: VOYA, Oct 89]

883 Smith, Jane B. **Library Media Center Programs for Middle Schools: A Curriculum-Based Approach**. Chicago: American Library Association, 1989. 150p. $26.00. ISBN 0-8389-0500-5. LC 88-7762.

School media specialists who are planning or evaluating middle school library media programs will find this work useful. It provides a step-by-step model for diverse sizes of libraries and addresses such issues as the role of the library media specialist, planning cooperatively with teachers, setting and meeting instructional goals, and meeting the needs of young adolescents. Recommended. [R: BL, 1 Apr 90; BR, May 90; SLJ, Jan 90; VOYA, Apr 90]

E +

884 **Tips and Other Bright Ideas for School Librarians**. Santa Barbara, Calif.: ABC-Clio, 1991. $24.95pa. ISBN 0-87436-605-4.

Over 1,200 succinct, imaginative ideas gleaned from the "Tips and Other Bright Ideas" column in *The Book Report* are to be found in this volume. Ideas concern curriculum involvement, reading motivation, bulletin boards, working with volunteers, computers, public relations, library management, and library skills. Among the suggestions are recycling reference materials for use in library instruction, teaching basic math using the Dewey Decimal Classification system, and teaching library skills to the non-college-bound student. Ideas are designed for middle and high school libraries, but many are adaptable to elementary schools. [R: SLJ, Jan 91]

885 Velleman, Ruth A. **Meeting the Needs of People with Disabilities: A Guide for Librarians, Educators, and Other Service Professionals**. Phoenix, Ariz.: Oryx Press, 1990. 288p. $37.50. ISBN 0-89774-521-3. LC 89-8570.

This revision of the author's *Serving Physically Disabled People* (1979) will help those seeking information and services for people with handicaps. The text covers civil rights of disabled persons, new technologies, rehabilitation, barrier-free environments (which include libraries), and more. Each chapter ends with a suggested reading list, and there is an extensive bibliography of books and periodicals. A directory of agencies and services concludes the volume. [R: LJ, 15 June 90]

E +

886 Woolls, Blanche. **Managing School Library Media Programs**. Englewood, Colo.: Libraries Unlimited, 1988. 181p. $24.50pa. ISBN 0-87287-590-3. LC 88-2689.

887 Biagini, Mary K. **A Model for Problem Solving and Decision Making: Managing School Library Media Programs**. Englewood, Colo.: Libraries Unlimited, 1988. 164p. $22.50pa. ISBN 0-87287-589-X.

The Woolls's handbook, designed for the beginning library media center manager, covers all types of day-to-day procedures, budgeting, services, marketing the media center, collection development, equipment, evaluating the program, professionalism, and much more. The 13 chapters include exercises and end notes. The sound advice given by this work makes it a worthwhile selection, especially for the new librarian.

Intended as a companion to Woolls's handbook, Biagini's work presents case studies that focus on some of the strategies treated in the management text, such as teaming with teachers in the educational process and planning a needs assessment. Part 1 describes a fictitious community and profiles its public and school libraries to demonstrate how a real situation is analyzed. Parts 2 and 3 contain case studies. Indexed. Both works are recommended. [R: BL, June 88; BR, Nov/Dec 88; SLJ, Jan 89; VOYA, Oct 88]

888 Woolls, Blanche. **Supervision of District Level Library Media Programs**. Englewood, Colo.: Libraries Unlimited, 1990. 228p. (School Library Management Series). $27.00. ISBN 0-87287-733-7.

This volume focuses on the role of the district level supervisor in all sizes of systems. A prologue provides a historical perspective for the position, followed by chapters on managing human resources, facilities and budgets, managing products of the media program (e.g., collection development, services, networking), presenting media programs to the community, and district services. The appendix includes such items as job descriptions, interview questions, and examples of forms in use in school districts. [R: VOYA, June 91]

E +

889 Zingher, Gary. **At the Pirate Academy: Adventures with Language in the Library Media Center**. Chicago: American Library Association, 1990. 132p. $15.00pa. ISBN 0-8389-3384-X. LC 90-1074.

Zingher concentrates on the instructional role of the media specialist and the integration of classroom and library activities related to the language arts. The first part examines thematic exploration and includes chapters on its historical, social, developmental, and literary perspectives. The second part is a sourcebook offering specific information on constructing a thematic unit, with chapters on villains and buddies, humor, special places and fantasy worlds, survival, and bedtime and nighttime. The work is well suited for use from kindergarten through grade 8. [R: SLJ, May 91; VOYA, June 91]

MEDIA SKILLS

E
890   Activities Almanac: Daily Ideas for Library Media Lessons. Santa Barbara, Calif.: ABC-Clio, 1990. 283p. $21.95pa. ISBN 0-87436-569-4.

Library skills activities related to famous people, historical events, and cultural activities (e.g., Pacific-American Heritage Week, Cartoon Art Appreciation Week) are arranged in calendar format. Black-and-white illustrations and an index enhance the contents, which have been compiled from articles published in *School Libraries Media Activities Monthly.*

E+
891   Bell, Irene Wood, and Jeanne E. Wieckert. **Basic Media Skills through Games. Volume 1. 2d ed. Englewood, Colo.: Libraries Unlimited, 1985. 389p. $28.50. ISBN 0-87287-438-9(v.1).

This title presents plans for teaching library skills in elementary and middle schools, using inexpensive materials readily available in most schools. The volume introduces children to the DDC system, the card catalog, reference books, and basic audiovisual equipment. The games are particularly well suited for developing the problem-solving abilities of students. Games increase motivation, help the socialization process, and integrate students with diverse ability.

E+
892   Berry, Margaret, and P. S. Morris. **Stepping into Research! A Complete Research Skills Activities Program for Grades 5-12. West Nyack, N.Y.: Center for Applied Research in Education, 1990. 338p. $27.95 spiralbound. ISBN 0-87628-800-X. LC 89-29997.

This work is designed "to develop a readiness for research" before students begin to organize and write research papers. It includes seven units, such as the card catalog, classifications systems, and a variety of standard reference tools. The units in turn are divided into 30 lessons, each of which follows the same format: lesson focus, teacher preparation, background information, concepts, vocabulary, objectives, materials needed, activities, and extended activities. Units cover basic skills but give scant attention to CD-ROMs and online searching. Appendixes include answer keys, unit tests, and a final test. Reproducible activity sheets accompany each lesson.

893   Cutlip, Glen W. **Learning and Information: Skills for the Secondary Classroom and Library Media Program. Englewood, Colo.: Libraries Unlimited, 1988. 134p. $19.50pa. ISBN 0-87287-580-6.

The library skills program, Learning and Information Model, integrates teaching with an equal amount of independent research, for it is designed, as Cutlip explains, to create "independent learners, not passive recipients of information." He provides arguments for such a program, an outline of its content, and steps to take in implementing it. This is an excellent guide for library media specialists attempting to integrate library skills programs into the general curriculum. [R: VOYA, Aug 89]

894   Gates, Jean Key. **Guide to the Use of Libraries and Information Sources. 6th ed. New York: McGraw-Hill, 1989. 348p. $17.95pa. ISBN 0-07-022999-6. LC 88-12700.

As with previous editions, Gates focuses on college library collections and follows the traditional approach to teaching the use of library and reference tools and the steps involved in preparing research papers. The volume is divided into five sections: a history of library development; the Dewey and Library of Congress classification systems; general reference tools, subdivided under dictionaries, encyclopedias, indexes, and so on; information sources in the subject fields; and the research paper. Two new features have been added to this revision: a brief description of CD-ROMs and their use in libraries, and a list of review questions at the end of each chapter. Citations of reference sources have also been updated in this edition. This standard work is recommended for use in high school library media centers. [R: ARBA 91]

895   Hackman, Mary H. **Library Media Skills and the Senior High School English Program. Englewood, Colo.: Libraries Unlimited, 1985. 120p. $23.50. ISBN 0-87287-419-2. LC 84-28895.

Hackman stresses a curriculum match between the English department and the library and provides a model for team teaching literature, composition, and the performing arts. She also discusses how to publicize services and how to create an environment where effective interaction can take place. [R: BL, July 85]

E+
896 Hart, Thomas L. **Instructions in School Library Media Center Use, K-12**. 2d ed. Chicago: American Library Association, 1985. 431p. $15.00pa. ISBN 0-8389-0418-1. LC 84-18405.

A large part of this work consists of extensive bibliographies of media skills materials – textbooks, instructional units, puzzles, games, and tests, as well as microcomputer software and audiovisual material. Although dated, the items cited remain useful for those who require suggestions for developing instructional programs. [R: SLJ, Feb 84; SLJ, Oct 85]

E+
897 **How to Use the Library: An Introduction**. Bronx, N.Y.: H. W. Wilson, 1989. 20 min. color videocassette. $49.00. ISBN 0-8242-0786-6.

Four middle school students debate how to proceed with their assignment. Should they search the library on their own or ask the librarian for help? The librarian intervenes and guides three students to the library catalog, *Readers' Guide*, and an almanac, respectively. The fourth student listens and consults all three. Many libraries will not hold the range of resources and equipment available to these students (e.g., *New York Times*, microfilm reader-printer), but this videocassette is useful for introducing middle school students to the library. [R: SLJ, Sept 90]

898 **Integrating Library Skills into the General Education Curriculum**. Maureen Pastine and Bill Katz, eds. Binghamton, N.Y.: Haworth Press, 1989. 334p. (*Reference Librarian*, no.24). $44.95. ISBN 0-86656-841-7. LC 89-31193.

This response to educational studies, similar to *A Nation at Risk* (National Commission on Excellence in Education, 1983), contains 24 articles by librarians who teach library skills. Starting with a survey of the process, the articles review current programs in high schools, community colleges, and colleges and universities. Nonacademic programs in public libraries are also included. End-user searching and cooperation between high schools and colleges in bibliographic instruction are among the programs examined. These examples of successful library skills programs should interest high school media specialists.

E
899 **Into the Curriculum: Lesson Plans for Library Media Skills**. Santa Barbara, Calif.: ABC-Clio, 1990. 318p. $21.95pa. ISBN 0-87436-567-8.

Compiled from articles paublished in *School Libraries Media Activities Monthly*, this work contains hundreds of library activities in lesson-plan format that complement what students are learning in math, chemistry, language arts, the social sciences, music, art, and physical education. A useful guide for elementary school media specialists.

E
900 **Media Production and Computer Activities**. Santa Barbara, Calif.: ABC-Clio, 1990. 265p. $21.95pa. ISBN 0-87436-568-6.

This volume describes dozens of successful projects that use computers and hands-on production techniques designed to teach library media skills (e.g., finding and identifying leaves and constructing a laminated chart on which to mount and label them). The ideas were gleaned from articles published over the last five years in *School Libraries Media Activities Monthly*. Recommended for elementary school media centers. [R: BR, Sept/Oct 90]

■ *Reference Readiness. See* entry 136.

E
901 Seaver, Alice R. **Library Media Skills: Strategies for Instructing Primary Students**. 2d ed. Englewood, Colo.: Libraries Unlimited, 1991. 165p. $21.50. ISBN 0-87287-857-0.

Seaver provides practical suggestions to assist the media specialist in planning cooperative media skills programs with teachers of children in kindergarten through grade 3. Sample activities are given in detail; individual and small group approaches are emphasized. Other topics include literature enrichment, evaluation of learning, and rewarding student achievement. A version of the book with an accompanying disk for AppleWorks contains exercises that can be customized for individual grade levels.

902   Smallwood, Carol. **Library Puzzles and Word Games for Grades 7-12**. Jefferson, N.C.: McFarland, 1990. 220p. $19.95pa. ISBN 0-89950-536-8. LC 90-52696.

The puzzles and games in this work are designed to introduce middle and high school students to reference tools "in a way that is memorable and fun." The problems presented require students to consult standard reference sources, such as dictionaries, encyclopedias, and almanacs, and to explore maps and the library catalog.

The four sections—crossword puzzles, word searches, multiple choice, and matchups—each contain 20 activities arranged in order of difficulty. The puzzles cover world history, geography, foreign languages, and other curricular areas. Answers are provided at the end of the book. Careful editing to correct typographical errors would have improved this work, which is approrpriate for grades 7 and up.

903   Stripling, Barbara K., and Judy M. Pitts. **Brainstorms and Blueprints: Teaching Library Research as a Thinking Process**. Englewood, Colo.: Libraries Unlimited, 1988. 181p. $22.50pa. ISBN 0-87287-638-1.

This outstanding work covers the teaching of library research as a thinking process: brainstorms; right-brained conceptual activities that encourage creative research projects; and blueprints, left-brain actions that organize the ideas. A 10-step process creates the structure for this function. Other features include imaginative alternatives to traditional term papers; sample assignments for various thought levels; suggested research topics; guidelines for organizing information, taking notes, outlining, compiling a bibliography, and writing; and reproducible exercises. Highly recommended. [R: BR, Jan/ Feb 89; VOYA, Feb 89]

PLANNING FACILITIES

904   Anderson, Pauline H. **Planning School Library Media Facilities**. Hamden, Conn.: Shoe String Press, 1990. 360p. $32.50; $22.00pa. ISBN 0-208-02253-8; 0-208-02254-6pa. LC 89-13801.

Planning a library facility is a time-consuming procedure that may appear to be overwhelming. Anderson discusses the various phases of the procedure that fall within four broad areas: the planning process, design, preconstruction and furnishings procurement, and construction and completion. Almost three-quarters of the text consists of case studies. The remainder outlines important steps to take in planning and completing the project, with advice about such matters as communication among the planning participants and working with the architect. The book has some shortcomings—poor editing and the need for more analysis of the case studies—but any library media specialist planning a facility will find this practical guide handy. [R: BL, 1 Apr 90; SLJ, Sept 90]

905   Fraley, Ruth A., and Carol L. Anderson. **Library Space Planning: A How-To-Do-It Manual for Assessing, Allocating and Reorganizing Collections, Resources and Facilities**. New York: Neal-Schuman, 1989. 196p. $35.00. ISBN 1-55570-040-3. LC 89-13311.

Designed for managers in all types of libraries, this update of a 1985 publication offers practical suggestions for the use of library space. Step-by-step instructions are given for planning, measuring the collection, assessing facilities, budgeting, and maintaining the library during the moving process. Special features include diagrams and charts, floor plans, sample bid specifications, and other helpful information. A bibliography and index conclude the volume. [R: LJ, 15 Apr 90]

E
906   Hart, Thomas L. **Creative Ideas for Library Media Center Facilities**. Englewood, Colo.: Libraries Unlimited, 1990. 75p. $18.50. ISBN 0-87287-736-1.

This small work describes 27 media center projects designed to help create an imaginative learning environment. Some ideas deal with the physical facility, such as theme-based decorations, while others suggest programs and activities. Colorful illustrations support the descriptions. A bibliography on the psychological impact on learning of light, color, and other environmental features completes the volume. [R: SLMQ, Spr 91]

PUBLICITY

907   Bradbury, Phil. **Border Clip Art for Libraries**. Englewood, Colo.: Libraries Unlimited, 1989. 126p. $26.00. ISBN 0-87287-744-2. LC 89-2306.

School librarians who produce lists, bookmarks, flyers, newsletters, and other promotional materials will want this work. It includes 120 pages of decorative borders and art work arranged in six topical sections, such as libraries and reading, holidays, and children's activities and literary characters.

A disk of border graphics for the Macintosh, under the same title, contains 75 border designs and 44 clip art illustrations from the hardcopy handbook. Graphics are in Encapsulated PostScript Format (EPSF), which can be used with ReadySetGo and Pagemaker or other programs that read EPSF files. Graphics can also be used with Macintosh drawing program, but the program Curator is needed to convert the files. [R: VOYA, Oct 89, Apr 90]

E +
908   Everhart, Nancy, and others. **Library Displays**. Metuchen, N.J.: Scarecrow, 1989. 112p. $19.50pa. ISBN 0-8108-2183-4. LC 88-35640.

Librarians creating displays will find many useful suggestions in this guide. Each of the first 2 sections presents 39 displays with a list of materials needed and assembly instructions, but only the first section is illustrated with black-and-white photographs of the completed project. The final section explains display-making techniques and the pros and cons of various media. The work emphasizes exhibits that are inexpensive and easy to construct. [R: VOYA, Dec 89]

E +
909   Laughlin, Mildred Knight, and Kathy Howard Latrobe. **Public Relations for School Media Centers**. Englewood, Colo.: Libraries Unlimited, 1990. 134p. $17.00. ISBN 0-87287-819-8. LC 90-13353.

Experienced library media specialists, professors of library media education, and coordinators of school media services contributed chapters to this guide to public relations. The text offers advice on how school media specialists, teachers, students, staff, administrators, community groups, public librarians, and local/national government officials should work together to meet specific goals. One chapter focuses on a multicultural environment. The volume concludes with activities for discussion and a bibliography. This work, intended as a textbook, is a useful guide for library media specialists at all levels. [R: SLJ, May 91; VOYA, Aug 91]

E +
910   Schaeffer, Mark. **Library Displays Handbook: Everything You Need to Know about Creating Effective Library Displays**. Bronx, N.Y.: H. W. Wilson, 1991. $39.00. ISBN 0-8242-0801-3. LC 90-49442.

Library Displays Handbook, a comprehensive guide, provides step-by-step instructions for dozens of ideas designed to meet different budget and skill levels—signs, posters, wall displays, bulletin boards, and exhibits. Alphabetically arranged materials include some 200 how-to illustrations (16 in full color) and photographs of finished projects to lead the reader through each stage of design and production. Recommended for all levels. [R: VOYA, June 91]

Military Science

☐ _____ ☐

See also **World Conflicts** in **History**.

911 **Almanac of United States Seapower 1989**. By Navy League of the United States. New York: Arco/Simon & Schuster, 1989. 184p. $14.95pa. ISBN 0-13-023599-7. LC 89-275.

This compilation of statistics and information on U.S. seapower contains sections on weapon systems; submarine and surface ships on active and reserve duty; aircraft serving the fleet; and the U.S. Marine Corps, Coast Guard, and Merchant Marine. Illustrations include black-and-white photographs, tables, and charts. A useful ready-reference work for secondary schools. [R: ARBA 91]

912 Dupuy, R. Ernest, and Trevor N. Dupuy. **The Encyclopedia of Military History: From 3500 B.C. to the Present**. 2d ed. New York: Harper & Row, 1986. 1524p. $50.00. ISBN 0-06-181235-8. LC 84-48158.

An authoritative encyclopedia, this massive volume provides a guide to the world's military history from ancient times to the present. The 2d edition expands coverage to include the Iran-Iraq war, the Soviet invasion of Afghanistan, and the wars in Lebanon and the Falkland Islands. Entries not only describe battles, campaigns, and the consequences of war but also tactics, strategy, and weaponry.

The work is arranged in 21 chapters, each covering a particular era (e.g., the end of the Middle Ages). The text begins with a succinct survey of the age, followed by a continent-by-continent assessment of wars and battles and a chronology of important events. Over 250 maps and line drawings of weapons and fortifications illustrate the text. A bibliography and extensive index conclude the volume. Recommended for high schools.

An Encyclopedia of Battles by David Eggenberger (Dover, 1967 [reprint]) provides brief descriptions of over 1,500 battles through the U.S. invasion of Grenada in 1983. *Great Battles of the World* by John Macdonald (Macmillan, 1985) examines 30 significant battles in world history, from Cannae, 216 B.C., to Dien Bien Phu, November 20, 1953. [R: ARBA 87]

913 Flintham, Victor. **Air Wars and Aircraft: A Detailed Record of Air Combat, 1945 to the Present**. New York: Facts on File, 1990. 415p. $40.00. ISBN 0-8160-2356-5. LC 89-23382.

This work recounts modern aviation history around the world and documents every operational use of aircraft in warfare from 1945 to the present, including civil wars, international police actions, and the abortive attempt to rescue American hostages in Iran in 1980. Arranged geographically and subdivided chronologically, the volume discusses all significant conflicts in which aircraft were involved. A table of units, listing numbers and types of aircraft that participated, bases from which they operated, roles they played (e.g., liaison, night fighter) and dates, supports the entry for each conflict. Over 200 black-and-white photographs and 100 maps illustrate the book.

Appendixes contain military aircraft designations (e.g., British, American, Soviet), a glossary, and a bibliography. A comprehensive index concludes the work. [R: ARBA 91; LJ, Jan 90; RBB, 1 May 90]

914 Foss, Christopher F. **Jane's AFV Recognition Handbook**. Alexandria, Va.: Jane's Information Group, 1987. 554p. $18.00pa. ISBN 0-7106-0432-7.

This pocket-sized book provides quick identification of, and concise information about, almost any armored fighting vehicle (AFV). Separate sections cover tanks, armored cars and reconnaissance vehicles, armored personnel carriers, tank destroyers, self-propelled guns, armored engines and recovery vehicles, and armored vehicle launching bridges.

Each entry begins with key recognition features and a small silhouette designed for quick field identification. Detailed information includes crew size, armament, ammunition, weight and measurements, engine, road and water speed, cruising range, fuel capacity, a brief development history, armament variants, and manufacturer. The only work of its kind, it has been accepted as the world's standard. [R: ARBA 88]

915 Lawrence, Robert W. **Strategic Defense Initiative: Bibliography and Research Guide**. Boulder, Colo.: Westview Press, 1987. 352p. $42.50. ISBN 0-8133-7229-1. LC 86-7811.

This bibliography opens with a summary of the main arguments for and against the Strategic Defense Initiative (SDI). Chapters cover different aspects of the topic, such as the history of various theories for defending against nuclear attacks and technical considerations for ballistic missile attacks and defense. Every chapter also contains abstracts of important publications on the topic (books, articles, and documents), some 80 in all. A long, annotated bibliography of additional material, a glossary, and an appendix of documents and treaties conclude the volume. For high schools. [R: ARBA 88; LJ, 1 May 87]

916 **Leadership: Quotations from the Military Tradition**. Robert A. Fitton, ed. Boulder, Colo.: Westview Press, 1990. 382p. $19.95. ISBN 0-8133-7867-2. LC 90-34115.
    Brave or eloquent words spoken by inspired leaders are contained in this volume. Most are quotations from military leaders to inspire their troops to greater effort, but others are by leaders in sports (e.g., Vince Lombardi) and historical figures (e.g., Aristotle). The main part of the book groups the quotations by subject; the second part contains readings on leadership. Indexed by author. [R: ARBA 91]

917 Luttwak, Edward, and Stuart L. Koehl. **The Dictionary of Modern War**. New York: Harper-Collins, 1991. 680p. $45.00. ISBN 0-06-270021-9. LC 90-55998.
    Students of military science and tactics will welcome this comprehensive guide, which contains 1,600 entries on every aspect of modern war: weaponry, the art of warfare, the use of deception, military organizations, and treaties. Based on thorough research, this scholarly work is "direct and uncompromising, compassionate and brilliant," according to one reviewer. Illustrations and an index support the text. [R: ARBA 92; RBB, 15 Sept 91]

918 **Reference Guide to United States Military History 1607-1815**. Charles R. Shrader, ed. New York: Facts on File, 1991. 277p. $50.00. ISBN 0-8160-1836-7. LC 90-25673.
    The first in a projected five-volume series, this work describes the organization, equipment, and military doctrines of the United States and its allies and opponents. Conflicts covered span from the founding of Jamestown to the War of 1812, which some historians call the "Second War for American Independence." This survey, which also covers relevant events and important persons, should be useful to high school students writing papers on military topics. [R: ARBA 92; LJ, 15 Apr 91; RBB, July 91]

919 Royle, Trevor, comp. **A Dictionary of Military Quotations**. New York: Simon & Schuster, 1989. 210p. $35.00. ISBN 0-13-210113-0. LC 90-34034.
    Over 3,500 statements on war by both the famous and the little-known are arranged under five subject headings, such as "Captains and Kings," and subdivided by person, battle, location, and topic. Some short poems are also included. There are indexes by author and subject. Some of the brief quotations evoke a feeling of pity or sorrow, while others provoke laughter.
    The print is small and hard to read. *The Dictionary of War Quotations* has a more attractive format, cites more quotes, and costs less, but Royle's dictionary is a worthwhile addition to high school libraries. [R: ARBA 91; LJ, July 90; WLB, Nov 90]

920 Shafritz, Jay, and others. **The Facts on File Dictionary of Military Science**. New York: Facts on File, 1989. 498p. $40.00. ISBN 0-8160-1823-5. LC 88-28648.
    This comprehensive dictionary of more than 5,000 terms and concepts covers the entire spectrum of military science and tactics from the age of Napoleon to the present, but it emphasizes modern warfare and Western military ideas and practices. Entries address weapons, equipment, procedures, operations, acronyms, abbreviations, and well-known military strategists. Longer articles include bibliographies. Recommended for high schools. [R: ARBA 90; BL, 1 Nov 89; LJ, July 89]

921 Taylor, Michael. **Encyclopedia of the World's Air Forces**. New York: Facts on File, 1989. 224p. $35.00. ISBN 0-8160-2004-3. LC 88-6970.
    From Comoros's single Cessna 402 to the flying power of the United States, the greatest in history, this comprehensive work covers the military air power of 147 nations. Entries, arranged alphabetically by country, vary from one-third of a page to six pages and include the following information: population, number of air force personnel, official air force name in the local language, location of headquarters, number of major air bases, number of airplanes (fixed-wing combat, fixed-wing noncombat, combat helicopters, and noncombat helicopters), aircraft by model, a narrative description, and one or more photographs of aircraft (most in color). Indexed. [R: BL, Apr 89; BR, Sept/Oct 89; LJ, Apr 89]

922 Waldman, Harry. **The Dictionary of SDI**. Wilmington, Del.: Scholarly Resources, 1988. 182p. $40.00; $19.95pa. ISBN 0-8420-2281-3; 0-8420-2295-3pa. LC 87-12477.

This dictionary attempts to clarify some of the major concepts related to SDI deployment. It defines over 800 terms and acronyms related to ballistic missile defense, arms control, research and development, countermoves to defense, and more. Roles of various U.S. allies and persons involved in the research and management aspects of SDI are also explained. Additional materials include illustrations of systems, a copy of the 1972 ABM treaty, and names of the Defensive Technologies Study Team. [R: ARBA 89; WLB, June 88]

■ *Warriors and Adventurers*. *See* entry 337.

923   **Weapons: An International Encyclopedia from 5000 B.C. to 2000 A.D.** By the Diagram Group. New York: St. Martin's Press, 1991. 336p. $27.95; $17.95pa. ISBN 0-312-03951-4; 0-312-03950-6pa. LC 89-27096.
    The 2,500 black-and-white drawings and other illustrations of weapons used by many cultures throughout the centuries make this a desirable acquisition for high school libraries. The text is arranged by weapon function and then from simple to complex. The lack of alphabetical sequence is offset by historical and regional indexes, which enable the reader to identify weapons for a specific era and place (e.g., the U.S. Civil War, the Crusades). Several chronologies also provide access to specific areas of interest. Recommended. [R: BL, July 91]

924   Wintle, Justin, comp. and ed. **The Dictionary of War Quotations**. New York: Free Press/ Macmillan, 1989. 506p. $29.95. ISBN 0-02-935411-0. LC 89-16818.
    This well-designed, well-organized volume contains quotations on war from ancient to modern times. The 4,000 quotations are divided into three sections: general quotations on the nature of warfare; those about specific battles and wars, arranged chronologically; and those about military commanders, arranged alphabetically by name. Entries range from brief statements to paragraphs to entire poems. Indexed by subject and author. This attractive work is recommended for high schools. [R: ARBA 91; LJ, 1 Mar 90]

Occult

See also **Mythology and Folkore**.

925   Clark, Jerome. **UFOs in the 1980s**. Detroit: Apogee Books/Omnigraphics, 1990. 234p. (UFO Encyclopedia, v.1). $65.00. ISBN 1-55888-301-0. LC 90-40291.
    Clark, vice-president of the Center for UFO Studies, has produced the first volume in a projected three-volume set designed to survey developments in the field of UFOs in the 1980s. An introductory essay on the history of the phenomena is followed by seven lengthy articles on such topics as "Extraterrestial Biological Entities," a survey of developments by country, profiles of individuals in the field, descriptions of a number of UFO organizations with directory information, and reviews of 11 periodicals focusing on ufology. A bibliography and index conclude this objectively written volume. Appropriate for high school libraries. [R: ARBA 91; BL, 15 Dec 90; LJ, 1 Nov 90]

926   **Encyclopedia of Occultism and Parapsychology**. 3d ed. Leslie Shepard, ed. Detroit: Gale, 1991. 2v. $295.00/set. ISBN 0-8103-4907-8. ISSN 1049-9636.
    Based on two earlier works and now substantially revised, the set includes all aspects of the occult sciences—magic, demonology, superstition, spiritism, mysticism, metaphysics, miracles, psychical science, and parapsychology. In addition to phenomena, entries cover individuals, terms, organizations, and publications. Bibliographies follow most entries. Cross-references and general and topical indexes provide access. [R: ARBA 92]

927   Guiley, Rosemary Ellen. **The Encyclopedia of Witches and Witchcraft**. New York: Facts on File, 1989. 421p. $45.00; $19.95pa. ISBN 0-8160-1793-X; 0-8160-2268-2pa. LC 89-11776.
    Witches and Witchcraft covers every aspect of the subject in 400 entries dealing with animals, beliefs, events, legends, myths, practices, rites, and places. It also recounts the lives of famous witches and witch hunters. There are survey articles on the history of witchcraft in particular countries. Because

some people equate witchcraft with Satanism and religion, the author has included essays that "distinguish the differences." Topics are described in factual terms, neither affirming or denying their reality. There are over 100 black-and-white illustrations, an excellent bibliogrpahy, and a detailed index.

Russell Robbins's *Encyclopedia of Witchcraft and Demonology* (Crown, 1959), a similar, older work, covers much the same material in more detailed, but less graphic, articles. [R: ARBA 90; BL, 1 Nov 89; BR, May/June 90; LJ, 1 June 89; SLJ, June 89]

928   Lasne, Sophie, and Andre Pascal Gaultier. **A Dictionary of Superstitions**. Englewood Cliffs, N.J.: Prentice-Hall, 1984. 355p. $10.95pa. ISBN 0-13-210873-9. LC 84-11717.

The nine chapters of this book have been grouped thematically by beliefs and practices, covering superstitions in such areas as minerals, plants, animals, the weather, the human body, stages of life, and clothing. The introduction explains the origins of superstitions and their motives and classifies them. Each section is prefaced by an overview. Indexed. [R: ARBA 86]

Political Science

DICTIONARIES AND ENCYCLOPEDIAS

See also **History**, **Military Science**, **Social Studies**, and **Statistics**.

929   Evans, Graham, and Jeffrey Newnham. **The Dictionary of World Politics: A Reference Guide to Concepts, Ideas and Institutions**. New York: Simon & Schuster, 1990. 449p. $55.00. ISBN 0-13-210527-6. LC 90-46772.

Definitions for over 600 terms and brief biographies of people associated with ideas and concepts make up this volume. Examples of the political terms included are Marxism/Leninism, the Kennedy Doctrine, neutralism and neutrality, and *Ostpolitik*. This work is an excellent choice for high school library media centers. [R: ARBA 92; LJ, Dec 90]

930   Lentz, Harris M., III. **Assassinations and Executions: An Encyclopedia of Political Violence, 1865-1986**. Jefferson, N.C.: McFarland, 1988. 275p. $29.95. ISBN 0-89950-312-8. LC 87-46383.

A unique reference source, this encyclopedia covers assassinations and executions of political leaders worldwide, beginning with the death of Abraham Lincoln. The chronological arrangement is far more telling than an alphabetical arrangement would have been; it reveals the dramatic increase in such deaths over the years, especially in the last half of the twentieth century (72 pages cover 1865-1940; 161 pages recount deaths for 1940-1986).

Brief entries of a sentence or more cover lesser-known victims; prominent persons are dealt with in more detail. Entries usually include manner of death, motive, assailant (when known), brief biographical information, immediate impact on the political scene, and fate of the assassin (if known). For assassination attempts that were unsuccessful, the victim's name is rendered in Roman type as opposed to boldface type for those who died. Recommended for high schools. [R: ARBA 89; BL, 15 Oct 88; WLB, Sept 88]

931   Plano, Jack C., and Milton Greenberg. **The American Political Dictionary**. 8th ed. New York: Holt, Rinehart and Winston, 1989. 608p. $15.50pa. ISBN 0-03-022932-4.

This standard work consists of definitions and explanations of over 1,200 terms, agencies, court cases, and important statutes drawn from American political life from the local to the national level. Arranged alphabetically within 14 chapters, it covers topics such as the U.S. Constitution, civil rights, legislative and judicial processes, business and labor, health, and education. A detailed index gives access to the text. High school libraries holding an earlier edition need not purchase this revision, since the principal change is an improved format.

932   Shafritz, Jay M. **The Dorsey Dictionary of American Government and Politics**. Chicago: Dorsey Press, 1988. 661p. $34.95; $18.95pa. ISBN 0-256-05639-0; 0-256-05589-0pa. LC 87-72401.

American national, state, and local government is the subject of this attractively illustrated volume. Some 4,000 entries profile important political figures and explain terms, laws, landmark court cases, concepts, and events. The work has copious cross-references, about 125 information boxes, and many brief bibliographies.

Appendixes provide an annotated U.S. Constitution, a list of bibliographic guides to government documents, and references to key concepts organized by subject. This authoritative dictionary is recommended for high school libraries. [R: ARBA 89; BL, 15 June 88; LJ, 15 Apr 88]

933 World Government. Peter J. Taylor, ed. New York: Oxford University Press, 1990. 256p. $45.00. ISBN 0-19-520861-7.

The introduction to *World Government* explains how nations are created, how they work, and how they relate to one another. The main text divides the world into 22 regions – Canada and the Arctic to Australasia – and describes the variety of government forms within each area. Boxes provide information on each nation's political style; cite its coups, civil wars, and internal conflicts; and list its memberships in international organizations. Photographs, maps, charts, tables, and diagrams illustrate the volume. Recommended for high schools. [R: ARBA 92; RBB, 15 Jan 91]

HANDBOOKS AND ALMANACS

934 Austin, Erik W., with Jerome M. Clubb. Political Facts of the United States since 1789. New York: Columbia University, 1986. 518p. $64.50. ISBN 0-231-06094-7. LC 86-2605.

This volume focuses on data about American political and economic life from 1789 to the early 1980s. Arranged by categories, the text includes chapters on national leadership; state politics; parties and elections; wealth, revenue, taxation, and public expenditures; and demographics. Information varies, but on the whole the work helps the reader understand the U.S. political system and the economic and historical forces that have shaped it. However, it lacks an index; the reader must rely on the table of contents to locate specific data. [R: ARBA 88; BL, 1 June 87; WLB, Mar 87]

935 Barone, Michael, and Grant Ujifusa, comps. Almanac of American Politics. Washington, D.C.: National Journal. biennial. $56.90. LC 70-160417.

Intended as a tool for evaluating the performances of members of Congress and the political climate of each state, this biennial provides voting records and ratings by organized groups (liberal, moderate, and conservative) for each member of Congress. It also includes an overview of election results, a voter profile, census data, and so on, for each state and congressional district. Entries for members of Congress also include a photograph, biographical data, political career data, directory information, committee assignments, election results, and campaign contributions and expenditures.

Congressional Quarterly publishes a similar handbook, *Politics in America*, which gives fewer details. The *Almanac* is a first choice for high schools.

936 Congressional Quarterly's Politics in America, 1992: The 102nd Congress. Phil Duncan, ed. Washington, D.C.: Congressional Quarterly, 1991. 1700p. $69.95; $39.95pa. ISBN 0-87187-599-3; 0-87187-641-8pa.

Politics in America provides a statistical profile of each state, brief information on the governor, and a map of congressional districts arranged alphabetically by state. For each member of Congress the book gives biographical data and a narrative assessment of personality, strengths, and weaknesses. It also lists committee assignments, election statistics, campaign financing, key votes, and interest group ratings.

The volume is comparable to the *Almanac of American Politics*, which includes more information. Both works are excellent, but the *Almanac* is preferable, since their costs are comparable.

937 Encyclopedia of the American Left. Mari Jo Buhle and others, eds. Hamden, Conn.: Garland, 1990. 928p. (Garland Reference Library of the Social Sciences, v.502). $95.00. ISBN 0-8240-4781-8. LC 90-30202.

The "Left" is identified as the social element that has sought, and continues to seek, fundamental changes in U.S. economic, political, and cultural systems. Entries cover over 600 figures (e.g., Eugene Debs, Helen Keller, Sinclair Lewis), events (e.g., Haymarket Incident, Greensboro Massacre), organizations (e.g., Industrial Workers of the World, Students for Democratic Action), ethnic and gay rights groups, periodicals, and institutions. A brief bibliography follows each entry. Special features include a bibliographic essay on American life; a list of acronyms, terms, and movements; over 100 illustrations;

and an overlay. This outstanding work is recommended for high schools. *Right Minds* is a comparable work concerning conservative thought. [R: ARBA 91; BL, Aug 90; LJ, 15 June 90]

938 The Facts on File World Political Almanac. Chris Cook, comp. New York: Facts on File, 1989. 432p. $40.00. ISBN 0-8160-1377-2. LC 88-11208.

This authoritative work contains data about international political organizations, civil conflicts, United Nations peacekeeping operations, major acts of terrorism, and bilateral/multilateral arms control agreements. There also are a chronology of the nuclear era and tables that compare nuclear arsenals. The main section profiles the political structure of all nations; heads of state/governments since 1945; legislatures and constitutions; political parties and elections; population, urbanization statistics, and trends; and treaties and other diplomatic agreements. Other features include a dictionary of political events, a biographical section, and a glossary. Indexed. This handbook is second only to the *Statesman's Year-Book* and *Europa Year Book* (Gale, annual), which are more extensive and more expensive. [R: ARBA 90; BL, 1 June 89; LJ, 15 Apr 89]

939 Political Quotations: A Collection of Notable Sayings on Politics from Antiquity through 1989. Daniel B. Baker, ed. Detroit: Gale, 1990. 509p. $39.95. ISBN 0-8103-4920-5.

Political quotations from Homer to George Bush and Margaret Thatcher can be found in this volume. The 4,000 numbered quotations, arranged chronologically within topical sections, are cited by speaker, source, and date. The topical arrangement is further enhanced by author/speaker and keyword indexes. This book, a valuable supplement to general works such as *Bartlett's Familiar Quotations*, is recommended for high school libraries. [R: ARBA 91; WLB, Dec 90]

940 Riddick, Floyd M., and Miriam H. Butcher. **Riddick's Rules of Procedure: A Modern Guide to Faster and More Efficient Meetings**. New York: Scribner's, 1985. 224p. $19.95. ISBN 0-684-18427-3.

Since most people find *Robert's Rules of Order* difficult to use, this simplified guide to parliamentary procedure is recommended. It discusses various processes alphabetically, making it easier to locate a specific rule. The reader can search under such entries as "Amendments and the Amending Process," "Main Motions," and "Debate." The table of contents and index also assist the user in finding appropriate headings. The work is authoritative; Riddick is a former parliamentarian of the U.S. Senate, and Butcher is a former president of the American Institute of Parliamentarians. [R: BL, 15 May 86; WLB, Mar 86]

941 The Scott, Foresman Robert's Rules of Order, 1990. 9th ed. New York: Scott, Foresman/Harper-Collins, 1990. 706p. $25.00; $10.95pa. ISBN 0-673-38735-6; 0-673-38734-8pa.

942 Robert's Rules of Order: Modern Edition. revised by Darwin Patnode. Nashville, Tenn.: Thomas Nelson, 1989. 155p. $19.95; $9.95pa. ISBN 0-8407-7199-1; 0-8407-7184-3pa. LC 89-2904.

There are several versions of *Robert's Rules of Order*, the standard guide to parliamentary procedure. The Scott, Foresman version, one of the best, includes charts, tables, and lists of motions and rules. The Patnode version updates the style and content of the original work (1876) with modern language and rules, provides definitions, and reorganizes the text in a more logical sequence. *Riddick's Rules of Procedure* provides parliamentary procedure in an alphabetical sequence, instead of the topical arrangement of these two. [R: ARBA 92]

943 Wolfe, Gregory. **Right Minds: A Sourcebook of American Conservative Thought**. Lake Bluff, Ill.: Regnery Gateway; distr., New York: Kampmann, 1987. 245p. $16.95. ISBN 0-89526-583-4. LC 86-20388.

This work, which begins with a foreword by William F. Buckley, Jr., contains a lengthy first section identifying important conservative writings classified under 22 headings, such as the Welfare state, urban studies, and education. Part 2, the biographical section, identifies conservatives from the founding of the Republic to the preseent. Part 3 lists journals, periodicals, publishers, think tanks, and groups that have taken a conservative stance. Indexed by name. Recommended for high schools. [R: ARBA 89]

944 The World Almanac of U.S. Politics. Sharilyn Jee, ed. New York: World Almanac/St. Martin's Press, 1989. 414p. $29.95. ISBN 0-88687-432-7. ISSN 1043-1535.

This useful, inexpensive work provides factual and descriptive information about federal, state, and local governments. Brief essays treat such topics as the electoral college, budget process, campaign financing, and political parties. Also covered are federal agencies; popular government programs;

congressional committees; and concise biographies of members of Congress, cabinet members, federal judges, and important executive branch persons.

The user can find here the demographic figures for every congressional district, the voting records of members of Congress on 10 key bills, presidential election results by county, and the high officials of all states and 50 large cities. A comprehensive name and subject index conclude the volume. *Almanac of American Politics*, this work's closest competitor, offers more information, but *World Almanac* will satisfy the needs of most high school students. [R: ARBA 91]

BIOGRAPHY

See also **Biography** and **History**.

945 Abrams, Irwin. **The Nobel Peace Prize and the Laureates: An Illustrated Biographical History, 1901-1987.** Boston: G. K. Hall, 1988. 269p. $40.00. ISBN 0-8161-8609-X. LC 88-16313.

Information about the Nobel Peace Prize and those who have received it is the focus of this volume. The book includes a section that explains the development of the prize and describes the process by which the Nobel Committee makes its selection.

Biographies of laureates are grouped by time period, with a short essay that explains historical events and conflicts prefacing each era. The profiles are accompanied by bibliographies and a black-and-white photograph of the honoree. The appendix contains Alfred Nobel's will and a list of trends in laureate selection. This work is appropriate for high schools. [R: ARBA 89; BL, 1 Jan 89; LJ, 15 Feb 89; SLJ, Feb 89; WLB, Mar 89]

946 **American Leaders, 1789-1991.** Washington, D.C.: Congressional Quarterly, 1991. 534p. $27.95. ISBN 0-87187-594-2. LC 90-22351.

This work describes people from all levels of government: presidents, vice presidents, justices of the Supreme Court, members of Congress, and governors of states. One section, an updated version of the publisher's now out-of-print book, *Members of Congress since 1789* (3d ed. 1985) (which is similar to *Biographical Directory of the American Congress*), lists all members of Congress, giving state represented, party affiliation, birth and death dates, and years in the Senate or House. Other sections provide similar information, arranged by categories.

Appendixes list Speakers of the House and presidents of the Senate. This convenient compilation of brief biographical data is recommended for high schools. [R: ARBA 92]

947 **Current Leaders of Nations.** Lansdale, Pa.: Current Leaders, 1990. 1v. (unpaged). $95.00 looseleaf w/binder; $39.00/yearly update. ISBN 0-9624900-0-8. (815 Scott Way, Lansdale, PA 19446).

This service provides a three-ring binder that contains reproducible profiles of leaders throughout the world. "Leaders" are defined as those who wield power, rather than heads of state, such as monarchs. When leadership changes, subscribers to the yearly update receive a new profile within one month.

Entries, arranged by the name of the country, include leader's name (with pronunciation), title, and portrait; basic data about the nation, with its location pinpointed on a small map; political background of the country; and information about the leader. Signed profiles give personal background, trace the leader's rise to power, describe leadership style and domestic/foreign policy, and give a mailing address and current bibliography. There is no index. This convenient compilation is recommended for grades 8 through 12. [R: ARBA 92; BR, Mar/Apr 91; LJ, Jan 91; RBB, 15 Jan 91; WLB, Jan 91]

948 O'Brien, Steven G. **American Political Leaders from Colonial Times to the Present.** Santa Barbara, Calif.: ABC-Clio, 1991. 473p. (Biographies of American Leaders). $65.00. ISBN 0-87436-570-8. LC 91-30755.

American Political Leaders is an excellent source of biographical information on more than 400 key American political figures. The sketches range from a few hundred to well over a thousand words, depending on the importance of the individual. Portraits are included in a number of the entries, as are short bibliogrpahies.

In addition to being accurate, the biographies are historically interpretative and provide the reader with more than a bland collection of facts and dates; they give meaning and significance to the life of each individual. Ranging from the well-known, such as Franklin Roosevelt, to the obscure (yet important), such as George Mason, the work includes most significant American political figures, not just those who held high office. A must buy for all high school and public libraries. [R: ARBA 92; LJ, 1 Oct 91; RBB, 15 Nov 91]

949   Who's Who in American Politics, 1991-92. 13th ed. New Providence, N.J.: R. R. Bowker, 1991. 2v. $199.95/set. ISBN 0-8352-3012-0. ISSN 0000-0205.

Over 24,000 individuals active in U.S. politics, from the president to local town officials, are listed in this standard work. It is valuable for information on persons below the top echelons, such as mayors and county officials. Over 2,500 people are new to this edition; entries for those in the 12th edition have been updated.

Information (based on questionnaires completed by the entrants) includes birth date and place, family information, education, political positions held, publications, memberships, voting residence, and mailing address. Updated biennially. Available online through Dialog, File 236.

950   Women in Congress, 1917-1990. By the Commission of the Bicentenary of the U.S. House of Representatives. Washington, D.C.: Government Printing Office, 1991. 266p. $21.00; $16.00pa. S/N 052-071-00919-1; S/N 052-071-00918-3pa.

From 1917 to date, 129 women have served in the U.S. Congress. This work provides a black-and-white portrait/picture and a short biography of the background and political career for each. Entries are arranged alphabetically, but there is no index.

INTERNATIONAL RELATIONS

See also **World Conflict** in **History**.
See **Military Science** for weapons.

951   Conetta, Carl, ed. Peace Resource Book, 1988-1989: A Comparative Guide to Issues, Organizations, and Literature. Cambridge, Mass.: Ballinger, 1988. 440p. $17.95pa. ISBN 0-88730-289-0. ISSN 9740-0885.

Peace Resource Book examines the world's military system, critiques arms control negotiations, and explains the ideology and strategy of the peace movement. It lists peace advocacy groups and describes pacifist educational programs. Indexing for the peace groups is both alphabetical and by zip code, enabling users to identify organizations in a certain location. A final section is a bibliography of peace-related reference works, books, pamphlets, and other material, arranged by subject. Order information is included. [R: ARBA 89; BL, 1 Feb 89]

952   Everyone's United Nations. 10th ed. By the Department of Public Information. New York: United Nations; distr., Lanham, Md.: UNIPUB, 1986. 484p. $14.95; $9.95pa. ISBN 92-1-100273-7; 92-1-100274-5pa.

This revision, the first in almost 7 years, covers more than 40 years of UN history. Since each volume serves as a continuation of previous editions, this work emphasizes the years 1978 to 1985 and gives accounts of the UN's role in such incidents as the Grenada intervention, the Falkland Island dispute, and the Iranian hostage crisis.

Following an introduction that explains the work's organizational structure, the volume focuses on the agency's role in world politics and relates social, economic, and legal events in which the UN was involved. Each of the UN intergovernmental organizations is covered by a separate chapter. The appendix contains the text of the United Nations Charter, the Statute of the International Court of Justice, and the Universal Declaration of Human Rights. Recommended for high schools, especially those that do not hold the *Yearbook of the United Nations*. [R: ARBA 87]

953   O'Toole, G. J. A. The Encyclopedia of American Intelligence and Espionage: From the Revolutionary War to the Present. New York: Facts on File, 1988. 539p. $50.00. ISBN 0-8160-1011-0. LC 87-30361.

This reference book is the first authoritative and comprehensive work on the history of American intelligence and espionage. Some 700 alphabetically arranged entries, varying in length from a few lines to several pages, cover major figures in the field (some 500 entries), American intelligence organizations and their roles in 9 wars, topics (e.g., covert action, cryptography), events or incidents (e.g., Bay of Pigs), and a few terms. A list of abbreviations, 150 black-and-white illustrations, a 10-page bibliography, and an index are included. Highly recommended for high schools. [R: ARBA 89; BL, 1 Jan 89; SLJ, May 89; WLB, Oct 88]

954   Plano, Jack C., and Roy Olton. The International Relations Dictionary. 4th ed. Santa Barbara, Calif.: ABC-Clio, 1988. 446p. $49.00; $18.00pa. ISBN 0-87436-477-9; 0-87436-478-7pa. LC 87-26943.

The 570 entries contained in this standard work define terms in international relations and foreign policy. Each entry has a "Significance" paragraph, often long, that places the term in historical perspective. Entries are grouped within topical sections rather than being in a single A to Z arrangement, under such categories as patterns of political organization; nationalism, imperialism, and colonialism; and ideology and communication. An 11-page guide to major concepts has been added to this edition. Recommended for high schools. [R: ARBA 89; BL, 1 Oct 88]

955   Thackrah, John Richard. **Encyclopedia of Terrorism and Political Violence**. New York: Routledge, Chapman & Hall, 1987. 308p. $37.50. ISBN 0-7102-0659-3. LC 87-4304.
This encyclopedia explains in clear and concise language complex topics related to terrorism and political violence. Entries include personalities, organizations, theories, institutions, and idealogies. Several nations with a history of terrorism receive special attention. A list of abbreviations and acronyms (in the front), a bibliography, and an index are provided. Suggested for high school level. [R: ARBA 88; BL, 1 Mar 88; WLB, Jan 88]

956   **United States Intelligence: An Encyclopedia**. Bruce Watson and others, eds. Hamden, Conn.: Garland, 1990. 792p. (Garland Reference Library of Social Science, v.589). $95.00. ISBN 0-8240-3713-8. LC 89-28206.
This source, which overlaps *Encyclopedia of American Intelligence and Espionage*, provides definitions for more terms and has more erudite analysis of the organizational structure of intelligence operations and techniques. Other features include an extensive list of acronyms (63 pages) and a list of federal laws and executive orders that govern intelligence operations. The other work, however, gives more space to biography than this volume. Appropriate for high schools. [R: ARBA 91; LJ, July 90; WLB, June 90]

957   **Yearbook of the United Nations**. New York: United Nations; distr., Lanham, Md.: UNIPUB. annual. $95.00. LC 47-7191.
This annual covers UN activities for the previous year. Part 1 summarizes important issues and actions. Part 2 provides brief accounts of the work of specialized agencies for the year. Appendixes list UN members and their dates of admission; outline UN structure; and provide copies of the United Nations Charter, the Statute of the International Court of Justice, and the Universal Declaration of Human Rights. Recommended for high schools.

FEDERAL GOVERNMENT

General Works

958   Turner, Mary Jane, and Sara Lake. **U.S. Government: A Resource Book for Secondary Schools**. Santa Barbara, Calif.: ABC-Clio, 1989. 317p. $39.95. ISBN 0-87436-535-X. LC 88-34956.
This work provides much information on U.S. government for teachers and their students. Among its numerous features are chapters on the purpose, theories, and organization of American government; biographies of founding fathers and others whose theories influenced them; chronologies of important documents and events, giving their significance; the text of such documents as the Mayflower Compact, the Declaration of Independence, and the Preamble to the Charter of the United Nations; lists of members of Congress and current Supreme Court judges; and statistics on demography and voting patterns.
Also included are an annotated list of reference books and online databases pertaining to the subject; other classroom materials, such as print, video, and computer sources, a glossary of terms; and a detailed index. Highly recommended for high school level. [R: ARBA 90; BL, 15 Sept 89; BR, Sept/Oct 89]

959   **United States Government Manual**. By Office of the Federal Register, National Archives & Records Service, General Services Administration. Washington, D.C.: Government Printing Office, 1935- . $21.00pa. S/N 069-000-00033-9.
The official handbook of the federal government, this irregularly published manual (usually biennial) provides comprehensive information on agencies of the three branches of government; quasi-official agencies; boards, committees, and commissions; and international organizations in which the U.S. participates. For each, the work names key officials, gives its purpose and a brief history,

describes its activities, and (when appropriate) lists directories for regional offices. Highly recommended for high schools.

960 **Washington Information Directory**. Washington, D.C.: Congressional Quarterly. annual. $69.95. ISSN 0887-8064.

This is a directory of thousands of names, addresses, and telephone numbers for the federal government and nonprofit/special interest organizations with offices in Washington. It is one of Congressional Quarterly's most useful publications. Arranged under 17 subject headings, entries provide directory information, organization's director or other appropriate contact person, and description. It also gives press telephone numbers, locator numbers, public information offices, foreign embassies, state and local government officials, labor unions, and Washington institutions (e.g., the Kennedy Center, the Corcoran Gallery). [R: ARBA 90]

Congress

961 **Biographical Directory of the American Congress, 1774-1989**. By the U.S. Congress, Joint Committee on Printing. Kathryn A. Jacob and B. A. Ragsdale, eds. Washington, D.C.: Government Printing Office, 1989. 2116p. $82.00. S/N 052-071-00699-1.

This revision of a standard work contains brief biographical entries for over 11,000 members of Congress, beginning with the First Continental Congress and ending in 1989. Information includes dates, education, occupation, party affiliation, positions held while in Congress, length of congressional service, and subsequent career achievements. Sources for additional information have been added to this edition. Also included are lists of cabinet members for each presidential administration and a chronological list (by state) of the members of each Congress. Recommended for high schools. [R: LJ, 15 May 90]

962 **Black Americans in Congress, 1870-1989**. Washington, D.C.: Government Printing Office, 1990. 176p. $16.00; $12.00pa. S/N 052-071-00892-6; 052-071-00891-8pa.

Since 1870, 66 African-Americans have served in the U.S. Congress. This work provides biographies of each, accompanied by a black-and-white portrait. Among those included are Hiram Revels, the first Black member of the U.S. Senate; Adam Clayton Powell, representative from New York; Barbara Jordan, representative from Texas; and Harold Washington, representative from Illinois and the first Black American to be elected mayor of Chicago.

963 **Congress A to Z: CQ's Ready Reference Encyclopedia**. Washington, D.C.: Congressional Quarterly, 1988. 612p. $80.00. ISBN 0-87187-447-4. LC 88-20336.

This extensive work provides clear explanations of the structure and operations of Congress. The alphabetically arranged entries include definitions of terms, profiles of committees, historical facts, biographies of selected past and present members, and essays on 30 basic topics (e.g., lobbying, appointment powers, campaign financing).

An alphabetical list of entries at the front of the book cites all articles, with more extensive essays in boldface type. The appendix contains historical lists of members, classified by sex and ethnic groups; historical statistics; and explanations of procedures, including how a bill becomes law.

Extensive indexes refer to all names, topics, and terms mentioned in the text. The most comprehensive encyclopedia available on the U.S. Congress, it is an indispensable sourcebook for high school libraries. Highly recommended. [R: ARBA 89; BL, 1 Mar 89; BR, Jan/Feb 89; SLJ, May 89; WLB, Nov 88]

964 **Congress and the Nation: A Review of Government and Politics. Volume VII: 1985-1988**. Colleen McGuiness, ed. Washington, D.C.: Congressional Quarterly, 1990. 1194p. $135.00. ISBN 0-87187-532-2. ISSN 1047-1324. LC 65-22351.

This excellent work chronicles Reagan's second term. Each of the first 15 chapters focuses on a topic (e.g., economic policy, energy and environment, law and justice), and the final chapter assesses the Reagan administration and his impact on the presidency. The 234-page appendix presents information such as political charts and statistics, members of Congress for the period, and committees and subcommittees with their chairs. [R: ARBA 91; BL, 15 Sept 90]

965 **Congressional District Atlas: One Hundredth Congress of the United States**. U. S. Bureau of the Census. Washington, D.C.: Government Printing Office, 1987. $33.00pa. S/N 003-024-06234-8.

The *Congressional District Atlas*, issued since 1960, will be reissued to reflect boundary changes resulting from the 1990 census. The present edition was issued on the 200th anniversary of the American Congress. It includes maps for each state, the District of Columbia, Puerto Rico, and other possessions. Maps depict counties, cities with 25,000 or more population, and congressional district boundaries. Tables list representatives from each state and cite county and congressional district. Recommended for high schools.

Congressional Districts in the 1980's (Congressional Quarterly, 1983) provides a detailed study of each of the nation's 435 congressional districts, giving population levels, where people live and work, how they voted in the past, racial or ethnic predominance, major industries, and more. The publisher is expected to issue a similar volume for the 1990s.

966   **Congressional Quarterly's Guide to Congress**. 4th ed. Washington, D.C.: Congressional Quarterly, 1991. 1200p. $159.00. ISBN 0-87187-584-5.

This extensive guide to Congress now has sections on the changing pressures on Congress including lobbying; the recent emphasis on the salaries, honoraria, and other benefits; and renewed interest in ethics. The work also provides biographies of everyone who has served a term in Congress, a glossary of terms, and full text of the Constitution and historic pre-Constitution documents. This is an important source, but *Congress A to Z* is less expensive.

967   **CQ Almanac**. Washington, D.C.: Congressional Quarterly. annual. $195.00. LC 47-41081.

The annual *CQ Almanac* provides a summary of legislative and political activity that receives detailed coverage in the publisher's *CQ Weekly Reports*. The almanac describes every bill that has emerged from committee markup and classifies it according to such major policy areas as the environment/energy, agriculture, leadership/ethics/campaign finance, and law/judiciary. Each bill's meaning is explained and the step-by-step action on it is given. Appendixes include special reports on important events, texts of presidential messages and vetoes, and lists of public bills enacted and Supreme Court decisions. Indexed by policy area, bill numbers, and votes.

The daily *Congressional Record* (Government Printing Office, 1873-) is the government's official record of debates and other proceedings on the floor of Congress. It is intended to be a verbatim record, but congressional representatives may edit their words or add material. A weekly index and annual cumulative indexes provide access. "History of Bills and Resolutions," a section of the index, leads to information on all stages of a bill's progress from introduction to defeat or passage.

968   **CQ's Guide to Current American Government**. Washington, D.C.: Congressional Quarterly. semiannual. $11.95pa. LC 61-16893.

Published twice yearly (spring and fall), this guide selects the best articles published in *CQ Weekly Reports* that examine current problems facing the administration and Congress. It is designed to help readers learn the facts and processes that underlie contemporary political development. Sidebar insets contain facts about each issue. Issue articles that describe major controversies and political battles also identify key players. A chart showing how bills are passed and an index complete the volume. Highly recommended for high schools. [R: Kliatt, Sept 90]

969   Davidson, Roger H., and Walter J. Oleszek. **Congress and Its Members**. 3d ed. Washington, D.C.: Congressional Quarterly, 1989. 458p. $32.95; $23.95pa. ISBN 0-87187-536-5; 0-87187-491-1pa. LC 89-9814.

Since this work's last edition (1985), it has been extensively revised to show the day-to-day activities of Congress and the influence that the President, lobbies, the media, and the home constituency have on it. The book deals with every facet of the lawmaking process, from getting into Congress to running for reelection—party politics, fund raising, the advantages of incumbency, campaign strategy, and the complex congressional committee and procedures process. Some 60 charts and tables and an index enhance its usefulness. Recommended for high school students.

See **Law** for federal courts.

970   **Historical Almanac of the United States Senate**. Washington, D.C.: Government Printing Office, 1989. 324p. $38.00. S/N 052-071-00857-8.

The vignettes contained in this handsome volume, called "Bicentennial Minutes," were delivered on the floor of the U.S. Senate by Senator Robert Dole of Kansas. Some narratives describe prominent former members of the "greatest deliberating body in the world," such as Daniel Webster, Henry Clay, and John C. Calhoun. Others focus on lesser-known persons, such as Hiram Revels, the first Black senator, and Rebecca Latimer Felton, the first female senator. Events such as the Senate's approach to the Alaska purchase are also recounted. Nearly 200 illustrations enhance the text.

971   **How Congress Works.** 2d ed. Washington, D.C.: Congressional Quarterly, 1991. 157p. $17.95pa. ISBN 0-87187-598-5. LC 91-11116.

This inexpensive guide provides an excellent introduction to congressional procedures. Its chapters explain the workings of party leadership in Congress, the legislative process, the committee system, and more. Each section includes charts, tables, and boxes to illustrate the subject. Recommended for high schools.

972   Hutson, James H. **To Make All Laws: The Congress of the United States, 1789-1989.** Washington, D.C.: Library of Congress; distr., Washington, D.C.: Government Printing Office, 1989. 120p. $9.50. S/N 030-000-00215-6.

In celebration of the bicentennial of the U.S. Congress, this handsome publication was prepared to accompany an exhibit at the Library of Congress. It covers such topics as the creation of Congress, elections, rules, floor action, and prerogatives. A section on milestones includes important actions on civil rights, the economy, environment, foreign policy, education, and exploration. Photographs, drawings, and political cartoons illustrate this excellent work. Appropriate for middle and high school levels. [R: LJ, 15 May 91]

973   **Official Congressional Directory, 1989-90.** By U.S. Congress. Washington, D.C.: Government Printing Office, 1989. 1241p. $20.00pa. S/N 052-070-06542-7.

This important directory includes biographical sketches of members of Congress; lists of representatives, arranged alphabetically within each state delegation, with their terms of office; committees, joint committees, and board membership; administrative assistants and secretaries; biographies of Supreme Court justices; foreign diplomatic representatives; maps of congressional districts; and much more. Recommended for high schools.

The First Ladies

E+

974   Klapthor, Margaret Brown. **The First Ladies.** 6th ed. Washington, D.C.: White House Historical Association; distr., Lincoln, Mass.: Sewall, 1989. 90p. $9.95pa. ISBN 0-912308-39-7. LC 89-050706.

Similar to its companion volume, *The Presidents of the United States*, this work is a joint project of the White House Historical Association and the National Geographic Society. Each entry consists of a two-page spread and a full-page portrait, usually in color, of the first lady. The text provides a readable account of her private and political life. Women who served as official hostesses but were not wives of presidents receive a brief profile and a small portrait. Suggested for upper elementary through high school levels. [R: ARBA 91]

975   Paletta, Lu Ann. **The World Almanac of First Ladies.** New York: World Almanac/St. Martin's Press, 1990. $21.95; $9.95pa. ISBN 0-88687-587-0; 0-88687-586-2pa. LC 89-78438.

Wives of presidents constitute the focus of this volume, but those who served as first lady and others who acted as hostesses for bachelors or widowers also receive attention. Entries contain basic facts (e.g., dates, burial site); an official portrait; and a "More Colorful Facts" section, which offers personal notes, nicknames, other occupations, and additional information. Comparative data, an index, and a chronology complete the volume. Appropriate for grades 7 through 12. [R: ARBA 92]

The Presidency

976   Beard, Charles A. **The Presidents in American History: George Washington to George Bush.** rev. ed. by William Beard and Detlev Vagts. Englewood Cliffs, N.J.: Julian Messner/Silver Burdett Press, 1989. 227p. $12.98; $5.95pa. ISBN 0-671-68574-0; 0-671-68575-9pa. LC 89-3241.

An update of the 1981 edition, this basic work provides brief biographical information and summaries of the achievements of each president. Each chronologically arranged article, two to seven pages, profiles a president but does not analyze his administration.

Presidents from Franklin D. Roosevelt through Ronald Reagan are covered in more detail than others. Additional material includes a biographical digest, which contains facts about each president, election data, and a list of vice-presidents and cabinet members for each administration. This is an important source for junior high and high school level. [R: ARBA 91; BR, Jan/Feb 90; VOYA, Apr 90]

E+
977   Blassingame, Wyatt. **The Look-It-Up Book of Presidents**. New York: Random House, 1990. 159p. $10.95; $5.95pa. ISBN 0-394-86839-0; 0-394-96839-5pa.

This excellent work focuses on the lives, careers, and administrations of U.S. presidents, Washington through Bush. Judiciously written chapters, two to six pages in length, are supported by black-and-white photographs, cartoons, and other illustrations. Students from upper elementary through junior high school levels will find this volume easy to use and more understandable than *The Presidents in American History*. [R: SLJ, May 90]

978   **The Bully Pulpit: Quotations from America's Presidents**. Elizabeth Frost, ed. New York: Facts on File, 1988. 282p. $27.95. ISBN 0-8160-1247-4. LC 87-24381.

Quotations of American presidents, selected "on the basis of their historical significance, intrinsic human interest, and colorful or eloquent language," focus on the presidential years but also include some statements made before and after. The quotations are taken from speeches, writings, and remarks overheard by others. The topical arrangement includes comments on the presidency, war, foreign affairs, democracy, slavery, and many other subjects. Dates and sources are cited, and author/subject indexes provide access. Recommended for secondary schools. [R: ARBA 89; BL, Aug 88; BR, May/June 88; WLB, May 88]

979   Cohen, Norman S. **The American Presidents: An Annotated Bibliography**. Pasadena, Calif.: Salem Press, 1989. 202p. $40.00. ISBN 0-89356-658-6. LC 89-10816.

The American Presidents, designed for high school students and college undergraduates, contains materials commonly held in good library collections. Following an introduction that sets the parameters of the work, Cohen cites general bibliographies and important treatises on the presidency. A section on each president cites and annotates recommended books about him, with emphasis on publications that have appeared since 1950. Annotations (50 to 100 words) often note strengths and weaknesses of the works listed. An author index concludes the volume. Recommended for high schools. [R: ARBA 91; BL, 15 May 90; LJ, 15 Mar 90]

980   **Congressional Quarterly's Guide to the Presidency**. Michael Nelson, ed. Washington, D.C.: Congressional Quarterly, 1989. 521p. $159.00. ISBN 0-87187-500-4. LC 89-7184.

This book, which completes the trio of guides to the three branches of U.S. government—*Guide to Congress* and *Guide to the U.S. Supreme Court*—provides an excellent survey of all aspects of the presidency. It is divided into chapters on the origins and development of the presidency (from Washington to Reagan), the selection and removal of the president (e.g., nominating process, presidential elections), the powers of the presidency, the president and the public (e.g., media, measurement of public support), the White House and the executive branch (e.g., housing, pay and perquisites, daily life), the chief executive and the federal government (e.g., Congress, Supreme Court, bureaucracy), and the president and the vice-president.

Many ready-reference boxes scattered throughout the text present organizational charts, lines of succession, the oath of office, and more. Selective bibliographies follow each chapter. The appendixes provide complete texts of several important documents (e.g., the Constitution, the Declaration of Independence) and a list of each president's cabinet. This outstanding work is recommended for high schools. [R: ARBA 91; LJ, 15 Mar 90; WLB, Apr 90]

981   Cunningham, Homer F. **The Presidents' Last Years: George Washington to Lyndon B. Johnson**. Jefferson, N.C.: McFarland, 1989. 335p. $25.95. ISBN 0-89950-408-6. LC 88-35089.

This work narrates the post-presidential years and deaths of 36 chief executives. These profiles, averaging 10 pages, appear in a variety of sources, but this is the only book that brings them together in one volume. Some anecdotes are well known, such as John Adams' last words, "Thomas Jefferson survives," when in fact, Jefferson had died earlier that same day. Others, such as the painful last years of Ulysses S. Grant, are less well known. High school libraries should consider this work as a supplementary purchase. [R: ARBA 90; BR, Nov/Dec 89]

E+
982   DeGregorio, William A. **The Complete Book of U.S. Presidents**. 2d ed. New York: Dembner Books; distr., New York: W. W. Norton, 1989. 740p. $29.95. ISBN 0-942637-17-8. LC 89-30971.

This new edition has been updated to include Ronald Reagan's second term and the beginning of George Bush's presidency. Due to the in-depth treatment of the personal life of each president, it complements Kane's *Facts about the Presidents*.

Each chapter (one for each president) follows a detailed format that can include up to 39 subheadings (e.g., physical description, childhood, education, religion, presidential nomination, major events of administration). The readable style and inclusion of a wide range of facts, political summaries, and personal data make this a popular work for grades 5 and up, for which it is highly recommended. [R: ARBA 91; BL, 1 Mar 90; LJ, Jan 90]

E+
983   Freidel, Frank. **The Presidents of the United States of America**. 12th ed. Washington, D.C.: White House Historical Association; distr., Lincoln, Mass.: Sewall, 1989. 91p. $9.95pa. ISBN 0-912308-37-0. LC 89-050707.

This work, which summarizes each president's administrative years, is a joint project of the White House Historical Association and the National Geographic Society. The volume was last updated in 1981. Each entry consists of a one-page, readable narrative on the verso and the official White House portrait on the recto; all are chronologically arranged. The table of contents lists the artist of each portrait, and the appendix lists vice-presidents. *The First Ladies* by Margaret Klapthor is a companion volume. Both are recommended for upper elementary grades through high school. [R: ARBA 91]

984   **Inaugural Addresses of the Presidents of the United States from George Washington, 1789, to George Bush, 1989**. bicentennial ed. Washington, D.C.: Government Printing Office, 1989. 350p. $16.00. S/N 052-071-00879-9.

Each inaugural address is preceded by a portrait of the president and a paragraph describing the events of the day. Also included is information for the five vice-presidents who succeeded to the presidency but were never inaugurated. The addresses constitute a valuable historical collection. Recommended for high schools. [R: LJ, 15 May 91]

E+
985   Kane, Joseph Nathan. **Facts about the Presidents: A Compilation of Biographical and Historical Information**. 5th ed. Bronx, N.Y.: H. W. Wilson, 1989. 419p. $49.00. ISBN 0-8242-0774-2. LC 89-5825.

This standard work, an update of the 1981 edition and its 1985 supplement, provides an authoritative compendium of facts, statistics, and anecdotes about the 40 men who have served as president. The first part consists of a chapter on each president, giving information about his life, family, career, and administration, each with a black-and-white portrait. The second part contains comparative data on such subjects as occupation, college, military experience, electoral votes, and presidential vetoes. Indexed. This is a basic source for students from grade 6 through high school. [R: ARBA 90; BL, 15 Nov 89; BR, May/June 90; VOYA, Apr 90]

986   Milkis, Sidney M., and Michael Nelson. **The American Presidency: Origins and Developments, 1776-1990**. Washington, D.C.: Congressional Quarterly, 1990. 350p. $19.95pa. ISBN 0-87187-542-X. LC 89-29377.

Fourteen chapters examine the constitutional precepts that created the presidency and established its social, economic and political powers, but only one chapter focuses on the office of vice-president. The work, which chronologically discusses presidents from George Washington to Ronald Reagan, covers numerous problems such as the presidential use of war powers, the New Deal, the use of the media, and the consequences of Watergate. High school social studies teachers will want this excellent work. [R: Kliatt, Sept 90]

E
987   Oakley, Ruth. **The Marshall Cavendish Illustrated History of the Presidents of the United States**. North Bellmore, N.Y.: Marshall Cavendish, 1990. 8v. $149.95/set. ISBN 1-85435-144-3. LC 89-17371.

This chronologically arranged set is designed for students in the upper elementary grades. Each volume opens with a survey of the era covered and concludes with a glossary and index; there is no comprehensive index to the set. Entries chronicle the highlights of each president's personal life and political career (through George Bush), review the historical events of the time, and show in map format the growth of the states and territories during his administration. Each volume is heavily illustrated with cartoons, photographs, and drawings from the period and contemporary watercolors prepared for the set.

Elementary school media centers may find the articles on presidents in encyclopedias and other less-expensive volumes adequate to their needs. Those who require additional information may wish to purchase this set. [R: BL, 1 Mar 91]

988 **Speeches of the American Presidents**. Janet Podell and Steven Anzovin, eds. Bronx, N.Y.: H. W. Wilson, 1988. 820p. $60.00. ISBN 0-8242-0761-0. LC 87-29833.

Chapters on each of the 40 presidents survey their rise to power and key events in their administrations, then reproduces 4 to 10 of their landmark and lesser-known addresses. Each speech, most of them complete, is prefaced by a description of the circumstances surrounding it. Among the 180 included are John F. Kennedy's "Ich Bin ein Berliner," Franklin D. Roosevelt's "Nothing to Fear but Fear Itself," and Dwight D. Eisenhower's "Don't Join the Bookburners." Suggested for middle and high school level. [R: BR, Jan/Feb 89; SLJ, May 89]

The Vice-Presidency

989 Dunlap, Leslie W. **Our Vice-Presidents and Second Ladies**. Metuchen, N.J.: Scarecrow, 1988. 397p. $35.00. ISBN 0-8108-2114-1. LC 88-4123.

Little is known about many of the men who have been a heartbeat away from the presidency. A few have gone on to the higher office, but most remain only a name in history books. This work consists of concise biographies of vice-presidents—John Adams to George Bush—and the women who have served as second ladies. Each chronologically arranged chapter begins with a resume of a vice-president's highest personal and political achievements, followed by an exposition of events and accomplishments throughout his life. Quotations and anecdotes add color to the narrative and give the reader some insight into the subject's personality and political style. The second ladies receive briefer coverage.

Each chapter ends with a bibliography of the primary sources and secondary accounts consulted by the author. An index, predominately by name, concludes the volume. No other work of this type is available on the subject. [R: ARBA 89; BL, 15 Feb 89; BR, Mar/Apr 89; VOYA, Apr 89]

STATE GOVERNMENT

990 **The Book of the States**. Lexington, Ky.: Council of State Governments, 1990. biennial. $42.50.

The biennial issues of this work provide comprehensive statistical information and other material on the 50 states and the District of Columbia, plus some data on American Samoa, Guam, the Northern Mariana Islands, Puerto Rico, the Virgin Islands, the Federated States of Micronesia, the Republic of the Marshall Islands, and the Republic of Palau. (The latter three are administered by the United States as trust territories.) Among the broad areas covered are state constitutions; state executive, legislative, and judicial branches; state elections; management and administration; finances; activities, issues, and services; and intergovernmental affairs. Indexed. *State Elective Officials and the Legislatures* (Council of State Governments, 1991), a directory of office holders, is published in odd-numbered years. [R: ARBA 91]

991 Elliot, Jeffrey M., and Sheikh R. Ali. **The State and Local Government Political Dictionary**. Santa Barbara, Calif.: ABC-Clio, 1988. 325p. $49.00; $19.95pa. ISBN 0-87436-417-5; 0-87436-512-0pa. LC 87-18722.

This dictionary focuses on the organization and function of state and local government. Arranged alphabetically in subject chapters, 290 entries define terms and analyze their significance. *See also* references and bibliographies for further reading are provided. Recommended for high schools. [R: ARBA 89; LJ, 15 Feb 88; RBB, 15 Jan 89]

■ *Facts about the States*. See entry 581.

LOCAL GOVERNMENT

992 **The Municipal Year Book**. Washington, D.C.: International City Management Association. annual. $77.50.

Annual volumes provide extensive comparative and descriptive data on all incorporated communities in the United States and Canada with over 25,000 inhabitants. The topical arrangement has profiles of each city, giving such information as per capita income, minority composition, mayor and council terms, salaries of municipal officers and public service employees, municipal employment data, tax structure, bond ratings, and local management and structure. The directory section lists individuals and organizations. [R: BL, 1 Dec 88]

☐ ———————————— **Social Studies** ———————————— ☐

BIBLIOGRAPHIES

See also **Geography**, **History**, and **Political Science**.

E+
993 **Educators Guide to Free Social Studies Materials**. Randolph, Wis.: Educators Progress Series. annual. $27.95. LC 61-65910.

This annual describes some 3,000 items chosen for their curriculum value. All titles are annotated, but not all are free; some producers require the borrower to pay postage and insurance charges. The arrangement is by format: films, filmstrips and slides, tapes, scripts, transcriptions, and printed material. Each is subdivided by broad subject (e.g., history, geography). Indexed. Recommended for all levels. [R: ARBA 85]

CURRENT EVENTS AND ISSUES

994 **The CQ Researcher**. Washington, D.C.: Congressional Quarterly. 48 issues. $285.00/yr.

Each week the *CQ Researcher* (formerly *Editorial Research Report*) gives authoritative information on a current topic, from politics and science to art and the social sciences. These reference aids, which include an overview of the topic and a bibliography, may be purchased individually or on a full subscription basis. Recent topics include school choice, animal rights, endangered species, Palestinians, quotas, and parental consent.

995 **Current Issues (Arlington): Critical Issues Confronting the Nation and the World**. Arlington, Va.: Close Up Foundation. annual. $11.95pa. ISSN 0161-6641. *Teacher's Guide*. $9.95 looseleaf. LC 78-643561. (44 Canal Center Plaza, Alexandria, VA 22314).

The Close Up Foundation "encourages responsible participation in the democratic process through educational programs in government and citizenship." Each issue of *Critical Issues* (published annually since 1976 for high school students) provides information on 20 or more domestic and foreign policy problems. Among the subjects included in the 1991 edition are the economy, the environment, health care, the Middle East, nuclear proliferation, and international trade. Background and history, outlook, key issues, and pro/con positions for each topic are given. The teacher's guide includes classroom activities, worksheets, and other materials. Recommended. [R: SLJ, Dec 84; WLB, Nov 84]

■ *Current News on File*. *See* entry 148.

■ *Editorials on File*. *See* entry 1258.

996   Flanders, Carl N. **Abortion**. New York: Facts on File, 1991. 256p. $22.95. ISBN 0-8160-1908-8. LC 90-42867.

997   Flanders, Stephen A. **Capital Punishment**. New York: Facts on File, 1991. 208p. $22.95. ISBN 0-8160-1912-6. LC 90-42868.
      Each of the volumes in the Library in a Book series is designed as a "one-stop source of information," giving background information in part 1 and a guide to sources in part 2. The first section includes a historical survey; statistics; attitudes and trends; a chronology (1965 through 1989 for *Abortion* and 1924 through 1989 for *Capital Punishment*); significant court cases, with background, legal issues, decisions, and impact; and biographical data for persons who have played leading roles in the controversy.
      The bibliographic section offers a generic library search (e.g., using the library catalog, indexes), a bibliographic essay on basic sources; and an annotated bibliography that cites books, articles, government documents, brochures and pamphlets, audiovisual materials, and more. Other features include lists of organizations (pro/anti abortion and anti-death penalty groups) and acronyms. *Abortion* offers a state-by-state survey of public funding of abortion and consent/notification laws. *Capital Punishment* provides state-by-state lists of laws on the subject and the annual number of executions since 1977. Indexed.
      The approach of these controversial topics is balanced and impartial. Volumes in the series include *Suicide* and *Eating Disorders*. For high school level. [R: BL, 1 Mar 90]

998   Gay, Kathlyn. **Bigotry**. Hillside, N.J.: Enslow, 1989. 144p. $16.95. ISBN 0-89490-171-0. LC 88-30428.
      This history of bigotry, prejudice, and racism covers minorities, the handicapped, women, homosexuals, and other groups, giving examples of actual occurrences drawn from newspaper, magazine, and historical accounts. The volume also addresses the progress made by various groups. Special features include a large number of photographs, bibliographies for further reading, and lists of national human relations and civil rights organizations. Indexed. Recommended for middle and high schools. [R: BR, Jan/Feb 90]

999   Hombs, Mary Ellen. **American Homeless: A Reference Handbook**. Santa Barbara, Calif.: ABC-Clio, 1990. 193p. $39.00. ISBN 0-874-36547-3. LC 90-30936.
      This useful handbook, part of the Contemporary World Issues series, surveys the problem of the homeless in America. It lists 61 organizations concerned with this issue, provides biographies of activists and leaders in the field, gives information about pertinent federal legislation/court cases, and excerpts relevant documents. The volume also includes a chronology of events related to the homeless from 1976 through 1989. The annotated bibliography of print and nonprint materials includes appropriate computerized databases. Highly recommended. [R: ARBA 91; BL, 15 Nov 90; LJ, 1 Oct 90]

1000 **Ideas in Conflict Series**. Hudson, Wis.: GEM/McCuen. 30v. $12.95/v; $388.50/set. (502 Second St., Hudson, WI 54016).
      The Ideas in Conflict Series, a current-issues series for high school students, collects and reprints articles, speeches, and other statements by recognized leaders on timely topics. The statements present different viewpoints on the issues and are designed to help readers develop critical thinking skills and formulate their own opinions on the subjects. Each title includes a bibliography, suggestions for discussion, and ideas for research on the topic.
      The four most recent titles are *Poison in Your Food*; *Born Hooked: Poisoned in the Womb*; *Firearms and Social Violence: The Other Arms Race*; and *Ending War Against the Earth*. Some of the topics covered in earlier volumes include religion and politics, teenage pregnancy, the religious right, artificial human reproduction, illiteracy, world hunger, AIDS, and the death penalty. [R: BL, 1 Mar 85]

1001 Magel, Charles R. **Keyguide to Information Sources on Animal Rights**. Jefferson, N.C.: McFarland, 1989. 281p. $39.95pa. ISBN 0-89950-405-1. LC 88-21574.
      This guide surveys the issue of animal rights, provides an annotated bibliography of 335 titles (chronologically arranged), and gives names and addresses of 182 worldwide animal welfare organizations. A bibliography of all works cited in the text concludes the volume. Indexed by author/subject. This comprehensive work is recommended for high schools. [R: WLB, Oct 89]

1002 Myers, Norman. **The Gaia Atlas of Future Worlds: Challenge and Opportunity in an Age of Change**. New York: Doubleday, 1991. 190p. $15.95pa. ISBN 0-385-26606-5. LC 90-39354.

The first section of this excellent atlas describes world problems, such as the effects of technological advances, population shifts, poverty, AIDS, and changes in the agricultural and space industries. The second section maps areas of crisis, and the third focuses on solutions to the problems and organizations, such as Oxfam and Greenpeace, that take an active role in solving them. Recommended for high schools. [R: SLJ, May 91]

■ *NBC News Rand McNally World News Atlas*. See entry 551.

1003 **New York Times: Current Events Edition**. Ann Arbor, Mich.: University Microfilms International, 1979- . monthly. 100 microfiche. $195.00/yr.
Subscribers receive a monthly microfiche containing the full text of some 600 items that have appeared in the *New York Times* (e.g., articles, news stories, presidential news conferences, major political speeches, Supreme Court decisions). An index accompanies each fiche; semiannual and annual cumulated indexes are also provided.

1004 **Opinions '90: Extracts from Public Opinion Surveys and Polls Conducted by Business, Government, Professional and News Organizations**. Edward Weilant and Chris John Miko, eds. Detroit: Gale, 1991. 3 issues plus hardcopy cumulation. $99.00/yr.
Opinions compiles the results of public opinion polls conducted by pollsters, market researchers, statisticians, and others. Each of the quarterly issues (including the cumulation) contains information, arranged by subject, on about 150 to 200 polls and surveys. Details for each are provided—scope, purpose, methodology, groups surveyed, and sample questions. Tables, charts, and graphs present the results. Indexed by poll name, group surveyed, and subject. The appendix lists the organizations, firms, and centers that conducted the surveys. For high school level. [R: BL, 15 Jan 91]

1005 **Opposing Viewpoints Series**. San Diego, Calif.: Greenhaven Press. $15.95/v.; $8.95pa./v. (Greenhaven Press, P.O. Box 289009, San Diego, CA 92198-0009).
Opposing Viewpoints Series presents a balanced debate, in pro/con format, of important current issues. Each volume covers one topic, with chapters divided into key questions; opposing viewpoints are presented for each. Issues include critical reading and thinking activities to sharpen the student's analytical skills. Each volume is supported by an index and bibliographies of current, accessible periodicals and books. Some of the newest titles in the 57 volumes available are *America's Children*, *The Environmental Crisis*, *Trade*, *Censorship*, *Immigration*, *Eastern Europe*, *Central America*, *Social Justice*, and *War on Drugs*. [R: BL, 1 Sept 84, 15 Jan 85; SLJ, Jan 85; SLJ, Dec 85]

1006 **The Reference Shelf**. Bronx, N.Y.: H. W. Wilson. 6 issues. $56.00/yr. $15.00/v.
Five volumes per year provide current opinions and information on social issues and trends; the sixth volume, *Representative American Speeches*, consists of the previous year's outstanding speeches on diverse topics by prominent public figures. The subject volumes contain excerpts from a wide range of publications (e.g., magazines, newspapers, books, government documents) selected to provide facts and different opinions on the issue. An introduction gives background information, and a bibliography facilitates further research.
Topics announced for 1991 include health care, the debate over animal rights, the state of U.S. education, affirmative action, and our future in space. Recent volumes, available for purchase individually, address Islamic politics and the modern world, the problem of waste disposal, race and politics, rock music in America, censorship, and religion in American life. These volumes are especially useful in the small high school library with limited current source material.

1007 **SIRS Critical Issues Series**. Boca Raton, Fla.: Social Issues Resources Series. 4v. $238.00/set; $17.00 (annual update). 42x microfiche included. Available on CD-ROM (*see* entry 1009).
The SIRS Critical Issues Series includes special volumes that cover significant issues that threaten society with massive disaster. Volumes published to date include *The AIDS Crisis* (2v., 1987) and *The Atmosphere Crisis* (2v., 1989). Each consists of reprinted articles that chronicle the issue's history and current developments, giving a variety of viewpoints. An index provides access to each volume, and updates add new material each year. Other publications include SIRS and SIRS Science Series. [R: BL, 1 Nov 89]

E+
1008   Smallwood, Carol. **Current Issues Resource Guide: Free and Inexpensive Materials for Librarians and Teachers.** Jefferson, N.C.: McFarland, 1989. 402p. $19.95pa. ISBN 0-89950-388-8. LC 88-43487.

This work addresses free and inexpensive sources ($16.00 or less) about current problems (e.g., the homeless, acid rain, age discrimination, aging, AIDS, air pollution, nuclear energy). The guide cites over 2,000 sources appropriate for preschool through high school levels. Specific titles are not listed, but catalogs and other selection aids are identified. The cumbersome arrangement (with materials in one section and the directory of sources in another) impedes this book's use, but worthwhile materials are cited. [R: ARBA 90; BR, Nov/Dec 89; VOYA, Dec 89]

1009   **Social Issues Resources Series (SIRS).** Boca Raton, Fla.: Social Issues Resources Series. 32v. $900.00/set looseleaf w/binder; $17.00 (annual supplements). 42x microfiche included. available on CD-ROM. $1,250.00 (32v., Critical Issues Series, Science Series, and Global Perspective).

Social Issues Resources Series (SIRS) provides timely information on a wide range of problems confronting society. The program consists of reprinted articles on 32 topics in looseleaf volumes. (Individual volumes are available for purchase.) The reprints are selected from more than 700 newspapers, magazines, government publications, and journals. Some of the topics are pollution, population, drugs, energy, food, privacy, family, crime, alcohol, aging, mental health, ethnic groups, death and dying, and human rights. Each volume contains an index, and a CD-ROM comprehensive index gives access to the entire series. Updates add new material each year. SIRS also publishes SIRS Critical Issues Series and the SIRS Science Series.

GLOBAL STUDIES

1010   **Background Notes on the Countries of the World.** By U.S. Department of State. Washington, D.C.: Government Printing Office, 1980- . leaflets. monthly. $58.00/current set; $18.00/yr. subscription for all new and revised *Notes*. S/N 708-014-00000-1.

Background Notes, consisting of 3- to 15-page leaflets on each of the countries of the world, provides concise information on the land, people, history, government, political conditions, economy, and foreign relations. Also included are travel notes, a small map, a list of government officials, and a reading list. These leaflets may be purchased separately, as a set, or by subscription for all new and revised notes issued over a year. In-print *Background Notes* are listed with stock number and price in the free *Subject Bibliography No. 093*. Recommended for middle and high schools.

1011   **Country Study Series.** By Department of the Army. Washington, D.C.: Government Printing Office. For a list of available titles, request the free *Subject Bibliography No. 166* (Superintendent of Documents, Government Printing Office, Washington, DC 20402).

Formerly entitled *Area Handbook Series*, these volumes, all similar in format and content, provide authoritative and reasonably current data on nations around the world. They are designed for persons who need a convenient compilation of basic information about a particular country (e.g., government, population, climate, social conditions, politics, economy, national security, recent legislation). Bibliographies are included.

New books and revised editions are announced in the *Monthly Catalog* and *U.S. Government Books*. A price list of all available titles appears in *Subject Bibliography No. 166*.

1012   **Illustrated Encyclopedia of World Geography.** New York: Oxford University Press, 1990. $45.00/v.

Volume 1, on the Earth's natural forces; volume 2, on world government; volume 3, which discusses the uninhabited parts of the world; and volume 4, covering plant life, are part of a planned 11-volume set. They show great promise as an update and expansion of such works as *Marshall Cavendish Illustrated Encyclopedia of the World and Its People* (Marshall Cavendish, c1978, 1981), now out of print. Introductory portions in each volume provide a global survey of the topic, such as origins of the Solar System and the Earth, its climate, geology, and so forth, for volume 1, and systems of government and human rights for volume 2. The remaining 200 pages of each, arranged by region, deal with the problems and uniqueness of each area. Generous coverage is provided for such topics as acid rain, climatic conditions, and political situations (e.g., apartheid in South Africa). Volumes are well written; informative; and attractively illustrated with color photographs, maps, and diagrams, making them a first choice for the middle school level and upward. Volumes on peoples and cultures, planet management, and the world economy are scheduled. [R: ARBA 92; LJ, Jan 91; RBB, 15 Jan 91; WLB, Mar 91]

1013   Kurian, George Thomas. **Encyclopedia of the First World**. New York: Facts on File, 1990. 2v. $145.00/set. ISBN 0-8160-1233-4. LC 89-11649.
   This set has a full range of social and economic information on the noncommunist countries that make up the industrial and postindustrial world. Included are the countries in Western Europe and North America, as well as Australia, New Zealand, and Japan. Using the same format as *Encyclopedia of the Third World*, each chapter contains data for one country (classified under more than 30 subheadings) that ranges from historical background, geographical features, climate, and weather to foreign policy, defense, and international commerce. Other topics covered are the political structure and government, legal system, law enforcement, economy, agriculture, manufacturing, labor, and education.
   The same publisher also produces the Facts on File National Profiles series, which contains identical material on clusters of countries at $35.00 per volume. Works in the series include *Australia and New Zealand*, *The Benelux Countries*, *The British Isles*, *Japan*, *North America*, and *Scandinavia*. [R: ARBA 91; BL, 1 Sept 90; LJ, Aug 90]

1014   Kurian, George Thomas. **Encyclopedia of the Third World**. 4th ed. New York: Facts on File, 1991. 3v. $225.00/set. ISBN 0-8160-2261-5.
   This authoritative set provides extensive information about 126 Third World nations. For each there is a basic fact sheet that gives location, area, population, ethnic composition, languages, religions, colonial experience, civil service, foreign policy, health, media, culture, and much more. An organizational chart of each country's governmental structure, a historical chronology, a bibliography of books and films, and an index are provided. Recommended for high schools.

E+
1015   **Lands and People**. Jean E. Reynolds, ed. in chief. Danbury, Conn.: Grolier, 1989. $184.50/set. ISBN 0-7172-8012-8. LC 88-21454.
   A standard work that has been revised many times, this set provides accurate and readable information on the countries of the world. The section for each country provides basic data; colorful maps and photographs; and a signed article about the people, land, economy, and history, presented attractively.
   The set is organized by continent, one per volume, with nations arranged alphabetically. The volume on Central and South America contains a 10,000-entry index, a reading list in which titles appropriate for young readers are starred, and 30 pages of facts and figures (e.g., the Earth's and continental extremes, significant geographic features, lists of rulers, important dates in history). The set includes a separate, paperbound copy of the index.
   Of the 261 articles in this edition, 146 have been revised or replaced. There are boxed facts and figures scattered throughout the set, a map of each country and a continent map highlighting its location, 1,660 photographs, and national flags. Articles usually emphasize history, with less information about geography and culture, but the set continues to meet social-studies needs for grades 5 and up. [R: ARBA 90]

E+
1016   Middleton, Nick. **Atlas of World Issues**. New York: Facts on File, 1989. 63p. $16.95. ISBN 0-8160-2022-1. LC 88-675216.
   This atlas introduces children in elementary and junior high schools to world events and problems, such as drought and starvation in Third World countries, the relationship between developed and backward nations, and the pros and cons of foreign aid. Topics covered in double-page spreads have colorful maps and pictures. This work, a companion to *Atlas of Environmental Issues*, provides objective essays easily understood by the intended audience. [R: ARBA 90; SLJ, Sept 89]

1017   Parisi, Lynn S., and Robert D. LaRue, Jr. **Global/International Issues and Problems: A Resource Book for Secondary Schools**. Santa Barbara, Calif.: ABC-Clio, 1989. 222p. $39.00. ISBN 0-87436-536-8. LC 89-30325.
   Four critical global issues are addressed in this book: peace and security, development (population, health, hunger, and food), environmental problems, and human rights. The work has chronologies, statistical data, biographies of key world figures (e.g., Mother Theresa, Lech Walesa, Desmond Tutu), bibliographies (e.g., books, videocassettes, games), and directories (e.g., student exchange services,

nonprofit organizations). An extensive glossary concludes the volume. Recommended. [R: ARBA 90; BR, May/June 90]

1018 **PCGlobe +**. Tempe, Ariz.: Comwell Systems, 1989. System requirements: IBM or compatible. $69.96. (2100 S. Rural Rd., Suite 2, Tempe, AZ 85282).

This program includes a database that provides information on 177 countries (e.g., population, age distribution, ethnic groups, religions, languages, life expectancy). Among its many features are the ability to calculate distances between cities, to manipulate the world map so that a selected country is at its center, and to create graphs. *PC USA* is a similar program for the United States.

1019 **Rand McNally World Facts & Maps**. Skokie, Ill.: Rand McNally, 1989. 208p. $9.95pa. ISBN 0-528-83336-7. LC 88-062041.

This inexpensive work contains a series of essays about 36 world hot spots (e.g., Sri Lanka, the Philippines, the Persian Gulf States, Lebanon, Northern Ireland); a gazetteer that features black-and-white maps for each country; population data; and information about the countries' geographies, economies, histories, and politics. Much of the data is contained in reference books such as *Statesman's Year-Book* and current world atlases, but this volume is a convenient compilation of world data and would be an asset in most high school libraries. [R: ARBA 90]

1020 **The Statesman's Year-Book Historical Companion**. John Paxton, ed. New York: St. Martin's Press, 1988. 356p. $45.00. ISBN 0-312-00047-2.

Commemorating the 125th year of publication of the *Statesman's Year-Book*, this valuable volume covers all of the sovereign nations of the world, providing a historical survey and bibliographic citations for each. The most important events for each country, gleaned from the *Year-Book*, are described in articles of one to three pages. The arrangement is alphabetical by the nation's current official name in English. The index refers the reader from an earlier name to the current one.

This is an excellent compendium of hard-to-find facts. Recommended for high schools. [R: ARBA 90; WLB, Mar 89]

1021 **The Statesman's Year-Book: Statistical and Historical Annual of the States of the World for the Year**. John Paxton, ed. New York: St. Martin's Press. annual. $75.00. LC 4-3776.

Published annually since 1864, *Statesman's Year-Book* is an important source for high school students who require social, political, economic, and historical data concerning the nations of the world. It provides concise information on each nation's history, area and population, climate, constitution and government, defense, international relations, economy, communications, justice, religion, education, and welfare. The United Nations and its agencies and other international organizations also receive attention. Thematic maps and indexes support each annual. [R: ARBA 92; RBB, 1 Nov 91]

E +
1022 **World Eagle: The Monthly Social Studies Resource**. Wellesley, Mass.: World Eagle. annual. 10 issues. $38.95/yr. (64 Washburn Ave., Wellesley, MA 02181).

A monthly looseleaf social studies resource service for grades 5 through high school, *World Eagle* presents charts, maps, graphs, tables, and brief digests on current national and worldwide topics: population, the developing world, trade, the economy, the budget, social programs, human rights, energy, education, employment, youth, and taxes. Most information comes from U.S. government sources. Duplication permission is given for school and library use. This is an excellent source of current national and world data. Other World Eagle publications include the following atlases of reproducible pages: *Europe Today*, *The Middle East*, and *Latin America Today*.

1023 **The World Factbook**. By Central Intelligence Agency. Washington, D.C.: Government Printing Office. annual. $23.00. S/N 041-015-00169-8.

The *Factbook* is similar to *Background Notes on the Countries of the World*, giving brief factual data and small location maps for each nation. It describes the typography and resources of the land, water, people, government, economy, communications, and defense. Almost 250 countries are covered in alphabetical order.

Gale reprints this annual as *Handbook of the Nations* ($95.00), and WANT Publishing reprints it as *Directory of World Leaders* ($95.00). ABC-Clio publishes the contents in abbreviated form in 4 publications for $35.00 each: *World Communications & Transportation Data*, *World Defense Forces Data*, *World Economic Data*, and *World Qualify of Life Indicators*. [R: RBB, 15 Apr 91]

AFRICAN STUDIES

1024   **Africa**. rev. ed. Sean Moroney, ed. New York: Facts on File, 1989. 2v. $95.00/set. ISBN 0-8160-1632-2. LC 88-28649.

High school libraries that require information on Africa may wish to consider these volumes, which belong to the Handbook of the Modern World series. Volume 1 provides 7- to 30-page entries for each African country, covering geography, population, constitutional system, recent history, economy, social services, mass media, and biographies of prominent people. Maps are included, and there are 40 pages of comparative data. Volume 2, designed to examine "critical political, economic, and social issues," contains essays of 15 to 25 pages written by subject specialists. A 75-page index completes this volume. Libraries purchasing the set may wish to circulate volume 2 and place volume 1 in the reference collection. [R: ARBA 90; BL, 15 Jan 90]

E+
1025   Murray, Jocelyn. **Africa**. New York: Facts on File, 1990. 96p. $17.95. ISBN 0-8160-2209-7. LC 90-2967.

Like others in the Cultural Atlas series, this work is designed for students in grades 6 through 9. Two-page spreads deal with such topics as wars, rituals, daily life, schools, religions, music, art, drama, geography, climate, and animal life. Outstanding illustrations, maps, and timelines appear on every page. A glossary, a gazetteer, and an index conclude the volume. [R: ARBA 92; BR, May/June 91]

1026   Pyatt, Sherman E. **Apartheid: A Selective Annotated Bibliography, 1977-1987**. Hamden, Conn.: Garland, 1990. 169p. $25.00. ISBN 0-8240-7637-0. LC 89-7710.

Pyatt's objective is to identify writings about "the effects of apartheid on the people of South Africa and its indirect effect on the world." Works in English published between 1977 and 1987 are arranged in seven chapters (e.g., economic and labor conditions, politics and government), then classified by format (e.g., monographs, periodical articles, U.S. documents). Among the periodicals cited are *Business Week*, *National Geographic*, and *Newsweek*. An appendix identifies South African laws and regulations concerning apartheid. Indexed by author and broad subject. [R: ARBA 91; LJ, 1 Mar 90; RBB, 15 June 90; WLB, May 90]

1027   Stewart, John. **African States and Rulers: An Encyclopedia of Native, Colonial and Independent States and Rulers Past and Present**. Jefferson, N.C.: McFarland, 1989. 395p. $45.00. ISBN 0-89950-390-X. LC 88-7945.

The most complete record available of historical and present-day African rulers, this work includes 1,139 country entries (arranged alphabetically by the official name of country) that give alternate names, location, capital, a chronological list of rulers with dates of power, and a historical survey. Cross-references from alternate names are also provided. The volume lists 10,500 rulers and is current to January 1989. High schools that require comprehensive reference information on Africa should consider this volume. [R: ARBA 90; BR, Nov/Dec 89; LJ, 15 May 89; WLB, Oct 89]

ASIAN STUDIES

1028   **The Cambridge Encyclopedia of India, Pakistan, Bangladesh, Sri Lanka, Nepal, Bhutan, and the Maldives**. Francis Robinson, ed. New York: Cambridge University Press, 1989. 520p. $49.50. ISBN 0-521-33451-9. LC 88-267737.

Focusing on the era since European colonization, especially the period of independence, this reliable reference work provides a history of those nations that make up the south Asian subcontinent. The major topical sections cover lands, peoples, histories before independence, postcolonial politics, foreign relations, economies, religions, societies, and cultures. Sections are further subdivided for specific topics, such as country. The signed articles include some 70 maps, color photographs, and brief bibliographies. A glossary, a list of maps and tables, and a detailed index conclude the volume. Recommended for high schools. [R: ARBA 91; BR, Jan/Feb 90; SLJ, May 90; WLB, Dec 89]

1029   Ulack, Richard, and Gyula Pauer. **Atlas of Southeast Asia**. New York: Macmillan, 1988. 171p. $95.00. ISBN 0-02-933200-1. LC 88-17543.

This work is made up of beautiful illustrations—color outline maps, charts, and photographs—that detail Southeast Asia in 4 chapters and its 10 nations in separate chapters. More a textbook than an atlas, the book contains one small-scale physical/political map for each country and a map of each capital. There are an index for the text and a bibliography. Recommended for high schools. [R: ARBA 90; BL, 15 Apr 89; LJ, 1 June 89]

AUSTRALIAN STUDIES

1030 The Concise Encyclopedia of Australia. 2d ed. John Shaw, ed. Buderim, Australia: David Bateman; distr., Boston: G. K. Hall, 1989. 848p. $54.95. ISBN 0-949135-23-2.

Libraries that need information on Australia will find this volume useful for ready-reference and, in some cases, more extensive use. Most articles are brief, but those that cover more important topics, such as aborigines and sheep, are four or five pages long. All subject areas are represented. Small black-and-white illustrations, maps, charts, and other visuals enhance the volume. The alphabetical arrangement is supported by an excellent subject index that pulls together related materials on broad areas. Appendixes provide a chronology; lists of such things as award winners, government officials, extinct animals, and sporting events; and glossaries of botanical and scientific terms. Recommended for high schools. [R: ARBA 90]

CANADIAN STUDIES

E+
1031 The Junior Encyclopedia of Canada. John H. Marsh, ed. Edmonton, Alta.: Hurtig, 1990. 5v. $202.95/set. ISBN 0-88830-334-3.

This completely new work, designed for Canadian students of all ages, provides excellent coverage of Canadian history, geography, biography, literature, arts, science, social sciences, politics, and cultures. The text is well written and enlivened by anecdotes. Broad-topic articles include suggested readings. Illustrations abound, with color and black-and-white photographs, computer-enhanced images, aerial photographs, maps, and charts. Highly recommended for libraries that need information about Canada. [R: ARBA 91]

Chinese Studies. *See*
The Atlas of China, entry 535.
Atlas of the People's Republic of China, entry 536.

EUROPEAN AND SOVIET STUDIES

1032 Atlas of Eastern Europe. By Central Intelligence Agency. Washington, D.C.: Government Printing Office, 1990. 39p. $16.00 spiralbound. S/N 041-015-001-70-1.

Part 1 of this atlas contains six topical maps of the region, covering geography, historical boundaries, demographics, economics, energy, and population. Part 2 provides maps and other information for the eight countries of the area, Albania through Yugoslavia. For each nation, there is a two-page spread that has basic statistical data (e.g., population, land, literacy), communications, language, religion, and climate; a historical timeline; and five maps that show the surrounding area, the country, population density, economic activity, and land use. A glossary of terms concludes the volume.

1033 Europe Today: An Atlas of Reproducible Pages. rev. ed. Wellesley, Mass.: World Eagle, 1990. 156p. $26.50pa. $26.50 looseleaf. ISBN 0-930141-34-2pa.; 0-930141-35-0 looseleaf. LC 90-675169. (64 Washburn Ave., Wellesley, MA 02181).

This compendium of reproducible maps, tables, graphs, and other current data on the nations of Europe and the Soviet Union includes topical sections on such things as the land; people, countries, and cities; and energy, education, and employment. The looseleaf version is more convenient for reproduction. Highly recommended for junior high and high school. [R: ARBA 91]

1034 Milner-Gulland, Robin, and Nikolai Dejevsky. Cultural Atlas of Russia and the Soviet Union. New York: Facts on File, 1989. 240p. $45.00. ISBN 0-8160-2207-0. LC 89-30982.

A volume of the publisher's Cultural Atlas series, this handsome work provides a concise history of Russia and the Soviet Union from ancient to modern times. It is divided into three parts: geographical background, historical periods, and regions and the republics of the Soviet Union. The section on historical periods is the longest and is arranged in chronological chapters. Two-page boxed articles cover topics of special interest (e.g., Ivan the Terrible, the Baroque Period). The section on regions and republics provides brief historical, geographical, and cultural data about 15 republics and 2 major cities. Detailed maps and color illustrations highlight the text. The volume includes a bibliography, a glossary, a gazetteer, and an index to the text and illustrations. This work is an excellent source for high school students. [R: BL, 15 Mar 90; BR, May/June 90]

1035   Warmenhoven, Henri J. **Global Studies: Western Europe**. 2d ed. Guilford, Conn.: Dushkin Publishing Group, 1991. 256p. $11.95pa. ISBN 0-56134-038-3.
      This volume, an outstanding value, contains essays on regions and countries of Western Europe, articles from the Associated Press on the area, a glossary, a bibliography, and an index. The work contains a wealth of factual data that is useful for high school students' reports and assignments. [R: SLJ, May 90]

JAPANESE STUDIES

1036   Collcutt, Martin, and others. **Cultural Atlas of Japan**. New York: Facts on File, 1988. 240p. $45.00. ISBN 0-8160-1927-4. LC 88-2967.
      An excellent reference source on Japan, this work correlates the disciplines of geography, history, archaeology, anthropology, and the arts. Cultural life is organized by historical periods, from prehistory to the present. Material is presented in text, illustrations, maps, and reference tables. The volume also includes a basic bibliography, lists of rulers and prime ministers, a glossary, a gazetteer, and an index. Highly recommended for secondary schools. [R: ARBA 89]

1037   **Kodansha Encyclopedia of Japan**. New York: Kodansha; distr., New York: Harper & Row, 1983. 9v. $780.00/set. ISBN 0-87011-620-7. LC 83-80778.
      This standard set provides 9,417 entries on all aspects of Japan's land and people (e.g., history, biography, culture). Some of the alphabetically arranged articles, written by experts, are long, but most range from 750 to 2,500 words, and all have bibliographies. Over 1,000 photographs, maps, charts, and diagrams illustrate the text. Generous cross-references and an analytical index in volume 9 provide access to the contents of the entire set. This is the most comprehensive encyclopedia on Japan available in English. [R: ARBA 84; RBB, 1 May 84]

1038   Perkins, Dorothy. **The Encyclopedia of Japan**. New York: Facts on File, 1991. 410p. $40.00. ISBN 0-8160-1934-7. LC 89-71499.
      The Encyclopedia of Japan contains 1,000 succinct, alphabetically arranged articles on all aspects of Japan's history, geography, and culture, from its ancient heritage to its current role as a world leader. Entries, which include both English and Japanese terms, emphasize the present but do not neglect earlier times. Photographs throughout the work illustrate a variety of subjects. Lists of all prime ministers and emperors, from the legendary Jimmu Tenno to the present, are included. A bibliography concludes the work. While less comprehensive than *Kodansha Encyclopedia of Japan*, this excellent work is recommended for high school library media centers that do not need as much depth in coverage. [R: ARBA 92; LJ, 1 Nov 90; RBB, 1 Feb 91; SLJ, July 91]

LATIN AMERICAN STUDIES

■ *The Atlas of Central America and the Caribbean*. See entry 534.

1039   **Latin America Today: An Atlas of Reproducible Pages**. rev. ed. Wellesley, Mass.: World Eagle, 1989. 153p. $26.50pa. $26.50 looseleaf. ISBN 0-930141-22-9pa.; 0-930141-24-5 looseleaf. LC 89-675053.
      Similar in purpose and format to *Middle East Today*, this is a compendium of maps, tables, graphs, and current data on the countries of Latin America. Designed for such junior high and high school courses as geography and international relations, the atlas contains valuable material on countries, cities, lands, peoples, trade, agriculture, energy, education, employment, and many other topics. The looseleaf version is the most convenient for purposes of reproduction. [R: ARBA 91]

1040   **MECC Dataquest: Latin America**. St. Paul, Minn.: Minnesota Educational Computing Corp., 1989. 2 disks plus guide. System requirements: Apple II family microcomputer. $59.00. (3490 Lexington Ave. N, St. Paul, MN 55126).
      This database, designed to support social studies curricula, provides geographic, demographic, political, social, cultural, and environmental information about Latin American nations, Puerto Rico,

and Guam. After choosing a category of interest, students may select a specific topic from a subdivision list. The guide provides instructional objectives, ideas for classroom use, a bibliography, and suggestions for adding U.S. data for comparison. Reproducible handouts explain the use of the database and give sample search topics. The program, which can be used by individuals, groups, or an entire class, is recommended for grades 7 through 12. [R: SLJ, Sept 90]

1041   Moss, Joyce, and George Wilson. **Peoples of the World: Latin Americans: The Culture, Geographical Setting, and Historical Background**. Detroit: Gale, 1989. 323p. $39.95. ISBN 0-8103-7445-5.

This volume surveys the history, geographical setting, and culture of 45 indigenous and national people of Latin America. The old cultures (Aztec, Incan, and Mayan) and contemporary populations of 24 nations are each covered in 3 to 11 pages. Special features include line drawings, photographs, and maps; a glossary of foreign and unusual terms; a selective bibliography; and a subject index. Despite a few misspellings that resulted primarily from confusion about the use of Portuguese and Spanish words, this work is recommended for junior high and high school levels. [R: ARBA 90; LJ, 15 Oct 89]

E +
1042   Swenson, Mary, and others, comps. **Directory of Central America Classroom Resources K-12**. 2d ed. St. Paul, Minn.: Central America Resource Center, 1990. 172p. $12.95pa. ISBN 0-961-7743-3-9.

This guide to classroom sources on Central America, Mexico, and the Caribbean is organized into nine sections. The annotated entries within each give grade level and order information and suggest curricular tools, books for supplemental reading, and audiovisual materials. A separate section contains a directory of embassies and other organizations from which information may be obtained. Potential buyers should be aware that many of the publications listed in this guide express views in opposition to current U.S. policy in Central America. [R: ARBA 91; BL, 15 Jan 91]

MIDDLE EAST STUDIES

1043   **Atlas of the Middle East**. Moshe Brawer, ed. New York: Macmillan, 1988. 140p. $60.00. ISBN 0-02-905271-8. LC 88-675435.

Encyclopedic information on the countries of the Middle East (except Algeria, Tunisia, and Morocco) is found in this excellent atlas. The work begins with maps that show the regions' physical, social, political, economic, and cultural geography. Next come an average of five pages of maps each for Bahrain, Cyprus, Egypt, Iran, Iraq, Israel, Jordan, Kuwait, Lebanon, Libya, Oman, Qatar, Saudi Arabia, South Yemen, Sudan, Syria, Turkey, United Arab Emirates, and Yemen. An index and a bibliography conclude the volume. [R: ARBA 90; LJ, 1 June 89; RBB, 1 Apr 89]

1044   **The Middle East**. Michael Adams, ed. New York: Facts on File, 1986. 865p. $50.00. ISBN 0-8160-1268-7. LC 86-29274.

This work contains essays on Middle Eastern demographics, politics, religions, culture, and current events, and gives a historical background. The well-balanced and perceptive text is supported by maps, charts, and tables. The work is a part of the Handbooks of the World series. Appropriate for high schools. [R: SLJ, May 89]

1045   **The Middle East Today: An Atlas of Reproducible Pages**. Wellesley, Mass.: World Eagle, 1989. 152p. $26.50pa.; $26.50 looseleaf. ISBN 0-930141-17-2; 0-930141-18-0 looseleaf. LC 88-65622.

Designed for use in junior high and high schools, this compendium of reproducible maps, tables, graphs, and other current data on the Middle East was gleaned from U.S. government publications, newspapers, and other sources. Classes concerned with global studies, geography, and international relations will find useful information on land use, people, the economy, food and nutrition, employment, education, energy, and many other topics. The looseleaf format is more convenient for reproduction. [R: ARBA 91]

NEW ZEALAND STUDIES

1046   **The Illustrated Encyclopedia of New Zealand**. Gordon McLauchlan, ed. Auckland, N.Z.: David Bateman; distr., Boston: G. K. Hall, 1989. 1448p. $76.00. ISBN 1-86953-007-1.

This greatly expanded revision of the *New Zealand Encyclopedia* (Auckland: Bateman, 1984) contains 2,500 readable and balanced articles for biography, history, geography, geology, the arts, and many other cultural areas. Most entries are brief, but major topics are covered by substantial essays. The work has over 2,000 color and 800 black-and-white photographs as well as sketches, maps, diagrams, and graphs. Statistics are current to 1988. A chronology of New Zealand's history and an index complete the volume. This attractive encyclopedia is recommended for secondary schools. [R: ARBA 91; LJ, 15 Oct 90; RBB, 15 Nov 90]

Sports

CHRONOLOGIES

E +
1047   Carruth, Gorton, and Eugene Ehrlich. **Facts and Dates of American Sports**. New York: Perennial Library/Harper & Row, 1988. 373p. $27.50; $12.95pa. ISBN 0-06-055124-0; 0-06-096271-2pa. LC 87-46126.

This chronology covers sports from 1540 (introduction of the horse into North America) to January 31, 1988 (Washington Redskins' Super Bowl victory). The calendar arrangement for each year notes sports events of all kinds. Brief descriptions of 10 memorable competitions, 38 tables of records and statistics for 11 major sports, and 222 brief biographies of major sports figures are located at appropriate places throughout the volume. A detailed index of names, individual sports, and general topics supports the text. This unique source is useful in any library. [R: ARBA 89]

E +
1048   Jarrett, William S. **Timetables of Sports History: Baseball**. New York: Facts on File, 1989. 90p. $17.95. ISBN 0-8160-1918-5.

1049   Jarrett, William S. **Timetables of Sports History: Basketball**. New York: Facts on File, 1990. 77p. $17.95. ISBN 0-8160-1920-7.

1050   Jarrett, William S. **Timetables of Sports History: Football**. New York: Facts on File, 1989. 82p. $17.95. ISBN 0-8160-1919-3.

1051   Jarrett, William S. **Timetables of Sports History: The Olympic Games**. New York: Facts on File, 1989. 96p. $17.95. ISBN 0-8160-1921-5.

These year-by-year chronologies, designed for young readers aged 10 and up, cover regular and postseason games, All-Star games, players, teams, stars, awards, honors, Halls of Fame, and much more. Each year is covered on a separate page, with columns for different aspects of the game (e.g., college, professional, postseason play).

Baseball presents a complete record of professional baseball from 1903, the first year of the World Series, through 1988. *Basketball* spans the history of the organized sport from 1891 through the 1989 season, covering college and professional games. *Football* narrates 100 years of professional and college football history. *The Olympic Games* covers all Olympiads from the Athens Games of 1896 to the 1988 Games in Seoul, listing who won medals in competitions from archery to yachting. [R: ARBA 90; ARBA 91; BL, Aug 89; BL, Dec 89; VOYA, Feb 90]

1052   Sparhawk, Ruth M., and others, comps. **American Women in Sport, 1887-1987: A 100-Year Chronology**. Metuchen, N.J.: Scarecrow, 1989. 149p. $20.00. ISBN 0-8108-2205-9. LC 89-6150.

American women's participation in sports events is described in four chapters: "The Pre-Organizational Era, 1887-1916"; "The Organizational Era, 1917-1970"; "The Competitive Period, 1957-1971"; and "The Title IX Era, 1972-1987." All major sports are covered (e.g., golf, archery, track, tennis, figure skating), as well as many minor ones. Each year-by-year section recognizes accomplishments.

A bibliography (books, newspapers, and periodicals) gives the names and addresses of organizations that provided information, and there are black-and-white photographs. A name index enables the reader to identify individual achievements, and a sports index accesses information about a specific sport. Suggested for middle school level and up. [R: ARBA 90; BL, 1 Jan 90; LJ, 15 Sept 89]

DICTIONARIES AND HANDBOOKS

■ *Career Opportunities in Sports*. See entry 334.

E +

1053   Condon, Robert J. **The Fifty Finest Athletes of the 20th Century: A Worldwide Reference.** Jefferson, N.C.: McFarland, 1990. 152p. $20.95. ISBN 0-89950-374-8. LC 89-43643.

The selection criteria for the top 50 athletes of the century (chosen by Condon) includes those who dominated a sport for at least a decade, who achieved an unsurpassed level of performance, or who have been judged the best ever to have competed in a sport. Fans will not be surprised to find Jack Nicklaus, Jesse Owens, and Muhammad Ali among the greats, but they may wonder why Hank Aaron, O. J. Simpson, and Chris Evert are not cited. Others such as Bo Jackson and Magic Johnson have not met the criteria and thus were not included. Many sports are represented, including soccer, skating, track, and swimming, but baseball players dominate, and the majority are U.S. citizens (43) and male (46).

Entries for each athlete provide personal information, career highlights, comparisons to other players in the same field, and a photograph. A reference and a circulating copy are suggested. [R: ARBA 92; BL, 15 Apr 91; VOYA, June 91]

E +

1054   **Guinness Book of Sports Records**. New York: Facts on File, 1991. 256p. $18.75; $12.95pa. ISBN 0-8160-2649-1; 0-8160-2650-5pa.

Facts and feats for more than 75 sports are included in this popular work. Arranged from acrobatics to yachting, each entry begins with a history of the sport, followed by world, United States, and (where applicable) Olympic records. Baseball, basketball, football, and other well-known sports are included as well as less-popular ones such as croquet and table tennis. Black-and-white photographs and numerous tables illustrate the volume. Indexed. Circulating and reference copies are recommended for grades 5 and up.

E +

1055   **The Information Please Sports Almanac**. Mike Meserole, ed. Boston: Houghton Mifflin. annual. $8.95pa.

Each edition of this sports annual recaps the year, November through October. An introduction surveys the year's highs and lows, followed by brief essays on individual sports (e.g., pro football, golf, hockey, college basketball) contributed by sports writers. Tables record end-of-season standings and championship series, award winners, and coaching changes. They also rank teams, coaches, and individual performers in various areas of achievement. Other sections include a necrology, lists of members of Halls of Fame, a directory of professional teams and governing organizations, and a chronology of parks and stadiums used by professional teams. Indexed. This compilation of sports information can be used by all school levels.

The Sports Address Book, edited by Scott Callis (Pocket Books, 1988), is a convenient compilation of addresses for major United States, Canadian, and international organizations, conferences, teams, publications, clinics, camps, Halls of Fame, and individuals. Over 50 major sports, as well as less publicized ones such as dog sledding, are included. [R: ARBA 91; WLB, Mar 90]

1056   Killpatrick, Frances, and James Killpatrick. **The Winning Edge: A Complete Guide to Intercollegiate Athletic Programs**. 7th ed. Alexandria, Va.: Octameron Press; distr., Chicago: Longman, 1989. 290p. $15.00. ISBN 0-945981-27-9.

The Winning Edge is directed toward the "better-than-average high school athlete who wants to keep competing while pursuing his or her college degree." Ten essays, each two to five pages in length, examine such topics as eligibility rules, self-appraisal, and financial aid. A 20-page summary chart, arranged alphabetically by state, lists 650 colleges and universities, giving addresses and telephone numbers, conference membership, availability of financial aid, athletic budget, and sports for men and women.

The largest part of the volume describes programs for 18 major sports, baseball to wrestling, and a number of minor ones, such as rodeo and water polo. The program descriptions list schools alphabetically by state and provide further information about the budget, coaching staff, size of stadium, and scholarships. In some listings, a code indicates the school's own evaluation of its programs. High school libraries may wish to consider this informative work. [R: BL, 1 Feb 90]

1057 Lessiter, Mike. **The College Names of the Games: The Stories behind 293 College Sports Teams**. Chicago: Contemporary Books, 1989. 342p. $7.95pa. ISBN 0-8092-4476-4. LC 88-39124.

1058 Lessiter, Mike. **The Names of the Games: The Stories behind the Nicknames of 102 Pro Football, Basketball, Baseball, and Hockey Teams**. Chicago: Contemporary Books, 1988. 126p. $4.95pa. ISBN 0-8092-4477-2. LC 88-17699.

Those who seek background information on the mascots and nicknames of college and professional athletic teams will find these books helpful. *The College Names of the Games* gives detailed information for some 293 college sports teams arranged by 32 major athletic conferences; there is a final chapter on independent schools. Each one-page entry gives school's name and nickname, a black-and-white replica of the mascot or logo, address, school colors, year founded, name and seating capacity of arena and stadium, and information on the origin/history of the nickname. *The Names of the Games* gives the same type of information for 102 professional teams. These are not essential purchases, but they will add interest to the sports reference section. [R: ARBA 90]

1059 **Masters Guide to Sports Camps**. national ed. Carol J. Bast, and others, eds. Grand Rapids, Mich.: Masters Press, 1987. 1v. (various paging). $24.95pa. ISBN 0-940279-00-2. LC 87-10994.

This book lists some 4,000 summer sports camps in the United States and Canada that offer 48 major and minor sports for children up to age 18. Each of the four geographical sections—Northeast, Midwest, South, and West—is arranged by sport and indexed by camp name. Information supplied by the camps includes the program; the staff, often with experience; site, housing, and meal facilities; dates; cost; and address and telephone number. Useful in middle and high schools. [R: ARBA 88; RBB, July 87; WLB, May 87]

E+
1060 **Racing on the Tour de France: And Other Stories of Sports**. Columbus, Ohio: Zaner-Bloser, 1989. 63p. $19.95pa. ISBN 0-88309-546-7.

The 18 articles in this book, drawn from the last 20 years of *Highlights for Children* magazine, cover children's activities and sports, even fencing and skydiving. Each of the three-page essays includes a history of the sport and the rules, equipment, and skills required to play it. Sidebars list facts, organizations, books about the sport, and further activities. Recommended for upper elementary and middle school levels. [R: SLJ, Mar 90]

1061 **Rules of the Game**. rev. ed. By the Diagram Group. New York: St. Martin's Press, 1990. 320p. $24.95. ISBN 0-312-04574-3.

Despite its British origin, the revised editions of *Rules of the Game* is a useful reference work that covers more than 150 sports. Each article, arranged under one of 13 headings (e.g., water, court, team), contains detailed coverage of objectives, playing area, equipment, rules, timing, scoring, participants, and officials. Color illustrations are numerous. A chart lists national and international governing bodies in the United States, Canada, and the United Kingdom for the sports included. General and sports indexes conclude the volume. A number of sports have been added to the revision (e.g., jujitsu, windsurfing, hang gliding), and articles that appeared in the earlier edition have been revised and updated. For high school libraries. [R: BL, 1 Jan 90]

■ *Sports and Recreation for the Disabled*. *See* entry 616.

1062 **Sports in America: Paradise Lost?** Oliver Trager, ed. New York: Facts on File, 1990. 224p. $29.95. ISBN 0-8160-2412-X. LC 89-49285.

A part of the Editorials on File series, this collection of editorials and cartoons from United States and Canadian newspapers deals with controversies in sports over the last five years, such as the Pete Rose gambling scandal, Ben Johnson and the widespread use of steroids, the Len Bias tragedy and drug abuse, the trials and tribulations of Mike Tyson, the recent football and baseball players' strikes, and Proposition 42 and academic standards among college athletes.

Each of the five chapters opens with an article that surveys the major issues of a particular sport or the Olympics. A boxed summary of the news story precedes several editorials that comment on it. The depth given these issues makes this a useful reference source for reports and research papers. Appropriate for high schools. [R: SLJ, May 91]

E+
1063   **Webster's Sports Dictionary**. Springfield, Mass.: Merriam-Webster, 1976. 512p. $15.95. ISBN 0-87779-067-1. LC 72-42076.

Webster's, a standard (if dated) and excellent reference source, defines some 7,000 terms in over 100 sports, from airplane and yacht racing to karate, roller derby, and frisbee competitions. Alphabetically arranged entries explain rules, specifications of playing areas, signals, equipment, and language. There are quotations from athletes and sportswriters, and over 200 drawings and diagrams illustrate equipment, playing areas, and body positions. Appendixes include abbreviations, illustrated referee signals for football and basketball, and instructions for scorekeeping in baseball and bowling.

1064   White, Jess R. **Sports Rules Encyclopedia**. 2d ed. Champaign, Ill.: Leisure Press/Human Kinetics, 1990. 732p. $42.00 ISBN 0-88011-363-4. LC 89-2280.

This current, comprehensive review of sports rules covers 51 areas, with only a few minor omissions. Rules are those of the sport's ruling body in the United States and in some cases are not those used by college or high school teams. Overall, this is the best survey of sports rules available. [R: ARBA 91]

BIOGRAPHY

E+
1065   Sullivan, George. **Great Lives: Sports**. New York: Scribner's/Macmillan, 1988. 273p. $22.95. ISBN 0-684-18510-5.

Students in grades 5 through 8 who require report material about outstanding athletes will find this a useful source. The alphabetically arranged biographies of 24 men and 5 women, representing 12 sports, highlight personal and athletic achievements. Photographs and short bibliographies are included. A table of athletes, arranged by time period, concludes the volume. [R: BL, 1 Jan 89; BR, May/June 89; SLJ, Jan 89]

BASEBALL

E+
1066   Aylesworth, Thomas G. **The Kids' World Almanac of Baseball**. New York: Pharos Books/ St. Martin's Press, 1990. 269p. $14.95; $6.95pa. ISBN 0-88687-463-7; 0-88687-563-3pa.

An informative and entertaining collection of data, this work contains an abundance of baseball trivia, lists, rules, and anecdotes. It also has biographies of superstars, a brief history of the World Series, records (e.g., oldest, youngest, shortest, tallest, most memorable), and advice on how to play to win. Numerous drawings illustrate the volume. Elementary and middle school sports fans will enjoy browsing through this inexpensive work. [R: Kliatt, Apr 90]

1067   **The Ballplayers: Baseball's Ultimate Biographical Reference**. Mike Shatzkin, ed. New York: William Morrow, 1990. 1230p. $39.95. ISBN 0-87795-984-6. LC 89-77086.

As the subtitle states, this work is primarily a biographical source and does not replace *The Baseball Encyclopedia* and other statistical works. *Ballplayers* covers people, places, organizations, and teams from the beginning of the sport through the 1989 season. More than 5,000 biographical sketches (a few sentences to several pages in length) profile major league players and managers; an additional 1,000 entries cover league executives; umpires; broadcasters; scouts; sports columnists; ballparks; stadiums; major and minor league teams; and players from the Japanese, Mexican, and Negro leagues.

Career information for players is comprehensive: nicknames, team affiliations, position, years in the major leagues, and summary statistics. When applicable, entries list awards, All-Star Game selections, World Series and League Championship statistics, and Hall of Fame information. Many off-the-field incidents (e.g., Pete Rose's suspension) are also included. Over 500 black-and-white photographs are scattered throughout the volume.

This work is especially useful for the unusual information it provides that other sources lack (e.g., the role Branch Rickey played in integrating baseball). Recommended. [R: ARBA 91; LJ, 1 Apr 90; RBB, 1 June 90; WLB, Sept 90]

E+
1068   The Baseball Encyclopedia: The Complete and Official Record of Major League Baseball. 8th rev. ed. Rick Wolff, ed. New York: Macmillan, 1990. 2781p. $49.95. ISBN 0-02-579040-4. LC 89-29902.

This work records major league baseball through the 1989 World Series. It provides player and pitcher registers (60 percent of the book); special achievements and awards; a chronological list of team standings, team rosters, player records, playoffs, and World Series games; rules; and sidelights.

This edition adds complete fielding records, a section on the start of the Negro League, and a new introductory history of the game. Virtually every record one might seek is contained in the volume, which is considered to be the basic reference work on baseball. [R: BL, 15 Nov 90; LJ, 1 Sept 90]

1069   The Complete Baseball Record Book. St. Louis, Mo.: Sporting News. annual. $14.95pa.

1070   Official Baseball Register. St. Louis, Mo.: Sporting News. annual. $11.95.

A comprehensive and authoritative work, the *Record Book* contains batting, baserunning, pitching, and fielding records for players, clubs, and leagues. Also included are the records of managers, umpires, All-Star games, the Championship series, and the World Series. The *Register* gives lifetime personal and statistical data for every active player and manager in the major leagues.

1071   Dickson, Paul. **The Dickson Baseball Dictionary**. New York: Facts on File, 1989. 438p. $35.00. ISBN 0-8160-1741-7. LC 88-23583.

This entertaining work contains words, phrases, and terms associated with baseball. Dickson consulted major baseball libraries in the preparation of this volume, and he quotes many well-known baseball writers, A definition is often followed by examples of use and a note explaining its etymology or first appearance.

Dickson's work includes 5,000 terms, compared to only 1,500 in *Fungoes, Floaters, and Fork Balls* by Patrick Ercolano (Prentice-Hall, 1987), a well-researched volume that also defines the rich vocabulary of baseball slang. Both are highly recommended for secondary schools. [R: ARBA 90; LJ, 15 Mar 89; WLB, May 89]

1072   Mote, James. **Everything Baseball**. New York: Prentice Hall Press, 1989. 429p. $14.95pa. ISBN 0-13-292889-2. LC 88-28816.

This unusual work, a celebration of baseball, attempts to identify all mentions of the sport by the arts from the nineteenth century to the present. The arrangement is by art form (e.g., books, movies, sheet music) with interesting articles and many illustrations. Highly recommended. [R: ARBA 91]

1073   Neft, David S., and Richard M. Cohen. **The Sports Encyclopedia: Baseball**. 9th ed. New York: St. Martin's Press, 1989. 629p. $16.95pa. ISBN 0-312-02644-7. LC 88-29854.

This standard work, one of the best on baseball, contains accurate, concise, and complete information through the 1988 season. The print is small, and there is no index, but the volume is a bargain. The records cover year-by-year rosters, with players' statistics for teams in each league and statistics for batters and pitchers by period since 1901. Baseball fans will welcome this guide, which offers a gold mine of information. [R: ARBA 91]

E+
1074   Schoor, Gene. **The History of the World Series**. New York: Morrow, 1990. 431p. $27.95. ISBN 0-688-07995-4.

Schoor's work covers each World Series game, 1904 through 1989, providing records and highlights for the series as a whole. An appendix lists series records. The narrative is less exciting than the games, but the content is sound, and baseball fans at all levels will appreciate its reference value. This work supersedes *The World Series* by John Devaney and Burt Goldblatt (Rand McNally, 1972), now out of print.

Sporting News publishes *The Series* (1988), which gives a year-by-year account of each World Series and lists game-by-game box scores. The same information is provided for the American and National League Championship series, beginning with 1969. [R: LJ, 15 Sept 90; WLB, Dec 90]

1075   Sugar, Bert Randolph, ed. **Baseballistics: The Absolutely, Positively, Greatest Book of Baseball Facts, Figures, and Astonishing Lists Ever Compiled**. New York: St. Martin's Press, 1990. 400p. $16.95pa. ISBN 0-312-03789-9. LC 89-27091.

This reasonably priced compendium, useful in all libraries requiring baseball statistics, is arranged in seven sections: batting, pitching, Hall of Fame, awards, All-Star games, miscellany, and team-by-team leaders. Libraries holding the *Baseball Encyclopedia*, the most basic reference source on the subject, will find unique features in *Baseballistics*: batting and pitching leaders for each team and players who have led their club throughout history. [R: ARBA 91; LJ, 15 June 90; RBB, 15 May 90]

1076 **Total Baseball**. John Thorn and P. Palmer, eds. New York: Warner Books, 1989. 2294p. $49.95. ISBN 0-446-51389-X.
This work rivals *Baseball Encyclopedia* in its impressive coverage of the sport. The book opens with 38 essays on a variety of topics (e.g., All-Star games, foreign-born players, Japanese baseball). The main section provides statistics for over a century of baseball, listing annual league leaders in numerous categories, ranking lifetime and single-season players, printing annual team rosters, and much more. Citation of the batting, field, and baserunning performance of over 13,000 players is a major feature of this work. Other sections include such statistics as hitting, runs batted in, times caught stealing, and times on base. Highly recommended. [R: WLB, Sept 89]

E +
1077 Weiner, Eric. **The Kids' Complete Baseball Catalog**. New York: Julian Messner, 1991. 254p. $15.98; $12.95pa. ISBN 0-671-70196-7; 0-671-70197-5pa. LC 90-45155.
This highly recommended work contains 13 chapters on such topics as baseball camps, Halls of Fame and museums, television and radio stations of each major league team, baseball card collecting, fan clubs, magazines and newsletters, videos and software, uniform suppliers, and sources of free items. The book is further enhanced by black-and-white photographs of past and present stars, and sidebar articles that include crossword puzzles, personal anecdotes, and quizzes. Indexed by personal name and subject. Young baseball fans will appreciate having a copy for circulation as well as reference. [R: WLB, May 91]

BASKETBALL

E +
1078 Neft, David S., and Richard M. Cohen. **The Sports Encyclopedia: Pro Basketball**. 3d ed. New York: St. Martin's Press, 1990. 589p. $17.95. ISBN 0-312-05162-X.
First published in 1975, this work contains a statistical and historical survey of professional basketball since 1896, when the first professional game was played in Trenton, New Jersey, through the 1988-1989 NBA season. Six sections, each covering about a decade, provide an essay on the season's highlights, year-by-year chronologies, and statistical data for the years. Player rosters provide year-by-year and lifetime statistics.
Each of the sections (except the earliest) lists players of the decade, providing for each nicknames, teams, birth year, height and weight, position, college, years as a player, and statistics. There are no photographs, and the volume is not indexed. This informative work is worthy of consideration, but it is less attractive and less readable than *The Official NBA Basketball Encyclopedia*. [R: ARBA 92]

E +
1079 **The Official NBA Basketball Encyclopedia: The Complete History and Statistics of Professional Basketball**. Zander Hollander and Alex Sachare, eds. New York: Villard/Random House, 1989. 766p. $29.95. ISBN 0-394-58039-7. LC 89-40201.
Entertaining and informational, this work traces basketball history "from the early years of barnstorming teams who played their games in dance halls" to modern times. Two chapters describe the sport before the NBA was formed; the history of the NBA through the 1988-1989 season follows. For each season, the work provides highlights, one or two black-and-white action photographs, final standings, playoff results, and individual records. Also included are summaries, results, records, and most valuable player awards for All-Star games. Separate chapters cover coaches, officials, players selected in ABA and NBA drafts, members of and electees to the Hall of Fame, and official NBA rules.
A major section of the volume, "All-Time Player Directory," lists 2,600 players with their nicknames, birth dates, heights and weights, colleges, seasons, teams, and statistics for each season, the playoffs, and All-Star games. The index cites all names included except those that appear only in the directory of draft lists. This is an attractive and readable work. [R: BL, 1 Mar 90; BR, Mar 90]

1080 **Official NBA Guide**. Edited by the Sporting News Staff. St. Louis, Mo.: The Sporting News. annual. $10.95pa. ISSN 0078-3862.

1081 **Official NBA Register**. Edited by the Sporting News Staff. St. Louis, Mo.: The Sporting News. annual. $10.95pa. ISSN 0739-3067.

The annual *Guide* provides a statistical summary of the past season, current rosters and schedules, NBA records and award winners, and season-by-season team and individual records since 1946-1947. This is an invaluable sports record.

The *Register* provides personal data and career statistics of every active professional player and rookie, plus a section of records and statistics for active coaches.

1082 Savage, Jim. **The Encyclopedia of the NCAA Basketball Tournament: Complete Independent Guide to College Basketball's Championship Event**. New York: Dell Publishing, 1990. 745p. $27.95. ISBN 0-440-50362-0.

The most comprehensive part of this history of the NCAA tournament consists of year-by-year accounts of the annual event, 1939 to 1990. A section on tournament highlights describes some of the most significant games and players for each year, and box scores for all games give individual and team records for the tournament. The remaining sections profile outstanding players and coaches (10 each) and give the win-loss records of every school that has played in the tournament. Unfortunately, the volume is not indexed. [R: RBB, 1 Mar 91]

CHEERLEADING

1083 **The All New Official Cheerleader's Handbook**. By the International Cheerleading Foundation Staff. New York: Simon & Schuster, 1987. $12.95pa. ISBN 0-671-61210-7.

This official guide, an update of the 1983 handbook, covers all aspects of cheerleading, from basic movements and routines to more complex stunts, formations, cheers, chants, and ideas for pep rallies and pep clubs. Randy Neil's *The Official Pompom Girl's Handbook* (St. Martin's Press, 1983) is an illustrated guide that gives conditioning exercises, routines, and advice on tryouts and teamwork. Both works are for grades 6 and up.

FOOTBALL

1084 **Football Register**. St. Louis, Mo.: The Sporting News. annual. $10.95pa. ISSN 0071-7258.

1085 **Pro Football Guide**. St. Louis, Mo.: The Sporting News. annual. $10.95pa.

The *Register* focuses on players and coaches. For each player are given age, weight, birthplace, education, awards, honors, records, and year-by-year performance statistics for his professional career. Information for each coach includes biographical data and a career summary. The annual's arrangement is alphabetical in each section.

Pro Football provides an annual compilation of data on all NFL clubs—statistics for the preceding year, all-time records, year-by-year standings, and the current season's schedule. Team listings include the player roster, draft picks, and front office facts.

1086 **Official NFL Record & Fact Book**. By the NFL Staff. New York: Workman. annual. $14.95pa.

This annual provides a detailed schedule of professional football games, indicating those that are nationally televised, playoff dates, other dates (e.g., when clubs can sign free agents, when the roster must be down to 45 players), rules, and other routine information. A four-page entry covers each team, giving conference, division, address, officials, record holders, last year's statistics, current roster, and coaching staff. Brief biographies are provided for coaches.

One section gives a detailed review of the previous season, listing trades, preseason and regular season standings, game results, and week-by-week game summaries. Also provided are awards; All-Pro teams; leaders in rushing, passing, and receiving; team and individual statistics; and a statistical history of the NFL. The Pro Football Hall of Fame and a chronology of the sport conclude the volume. Recommended. [R: ARBA 89]

1087 Smith, Myron J., Jr. **The Pro Football Bio-Bibliography**. West Cornwall, Conn.: Locust Hill Press, 1989. 288p. $25.00pa. ISBN 0-933951-23-X. LC 88-37741.

This bibliography, arranged alphabetically, cites biographical materials on some 1,400 persons associated with professional football since the formation of the National Football League in 1920. Most biographees listed are players, but a few are coaches and executives. Sources include books, articles, league publications, and annuals; newspaper articles are excluded. Only brief biographical data is provided—name and nicknames, position, and team. Appropriate for middle and high school levels. [R: ARBA 90; RBB, Aug 89]

GOLF

1088   Lopez, Nancy. **The Complete Golfer**. Chicago: Contemporary Books, 1989. 224p. $11.95pa. ISBN 0-8092-4711-9. LC 88-39398.
Fundamentals of golf (from purchasing the correct clubs to playing the game) for all players are well presented in this book. Lopez also covers the psychology of competition and the importance of exercise and good nutrition. There are vignettes of players, with comments about their games and personalities. Black-and-white photographs, with helpful captions, illustrate grip, stance, ball position, specialty shots, and other basics. [R: BR, Nov/Dec 89]

1089   Morrison, Ian. **The Hamlyn Encyclopedia of Golf**. Topsfield, Mass.: Salem House, 1986. 175p. $21.95. ISBN 0-600-50218-X.
High-quality photographs (half in color) lavishly illustrate this handsome volume, which includes many amusing incidents in players' careers. The text also covers golf terms, slang, records and statistics through mid-1986, histories of major tournaments worldwide, rules, and famous courses.
The author is British and so is the spelling, but the United States contribution to the sport is not slighted. Appropriate for high schools. [R: ARBA 87]

GYMNASTICS

1090   **Gymnastics Safety Manual: The Official Manual of the United States Gymnastics Safety Association**. 2d ed. Eugene Wettstone, ed. State College, Pa.: Pennsylvania State University Press, 1979. $14.95; $7.95pa. ISBN 0-271-00242-5; 0-271-00244-1pa. LC 79-65860.
Gymnastics instructors and their students should use this official manual, which has been prepared by experts. It includes checklists of basic safety rules on equipment and techniques.

HOCKEY

1091   **Hockey Guide**. St. Louis, Mo.: The Sporting News. annual. $10.95pa. ISSN 0278-4955.

1092   **Hockey Register**. St. Louis, Mo.: The Sporting News. annual. $10.95pa. ISSN 0090-2292.
These annual publications thoroughly cover the National Hockey League. The *Guide* reviews the previous season and playoffs, and gives the current season's schedule and entry draft; complete team directories, including managers, team rosters, and records; and team and player statistics for every North American hockey league and American college team.
The *Register* provides career information for all players during the previous season, with names listed alphabetically in separate sections for forwards/defenders and goaltenders. Each entry gives vital statistics, injuries, shooting side, and career statistics.

1093   **The National Hockey League Official Guide & Record Book**. Philadelphia: Running Press. annual. $15.95. ISSN 0828-6647. LC 88-42749.
This official publication of the National Hockey League (NHL) provides in-depth coverage for the sport. Part 1 analyzes each of the 21 teams in the league; provides an outlook for the season; and gives draft information, team records over the past 20 years, the team's playoff history, club and individual records, and a summary of the previous year's scoring and highlights. Part 2 consists of a history of the NHL and a variety of team awards and records. A history of the Stanley Cup competition and statistical records of the players conclude the volume. [R: ARBA 91]

HORSEMANSHIP

1094   Pervier, Evelyn. **Horsemanship: Basics for Beginners**. New York: Arco/Simon & Schuster, 1984. 95p. $5.95pa. ISBN 0-668-05935-4. LC 83-10004.

1095   Pervier, Evelyn. **Horsemanship: Basics for Intermediate Riders**. New York: Arco/Simon & Schuster, 1984. 94p. $5.95pa. ISBN 0-668-05942-7. LC 83-10003.

1096   Pervier, Evelyn. **Horsemanship: Basics for More Advanced Riders**. New York: Arco/Simon & Schuster, 1984. 94p. $5.95pa. ISBN 0-668-05950-8. LC 83-10002.

These three volumes present a sequential course of instruction on horse riding, ownership, and care. Each volume covers information appropriate to the level of the rider, illustrated with black-and-white photographs.

Beginners includes buying a horse, care and stabling, and basic riding techniques. *Intermediate* provides information on schooling, trailering, and routine healthcare. *Advanced* offers more refined techniques and information on show preparation, breeding, and raising a foal. For grades 5 and up. [R: BL, 1 June 84]

1097   Rodenas, Paula. **The Random House Book of Horses and Horsemanship**. New York: Random House, 1991. 180p. $17.95. ISBN 0-394-88705-0. LC 86-42934.

This new guide, which includes an introduction by Walter Farley, covers the history, anatomy, and life cycle of horses, as well as horsemanship. Breeds are described and illustrated. There also are illustrations that show equipment and proper horsemanship techniques. Professionals—farriers, stunt riders, and veterinarians—describe their work with horses. Addresses of associations and protection agencies conclude the volume. [R: BR, Sept/Oct 91]

OLYMPIC GAMES

1098   Greenberg, Stan. **Olympic Games: The Records**. New York: Guinness Superlatives; distr., New York: Sterling Publishing, 1987. 176p. $17.95. ISBN 0-85112-896-3.

This work lists the gold, silver, and bronze medal winners of every event of the Olympics from 776 B.C. to A.D. 1988. Special features include a narrative with highlights of each of the summer and winter olympics, and in-depth profiles of some of the all-time heroes of the contests. Black-and-white photographs illustrate the volume. Indexed. [R: ARBA 89]

E+
1099   Mallon, Bill. **The Olympic Record Book**. Hamden, Conn.: Garland, 1988. 522p. $38.00. ISBN 0-8240-2948-8. LC 87-22511.

Unlike most others on the subject, which focus on U.S. athletes, Mallon's work records the feats of athletes of all nations in the summer and winter Olympic games. The volume begins with general records (e.g., most medals won by an individual, most years winning a medal) followed by records of particular sports, name of international governing body, number of countries affiliated, year formed, year sport apeared in the Olympics, historical synopsis of the event in Olympic competition, and all medal winners.

The Olympic history and overall success of each participating nation is presented. A third section summarizes each set of games, giving sites, dates, and other information about them. Despite the lack of an index, this guide is recommended for all levels. [R: ARBA 89; LJ, 1 Apr 88; WLB, June 88]

E+
1100   Page, James A. **Black Olympian Medalists**. Englewood, Colo.: Libraries Unlimited, 1991. 190p. $27.50pa. ISBN 0-87287-618-7. LC 90-46660.

This work contains profiles of 471 Black athletes, past, present, and worldwide, who have won a medal in either individual or team Olympic competition. Entries are prefaced with information on the subject's country; dates; birthplace; medals (by type and event for each Olympiad); and, for individual events, time, distance, or point total. The sketches describe the subjects' development and achievements, give information on their lives after their competitive career, and cite sources (excluding newspapers) for further information. Data is more complete on some athletes than others.

Appendixes list athletes by event and country. Indexed by name, institution, teams, and other sports events mentioned in the profiles. Highly recommended. [R: ARBA 92; LJ, 15 June 91; VOYA, Oct 91]

RODEO

1101 **Official Professional Rodeo Media Guide, 1990**. Steve Fleming, ed. Colorado Springs, Colo.: Professional Rodeo Cowboy Association, 1990. 287p. $10.00pa.

The most comprehensive guide of its kind, this work contains history, statistics, and biography related to professional rodeo. Profiles include champion and near-champion competitors, clowns, bullfighters, and others important to the report. A table lists winners and prize money throughout rodeo history; a section explains the circuit system. Illustrations are numerous. Recommended. [R: ARBA 91]

1102 **Professional Rodeo Official Handbook, 1987**. Boulder, Colo.: Johnson Books, 1987. 254p. $10.95pa. ISBN 1-55566-015-0.

This work contains more information about rodeo than any other source. Produced by the Professional Rodeo Cowboys Association (PRCA), it contains reports on champions and others connected with the sport (e.g., clowns, announcers, sponsors), rodeo history, the National Finals Rodeo, and the circuit system. There are many action shots and portraits of the best riders. [R: ARBA 88; LJ, Aug 87]

SOCCER

E+
1103 Rollin, Jack. **The World Cup, 1930-1990: Sixty Glorious Years of Soccer's Premier Event**. New York: Facts on File, 1990. 191p. $24.95. ISBN 0-8160-2523-1.

The growing interest in soccer is likely to increase when the World Cup is held in the United States for the first time in 1994. The first section of this work, which surveys the competition, covers each of the 14 previous tournaments (starting in 1930), reports events on and off the field, provides basic statistics for each game, and provides several black-and-white photographs. Two-page biographies of 21 famous players comprise the second section; a third covers all teams that made the 1990 finals.

Appendixes include World Cup records, World Cup trivia, FIFA-affiliated countries, and "Looking Ahead: USA 1994." Indexed by personal name. This handbook is useful at all levels. [R: ARBA 92]

WRESTLING

1104 Chapman, Mike. **Encyclopedia of American Wrestling**. Champaign, Ill.: Leisure Press/Human Kinetics, 1990. 533p. $23.95pa. ISBN 0-88011-342-1. LC 89-2701.

This volume covers amateur wrestling, not the theatrical version seen on television. It includes American champions in the Olympics, World Championships, other world meets, the AAU National Freestyle Championships, the U.S. Freestyle Senior Open, the Greco-Roman Nationals, the Collegiate Nationals, the Midland Championships, the Junior Nationals, the Junior World Tournaments, special honors and awards, Halls of Fame, and other issues related to the sport. [R: ARBA 91]

□ —————————— # Statistics —————————— □

UNITED STATES

See also **Almanacs and Fact Books** in **General Reference**.

1105 Biracree, Tom, and Nancy Biracree. **Almanac of the American People**. New York: Facts on File, 1988. 336p. $29.95; $12.95pa. ISBN 0-8160-1821-9; 0-8160-2329-8pa. LC 88-3882.

This volume presents well-documented facts about the average American and answers such questions as who goes to college and how the increased number of women in the work force affects spending patterns and housing trends. The text is based on government publications, magazine surveys, and statistics gathered by industrial and professional organizations.

The first chapter covers ethnicity, health, education, crime, and other aspects of American life. Chapters 2 through 9 deal with residence, money, love life (some quite explicit), children, property, food, and recreation. The reader should be aware that this work, which complements standard almanacs, is based on 1985 and 1986 data. [R: ARBA 89; BL, 1 Apr 89; BR, Mar/Apr 89; WLB, Jan 89]

1106   Bogue, Donald J. **Population of the United States: Historical Trends and Future Projections**. New York: Free Press/Macmillan, 1985. 728p. $125.00. ISBN 0-02-904700-5. LC 84-18688.

This volume provides extensive demographic data for the United States, including census information available through July 1, 1984, and future projections. The readable text evaluates the statistical information and provides a broad portrait of social and economic changes from 1790 to 1980, illustrated by graphs and pie charts. Twelve chapters cover such topics as nativity and ethnicity and school enrollment. Terms are defined, and the bibliography is excellent. Indexed. [R: LJ, 15 Apr 86]

1107   Boyer, Richard, and David Savageau. **Places Rated Almanac: Your Guide to Finding the Best Places to Live in America**. Chicago: Rand McNally, 1989. 421p. $16.95pa. ISBN 0-13-677006-1. LC 89-22971.

Places Rated provides excellent profiles and rankings of 329 metropolitan areas. Ratings are based on nine quality-of-life factors: climate and terrain, housing, health care, crime, transportation, education, the arts, recreation, and economics. The top 10 areas are listed for each category. Scores based on all factors determine the overall rank for each location. A summary section lists each area according to its quality and then alphabetically, giving the rank of each site. Previous editions were compiled in 1981 and 1985. Recommended for high schools. [R: ARBA 91; WLB, Feb 90]

1108   **County and City Data Book, 1988: A Statistical Abstract Supplement**. 11th ed. By Bureau of the Census. Washington, D.C.: Government Printing Office, 1989. 958p. $36.00. S/N 003-024-06709-9.

A variety of detailed statistics for counties, SMSAs, and cities of 25,000 or more are included in this supplement to *Statistical Abstract of the United States*. Data can be found on population, marriage, divorce, employment, income, housing, retail trade, and more. State maps show county outlines, SMSAs, and cities. A new edition, based on the 1990 census, should appear soon. A CD-ROM version of the *County and City Data Book* is available from the Bureau of the Census for $125.00.

1109   **Historical Statistics of the United States: Colonial Times to 1970**. bicentennial ed. By Bureau of the Census. Washington, D.C.: Government Printing Office, 1976. 2v. $56.00/set. S/N 003-024-00120-9.

Intended as a supplement to *Statistical Abstract of the United States*, this set provides a survey of American history, 1610 to 1970, in some 12,500 tables. Beginning dates of topics vary, depending on when statistical gathering began. Most data relate to the country as a whole.

The statistics are presented in 24 chapters that cover topics such as population, immigration, migration, slavery, economic facts, and business enterprises. Sources are cited for each table. There is detailed indexing by subject and time period.

1110   **State and Metropolitan Area Data Book: A Statistical Abstract Supplement: Regions, Divisions, States, Metropolitan Areas (SMSAs) by Population-Size, Class**. By Bureau of the Census. Washington, D.C.: Government Printing Office, 1987. 723p. $28.00. S/N 003-024-06334-4.

A supplement to *Statistical Abstract of the United States*, this work presents statistical data for state and metropolitan areas, arranged in three categories: SMSAs; cities within SMSAs; and regions, divisions, and states. These are then subdivided by broad areas. Introductory materials include extensive explanations of terminology, concepts, and sources of data. Appendixes rank states by socioeconomic indicators. This reliable source is recommended for high schools. A new edition, based on the 1990 census, should be available soon.

1111   **State Rankings, 1991: A Statistical View of the 50 United States**. Kathleen O'Leary Morgan and others, eds. Lawrence, Kans.: Morgan Quitno, 1991. 347p. $39.95pa. ISBN 0-9625531-1-5. (P.O. Box 1656, Lawrence, KS 66044).

A revision of *U.S. Statistical Rankings*, published by another company since 1967, this work consists of tables that rank the 50 states in areas such as population, health, land, crime, transportation, and education. All information is drawn from *Statistical Abstract of the United States* or *Federal Expenditures of States* and converted into tables, such as "Daily Per Capita Fresh Water Withdrawal in

1985" in the chapter on energy. This work's coverage is more comprehensive than that found in *State and Metropolitan Area Data Book*.

Individual state guides that give state rankings for each of the categories are available from the publisher. High schools may wish to purchase the guide for their state instead of the complete publication. [R: ARBA 92; RBB, 15 June 90]

1112 **Statistical Abstract of the United States**. Washington, D.C.: Government Printing Office, 1878- . annual. $34.00; $28.00pa. S/N 003-024-07261-1; 003-024-07260-2pa.

This is the most important annual compendium of U.S. social, political, and economic statistics derived from governmental and nongovernmental agencies. Some 1,600 tables are grouped in 35 broad subject categories. In addition to standard political, demographic, and economic topics, new ones are continually added (e.g., microcomputer use in schools, seat belt usage). The source for each statistical table is provided, making the annual an informal index to the government agencies responsible for collecting statistics on a given topic. A detailed index of more than 40 pages gives access to the information. This material is available on microfiche and in microform. It is also available online.

The statistics concern the United States as a whole; smaller areas are covered by supplements, such as *State and Metropolitan Area Data Book* and *County and City Data Book*. *Historical Statistics of the United States* details developments to 1970. All of these important publications are highly recommended for high schools.

1113 Thomas, G. Scott. **The Rating Guide to Life in America's Small Cities**. Buffalo, N.Y.: Prometheus Books, 1990. 538p. $34.95; $16.95pa. ISBN 0-87975-599-7; 0-87975-600-4pa. LC 89-77457.

Current as of June 15, 1989, this guide rates 219 small cities (15,000 to 50,000 inhabitants). Its content is similar to that of *Places Rated Almanac*, which covers big cities.

Ten sections include climate, housing, health care, sophistication, urban proximity, and so forth, covering a total of 50 measures. Using a 20-point system, Thomas rates cities on each factor and lists the 10 best and 10 worst in each of the categories. A national report card on all cities is arranged from most to least desirable, followed by an alphabetical listing by state and then city, giving scores for each location. [R: ARBA 91; BL, 15 June 90; WLB, June 90]

THE WORLD

1114 Showers, Victor. **World Facts and Figures**. 3d ed. New York: John Wiley, 1989. 721p. $74.95. ISBN 0-471-85775-0. LC 88-31698.

The comparative rankings of world geographic and cultural characteristics cited by this work have increased from 15 categories in the 2d edition (1979) to 45 in the current one; the number of cities covered has increased from 2,045 to 2,644. Rankings of such things as education, commerce, transportation, and communications cite statistics gleaned from a wide variety of sources. [R: ARBA 90; RBB, 1 Oct 89]

1115 **World Economic Data**. 3d ed. Timothy S. O'Donnell and others, eds. Santa Barbara, Calif.: ABC-Clio, 1991. 261p. $35.00. ISBN 0-87436-658-5. ISSN 0891-4125.

This fact book contains reliable data about the world's economy. Part 1 gives information on 171 nations, including budgets, international liquidity, imports/exports, trading partners, tourism, natural resources, and natural gas production. U.S. economic indicators, covered in part 2, include business cycles, gross national production, employment, energy, inflation, banking, gold, stocks, and bonds. World currency rates and data on U.S. foreign trade by region and nation also appear. Highly recommended for high schools. [R: ARBA 90; BR, May 90]

1116 **World Statistics in Brief: United Nations Statistical Pocketbook**. 12th ed. By the Department of International Economics and Social Affairs, Statistical Office. Lanham, Md.: UNIPUB, 1990. (Statistical Papers, Series V, no.9). $7.50. S/N E.90.XVII.5.

This work contains the most commonly sought statistics for 167 UN members, such as demography, labor force, national wealth, agriculture and industry, trade, finance, tourism, transportation, communications, education, health, and nutrition. The data, based on compilations published by the United Nations and its agencies, usually cover the last 10 years. Notes explain terms, time periods, and gathering methods. An annotated bibliography completes the volume.

1117 World Tables. Baltimore, Md.: Johns Hopkins University Press, 1991. 653p. $34.95pa. ISBN 0-8018-4252-2. ISSN 1043-5573.

Published for the World Bank, this work has world economic and social statistics. The sixth in the series, it opens with a comparison of nations according to several economic indicators—Gross National Product (GNP), consumption per capita, and contributions of different sectors to economic growth.

Statistical data is organized by country, Algeria to Zimbabwe, providing population, GNP, price, manufacturing, monetary holdings, national budget, foreign trade, balance of payments, external debt, and selected social indicators. All data is for the period 1969 through 1989. Nations included are limited to those that belong to the World Bank. The information is also available on IBM-compatible diskettes.

Women's Studies

ATLASES

1118 Gibson, Anne, and Timothy Fast. The Women's Atlas of the United States. New York: Facts on File, 1986. 248p. $60.00. ISBN 0-8160-1170-2. LC 86-675059.

This attractive atlas presents a detailed picture of women in America, covering such topics as demography, employment, education, family relationships, health, crime, and politics, all drawn from the 1980 U.S. Census. Clear explanations of how to read the various maps make this an ideal selection for young adults. *Atlas of American Women* by Barbara Gimla Shortridge (Macmillan, 1987) covers much the same material, but is less attractive in format and lacks the lucid explanations offered by the other atlas. The content of both works is dated by the 1990 census. [R: ARBA 88; BL, May 87; LJ, 1 Apr 87; WLB, Apr 87]

BIBLIOGRAPHIES

1119 Loeb, Catherine R., and others. Women's Studies, 1980-1985: A Recommended Core Bibliography. abridged ed. Englewood, Colo.: Libraries Unlimited, 1987. $23.50. ISBN 0-87287-598-9. LC 87-17015.

This work abridges *Women's Studies: A Recommended Core Bibliography 1980-1985* (Libraries Unlimited, 1987) for a nonspecialist audience of high school and undergraduate students and their teachers. The 645 annotated, critical annotations are arranged in broad subject areas, such as law, sports, and feminist theory. This is an excellent source for identifying the best materials for a high school women's studies collection. [R: ARBA 88; BL, 1 June 88; BR, Mar/Apr 88]

1120 Mumford, Laura Stempel. Women's Issues: An Annotated Bibliography. Pasadena, Calif.: Salem Press, 1989. 163p. $40.00. ISBN 0-89356-654-3. LC 89-10831.

Women's Issues, designed for high school students and college undergraduates, focuses on materials usually available in "good" library collections. Following an introduction that sets the parameters of the work, Mumford lists general works about women. The main part of the annotated bibliography is arranged under broad subject areas such as history, politics, and education; health issues and sexuality; family, home, and relationships; violence against women; and women and the arts. Selected materials, which include books and chapters in books, reflect divergent, often opposing viewpoints. Recommended. [R: ARBA 91; RBB, 15 May 90]

1121 Reese, Lyn, and Jean Wilkinson, comps. and eds. Women in the World: Annotated History Resources for the Secondary Student. Metuchen, N.J.: Scarecrow, 1987. 220p. $22.50. ISBN 0-8108-2050-1. LC 87-16436.

This attractive bibliography, which presents the role of women in world history and their contributions to culture and economics, is designed to stimulate the interest of secondary students and their teachers. Graphics and quotations are interspersed among annotated sources, which are divided mainly by continent. An additional section lists cross-cultural materials. Bibliographic citations, grouped in each section under such categories as autobiogrpahy/biography, first-person accounts, and fiction, are annotated and give reading level, time period, place, theme, description, and suggested uses. [R: ARBA 88; BL, 1 May 87; VOYA, Apr 88]

1122   Sweeney, Patricia E. **Biographies of American Women: An Annotated Bibliography**. Santa Barbara, Calif.: ABC-Clio, 1990. 290p. $60.00. ISBN 0-87436-070-6. LC 89-28277.

A useful reference tool for the secondary level, this bibliography identifies 1,291 English-language biographies (each at least 50 pages long) of 700 American women of all eras and endeavors. Those included range from Mary Todd Lincoln to Belle Starr, from Mahalia Jackson to Gene Stratton-Porter. Biographies, listed alphabetically by the subject's name, are critically annotated. Indexing is by profession, vocation, and name. [R: ARBA 91; RBB, Aug 90]

ENCYCLOPEDIAS AND HANDBOOKS

1123   Clark, Judith Freeman. **Almanac of American Women in the 20th Century**. New York: Prentice Hall Press, 1987. 274p. $24.95. ISBN 0-13-022658-0. LC 86-43172.

The almanac is composed of short date-and-event entries interspersed with essays on such topics as early labor activists and organizers, or biographies of noted individuals from various professions. The content of this work is excellent, but its usefulness as a reference tool is limited because it is indexed only by name. [R: ARBA 89; BL, 15 Oct 87; LJ, Aug 87]

1124   **Handbook of American Women's History**. Angela Howard Zophy, ed. Hamden, Conn.: Garland, 1990. 763p. (Garland Reference Library of the Humanities, v.696). $95.00. ISBN 0-8240-8744-5. LC 89-17120.

Signed articles averaging 300 words cover women's movements, historical events, literary works, and famous individuals. Each article is supported by a short bibliography. The volume emphasizes the nineteenth and twentieth centuries, with proportionately less coverage of frontier times. Minority women also receive less attention. Despite these inadequacies, this manual has valuable information. Recommended for high schools. [R: ARBA 91; LJ, 1 Mar 90; RBB, 15 Mar 90]

1125   Partnow, Elaine, comp. and ed. **The Quotable Women: 1800-1981**. rev. ed. New York: Facts on File, 1984. 608p. $35.00. ISBN 0-8160-2134-1.

1126   Partnow, Elaine, with Claudia B. Alexander, comps. and eds. **The Quotable Woman from Eve to 1799**. New York: Facts on File, 1985. 533p. $29.95. ISBN 0-87196-307-8. LC 82-15511.

Of the many books of quotations, only these two are devoted solely to women. The 1984 volume contains 20,000 quotations from more than 2,500 women who lived from biblical to contemporary times. *Eve to 1799* expands the quotations drawn from the ancient era, reacquainting us with some of the world's most famous women.

Each volume organizes the quotations chronologically by the birthdate of the speaker. A subject index and biographical-fact index by author (dates, nationality, profession, family relations, and honors) provide additional access. Both works are recommended for middle and high schools. [R: ARBA 86; BL, 15 May 85; LJ, Dec 84; WLB, Apr 85]

1127   **Statistical Handbook on Women in America**. Cynthia Taeuber, comp. and ed. Phoenix, Ariz.: Oryx Press, 1991. 385p. $54.50. ISBN 0-89774-609-0. LC 90-41624.

The 437 tables in this volume, drawn from a variety of federal publications, illustrate trends in life patterns of women since World War II. The entries cover demographics, education, crime, employment, economic status, health, political behavior, and life style. Some articles address these topics by such factors as race, age, and marital status. A survey essay introduces each topical section, and an index offers excellent access to specific subjects. This is the only work that brings together this kind of data about women. [R: ARBA 92; LJ, 1 May 91]

1128   **Women's Studies Encyclopedia**. Helen Tierney, ed. Westport, Conn.: Greenwood Press, 1989-1991. $59.95/v. LC 88-32806.

This encyclopedia is the first to address women's studies. *Volume 1: Views from the Sciences* (of a projected 3-volume set) surveys subjects pertaining to natural, behavioral, and social sciences; health and medicine; politics; law, economics; and linguistics. *Volume 2: Literature Arts and Learning* reviews the role of women in literature, the arts, and education. The third volume will cover history, philosophy, and religion.

Articles range from 750 to 1,500 words each and reflect a variety of feminist approaches. Each entry defines terms and includes a brief bibliography for further study. Copious cross-references and a subject index appear in each volume. [R: ARBA 90; ARBA 92]

INDEXES

1129 Index to Women of the World from Ancient to Modern Times: Biographies and Portraits. Norma O. Ireland, ed. Metuchen, N.J.: Scarecrow, 1970. 573p. $32.50. ISBN 0-8108-2012-9. LC 75-120841.

1130 Index to Women of the World from Ancient to Modern Times: A Supplement. By Norma O. Ireland. Metuchen, N.J.: Scarecrow, 1988. 774p. $79.50. ISBN 0-8108-2092-7. LC 87-35934.
The basic volume, published in 1970, indexes some 13,000 women cited in 945 collective biographies, a few magazines, and general and specialized compilations. The supplement gives further sources for women listed in the first volume and adds many contemporary individuals, covering 380 books from the 1970s and early 1980s. The index, alphabetically arranged by name, gives birth and death dates, field of activity, and references to sources. There are no subject or occupational indexes. The introduction to the supplement states that books for young people are included, but the list of those indexed does not indicate the reading level. [R: BL, 1 June 89; VOYA, Apr 89; WLB, Apr 89]

1131 Manning, Beverley. We Shall Be Heard: An Index to Speeches by American Women, 1978 to 1985. Metuchen, N.J.: Scarecrow, 1988. 620p. $62.50. ISBN 0-8160-2122-2. LC 88-6644.
The title notwithstanding, this update of the author's 1980 book, *Index to American Speeches, 1928-1985*, includes references to speeches given over a century ago. The main part, the author index, cites 2,500 women, with references to books and periodicals in which the speech can be found. Indexes by subject and title refer to the author index.
The speakers, who address a wide variety of topics, include feminists (e.g., Gloria Steinem), wives of presidents (e.g., Betty Ford), historical figures (e.g., Elizabeth Cady Stanton), and contemporary political figures (e.g., Barbara Jordan). Since congressional hearings are indexed, access to congressional publications is necessary to obtain the text of such speeches. The hearings, however, are only a minor part of the sources indexed. [R: ARBA 90; BL, 1 May 89]

BIOGRAPHY

■ *American Women in Sport*. See entry 1052.

■ *American Women Writers*. See entry 1589.

■ *A Biographical Dictionary of Women Artists in Europe and America since 1850*. See entry 1357.

■ *Black American Women in Literature*. See entry 1577.

1132 The Continuum Dictionary of Women's Biography. rev. ed. Jennifer Uglow, ed. New York: Continuum; distr., New York: Harper & Row, 1989. 621p. $39.50. ISBN 0-8264-0417-0. LC 88-28224.
A revision of *International Dictionary of Women's Biography* (1982), this work updates profiles from the earlier edition and adds 250 new subjects. The one- to two-paragraph entries cover rulers, social reformers, writers, scholars, entertainers, and others from ancient to contemporary times. "Additional Reference Sources" is a guide to general works and other biographies. A subject index identifies women associated with various occupations and groups. This reliable work is recommended for high schools. [R: BL, 1 Sept 89; WLB, Oct 89]

■ *The Encyclopedia of British Women Writers*. See entry 1601.

E +
1133 Kulkin, Mary-Ellen. Her Way: A Guide to Biographies of Women for Young People. 2d ed. Chicago: American Library Association, 1984. 415p. $35.00. ISBN 0-8389-0396-9. LC 83-22375.
Her Way consists of 1,000 short profiles of important historical women, followed by a graded and annotated list of biographies suitable for students from elementary level through high school. Kulkin

sought biographies that were free of sexist or racist bias, but that were also well written and of interest to young readers. Appended are lists by nationalities other than American and Americans classified by ethnic groups and by vocation and avocation. Author/title and subject indexes. [R: ARBA 85; BL, 15 June 84; SLJ, May 85; WLB, Sept 84]

■ *Modern American Women Writers*. *See* entry 1593.

1134 **Notable American Women, 1607-1950: A Biographical Dictionary**. E. T. James, J. W. James, and P. S. Boyer, eds. Cambridge, Mass.: Belknap Press/Harvard University Press, 1971. 3v. $45.00 pa./set. ISBN 0-674-62734-2. LC 76-152274.

1135 **Notable American Women: The Modern Period**. Barbara Sicherman and Carol H. Green, eds. Cambridge, Mass.: Belknap Press/Harvard University Press, 1980. 773p. $48.00; $19.95pa. ISBN 0-674-62732-6; 0-674-62733-4pa. LC 80-18402.
Modeled after *Dictionary of American Biography*, this work consists of 1,359 long, signed articles in the original set and 442 more (women born between 1857 and 1943 and deceased by 1975) in the supplement. Length of the articles depends upon prominence, complexity of career, or availability of materials. Only one group of women—wives of U.S. presidents—is included on the basis of husband's position. Most were chosen because they had been influential in their fields or had made innovative contributions to society.
Notable American Women supplements *Dictionary of American Biography*, which lists only 700 women (among more than 17,000 entries). Of these, *NAW* excludes 179 because they have lost significance. [R: ARBA 82; Kliatt, winter 84]

1136 Opfell, Olga S. **The Lady Laureates: Women Who Have Won the Nobel Prize**. 2d ed. Metuchen, N.J.: Scarecrow, 1986. 316p. $32.50. ISBN 0-8108-1851-5. LC 85-19670.
This update of the 1978 edition provides biographical portraits of the 20 women who have won the Nobel Prize, from Bertha von Suttner, who won the Peace prize in 1905, to Barbara McClintock, awarded the Science prize in 1983. Marie Curie is the only two-time winner. The well-written biographies include anecdotes and quotations from friends, colleagues, and family.
The volume begins with an essay on Alfred Nobel and the history of his prize. Chapters that describe the winners also address the struggle of women to attain equal consideration with men in education and the awarding of high honors. A chronology of events about the prize from 1883 to 1984 and a bibliography of sources for each recipient conclude the volume. [R: ARBA 87]

1137 Opfell, Olga S. **Queens, Empresses, Grand Duchesses and Regents: Women Rulers of Europe, A.D. 1328-1989**. Jefferson, N.C.: McFarland, 1989. 282p. $25.95. ISBN 0-89950-385-3. LC 88-43484.
This volume includes lively biographical sketches of 40 women who have served as reigning monarchs or ruling regents in Europe. Consorts are excluded. Four- to eight-page essays on each ruler, arranged alphabetically, include a portrait of the subject and a selective bibliography. Indexed. Recommended for secondary schools. [R: ARBA 90]

1138 Tinling, Marion. **Women Remembered: A Guide to Landmarks of Women's History in the United States**. Westport, Conn.: Greenwood Press, 1986. 796p. $79.95. ISBN 0-313-23984-3. LC 85-17639.
The historic sites that commemorate U.S. women and their achievements constitute the focus of this outstanding work. Sites, such as homes, monuments, memorials, workplaces, markers, and plaques, are arranged by geographic region and then by state, city, and personal name. For each location are given directions, hours, notations of inclusion in *Notable American Women*, and whether the site appears on the historic register. Next come one or more paragraphs of biographical information. Those profiled range from the famous, such as Susan B. Anthony, to the obscure, such as Marie Therese Metoyer, an eighteenth-century emancipated slave of Bermuda and Melrose, Louisiana.
Other features include photographs, a classified list of women, a chronology of significant dates in women's history, and a bibliographic essay. Indexed. This interesting work is worthy of consideration by all secondary schools. [R: ARBA 87; LJ, 1 Oct 86; RBB, 15 Dec 86; WLB, Dec 86]

1139 Who's Who of American Women: A Biographical Dictionary of Notable Living American Women. Chicago: Marquis Who's Who. biennial. $210.00.

Directory-type biographical entries for some 25,000 women are included in this biennial, a companion volume to *Who's Who in America*. Criteria for inclusion are based on "demonstrated accomplishments," position attained, or noteworthy achievement. No supplementary indexes are provided, but biographees are listed in the *Marquis Who's Who Index*.

■ *Women in Congress, 1917-1990*. *See* entry 950.

■ *Women into the Unknown*. *See* entry 599.

□ —————————— **Children's Literature** —————————— □

GENERAL WORKS

See also **Books** under **Media Sources**.
See **Literature** for **Reading Guidance**.

1140   Donelson, Kenneth L., and A. P. Nilsen. **Literature for Today's Young Adults**. 3d ed. Glenville, Ill.: Scott, Foresman, 1989. 561p. $29.95. ISBN 0-673-38400-4. LC 88-31250.

As in the previous edition, the introduction to this excellent work surveys the field of young adult literature and its literary aspects. The second part focuses on books and authors by genre, and part 3 discusses the role of the youth librarian, the evaluation of books, and censorship. The fourth part provides a history of young adult reading habits from 1800 to the present.

The format of the 3d edition (last revised in 1985) has been improved by the addition of color at the beginning of each chapter and in headings and subheadings. The treatments of radio/television and adolescent psychology have been expanded, and the books covered have been updated. The list of suggested teaching activities at the end of each chapter has been replaced by a teacher's manual.

This work, intended as a textbook, offers fresh and worthwhile guidance to those who promote reading among young adults aged 12 to 20. Highly recommended for middle and high schools. [R: VOYA, Dec 89]

E +
1141   Huck, Charlotte S. **Children's Literature in the Elementary School**. 4th ed. New York: Holt, Rinehart, 1987. 780p. $29.50. ISBN 0-03-041770-8.

Chapters of this standard textbook on the use of children's literature in the classroom provide thorough coverage of the basic genres, analysis and evaluation of children's books, child development, and topics that encourage the use of books with children. The bibliographies are current through 1986. This is an excellent source for librarians and teachers at elementary and middle school levels.

E +
1142   Norton, Donna E. **Through the Eyes of a Child: An Introduction to Children's Literature**. 3d ed. New York: Macmillan, 1991. 754p. $31.50. ISBN 0-675-21144-1. LC 90-60624.

Intended as a text for those interested in evaluating, selecting, and sharing children's literature, this work surveys artists and illustrators, picture books, traditional literature, modern fantasy, poetry, contemporary realistic fiction, multicultural literature, and nonfiction. Each chapter contains black-and-white and color illustrations from children's books; chronologies; and boxes with "Flashbacks" (interesting historical notes), "Issues" (e.g., racism in Mark Twain), and "Through the Eyes of ..." (comments by authors, illustrators, and authorities on children's literature). There are charts on such topics as the characteristics of various literary genres and the relationship of reading interest to developmental level. Chapters also include suggested activities and extensive bibliographies.

Appendixes list book selection aids, books for professional reading, and award books. Readability scales are explained, and a directory of publishers is provided. Indexed by author/illustrator/title and subject. Highly recommended.

E +
1143   Smith, Lillian H. **The Unreluctant Years: A Critical Approach to Children's Literature**. Chicago: American Library Association, 1991. 183p. $25.00. ISBN 0-8389-0557-9. LC 90-23850.

This reprint of a children's literary classic that appeared in 1953 is as timely today as it was almost four decades ago. (This volume has a new introduction by Kay E. Vandergrift.) Smith considered children's books as literature and applied critical standards and the interests of children in identifying quality. Librarians responsible for selecting and using books for children will want to read and reread this slim, perceptive work.

E +
1144   Stott, Jon C., and R. E. Jones. **Canadian Books for Children: Guide to Authors and Illustrators**. Toronto: Harcourt Brace Jovanovich, 1988. 246p. $19.95pa. ISBN 0-7747-3081-1.

The main section of this work consists of articles about 105 Canadian authors and illustrators, the majority of whom are still active. The entries, ranging in length from a short paragraph to almost five pages, are critical and include complete bibliographies of the author/illustrator's works. A reference section cites standard critical sources. Special features include black-and-white reproductions of illustrations, a list of stories for the language arts curriculum, a selective list of recommended Canadian books for kindergarten through grade 8, and a list of award books.

E +
1145   Sutherland, Zena, Dianne L. Monson, and May Hill Arbuthnot. **Children and Books**. 7th ed. Glenville, Ill.: Scott, Foresman, 1986. 768p. $28.95.

An outstanding work, this standard textbook for courses in children's literature also serves as a handbook and selection aid for the field. Arranged in five major sections, it provides extensive information on all aspects of children's literature. The introductory section surveys developmental needs and interests, trends, and evaluation criteria. The second section treats picture books and their authors and illustrators, and the third section focuses on books and authors for older children. The last two sections discuss the use of books with children and current issues in children's literature.

Bibliographies appear throughout the text and in the appendix, which also includes a section on awards and a pronunciation guide. Indexed by subject and by author-title-illustrator. An essential holding for elementary and junior high school libraries. [R: BL, 1 Apr 86; SLJ, Mar 86]

E +
1146   Vandergrift, Kay E. **Children's Literature: Theory, Research, and Teaching**. Englewood, Colo.: Libraries Unlimited, 1990. 277p. $32.50. ISBN 0-87287-749-3. LC 89-29959.

While this work treats the study of children's literature as an academic discipline, it is useful to practitioners who select and use literature with children. The first three chapters survey literary theory, research, and teaching the field. Succeeding chapters provide course syllabi with numerous examples, worksheets that can be used in evaluating books or instructional media, and ideas for continuing education activities relevant to children's literature (e.g., in-service workshops, institutes). An extensive bibliography includes works about literary theory, research, and teaching children's literature. A detailed general index includes all titles mentioned in the text. Recommended.

BIBLIOGRAPHIES ABOUT

E +
1147   Hendrickson, Linnea. **Children's Literature: A Guide to the Criticisms**. Boston: G. K. Hall, 1987. 696p. (Reference Publications in Literature). $39.50. ISBN 0-8161-8670-7. LC 86-19455.

A critical guide to children's literature, this bibliography identifies books, articles, unpublished dissertations, and ERIC documents that have appeared since 1960. Citations, grouped under authors and their works or subjects, themes, and genres, are indexed by author, title, subject, and critic. A brief annotation describes each item but does not evaluate it. Students of children's literature, teachers, and librarians will find this bibliography useful. [R: BL, 15 June 87]

E
1148   Marantz, Sylvia S., and Kenneth A. Marantz. **The Art of Children's Picture Books: A Selective Reference Guide**. Hamden, Conn.: Garland, 1988. 165p. $27.00. ISBN 0-8240-2745-0. LC 88-1704.

The Art of Children's Picture Books lists 451 carefully chosen books, articles, and audiovisuals that appeared through 1987. The introduction focuses on picture books as a visual art. The bibliography is arranged in six parts: the history of children's picture books; how a picture book is made; criticisms of children's picture books; artists anthologized; books, articles, and audiovisual materials on individual picture book artists; and guides and aids to further research. Each entry includes full bibliographic data and a brief annotation. Indexing by artist, author/editor/compiler, and title and a directory of institutions holding outstanding collections of picture books complete this excellent bibliography. [R: ARBA 89; BL, 1 Apr 89]

BIBLIOGRAPHIES OF

See also **Books** in **Media Sources**.

E+
1149   Anderson, Vicki. **Fiction Sequels for Readers 10 to 16: An Annotated Bibliography of Books in Succession**. Jefferson, N.C.: McFarland, 1990. 150p. $19.95pa. ISBN 0-89950-519-8. LC 89-43686.

Anderson defines sequels as books that have the same characters and similar themes but that can stand alone. This bibliography lists some 1,500 such titles appropriate for children over 10; most were published after 1960, but some are nineteenth-century classics. Sequels were selected for their type, suitability for the age level, and availability, not for their literary quality.

Entries, arranged alphabetically by author, include title, book's numerical position in the sequence, publisher, date, and a brief annotation. A title index lists each work's author and its place in the series.

A similar work, *Sequences: An Annotated Guide to Children's Fiction in Series* by Susan Roman (American Library Association, 1985), is now out of print. *Fiction Sequels* is far more comprehensive, but *Sequences* provides more information about each series. [R: ARBA 92]

E
1150   Apseloff, Marilyn Fain, comp. **They Wrote for Children Too: An Annotated Bibliography of Children's Literature by Famous Writers for Adults**. Westport, Conn.: Greenwood Press, 1989. 202p. (Bibliographies and Indexes in World Literature, no.20). $37.95. ISBN 0-313-25981-X. LC 89-2194.

This bibliography lists picture books, stories, poetry, drama, and nonfiction for children by famous authors usually associated with adult literature. Works that have been ably adapted for children are also included. Entries, arranged chronologically from ancient times (e.g., the *Aeneid*) to the twentieth century, usually include author, title, illustrator, publisher, date, type of work, paging, age level, country of author's origin (most are American or English), and an annotation. Adapter or reteller and awards are cited when applicable. This is a useful, though not an essential, purchase for elementary school libraries. [R: ARBA 90; RBB, 1 Nov 89]

1151   **Best Books for Junior High Readers**. John T. Gillespie, ed. New Providence, N.J.: R. R. Bowker, 1991. 567p. $39.95. ISBN 0-8352-3020-1. LC 91-13521.

This bibliography of books recommended for students in grades 7 through 9 "was established to help librarians and media specialists meet curricular needs and the personal interests of their students" (p. xv). Anticipated uses include collection development and evaluation, reading guidance, and the compilation of bibliographies. Each of the 5,674 entries is composed of bibliographic information, a brief annotation, citations to reviews published since 1985, and DDC numbers for nonfiction titles. Author, title, and subject/grade level indexes are included in the appendix.

The extensive and detailed table of contents outlines the book's arrangement by broad categories. Often the arrangement within each area follows the traditional mode of alphabetizing by the author's last name. But this can be superseded by other arrangements where deemed appropriate; for example, history is primarily chronological, and geographical titles are grouped by location. The stipulation that titles listed be in print in 1990 necessarily limits selection. The fiction section, especially, includes a wide and almost exhaustive selection of appropriate authors. Also, Gillespie does a nice job of separating fantasy and science fiction categories. Titles are often gathered together from diverse classification areas under pertinent subject headings.

Gillespie has compiled two companion bibliographies to this work: *Best Books for Children* (4th ed. Bowker, 1990) and *Best Books for Senior High Readers* (Bowker, 1991). [R: RBB, 15 Sept 91; SLJ, Aug 91]

E
1152   **BookBrain Grades 1-3**. Phoenix, Ariz.: Oryx Press, 1989. $195.00 w/64-page manual.

E
1153   **BookBrain Grades 4-6, Version 3.0**. Phoenix, Ariz.: Oryx Press, 1990. $195.00 w/64-page manual.

1154   **BookBrain Grades 7-9, Version 2.0**. Phoenix, Ariz.: Oryx Press, 1990. $195.00 w/64-page manual.

Each of these programs requires an Apple II computer (includes the Apple IIGS) with 64K RAM and single or duel disk drives, or an IBM PC/XT/AT or compatible computer with 256K, DOS 3.0 or higher, and monochrome or color graphics adapter.

BookBrain (*BB*), similar to *BookWhiz*, is a reader's adviser based on the best books contained in standard lists and other titles judged to be appealing to children at each grade level. Each program contains annotated citations with a list of similar titles.

BB for grades 1 to 3 includes 950 annotated titles and lists 1,200 additional books; that for grades 4 to 6 has 1,000 annotations plus 1,400 others; and that for grades 7 to 9 includes 800 annotated citations and 1,000 more titles. The user accesses the program by answering a group of multiple-choice questions that gives a reading profile. Books can be selected by subject or by inputting an author or title. In either case, suggested titles are matched to the reading profile. The user can select up to five books to compile a printed reading list.

BB includes fiction titles only, while the BookWhiz series also has nonfiction titles. Both permit students to rate books, but *BB* also allows them to enter comments. Both are user-friendly. [R: WLB, Jan 90; WLB, Nov 90]

E
1155   **BookWhiz, Jr.** Princeton, N.J.: Educational Testing Service, Library and Reference Service, 1990. $195.00.

E+
1156   **BookWhiz.** Princeton, N.J.: Educational Testing Service, Library and Reference Service, 1990. $195.00.

1157   **BookWhiz for Teens.** Princeton, N.J.: Educational Testing Service, Library and Reference Service, 1990. $195.00.

All of these programs require Apple/Apple II family computers or IBM-compatible units. *BookWhiz, Jr.* is designed for grades 3 to 6, and *BookWhiz* and *BookWhiz for Teens* are designated respectively for grades 6 to 9 and 9 to 12. The student reads a story and then chooses from the programs' seven genres: funny; animals; mystery and adventure; sports, games, and amazing feats; biography and stories from the past; fantasy and magic; and growing up. After the user selects a category and chooses a certain length, level of difficulty, and gender of characters, the program responds with 5 to 10 annotated book titles.

The program, which includes 1,007 fiction and nonfiction titles, permits several adaptations: insertion of local call numbers, addition or deletion of titles, modification of levels of difficulty, and student ratings of titles. Each genre is on a different color disk; an "All Star Books" disk holds 50 of the most popular titles from all colored disks. [R: SLJ, June 90; WLB, June 90]

E+
1158   Dreyer, Sharon Spredemann. **The Bookfinder 4: When Kids Need Books: Annotations of Books Published 1983 through 1986.** Circle Pines, Minn.: American Guidance Service, 1989. 642p. $75.00; $34.95pa. ISBN 0-913476-50-1; 0-913476-51-Xpa. LC 89-83797. (Circle Pines, MN 55014-1796).

Counselors, psychologists, teachers, librarians, and other professionals seeking books that can help children ages 2-15 cope with problems will find this an indispensable series. The first *Bookfinder* (1977) covered 1,031 books published through 1974; *Bookfinder 2* (1981) listed 723 books from 1975 to 1978; and *Bookfinder 3* (1985) presented 725 books published from 1979 to 1982. This latest addition to the series has 731 titles published from 1983 to 1986.

Titles, arranged alphabetically by author under main and secondary subject headings, deal with some 450 psychological, behavioral, and developmental themes. The detailed annotation that follows each entry provides a synopsis; a commentary on the book's strengths, weaknesses, literary merit, and illustrations; qualifications of the author; sequels; approximate age level; and other formats (e.g., film, cassettes, braille, large print). A first choice for elementary and middle school libraries. [R: BL, 1 Mar 90]

E
1159   **Exciting, Funny, Scary, Short, Different and Sad Books Kids Like about Animals, Science, Sports, Families, Songs and Other Things.** Frances Laverne Carroll and Mary Meacham, eds. Chicago: American Library Association, 1984. 192p. $12.50pa. ISBN 0-8389-0423-8. LC 84-20469.

The titles identified by this bibliography should help librarians meet the everyday demands of children for books in a particular category (e.g., a funny book, a short book, a book about snakes).

The 1,000 selections for readers in grades 2 through 5 are arranged by 100 popular topics. Bibliographic information is provided for each title, and annotations are designed to appeal to children. Despite the work's age, librarians and teachers continue to find it useful. [R: ARBA 86; SLJ, Sept 85; WLB, May 85]

E+
1160   Hearne, Betty. **Choosing Books for Children: A Commonsense Guide**. rev. ed. New York: Delacorte/Dell, 1990. 228p. $9.95. ISBN 0-385-30108-1. LC 89-71459.

This well-written volume, by the editor of *Bulletin of the Center for Children's Books*, will help parents, teachers, and librarians choose appropriate literature for children at various stages of development. A revision of a 1981 edition, it includes over 300 annotated selections published from 1970 to 1990, with the exception of a few old favorites. Introductions to the chapters have been expanded and enriched, and two new chapters have been added: one about young adult literature, and the other on literacy and children's literature. Indexed by author/illustrator and subject. [R: ARBA 91; SLJ, May 91]

1161   Horner, Catherine Townsend. **The Single-Parent Family in Children's Books: An Annotated Bibliography**. 2d ed. Metuchen, N.J.: Scarecrow, 1988. 339p. $32.50. ISBN 0-8108-2065-X. LC 87-26403.

Laypersons, teachers, and professionals interested in identifying reading materials for children of nontraditional homes will welcome this bibliography. Horner annotates and rates 596 fictional and 26 nonfictional titles, published between 1965 and 1986, that focus on single-parent families, unmarried mothers and homes broken by divorce, separation, desertion, or death. Titles are annotated, and bibliographical and order information is provided. A useful bibliography for professionals at the upper elementary and middle school levels. [R: ARBA 89; BR, Nov/Dec 88; RBB, Aug 88; VOYA, Dec 88]

E+
1162   Lynn, Ruth Nadelman. **Fantasy Literature for Children and Young Adults: An Annotated Bibliography**. 3d ed. New Providence, N.J.: R. R. Bowker, 1989. 771p. $44.95. ISBN 0-8352-2347-7. LC 88-8162.

A valuable source for those working with children in grades 3 through 12, this volume lists 3,300 fantasy novels and story collections (1,600 more than the 2d edition, published as *Fantasy for Children*). Part 1 cites works published in English between 1900 and 1988. These are arranged in 10 topical chapters such as allegorical fantasy and witchcraft and sorcery. Each title receives a one-sentence annotation, review citations, a designation of quality, and estimated grade level. Part 2, the research guide, lists secondary works divided into chapters on reference and bibliography, history and criticism, teaching resources, and author studies. Title and subject indexes support the text. Also of note is the older *Reference Guide to Modern Fantasy for Children*, edited by Pat Pfieger and Helen M. Hill (Greenwood Press, 1984). That work treats 36 American and British writers and 100 books of the nineteenth and twentieth centuries. [R: ARBA 90; BR, Nov/Dec 89; LJ, 1 Feb 89; RBB, 1 May 89; VOYA, Aug 89]

1163   Nilson, Lenore, comp. **The Best of** *Children's Choices*. Ottawa: Citizens' Committee on Children, 1988. 114p. $8.95pa. ISBN 0-9690205-5-4.

This selection was gleaned from the first five volumes of *Children's Choices of Canadian Books*, which is based on reviews by children. Titles, arranged in three sections according to the levels of their readers, are briefly annotated, with setting and age level provided. Symbols indicate relative popularity of each title, easy readers, and books available in French editions. This is a useful list of Canadian books that children have selected as their favorites. [R: ARBA 90; CLJ, Aug 89]

E
1164   Roberts, Patricia L. **Alphabet Books as a Key to Language Patterns: An Annotated Action Bibliography**. Hamden, Conn.: Library Professional Publications/Shoe String Press, 1987. 263p. $27.50. ISBN 0-208-02151-5. LC 87-3216.

Roberts' introduction, a comprehensive essay on language patterns and their relationship to children's language and learning skills, explains her approach to alphabet books. For each of almost 500 titles, including some in which the alphabet is used to organize a topic (e.g., *Ancient Egypt from A to Z*), she describes the book's approach, provides response activities, and gives the specific language pattern used. Some titles are recommended. Indexed by author and title. Of interest primarily to those involved in early childhood education, this bibliography also has use as a selection aid. [R: ARBA 89; BL, 1 Oct 87]

E+
1165 Strickland, Charlene. **Dogs, Cats, and Horses: A Resource Guide to the Literature for Young People**. Englewood, Colo.: Libraries Unlimited, 1990. 225p. $26.50. ISBN 0-87287-719-1. LC 90-6597.

Books about dogs, cats, and horses are perennial requests in libraries serving children and young adults. Strickland's excellent guide will help school media specialists develop core collections of quality titles for these topics and assist them in guiding readers to exciting and entertaining books. The annotated bibliography consists of 630 selected titles, fiction and nonfiction for grades 1 to 12, that were published since 1970. Classic works are also included if still in print. All books cited portray animals as companions; fairy tales and fantasies are excluded.

Citations include bibliographic data, illustrator and type of illustrations, subject tracings, and audience appeal (boys, girls, both, and age levels). Setting, period, and sequels are included for fiction. The bibliography is highly recommended.

A disk version offers subject access through numerous descriptors and is available in three formats: Apple for AppleWorks ($26.00), Mac for Microsoft Works ($27.00), and IBM-ASCII comma delimited files ($26.25). The disk can be tailored to a library's collection and is useful for producing reading lists for specific age groups or subject categories. [R: ARBA 91]

E+
1166 Wear, Terri A. **Horse Stories: An Annotated Bibliography of Books for All Ages**. Metuchen, N.J.: Scarecrow, 1987. 277p. $29.50. ISBN 0-8108-1998-8. LC 87-13050.

"Have you got any good horse stories?" is a request not easily filled if the patron is already widely read on the topic. When all else fails, this bibliography is a good place to turn for ideas. "Horse stories" is interpreted broadly to include donkeys, mules, merry-go-round horses, rocking horses, and toy horses. Most westerns are excluded as they are not specifically about horses. Titles listed are briefly annotated (usually one sentence). Series and sequels are noted, and out-of-print works are so indicated. Indexed by title and subject. [R: ARBA 89; BR, May/June 88; RBB, 1 May 88; VOYA, Oct 88]

E
1167 Wilson, George, and Joyce Moss. **Books for Children to Read Alone: A Guide for Parents and Librarians**. New Providence, N.J.: R. R. Bowker, 1988. 184p. $39.95. ISBN 0-8352-2346-9. LC 88-10430.

The educators who created this work discovered that most of the 2,500 children's books published annually are intended to be read to children. The purpose of this guide is to identify books suitable for prekindergarten through third grade children to read for themselves. The 350 titles, published from the early 1950s through 1985, are arranged by level.

The first chapter contains wordless (or near-wordless) books; succeeding chapters are divided by intervals of half a grade. Each of the seven chapters begins with a list of the books included, divided into easy, average, and challenging sections. The annotated entries that follow describe the story, comment on illustrations, and identify genre and subject. Indexing is by subject, author, title, and readability level. Highly recommended. [R: ARBA 89; BL, 1 Apr 89; LJ, Dec 88; SLJ, Apr 89]

DICTIONARIES AND ENCYCLOPEDIAS

E+
1168 Carpenter, Humphrey, and Mari Prichard. **Oxford Companion to Children's Literature**. New York: Oxford University Press, 1984. 586p. $45.95. ISBN 0-19-211582-0. LC 83-15130.

This work, though designed for those who work with children from grade 5 through middle school and above, also has reference value for the children themselves. The 2,000 entries, written in a lively style, cover authors, illustrators, fictitious characters, children's magazines, films, and comic strips. Moreover, the volume provides plot summaries, discusses genres, and includes other topics relevant to nineteenth- and twentieth-century children's books (primarily from the English-speaking world). [R: ARBA 85; BL, 15 Apr 84; LJ, 15 Apr 85; SLJ, Aug 84; WLB, Oct 84]

INDEXES

See **Mythology and Folklore** for indexes to fairy tales and myths.

■ *Children's Book Review Index. See* entry 218.

■ *Children's Book Review Index: Master Cumulation, 1965-1984. See* entry 219.

■ *Children's Magazine Guide. See* entry 220.

1169   *Horn Book* **Index, 1924-1989**. By Serenna F. Day. Phoenix, Ariz.: Oryx Press, 1990. 534p. $65.00. ISBN 0-89774-156-0. LC 90-38195.

Since *Horn Book Magazine* began in 1924 "to blow the horn for fine books for boys and girls," it has reviewed 400-500 books per year and published articles on writers, illustrators, and trends in children's literature. This access tool covers the magazine's 66 years. A name/title index and a subject index cite volumes and pages in *Horn Book* for over 80,000 references. [R: ARBA 91]

E
1170   Lima, Carolyn W., and John A. Lima. **A to Zoo: Subject Access to Children's Picture Books**. 3d ed. New Providence, N.J.: R. R. Bowker, 1989. 939p. $44.95. ISBN 0-8352-2599-2. LC 89-15916.

When children, preschool through second grade, request "a book about...," *A to Zoo* will supply many suggestions. Now in its 3d edition, it has become a standard tool for reader guidance and selection, compiling bibliographies, and planning story hours. The 11,500 indexed titles (fiction and nonfiction) are based on the San Diego Public Library's picture-book collection and a number of other sources, including review literature.

The five sections are an alphabetical list of 700 subject headings, with cross-references; the main division, which lists titles under subject headings; a list of the picture books by author, with full bibliographic information and heading under which each title is classified; a title index; and an illustrator index.

Coverage provided by this work has almost tripled since it began in 1982. The first edition included 4,400 picture books arranged under 543 headings; the subsequent edition expanded coverage to 8,500 titles under 600 headings. The revision adds new titles to replace deleted ones. Highly recommended. [R: ARBA 90; BL, 1 Feb 90; SLJ, Nov 89]

E +
1171   **Olderr's Young Adult Fiction Index**. Steven Olderr and Candace P. Smith, eds. Chicago: St. James. annual. $50.00.

The first annual volume of this new index lists 852 hardback and paperback books for junior and senior high school students (grades 6-12), published in the United States in 1988 and reviewed in *Booklist*, *VOYA*, *Publishers Weekly*, and *School Library Journal*. The main entry section includes complete bibliographic data, level, subject headings (up to nine), main characters (up to three), and citations to reviews.

A second part provides a subject, title, and character list, and refers to the first part. A separate section lists the best books of the year in the editors' judgment, based on the reviews consulted. The index should be useful to those responsible for collection development and readers' advisory work. [R: ARBA 90; VOYA, June 90]

BIOGRAPHY

E +
1172   **American Writers for Children since 1960: Poets, Illustrators, and Nonfiction Authors**. Glenn E. Estes, ed. Detroit: Gale, 1987. 430p. (Dictionary of Literary Biography, v.61). $103.00. ISBN 0-8103-1739-7. LC 87-14352.

This volume contains 32 biographies of poets, illustrators, and nonfiction writers for children. Four- to sixteen-page biographies provide background information, describe many of the author's works in detail, and include bibliographies of books by and about the subject. Illustrations include reproductions of dust jackets in black-and-white, facsimile reproductions of pages from the original manuscripts, and photographs of the biographees. Illustrators dominate and include Maurice Sendak, Marcia Brown, and Tomie de Paola.

Other volumes in the Dictionary of Literary Biography series that focus on children's writers are *American Writers for Children before 1900*, edited by Glenn E. Estes (Gale, 1985); *American Writers for Children, 1900-1960*, edited by John Cech (Gale, 1983); and *American Writers for Children since 1960: Fiction*, edited by Glenn E. Estes (Gale, 1986). [R: ARBA 88]

1173 Authors & Artists for Young Adults. Agnes Garrett and Helga P. McCue, eds. Detroit: Gale, 1988- . $59.00/v. ISSN 1040-5682. LC 89-641100.

This series is designed to bridge the gap between *Something about the Author* for children, and *Contemporary Authors* for adults. Each volume features 18 to 20 contemporary and classic creative artists—authors, songwriters, movie producers, screenwriters, and editors. Among those included in the five volumes published to date are Lois Duncan, James Herriot, Gary Larson, Toni Morrison, and Richard Peck.

Articles of six or more pages contain personal information, awards and other credits, a complete list of publications, works in progress, and a bibliography of additional sources. Each essay provides the usual biographical data, plus a critical evaluation of the author's work. Scattered through the sketches are anecdotes and quotations from the writer or artist. In addition to lists of the person's most prestigious awards, there are notations of titles cited in "School Library Journal Best Books" and other noteworthy listings. The volume also lists novels and short stories made into television programs or motion pictures.

Illustrations (black-and-white photographs, stills from films or theatrical productions, and book or magazine covers) support the text. The set is a worthwhile addition to secondary libraries, if not an essential holding. [R: ARBA 90; BL, 15 May 89; EL, Nov-Dec 89; SLMQ, summer 89; WLB, Jan 89; WLB, Mar 89]

E +

1174 Children's Authors and Illustrators: An Index to Biographical Dictionaries. 4th ed. Joyce Nakamura, ed. Detroit: Gale, 1987. 799p. $140.00. ISBN 0-8103-2525-X. LC 86-27035.

This index provides access to biographical information on over 25,000 authors and illustrators of books for children. The citations also appear in the eight-volume *Biography and Genealogy Master Index* (Gale, 1989), of which this guide is a spinoff.

E +

1175 Children's Literature Review: Excerpts from Reviews, Citations, and Commentary on Books for Children and Young People. Detroit: Gale, 1976- . $92.00/v. ISSN 0362-4145. LC 75-34953.

Each volume in this ongoing series contains biographical/critical information about 10-14 children's authors, commentaries excerpted from reviews and other articles, comments by the authors, their portraits, and illustrations from their books. Selected volumes feature essays written especially for the series by such noted critics and authors as Zena Sutherland, John Rowe Townsend, Sheila A. Egoff, and Rudine Sims. Cumulative indexes to authors and titles appear in each volume. Appendixes identify the sources from which material has been drawn. [R: ARBA 90; BL, 1 Feb 89]

E

1176 Eden, Cooper. The Glorious ABC: With Illustrations by the Best Artists from the Past. New York: Atheneum, 1990. 46p. $14.95. ISBN 0-689-31604-4. LC 90-30566.

Short biographies of illustrators of alphabet books for the period 1900 to 1930 are accompanied by their illustrations. Included are Leslie Brooke, Randolph Caldecott, Beatrix Potter, Kate Greenaway, and a number of lesser-known artists. This attractive work is suitable for children in elementary school and adults interested in children's literature. [R: SLJ, Dec 90]

E +

1177 Gallo, Donald R., comp. and ed. Speaking for Ourselves: Autobiographical Sketches by Notable Authors of Books for Young Adults. Urbana, Ill.: National Council of Teachers of English, 1990. 231p. $12.95pa. ISBN 0-8141-4625-2. LC 89-48918.

This work provides an informal look at 87 authors of young-adult fiction, from Joan Aiken to Paul Zindel, written in their own words. Three-page portraits are accompanied by photographs and bibliographies of major works. Most autobiographies explain why authors chose a writing career, why they prefer particular genres, and what inspired them to write certain books. The personal information this work contains should stimulate students' interest in these popular authors. Recommended for elementary and junior high levels. [R: ARBA 91; BL, 1 June 90; EL, Sept/Oct 90; SLJ, May 90]

E+
1178 **Illustrators of Children's Books: 1744-1945**. Bertha E. Mahoney and others, eds. Boston: Horn Book, c1947, 1961. 527p. $35.95. ISBN 0-87675-015-3.

1179 **Illustrators of Children's Books: 1946-1956**. Ruth Hill Viguers and others, eds. Boston: Horn Book, 1958. 299p. $30.95. ISBN 0-87675-016-1. LC 57-31264.

1180 **Illustrators of Children's Books: 1957-1966**. Lee Kingman and others, eds. Boston: Horn Book, 1968. 295p. $30.95. ISBN 0-87675-017-X.

1181 **Illustrators of Children's Books: 1967-1976**. Lee Kingman and others, eds. Boston: Horn Book, 1978. 295p. $35.95. ISBN 0-87675-018-8. LC 78-13759.
This standard series contains biographies and bibliographies of outstanding illustrators of children's books. Each book also includes essays on the history and evolution of the art of illustrating children's books. The 1967-1976 volume contains a cumulative index for the series.

E+
1182 **Junior Book of Authors**. 2d ed. Stanley J. Kunitz and Howard Haycraft, eds. Bronx, N.Y.: H. W. Wilson, 1951. 309p. $32.00. ISBN 0-8242-0028-4. LC 51-13057.

E+
1183 **More Junior Authors**. Muriel Fuller, ed. Bronx, N.Y.: H. W. Wilson, 1963. 235p. $28.00. ISBN 0-8242-0036-5. LC 63-11816.

E+
1184 **Third Book of Junior Authors**. Doris de Montreville and Donna Hill, eds. Bronx, N.Y.: H. W. Wilson, 1972. 320p. $32.00. ISBN 0-8242-0408-5. LC 75-149381.

E+
1185 **Fourth Book of Junior Authors & Illustrators**. Doris de Montreville and Elizabeth D. Crawford, eds. Bronx, N.Y.: H. W. Wilson, 1978. 370p. $38.00. ISBN 0-8242-0568-5. LC 78-115.

E+
1186 **Fifth Book of Junior Authors & Illustrators**. Sally Holmes Holtze, ed. Bronx, N.Y.: H. W. Wilson, 1983. 357p. $40.00. ISBN 0-8242-0694-0. LC 83-21828.

E+
1187 **Sixth Book of Junior Authors & Illustrators**. Sally Holmes Holtze, ed. Bronx, N.Y.: H. W. Wilson, 1989. 345p. $40.00. ISBN 0-8242-0777-7. LC 89-14815.
Those seeking information on the most important creators of juvenile and young adult literature can rely on this ongoing set, which began in 1934. With the addition of the 250 biographical and auto-biographical profiles of prominent authors and illustrators contained in the *Sixth Book*, the set now contains over 1,500 entries. It should be noted that the first three books treat authors only; beginning with the *Fourth Book*, illustrators receive attention.
Essays focus on the lives and careers of notables from Hans Christian Andersen, Randolph Caldecott, Kate Greenaway, and A. A. Milne to those who have recently achieved prominence. Each volume contains an index to all previous works in the series. Highly recommended.

1188 Loertscher, David V., and Lance Castle. **A State-by-State Guide to Children's and Young Adult Authors and Illustrators**. Castle Rock, Colo.: Hi Willow Research and Publishing; distr., Englewood, Colo.: Libraries Unlimited, 1991. 344p. $29.00 looseleaf w/binder. ISBN 0-931510-33-3.
Entries for over 6,000 authors and illustrators are arranged by state of birth (not current location or "adopted" state) and then alphabetically by author. For each name, information includes birth/death dates; place of birth; sample titles; directory information; and references to biographical data in over 100 sources, such as the Wilson *Junior Author* series and *Something about the Author*.
The content is also available on disk (Apple for AppleWorks, $22.00; Mac for Microsoft Works, $22.50; and IBM-ASCII comma delimited file, $23.00), which permits the creation of lists by states or "adopted" states. [R: ARBA 92]

E+
1189 Munroe, Mary, and Judith Banja. **The Birthday Book**. New York: Neal-Schuman, 1991. 499p. $49.95. ISBN 1-55570-051-9. LC 90-20019.

The Birthday Book includes 7,219 American authors and illustrators of books that appeal to young people. They are listed by birth month, birth year, and place of birth. The work, however, is far more than a calendar of birthdays. It also provides biographical information for the arranged alphabetically listees and cites biographical and bio-bibliographical sources for each author. This excellent work should be useful both in supplying ideas for programming and for biographical material. [R: ARBA 92; RBB, 15 May 91; VOYA, Oct 91; WLB, May 91]

1190 **Presenting Children's Authors, Illustrators and Performers**. Barbara O. Greenwood, ed. Markham, Ontario: Pembroke, 1990. 200p. $24.95pa. ISBN 0-921217-45-5.

Librarians and educators interested in Canadian children's authors, illustrators, and performers will welcome this volume. The work reprints 37 sketches that appeared in the Canadian Society of Children's Authors, Illustrators and Performers newsletter from 1979 through 1989. Information has been updated when appropriate. Profiles include biographical and personal information and artists' comments on the children's literature field.

E+
1191 Roginski, Jim. **Behind the Covers: Interviews with Authors and Illustrators of Books for Children and Young People**. Englewood, Colo.: Libraries Unlimited, 1985. 249p. $23.50. ISBN 0-87287-506-7. LC 85-18129.

1192 Roginski, Jim. **Behind the Covers: Interviews with Authors and Illustrators of Books for Children and Young People. Volume II**. Englewood, Colo.: Libraries Unlimited, 1989. 261p. $27.50. ISBN 0-87287-627-6. LC 85-18129.

Unlike traditional biographical sources in narrative format, these volumes consist of interviews with authors and illustrators, 22 in the original volume and 21 in the second. Entries use a similar format; each begins with a biographical profile followed by an interview that explores the artist's philosophy of writing and approach to work. The interviews for the first volume were conducted in 1983 and 1984, and those for volume 2 took place in 1987. A complete bibliography, a list of awards and honors, the location of libraries owning original manuscripts and artwork, and a selection of additional sources conclude each entry. These volumes are worthy companions to *Something about the Author* and *American Writers for Children since 1960*. [R: ARBA 86; ARBA 90]

E+
1193 Rollock, Barbara. **Black Authors and Illustrators of Children's Books: A Biographical Dictionary**. Hamden, Conn.: Garland, 1988. 130p. (Garland Reference Library of the Humanities, v.660). $27.00. ISBN 0-8240-8580-9. LC 87-25748.

This work contains profiles of 115 Black authors and illustrators—British, African, Canadian, and American—whose works appeared from the early 1930s to date. Concise biographical sketches, ranging from 30 to 350 words, include a bibliography of each author's books for children. A short list of bibliographical sources and references and some 50 black-and-white photographs of author/illustrators and book covers support the text. [R: ARBA 89; BL, 1 Apr 89; SLJ, Nov 88]

E+
1194 **Something about the Author Autobiography Series**. Adele Sarkissian, ed. Detroit: Gale, 1986- . $74.00/v. ISSN 0085-6842. LC 86-641293.

This companion set to *Something about the Author*, which began in 1986, is the only ongoing series in which juvenile authors discuss their lives, careers, and published works. Each volume contains essays by 20 established writers or illustrators (e.g., Evaline Ness, Nonny Hogrogian, Betsy Byars, Jean Fritz) who represent all types of literature, preschool to young adult.

The authors/illustrators are given the freedom to express what they want to say, without a set format for the essay. Some articles focus on biographical information, while others emphasize the writing career. Most, however, address young readers and provide family background, discuss the writing experience, and cite some factors that influenced it. Illustrations include portraits of the authors as children and more recent action pictures and portraits. There are cumulative indexes by authors, important published works, and geographical locations mentioned in the essays. [R: ARBA 91]

E +
1195 **Something about the Author: Facts and Pictures about Contemporary Authors and Illustrators of Books for Young People.** Anne Commire, ed. Detroit: Gale, 1971- . $74.00/v. ISSN 0267-816X. LC 72-27107.

This attractive and useful series, the only ongoing work focusing on the lives and writings of authors and illustrators of children's books, is an essential purchase for elementary and middle school libraries. It now covers over 6,000 contemporary notables and major creators of children's books. Each new volume adds about 100 profiles.

The essays include career and personal data, a bibliography of the author's works, information on works in progress, and references to further information. A section called "Sidelights" provides quotations by the author (letters, diaries, memoirs, and other sources), a list of hobbies and special interests, and a chronology of the author's personal life.

For authors and illustrators who have remained productive over a long period of time, sketches are often revised for later volumes; obituaries for those in earlier volumes are also included. [R: ARBA 89]

E +
1196 **Twentieth Century Children's Writers.** 3d ed. Tracy Chevalier, ed. Chicago: St. James, 1989. 1288p. $85.00. ISBN 0-912289-95-3.

This edition of an outstanding work contains biographical data and critical essays on over 800 English-language authors of children's fiction, nonfiction, drama, and poetry. All essays are new or updated. Among the authors added are Arna Bontemps, Anita Desai, Anne McCaffrey, and Lois Lowry. A panel of authorities on children's literature selected the biographees.

Each entry, a half page to a page in length and written and signed by a subject specialist, consists of a short biography, a bibliography of publications, and a critical essay. Many articles also cite the location of manuscripts and provide authors' comments about their work. The title index lists all books cited in the entries.

The appendix contains similar articles on 40 prominent nineteenth-century children's authors (e.g., Howard Pyle, Louisa May Alcott). Another lists 70 foreign-language writers whose children's books are available in English, with their nationality and a list of their translated works. Highly recommended. [R: ARBA 90; LJ, 15 May 90, June 90]

E +
1197 Ward, Martha E., and others. **Authors of Books for Young People.** 3d ed. Metuchen, N.J.: Scarecrow, 1990. 780p. $59.95. ISBN 0-8108-2293-8. LC 90-32569.

This edition, which expands the previous one (1979) by 297 entries, includes brief biographies of 3,708 authors and illustrators for young adults. Entries give dates and a few sentences about the author, and cite several sources. The work's claim to fame is that it lists more authors than any other one-volume source. Other dictionaries, such as *Twentieth Century Children's Writers* and Wilson's *Junior Book of Authors* focus on the most outstanding writers and illustrators and contain more information about those listed. [R: ARBA 91; BL, 1 May 91]

E +
1198 **Writers for Young Adults: Biographies Master Index: An Index to Sources of Biographical Information....** 3d ed. Joyce Nakamura, ed. Detroit: Gale, 1989. 183p. $92.00. ISBN 0-8103-1833-4. LC 84-21144.

Writers for Young Adults provides 45,000 citations to almost 16,000 authors treated in some 600 biographical dictionaries. The index, moreover, includes references to biographies of writers of adult fiction and nonfiction whose works are considered suitable for young people. Citations are arranged alphabetically by author. The index is a spinoff of *Biography and Genealogy Master Index* (Gale, 1989). [R: ARBA 90; VOYA, Oct 89]

AWARDS

E +
1199 **Award-Winning Books for Children and Young Adults.** By Betty L. Criscoe. Metuchen, N.J.: Scarecrow. annual. $37.50. LC 90-38848.

This annual is designed to assist librarians, teachers, and others in selecting quality books for children and adolescents. All award books and runners-up printed in English throughout the world are listed. Entries provide the name of the award, its address and background, complete bibliographic data for the book, a brief summary, other awards the book has won, and grade level. Small black-and-white photographs of each winner are provided. Appendixes list publishers of the books with addresses and the award-winning books by age/grade level and genre. [R: ARBA 91; BL, 1 Oct 90; SLJ, May 91]

E+
1200   **Children's Literature Awards and Winners: A Directory of Prizes, Authors, and Illustrators**. 2d ed. Dolores Blythe Jones, ed. Detroit: Neal-Schuman with Gale, 1988. 671p. $94.00. ISBN 0-8103-2741-4. LC 84-643512.

Current and discontinued awards for children's books in the United States, other English-speaking countries, and worldwide are the focus of this volume. Information on the 211 awards (an increase of 67 over the original edition of 1983) is followed by a chronological list of award-winning titles and runners-up. In all, the book cites more than 5,000 books and nearly 7,000 authors and illustrators. The title index and author/illustrator index list award-winning and runner-up books.

Children's Books: Awards & Prizes, Including Prizes and Awards for Young Adult Books, compiled and edited by the Children's Book Council (Children's Book Council, 1986), which is updated and reissued about every five years, is a similar work. Awards are grouped in four general categories: U.S. awards selected by adults, U.S. awards selected by young readers, British Commonwealth awards, and international and multinational awards. [R: ARBA 89; RBB, 15 Dec 88]

E+
1201   **The Newbery and Caldecott Awards: A Guide to the Medal and Honor Books**. By Association for Library Services to Children. Chicago: American Library Association. annual. $12.00pa.

This annual guide lists all Newbery and Caldecott award-winning titles and honor books from the beginning of the awards (1922 and 1938, respectively) to 1991. For the first time, the 1991 edition includes brief descriptive annotations for each work and a black-and-white illustration from the latest winners. A feature article treats the various art media used in Caldecott winners. [R: ARBA 92]

E+
1202   **Newbery Medal Books: 1922-1955**. Bertha Mahony Miller and Elinor Whitney Field, eds. Boston: Horn Book, 1955. 458p. $22.95. ISBN 0-87675-000-5. LC 55-13968.

E+
1203   **Caldecott Medal Books: 1938-1957**. Bertha Mahony Miller and Elinor Whitney Field, eds. Boston: Horn Book, 1957. 329p. $22.95. ISBN 0-87675-001-3. LC 57-11582.

E+
1204   **Newbery and Caldecott Medal Books: 1956-1965**. Lee Kingman, ed. Boston: Horn Book, 1965. 300p. $22.95. LC 65-26759.

E+
1205   **Newbery and Caldecott Medal Books: 1966-1975**. Lee Kingman, ed. Boston: Horn Book, 1975. 321p. $22.95. ISBN 0-87675-003-X. LC 75-20167.

E+
1206   **Newbery and Caldecott Medal Books: 1976-1985**. Lee Kingman, ed. Boston: Horn Book, 1986. 376p. $24.95. ISBN 0-87675-004-8. LC 86-15223.

Each volume covers the award-winning books and their authors and illustrators for a given time period. Entries give a summary of the plot, excerpts from the recipient's acceptance speech at the Newbery/Caldecott Award dinner, and a profile of the author or illustrator. Well-known authorities have contributed several essays about children's literature to each collection. Barbara Baden, Zena Sutherland, and Ethel L. Heins wrote the essays in the 1986 volume.

Information about these books and their creators can be found in many other sources, such as *Something about the Author*, but this series is a worthwhile acquisition for libraries serving children and young adults. [R: BL, July 87]

PLOT OUTLINES

See also **Storytelling and Activities** in **Children's Literature**.

E +

1207 Beacham's Guide to Literature for Young Adults. Kirk Beetz and Suzanne Niemeyer, eds. Washington, D.C.: Beacham, 1990. 4v. $189.00/set. ISBN 0-933833-16-4. LC 89-1804. (210 S St. NW, Washington, DC 20018).

Students, teachers, and librarians will welcome this excellent set, which surveys and analyzes outstanding books for young adult readers. Among the more than 200 titles (novels, short story collections, nonfiction works, and biographies) the reader will find many that tell of earlier times and places and others that examine the age-old problem of growing up. Some portray a stable and secure world, while others treat issues that challenge today's young people. School reading lists frequently cite titles examined in the set.

For each book, the guide provides biographical information about the author and a description of the book's setting, an analysis of its theme and characters, an assessment of its literary quality, its relevance to today's society, suggested topics for assignments and discussions, and a bibliography of critical reviews. A thematic index supports the alphabetical arrangement. Appropriate for upper elementary through high school levels. [R: BL, July 90; VOYA, Apr 91; WLB, June 90]

1208 Gillespie, John T., and Corinne J. Naden. Seniorplots: A Book Talk Guide for Use with Readers Ages 15-18. New Providence, N.J.: R. R. Bowker, 1989. 386p. $39.95. ISBN 0-8352-2513-5. LC 88-27333.

Like *Juniorplots 3* and *Introducing Bookplots 3* for young students, this work provides book talk guidance for presentations to grades 9 through 12. The work groups 1,050 titles under themes and genres popular with the age group and then highlights 80 of the best fiction and nonfiction titles. Provided are plots, characters, settings, suggested passages for reading aloud, and similar books of interest. Highly recommended for high schools. [R: ARBA 90; LJ, 15 June 89; RBB, 1 May 89; SLJ, July 89]

E +

1209 Gillespie, John T., with Corinne J. Naden. Juniorplots 3: A Book Talk Guide for Use with Readers Ages 12-16. New Providence, N.J.: R. R. Bowker, 1987. 352p. $29.95. ISBN 0-8352-2367-1. LC 87-27305.

Teachers and librarians preparing book talks for students in grades 6 through 10 will find this work indispensable. The volume introduces 80 fiction and nonfiction books arranged by genre (e.g., science fiction, adventure, mystery). Each entry provides theme, characters, setting, passages suggested for reading aloud, and similar books that the speaker could mention to the audience. Highly recommended as a book talk guide and for book selection.

Earlier volumes in this series include *Juniorplots: A Book Talk Manual for Teachers and Librarians* by John T. Gillespie and Diana L. Lembo (R. R. Bowker, 1967) and *More Juniorplots: A Guide for Teachers and Librarians* by John T. Gillespie (R. R. Bowker, 1977). [R: ARBA 89; RBB, 1 June 88; SLJ, Sept 88]

E +

1210 Spirt, Diana L. Introducing Bookplots 3: A Book Talk Guide for Use with Readers Ages 8-12. New Providence, N.J.: R. R. Bowker, 1988. 352p. $39.95. ISBN 0-8352-2345-0.

This highly recommended volume focuses on book talk material for grades 3 through 8. The work contains 90 plot and theme summaries of books chosen for their quality and wide appeal. Fiction and nonfiction titles are arranged under life-goal themes (e.g., making friends, developing values, getting along in the family, understanding social problems). Suggestions about how to review each book and a list of related materials are included. A "Reading Ladder" section arranges titles by age level and difficulty. The guide also is useful as a selection aid.

Two earlier volumes also are available, *Introducing Books: A Guide for the Middle Grades* by John T. Gillespie and Diana L. Lembo (R. R. Bowker, 1970) and *Introducing More Books: A Guide for the Middle Grades* by Diana L. Spirt (R. R. Bowker, 1978). [R: ARBA 89; RBB, 1 Sept 88; SLJ, Sept 88]

E
1211 Thomas, Rebecca L. **Primaryplots: A Book Talk Guide for Use with Readers Age 4-8**. New Providence, N.J.: R. R. Bowker, 1989. 392p. $39.95. ISBN 0-8352-2514-3. LC 88-34054.

This addition to the Bowker book talk series will help those who wish to introduce young children to picture and early-reading books. It contains profiles of 150 recommended titles published between 1983 and 1987. Titles are grouped in eight categories with such headings as "Developing a Positive Image," "Enjoying Family and Friends," and "Analyzing Illustrations."

Each entry provides bibliographic information, suggested grade or reading level, plot and theme summaries, related titles, and sources of additional information about the author and illustrator. Indexed by author, title, illustrator, and subject. Highly recommended as a book talk and selection aid for libraries serving preschool and primary grades. [R: ARBA 90; LJ, 15 Apr 89; RBB, July 89]

PLAYS

E+
1212 Karp, Rashelle S., and June H. Schlessinger. **Plays for Children and Young Adults: An Evaluative Index and Guide**. Hamden, Conn.: Garland, 1991. 580p. (Garland Reference Library of Social Science, v.543). $78.00. ISBN 0-8240-6112-8. LC 90-44195.

This work is designed "to provide enough detailed and evaluative information about specific plays for children and young adults (ages 5-18) to enable those producing them to make effective decisions." It includes 3,560 plays, playlets, choral readings, scenes, monologues, musical reviews, readers' theater, and skits published between 1975 and February 1989. Plays included are taken from *Play Index*, 1978-1982 and 1983-1987; the catalog of Dramatist Play Service; *Plays: The Drama Magazine for Young People, 1975-1984*; and plays from individual publishers.

Each entry indicates the intended grade level, whether the play can be successfully produced at that level, and whether it received positive or negative reviews. Given, too, are the author, the full title, a cast analysis, playing time, a brief description of the stage setting, number of acts, a brief plot summary, an evaluation of the play, royalty information, the source document, subjects and themes, and type of play. Indexed by author/original title, cast, grade level, subject/play type, and playing time. Recommended. [R: ARBA 92; BL, 15 Apr 91; JOYS,, summer 91; LJ, 1 Mar 91]

POETRY

E+
1213 Brewton, John E., and Sara W. Brewton, comps. **Index to Children's Poetry**. Bronx, N.Y.: H. W. Wilson, 1942. 966p. $48.00. ISBN 0-8242-0021-7. *First Supplement*. 1954. 405p. $35.00. ISBN 0-8242-0022-5. *Second Supplement*. 1965. 453p. $35.00. ISBN 0-8242-0023-3. LC 42-20148.

E+
1214 Brewton, John E., Sara W. Brewton, and G. Meredith Blackburn, III, comps. **Index to Poetry for Children and Young People: 1964-1969**. Bronx, N.Y.: H. W. Wilson, 1972. 574p. $43.00. ISBN 0-8242-0435-2. LC 71-161574.

E+
1215 Brewton, John E., G. Meredith Blackburn, III, and Lorraine A. Blackburn, comps. **Index to Poetry for Children and Young People: 1970-1975**. Bronx, N.Y.: H. W. Wilson, 1978. 471p. $43.00. ISBN 0-8242-0621-5. LC 77-26036.

E+
1216 Brewton, John E., G. Meredith Blackburn, III, and Lorraine A. Blackburn, comps. **Index to Poetry for Children and Young People: 1976-1981**. Bronx, N.Y.: H. W. Wilson, 1983. 350p. $43.00. ISBN 0-8242-0681-9. LC 83-10459.

E+
1217 Blackburn, G. Meredith, III, comp. **Index to Poetry for Children and Young People: 1982-1987: A Title, Subject, Authors, and First Line Index**.... Bronx, N.Y.: H. W. Wilson, 1989. 408p. $48.00. ISBN 0-8242-0773-4. LC 89-5342.

Each of the five volumes in this series provide indexing to poems for children and young adults by author, title, subject, and first line. Since it began almost 50 years ago, the series has provided access to over 66,000 poems contained in 727 poetry collections. The latest index (1989) includes 8,500 poems in 110 collections published between 1982 and 1987.

The index includes all types of anthologies, ranging from those intended for preschool children to collections of more than one poet, selections from the works of a single author, anthologies with a theme, books of poetry and prose, and comprehensive collections. An analysis of the books indexed outlines the contents of each collection, the number of authors and poems, and the suggested grade level. These indexes (at least the last several volumes) are an essential holding in school libraries for use in reference and book selection on all levels. [R: ARBA 90]

E +
1218   Olexer, Marycile E. **Poetry Anthologies for Children and Young People**. Chicago: American Library Association, 1985. 285p. $40.00. ISBN 0-8389-0430-0. LC 85-6033.

Olexer's guide analyzes some 300 poetry collections with a central theme or character, for preschool through ninth grade. Anthologies, with full bibliographic data, are arranged under three grade-level groupings: preschool through grade 3, grades 4 through 6, and grades 7 through 9. Critical annotations (about 350 words) analyze the contents of each anthology, evaluate its uses, cite similar titles that can be substituted, and provide a sample poem from each collection. Indexed by author/title and subject. Highly recommended. [R: ARBA 86; BL, 1 Jan 86; SLJ, May 86; WLB, Dec 85]

E +
1219   **Oxford Book of Children's Verse in America**. Donald Hall, ed. New York: Oxford University Press, 1985. 319p. $24.95; $9.95pa. ISBN 0-19-503539-9; 0-19-506761-4pa.

If poetry anthologies are to be added to the reference collection, the *Oxford Book* is a good choice. It consists of some 250 popular American poems for children, some well-known and some not, from all periods of history. Along with poets of the past (e.g., Clement Clark Moore, Mary Mapes Dodge, James Whitcomb Riley) are some who are modern (e.g., Langston Hughes, John Ciardi, David McCord). [R: SLJ, May 86]

E
1220   **Oxford Dictionary of Nursery Rhymes**. Ione Opie and Peter Opie, eds. New York: Oxford University Press, 1951. $47.50. ISBN 0-19-869111-4.

Nursery rhymes, songs, and riddles comprise this comprehensive and authoritative work. The 550 entries, arranged alphabetically by keyword, give the standard version of each rhyme followed by other known versions. Indexing is by notables associated with the rhymes and first lines.

E +
1221   **The Oxford Treasury of Children's Poems**. Michael Harrison and Christopher Stuart-Clark, eds. New York: Oxford University Press, 1988. 174p. $17.95. ISBN 0-19-276055-6. LC 88-42849.

Some 150 poems by English-speaking poets from William Butler Yeats to Shel Silverstein make up this collection. Poems are loosely grouped by subject (e.g., cars, night, shadows). Illustrations by a number of artists add little to the work, which otherwise is excellent. [R: BL, 15 Nov 88; SLJ, May   89]

E +
1222   Smith, Dorothy B. **Subject Index to Poetry for Children and Young People, 1957-1975**. Chicago: American Library Association, 1977. $45.00. ISBN 0-8389-0242-1. LC 77-3296.

A supplement to *Subject Index to Poetry for Children and Young Adults*, compiled by Violet Sell (American Library Association, 1957, o.p.), this work provides subject access to poems in 263 poetry collections published between 1957 and 1975. Poems are entered under some 2,000 subject headings, based on the 10th edition of Sears. Suggested age levels are included for each citation. Brewton's indexes to poetry provide indexing for more recent collections.

STORYTELLING AND ACTIVITIES

See **Library Science** for **Media Skills**.
See **Literature** for **Reading Guidance**.
See **Plot Outlines** in **Children's Literature** for
booktalks.

E
1223   Bauer, Caroline Feller. **Handbook for Storytellers**. Chicago: American Library Association,
1977. 381p. $25.00pa. ISBN 0-8389-0293-6. LC 76-56385.
    Drawing on her own experience as a librarian, storyteller, radio performer, and college professor,
Bauer has produced a storytelling handbook of the first order. Divided into four parts, the book covers
planning, preparation, and promotion; sources for storytelling; multimedia storytelling; and programs
for specific age and interest groups. This is a good basic source for the storytelling collection.

E
1224   **Books to Read Aloud with Children through Age 8**. By Child Study Children's Book Committee
at Bank Street College. New York: Child Study Children's Committee, Bank Street College, 1989. 59p.
$4.00pa.
    Suggested classics to read aloud with (not to) young children are listed herein, from the old favorite
Goodnight Moon and the Babar books to the more current *The Best Town in the World* by Byrd
Baylor. There is a generous mix of story types, all carefully chosen to help foster a lifelong love of
books. Unfortunately, dates are not supplied to tell the user whether the titles are new or reprints of old
books. [R: ARBA 91]

E
1225   Cullum, Carolyn N. **The Storytime Sourcebook: A Compendium of Ideas and Resources for
Storytelling**. New York: Neal-Schuman, 1990. 177p. $24.95pa. ISBN 1-55570-067-5. LC 90-49657.
    This work assists librarians, teachers, and others in planning storytime. It includes 100 alphabet-
ically arranged story-hour topics (e.g., dragons, ecology, ghosts, holidays) with suggested materials and
activities for children ages three to seven. Categories under each include such things as filmstrips or
film, books, fingerplays, and crafts. A bibliography provides complete data and prices for 445 picture
books, 351 filmstrips, and 93 16mm films. The appendix includes a directory of publishers and audiovisual distributors. Indexed by title, author, craft, activity, and song. [R: ARBA 92]

E
1226   Doll, Carol A. **Nonfiction Books for Children: Activities for Thinking, Learning, and Doing**.
Englewood, Colo.: Teacher Ideas Press/Libraries Unlimited, 1990. 117p. $19.50. ISBN 0-87287-710-8.
LC 90-13370.
    This slim volume suggests creative ways in which teachers can use nonfiction books to enrich the
curriculum for elementary school students. Some 60 books are divided into 9 groups (e.g., information
picture books, how-to books, contemporary issues). For each, the guide gives bibliographic data, a
content summary, grade level, pertinent curricular area, objectives, and detailed plans for the activities.
Appendixes provide a bibliography of selected sources and a list of titles chosen from the 1989 booklists
of the National Council for the Social Sciences and the National Science Teachers Association. Indexed
by grade level and subject/activity. [R: ARBA 91; SLJ, July 91]

1227   Freeman, July. **Books Kids Will Sit Still For: The Complete Read-Aloud Guide**. 2d ed. New
Providence, N.J.: R. R. Bowker, 1990. 660p. $34.95. ISBN 0-8352-3010-4. LC 90-2373.
    This work offers inventive ways to introduce children to books. There are chapters on storytelling,
using nonfiction and biography; booktalks; creative dramatics, pantomime, and readers' theater; and
ways to celebrate books, such as debates, awards, and workshops. The main body of the guide recommends 2,100 read-aloud books tested through the author's 15 years as a school librarian and educator.
    Each entry includes a brief plot summary, numerous suggested activities, related titles, and a
subject designation. Organization is by age level for fiction, with separate sections for works of fantasy,
poetry, nonfiction, and picture books. [R: ARBA 92; JOYS, Spring 91; RBB, 15 Feb 91]

1228   Gomberg, Karen C. **More Books Appeal: Keep Young Teens in the Library**. Jefferson, N.C.:
McFarland, 1990. 152p. $14.95pa. ISBN 0-89950-476-0.

A sequel to the author's *Books Appeal* (McFarland, 1987), this work suggests ways of getting and keeping seventh and eighth graders in the library. Chapters focus on different types of activities: "Publicity," "Fun with Book Lists," "Quiet Mental Games," "Contest and Action Games," "Reference Books," and "Fiction Crossword Puzzles." Suggested activities include some that are easy to organize and others that are arduous. [R: VOYA, Oct 90]

E+
1229 Hall, Susan. **Using Picture Storybooks to Teach Literary Devices: Recommended Books for Children and Young Adults**. Phoenix, Ariz.: Oryx Press, 1990. 168p. $24.95pa. ISBN 0-89774-582-5. LC 89-8574.
This work is designed for educators and librarians who wish to use quality picture books to teach literary devices in second grade through junior high. The main body of the work lists and defines 30 literary terms, from alliteration to understatement, and cites 273 picture books, published between 1980 and 1988, that effectively illustrate satire, allusion, puns, imagery, paradox, simile, analogy, and other literary devices. A separate section suggests ways in which these literary elements can be taught. An alphabetical list of all titles cited and an author/title/illustrator index conclude the volume. [R: ARBA 91]

E
1230 Jenkins, Christine, and Sally Freeman. **Novel Experiences: Literature Units for Book Discussion Groups in the Elementary Grades**. Englewood, Colo.: Teacher Ideas Press/Libraries Unlimited, 1991. 231p. $23.00pa. ISBN 0-87287-730-2.
Designed as a guide to literature discussion groups, such as Junior Great Books, this work includes 35 literature units for new titles (e.g., *The Beast in Ms. Rooney's Room*) and classics (e.g., *Homer Price*) for grades 2 through 6. Related titles accompany each unit. Despite some criticisms, such as the repetition of activities in different units, the work is clearly written and will be helpful to libraries and teachers planning book discussion programs. [R: SLJ, June 91]

E
1231 Kallevig, Christine P. **Folding Stories: Storytelling and Origami Together as One**. Newburgh, Ind.: Storytime Ink, 1991. 92p. $11.50pa. ISBN 0-9628769-0-9. LC 91-90852. (P.O. Box 813, Newburgh, IN 47629).
Seven paperfold stories, or "storigami," as the author calls them, comprise this small work, which is designed for those new to origami and storytelling. The clear instructions and text include suggestions for discussions and related activities. A glossary, a detailed index, and a bibliography conclude this work. Recommended for preschool and elementary levels. [R: SLJ, June 91]

E+
1232 Kelly, Joanne. **The Battle of Books: K-8**. Englewood, Colo.: Libraries Unlimited, 1990. 199p. $23.50. ISBN 0-87287-779-5.
Detailed instructions for the popular reading game, "The Battle of Books," created in 1938, make up this work. The contest requires teams to answer questions based on the plots, settings, and characters of books. Over 850 questions on popular contemporary novels, award books, and classics are included in Kelly's work. The questions on index cards are arranged by grade level, then by difficulty. Kelly suggests skits for a number of the books and provides reproducible publicity ideas, scorecards, bookmarks, and certificates.
Disk versions allow teachers or librarians to add questions, to tailor the game to groups of various sizes or to different age levels, and to record dates and groups with whom specific questions were used. The written skits are contained in a word-processing program.
The computer disk alone may be purchased in AppleWorks, Microsoft Works or ASCII comma delimited file formats for around $26.00 each. A book and disk is $40.00.

1233 Korbin, Beverly. **Eyeopeners! How to Choose and Use Children's Books about Real People, Places, and Things**. New York: Viking Penguin, 1988. 317p. $16.95; $7.95pa. ISBN 0-670-82073-3; 0-14-046830-7pa. LC 88-40115.
The first part of this work addresses ways in which children can be introduced to books and taught to read critically. The next section cites over 500 nonfiction books, arranged by subject, with analyses of each and suggested projects to link the books to the child's life. Korbin lists topics with which children should be familiar and problems they may encounter, such as divorce, alcoholism, nontraditional families, and disabilities. All books listed were in print at the beginning of 1988. This unique title

will introduce many new ideas to those who work with children. [R: ARBA 89; BL, 1 Oct 88; SBF, May/June 89; SLJ, Feb 89]

E
1234 Laughlin, Mildred K., and C. L. Swisher. **Literature-based Reading: Children's Books and Activities to Enrich the K-5 Curriculum.** Phoenix, Ariz.: Oryx Press, 1990. 149p. $29.50pa. ISBN 0-89774-562-0. LC 90-36415.
Chapters, divided by level, explain the use of literature in teaching reading. Well-organized units for each level include objectives; a wide variety of introductory and follow-up activities; and a bibliography of recommended fiction, poetry, biographies, and other nonfiction books. This helpful work on whole-language learning will interest teachers, reading specialists, and librarians. [R: SLMQ, Spring 91]

E+
1235 McDonald, Margaret R. **The Skit Book: 101 Skits for Kids.** Hamden, Conn.: Shoestring Press, 1990. 147p. $25.00; $15.00pa. ISBN 0-208-02258-9; 0-208-02283-Xpa. LC 89-29654.
In this work, skits, short routines based on one idea, are arranged in categories (e.g., trick endings, word play, those based on songs or stories). McDonald gives directions for the scene, action, essential characters, and ending, but leaves the remainder open to adaptation and variations. Elementary and middle school students and their teachers will enjoy producing these short plays. [R: BL, 1 June 90; SLJ, June 90]

E
1236 McElmeel, Sharron L. **An Author a Month (for Nickels).** Englewood, Colo.: Teacher Ideas Press/Libraries Unlimited, 1990. 172p. $24.00pa. ISBN 0-87287-827-9.

E
1237 McElmeel, Sharron L. **An Author a Month (for Pennies).** Englewood, Colo.: Teacher Ideas Press/Libraries Unlimited, 1988. 224p. $24.50pa. ISBN 0-87287-661-6.
Each volume suggests creative ideas for building reading and writing skills by using the works of 12 favorite children's authors. The books also provide photographs, biographical information, a bibliography, and hundreds of activity suggestions. Recommended for elementary schools.

E
1238 McElmeel, Sharron L. **Bookpeople: A First Album.** Englewood, Colo.: Teacher Ideas Press/Libraries Unlimited, 1989. 176p. $17.00pa. ISBN 0-87287-720-5. LC 89-20556.

E+
1239 McElmeel, Sharron L. **Bookpeople: A Second Album.** Englewood, Colo.: Teacher Ideas Press/Libraries Unlimited, 1989. 200p. $18.00pa. ISBN 0-87287-721-3.
These sources are part of a series that began with *An Author a Month (for Pennies)*. They are designed to assist elementary teachers and media specialists in finding creative uses for books. Each album covers some 40 authors and illustrators. Every entry includes an author/illustrator poster page with a black-and-white photograph of the subject on one side and information about the individual on the back, a selective list of works, and suggestions for using the book to stimulate reading and writing. Copyright permission to duplicate the material for use in a single school is given.
The first album focuses on authors and illustrators of picture books; the second concentrates on authors popular with children from grade 3 through 9. An index to the series completes each work. Highly recommended. [R: ARBA 91]

E
1240 Moss, Joy F. **Focus Units in Literature: A Handbook for Elementary School Teachers.** Urbana, Ill.: National Council of Teachers of English, 1984. 288p. $15.95pa.
Thirteen units focus on introducing books on a wide variety of subjects. Within each unit there are bibliographies for the topic; suggested books to read aloud and individually; sample questions for promoting classroom discussions; examples of student responses; and additional classroom activities involving writing, dramatization, art, dance, and music. Units include toy animals, pig tales, the sea, folklore patterns, friendship, giants, and dragons.

E
1241   **National Directory of Storytelling**. 1990 ed. Jonesborough, Tenn.: NAPPS, 1990. 74p. $7.95pa.
This directory, published by the National Association for the Preservation and Perpetuation of Storytelling, lists U.S. persons, places, and events connected with storytelling. Among those cited are storytellers, organizations, conferences, festivals, centers, institutes/educational opportunities, and books about the art. For storytellers listed (they paid a fee to be included), the slim volume gives addresses, telephone numbers, and information about their repertoires. Advertisements that publicize workshops, programs, and publications keep the cost of the directory low. Recommended for schools with an interest in the art. [R: ARBA 91]

E
1242   Painter, William M. **Story Hours with Puppets and Other Props**. Hamden, Conn.: Shoe String Press, 1990. 187p. $27.50. ISBN 0-208-02284-8. LC 90-6554.
The author suggests ideas for story hours in which the storyteller/reader tells the tale as the puppets act it out. The text gives advice on planning, setting up a collection, and gathering props, but most chapters (4 through 24) treat specific story types, such as puppets and Mother Goose, and suggest ways to use the puppets and props. A quick reference section lists titles by chapter, with suggestions for each story.

E
1243   Pellowski, Anne. **The World of Storytelling: A Guide to the Origins, Development, and Applications of Storytelling**. rev. ed. Bronx, N.Y.: H. W. Wilson, 1990. 311p. $32.00. ISBN 0-8242-0788-2. LC 90-31151.
Anyone interested in the background of storytelling will welcome this guide, an update of a 1977 work. Pellowski reviews the oral tradition from which literature for children grew; addresses the controversy between storytellers and folklorists; discusses the types, formats, and styles of storytelling; and covers the training of storytellers. The new edition incorporates recent research and offers the author's own insights gained from teaching and practicing the art. An index and a bibliography of training manuals and story collections conclude the volume. This excellent guide is highly recommended. [R: SLJ, Oct 90; SLJ, May 91]

E
1244   Sitarz, Paula Gaj. **More Picture Book Story Hours: From Parties to Pets**. Englewood, Colo.: Libraries Unlimited, 1990. 166p. $20.00pa. ISBN 0-87287-764-7. LC 89-78336.
This sequel to *Picture Book Story Hours* (Libraries Unlimited, 1986) contains a collection of tested program plans for preschoolers. There are ideas for 22 programs (e.g., "Let's Go on a Picnic"; "Goodnight, Sleep Tight"; "How Does Your Garden Grow"), details on the activity, and which books to read aloud or use for book talks. Other suggestions include using flannel boards, action rhymes, finger plays, films, and filmstrips. A bibliography of other works concludes this book of fresh, creative ideas for those who work with young children.

E
1245   Trelease, Jim. **The New Read-Aloud Handbook**. 1989 ed. New York: Viking Penguin, 1989. 290p. $9.95pa. ISBN 0-14-046881-1. LC 89-31925.
As in the previous editions of this classic handbook, the first half contains chapters on why and how to read aloud. The second half lists and annotates 300 suggested in-print titles grouped by category or type. The age/grade level and related titles are given for each book. Indexed by author/illustrator only. Highly recommended. [R: ARBA 91]

E+
1246   Wilson, Mary E. **Representing Children's Book Characters**. Metuchen, N.J.: Scarecrow, 1989. 174p. $25.00. ISBN 0-8108-2169-9. LC 88-31286.
Wilson suggests over 200 ideas for incorporating book characters into plays and other activities, including Mother Goose rhymes, fables, folk and fairy tales, picture books, fiction, biography, and nonfiction. Chapters cover the dramatization of 15 titles, such as *Charlie and the Chocolate Factory*, and production needs, such as making costumes. Appendixes provide scripts and programs, and indexes give access by subject and author/title/characters. [R: SLJ, June 90]

Communication

☐ _____ _____ ☐

GENERAL WORKS

See **Library Science** for **Censorship**.

1247 Hudson, Robert V. **Mass Media: A Chronological Encyclopedia of Television, Radio, Motion Pictures, Magazines, Newspapers, and Books in the United States**. Hamden, Conn.: Garland, 1987. 435p. (Garland Reference Library of Social Science, v.310). $39.95. ISBN 0-8240-8695-3. LC 85-45153.

This history of mass media in America is arranged in 16 sections, beginning with "Founding Period, 1638-1796," and ending with "Economic and Legal Challenges, 1973-1985." Each section is subdivided by media (e.g., books, radio, television); events, organizations, and historical notables are then treated chronologically within each subsection. Entries range from a few sentences to several pages. A detailed index enables the reader to access the wealth of material this work contains. Recommended for high schools. [R: ARBA 88; WLB, Oct 87]

1248 **Webster's New World Dictionary of Media and Communications**. By Richard Weiner. Englewood Cliffs, N.J.: Prentice-Hall, 1990. 533p. $29.95. ISBN 0-13-969759-4. LC 90-31012.

This comprehensive and well-designed dictionary defines 30,000 terms, including jargon and slang, covering a wide range of areas (e.g., communications, technology, marketing, journalism), 27 fields in all. High school students who need such material will find this a useful dictionary. [R: ARBA 92; BL, 1 Sept 90; BR, Nov/Dec 90; LJ, 15 Apr 91]

CALLIGRAPHY

1249 Folsom, Rose. **The Calligraphers' Dictionary**. London: Thames & Hudson; distr., New York: W. W. Norton, 1990. 144p. $24.95. ISBN 0-500-01489-2. LC 89-52098.

Folsom's excellent dictionary, containing 1,500 entries, views calligraphy broadly to include all written processes as they relate to handwriting—materials, forms, concepts, places, important persons, and a few notable artifacts. This work is handsomely designed and a browser's delight. [R: BL, 15 Apr 91]

COPYRIGHT

E+
1250 Sinofsky, Esther R. **Off-Air Videotaping in Education**. New Providence, N.J.: R. R. Bowker, 1984. 163p. $39.95. ISBN 0-8352-1755-8.

What comprises legal off-air videotaping by nonprofit educational institutions? This and other questions related to infringement of copyright laws are clearly explained. Also included are a directory of educational media producers and their policies, Public Broadcasting Services taping guidelines, commonly asked questions with answers, and a glossary of terms.

FORENSICS

■ _Communicators_. _See_ entry 337.

1251 **National Debate Topic for High Schools, Pursuant to Public Law 88-246**. Compiled by Congressional Research Service, Library of Congress. Washington, D.C.: The Senate. annual. Request from appropriate senator or the Secretary of the Senate (Senate Document Room, The Capitol, Washington, DC 20510).

The Library of Congress, required by law to compile materials relevant to annual high school and college debate topics, provides this important collection of data as a senate document. Materials related to the college topic are published as a house document. Each collection consists of background information on the issue; excerpts from pertinent books, articles, and government publications; and bibliographies of other material on the topic.

1252 Subject Bibliography No. 176: College Debate Topic. Washington, D.C.: Government Printing Office. free looseleaf. (request from Superintendent of Documents, Government Printing Office, Washington, DC 20402).

Subject Bibliography No. 176 in GPO's important free Subject Bibliographies series lists available government documents pertaining to the year's college debate topic. Bibliographies of material on the annual high school debate topic are published in *The Forensic Quarterly* (155 Communications Studies Building, University of Iowa, Iowa City, IA 52242). *New York Times File: Critical Issues* provides articles on microfiche for the National Federation of State High School Associations' debate topic each year.

1253 Sutton, Roberta Briggs. **Speech Index**. 4th ed. Metuchen, N.J.: Scarecrow, 1966. 947p. $59.50. ISBN 0-8108-0138-8. LC 66-13747.

1254 Mitchell, Charity. **Speech Index: Fourth Edition Supplement, 1966-1980**. Metuchen, N.J.: Scarecrow, 1982. 466p. $45.00. ISBN 0-8108-1518-4. LC 81-23282.

Speech Index provides access to collections of published orations by author, subject, and type of speech. The main volume includes all material in three previous volumes (1935-1962), with added indexing for 1962-1965. Mitchell's update cumulates the 1966-1970 and 1971-1975 supplements to the 4th edition and adds indexing for speeches published in books during the 1975-1980 period. [R: ARBA 83]

1255 Vital Speeches of the Day. Mount Pleasant, S.C.: City News Publishing. semimonthly. $30.00/yr. (389 Highway 17 By-Pass, Mount Pleasant, SC 39465).

Each semimonthly issue contains the full text of some 12 to 15 addresses on public issues delivered by important figures. The editors attempt to select speeches pertaining to all sides of controversial issues. An annual index is published in November; the serial is also indexed in *Readers' Guide to Periodical Literature*. Recommended for high schools.

■ *We Shall Be Heard: An Index to Speeches by American Women, 1978 to 1985. See* entry 1131.

JOURNALISM

1256 Biographical Dictionary of American Journalism. Joseph McKerns, ed. Westport, Conn.: Greenwood Press, 1989. 820p. $95.00. ISBN 0-313-23818-9. LC 88-25098.

Using the format of *Dictionary of American Biography*, this source provides biographical essays, contributed by 133 subject specialists, on some 500 deceased or retired American journalists. Readable profiles give dates, a summary of achievements, a chronological narrative of the person's life, and a bibliography of works by and about the subject. Indexing includes names of publications or broadcast companies and other topics related to the biographees. The appendix lists the subjects by media, professional field, and Pulitzer prizes won. [R: ARBA 90; BL, 1 Sept 89; LJ, 15 June 89; WLB, Nov 89]

1257 Black, Jim N. **Managing the Student Yearbook: A Resource for Modern Yearbook Management and Design**. Dallas, Tex.: Taylor, 1983. 272p. $19.95. ISBN 0-87287-333-9. LC 83-3930.

Taylor, a large publisher of school annuals, provides this guide, which is composed of useful information on various aspects of planning and producing a school yearbook. Indexed. High schools and others publishing a yearbook will require this helpful resource. [R: SLJ, Jan 84]

1258 Editorials on File. New York: Facts on File. semimonthly. $345.00/yr. Available on microfiche.

This subscription service consists of editorials and editorial cartoons on various topics in the news. The editors attempt to balance liberal, conservative, and moderate positions drawn from 150 newspapers in all 50 states, the District of Columbia, and Canada. Each issue contains some 200 editorials plus cartoons on 10 to 12 important issues. Subjects are introduced by brief factual surveys. Indexed once each month and cumulated on a quarterly, six-month, nine-month, and annual basis. Subscription cost includes a binder.

Editorials on File Books offer compilations of editorial opinions on key issues. Recent compilations include *America's Children: New Generation, New Troubles* and *Poverty in America: The Forgotten Millions*.

1259 Gale Directory of Publications and Broadcast Media. Detroit: Gale. annual. $265.00/yr. ISSN 0892-1636. LC 1-31589.

Long known as *Ayer Directory of Publications* and later *ISM Directory of Publications*, this annual has had a variety of publishers. When Gale became its publisher, the name was changed to the current title and broadcast media were added. The aim is to supply directory information for magazines, newspapers, radio and television stations, and cable companies in Canada and the United States and its territories and possessions.

Entries, arranged by state and province and then city, begin with brief demographics. For periodicals, the listings give title, publisher, address, telephone and fax numbers, content, date established, frequency, contact persons, subscription price, advertising rates, circulation, and special notes. Broadcast media entries give complete contact information and other data useful to marketing and advertising professionals: station call letters and channel, Area of Dominant (AOD) influence, mailing address, telephone and fax numbers, network affiliation, top three local programs with air time, and more. A master alphabetical/keyword index provides access.

1260 Garst, Robert E., and Theodore M. Bernstein. **Headlines and Deadlines: A Manual for Copy Editors**. 4th ed. New York: Columbia University Press, 1981. 1v. $36.50. ISBN 0-231-04816-5.

Headlines and Deadlines treats the mechanics of copyediting, headlines, and other important topics confronting editors.

1261 Taft, William H. **Encyclopedia of Twentieth-Century Journalists**. Hamden, Conn.: Garland, 1986. 408p. (Garland Reference Library of the Humanities, v.493). $41.95. ISBN 0-8240-8961-8. LC 84-48011.

This lucid volume contains more than 750 profiles of the most famous journalists, publishers, columnists, cartoonists, radio/television broadcasters, and so forth. Those included are award winners past and present (e.g., Edward R. Murrow, Walter Cronkite, Barbara Walters, Gene Siskel, Katherine Graham). Entries range from a short paragraph to several pages. While many of those treated can be found elsewhere, this is an excellent compilation. [R: ARBA 87; LJ, 1 June 86; WLB, Sept 86]

PUBLISHING

See also **Publishers Directories** in **Media Sources**.

E +
1262 The Children's Writing and Publishing Center. Fremont, Calif.: Learning Company, 1989. System requirements: Apple II +, IIe, IIC, IIG; IBM-PC, Tandy 100, or compatible; minimum 128K RAM. $89.95 (Apple); $99.95 (IBM). lab packs $159.95 and $169.95 respectively; $699.00 site license. ICLAS/Novell network version. (6493 Kaiser Dr., Fremont, CA 94555).

This simple tool for teaching desktop publishing features a built-in word processor, 137 pictures, and 32 predesigned headings. The program is designed for ages 7 through 14. The school edition offers suggestions for classroom activities and story starters, and the documentation includes teaching ideas.

1263 Literary Market Place: The Directory of the American Book Publishing Industry. New Providence, N.J.: R. R. Bowker. annual. $124.95pa. ISSN 0075-9899. LC 41-51571.

The 1991 *LMP* lists over 13,000 publishing-related activities and some 30,000 personnel associated with United States and Canadian companies and services. Among the 18 areas included are major publishers and small presses, book clubs, associations, book trade events and conferences, literary awards and contests, services, suppliers, book review media, jobbers, export and import companies, and magazine and newspaper publishers. Complete directory information is provided for each listing. This annual is the best directory for the world of publishing. [R: ARBA 92]

RADIO

1264 Pitts, Michael R. **Radio Soundtracks: A Reference Guide**. 2d ed. Metuchen, N.J.: Scarecrow, 1986. 337p. $32.50. ISBN 0-8108-1875-2. LC 85-30409.

Radio Soundtracks identifies tape recordings and records of programs from the "golden age of radio," the late 1920s to the early 1960s. Part 1, the largest section, lists 1,040 tape recordings arranged by program, giving network, length, stars, and a sentence or more of commentary. Part 2 lists radio specials on tape, and parts 3 and 4 list records of radio programs and performer's radio appearances, giving the same information as the first section. Part 5, "Compilation Record Albums," consists of excerpted recordings. In all, 2,744 recordings are listed. The appendix cites companies that will supply the recordings. Indexed. [R: ARBA 87; BL, 1 Oct 86]

1265 **The Radio Amateur's Handbook**. 15th ed. Newington, Conn.: American Radio Relay League; distr., New York: Harper & Row, 1983. 416p. $23.95. ISBN 0-06-181366-4. LC 82-48666.

This comprehensive and authoritative handbook offers instructions and information needed to participate in ham-radio activities. Its contents cover fundamental principles, rules and regulations, and other technical data, as well as instructions for building receivers, transmitters, and other equipment. [R: BL, 1 Sept 84]

■ *World Communication and Transportation Data*. *See* entry 2180.

TELEVISION AND VIDEO

See **Film Study** for **Motion Pictures**.

■ *Blacks in American Film and Television*. *See* entry 1311.

1266 Brooks, Tim, and Earle Marsh. **The Complete Directory to Prime Time Network TV Shows, 1946-Present**. 4th ed. New York: Ballantine/Random House, 1988. 1063p. $16.95pa. ISBN 0-345-35610-1. LC 87-91863.

This volume provides a historical survey of network television, including technical changes and trends in programming, beginning with "Vaudeo" (1946-1957) to the "soaps" of the 1980s. The main body of the work lists all prime-time, regular and network series, and top syndicated programs aired primarily in the evenings.

Each entry includes dates for the first and last broadcasts; days, times, and networks; names of regular casts and guests; and a description of the series. The 4th edition covers hundreds of new programs on ABC, CBS, NBC, and Fox.

Appendixes provide prime-time network schedules for each season, 1946-1947 through 1987-1988; lists of Emmy Award winners; the top 100 series of all times; and hit theme songs from the series. Indexed by personalities and performances. This work and *Syndicated Television* offer a complete history of television programming. [R: ARBA 90]

1267 Castleman, Harry, and Walter J. Podrazik. **Harry and Wally's Favorite TV Shows**. New York: Prentice Hall Press, 1989. 628p. $14.95. ISBN 0-13-933250-2. LC 89-3953.

A fascinating guide to 4 decades of television, this work rates and describes over 2,100 television programs currently being aired, from 1950s reruns through the fall 1989 schedule. The work emphasizes prime-time comedy and drama, rates each show on a zero- to four-star scale, and indicates which are available on home-video tapes. Commentaries, ranging from a few lines to a full page, give the original telecast date, number of episodes, producer, and stars. [R: ARBA 91; BL, 1 Mar 90; WLB, Feb 90]

■ *Communicators*. *See* entry 337.

■ *Contemporary Theater, Film, and Television*. *See* entry 1791.

1268 Erickson, Hal. **Syndicated Television: The First Forty Years, 1947-1987**. Jefferson, N.C.: McFarland, 1989. 418p. $45.00. ISBN 0-89950-410-8. LC 89-42583.

Within each chronologically arranged decade, *Syndicated Television* is organized by genre from adventure/mystery to women's programs. Each entry is described in three lines to a page, written in an informal, readable style. A comprehensive index accesses the information by title, cast (including minor personalities), producers, writers, and other such factors. This work complements *The Complete Directory to Prime Time Network TV Shows*. [R: ARBA 90; BL, 15 Dec 89; LJ, Aug 89; WLB, Nov 89]

1269   Jones, Glenn. **Jones Dictionary of Cable Television Terminology**. 3d ed. Englewood, Colo.: Jones 21st Century, 1988. 108p. $14.95. ISBN 0-9453-7300-7. (9697 E. Mineral Ave., Englewood, CO 80112).

This dictionary focuses on cable television and related computer and satellite terms. Over 1,600 definitions, written in nontechnical language, are generously cross-referenced. Acronyms are connected to their full titles. Useful for students studying the media, physics, and computer technology. [R: ARBA 89; BR, Nov/Dec 88]

E+

1270   Langman, Larry, and Joseph A. Molinari. **The New Video Encyclopedia**. Hamden, Conn.: Garland, 1990. 312p. (Reference Library of the Humanities, v.1221). $49.95. ISBN 0-8240-8244-3. LC 90-3608.

A comprehensive work, this encyclopedia defines terms and jargon that cover a broad range of video equipment, emerging technologies, and products developed during the last few years. The arrangement is alphabetical with generous cross-references. This unique reference tool is useful for all levels. [R: ARBA 92; LJ, 1 Feb 91; RBB, 15 Feb 91]

1271   **Leonard Maltin's TV Movies and Video Guide**. Leonard Maltin, ed. New York: New American Library/Dutton. annual. $12.95; $5.95pa.

Each of 18,500 movies in this standard source has basic information (e.g., director, stars, release date, running time), a short synopsis, a critical evaluation, and a rating. The entries are lively and fun to read. The paperback edition is published by Signet. [R: Kliatt, Nov 89]

1272   Shapiro, Mitchell. **Television Network Prime-Time Programming, 1948-1988**. Jefferson, N.C.: McFarland, 1989. 743p. $45.00. ISBN 0-89950-412-4. LC 89-45006.

Tables and timelines cover prime-time programming (7 p.m. to 11 p.m., Eastern Standard Time) of commercial networks, 1948 to 1988. The work is divided into seven chapters, one for each day of the week, that provide the program's name and type, episode running time, and previous/new times for every month of the 40-year span. This work complements *The Complete Directory to Prime Time Network TV Shows*. [R: ARBA 90; WLB, Nov 89]

■ *World Communications and Transportation Data*. *See* entry 2180.

WRITING AND REPORTS

See also **Media Skills** in **Library Science**.
See **Usage and Grammar** in **Language** for usage.

1273   **Bud's Easy Term Paper Kit**. 8th ed. Lawrence, N.Y.: Lawrence House, 1988. 24p. $4.50pa. ISBN 0-9609436-4-1. (P.O. Box 329, Lawrence, NY 11559).

Subtitled "Everything You Need to Write, Type or Word Process an A+ Paper," this pamphlet is not a reference book in the true sense of the term. It provides excellent step-by-step instructions on writing term papers: preparing footnotes, endnotes, author-page citations, author-date citations, bibliographies, and tables using MacWrite, Word Perfect, AppleWorks, PFS Write, and Microsoft Word software. Formats conform to the *MLA Handbook*, the *Publication Manual of the American Psychological Association*, and *The Chicago Manual of Style*. Instructions include samples of citation styles. [R: BL, 1 Apr 91]

■ *Communicators*. *See* entry 337.

1274   Campbell, William Giles. **Form and Style: Theses, Reports, Term Papers**. 8th ed. Boston: Houghton Mifflin, 1990. 279p. $19.16pa. ISBN 0-395-43204-9.

A standard college guide, this handbook incorporates the bibliographic style of the *MLA Handbook* and *The Chicago Manual of Style*. It also surveys the *Publication Manual of the American*

Psychological Association. Campbell contains eight sections that address computer software, CD-ROM and online databases, and the use of computers in paper preparation. A glossary of terms, a list of abbreviations, and an index conclude the volume. [R: BL, 1 Apr 91]

1275 **The Chicago Manual of Style**. 13th ed. Chicago: University of Chicago Press, 1982. 737p. $37.50. ISBN 0-226-10390-0. LC 82-2832.
The 13th edition of this style manual, widely accepted by publishers, writers, colleges, and universities, is a required holding for most high school libraries. The book provides extensive coverage of footnote/bibliographic form, organization, and manuscript preparation. It recommends the author-date method of documentation as the most practical, with endnotes as the preferred form. *A Manual for Writers of Term Papers, Theses and Dissertations* abridges this work. [R: ARBA 83; BL, 15 Dec 82; LJ, 1 Nov 82; WLB, Nov 82]

1276 **Harbrace College Handbook**. 11th ed. By John C. Hodges and others. San Diego, Calif.: Harcourt Brace Jovanovich, 1990. 576p. $19.75. ISBN 0-15-531862-4.

1277 **Prentice-Hall Handbook for Writers**. By Glenn H. Legget and others. Englewood Cliffs, N.J.: Prentice-Hall, 1988. 608p. $18.67. ISBN 0-13-695271-2.
Intended for high school and college students, each of these guides to English usage contains substantial sections on writing research papers. *Harbrace* and *Prentice-Hall* cover the Modern Language Association and American Psychological Association documentation styles and provide excellent examples. Recommended for high schools. [R: BL, 1 Apr 91]

E +
1278 James, Elizabeth, and Carol Barkin. **How to Write a Great School Report**. New York: Lothrop, 1983. 167p. $16.95pa. ISBN 0-688-02278-2. LC 83-764.

E +
1279 James, Elizabeth, and Carol Barkin. **How to Write a Good Term Paper**. New York: Lothrop, 1980. 94p. $10.88. ISBN 0-688-02283-9.
This work on school reports, recommended for grades 5 and up, provides clear directions on all stages of the assignment. The section on reference books, however, is too advanced for children at the lower grade level.
The manual on writing term papers begins with choosing a topic and continues through setting a schedule, doing research, taking notes, organizing materials, making an outline, and writing the paper. Like the other, it gives clear and succinct directions for students from grade 5 through middle school. [R: BL, 15 Jan 84; SLJ, Feb 84]

1280 Markham, Roberta H., and Marie T. Waddell. **10 Steps in Writing the Research Paper**. 4th ed. Hauppauge, N.Y.: Barron's Educational Series, 1989. 140p. $7.95pa. ISBN 0-8120-4151-8. LC 88-7408.
This detailed guide may overwhelm some students; nonetheless, it is a cogent work, covering the research paper in depth. Since this manual appeared in 1965, it has been considered a standard of its genre. New information in this edition includes the use of online computer searching; the citation of material from software, videotape, television, and radio; and documentation through parenthetical referencing. One perceptive chapter addresses plagiarism. Sample papers demonstrate two popular styles of documentation, one using traditional footnotes, and the other using parenthetical referencing. Recommended for high schools. [R: BR, Sept/Oct 89]

E +
1281 McInerney, Claire. **Tracking the Fact: How to Develop Research Skills**. Minneapolis, Minn.: Lerner, 1990. 64p. $9.95. ISBN 0-8225-2426-0. LC 90-5454.
Designed for students in grades 4 through 7, this small volume covers the major steps in researching and writing papers and executing research projects. With emphasis on the importance of planning and preliminary research, the book treats primary sources, interviews, and secondary accounts. It also covers basic library skills, traditional works such as *Readers' Guide*, and the new technologies. The manual has sections on note cards, preparing the final draft, and making bibliographies. Excellent examples, numerous charts, and outlines are provided. A bibliography and index complete the guide. Recommended for elementary and middle school levels. [R: BR, Mar/Apr 91; SLJ, Jan 91]

1282 Miller, Joan I., and Bruce Taylor. **The Punctuation Handbook**. West Linn, Oreg.: Alcove Publishing, 1989. 89p. $4.95pa. ISBN 0-937473-14-6. LC 88-35148.

This small volume explains the rules of punctuation in lucid language, illustrated with simple examples. Guidelines for using the "17 marks" (apostrophe through vigule) are followed by a section on capitalization, examples of proofreaders' marks, and a glossary of terms used in the text. Recommended for secondary schools. [R: ARBA 90]

1283 **MLA Handbook for Writers of Research Papers**. By Joseph Gibaldi and Walter S. Achtert. New York: Modern Language Association of America, 1988. 248p. $9.95pa. ISBN 0-87352-379-2. LC 88-5195.

This update of a standard work, first published in 1977, has high school and college students as its primary audience. The manual is divided into six chapters: research and writing, the mechanics of writing, the format of the research paper, preparing the list of works cited, documenting sources, and abbreviations and reference works. It gives rules on abbreviations, footnotes, bibliographies, and other matters of style, and it recommends parenthetical documentation and the use of a works-cited page rather than a bibliography. Also provided are examples that illustrate rules, sample pages, and an index. [R: ARBA 89; BL, 1 Apr 91]

1284 **Publication Manual of the American Psychological Association**. 3d ed. Washington, D.C.: American Psychological Association, 1983. 208p. $16.50pa. ISBN 0-912704-57-8. LC 83-2521.

Widely used by students in disciplines other than psychology, this style manual, which dates from 1952, is divided into five chapters that cover the content and organization of a manuscript, the expression of ideas, APA editorial style, typing instructions and sample papers, and submitting the manuscript and proofreading. The appendix contains suggestions for writing papers, theses, and dissertations. The work is indexed and well illustrated with sample pages. This style manual is not generally used in high schools, but students going to college should know about it. [R: BL, 1 Apr 91]

1285 Strunk, William, Jr., with E. B. White. **The Elements of Style**. 3d ed. New York: Macmillan, 1979. 92p. $9.75. ISBN 0-02-418190-0. LC 78-18444.

"Will Strunk loved the clear, the brief, the bold, and his book is clear, brief, and bold." This small volume, revised by award-winning children's writer and essayist White, is a valuable addition to any library. It is prescriptive, conservative, and humorous; in sum, it is the best book available on how to write English prose. Rules of good usage are stated, followed by incorrect and correct examples. [R: ARBA 80; LJ, 15 May 79]

1286 Turabian, Kate L. **A Manual for Writers of Term Papers, Theses and Dissertations**. 5th ed. Revised by Bonnie B. Honigsblum. Chicago: University of Chicago Press, 1987. 300p. $22.00; $8.95pa. ISBN 0-226-81624-9; 0-226-81625-7pa. LC 86-19128.

This well-known and widely used handbook abridges *The Chicago Manual of Style*. The 13 chapters treat such topics as parts of the paper; abbreviations and numbers; spelling and punctuation; capitalization, quotations, and underlining; illustrations; and footnotes and bibliographies.

This edition includes a new chapter entitled "Parenthetical References and Reference Lists." The chapter on preparing the paper incorporates new information on word processing. Sample pages serve as models for the title page, table of contents, and other sections of the paper. This volume continues to be a standard guide for writing term papers. Recommended for high schools. [R: ARBA 88; BL, 1 Oct 87, 1 Apr 91; Kliatt, Sept 87; WLB, Sept 87]

1287 **The Writer's Handbook**. Boston: The Writer. annual. $27.95. LC 36-28596.

Those seeking suggestions on how to write fiction and nonfiction in various formats and how to market the finished product will welcome this standard handbook. Articles on writing and manuscript preparation make up much of each annual. The main part of the book is a market guide, mainly to the periodical field but including radio, television, and book publishing as well. For each publisher the entry provides name, address, editor, editorial requirements, type of material sought, payment rate, and other useful information. A list of literary agents and organizations for writers is also included. This work is far more than a directory of publishers. Its articles on how to write for specific markets make it a first choice of publications of its kind. [R: ARBA 91]

1288 **The Writer's Market: Where and How to Sell What You Write**. Cincinnati, Ohio: Writer's Digest Books. annual. $24.95. ISSN 0084-2729. LC 31-20772.

Published annually since 1926, this guide to markets for prospective writers covers over 4,000 outlets from book and magazine publishers to script producers and greeting card companies. Each entry offers name and address, type of material sought, editorial needs, submission requirements, payment rates, and other useful data. Essays in the 1991 edition offer advice on pricing, researching the market, establishing copyright, and self-promotion. [R: ARBA 91]

Decorative Arts

ARTS AND CRAFTS

1289 The Facts on File Dictionary of Design and Designers. By Simon Jervis. New York: Facts on File, 1984. 544p. $35.00. ISBN 0-87196-891-6.

Biographical and topical entries comprise this volume. Entries on European and North American designers from the fifteenth century to the present focus on major contributions but also provide dates and background information. Other entries cover design schools, movements, periodicals, and specific items (e.g., textiles, glass, ceramics, furniture). The alphabetically arranged dictionary is generously cross-referenced. [R: ARBA 85; LJ, Aug 84]

E +
1290 Heim, Mary Ellen. Make It II: An Index to Projects and Materials, 1974-1987. Metuchen, N.J.: Scarecrow, 1989. 552p. $42.50. ISBN 0-8108-2125-7. LC 88-11503.

This index, a supplement to *Make It: An Index to Projects and Materials* by Joyce Shields (Scarecrow, 1974), is a guide to almost 20 years of projects published in books from 1974 to 1987. It indexes over 35,000 projects for children, adults, or adults working with children. Indexed. Useful for school libraries at all levels. [R: ARBA 90]

1291 The Oxford Companion to the Decorative Arts. Harold Osborne, ed. New York: Oxford University Press, c1975, 1985. 865p. $19.95pa. ISBN 0-19-281863-5. LC 84-19072.

Another in the Oxford Companion series, this reprint of a 1975 work concerns items that are intended to be functional but are "prized for quality of their workmanship and the beauty of their appearance." Unsigned entries cover ceramics, textiles, wood and metal work, glass, clocks, leather, enamels, lacquer, toys, lace, embroidery, and other materials and objects. Coverage is worldwide, with emphasis on the Western world. The authoritative articles, some lengthy, end with numbers that refer to items in an extensive bibliography. The work should be used in conjunction with *Oxford Companion to Art* and *Oxford Companion to Twentieth-Century Art*.

1292 The Penguin Dictionary of Decorative Arts. rev. ed. By John Fleming and Hugh Honour. New York: Viking Penguin, 1990. 935p. $40.00. ISBN 0-670-82047-4.

A revision of the 1974 work, this dictionary emphasizes the decorative arts of Europe and North America since the Middle Ages, discussing all styles and the artists who created them. Some 5,000 entries, 600 new to this edition, are illustrated with over 1,000 black-and-white photographs and 67 color plates. Styles, techniques, and individual pieces (e.g., furniture, costume, china, glass) are well covered.

Its competitor, *The Oxford Companion to the Decorative Arts*, has more entries, but they are shorter, with fewer illustrations. The volumes complement each other. [R: BL, Aug 90; LJ, 1 June 90]

FASHION AND COSTUME

1293 Fairchild's Dictionary of Fashion. 2d ed. By Charlotte Mankey Calasibetta. New York: Fairchild Books, 1988. 749p. $50.00. ISBN 0-87005-635-2.

An update of a 1982 dictionary, this work defines over 15,000 cultural and artistic terms related to fashion from classical to modern times. Over 500 black-and-white drawings, 16 pages of full-color illustrations, and a biographical index of designers support the concise definitions. Recommended for high school libraries requiring a reference tool on fashion. [R: ARBA 89; BL, 15 Dec 88]

1294 Racinet, Albert. **The Historical Encyclopedia of Costumes**. New York: Facts on File, 1988. 320p. $40.00. ISBN 0-8160-1976-2.

This work condenses Racinet's classic six-volume set, *History of World Costume* (1876-1888), and translates it into English for the first time. Its text and 2,000 illustrations, most in full color, cover worldwide costumes from ancient Egypt to nineteenth-century Europe—royalty, the working class, soldiers, and the poor. High school libraries should consider acquiring this volume. [R: ARBA 89; BL, 15 Feb 89; LJ, Dec 88]

1295 Stegemeyer, Anne. **Who's Who in Fashion**. 2d ed. New York: Fairchild Books, 1988. 243p. $25.00. ISBN 0-87005-574-7. *Supplement*. 1991. 72p. $15.00pa. ISBN 0-87005-746-4. LC 87-82511.

Some 200 established international fashion designers, promising newcomers, and influential persons in related fields are the focus of this work. The supplement includes some 50 additional newcomers. Most entries are short; only the famous receive a page or more of space and several illustrations. All articles conclude with a bibliography of works suggested for further reading. Black-and-white photographs and 16 pages of full-color plates illustrate the volume, which is appropriate for high school libraries. [R: ARBA 90]

1296 Wilcox, Ruth Turner. **The Dictionary of Costume**. New York: Macmillan, c1963, 1977. 406p. $50.00. ISBN 0-684-15150-2. LC 68-12503.

E+
1297 Wilcox, Ruth Turner. **Five Centuries of American Costume**. New York: Macmillan, c1963, 1977. 207p. $17.50. ISBN 0-684-15161-8. LC 63-9768.

E+
1298 Wilcox, Ruth Turner. **Folk and Festival Costumes of the World**. New York: Macmillan, c1965, 1977. 1v. $45.00. ISBN 0-684-15379-3. LC 65-23986.

1299 Wilcox, Ruth Turner. **The Mode of Costume**. New York: Macmillan, c1958, 1974. 1v. $32.00. ISBN 0-684-13913-8.

Wilcox, an authority on costume, has written several standard works on the subject. *The Dictionary of Costume* contains 3,200 entries on articles of clothing worldwide and from all periods—jewelry, underclothing, fabrics, lace, folk costume, high fashion, academic and military dress, tailoring, and dressmaking tools and terms. There are also 60 brief biographies of notables.

Five Centuries of American Costume, which focuses on the people of North and South America, presents costumes from the sixteenth to the twentieth century and includes clothing of Native Americans, the military, and children.

Folk and Festival Costumes of the World describes and illustrates traditional costumes from 150 countries. The arrangement is alphabetical by country, with one page of text accompanying a facing plate of six or more black-and-white drawings. *The Mode of Costume* surveys the history of fashion from 3000 B.C. (ancient Egypt) to 1958. Drawings illustrate the text.

1300 Yarwood, Doreen. **Costume of the Western World: Pictorial Guide and Glossary**. New York: St. Martin's Press, 1980. 192p. price not reported. ISBN 0-312-17013-0.

The first part consists of 10 chapters that briefly trace the development of costume in England, western Europe, and North America from the middle ages to contemporary times. The second and main portion is a glossary of 600 terms covering apparel, fabric, accessories, and other aspects of costume. Definitions are supported by monochrome illustrations. [R: ARBA 82]

FURNITURE AND INTERIOR DESIGN

1301 Boyce, Charles. **Dictionary of Furniture**. New York: Facts on File, 1985. 331p. $35.00. ISBN 0-8160-1042-0. LC 83-20753.

More than 2,000 entries cover furniture styles, movements, periods, and cabinetmakers, from ancient times through the postmodern era and from all regions of the world. The alphabetically arranged entries are illustrated by over 400 line drawings showing furniture design and decorative detail. [R: ARBA 86; LJ, 1 Mar 86]

1302 Dizik, A. Allen. **Concise Encyclopedia of Interior Design**. 2d ed. New York: Van Nostrand Reinhold, 1988. 220p. $39.95. ISBN 0-442-22109-6. LC 88-5560.

Intended for students and others interested in interior design, this work contains brief entries on such topics as furniture periods, room arrangement, fabrics, wall and floor coverings, lighting, architecture, antiques, and construction. Many items are covered by a one-sentence definition, but others receive two to four pages. Special features include generous cross-references, charts and tables (e.g., types of carpet fibers, calculating wallpaper measurements, periods and styles of furniture), and four pages of line drawings. This work is recommended for high schools requiring a reference tool on the subject. [R: ARBA 89; BL, 15 Dec 88]

1303 Gloag, John. **A Complete Dictionary of Furniture**. Revised by Clive Edwards. Woodstock, N.Y.: Overlook Press; distr., New York: Viking Penguin, 1991. 828p. $35.00. ISBN 0-87951-414-0. LC 90-43790.

This revised and expanded edition of Gloag's classic work, first published in 1952, contains some 3,000 entries about furniture made in England since 1100 and in North America since 1650. Entries, ranging from a sentence to two or more pages in length, cover styles, woods, fabrics, locks and other hardware, furniture makers, and furniture parts. Other features include a list of furniture makers in Great Britain and America; a bibliography; and tables that outline types of furniture, materials and craftsmen employed, and influences that affected design over eight and a half centuries. [R: ARBA 92; RBB, 15 Mar 91]

SEWING AND NEEDLEWORK

1304 **The Complete Book of Needlecrafts**. Radnor, Pa.: Chilton Book, 1990. 240p. $24.95. ISBN 0-8019-8081-X.

This beautifully produced work focuses on a variety of projects, from belts to wall hangings, that involve the use of applique, embroidery, needlepoint, patchwork, and quilting. Most projects are designed for hand work rather than the sewing machine. Techniques are discussed briefly, and projects are attractively illustrated with color photographs. Useful for both the beginner and the more advanced individual. [R: BR, 1 June 90; Kliatt, June 90; LJ, 1 June 90]

1305 **The Complete Step-by-Step Guide to Home Sewing**. Jeanne Argent, ed. Radnor, Pa.: Chilton Book, 1990. $26.95pa. ISBN 0-8019-8080-1. LC 89-27169.

An excellent guide to home sewing projects, this volume offers step-by-step instructions and time-saving tips for giving professional-looking finishes to curtains, cushions, bed linens, lampshades, upholstery, and other household items. Some projects are for beginners, but many are designed for those who are experienced. Attractive color illustrations enhance the book's value. Recommended for high schools with a need for instructions on home furnishings. [R: BR, Sept/Oct 90; LJ, 15 June 90]

1306 Compton, Rae. **The Illustrated Dictionary of Knitting**. Loveland, Colo.: Interweave Press, 1988. 272p. $18.95pa. ISBN 0-934026-41-6.

This work provides extensive coverage of terms, styles, patterns, stitches, yarn features, conversion charts, and equipment. The 700 alphabetically arranged entries include diagrams, easy-to-follow instructions, and black-and-white and color photographs. [R: ARBA 90]

1307 Meyers, Belle. **Knitting Know-How: An Illustrated Encyclopedia**. New York: HarperCollins, c1979, 1982. $10.95pa. ISBN 0-06-463564-3. LC 80-7857.

Knitting fundamentals and stitches are covered in alphabetically arranged entries. Other features include charts for needle sizes and metric conversion; instructions in planning and executing original designs; and clear, well-placed, black-and-white illustrations. [R: ARBA 82; LJ, 1 Sept 81]

1308 **The Vogue/Butterick Step-by-Step Guide to Sewing Techniques**. Englewood Cliffs, N.J.: Prentice-Hall, 1989. 415p. $24.95. ISBN 0-13-944125-5.

This sewing guide provides step-by-step instructions for over 500 dressmaking procedures used in the patterns produced by Butterick and Vogue. Arrangement is by 47 broad sewing areas (e.g., linings, pleats, facings, collars, zippers, buttonholes). This visual encyclopedia is recommended for high schools. [R: BL, 1 Nov 89; LJ, July 89]

TEXTILES

1309 **Encyclopedia of Textiles**. 3d ed. By the editors of *American Fabrics and Fashions Magazine*. New York: French & European Publications, 1980. 656p. $39.95. ISBN 0-8288-2376-6. LC 79-26497.

Well-illustrated entries define terms and cover topics concerning design, fabrics, and production techniques. *Fairchild's Dictionary of Textiles*, edited by Isabel B. Wingate (6th ed. Fairchild Books, 1979), is another authoritative and comprehensive dictionary for the textile industry. Both works are recommended for high schools requiring information on the topic.

☐ —————————————— **Film Study** —————————————— ☐

DICTIONARIES AND ENCYCLOPEDIAS

■ *Authors & Artists for Young Adults*. See entry 1173.

1310 **The BFI Companion to the Western**. Edward Buscombe, ed. New York: Atheneum, 1988. 432p. $50.00. ISBN 0-689-11962-3.

This encyclopedia compares the western movie to the real West. A lengthy historical essay traces the development of the genre from silent films through the 1980s, followed by some 800 entries that cover themes, characters, weapons, actors, geography, and many other topics. For such entries as the Dalton Gang, Bat Masterson, prostitution, and the Springfield rifle, the text gives historical/biographical information and names of films in which the topic or person played a role.

Brief biographical data is provided for more than 400 actors, scriptwriters, directors, and others connected with westerns. A separate entry deals with each film considered to be a classic. This cultural/historical dictionary is highly recommended for secondary schools. [R: ARBA 89; LJ, 1 Apr 89; WLB, Mar 89]

1311 Bogle, Donald. **Blacks in American Film and Television: An Encyclopedia**. Hamden, Conn.: Garland, 1988. 510p. (Garland Reference Library of the Humanities, v.604). $65.00. ISBN 0-8240-8715-1. LC 87-29241.

This reference work, filled with facts and strong opinions, provides highly critical evaluations of over 260 films (Hollywood and independent) and over 100 television series, specials, and programs featuring Black performers. A profile section traces the careers of some 100 Black actors and a few directors. Excellent illustrations, a bibliography, and a substantial index support the text. Recommended for high schools. [R: ARBA 89; BL, 1 Oct 88; LJ, 1 Sept 88]

■ *Contemporary Theater, Film, and Television*. See entry 1791.

1312 Ellrod, J. G. **Hollywood Greats of the Golden Years: The Late 1920s through the 1950s**. Jefferson, N.C.: McFarland, 1989. 222p. $27.50. ISBN 0-89950-371-3. LC 89-42713.

This work has biographies of 81 men and women who "personified the Golden Age of Hollywood"—the late 1920s to the mid-1950s. All were deceased by 1989. The 81 alphabetically arranged entries for such stars as Fred Astaire, Joan Crawford, Spencer Tracy, Marilyn Monroe, and Mae West are 2 to 4 pages in length and include career milestones, a chronologically arranged list of film credits, and 2 or more movie stills. Indexed. The work provides a concise survey of three decades of American motion picture entertainment. [R: ARBA 90]

1313 Halliwell, Leslie. **Halliwell's Film Guide**. New York: HarperCollins. annual. $19.95pa. LC 89-54159.

1314 Halliwell, Leslie. **Halliwell's Filmgoer's and Video Viewer's Companion**. 9th ed. New York: HarperCollins, 1990. 786p. $19.95pa. ISBN 0-06-096392-1. LC 89-45916.

Both titles are standard reference works. The *Film Guide* covers 16,000 films and television movies produced in the United States and the United Kingdom. For each it lists writers, producers, directors, and principal characters; Academy Award nominations; and awards. The entries provide a plot synopsis, critical evaluation and quotations from contemporary reviews, a 0- to 4-star rating system, running time, and availability on videotape.

The primary purpose of the *Companion* is to give brief biographical entries for actors, directors, writers, bit players, silent stars, cinematographers, and others involved in the history of film and video. Entries for general topics, such as definitions of terms, themes and subjects, historical figures frequently depicted in film, and important films are also included. Both volumes are profusely illustrated with movie stills. [R: ARBA 90]

1315 International Dictionary of Films and Filmmakers. [Volume] 1: Films. 2d ed. Nicholas Thomas, ed. Chicago: St. James Press, 1990. 1105p. $105.00. ISBN 1-55862-037-0.

1316 International Dictionary of Films and Filmmakers. Volume 2: Directors. 2d ed. Nicholas Thomas, ed. Chicago: St. James Press, 1991. 958p. $115.00. ISBN 1-55862-038-9. LC 90-64265.

These are the first two volumes in a projected five-volume set; the remaining books will include actors and actresses, writers and production artists, and a title index; they are scheduled for publication at six-month intervals in 1992 and beyond.

Films contains entries for some 650 films (150 new to this edition), giving comprehensive credits; cast lists with roles played; major awards; an extensive bibliography of books, articles, and contemporary reviews; and a review by a recognized film critic.

Directors discusses 480 international directors. Each entry has a brief biography; a complete filmography; a selected bibliography; and a signed essay that covers such topics as the major themes in the director's work. Eighty entries are new; sixty have been dropped or (in the case of animators) moved to the volume on writers and production artists. Recommended for high schools that offer film studies courses. [R: ARBA 91; ARBA 92; LJ, 1 Sept 90; RBB, 15 Oct 90; SLJ, May 91; WLB, Oct 90]

1317 Konigsberg, Ira. The Complete Film Dictionary. New York: New American Library, 1987. 420p. $24.95; $12.95pa. ISBN 0-453-00564-0; 0-452-00980-4pa. LC 87-5747.

An excellent source for high schools, this dictionary covers all aspects of the film industry—technology, production, distribution, economics, history, and criticism. Over 3,500 clear, easy-to-understand entries also address the artistic approach to film making by genre: fictional, documentary, and experimental. Line drawings and motion-picture stills complement the text.

Filmmaker's Dictionary by Ralph S. Singleton (Lone Eagle, 1990) is a more recent work, containing 1,500 terms, but Konigsberg is a better choice. [R: ARBA 89; BL, 15 Jan 88; LJ, Dec 87; SLJ, Sept 88; SLJ, May 88]

1318 Langman, Larry, and Edward Borg. Encyclopedia of American War Films. Hamden, Conn.: Garland, 1989. 696p. (Garland Reference Library of the Humanities, v.873). $95.00. ISBN 0-8240-7540-4. LC 89-1491.

This work covers some 3,000 films—features, documentaries, short subjects, serials, and cartoons—pertaining to war, which is broadly defined to include spies, refugees, and the homefront. For each film, information includes studio, release date, director, screenwriter, selective credits, an annotation, and an analysis that addresses its technical strengths, weaknesses, and overall importance to film history.

Appendixes contain a selective list of film biographies, a list of war movies that have received Academy Awards, and a list of wars depicted on film. There is no index. High schools with courses in film history or popular culture should consider this work. [R: ARBA 90; BL, 1 Mar 90; LJ, Dec 89; WLB, Dec 89]

1319 McCarty, John. The Modern Horror Film: 50 Contemporary Classics. New York: Carol Publishing Group, 1990. 256p. $15.95. ISBN 0-8065-1164-8.

Fifty classic horror films produced during the past thirty years are listed in this excellent volume. For each, McCarty discusses its importance, background, actors, producers, directors, writers, and composers. He also appraises the film's strengths, weaknesses, and impact on later movies. Among those addressed are *Jaws*, *The Shining*, *The Exorcist*, *Psycho*, and *The Curse of Frankenstein*. Photographs are scattered throughout the volume. There is no index. [R: SLJ, Nov 90]

1320 Nowlan, Robert A., and Gwendolyn Wright Nowlan. Movie Characters of Leading Performers of the Sound Era. Chicago: American Library Association, 1990. 396p. $47.50pa. ISBN 0-8389-0480-7. LC 88-37686.

This work addresses the major movie roles played by some 400 actors and actresses. Arranged alphabetically by performer, entries provide a brief portrait; key roles played with character name and description, movie title, date, studio, and directors; and character names, movie titles, and dates for other roles played. Information is accurate and useful, but the lack of an index hampers the volume's use as a quick-reference tool. [R: ARBA 91; LJ, 1 June 90; RBB, 15 June 90]

1321 Segrave, Kerry, and Linda Martin. **The Post-Feminist Hollywood Actress: Biographies and Filmographies of Stars Born after 1939**. Jefferson, N.C.: McFarland, 1990. 313p. $39.95. ISBN 0-89950-387-X. LC 90-42755.

This volume focuses on women of the film industry who were in their twenties at the advent of the women's liberation movement. It provides brief biographies, their sources, and complete filmographies of 50 actresses. The information includes milestones in their private lives (e.g., income, marriages, divorces, children) and quotations that relate to the feminist movement.

The chronologically arranged filmographies include the name of each character played and the billing order of the stars. The appendixes present gender-related statistics (e.g., first five billed characters, percentage of films with one gender in a major role). Indexed by stars, film, and topics (e.g., assertiveness, feminism, nudity, rape, sexuality, prostitution). [R: ARBA 91; BL, 1 May 90; LJ, Jan 90]

1322 Siegel, Scott, and Barbara Siegel. **The Encyclopedia of Hollywood**. New York: Facts on File, 1990. 499p. $40.00; $16.95pa. ISBN 0-8160-1792-1; 0-380-71202-4pa. LC 89-11799.

This who's who of past and present stars, producers, directors, cinematographers, and other film-makers offers a survey of the American industry in some 700 brief entries, many with black-and-white photographs. The work also offers succinct summaries of famous movies and discusses the various film genres, technical advances, and behind-the-scenes activities involved in producing movies. The paper-back edition is available from Avon Books. *Halliwell's Filmgoer's and Video Viewer's Companion* is more comprehensive in its coverage of actors, but its articles are shorter than those contained in the encyclopedia. [R: ARBA 91; BL, 1 May 90; BR, Sept/Oct 90]

1323 Stanley, John. **Revenge of the Creature Features Movie Guide: An A to Z Encyclopedia to the Cinema of the Fantastic....** 3d ed. Pacifica, Calif.: Creatures at Large Press, 1988. 420p. $40.00; $11.95pa. ISBN 0-940064-05-7; 0-940064-04-9pa. LC 87-91426.

This guide covers 4,000 motion pictures and made-for-television films in which extrahuman forces play a major role—monsters, psychological terror, psychic phenomena, supernatural forces, mytho-logical creatures, and fantasies. There are interpretations of Frankenstein and Dracula as well as science fiction characters, mutant insects, supervillians, and superheroes. Each entry includes major cast credits, director, and a synopsis supported by movie stills and photographs. Standard guides such as *Halliwell's Film Guide* do not include many of the lesser-known, unusual movies found here. [R: ARBA 90; BL, 1 Jan 89]

FILMOGRAPHIES

1324 Drew, Bernard A. **Motion Picture Series and Sequels: A Reference Guide**. Hamden, Conn.: Garland, 1990. 412p. (Garland Reference Library of the Humanities, v.1186). $50.00. ISBN 0-8240-4248-4. LC 90-3321.

The practice of continuing a successful format is as old as movie making. This volume focuses on over 900 series and sequels, silent and sound, filmed since 1899. Entries contain a brief plot summary, studio, year, director, major performers, and (when appropriate) alternate titles and citations to literary and other sources. A bibliography of film history and an individual title index complete the volume. [R: ARBA 91; WLB, Nov 90]

1325 Dye, David. **Child and Youth Actors: Filmographies of Their Entire Careers, 1914-1985**. Jefferson, N.C.: McFarland, 1988. 310p. $24.95. ISBN 0-89950-247-4. LC 87-46441.

This work covers 550 major and minor child/teenage actors who performed in at least two films, television movies or series, or stage productions, 1914 to 1985. Most are from the United States. Alphabetically arranged entries give place and date of birth; a chronological list of media performances; studio name, name of characters played, and other information about the film, television, or stage performance; and, when appropriate, the adult career. Cross-references direct the reader from the real name to the professional one. Lists of all actors in Our Gang/Little Rascals and the Mickey Mouse Club are provided. Small black-and-white photographs appear throughout the book. Indexed by title. This unique source contains information not found elsewhere. [R: ARBA 89; RBB, 1 Jan 89; VOYA, Dec 88]

1326   Enser, A. G. S. **Filmed Books and Plays: A List of Books and Plays from Which Films Have Been Made, 1928-86.** rev. ed. Brockfield, Vt.: Gower Publishing, 1987. 770p. $59.95. ISBN 0-566-03564-2. LC 87-157.
   The latest edition of this work updates and adds to previous editions covering 1928-1974 and 1975-1983. The title index, arranged alphabetically, includes the film's producer/distributor and the date, author, title, and publisher of the book on which the film is based. Film titles that differ from book titles are italicized. An author index lists, for each writer, the works that have been filmed, with a reference to the movie title if it is different. A change of original title index also supports the title section.
   A related work, *Short Stories on Film and Video*, by Carol A. Emmens (2d ed. Libraries Unlimited, 1985) names some 1,400 films (1920-1984) that were based on short stories. [R: ARBA 88]

1327   Parish, James R., and Michael R. Pitts. **The Great Detective Pictures.** Metuchen, N.J.: Scarecrow, 1990. 616p. $59.95. ISBN 0-8108-2286-5. LC 90-8551.

1328   Parish, James R., and Michael R. Pitts. **The Great Science Fiction Pictures.** Metuchen, N.J.: Scarecrow, 1977. 390p. $32.50. ISBN 0-8108-1029-8.

1329   Parish, James R., and Michael R. Pitts. **The Great Science Fiction Pictures II.** Metuchen, N.J.: Scarecrow, 1990. 489p. $49.50. ISBN 0-8108-2247-4. LC 89-24058.
   These volumes in the authors' Great Pictures series are similar in format. *Great Detective Pictures* includes some 350 feature-length films, serials, and made-for-television movies, which range from the best to the worse. Arranged alphabetically by title, each entry gives name of production company, year released, running time, production credits, cast credits with character names, a synopsis, and critical commentary.
   The Great Science Fiction Pictures and its sequel cover some 800 films and radio and television shows, with the same types of information for each. All volumes are illustrated with black-and-white movie stills, chronological lists of films covered, and brief bibliographies. [R: ARBA 91; LJ, 15 Mar 90]

1330   Rothwell, Kenneth S., and Annabelle Henkin Melzer. **Shakespeare on Screen: An International Filmography and Videography.** New York: Neal-Schuman, 1990. 404p. $59.95. ISBN 1-55570-049-7. LC 90-31509.
   This handbook describes 750 films and videos produced since 1899. Entries, arranged alphabetically by play and then by date of production, give country and year of release; information about color, length, type of film, and language; credits; distribution and availability (with price); and citations to reviews.
   Additional material includes a list of documentaries about Shakespeare; an extensive annotated bibliography; and indexing by play, series and genre, year of production or release, and names (actors, production staff, authors, critics, and editors). [R: ARBA 92; BL, 15 Mar 91]

HANDBOOKS

E +
1331   Andersen, Yvonne. **Make Your Own Animated Movies and Videotapes.** rev. ed. Boston: Little, Brown, 1991. 176p. $19.95. ISBN 0-316-03941-1. LC 90-33756.
   This updated version of Andersen's 1970 work bears little resemblance to the original volume. The advances of the last two decades are reflected in the instructions for movie, videotape, and computer animation. Areas include flip books, cutouts, clay animation, puppetry, and soundtracks. This basic information is useful for grades 5 through 12. [R: SLJ, May 91]

1332   Andrew, Geoff. **The Film Handbook.** Boston: G. K. Hall, c1989, 1990. 362p. $15.95pa. ISBN 0-8161-9093-3. LC 89-77760.
   This attractive, easy-to-use book, a volume in the Handbook of the Performing Arts series, focuses on outstanding directors. Entries, arranged alphabetically by name, provide factual information about the directors; critiques of their work; suggestions for further reading; and lists of all their films, with data and major actors for each. Coverage is international. A databank section includes

a glossary and bibliography, followed by a comprehensive index. Recommended for high schools. [R: ARBA 91; BR, Jan/Feb 91]

1333 Handbook of American Film Genres. Wes D. Gehring, ed. Westport, Conn.: Greenwood Press, 1988. 405p. $55.00. ISBN 0-313-24715-3. LC 87-31784.

Students who require an introduction to the concept and classification of film genres and critical and historical literature on filmmaking will find this volume of use. Nineteen chapters group types into five broad categories: action/adventure, comedy, fantasy, songs and soaps, and nontraditional. Each chapter consists of essays that define and analyze the genre, a bibliographic essay on secondary literature, and a selective filmography that lists significant examples of the genre. Indexed by name and title. High schools that support strong film-study programs may wish to consider this scholarly work. [R: BL, 1 Nov 88]

1334 Nowlan, Robert A., and Gwendolyn Wright Nowlan. **Cinema Sequels and Remakes, 1903-1987**. Jefferson, N.C.: McFarland, 1989. 954p. $75.00. ISBN 0-89950-314-4. LC 88-42640.

Cinema Sequels and Remakes covers silent and sound films—drama, adventure, romances, comedy, and thrillers—that have at least one English-language sound remake or sequel. Some films have had several remakes (e.g., *Here Comes Mr. Jordan* has three), and sequels are common (e.g., *Rocky*, *Superman*, *The Pink Panther*). The arrangement is alphabetical by the primary film, with *see* references for later titles to the original.

The well-written and entertaining entries include studio, country, release date, cast, credits, story summary, and a comparison of the remakes or sequels. Other media (e.g., novels, plays) on which the film is based are identified when applicable. Black-and-white movie stills illustrate the volume. An extensive index lists actors, directors, and others involved in making the film; titles of other works on which the film is based; and song titles in the films. [R: ARBA 90]

☐ —————————— # Fine Arts —————————— ☐

CATALOGS

1335 Catalog of Fine Art Reproductions. Sandy Hook, Conn.: Shorewood Fine Art Reproductions, 1990. 216p. $18.00 looseleaf w/binder. (27 Glen Rd., Sandy Hook, CT 06482).

This catalog lists over 800 images that span 3,000 years of visual art history and that are available from Shorewood Fine Art Reproductions. It is illustrated in full-color, with reproductions of works by da Vinci, Rembrandt, Dali, Van Gogh, Picasso, Homer, Monet, and Wyeth, among others. Shorewood also offers *Artists' Biographies for the Art Reference Guide* (1986).

1336 Catalogue of Reproductions of Paintings, 1860 to 1979. 11th ed. Paris: Unesco; distr., Lanham, Md.: UNIPUB, 1981. 368p. $14.95pa. ISBN 92-3-001924-0.

The choice of prints selected for this catalog is based on the significance of the artist, the importance of the painting, and the quality of the reproduction. Arranged by artist, the entries include a small reproduction in black-and-white; name of the artist with life dates and place of birth; and title of the original and its date, medium, size, and location. For the reproductions, information includes the printing process, size, publisher, price, and Unesco archives number. An index by painter and a list of publishers and printers complete each volume.

DICTIONARIES AND ENCYCLOPEDIAS

1337 Baigel, Matthew. **Dictionary of American Art**. New York: Harper & Row, 1979. 390p. $18.50; $10.95pa. ISBN 0-06-433254-3; 0-06-430078-1pa. LC 78-24824.

Reprinted with corrections in 1982, this work covers some 725 major American painters, sculptors, printmakers, photographers, artistic movements, and other topics from the sixteenth to the twentieth century. Biographies, about a column in length, cover the artist's style and achievements; bibliographies are appended to each entry.

■ *Career Opportunities in Art*. See entry 333.

1338   International Dictionary of Art and Artists. James Vinson, ed. Chicago: St. James Press, 1990. 2v. $250.00/set. ISBN 1-55862-055-9.

Volume I: Works of Art presents an "art gallery" of 500 works, chronologically arranged, produced in Western Europe and the Americas from the early Renaissance to the present. Information for each full-page reproduction includes artist's name; location, size, and date of the work; a selective bibliography of books and articles; and a signed critical essay that describes and evaluates technique, style, the artist's school of art, and anecdotes about the work. Indexed by location and artist.

Volume II: Artists contains entries for 500 painters, sculptors, engravers, and other artists from the same era and areas. Information provided for each consists of a short biography, a list of museums and private collections where works are held, an extensive bibliography of books and articles by and about the artist, a signed critical essay, and a black-and-white photograph of a representative work.

This is an excellent set, but its price is high and it lacks color. The volumes are available separately, so if one is chosen, *Artists* is preferable, although they complement each other. [R: ARBA 91; BL, 1 Jan 91; BR, Mar/Apr 91; WLB, Dec 90]

1339   Janson, Horst W., and Anthony F. Janson. History of Art. 4th ed. New York: Harry Abrams, 1991. 856p. $55.00. ISBN 0-8109-3401-9. LC 72-15717.

A standard art history, this work surveys Western painting, sculpture, and architecture from the earliest times to the present. Although it is a textbook, this handsomely illustrated volume is also an excellent reference source for high schools. *History of Art for Young People* is more suitable for younger students.

E +
1340   Janson, Horst W., and Anthony F. Janson. History of Art for Young People. 3d ed. New York: Harry Abrams, 1987. 472p. $29.95. ISBN 0-8109-1098-5.

This work is a rewritten version of *History of Art* for young readers, grades 5 to 9. In addition to a lucid text, the work includes 434 outstanding plates; maps; a glossary; a synoptic table that lists events in political history, religion, literature, science, architecture, and painting; and an index. Recommended for elementary and middle schools.

1341   Lahti, N. E. Plain Talk about Art. 2d ed. Brooklyn, N.Y.: York Books, 1989. 163p. $9.95pa. ISBN 0-9620147-0-2. LC 88-050220.

This dictionary, intended for laypersons, identifies some 900 art terms that span all eras. Although international in scope, it emphasizes West European and American art. The text is clear, succinct, and nontechnical. No biographies are included, but artists are often mentioned in articles about periods and schools. A section on the language of color and a bibliography are included. This inexpensive work provides unsophisticated readers with a good introduction to the art world. Recommended for high schools. [R: ARBA 90; BL, 15 Jan 89]

1342   Mills, John. The Encyclopedia of Sculpture Techniques. New York: Watson-Guptill, 1990. 239p. $32.50. ISBN 0-8230-1609-9. LC 89-25058.

Terms related to sculpture techniques are defined in depth in this authoritative volume. Alphabetically arranged entries cover traditional, contemporary, and experimental practices, illustrated by 260 black-and-white photographs and line drawings. This practical guide for studio use is designed for the novice sculptor. [R: ARBA 91]

1343   The Oxford Companion to Twentieth Century Art. Harold Osborne, ed. New York: Oxford University Press, 1988. 800p. $50.00; $21.50pa. ISBN 0-19-866119-3; 0-19-282076-1pa.

Intended as a layperson's guide through the dense and confusing jungle of contemporary art, this volume attempts to explain modern artists, movements, and trends. Bibliographies and some 300 illustrations are included. Coverage extends to 1980 and emphasizes the art and artists of Great Britain, but the book also deals with Europe, Africa, Latin America, Australia, and the Soviet Union.

1344   The Oxford Dictionary of Art. Ian Chilvers and Harold Osborne, eds. New York: Oxford University Press, 1988. 548p. $49.95. ISBN 0-19-866133-9. LC 88-5138.

This work is based on three standard art reference works: *Oxford Companion to Art* (1970), *Oxford Companion to the Decorative Arts*, and *The Oxford Companion to Twentieth Century Art*, but it does not substitute for any of them. The 3,000 entries extracted from the other volumes have been rewritten and updated, and 300 new ones have been added. The work addresses all aspects of Western art—terms, movements, museums, and biographies of artists, dealers, patrons, scholars, and collectors. Architecture, illustrations, and bibliographies are excluded. This is a good, basic work for the high school library media center. [R: ARBA 89]

1345 Oxford Illustrated Encyclopedia of the Arts. John Julius Norwich, ed. New York: Oxford University Press, 1990. 502p. $45.00. ISBN 0-19-869137-8. LC 89-71125.

This work, the fifth of a projected eight-volume set, can stand alone as a general study of the fine arts. It covers music, literature, drama, painting, sculpture, architecture, cinema, and decorative and applied arts. Entries of one to three paragraphs survey the major works, performances, and so forth, of architects, writers, composers, performers, and other artists. Technique or style and country or period are provided. The volume includes modern individuals in the arts (e.g., Margaret Atwood, Steven Spielberg, Luciano Pavorotti) as well as famous artists of the past.

The work has internal cross-referencing and *see* references and beautiful, well-chosen illustrations in black-and-white and color (e.g., photographs, charts, diagrams). There are no references to other volumes in the set. This survey of the fine arts is highly recommended for high schools. [R: ARBA 91; BL, 1 Apr 91; LJ, 15 Feb 91]

DIRECTORIES

1346 American Art Directory. New Providence, N.J.: R. R. Bowker. annual. $159.95. ISSN 0065-6968. LC 99-1016.

American Art Directory supplies information for some 7,000 art institutions in the United States and Canada. For 2,500 art museums, libraries, and other organizations, it identifies collections, funding sources, exhibitions, and key personnel. For 1,700 art schools, it provides enrollment, entrance requirements, degree programs, and similar details. Other entries include state art councils, exhibition opportunities, art education administrators, magazines, newspaper art editors and critics, and scholarships. Subject, personnel, and institutional indexes conclude each annual volume. [R: ARBA 92]

1347 Artist's Market: Where & How to Sell Your Artwork. Lauri Miller, ed. Cincinnati, Ohio: Writer's Digest Books. annual. $21.95. ISSN 0161-0546.

This annual guide provides access to market opportunities available to freelance artists in both fine and commercial art fields. The volume provides information on pricing, researching the market, self-promotion, establishing copyright, and business practices for the field. Markets include advertising agencies, art/design studios, book publishers, businesses, galleries, greeting cards and paper products, magazines, newspapers, and clip art firms. Some sections are broken down by geographical area.

Entries include directory information, date of establishment, company description, and submission requirements. An asterisk marks companies receptive to unsolicited material. This is the standard source for information on selling art work. [R: ARBA 91; SLJ, Jan 91]

1348 A Guide to National and State Arts Education Services. John McLaughlin, ed. New York: American Council for the Arts, 1987. 84p. $14.95pa. ISBN 0-915400-60-X. LC 87-18712.

Designed to help educators locate art-related resources on the state and national level, this guide lists 191 organizations arranged in 6 sections: state arts agencies, departments of education, arts education alliances, and national art educational associations, arts service organizations, and education associations. The state sections are arranged alphabetically by state, but the national sections are arranged alphabetically by organization name.

Entries provide directory information, a contact person, goal statement, publications, art education services, and fields served (e.g., dance, visual art, creative writing). Among the art education services offered are advocacy, consulting, curriculum development, speaker's bureaus, and teacher workshops. Indexing is by organization and personnel. [R: ARBA 89]

1349 Shore, Irma, and Beatrice Jacinto, comps. **Access to Art: A Museum Directory for Blind and Visually Impaired People**. New York: American Foundation for the Blind and Museum of American Folk Art, 1989. 127p. $11.95pa. ISBN 0-89128-156-8. LC 88-34393.

To compile this directory, a questionnaire about services provided to the blind and visually impaired was sent to all members of the American Association of Museums. The directory is a state-by-state list of museums that provide access through cassettes, trained guides, braille, or large-print labels.

Most are art museums, but some are general, scientific, natural history, or historical facilities. A bibliography on the blind and art includes art books on cassette and in braille or large print. [R: ARBA 90]

BIBLIOGRAPHIES

1350 **ArtsAmerica Fine Art Film & Video Source Book 1987**. Greenwich, Conn.: ArtsAmerica, 1987. 79p. $12.95pa.

This excellent volume lists 750 documentary films and videos on art that are available for purchase or rental. Entries, arranged by time period and then by discipline and country (artists are designated by country of birth), contain basic production data, order/rental information, and a 100- to 200-word annotation. Also included are citations of films about museum collections, techniques of art production, and items spanning more than two centuries. Indexing is by artist or architect, title, and distributor. Two inexpensive supplements of eight pages each are available. Highly recommended for high schools. [R: ARBA 89]

HANDBOOKS

E+
1351 Burroughs, Lea. **Introducing Children to the Arts: A Practical Guide for Children's Librarians and Educators**. Boston: G. K. Hall, 1988. 306p. $38.50. ISBN 0-8161-8818-1. LC 88-14770.

This volume covers seven fields of the arts: architecture, art, dance, music, poetry, story, and theater. For each there is a survey of its history, a description of its internal structure, and suggested program ideas that offer children an opportunity to experience and understand the form. A filmography and a bibliography are provided for every field; the bibliography includes older works considered to be classics and recent books that help develop children's cultural literacy. [R: ARBA 89; BL, 1 Jan 89]

1352 Mayer, Ralph. **The Artist's Handbook of Materials and Techniques**. 5th ed. Revised and updated by Steven Sheehan. New York: Viking, 1991. 761p. $30.00. ISBN 0-670-83701-6. LC 90-50357.

Designed to present a wide range of artists' materials and techniques, Mayer's handbook includes chapters that explain painting with oil, tempera, watercolor, and gouache. Others deal with specific kinds of paintings, such as murals, and the chemistry of materials, solvents, and thinners. Appendixes provide technical data, such as oil absorption and conversion factors. There is a detailed index. [R: ARBA 92]

INDEXES

1353 Havlice, Patricia Pate. **World Painting Index**. Metuchen, N.J.: Scarecrow, 1977. 2v. $99.50/set. ISBN 0-8108-1016-6. LC 76-52407.

1354 Havlice, Patricia Pate. **World Painting Index: First Supplement, 1973-1980**. Metuchen, N.J.: Scarecrow, 1982. 2v. $62.50/set. ISBN 0-8108-1531-1. LC 82-3555.

World Painting Index supplements three volumes by Isabel and Kate Monro: *Index to Reproductions of European Paintings* (1956) and *Index to Reproductions of American Paintings* (H. W. Wilson, 1948) and its supplement (1964). The 1977 Havlice work indexes paintings reproduced in books published from 1940 to 1975; the supplement indexes books published between 1973 and 1980.

In each set, the first volume contains a numbered bibliography of sources, arranged by main entry. The main part lists painters and their works with codes that refer to the bibliographies. The second volume consists of a list of the paintings, arranged alphabetically by title, with references to the artist list in the first volume. Havlice's works are not indexed by subject, as are those by the Monros.

Index to Reproductions of American Paintings Appearing in More Than 400 Books, Mostly Published since 1960, by Lyn Wall Smith and Nancy Dustin Wall Moure (Scarecrow, 1977) indexes some 30,000 works arranged by artist and extends the Monro indexes cited above. [R: ARBA 84]

BIOGRAPHY

1355 **Contemporary Artists**. 3d ed. Colin Naylor, ed. Chicago: St. James Press, 1989. 1059p. $135.00. ISBN 0-912289-96-1.

The international scope of this biographical directory and its critical essays distinguishes it from other sources such as *Dictionary of Contemporary American Artists* and *Who's Who in American Art*. Naylor's work provides reliable and in-depth information for 850 artists worldwide who are currently active. Previous editions had included a number of deceased artists and some still living but inactive. Some 200 who died before 1960 were dropped from this edition, and 40 new artists have been added.

Entries include a short profile, lists of exhibitions and collections in which the artist is represented, references to sources by and about the artist, signed critical essays by one of 120 contributors, and a comment by the artist on his or her own works. Highly recommended. [R: ARBA 90; BL, July 89; LJ, 1 Sept 89]

1356 Cummings, Paul. **Dictionary of Contemporary American Artists**. 5th ed. New York: St. Martin's Press, 1988. 738p. $65.00. ISBN 0-312-00232-7. LC 82-7337.

Cummings's standard reference work focuses on American artists active in the last 50 years. For some 900 artists, the entries provide dates, education, teaching background, commissions, awards, address, dealer's address, exhibitions (one-person and group), collections, and a bibliography. An index, a name pronunciation guide, a key to museums and institutions cited, a gallery list, and a 50-page bibliography complete the volume. Some 125 black-and-white reproductions are scattered throughout the work.

Although the title implies living artists, about one-fourth of those included are deceased, some for several decades, and few young artists are included. Since there is no critical information, *Contemporary Artists* is a better choice, but its cost is more than double that of Cummings. [R: ARBA 89; BL, 15 Sept 88]

1357 Dunford, Penny. **A Biographical Dictionary of Women Artists in Europe and America since 1850**. Philadelphia: University of Pennsylvania Press, 1989. 340p. $89.95. ISBN 0-8122-8230-2. LC 89-16663.

Some 750 concise biographies of living and deceased female artists in Europe and America after 1850 are found in this volume. Written in a lively style, the work provides basic biographical data (e.g., place and date of birth, education, prizes) but also gives details about the artist's life, including her struggles and determination to succeed under difficult circumstances. This work serves as a worthy supplement to *Who's Who in American Art*. [R: ARBA 91; LJ, 15 June 90; RBB, 1 Sept 90]

1358 Goulart, Ron. **The Great Comic Book Artists**. New York: St. Martin's Press, 1986. 128p. $12.95pa. ISBN 0-312-34557-7. LC 86-3711.

1359 Goulart, Ron. **The Great Comic Book Artists. Volume 2**. New York: St. Martin's Press, 1989. 112p. $12.95pa. ISBN 0-312-01768-5. LC 86-3711.

Summaries of the careers of comic-book artists, historical and contemporary, comprise these volumes (60 in volume 1 and 56 in volume 2). Each one-page essay contains biographical, critical, and career information, supported by a black-and-white illustration of the artist's work on the opposite page. Students interested in a career in the field will enjoy this brief introduction to the world of comic-book artists. [R: ARBA 87; ARBA 91; LJ, 15 June 86; VOYA, Dec 89]

1360 **Who's Who in American Art 1991-92**. 19th ed. New Providence, N.J.: R. R. Bowker, 1991. 1404p. $159.95. ISBN 0-8352-2897-5. ISSN 0000-0191. LC 36-27014.

Almost 11,300 entries, some 600 new to this edition, provide basic biographical data for artists in all media as well as critics, curators, administrators, librarians, historians, collectors, dealers, and other art professionals. Each entry includes personal, educational, and career information. For artists, the sketches also provide data on museums that hold their works, books and articles by and about them, the media in which they work, their dealers, and agents.

Indexing is by name, geographic location, and more than 50 professional categories (e.g., mosaic artist, writer). A necrology lists all persons in earlier editions who have died between 1953 and 1989. Updated biennially, this work is also available online through Dialog and ORBIT Search Service. [R: ARBA 92]

1361 World Artists, 1950-1980. Claude Marks, ed. Bronx, N.Y.: H. W. Wilson, 1984. 912p. $78.00. ISBN 0-8242-0707-6. LC 84-13152.

1362 World Artists, 1980-1990. Claude Marks, ed. Bronx, N.Y.: H. W. Wilson, 1991. 416p. $50.00. ISBN 0-8242-0827-7. LC 91-13183.

Marks provides profiles and critical commentaries for world-renowned artists (312 in the foundation volume and 120 in the second) who represent a variety of styles and movements in painting, sculpture, and the graphic media. The evaluations cite statements by critics and reviewers and often quote the artists. Each essay is followed by lists of the artist's works, major exhibits, and a bibliography of reviews. These authoritative and readable volumes are recommended for high schools. [R: ARBA 92; WLB, Oct 91]

ARCHITECTURE

1363 America's Architectural Roots: Ethnic Groups That Built America. Dell Upton, ed. Washington, D.C.: Preservation Press, 1986. 193p. $9.95pa. ISBN 0-89133-123-9. LC 86-25165.

This volume in the Building Watchers Series focuses on the construction style of 22 ethnic groups, primarily in the United States. Each chapter begins with a short essay about the immigrants and why they came to America, followed by a description of their building designs and construction methods. These include homes, farm buildings, and religious structures, all profusely illustrated. This small volume is recommended for high schools. [R: ARBA 88; BL, 15 Apr 87]

1364 Blemenson, John J. **Identifying American Architecture**. rev. ed. New York: W. W. Norton, c1981, 1990. 136p. $19.95pa. ISBN 0-393-30610-0. LC 80-28103.

A reprint of a 1981 work, this volume identifies characteristics of 39 architectural styles that are arranged chronologically from Spanish Colonial to Art Moderne. For each style there are three or four illustrations, specific architectural details keyed to the illustrations, and a descriptive paragraph. An index of terms and a pictorial glossary complete the volume. The many photographs and illustrations make this an excellent choice for middle and high school students.

Encyclopedia of American Architecture by W. D. Hunt (McGraw-Hill, 1980) presents an authoritative survey of the history of architecture, providing broad coverage in nontechnical language. It, too, is well illustrated (500 illustrations and 16 pages of color plates). *The World Atlas of Architecture*, edited by John J. Norwick (G. K. Hall, 1984), provides a visual and textual history of architecture primarily of the Western world from early civilization to the present; some attention is given to non-European architecture.

1365 Built in the U.S.A.: American Buildings from Airports to Zoos. Diane Maddex, ed. Washington, D.C.: Preservation Press, 1985. 189p. $8.95pa. ISBN 0-89133-118-2. LC 84-26473.

Forty-two types of buildings, arranged alphabetically from airports to zoos, are described and illustrated with black-and-white photographs. Structures range from common ones (e.g., banks, libraries) to the more unusual (e.g., decorated sheds). Articles provide historical background, importance, and function for each. There are a selective bibliography and a directory of organizations concerned with specific types of structures. This work is a companion volume to *What Style Is It?* (Preservation Press, 1984). [R: ARBA 86; BL, 15 June 85; LJ, 15 May 86]

E
1366 Maddex, Diane. **Architects Make Zigzags: Looking at Architecture from A to Z**. Washington, D.C.: Preservation Press, 1986. 64p. $8.95pa. ISBN 0-89133-121-2. LC 84-9679.

This delightful little volume, published by the National Trust for Historical Preservation, consists of 26 architectural terms, *architect* to *zigzag*, defined in language understandable to elementary school children. Presented in two-page spreads, each word is defined and illustrated in black-and-white drawings by Roxie Munro. Actual structures are portrayed, and the location, date, and architect are given. This attractive work will introduce children to architecture and the concepts of preservation and is highly recommended for elementary grades. [R: BL, 15 Nov 86]

1367 Master Builders: A Guide to Famous American Architects. Diane Maddex, ed. Washington, D.C.: Preservation Press, 1985. 203p. (Building Watchers Series). $9.95pa. ISBN 0-89133-111-5. LC 85-16982.

Arranged chronologically, this excellent volume provides biographies (each by a different author) of 40 architects, beginning with William Thornton, designer of the U.S. Capitol. The profiles, averaging four to six pages each, emphasize the individual's major achievements and influence on the field; each includes a portrait and several illustrations of buildings the architect designed. Additional sections include a listing of 67 other historic architects with brief paragraphs about each, a bibliography for further reading, and an index. [R: ARBA 87]

1368   Nabokov, Peter, and Robert Easton. **Native American Architecture**. New York: Oxford University Press, 1989. $65.00; $25.00pa. ISBN 0-19-503781-2; 0-19-506665-0pa. LC 88-9944.

Native American Architecture examines American Indian architecture in all of North America above Mexico. It describes materials and techniques with words, line drawings, and photographs. Separate chapters cover wigwams and long houses; mounds, towns, and chickee; earth lodges, grass houses, and tepees; pit houses and extended tepees; winter houses, igloos, and tents; plank houses; earth, wood, and fiber houses; hogans, kis, and ramadas; and pueblos. Other forms, such as ceremonial structures and sweat lodges, are also mentioned.

The fascinating and informative text makes this a reference book that can be placed in the circulating collection. It is recommended for the secondary level. [R: ARBA 90]

1369   Phillips, Steven J. **Old-House Dictionary: An Illustrated Guide to American Domestic Architecture (1600-1940)**. Lakewood, Colo.: American Source Books, 1989. 239p. $16.95pa. ISBN 0-9621333-6-1. LC 88-83158.

This work has 450 line drawings and clear, precise definitions of 1,500 terms. Definitions note synonyms, but there is no cross-referencing; the topic index is entitled "Cross References." The emphasis on illustration is an asset; it makes the volume useful as a reverse dictionary for those who know what something looks like but do not know its name. [R: ARBA 90; BL, Aug 89; LJ, 1 Feb 89]

1370   Yarwood, Doreen. **A Chronology of Western Architecture**. New York: Facts on File, 1987. 353p. $35.00. ISBN 0-8160-1861-8. LC 87-13652.

This work offers a visual presentation of Western architecture, from the ancient Greek mainland and islands to the modern United States, Australia, and Europe. Some 80 sections that vary from 1 to 6 or more double-page spreads cover several centuries for the earlier eras and shorter spans for the later periods. The text includes sections on such subjects as castle building and town defenses, town planning in the eighteenth and nineteenth centuries, and modern architecture.

A general heading that gives date and general style introduces each double-page spread, which includes two columns of text that explain cultural and technological trends of the period. The left margin identifies the countries and area covered. Excellent line drawings and other illustrations extend across the pages. The right margin provides information about events and people. This attractive work is highly recommended for secondary schools. [R: ARBA 89; BL, 15 Mar 88; LJ, 1 Apr 88; SLJ, May 88]

PHOTOGRAPHY

1371   **American Photographers: An Illustrated Who's Who among Leading Contemporary Americans**. Les Krantz, ed. New York: Facts on File, 1989. 352p. $40.00. ISBN 0-8160-1419-1. LC 89-1435.

This beautiful work surveys the lives of over 1,000 current photographers from the worlds of fashion, advertising, and photojournalism. Biographical information includes name, address, telephone number, field of specialization, and major awards and exhibits. The volume is illustrated with over 300 black-and-white and 109 color photographs. The index cross-references photographers by location and specialty. A list of stock photography agencies and an index of illustrations conclude the work. Appropriate for high school level. [R: ARBA 90; BR, Jan/Feb 90]

1372   **Contemporary Photographers**. 2d ed. Colin Naylor, ed. Chicago: St. James Press, 1988. 1145p. $120.00. ISBN 0-912289-79-1.

This volume covers 750 of the "best and most prominent" contemporary photographers and those of earlier times whose works are still popular. Selections were made by a 20-member advisory board, many of whom are distinguished photographers and critics.

Entries open with basic information on date and place of birth, marriage and family, education, photographic studies and teachers, positions held, honors, awards, agent's name and address, and current address or date and place of death (whichever is applicable). This is followed by information about exhibits and museums with major holdings and publications by and about the photographer. A signed essay by one of 175 contributors and comments by the biographee about photography and works, conclude the entry. Most entries also include a sample black-and-white photograph. Recommended for high schools with photography programs. [R: ARBA 89; BL, 1 Sept 88]

1373 **The Guide to Photography Workshops and Schools, 1991.** 2d ed. Lawrence H. Caplan and Dorlene V. Kaplan, eds. Coral Gables, Fla.: Shaw Associates, 1990. 278p. $16.95pa. ISBN 0-945834-09-8. LC 89-61941.

Workshops and tours are the major focus of this directory. The 2d edition contains a new section on photography schools. Other sections cover residencies/retreats and professional organizations. The book provides addresses, telephone numbers, contact persons, dates, and other standard information for tours, workshops, and schools. Indexed by type of program/activity and geographical location. Recommended for high schools with strong art programs. [R: LJ, Jan 91]

1374 **Photographer's Market: Where & How to Sell Your Photographs.** Sam A. Marshall, ed. Cincinati, Ohio: Writer's Digest Books. annual. $21.95pa. ISSN 0147-247X.

Young adults who hope to find a market for their photography should seek help from this standard directory. It provides information on all types of markets (e.g., book publishers, advertising agencies, greeting card companies, galleries, magazines, newspapers). Entries include basic directory information, data on the company, and submission requirements. The work also gives information on self-promotion, pricing, business practices in the field, and establishing copyright. Those companies receptive to unsolicited material are so indicated. [R: ARBA 91; SLJ, June 91]

1375 Pinkard, Bruce. **The Photographer's Bible: An Encyclopedic Reference Manual.** New York: Arco/Simon & Schuster, 1982. 352p. $24.95. ISBN 0-668-05781-5. LC 82-20658.

Alphabetically arranged entries, from brief definitions to several pages of text, cover technical aspects of photography and individuals in the field. Diagrams, charts, tables, color photographs, and 260 black-and-white reproductions supplement the text. Appendixes list people mentioned and provide a directory of associations, publishers, galleries and museums, photographic schools and workshops, and sources of equipment. Although somewhat dated, this is a good general reference source for middle and high school level. [R: ARBA 84; BL, 1 Feb 84]

1376 **Prentice-Hall Pocket Encyclopedia [of] Creative Photography.** Michael Langford, ed. Scarborough, Ont.: Prentice-Hall Canada, 1991. 240p. $14.95pa. ISBN 0-13-718446-8.

Designed as a practical guide and a ready-reference tool, this work is lavishly illustrated with color and black-and-white photographs and drawings. Chapter 1 illustrates the way each different type of photographic apparatus works; chapter 2 teaches the use of light and color. The third chapter shows that not all pictures are a simple matter of point and shoot. Individual sections cover the specialized requirements for shooting a wide variety of photographs, from crowd shots to landscapes. Chapter 4 is a simplified guide to doing film processing. The different techniques for processing black-and-white films, color negatives, and color slides are all explained in clear and concise terms. A chapter on special effects covers the gamut from special filters and films to solarization and manipulated colors. Completing the book are a 6-page appendix that identifies common photograph problems, an 800-word glossary, and a complete index.

1377 Willis-Thomas, Deborah. **An Illustrated Bio-Bibliography of Black Photographers 1940-1988.** Hamden, Conn.: Garland, 1989. 483p. $85.00. ISBN 0-8240-8389-X. LC 88-11200.

A continuation of *Black Photographers 1840-1940* (1985), this volume includes Black photographers not listed in the earlier work. Most of the photojournalists, studio owners, and commercial and fine art photographers within are from the United States, but a few are foreign. For some the information is meager, but for others it is extensive, with birth date, date of first activity, or both; collections that own works; exhibitions; and a bibliography of exhibition catalogs, monographs by and about the photographer, and citations of articles and reviews in newspapers and magazines. One or two paragraphs about the person's life and works are also provided.

A section of over 200 pages of black-and-white photographs, arranged alphabetically by photographer, illustrates the book. The entries in the first part contain cross-references to this section. A four-page bibliography of books and articles by and about Black photographers concludes the volume. Recommended for high schools, especially those with photography or Black studies programs. [R: ARBA 90; LJ, 15 June 89; RBB, 1 Sept 89]

Language

□   □

GENERAL WORKS

See **Handicapped** for sign language.
See **Hobbies and Games** for **Word Games**.
See **Writing and Reports** in **Communications** for formal writing.

1378 **The Cambridge Encyclopedia of Language**. By David Crystal. New York: Cambridge University Press, 1987. 472p. $39.50. ISBN 0-521-26438-3. LC 86-32637.

This work, the first encyclopedic survey of its kind, covers language and the many branches of linguistic science. More than 60 essays, all generously cross-referenced, discuss the major areas of language study. Hundreds of tables, charts, maps, and other illustrations support the text. Appendixes include a glossary of over 1,000 linguistic terms, a table of the world's languages, and an extensive bibliography. Indexed by language, author, and subject. This outstanding work is recommended for high school libraries. [R: ARBA 89]

1379 Katzner, Kenneth. **The Languages of the World**. rev. ed. New York: Routledge, Chapman & Hall, c1986, 1990. 376p. $13.95. ISBN 0-415-04604-1.

This survey of the world's languages, a partial revision and update of the 1975 edition, is arranged in three parts. The first consists of a chart of the major language families; the second, the main body of the work, briefly describes some 200 languages arranged by geographical areas (e.g., Europe, Asia, Middle East); and the third provides a country-by-country language survey, listing major and minor languages for each, with figures showing distribution. Recommended for high school libraries. This work is now available on CD-ROM (National Textbook, $950.00). [R: ARBA 88]

ENGLISH AS A SECOND LANGUAGE

1380 Collin, P. H., and others. **Beginner's Dictionary of American English Usage**. Lincolnwood, Ill.: National Textbook, 1986. 279p. $7.95; $4.95pa. ISBN 0-8325-0440-8; 0-8325-0439-4pa.

Directed toward beginning or low intermediate learners of English as a second language, this dictionary offers 4,000 entries. Pronunciation is shown in symbols of international phonetic transcription. Other features include at least one sentence that shows usage and shaded boxes that provide grammatical advice, usage notes, and idioms. [R: ARBA 87]

1381 **Collins COBUILD English Language Dictionary**. John Sinclair and others, eds. New York: HarperCollins, c1987, 1989. 1703p. $35.00. ISBN 0-00-375021-3.

This revolutionary dictionary is based on a seven-year computer study sponsored by Birmingham University in England, which analyzed contemporary English usage in a group of standard texts. (COBUILD is the name of the database used for this purpose.) It is designed for learners of English, but others may benefit from it.

The dictionary contains 70,000 entries, a small number when compared to other abridged or desk-type dictionaries, but emphasis is placed on 2,000-3,000 words identified by the analysis as the central core of the language. More space is devoted to this group of words than is found in traditional dictionaries. Some standard information, such as syllabication and etymological notes, has been replaced by data the editors consider to be more useful.

Alphabetically arranged entries consist of pronunciation (using the International Phonetic Alphabet), definition, and usage samples (in greater numbers than in standard works). The dictionary uses British spelling and definition variations, but when applicable, entries are labeled "used in British English," or "used in American English." Notes included at the side of each column contain synonyms, information on grammar, and syntactic data. This work supplements standard dictionaries and constitutes a major source for ESL programs. [R: RBB, 1 Apr 90]

1382 **Eng'lish Lan'guage and O'ri·en·ta'tion Pro'grams in the United States**. 9th ed. New York: Institute of International Education, 1988. 214p. $21.95pa. ISBN 0-87206-161-2. LC 78-101308.

This comprehensive directory identifies English-language programs for foreign students who hope to study in the United States. The listings are divided into three sections. "Programs" names those that offer 15 hours or more of instruction per week; "Courses" lists institutions that have regular classes for foreign students; and "Secondary Schools" includes high schools that provide language instruction for foreign students. [R: ARBA 90]

E+

1383 **Everyday American English Dictionary**. Richard A. Spears, ed. Lincolnwood, Ill.: National Textbook, 1984. 389p. $7.95; $4.95pa. ISBN 0-8325-0339-8; 0-8325-0337-1pa.

A basic dictionary designed for new learners of English as a second language, this work includes 5,500 words that focus on everyday life and the most commonly used vocabulary. Pronunciation is given in the International Phonetic Alphabet. Brief definitions in basic English are frequently accompanied by examples of usage. [R: ARBA 85; BL, 15 June 84]

1384 Maclin, Alice. **Reference Guide to English: A Handbook of English as a Second Language**. 2d ed. New York: Holt, Rinehart and Winston, 1987. 496p. $15.50. ISBN 0-03-004193-7. LC 80-29208.

This valuable reference source is directed toward nonnative English speakers, intermediate and advanced, and the difficulties they normally face in writing and speaking the language. It includes colloquialisms, jargon, idioms, irregular verbs, tenses, gender, use of articles, punctuation, word formation, and many other topics. A detailed index concludes the volume.

UNABRIDGED DICTIONARIES

1385 **Oxford English Dictionary**. 2d ed. J. A. Simpson and E. S. C. Weiner, eds. New York: Oxford University Press, 1989. 20v. $2,750.00/set. ISBN 0-19-861186-2. LC 88-5330.

Revision of the *Oxford English Dictionary* (*OED 2*), a premier publishing event of the twentieth century, brings this authoritative historical record of the language up to date. The initial work, completed in 1928 after more than seven decades of planning and compiling, was supplemented in 1972 (A-G), 1976 (H-N), and 1982 (O-Scz).

OED 2 treats over 500,000 words, providing spellings, pronunciations (using the International Phonetic Alphabet instead of the original pronunciation system), parts of speech, kinds of terms, statuses and morphologies, and meanings. The latter are chronologically arranged from the word's recorded appearance to contemporary times. Illustrative quotations, 2.4 million of them, reflect usage and changes in meaning throughout the word's history. The revision merges all words contained in the original work and its supplements, with the addition of some 5,000 new words that have entered the language during the last decade.

Most high school libraries, of course, cannot afford *OED 2*, but students should know about it and its importance as the ultimate English-language dictionary. Many school libraries may hold *The Compact Edition of the Oxford English Dictionary* (Oxford University Press, 1987), a miniaturization of the original 1928 edition, which requires the use of a magnifying glass, or *The Shorter Oxford English Dictionary on Historical Principles* (Oxford University Press, 1973), based on the original. [R: ARBA 90; BL, 15 Dec 89; LJ, 15 Apr 90; WLB, June 89]

E+

1386 **The Random House Dictionary of the English Language**. 2d unabridged ed. Stuart Berg Flexner, ed. in chief. New York: Random House, 1987. 2478p. $89.95. ISBN 0-394-50050-4. LC 87-4500.

This comprehensive dictionary, first published in 1966, emphasizes current language. The 2d edition indicates changes in pronunciation, usage, and definitions. Some 50,000 new words coined over the last 2 decades and 75,000 new definitions are included in the more than 300,000 entries. The revision also contains more sample sentences, usage notes, synonyms and antonyms, and illustrations. Coverage of regional English has been expanded, and dates when words entered the language have been added.

The work opens with essays on the history of the English language, changes in usage, U.S. dialects, and pronunciation, followed by an extensive exposition on how to use the dictionary. Definitions are arranged according to their frequency of use. On the whole, definitions are clear and accurate; examples of usage are helpful; and the dictionary's efforts to include very current terminology, gender-neutral definitions, and modern tendencies in spelling have been achieved. Biographical and geographical entries, listed in the main alphabet, reflect updating in information and population figures. The appendix contains such material as lists of signs and symbols; a directory of colleges and universities;

copies of the Declaration of Independence and the U.S. Constitution; basic foreign-language dictionaries for French, Spanish, Italian, and German; a style manual with sections on writing term papers and resumes; and an atlas.

Despite this work's extensive coverage of the language, it does not compare in comprehensiveness or authority with *Webster's Third*. Nonetheless, it is recommended for all levels of school libraries. [R: ARBA 88; BL, 15 Feb 88; LJ, 15 Nov 87; WLB, Dec 87; WLB, Feb 88]

1387 **Webster's Third New International Dictionary of the English Language**. Philip Babcock Grove and the Merriam-Webster editorial staff, eds. 3d unabridged ed. Springfield, Mass.: Merriam-Webster, 1981. 2662p. $99.95. ISBN 0-87779-206-2.

1388 **12,000 Words: A Supplement to** *Webster's Third New International Dictionary*. Springfield, Mass.: Merriam-Webster, 1986. 212p. $10.95. ISBN 0-87779-207-0. LC 86-12598.

The current edition of this prestigious work, first published in 1828, appeared in 1961. Due to periodic revision, a new copyright is issued about every five years.

The 3d edition is different from previous ones by being nondidactic: the new objective is to record the language, not to limit coverage to what linguists consider correct usage. Labels such as "slang" are used sparingly, and the description "colloquial" has been replaced by "substandard" or "nonstandard." There are many deletions: gazetteer and biographical entries, foreign words and phrases, literary allusions, and words that became obsolete before 1755.

The 464,000 entries include 50,000 new words and 50,000 new meanings for old words. Illustrative quotations are taken from contemporary sources, but citations are incomplete. Definitions, listed in historical order, are usually clear and easily understood. Etymologies and pronunciations are included. *Webster's Ninth Collegiate Dictionary* is an abridged version of this work.

Webster's Third is supplemented by *12,000 Words*, which covers new words and meanings that have entered the language since the parent dictionary was published. Two earlier supplements, which this work supersedes, are *6,000 Words* (1976) and *9,000 Words* (1983). It is recommended for all libraries that hold *Webster's Third* and is useful in its own right. [R: ARBA 88; BL, 1 Sept 87]

E+
1389 **The World Book Dictionary**. Clarence L. Barnhart and Robert K. Barnhart, eds. Chicago: World Book Encyclopedia, 1990. 2v. $79.00/set. ISBN 0-7166-0291-1. LC 90-71023.

Designed as a complement to *The World Book Encyclopedia* this excellent word book is updated annually. The 225,000 entries are directed toward approximately the same audience as its companion; upper elementary through high school students and adults at a popular level. Its scope is essentially that of the typical collegiate dictionary, but it offers simplified treatment. Included are foreign words and phrases in general use, idioms, and new words; obsenities, vulgar words, and proper nouns (biographical and geographical entries) are omitted. Synonyms, example sentences, and word origins are given for each word.

Definitions, arranged by frequency of meaning, are written with a controlled vocabulary adjusted to the reading level of the prospective reader. Special features include black-and-white illustrations, a section on the history of the English language, word exercises, vocabulary inventories, spelling rules, foreign-language alphabets and rules of pronunciation, and a style manual. Recommended for elementary and secondary schools. [R: ARBA 92]

DESK DICTIONARIES

1390 Lemay, Harold, and others. **The Facts on File Dictionary of New Words**. New York: Facts on File, 1988. 163p. $19.95. ISBN 0-8160-2088-4.

1391 Lemay, Harold, and others. **The New New Word Dictionary**. rev. ed. New York: Ballantine/Random House, 1988. 128p. $2.95pa. ISBN 0-345-35696-9. LC 88-72270.

The Facts on File Dictionary of New Words is a revised and expanded edition of Ballentine's *New New Word Dictionary* (Ballentine, 1985), while the 1988 *New New Word Dictionary* is a revision of the earlier edition. Both include new words, catch phrases, slogans, terms, acronyms, and initialisms, with 500 word and phrase entries in *Facts on File* and a more limited number in *New New*. Entries give pronunciation, part of speech, brief definition, and cross-references to related words. Both are recommended for high schools. [R: ARBA 90; BR, Nov/Dec 89; Kliatt, Apr 89; WLB, Oct 89]

1392 The New Merriam-Webster Dictionary for Large Print Users. Boston: G. K. Hall, 1989. 1106p. $35.00. ISBN 0-8161-4754-X. LC 89-15437.

A revision of the first large-print dictionary (1977), this work consists of 60,000 entries that provide definitions, some usage labels, and ethnologies. It conforms to the standards of the National Association for the Visually Handicapped, with guide words printed in 18-point boldface type, entries in 14-point boldface, and definitions in 12-point. Recommended for secondary schools that serve visually impaired students. [R: ARBA 91]

1393 Random House Webster's College Dictionary. New York: Random House, 1991. 1611p. $18.00. ISBN 0-679-40110-5. LC 90-21963.

This abridged and updated version of the *Random House Dictionary of the English Language*, 2d ed. is the retitled successor to the *Random House College Dictionary*, 2d ed. (1975). It now joins *Webster's Ninth New Collegiate* and *Webster's New World*, 3d ed. as a top-rated desk dictionary. The work's authority and attractive format make it a worthy competitor.

The impressive word count of 180,000 entries gives special attention to recently coined words, slang, dialect, and scientific terms. The clear definitions describe the language as it is used, but usage notes and labels often express the purist viewpoint on word status. Etymologies date the first use of most words.

The addition of the word "Webster" to the dictionary's title is a marketing device and does not indicate a change in company ownership. The name is in the public domain and may be used by any publisher. Recommended for high schools. [R: BL, July 91; LJ, 15 June 91]

E+
1394 Third Barnhart Dictionary of New English. Robert K. Barnhart and Sol Steinmetz with Clarence L. Barnhart, eds. Bronx, N.Y.: H. W. Wilson, 1990. 565p. $49.00. ISBN 0-8242-0796-3. LC 90-33483.

The present volume—an update of the *First* and *Second Barnhart Dictionary of New English*, now out of print—covers 12,000 new terms that have come into use during the last 30 years. Some entries update information contained in earlier editions. Each entry includes at least one quotation that helps the reader understand the meaning of the term. Pronunciation, etymology, and usage notes are provided where necessary. The editors, themselves distinguished lexicographers, have called upon scholars throughout the world to assist them in making this the most authoritative dictionary of new words to date. Highly recommended for all levels as a supplement to other dictionaries. [R: ARBA 91; BL, 1 Dec 90; LJ, 1 Oct 90; WLB, Oct 90]

1395 Webster's New Ideal Dictionary. 2d ed. Springfield, Mass.: Merriam-Webster, 1989. 658p. $9.95. ISBN 0-87779-449-9. LC 89-34610.

The *New Ideal*, a concise version of *Webster's Ninth New Collegiate Dictionary*, is an "ideal" work for those who do not require comprehensive word treatment. It includes 60,000 words and phrases, about half the number generally found in a desk-type dictionary. With far fewer pages, larger type, heavier paper, and better spacing on the page, it is easy to read and handle. It focuses on the most commonly used words, omitting obsolete, rare, and highly technical words. Definitions are fewer and shorter, although generally adequate for basic use, and the inclusion of etymologies, illustrations, and usage notes is less frequent. Entries include the essentials: pronunciation, parts of speech, division points, capitalization, and irregular verb forms.

All Merriam-Webster dictionaries are conservative in their approach to language and are reluctant to show current usage and spelling and to include new words; this one is no exception. Recommended as an added source for junior and senior high schools. [R: ARBA 91]

1396 Webster's New World Dictionary of American English. 3d ed. Victoria Neufeldt, ed. New York: Webster's New World; distr., New York: Prentice Hall Press, 1988. 1574p. $17.95 (thumb-indexed volume). ISBN 0-13-947169-3. LC 88-1712.

This highly regarded dictionary, first published in 1953 and frequently revised, emphasizes the English language as used in the United States. It is an authoritative work noted for its clarity and currency.

This edition's 170,000 entries (12,000 more than in the previous edition) arrange definitions in historical order and provide etymologies, pronunciation, irregularly formed plurals, spelling variations, and capitalization. More than 11,000 words or meanings of U.S. origin are identified by a star preceding the word. Usage labels (e.g., slang, vulgar) or comments (e.g., nonstandard) are added where appropriate, and short phrases illustrate meaning. Synonyms indicating shades of meaning, antonyms, and frequent usage notes are among other useful features.

A few well-drawn illustrations are provided. The main alphabet also includes foreign terms and phrases, biographical and geographical entries, literary references, abbreviations, and acronyms. Swear words and racial slurs, omitted from previous editions, have been added and labeled as slang or vulgar. The appendix contains a style manual and a section on signs and symbols.

Webster's New World Dictionary's special strengths are its emphasis on the current language, clear and easily understood definitions, and readable typeface. It is highly recommended for high schools. [R: ARBA 89; BL, 1 Mar 89; WLB, Dec 88]

1397 **Webster's Ninth New Collegiate Dictionary**. Springfield, Mass.: Merriam-Webster, 1991. 1563p. $16.95; $17.95 (thumb indexed). ISBN 0-87779-508-8; 0-87779-509-6 (thumb indexed). LC 89-38961.

Based on *Webster's Third International Dictionary*, this desk dictionary reflects the permissive-usage philosophy of the parent. The almost 160,000 entries, which include 22,000 new words and meanings, list all definitions in historical order but emphasize contemporary pronunciation, meaning, and usage. New to this edition is a dating system that indicates the first use of the word and each additional meaning. It also briefly explains words often misused or that have disputed usage.

Due to its continuous revision policy, *Webster's Ninth* is copyrighted annually. One of the best abridged dictionaries available, it is a first choice for middle and high school libraries. [R: ARBA 91]

JUVENILE DICTIONARIES

E

1398 **The American Heritage First Dictionary**. By Stephen Krensky. Boston: Houghton Mifflin, 1986. 340p. $11.95. ISBN 0-395-42530-1. LC 86-7363.

E+

1399 **The American Heritage Children's Dictionary**. Boston: Houghton Mifflin, 1986. 848p. $13.95. ISBN 0-395-42529-8. LC 86-7349.

E+

1400 **The American Heritage Student's Dictionary**. Boston: Houghton Mifflin, 1986. 992p. $12.95. ISBN 0-395-40417-7. LC 86-7337.

The *First Dictionary*, a revision of *My First Dictionary* (Houghton Mifflin, 1980), contains 1,700 entries chosen from first primers, reading textbooks, and common vocabulary. The six or seven words defined on each page are used in sample sentences; only a few words are illustrated. The work also includes sections on word games and homonyms. Recommended for preschool and primary grades.

Children's Dictionary, for elementary grades, features a large, easy-to-read typeface and clearly written definitions. Each word is followed by the part of speech, synonyms, antonyms, and historical notes set off by color blocks. Each different sense of the word is followed by an illustrative sentence. Some 1,500 color illustrations, drawings, and photographs help to clarify word meanings. *Children's Dictionary* is more comprehensive than the *Macmillan Dictionary for Children*. Highly recommended.

Student's Dictionary, intended for students in grades 6 through 9, contains concise, readable definitions enhanced by frequent sentence or phrase illustrations. Margin notes, which include related matter such as word histories, are a special feature. Slang is clearly labeled as such, and many notes explain correct word usage. Line drawings that illustrate words and notes are located in a wide column on each page. There are a number of appendixes, including a style manual and a guide to the metric system. *Student Dictionary* is recommended, but it falls behind the *Scott, Foresman Advanced Dictionary* and the *Macmillan Dictionary for Students* in overall quality. [R: ARBA 88; BL, 15 Feb 87, BL, 15 Jan 90]

E

1401 **Childcraft Dictionary**. Chicago: World Book, 1989. 900p. $25.00. ISBN 0-7166-1489-8. LC 88-50694.

World Book published a dictionary with this title in 1982 (a version of *Macmillan Dictionary for Children*), but the current *Childcraft Dictionary* is original, not based on any other work. Children in grades 3 through 6 should be able to use and learn from this attractive and current dictionary. Entry words are in boldface type; definitions are clear; and illustrations are of good quality. Language facts and word history sections appended to many entries enhance clarity and interest. Homophones, synonyms, antonyms, plurals, adjective forms, and idioms all receive adequate treatment. *Childcraft*

Dictionary does not replace standard elementary school dictionaries, but it deserves a place on elementary school library shelves. [R: ARBA 90]

E
1402   Eastman, Philip D. **The Cat in the Hat Beginner Book Dictionary**. Random House, 1964. 133p. $8.99. ISBN 0-394-91009-0. LC 64-1157.
   The Cat in the Hat ... Dictionary provides a sense of fun with words and serves as both a wordbook (words identified visually and usually grouped thematically) and a dictionary. It defines more than 1,000 words with humorously captioned pictures. The background color changes with each letter of the alphabet. Pages, in two columns with two to four entries each, are relatively uncluttered. This work, the prototype for many later works, is also produced in French and Spanish.

E
1403   Hayward, Linda. **The Sesame Street Dictionary**. New York: Random House, 1980. 256p. $15.95. ISBN 0-394-84007-6. LC 80-11644.
   The Sesame Street Dictionary is as much a mainstay to librarians as the television program has been to children. Designed for preschool through grade 3, it briefly defines 1,300 words and illustrates them in amusing sentences and pictures, often in balloons coming out of character's mouths. The dictionary builds vocabulary and reading readiness for the very young and serves as a beginning dictionary for children in the primary grades. Highly recommended. [R: ARBA 81]

E
1404   Hillerich, Robert L. **The American Heritage Picture Dictionary**. Boston: Houghton Mifflin, 1986. 144p. $9.95. ISBN 0-395-42531-X.
   Preschool children will enjoy this workbook/dictionary containing some 900 entries. The work is intended to be enjoyed as a picture book while promoting reading and writing. In each of the columns (two per page), there are two or three entries with a brief, simple definition or a picture illustrating the word. Many of the illustrations are of scenes (rather than objects) that depict multiracial and multiage characters. A group of topical pictures (e.g., supermarkets, zoos) conclude the volume. Recommended. [R: BL, 15 Feb 87; BL, 15 Jan 90]

E+
1405   **The Lincoln Writing Dictionary for Children**. San Diego, Calif.: Harcourt Brace Jovanovich, 1988. 901p. $17.95. ISBN 0-15-152394-0.
   A handsome new dictionary, this work helps young people meet their writing needs. Entries for 35,000 words offer clear, readable definitions; pronunciation; part of speech; and other word forms. Interspersed in the work are some 600 essays on writing and over 4,000 quotations from the works of 500 authors, many of whom are familiar to young people. Reproductions of paintings, photographs, and drawings in color and black-and-white illustrate the volume. The essays on writing and word histories are highlighted in boxes. Synonyms and obsolete words are omitted, and etymologies are few. There are, however, over 600 biographical and geographical entries in the main alphabet.
   This work is recommended for children in the upper elementary grades, but older students could benefit from its readability and emphasis on good writing. Its format and title, however, may hinder its use in junior high schools. [R: ARBA 89; RBB, 1 Mar 89]

E
1406   **Macmillan Dictionary for Children**. rev. ed. Judith S. Levey, ed. New York: Macmillan, 1989. 864p. $14.95. ISBN 0-02-761561-8. LC 89-60916.
   This excellent dictionary, identical in content to the *Macmillan School Dictionary*, was last revised in 1982. Designed for grades 3 through 6, it is a good choice for elementary school libraries.
   Clear definitions for 35,000 words include frequent color pictures to assist in clarifying meaning. Syllabication, pronunciation, parts of speech, and different word forms are provided. Pronunciation guides are clear and well placed, and highlighted guidewords assist the reader in finding the proper page. There are also a 10-page section on how to use a dictionary and a reference section that consists of U.S. and world history timelines, pictures of the presidents, national flags, world maps, and tables of weights and measures. [R: ARBA 90; SLJ, May 90]

E
1407   **Macmillan First Dictionary**. rev. and expanded ed. Judith S. Levey, ed. in chief. New York: Macmillan, 1990. 402p. $12.95. ISBN 0-02-761731-9.

A revision of *Macmillan Very First Dictionary* (1983), this work focuses on the most common words in the English language. An introduction outlines the development of words and explains how to use a dictionary. Simple definitions for each of the 2,200 words are often supported by illustrative sentences. Nearly 550 pictures in color explain concepts and abstract words. Recommended for grades 1 through 3. [R: BL, 15 Jan 90]

1408 **My First Dictionary**. Glenville, Ill.: Scott, Foresman, 1989. 1v. $11.95. ISBN 0-673-28497-2.
This work defines more than 4,000 words that children encounter while reading books. Definitions have sample sentences or illustrations or both. Multiple forms of a word (e.g., noun, verb) are numbered in one entry; homonyms are treated in separate entries. Alternative word forms—plurals, past tense, comparatives, and superlatives—conclude many definitions. Large type and boldfaced lettering are featured throughout this dictionary, which is intended for the primary grades. Highly recommended. [R: BL, 1 Jan 90; BL, 15 Jan 90]

E
1409 **My First Muppet Dictionary**. New York: Macmillan, 1989. 112p. $9.95. ISBN 0-02-689153-0.
My First Muppet Dictionary, a junior version of *Sesame Street Dictionary*, includes more than 500 early vocabulary words. Pages have six entries, each with a simple definition, sample sentence, and picture. Each letter is presented in a different background color. Recommended for preschool and primary grades. [R: BL, 15 Jan 90]

E
1410 **My First Picture Dictionary**. Glenville, Ill.: Scott, Foresman, 1990. 312p. $13.95; $10.95pa. ISBN 0-673-12489-4; 0-673-28452-2pa.

E
1411 **My Pictionary**. Glenville, Ill.: Scott, Foresman, 1990. 144p. $10.95; $8.50pa. ISBN 0-673-12488-6; 0-673-28451-4pa.

1412 **My Second Picture Dictionary**. Glenville, Ill.: Scott, Foresman, 1990. 448p. $15.95; $12.95pa. ISBN 0-673-28453-0; 0-673-12490-8pa.
These three works are correlated to meet the needs of children in kindergarten through second grade. *My Pictionary* gives 850 words for kindergarten level; *My First Picture Dictionary* includes 1,500 words for first grade; and *My Second Picture Dictionary* provides 4,000 words for second grade. Each has been published in part under the titles *Good Morning Words*, *Words for New Readers*, and *My First Dictionary*.
Pictionary groups words under headings (e.g., people, animals, seasons), pictures every word, and provides an index for adult use. *First Picture Dictionary* lists different forms of the word, numbers separate meanings, uses words in sentences, and illustrates about three-fourths of those cited. *Second Picture Dictionary* is similar in format to the former, but with fewer pictures; words are defined and used in sentences. Various types of illustrations—cartoons, photographs, and art prints (in the last work)—are used in the books. These appealing works are recommended. [R: ARBA 91]

1413 **Scott, Foresman Advanced Dictionary**. By E. L. Thorndike and Clarence L. Barnhart. Glenview, Ill.: Scott, Foresman, 1988. 1302p. $17.95. ISBN 0-673-12385-5.

E+
1414 **Scott, Foresman Beginning Dictionary**. By E. L. Thorndike and Clarence L. Barnhart. Glenview, Ill.: Scott, Foresman, 1988. 770p. $17.95. ISBN 0-673-12383-9.

E+
1415 **Scott, Foresman Intermediate Dictionary**. By E. L. Thorndike and Clarence L. Barnhart. Glenview, Ill.: Scott, Foresman, 1988. 1098p. $17.50. ISBN 0-673-12384-7.
The "Thorndike" dictionaries, as they are sometimes called, have been published for more than 50 years and have for generations ranked among the top juvenile dictionaries. These three continue the tradition set by their predecessors.
The *Beginning Dictionary*, as the name indicates, is directed toward elementary students, but it is also useful in middle schools. Basic vocabulary words are clearly defined for its audience; word histories are also provided. Geographical names are incorporated into the main alphabet; personal names are omitted. There are some 50 pages of vocabulary exercises.

The *Intermediate Dictionary*, intended for junior high level, contains lucid definitions of 68,700 words (80,800 definitions) with illustrations (e.g., line drawings, cartoons) on every page. Word histories, illustrative sentences for all meanings (43,700), and exercises accompany the definitions.

The *Advanced Dictionary*, also published as *Thorndike-Barnhart Student Dictionary*, contains over 100,000 entries and is designed for students in grades 7 through 12. This edition, a colorful and attractive volume, includes entries for 7,500 new words, 18,000 etymologies, and 900 usage notes. Word-family and language-origin boxes are scattered throughout the text. Dictionaries in the Scott, Foresman series are first choices for school libraries. [R: ARBA 90; WLB, Mar 89]

E
1416 **Webster's Elementary Dictionary**. Springfield, Mass.: Merriam-Webster, 1990. 600p. $18.95. ISBN 0-8123-6247-0.

1417 **Webster's School Dictionary**. Springfield, Mass.: Merriam-Webster, 1980. 1184p. $12.95. ISBN 0-87779-280-1.

The *Elementary Dictionary*, which contains over 32,000 entries, 600 illustrations in full color, and thousands of usage examples, is designed for children in grades 4 through 6. The *School Dictionary*, designed for grades 9 through 12, includes 85,000 entries and 91,000 definitions. An appendix includes sections on biography, geography, signs and symbols, chemical elements, and writing. *Webster's Intermediate Dictionary* (Merriam-Webster, 1977) for grades 6 through 8, is available in a large-type edition only. It includes 65,000 words.

The dictionaries are attractively formatted, and definitions can be easily understood by the intended audience. Recommended.

PICTURE DICTIONARIES

1418 Bragonier, Reginald, Jr., and David Fisher. **What's What: A Visual Glossary of the Physical World**. rev. ed. Maplewood, N.J.: Hammond, 1990. 581p. $34.95. ISBN 0-8437-3322-5. LC 89-51862.

This visual glossary, which appeared in 1981, is similar to the *Facts on File Visual Dictionary*. *What's What*, however, contains more than 1,000 pictures, including 20 new illustrations, 150 that are updated, and reprints of hundreds of others. Component parts of the thematically arranged illustrations are identified and labeled. Among the new items are a copier, fax machine, cellular telephone, personal computer, microwave oven, and CD player, as well as the human circulatory system. Thousands of component parts are indexed. Recommended for secondary schools. [R: ARBA 91; BL, 15 Sept 90; WLB, Sept 90]

E +
1419 **The Facts on File Junior Visual Dictionary**. By Jean-Claude Corbeil and Ariane Archambault. New York: Facts on File, 1989. 159p. $18.95. ISBN 0-8160-2222-4.

In the style of the author's *Facts on File Visual Dictionary* for adults, this juvenile work pictures well-known objects in color and identifies their parts. For example, 15 parts of an electric guitar are labeled. The table of contents lists the themes under which items are arranged (e.g., clothing, farms, food, the human body). Pictures, captioned at the top, are of good quality, making the work attractive. Recommended. [R: ARBA 90; BL, 15 Jan 90; SLJ, Apr 90; SLJ, May 90; SLJ, June 90]

E +
1420 **The Facts on File Visual Dictionary**. By Jean-Claude Corbeil. New York: Facts on File, 1986. 797p. $29.95. ISBN 0-8160-1544-9. LC 86-6261.

Thousands of objects and their parts are labeled in this graphic presentation. The aims are to indicate "the specialized vocabulary currently used in every field," and to "look up the word from the picture" and "find the picture from the word." Under measuring devices, for example, there are drawings for devices that measure time (e.g., hourglass, sundial, grandfather clock), pedometers, horizontal seismographs, and others. Each page is captioned, and each item and its parts is clearly labeled. The table of contents lists over 40 topical sections with their subsections. There are general, topical, and specialized (e.g., athletics, automobile, baseball, bicycle, camping) indexes. [R: ARBA 87]

E
1421 **Macmillan Picture Wordbook**. Judith S. Levey, and others, eds. New York: Macmillan, 1990. 58p. $8.95. ISBN 0-02-754641-2. LC 90-8274.

This word book, also issued as *Macmillan/McGraw Hill Picture Word Book*, contains captioned pictures suitable for children ages two to six or for ESL students in the elementary grades. The colorful illustrations are arranged in categories (e.g., home, clothes, fall/winter). There also is an alphabetical word list. Recommended. [R: ARBA 92; RBB, 15 June 91]

1422 **The Oxford-Duden Pictorial English Dictionary**. John A. Pheby, ed. New York: Oxford University Press, 1984. 1v. $14.95pa. ISBN 0-19-864155-9.

The purpose of this work, based on the German *Duden Bildworterbuch*, is to enable readers to determine the English-language term for objects they can identify visually. The 384 illustrations are grouped in 11 broad categories (e.g., the Earth, man and his social environment). Objects are labeled with the English-language term (British spellings and American equivalent for most). French and German versions are also available.

1423 Scarry, Richard. **Richard Scarry's Best Word Book Ever**. New York: Western/Golden Press, 1963. 91p. $6.95. ISBN 0-307-15510-2. LC 63-24822.

Challenging and often humorous story-pictures in color have made this word book for preschool children a popular choice for almost three decades. Each object in the illustration is labeled. *The Sesame Street Word Book* (Western/Golden Press, 1983) is a similar work that identifies words from some 1,000 objects and feelings.

AMERICANISMS AND SLANG

1424 **A Concise Dictionary of Slang and Unconventional English: From** *A Dictionary of Slang and Unconventional English* **by Eric Partridge**. Paul Beale, ed. New York: Macmillan, 1990. 534p. $35.00. ISBN 0-02-605350-0. LC 90-38042.

High school library media centers that do not own the 8th edition of Partridge's scholarly *Dictionary of Slang and Unconventional English* should consider purchasing this concise version of it. Beale, chosen by Partridge to succeed him as editor, has reduced the original 1,400 pages to 534 by omitting words and phrases that originated prior to the twentieth century, but he has added 1,500 new expressions from the 1980s.

Like the parent work, the *Concise Dictionary* emphasizes British and Commonwealth slang. Each entry usually includes the part of speech; indicates whether the usage is current; and gives the definition, date of appearance, and source for the earliest recorded use of the expression. The use of unusual abbreviations and variations in the order of information given within the entry make the source difficult to use. Nonetheless, based as it is on a classic work, the dictionary should be considered by libraries that require an authoritative source for British slang of this century. [R: BL, 1 Apr 91]

1425 Dickson, Paul. **Slang! The Topic-by-Topic Dictionary for Contemporary American Lingoes**. New York: Simon & Schuster, 1990. 295p. $9.95pa. ISBN 0-671-67251-7. LC 89-49628.

This inexpensive dictionary of current American slang classifies 3,900 terms under 24 subject categories, from auctioneering to yuppie slang. In compiling the work, Dickson used the Tamony Collection of slang at the University of Missouri and drew upon the expertise of over 200 consultants.

Emphasis of the book is on definitions, with little attention given to etymologies. Some entries offer illustrative examples of use from the media. Sources are listed at the end of each chapter and in a comprehensive bibliography at the end of the volume. There is a detailed index.

Slang is recommended as a supplement to other current works, such as Chapman's *New Dictionary of American Slang*, a basic source for high school libraries. [R: ARBA 91; BL, 1 June 90; Kliatt, Apr 90; LJ, 1 Apr 90]

E+

1426 **Dictionary of American Idioms**. 2d ed. Adain Makkai and others, eds. Hauppauge, N.Y.: Barron's Educational Series, 1987. 398p. $11.95pa. ISBN 0-8120-3899-1. LC 84-9247.

Similar to *NTC's American Idioms Dictionary*, this work would be especially useful to students who speak English as a second language; its 5,000 words and phrases duplicate as well as supplement the competition. Expressions are defined in clear, formal language, and cross-references are generously used. Since neither work is expensive, secondary school libraries should have both. [R: ARBA 89; BR, Sept/Oct 88]

1427 Dictionary of American Regional English. Volume 1, A-C. Frederic G. Cassidy, ed. Cambridge, Mass.: Harvard University Press, 1985. 903p. $66.00. ISBN 0-674-20511-1. LC 84-29025.

The first of a projected 5-volume set and the only work of its kind, this dictionary represents an effort to systematically record the variations in English spoken in different sections of the United States. It includes unusual meanings for common terms, regional colloquialisms, and words found only among particular social or ethnic groups. None are found in standard dictionaries.

Each entry gives definition, part of speech, variant spellings, pronunciation, alternative forms, usage labels, and cross-references. The work has dated quotations that illustrate the word's evolution and computer-generated maps that show geographical distribution of the word's usage. This work, no doubt, will become a classic. [R: ARBA 86; BL, 1 Apr 86; LJ, 1 Nov 85; LJ, 15 Apr 86; WLB, Nov 85]

■ *Facts on File Dictionary of 20th Century Allusions*. *See* entry 169.

■ *Grand Allusions*. *See* entry 170.

1428 New Dictionary of American Slang. Robert L. Chapman, ed. New York: Harper & Row, 1986. 485p. $27.50. ISBN 0-06-181157-2. LC 86-45086.

A worthy successor to Wentworth and Flexner's *Dictionary of American Slang* (2d ed. Crowell, 1975), now out of print, Chapman's work provides slang from all periods, plus hundreds of new terms coined during the past two decades that reflect the drug scene, the computer age, the yuppie generation, and many other facets of society. Other entries update information contained in the earlier work.

Entries provide pronunciation, word-class and dating labels, definitions, illustrative phrases, and cross-references. Like others of its kind, this dictionary contains taboo or vulgar words and similar non-standard terms that are not found in general dictionaries of English. [R: ARBA 88; BL, 15 Dec 86]

1429 Rawson, Hugh. **Wicked Words.** New York: Crown, 1989. 435p. $24.95. ISBN 0-517-57334-2. LC 89-672.

Wicked Words challenges the adage: "Sticks and stones may break my bones, but names will never hurt me." It focuses on insults, curses, and other degrading invectives. Rawson, who used standard slang dictionaries and other sources to compile this unusual work, defines and traces the history of more than 1,000 acerbic words and phrases. Entries often include additional insulting words; for example, under *blockhead*, one finds, *addlehead*, *airhead*, *hardhead*, and *pointed or pointy head*. Thoroughly researched and very readable, this work is an appropriate selection for high school libraries. [R: BL, 1 Jan 90]

1430 Similes Dictionary: A Collection of More Than 16,000 Comparison Phrases.... Elyse Sommer and Mike Sommer, eds. Detroit: Gale, 1988. 950p. $68.00. ISBN 0-8103-4361-4. LC 87-36109.

This work explains over 16,000 similes or comparative phrases (e.g., "crazy as a bedbug," "fading like young joy," "smart as a whip"), all arranged in 558 thematic categories, such as anger, ability, happiness, duty, and intelligence. These figurative expressions are taken from a wide range of sources listed in the bibliography. Numerous cross-references and an alphabetical list of the similes follow each group. [R: ARBA 90]

1431 Spears, Richard A. **NTC's American Idioms Dictionary.** Lincolnwood, Ill.: National Textbook, 1987. 463p. $9.95pa. ISBN 0-8442-5450-9. LC 86-63996.

This work, which opens with a long exposition on how to use the dictionary, provides extensive coverage of American idioms. The main entry gives the full form of the idiom, followed by variant and shorter versions. Additional access is provided by the 100-page phrase finder index. Special types of phrases (e.g., slang, folksy, informal) are so labeled, but Spears makes "no attempt to instruct the user in English grammar." Entries include one or more definitions and examples of usage. Recommended for secondary schools. [R: ARBA 88; BL, 1 Oct 87]

1432 Thesaurus of American Slang. Robert Chapman, ed. New York: Harper & Row, 1989. 489p. $22.50. ISBN 0-06-016140-X. LC 89-45029.

This work differs from conventional compendia of slang, such as *New Dictionary of American Slang*. The *Thesaurus* gives definitions, parts of speech, and illustrative sentences that use slang terms and terms of standard speech. Then it lists their slang synonyms (the main body of the entry) and refers to related or similar terms. Indexing by slang term provides access to its word entry or cluster of synonyms. Many of the slang words refer to sex, drugs, alcohol consumption, and body functions. [R: BL, 15 Feb 90; WLB, Jan 90]

EPONYMS

1433 Beeching, Cyril Leslie. **A Dictionary of Eponyms**. 3d ed. London: Library Association; distr., American Library Association, 1989. 218p. $28.50. ISBN 0-85365-559-6.

Eponyms are words derived from names of people. The 3d edition of this British work explains the origin of 511 numbered entries, an increase of 111 over the previous edition (1983). Explanations are clearly written and often amusing. A subject index enables the reader to find eponyms on a particular subject.

The Dictionary of Eponyms: Names That Became Words by Robert Hendrickson (Stein and Day, 1985), a reprint of a work published in 1972, contains 3,500 words named after people and animals. Beeching is less expensive and includes many words that have emerged over the last two decades. [R: ARBA 91; BL, 15 Dec 90; Kliatt, Jan 89]

1434 **Webster's New World Dictionary of Eponyms: Common Words from Proper Names**. By Auriel Douglas. New York: Prentice Hall Press, 1990. 238p. $7.95pa. ISBN 0-13-949926-1. LC 90-12181.

This pocket-sized paperback presents shelving problems, but it contains some 800 interesting descriptions of common words derived from proper names. Definitions of the word, the name of the person from whom it "descended," and brief information about that person make up the entries. [R: ARBA 91]

ETYMOLOGY

1435 **The Barnhart Dictionary of Etymology**. Robert K. Barnhart, ed. Bronx, N.Y.: H. W. Wilson, 1988. 1284p. $59.00. ISBN 0-8242-0745-9. LC 87-27994.

This work, the first scholarly etymological dictionary to appear in almost 25 years, is edited by Robert K. Barnhart, who coedited several well-known works with Clarence Barnhart, his father. These include *The World Book Dictionary* and *Third Barnhart Dictionary of New English*. Several eminent U.S. language scholars have ably assisted him.

The 30,000 entries focus on current U.S. English and provide spelling variations, pronunciation, part of speech, a short definition, date of first recorded use in English, information about the language from which the word evolved, and (in some cases) comments on the word's history. Words of U.S. origin are so indicated. The work includes scientific and technical words, regional English, slang, product names, and recent words. Recommended for high schools. [R: ARBA 89; BL, 15 Dec 88; LJ, 15 Apr 89]

1436 Ciardi, John. **Good Words to You: An All-New Dictionary and Native's Guide to the Unknown American Language**. New York: Harper & Row, 1987. 343p. $19.95. ISBN 0-06-015691-0. LC 86-45647.

Ciardi, the late American editor and poet, has provided this delightful book on the American language. Its predecessors are *A Browser's Dictionary and Native's Guide to the Unknown American Language* (Harper & Row, 1980) and *A Second Browser's Dictionary* (1983, now out of print). He said of his books that they are for "those who will be pleased to ramble beyond the standard dictionaries to a more intimate conversation with words and phrases and their origins and shifting histories." Whether one wishes to know how "long in the tooth" came to mean getting on in years or the origin of the term *hinterland*, the volumes will supply an authoritative explanation, presented with wit and charm.

This volume and *Browser's Dictionary*, which is still available, should appeal to middle and high school students, for whom they are highly recommended. [R: ARBA 89]

E+
1437 Freeman, Morton S. **The Story behind the Word**. Philadelphia: ISI Press, 1985. 294p. (Professional Writing Series). $19.95; $14.95pa. ISBN 0-89495-046-0; 0-89495-047-9pa.

The origins of *robot*, *sideburns*, *jinx*, *denim*, *humble pie*, and *tinker's damn* are among the many stories Freeman tells about words. The stories are written in a delightful style that will be enjoyed by students from middle school onward. [R: ARBA 86; BL, 1 Apr 86; BR, May/June 86; Kliatt, Winter 86; WLB, Dec 85]

E+
1438 Limburg, Peter R. **Stories behind Words: The Origins and Histories of 285 English Words**. Bronx, N.Y.: H. W. Wilson, 1986. 288p. $35.00. ISBN 0-8242-0718-1. LC 85-26398.

Limburg's work explains the evolution of 285 words, how they entered the language, and how their meaning changed over the centuries. The entries are arranged in seven chapters, each related to a theme: mood and character, democracy and aristocracy, religion, sorcery and superstition, eating and drinking, dress, and names (e.g., Cardigan, Boycott, Sandwich) that have become words. Children and young people, upper elementary through high school, will be intrigued with this delightful work. [R: ARBA 88]

1439   Morris, William, and Mary Morris. **Morris Dictionary of Word and Phrase Origins**. 2d ed. New York: Harper & Row, 1988. 669p. $28.00. ISBN 0-06-015862-X. LC 87-45651.

The Morrises, well-known lexicographers, published a dictionary of the same title in 1977, a revision of a three-volume work published between 1962 and 1971. This new revision, which provides histories of interesting words and phrases in the English language, is similar in concept to several books by John Ciardi. Like Ciardi's works, the etymologies and phrase origins are presented in a readable style, making them a joy to browse. For libraries holding the first edition, this is not an essential purchase; others should consider it. [R: ARBA 89; BL, 1 Oct 88]

1440   Rees, Nigel. **Why Do We Say...? Words and Sayings and Where They Come From**. London: Blandford Press; distr., New York: Sterling Publishing, 1987. 224p. $17.95. ISBN 0-7137-1944-3.

Why Do We Say...? answers that question for some 500 expressions, such as "sowing his wild oats," and "one's name is Mudd." Interesting explanations are arranged by key word, but the text is not indexed. This work is similar to the Laurence Urdang works *A Hog on Ice* (Harper & Row, 1985), *Heavens to Betsy* (Harper & Row, 1986), *Thereby Hangs a Tale* (Harper & Row, 1985), *Horsefeathers* (Harper & Row, 1987), and *The Whole Ball of Wax and Other Colloquial Phrases* (Perigree Books/ Putnam, 1988), all of which deserve a place on high school library shelves. [R: ARBA 89]

1441   **Webster's Word Histories**. Springfield, Mass.: Merriam-Webster, 1989. 526p. $14.95. ISBN 0-87779-048-5. LC 89-23427.

This excellent and highly readable work explains the probable origin of some 1,500 words and traces the history of each. The articles are substantial, some almost two pages in length. The treatment is more detailed than that given by *Morris Dictionary of Word and Phrase Origins*, but the latter is more comprehensive. Entries in *The Barnhart Dictionary of Etymology* are briefer. All are worth-while additions to high school libraries. [R: ARBA 91; BL, 1 Dec 89; VOYA, Mar/Apr 90; WLB, Jan 90]

FOREIGN PHRASES

1442   Guinagh, Kevin. **Dictionary of Foreign Phrases and Abbreviations**. 3d ed. Bronx, N.Y.: H. W. Wilson, 1982. 288p. $40.00. ISBN 0-8242-0675-4. LC 82-8486.

This work represents a substantial revision of the 2d edition, which appeared in 1972. Foreign expressions, proverbs, mottoes, maxims, abbreviations, and more are listed in a single alphabet. Languages covered include French, German, Greek, Hebrew, Irish, Italian, Latin, Portuguese, Russian, and Spanish. Entries for the over 5,000 phrases and abbreviations commonly used in English often give brief explanations of obscure meaning or items of particular historical interest. [R: ARBA 84; BL, 1 Dec 83; WLB, Apr 83]

1443   **The Harper Dictionary of Foreign Terms**. 3d ed. Eugene Ehrlich, ed. New York: Harper & Row, 1987. 423p. $20.00. ISBN 0-06-181576-4. LC 86-46061.

This revision of C. O. Sylvester Mawson's *Dictionary of Foreign Terms*, last updated in 1979, includes over 15,000 words and phrases in some 50 languages for a variety of fields (e.g., food, the arts, business, diplomacy, history). The new edition adds expressions from Japanese, Russian, and other languages, to which an English index gives access. Unfortunately, there is no guide to pronunciation. This is the standard one-volume source for foreign terms often used in English. Recommended for high schools. [R: ARBA 88; RBB, 15 Nov 87]

RHYMES

1444   Espy, Willard R. **Words to Rhyme With: For Poets and Song Writers....** New York: Facts on File, 1986. 656p. $50.00. ISBN 0-8160-1237-7. LC 85-31216.

The 80,000 rhyming words in this book are divided by sound into single, double, and triple rhyme lists, arranged in each section by initial vowels. Syllables are spelled phonetically. This reference tool is so complex that its use is restricted to high school students. It is the most comprehensive rhyming dictionary available. [R: ARBA 87; LJ, 15 Sept 86; WLB, Nov 86]

E+

1445   Israel, Peter, and Peg Streep. **The Kid's World Almanac Rhyming Dictionary: A Guide for Young Poets and Songwriters.** New York: Pharos Books/St. Martin's Press, 1991. 134p. $12.95. ISBN 0-88687-576-5. LC 90-42407.

The introduction provides instruction on rhymes and using the book. In the main body, two or three entries appear on every page, giving alternate spellings (where appropriate), a list of rhyming words, and a list of harder words in paragraph form. Some entries include tips, quizzes, a black-and-white illustration, and warnings against using certain rhyming sounds. The index lists entries and alternate spellings with pronunciation, but not every word listed is included. Despite the fact that the authors give a simplistic treatment of poetry, the dictionary is recommended and will be useful to elementary and junior high students. [R: BL, 1 June 91]

1446   **Webster's Compact Rhyming Dictionary.** Springfield, Mass.: Merriam-Webster, 1987. 382p. $4.95. ISBN 0-87779-185-6. LC 86-33165.

This dictionary arranges some 50,000 words by rhyming sounds, all in one alphabet. To use it, one looks up the sound that needs to rhyme and then finds a list of words with similar sounds, arranged by one, two, or three syllables. Alternate spellings of sounds are cross-referenced. Pronunciation is based on *Webster's Ninth New Collegiate Dictionary*. Recommended for middle and high schools. [R: ARBA 88]

1447   Young, Sue. **The New Comprehensive American Rhyming Dictionary.** New York: William Morrow, 1991. 622p. $24.95. ISBN 0-688-10360-X. LC 90-19165.

Organized by vowel sounds and final syllables expressing those sounds, this work uses its own easy-to-use pronunciation system. Young's dictionary, which deserves a place beside more standard works, offers many more phrases and slang terms and does not emphasize matching the consonant sound preceding an accented vowel, as other dictionaries do. This is an imaginative, practical work. Recommended for high schools. [R: BL, 15 June 91; WLB, June 91]

SPELLING AND PRONUNCIATION

E+

1448   Chang, Sam H., with Frank T. Phipps. **The Spelling Bee Speller.** Akron, Ohio: Hondale, 1984. 3v. $19.95pa./set. ISBN 0-942462-01-7. LC 81-90754.

These study guides were prepared for spelling bee participants in grades 3 through 8. Volume 1, *The First Round*; volume 2, *The Middle Round*; and volume 3, *The Final Round*, contain 1,000 words each that are commonly used in spelling bees.

Words, grouped according to similarities in meaning and sound, are shown in phonetic letters with diacritical markings (not spelled), followed by a definition and a simple sentence that uses the word. The correct spelling for all words on facing pages is provided at the bottom of the right-hand page. Recommended for elementary and middle school libraries. [R: ARBA 85; SLJ, May 84; WLB, May 84]

1449   **NBC Handbook of Pronunciation.** 4th ed. By Eugene Ehrlick and Raymond Hand, Jr. New York: HarperCollins, 1991. 539p. $10.95pa. ISBN 0-06-096574-6. LC 90-55604.

This standard handbook provides pronunciation for 21,000 difficult proper names and words commonly "used by educated persons in the greater part of the United States." Those names no longer in use have been deleted, and outdated pronunciations have been replaced. The dictionary is intended as a quick-reference source for broadcasters, but it is equally useful to others. A respelling system indicates current pronunciations. Recommended for high schools. [R: ARBA 86; BL, 1 Oct 84]

1450 **Webster's Instant Word Guide**. Springfield, Mass.: Merriam-Webster, 1980. 384p. $4.95. ISBN 0-87779-273-9.

This compact volume contains 35,000 spelled and divided words, including words of similar spelling or pronunciation and hard-to-spell U.S. place-names. The appendix lists 1,500 abbreviations, punctuation rules, and weights and measures with metric equivalents. This is an ideal handbook for those needing a quick-reference guide to spelling. [R: ARBA 81]

SYNONYMS

1451 **The Doubleday Roget's Thesaurus in Dictionary Form**. rev. ed. New York: Doubleday, c1977, 1987. 804p. $13.95. ISBN 0-385-23997-1. LC 76-7696.

Despite the words "Roget" and "thesaurus" in the title, which may imply a classified arrangement, the entry words in this volume are listed in alphabetical order. Some 250,000 synonyms and antonyms, including slang, are provided, but with little guidance in word selection. This work's arrangement will appeal to those who find *Roget's International Thesaurus* awkward to use.

1452 **Facts on File Student's Thesaurus**. Paul Hellweg, ed. New York: Facts on File, 1991. 287p. $24.95. ISBN 0-8160-1634-8. LC 90-3185.

Designed for students in middle school and junior high, this thesaurus incorporates entries for more than 5,000 of the most commonly used works in English, with synonyms, antonyms, and sample sentences for each meaning. For ordinary words that may have 25 or more synonyms, this work lists only the most obvious. This clear and easy-to-use work is recommended. [R: ARBA 92; RBB, 15 Jan 90]

1453 Hook, J. N. **The Appropriate Word: Finding the Best Way to Say What You Mean**. New York: Addison-Wesley, 1990. 259p. $18.95; $12.45pa. ISBN 0-201-52323-X; 0-201-57703-8pa. LC 89-18616.

Some 2,300 entries cover around 4,000 words with synonyms and comparative or contrasted words. Clear and yet humorous explanations are enhanced by a unique set of symbols and terms. "Weed" indicates words used inappropriately; FF (Family and Friend) and SWE (Standard Written English) point out differences in appropriateness of word usage. This work contains sound advice for students and serves as a worthy companion to more standard works. [R: ARBA 91]

1454 **Illustrated Reverse Dictionary**. John Ellison Kahn, ed. Pleasantville, N.Y.: Reader's Digest; distr., New York: Random House, c1990, 1991. 608p. $25.00. ISBN 0-89577-352-X. LC 90-39606.

Although akin to a thesaurus, this attractive book is not a dictionary in the true sense. Its purpose is to jog users' memories and help them find the right words through synonyms, common phrases, antonyms, and word association. It groups associated words and phrases under a single access point. Each of the 70,000 words included is defined and related to its access word. Quick reference charts define words for a subject (e.g., deciduous trees, embroidery stitches). Over 400 color illustrations, diagrams, charts, and photographs help to clarify the text.

Students and other users must be encouraged to try this new work, since it is unlike traditional thesauri or synonym dictionaries. The *Reverse Dictionary* has enough to offer through its new format to deserve a recommendation for secondary schools. [R: BL, 15 Apr 91]

1455 **Roget's II: The New Thesaurus**. expanded ed. By the editors of the *American Heritage Dictionary*. Boston: Houghton Mifflin, 1988. 1v. (unpaged). $12.95; $4.95pa. ISBN 0-395-48317-4; 0-395-48318-2pa. LC 88-8842.

Unlike the traditional Roget thesauri, *Roget's II* is alphabetically arranged to provide "rapid access to synonyms, which are grouped by precise meaning." This work, which can stand alone without the support of a general dictionary, offers brief definitions of words, parts of speech, synonyms, near-synonyms, antonyms, near-antonyms, and idioms, but provides no index. A system of secondary entries cross-references words to 17,000 main entries.

Whether this revamped method of organizing a synonym dictionary is more useful than the conventional classified system of *Roget's International Thesaurus* or the alphabetically arranged *Webster's Collegiate Thesaurus* remains moot; *Roget's II* is worth a try. Recommended for high school libraries. [R: ARBA 90; RBB, 15 Jan 89]

1456 Roget's International Thesaurus. 4th ed. By Peter M. Chapman. New York: HarperCollins, 1977. 1347p. $14.95; $15.95 (thumb indexed); $10.05pa. ISBN 0-690-00011-3; 0-690-00011-1 (thumb indexed); 0-06-091169-7pa.

Like its ancestor, the pioneering work of Peter Mark Roget (1852), this volume classifies thought under 990 categories, thereby offering the user a variety of ways to express an idea. Boldface type indicates the most commonly used terms. The index of over 250,000 entries is essential for the use of the thesaurus. [R: ARBA 78; WLB, Jan 78]

E+

1457 Ryan, Elizabeth A. **Student Thesaurus.** Mahwah, N.J.: Troll Associates, 1990. 160p. $14.89; $6.95pa. ISBN 0-8167-1914-4; 0-8167-1856-3pa. LC 89-20305.

Designed for children in the middle grades, this thesaurus arranges more than 2,000 words alphabetically. At least three synonyms are given for each main entry word, printed in boldface type; antonyms that follow are printed in red. Two or more humorous line drawings, which show meaning, are included on every page.

This dictionary contains about the same number of entries as *A First Thesaurus* and includes more than *In Other Words*. *Student Thesaurus* is a good supplementary work, but it is not an essential purchase for elementary and middle schools. [R: BL, 15 Apr 90]

E

1458 Scott, Foresman Beginning Thesaurus. By Andrew Schiller and William A. Jenkins. Glenview, Ill.: Scott, Foresman, 1988. 240p. $9.95. ISBN 0-673-12493-2.

1459 Scott, Foresman Junior Thesaurus. By Andrew Schiller and William A. Jenkins. Glenview, Ill.: Scott, Foresman, 1988. 447p. $11.95. ISBN 0-673-12494-0.

Beginning Thesaurus, designed for children 8 to 12 for use on their own, contains some 100 alphabetically arranged base words in boldface, with secondary synonyms entered in regular type. Simple definitions and synonyms are provided for each word; antonyms appear in blue at the end of the entry. The over 1,000 synonyms and antonyms are enhanced by full-color illustrations.

Junior Thesaurus, a similar work for ages 10 to 14, gives at least a page of synonyms for the entry word. One reviewer recommends it over the *Beginning Thesaurus*, since most of the material contained in the latter can be found in standard children's dictionaries. Both works are recommended, however, and are excellent introductions to this type of reference tool. [R: ARBA 90]

1460 Webster's Collegiate Thesaurus. Springfield, Mass.: Merriam-Webster, 1976. 944p. $12.95. ISBN 0-87779-069-8. LC 75-45167.

Despite the word *thesaurus* in its title, this work is arranged alphabetically rather than in a classified arrangement. The 20,000 entries list synonyms, related words, contrasted words (near-synonyms), and antonyms—some 100,000 in all. A concise definition after each entry is helpful, but differences in word usage is not explained, a disadvantage for many. *Webster's New Dictionary of Synonyms* is more helpful in this regard.

Webster's School Thesaurus (Merriam-Webster, 1978), similar in format, is directed toward junior high and high school levels. It includes 43,000 entries for synonyms, antonyms, idiomatic expressions, related words, and contrasted words. [R: ARBA 77]

1461 Webster's Compact Dictionary of Synonyms. Springfield, Mass.: Merriam-Webster, 1987. 374p. $4.95. ISBN 0-87779-186-4. LC 86-33138.

This inexpensive dictionary contains more than 700 synonym paragraphs designed to assist users in selecting the right word for a given context. Each entry presents a group of synonyms, lists the meaning of each, the distinguishing connotations, and an example of usage. Although limited in its scope, this authoritative dictionary treats those words most commonly requiring differentiation. The volume's ease of use and clear definitions make it an excellent choice for secondary schools. [R: ARBA 88]

1462 Webster's New Dictionary of Synonyms. Springfield, Mass.: Merriam-Webster, c1973, 1984. 942p. $14.95. ISBN 0-87779-241-0.

This synonym dictionary is an outstanding work, easier to use and more precise and complete than any other reference source of its kind. Synonyms and similar words, alphabetically arranged, are carefully defined, discriminated, and illustrated with thousands of quotations. The entries also include antonyms and analogous words. Highly recommended.

E
1463   Wittels, Harriet, and Joan Greisman. **A First Thesaurus**. New York: Golden Book/Western Publishing, 1985. 126p. $5.95pa. ISBN 0-307-15835-7. LC 84-82602.

A good basic thesaurus for children in grades 3 through 6, this dictionary provides 2,000 alphabetically arranged entry words, listing synonyms from the simplest to the most sophisticated. If the word has more than one meaning, separate entries are provided. Antonyms, printed in red, follow synonyms. The work is also useful to older children learning English as a second language. [R: ARBA 87; SLJ, Feb 86]

USAGE AND GRAMMAR

See also **Writing and Reports** in **Communications**.

1464   Bryson, Bill. **The Facts on File Dictionary of Troublesome Words**. rev. ed. New York: Facts on File, 1987. 192p. $22.95. ISBN 0-8160-1933-9. LC 87-33046.

This concise dictionary, which first appeared in 1984, explains the differences in meaning between words often confused with each other, and provides examples of their use from carefully edited sources such as the *New York Times*. Alphabetically arranged entries, with frequent cross-references, are often humorous. A bibliography of usage and style manual, a guide to punctuation, and a glossary of grammar terms conclude the volume. Recommended for high schools. [R: ARBA 89; BL, 15 Nov 88]

1465   Follett, Wilson. **Modern American Usage**. Jacques Barzun and others, comps. and eds. New York: Hill and Wang, c1966, 1979. 436p. $10.95pa. ISBN 0-8090-1039-X.

Despite its age, this standard guide to the language deserves a place on library shelves. Follett, a famous U.S. language scholar and champion of good usage, provides sound advice concerning the use and misuse of U.S. English. He also challenges readers to think for themselves. [R: ARBA 75]

1466   Fowler, Henry Watson. **A Dictionary of Modern English Usage**. 2d ed. Revised and enlarged by Ernest Gowers. New York: Oxford University Press, c1965, 1987. 725p. $24.95; $10.95pa. ISBN 0-19-869115-7; 0-19-281389-7pa.

This classic British work, one of the most quoted dictionaries of its kind, is an authoritative guide to proper use of the English language. The 2,000 entries deal extensively with grammar and syntax, use and misuse of words, and disputed spellings and pronunciations. It also contains information on etymology and comparisons between British and American usage. Gowers's revision deletes some obsolete terms and adds newer entries.

1467   Freeman, Morton S. **The Wordwatcher's Guide to Good Writing & Grammar**. Cincinnati, Ohio: Writer's Digest Books, 1990. 296p. $15.95pa. ISBN 0-89879-436-6. LC 90-12514.

In a conversational style, this volume addresses common problems such as usage, pronunciation, and spelling, but it does not answer all questions. However, its well-organized format and readability make it a good choice for middle and high school libraries. [R: ARBA 91; BL, 15 Oct 90]

1468   Lewis, Norman. **The New American Dictionary of Good English: An A-Z Guide to Grammar and Correct Usage**. New York: New American Library, 1987. 294p. $4.95pa. ISBN 0-451-15023-6. LC 87-62469.

The small size and paperback format of this work may suggest to some librarians that it should not be placed in the reference collection. However, it does provide cogent explanations for troublesome words (e.g., lie and lay, farther and further) and words often confused with each other (e.g., feeble-minded and moronic). There are occasional self-tests for readers to determine their understanding of word differences. Parts of speech are also treated, making this a useful grammar book. [R: ARBA 89; Kliatt, Apr 88]

1469   Morris, William, and Mary Morris. **Harper Dictionary of Contemporary Usage**. 2d ed. New York: Harper & Row, 1985. 641p. $22.50. ISBN 0-06-181606-X. LC 83-48797.

This work treats virtually all aspects of the language, including idioms, slang, vulgar words, and regionalisms, providing valuable guidance in its use. This revision updates the 1975 edition and reflects current trends in usage, including new words and phrases. The editors consulted a panel of writers, editors, and philologists, who have offered their opinions on debatable points. Comments are often lively. Highly recommended for junior high and high school libraries. [R: ARBA 86; BL, 1 Nov 86]

1470   The Painless Path to Proper English Usage. Stan Malotte, ed. New York: St. Martin's Press, c1986, 1987. 127p. $8.95pa. ISBN 0-312-00714-0. LC 87-4469.

This work presents 126 pairs of frequently confused words (e.g., everyday and every day, that and which) in brief paragraphs. It also include mnemonic devices and cartoon illustrations. Junior high and high school students will find this slim volume a helpful tool. [R: ARBA 89]

1471   Phythian, B. A. A Concise Dictionary of Confusables: All Those Impossible Words You Never Get Right. New York: John Wiley, 1990. $10.95pa. ISBN 0-471-52880-3. LC 90-35359.

Phythian, a British headmaster, has produced a commendable work that attempts to clarify differences in meaning between words that are often confused with one another. Some 2,000 words have been selected for inclusion. Alphabetically arranged entries are clear and informative. This work will not replace other standard usage dictionaries, but it is a useful supplement to them. Recommended for secondary schools. [R: BL, 1 Jan 91]

1472   Roberts, Philip Davies. Plain English: A User's Guide. New York: Viking Penguin, 1987. 191p. $5.95pa. ISBN 0-14-008407-X.

Plain English, a useful quick-reference guide for high school students, covers all aspects of usage—grammar, vocabulary, topography, dialect, and style—and includes information on letter writing, irregular verbs, and definitions of grammatical terms. Common errors are discussed and variations between British and American English noted. Despite its British bias, this work is recommended. [R: ARBA 89]

1473   Urdang, Laurence. The Dictionary of Confusable Words. New York: Facts on File, 1988. 391p. $35.00. ISBN 0-8106-1650-X. LC 88-045090.

Of British imprint, with some changes for American readers, this dictionary defines everyday terms often confused with each other (e.g., *atomic* and *nuclear*, *motor* and *engine*). They are drawn from science, art, business, and specialized areas. The major shortcoming is Urdang's occasional use of technical language, but overall this is a worthwhile addition to high school libraries. [R: ARBA 89; BL, 15 Nov 88]

1474   Webster's Dictionary of English Usage. Springfield, Mass.: Merriam-Webster, 1989. 978p. $18.95. ISBN 0-87779-032-9. LC 88-37248.

Middle and high school libraries should hold this 500-entry dictionary, which emphasizes the current use of English. Entries vary from a few lines to several pages, treating such terms as "ain't," "hopefully," "you know," "irregardless," "prioritize," and "underwhelm." The work covers both historical and contemporary perspectives, grammar, and pronunciation. Other articles deal with general usage. Spelling and pronunciation variations are explained. The dictionary also includes some 20,000 illustrative quotations from past and contemporary sources.

Webster's will not replace other standards in the field, such as *Harper Dictionary of Contemporary Usage* and *Dictionary of Modern English Usage*, but it is a current, reliable source. Highly recommended. [R: ARBA 90; BL, 15 Sept 89; WLB, June 89]

1475   The World Almanac Guide to Good Word Usage. Martin H. Manser with Jeffrey McQuain, eds. New York: World Almanac/St. Martin's Press, 1989. 274p. $19.95. ISBN 0-88687-570-6. LC 89-33731.

This guide has the advantage over similar works by being more current, less dogmatic, less technical, and easier to understand. Edwin Newman, considered an authority on the language, wrote the introduction and gave the book his endorsement.

The guide covers five main problem areas: spelling, pronunciation, grammar and punctuation, usage, and buzzwords. Entries focus on the usage question and give examples of correct usage. This dictionary, along with *Webster's Dictionary of English Usage*, is recommended. [R: ARBA 91]

CHINESE DICTIONARIES

E+

1476   The Facts on File English/Chinese Visual Dictionary. By Jean-Claude Corbeil and Mein-ven Lee. New York: Facts on File, 1988. 823p. $35.00. ISBN 0-8160-2043-4. LC 88-16609.

A part of the Facts on File Visual Dictionary series, this work contains illustrations of more than 2,000 objects and their parts, with clearly identified terminology in English and Chinese. Students from grades 7 through adult can look up a word from a picture or find a picture from a word. Indexed in Chinese and English. Other dictionaries in this series cover French and Spanish. [R: ARBA 90; BR, Nov/Dec 89]

FRENCH DICTIONARIES

E+
1477 **The Ashley Dictionary**. Toronto: Editions Renyi, 1989. unpaged. $19.95. ISBN 0-921606-00-1.

E+
1478 **Dictionnaire Français**. Toronto: Editions Renyi, 1989. unpaged. $19.95. ISBN 0-921606-02-8.
These dictionaries, intended for children ages 8 to 13, present 3,300 alphabetically arranged and numbered words. *The Ashley Dictionary* lists words in French with English equivalents; *Dictionnaire Français* gives words in English with French equivalents. The latter work also includes a French index keyed to the English word number, making it useful as a French-English dictionary. Brightly colored cartoons illustrate both volumes. [R: ARBA 90]

1479 **Concise Oxford French Dictionary**. 2d ed. French-English section by H. Ferrar. English-French section by J. A. Hutchinson and J. D. Biard. New York: Clarendon Press/Oxford University Press, 1985. 912p. $32.50; $11.95pa. ISBN 0-19-864126-5; 0-19-864157-5pa. LC 80-40695.
The *Concise Oxford* is an excellent choice for secondary level. The French-English section, the larger portion, provides full definitions and phonetic pronunciations; the English-French section (which uses British spellings) gives only French equivalents. Labels indicate how meaning changes with use and identify vulgar and popular expressions.

1480 Eastman, Philip D. *Cat in the Hat* **Beginner Book Dictionary in French and English**. New York: Random House, 1965. 133p. $14.95. ISBN 0-394-81063-5. LC 65-22650.
This French-language version of *Cat in the Hat Beginner Book Dictionary* is the same work with added translations of each caption printed in a different color. It also provides a guide to pronunciation.

E+
1481 **The Facts on File English/French Visual Dictionary**. By Jean-Claude Corbeil and Ariane Archambault. New York: Facts on File, 1987. 924p. $35.00. ISBN 0-8160-1545-7. LC 87-9037.
This bilingual treatment of English and French is part of the Facts on File Visual Dictionary series. Each page contains line drawings with objects and their parts labeled in the two languages. Separate indexes provide general access and thematic/specialized indexing in French and English. The dictionary is especially valuable for identifying objects encountered in everyday life but rarely included in traditional dictionaries. Although limited to nouns, this is a clear, useful, and entertaining work. Another dictionary in the series covers Chinese. [R: ARBA 88; SLJ, May 88]

E
1482 Lipton, Gladys C. **Beginning French Bilingual Dictionary: A Beginner's Guide in Words and Pictures**. 2d ed. Hauppauge, N.Y.: Barron's Educational Series, 1989. 385p. $4.95pa. ISBN 0-8120-4273-5. LC 89-6800.
This dictionary is designed for elementary school students who have just begun to learn French. It provides short, simple definitions; masculine and feminine articles; an example sentence that uses the word (with translation); and one or two small drawings on every page. Pronunciation is given in the phonemic alphabet, an easier system to use than the International Phonetic Alphabet. The appendix contains lists of days, months, personal names, classroom expressions, numbers, conversion tables, grammar terms, and a brief French verb supplement. The work does have two disadvantages: small print and sample sentences that express sex-role stereotypes. [R: ARBA 90]

1483 **The Oxford-Duden Pictorial French-English Dictionary**. New York: Clarendon Press/Oxford University Press, 1983. 1v. (various paging). $49.95. ISBN 0-19-864153-2. LC 83-4262.
Based on the 3d edition of the German Bildworterbuch (published as three volumes of the Duden series of German picture dictionaries), this dictionary contains labeled illustrations (in French and English) of specific objects and their component parts. No written definitions are provided. The

arrangement is by broad category such as recreation, animals and plants, and communications and information technology. Indexed in French and English. [R: ARBA 84; SLJ, Dec 83]

GERMAN DICTIONARIES

1484 The Oxford Duden German Dictionary: German-English, English-German. Edited by the Dudenredaktion and the German Section of the Oxford University Press Dictionary Department. New York: Clarendon Press/Oxford University Press, 1990. 1696p. $24.95 (thumb indexed). ISBN 0-19-864171-0. LC 90-30292.

The editors of this new German dictionary, which took more than a decade to compile, have made a concerted effort to overcome some of the shortcomings of bilingual dictionaries. "Sense indicators" are used to clarify variant meanings and to make the transition from one language to the other easier and more accurate. Sentences and phrases are frequently used, and subject labels indicate special vocabulary for a field. The publisher's claim that this work contains the "fullest and most up-to-date coverage" of any one-volume dictionary is most likely justified. [R: ARBA 91]

1485 The Oxford-Duden Pictorial German-English Dictionary. Edited by Dudenredaktion and the German Section of the Oxford University Press Dictionary Department. New York: Clarendon Press/Oxford University Press, 1979. 1v. (various paging). $49.95. ISBN 0-19-864135-4.

This Duden pictorial dictionary, similar to those for English and French, includes illustrations for objects, with German and English terms keyed to the pictures. Some 28,000 objects are arranged by 384 activity categories (e.g., playgrounds, department stores, steel production). All terms are indexed in German and English. [R: ARBA 81]

JAPANESE DICTIONARIES

1486 Basic Japanese-English Dictionary. By the Japan Foundation. New York: Oxford University Press, 1989. 958p. $16.95pa. ISBN 0-19-864162-1. LC 88-30642.

Considered the best of its type, this dictionary is designed for nonnative students of the language. Some 3,000 of the most common words and phrases are arranged on the basis of pronunciation with sentences in Japanese script (*hiragana*, *katakana*, *kanji*, and *romanization*) in the left column and English equivalents on the right. The appendix includes a section on Japanese grammar. Recommended. [R: ARBA 90]

LATIN DICTIONARIES

1487 Simpson, D. P., comp. **Cassell's Latin Dictionary: Latin-English, English-Latin**. New York: Macmillan, 1977. 883p. $23.95; $9.95pa. ISBN 0-02-522580-4; 0-02-522630-4pa. LC 77-7670.

As are all Cassell's dictionaries, this is a standard work and a good choice for libraries that require a basic Latin dictionary. The 30,000 entries include geographical and proper names, etymological notes, and illustrative quotations.

RUSSIAN DICTIONARIES

1488 Katzner, Kenneth. **English-Russian, Russian-English Dictionary**. New York: John Wiley, 1984. 904p. $94.95; $29.95pa. ISBN 0-471-86763-2; 0-471-84442-Xpa. LC 82-24747.

This work is recommended for high schools with Russian language programs. It is the first English-Russian, Russian-English dictionary published in the United States and intended for English-speaking users. Russian entries show stress, part of speech, gender, irregularities, usage, synonyms, and morphological changes. Explanatory notes are in English. In addition to standard vocabulary, the work includes colloquial and idiomatic expressions, acronyms, and abbreviations. [R: ARBA 85]

1489 The Oxford English-Russian Dictionary. P. S. Falla, ed. New York: Clarendon Press/Oxford University Press, c1984, 1991. 1052p. $27.50. ISBN 0-19-864118-0. LC 83-17344.

1490   **The Oxford Russian-English Dictionary.** 2d ed. By Marcus Wheeler. New York: Clarendon Press/Oxford University Press, c1984, 1990. 930p. $75.00; $27.50pa. ISBN 0-19-864154-0; 0-19-864167-2pa. LC 83-13447.

This paperback reprint of a 1984 set is directed toward English-speaking users, but with a British bias. The *Russian-English Dictionary* contains 70,000 entries, including colloquial vocabulary, idioms, and some technical language. The *English-Russian Dictionary* contains 90,000 English words, phrases, and other vocabulary items. Recommended for all high school libraries that require Russian-language dictionaries. [R: ARBA 85]

SPANISH DICTIONARIES

1491   **The American Heritage Larousse Spanish Dictionary: Spanish/English, English/Spanish.** Boston: Houghton Mifflin, 1986. 572p. $21.95; $3.95pa. ISBN 0-395-32429-7; 0-317-65694-5pa. LC 86-7202.

This high-quality Spanish dictionary features Latin American usage as well as conventional European Spanish on which most dictionaries focus. Useful features of the work include careful discrimination of synonyms and keyed references to the irregular verb table at the beginning of the volume. [R: ARBA 88]

1492   Castillo, Carlos, and others, comps. **The University of Chicago Spanish Dictionary: A New Concise Spanish-English and English-Spanish Dictionary ... Diccionario de la Universidad de Chicago Inglés-Español y Español-Inglés.** 4th ed. Revised by D. Lincoln Canfield. Chicago: University of Chicago Press, 1987. 475p. $19.95; $6.95pa. ISBN 0-226-10400-1; 0-226-10402-8pa. LC 86-24886.

Compiled for the use of American learners of Spanish and Spanish-speaking learners of English, this work makes a special effort to include references to usage in the United States and Spanish America. It provides a short history of the language, a list of 500 common Spanish-English idioms and proverbs, and a similar English-Spanish section. More than 32,000 entries give pronunciation, part of speech, definitions, and occasional examples of usage. This excellent work is recommended for secondary schools. [R: ARBA 88]

1493   **Collins Spanish-English, English-Spanish Dictionary. Collins Diccionario Español-Inglés, Inglés-Español.** 2d ed. By Colin Smith. Don Mills, Ont.: Collins; distr., New York: Prentice Hall Press, 1989. 1v. (various paging). $21.95. ISBN 0-671-67839-6.

This dictionary, first published in 1971, emphasizes British English and Latin American usage, but it is an excellent work that includes thousands of phrases and expressions grouped according to their function in speech. A special section deals with Spanish and English verbs. Recommended for high school libraries. [R: ARBA 90]

E

1494   Eastman, P. D. *Cat in the Hat* **Beginner Dictionary in Spanish and English.** New York: Random House, 1966. 133p. $14.95. ISBN 0-394-81542-4. LC 66-10688.

This book, the Spanish-language version of *Cat in the Hat Beginner Book Dictionary*, reprints the original work, adds Spanish translations of the captions (printed in a different color), and provides a guide to pronunciation.

□ _____ # Literature _____ □

BIBLIOGRAPHIES

See **Children's Literature** for juvenile literature.

1495   Hartman, Donald K., and Jerome Drost, comps. **Themes and Settings in Fiction: A Bibliography of Bibliographies**. Westport, Conn.: Greenwood Press, 1988. 223p. (Bibliographies and Indexes in World Literature, no.14). $39.95. ISBN 0-313-25866-X. LC 88-25082.

This annotated bibliography of bibliographies cites over 1,400 works that provide access to literature and literary criticism. The major section, arranged alphabetically, lists bibliographies of themes and settings in fiction, published between 1900 and 1985. Full bibliographic data and a brief annotation are given for each title. Another section cites other reference tools that list bibliographies. Indexing is by title and subject. Recommended for high schools that require such treatment of world literature. [R: ARBA 90]

1496   Husband, Janet, and Jonathan F. Husband. **Sequels: An Annotated Guide to Novels in Series**. 2d ed. Chicago: American Library Association, 1990. 576p. $35.00. ISBN 0-8389-0533-1. LC 90-180.

This revised edition of a 1982 reference book updates sequence novels through 1989 and includes well-known writers from most popular genres (e.g., Margaret Drabble, Sara Parentsky, Tom Clancy, Philip Roth, Antonia Fraser, Larry McMurtry, Belva Plain). Science Fiction is not as well covered as other genres. Criteria for inclusion are books that show development of plot or characters from title to title, that share a cast of characters, or that are viewed as a series by the author.

Entries, arranged alphabetically by author, list titles in plot order (which does not necessarily coincide with publication date), with a one-sentence annotation for each. Indexed by title and subject (name of main characters, location, and genre). It should be noted that some titles are out of print. [R: ARBA 92; BL, 15 Mar 91]

1497   **Research Guide to Biography and Criticism**. Walton Beacham, ed. Washington, D.C.: Research Publishing, 1985. 2v. $125.00/set. ISBN 0-933833-00-8. LC 85-2188.

This work is designed to assist high school students and college undergraduates in "narrowing and researching topics for terms papers and essay exams and to provide librarians with a tool that will help them lead students to valuable, accessible resources." For each author, an entry provides a chronology of the writer's life, a selective bibliography of works, and a short essay on biographical sources found in most libraries. Recommended for high schools. [R: ARBA 87]

DICTIONARIES AND ENCYCLOPEDIAS

1498   Baldick, Chris. **The Concise Oxford Dictionary of Literary Terms**. New York: Oxford University Press, 1990. 246p. $19.95. ISBN 0-19-811733-7. LC 89-71330.

This work defines more than 1,000 literary terms, old and new, often omitted or not clearly defined in general dictionaries. Most terms are drawn from English, but frequently used foreign words and phrases are included. Those looking for the meaning of "purple patches" or "beat writers" will find those definitions and more, often with a touch of humor. Frequent illustrative examples are provided. Recommended for high schools. [R: ARBA 91; BL, 1 Oct 90; LJ, 1 June 90; WLB, Dec 90]

1499   Beckson, Karl, and Arthur Ganz. **Literary Terms: A Dictionary**. 3d ed. New York: Farrar/Noonday, 1989. 308p. $8.85pa. ISBN 0-374-52177-8. LC 88-34368.

First published under the title *A Reader's Guide to Literary Terms* (1960) and last revised in 1975, this dictionary defines terms, concepts, and theories concerning various aspects of literary history and criticism. Alphabetically arranged terms are clearly and concisely defined with frequent illustrative quotations/excerpts from literature. Sources for further reading are given. The volume concludes with a list of terms arranged by broad categories. There is no index, but within a definition, boldface type indicates that the word used is defined in its own entry. This work is useful on the senior high school level. [R: BL, 1 Dec 89]

■ *Benet's Reader's Encyclopedia of American Literature*. *See* entry 1579.

E +
1500   **Brewer's Dictionary of Phrase and Fable**. 14th ed. By Ivor H. Evans. New York: Harper & Row, 1989. 1220p. $35.00. ISBN 0-06-016200-7. LC 89-45161.

A work that originated in the eighteenth century, this delightful volume contains 15,000 brief entries, 300 new to this edition. Other entries remain largely unchanged. The work includes miscellaneous information about literary characters and allusions, historical people, and literary terms. The material ranges from Greek mythology and the Bible to twentieth-century events.

Old and new expressions are another feature. Under a noun such as "dog," for example, one finds: "to lead a dog's life," "to put on the dog," "to rain cats and dogs," and "you can never scare a dog away from a greasy hide," each with an explanation of its meaning. Numerous lists provide such things as the dying words of famous people, symbols of saints, and flowers and trees in symbolism.

New to this edition is a selective index that gives *see* and *see also* references and groups similar entries under topical headings. This "almsbasket of words," as Ebenezer Brewer (the original compiler) called it, is a classic that all libraries should hold. [R: BL, 15 Mar 90]

1501   **The Cambridge Guide to Literature in English**. Ian Ousby, ed. New York: Cambridge University Press, 1988. 1109p. $39.50. ISBN 0-521-26751-X. LC 87-33129.

This volume deals with the literature of Great Britain, Ireland, Australia, New Zealand, South Africa, Nigeria, and the West Indies. More than 3,100 entries cover authors, titles, characters, and literary terms; they vary in length from a few lines to several columns. Most include critical comments.

The volume resembles *Benet's Reader's Encyclopedia*, which discusses world literature in English. High schools requiring additional studies of literature of the English-speaking world will find the *Cambridge Guide* a worthwhile purchase. [R: ARBA 89; BR, May/June 89]

1502   **Columbia Dictionary of Modern European Literature**. 2d ed. Jean-Albert Bede and William Edgerton, eds. New York: Columbia University Press, 1980. 895p. $125.00. ISBN 0-231-03717-1. LC 80-17082.

This standard work, a revision of the 1947 edition, contains survey articles on 33 national literatures and entries on 1,853 individual authors, contributed by over 500 subject specialists. The concise articles are followed by brief bibliographies of additional sources. This is a good basic reference tool for high school libraries. [R: ARBA 82]

1503   **Cyclopedia of Literary Characters II**. Frank N. Magill, ed. Pasadena, Calif.: Salem Press, 1990. 4v. $300.00/set. ISBN 0-89365-517-2. LC 90-8550.

Similar to the original work published in 1963 to accompany *Masterplots*, this set covers some 5,000 characters in 1,437 works from the following volumes of *Masterplots II: American Fiction, British and Commonwealth Fiction, World Fiction*, and *Drama*, plus 20 works selected from the *Short Story* volumes. Arranged alphabetically by title, characters for each work are listed in order of importance. Central characters are described more fully, and pronunciations for names are provided when necessary. Indexed by title, author, and character.

The set enables the reader to become familiar with personalities from important works or to identify the books in which specific characters appear. Libraries holding *Cyclopedia* (Harper & Row, 1963) should not expect *Cyclopedia II* to replace it, recommended for high schools. [R: ARBA 91; BL, 1 Jan 91; LJ, Dec 90; WLB, Dec 90]

1504   **Encyclopedia of World Literature of the 20th Century**. 2d ed. Leonard S. Klein, ed. New York: Frederick Ungar, 1983-1984. 5v. $310.00/set. ISBN 0-8044-3135-3. LC 81-3357.

This set is a rich source of biographical and critical information on this century's writers worldwide. It contains 1,700 well-written articles on national literatures (European, American, Asian, and African), literary movements, and authors, arranged alphabetically. The set is especially valuable for its biographical/critical articles on European authors, including little-known ones. Photographs of individuals and a bibliography support each entry. The index, in a separate volume, supplements the extensive cross-referencing. Highly recommended. [R: ARBA 84; ARBA 85; ARBA 86; BL, 15 Jan 83; BL, 15 Oct 85]

1505   Freeman, William. **Dictionary of Fictional Characters**. Revised edition by Fred Urquhart. Boston: The Writer, c1974, 1985. 597p. $15.00pa. ISBN 0-87116-085-4. LC 73-18065.

A revision of the original edition (1963), this volume identifies some 20,000 characters in 2,000 classic and modern. British and American novels, short stories, poems, plays, and operas. Each character is identified within the context of the work in which it appears and the relationship of each to other characters. Separate author and title indexes enable the reader to find the characters of a particular work. Magill's *Cyclopedia of Literary Characters* provides more information about each character, but Freeman's work is more extensive.

1506 Harris, Laurie Lanzen. **Characters in 20th Century Literature**. Detroit: Gale, 1990. 480p. $49.95. ISBN 0-8103-1847-4.
This work lists 250 living authors and those who have died since 1899. Over half of these individuals were active after 1960. Special attention is given to minority writers and authors from emerging nations.
The entries contain basic factual data (e.g., dates, nationality, principal genres) and a brief essay on one or more of the author's works—plot summary, commentary on the theme, and the role of the characters. Bibliographies of other criticisms and indexing by character and title support the essays. High school libraries holding the various *Masterplots* volumes do not need this work, but others should consider it. [R: ARBA 91; BL, 1 Mar 90]

1507 Holman, C. Hugh, and William Harmon. **A Handbook to Literature**. 5th ed. New York: Macmillan, 1986. 647p. $27.50. ISBN 0-02-553430-0. LC 85-24133.
Since it first appeared in 1936, this standard work has been known as "Thrall and Hibbard," the names of its original compilers. An important literary handbook, it contains entries on literary terms, concepts, schools, and movements.
The current edition includes 1,500 words and phrases, alphabetically arranged, with entries that range from a sentence to several pages. Entries from the previous edition have been revised and updated and over 100 new ones added. Author, short title, and date of the source used in establishing the definitions are cited at the end of each item.
An "Outline of Literary History" and appendixes that list Nobel prizes for literature and Pulitzer prizes for fiction, drama, and poetry complete the volume. Authors mentioned in entries are indexed. Highly recommended for high school libraries. [R: ARBA 87; WLB, Dec 86]

1508 **The Illustrated Dictionary of Western Literature**. Michael Legat, ed. New York: Continuum; distr., New York: HarperCollins, 1987. 352p. $29.95. ISBN 0-8264-0393-X. LC 87-19991.
Libraries holding *Benet's Reader's Encyclopedia*, *Oxford Companion to American Literature*, *Oxford Companion to English Literature*, and other standard literary dictionaries may not need this compilation of English-language authors and their works. However, it is attractive and would be a useful addition to high school reference collections.
About half of the 2,000 entries cover authors of serious literature, but the work includes a few popular authors, such as Judy Blume and Barbara Cartland. The other half covers literary movements and terminology and specific books, plays, and poems. Author entries usually provide dates, birthplace, nationality, major works, themes (where appropriate), and information on the person's life. All authors included were born before 1940.
Entries for literary works give only author and publication date; few describe the plot or indicate the work's importance. Terms and movements are clearly defined. Appendixes give examples of types of verse and a chronological list of all authors covered. Excellent illustrations consist of photographs, drawings, color reproductions of paintings, title pages of early works, and motion picture stills. [R: ARBA 89]

1509 Manguel, Alberto, and Gianni Guadalupi. **The Dictionary of Imaginary Places**. San Diego, Calif.: Harcourt Brace Jovanovich, 1987. 454p. $14.95pa. ISBN 0-15-626054-9. LC 86-26063.
The Dictionary of Imaginary Places, an update of a 1981 work, provides descriptions, illustrations, and maps of fanciful worlds (e.g., Middle Earth, Lilliput, Narnia). Excluded are heavens and hells, future places, worlds that mimic real places, and other planets. This work is a good reference source and fun to browse. [R: ARBA 88]

E+
1510 Pringle, David. **Imaginary People: A Who's Who of Modern Fictional Characters**. New York: World Almanac/St. Martin's Press, c1987, 1988. 518p. $24.95. ISBN 0-88687-364-9. LC 88-60375.
Covering roughly the period from Daniel Defoe to the present, this unique volume identifies 1,300 fictitious characters, human and nonhuman (e.g., Lassie, R2D2), who have appeared in novels, short

stories, poetry, plays, films, television, operas, ballets, radio, pop songs, and comic strips. Enduring popularity is the criterion for inclusion. The British author has omitted some names Americans might expect to find, but overall coverage of American and British literature and popular culture is excellent.

Generally speaking, the characters are arranged alphabetically by last name, but some appear under a single name (e.g., Dracula, Winnie-the-Pooh), best-known form of name (e.g., Minnie Mouse), or designation (e.g., She-Who-Must-Be-Obeyed). Generous use of cross-references assists the reader in locating a desired character.

Entries vary in length, but each describes the character's creation, inclusion in other works, adaption by other media, and other "career" information. Pringle also provides 60 black-and-white illustrations of sources used in preparing the work. Recommended for upper elementary through high school levels. [R: ARBA 90; BL, 1 Mar 89; SLJ, Jan 89; SLJ, May 89]

1511 Stephens, Meic, comp. **A Dictionary of Literary Quotations**. New York: Routledge, Chapman & Hall, 1990. 193p. $25.00. ISBN 0-415-04129-5.

The more than 3,000 quotations collected are literary because they refer to reading, writing, journalism, and other topics related to books. Most of those quoted are English-language writers, but a few are foreign authors (e.g., Camus, Pasternak) and some are not writers at all (e.g., Napoleon). Sources include speeches, diaries, interviews, and the subject's own writings.

The arrangement is under 180 topics (e.g., censorship, joys of reading) also accessed by many cross-references and a detailed subject index. Since there is little duplication with *Bartlett's Familiar Quotations* and other standard works, this compilation is a useful supplement to them. [R: ARBA 91; RBB, 15 June 90; WLB, June 90]

DIGESTS AND SURVEYS

1512 **Masterplots II: American Fiction Series**. Frank N. Magill, ed. Pasadena, Calif.: Salem Press, 1986. 4v. $325.00/set. ISBN 0-89356-456-7. LC 86-1910.

This set is criticized by many English teachers as a shortcut to writing critical papers, but it is accepted by others as a worthwhile aid to teaching literary appreciation. It focuses on lesser-known works of well-known authors and outstanding works by others who are obscure. In all, there are 366 articles about 198 authors (53 women, 32 Blacks, and 34 Latin Americans, Carlos Fuentes and Gabriel Garcia Marquez among them). None of the works are treated in other *Masterplots* sets.

Essays begin with headnotes that list author, type of plot, time and locale, first publication date, and principal characters. This is followed by a plot summary, an analysis of the book's critical reception and contributions to its genre, and a list of suggested readings about it. The signed articles, well written and balanced with descriptive and critical comments, are four to five pages long.

Two other sets in the series, both edited by Frank Magill, may be needed by some high school library media centers: *Masterplots II: British and Commonwealth Fiction Series* (Salem Press, 1987) and *Masterplots II: World Fiction Series* (Salem Press, 1988). [R: ARBA 87; BL, 15 Oct 86; LJ, 1 Sept 86]

1513 **Masterplots II: Short Story Series**. Frank N. Magill, ed. Pasadena, Calif.: Salem Press, 1986. 6v. $400.00/set. ISBN 0-89356-461-3. LC 86-22025.

Following the same format of providing factual information, plot summary, and criticism as used in other *Masterplots* sets, this work covers 732 stories by 275 authors. Included are old masters of the genre (e.g., Edgar Allen Poe), contemporary writers (e.g., Joyce Carol Oates), and foreign authors whose books have been translated into English (e.g., Yukio Mishima). The works are arranged alphabetically by story title. Author access is provided by an index in the last volume, which also includes an extensive annotated bibliography of older works and recent criticism of the short story genre. [R: ARBA 88]

1514 **Survey of Contemporary Literature**. rev. ed. Frank N. Magill, ed. Pasadena, Calif.: Salem Press, 1977. 12v. $350.00/set. ISBN 0-89356-050-2. LC 77-79874.

This set reprints synopses/criticisms that originally appeared in *Masterplots Annuals*, 1945-1976, and *Survey of Contemporary Literature Supplements*. It covers over 1,000 fiction works, 400 biographies and memoirs, 250 poetry collections, 210 history titles, 80 books of drama, 70 volumes of essays, and 200 works on current affairs. The arrangement is alphabetical by title; author access is provided by the index in volume 12.

BIOGRAPHY

■ *Authors and Artists for Young Adults. See* entry 1173.

1515 **Black Writers: A Selection of Sketches from** *Contemporary Authors*. Linda Metzger and others, eds. Detroit: Gale, 1989. 619p. $80.00. ISBN 0-8103-2772-4.

High school libraries unable to afford *Contemporary Authors* will find this bio-bibliographic guide useful. It includes over 400 Black writers, predominately American, who have gained prominence during the twentieth century – novelists, poets, playwrights, essayists, and historians. Also included are individuals whose major contributions are not literary (e.g., civil rights leaders, educators, journalists, politicians, entertainers). Among those in this category are Desmond Tutu and Booker T. Washington.

Many entries duplicate those in *Contemporary Authors*, especially ones drawn from recent volumes, but others have been updated or substantially revised. Some older entries found in other Gale publications, such as *Dictionary of Literary Biography*, also have been duplicated in this work.

Like *Contemporary Authors*, the table of contents contains brief notes on each author's significance; alphabetically arranged entries provide biographical information, lists of writings and works in progress, and frequent comments by the biographees. Articles vary according to the writer's importance: a half column for some, but 10 or 12 pages for the likes of James Baldwin and Toni Morrison. There is no index. Highly recommended for high schools. [R: ARBA 90; BL, Apr 89; WLB, Mar 89]

1516 **Contemporary Authors**. Susan Trosky, ed. Detroit: Gale, 1962- . 134v. (ongoing). $104.00/v. ISSN 0010-7468. LC 62-52046.

1517 **Contemporary Authors New Revision Series**. James G. Lesniak, ed. Detroit: Gale, 1987- . 34v. (ongoing). $104.00/v.

An ongoing series, this work provides basic personal, career, and publication information for some 91,000 authors to date, many of whom are not profiled elsewhere. Each new volume adds about 900 new entries. All types of writers receive attention, except those in highly technical fields. Also included are persons prominent in communications: newspaper and television reporters and correspondents, columnists, editors, photojournalists, screenwriters, and scriptwriters. In addition, *Contemporary Authors* covers those deceased since 1900 whose works still attract interest. Cumulative indexes appear in alternate volumes and refer to the volumes in the set and to authors included in Dictionary of Literary Biography or any of the other Gale Literary Criticism series.

The *Contemporary Authors New Revision Series* is a separate set that contains updated profiles of authors who have been highly productive since they appeared in *Contemporary Authors*. Both series are recommended as basic sources for high schools. [R: ARBA 92]

1518 **Contemporary Novelists**. 4th ed. D. L. Kirkpatrick, ed. New York: St. Martin's Press, 1986. 1003p. $70.00. ISBN 0-312-16731-8. LC 86-13904.

This work covers some 600 leading novelists. Alphabetically arranged entries consist of brief biographical profiles, bibliographies of primary sources, and critical essays about each author's works. Some 120 entries have been added since the last revision in 1982, and others have been updated. Eleven authors who have died since the first edition appeared in 1960 are included in the appendix. Indexed by title. High schools will welcome this excellent reference tool. [R: ARBA 87]

1519 **Dictionary of Literary Biography Series**. Detroit: Gale, 1978- . $108.00/v.

The Dictionary of Literary Biography (DLB) is a series in which each volume focuses on a specific literary movement or periods in a national literature (American, English, Canadian, German). Major writers are discussed in long, definitive essays by well-known scholars; numerous illustrations and bibliographies of works by and about the subject are included. Writers of less importance are covered by shorter articles. The essays consist primarily of chronologically arranged personal and career summaries, with attention given to all major works. Recent volumes in the series address American short story writers, literary biographers, and poets; British publishing houses, prose writers, and poets; and Spanish poets. [R: ARBA 92]

1520 **European Authors, 1000-1900: A Biographical Dictionary of European Literature**. Stanley J. Kunitz and Vineta Colby, eds. Bronx, N.Y.: H. W. Wilson, 1967. 1016p. $68.00. ISBN 0-8242-0013-6. LC 67-13870.

As do other volumes in the Wilson Authors series, this one focuses on a wide range of influential writers: historians, theologians, philosophers, educators, critics, and literary figures. Profiles of 967 authors summarize each person's life and examine the principal works translated into English. All authors were born after A.D. 1000 and were deceased prior to 1925. French and German writers dominate, followed by Russian authors. Portraits accompany about one-third of the sketches.

1521 European Writers. George Stade and others, eds. New York: Scribner's, 1983-1991. 14v. $1060.00/set. ISBN 0-684-19267-5. LC 83-16333.

This set was designed to complement Scribner's other compilations devoted to world authors: *American Writers*, *British Writers*, and *Ancient Writers: Greece and Rome*. More recently, the three-volume *Latin American Writers* was added to the series.

The first 13 volumes of *European Writers* are divided into 4 chronologically arranged subsets: *The Middle Ages and the Renaissance*, *The Age of Reason and the Enlightenment*, *The Romantic Century*, and *The Twentieth Century*. Volume 14 is the index to the entire set. The series contains a total of 261 essays, 248 of which treat individual writers who range chronologically from the fourth-century Christian poet Prudentius to the twentieth-century Czechoslovakian writer Milan Kundera. Four essays cover anonymous works (e.g., *Beowulf*), and the remaining nine essays focus on themes and genres (e.g., "The Cid in Epic and Ballad"). The editors chose not only prominent creative writers but also noted scholars and thinkers in such disciplines as history, religion, philosophy, music, psychology, and literary criticism. The first volume of each subset includes an introductory essay and a chronology of the period covered. Articles on individual writers, contributed primarily by scholars from the United States and Great Britain, then appear in chronological sequence by the author's date of birth. Generally, they discuss the authors' lives and works against the broader backdrop of the social, political, and cultural milieu in which they lived. In addition, the essays provide critical analyses of the writers' major works and discuss their style, thematic concerns, and literary relationships with other authors. Although scholarly, the highly readable essays are written on a level appropriate to the general audience for which this set is intended. Following each essay is a selective bibliography of primary and secondary works. Cross-references guide the user from both original and translated titles to the appropriate author and subheading. Index references locate the pertinent passage by volume, page number, and column.

Prefacing the index are a volume-by-volume table of contents to the set; an alphabetical list of all the writers and other subjects accorded separate essays; and a list that categorizes the authors and anonymous works by language. In addition, the index volume includes a seven-page bibliography of general works arranged according to the chronological periods covered by the subsets. The essays in this series provide excellent introductions to the writings and ideas of the foremost European authors and thinkers for 16 centuries.

1522 Index to the Wilson Authors Series. rev. ed. Bronx, N.Y.: H. W. Wilson, 1991. 104p. $25.00. ISBN 0-8242-0820-0. LC 86-5486.

The index provides access to more than 8,600 profiles in the 10-volume Wilson Author series: *American Authors, 1600-1900*; *British Authors before 1800*; *British Authors of the Nineteenth Century*; *European Authors, 1000-1900*; *Greek and Latin Authors, 800 B.C.-A.D. 1000*; *Twentieth Century Authors* and *First Supplement*; *World Authors, 1950-1970*; *World Authors, 1970-1975*; and *World Authors, 1975-1980*. Each citation gives birth and death dates and provides cross-references to variant forms of the author's name.

1523 Major 20th-Century Writers: A Selection of Sketches from *Contemporary Authors*. Bryan Ryan, ed. Detroit: Gale, 1991. 4v. $295.00/set. ISBN 0-8103-7766-7. LC 90-84380.

High school libraries unable to afford the continuing commitment to the Contemporary Authors series should consider this set, which focuses on some 1,000 of the "most influential" and frequently studied writers of our times. Most entries are updated versions of articles in the parent set, but about 40 are new.

Most essays address novelists, poets, and playwrights, but some 300 cover nonfiction writers, journalists, and popular authors. United States and British writers dominate, but some from other English-speaking countries, or whose works have been translated into English, are included. Among those who appear are serious literary figures (e.g., Eudora Welty, Gertrude Stein), popular writers (e.g., Barbara Cartland, Sidney Sheldon), children's writers (e.g., Dr. Seuss, Maurice Sendak), journalists (e.g., Norman Cousins, George Will), eminent thinkers (e.g., Bertrand Russell, Mahatma Gandhi), and prominent world leaders (e.g., Winston Churchill, John F. Kennedy).

Profiles follow the Contemporary Authors format and include birth/death dates, family data, political and religious affiliation, education, address, and name and address of agent; career history (e.g., vocational accomplishments, awards, honors); a complete bibliography; works in progress;

insights into the author's life and personality; hobbies/other interests; and a bibliography of bio-graphical/critical articles and books. Recommended for high school library media centers. [R: ARBA 92; BL, 15 mar 91]

1524 Popular World Fiction, 1900-Present. Walton Beacham and Suzanne Niemeyer, eds. Washing-ton, D.C.: Beacham, c1987, 1988. 4v. $249.00/set. ISBN 0-933833-08-3. LC 87-19545.

This set deals with 176 fiction writers—foreign authors whose works have been translated into English and American writers whose reputations were established after 1900. The term "popular" is broad and vague, however, because the set places Edgar Rice Burroughs, Louis L'Amour, and Sidney Sheldon in company with Isaac Bashevis Singer, Ernest Hemingway, and Robert Penn Warren. Most authors included are found on high school reading lists, but some are not treated in standard reference works.

Alphabetically arranged essays, 7 to 10 pages in length, emphasize the writings and career of each author with only brief information about their lives. Each essay describes the author's writings and their reception; the essays have little critical depth. The analyses provide theme, characters, social concerns, and techniques for one to four titles. A bibliography of additional works and secondary sources support each entry.

Each volume includes appendixes for the entire set that arrange the titles by broad themes and social issues and authors by genre. The last volume contains an author and title index to the set. The work is suggested as an optional purchase for high school libraries. [R: ARBA 89]

1525 Twentieth Century Authors: A Biographical Dictionary of Modern Literature. Stanley J. Kunitz and Howard Haycraft, eds. Bronx, N.Y.: H. W. Wilson, 1942. 1577p. $85.00. ISBN 0-8242-0049-7. LC 43-51003.

1526 Twentieth Century Authors: A Biographical Dictionary of Modern Literature. First Supple-ment. Stanley J. Kunitz, ed. Bronx, N.Y.: H. W. Wilson, 1955. $75.00. ISBN 0-8242-0050-0. LC 43-51003.

The initial volume and its supplement, which belong to the Wilson Authors series, include 2,550 writers worldwide whose works have been published in English. Those in the main volume were active between 1900 and 1942; the supplement contains updated entries for authors covered in the main volume and profiles of writers who gained prominence between 1942 and 1955. The volumes emphasize biographical and critical information.

1527 World Authors, 1950-1970: A Companion Volume to Twentieth Century Authors. John Wake-man, ed. Bronx, N.Y.: H. W. Wilson, 1975. 1593p. $95.00. ISBN 0-8242-0419-0. LC 75-172140.

1528 World Authors, 1970-1975: A Biographical Dictionary. John Wakeman, ed. Bronx, N.Y.: H. W. Wilson, 1980. 893p. $78.00. ISBN 0-8242-0641-X. LC 79-21874.

1529 World Authors, 1975-1980. Vineta Colby, ed. Bronx, N.Y.: H. W. Wilson, 1985. 829p. $80.00. ISBN 0-8242-0715-7. LC 85-10045.

1530 World Authors, 1980-1985. Vineta Colby, ed. Bronx, N.Y.: H. W. Wilson, 1991. 938p. $80.00. ISBN 0-8242-0797-1. LC 90-49782.

A part of the Wilson Authors series, these volumes continue *Twentieth Century Authors* and its *First Supplement*. The four *World Authors* volumes cover prominent writers whose works have been published in English: 950 in the volume for 1950-1970; 348 in the 1970-1975 volume; 379 in the 1975-1980 book; and 320 in the 1980-1985 volume.

The series focuses on novelists, poets, and dramatists, with some attention given to historians, philosophers, and others of interest. Sketches describe their lives and careers and evaluate their principal works. Portraits are included for many authors. [R: ARBA 86; ARBA 92]

CRITICISM

1531 Contemporary Literary Criticism: Excerpts from Criticism of the Works of Today's Novelists, Poets, Playwrights, Short Story Writers, Scriptwriters, and Other Creative Writers. Roger Matuz and others, eds. Detroit: Gale, 1973- . 67v. (ongoing). $104.00/v.

1532 Twentieth-Century Literary Criticism: Excerpts from Criticism of the Works of Novelists, Poets, Playwrights, Short Story Writers, and Other Creative Writers. Paula Kepos and others, eds. Detroit: Gale, 1978- . 41v. (ongoing). $104.00/v.

1533 Nineteenth-Century Literary Criticism: Excerpts from Criticism of the Works of Novelists, Poets, Playwrights, Short Story Writers, Philosophers, and Other Creative Writers. Laurie O. Mauro, ed. Detroit: Gale, 1981- . 32v. (ongoing). $104.00/v.

These series, each of which focuses on a specific period, provide critical excerpts from a variety of sources that offer contrasting evaluations of an author or a given work. In addition to the critiques, the following are included for each author: a portrait, a biographical/critical introduction written by Gale editors, a list of principal works, and citations of critical books and articles. In each volume, an appendix lists works from which critical comments have been drawn.

Authors included in *Contemporary Literary Criticism* are still living or died after December 31, 1959. Those included in *Twentieth-Century Literary Criticism* died between 1900 and 1959; those in *Nineteenth-Century Literary Criticism* had died by 1899.

Other Gale literary criticism series include Literature Criticism from 1400-1800, Shakespearean Criticism, and Short Story Criticism. [R: ARBA 92]

1534 Cyclopedia of World Authors II. Frank N. Magill, ed. Pasadena, Calif.: Salem Press, 1989. 4v. $300.00/set. ISBN 0-89356-512-1. LC 89-10659.

This work does not supersede the *Cyclopedia of World Authors* (Salem Press, 1974), but continues the coverage of the basic set. For about one-fourth of the entries, the information updates that found in the earlier work; the remainder are new. Brief biographical and critical information on over 700 authors is contained in entries of some 1,000 words, followed by a bibliographic essay that highlights additional critical evaluations. Most of those included are English-language writers, but some are European, Latin American, or Asian. *Masterplots II* contains plot summaries of about 80 percent of the books treated in this set. Recommended for high schools. [R: ARBA 91; BL, 1 Mar 90; BL, 1 Jan 91; WLB, 1 Feb 90]

1535 Great Writers of the English Language. North Bellmore, N.Y.: Marshall Cavendish, 1989. 14v. $399.95/set. ISBN 1-85435-000-5. LC 88-21077.

This set profiles the lives and times of 56 of the most influential authors and poets in the English language. Each volume focuses on from 2 to 4 authors, except volume 13, which covers 11 poets.

The chapter on each writer follows a uniform format, beginning with "The Writer's Life," giving background and personality, followed by "The Writer at Work," an examination of the author's hopes, aspirations, and career. "Sources of Inspiration" covers events that influenced the writer's career, and "The Reader's Guide" gives a summary of one of the writer's major works, exploring its characters, themes, and ideas. The author's other writings, literary devices and themes are also treated. Illustrations are an outstanding feature. In addition to a full-page portrait of each writer, there are 40 to 50 reproductions of paintings, photographs, posters, and drawings for each.

A three-part index in the last volume consists of a general index, an index of authors with subsections for life and works, and an index of all titles named. A glossary of 100 terms concludes the volume. The set is not a substitute for the Wilson Authors series or the various sets published by Gale, but it is a worthwhile source that high schools should consider. [R: ARBA 91; BL, 15 Feb 90]

1536 Harris, Laurie Lanzen. Characters in 20th-Century Literature. Detroit: Gale, 1990. 480p. $49.95. ISBN 0-8103-1847-4. LC 89-25709.

This volume on twentieth-century literature emphasizes characters that appeared in post-1960 novels, short stories, and dramas. The arrangement is alphabetical by author, giving dates, nationality, principal genre, and writing style. The critical essays that follow cover each work chronologically, describing the characters and how they personify the theme. A bibliography for each author, character and title indexes, and chronologies support the text. There is not a great deal here that cannot be found in similar works, but it is a worthwhile purchase for grades 9 through 12. [R: ARBA 91; BL, 1 Mar 90; BR, Sept/Oct 90]

1537 Masterpieces of World Literature. Frank N. Magill, ed. New York: HarperCollins, 1989. 957p. $35.00. ISBN 0-06-016144-2. LC 89-45052.

High school libraries unable to purchase the more extensive critical surveys by Magill or the *Cyclopedia of Literary Characters* may wish to consider this volume. The work, arranged alphabetically by title, contains plot summaries, character portrayals, and critical evaluations of 270 classics of world literature (novels, plays, stories, poems, and essays), all reprints from other Magill guides. Indexing provides access by author and original title. [R: BL, 1 Feb 90; WLB, Jan 90]

1538   Shields, Nancy E. **Index to Literary Criticism for Young Adults**. Metuchen, N.J.: Scarecrow, 1988. 410p. $32.50. ISBN 0-8108-2112-5. LC 87-37666.

This index provides a short cut to locating critical material on 4,000 authors found in Scribner's *American Writers* and *British Writers*; H. W. Wilson's *Twentieth Century Authors* and its *First Supplement*; and the Gale series *Contemporary Literary Criticism*, *Twentieth-Century Literary Criticism*, *Nineteenth-Century Literary Criticism*, and *Literary Criticism from 1400 to 1800*.

Authors are listed alphabetically with reference to the works that cite them. Cross-references for pseudonyms, multiple pen names, and variant spellings are included. Since each of the indexed works has its own index, this work is optional for high school libraries. [R: ARBA 89; BL, 15 Sept 88; VOYA, Dec 88; WLB, Sept 88]

DRAMA

See also **Theater and Dance**.

1539   Carpenter, Charles A. **Modern Drama Scholarship and Criticism 1966-1980: An International Bibliography**. Toronto and Buffalo, N.Y.: University of Toronto Press, 1986. 587p. $75.00. ISBN 0-8020-2549-8.

The more than 2,700 "publications on world drama since Ibsen" listed within have been gleaned from 1,600 journals, thousands of books, and numerous reference works. Designed for students of modern dramatic literature, it emphasizes plays and playwrights, not players and performances. The work is arranged by national literature/language groups (e.g., American, British and Irish, Hispanic, East European) and then alphabetically by playwright. High schools with strong programs in drama should consider this work. [R: ARBA 87]

1540   Connor, Billie M., and Helene G. Mochedlover. **Ottemiller's Index to Plays in Collections: An Author and Title Index to Plays Appearing in Collections Published between 1900 and 1985**. 7th ed. Metuchen, N.J.: Scarecrow, 1988. 564p. $42.50. ISBN 0-8108-2081-1. LC 87-34160.

Ottemiller's is the standard index to collections of full-length plays in English and English translations of foreign plays. Some types of plays are omitted: one-act, radio and television, holiday and anniversary, and those written for children.

The 7th edition constitutes a substantial revision of the 6th. Publication dates of collections, extended 10 years, now cover 1900 to 1985. The scope has been expanded to include collections in English published outside the United States. *Ottemiller's* now analyzes 1,350 collections (251 more than the 6th edition) and covers plays by 2,555 authors. The arrangement is by playwright, with lists of plays and collections in which each is designated by symbols. A list of collections analyzed and key to symbols and a title index complete the volume, which is highly recommended for high schools. [R: ARBA 89]

1541   **Contemporary Dramatists**. 4th ed. D. L. Kirkpatrick, ed. Chicago: St. James Press, 1988. 785p. $85.00. ISBN 0-912289-62-7.

Three hundred significant living dramatists who write in English are listed in this work. Alphabetically arranged entries consist of a biography, a chronological bibliography of all produced and published plays, a bibliography of all other published works, and a signed critical essay.

Brief entries are contained in a supplementary section on writing for screen, radio, and television; musical librettists; theater groups; and seven recently deceased dramatists considered contemporary. An index to all listed plays concludes the volume. This major biographical source is recommended for high schools. [R: ARBA 89; BL, 1 Dec 88; LJ, 1 Mar 83]

1542   **Masterplots II: Drama Series**. Frank N. Magill, ed. Pasadena, Calif.: Salem Press, 1990. 4v. $325.00/set. ISBN 0-89356-491-5. LC 89-10989.

The *Drama Series* examines 327 words of twentieth-century drama by 148 authors, most of whom write in English. Some 70 of the plays have been translated into English from another language.

Entries, arranged alphabetically by title, have playwright's life dates, time and place of drama's first performance, setting, principal characters, and plot summary. A critical commentary treats the ideas and issues with which the play deals, appraises its place among the author's works, and evaluates its influence on the field of drama. Indexed by author and title. Some high schools with advanced placement programs or courses on twentieth-century drama will require this work. [R: ARBA 91; BL, 1 Sept 90; WLB, June 90]

1543 Taylor, Thomas J. **Restoration Drama**. Pasadena, Calif.: Salem Press, 1989. 156p. $40.00. ISBN 0-89356-657-8.

Restoration Drama includes references to critical reviews of drama that reflects the changing social and political life of London between 1660 and 1700. Informative annotations refer to the most important criticisms for the period. [R: LJ, 1 May 90; LJ, 1 June 90; WLB, May 90]

GENRE

1544 **Anatomy of Wonder: A Critical Guide to Science Fiction**. 3d ed. Neil Barron, ed. New Providence, N.J.: R. R. Bowker, 1987. 874p. $39.95. ISBN 0-8352-2312-4. LC 87-9305.

Highly recommended for high school libraries, this annotated bibliography identifies the best in science fiction from earliest times through 1986. The 3d edition expands coverage of the 2d; the number of contributors has increased from 14 to 24; the recognition of foreign science fiction has grown from 6 to 13 countries; and the bibliography has doubled.

The 2,650 annotated citations are arranged in three parts: English language, foreign language, and research aids. The English-language section is divided by date (up to the early twentieth century, 1918-1938, 1939-1963, and 1964-1986), with a separate section for children's and young adult literature. The foreign language section is arranged by country. Each entry includes author or editor (pseudonyms are identified), author's nationality, title, publisher, year of first edition, concise plot summary with critical comments and comparisons, and awards. The editor identifies books recommended for a core collection.

The section on research aids lists reference works, histories and criticisms, author studies, books about science fiction in motion pictures and television, science fiction magazines, and major science fiction libraries and collections. A core list of science fiction reference books completes the volume. [R: ARBA 89]

1545 **The Encyclopedia of American Comics**. Ron Goulart, ed. New York: Facts on File, 1990. 408p. $39.95; $19.95pa. ISBN 0-8160-1852-9; 0-8160-2582-7pa. LC 90-2974.

This encyclopedia provides coverage of comic strips, comic books, and the artists who created them, from the appearance of the Katzenjammer Kids in 1897 to the present. Goulart, an authority on the genre and the creator of the *Star Hawks* strip for United Features Syndicate, wrote about two-thirds of the 650 alphabetically arranged entries; others involved in the industry contributed the remaining third.

Articles about specific strips give their history, development, content, and distribution. Those about artists trace their careers and evaluate the contribution of each to the field. Over 100 black-and-white reproductions illustrate the volume, which is recommended for high schools. [R: ARBA 92; BR, May/June 91; LJ, Jan 91; SLJ, Mar 91]

1546 **Fantasy Literature: A Reader's Guide**. Neil Barron, ed. Hamden, Conn.: Garland, 1990. 586p. (Garland Reference Library of the Humanities, v.874). $49.95. ISBN 0-8240-3148-2. LC 89-23693.

1547 **Horror Literature: A Reader's Guide**. Neil Barron, ed. Hamden, Conn.: Garland, 1990. 596p. (Garland Reference Library of the Humanities, v.1220). $49.95. ISBN 0-8240-4347-2. LC 89-27454.

These volumes are modeled on Barron's *Anatomy of Wonder*, a standard work on science fiction. *Fantasy Literature* covers the genre from *The Odyssey* to 1988. It includes extensive annotations for reference works and other library resources, criticism, film, art, awards, and selected fantasy titles (the most important of which are starred). The annotations include synopses and recommended editions.

Horror Literature, which covers Gothic romances and early modern and contemporary horror fiction, contains the same type of sources and information. Both works are recommended for high schools that require reference tools that address these kinds of literature. [R: ARBA 91; BL, July 90; LJ, 1 Feb 90]

1548 Fletcher, Marilyn P., comp. and ed. **Readers' Guide to Twentieth-Century Science Fiction**. Chicago: American Library Association, 1989. 673p. $60.00. ISBN 0-8389-0504-8. LC 88-7815.

This work provides biographical and critical information for more than 150 science fiction writers. Biographies (brief for some, but several pages for major authors) include basic data, factors that influenced the development as a writer, an analysis of themes and styles that characterize the author's work, and plot summaries for up to six of the author's most important works. The appendixes contain lists of science fiction magazines and journals, Nebula and Hugo winners through 1986, and a title index.

This guide is more limited in scope than *Anatomy of Wonder*, but each entry provides more biographical and critical material. Caveats include unevenness in the entries and inadequate proofreading. Overall, however, the work has value for high school libraries that need biographical materials and plot summaries for the genre. [R: ARBA 90; BL, 15 Feb 90; BR, May/June 90; LJ, Jan 90; VOYA, Dec 89; WLB, Mar 90]

1549 Handbook of American Popular Literature. M. Thomas Inge, ed. Westport, Conn.: Greenwood Press, 1988. 408p. $55.00. ISBN 0-313-25405-2. LC 87-32294.

An outgrowth of Inge's *Handbook of Popular Culture* (1982), this work includes 15 essays, 10 of which have been revised and updated since the earlier work appeared, and 5 original to this edition. Each essay, written by a specialist, focuses on a particular genre (e.g., detective novels, fantasy, Gothic novels), and covers the historical development of the literature and reference works, research centers, and useful publications relevant to it. Appropriate for middle and high schools. [R: ARBA 89; BL, 15 Nov 88; LJ, 15 Oct 88; WLB, Jan 89]

1550 Keating, H. R. F. **Crime & Mystery: The 100 Best Books**. New York: Carroll & Graf, 1987. 219p. $15.95. ISBN 0-88184-345-8. LC 87-17377.

Two-page critiques of the 100 mystery novels the author "has enjoyed the most" make up this delightful volume. The chronological arrangement includes well-known authors (e.g., P. D. James, Ellery Queen) as well as some lesser renown. Keating, himself a mystery writer, has produced well-written and often humorous essays that will interest any fan of the genre. [R: ARBA 89; BL, 15 Dec 87; LJ, 15 Nov 87]

1551 McCormick, Donald, and Katy Fletcher. **Spyfiction: A Connoisseur's Guide**. New York: Facts on File, 1990. 346p. $23.95. ISBN 0-8160-2098-1. LC 89-29524.

Spyfiction updates McCormick's *Who's Who in Spy Fiction* (1978) with the addition of many new authors and the deletion of others of little interest. Entries detail more than 200 writers of the genre, providing pseudonyms; nationality; birthplace; birth and death dates; a bibliography of spy fiction; major characters; a biographical profile; critical analysis (e.g., plot summaries, writing characteristics); and author's work in film, radio, and television.

Eight essays treat such topics as the history of American spy fiction, the future of the genre, screen adaptations, and the use of real events in writing spy fiction. The index links pseudonyms and real names, which are not provided by cross-references in the text. [R: ARBA 91; BL, 15 June 90]

1552 The New Encyclopedia of Science Fiction. James Gunn, ed. New York: Viking, 1988. 524p. $24.95. ISBN 0-670-81041-X. LC 87-40637.

This comprehensive volume contains 529 articles on science fiction writers and illustrators, over 250 entries on film and television shows, and 96 topical essays (e.g., comic books, lost worlds, monster movies, time travel). Articles on minor writers consist of only a few sentences, but those for renowned authors such as Robert Heinlein analyze chief plot elements, comment on the writer's development, and conclude with bibliographies of works not mentioned in the entry. Films and television essays supply criticism and appraise their artistic merits.

The list of 107 distinguished contributors includes Arthur C. Clarke, E. F. Bleiler, and a number of Hugo award winners. This is the only work that treats science fiction in its written and film formats. [R: BL, 1 Jan 89; LJ, 15 Nov 88]

1553 Pringle, David. **Modern Fantasy: The Hundred Best Novels: An English-Language Selection, 1946-1987**. New York: Peter Bedrick; distr., New York: HarperCollins, 1989. 284p. $17.95; $8.95pa. ISBN 0-87226-328-2; 0-87226-219-7pa. LC 89-33072.

High school library media centers that serve modern fantasy buffs will welcome this work. Pringle focuses on horror and "absurdist metafiction," such as the works of John Updike and Angela Carter, published from 1946 to 1987. He excludes children's books, Latin American and light fantasy, and multivolume sets (except for a few standards, such as those by J. R. R. Tolkien, C. S. Lewis, and Ursula K. Le Guin).

The arrangement of the 100 best novels is chronological by publication date and includes a two-page entry for each, giving a plot summary, information about the author, publication history, and comments by Pringle. Indexed by author. [R: VOYA, Apr 90]

1554   Rosenberg, Betty, and Diana Tixier Herald. **Genreflecting: A Guide to Reading Interests in Genre Fiction**. 3d ed. Englewood, Colo.: Libraries Unlimited, 1991. 345p. $33.50. ISBN 0-87287-930-5. LC 91-28074.

The purpose of *Genreflecting*, which has been expanded to reflect the newest popular fiction, is to assist the librarian in identifying books of interest to a wide audience. The work is divided into six chapters: westerns, thrillers, romances, science fiction, fantasy, and supernatural/horror. Each chapter discusses themes and types and then describes a variety of topics appropriate to the category: best authors, anthologies, bibliographies, criticism, films, magazines, publishers, reviews, associations, and awards. Indexes of genre authors and secondary materials conclude the volume.

E+

1555   Rovin, Jeff. **Encyclopedia of Superheroes**. New York: Facts on File, 1985. 443p. $35.00; $19.95pa. ISBN 0-8160-1168-0; 0-8160-1879-5pa. LC 85-10329.

1556   Rovin, Jeff. **Encyclopedia of Super Villains**. New York: Facts on File, 1987. 416p. $29.95; $19.95pa. ISBN 0-8160-1356-X; 0-8160-1899-5pa. LC 87-8831.

These entertaining companion volumes cover larger-than-life fictitious crime fighters and their arch-foes, super villains. The "good guys" must possess at least one super power, fight for the common good, and wear a costume. The "bad guys" must be a threat to society and have at least one distinguishing feature. Both types are drawn from literature, legend, radio, movies, and television, but most stem from comic books.

The "biographies" of 1,300 superheroes, arranged alphabetically by "real" name, provide such information as a chronology of appearances, companion (if any), occupation, costume, tools and weapons, special powers, media, and representative quotations. Illustrations, several appendixes (e.g., superhero teams, minor superheroes), and an index support the volume.

The alphabetically arranged "biographies" of villains give similar information: "real" name, name of any companions or henchmen, first appearance, description of costume or distinguishing feature, explanation of how the character came to acquire the evil role, and typical quotations. The work contains 140 illustrations, 32 in full color, and an index. Both books are recommended for reference, browsing, and just plain fun. [R: ARBA 86; BR, Jan/Feb 89; BR, Nov/Dec 89; Kliatt, Jan 89]

1557   **Twentieth-Century Crime and Mystery Writers**. 2d ed. John M. Reilly, ed. New York: St. Martin's Press, 1985. 1094p. $85.00. ISBN 0-312-82418-1. LC 84-40813.

The 2d edition of this highly acclaimed work includes 640 entries on English-language crime and mystery writers of the century. Of this number, 109 are new and the remaining entries from the original edition have been revised and updated. Each entry includes brief biographical data, a bibliography of works by and about the author, a signed critical essay, a list of manuscript collections, and (when possible) comments from the author about the work. Appendixes on influential nineteenth-century and foreign-language writers and a title index conclude the volume. This comprehensive, well-organized work is recommended for high schools. [R: ARBA 86]

1558   **Twentieth-Century Romance and Historical Writers**. 2d ed. Lesley Henderson, ed. Chicago: St. James Press, 1990. 856p. $95.00. ISBN 0-912289-97-X.

The 2d edition of this work (formerly entitled *Romance and Gothic Writers*) has expanded to include writers of historical fiction. It contains 530 authors (an addition of 200), giving biographical data; a list of works; some comments by the author; and a short, signed critical essay, with emphasis on the writer's style and contribution to the genre. Entries range from 500 to 1,000 words.

The included authors, selected by a panel of advisers, are an eclectic group. They range from popular writers (e.g., Irving Stone, James Michener) and prominent people generally associated with the west (e.g., Louis L'Amour, Zane Gray) to critically acclaimed individuals (e.g., Robert Penn Warren, William Golding). This is the most comprehensive work available on historical and romance novels. [R: ARBA 91; LJ, 15 May 90]

1559   **Twentieth-Century Science Fiction Writers**. 2d ed. Curtis C. Smith, ed. Chicago: St. James Press, 1986. 933p. $85.00. ISBN 0-912289-27-9.

This science fiction bio-bibliography treats over 600 authors, including 35 foreign writers whose works have been translated into English. Some writers were dropped from the 1981 edition to make room for new ones. Each signed entry of 1,000 or more words contains detailed biographical data, a critical analysis of major works, and a complete bibliography of science fiction and other writings by the author. [R: ARBA 87; BL, 15 Mar 87]

POETRY

See **Language** for **Rhymes**.

1560   **The Columbia Granger's Index to Poetry**. 9th ed. Edith P. Hazen and Deborah J. Fryer, eds. New York: Columbia University Press, 1990. 2082p. $175.00. ISBN 0-231-07104-3. LC 90-1334.

Since this work's appearance in 1904, librarians have regarded it as a standard reference tool that is valuable for identifying and locating poems contained in selected anthologies. The latest edition indexes poems published in over 550 volumes, of which 50 are collections of poetry translated from other languages. Indexed by first line, title, author, and subject. With the previous edition, the editors abandoned the practice of indexing only in-print anthologies; they now index older collections no longer available that the library still may hold. Anthologies recommended for first purchase are highlighted. Recommended for high schools.

A capsule review of each anthology indexed is provided by *The Columbia Granger's Guide to Poetry Anthologies* by William Katz and Linda Sternberg Katz. [R: ARBA 91]

1561   **Contemporary Poets**. 4th ed. James Vinson and D. L. Kirkpatrick, eds. New York: St. Martin's Press, 1985. 1071p. $70.00. ISBN 0-312-16837-3. LC 85-22249.

Concise biocritical essays of some 850 living poets, and others who have died since 1950, comprise the contents of this volume. The 4th edition adds over 70 new entries, drops those on poets no longer of interest, and revises others carried over from the last edition. Alphabetically arranged entries, up to several pages in length, provide brief biographical data and a list of publications. The remainder of the entry consists of a signed critical analysis about the poet's work and comments by the poet. [R: ARBA 87; BL, 15 June 86]

1562   Deutsch, Babette. **Poetry Handbook: A Dictionary of Terms**. 4th ed. New York: HarperCollins, c1976, 1982. 309p. $8.95pa. ISBN 0-06-463548-1.

Designed for the student and the budding poet, this reprint of a 1974 handbook provides explanations and illustrations of the technical side of poetry. Lines, stanzas, and complete poems illustrate terms and techniques.

1563   Hoffman, Herbert H., and Rita L. Hoffman. **International Index to Recorded Poetry**. Bronx, N.Y.: H. W. Wilson, 1983. 529p. $75.00. ISBN 0-8242-0682-7. LC 83-16659.

This is a comprehensive guide to poetry for all ages in recordings; 2,300 poets on 1,700 tapes, cassettes, and films, in over 20 languages, are represented. The main entries are under the author's name, with citations to specific poems and their recording media. Other access points include first line, title, reader, and a register of poets by language. The list of recordings analyzed (to which the main entry refers by code) gives full bibliographic data: title or recording, serial number, manufacturer's name and address, format, and name of reader.

1564   Jason, Philip K. **Nineteenth Century American Poetry**. Pasadena, Calif.: Salem Press, 1989. 251p. $40.00. ISBN 0-89356-651-9. LC 89-10804.

This bibliography in the Magill Bibliographies series, directed toward senior high school students and college undergraduates, locates background reading and research materials about nineteenth-century American poetry. The first section covers general criticism, followed by sections on individual poets arranged chronologically by date of birth. Citations are well annotated. [R: ARBA 91; LJ, 1 May 90; LJ, 1 June 90; WLB, May 90]

1565   Katz, William, and Linda Sternberg Katz. **The Columbia Granger's Guide to Poetry Anthologies**. New York: Columbia University Press, 1991. 231p. $52.00. ISBN 0-231-07244-9. LC 90-2469.

The authors provide a capsule review of each of the anthologies indexed in the 9th edition of *Columbia Granger's Index to Poetry*. Reviews describe the scope and organization of each anthology and judge its value in terms of originality and poetic quality. This guide is arranged in 61 categories (e.g., African, American twentieth century, ballads, humorous and nonsense, love). A valuable list of 10 "must-purchase anthologies" and 34 other highly recommended ones are listed in the appendix. High school libraries with tight budgets will welcome the advice this work provides. [R: ARBA 92; WLB, May 91]

1566   Leo, John R. **Modern and Contemporary**. Boston: G. K. Hall, 1989. 546p. (Guide to American Poetry Explication, v.2). $50.00. ISBN 0-8160-8918-9. LC 89-2195.

1567   Ruppert, James. **Colonial and Nineteenth Century**. Boston: G. K. Hall, 1989. 239p. (Guide to American Poetry Explication, v.1). $35.00. ISBN 0-8161-8919-6. LC 89-2196.
   The first two volumes in a projected five-volume set (the others to cover British poetry), these works revise the 3d edition of *Poetry Explication* by Joseph M. Kuntz and Nancy C. Martinez (G. K. Hall, 1980). All poets included in the earlier guide and its predecessors are included; material is added through 1987.
   The volumes are arranged by the poet's name, then by poems. These are followed by the last name of the critic, which refers to the work's bibliography. Volume 1 covers 43 poets, while volume 2 provides 1,988 references to explications for some 350 poets. Some high school libraries may require this work. [R: ARBA 90; RBB, 1 Oct 89]

■ *The New Comprehensive American Rhyming Dictionary*. *See* entry 1447.

1568   **Princeton Encyclopedia of Poetry and Poetics**. rev. ed. Alexander Preminger and others, eds. Princeton, N.J.: Princeton University Press, 1974. 906p. $89.00; $24.95pa. ISBN 0-691-06280-3; 0-691-01317-9pa. LC 63-7076.

1569   **The Princeton Handbook of Poetic Terms**. Alexander Preminger and others, eds. Princeton, N.J.: Princeton University Press, 1986. 309p. $35.00; $9.95pa. ISBN 0-691-06659-0; 0-691-01425-6pa. LC 85-43380.
   The 1,034 entries in the authoritative and scholarly *Princeton Encyclopedia* range from a few sentences to long surveys and cover history, techniques, poetics and criticism, and other theoretical topics. The work covers all periods and most languages, but does not include poets, poems, and allusions per se. High school libraries requiring in-depth coverage of poetry should make this work a first choice.
   The Princeton Handbook is an updated, but abbreviated, version of the parent work that places emphasis on "prosodic and poetic terms." The work offers 402 entries on poetic forms, prosody, rhetoric, genre, and topics such as poetry reading. Libraries not needing the full coverage offered by the parent volume may wish to consider this abridgment of it. [R: ARBA 88; BL, July 87]

1570   Williams, Miller. **Patterns of Poetry: An Encyclopedia of Forms**. Baton Rouge, La.: Louisiana State University Press, 1986. 203p. $32.50; $14.95pa. ISBN 0-8071-1253-4; 0-8071-1330-1pa. LC 85-23717.
   Despite its subtitle, *Patterns of Poetry* is not an encyclopedia; moreover, it is arranged in chapters instead of alphabetically. The main sections cover fully and loosely defined traditional stanza patterns, traditional poems of set and indefinite length, nonspecific forms and formal elements, and variations in the stanzas and poems.
   A detailed index gives easy access to poetic terms, which are clearly defined and illustrated. Because the content is excellent, this work is suggested for high school libraries.

SHORT STORIES

1571   May, Charles E. **Twentieth Century European Short Story: An Annotated Bibliography**. Pasadena, Calif.: Salem Press, 1989. 178p. $40.00. ISBN 0-89356-656-X. LC 89-10853.
   This bibliography, a part of the Magill Bibliographies series directed at high school students and college undergraduates, brings together critiques of important European writers of short fiction. Succinct and well-written annotations are provided for the entries, which are arranged alphabetically by author. [R: ARBA 91; LJ, 1 May 90; LJ, 1 June 90; WLB, May 90]

1572   **Short Story Criticism: Excerpts from Criticisms of the Works of Short Fiction Writers**. Thomas Votteler, ed. Detroit: Gale, 1988- . 8v. (ongoing). $79.00/v. ISSN 0895-9439.

Similar in format to Gale's other sets of literary criticism, this series covers all nationalities and periods of literary history. Volumes provide excerpts from critical reviews of the works of great short story writers, supplemented by biographical information and bibliographic sources. Each volume covers 15 to 20 authors.

The small number of authors contained in each volume makes this an expensive purchase. Masterplots II: Short Story Series is far more comprehensive but has briefer analyses than *Short Story Criticism*. [R: ARBA 89; BL, 1 Feb 89; BR, Sept/Oct 88; SLJ, May 89]

1573 **Short Story Index: An Index to Stories in Collections and Periodicals**. Juliette Yaakov, ed. Bronx, N.Y.: H. W. Wilson. annual. $85.00/yr. ISSN 0360-9774. LC 75-649762.

1574 **Short Story Index 1984-1988: An Index to Stories in Collections and Periodicals**. Juliette Yaakov, ed. Bronx, N.Y.: H. W. Wilson, 1989. 1195p. $125.00. ISSN 0360-9774. LC 75-649762.

The annual *Short Story Index*, published each September, indexes stories published in collections and magazines during the year and lists them in a single alphabet by author, title, and subject. The list of collections indexed, which also serves as a selection aid, provides full bibliographic information needed to locate any cited story.

Five-year cumulations replace annual volumes. The latest, *Short Story Index 1984-1988*, indexes 32,400 stories in some 1,250 recent collections. Five-year cumulations are also available starting from the 1950-1954 period; a single volume indexes short stories published in collections from 1900 to 1949. [R: ARBA 90]

READING GUIDANCE

See also **Children's Literature** and **Young Adult** Lists under **Books** in **Media Sources**.

1575 Davis, Barbara Kerr. **Read All Your Life: A Subject Guide to Fiction**. Jefferson, N.C.: McFarland, 1989. 286p. $24.95. ISBN 0-89950-370-5. LC 89-42709.

This work is intended as a guide for book discussion groups, but readers seeking guidance in organizing a reading plan for serious fiction also can use it. Titles are arranged in 5 broad categories—self, family, society and politics, religion, and philosophy—which in turn are divided into 43 subject areas, such as mid-life crisis, first love, and the dark side of humankind. Each section begins with a brief, readable, informative essay, followed by eight recommended titles, with excerpts, discussion questions, and additional suggested novels. Recommended for high schools. [R: ARBA 90; BL, 15 Nov 89]

1576 **Good Reading: A Guide for Serious Readers**. 23d ed. Arthur Waldhorn and others, eds. New Providence, N.J.: R. R. Bowker, 1990. 465p. $39.95. ISBN 0-8352-2707-3. LC 89-17317.

Good Reading, which attempts to identify good fiction and nonfiction, is directed toward the serious adult reader. Three thousand briefly annotated titles, arranged under five major subject headings (historical periods, regional and American minority cultures, literary types, humanities and social sciences, and sciences), comprise the latest edition. The core list of "101 Significant Books" featured in earlier editions has been supplemented with new lists of suggested books to be read before entering college, while on vacation, and after retirement.

AMERICAN LITERATURE

Bibliographies

1577 Glikin, Ronda. **Black American Women in Literature: A Bibliography, 1976 through 1987**. Jefferson, N.C.: McFarland, 1989. 251p. $35.00. ISBN 0-89950-372-1. LC 88-43488.

Citations to current works by 300 Black American women and biographical/critical material about them are found in this volume. Approximately 4,300 entries (from 80 periodicals and 200 books) cover scholarly and popular works published between 1976 and 1988. The arrangement is alphabetical by author. Appendixes list books and articles that deal with Black writers, arranged by category (e.g., general, autobiography, fiction, etc.), and a list of authors cited in the text, arranged by genre. Indexed by name/title. [R: ARBA 90; BL, 15 Sept 89; BR, Nov/Dec 89; VOYA, Dec 89]

1578 Werner, Craig. **Black American Women Novelists: An Annotated Bibliography**. Pasadena, Calif.: Salem Press, 1989. 286p. $40.00. ISBN 0-89356-651-1. LC 89-10826.

This bibliography, a part of the Magill Bibliographies series, surveys criticism of Black women novelists and their most important works. It also identifies critical reviews that will help students better understand their writings. Well-written annotations accompany each citation. [R: ARBA 91; LJ, 1 May 90; LJ, 1 June 90; WLB, May 90]

Dictionaries and Encyclopedias

1579 **Benet's Reader's Encyclopedia of American Literature**. George Perkins, Barbara Perkins, and Phillip Leininger, eds. New York: HarperCollins, 1991. 1176p. $45.00. ISBN 0-06-270027-8. LC 91-55001.

This handy volume provides information pertinent to the study of American literature, encompassing as it does Canada, the United States, and Latin America. It is an update and revision of *The Reader's Encyclopedia of American Literature* (1962) and the 3d edition of *Benet's Reader's Encyclopedia* (HarperCollins, 1987), adding 1,500 new articles. Entries range from brief identifications to extensive surveys. More than 130 scholars have produced the signed entries. Cross-references are adequate but might have been enhanced by an index.

There appears to be some imbalance throughout the work. Native American literature is treated both in overview and in entries for specific tribes, and feminist literature is covered with an overview and through individual authors. However, the body of gay and lesbian literature is largely neglected (although some authors are represented). Nonetheless, this volume is highly recommended for its scope and ready-reference value. It will likely remain a standard for years to come.

1580 **The Cambridge Handbook of American Literature**. Jack Salzman, ed. New York: Cambridge University Press, 1986. 286p. $22.95. ISBN 0-521-30703-1. LC 86-2587.

The Cambridge Handbook is an excellent guide to eminent American writers, literary movements, and literary journals. The handbook also provides plot summaries of major works and side-by-side chronologies of American history and literature.

This work is a less expensive alternative to *Oxford Companion to American Literature*. Both contain similar entries and offer literary and social chronologies, but *The Cambridge Handbook* focuses on the most significant (750 entries), while *Oxford* is more comprehensive (5,000 entries). It is unlikely that most high school libraries will need both. [R: ARBA 87; LJ, 15 Sept 86; RBB, 15 Apr 87; WLB, Dec 86]

1581 Conn, Peter. **Literature in America: An Illustrated History**. New York: Cambridge University Press, 1989. 587p. $29.95. ISBN 0-521-30373-7.

Advanced high school students will find the biographical and critical material contained in this work useful. Information on writers' styles and contributions to the field is excellent, but the text is too sophisticated for many students to understand. Parallel literary and historical chronologies are a special feature. [R: SLJ, May 90]

1582 **Dictionary of American Literary Characters**. Benjamin Franklin and others, eds. New York: Facts on File, 1990. 542p. $60.00. ISBN 0-8160-1917-7. LC 89-25820.

This ambitious work identifies 11,000 characters from American novels published between 1789 and 1980. Characters are selected from great literature (e.g., John Steinbeck's *Grapes of Wrath*), works important to their times (e.g., Upton Sinclair's *The Jungle*), and significant popular novels (e.g., Margaret Mitchell's *Gone with the Wind*). Many of those included are well known, but others are obscure. Real people who appear as characters in the novels and a few animals are included. An appendix lists series characters (e.g., Tarzan, Charlie Chan), and the index, in three levels, lists all authors represented, their novels, and the characters.

High school libraries may not require the depth of coverage found in this work, but it is a convenient compilation to hold. Several standard sources, such as *Benet's Reader's Encyclopedia* and *Brewer's Dictionary of Phrase and Fable*, identify characters from novels by America's most significant writers. [R: ARBA 91; BL, 1 Mar 90; BR, Sept/Oct 90]

1583 Hart, James D. **The Oxford Companion to American Literature**. 5th ed. New York: Oxford University Press, 1983. 896p. $49.95. ISBN 0-19-503074-5. LC 81-22469.

1584   Hart, James D. **The Concise Oxford Companion to American Literature**. New York: Oxford University Press, 1986. 497p. $24.95. ISBN 0-19-503982-3. LC 86-8510.

Hart's standard works cover American literary and popular authors from colonial times to the present and treat major social and cultural movements reflected in American literature. The full volume provides alphabetically arranged short biographies of authors, explaining their styles and interests; summarizes over 1,000 novels, short stories, essays, poems, plays, biographies, tracts, narratives, and histories; defines literary terms; and gives other useful information about American literature.

The abridged version contains about half as much information as the parent work, placing emphasis on older and some recent literature. It includes 2,000 brief articles that cover the same types of material. High school libraries should hold one of these volumes, preferably the full work. [R: ARBA 84; ARBA 87]

1585   **A Literary History of the American West**. J. Golden Taylor and others, eds. Fort Worth, Tex.: Texas Christian University Press; distr., College Station, Tex.: Texas A & M University Press, 1987. 1353p. $79.50. ISBN 0-87565-021-X. LC 85-50538.

This monumental work provides extensive coverage of the movements, trends, and genre of western literature, including biographies of several hundred authors and a critical analysis of the works of each. The major divisions are "Encountering the West," subdivided into such topics as "Across the Wide Missouri," and "Precursors of the Western Novel." An analytical section, divided geographically, contains biographies and critical reviews of over 40 major authors (e.g., Mark Twain, Paul Horgan, Bernard De Voto). "Rediscovering the West" includes essays on Indian poetry, western movies, television, and film.

Written by subject specialists, each of the 80 authoritative essays concludes with a bibliography of primary sources and secondary accounts. A list of 126 major reference works and an index conclude the volume. Recommended for high schools with an interest in western literature. [R: ARBA 89; BL, Aug 89; LJ, 15 Apr 88]

1586   Ruoff, A. LaVonne Brown. **American Indian Literatures: An Introduction, Bibliographic Review, and Selected Bibliography**. New York: Modern Language Association of America, 1990. 200p. $45.00; $19.50pa. ISBN 0-87352-187-0; 0-87352-188-9pa. LC 90-13438.

Covering the period 1500 to the present, this scholarly, comprehensive work surveys the Native American oral tradition and written literature, a long-neglected area. The work opens with an introduction to the literature, followed by a section containing essays on bibliographies and research guides; anthologies, collections, and re-creations; and scholarship and criticism. An extensive classified bibliography cites all works mentioned in the essays and additional titles. When an Indian author is named anywhere in the text, the individual's tribal affiliation is given in parentheses. High schools with American Indian enrollment should consider this work. [R: ARBA 92; BL, 1 Mar 91]

Digests and Surveys

1587   **Masterplots: Revised Category Edition, American Fiction Series**. Frank N. Magill, ed. Pasadena, Calif.: Salem Press, 1985. 3v. $120.00/set. ISBN 0-89356-500-8. LC 85-1936.

Many teachers believe that *Masterplots*, now more than 40 years old, does not belong on library shelves, since students are likely to use its synopses and criticisms rather than read the actual books, but this question is a matter for local decision. This set, a reprint with some update and minor editorial changes, deals with 343 novels and collections of short stories. Each work receives uniform treatment: type, author with life dates, time and locale, first date of publication, principal characters, plot summary, and critical remarks. Most authors and books included are standard fare on high school reading lists. [R: ARBA 86]

Biography

1588   **American Authors, 1600-1900: A Biographical Dictionary of American Literature**. Stanley J. Kunitz and Howard Haycraft, eds. Bronx, N.Y.: H. W. Wilson, 1938. $65.00. ISBN 0-8242-0001-2. LC 38-27938.

One of the well-known Wilson Authors series, this volume contains biographies of 1,300 authors who contributed to the development of American literature, from the founding of Jamestown (1607) to the end of the nineteenth century. Each essay describes the author's life, discusses past and present significance, and evaluates principal works. Some 400 portraits illustrate the volume.

1589 American Women Writers: A Critical Reference Guide from Colonial Times to the Present.
Lina Mainiero, ed. New York: Ungar, 1979-1982. 4v. $75.00/v. ISBN 0-8044-3150-7. LC 82-40286.

This set contains biocritical essays on over 1,000 American women authors of literary, popular, and juvenile fiction and nonfiction, from colonial times to the present. Entries consist of brief biographical data; an essay on the author's significance and overall contribution, major works, themes, and style; and a list of works by and about her. This comprehensive source is recommended for high school libraries. [R: ARBA 84]

1590 Biographical Dictionary of Hispanic Literature in the United States: The Literature of Puerto Ricans, Cuban Americans, and Other Hispanic Writers. Nicolas Kanellos, ed. Westport, Conn.: Greenwood Press, 1989. 374p. $49.95. ISBN 0-313-24465-0. LC 88-37288.

This work focuses on 50 important, contemporary Hispanic literary figures from Cuba, Puerto Rico, and Central and South America. Cuban writers predominate. Mexican-American writers are excluded, since they are covered in *Chicano Literature*.

The introduction surveys Hispanic literature. Each signed biography, arranged alphabetically, includes a two- to three-page profile, an analysis of the author's major themes, a brief critical review, and a bibliography of works by and about the writer. A general bibliography, an author-title index, and a list of contributors conclude the volume.

Despite the limited selection (some well-known authors are omitted), this is a reference tool worthy of consideration by secondary school libraries supporting Hispanic studies programs. [R: ARBA 90; BL, 1 Nov 89]

1591 Chicano Literature: A Reference Guide. Julio A. Martinez and Francisco A. Lomeli, eds. Westport, Conn.: Greenwood Press, 1985. 492p. $55.00. ISBN 0-313-23691-7. LC 83-22583.

As defined by the editors, Chicano literature is that which has been "written since 1848 by Americans of Mexican descent or by Mexicans in the United States who write about the Chicano experience." Thirty entries consist of biographical/critical articles about literary figures, and the remaining ten treat literary genres and topics such as Chicano philosophy. Entries include selective bibliographies. High school libraries that serve a Hispanic population should consider this work. [R: ARBA 86; BL, 1 Jan 86; LJ, 15 Apr 86]

1592 Concise Dictionary of American Literary Biography. Detroit: Gale, 1987-1989. 6v. $350.00/set. ISBN 0-8103-1818-0.

Similar in format to *Dictionary of Literary Biography*, this biographical/critical set includes American authors most frequently studied in high school and college literature courses. Organized chronologically in order to emphasize the historical development of American literature, each volume focuses on a historical period and covers 30 to 40 writers from all genres. Articles on 200 authors (selected from the 2,300 American authors in the parent set) have been updated and expanded for this edition. Also provided are an annotated bibliography of secondary works and a "contextual map" that shows how each author fits into the literary, social, and cultural context of the times.

Volumes may be purchased separately in order to meet a specific curricular need. They are titled as follows: *Colonization to the American Renaissance, 1640-1865*; *Realism, Naturalism, and Local Color, 1865-1917*; *The Twenties, 1917-1929*; *The Age of Maturity, 1929-1941*; *The New Consciousness, 1941-1968*; and *Broadening Views, 1968-1988*. [R: ARBA 89; ARBA 90; ARBA 91; SLJ, May 89]

■ *Hispanic Writers*. See entry 1619.

1593 Modern American Women Writers. Lea Baechler and A. Walton Litz, eds. New York: Scribner's, 1991. 583p. $85.00. ISBN 0-684-19057-5. LC 90-52917.

This work focuses on 41 representative American women who have published since 1870. Among those included are Anne Tyler, Alice Walker, and Emily Dickinson. The essays, ranging from 8 to 22 pages, emphasize the social and historical environment in which each wrote. *American Women Writers: A Critical Reference Guide from Colonial Times to the Present* covers all the women included here, but this work provides greater depth of criticism and more current bibliographies. Recommended for high schools. [R: ARBA 92; LJ, 15 June 91]

1594 Roses, Lorraine Elena, and Ruth Elizabeth Randolph. **Harlem Renaissance and Beyond: Literary Biographies of 100 Black Women Writers 1900-1945**. Boston: G. K. Hall, 1990. 413p. $45.00. ISBN 0-8161-8926-0. LC 89-38731.

The lives and works of 100 Black women writers are chronicled in this volume – novelists, short-story writers, playwrights, poets, essayists, critics, historians, journalists, and editors. This is the only biographical guide that focuses on Black women writers in the first half of the twentieth century. *Afro-American Writers from the Harlem Renaissance to 1940*, a volume in the Dictionary of Literary Biography series, includes only eight women.

Most profiles are 1 to 2 pages in length, but significant writers, such as Zora Neale Hurston, receive 10 or more. Bibliographies of primary and secondary works support all entries, many of which include photographs. Appendixes list writers by genre, geographic location, dates, and titles. A general bibliography concludes the volume. This work covers a neglected area, and high school libraries should consider it. [R: ARBA 91; BL, 15 Jan 90; LJ, Dec 89]

Criticism

1595 **American Writers**. Leonard Unger and A. Walton Litz, eds. New York: Scribner's, 1974-1981. 4v. with 2 supplements (2v. ea.). $625.00/set. ISBN 0-684-17322-0.

The 156 critical essays in the main set, written by distinguished scholars, cover American writers from the seventeenth century to the present – novelists, poets, short story writers, playwrights, critics, and philosophers. For a famous author, a 12- to 15-page essay provides an in-depth analysis of the writer's style, the social and cultural context in which the author wrote, and themes and viewpoints of major works. There are no biographical sketches or plot summaries. Each entry concludes with a chronological list of the author's writings and a selective list of critical reviews. An author, title, and subject index gives access to the set. Supplements 1 and 2 augment the 4 base volumes with essays on 59 additional writers.

Other sets in the series include *Science Fiction Writers* (Scribner's, 1982), *Supernatural Fiction Writers* (Scribner's, 1985), *Modern American Writers* (Scribner's, 1990), and *African Writers* (Scribner's, 1991).

ENGLISH LITERATURE

Bibliographies

1596 Mazzeno, Laurence W. **The Victorian Novel: An Annotated Bibliography**. Pasadena, Calif.: Salem Press, 1989. 222p. $40.00. ISBN 0-89356-653-5. LC 89-10794.

This bibliography, a part of the Magill Bibliographies series, focuses on the criticism of Victorian novels most frequently read at high school and undergraduate levels. Arranged alphabetically by author and title, it refers to accessible works that address the author's career and achievements, often providing a comparison with contemporaries or novelists of other periods. Each entry includes a well-written annotation. [R: ARBA 91; LJ, 1 May 90; LJ, 1 June 90; WLB, May 90]

Dictionaries and Encyclopedias

1597 **The Oxford Companion to English Literature**. 5th ed. Margaret Drabble, ed. New York: Oxford University Press, 1985. 1155p. $49.95. ISBN 0-19-866130-4.

1598 **The Concise Oxford Companion to English Literature**. Margaret Drabble and Jenny Stringer, eds. New York: Oxford University Press, 1987. 640p. $24.95. ISBN 0-19-866140-1. LC 87-1595.

Drabble, a noted novelist and critic, has produced a substantial revision of the indispensable *Oxford Companion to English Literature* and its concise version. The work was created by Paul Harvey in 1932 and last revised in 1967.

The full volume contains over 9,000 entries: some 2,000 plot summaries and outlines of novels, plays, poems, and so forth; over 3,000 concise biographies (for authors born before 1940); entries for literary characters; surveys of literary and artistic movements; and lists of prizes, periodicals, newspapers, and other publications. The revision includes allusions, which Harvey excluded because he believed that *Brewer's Dictionary of Phrase and Fable* and other standard sources adequately covered them. Artists and composers also receive attention. Highly recommended for high school libraries.

The concise volume, an abridgment of the 5th edition, emphasizes basic information rather than evaluation and provides briefer treatments of all entries. It is recommended for libraries that cannot afford the full volume. [R: ARBA 86; BL, 1 Mar 88; SLJ, May 88]

Biography

1599 **British Authors before 1800: A Biographical Dictionary**. Stanley J. Kunitz and Howard Haycraft, eds. Bronx, N.Y.: H. W. Wilson, 1952. 584p. $53.00. ISBN 0-8242-0006-3. LC 52-6758.

1600 **British Authors of the Nineteenth Century: A Biographical Dictionary**. Stanley J. Kunitz and Howard Haycraft, eds. Bronx, N.Y.: H. W. Wilson, 1936. 677p. $55.00. ISBN 0-8242-0007-1. LC 36-28561.

These works contain more than 1,650 biographical profiles (650 before 1800 and 1,000 during the nineteenth century) of writers, philosophers, theologians, critics, and others who achieved eminence in British literature before the twentieth century. Articles focus on their lives and most influential writings. Portraits accompany many of the entries. Recommended for high schools.

1601 **An Encyclopedia of British Women Writers**. Paul Schlueter and Jane Schlueter, eds. Hamden, Conn.: Garland, 1988. 516p. (Garland Reference Library of the Humanities, v.818). $75.00. ISBN 0-8240-8449-7. LC 88-21393.

Some 375 British women writers, from Marie de France and Eleanor of Aquitaine to Mary Drabble and P. D. James, constitute the focus of this work. It is not limited to women known primarily for their writings; also included are authors of diaries, translators, social activists, feminists, scientists, and other professionals.

Alphabetically arranged entries written by over 100 contributors range in length from one-half to three pages. Each essay opens with a factual summary (e.g., parentage, marriage) and ends with a bibliography of works by and about the author. The entry's emphasis is on the author's writing career. Indexing is by subject, profession, genre, and author name. Appropriate for high school libraries. [R: ARBA 89; BL, 1 Apr 89; WLB, Feb 89]

Criticism

1602 **British Writers**. Ian Scott Kilvert, ed. 8 v. New York: Scribner's, 1979-1984. $625.00/set. ISBN 0-684-18253-X.

The 153 essays in this set, the companion to *American Writers*, cover authors who have made a significant contribution to British literature from the fourteenth century to the present. Each of the chronologically arranged volumes contains an introductory essay and a chronology of major political and literary events of the period. In each volume, a topical essay addresses a major contribution or movement of the era (e.g., "The English Bible" in volume 1, "Poets in World War II" in volume 7).

Articles about authors (10,000 to 15,000 words) are followed by a complete list of their writings and a selected list of major critical reviews. The scholarly articles, often by well-known figures, are signed (e.g., T. S. Eliot contributed the article on George Herbert). An author, title, and subject index appears in the last volume of the set. *Supplement I* (1987) extends coverage to writers who have become prominent since World War II. This superior set is highly recommended for high schools.

1603 Kloesel, Christian J. W. **English Novel Explication: Supplement IV**. Hamden, Conn.: Shoe String Press, 1990. 351p. $55.00. ISBN 0-208-02231-7. LC 84-137107.

The earlier supplements covered 1972-1974 (1976), 1975-1979 (1980), and 1980-1985 (1986). *Supplement IV* extends coverage from 1986 through 1989. All serve as continuations of Inglis F. Bell and Donald Baird's *The English Novel, 1518-1956* (subsequently updated in 1973 by Helen Palmer and Jane Dyson as *English Novel Explication*), which listed critical reviews to 1972.

Writers covered in *Supplement IV* range from standard authors, such as Charles Dickens, to popular contemporary writers, such as Dick Francis and P. D. James. The arrangement is alphabetical by author and then by book title. Indexed by author/title. High schools with advanced placement English programs and that own the earlier volumes should consider this update. [R: ARBA 91; BL, 1 Nov 90]

Shakespeare

1604 Boyce, Charles. **Shakespeare A to Z: The Essential Reference to His Plays, His Poems, His Life and Times, and More.** New York: Facts on File, 1990. 742p. $45.00. ISBN 0-8160-1805-7. LC 90-31239.

Almost 3,000 entries describe Shakespeare's characters and the actors who have interpreted them, from the sixteenth century to date; famous theaters; film directors of Shakespeare; composers who wrote music for the plays; contemporaries of Shakespeare; persons who have written about him; literary and theatrical terms; historical references; places; Shakespeare himself; and each of the plays. Entries vary from a few sentences to three or more pages for major characters, and nine pages for plays such as *Hamlet*. Entries for plays summarize each scene and give historical sources of the play, famous productions, and a brief commentary. Some 50 black-and-white photographs and line drawings illustrate the volume.

Shakespare Handbook has more attractive illustrations, but the text is not as accessible as the A to Z arrangement of Boyce's work. High school library media centers will find the latter an excellent choice for their collections. [R: ARBA 92; BL, 15 Mar 91]

1605 Cahn, Victor L. **Shakespeare the Playwright: A Companion to the Complete Tragedies, Histories, Comedies, and Romances.** Westport, Conn.: Greenwood Press, 1991. 828p. $75.00. ISBN 0-313-27493-2.

This work, a study guide to Shakespeare's 37 plays, includes quotes, paraphrases, and critical comments. Cahn's straightforward approach makes this volume an excellent source for high school and college students. Bibliographies conclude each chapter and the book. Recommended. [R: LJ, Dec 90]

1606 Macrone, Michael. **Brush Up Your Shakespeare!** New York: Harper & Row, 1990. 235p. $15.00. ISBN 0-06-016393-3. LC 89-46105.

This unique volume is an excellent reference work and a joy to read. The first and longest section focuses on hundreds of the most memorable Shakespearean phrases, arranged alphabetically by key word. Each is presented in context with interesting commentaries. The second section lists household words originated by Shakespeare, and the third identifies phrases often mistakenly attributed to the Bard. The final section lists titles by other authors and artists that are based on Shakespeare (e.g., *Kiss Me, Kate*). [R: ARBA 91]

1607 Onions, C. T. **A Shakespeare Glossary.** 3d ed. Revised by Robert D. Eagleson. New York: Clarendon Press/Oxford University Press, 1986. 326p. $24.95; $8.95pa. ISBN 0-19-811199-1; 0-19-812521-6pa. LC 84-7912.

Most students require assistance with the language of the seventeenth century, for many words today mean something quite different from what they meant back then. Relying on textual studies and computer-generated concordances of Shakespeare, the current edition has updated Onion's glossary and added many new entries. After a word is defined, one or more examples of Shakespeare's use of it are cited; they are taken from the *Riverside Shakespeare* (Houghton Mifflin, 1974), edited by G. Blakemore Evans and others. Recommended for high schools. [R: ARBA 88]

1608 **The Quotable Shakespeare: A Topical Dictionary.** Charles DeLoach, comp. Jefferson, N.C.: McFarland, 1988. 544p. $39.95. ISBN 0-89950-303-9. LC 87-35362.

This work identifies Shakespearean quotations that "contain ... a philosophical axiom, a general truth or a fundamental principle"; also included are some that will inspire and delight readers. The volume contains 6,516 numbered quotations arranged alphabetically under 1,000 topics. Each entry from a play cites character's name; quotation; and title of play, act, scene, and line as it appears in *Riverside Shakespeare*, edited by G. Blakemore Evans and others (Houghton Mifflin, 1974). Poetry quotations are identified by line or sonnet number. The indexes provide approaches to the content by play title, sonnet, character, and topic (which also serves as a partial keyword index). This unique source is an appropriate addition to high school libraries. [R: ARBA 89; BL, 1 Nov 88; BR, Nov/Dec 88]

1609 **The Shakespeare Handbook.** By Levi Fox. Boston: G. K. Hall, 1987. 264p. $29.95. ISBN 0-8161-8905-6. LC 87-16990.

Intended as "a companion reference source for students" and others interested in Shakespeare, this handbook contains background information for those needing help in understanding the Bard. It consists of a brief chronology and chapters that cover the Elizabethan world, Shakespeare's Life, Elizabethan and Jacobean theater, the plays, Shakespeare in performance, the poetry, music and song, and Shakespeare on film. The longest section covers every play in double-page spreads. For each, there is a list of characters and a commentary on the text—its source, themes, derivations, and imagery.

Attractive color and black-and-white illustrations enliven most pages of the lucid text, and the information reflects the latest research on Shakespeare. The overall quality of the work is uneven, but libraries serving high school students should consider it.

■ *Shakespeare on Screen*. *See* entry 1330.

1610 **William Shakespeare: His World, His Work, His Influence.** John F. Andrews, ed. Scribner's, 1985. 3v. $225.00/set. ISBN 0-684-17851-6. LC 85-8305.

This beautiful set, produced under the supervision of the editor of *Shakespeare Quarterly*, will interest many high school libraries. Volume 1, *His World*, presents articles on life in Elizabethan England; volume 2, *His Work*, focuses on comedies, tragedies, sonnets, and other poems; and volume 3, *His Influence*, deals with Shakespeare's influence on drama and the modern theater. Articles also cover his treatment of history, the teaching of Shakespeare, and Shakespeare-related institutions.

All essays, contributed and signed by American and British scholars, conclude with a bibliography. Most articles are illustrated with black-and-white drawings and photographs. The last volume contains an index to the set. This is an important source that could become a classic. High school libraries able to afford its high cost should consider it a first purchase. [R: ARBA 86; BL, 1 Mar 86]

AUSTRALIAN LITERATURE

1611 Wilde, William H., and others. **The Oxford Companion to Australian Literature.** New York: Oxford University Press, c1985, 1986. 760p. $39.95. ISBN 0-19-554233-9.

This comprehensive guide to the literature and culture of Australia is an outstanding reference work. Over 3,000 entries provide an overview of the country's literary life from the first English settlement in 1788 to the early 1980s. Authors, important literary works, characters, and topics related to literature, art, and history are included. The alphabetically arranged essays, most of which are brief, are well written and interesting. This is not an essential holding for most high schools, but it is a lively volume for those that require material on Australia. [R: ARBA 88]

CANADIAN LITERATURE

1612 **Oxford Companion to Canadian Literature.** William Toye, ed. New York: Oxford University Press, 1983. 843p. $49.95. ISBN 0-19-540283-9.

This work consists of 750 signed articles on English and French Canadian literature. Entries for authors and genres predominate, but there also are articles on specific titles, publishers, periodicals, and other literary topics. Survey essays treat broad areas, such as humor and satire, travel literature, and mystery and crime. Emphasis is on modern times, particularly for the period since 1940. High school libraries with an interest in Canadian intellectual and cultural life should hold this volume. [R: ARBA 85]

CLASSICAL LITERATURE

1613 Forman, Robert J. **Classical Greek and Roman Drama: An Annotated Bibliography.** Pasadena, Calif.: Salem Press, 1989. 239p. $40.00. ISBN 0-89356-659-4. LC 89-10805.

A part of the Magill Bibliographies series designed for senior high school students and college undergraduates, this bibliography examines the evolution of classical drama. The citations include the best-known critical works and focus on those most likely to be available to students. Each entry includes a well-written annotation. [R: ARBA 91; LJ, 1 May 90; LJ, 1 June 90; WLB, May 90]

1614 Grant, Michael. **Greek and Latin Authors, 800 B.C.-A.D. 1000.** Bronx, N.Y.: H. W. Wilson, 1980. 490p. $60.00. ISBN 0-8242-0640-1. LC 79-27446.

This excellent biographical dictionary, one of the Wilson Authors series, contains brief profiles of 376 writers who contributed to the rich and varied literature of the classical world. Each essay contains critical comments and a bibliography of the best editions and translations. The appendix lists authors chronologically by century. Grant is a renowned classical scholar. [R: ARBA 81]

1615 **The Oxford Companion to Classical Literature**. 2d ed. M. C. Howatson, ed. New York: Oxford University Press, 1989. 615p. $45.00. ISBN 0-19-866121-5. LC 86-27330.

Updating the 1937 work edited by the distinguished Paul Harvey, this revision is likely to become a worthy successor. It covers classical literature from the appearance of the Greeks, around 2200 B.C., to the close of the Athenian philosophy schools in A.D. 529. It includes articles on authors, major works, historical notables, mythological figures, and topics of literary significance. Short summaries of major works, chronologies, charts, and maps are special features. [R: ARBA 90; BL, 1 Nov 89; WLB, Sept 89]

FRENCH LITERATURE

1616 Dolbow, Sandra W. **Dictionary of Modern French Literature: From the Age of Reason through Realism**. Westport, Conn.: Greenwood Press, 1986. 365p. $49.95. ISBN 0-313-23784-0. LC 85-15492.

Articles cover all major authors of the Regency period (which began in 1715) to 1980, including historians, dramatists, poets, and philosophers. Essays that cover significant authors (e.g., Rousseau, Voltaire) are six or more pages in length, but most are only one or two pages long. All have appended bibliographies that cite English-language items published between 1980 and 1985. Appendixes provide a chronology of important literary and historical events and a list of entries, grouped by subject. [R: ARBA 87; BL, 15 Oct 86; LJ, 1 Oct 86]

GERMAN LITERATURE

1617 **The Oxford Companion to German Literature**. 2d ed. Henry Garland and Mary Garland, eds. New York: Oxford University Press, 1986. 1020p. $55.00. ISBN 0-19-866139-8.

This outstanding work focuses on German literature and gives a concise summary of the political and cultural background necessary to understand it. Entries cover significant writers, important works with plot summaries, major genres, literary movements, characters, historical figures and events, literary devices, artists, philosophers, historians, literary critics, and journals. First lines of hymns, folk songs, and poems also appear. Major writers of the former German Democratic Republic are well represented. [R: ARBA 88; BL, 15 Mar 87]

HISPANIC LITERATURE

1618 Foster, David William, comp. **Handbook of Latin American Literature**. Hamden, Conn.: Garland, 1987. 608p. (Garland Reference Library of the Humanities, v.669). $50.00. ISBN 0-8240-8559-0. LC 86-22860.

These surveys of the national literature of 21 Latin American nations are intended for the general reader. Most entries follow a historical approach, focusing on the development of the literature and its relationship to the culture, with attention given to major writers and the dominant themes of the country's literary tradition. Recommended for high schools. [R: ARBA 88; LJ, 15 May 87]

1619 **Hispanic Writers: A Selection of Sketches from *Contemporary Authors***. Bryan Ryan, ed. Detroit: Gale, 1991. 514p. $75.00. ISBN 0-8103-7688-1. LC 90-83635.

Some 40 percent of those included in *Hispanic Writers* have appeared in *Contemporary Authors* (CA), and many others, according to the publisher, will be covered in CA's future volumes. High school libraries with a strong interest in Hispanic literature, including those holding sets of CA, may wish to acquire this volume, which contains many important authors now deceased who are unlikely candidates for the "contemporary" set.

Over 400 writers (European, Mexican, South American, Central American, and American Hispanics) are treated in this volume. Entries, similar to others in CA and its spinoffs, summarize personal and career information, followed by bibliographies and concise essays on the author's works. [R: ARBA 92; WLB, Jan 91]

1620 **Latin American Literature in the 20th Century: A Guide**. New York: Crossroad/Ungar/Continuum, 1986. 278p. $12.95pa. ISBN 0-8044-6361-1. LC 85-24534.

This handbook contains surveys of the literature of 20 Latin American countries, Argentina to Venezuela, drawn from the 5-volume *Encyclopedia of World Literature of the 20th Century*. Each section treats the precursors of the current literature and examines the works of several important writers, giving a biographical profile of each, a survey of the writings, and a bibliography. Highly recommended. [R: ARBA 88]

1621 **Latin American Writers**. Carlos A. Sole and Maria Isabel Abreau, eds. New York: Scribner's, 1989. 3v. $250.00/set. ISBN 0-684-18463-X. LC 88-35481.

Latin American writers who represent many literary genres are included in this set. The essays cover 176 authors from the colonial period to the present, and each entry contains a short biography, an evaluation of the writer's works and style, and a bibliography of the author's writings. The arrangement is chronological with indexing by name and country. Recommended for high school libraries. [R: ARBA 90; BR, Mar 90; SLJ, May 90]

1622 **Oxford Companion to Spanish Literature**. Philip Ward, ed. New York: Oxford University Press, 1978. 629p. $39.95. ISBN 0-19-866114-2.

Another of the excellent Oxford Companion series, this work covers all aspects of the literature of Spain, Central and South America, the Philippines, and other Spanish-speaking regions, as well as minority languages of Spain and major writers in Basque, Catalan, and Galician. The literatures of Portugal and Brazil are excluded. Entries treat authors, literary movements, journals, and other topics and provide plot summaries of significant books. [R: ARBA 80]

SCANDINAVIAN LITERATURE

1623 **Dictionary of Scandinavian Literature**. Virpi Zuck, ed. Westport, Conn.: Greenwood Press, 1990. 792p. $99.50. ISBN 0-313-21450-6. LC 89-11970.

This dictionary represents the first attempt to compile (in English) a comprehensive work of the literature of five Nordic languages plus Faroese, Inuit, and Sami. The volume consists of 400 articles that cover authors and other topics. Entries for writers list their major works, English translations, and literary criticism. A bibliography arranged by subject and an index conclude the work. Persons of Scandinavian descent should welcome this reference tool. [R: ARBA 92; LJ, 1 May 90; LJ, 15 Apr 91]

SLAVIC LITERATURE

1624 **Handbook of Russian Literature**. Victor Terras, ed. New Haven, Conn.: Yale University Press, 1985. 558p. $55.00; $24.95pa. ISBN 0-300-03155-6; 0-300-04868-8pa. LC 84-11871.

This alphabetically arranged handbook, containing almost 1,000 signed articles, was prepared by American scholars. It treats the authors, critics, theorists, history, terminology, literary movements, journals, publishers, societies, and organizations of Russian literature. Essays on authors cite their principal works and their most important translations. Most entries end with a bibliography; a general bibliography and an index conclude the volume. [R: ARBA 86; BL, 15 May 85; LJ, 1 June 85]

1625 Kasack, Wolfgang. **Dictionary of Russian Literature since 1917**. New York: Columbia University Press, 1988. 502p. $55.50. ISBN 0-231-05242-1. LC 87-20838.

A translation of Kasack's *Lexikon der russischen Literatur ab 1917* (1976) and its supplement (1986), this major work contains entries for Russian (not Soviet) literature, including 619 authors, literary scholars, and translators of belles-lettres. The biographical section provides the usual data, plus membership in the Communist Party, date of emigration (if applicable), pseudonyms, and position in the writer's union. Journals, movements, and other literary topics also receive attention. A separate section lists the author's works. Indexed by name and subject.

More authors are included in this work than in Victor Terras's *Handbook of Russian Literature*. Most high schools will not require a reference book on Russian literature, but those that do will find this authoritative work useful. [R: ARBA 89]

☐ # **Music** ☐

CHRONOLOGIES

■ *The New Penguin Guide to Compact Discs and Cassettes: Yearbook*. *See* entry 37.

■ *Opus*. *See* entry 38.

■ *Spectrum*. *See* entry 39.

1626   Burbank, Richard. **Twentieth Century Music: Orchestral, Chamber, Operatic, & Dance Music, 1900-1980**. New York: Facts on File, 1984. 485p. $50.00. ISBN 0-87196-464-3. LC 80-25040.
    This attractive work, a chronology of musical events of the first 80 years of this century, is arranged by year and then by 5 headings: opera; dance; instrumental and vocal music; births, deaths, and debuts; and related events. The sections that cover compositions cite their premieres with conductors, casts, dancers, choreographers, orchestras, and performance locations. The fourth section, among other things, summarizes the contributions of deceased dancers and musicians. Related events include developments in the film and recording industries. Many illustrations and a detailed index are provided. [R: ARBA 85; BL, 1 Nov 85; WLB, Sept 84]

DICTIONARIES AND ENCYCLOPEDIAS

E+
1627   Ardley, Neil. **Music: An Illustrated Encyclopedia**. New York: Facts on File, 1986. 192p. $18.95. ISBN 0-8160-1543-0. LC 86-6279.
    A comprehensive introduction to all aspects (technical, historical, geographical, and biographical) of classical and popular music, this work is an excellent addition to any collection serving children in grades 5 through 8. It provides chapters on such varied topics as musical instruments, folk and ethnic music, opera and ballet, theory and notation, and music making.
    Numerous illustrations, three or four to a page, include black-and-white and color photographs of musicians and musical events, detailed drawings of instruments, and diagrams of theory and sound systems. This handsome work is highly recommended. [R: ARBA 87; BL, 15 Dec 86; SLJ, May 87]

1628   Blom, Eric, and David Cummings, comps. **The New Everyman Dictionary of Music**. 6th ed. Toronto: Fitzhenry & Whiteside, 1988. 876p. $19.95pa. ISBN 0-88902-876-1.
    Edited by Blom in 1971 and revised by Cummings, this work contains entries for musical terms, orchestras, composers, and performers. All original articles retained have been revised. Entries for obscure musicians no longer of interest have been dropped, and 1,500 new ones have been added. Biographies of composers list major works; well-known compositions are also entered separately under their own titles. This inexpensive dictionary is suggested for high schools. [R: ARBA 90; LJ, July 89]

1629   **Heritage of Music**. Michael Raeburn and Alan Kendall, eds. New York: Oxford University Press, 1989. 4v. $195.00/set. ISBN 0-19-520493-X. LC 85-21429.
    This history of Western music consists of broad chapters that usually focus on one or more major composers of a particular period and the times in which they lived. Each of the four volumes, chronologically arranged, cover an era: classical music and its origin, the Romantic period, the nineteenth-century legacy, and music of the twentieth century. Profiles of relevant composers are appended to the end of each volume, the last of which contains an index to this handsome set. This excellent survey of musicology shows how music reflects the times and events of composers' lives. [R: ARBA 90; LJ, 15 Oct 89; RBB, 15 Dec 89]

1630   **The New Grove Dictionary of American Music**. H. Wiley Hitchcock and Stanley Sadie, eds. New York: Stockton Press/Grove's Dictionaries of Music, 1986. 4v. $695.00/set. ISBN 0-943818-36-2. LC 86-404.
    A spinoff of *The New Grove Dictionary of Music and Musicians*, this set contains 5,000 articles on all aspects of American music, popular and classical. Some entries revise and expand those in the

original set, but others were written especially for this work. This significant publication is the definitive work on American music. [R: ARBA 88]

1631 The New Grove Dictionary of Music and Musicians. 6th ed. Stanley Sadie, ed. New York: Stockton Press/Grove's Dictionaries of Music, 1980. 20v. $2,300.00/set. ISBN 0-333-23111-2. LC 79-26207.

The latest edition of this standard, comprehensive work contains 22,500 articles that include biographies of composers, writers, publishers, and instrument makers; terms; instruments; musical works; and music history. The emphasis, however, is on biographical entries, of which there are 16,500. The set covers popular, folk, and classical music from earliest times to the present. Over 3,000 illustrations (tables, technical diagrams, family trees, musical autographs, and portraits), 500 pages of bibliographies, and a detailed index support the work. This is the best work available on music and musicians, but most high school library media centers do not require the extensive coverage it provides. [R: ARBA 81]

1632 The New Harvard Dictionary of Music. 3d rev. ed. Don Michael Randel, ed. Cambridge, Mass.: Belknap Press/Harvard University Press, 1986. 942p. $35.00. ISBN 0-674-61525-5. LC 86-4780.

The latest edition of this work, a standard for more than 40 years, contains some 6,000 terms, concepts, and histories for many kinds of music, including jazz and rock, and the music of Africa, Asia, Latin America, and the Near East. Descriptions of musical instruments, 250 musical examples, and black-and-white drawings are provided. Biographical entries are omitted. Longer articles have bibliographies. Recommended for high schools. [R: ARBA 87; BL, 1 Mar 87; LJ, Jan 87; LJ, 15 Apr 87]

1633 The New Oxford Companion to Music. Denis Arnold, ed. New York: Oxford University Press, 1983. 2v. $125.00. ISBN 0-19-311316-3.

This work is based on the standard *Oxford Companion to Music* (10 editions, 1938-1970); nonetheless, the text has been extensively rewritten. Some 6,600 articles, ranging from 50 words to several pages, provide international coverage. Entries for composers predominate, but those for individual works are numerous. Other essays cover musical theory, instruments, styles, forms, and terms. Illustrations, which consist of black-and-white photographs, line drawings, and musical examples, are scattered throughout the set. Recommended for high schools. [R: ARBA 84]

1634 The Norton/Grove Concise Encyclopedia of Music. Stanley Sadie and Alison Latham, eds. New York: W. W. Norton, 1988. 850p. $40.00. ISBN 0-393-02620-5.

High schools that do not need (or are unable to afford) the 10-volume *New Grove Dictionary of Music and Musicians*, on which this volume is based, will find this authoritative (and in some cases, updated) work useful. The 10,000 alphabetically arranged entries, written by subject specialists, cover all areas of music (e.g., composers, instrumentalists, performers, terminology). There are 1,000 entries under names of individual works. The emphasis is on classical music, but some attention is given to rock and popular music. Illustrations include pictures of instruments, diagrams for the symphony orchestra, and music examples. [R: ARBA 90; LJ, Jan 89; RBB, 1 Apr 89]

E+
1635 The Oxford Junior Companion to Music. 2d ed. Michael Hurd, ed. New York: Oxford University Press, 1979. 353p. $35.00. ISBN 0-19-314302-X.

E+
1636 The Oxford First Companion to Music. Kenneth McLeish and Valerie McLeish, eds. New York: Oxford University Press, 1982. 1v. (various paging). $25.00. ISBN 0-19-314303-8.

These two beautifully illustrated volumes are recommended for grades 5 through 8. Each contains entries about people, places, musical styles, instruments, and terminology for classical, jazz, and popular music worldwide. *First Companion* contains fewer articles than the *Oxford Companion*, which is preferred, but both are recommended. [R: ARBA 81; ARBA 83]

BIOGRAPHY

■ *Authors and Artists for Young Adults*. See entry 1173.

1637   **Baker's Biographical Dictionary of Musicians**. 8th ed. Revised by Nicolas Slonimsky. New York: Schirmer Books/Macmillan, 1992. 2115p. $125.00. ISBN 0-02-872415-1. LC 91-24591.

Since this work appeared in 1900, it has become a classic in its field. More than 13,000 entries cover musicians both living and deceased, classical and popular, worldwide and historical: composers, singers and other performers, instrumentalists, conductors, critics, librettists, impressarios, instrument makers, scholars, and patrons. Those included range from Bach, Luciano Pavarotti, and Handel to Loretta Lynn and Elvis Presley. The profiles, from a few lines to multi-page accounts, are enlightening and entertaining.

This important work is recommended for high schools. *The Concise Baker's Biographical Dictionary of Musicians* also is recommended, but the original work is preferable. [R: ARBA 86; BL, 1 Sept 85; LJ, 15 Apr 85; WLB, May 85]

1638   **Contemporary Musicians: Profiles of the People in Music**. Michael L. LaBlanc, ed. Detroit: Gale. semiannual. $52.95/v. ISSN 1044-2197.

Each volume in this series includes 80 to 100 performers and writers from a variety of musical fields: pop, rock, rap, jazz, rhythm and blues, folk, new age, country, gospel, and reggae. Entries include biographical and professional highlights, a photograph, a critical essay on contributions, and a selective bibliography. Music fans will welcome these straightforward evaluations of musicians and their music. (As of June 1991, five volumes had been published.) [R: ARBA 90; BR, Jan/Feb 90; RBB, 1 Nov 89; WLB, Nov 89]

1639   Ewen, David. **American Songwriters: One Hundred Forty-Six Biographies of America's Greatest Popular Composers & Lyricists**. Bronx, N.Y.: H. W. Wilson, 1986. 489p. $56.00. ISBN 0-8242-0744-0. LC 86-24658.

This work is filled with 146 composers and lyricists who created the best-known American popular songs (e.g., Irving Berlin, George M. Cohan, Bob Dylan, Stephen Foster, George Gershwin, Oscar Hammerstein, II). The text narrates the performance history of more than 5,500 of their songs, providing the background, movie or Broadway shows in which they were performed, and who recorded them. A great deal of attention is given to the critical reception of specific songs and statistics, such as appearances on "Your Hit Parade" and successive Broadway performances. Indexing is by song only.

This work supersedes Ewen's *Popular American Composers* (1962) and its *First Supplement* (1973). Recommended for secondary schools. [R: ARBA 88]

1640   Floyd, Samuel A., Jr., and Marsha J. Reisser. **Black Music Biography: An Annotated Bibliography**. White Plains, N.Y.: Kraus International, 1987. 302p. $35.00. ISBN 0-527-30158-2. LC 86-27827.

This major contribution to the field consists of an extensively annotated bibliography of 147 monographs on 87 Black composers and performers. It covers the period from Blind Tom (born in 1849) to Michael Jackson and treats musicians who represent all types of musical activity. The lengthy annotations make this work an informational source as well as a bibliographic tool. References to book reviews are listed, and discographies are provided where appropriate. Indexed by author, title, and subject. [R: ARBA 88]

1641   **Great Composers, 1300-1900**. David Ewen, comp. and ed. Bronx, N.Y.: H. W. Wilson, 1966. 419p. $53.00. ISBN 0-8242-0018-7. LC 65-24585.

1642   **Composers since 1900**. David Ewen, comp. and ed. Bronx, N.Y.: H. W. Wilson, 1969. 639p. $58.00. ISBN 0-8242-0400-X. LC 72-102368.

1643   **Composers since 1900. First Supplement**. David Ewen, comp. and ed. Bronx, N.Y.: H. W. Wilson, 1981. 328p. $40.00. ISBN 0-8242-0664-9. LC 81-14785.

This series profiles major and less well known composers who have shaped the international development of music over the last seven centuries. The foundation volume covers 200 composers for the period 1300-1900; *Composers since 1900* and the supplement add 267 biographical sketches. The latter also contains new material on some composers included in the first volume. For the two volumes on the twentieth century, Ewen interviewed many of the subjects. Each entry provides biographical and critical information, a list of major works, recommended sources about the composer, and (usually) a portrait.

1644 The Great Composers I. North Bellmore, N.Y.: Marshall Cavendish, 1987. 11v. $329.95/set. ISBN 0-86307-776-5. LC 86-31294.

1645 The Great Composers II. North Bellmore, N.Y.: Marshall Cavendish, 1990. 5v. $179.95/set. ISBN 1-85435-300-4.

The lives and works of over 40 outstanding composers of the seventeenth to the twentieth centuries are discussed in these beautiful sets. Set I devotes a full volume to Mozart, Beethoven, and Tchaikovsky. Other volumes in both sets each treat several composers.

Coverage of each composer includes life, a review of the times in which the individual lived, and a listener's guide for one or more works. The guide contains the historical background of the composition; program notes; and explanations of movements, melodic themes, and other parts of the composition.

Several volumes include special features; for example, volume 10 in set I contains "A Beginner's Guide to the Opera," which provides a brief history of opera, profiles noted singers, defines terms, and describes great opera houses throughout the world. Color illustrations include portrait of the composer and members of the family; paintings of opera houses, palaces, opera sets, and costumes; and pictures of musical instruments, scores, and many other items. The last volume in each set is a comprehensive index. Recommended for high school libraries. [R: BL, 1 Apr 88; WLB, Mar 88]

1646 Musicians since 1900: Performers in Concert and Opera. David Ewen, comp. and ed. Bronx, N.Y.: H. W. Wilson, 1978. 974p. $75.00. ISBN 0-8242-0565-0. LC 78-12727.

This volume contains biographical sketches of 432 twentieth-century artists of the concert hall and opera—performers, conductors, and instrumentalists. Essays of varying length provide career and personal information in a readable style. When possible, profiles are based on personal interviews. [R: ARBA 80]

1647 Slonimsky, Nicolas. The Concise Baker's Biographical Dictionary of Musicians. New York: Schirmer Books/Macmillan, 1988. 1407p. $35.00. ISBN 0-02-872411-9. LC 87-32328.

Baker's Biographical Dictionary of Musicians is a standard, authoritative, one-volume work. This concise version, based on the 7th edition (1984), is about half the size of the original, "giving prominence to great figures of music but eliminating the secondary entries." Articles for music critics, theorists, librarians, church organists, and many popular musicians have been deleted. The remaining 6,300 entries have been shortened, primarily in the listing of compositions and writings. Bibliographies also have been omitted, but Slonimsky's delightful wit is retained. The concise version is recommended for high schools that require a biographical source for performers, composers, and other musicians for all time periods, but those able to purchase the full version should do so. [R: ARBA 89; BL, 15 May 89; LJ, 1 Mar 89]

BANDS

1648 Band Music Guide: Alphabetical Listing of Titles and Compositions of All Band Music. 8th ed. Northfield, Ill.: Instrumentalist, 1982. 408p. $28.00. ISBN 0-686-29239-1.

Some 15,000 band compositions and arrangements are grouped under 5 headings: band titles, collections, solos and ensembles, band books, and marching routines. For each piece of music, the guide gives composer/arranger, publisher, and degree of difficulty. A composer index and directory of publishers complete the volume. Other reference guides from the publisher include *Woodwind Music Guide: Ensemble Music in Print*; *Woodwind Music Guide: Solo and Study Material in Print*; *Brass Ensemble Music Guide*; and *Brass Solo and Study Material Music Guide*.

1649 Dvorak, Thomas L., with Cynthia Crump Taggart and Peter Schmalz. Best Music for Young Bands: A Selective Guide to the Young Band/Youth Wind Ensemble Repertoire. Brooklyn, N.Y.: Manhattan Beach Music, 1986. 50p. $19.95pa. ISBN 0-931329-02-7. LC 86-12443.

In an attempt to provide the best music for young musicians, this bibliography lists suggestions in three groups: concert works for the band, concert marches for the band, and concert pieces for the wind ensemble. Works are arranged alphabetically by composer in each section, with title, degree of difficulty, timing, publisher, and an annotation for each entry. [R: ARBA 88]

1650 Holston, Kim R., comp. **The Marching Band Handbook: Competitions, Instruments, Clinics, Fund-Raising, Publicity, Uniforms, Accessories, Trophies, Drum Corps, Twirling, Color Guard, Indoor Guard, Music, Travel, Directories, Bibliographies, Index**. Jefferson, N.C.: McFarland, 1984. 201p. $18.95pa. ISBN 0-89950-105-2. LC 84-25575.

School libraries that support band programs will find some value in this handbook, although it is uneven in quality and needs updating. There are entries for a wide variety of topics, as the subtitles explain, but the main body of the book identifies sources for supplies, services, and other band needs. Some topical articles include brief bibliographies; a general bibliography concludes the volume. [R: ARBA 85; BL, 15 May 85]

CHORAL

1651 White, Perry J. **Twentieth-Century Choral Music: An Annotated Bibliography of Music Suitable for Use in High School Choirs**. 2d ed. Metuchen, N.J.: Scarecrow, 1990. 214p. $25.00. ISBN 0-8108-2394-2. LC 90-20005.

White's bibliography, a revision of his 1983 work, focuses on twentieth-century choral music of high quality and lasting value. The 2d edition adds 120 new pieces, most of which have been published since 1980. Each of the 360 entries evaluates the piece's appropriateness for performance by junior and senior high school ensembles of varying size, skill, and maturity. The entries also provide composer, title, voicing, accompaniment (or a capella), text, range (for each part), difficulty, style, comments, publisher, date, and level (junior high through college). A directory of musical publishers, a composer index, and a title index complete the volume. Highly recommended for secondary level. [R: ARBA 92; RBB, 1 June 91]

CLASSICAL

1652 Kramer, Jonathan D. **Listen to the Music: A Self-Guided Tour through the Orchestral Repertoire....** New York: Schirmer Books/Macmillan, 1988. 816p. $32.50. ISBN 0-02-871841-0. LC 88-9248.

The short essays contained in this volume analyze 290 frequently performed works (mostly orchestral) by 52 composers (e.g., Bach, Beethoven, Brahms, Mozart) as well as modern composers, such as Aaron Copland. Most entries, taken from notes the author wrote for the Cincinnati Symphony Orchestra (1980 to 1989), provide information about the composers and their times, rather than a critique of their music. There is a glossary of music terms used in the book. This basic work contains introductory material on the classical composers and should be considered by middle and high school libraries. [R: ARBA 90; RBB, 1 Dec 89]

1653 Rosenberg, Kenyon C. **A Basic Classical and Operatic Recordings Collection for Libraries**. Metuchen, N.J.: Scarecrow, 1987. 255p. $27.50. ISBN 0-8108-2041-2. LC 87-12747.

1654 Rosenberg, Kenyon C. **A Basic Classical and Operatic Recordings Collection on Compact Disc for Libraries: A Buying Guide**. Metuchen, N.J.: Scarecrow, 1990. 375p. $39.50. ISBN 0-8108-2322-5. LC 90-8317.

Librarians who select classical and operatic recordings will welcome these works. The 1987 volume opens with an excellent survey of evaluation and selection. Each recording cited is ranked A (required in every library), B (useful in medium-sized libraries), or C (recommended for large libraries). Arranged alphabetically by composer, each entry comments on the individual's life and musical works and lists recommended recordings, with full descriptive data for each. Translations of foreign-language titles are provided.

In the supporting guide. Rosenberg suggests 1,208 compact disc recordings for libraries building a collection of "serious music" in that format. Arranged alphabetically by composer, entries include playing time and the nature of the recording. Indexed by title and popular association (e.g., radio/television show themes). [R: ARBA 91; LJ, Sept 15, 1990; RBB, 15 Oct 90]

INSTRUMENTS

E+

1655 Andre Previn's Guide to the Orchestra. Andre Previn, ed. New York: Putnam, 1983. 192p. $17.95. ISBN 0-399-12865-4. LC 83-4587.

Colorful and informative, this is a worthwhile introduction to contemporary musical instruments. Chapters cover families of instruments (e.g., strings, woodwinds) and explain how they are designed and played. The work is supported by an abundance of photographs and drawings that show instrument details. The language is lively and technical terminology is studiously avoided; terms that must be used are defined in a glossary. The book is well organized, but it lacks an index. [R: ARBA 85; BL, 15 Feb 84; LJ, 1 Feb 84; VOYA, Apr 84]

OPERA

1656 The Definitive Kobbe's Opera Book. rev. ed. Earl of Harewood, ed. New York: Putnam, 1987. 1404p. $35.00. ISBN 0-399-13180-9. LC 86-187705.

1657 Kobbe's Illustrated Opera Book: Twenty-Six of the World's Best-Loved Operas. Earl of Harewood, ed. New York: Putnam, 1989. 160p. $34.95. ISBN 0-399-13475-1.

The Definitive Kobbe's covers 319 operas and updates the 1976 edition, entitled *The New Kobbe's Complete Opera Book*. Each of the three parts — "Opera before Gluck (1600-1800)," "The Nineteenth Century," and "The Twentieth Century" — is arranged chronologically by the composer's birthdate. For each opera, the work provides a chronological list of important performances, with location and performers; a list of characters with voice and a description of the role; and a lengthy synopsis. A detailed index to composers, operas, and major characters gives easy access to the volume.

Unlike *The Definitive Kobbe's Opera Book*, which provides extensive coverage, *Illustrated Opera Book* describes only 26 of the "best-loved" operas. The essays are shorter than those contained in the parent volume, but the book is profusely illustrated with beautiful plates, most in color. This work, suitable for opera beginners, is a good choice for high schools. [R: BL, 15 Jan 90; LJ, 1 Feb 90]

1658 Hamilton, Mary. **A-Z of Opera**. New York: Facts on File, 1990. 223p. $22.95. ISBN 0-8160-2340-9. LC 90-3115.

This volume, designed for "first-time attenders" of performances, contains some 850 brief entries for individual operas, composers, performers, conductors, major opera companies, and terms. Entries give the date of each opera's first performance and a plot outline. Some 75 black-and-white photographs and line drawings illustrate the entries. The British emphasis and spelling do not hamper this dictionary's usefulness. [R: ARBA 92; BR, May/June 91; RBB, Mar 91]

1659 The Harper's Dictionary of Opera and Operetta. James Anderson, ed. New York: HarperCollins, 1990. 691p. $35.00. ISBN 0-06-016488-3. LC 89-46515.

Despite its title, *Harper's Dictionary* focuses on operas that have been prominent during the twentieth century; it contains few operettas. The 5,000 entries cover composers; operas and operettas; opera houses, companies, conductors, singers, librettists, designers, and critics; and others connected with the field. Some 100 panels highlight interesting facts about specific operas. A list of all opera recordings and a comparative operatic chronology are special features. Suggested for high school level. [R: ARBA 91; BL, 15 Jan 91]

1660 Lazarus, John. **Opera Handbook**. Boston: G. K. Hall, c1987, 1990. 242p. $25.00. ISBN 0-8161-9094-1. LC 89-77758.

This attractive book, a volume in the G. K. Hall Performing Arts Series, treats opera for each country in a separate chapter — Italy, France, Great Britain, Germany, Russia, and the United States. There is also a general chapter for other countries in Europe. Each entry, selected from operas most frequently performed in the 1980s, gives a plot summary, factual data, critiques, and guidance for listeners. A "Databank" section provides brief biographies of contemporary opera singers. Indexed. This volume is suggested for high school level.

Other volumes in the series include *The Film Handbook*, *The Jazz Handbook*, and *The Dance Handbook*. [R: ARBA 91; BR, Jan/Feb 91; BL, 1 Sept 90; LJ, July 90]

POPULAR

General

1661 Gammond, Peter. **The Oxford Companion to Popular Music**. New York: Oxford University Press, 1991. 739p. $39.95. ISBN 0-19-311323-6. LC 90-4209.

This *Oxford Companion*, which defines "popular" as music that is neither serious nor classical, covers the English-speaking world from the 1950s to the present. Brief entries focus primarily on musicians (performers, composers, and others) and emphasize their careers. Others cover songs, famous theaters and clubs, types of music (e.g., jazz, soul, blues), musicals, and light opera.

Most topics receive only a paragraph (about 60 words), but entries for famous musicians, composers, and their compositions run for a page or more. Brief bibliographies support some articles, but the work lacks a general bibliography and an index. As are most other Oxford Companions, this is a worthwhile reference work. Appropriate for high school library media centers. [R: ARBA 92; BL, 1 Apr 91]

1662 **The Marshall Cavendish Illustrated History of Popular Music**. Ashley Brown, ed. North Bellmore, N.Y.: Marshall Cavendish, c1988, 1990. 21v. $499.00/set. ISBN 1-85436-015-3. LC 88-21076.

This work identifies "popular music" as rock, blues, and soul and covers the period from the mid-1950s to the present. The first 10 volumes treat the 1950s and 1960s; the second 10 address the 1970s and 1980s. Each volume has an index, but the final volume contains a comprehensive index to the entire set, plus the annual *Billboard* list of the top songs of each year.

Most of the historically arranged articles cover performers, but some deal with topics such as social phenomena, musical styles, regional music, and the economics of the music business. Performers include not only the well known (e.g., the Beatles, Elvis Presley, the Rolling Stones, the Beach Boys) but also numerous soul and blues singers and Jamaican musicians known primarily to fans of the genre. Some 4,000 photographs, most in color, illustrate the set. Each volume contains a chronology of musical events and a list of British and American hit singles of the era.

The set's coverage of the origins of rock evokes high praise, but its treatment of the 1980s does not fulfill expectations. The work is suggested for high school libraries that require an extensive reference tool on the topic. [R: ARBA 91; WLB, June 90]

1663 **The Penguin Encyclopedia of Popular Music**. Donald Clarke, ed. New York: Viking Penguin, 1989. 1378p. $40.00. ISBN 0-670-80349-9.

Some readers may find the informal approach provided by this source a deterrent to its use as a reference tool. The lively and often humorous entries describe individuals, groups, trends, and genres. The brief biographical information and perceptive commentaries deserve praise, but the incomplete discographies constitute a weakness. Secondary school students interested in popular music will enjoy browsing this informative and entertaining work. [R: ARBA 91; VOYA, Apr 90]

1664 Stambler, Irwin. **Encyclopedia of Pop, Rock and Soul**. rev. ed. New York: St. Martin's Press, 1989. 881p. $35.00. ISBN 0-312-02573-4. LC 88-29860.

This revision of the author's 1976 work offers 500 alphabetically arranged entries for individual performers and groups, both representative and influential, plus record producers, rock festivals, musicals, and other forms of popular music. Biographical essays of musicians, averaging 800 to 1,000 words each, include interview quotations and selective discographies. This volume is a first choice for pop, rock, and soul fans. [R: ARBA 90; LJ, 15 Feb 89; RBB, 15 June 89]

Country

1665 Dellar, Fred, and others. **The Harmony Illustrated Encyclopedia of Country Music**. rev. ed. New York: Harmony Books/Crown, 1986. 208p. $22.95; $13.95pa. ISBN 0-517-56502-1; 0-517-56503-Xpa. LC 86-18423.

An extensive revision of a 1977 publication, this profusely illustrated volume, considered a major classic in its field, describes the careers of country music's most famous performers. Its 450 entries emphasize career information and major recordings, with few evaluative comments. Color reproductions of album covers and promotional photographs make this an attractive work. The appendix mentions stars of the past in short paragraphs. [R: ARBA 88; WLB, Sept 87]

Jazz

1666 Case, Brian, and Stan Britt. **The Harmony Illustrated Encyclopedia of Jazz**. Revised and updated by Chrissi Murray. New York: Harmony Books/Crown, 1986. 208p. $13.95pa. ISBN 0-517-56443-2. LC 86-15040.

The 3d edition of this informative work covers 450 jazz musicians and a few topics. The biographical entries provide compact career information, assess the subject's contribution, often list significant recordings, and conclude with discographies of recordings. The appendix provides briefer entries for 100 less-prominent jazz musicians. Indexed. [R: ARBA 88]

1667 Feather, Leonard G. **The Encyclopedia of Jazz**. New York: Da Capo Press, c1960, 1984. 527p. $19.95pa. ISBN 0-306-80214-7. LC 83-26164.

1668 Feather, Leonard G. **The Encyclopedia of Jazz in the Sixties**. New York: Da Capo Press, c1966, 1986. 312p. $14.95pa. ISBN 0-306-80263-5. LC 85-31125.

1669 Feather, Leonard G. **The Encyclopedia of Jazz in the Seventies**. New York: Da Capo Press, c1976, 1987. 393p. $16.95pa. ISBN 0-306-80290-2. LC 87-517.

These volumes constitute an unsurpassed source of biographical information about jazz musicians, especially those who gained prominence between 1950 and 1975. Each volume contains alphabetically arranged essays, 2,000 in all, that provide life dates, instrument played, musical education, career highlights, and recordings. They often quote the subject, reviewers, or other musicians. Other features include photographs of artists, award winners, and a list of jazz films. [R: ARBA 88]

1670 McRae, Barry. **The Jazz Handbook**. Boston: G. K. Hall, c1987, 1989. 272p. $25.00. ISBN 0-8161-9096-8. LC 89-77757.

Jazz Handbook, a volume in the G. K. Hall Performing Arts Series, focuses on performers from the earliest times through the 1980s. Each entry covers the musician's background, career, and influence in the field; lists films, television appearances, and books about the individual; and provides a critical discography. A "Databank" section includes a glossary and bibliography. Indexed. This attractive, easy-to-use work is appropriate for high schools.

Other volumes in the series include *Opera Handbook*, *The Film Handbook*, and *The Dance Handbook*. [R: ARBA 91; BR, Jan/Feb 91; LJ, July 90; RBB, 1 Sept 90]

1671 **The New Grove Dictionary of Jazz**. Barry Kernfeld, ed. New York: Stockton Press/Grove's Dictionaries of Music, 1988. 2v. $350.00/set. ISBN 0-935859-39-X. LC 87-25452.

This work is a spinoff from the monumental *New Grove Dictionary of Music and Musicians*, but few of its articles have been drawn from the parent set. Most of the 4,500 signed essays, which explore all aspects of jazz, were specially prepared for this work.

The 250 contributors from 25 nations provide encyclopedic coverage for mainstream and progressive jazz, theory, instrumentation, performers, composers, bands, and film. More than 3,000 biographies predominate. Entries for broad topics are extensive, while others are little more than definitions or identifications. This excellent work, which is likely to become the standard source for the field, is recommended for high schools. [R: ARBA 90; LJ, 15 Apr 89; RBB, 15 Apr 89; WLB, Feb 89]

Musicals

1672 Gänzl, Kurt, and Andrew Lamb. **Gänzl's Book of the Musical Theatre**. New York: Schirmer Books/Macmillan, 1989. 1373p. $75.00. ISBN 0-02-871941-7. LC 88-18588.

Musical theater, as defined by this work, includes operetta, comic opera, musical comedy, and the modern-day musical. Each of the 198 entries is 4 to 6 pages in length and provides information on significant stage and film productions, the cast of characters, and a summary of each act (including the songs sung). There are 32 pages of black-and-white photographs of productions.

International in coverage, the volume is arranged by country: Great Britain (from *The Beggar's Opera* in 1782 to *Phantom of the Opera* in 1987); France (including *Les Miserables*); United States (from *Robin Hood* in 1890 to *La Cage Aux Folles* in 1983); Australia, Hungary, and Germany (from 1865 to 1964); and Spain. The work admittedly contains both well-known musicals and obscure ones that have historical significance, or that have won the author's favor.

A discography of recordings concludes the volume. For each musical, the entry includes the original-cast recording and the soundtracks in the original language and translation. Indexed by author, title, composer, lyricist, and song title. [R: ARBA 90]

1673 Lynch, Richard Chigley, comp. **Broadway on Records**. Westport, Conn.: Greenwood Press, 1987. 347p. $42.95. ISBN 0-313-25523-7. LC 87-11822.
    Lynch's discography includes 459 recordings of Broadway and Off-Broadway musicals, from *The Band Wagon* (1931) through *Me and My Girl* (1986). For each musical the work provides opening dates, theater, record label and number, composer, lyricist, musical director, cast, songs, and cast members who perform each song. The entry specifies whether the recording is monaural or stereophonic, and whether it is available on CD. Indexing is by performer and technical personnel, not by individual song. [R: ARBA 89; RBB, 1 Feb 88; WLB, Mar 88]

Rock

1674 **Encyclopedia of Rock**. Phil Hardy and Dave Laing. Revised by Stephen Barnard and Don Perretta. New York: Schirmer Books/Macmillan, 1988. 480p. $50.00. ISBN 0-02-919562-4.
    This revised and updated edition of a British work first published in 1975 includes developments over the past decade. Over 3,500 entries about solo artists, bands, musical styles, people, places, and events comprise the volume. Black-and-white and color photographs scattered throughout the text make this an attractive work, but it lacks discographies, which *The Harmony Illustrated Encyclopedia of Rock* includes. The entries are much shorter than those contained in *Encyclopedia of Pop, Rock and Soul*, but far more artists are found herein than in the other volumes. [R: ARBA 90; RBB, 15 June 89]

1675 **The Harmony Illustrated Encyclopedia of Rock**. 6th ed. Mike Clifford, ed. New York: Harmony Books/Crown, 1988. 208p. $14.95pa. ISBN 0-517-57164-1. LC 88-21473.
    This is not the definitive work on rock music, but it is an attractive and valuable source, similar to the *Encyclopedia of Rock*. Over 700 colorfully illustrated entries profile established British and American artists, giving background information, career highlights, and discographies of outstanding recordings. Illustrations are of individuals, groups, and album covers. [R: ARBA 90; BL, 15 June 89; VOYA, June 89]

SONGS

1676 Bianco, David. **Heat Wave: The Motown Fact Book**. Ann Arbor, Mich.: Pierian Press, 1988. 542p. $45.00. ISBN 1-56075-011-1. LC 86-60558.
    This work provides comprehensive coverage for 5,500 Motown recordings released in the United States and the United Kingdom from 1959 through 1986, 6,700 artists who performed on the recordings, and 8,599 references to songs and record titles. The short biogrpahical entries for stars who made their reputations on Motown records include complete Motown discographies, selected discographies for non-Motown recordings, and short bibliographies of books and articles for some artists.
    Separate chronologies for U.S. and U.K. recordings include label and record number, date of release, title and artists, and availability on compact disc or cassette. The chronologies are indexed by name (individuals and groups), song and record titles, date, and record number. The appendix lists five labels related to Motown and records produced under these labels. [R: ARBA 89; BL, 1 Jan 89; WLB, Oct 88]

1677 Bronson, Fred. **The Billboard Book of Number One Hits**. rev. ed. New York: Billboard Books/Watson-Guptill, 1988. 712p. $16.95pa. ISBN 0-8230-7545-1. LC 88-14707.
    The Billboard popularity charts began in 1940, but Bronson did not begin his coverage until 1955, with the appearance of "Rock around the Clock." From that time up to June 18, 1988 ("Together Forever"), every song that attained the position of number one is listed chronologically, giving artist or group, label, writer, producer, date it became number one, a list of the top five songs on that date, length of time on the chart, an explanatory note about the artist, biographical data, quotations from the artist, and a black-and-white photograph.
    A table of contents lists the songs in chronological order. Additional features include lists of the most number ones by writer, producer, label, and artist; an artist index; and a title index. [R: ARBA 90]

E+
1678 Delamar, Gloria T. **Rounds Re-Sounding: Circular Music for Voices & Instruments: An Eight-Century Reference**. Jefferson, N.C.: McFarland, 1987. 347p. $35.00. ISBN 0-89950-203-2. LC 85-43576.

This unusual volume focuses on 600 rounds, spanning 8 centuries. The introductory materials provide a history of rounds and suggest ways to use them in chroal performances and for fun. The arrangement by 27 categories includes foreign language rounds and parodies, variations and retrogrades. One or two musical selections per page provide notations and words, with entry points for each voice or group. Music teachers and students at all grade levels will welcome this work. [R: SLJ, May 88]

1679 Gargan, William, and Sue Sharma. **Find That Tune: An Index to Rock, Folk-Rock, Disco & Soul in Collections. Volume 1**. New York: Neal-Schuman, 1984. 303p. $47.50. ISBN 0-918212-70-7. LC 82-22346.

1680 Sharma, Sue, and William Gargan. **Find That Tune: An Index to Rock, Folk-Rock, Disco & Soul in Collections. [Volume 2]**. New York: Neal-Schuman, 1989. 387p. $49.95. ISBN 1-55570-019-5. LC 82-22346.

Find That Tune helps the searcher locate sheet music for the popular music field. Volume 1 indexes 4,000 songs in 203 collections, covering music from 1950 to 1981; volume 2 indexes 4,000 songs from 1982 to 1985.

Both volumes have the same arrangement. Part 1 lists indexed collections alphabetically by title. Part 2 lists songs alphabetically by title, giving composer and lyricist, performers, publisher, and date, with references to collections in part 1. Part 3 lists first lines of songs, with references to the title index. Part 4 indexes composers and lyricists, with titles of songs under each; and part 5 lists performers and groups, with songs listed under each. [R: ARBA 85; ARBA 90]

1681 Havlice, Patricia P. **Popular Song Index. Third Supplement**. Metuchen, N.J.: Scarecrow, 1989. 875p. $59.95. ISBN 0-8108-2202-4. LC 89-6414.

This work, a standard since its base volume appeared in 1975, updates *Song Index* by Minnie Earl Sears (H. W. Wilson, o.p.). The base volume indexes some 32,000 folk songs, pop tunes, spirituals, hymns, sea chanteys, children's songs, and other categories that are contained in 3,101 collections that were published from 1940 through 1972. Three supplements index an additional 407 collections published between 1970 and 1975, 1974 and 1981, and 1979 and 1987.

The volumes index song titles and first lines in one alphabet, locating them in collections. Each volume is also indexed by composer and lyricist. The overlap with *Find That Tune*, which provides better coverage of rock, folk, and country music, is slight. [R: ARBA 90]

1682 Jacobs, Dick. **Who Wrote That Song?** White Hall, Va.: Betterway, 1988. 415p. $29.95; $19.95pa. ISBN 1-55870-108-7; 1-55870-100-1pa. LC 88-19351.

This song index lists over 11,000 popular songs by 5,000 composers and lyricists. Most are twentieth-century compositions, but a few are classical works recorded in popular style.

"The Songs," arranged alphabetically by title, provides for each song composer, lyricist, artist who introduced or popularized it, Broadway show or film in which it was sung, and other performers who recorded or revived it. "The Songwriters" lists composers and lyricists with their songs. "The Award Winners" lists Academy, Grammy, and Songwriter Hall of Fame awards. [R: ARBA 90; LJ, Jan 89; RBB, 1 Mar 89]

■ *The Kid's World Almanac Rhyming Dictionary*. See entry 1445.

1683 Lax, Roger, and Frederick Smith. **The Great Song Thesaurus**. 2d ed. New York: Oxford University Press, 1989. 774p. $75.00. ISBN 0-19-505408-3. LC 88-31267.

Over 11,000 of the best-known songs of the English-speaking world are identified in this work. The main section consists of song titles arranged alphabetically; for each are provided lyricist, composer, year of composition, musical or film in which the song was featured, performer associated with it, and other facts of interest.

Eight other sections include "Lyric Key Lines," new to this edition, which indexes songs by their best-known lines; British song titles; "The Greatest Hits," a chronological list of notable hits from 1958 through 1986, in which many songs are placed in historical context; a chronological list of award-winning songs; "Themes, Trademarks, and Signatures"; a thematic index arranged by over 2,000 headings; "American and British Theatre, Film, Radio, and Television," which associates songs with their source of popularity; and notes on significant lyricists and composers. This work stands alone as the only reference source of its kind. [R: ARBA 90]

E +
1684 **National Anthems of the World**. 7th ed. W. L. Reed and M. J. Bristow, eds. London: Blandford; distr., New York: Sterling Publishing, c1987, 1988. 512p. $75.00. ISBN 0-7137-1962-1.

In a rapidly changing world, national anthems change to reflect developments in the country, which is the reason for this volume's update. It was published in 1985.

For each of the 172 alphabetically arranged nations, the anthem is provided along with the musical score for piano, lyrics in the native language, and a brief history of the composition. For Chinese, Japanese, and other non-Latin alphabets, a transliterated, phonetic version is provided for singers unfamiliar with the language. Additional verses in the original language and in English are included at the end of the anthem.

The authors, who are responsible for adapting or arranging many of the anthems for piano, were assisted by many embassies, governments, scholars, and educational institutions in compiling this work. [R: BL, 15 Sept 88]

E +
1685 Peterson, Carol Sue, and Ann D. Fenton, comps. **Index to Children's Songs**. Bronx, N.Y.: H. W. Wilson, 1979. 318p. $36.00. ISBN 0-8242-0638-X. LC 79-14265.

In this book, the contents of 198 children's song collections (5,000 songs) published between 1909 and 1977 are alphabetically arranged in a single alphabet by title and first line. The subject index lists song titles under more than 1,000 subject headings. A list of collections indexed concludes the volume. [R: ARBA 80]

Mythology and Folklore

GENERAL WORKS

1686 **Bulfinch's Mythology**. New York: HarperCollins, 1991. 732p. $35.00. ISBN 0-06-270025-1. LC 91-55002.

This classic work contains the myths of Greece, Rome, and the Far East; Norse and Germanic myths; and the legends of Arthur and Charlemagne. The appendix relates some 60 archaeological finds to sites mentioned in the myths.

1687 Thompson, Stith. **The Folktale**. Berkeley, Calif.: University of California Press, c1946, 1977. 510p. $13.95pa. ISBN 0-520-03537-2. LC 76-42715.

Thompson's classic work is a guide to kinds of folktales and methods of studing folklore. The work includes extensive bibliographies and indexing by types of tale and motifs, arranged according to Thompson's *Motif-Index of Folk Literature* (Indiana University Press, 1955-1958).

1688 **The World of Myth: An Anthology**. David A. Leemings, ed. New York: Oxford University Press, 1990. 416p. $24.95. ISBN 0-19-505601-9. LC 89-48070.

Myths are divided into four sections: the cosmos, the gods, the heroes, and places and objects. Each part is supported by concise commentaries and a bibliography. This collection of myths is a good introductory work. Recommended for high schools. [R: BL, 1 Oct 90; LJ, 1 Oct 90]

DICTIONARIES AND ENCYCLOPEDIAS

1689 Allardice, Pamela. **Myths, Gods and Fantasy**. Santa Barbara, Calif.: ABC-Clio, 1991. 232p. $35.00. ISBN 0-87436-660-7.

The concise alphabetically arranged entries in this dictionary include gods, goddesses, and creatures worldwide. Greek, British, and other European mythologies are well covered, along with African, Australian Aboriginal, Chinese, Egyptian, Eskimo, Japanese, Mayan, Micronesian, North

American, and many others. This informative volume is suggested for high school libraries. [R: ARBA 92; LJ, Aug 91]

1690 Bell, Robert E. **Dictionary of Classical Mythology: Symbols, Attributes & Associations**. Santa Barbara, Calif.: ABC-Clio, 1982. 390p. $51.50. ISBN 0-87436-305-5. LC 81-19141.

This excellent work consists of over 1,000 entries that name mythological characters, summarize each myth, and explain the meaning of the symbol. Bell often cites *Loeb Classical Library*. A "Guide to Persona," which identifies all topical entries associated with a given character, concludes the volume. Highly recommended. [R: ARBA 83]

1691 Bell, Robert E. **Place-Names in Classical Mythology: Greece**. Santa Barbara, Calif.: ABC-Clio, 1989. 350p. $51.50. ISBN 0-87436-507-4. LC 88-16870.

Places associated with the legends, festivals, temples, and relationships of Greek mythology as told by Homer and others are identified in terms of modern Greek cities, shrines, and historical geography. Entries provide the original and modern names of places associated with figures such as Ajax and Electra and describes ruins that have survived. An appendix compares modern and ancient names. An index of deities lists sites associated with each. [R: ARBA 90; BL, July 89; WLB, May 89]

1692 Briggs, Katharine M. **An Encyclopedia of Fairies: Hobgoblins, Brownies, Bogies, and Other Supernatural Creatures**. New York: Pantheon, c1976, 1977. 481p. $16.95pa. ISBN 0-394-73467-X. LC 76-12939.

Folk creatures, such as those named in the book's subtitle, and the authors who wrote about them are found in this British work. The type and motif indexes are based on Stith Thompson's *Motif-Index of Folk Literature* (Indiana University Press, 1955-1958). [R: ARBA 78]

1693 Cohen, Daniel. **The Encyclopedia of Monsters**. New York: Dorset Press, 1990. 287p. $17.95. ISBN 0-88029-442-6.

The 100 strange creatures described by this work are grouped into 8 categories: humanoids, land monsters, monster birds and bats, phantoms, river and lake monsters, sea monsters, visitors from outer space, and weird creatures in folklore. Monsters created in film and literature are excluded. Entries provide the creature's background and the evolution of its legend, a description of its personality and physical appearance, sightings and their locations, controversies related to the sightings, and organized attempts to find it.

1694 Cotterell, Arthur. **The Macmillan Illustrated Encyclopedia of Myths and Legends**. New York: Macmillan, 1989. 260p. $29.95. ISBN 0-02-580181-3. LC 89-8282.

This handsome volume is divided into three sections: cultural areas, characters and concepts, and a "micropedia." The cultural section covers the religion, mythology, and legends of 18 areas of the world, Egypt to Oceania, and provides a map, a chronology, color photographs, and an identification symbol for each region.

The second section identifies heroes and deities, arranged alphabetically, giving their myths and the area symbol. Tables of concepts (e.g., quests, afterlife) are scattered throughout the section; names of heroes and deities are cross-referenced to themes and topics listed in the micropedia in the third section.

The micropedia contains short entries for names and places, arranged alphabetically, and again links the subjects to their cultural areas with identification symbols. A list of books for further reading completes the volume. Recommended for junior and senior high schools. [R: ARBA 91; BL, 1 Feb 90; LJ, 1 Feb 90]

1695 Craig, Robert D. **Dictionary of Polynesian Mythology**. Westport, Conn.: Greenwood Press, 1989. 409p. $49.95. ISBN 0-313-25870-2. LC 89-7479.

The *Dictionary of Polynesian Mythology* emphasizes Cook Island, Hawaii, the Marquesas Islands, New Zealand, Samoa, Tahiti, and Tonga. The introduction offers a survey and a pronunciation guide. Entries briefly identify significant characters and events and cite sources. The appendix groups gods and goddesses by categories, and the index refers to characters, animals, people, and other subjects. For middle and high school levels. [R: ARBA 90]

1696 Ellis, Peter Berresford. **A Dictionary of Irish Mythology**. Santa Barbara, Calif.: ABC-Clio, 1989. 240p. $41.50. ISBN 0-87436-553-8. LC 89-160.

This volume, intended for the general reader and high school/college students, explains events, beings, places, and objects found in Irish mythology. The introduction provides an excellent historical and bibliographic essay about the subject. Entries, varying from a few words to several pages, often include a synopsis of the myth. Since most books on mythology contain scant information about Irish myths, this is a useful reference tool. [R: ARBA 90; BR, Nov/Dec 89; RBB, 1 Nov 89; WLB, Oct 89]

1697   **Funk and Wagnalls Standard Dictionary of Folklore, Mythology and Legend**. Marie Leach, ed. San Franciso, Calif.: HarperSanFrancisco, c1973, 1984. $34.95pa. ISBN 0-06-250511-4.

This reissue of a two-volume set, published in 1949-1950, is a standard reference work. Survey articles discuss regions and special topics—fairy tales, ballads, and dances—and concise essays treat gods, heroes, folk tales, customs, beliefs, superstitions, motifs, and other topics related to world culture.

1698   Grimal, Pierre. **The Dictionary of Classical Mythology**. Cambridge, Mass.: Basil Blackwell, 1986. 603p. $50.00. ISBN 0-631-13209-0.

1699   Grimal, Pierre. **A Concise Dictionary of Classical Mythology**. Cambridge, Mass.: Basil Blackwell, 1990. 350p. $34.95. ISBN 0-631-16696-3.

First published in French (1951), this excellent English translation by A. R. Maxwell-Hyslop is an interesting and attractive volume. Intended for college students studying the humanities, the dictionary nonetheless is useful on the high school level. The work indicates variant spellings, gives alternative versions of many myths, provides genealogical charts, cites classical authors, and lists relevant editions of myths. The volume is handsomely illustrated and indexed. This competent and authoritative dictionary is a worthwhile addition to library reference shelves.

The condensed version of this work may be adequate for some libraries. The author has shortened the entries by excluding minor variants of the myths and concentrating on the major versions of others. [R: ARBA 87; BL, 15 Jan 91; LJ, 15 Sept 90]

1700   Lurker, Manfred. **Dictionary of Gods and Goddesses, Devils and Demons**. New York: Routledge, Chapman & Hall, 1987. 451p. $45.00; $15.95pa. ISBN 0-7102-0877-4; 0-7102-1106-6pa. LC 86-21911.

A translation of a German work published in 1984, this dictionary provides an alphabetical list of world deities and demons, some 1,800 in all. The text does not recount their exploits but emphasizes their symbolic value, their attributes and motifs, and the meanings and origins of their names.

The appendixes arrange the deities according to the function of each and other aspects (e.g., fertility, death) and list each by symbol (e.g., owl, trident). Drawings and photographs illustrate the volume, which is supported by a bibliography. This authoritative work is suggested for high schools. [R: ARBA 88; BL, 1 Feb 88; WLB, Dec 87]

1701   **Man, Myth & Magic: The Illustrated Encyclopedia of Mythology, Religion, and the Unknown**. rev. ed. Richard Cavendish, ed. in chief. North Bellmore, N.Y.: Marshall Cavendish, 1983. 12v. $399.95/set. ISBN 0-86307-041-8. LC 82-13041.

Man, Myth & Magic attempts to explain how cultures throughout history have interpreted the unknown. A bibliography of books and articles in the first volume is arranged in categories such as hero's quests, ghosts, and magic. Alphabetically arranged articles, ranging from several paragraphs to 30 pages, treat major faiths, philosophies, legends, witchcraft, and the supernatural. The more substantial articles are signed and cite sources for further study. A profusion of color illustrations located throughout the set include many that depict torture and diabolic rituals. [R: ARBA 85; BL, 1 May 84; WLB, Nov 83]

1702   Mercatante, Anthony. **The Facts on File Encyclopedia of World Mythology and Legend**. New York: Facts on File, 1988. 807p. $95.00. ISBN 0-8160-1049-8. LC 84-21218.

This outstanding work encompasses myths, legends, folklore, and fables around the world and throughout the ages. Over 3,000 entries, enhanced by over 400 black-and-white illustrations, comprise the encyclopedia. Concise and well-written articles describe the subject (e.g., historical characters, saints, rulers, sacred relics, animals), provide historical notes, and indicate works in which the subject appears. Brief plot summaries and cross-references are numerous.

The extensive annotated bibliography is arranged by culture and nation, subject, and type of collection. A key to variant spellings and general, cultural, and ethnic indexes conclude the volume, which is recommended for high school level. [R: ARBA 89; BR, Nov/Dec 88]

1703   Monaghan, Patricia. **The Book of Goddesses & Heroines**. rev. ed. St. Paul, Minn.: Llewellyn, c1981, 1990. $17.95pa. ISBN 0-87524-573-9. LC 89-77418.

A glossary of goddesses and heroines first published in 1981, this work has been increased by 250 and now includes 1,533 entries representing many cultures. Entries, which range from a sentence to over 600 words, are more detailed than many found in similar works.

The volume, which is illustrated with black-and-white photographs, includes a bibliography and several indexes in which goddesses and heroines are listed by cultural/geographic areas, symbolic representations, and alternative names. The depth of coverage offered by this work makes it a desired dictionary for high schools. [R: ARBA 91; RBB, 15 Sept 90]

E +
1704   Rovin, Jeff. **The Encyclopedia of Monsters**. New York: Facts on File, 1989. 390p. $35.00. ISBN 0-8160-1824-3. LC 89-30417.

Beasts, fiends, specters, werewolves, mummies, and monsters of all types and times come to life and haunt the pages of this excellent work. The introduction gives a short history of monsters since 4000 B.C. and identifies them as characters unknown to science who arise to frighten human beings. They may appear in motion pictures, television, literature, comic books, mythology, folklore, religion, toys, computer games, or even bubble-gum trading cards.

Each entry gives the monster's name, nickname, species, gender, and size. It also provides a life story (which includes a description of its features and powers), a picture, and comments by the author. The appendix contains brief information about the monster's first appearance and location, pictures of some characters, and reproductions of comic-book covers. There is a detailed index.

Librarians may wish to purchase a second copy for the circulating collection, since this work is likely to be a popular holding at all levels. [R: ARBA 90; LJ, 1 Sept 89; RBB, 15 Nov 89]

1705   Senior, Michael. **The Illustrated Who's Who in Mythology**. New York: Macmillan, 1985. 223p. $45.00. ISBN 0-02-923770-X. LC 85-18814.

This encyclopedia covers myths from many cultures: Greek, Egyptian, Hindu, Hebrew, Indian, Mayan, Japanese, Russian, and Scandinavian, among others. The introduction addresses mythology and its relationship to religion, history, and folklore. Some 1,200 alphabetically arranged entries briefly describe mythological subjects, often referring to the source of the myth. The thematic index, containing such topics as the creation of man, the flood, and the underworld, refers the reader to appropriate myths. Recommended for secondary schools. [R: ARBA 87]

HANDBOOKS

1706   Bierhorst, John. **The Mythology of North America**. New York: Morrow, 1985. 259p. $13.00; $6.95pa. ISBN 0-688-04145-0. LC 85-281.

This work, which provides a survey of North American Indian mythology, identifies 11 mythological regions and their tales. Bierhorst examines recurring patterns and themes, describes the unique characteristics of the myths, and compares their themes and elements to mythologies of other cultures. Illustrations, maps, and an index are included. One reviewer thought some allusions were sexual and bawdy. [R: BL, 15 June 85; SLJ, Aug 85]

1707   Emrich, Duncan. **Folklore on the American Land**. Boston: Little, Brown, 1988. 707p. $12.95pa. ISBN 0-316-23721-3. LC 72-161865.

This work covers many aspects of American folklore—rhymes and ditties from childhood; children's folktales; street cries and epithets; legends and tales (including Santa Claus, "tall" tales, and Jack tales); folksongs and ballads; folk beliefs; and superstitions. Duncan includes representative examples. An extensive bibliography, a general index, and a song index conclude the volume. For high school level. [R: BR, May/June 89]

1708   **The Folklore of American Holidays**. 2d ed. Hennig Cohen and Tristram Potter Coffin, eds. Detroit: Gale, 1991. 461p. $85.00. ISBN 0-8103-7602-4.

This is a massive compilation of more than 400 beliefs, legends, superstitions, proverbs, riddles, poems, songs, dances, plays, pageants, fairs, foods, and processions associated with over 100 American calendar customs and festivals. The entries, in calendar arrangement, range from less than one-half page to 30 (Christmas) and include ideas for holiday programs. A five-part index provides access by subject; ethnic and geographical area; collectors, informants, and translators; song titles and first lines; and motifs and tale types.

1709   Martin, Laura C. **Garden Flower Folklore**. Chester, Conn.: Globe Pequot Press, 1987. 273p. $19.95. ISBN 0-87106-766-8. LC 87-17394.

This companion volume to *Wildflower Folklore* (East Woods Press, 1984) provides fascinating histories, legends, and superstitions surrounding more than 100 popular flowers. Full-page pen-and-ink drawings of each flower are accompanied by several pages of text that relate folklore about each, describe the botanical species, and give cultivation information. Browsers will welcome this delightful volume. [R: ARBA 88; BL, 1 Nov 87]

1710   **Mythical and Fabulous Creatures: A Sourcebook and Research Guide**. Malcolm South, ed. Westport, Conn.: Greenwood Press, 1987. 393p. $49.95. ISBN 0-313-24338-7. LC 88-14964.

Mythical and fantastic creatures are discussed in this outstanding work. The introduction surveys the place of imaginary creatures in literature and art, provides a glossary, and illustrates several.

Part 1 examines birds and beasts (e.g., the phoenix, dragons, unicorns, griffins), human-animal composites (e.g., centaurs, manticores, mermaids, harpies, gorgons, sphinxes), creatures of darkness (e.g., vampires, werewolves), and giants and fairies. Each 20- to 30-page essay provides extensive information about the origin of the creatures and their treatment in myths, folklore, literature, film, sculpture, and art from classical to modern times. Each essay concludes with a bibliography.

Part 2 contains a general bibliography and covers a miscellany of other beings that do not fit into the categories in part 1 (e.g., Cerberus, the three-headed dog that guards the gates of Hades; Pegasus, the flying horse). This outstanding work is highly recommended. [R: ARBA 88; BR, May/June 89; LJ, 15 June 87; RBB, July 87]

INDEXES

E+
1711   Ireland, Norma O., comp. **Index to Fairy Tales, 1949-1972: Including Folklore, Legends and Myths in Collections**. Westwood, Mass.: F. M. Faxon and Metuchen, N.J.: Scarecrow, 1973. 741p. $22.50. LC 26-11491.

1712   Ireland, Norma O., comp. **Index to Fairy Tales, 1973-1977: Including Folklore, Legends and Myths in Collections**. Westwood, Mass.: F. W. Faxon and Metuchen, N.J.: Scarecrow, 1979. 259p. $20.00. LC 79-16150.

1713   Ireland, Norma O., and Joseph W. Sprug, comps. **Index to Fairy Tales, 1978-1986: Including Folklore, Legends and Myths in Collections. Fifth Supplement**. Metuchen, N.J.: Scarecrow, 1989. 575p. $49.50. ISBN 0-8108-2194-X. LC 89-6042.

The basic *Index to Fairy Tales, Myths and Legends*, compiled by Mary H. Eastman (Boston: F. W. Faxon, 1926), and its *First Supplement* (1937) and *Second Supplement* (1952) are now out of print. The third supplement (1973) indexes 406 collections under 3,000 headings; the fourth supplement (1979) indexes 130 collections.

The fifth supplement indexes 262 collections published between 1978 and 1986 under 2,000 subject headings. It has added a number of headings that reflect current times and the changing interests of children. All volumes begin with a list of collections analyzed, followed by a subject-title index. [R: ARBA 91]

Philosophy

1714 Encyclopedia of Philosophy. Paul Edwards, ed. New York: Free Press/Macmillan, 1973. 4v. $400.00/set. ISBN 0-02-894950-1. LC 67-10059.

International in scope and authority, covering Eastern and Western philosophy for all periods of time, this outstanding work is highly recommended for advanced high school students. The set analyzes relevant themes in history, psychology, religion, the sciences, and other fields. The 1,430 signed articles range in length from very short to some 65,000 words. Copious annotated bibliographies, both for the general reader and the specialist, follow each article. The last volume is an analytical index.

1715 Masterpieces of World Philosophy. Frank N. Magill and John Roth, eds. New York: Harper-Collins, 1990. 800p. $40.00. ISBN 0-06-016430-1. LC 89-46545.

This work, based on the 5-volume set *World Philosophy*, consists of 100 explanatory essays on the world's most important works of philosophy. Each analytical article includes title, type of work, date of first publication, principal ideas advanced, pertinent literature, and additional recommended readings. The books, arranged by title, include *The Social Contract* by Rousseau, *Being and Nothingness* by Sartre, and *Novum Organum* by Bacon. A glossary of terms and an index complete the volume. [R: RBB, 15 Jan 91]

Quotations

1716 Andrews, Robert. The Concise Columbia Dictionary of Quotations. New York: Columbia University Press, 1989. 343p. $19.95. ISBN 0-231-06990-1. LC 89-593.

This work, originally published in London as *The Rutledge Dictionary of Quotations* (1987), emphasizes quotations drawn from contemporary culture. It is a worthwhile supplement to such standard works as Bartlett's *Familiar Quotations*. Arranged alphabetically by subject, the work has additional access in the form of subject and author indexes. The name, life dates, and profession of the person quoted are given, but no sources appear. Foreign quotations appear in both the original language and English translation. Appropriate for high schools. [R: ARBA 90; RBB, 15 Sept 89; WLB, Sept 89]

1717 Barnes & Noble Book of Quotations. rev. ed. Robert I. Fitzhenry, ed. New York: Barnes & Noble Books/HarperCollins, 1987. 412p. $7.95pa. ISBN 0-06-463720-4. LC 86-45096.

Designed as a pocket reference, this work focuses on the most commonly heard quotations, providing limited information about their sources (person quoted only). The 5,500 quotations are arranged by subject. Indexed by subject in the front of the book and by person quoted in the back. [R: ARBA 88]

1718 Bartlett, John. Familiar Quotations. 15th ed. Emily Morison Beck, ed. Boston: Little, Brown, 1980. 1540p. $35.00. ISBN 0-316-08275-9. LC 80-17076.

The best known of the quotation books, Bartlett's began in 1855, and with the publication of the 15th edition, celebrated 125 years of renown. More than 3,000 persons (including 400 new ones) are cited in some 22,500 quotations. Arrangement is chronological, usually by birth date of the person quoted, with indexing by author, subject, and keyword (602 pages). Emphasis is on British and American quotations, with the Bible and Shakespeare amply represented. Exact references to original sources and helpful historical footnotes are provided.

The 16th edition of this title, edited by Justin Kaplan, is scheduled for publication in the fall of 1992. Due to deletions in each revision, earlier editions should be retained. This is a basic reference source for grades 7 and up. [R: ARBA 82; BL, 1 May 81; LJ, 1 Nov 80]

■ *Brush Up Your Shakespeare! See* entry 1606.

■ *The Bully Pulpit: Quotations from America's Presidents*. See entry 978.

1719 Camp, Wesley D. **What a Piece of Work Is Man! Camp's Unfamiliar Quotations from 2000 B.C. to the Present**. Englewood Cliffs, N.J.: Prentice-Hall, 1990. 470p. $12.95pa. ISBN 0-13-952102-X. LC 89-37207.
    Ranging from the Bible to the Marquis de Sade, this quotation book omits the well known and focuses on the unfamiliar, or at least the little known. The text is arranged alphabetically (X is omitted) and then by topics and qualities (e.g., actors, anxiety, atheism). Unfortunately, there are no name, subject, or keyword indexes; the user must rely solely on the table of contents. Despite this lacuna, Camp's work is recommended. [R: ARBA 91; WLB, Oct 90]

■ *The Complete Book of Bible Quotations*. See entry 1766.

1720 **The Concise Oxford Dictionary of Proverbs**. J. A. Simpson, ed. New York: Oxford University Press, 1982. 256p. $24.95; $7.95pa. ISBN 0-19-866131-2; 0-19-281880-5pa.
    Over 1,000 proverbs commonly used in Great Britain during the twentieth century, and some that originated elsewhere, appear in this work. Each is entered under the first significant word, with cross-references from other key words in the saying. Chronologically arranged illustrations show its first and notable usages and current examples. Since proverbs are excluded from quotations books, this dictionary and others, such as *Facts on File Dictionary of Proverbs*, are useful supplements to them. [R: ARBA 84]

■ *A Dictionary of Literary Quotations*. See entry 1511.

■ *A Dictionary of Military Quotations*. See entry 919.

■ *A Dictionary of Quotations from the Bible*. See entry 1767.

■ *The Dictionary of War Quotations*. See entry 924.

1721 Fergusson, Rosalind, comp. **The Facts on File Dictionary of Proverbs**. New York: Facts on File, 1983. 331p. $27.95. ISBN 0-87196-298-5. LC 83-5621.
    More than 7,000 proverbs, drawn from all nations and all time periods, are listed in this collection. The arrangement is by 188 general categories subdivided by specific topics. Unlike *The Concise Oxford Dictionary of Proverbs*, this work does not trace the saying's history, but notes often clarify its meaning. Frequent cross-references and indexing by keyword provide access. [R: ARBA 84; BL, 1 June 84; WLB, Nov 83]

1722 **Home Book of Quotations, Classical and Modern**. 10th ed. Burton Egbert Stevenson, ed. New York: Dodd, Mead, c1967, 1984. 2816p. $34.95. ISBN 0-396-08340-4. LC 67-13583.
    This standard work, first published in 1934 and last updated in 1967, is the most extensive of the quotation books, containing some 50,000 quotations. Arranged alphabetically by subject and subdivided by narrower topics, it is indexed by author and leading word (usually noun, but sometimes by verb or adverb). Exact citations to sources are provided. [R: ARBA 85; BL, 15 Sept 84]

■ *Isaac Asimov's Book of Science and Nature Quotations*. See entry 2121.

■ *Leadership: Quotations from the Military Tradition*. See entry 916.

1723 **The Macmillan Dictionary of Quotations**. New York: Macmillan, 1989. 790p. $35.00. ISBN 0-02-511931-1. LC 89-12237.
    Macmillan includes some 20,000 historical and modern quotations, grouped under 1,100 headings. About 100 quotations are biographical, with those by and about several individuals (e.g., Mark Twain, Shakespeare) interspersed among subject headings. Quotations, selected for their interest, relevance, and wit, include those that "many people know—or, at least, half remember." Indexing is by keyword and name of person quoted. This is an excellent supplement to standard works [R: ARBA 91; LJ, Jan 90; RBB, 15 Jan 90]

1724 **Magill's Quotations in Context. First Series**. Frank N. Magill, ed. Englewood Cliffs, N.J.: Salem Press, 1965. 2v. $75.00/set. ISBN 0-89356-132-0. LC 65-21011.

1725   Magill's Quotations in Context. Second Series. Frank N. Magill, ed. Englewood Cliffs, N.J.: Salem Press, 1969. 2v. $75.00/set. ISBN 0-89356-136-2. LC 65-21011.

Magill goes beyond the identification of a quotation's source to provide background information and a summary of the original context. Two thousand quotations in the *First Series* and 1,500 in the *Second Series* come from the classics, fiction, poetry, drama, and nonfiction. Entries, arranged alphabetically by key word, give source, author, date of first appearance, and type of work, followed by explanations and comments. The value of the work is not in its number of quotations, which are far fewer than in most one-volume works, but in the unique information the volumes provide.

1726   The Oxford Book of Aphorisms. John Gross, ed. New York: Oxford University Press, 1983. 383p. $29.95; $9.95pa. ISBN 0-19-214111-2; 0-19-282015-Xpa.

Aphorisms, maxims, quotations, and pensées from ancient times to the present comprise this volume. Entries, arranged under subjects such as good and evil, provide the originator, source, and date for the sayings (if known). [R: ARBA 84; BL, 1 Apr 83; LJ, 15 Mar 83; WLB, Sept 83]

1727   The Oxford Dictionary of Modern Quotations. Tony Augarde, ed. New York: Oxford University Press, 1991. 371p. $29.95. ISBN 0-19-866141-X. LC 90-26588.

This new collection of quotations focuses on persons of the twentieth century. The 5,000 quotations are arranged alphabetically by personal name, from Abbott and Costello (their "Who's on First" routine) to Frank Zappa. Some quotations were uttered by persons from popular culture, such as Sonny Bono, and others come from writers, such as James Baldwin. It should be noted, however, that about half the people quoted are from Great Britain and are not widely known in this country. Exact sources are provided, and there is an extensive keyword index. This dictionary will supplement Bartlett's *Familiar Quotations* and other standard sources. [R: ARBA 92; BL, 1 May 91; SLJ, Nov 91; WLB, Sept 91]

1728   The Oxford Dictionary of Quotations. 3d ed. New York: Oxford University Press, 1979. 907p. $49.95. ISBN 0-19-211560-4. LC 79-40699.

Some 40,000 quotations, chosen for their popularity and usefulness to readers, are arranged alphabetically by the author quoted, with separate sections for anonymous sayings, ballads, and biblical quotations. The keyword index (over 300 pages) provides comprehensive access to the quotations. This standard work is recommended for high schools. [R: ARBA 81]

■ *Political Quotations*. *See* entry 939.

■ *The Quotable Shakespeare*. *See* entry 1608.

■ *The Quotable Woman*. *See* entries 1125 and 1126.

1729   Rawson, Hugh, and Margaret Miner. The New International Dictionary of Quotations. New York: E. P. Dutton, 1988. 406p. $4.50pa. ISBN 0-451-15153-4. LC 85-31132.

Some 7,500 quotations that cover all time periods are arranged by subject. The compilers have included "more quotes from well-known writers; relatively more prose compared to poetry; relatively more quotes from doers ... as opposed to literary figures." They also admit to having selected more American material than foreign and having given special attention to quotations from "women, minority leaders, scientists, and others who have addressed topics of special importance to our times." The dictionary provides the author and title of sources cited, and notes often place the quotation in historical context or give background information. Indexing is by author; there is no keyword index. [R: ARBA 87; BL, 1 Oct 86; LJ, 15 May 86]

1730   Respectfully Quoted: A Dictionary of Quotations Requested from the Congressional Research Service. Suzy Platt, ed. Washington, D.C.: Library of Congress, 1989. 520p. $29.00. ISBN 0-8444-0538-8. LC 86-600157.

Members of Congress often turn to the Congressional Research Service (CRS) of the Library of Congress to verify quotations they intend to use in speeches or writing. Similar to most libraries, which often build reference files of frequently asked questions, CRS has kept a record of these requests with their verifications. *Respectfully Quoted* stems from this file. It contains 2,100 quotations arranged by subject, key word, and author, A reliable compilation of popular quotations, it is a worthwhile purchase for any secondary school library. [R: ARBA 90; BL, July 89; LJ, 15 Apr 90]

1731 Safire, William, and Leonard Safir, comps. and eds. **Leadership: A Treasury of Great Quotations**. New York: Simon & Schuster, 1990. 258p. $19.95; $8.95pa. ISBN 0-671-67536-2; 0-671-73292-7pa. LC 89-29598.

1732 Safire, William, and Leonard Safir, comps. and eds. **Words of Wisdom**. New York: Simon & Schuster, 1989. 432p. $19.95; $10.95pa. ISBN 0-671-67535-4; 0-671-67587-8pa. LC 88-31336.

Leadership contains some 1,000 quotations gleaned from the writings of a variety of historical and current notables. Arranged under 306 subject headings, the categories include broad concepts, such as authority, and specific business areas, such as truth in advertising.

Words of Wisdom quotes the Bible and persons from Benjamin Franklin to Robert Redford, arranged under topics such as ability and youth. Both works contain *see* references and indexing by name and subject, but neither gives quotation sources. Neither collection is a first choice as a quotation book, but both are worthwhile purchases for high school libraries. [R: ARBA 91]

1733 Shipps, Anthony W. **The Quote Sleuth: A Manual for the Tracer of Lost Quotations**. Urban, Ill.: University of Illinois Press, 1990. 194p. $24.95. ISBN 0-252-01695-5. LC 89-77126.

This guide will help librarians plan an organized search to find quotations. General quotation books, as well as single-subject and single-author works, are evaluated and compared. Chapters also treat language dictionaries with illustrative quotations, concordances, and indexes to first lines of poetry. An annotated bibliography of all sources cited in the text and a comprehensive index complete the volume. [R: BL, 15 June 90; BR, Nov/Dec 90]

1734 Simpson, James B., comp. **Simpson's Contemporary Quotations**. Boston: Houghton Mifflin, 1988. 495p. $19.95. ISBN 0-395-43085-2. LC 87-37867.

Similar to *Wit and Wisdom of the 20th Century*, Simpson has sought quotable material from contemporary times. Both titles are small quotation books that are worthy additions to library shelves. This work consists of some 10,000 quotations from 4,000 clever minds, all arranged under 3 major headings—the world, humankind, and communications and the arts—and subdivided by topics such as law, love, religion, sports, and theater. Indexed by author and subject/keyword. [R: ARBA 89; LJ, 15 June 88; RBB, Aug 88]

1735 **Webster's New World Dictionary of Quotable Definitions**. 2d ed. Eugene E. Brussell, ed. New York: Simon & Schuster, 1988. 674p. $14.95pa. ISBN 0-13-948159-1. LC 88-15087.

This delightful volume, a revision of a 1970 work, adds almost 5,000 new quotable definitions (e.g., "education—the progressive discovery of our ignorance"). The arrangement is alphabetical, with subject and names listed together; indexing is by author. Those quoted run from Aristotle to Frank Zappa; definitions range from scholarly to popular and from literary to folk. This entertaining volume will be of special interest to students in creative writing courses, but it will be enjoyed by everyone. [R: ARBA 89; BR, May/June 89]

1736 **The Wit and Wisdom of the 20th Century: A Dictionary of Quotations**. Frank S. Pepper, ed. New York: Peter Bedrick Books, 1987. 406p. $19.95; $10.95pa. ISBN 0-87226-165-4; 0-87226-166-2pa. LC 87-47755.

Arranged by one-word headings (e.g., aviation, birthday, computers, dictatorships, luxury), this small volume of quotations focuses on the wit and wisdom of contemporary minds. The subject headings listed in the front and the author index provide access. This is a worthwhile collection and a worthy supplement to standard works. [R: ARBA 88; BL, 15 Feb 88; BR, Mar/Apr 88]

Religion

BIBLIOGRAPHIES

See also **Mythology and Folklore** and **Occult**.
See also **Jews** in **Ethnic Minorities**.

E
1737　**Books for Catholic Elementary Schools**. Eileen Noonan, ed. Haverford, Pa.: Catholic Library Association, 1987. 16p. $5.00pa. ISBN 0-87507-041-8. (461 W. Lancaster Ave., Haverford, PA 19041).

1738　**Books for Religious Education in Catholic Secondary Schools**. Eileen Noonan, comp. Haverford, Pa.: Catholic Library Association, 1986. 18p. $5.00pa. ISBN 0-318-41052-4.

E
1739　Pearl, Patricia. **Religious Books for Children: An Annotated Bibliography**. rev. ed. Portland, Oreg.: Church and Synagogue Library Association, 1988. 36p. $6.95pa. ISBN 0-915324-21-0. LC 83-7339. (P.O. Box 19357, Portland, OR 97219).

Noonan's bibliographies provide a core collection for Catholic schools in all curricular areas. The Catholic Library Association also publishes *The Catholic Periodical and Literature Index*, a bimonthly. Pearl's annotated list of 400 books is limited to books on religion for preschool through grade 6.

ATLASES

1740　Bahat, Dan, with Chaim T. Rubinstein. **The Illustrated Atlas of Jerusalem**. New York: Simon & Schuster, 1990. 152p. $95.00. ISBN 0-13-451642-7. LC 90-675114.

This atlas of Jerusalem, the holy city of Jews, Christians, and Muslims and the cause of religious and political conflict for centuries, depicts the history of the citadel from 1000 B.C. to the present. Beginning with a section of topographical maps, the atlas provides over 400 4-color maps, charts, drawings, and photographs. This excellent work reflects the knowledge gained from archaeological digs, historical writings for each period, Biblical texts, and contemporary essays. For high school level. [R: ARBA 91; LJ, Aug 90; RBB, 15 Nov 90; WLB, Nov 90]

DICTIONARIES AND ENCYCLOPEDIAS

1741　**Abingdon Dictionary of Living Religions**. Keith　Crim, ed. Nashville, Tenn.: Abingdon Press, 1981. 830p. $39.95. ISBN 0-687-00409-8. LC 81-1465.

In this work are extensive articles on each major religious tradition worldwide and briefer essays on beliefs, notables, sacred books, and other topics—some 1,600 entries in all. Articles are signed, and most are supported by brief bibliographies. Illustrations include color plates and maps and around 150 black-and-white photographs and drawings. This guide to the historical development of beliefs and religious practices is less technical than *Dictionary of Comparative Religion* and suitable for high school students.

Handbook of Living Religions, edited by John R. Hinnells (Viking, 1986), summarizes practices and beliefs of 13 living religions, including Baha'ism, Christianity, Hinduism, Islam, Judaism, and Sikhism. [R: ARBA 82]

1742　**Dictionary of Comparative Religions**. S. G. F. Brandon, gen. ed. New York: Macmillan, 1970. 704p. $60.00. ISBN 0-684-15561-3. LC 76-11390.

The concise entries in this standard work cover the iconography, philosophy, anthropology, and psychology of primitive, ancient, Asian, and Western religions. Bibliographies end most articles. There are a detailed subject index and a synoptic index that groups articles related to each religious group or an individual country. Although highly technical, the work is recommended for high school libraries. [R: ARBA 71]

1743   The Encyclopedia of Judaism. Geoffrey Wigoder, ed. New York: Macmillan, 1989. 768p. $75.00. ISBN 0-02-628410-3. LC 89-8184.

Judaism focuses on the most important terms, traditions, institutions, and individuals associated with the religion. More than 1,000 current, well-written articles contributed by scholars are enhanced by superb pictures and illustrations, extensive cross-referencing and indexing, and boxes that highlight important data. Articles vary in length according to their importance and range from a few paragraphs to several pages.

This attractive, carefully prepared work provides a concise introduction to many topics related to Judaism. It is highly recommended for secondary schools requiring a reference source on the topic. [R: ARBA 91; LJ, 1 Feb 90; RBB, 1 Mar 90]

1744   The Encyclopedia of World Faiths: A Illustrated Survey of the World's Living Religions. Peter Bishop and Michael Darnton, eds. New York: Facts on File, 1987. 352p. $40.00. ISBN 0-8160-1860-X.

This authoritative survey of the world's living religions examines the nature of each faith and religious beliefs among Western societies, primitive people, and the modern world. It provides extensive coverage of Christianity, Judaism, Islam, Babism, Hinduism, Buddhism, Zoroastrianism, Sikhism, Jainism, the Baha'i faith, Confucianism, Taoism, and Shintoism. Each faith is described in terms of six dimensions: ritual, myth, doctrine, ethics, social structure, and experience.

In order to enable the reader to compare practices and beliefs, color sections present themes such as faith and life, gods and gurus, prophets and teachers, death and afterlife, and festivals. More than 240 photographs and illustrations (162 in full color), a bibliography, a glossary, and an index support the text. Recommended. [R: ARBA 89; BR, Sept/Oct 88; LJ, 15 Mar 88; RBB, Aug 88]

1745   The Facts on File Dictionary of Religions. John R. Hinnells, ed. New York: Facts on File, 1984. 550p. $40.00. ISBN 0-87196-862-2. LC 83-20834.

Most entries concern the world's major religions—Christianity, Buddhism, Islam, Judaism, and Hinduism—but new religious movements and cults, primitive religions, and secular alternatives to traditional forms of worship also receive attention. Some three-fourths of the entries are for non-Christian religions. The 1,150 concise entries, contributed by 29 scholars worldwide, define terms, concepts, beliefs, groups, and rituals. The synoptic index and cross-references connect topics otherwise separated by the alphabetical format. Extensively indexed. This work is similar to *Dictionary of Comparative Religions* but complements it rather than replaces it. [R: ARBA 85; LJ, 1 Sept 84; LJ, 15 Apr 85; WLB, Oct 84]

1746   Glasse, Cyril. The Concise Encyclopedia of Islam. San Francisco: Harper & Row, 1989. 472p. $59.95. ISBN 0-06-063123-6. LC 88-45658.

The author of this work, an American Moslem, seeks to explain the social, religious, and ritualistic practices of Islam. Brief articles treat Islamic philosophy, history, science, medicine, ethnography, laws, calendar, centers of culture, and other matters concerning the faith. Biographical entries profile rulers, leaders, and prophets. Appendixes include several useful features: maps of the pre-Islamic world and the spread of Islam, diagrams of the Hajj (pilgrimage to Mecca), a chronology, branches of the religion, and a genealogical table.

Despite the excellent quality of this work's content, the print is poor, and the binding's weak. Libraries purchasing the volume should expect to rebind it almost immediately. However, it satisfies a critical need for a reliable source on this important topic. [R: ARBA 91]

1747   MacGregor, Geddes. Dictionary of Religion and Philosophy. New York: Paragon House, 1989. 696p. $35.00. ISBN 1-55778-019-8. LC 89-3404.

Despite this work's broad title, its primary focus is on the Judeo-Christian religious tradition. Philosophy is largely secondary, but major concepts are included. Concise, alphabetically arranged entries include historical figures, terms, and events in religion and philosophy. Selective bibliographies grouped by major headings complete the volume. This handy, accurate, and clearly written work is appropriate for high school level. [R: ARBA 91; RBB, 15 May 90; WLB, Apr 90]

■ *Man, Myth & Magic. See* entry 1701.

1748   Melton, J. Gordon. The Encyclopedia of American Religions. 3d ed. Detroit: Gale, 1989. $165.00. ISBN 0-8103-2841-0.

The 3d edition of this work (the previous editions were in 1979 and 1985) divides 588 United States and Canadian religious bodies into 22 "families." For each, Melton provides a historical narrative that identifies key figures, events, and doctrinal characteristics; he also offers a directory that gives names, addresses, membership statistics, and publication data for each body. Separate indexes provide access by organization and institution, publications, geography, personal name, educational institution, and subject. [R: ARBA 91]

1749 Melton, J. Gordon, and others. **New Age Encyclopedia: A Guide to Beliefs, Concepts, Terms, People, and Organizations....** Detroit: Gale, 1990. 586p. $59.50. ISBN 0-8103-7159-6. ISSN 1047-2746.
An introductory essay traces the historical development of the New Age movement and its current patterns and trends. The main part provides 325 alphabetically arranged entries on a broad range of topics, such as persons, organizations, concepts, beliefs, and opposition to New Age beliefs. Among the topics included are New Age music, Shirley MacLaine, yoga, crystals, channeling, rolfing, aromatherapy, and Feldenkrais. A chronology of the movement and a name and keyword index complete the volume. Melton provides an impartial approach to a controversial area. [R: ARBA 91; LJ, Aug 90; RBB, 15 Sept 90; WLB, Oct 90]

1750 **New Catholic Encyclopedia.** By an editorial staff at the Catholic University of America. Palatine, Ill.: Publishers Guild, 1981. 17v. $750.00/set. ISBN 0-07-010235-X. LC 66-22292.
The emphasis of this set is on the church in the United States and the English-speaking world. The main set provides coverage through the close of Vatican II; the supplements include articles on more current issues and biographies of notables who died after 1965. Volume 18, the latest supplement, covers the years 1978-1988.
Most of the 17,000 entries are long and scholarly. With both Catholic and non-Catholic scholars contributing, this work is objective, ecumenical, and readable. Scholarly bibliographies support each article, and the analytical index contains some 250,000 entries. [R: ARBA 80]

HANDBOOKS

1751 Deedy, John. **The Catholic Fact Book.** Chicago: Thomas More Press, 1986. 412p. $24.95; $15.95pa. ISBN 0-88347-186-8; 0-88347-252-Xpa.
This work contains a wealth of information about the Roman Catholic Church. Arrangement is in seven sections: history, basic tenets, church teachings, organization, saints, modern biography, and terms in common use. The biographical section includes twentieth-century individuals, some controversial. High school libraries with a need for a reference tool on Catholicism but unable to afford the *New Catholic Encyclopedia* should consider this work. [R: ARBA 88]

1752 Himelstein, Shmuel. **The Jewish Primer: Questions and Answers on Jewish Faith and Culture.** New York: Facts on File, 1990. 256p. $21.95. ISBN 0-8160-2322-0. LC 90-2951.
The Jewish primer provides simple, forceful explanations of the faith and practices of Judaism. Reform and Conservative forms are briefly covered, but the work's emphasis is on traditional Orthodox beliefs. Himelstein offers succinct discussions of dietary laws, marriage and divorce, holy days, the sabbath, sacred writings, Jewish life, and many other topics, all in question-and-answer format and supported by a subject index. This is an excellent introduction to the tenets of traditional Judaism. [R: BL, 15 May 90; LJ, 15 Apr 90]

1753 Mead, Frank S. **Handbook of Denominations in the United States.** 9th ed. Nashville, Tenn.: Abingdon Press, 1990. 316p. $13.95. ISBN 0-687-16572-5. LC 90-32830.
The history, doctrines, governance, statistics, and auxiliary institutions of 225 religious groups in the United States make up the latest edition of this standard handbook, which was last revised in 1985. Many of the essays on individual denominations have been updated to reflect changes, with more attention given to evangelicalism and fundamentalism.
New features include essays on religious movements and ecclesiastical terms (e.g., *catholic*, *episcopal*), and an appendix that lists American evangelical and pentecostal groups. Other features include a list of denomination headquarters, a glossary, and a bibliography. Indexed. [R: ARBA 91]

1754 Melton, J. Gordon. **Encyclopedic Handbook of Cults in America.** Hamden, Conn.: Garland, 1986. 272p. (Garland Reference Library of Social Sciences, v.213). $24.95. ISBN 0-8240-9036-5. LC 83-48227.
Following an essay on the definition and history of cults in the United States, this work treats 28 groups: older cults, such as the Rosicrucians and Theosophy; the New Age movement; and newer cults,

such as the Unification Church and the Rajneesh Foundation. For each group, the text covers its major figures, beliefs, organizational structure, and controversies. A bibliography of books about the cult by both members and nonmembers concludes each entry. Indexed. These unbiased essays about a popular topic make this a worthwhile source on the subject. [R: ARBA 87; RBB, 15 Dec 86]

1755   Nielsen, Niels, and others. **Religions of the World**. 2d ed. New York: St. Martin's Press, 1988. 736p. $37.30. ISBN 0-312-00308-0. LC 87-60523.
       Intended as an undergraduate textbook, this extensive and authoritative work provides outstanding coverage of world religions. The first of eight chapters introduces religious concepts and questions, the unexplained in myth and legend, and religions of the ancient world. The remaining chapters explore the major living religions and their development, beliefs, settings, customs, and relations to art and everyday life. Special features include maps, timelines, and a detailed index.

1756   **Religions on File**. By the Diagram Group. New York: Facts on File, 1990. 1v. (various paging). $145.00 looseleaf w/binder. ISBN 0-8160-2224-0. LC 89-48398.
       Some 650 reproducible maps, charts, blueprints for houses of worship, creeds and texts, social and religious hierarchy diagrams, calendars, ritual objects and symbols, and other religious items comprise this collection. Included are ancient religions (e.g., Egyptian, Greek), Hinduism, Buddhism and other Asian religions, Judaism, Christianity, and Islam. A detailed table of contents and index provide access. Junior and senior high school classes in current events, geography, history, literature, and social studies will welcome this excellent "on file" collection, which is copyright-free and designed to be reproduced on standard photocopy machines. [R: ARBA 91; BR, Sept/Oct 90; RBB, Aug 90]

1757   **Yearbook of American and Canadian Churches**. Constance H. Jacquet, ed. Nashville, Tenn.: Abingdon Press. annual. $27.95pa. ISSN 0195-9034. LC 16-5726.
       Published over a period of 70 years, this valuable reference yearbook provides accurate statistics and other timely data on over 250 religious groups in North America. The statistical information contained in the 1989 edition was reported in 1987 and 1988.
       For each group, the work gives the names, addresses, and leadership personnel for its headquarters and divisions, as well as a brief history of the denomination. Also provided are directory data for theological seminaries, national and international cooperative organizations, service agencies, colleges and universities, and periodicals published by each church. A calendar for church use gives dates through 1993 for conferences and other meetings. Indexed by topic and church name.

BIBLE STUDIES

1758   **Baker Encyclopedia of the Bible**. Walter A. Elwell and others, eds. Grand Rapids, Mich.: Baker Book House, 1988. 2v. $79.95/set. ISBN 0-8010-3447-7. LC 88-19318.
       This two-volume set, which takes a conservative Protestant stance, provides comprehensive treatment of the books of the Bible, theological topics, life in ancient times, biblical persons and places, and modern religious notables. Most entries are lengthy, and all are well written in nontechnical language. The book does not supply a pronunciation guide, and illustrations are limited to a few black-and-white maps. Nevertheless, the work is attractive and informative. [R: ARBA 90]

1759   **The Books of the Bible**. Bernhard W. Anderson, ed. New York: Scribner's, 1989. 2v. $175.00/ set. ISBN 0-684-18487-7. LC 89-10074.
       Descriptive and interpretive essays on the books of the Bible appear in this excellent work. Volume 1 covers the 39 books of the Old Testament/Hebrew Bible; volume 2 contains essays on the Apocrypha and the 27 books of the New Testament. Several general articles, such as "Introduction to the Old Testament" and "The Apocrypha: A Window into the Ancient World," provide broad historical insights.
       Each essay, written and signed by a renowned scholar, addresses the Bible as literature, with some attention to the oral traditions from which it evolved. References cite numerous standard translations of Biblical texts, and a bibliography for further study supports each essay. Each volume includes a chronology and index, but the set lacks maps and illustrations.
       General readers, students, teachers, and clergy should profit from this study of the books of the Bible, which is a scholarly humanist work, not a learned theological treatise. Highly recommended for high schools.

Asimov's Guide to the Bible by Isaac Asimov (Avon, 1976, 1982) provides interesting interpretations in terms of history and science and gives the relevant research findings of a number of disciplines.

1760 Brown, Raymond E. **Responses to 101 Questions on the Bible**. Mahwah, N.J.: Paulist Press, 1990. 224p. $9.95; $5.95pa. ISBN 0-8091-0443-1; 0-8091-3188-9pa.

Brown, a popular platform speaker, based the contents on questions most frequently asked at his lectures by laity and clergy. Questions, arranged by broad theme, receive scholarly responses that reflect a middle-of-the-road Roman Catholic position. A final section outlines the Catholic approach to the Bible. Even non-Catholics will find this work informative. [R: LJ, Aug 90]

1761 Douglas, J. D., and Merrill C. Tenney. **NIV Compact Dictionary of the Bible**. Grand Rapids, Mich.: Zondervan, 1989. 668p. $14.95. ISBN 0-310-33180-3. LC 88-29690.

The *NIV Compact Dictionary*, a condensed version of *New International Dictionary of the Bible*, a large one-volume work published in 1987, uses the New International Version (NIV) of the Bible (1978) as its textual source. This readable and inexpensive work, Protestant in approach, provides information on Biblical culture, persons, places, events, concepts, doctrines, and literature. The introductory material includes a 23-page survey of the Bible and life in ancient times. A list provides scripture references for persons not included in the dictionary. [R: ARBA 90]

1762 **The Eerdmans Bible Dictionary**. Allen C. Myers, ed. Grand Rapids, Mich.: William B. Eerdmans, 1987. 1094p. $32.50. ISBN 0-8028-2402-1. LC 87-13239.

Eerdmans, an expanded and updated translation of a Dutch Bible dictionary (1975), contains almost 5,000 entries. Articles cover all persons and places mentioned in the Bible, explain important Biblical concepts, and examine the background and contents of each book of the Bible.

Coverage, which includes canonical and apocryphal books, reflects recent archaeological discoveries and literary, historical, and sociological studies. Forty-eight persons from a variety of evangelical denominations have contributed the unsigned articles. Bibliographies support major articles; there are a limited number of illustrations, but there are tables, charts, and a 12-page collection of colored maps from Hammond.

This work is not as scholarly as *Harper's Bible Dictionary*, but it is a good dictionary that reflects a Protestant stance. [R: ARBA 89; RBB, 15 Jan 88; WLB, Nov 87]

1763 **The Harper Atlas of the Bible**. James B. Pritchard, ed. San Francisco, Calif.: Harper & Row, 1987. 254p. $49.95. ISBN 0-06-181883-6. LC 86-675550.

This work presents biblical geography and social and cultural history in topical entries, all illustrated by full-color maps, charts, diagrams, photographs, and drawings. The chronological arrangement, extending from prehistoric times to A.D. 135, relates the Bible to ancient history, including major events, customs, beliefs, and everyday life. The maps, presented in a curved-Earth format, are supported by an index that lists all place-names shown.

Other features include an extensive chronology and a biographical section entitled "People of the Bible," which provides brief information about major personalities and cites the books of the Bible in which they appear.

Two other recommended atlases, both less expensive than *Harper*, are *The Macmillan Bible Atlas* by Yohanan Aharoni and Michael Avi-Yonah (rev. ed. Collier/Macmillan, 1977), and *The Oxford Bible Atlas* edited by Herbert G. May (3d ed. Oxford University Press, 1985). [R: ARBA 89; LJ, 15 Apr 88; RBB, 15 Feb 88]

1764 **Harper's Bible Commentary**. James L. Mays and others, eds. New York: Harper & Row, 1988. 1326p. $32.50. ISBN 0-06-065541-0. LC 88-95148.

Produced under the auspices of the Society of Biblical Literature, this Bible commentary is a companion volume to *Harper's Bible Dictionary*, to which it frequently is cross-referenced. The eight main sections contain long essays that focus primarily on Biblical meaning and interpretation (e.g., "The Bible Story: Genesis to Esther"; "Psalms and Wisdom"). Shorter articles treat special topics, such as women in Genesis and Jeremiah's symbolic action. The 79 contributors—Protestant, Catholic, and Jewish scholars—were chosen for their subject competence. Numerous black-and-white illustrations and 16 color maps support the text.

Other standard commentaries include the Protestant work, *The Interpreter's One-Volume Commentary on the Bible*, edited by Charles M. Laymon (Abingdon Press, 1971), and the Roman Catholic study, *The New Jerome Biblical Commentary*, edited by Raymond E. Brown and others (Prentice-Hall, 1989). [R: ARBA 89; BL, 1 Dec 89]

1765   **Harper's Bible Dictionary**. Paul J. Achtemeier and others, eds. San Francisco, Calif.: Harper & Row, 1985. 1178p. $28.50; $30.95 (thumb indexed). ISBN 0-06-069862-4; 0-06-069863-2 (thumb indexed.

This work, a cooperative project between the publisher and the Society of Biblical Literature, replaces earlier handbooks that bore the same title. The 3,700 alphabetically arranged articles, written and signed by 179 Protestant, Catholic, and Jewish scholars, cover all important persons and places in all books of the Bible, including the Apocrypha. Also included are theological terms, archaeological sites, and words used in the Bible in important or unusual ways.

Most entries are concise, but articles on major topics are several pages in length. The dictionary is generously illustrated with black-and-white and color photographs, line drawings, charts, and maps. Major essays are supported by bibliographies. Highly recommended. [R: ARBA 86]

1766   Levine, Mark L., and Eugene Rochlis. **The Complete Book of Bible Quotations**. New York: Pocket Books/Simon & Schuster, c1986, 1989. $14.95pa. ISBN 0-671-70551-2.

1767   Miner, Margaret, and Hugh Rawson. **A Dictionary of Quotations from the Bible**. New York: New American Library, 1988. 305p. $18.95; $4.95pa. ISBN 0-453-00631-1; 0-415-16550-0pa.

Both quotation books are based on the King James version of the Bible. Levine's compendium, the larger of the pair, arranges 5,000 quotations under 800-plus subject headings. Quotations were selected for their beauty, significance, and suitability for illustrating concepts. Miner's collection arranges some 3,000 quotations under about 400 board subjects, with frequent explanatory notes. Both dictionaries are indexed by keyword.

Another recommended source, *Biblical Quotations*, edited by Jennifer Speake (Facts on File, 1983), arranges quotations in the order of the books of the Bible, from Genesis through Revelation (including the Apocrypha), then by chapter and verse. [R: BL, 15 Jan 87; BL, 15 Apr 89]

1768   **The Lion Encyclopedia of the Bible**. rev. ed. Pat Alexander and others, eds. Batavia, Ill.: Lion Publishing, 1986. 352p. $24.95. ISBN 0-7459-1113-7.

This work, a revision of *Eerdmans' Family Encyclopedia of the Bible* (1978), provides a wealth of concise, easy-to-read information on all aspects of the Bible (e.g., people, places, key teachings, archaeology). It also includes a narrative section on everyday life in biblical times, illustrations, maps, and an index. This encyclopedia is directed toward students of junior high school age and above. [R: BL, 15 Jan 87; BL, 1 Dec 89]

1769   **The Revell Bible Dictionary**. Old Tappan, N.J.: Fleming H. Revell, 1990. 1156p. $29.95. ISBN 0-8007-1594-2. LC 90-33002.

This Bible dictionary, designed for young people, reflects the religious position of conservative, fundamentalist Protestants. Its 2,000 alphabetically arranged entries, which vary from a sentence to several pages, cover books of the Bible, major persons and events, and theological ideas.

Special features include information boxes scattered throughout the volume, which provide study guides, chronologies, tables, and other data; 1,700 drawings and color photographs of artifacts, sites, and reproductions of paintings; the "Identiquick," which gives brief identifications and pronunciations for proper names; and a section of color maps. This attractive work is recommended for libraries that need a Bible dictionary with a fundamentalist bias. [R: ARBA 91; LJ, Dec 90; RBB, 15 Dec 90]

BIOGRAPHY

1770   Bowden, Henry W. **Dictionary of American Religious Biography**. Edwin S. Gaustad, ed. Westport, Conn.: Greenwood Press, 1977. 572p. $45.00. ISBN 0-8371-8906-3. LC 76-5258.

Patterned after the *Dictionary of American Biography* and other scholarly subject biographies, this volume presents sketches of 425 persons from all denominations who played a significant role in American history, from ordained ministers to cultists, freethinkers, and laypersons. For each, information includes dates, education, and career, but the focus is on the person in terms of time and place. Bibliographies cite works by and about each subject. [R: ARBA 78]

1771   Kelly, J. N. D. **The Oxford Dictionary of Popes**. New York: Oxford University Press, 1986. 347p. $29.95; $8.95pa. ISBN 0-19-213964-9; 0-19-282085-0pa.

This scholarly and objective work, arranged chronologically, covers the 264 Popes who followed Peter. Entries include each Pope's family, educational background, prepapal career, and activities in office, followed by a selective bibliography. An appendix refutes the fable that an Englishwoman named Joan was elected Pope in 855. An extensive index provides excellent topical access. [R: ARBA 87]

1772 **Twentieth-Century Shapers of American Popular Religions**. Charles H. Lippy, ed. Westport, Conn.: Greenwood Press, 1989. 494p. $65.00. ISBN 0-313-25356-0. LC 88-15487.

This excellent volume provides biographies for 64 important individuals in popular religion. Signed articles, contributed by scholars, address positive and negative aspects of each person's life, appraise their contributions and importance to the field, give a summary of criticism, and provide a bibliography of works by and about each biographee. Appropriate for high school reference collections. [R: ARBA 90; LJ, 15 Mar 89; RBB, 15 June 89]

CUSTOMS

See also **Holidays and Special Days**.

1773 Cardozo, Arlene Rossen. **Jewish Family Celebrations: The Sabbath, Festivals, and Ceremonies**. New York: St. Martin's Press, 1982. 288p. $17.50; $8.95pa. ISBN 0-312-44231-9; 0-312-44232-7pa. LC 82-5566.

Festivals and celebrations, arranged by seasons of the year, and life cycle ceremonies (e.g., births, deaths, bar and bat mitzahs, weddings) are the focus of this volume. Entries explain the celebration's origin, development, and significance, and describe its ceremonies and traditions. [R: ARBA 84]

SAINTS

1774 **The Book of Saints: A Dictionary of Servants of God**. 6th ed. Compiled by the Benedictine Monks of St. Augustine's Abbey, Ramsgate. Wilton, Conn.: Morehouse, 1989. 605p. $34.95. ISBN 0-8192-1501-5. LC 89-33515.

This work, considered one of the best hagiographical reference works, has been revised and updated to reflect the 1969 changes in the Roman calendar. Each of the some 10,000 entries includes the saint's name, appellation, feast day, dates, liturgical group, rank (saint or blessed), religious order, and life. Those deleted from the calendar in 1969 are included with reasons for their removal. Special features include illustrations of saints and symbols, a list of patron saints, and a list of pre-Christian prophetesses (sibyls) often depicted in Christian art. [R: ARBA 91]

1775 Farmer, David Hugh. **The Oxford Dictionary of Saints**. 2d ed. New York: Oxford University Press, 1987. 478p. $12.95pa. ISBN 0-19-282038-9. LC 86-19263.

The original plan of this hagiography called for the treatment of all saints who died before 1530, plus representatives from Ireland, Scotland, and Wales. As the work progressed, however, the terminal date was extended to include those listed in the 1969 Roman calendar, others important in the history of the church, all those honored by the Anglican Church, and Eastern (Greek and Russian) saints. Its content, therefore, came to include all important martyrs and saints of the Christian church.

Entries, which vary from 30 words for obscure saints to almost 1,000 words for the well known, are followed by brief bibliographies. The appendixes contain a short list of unsuccessful candidates for canonization, the principal patronage of each saint (if any), symbols of various saints, and a calendar of feast and special days. The index cites all places in Great Britain associated with particular saints.

Dictionary of Saints by John J. Delaney (Doubleday, 1980) provides concise information on saints and those who are termed "blessed" and "venerable," including those dropped from the liturgical calendar. *Butler's Lives of the Saints*, edited by Michael Walsh (Harper & Row, 1985), based on Alban Butler's 1966 work, has sketches of saints of many nationalities, arranged by the calendar. [R: ARBA 88]

□ _____ # Theater and Dance _____ □

THEATER

Dictionaries and Encyclopedias

See **Literature** for **Drama**.
See **Music** for **Opera**.
See also **Fashion and Costume** in **Decorative Arts**.

1776   Bloom, Ken. **Broadway: An Encyclopedic Guide to the History, People and Places of Times Square**. New York: Facts on File, 1991. 442p. $50.00. ISBN 0-8160-1249-0. LC 90-32632.
This is a fascinating work about Times Square, the heart of American theater. The book spans more than a century of the history of Broadway. For each major Broadway theater, the Ambassador to the Zeigfield, it provides complete information on shows and their performance times. Biographies of stars, playwrights, composers, directors, and producers are also included. The Broadway "scene" is covered as well—Sardi's restaurant, the Astor Hotel, the Latin Quarter nightclub, and other locations associated with the theater. [R: ARBA 92; LJ, 1 Nov 90; SLJ, July 91]

1777   Bordman, Gerald. **The Oxford Companion to American Theatre**. New York: Oxford University Press, 1984. 734p. $55.00. ISBN 0-19-503443-0. LC 83-26812.

1778   Bordman, Gerald. **The Concise Oxford Companion to American Theatre**. New York: Oxford University Press, 1987. 451p. $29.95; $13.95pa. ISBN 0-19-505121-1; 0-19-506327-9pa.
Some 3,000 alphabetically arranged entries appear in this lucid work. Many entries provide information on persons associated with the American theater, such as playwrights, performers, producers, composers, librettists, choreographers, and designers. Performers from vaudeville, minstrel shows, and other forms of popular theater are treated along with those of the legitimate stage. More than 1,000 entries for individual plays and musicals give plot summaries and brief commentaries. Others cover theaters, organizations, and terminology. This work is a worthwhile supplement to *Oxford Companion to the Theatre*, a standard reference tool on the subject.
The abridged version eliminates many entries for minor plays and individuals while retaining those of the greatest general interest. It also contains updated information for 2,000 articles carried over from the parent volume. [R: ARBA 85]

1779   **Cambridge Guide to World Theatre**. Martin Banham, ed. New York: Cambridge University Press, 1988. 1104p. $49.50. ISBN 0-521-26595-9. LC 88-25804.
High schools with active drama departments will welcome this work, which contains signed, alphabetically arranged articles on theatrical history and tradition for countries and cultures throughout the world. Everything from Shakespearean performers, Greek drama, and Broadway musicals to mime, jugglers, actors, directors, playwrights, designers, censorship, and criticism is covered. Cross-references connect related articles, and over 500 black-and-white illustrations support the volume. Indexed.
The *Cambridge Guide* is similar to the *Oxford Companion to the Theatre*, but it defines theater in a broader sense than does the *Oxford Companion* and also offers broader coverage of world theater. Highly recommended. [R: ARBA 90; LJ, 1 Apr 89; RBB, 1 June 89; SLJ, May 89]

■ *Gänzl's Book of the Musical Theatre*. *See* entry 1672.

1780   Hodgson, Terry. **The Drama Dictionary**. New York: New Amsterdam, 1989. 432p. $35.00. ISBN 0-941533-40-9.
Entries in this work vary in length from a few lines to several pages; they define 1,300 terms commonly heard in the theater. Some 30 line drawings add interest. For many entries there are suggestions for further reading. The author intends to provide a useful source on dramatic practice, theory, and criticism rather than exhaustive coverage of terminology. High school students who wish to acquire a working vocabulary of the theater will find this source useful. [R: ARBA 90; RBB, 1 Apr 89]

1781   **International Guide to Children's Theatre and Educational Theatre: A Historical and Geographical Sourcebook**. Lowell Swortzell, ed. Westport, Conn.: Greenwood Press, 1990. 381p. $59.95. ISBN 0-313-24881-8. LC 89-12059.

Alphabetically arranged, this work surveys the children's theater movement in 45 countries, Australia to Zimbabwe, providing information on important plays and productions, influential dramatists, directors, designers, performers, teachers, and artistic/educational goals. An index and a bibliography of books, articles, and dissertations conclude the volume. Suggested for middle and high school level. [R: ARBA 91; BR, Nov/Dec 90]

1782   Loney, Glenn. **20th Century Theatre**. New York: Facts on File, 1983. 2v. $75.00/set. ISBN 0-87196-463-5. LC 81-19587.

For retrospective coverage of major theater productions, this work is excellent. Volume 1 consists of a chronology of United States and British productions from 1900 to 1979. Within each year, theatrical activities are arranged in five categories: American premieres, British premieres, revivals and repertoires, births/deaths/debuts, and theater/productions (a miscellaneous section). Production photographs illustrate almost every page. Volume 2 presents a chronologically arranged bibliography and a name/title/subject index. [R: ARBA 84]

1783   McCaslin, Nellie. **Historical Guide to Children's Theater in America**. Westport, Conn.: Greenwood Press, 1987. 348p. $55.00. ISBN 0-313-24466-9. LC 85-12684.

McCaslin provides a historical survey of 80 years of children's theater in America, beginning with a theater founded in 1903 by a settlement house on New York's Lower East Side. Part 1 covers children's theater from the early attempts at professionalism to today's budgetary and equity-contract problems and the omnipresent need for good scripts.

Part 2 provides an alphabetical list of production companies and associations that have made significant contributions to the field. For each group, there is a short essay on its origin, development, purpose, goals, physical plant, and touring operation. The appendixes include a chronology of events, a list of persons who have made significant contributions, and a geographical directory of companies and associations. [R: ARBA 88; RBB, 15 Nov 87]

1784   Mordden, Ethan. **The Fireside Companion to the Theatre**. New York: Simon & Schuster, 1988. 313p. $24.95; $12.95pa. ISBN 0-671-67188-X; 0-671-62553-5pa.

The Fireside Companion to the Theatre focuses on theatrical terminology, people, movements, and some plays, arranged alphabetically from Abbey Theatre through *Zoo Story*. The concise entries are supported by an abundance of illustrations and cross-references. This attractive work is appropriate for high school level. [R: Kliatt, Apr 88]

1785   **The Oxford Companion to the Theatre**. 4th ed. Phyllis Hartnoll, ed. New York: Oxford University Press, 1983. 934p. $49.95. ISBN 0-19-211546-4.

This valuable work, international in scope, covers all time periods. It focuses on the legitimate stage, with little attention given to popular theater. Entries include terms, theater companies and buildings, acoustics, lighting, stage technology, performers, playwrights, copyright, and other topics. Nearly 100 pages of plates display some 400 illustrations. This is an excellent one-volume reference on world theater. [R: ARBA 84; BL, 1 Nov 84]

■ *Shakespeare A to Z*. See entry 1604.

Handbooks

1786   **The *Back Stage* Handbook for Performing Artists**. Sherry Eaker, comp. and ed. New York: Back Stage Books/Watson-Guptill, 1989. 239p. $18.95pa. ISBN 0-8230-7508-7. LC 88-34446.

This work discusses the business side of the performing arts and practical advice for beginning and veteran actors, singers, dancers, and models. Its 32 "how-to" and "who-to-contact" articles, which have appeared in issues of *Back Stage*, are arranged in 6 categories: basic tools, training, finding work, getting the show on the road, working in the theater, and off the main stage. Among the topics covered are agents, photographers, resumes, and auditions. Several essays alert the reader to shady practices and exploitation schemes. [R: ARBA 90; LJ, 15 June 89]

1787   **The Best Plays**. Otis L. Guernsey, Jr. and Jeffrey Sweet, eds. New York: Applause Theatre Books. annual. $37.95; $19.95pa. LC 20-21432.

This series, also known as the *Burns Mantle Theater Yearbook*, has been published since 1926. Contents vary, but more recent annuals provide digests and critical comments on selected plays and list productions of the year: plays produced in New York with theater, cast, technical personnel, and a brief plot summary; plays produced outside of New York; and Shakespearean festivals. Other sections provide theater statistics, prizes and awards, and actors with place and date of birth. Indexed. [R: BL, 15 Feb 85]

1788   **The Book of a Thousand Plays**. Steve Fletcher and Norma Jopling, comps. and eds. New York: Facts on File, 1989. 352p. $24.95. ISBN 0-8160-2122-8. LC 88-38121.

The Book of a Thousand Plays identifies the most popular plays performed in the last century. For each of the 1,000 alphabetically arranged English-language plays, musicals, and operettas, information includes author/playwright, genre, city and year of first performance, a synopsis, and a list of characters. Indexed by author/playwright. [R: ARBA 90; RBB, 1 Nov 89; SLJ, May 90]

1789   Willis, John. **Theatre World**. New York: Crown. annual. $40.00.

This annual survey of the American theater, published for almost 50 years, places emphasis on Broadway productions, with some attention given to off-Broadway plays, regional theater, and touring companies. Casts, dates of opening and closing, and other descriptive data are given, but there are no critical comments. Biographical sketches of outstanding performers, producers, and other theatrical notables are included. Indexed.

Indexes

E +

1790   **Play Index, 1983-1987: An Index to 3,964 Plays**. Juliette Yaakov and John Greenfieldt, eds. Bronx, N.Y.: H. W. Wilson, 1988. 522p. $55.00. ISSN 0554-3037. LC 64-1054.

The latest edition of this index provides comprehensive coverage of 3,964 plays contained in collections or published separately from 1983 to 1987. Six additional cumulations cover the period from 1949 through 1982.

Included are all types of works, from puppet plays to classical drama. Author, title, subject, and dramatic style entries are arranged in a single alphabet, with additional sections for cast analysis (number and gender of characters), a list of collections analyzed, and a directory of publishers. The author entry contains a descriptive note and indicates size of cast and number of sets required. Symbols note plays suitable for children and young people. This index is an excellent source for locating published plays. [R: ARBA 89]

■ *Plays for Children and Young Adults*. See entry 1212.

Biography

■ *Authors and Artists for Young Adults*. See entry 1173.

1791   **Contemporary Theater, Film, and Television**. Linda S. Hubbard, Owen O'Donnell, and Sara J. Steen, eds. Detroit: Gale. annual. $110.00/v. ISSN 0749-064X.

This series, which now consists of seven volumes, began in 1984 as a continuation of *Who's Who in the Theatre*. It provides biographical and career information on currently popular theater, film, and television performers, directors, producers, writers, designers, managers, choreographers, technicians, composers, executives, dancers, and critics. Each volume covers some 700 individuals, many with photographs.

Entries, similar in format to *Contemporary Authors* gives complete career credits for work in the three media, plus information on recordings, awards, and memberships. Personal information includes birthdate, original name, parents and spouses, education, political and religious affiliations, and address. Each volume contains a cumulative index for all previous annuals.

1792   Morley, Sheridan. **The Great Stage Stars: Distinguished Theatrical Careers of the Past and Present**. New York: Facts on File, 1986. 425p. $29.95. ISBN 0-8160-1401-9. LC 85-27548.

Biographies of 200 past and present stars of the American and British stage comprise this volume. Emphasis is on those who have had long and distinguished careers. The author quotes frequently from the actors and from reviews that seem to capture the essence of a performance. Entries, many with photographs, run two or three pages. [R: ARBA 87; LJ, 1 Apr 86]

DANCE

E+
1793   Balanchine, George, and Francis Mason. **101 Stories of the Great Ballets**. New York: Anchor Books/Doubleday, 1989. 541p. $9.95pa. ISBN 0-385-03398-2. LC 74-9140.

A new edition of *Balanchine's New Complete Stories of the Great Ballets* (Doubleday, 1975), this work narrates the stories of 101 of the most popular ballets up to 1975. For the alphabetically arranged titles, each entry provides information on music, orchestration, choreography, design, date and place of premiere, and principal dancers. Critical notes follow the detailed synopses. [R: ARBA 90]

1794   Koegler, Horst. **The Concise Oxford Dictionary of Ballet**. New York: Oxford University Press, 1982. 459p. $17.95pa. ISBN 0-19-311330-9.

Over 5,000 alphabetically arranged entries that cover all aspects of ballet for the last four centuries are to be found in this volume. Included are choreographers, dancers, composers, terms, sets, costumes, and literary sources of ballet. Ethnic, ballroom, and modern dance also receive attention. This revision of a 1977 work contains much information on the subject. [R: ARBA 84]

1795   Robertson, Allen, and Donald Hutera. **The Dance Handbook**. Boston: G. K. Hall, c1988, 1990. 278p. $25.00; $16.95pa. ISBN 0-8161-9095-X; 0-8161-1829-9pa. LC 89-77759.

Western ballet and modern dance are the concerns of this small, informative work, a volume in the Performing Arts series. The book consists of 200 main entries for choreographers, dancers, and ballets, grouped into 8 chronological sections. Each entry contains factual data, a critical evaluation, cross-references to related topics, and a bibliography. This unpretentious guide is not comprehensive, but it offers a great deal of useful information on dance.

Other volumes in the series include *Opera Handbook*, *The Jazz Handbook*, and *The Film Handbook*. [R: ARBA 91; BR, Jan/Feb 91; LJ, July 90; RBB, 1 Nov 90]

1796   Warren, Gretchen Ward. **Classical Ballet Techniques**. Tampa, Fla.: University of South Florida Press; distr., Gainesville, Fla.: University Presses of Florida, 1989. 395p. $85.00; $39.95pa. ISBN 0-8130-0895-6; 0-8130-0945-6pa. LC 89-31141.

This volume covers the theory, tradition, and movements of classical ballet; defines the vocabulary of the field; and suggests ways in which ballet should be taught. Over 2,600 black-and-white photographs illustrate correct and incorrect movements, poses, and exercises. Other features include a glossary, a pronunciation guide, a selective bibliography, and an essay on classroom etiquette. Indexed. [R: ARBA 91; LJ, Jan 90; RBB, 1 Nov 90]

Part V
Science and Technology

□ _____ **Astronomy** _____ □

GENERAL WORKS

E
1797   Asimov, Isaac. **Isaac Asimov's Library of the Universe**. Milwaukee, Wis.: Gareth Stevens, 1988-1990. 33v. $394.35/set. ISBN 1-55532-420-7.

This colorful set introduces children to the wonders of the universe, from its origins to recent scientific discoveries. Each book consists of 2-page spreads that cover 12 topics, followed by fact files, lists for further reading, additional sources of information, and a glossary. These are supported by spectacular photographs and drawings. Phonetic spellings in parentheses follow every difficult name or word.

Caveats include some contradictory statements in the text and captions, inconsistencies in providing pronunciations, and a cluttered page format. Kudos include informative text, beautiful illustrations, and imaginative analogies between familiar objects and the subject. Appropriate for ages 8 through 12. [R: ARBA 91; RBB, 1 Sept 90]

ATLASES

1798   **The Cambridge Atlas of Astronomy**. 2d ed. Jean Audouze and G. Israel, eds. New York: Cambridge University Press, 1988. 431p. $90.00. ISBN 0-521-36360-8. LC 84-73453.

This beautiful compendium is well worth the cost. It takes the reader on a stunning journey through the solar system and beyond it to stars and galaxies, providing an up-to-date survey of recent knowledge gained from satellite-based imagery and voyages to the moon, Venus, and Mars. The atlas is divided into five major sections on the sun, the solar system, the stars and the galaxies, the extragalactic domain, and the scientific perspective. It includes 350 color and 450 black-and-white photographs, and 350 color diagrams. Three sky maps conclude the volume. Recommended for advanced high school students. [R: ARBA 90; BL, 1 May 89; SBF, Sept/Oct 89]

E
1799   **Rand McNally Children's Atlas of the Universe**. Skokie, Ill.: Rand McNally, 1990. 93p. $14.95. ISBN 0-528-83408-8. LC 90-53622.

This is an attractive atlas of the planet Earth, celestial bodies of our solar system, and the Milky Way and other galaxies. It includes beautiful satellite photographs and drawings, informative text that provides historical and physical descriptions of each entity, and fact boxes that contain pertinent data. Star charts map the constellations through each of the four seasons. A glossary and detailed index conclude the volume. The large type, spectacular photographs, and easy accessibility make this an excellent selection for the elementary level. [R: BL, 1 Feb 91; SLJ, May 91]

1800   Vehrenberg, Hans. **Atlas of Deep-Sky Splendors**. 4th ed. New York: Cambridge University Press, 1983. 242p. $57.50. ISBN 0-521-24834-0. LC 83-7656.

High-quality photographs of deep-space objects—galaxies, star clusters, and nebulas—are the hallmark of this excellent atlas designed for the amateur astronomer. The 113 charts of star fields show more than 400 nonstellar objects. Star charts, small finder charts, and a list of the objects in the photographs appear on the right-hand page; the left-hand page contains commentary and photographs of selected objects in the chart. The text of this edition has been updated with the addition of lesser-known objects and many photographs. For secondary schools. [R: ARBA 85; SBF, May/June 85]

1801   Wray, James D. **The Color Atlas of Galaxies**. New York: Cambridge University Press, 1988. 189p. $79.50. ISBN 0-521-32236-7. LC 86-13715.

Unlike earlier black-and-white atlases that classify galaxies by type and shape (e.g., spirals, elliptical), Wray approaches the development of galaxies by analyzing their color. (A star changes color as it evolves through the stages of its life.) The 600 galactic photographs, made at the McDonald Observatory in Texas and two observatories in South America, are arranged by New General Catalogue (NGC) number.

Entries include observational and photometric data; star type; radial velocity; and a paragraph of descriptive text, containing comments on the stage of galactic evolution, stellar population, and other information. Recommended for high schools. [R: ARBA 90]

DICTIONARIES AND ENCYCLOPEDIAS

■ *The Air and Space Catalog*. *See* entry 2187.

1802   Angelo, Joseph A., Jr. **The Extraterrestrial Encyclopedia**. rev. ed. New York: Facts on File, 1991. 272p. $40.00. ISBN 0-8160-2276-3. LC 83-5599.

This revision of a 1985 work contains a variety of articles about the universe, updated to include events and discoveries that have occurred during the past few years—the Challenger disaster, the loss of the Soviet Mars probe (Probos 1), the flyby of Uranus and Neptune by Voyager 2, the Magellan probe of Venus, the deployment of the Hubble telescope, and the development of space programs by other nations. The alphabetically arranged, lucid explanations are attractively formatted and supported by 16 color and 150 black-and-white photographs, drawings, and diagrams. For grades 7 and up.

1803   **The Facts on File Dictionary of Astronomy**. 2d ed. Valerie Illingworth, ed. New York: Facts on File, 1985. 437p. $24.95; $12.95pa. ISBN 0-8160-1357-8; 0-8160-1892-8pa. LC 85-20409.

The revised edition of this excellent work updates articles appearing in the first (1979) and adds 250 new entries, bringing the total to 2,300. Essays contain full information about different types of celestial bodies and the instruments used to investigate them. The text also cites organizations, agencies, and observatories, all supported by 85 relevant diagrams, illustrations, and tables. This work is recommended for high school libraries. [R: ARBA 87; RBB, 1 Oct 86; SBF, Nov/Dec 86]

1804   **The Guinness Book of Astronomy**. By Patrick Moore. New York: Facts on File, 1988. 288p. $19.95. ISBN 0-8160-2568-1. LC 83-146472.

"The Solar System," the largest of the five sections of this British work, remains relatively unchanged from its 1983 edition. It covers planets, meteors, comets, the Earth's moon, and other travelers around the Sun. Each chapter includes a data box that lists facts, "firsts" (e.g., first attempted lunar probe), features, and other data. Sections 2 and 3 describe different types of stars and provide detailed star charts. Other sections cover telescopes/observatories, a history of astronomy, and biographies of astronomers. An index and illustrations (primarily drawings and black-and-white photographs) support the text. [R: ARBA 90; RBB, 1 Mar 89]

1805   Moore, Patrick. **Patrick Moore's A-Z of Astronomy**. New York: W. W. Norton, c1986, 1987. 240p. $13.50pa. ISBN 0-393-30505-8. LC 87-11017.

This dictionary, an updated and expanded revision of an earlier British work, is aimed primarily at amateur astronomers. It includes 400 concise, nontechnical entries, current to mid-1985, that define basic astronomical terms and identify observatories and astronomers. Historical notables, events, and landmark astronomy publications are also included. Black-and-white photographs, charts, and diagrams, at least one per page, illustrate this basic work. For middle and high school levels. [R: ARBA 89]

E+

1806   Room, Adrian. **Dictionary of Astronomical Names**. New York: Routledge, Chapman & Hall, 1988. 282p. $27.50. ISBN 0-415-01298-8. LC 87-31670.

The origins of the names of stars, planets, and other celestial bodies comprise the focus of this readable work. A glossary and a lengthy history of astronomical names (ancient terms from Greek, Latin, and Arabic, and others derived from personal names since the sixteenth century) introduce the volume. Entries in the main body, arranged by popular name, give the origin of each name; the namer, if known; cross-references to related terms; and any alternative names. Appendixes provide lunar crater and asteroid names. Recommended for all levels. [R: ARBA 90]

E +

1807 Schweighauser, Charles A. **Astronomy from A to Z: A Dictionary of Celestial Objects and Ideas**. Springfield, Ill.: Illinois Issues, 1991. $14.95. LC 91-7124. (available from Illinois Issues, K-80 A, Sangamon State University, Springfield, IL 62794-9243).

This dictionary, designed for laypersons, resulted from a series of articles published in Illinois weekly newspapers that were made available to those attending star parties at the Sangamon State University Observatory. Personal names, terms and phrases used in astronomy, and names of constellations and planets comprise the 106 entries. Excellent black-and-white drawings and photographs accompany many articles. The volume concludes with a list of major constellations that show their star configurations, and notes on how to locate them in the night sky. The lack of cross-references and an index is unfortunate, but otherwise the work is excellent. [R: Choice, July/Aug 91; LJ, 1 Sept 91; RBB, 1 June 91; SBF, May 91]

■ *Space Almanac*. *See* entry 2196.

FIELD GUIDES AND HANDBOOKS

E +

1808 Brown, Peter Lancaster. **Star & Planet Spotting: A Field Guide to the Night Sky**. New York: Sterling Publishing, c1974, 1990. 148p. $8.95pa. ISBN 0-8069-7268-8. LC 89-26176.

First published in 1974 and updated in 1990, this small, inexpensive volume contains a wealth of material. The introduction provides a brief history of astronomy, describes celestial objects, and gives suggestions for sky watching. Star charts comprise a large part of the remaining pages, but the guide also includes sections on locating the brightest planets, stars, and deep-sky objects, and other information of interest to hobbyists of all ages. [R: ARBA 91]

1809 Chartrand, Mark R. **Skyguide: A Field Guide for Amateur Astronomers**. Racine, Wis.: Western Publishing, 1982. 280p. $9.95pa. ISBN 0-307-13667-1. LC 81-70086.

Presented in two-page spreads (one page of text and a facing page of illustrations), this work covers the Sun, Moon, planets, stars, galaxies, nebulas, astronomical coordinates, and other topics. Special features include tables and lists of celestial objects for amateur viewing; data on sun and planet positions; seasonal sky maps; and 88 individual constellation charts (arranged alphabetically) that supply pronunciation, origin, special objects for viewing, and notes on major stars. One of the dependable Golden Field Guides, this volume is especially useful to the beginning sky watcher.

E +

1810 Pasachoff, Jay M. **Peterson First Guide to the Solar System**. Boston: Houghton Mifflin, 1990. 128p. $4.95pa. ISBN 0-395-52451-2. LC 89-24744.

An abridgment of the author's *Field Guide to the Stars and Planets* (2d ed. Houghton Mifflin, 1983), this small volume is one of the best books for the beginning sky watcher. It contains a clearly written text, beautiful illustrations, and up-to-date information gathered by spacecraft over the last two decades. Coverage of the Sun, planets, comets, asteroids, and meteors should capture the interest of students from upper elementary grades through high school. [R: ARBA 91]

1811 **Universe Guide to Stars and Planets**. By Ian Ridpath. New York: Universe Books, 1984. 384p. $19.50; $10.95pa. ISBN 0-87663-366-1; 0-87663-859-0pa. LC 84-24133.

Monthly maps for the northern and southern hemispheres and individual star maps for each of the 88 constellations comprise a large part of this competent guide to observing the night skies. Other features include the allegorical histories of the constellations; characteristics of their brightest members (degree of brightness, color, size, and distance); photographs of famous clusters, nebulas, and galaxies; and an explanation of the nature of the solar system. Recommended for secondary schools. [R: ARBA 86; LJ, 15 Oct 85]

INDEXES

1812 **Quick Reference Guide to Astronomy Magazine, 1973-1990**. Los Angeles, Calif.: Geoimages Publishing, 1990. 74p. $8.00pa. ISBN 0-9623093-1-1. LC 89-82074. (P.O. Box 45677, Los Angeles, CA 90045).
   This quick index provides subject access to articles, photographs, and special issues of *Astronomy* magazine. Appendixes include a glossary of astronomical terms, explanations of time and position measurement, and the electromagnetic spectrum. Libraries that hold a long run of this popular magazine will want to consider this inexpensive index. [R: ARBA 92; BL, 1 Apr 91]

PLANETOLOGY

1813 **Planetary Exploration Series**. David Hughes, ed. New York: Facts on File, 1989. 6v. $13.95/v.; $65.00/set. ISBN 0-8160-2051-5.

E+
1814 Cattermole, Peter. **Mars**. ISBN 0-8160-2047-7.

E+
1815 Halliday, Ian. **Saturn**. ISBN 0-8160-2049-3.

E+
1816 Hughes, David. **The Moon**. ISBN 0-8160-2046-9.

E+
1817 Levasseur-Regourd, Arny Chantal. **Our Sun and the Inner Planets**. ISBN 0-8160-2045-0.

E+
1818 Petersen, Carolyn Collins. **Jupiter**. ISBN 0-8160-2048-5.

E+
1819 Yeomans, Donald K. **The Distant Planets**. ISBN 0-8160-2050-7.
   This excellent series provides a vivid description of our solar system and how it evolved, including the Sun, satellites, and Saturn's rings. Each book, written by an expert, combines clear, informative text with 20 spectacular full-color illustrations drawn by Don Davis, a space artist of the Hansen Planitarium in Utah. The series is highly recommended for upper elementary and junior high school students. [R: BL, 1 June 90; BR, Sept/Oct 90]

Biology

See also **Environmental Science**.

1820 **Chambers Biology Dictionary**. Peter M. B. Walker, ed. New York: Cambridge University Press, 1989. 324p. $34.50; $14.95pa. ISBN 1-85296-152-X; 1-85296-153-8pa.
   This work defines over 10,000 terms drawn from the *Chambers Science and Technology Encyclopedia*. Most are taken from zoology, but other fields (e.g., genetics, botany, behavioral science) are covered in brief entries. Some 100 longer essays, however, treat topics of current interest (AIDS, genetic manipulation, photosynthesis). Over 80 diagrams illustrate complex subjects. This basic dictionary is appropriate for advanced high school students. [R: ARBA 90]

1821 **Encyclopedia of Bioethics**. Warren T. Reich, ed. New York: Free Press/Macmillan, 1978. 4v. $250.00/set. ISBN 0-02-926060-4. [Also available as 4v. in 2. $190.00/set. ISBN 0-02-925910-X.]
   This important set was the first to deal with ethical problems that stem from life/death/health issues (e.g., human experimentation, genetic intervention, organ transplant, abortion). The set,

the product of over 300 editors and contributors, includes 315 signed, judicious, and authoritative articles.

The last volume contains a topical classification of all entries and over 30 codes of the health care professions. This unique and scholarly work, a significant achievement, is recommended for high school libraries. The two-volume edition is a more compact version, not an abridgment. [R: ARBA 80]

1822   **The Facts on File Dictionary of Biology**. rev. ed. Elizabeth Tootill, ed. New York: Facts on File, 1988. 326p. $24.95; $12.95pa. ISBN 0-8160-1865-0; 0-8160-2368-9pa. LC 88-045476.

An expansion and update of the 1981 edition, this dictionary contains the most important and commonly used biological terms. Coverage is extensive for traditional fields and new, rapidly changing ones such as molecular biology and genetics. Definitions for over 3,000 terms, written in clear, nontechnical English, include an abundance of cross-references. Forty line drawings illustrate such basic elements as DNA, cells, plant and animal structure. Recommended for high schools. [R: ARBA 89]

1823   **The Life Sciences on File Collection**. By the Diagram Group. New York: Facts on File, 1986. 1v. $145.00 looseleaf w/binder. ISBN 0-8160-1284-9. LC 85-29359.

This set of reproducible charts and diagrams contains more than 300 drawings keyed to the study of biology, zoology, and botany. The contents, arranged by broad areas, include such topics as reproduction, evolution, nutrition, respiration, and plant and animal growth. Drawings are clear and well captioned. A detailed table of contents and an index provide access to the subject matter. Designed primarily for college level, the collection contains enough basic material to warrant selection for high school libraries.

1824   Margulis, Lynn, and Karlene V. Schwartz. **Five Kingdoms: An Illustrated Guide to the Phyla of Life on Earth**. 2d ed. New York: W. H. Freeman, 1988. 376p. $37.95; $24.95pa. ISBN 0-7167-1885-5; 0-7167-1912-6pa. LC 87-210.

This book presents taxonomic studies in simple language that should appeal to its target audience—science students and laypersons. The authors have succeeded in producing a work that helps beginning biology students understand the broad spectrum of life on Earth.

Each of the five chapters—Prokaryotae, Protoctista, Fungi, Animalia, and Plantae—begins with a discussion of the evolutionary relationships among the phyla described. A two-page analysis of each phylum follows the introduction, and each section includes illustrations of several phyla (a photograph and an anatomical drawing): 17 prokaryotea, 27 protoctista, 5 fungi, 37 animals, and 10 plants.

The volume concludes with an extensive index, a glossary of 734 terms, and a list of 1,000 genera with phylum and common names. This excellent work is highly recommended for high schools. [R: ARBA 89]

Botany

DICTIONARIES, ENCYCLOPEDIAS, AND HANDBOOKS

1825   **The Facts on File Dictionary of Botany**. Elizabeth Tootill and Stephen Blackmore, eds. New York: Facts on File, 1984. 390p. $24.95. ISBN 0-87196-861-4. LC 83-25309.

This British work, published in the United Kingdom as *The Penguin Dictionary of Botany*, clearly explains 3,000 terms used in major areas of botany, horticulture, and microbiology. Some 35 line drawings and charts illustrate the dictionary, which is appropriate for high school use. [R: ARBA 85]

1826   Lyons, Janet, and Sandra Jordan. **Walking the Wetlands: A Hiker's Guide to Common Plants and Animals of Marshes, Bogs, and Swamps**. New York: John Wiley, 1989. 222p. $12.95pa. ISBN 0-471-62087-4.

Fifty-nine plants and forty-two animnals commonly found in freshwater wetlands in the eastern United States are illustrated and described in this highly recommended guide. The black-and-white illustrations are skillfully drawn. Informative essays examine uses of wetland flora and fauna, animal-plant relationships, and the ecological importance of the organisms. Appendixes include wetland areas in the National Park and Wildlife Refuge System, a glossary, a bibliography, and an index. [R: SBF, May/June 90]

1827 **The Marshall Cavendish Illustrated Encyclopedia of Plants and Earth Sciences**. David M. Moore, ed. North Bellmore, N.Y.: Marshall Cavendish, 1988. 10v. $299.95/set. ISBN 0-86307-901-6. LC 87-23927.

This set, prepared by more than 120 botanists and geologists, is the first multivolume encyclopedia on plants and the geological basis of botanical communities. Volumes 1, 2, and part of 3 contain an alphabetical list, by scientific and common name, of the most important plants. One-paragraph entries, many with color photographs, describe the plants and explain their use. A number of longer entries focus on major crops or botanical groups.

The remainder of volume 3, and all of volumes 4 and 5, consist of surveys of more than 300 flowering families. The essays, a page or more in length, are arranged in taxonomic order and give number of genera and species, distribution, description, and economic and scientific importance. Distribution maps and beautiful paintings of representative flowers, fruits, and foliage illustrate the text.

Volumes 6 and 7 cover plant ecology; the history of the exploration of the plant world; the development of methodologies to study plant ecology; the methods and results in plant geography, ecology, paleobotany, and evolution; and the world's vegetation types and zones. Volumes 8 and 9 comprise a textbook on geology as it relates to evolution and plant distribution. Volume 10 contains an alphabetical and thematic index, a glossary, and an extensive bibliography. This outstanding work is recommended for high schools. [R: ARBA 89; BL, 1 June 89; WLB, Oct 89]

■ *Official Wildlife Fund Guide to Endangered Species of North America*. See entry 2222.

■ *Oxford Illustrated Encyclopedia*. See entry 1888.

1828 **Popular Encyclopedia of Plants**. Vernon H. Heywood, ed. New York: Cambridge University Press, 1982. 368p. $42.50. ISBN 0-521-24611-3. LC 81-21713.

Economically important plants and their products comprise the focus of this work. Some 2,200 brief articles and 21 longer essays are supported by more than 800 illustrations. Special features include a 240-term glossary and indexing by common and scientific names. Appropriate for high schools. [R: ARBA 83; BL, 1 Sept 84; LJ, 15 June 82; SLJ, Sept 82]

FLOWERING PLANTS

See also **Horticulture**.

1829 Duft, Joseph F., and Robert K. Moseley. **Alpine Wildflowers of the Rocky Mountains**. Missoula, Mont.: Mountain Press, 1989. 200p. $9.95pa. ISBN 0-87842-238-2. LC 89-30719.

This volume on wildflowers of the Rocky Mountains (from the Canadian border to New Mexico) devotes about 100 pages to describing over 300 species and 100 similar varieties, giving plant size, habitat, and an illustration of each. The section is arranged by Latin name and genus within each family. The common name in large print accompanies each entry. Photographs, which make up the remainder of the work, are grouped by color to aid in identification, and give common and scientific names.

Other features include line drawings of floral anatomy, a glossary of terms, and an index of common and botanical names. Since the book is intended as a guide for hikers and tourists, it is small, thereby presenting a shelving problem for libraries. [R: ARBA 91]

1830 Elias, Thomas S., and Peter A. Dykeman. **Field Guide to North American Edible Wild Plants**. New York: Outdoor Life Books; distr., New York: Van Nostrand Reinhold, 1982. 286p. $19.95pa. ISBN 0-442-22254-8. LC 82-18785.

The introduction provides an overview of edible wild plants and warns of the dangers of wild foraging. The main body of the work focuses on season-by-season identification of some 200 such plants and their harvesting and preservation. The illustrations consist of over 400 photographs, most in color. Entries provide scientific and common names, fruit, edible season, and habitat. Related edible species and similar poisonous plants are also discussed. Twenty poisonous plants are described and illustrated in a separate section. Tables of nutritional value of plants and indexing by scientific and common names complete the volume. Recommended for high schools. [R: ARBA 84]

1831 Forey, Pamela. **Wild Flowers**. New York: Gallery Books/W. H. Smith, 1990. 239p. $9.98 spiral-bound. ISBN 0-8317-6961-0.

This manual, a part of the American Nature Guide series, provides information about some 500 wildflower species arranged by plant family. After each group is introduced, it is described and illustrated by beautiful watercolor paintings, two or three to a page. The text is lucid and nontechnical. A glossary and an index by common name complete the volume. [R: ARBA 91]

E +
1832 Houk, Rose. **Eastern Wildflowers: A Photographic Celebration from New England to the Heartland**. San Francisco, Calif.: Chronicle Books, 1989. 108p. $16.95pa. ISBN 0-87701-594-5. LC 88-30436.

This beautiful book, a collection of 60 color photographs chosen for their artistic (rather than botanical) value, is an excellent introduction to wildflowers. The commentaries provide more historical and cultural information than scientific data. Each of the four geographical sections — New England, Coastal Plain and Piedmont, Appalachian Mountains, and Heartland (Midwest) — begins with a brief survey of the history, geography, climate, and ecology of the region. This is followed by 8 to 10 full-page photographs of indigenous wildflowers, with a description of each. Recommended for all levels. [R: ARBA 90; BL, 15 Apr 89]

E +
1833 **The National Wildflower Research Center's Wildflower Handbook**. Annie Paulson, ed. Austin, Tex.: Pacesetter Press, 1989. 337p. $9.95pa. ISBN 0-87719-167-0. LC 89-4346.

This work focuses on the use of native plants in landscaping projects, from prairie restoration and roadside planting to backyard gardens. The opening chapters explain how to organize a roadside flower project, establish a buffalo grass lawn, and implement other landscaping ideas. The main body of the manual cites ways and means of obtaining additional information (arranged by state and region) — books, wildflower societies, sources of plants and seeds, and more. Recommended for all levels. [R: ARBA 90; BL, 15 May 89]

E +
1834 Niering, William A., and Nancy C. Olmstead. **The Audubon Society Field Guide to North American Wildflowers, Eastern Region**. New York: Alfred A. Knopf/Random House, 1979. 863p. $14.95. ISBN 0-394-50432-1. LC 78-20383.

E +
1835 Spellenberg, Richard. **The Audubon Society Field Guide to North American Wildflowers, Western Region**. New York: Alfred A. Knopf/Random House, 1979. 862p. $14.95. ISBN 0-394-50431-3. LC 78-20384.

These field guides describe 600 wildflower species arranged by color, with notes on some 400 others. The 700-plus color photographs in part 1 are keyed to their identifications and descriptions in part 2. These excellent, beautiful volumes are highly recommended for all levels. [R: ARBA 80; BL, 1 Dec 80]

E +
1836 Prance, Ghillean T. **Wildflowers for All Seasons**. New York: Crown, 1989. 208p. $35.00. ISBN 0-517-57007-6.

This work is composed of beautiful and botanically accurate watercolor paintings by Anna Vojtech that are supported by perceptive comments on the ecology, folklore, medicinal uses, and chemical properties of each plant. The 129 paintings of coastal and interior New England plants are arranged in four sections, one for each season. Indexes are by scientific and common names.

Since the wildflowers shown are only a sample of those in the region, this work is not useful as a guide. Nonetheless, it is a worthwhile holding in any school media center. [R: ARBA 90]

1837 Runkel, Sylvan T., and Dean M. Roosa. **Wildflowers of the Tallgrass Prairie: The Upper Midwest**. Ames, Iowa: Iowa State University Press, 1989. 279p. $24.95pa. ISBN 0-8138-1979-2. LC 87-34482.

The tallgrass prairie that once consisted of 221,000 square miles of the midwestern section of North America has been reduced to only 1 percent of its former size. Drab grasses form the basis of this ecosystem, but wildflowers dot the prairie landscape with glorious color.

This book contains 129 beautiful, full-page photographs of prairie wildflowers, many of which are rare. A page of commentary on each gives descriptive, ecological, and herbalist information. The arrangement is by season of bloom. This is not a guide book, but its beauty and data make it a worthwhile purchase for secondary schools, especially those in the remaining prairie area. [R: ARBA 90]

NONFLOWERING PLANTS

1838   Huffman, D. M., and others. **Mushrooms and Other Fungi of the Midcontinental United States**. Ames, Iowa: Iowa State University Press, 1989. 326p. $14.95pa. ISBN 0-8138-1168-6. LC 89-9250.

The midwest prairie, a mushroom hunter's paradise, receives the attention of this excellent guide to edible and inedible fungi. The introduction describes mushroom biology, explains how to identify the fungi, and lists the different kinds found in each season. The text covers 250 of the most common, showy species; describes each mushroom in nontechnical language; and illustrates them with excellent color photographs. The number treated is only a fraction of the species that grow in the area, but the volume is a good guide for the beginner. [R: ARBA 90]

1839   Phillips, Roger. **Mushrooms of North America**. Boston: Little, Brown, 1991. 319p. $39.95; $24.95pa. ISBN 0-316-70612-4; 0-316-70613-2pa. LC 89-37050.

Amateur and professional mycologists will welcome this beautifully illustrated and informative volume. The more than 1,000 photographs were shot in a studio rather than in the field so as to capture external and internal detail. Specimens representing various stages of growth are included. Each mushroom is described in detail (cap, gills, stem, and spores), and explanations are given about where and when it can be found and whether it is edible. Highly recommended for high schools. [R: ARBA 92; LJ, 15 June 91]

TREES AND SHRUBS

E+
1840   Brockman, C. Frank. **Trees of North America: A Field Guide to the Native and Introduced Species North of Mexico**. New York: Golden Books/Western Publishing, 1968. 208p. $9.95. ISBN 0-307-13658-2. LC 68-23532.

Almost 600 species of North American trees are described and illustrated in this excellent guide, another of the Golden Field Guides. Distribution maps are also provided. Suggested for grades 6 and up.

E+
1841   Burnie, David. **Tree**. New York: Alfred A. Knopf/Random House, 1988. 64p. $15.00. ISBN 0-394-89617-3. LC 88-1572.

The introduction to this excellent work explains the role of trees in history and culture and describes the three categories of trees (needle-leaved, broad-leaved, and palm). Two-page, poster-format chapters cover all phases of a tree's life from birth to death: anatomy, physiology, growth and development, and reproduction. Other chapters treat ecosystems, lumber production, uses of wood, tree diseases, and pollution. Superb photographs illustrate this small volume. Recommended for upper elementary grades through high school. [R: BL, 1 Dec 88; SLJ, Dec 88]

1842   Collingwood, G. H., and Warren D. Brush. **Knowing Your Trees**. rev. ed. Washington, D.C.: American Forestry Association, 1984. 392p. $9.50. ISBN 0-00-001918-6. LC 78-52994.

This volume describes 188 species of trees that grow in the United States. Photographs show winter and summer forms and details of leaves, bark, flowers, and fruit. Distribution maps and a map of hardiness zones also are provided. Recommended for middle and high schools.

1843   Kricher, John C. **A Field Guide to Eastern Forests: North America**. Boston: Houghton Mifflin, 1988. 368p. (Peterson Field Guide Series). $22.95; $14.95pa. ISBN 0-395-35346-7; 0-395-47953-3pa. LC 87-35247.

Unlike some earlier Peterson Field Guides that deal with one species (e.g., birds, flowers, trees), Kricher's guide considers all species, from insects to trees, in a particular habitat and the interaction among them. The attempt is to interpret nature, not to identify species.

The arrangement, by observable patterns (e.g., disturbance and pioneer plants, patterns of spring), suggests how to identify the patterns. Species included are indigenous to the area or groups studied. Chapters end with an ecological questionnaire; drawings illustrate each section. *The Audubon Society's Eastern Forest* (Alfred A. Knopf, 1985), a similar work, is illustrated with photographs instead of drawings. [R: ARBA 89; LJ, Dec 88; WLB, Dec 86]

1844   Lauriault, Jean. **Identification Guide to the Trees of Canada**. Markham, Ont.: Fitzhenry & Whiteside, 1989. 479p. $25.00. ISBN 0-88902-564-9.

For each of the 149 tree species of Canada, this guide provides the family name (English, French, and Latin), distribution, description, and interesting facts. A range map and a detailed line drawing that shows leaves, fruit, and twigs accompany each entry. A unique identification system enables the user to classify an unknown tree according to leaf shape, arrangement, margin, and vein pattern. Numbers refer the reader to the descriptive entries and illustrations. Recommended for libraries requiring botanical information on Canada. [R: ARBA 91]

1845   Phillips, Roger, and Martyn Rix. **Shrubs**. New York: Random House, 1989. 288p. $22.95pa. ISBN 0-679-72345-5.

Over 1,900 shrubs are identified in this quick-reference source. The brief information gives genus and species, common and family names, hybridization, parentage, place of origin, a brief description, and where the plant thrives. Excellent pictures of leaves, flowers, and stem conformations make this volume useful for identification. Indexed by scientific and common name. [R: ARBA 90; BL, 15 Mar 89; LJ, 15 Apr 89]

1846   Preston, Richard J., Jr. **North American Trees Exclusive of Mexico and Tropical Florida**. 4th ed. Ames, Iowa: Iowa State University Press, 1989. 407p. $39.95; $19.95pa. ISBN 0-8138-1171-6; 0-8138-1172-4pa. LC 89-1944.

This work provides descriptions and botanical keys to identify all American trees north of Mexico and tropical Florida. Line drawings of leaves, twigs, fruit, flowers, and bark illustrate each tree, and distribution maps indicate the range of each species. A detailed glossary and index are included. This is an excellent guide for high school students. [R: ARBA 90]

ACTIVITIES

E +
1847   Bonnet, Robert L., and G. Daniel Keen. **Botany: 49 Science Fair Projects**. Blue Ridge Summit, Pa.: TAB Books, 1989. 160p. $16.95; $9.95pa. ISBN 0-8306-9277-0; 0-8306-3277-8pa.

E +
1848   Bonnet, Robert L., and G. Daniel Keen. **Botany: 49 More Science Projects**. Blue Ridge Summit, Pa.: TAB Books, 1990. 170p. $16.95; $9.95pa. ISBN 0-8306-7416-0; 0-8306-3416-9pa.

Science fair projects or classroom demonstrations that do not require expensive or sophisticated equipment comprise these volumes. Subjects include photosynthesis, plant tropisms, germination, hydroponics, transport of food and water, fungi and simple plants, and plant dispersal. Background information, photographs, diagrams, and suggestions for further study all support the projects. Recommended for grade school and junior high levels. [R: SBF, May/June 90]

☐ _____ **Chemistry** _____ ☐

See also **Activities** under **Science in General**.

■ *The Biographical Dictionary of Scientists*. See entry 2130.

1849 **Chemistry: The Periodic Table**. St. Paul, Minn.: Minnesota Educational Computing Corp., 1988. 3 disks and guide. System requirements: Apple II computer. $59.00.

This program, designed to strengthen student awareness of the periodic table and its organization, is a useful reference tool for individuals and an excellent visual aid for classroom instruction. It offers information about the 92 natural elements, listing 27 properties for each (e.g., atomic number, periods, state, atomic radius). Searches can be conducted by element, group, or period. Recommended for high schools. [R: SLJ, Dec 89]

1850 **Concise Chemical and Technical Dictionary**. 4th ed. H. Bennett, ed. New York: Chemical Publishing, 1986. 1271p. $105.00. ISBN 0-8206-0310-4.

Some 100,000 terms, including chemicals, drugs, trade names, and property products, that cover all fields of scientific and technical development are briefly described in this handbook. It is intended for the beginning student, but some knowledge of chemistry is required to understand several definitions. Useful features include pronunciation of chemical words and vitamin values for important foodstuffs. Recommended for high schools. [R: ARBA 87]

1851 **A Concise Dictionary of Chemistry**. new ed. New York: Oxford University Press, 1990. 314p. $8.95pa. ISBN 0-19-286110-7. LC 90-38630.

This handy, compact dictionary is derived from an earlier publication of the Oxford University Press entitled *Concise Science Dictionary*. Its scope includes all areas of chemistry and many of the terms used in biochemistry. There are over 3,000 entries, many of which reflect recent advances in techniques, concepts, and materials. Most of the entries are lengthy explanatory concepts. Some refer the reader to another entry which indicates that they are synonyms or abbreviations, or that they are discussed more fully in one of the longer articles. The use of asterisks placed before words in an entry is useful, as it allows the reader to locate the word elsewhere in the dictionary for further explanation or clarification. The inclusion of diagrams, the tables of SI (International System of Units) measurements, appendixes of fundamental constants, the solar system, and the periodic table are also invaluable. This dictionary would be a worthy purchase.

1852 **CRC Handbook of Chemistry and Physics, 1987-1988: A Ready-Reference Book of Chemical and Physical Data**. 71st ed. Robert C. Weast, ed. Boca Raton, Fla.: CRC Press, 1990. 1v. $99.50. ISBN 0-8493-0471-7. LC 13-11056.

CRC Handbook has been a standard reference work for chemistry and physics since it started in 1913. It provides basic tables for these fields and for mathematics, and it includes inorganic and organic compounds, conversion factors, data on planets, Hofmann ellipse transfer data, and much more. Most of the tables do not require updating with every revision, but many are periodically revised and new ones are added. Indexed by primary, secondary, and tertiary categories. High school libraries should hold this work or *Lange's Handbook of Chemistry*.

1853 **The Facts on File Dictionary of Chemistry**. rev. ed. John Daintith, ed. New York: Facts on File, 1988. 249p. $24.95; $12.95pa. ISBN 0-8160-1866-9; 0-8160-2368-9pa. LC 88-045477.

Designed for high school students and college undergraduates, this dictionary uses nontechnical language to identify terms, reactions, techniques, and applications likely to need definition by the intended reader. The revision adds some 300 terms to the 2,200 contained in the first edition (1981) and illustrates chemical reactions with almost 50 line drawings.

The appendix provides tables of chemical elements with symbols, proton numbers, and atomic weights; lists of physical constants and elementary particles; the Greek alphabet; and the periodic table. Recommended as a first choice for high schools. [R: ARBA 89; BR, May/June 89; RBB, 1 Jan 89]

1854 **Hawley's Condensed Chemical Dictionary**. 11th ed. Irving N. Sax and Richard J. Lewis, Sr., eds. New York: Van Nostrand Reinhold, 1987. 1288p. $52.95. ISBN 0-442-28097-1. LC 86-23333.

Definitions of chemical terms, short retrospective biographies of outstanding scientists, and information about American technical societies comprise this standard work. Entries for compounds give other commonly accepted names, molecular formulas, properties, sources of occurrence, commercial grade available, hazards, uses, and shipping regulations. Recommended for high schools with advanced science programs. [R: ARBA 86]

1855 **Lange's Handbook of Chemistry**. 13th ed. John A. Dean, ed. New York: McGraw-Hill, 1985. 1v. (various paging). $78.00. ISBN 0-07-016192-5.
A standard reference source periodically updated since it appeared in 1934, *Lange's Handbook* still serves as the practicing chemist's Bible. It contains a vast amount of information covering mathematics, general information and conversion tables, atomic and molecular structure, inorganic and analytical chemistry, electrochemistry, organic chemistry, spectroscopy, thermal properties, physical properties, and other data. High schools with advanced classes in chemistry should hold this volume or *CRC Handbook of Chemistry and Physics*. [R: ARBA 86; BL, 1 Feb 86]

1856 **Rapid Guide to Hazardous Chemicals in the Workplace**. 2d ed. Richard J. Lewis, ed. New York: Van Nostrand Reinhold, 1990. 286p. $24.95pa. ISBN 0-442-23804-5. LC 89-25087.
The updated version of this handbook is an authoritative work incorporating the extensively changed Occupational Safety and Health Administration (OSHA) Permissible Exposure Limits (PELs) and the transition and final rules that become effective December 31, 1993. The work also includes updated workplace control recommendations from the American Conference of Governmental Industrial Hygienists and the German Research Society, and U.S. Department of Transportation hazard numbers for 800 of the most frequently used industrial hazardous materials. These substances are arranged alphabetically by common chemical names, giving identification, standards and recommendations, safety profiles, and physical properties. [R: ARBA 91]

1857 Shugar, Gershon J., and John A. Dean. **The Chemist's Ready Reference Handbook**. New York: McGraw-Hill, 1990. 1v. (various paging). $76.50. ISBN 0-07-057178-3. LC 89-8166.
This compendium of data, written by experts, is designed for levels of practicing laboratory chemists. Practical suggestions for conducting safe and successful experiments are emphasized. Indexed.
This is an advanced work, but it would be useful to chemistry teachers and students with some background in chemistry. [R: ARBA 91]

Computers and Electronics

DICTIONARIES AND ENCYCLOPEDIAS

See also **Computer Software** in **Media Sources,** and **Computers** under **Instructional Technology** in **Education**.

1858 Covington, Michael, and Douglas Downing. **Dictionary of Computer Terms**. 2d ed. Hauppauge, N.Y.: Barron's Educational Series, 1989. 333p. $8.95pa. ISBN 0-8120-4152-6. LC 88-39671.
Nontechnical definitions of over 1,000 commonly used computer terms make up this compact dictionary. Terms relate to hardware, software, programming languages, operating systems, electronics, and logic circuits. Definitions include principles of use, applications, and practical examples. This edition was revised to include many terms of recent origin, such as those related to desktop publishing. Highly recommended for junior and senior high schools. [R: ARBA 90]

1859 Danuloff, Craig, and D. McClelland. **Encyclopedia Macintosh**. Alameda, Calif.: SYBEX, 1989. 782p. $26.95. ISBN 0-89588-628-6.
This encyclopedia, designed for all levels of Macintosh users, is divided into five parts. The first three cover such topics as system software and utilities, applications, and hardware (e.g., AppleTalk, modems, RAM). The fourth part lists resources—books, bulletin boards, magazines, user groups, and

vendors. The last section consists of a glossary and index. Special features include illustrations, sample screens, and charts for various hardware packages. [R: BL, 15 Mar 90]

1860   **Dictionary of Computing**. 3d ed. New York: Oxford University Press, 1990. 510p. $39.95; $10.95pa. ISBN 0-19-853825-1; 0-19-386131-Xpa.

1861   **Que's Computer User's Dictionary**. By Bryan Pfaffenberger. Carmel, Ind.: Que, 1990. 448p. $9.95pa. ISBN 0-88022-540-8. LC 90-60375.

In a field that is constantly evolving, an up-to-date dictionary is essential. Beginning with *abelian group* and ending with *ZIF socket*, this excellent work, which has become a standard, treats terms concerning computers, electronics, mathematics, and logic. The definitions in this authoritative and reliable work are clearly written and easy to understand. An asterisk in front of a word indicates that it has an entry of its own. Highly recommended for high schools.

Que's Computer User's Dictionary appears in paperback format only and is filled with practical, current information. Recommended as a desk reference for computer users. [R: ARBA 91]

1862   Douglas-Young, John. **Illustrated Encyclopedic Dictionary of Electronics**. 2d ed. Englewood Cliffs, N.J.: Prentice-Hall, 1987. 692p. $42.95; $16.95pa. ISBN 0-13-450701-0; 0-13-451006-2pa. LC 86-21272.

This clearly written and profusely illustrated volume defines thousands of electronic terms. Cross-referencing links terms with larger concepts or subjects treated in more detailed entries. The principal concepts are covered in long articles of seven or eight pages. Illustrations include drawings, schematics, diagrams, and tables. A first choice for high school libraries requiring a reference tool for the field. [R: ARBA 89; BL, 15 Dec 88; BR, Nov/Dec 88]

1863   **Encyclopedia of Electronics**. 2d ed. Stan Gibilisco and Neal Sclater, eds. Blue Ridge Summit, Pa.: TAB Books, 1990. 960p. $69.50. ISBN 0-8306-3389-8. LC 89-77660.

Well written and well designed, this encyclopedia updates the 1985 edition and is directed toward both laypersons and scientists. The work contains over 3,000 long, detailed articles, ranging from a paragraph to over a page, that explain electronic terms. Every page includes one or more simple line drawings that give added support to the clear explanations, which are written in plain English. Only those computer terms that are important to the wide field of electronics are included. This impressive work is recommended for high schools. [R: ARBA 91; BL, 1 Nov 90]

1864   Freedman, Alan. **The Computer Glossary: The Complete Illustrated Desk Reference**. 5th ed. New York: AMACOM; distr., Detroit: Gale, 1989. 776p. $34.95. ISBN 0-8144-7709-7. LC 88-26235.

Some 3,500 well-defined terms illustrated by 400 diagrams, flow charts, drawings, and photographs constitute this outstanding work. General terms are defined in simple language; technical terms are explained in a specialized vocabulary. Terms and concepts, drawn from the whole field, include many vocabulary entries not found in similar reference work. Highly recommended for high schools. [R: ARBA 91]

1865   Hordeski, Michael F. **Illustrated Dictionary of Microcomputers**. 3d ed. Blue Ridge Summit, Pa.: TAB Books, 1990. 442p. $29.95; $19.95pa. ISBN 0-8306-7368-7; 0-8306-3368-5pa. LC 89-48453.

Detailed definitions of some 1,500 computer hardware and software terms comprise this excellent dictionary, recommended for advanced high school students. Terms gleaned from periodicals, industry presentations, and product manuals include common language and jargon known only to programmers and engineers. Frequent cross-references and diagrams make this a useful tool for students whose hobbies involve computer technology, electronic devices, and related areas. [R: ARBA 91; BR, Mar/Apr 91]

1866   **McGraw-Hill Personal Computer Programming Encyclopedia: Languages and Operating Systems**. 2d ed. William J. Birnes and others, eds. New York: McGraw-Hill, 1989. 832p. $95.00. ISBN 0-07-005393-6. LC 88-8410.

High school students who design and write programs for personal computers will welcome this update of the 1985 edition. The opening essays on special applications, which cover such topics as local area networks, artificial intelligence, and desktop publishing, are designed for the beginner. Succeeding articles, which require more advanced knowledge, deal with 17 microprocessors, 28 programming languages (e.g., COBOL), 9 software command languages (e.g., dBase II), and 12 operating systems (e.g., CP/M). The index of high-level language keywords defines terms employed in all programs and enables the user to interface statements used in one command language with those of another. There is also a glossary of 1,700 terms intended for beginning programmers. A subject index and a bibliography of books and manuals support the volume. [R: BL, 1 June 89; SBF, Mar/Apr 89, Sept/Oct 89]

1867   Turner, Rufus P., and Stan Gibilisco. **The Illustrated Dictionary of Electronics**. 5th ed. Blue Ridge Summit, Pa.: TAB Books, 1991. 723p. $39.95; $26.95pa. ISBN 0-8306-7345-8; 0-8306-3345-6pa. LC 90-22674.

This work, recommended for any high school requiring a reference tool on electronics, updates the 1985 edition. It deals with electronics in the broadest sense, covering standard terminology as well as jargon and related trade terms. There are 27,000 entries in all. Definitions are concise, cross-referenced, and illustrated with line drawings, which usually are more informative than photographs. Recommended for high schools. [R: ARBA 92; RBB, 1 May 91]

DIRECTORIES

1868   **Dial-A-Fax Directory**. 3d ed. Jenkintown, Pa.: Dial-A-Fax Directories; distr., Grosse Pointe, Mich.: Moonbeam, 1989. 1764p. $94.00pa. ISBN 0-945622-00-7. ISSN 0896-9434. LC 87-656600.

This state-by-state and province-by-province directory of company and individual fax numbers for the United States and Canada includes separate sections for public fax numbers and state and federal fax numbers. Twenty-four-hour directory service for new numbers is available to subscribers. [R: ARBA 91]

1869   Glossbrenner, Alfred. **Alfred Glossbrenner's Master Guide to Free Software for IBMs and Compatible Computers**. New York: St. Martin's Press, 1989. 530p. $18.95pa. ISBN 0-312-02157-7. LC 88-11474.

Sources of free or low-cost alternatives to commercial software are discussed in this guide. Examples include computer user groups, downloading software from online bulletin boards, and vendors. The author compares the differences between free public domain software and low-cost shareware; the potential problems of compatibility are discussed. A section entitled "Core Collection for All PC Users" includes the best alternate utility programs, word processors, spreadsheets, printer programs, communications software, and more. [R: ARBA 90]

HANDBOOKS

E+
1870   **Consumer Guide Computer Buying Guide**. new ed. Lincolnwood, Ill.: Publications International, 1989. 160p. $7.95pa. ISBN 0-451-82211-0.

An updated version of the 1987 edition, this work reviews the most widely used personal computers for home, office, and classroom. Hardware ranges in price from $1,000 to $6,000. Software, chosen for its usefulness and popularity, is also covered. The evaluations are helpful to the first-time buyer as well as the experienced user who wishes to upgrade a system. A glossary of terms is included. In a rapidly changing field, updating is essential; it is assumed that this work will be revised regularly. Recommended for all levels. [R: ARBA 90]

1871   Fenton, Erfert, and C. Morrissett. **Canned Art: Clip Art for the Macintosh**. Berkeley, Calif.: Peachpit Press, 1990. 840p. $29.95. ISBN 0-938151-16-9. LC 89-72207.

This volume identifies Macintosh clip art (15,000 public domain chips) available from 37 companies. All standard graphs are represented, including Paint, PICT, EPS, and TIFF. Arranged alphabetically by vendor, this directory provides address, telephone/fax numbers, a reproduction of the art, and (in some cases) coupons and special offers from the vendors. Indexing is by subject. [R: ARBA 91; SLJ, Sept 90]

1872   Glossbrenner, Alfred. **The Complete Handbook of Personal Computer Communication**. 3d ed. New York: St. Martin's Press, 1989. 405p. $19.95pa. ISBN 0-312-03312-5.

The first part of this completely revised work discusses TYMNET, Telenet, and other communications networks. Part 2 summarizes online utilities and describes CompuServe and other services. Part 3 surveys brochures for libraries and information centers, and part 4 explains E-Mail, Telex, and similar systems. This practical handbook is appropriate for high schools.

1873 Haynes, Collin. **The Computer Virus Protection Handbook**. San Francisco, Calif.: SYBEX, 1990. 192p. $24.95pa. includes disks (ViruScan and Virus Simulation Suite). ISBN 0-89588-696-0. LC 90-70167.

Managers responsible for electronic systems should know about computer viruses and how they can enter and affect their facilities. The first three chapters describe the problem. Chapter 4 explains how to use the accompanying software, which demonstrates viruses in action. Other chapters discuss malfunctions that may be mistaken for viruses, instructions on what to do should one appear, prevention measures, some of the famous viruses that have affected MS-DOS and Macintosh systems, and suggestions on formulating a disaster plan. The final chapter instructs the reader on how to use the ViruScan program, the most widely used virus identification and removal program. [R: LJ, Dec 90]

1874 LaPier, Cynthia B. **The Librarian's Guide to WordPerfect 5.0**. Westport, Conn.: Meckler, 1990. 177p. $39.50. ISBN 0-88736-493-4.

This instructional manual is designed for those who have no knowledge of WordPerfect and only limited word processing experience. The first part explains the function keys and other basics. Part 2 covers document creation, bar graphs, columns, and program specifics. Since there are only minor differences between WordPerfect 5.0 and 5.1, this guide will assist any new user of the system. [R: BL, 1 Jan 91; LJ, 1 Mar 91]

1875 **The Macintosh Bible: Thousands of Basic and Advanced Tips, Tricks, and Shortcuts Logically Organized and Fully Indexed**. 3d ed. Berkeley, Calif.: Goldstein & Blair; distr., Emeryville, Calif.: Publishers Group West, 1991. 1115p. $28.00pa.; $38.00 w/disk. ISBN 0-940235-11-0; 0-940235-13-7 w/disk.

As the subtitle states, this reference for Macintosh owners contains a plethora of information. The purchase price also includes two updates. Schools owning this type of computer will find this book a useful acquisition.

1876 **Microcomputer Applications Handbook**. William J. Birnes, ed. New York: McGraw-Hill, 1989. 645p. $79.95. ISBN 0-07-005397-9. LC 89-12714.

High school students and teachers requiring a guide to personal computer operations will find this an excellent reference source. The handbook includes computer hardware, operating systems, programming languages, and application software. Technical descriptions of hardware technology emphasize peripheral devices such as printers. Operating systems covered include Macintosh, PC-based DOS, OS/2, and Unix-Xenix. Application software descriptions address desktop publishing, word processing, graphics, and games. Pascal, Fortran, COBOL, BASIC, and other high-level programming languages are also discussed. [R: ARBA 90; SBF, May/June 90]

1877 Nimerscheim, Jack. **The First Book of MS-DOS**. 2d ed. Carmel, Ind.: Howard W. Sams, 1990. 292p. $16.95. ISBN 0-672-27341-1. LC 90-61020.

Nimerscheim has attempted to strike a balance between a lengthy, technical guidebook and a quick reference manual that is too brief for practical use. He has written a book that explains and clarifies difficult concepts in a concise format. It begins with an explanation of the basic components of a personal computer, progresses to topics such as formatting disks and copying files, and advances to the basics of writing short programs and batch files. Overall, it provides a readable survey of DOS through release 4.0. The work is more an instructional manual than a reference work, but it will meet the reference needs of the novice as well as the more experienced computer user.

1878 **Personal Computer Buying Guide: Foolproof Advice on How to Buy Computer Software and Hardware**. By Olen R. Pearson and the editors of *Consumer Reports* Books. Fairfield, Ohio: Consumer Reports Books, 1990. 224p. $10.95pa.

This general guide to personal computers is designed for the first-time buyer or owner planning to upgrade or replace an old system. It provides information on how to determine needs and find equipment that meets them. Written in a user-friendly style, the work offers advice on getting the most value for the money spent. [R: BL, 15 Feb 91]

1879 Timms, Howard. **Measuring and Computing**. New York: Franklin Watts, 1989. 36p. (Today's World Series). $12.40. ISBN 0-531-17188-4.

The series to which this work belongs is intended for junior high school students. *Measuring and Computing* surveys the history and uses of measuring, relating computing to the mass production process and emphasizing that the computer's function is to measure. Numerous diagrams and photographs, a glossary, and an index support this outstanding slim volume. Highly recommended. [R: SBF, May/June 90]

BIOGRAPHY

1880 Slater, Robert. **Portraits in Silicon**. Cambridge, Mass.: MIT Press, 1987. 374p. $32.50; $10.95pa. ISBN 0-262-19262-4; 0-262-69131-0pa. LC 87-2868.
These readable biographies of 31 individuals who have played leadership roles in the history of the computer revolution are based on personal interviews. Beginning with the inventors who built the first computers, the work continues with those who developed more powerful hardware and software. The last group covered is those who established companies to bring computers to everyone. Recommended for high school libraries. [R: ARBA 89; BL, 1 Feb 88; SBF, Jan/Feb 88]

ACTIVITIES

1881 Bonnet, Robert L., and G. Daniel Keen. **Computers: 49 Science Fair Projects**. Blue Ridge Summit, Pa.: TAB Books, 1990. $16.95; $9.95pa. ISBN 0-8306-7524-8; 0-8306-3524-6pa. LC 90-43540.
The projects in this volume, designed for students in grades 6 through 9, address programming rather than the use of the computer as a tool. Most projects require some programming knowledge and focus on such subjects as computer concepts, databases, statistics, and probability. The "Stop" message is a useful feature that signals the need for adult supervision. The book is best suited to computer application students and hobbyists. [R: BL, 1 Feb 91; BR, Mar/Apr 91]

□ _____ Earth Sciences _____ □

ATLASES

1882 **Rand McNally Atlas of Earth Mysteries**. Philip Whitfield, ed. Chicago: Rand McNally, 1990. 239p. $39.95. ISBN 0-528-83394-4. LC 89-43714.
What causes tidal waves and typhoons? How do migrating eels reach the Sargasso Sea? What causes devastating earthquakes? The *Atlas of Earth Mysteries* examines these and many other intriguing phenomena of our planet (e.g., wind, tornadoes, lightning, plate tectonics). Maps, photographs, and text illustrate how these forces gain and expend their power and show unique environments such as the Iraq marshlands, volcanic islands, and the Okavango basin in northern Botswana. Highly recommended for high schools. [R: WLB, Mar 91]

E+
1883 Wood, Robert Muir. **Atlas of the Natural World**. New York: Facts on File, 1990. 64p. $16.95. ISBN 0-8160-2131-7.
Designed for students from upper elementary grades through junior high school, this atlas begins with an introduction about the Earth's atmosphere, soils, and vegetation, followed by an explanation of the ecosystem. Among the topics covered are the origin of the Earth, dinosaurs, the Ice Age, and disasters (e.g., hurricanes, fires, volcanic eruptions). Each page includes colorful graphics. Recommended. [R: ARBA 92; RBB, July 91]

DICTIONARIES AND ENCYCLOPEDIAS

E+
1884 Ballard, Robert D. **Exploring Our Living Planet**. Washington, D.C.: National Geographic Society, 1983. 366p. $21.95. ISBN 0-87044-397-6. LC 83-2336.
Students from the fifth grade through high school will find this well written and superbly illustrated volume appealing. Color photographs, maps, diagrams, and other visual aids support the lucid

text, which discusses tectonic, crustal, and surface evolution and its effect on life on our planet. [R: SLJ, May 84]

1885   The Cambridge Encyclopedia of Earth Sciences. David G. Smith, ed. New York: Cambridge University Press, 1981. 496p. $47.50. ISBN 0-521-23900-1. LC 81-3313.

This work, which surveys many earth science fields, is divided into broad subject areas (e.g., physics and chemistry of the earth, crustal processes and environment, extraterrestrial geology). Some of the heavily illustrated text (color and black-and-white photographs, drawings, maps, and diagrams) is too advanced for most high school students, but many articles are suitable for young adult readers. [R: ARBA 83]

1886   Magill's Survey of Science: Earth Science Series. Frank N. Magill, ed. Pasadena, Calif.: Salem Press, 1990. 5v. $400.00/set. ISBN 0-89356-606-3. LC 89-10923.

The volumes of this series include 377 articles on physical and economic geology, geochemistry, geophysics, paleontology, oceanography, and related subjects. Current issues such as the greenhouse effect, ozone depletion, and hazardous waste are among the problems covered.

Clear, concise, alphabetically arranged entries include an introduction, a list of key terms, a summary of the topic, an explanation of the methods of study, a bibliography, and cross-references. Each volume contains an index to the set; the last volume contains a subject/keyword index and a glossary. Highly recommended for high schools. [R: ARBA 91; LJ, 15 Sept 90; RBB, 1 Sept 90]

■ *The Marshall Cavendish Illustrated Encyclopedia of Plants and Earth Sciences*. *See* entry 1827.

1887   McGraw-Hill Dictionary of Earth Sciences. 3d ed. Sybil P. Parker, ed. New York: McGraw-Hill, 1984. 837p. $46.95. ISBN 0-07-045252-0. LC 83-20362.

This spinoff from the *McGraw-Hill Dictionary of Scientific and Technical Terms* covers basic terminology used in some 18 disciplines, including climatology, geology, mapping, paleontology, and petrology. Each of the 15,000 entries briefly defines a term and identifies the field from which it comes. Recommended for advanced high school students. [R: ARBA 85; LJ, July 84]

1888   Oxford Illustrated Encyclopedia. Volume 1: The Physical World. Harry Judge and others, eds. New York: Oxford University Press, 1985. 384p. $45.00. ISBN 0-19-869129-7. LC 85-4876.

Each of the volumes in this set, which covers a broad area of knowledge, can stand alone. *The Physical World* contains concise entries, alphabetically arranged, that deal with geology, climatology, mineralogy, and oceanography. The text is supported by maps, photographs, tables, and diagrams. The color and black-and-white pictures are excellent. Indexed. This attractive volume is recommended for high school level.

Other volumes in the set include *The Natural World*, *World History from Earliest Times to 1800*, *World History from 1800 to the Present Time*, and *The Arts*. [R: ARBA 86]

HANDBOOKS

1889   Earth Science on File. By David Lambert. New York: Facts on File, 1988. 1v. (various paging). $145.00 looseleaf w/binder. ISBN 0-8160-1625-9. LC 88-21322.

This collection of reproducible materials consists of more than 1,000 charts of geomorphic principles and phenomena, such as the Earth's formation, volcanoes, minerals, earthquakes, glaciers, types of rainfall, river formation, and geological ages. The drawings are grouped in several sections: "Earth and Space," "Shaping the Surface," "The Restless Rock," "Earth History," "Air and Ocean," "Resources," and "Maps, Tables and Scales." This is a valuable collection for grades 7 through 12. [R: ARBA 89; BL, June 89; BR, May/June 89; SBF, Sept/Oct 89]

1890   The Earth's Natural Forces. K. J. Gregory, ed. New York: Oxford University Press, 1990. 256p. $45.00. ISBN 0-19-520860-9.

A profusely illustrated volume in The Illustrated Encyclopedia of World Geography series, this work surveys the Earth's regions and describes the geographical forces, climate, and natural phenomena (e.g., hurricanes) that created and modified the Earth's surface. Color maps depict the land, showing topographical features, and color photographs display the results of natural forces. Suggested for high schools. [R: ARBA 92; LJ, Jan 91; RBB, 15 Jan 91; WLB, Mar 91]

CLIMATE AND WEATHER

■ *The Air and Space Catalog. See* entry 2187.

1891 Day, John A., and Vincent J. Shaefer. **Peterson First Guide to Clouds and Weather**. Boston: Houghton Mifflin, 1991. 128p. $4.95pa. ISBN 0-395-56268-6. LC 90-13379.

This small, worthwhile book is mostly visual, with beautiful pictures of clouds and optical effects such as rainbows and halos. The authors gently remind readers to take better care of the atmosphere, putting special emphasis on acid rain, ozone depletion, and global warming. However, the guide covers weather forecasting insufficiently; computers are not even mentioned. On the weather map, the station chosen to be expanded and fully explained has a pressure reading that does not fit the isobars. However, the book does an outstanding job on clouds and visual effects.

1892 **Meteorology Source Book**. Sybil P. Parker, ed. New York: McGraw-Hill, 1989. 304p. (McGraw-Hill Science Reference Series). $45.00. ISBN 0-07-045511-2. LC 88-15076.

A spinoff from the *McGraw-Hill Encyclopedia of Science and Technology*, this volume includes sections covering the atmosphere; atmospheric optical and electrical phenomena; climate; micrometeorology; hydrometeorology; weather; instrumentation, observation, and forecasts; and weather modification. Photographs, maps, and drawings illustrate this work, which has merit for advanced high school students. Those holding the parent set, however, need not purchase this volume. [R: ARBA 89]

1893 Pearce, E. A., and Gordon Smith. **The Times Books World Weather Guide**. enlarged ed. New York: Times Books/Random House, 1990. 480p. $17.95pa. ISBN 0-8129-1881-9. LC 90-50319.

Seasonal weather conditions for almost 500 cities worldwide make up the content of this volume, an update of the 1984 edition. The introductory material contains explanations of weather conditions, charts of heat and humidity, the windchill index, and a glossary of terms. The main body of the work, arranged by continent and then by nation and city, includes a survey of the country's climate, followed by charts for cities.

The text gives average high/low and record high/low in Fahrenheit and Celsius, relative humidity for mornings and afternoons, average precipitation, and average number of days per month with 0.01 inch or more of rain. Maps showing climatic regions are scattered throughout the text. This inexpensive source is recommended for middle and high schools. [R: BL, 1 Apr 91]

1894 **Weather Almanac**. 6th ed. James A. Ruffner and Frank A. Bair, eds. Detroit: Gale, 1990. 811p. $120.00. ISBN 0-8103-2843-7. LC 81-644322.

This comprehensive collection of U.S. weather information, which focuses on climate and air quality, provides safety rules for environmental hazards associated with storms, earthquakes, volcanoes, and weather extremes. It also includes a list of all earthquakes in the country's history, a meteorological primer for the amateur weather forecaster, and a glossary of weather trends.

A major section of the work gives a weather history for cities from 1951 to 1980 and provides a verbal summary of the year's average weather conditions throughout the year. This work is more detailed in coverage than *The Weather Handbook*, but it is also more expensive.

1895 **The Weather Handbook**. rev. ed. McKinley Conway and Linda Liston, eds. Norcross, Ga.: Conway Data, 1990. 548p. $39.95. ISBN 0-910436-29-0. LC 90-82037. (40 Technology Park, Norcross, GA 30091).

Averages and extremes in temperature, precipitation, snowfall, relative humidity, and other weather information for selected U.S. cities make up this handbook. *Weather Almanac*, its closest competitor, provides a textual summary of the climate in each area, while *Handbook* readers must glean such information from quantitative tables. The *Handbook's* advantages are its coverage of twice as many U.S. cities as *Weather Almanac* and its lower price tag. [R: ARBA 92; WLB, Dec 90]

FOSSILS AND PREHISTORIC LIFE

E
1896 Benton, Michael. **The Dinosaur Encyclopedia**. New York: Julian Messner, 1984. 192p. $10.79; $6.95pa. ISBN 0-671-53131-X; 0-671-51046-0pa.

This small and colorful work is an alphabetically arranged guide to dinosaurs. For each reptile it provides an outline, a ruler (indicating length), common name, pronunciation, period extant, and range. Descriptive entries tell where skeletons have been found, and some include an artist's conception of the creature. A chronology, facts and theories about dinosaurs, an index, and a glossary all support the volume. Recommended for elementary schools. [R: BL, July 85; SLJ, May 86]

E+
1897 The Dinosaur Data Book: The Definitive, Fully Illustrated Encyclopedia of Dinosaurs. By David Lambert and the Diagram Group. New York: Avon, 1990. 320p. $12.95pa. ISBN 0-380-75896-2.

This stimulating reference book answers many questions about dinosaurs – known genera, their families, distribution, anatomy (e.g., brain size, sense organs), reproduction, feeding habits, and theories about their extinction. It also contains information on fossil collecting and bibliographies of dinosaurs found in cartoons, fiction, the comics, and film. This inexpensive work is recommended for all levels. [R: Kliatt, Sept 90; SBF, Nov/Dec 90]

E+
1898 The Field Guide to Prehistoric Life. By David Lambert and the Diagram Group. New York: Facts on File, 1985. 256p. $24.95. ISBN 0-8160-1125-7. LC 84-21237.

Major forms of prehistoric life are identified in a field-guide format, which describes and locates them in time and place. Chapters focus on fossil plants, invertebrates, fishes, amphibians, reptiles, birds, and mammals. A chapter on fossil hunting includes a list of famous fossil hunters, with notes on their most important finds, and a list of worldwide museums containing notable fossil collections. A short bibliography; an index; and hundreds of outstanding illustrations, maps, and charts support the text. Highly recommended for upper elementary grades upward. [R: ARBA 86; BL, 15 June 85; Kliatt, Jan 89]

E
1899 Kricher, John C. **Peterson First Guide to Dinosaurs.** Boston: Houghton Mifflin, 1990. 128p. $4.95. ISBN 0-395-52440-7. LC 89-26697.

This introduction to dinosaur life contains brief descriptions of over 100 dinosaurs and other reptiles of the Mesozoic period, including the antecedents of mammals and birds. Each is illustrated by a color painting.

The information is sound, but the work is poorly organized, and there are inconsistencies in the type of information provided for each group (geographic distribution, approximate weight, time ranges, and scale object to indicate relative size). However, this inexpensive guide is worthy of consideration by elementary schools. [R: ARBA 91; LJ, July 90]

1900 MacFall, Russell P., and Jay C. Wollin. **Fossils for Amateurs: A Guide to Collecting and Preparing Invertebrate Fossils.** 2d ed. New York: Van Nostrand Reinhold, 1983. $19.95pa. ISBN 0-442-26350-3. LC 82-21796.

A well-rounded guide, this excellent volume covers all aspects of fossil hunting, from the search to selling and displaying the specimens. Invertebrate fossils and a few plant fossils receive extensive treatment – how they were formed; where they are found; and their description, nomenclature, and classification. Other features include advice on planning field trips and an illustrated key based on shape, helpful in field identification. Amateur paleontological societies, museums and other fossil displays, fossil dealers, and maps of fossil areas complete the volume. Indexed. Recommended for secondary level. [R: ARBA 85; SBF, Mar/Apr 85]

1901 The Macmillan Illustrated Encyclopedia of Dinosaurs and Prehistoric Animals: A Visual Who's Who in Prehistoric Life. Dougal Dixon and others, eds. New York: Macmillan, 1988. 312p. $39.95. ISBN 0-02-580191-0. LC 88-1800.

This compendium is arranged in chapters on fishes, amphibians, reptiles, birds, therapsids (mammal-like reptiles), mammals and other species.

A typical entry includes the time the creature lived, locality, size, physical appearance, diet, how it differed from other members of the same family, and how it compares to animals living today. Other commendable features of the work include an attractive format, excellent four-color illustrations, a glossary, a bibliography, and an index. This volume, which is of British origin, is recommended for high schools. [R: ARBA 89; BL, 15 Mar 89; LJ, 15 Feb 89; SBF, Sept/Oct 89]

1902 Paul, Gregory S. **Predatory Dinosaurs of the World.** New York: Simon & Schuster, 1988. 464p. $22.95. ISBN 0-671-61946-2. LC 88-23052.

Predatory or carnivorous dinosaurs, from the small dinosaurlet to the Tyrannosaurus Rex, are the focus of this work. The introduction evokes controversial issues about these dinosaurs and treats their physiology, behavior, and other characteristics.

The main body of the work addresses 70 genera and 102 species, giving data on size, weight, age, place of occurrence, and other information, in entries from a paragraph to several pages. Carefully drawn black-and-white representations of dinosaurs in their own habitat and specific body parts illustrate the volume. This informative volume is recommended for high schools. [R: ARBA 90]

■ *Rocks, Minerals, and Fossils of the World*. See entry 1909.

E
1903 The Rourke Dinosaur Dictionary. By Joseph Hincks. Vero Beach, Fla.: Rourke, 1989. 96p. $26.60. ISBN 0-86592-049-4. LC 88-4612.

Over 125 species of dinosaurs, including some that are obscure (e.g., Opisthocoelicaudia, Tuojiangosaurus) are included in this work. Entries give pronunciations, measurements, locations, time periods, a one- or two-paragraph description, and other interesting data. Pictures (some of poor quality), a glossary, and a chart support the text. The work is not outstanding, but it is suggested as a supplementary selection for grades 4 through 6. [R: ARBA 91; SLJ, July 90]

E +
1904 Sattler, Helen Roney. **The New Illustrated Dinosaur Dictionary**. 352p. New York: Lathrop, Lee & Shepard, 1990. $24.95; $14.95pa. ISBN 0-688-08462-1; 0-688-10043-0pa. LC 90-3313.

An introduction provides a classification table of dinosaurs, a multipage pictorial chart showing relationships among them, and maps of the world as it may have been during the Mesozoic age. The main body of the work contains alphabetically arranged entries describing each dinosaur's physical appearance, specifying its family and eating habits, and indicating the fossil material found. Line drawings illustrate the dinosaur's distinguishing features.

Sattler's work is narrower in scope and less detailed than *The Dinosaur Encyclopedia*, but more dinosaurs are treated as well as some reptiles often confused with them. [R: BL, 15 Jan 90; SBF, Mar 91]

1905 Thompson, Ida. **The Audubon Society Field Guide to North American Fossils**. New York: Alfred A. Knopf, 1982. 846p. $17.95. ISBN 0-394-52412-8. LC 81-84772.

The main body of this authoritative guide consists of color plates of 420 fossils arranged by shape, including vertebrates, invertebrates, insects, and plants found in North America north of Mexico. The text, which is keyed to the plates, provides a physical desciption of each, and gives scientific name, age, and location. Other sections cover general geologic topics such as time, crustal and glacial formations and evolution, and fossil formation. A glossary and index are provided. Recommended for middle school and high school levels. [R: ARBA 83]

MINERALOGY AND GEMSTONES

1906 Chesterman, Charles W. **The Audubon Society Field Guide to North American Rocks and Minerals**. New York: Alfred A. Knopf, 1978. 850p. $17.95. ISBN 0-394-50269-8. LC 78-54893.

Visual identification of 232 mineral species (including 20 that are used as gemstones) and 40 types of rock comprise the main section of this guide. Specimens are keyed to 794 full-color photographs and smaller drawings that show structure and crystal habit. Field identification is based on color, crystal habit, forms and class, and texture. More precise identification is given by additional keys to such things as hardness and streak, and complete physical descriptions are given for each rock and mineral. A glossary and index complete the volume.

Rock Hunter's Guide: How to Find and Identify Collectible Rocks by Russell P. MacFall (Crowell, 1989) explains how to collect rocks, discusses tools and identification of rocks, and presents a state-by-state list of rock hunting sites. [R: ARBA 80]

E
1907 Jackson, Julia A. **Gemstones: Treasures from the Earth's Crust**. Hillside, N.J.: Enslow, 1989. 104p. $17.95. ISBN 0-89490-201-6. LC 88-1380.

The background and descriptive information on gemstones contained in this small volume is geared to children in the upper elementary grades. Maps showing locations, and color and black-and-white photographs of gemstones are useful features. Some of the latter, however, are of poor quality. A glossary of terms and a list of books for further reading support the text, but there is no index. [R: SBF, Nov/Dec 89]

1908   O'Donoghue, Michael. **Rocks and Minerals**. New York: Gallery Books/W. H. Smith, 1990. 224p. $9.98 spiralbound. ISBN 0-8317-6964-5.

Intended for the novice collector, this manual in the American Nature Guide series provides basic information on collecting, cleaning, and displaying rocks and minerals. For some 300 of those most commonly found it gives chemical composition, crystal systems, hardness, color, luster, and excellent photographs. This work provides a good introduction to a fascinating subject. [R: ARBA 91]

1909   Pellant, Chris. **Rocks, Minerals, and Fossils of the World**. Boston: Little, Brown, 1990. 175p. $17.95. ISBN 0-316-69796-6. LC 89-63627.

High school rockhounds will find this a useful guide. Some 150 rocks are classified by type – igneous, metamorphic, or sedimentary. Identifying characteristics (crystal shape, color, luster, cleavage, and hardness) are provided for over 250 minerals. Fossils, which receive the most attention, are organized by such types as trilobites, corals, and crinoids. The work's strength lies in its beautiful photographs, which are equally useful for identification. [R: ARBA 91; BL, 15 June 90; Kliatt, Sept 90]

1910   Roberts, Willard Lincoln, and others. **Encyclopedia of Minerals**. 2d ed. New York: Van Nostrand Reinhold, 1990. 979p. $99.95. ISBN 0-442-27681-8. LC 89-5633.

This revision of a 1974 work, a basic reference tool on the subject, includes more than 400 new minerals discovered during the interim and expanded knowledge about others. The volume covers 3,200 minerals in all, giving chemical composition, hardness, density, cleavage, description, mode of occurrence, and references to additional sources. Black-and-white photographs and drawings support the text. A section of outstanding color photographs of over 300 minerals is a special feature. This encyclopedia is considered to be the best of its kind in English. [R: ARBA 91]

OCEANOGRAPHY

1911   **The Facts on File Dictionary of Marine Science**. Barbara Charton, ed. New York: Facts on File, 1988. 325p. $24.95; $12.95pa. ISBN 0-8160-1031-5; 0-8160-2369-7pa. LC 82-15715.

This work offers comprehensive coverage of marine science, providing almost 2,000 entries for ecosystems, seas, currents, tides, seabirds, marine plants and animals, seafloor features, reefs, and water chemistry. Definitions, which range from a few lines to a page or more, are supported by some 75 black-and-white illustrations. The appendix provides a table of geologic time periods, a chronology of significant events in marine history, a taxonomic chart, and a list of agencies involved in marine research.

Another recommended work is *Ocean and Marine Dictionary* by David F. Tver (Cornell Maritime Press, 1979), which contains some 8,000 short entries. Charton's work, however, is the better choice for high school libraries. [R: ARBA 89; BR, May/June 89; LJ, 15 June 88; RBB, 1 Oct 88]

1912   Groves, Don. **The Oceans: A Book of Questions and Answers**. New York: John Wiley, 1989. 203p. $12.95. ISBN 0-471-60712-6. LC 88-32625.

Written for the nonspecialist, this work, arranged in 7 broad chapters, answers some 100 questions commonly asked about the oceans, such as what currents they have. It treats topics related to all areas of oceanography: ocean engineering, physics, chemistry, geology, meteorology, and the global ocean. A glossary and other aids assist in understanding technical aspects of the articles. An extensive bibliography and index conclude this work. Highly recommended for grades 9 and up. [R: BL, 15 Apr 89; BR, Nov/Dec 89; WLB, Sept 89]

■ *Meteorology Source Book*. See entry 1892.

1913   **The Times Atlas and Encyclopaedia of the Sea**. Alistair Couper, ed. New York: HarperCollins, 1989. 272p. $65.00. ISBN 0-06-016287-2. LC 89-67164.

This work, a revision of *Atlas of the Oceans* (Van Nostrand Reinhold, 1983), also edited by Couper, is a significant reference that received the Dartmouth Medal the year it was published. It covers physical and biological oceanography, resources, uses, laws of the ocean, and many other topics. Concise and readable articles are divided into four sections: the ocean environment (e.g., geography, ocean basin, atmosphere), resources of the ocean (e.g., fisheries, offshore oil, minerals), ocean trade (e.g., ports, collisions), and the world oceans (e.g., health, pollution, territorial claims). Each section, consisting of 4 to 12 articles, contains 2-page essays illustrated by 142 full-color photographs and 320 multicolor charts, graphs, diagrams, and drawings. Other features are statistics, shipping routes, distance charts, a glossary of terms, a bibliography, and an index.

Libraries holding the original work may not wish to replace it, since revision is slight; some graphics and statistical tables have been updated, but most materials remain unchanged. This excellent work, or its predecessor, is highly recommended for secondary schools. [R: BL, 1 Feb 90; LJ, 15 Nov 89; WLB, Feb 90]

Food and Nutrition

1914 **Better Homes and Gardens New Cook Book**. 10th ed. Des Moines, Iowa: Meredith Press, 1989. 472p. $24.95; $12.95pa. ISBN 0-696-00891-2; 0-696-00826-2pa. LC 88-80967.

This revision of a standard cookbook reflects the current emphasis on better nutrition. It offers more than 1,300 recipes (many of which feature reduced sugar, salt, and fat), gives microwave variations for some, and indicates those that are fast and easy. Special features include an alphabetical table of contents, arranged in 18 categories of recipes; useful charts; and over 400 photographs of a variety of cooking procedures. Indexed. Suggested for secondary schools. [R: BR, Jan/Feb 90; BL, 1 Nov 89]

E
1915 **Better Homes and Gardens New Junior Cook Book**. rev. ed. Des Moines, Iowa: Better Homes and Gardens Books/Meredith Press, 1989. 96p. $8.95. ISBN 0-696-01147-6.

The *New Junior Book*, which updates an earlier edition (1972), reflects a greater awareness of healthier eating habits, preparation of food from scratch instead of mixes, and the use of microwaves in food preparation. Among the more enticing recipes are several for Americanized ethnic foods.

1916 Bosco, Dominick. **The People's Guide to Vitamins and Minerals from A to Zinc**. rev. ed. Chicago: Contemporary Books, 1989. 351p. $11.95pa. ISBN 0-8092-4582-5. LC 88-31771.

Detailed articles, written in a readable style, present newly discovered facts about vitamins and minerals and how they affect the human body. This well-researched volume describes positive and toxic effects. The work concludes with an extensive bibliography and a comprehensive index. [R: ARBA 90; LJ, 1 Nov 89]

1917 Brody, Jane. **Jane Brody's Good Food Gourmet: Recipes and Menus for Delicious and Healthful Entertaining**. New York: W. W. Norton, 1990. $25.00. ISBN 0-393-02878-X.

The well-known nutritionist/writer has published a number of important works related to healthful eating. *Jane Brody's Nutrition Book* (W. W. Norton, 1981), the first of her publications, surveys current scientific knowledge regarding human nutrition. *Good Food Gourmet*, designed as a cookbook, also includes sound advice on meeting nutritional needs. Her other works include *Jane Brody's Good Food Book* (W. W. Norton, 1985) and *Parents Guide to Feeding Your Kids Right* (Prentice-Hall, 1989).

1918 Catsberg, C. M. E., and G. J. M. Kempen-van Dommelen. **Food Handbook**. Chichester, England: Ellis Horwood; distr., New York: Van Nostrand Reinhold, 1990. 382p. $74.95. ISBN 0-7476-0054-6. LC 89-19911.

This handbook contains information on food production, technology, preservation, quality, nutrition, and consumption. Some chapters focus on specific types of food (e.g., seafood, eggs, chocolate, vinegar, margarine). Illustrations and an index support the text. [R: ARBA 91]

1919 **Complete Book of Vitamins & Minerals**. By the editors of *Consumer Guide*. Lincolnwood, Ill.: Publications International, 1989. 320p. $12.95pa. ISBN 0-88176-497-3.

The body's nutrient requirements and the need for a proper diet are the themes of this medically sound guide. Vitamins and minerals are covered in separate sections; for each the book gives food sources, dietary requirements, functions, and other data. A section entitled "Supplement Product Profiles" addresses commercial products, providing trade name, producer, form, dosage, contents, a safety evaluation, and precautions. [R: ARBA 89]

E+
1920 **Cooking A to Z**. Jane Horn, ed. San Ramon, Calif.: Ortho Books, 1988. 631p. $32.95. ISBN 0-89721-147-2. LC 87-072103.

Any high school library should have this well-organized and beautifully illustrated work, which deserves a place on the shelf with *The Joy of Cooking*. The alphabetically arranged book contains over 600 easy-to-follow recipes and almost 500 entries that define cooking terms or describe and illustrate cooking techniques. The volume also gives information about maintaining kitchen equipment, consumer advice, and suggestions for selecting ingredients. Margin notes contain helpful suggestions on preparation and cooking. Entries range from a paragraph to 10 pages. Four-color photographs illustrate almost every page. [R: ARBA 90; LJ, 15 Feb 89; RBB, 15 Mar 89; WLB, Feb 89]

1921 Dunne, Lavon J. **Nutrition Almanac**. 3d ed. New York: McGraw-Hill, 1990. 340p. $15.95pa. ISBN 0-07-034912-6. LC 89-33019.

Eight major sections explain how the body uses nutrients, the consequences of nutrient imbalance, the benefits of herbs, how drinking polluted water affects health, dosage levels of vitamin and mineral supplements, and much more. Special features include recipes for healthful foods; a table of food composition, which analyzes 600 foods; and a nutrient allowance chart, which relates nutrient needs to body size, metabolism, and caloric requirements. A lengthy bibliography and an extensive index conclude this excellent volume. [R: ARBA 91]

1922 **Foods and Food Production Encyclopedia**. Douglas M. Considine, ed. in chief. New York: Van Nostrand Reinhold, 1982. 2560p. $264.95. ISBN 0-442-21612-2. LC 81-19728.

Some 1,201 entries cover the three stages of food production: the food-growth cycle, plant and animal growth, and raw-food processing into refined and complex products. Subtopics provide worldwide coverage of fruits and vegetables, oils and seeds, grain, livestock and poultry, and fishes and seafood, as well as their processing, the use of chemicals, nutrients and other food ingredients, and many other topics.

This massive, authoritative volume has a broad subject approach; it brings together information on narrow topics within general articles (e.g., all aspects of milk and dairy products in one entry). Articles are written in a nontechnical style, making the information useful to high school students with an interest in the food-production chain. Indexed. [R: BL, 1 Sept 83]

E+
1923 George, Jean Craighead. **The Wild, Wild Cookbook: A Guide for Young Wild-Food Foragers**. New York: HarperCollins, 1982. 192p. $12.89. ISBN 0-690-04315-5. LC 82-45187.

George, the well-known naturalist, aims this guide at young food foragers in grades 5 to 7. Thirty-nine wild food plants found in cities, along roadsides, and in the wild are introduced. Each has its common and botanical name, a detailed outline drawing, a description of the plant and its habitat, nutritional content, and clearly written recipes for its use. George advises adult supervision in plant identification. [R: SLJ, Mar 83]

1924 Griffith, H. Winter. **Complete Guide to Vitamins, Minerals & Supplements**. Tucson, Ariz.: Fisher Books, 1988. 510p. $14.95pa. ISBN 1-55561-006-4. LC 87-25156.

Most of the material in this work, written by a physician, is presented in chart format. The introduction surveys all nutrients and their importance in maintaining good health. The chart section covers vitamins, minerals, amino and nucleic acids, other supplements, and medical herbs. The charts on the latter topic indicate effects, claimed (but unproven) benefits, warnings and precautions, toxicity, and adverse reactions or overdose symptoms. Another section rates the toxicity of herbs.

Supplementary products are covered in an alphabetically arranged section that gives information on dosage, benefits, deficiency symptoms, natural food sources, possible side effects, overdosage, medical test effects, interaction with medication, and reports about claims made (proven and unproven). This work is more extensive than the *Complete Book of Vitamins and Minerals*; both are recommended. [R: ARBA 89; LJ, 15 Feb 88; RBB, 15 June 88]

1925 Hendler, Sheldon Saul. **The Doctors' Vitamin and Mineral Encyclopedia**. New York: Simon & Schuster, 1990. 496p. $24.95. ISBN 0-671-66784-X. LC 89-26367.

This comprehensive work opens with a survey of "micronutrition," followed by an extensive analysis of 160 vitamins, minerals, herbs, acids, and other supplements, from vitamin A to zinc. Clear and concise entries include appropriate dosage, best sources, and forms of each supplement or substance. The final section lists supplements recommended for specific needs. This impartial and well-documented work, written by a medical doctor involved in research, is highly recommended for high schools. [R: ARBA 91; LJ, 1 Apr 90]

1926   Herbst, Sharon Tyler. **Food Lover's Companion: Comprehensive Definitions of Over 3000 Food, Wine and Culinary Terms**. Hauppage, N.Y.: Barron's Educational Series, 1990. 582p. $10.95pa. ISBN 0-8120-4156-9. LC 89-140.

This small, inexpensive volume contains a wealth of information on food. Entries, ranging from a sentence to 2 pages, define over 3,000 terms on dishes and sauces, kitchen equipment, styles of preparation, foreign foods, brand names, and more. Other features include pronunciations for foreign words, an additives directory, substitutes for ingredients, an herb and spice chart, and illustrations of meat cuts. Highly recommended. [R: ARBA 91; BL, 1 June 90]

1927   Kraus, Barbara. **Calories and Carbohydrates**. 9th ed. New York: New American Library/ Dutton, 1991. 385p. $9.95; $4.99pa. ISBN 0-452-26559-2; 0-451-16923-9pa.

This frequently updated volume lists calories and carbohydrates for over 8,000 brand names and basic foods, arranged alphabetically. Fast-food restaurant menus and popular frozen foods are included. For each item, a brief entry gives portion size and number of calories or carbohydrates. The update adds new products and includes the latest nutritional information.

1928   **Larousse Gastronomique**. Jenifer Harvey Lang, ed. New York: Crown, 1988. 1193p. $60.00. ISBN 0-517-57032-7. LC 88-1178.

First published in 1938 and revised in 1971, this work is considered "the world's greatest culinary encyclopedia." It is the essential guide for anyone interested in classic French cuisine and "the best in cooking" worldwide.

Lang, in translating the French text, has used American terms and measurements and added American regional cuisine. The volume contains 4,000 recipes and articles on general topics, such as utensils, customs, chefs, sauces, and cooking techniques. Some 1,000 photographs and drawings, most in color, make this a work of art as well as gastronomy. [R: ARBA 89]

■ *The Marshall Cavendish Encyclopedia of Health*. *See* entry 1987.

1929   McGee, Harold. **On Food and Cooking: The Science and Lore of the Kitchen**. New York: Scribner's, 1984. 684p. $45.00; $18.95pa. ISBN 0-684-18132-0; 0-02-034621-2pa. LC 84-42667.

Clearly written entries survey the origin and use of different kinds of food and explain their composition and characteristic reaction to cooking. The three parts are foods, food and the body, and principles of cooking. Foods, the main section, is arranged by food types, with a chapter on additives. Special features include informative anecdotes, 200 diagrams and illustrations, a chemical primer, and an extensive bibliography. Indexed. This is an impressive volume in scope and detail. [R: ARBA 86]

E

1930   Moore, Carolyn E., and others. **Young Chef's Nutrition Guide and Cookbook**. Hauppauge, N.Y.: Barron's Educational Series, 1990. 281p. $11.95 spiralbound. ISBN 0-8120-5789-9. LC 89-18218.

The recipes in this cookbook for beginners reflect changes in nutritional awareness and eating habits. In addition to ingredients and food value, each recipe lists utensils and indicates the level of skill required. Recommended for students in grades 4 to 6. [R: BL, 1 Jan 90; Kliatt, Sept 90; SLJ, Aug 90]

1931   Mott, Lawrie, and Karen Snyder. **Pesticide Alert: A Guide to Pesticides in Fruits and Vegetables**. San Francisco, Calif.: Sierra Club Books; distr., New York: Random House, 1987. 179p. $15.95; $6.95pa. ISBN 0-87156-728-8; 0-87156-726-1pa. LC 87-42965.

Designed to inform the public about pesticides and food, this work presents factual data on the 5 pesticides most frequently found in 26 fruits and vegetables. The bad news is that 68 percent of produce is coated with, or contains the residue of, pesticides; the good news is that surface residues can be reduced by washing. Organizations that may be consulted for further information and involvement are also listed. Excellent illustrations, a glossary, indexes by pesticides and produce type, and suggestions for further reading all enhance this informative, thought-provoking volume. [R: ARBA 89; BL, 15 Sept 90; LJ, 1 June 90]

1932 The Mount Sinai School of Medicine Complete Book of Nutrition. Victor Herbert, Genell J. Subak-Sharpe, and Delia A. Hamock, eds. New York: St. Martin's Press, 1990. 796p. $35.00. ISBN 0-312-05129-8. LC 90-8624.

Compiled by a group of some 60 physicians, dieticians, and other health professionals, this extensive volume covers all aspects of nutrition. Part 1 summarizes the basic concepts of a healthy diet; part 2 focuses on specific categories of foods. Part 3 deals with nutritional needs at different stages of life, while parts 4 and 5 cover nutrition-related problems and the use of diet in treating various diseases. The final part offers practical advice on applying the information in daily living. This work is recommended for high schools. [R: ARBA 92; LJ, 15 Apr 91]

1933 Rinzler, Carol Ann. The Complete Book of Herbs, Spices, and Condiments: From Garden to Kitchen to Medicine Chest. New York: Facts on File, 1990. 199p. $19.95. ISBN 0-8160-2008-6. LC 89-23465.

For each of the 112 entries on herbs, spices, and condiments, this work gives 1 or 2 pages of information about food preparation, cooking, nutritional value, chemical properties, medicinal benefits, how it can be grown and used, and possible side effects. A final section covers hazardous herbs. Indexed. Thirty-six line drawings illustrate the book, which is filled with fascinating information. [R: ARBA 91; BL, 1 June 90; LJ, Feb 90]

1934 Rombauer, Irma, and Marion R. Becker. The Joy of Cooking. rev. ed. Indianapolis, Ind.: Bobbs-Merrill, 1975. 915p. $16.95. ISBN 0-672-51831-7.

Considered one of the best American cookbooks, *Joy of Cooking* provides excellent recipes, step-by-step instructions, and tips on food selection and preparation. The book's exhaustive coverage of clearly written recipes (4,500), old and new, national and regional, is enhanced by some 1,000 line drawings. Additional features include charts of meat cuts, carving instructions, measurement tables, ingredient substitutions and equivalents, high-altitude cooking adjustments, definitions of cooking terms, nutrition tables, and table settings. Thoroughly indexed. Highly recommended.

E +
1935 Spence, Annette. Nutrition. New York: Facts on File, 1988. 128p. $18.95. ISBN 0-8160-1670-4. LC 87-20203.

Nutrition, a volume in the Encyclopedia of Good Health, relates eating habits to one's growth and development. The work provides essential, scientifically accurate information about nutrition in an easily understood style for young people ages 10 and up. Pictures, drawings, charts, and diagrams illustrate the text, which also is supported by a glossary, a bibliography, and an index. [R: ARBA 90; BR, Sept/Oct 89; RBB, Aug 89]

■ *The Surgeon General's Report on Nutrition and Health. See* entry 1995.

1936 Webb, Denise. The Complete "Lite" Foods Calorie, Fat, Cholesterol, and Sodium Counter. New York: Bantam, 1990. 482p. $4.95pa. ISBN 0-553-28471-1.

Webb hopes to educate the general public on reading food labels. The main section rates "lite" products, indicating serving size, calories, sodium content, grams of fat, percentage of calories from fat, and whether the designation of "lite" is justified. Appendixes list food companies that produce "lite" products and a bibliography of materials on the topic. An index and glossary conclude this very helpful source. [R: BL, 1 May 90; VOYA, Oct 90]

1937 Winick, Myron, and others, comps. and eds. The Columbia Encyclopedia of Nutrition. New York: Putnam, 1988. 349p. $12.95pa. ISBN 0-399-51573-9. LC 87-10782.

Written in a conversational style, this volume speaks to laypeople with limited knowledge of disease prevention and the promotion of good health. The Institute of Human Nutrition within Columbia University's College of Physicians and Surgeons sponsored this scholarly work, which has been compiled by a physician and three scientists.

More than 100 alphabetically arranged articles, 1 to 10 pages in length, cover diet and its relationship to pregnancy, hypertension, obesity, allergies, breast feeding, and infection. Numerous tables and lists (e.g., average cholestrol readings, drugs that affect nutrition) are provided. Lucid articles reflect the latest scientific knowledge on this subject. Recommended for secondary schools. [R: ARBA 89; BL, 15 Sept 88; LJ, June 88]

Health and Family

AGING

See also **Handicapped**.

1938 **Aging America: Trends and Projections**. 1987/1988 edition. U.S. Congress. Washington, D.C.: Senate Special Committee on Aging, n.d. free. (Senate Special Committee on Aging, U.S. Senate, Washington, DC 20402).
Compiled by the Senate Special Committee on Aging, this free report contains statistics and projections on such topics as the aging population, economic status, retirement and labor, health, social characteristics, and federal and private spending. This report forecasts that by 2028, one-third of the American population will be 55 or older, and it emphasizes the increasing need for planning for this demographic change. Numerous charts, tables, and maps illustrate the text. [R: LJ, 15 May 91]

1939 Langone, John. **Growing Older: What Young People Should Know about Aging**. Boston: Little, Brown, 1990. 172p. $14.95. ISBN 0-316-51459-4. LC 90-38434.
This excellent source attempts to raise teenagers' awareness of the aging process and society's attitude toward the elderly. Our youth-oriented society is contrasted with others that honor their elders. Other topics covered include theories on biological aging, illnesses commonly found in older people, economic issues facing the elderly and society as a whole, and genetic engineering that some day may diminish or stop the aging process.
This work not only will give students a greater understanding of older members of their own families but also will provide data for reports on the subject. Recommended for middle and high school levels. [R: SLJ, Jan 91]

ALTERNATIVE HEALTH CARE

1940 Drury, Nevill, and Susan Drury. **The Illustrated Dictionary of Natural Health**. New York: Sterling Publishing, 1989. 304p. $12.95pa. ISBN 0-8069-6924-5.
This dictionary, which defines words related to natural healing, is divided into three sections: healing plants; alternative health therapies; and diet, nutrition, and body functions. Each section briefly defines terms and lists various treatments, alphabetically arranged. Warnings against radical health fads are numerous. The work provides drawings, black-and-white photographs, and a bibliography, but not an index. [R: ARBA 90; BL, 15 June 89; LJ, 1 May 89; SLJ, Sept 89]

1941 Murray, Michael T., and Joseph E. Pizzorno. **An Encyclopedia of Natural Medicine**. Rocklin, Calif.: Prima Publications & Communications; distr., New York: St. Martin's Press, 1991. 609p. $28.95; $18.95pa. ISBN 1-55958-092-5; 1-55958-091-7pa.
The authors, doctors of naturopathic medicine, combine natural treatment with modern scientific knowledge to explain the basic principles of health. The text describes problems and suggests therapies for 62 conditions, such as varicose veins. Therapies range from changes in life style and diet to vitamins and treatment for psychological problems. Each problem addresses the causes of the disease and includes an extensive bibliography. [R: LJ, 1 May 91]

1942 Olsen, Kristin Gottschalk. **The Encyclopedia of Alternative Health Care**. New York: Pocket Books/Simon & Schuster, 1989. 325p. $8.95pa. ISBN 0-671-66256-2.
This guide covers 33 healing arts, ranging from acupuncture to yoga, and including biofeedback, herbalism, and rolfing. There are chapters on such topics as choosing and working with practitioners, but the main body of the work provides alphabetically arranged essays on health-care therapies. For each technique, the author provides the history and development of the treatment, what happens in a

typical session, how the treatment is purported to work, and what cautions one should take. A bibliography and list of resource agencies conclude the volume. [R: ARBA 91; BL, 15 Mar 90; LJ, Jan 90]

CHILD ABUSE

E+
1943   Clark, Robin E., and Judith Freeman Clark. **The Encyclopedia of Child Abuse**. New York: Facts on File, 1989. 328p. $45.00. ISBN 0-8160-1584-8. LC 88-30880.

Due to the current public and professional concern about child abuse, reference tools such as this have become a necessity for those who work with children. Ranging from a brief identification to several paragraphs, entries for the nonspecialist cover medical terms, legal expressions, important legal acts and decisions, psychological concepts, and organizations. Appendixes include a directory of organizations, state-by-state reporting laws, child welfare laws, and a number of other useful listings. A bibliography and index conclude the volume. Recommended for professional collections at all levels. [R: ARBA 90; BL, 15 Oct 89]

E+
1944   Iverson, Timothy J., and Marilyn Segal. **Child Abuse and Neglect: An Information and Reference Guide**. Hamden, Conn.: Garland, 1990. 220p. $34.00. ISBN 0-8240-7776-8. LC 89-71495.

This work not only provides a realistic survey of the problems of child abuse and neglect and the characteristics of abused children and their families but also cites resource materials for professionals. The first chapter examines the historical and cultural perceptions of the issue and presents theories about its causes. Current definitions of maltreatment and the problems of research in the area are also covered. Later chapters address reporting, intervention practices and processes, indications of abuse and neglect, legal aspects of the problem, and preventive programs. Administrators, teachers, and librarians at all levels will welcome this work. [R: ARBA 91]

1945   Layman, Richard. **Current Issues: Child Abuse**. Detroit: Omnigraphics, 1990. 122p. $35.00. ISBN 1-55888-271-5. LC 90-48200.

Child Abuse, the first volume is a series designed "to provide in an orderly way the information necessary to discuss and pursue matters of public concern," surveys the problem, defines relevant terminology, and reports interviews with experts. The series generally focuses on contemporary issues in the United States and the world. Future volumes will address gun control, the environment, the Freedom of Information and Privacy acts, genetic engineering, and capital punishment. Recommended for high schools. [R: BL, 1 Feb 91]

DEATH AND DYING

See also **Mental Health** in **Health and Family**.

1946   **Encyclopedia of Death**. Robert Kastenbaum and Beatrice Kastenbaum, eds. Phoenix, Ariz.: Oryx Press, 1989. 295p. $74.50. ISBN 0-89774-263-X. LC 89-9401.

This encyclopedia contains 130 succinct and cogent articles about death and dying. They analyze such issues as attitude toward death, the representation of death in literature and mythology, violent death, bereavement counseling, hospice care, funeral rites, and the meaning of death. Balanced treatment of opposing opinions is provided for controversial issues such as gun control, euthanasia, the death penalty, and prolonging life. Articles of one to several pages end with bibliographies of current material. Frequent cross-references, a 14-category guide to topics, and a subject index all provide outstanding access to the text. This important work is recommended for high schools. [R: ARBA 90; BL, 15 Feb 90; WLB, Jan 90]

1947   Evans, Glen, and Norman L. Farberow. **The Encyclopedia of Suicide**. New York: Facts on File, 1988. 434p. $45.00. ISBN 0-8160-1397-7. LC 88-11173.

Patterned after *Encyclopedia of Alcoholism* and *Encyclopedia of Drug Abuse*, this encyclopedia helps meet a growing demand for information about the psychological, political, legal, socioeconomic, and sociological aspects of suicide. Over 500 alphabetically arranged entries, which range from a few sentences to extensive coverage, contain facts and theories about self-destructive behavior. There is an introductory essay on the history of suicide.

Appendixes provide suicide statistics by race, age, geographic area, marital status, months of occurrence, and methods of suicide; a directory of agencies concerned with the problem; a directory of suicide prevention centers; and major English-language journals. A bibliography and index conclude the volume. Recommended for high schools. [R: ARBA 89; BL, 15 Nov 88; LJ, Aug 88; SLJ, May 91]

1948   Flanders, Stephen A. **Suicide**. New York: Facts on File, 1991. 192p. $22.95. ISBN 0-8160-1909-6.

Given the alarming increase in teenage suicides, this volume in the Library in a Book series addresses a subject of particular relevance to today's high school students. While extensive research has failed to determine the exact reasons for suicide, social scientists and psychologists have learned a great deal about it in recent years. This work reflects their findings.

The Encyclopedia of Suicide provides far more information on this tragic social phenomenon, but this compact reference work contains the latest knowledge about the subject. It surveys the history and social implications of suicide, demographic trends, and the emotional and psychological impact on a family. It also includes a chronology of major events related to suicide, geographical information, organization leaders and other key figures, a glossary of important terms, an analysis of legal issues, major court cases, and an extensive bibliography. Indexed. Recommended for high schools.

E +
1949   Pyle, Marian S. **Death and Dying in Children's and Young People's Literature: A Survey and Bibliography**. Jefferson, N.C.: McFarland, 1988. 187p. $20.95. ISBN 0-89950-335-7. LC 87-46386.

Pyle explores the theme of death and dying in literature for children and young adults in this excellent work. She provides synopses of 140 books published from 1938 to 1985 that, in her judgment, deal with the subject in a proper manner. Chapters cover death in folklore and nursery rhymes; death of a pet, a friend, or a relative; and one's own death. The bibliographic essays are supported by an index to specific topics. [R: BR, Nov 88; VOYA, Feb 89]

DRUGS AND SUBSTANCE ABUSE

E +
1950   Berger, Gilda, and Melvin Berger. **Drug Abuse A-Z**. Hillside, N.J.: Enslow, 1990. 143p. $15.95. ISBN 0-89490-193-1. LC 89-1512.

Using a dictionary approach, this volume in the A-Z Reference series describes more than 1,000 drug-related terms in lucid and readable articles that vary from a few sentences to several paragraphs. The work also includes federal legislation that regulates drugs and a few additional references and agencies that will provide further information. This small volume is highly recommended for all levels. [R: ARBA 91; BR, May/June 90; SBF, May/June 90; VOYA, June 90]

1951   Evans, Glen, and others. **The Encyclopedia of Drug Abuse**. 2d ed. New York: Facts on File, 1991. 370p. $45.00. ISBN 0-8160-1956-8.

The first edition of this work, under the authorship of Robert O'Brien and Sidney Cohen (1984), was acclaimed as an outstanding reference source and highly recommended for students, seventh grade and up. The work has now been completely revised, with over 500 entries on all aspects of drug abuse. The text, alphabetically arranged, treats topics and terms related to biological, medical, social, and legal factors regarding drugs and their abuse; organizations and government agencies concerned with drug abuse and related diseases; drugs and pregnancy; abuse among specific social groups; and treatment options.

Appendixes include glossaries of street language and slang, tables of drug laws and patterns of usage, and sources of information. A bibliography and subject index conclude the volume. Highly recommended for middle and high schools.

1952   Fay, John J. **The Alcohol/Drug Abuse Dictionary and Encyclopedia**. Springfield, Ill.: Charles C. Thomas, 1988. 167p. $19.25. ISBN 0-398-05491-6. LC 88-4947.

The sophisticated language of professionals and the slang of the drug subculture are covered in this work. Entries for over 1,400 terms, phrases, and concepts related to alcohol and drug abuse vary from short identifications to several paragraphs. Appendixes list the jargon of street users, state agencies for alcohol and drug control, drug-poison information centers, and abuse resource agencies. Also provided is a generic name/brand name cross-reference directory for commonly abused substances. A bibliography concludes this excellent work. Recommended for high schools. [R: ARBA 90]

1953   Gilbert, Sara D. **Get Help: Solving the Problems in Your Life**. New York: William Morrow, 1989. 130p. $12.95; $7.95pa. ISBN 0-688-08010-3; 0-688-08928-3pa. LC 88-32352.

Organizations that provide help for troubled teenagers, at little or no cost, are presented in this directory. Arranged by broad category (e.g., substance abuse, addiction), each entry gives address, telephone number, a brief description, and an indication of the kind of help provided (e.g., information, direct help, referrals). The guide also supplies instructions on how to ask for help or locate information and criteria for evaluating resources or services. An alphabetical list of agencies and a subject index conclude the volume. [R: ARBA 90; BL, 15 June 90]

1954   Nordquist, Joan, comp. **Substance Abuse I: Drug Abuse: A Bibliography**. Santa Cruz, Calif.: Reference and Research Services, 1989. 68p. (Contemporary Social Issues: A Bibliographic Series, no.16). $15.00pa. ISBN 0-937855-31-6.

1955   Nordquist, Joan, comp. **Substance Abuse II: Alcohol Abuse: A Bibliography**. Santa Cruz, Calif.: Reference and Research Services, 1989. 68p. (Contemporary Social Issues: A Bibliographic Series, no.17). $15.00pa. ISBN 0-937855-32-4.

These bibliographies, designed to provide access to current literature on two of today's critical problems, cite books, articles, government documents, and pamphlets. *Drug Abuse* includes 500 entries, and *Alcohol Abuse* has 800 titles. Each volume addresses a variety of spinoff problems: crime, drugs in the workplace, alcohol use and abuse among specific populations, and alcohol abuse and the family. Neither work is annotated, but both are recommended for high school students writing papers on the issue or suffering from substance abuse. [R: ARBA 91]

1956   O'Brien, Robert, and Morris Chafetz. **The Encyclopedia of Alcoholism**. 2d ed. New York: Facts on File, 1991. 400p. $45.00. ISBN 0-8160-1955-X.

This new edition, well received when its predecessor appeared in 1983, includes over 100 new entries and updated coverage for some 500 articles carried over from the earlier work. The main part, arranged alphabetically, covers a broad spectrum of topics and terms (e.g., alcoholic beverages, legal aspects, effects on the body, psychological and sociological effects, treatment, organizations). Clearly written entries range from a short identification to multipage articles.

Tables and graphs provide data on legal drinking age by state; alcohol use by such factors as age, race, and sex; tax revenues; and demographic correlation with drinking. The appendix includes extensive lists of national and state organizations and agencies. A lengthy bibliography and subject index conclude the volume. Highly recommended for middle and high schools. [R: ARBA 92; RRB, 1 Nov 91; WLB, Nov 91]

1957   **Peterson's Drug and Alcohol Programs and Policies at Four-Year Colleges**. Janet Carney Schneider and Bunny Porter-Shirley. Princeton, N.J.: Peterson's Guides, 1989. 445p. $19.95pa. ISBN 0-87866-731-8. LC 89-8743.

Parents or students who wish to know the attitude of specific colleges toward drugs and alcohol will find answers in this guide. Profiles of some 900 American colleges identify each institution's drug- and alcohol-education program and indicate how chemically dependent students and staff are identified, types of services provided to help them, and disciplinary action taken when the rules are broken.

The volume also gives other information about each college: founding date, degrees awarded, enrollment and faculty size, and fraternities and sororities (with their memberships). A comparative table of drug and alcohol matters, a directory of related programs, and other useful data conclude the volume. General college directories contain brief information about the topic, but this guide provides better coverage of the issue. [R: ARBA 90; BL, 1 Jan 90; WLB, Dec 89]

1958   Ryan, Elizabeth. **Straight Talk about Drugs and Alcohol**. New York: Facts on File, 1989. 160p. $16.95. ISBN 0-8160-1525-2.

This volume focuses on research about drugs and alcohol; it has interviews with young substance abusers. It explains the use and abuse of drugs in society today, the reasons why teenagers turn to them, the long- and short-term physical effects of drugs, and advice on how to avoid the drug and alcohol scene. This small work makes an excellent contribution to the literature on this problem. There is a Spanish-language edition available. [R: BL, Apr 89; SLJ, May 89; WLB, May 89]

E+
1959   Shulman, Jeffrey. **The Drug-Alert Dictionary and Resource Guide**. Fredrick, Md.: Twenty-First Century Books, 1991. 91p. $14.95. ISBN 0-941477-85-1. LC 90-46534.

A part of the Drug-Alert series, which is designed to give young readers easily understood and comprehensive information, this volume serves two purposes: it defines the most important drug-related terms, concepts, and issues, and it gives directory information for organizations and other resources. Most definitions are short, but some longer entries also include a boxed facts and figures section, highlighted in blue. *See* references are frequently used.

The resources section includes private organizations (e.g., MADD, Alcoholics Annonymous, Toughlove) and federal and state government agencies, the latter arranged by state. This clearly written and well-organized guide is designed for children 8 to 12. [R: ARBA 92; BL, June 91]

E+
1960   Spence, Annette. **Substance Abuse**. New York: Facts on File, 1989. 128p. $18.95. ISBN 0-8160-1669-0. LC 87-21142.

A volume in the Encyclopedia of Good Health, this work provides hard facts about the effects of drugs, alcohol, and tobacco products. The small book gives an excellent survey of the subject in easy-to-understand entries, supported by good illustrations, a glossary, a bibliography, a list of contact agencies, and an index. Recommended for ages 10 and up. [R: ARBA 90; BL, Aug 89; BR, Sept/Oct 89]

E+
1961   **Substance Abuse & Kids: A Directory of Education, Information, Prevention, and Early Intervention Programs**. Phoenix, Ariz.: Oryx Press, 1989. 466p. $65.00pa. ISBN 0-89774-583-3. LC 89-8848.

This important directory is intended for school personnel and anyone else who is trying to save children from drugs. Listings, current as of June 1, 1989, include programs designed to help children avoid drugs and to assist those already addicted. The work also covers a wide range of behavioral disorders (e.g., codependency, eating disorders, kleptomania, submission to cults).

All listings give name, address, telephone number, contact person, and age/grade of its clientele. Some also provide hotline number, specialties (e.g., particular ethnic groups), staff/client ratio, follow-up programs, and other useful information. Three indexes provide access to age/grade level, addiction/disorder, and program services offered (e.g., speakers, family counseling). [R: ARBA 90; BL, 15 Mar 89; VOYA, Apr 90]

1962   **Substance Abuse Residential Treatment Centers for Teens**. Phoenix, Ariz.: Oryx Press, 1990. 286p. $45.00pa. ISBN 0-89774-585-X. LC 89-26553.

This directory lists over 1,000 residential treatment programs for young people between the ages of 9 and 19 who have drug, alcohol, and behavior problems. Arranged by state and city, the directory includes name, address, telephone and hotline numbers, affiliations and accreditation, addiction or disorder treated, treatment method employed, program setting, staff size, admission requirements and fees, and other services. Programs are not evaluated. Indexes provide access by name of treatment center, addiction/disorder, and treatment method. [R: ARBA 91; VOYA, Apr 90; WLB, Apr 90]

FAMILY

E
1963   Biracree, Tom, and Nancy Biracree. **The Parents' Book of Facts: Child Development from Birth to Age Five**. New York: Facts on File, 1989. 240p. $19.95. ISBN 0-8160-1412-4.

Intended for parents, this work focuses on the physical, mental, and emotional development of children from infancy to the age of five. The child development and health information given is useful, however, for those involved in preschool programs. A "What You Should Know About" section gives charts and brief articles on a wide variety of topics. [R: BR, Nov/Dec 89; LJ, 15 Apr 89]

1964   Cline, Ruth K. J. **Focus on Families: A Reference Handbook**. Santa Barbara, Calif.: ABC-Clio, 1990. 233p. $35.00. ISBN 0-87436-508-2. LC 89-17937.

The Teenage Perspectives series, to which *Focus on Families* belongs, provides access to information of interest to adolescents. This work covers adoption, single-parent families, grandparents and other relatives, siblings, stepfamilies, divorce, children of divorce, and child abuse.

Each chapter provides background information; definitions of terms; statistics; and briefly annotated citations of fiction, nonfiction, articles, and nonprint materials. Some chapters describe support organizations, many with telephone numbers for hotlines and treatment centers. Author, subject, and title indexes give access to the text. Despite the inclusion of some dated material, this work is recommended for secondary schools, since no comparable guide is available. [R: ARBA 91; BL, 15 June 90; BR, Sept/Oct 90]

1965   DiCanio, Margaret. **The Encyclopedia of Marriage, Divorce and the Family**. New York: Facts on File, 1989. 607p. $45.00. ISBN 0-8160-1695-X. LC 89-11838.

This encyclopedia provides current information on important (and sometimes controversial) issues, reflecting changes in family life over the past 25 years. There are broad essays on marriage, divorce, and family, each several pages in length, and shorter entries for specific topics such as dual-career marriages, cohabitation, the elderly, sudden death syndrome, eating disorders, and Caesarean sections. The articles are scholarly but written in jargon-free language suitable to the high school level.

Appendixes contain a variety of useful sections: a consumer guide to family counseling and mental health services, divorce procedures, choosing a divorce attorney, and sample antenuptial and living-together agreements. The extensive bibliography (more than 500 items) is arranged by author, but a subject arrangement would have been more useful. A detailed index concludes the volume. Highly recommended for high school libraries, especially those supporting a family-life curriculum. [R: ARBA 90; BL, 1 Jan 90; BR, May/June 90; WLB, Nov 89]

1966   **Encyclopedia of Adolescence**. Richard M. Lerner and others, eds. Hamden, Conn.: Garland, 1991. 2v. (Garland Reference Library of the Social Sciences, v.495). $150.00. ISBN 0-8240-4378-2. LC 90-14033.

The latest research is reflected in this outstanding set, which covers all aspects of adolescence and ranges across disciplines from education and psychology to history and medicine. More than 200 entries cover such topics as eating disorders, drug dependency, cystic fibrosis, phobias, teenagers as parents, academic achievement, and important figures in theory development (e.g., Freud). All are contributed by scholars and other subject specialists. Charts frequently illustrate the text, and bibliographies support all entries. Cross-references and a subject index provide access. Highly recommended for secondary schools. [R: ARBA 92; LJ, 15 May 91; WLB, May 91]

1967   Franck, Irene, and David Brownstone. **The Parent's Desk Reference**. New York: Prentice Hall Press, 1991. 615p. $29.95. ISBN 0-13-649989-9. LC 90-27359.

This outstanding reference work is aptly named. The more than 2,500 entries contain information on a broad spectrum of educational, medical, social, and personal concerns that pertain to parents or their children. Subjects include pregnancy and childbirth; nutrition and infant care; genetic and common disorders of childhood or pregnancy; education and special education concerns; educational, medical, and psychological tests; family law and social services; and key social problems relating to children. Almost every term, problem, disease, syndrome, or acronym that parents might encounter is included. Cross-references abound.

The most significant entries have an appended bibliography and a list of public and private organizations where parents may seek additional help or information. Sensitive topics, such as abortion, homosexuality, and AIDS, are treated impartially. A special boxed section in many entries offers detailed information about a specific term, disease, or condition.

The last part of the book contains an outstanding special-help section that encompasses topics that the authors feel needed further elucidation. Advice on helping a child become a good reader, writer, mathematician, and test-taker is presented. Three areas furnish a list of organizations that offer assistance to special children and help with substance abuse. An alphabetized directory of all the hotlines, helplines, and related organizations cited in the text concludes this valuable contribution to parenting literature. Librarians in school, public, and academic libraries should definitely purchase this encyclopedia. [R: ARBA 92; RBB, Aug 91]

1968   Gouke, Mary Noel, and Arline McClarty Rollins. **One-Parent Children, the Growing Minority: A Reference Guide**. Hamden, Conn.: Garland, 1990. 494p. (Reference Books on Family Issues, v.14; Garland Reference Library of Social Science, v.344). $50.00. ISBN 0-8240-8576-0. LC 84-48876.

The dramatic growth of single-parent households during the last two decades has also swollen the literature on the issue. This comprehensive bibliography includes 1,100 citations. Annotations focus on the results of research without a description of the methodology used. The citations are indexed by subject, author, and geographic area. [R: ARBA 91]

HOMOSEXUALITY

1969 **Encyclopedia of Homosexuality**. Wayne R. Dynes and others, eds. Hamden, Conn.: Garland, 1990. 2v. (Garland Reference Library of Social Science, v.492). $150.00/set. ISBN 0-8240-6544-1. LC 89-28128.

Homosexuality is covered broadly in this extensive work. The 770 biographical, topical, and thematic articles, arranged alphabetically by topic, cover historical, medical, psychological, socio-logical, and transcultural information. A subject cross-reference guide in the front of the volume and a detailed subject index provide access.

The focus of the work is Western, but African, Eastern, and other groups receive coverage. Articles deal with contrasting viewpoints and conclude with bibliographies. Most entries are readable at a high school level, but others require some technical background. This work provides a masterful survey of a controversial topic. [R: ARBA 91; BL, 15 May 90; LJ, Jan 90; WLB, May 90]

THE HUMAN BODY

1970 Covington, Timothy R., and J. Frank McClendon. **Sex Care: The Complete Guide to Safe and Healthy Sex**. New York: Pocket Books/Simon & Schuster, 1987. 402p. $8.95pa. ISBN 0-671-52398-8.

This highly recommended source, containing strongly written and nonjudgmental essays on sex care, is designed for laypersons. It opens with an article on male and female anatomy, followed by a section on contraception and contraceptive methods (e.g., proper use, safety, effectiveness, adverse effects), including IUDs, condoms, creams, gels and foams, sterilization, abstinence, and the rhythm method. Another section on sexually transmitted diseases gives information on prevention; symptoms; and treatments for gonorrhea, syphilis, herpes, PID, and AIDS. The last section provides frank and objective coverage of sexual health: PMS, abortion, toxic shock syndrome, and sexual hygiene. [R: ARBA 89]

E+
1971 Crocker, Mark. **The Body Atlas**. New York: Oxford University Press, 1991. 64p. $16.95. ISBN 0-19-520845-5.

The basic facts and concepts concerning body "machinery"—the digestive, respiratory, immune, and nervous systems; muscles; the skeleton; and vital organs—are explained and illustrated. Organized thematically, pages contain a mixture of entertaining and instructive text, question-and-answer boxes, historical vignettes, and practical tips, with full-color body maps, diagrams, and other images. Comparisons are made to common objects (e.g., the elbow and knee joints to a door hinge). Among the many illustrations are drawings of male and female bodies at various stages of development. A useful source for grades 5 through 8.

1972 Hole, John W., Jr. **Human Anatomy and Physiology**. 5th ed. Dubuque, Iowa: Wm. C. Brown, 1990. 947p. $41.00. ISBN 0-697-05779-8. LC 89-50307.

Designed for the student who has a limited background in the physical and biological sciences but who aspires to a career in the health sciences, this standard source is an appropriate selection for high school level. Technical and clinical terms are used sparingly, and those that appear in the text are defined in the glossary. Every page bears a table, summary chart, flow chart, or other diagram to illus-trate the text. [R: ARBA 91]

1973 **The Human Body on File**. By the Diagram Group. New York: Facts on File, 1983. 300p. $145.00 looseleaf w/binder. ISBN 0-87196-706-5. LC 82-12104.

This collection of anatomical drawings, printed in black and white, is designed for classroom use and is reproducible for free. The collection begins with a survey of the body and includes drawings of joints, bone structure, muscles, nerves, veins and arteries, and the lymphatic system. Additional sections focus on particular parts of the body (e.g., head, spine, organs). A final section traces human development from birth to age 15 and includes charts and graphs of blood pressure, temperature, menstrual cycles, growth, and weight. Identifying captions on the bottom of each page are keyed to numbers marked on the diagram. An index includes all terms used in the drawings. [R: BL, 15 Apr 84; SLJ, May 85; WLB, Nov 83]

1974 Kittredge, Mary. **The Human Body: An Overview**. New York: Chelsea House, 1989. 144p. $17.95. ISBN 0-791-00019-2. LC 89-9877.

This work opens with a survey of research on the human body and the individuals who have contributed to our understanding of how it works. The text is then divided into systems, with a detailed explanation of each. The final chapter, "The Body of the Future," looks at the direction in which research is taking us. Diagrams, black-and-white photographs, and an index support the volume. Recommended for middle and high schools. [R: SLJ, Mar 90]

E+

1975   Spence, Annette. **Human Sexuality**. New York: Facts on File, 1989. 124p. $18.95. ISBN 0-8160-1666-6. LC 87-20122.

This volume in The Encyclopedia of Good Health offers clear, straightforward information and frank advice to enable adolescents to make appropriate choices regarding sexual activity. The book explains physical and emotional changes that all teenagers experience and the peer pressure they are likely to encounter. Included are illustrations, a glossary of terms, contact agencies with addresses, and an index. Suggested for ages 10 and up. [R: ARBA 90; BL, Aug 89; BR, Sept/Oct 89]

1976   Treboux, Dominique, and Elizabeth I. Lopez. **T.A.P.P. Sources: A National Directory of Teenage Pregnancy Prevention Programs**. Metuchen, N.J.: Scarecrow, 1989. 557p. $42.50. ISBN 0-8108-2277-6. LC 89-24282.

T.A.P.P. Sources lists over 500 teenage pregnancy prevention programs, arranged by state. For each program the directory provides name, address, affiliation, contact person, type of agency, scope, staff size, years in operation, fees, target population, goals, parental notification requirements, funding sources, services (direct, indirect, and special), and a critical annotation. School-based and family-planning clinics are highlighted.

An introductory chapter describes the major types of pregnancy prevention programs and the approach of each to the issue. Another chapter emphasizes the importance of including teenage sex-role stereotyping in prevention programs. The Women's Action Alliance initiated the Teenage Pregnancy Prevention Program that produced this manual. [R: ARBA 91; RBB, 15 May 90; VOYA, June 90; WLB, May 90]

MEDICINE

1977   **AIDS and Women: A Sourcebook**. Sarah Barbara Watstein and Robert Anthony Laurich, eds. Phoenix, Ariz.: Oryx Press, 1991. 159p. $36.50. ISBN 0-89774-577-9. LC 90-7732.

This volume focuses on women and AIDS. It contains information about this epidemic and its consequences that was gathered from popular and scientific articles, books, brochures, editorials, research reports, and government documents published in the 1980s. Fourteen chapters cover transmission, risk factors, prevention, demographics, occupational issues, and resources for support and education. Also included is information on AIDS and prostitution, women in prison, and specific ethnic groups.

Each chapter opens with a survey of the subject treated, followed by a list of annotated sources. Appendixes include audiovisual resources; hotlines; addresses of organizations that provide information and support services; a glossary; and indexing by author, title, and subject. For high school level. [R: ARBA 92; RBB, 15 Mar 91]

1978   **AIDS: Plague or Panic?** Oliver Trager, ed. New York: Facts on File, 1988. 192p. $29.95. ISBN 0-8160-1938-X.

This useful source, which resulted from the Editorials on File series, consists of editorials on AIDS published in North American newspapers from 1983 to 1987. The reprints are arranged by subject area: research and public health, education, law, American life-styles, and the Reagan administration's response to AIDS. Indexed. [R: BR, Mar/Apr 89; SBF, Sept 89]

1979   **The American Medical Association Encyclopedia of Medicine**. Charles Clayman, ed. New York: Random House, 1989. 1184p. $44.45. ISBN 0-394-56528-2. LC 88-29693.

Recommended for high school level, this excellent work describes (in nontechnical language) diseases, symptoms, conditions, medications, new drugs, tests and procedures, and conflicting or varying opinions. It also defines medical terminology. More than 5,000 entries are arranged in three major sections: "Medicine Today"; "The A to Z of Medicine"; and "Drug Glossary."

The first section provides essays on such topics as staying healthy, prenatal technology, and new diseases. The second and largest defines terms and diseases in alphabetically arranged entries that range from a sentence to three pages. The final part lists some 2,500 generic and brand-name drugs, vitamins, and minerals.

Even the most common complaints (e.g., tiredness, diarrhea, headaches) are discussed in terms of their most likely causes. The articles are supported by over 2,200 2-color illustrations, which include anatomically correct drawings, photographs, charts, and tables. [R: BL, 1 Sept 89; LJ, 15 June 89; WLB, Jan 91]

1980 Bendiner, Jessica, and Elmer Bendiner. **Biographical Dictionary of Medicine**. New York: Facts on File, 1990. 284p. $40.00. ISBN 0-8160-1864-2. LC 89-23604.

This volume contains some 500 biographies of noted individuals involved with biomedical science. Entries, from one paragraph to two pages in length, give information on the biographees' lives but emphasize their contributions to medical science. Louis Pasteur, Sister Kenny, Karl Menninger, Jonas Salk, Benjamin Spock, Elisabeth Kubler-Ross, and the Mayo brothers are all included, as well as many who are not as familiar. The work has a brief bibliography, a chronology, and subject and name indexes. This source will be useful for high school students writing about some aspect of medical history. [R: ARBA 92; BL, 1 Mar 91]

1981 **Black's Medical Dictionary**. 36th ed. C. W. H. Havard, ed. Totowa, N.J.: Barnes & Noble Books, 1990. 750p. $54.50. ISBN 0-389-20901-5.

The latest revision, similar to its predecessors, describes 4,500 medical terms in clear and concise language. Each entry surveys a particular disease and often describes it from the patient's point of view. The work also defines terms drawn from related fields (e.g., genetics, nutrition, speech therapy). This heavy tome, although prepared for physicians, can be understood by intelligent laypersons. Teachers, librarians, and other professionals should have a good medical dictionary available to them; *Black's* is an excellent choice.

1982 Dollinger, Malin, and others. **Everyone's Guide to Cancer Therapy: How Cancer Is Diagnosed, Treated, and Managed on a Day-to-Day Basis**. Kansas City, Mo.: Andrews & McMeel, 1991. 656p. $29.95. ISBN 0-8362-2418-3.

This comprehensive, readable, and authoritative work, which contains the latest research findings, is arranged in four sections: diagnosis and treatment, therapy and management, supportive care, and developments in assessment. Every aspect of cancer is covered, such as early detection, stages of the disease, and risk factors. Appendixes include a glossary of medical terms; a list of anticancer drugs and their side effects; and a directory of cancer centers, associations, and support groups. Highly recommended. [R: LJ, 15 May 91]

1983 Flanders, Stephen A., and Carl N. Flanders. **AIDS**. New York: Facts on File, 1991. 248p. $22.95. ISBN 0-8160-1910-X. LC 90-42577.

AIDS, a volume in Facts on File's Library in a Book series, provides beginning research on this alarming epidemic. Similar to others in the series, such as *Eating Disorders* and *Suicide*, it is arranged in two parts: background information and bibliography.

The volume opens with a history of the disease, followed by a chronology of the last decade of AIDS developments and research. Significant court cases related to the disease and biographies of prominent people associated with the problem complete the first section. The sources section describes a generic library search and contains a bibliographic essay on basic sources and an annotated bibliography of books, articles, government publications, pamphlets and brochures, and audiovisual material. A list of organizations, a glossary of terms related to AIDS, and an index conclude the book. Recommended for high schools. [R: ARBA 92]

1984 Gaffney, Maureen. **Using Media to Make Kids Feel Good: Resources and Activities for Successful Programs in Hospitals**. Phoenix, Ariz.: Oryx Press, 1988. 253p. $39.50. ISBN 0-89774-345-8. LC 86-43113.

This work will help librarians and teachers better understand the needs of children about to be hospitalized or who have just returned from the experience. As the introduction explains, the book stems from a research project on the use of media with hospitalized children in eight hospitals over a four-year period. Sections that follow evaluate the films used, with the researcher's opinion on why a particular film succeeded or failed. Art activities used with the children are described, and a survey of television options given children in Canadian children's hospitals is reported. A glossary, an index, and a bibliography conclude the volume. [R: ARBA 90]

1985 **Laboratory Test Handbook**. 2d ed. David S. Jacobs and others, eds. Baltimore, Md.: Williams & Winkins, 1990. 1244p. $39.95pa. ISBN 0-683-04368-4.

This stout volume describes routine and specialized tests in a uniform format, giving test name and synonyms, patient care recommendations, specimen requirements, reference range, interpretive information, and references to additional data. A glossary of acronyms and abbreviations and an index by key word and subject complete the work. The clear explanations and easy access via cross-referencing and extensive indexing make this an excellent source for persons with little technical knowledge. [R: ARBA 91]

E +
1986 **Learning AIDS 1989: An Information Resources Directory**. 2d ed. Trish Halleron and others, eds. New Providence, N.J.: R. R. Bowker, 1989. 270p. $24.95pa. ISBN 0-9620363-1-5. ISSN 1043-8564.

Prepared by the American Foundation for AIDS Research (AmFAR), *Learning AIDS* evaluates over 1,000 educational items about AIDS that target 21 specific audiences, such as children and adolescents, parents, educators, administrators, counselors, and minorities. Materials reviewed include brochures, pamphlets, videos, instructional programs, posters, and public service campaigns.

The review panel of 35 experts, including health-care professionals and educators, applies the following criteria to each item: accuracy and currency, level of communication and instructional method employed, quality, and overall effectiveness of presentation. Recommended for all levels. [R: ARBA 90; LJ, 1 Sept 89; VOYA, Dec 89; WLB, Nov 89]

E +
1987 **The Marshall Cavendish Encyclopedia of Health**. Angela Sheehan, ed. North Bellmore, N.Y.: Marshall Cavendish, 1991. 14v. $289.95. ISBN 1-85435-203-2. LC 89-17336.

The short volumes (60 pages each) focus on a medical/health topic (e.g., parts of the body, disease) or a mental health problem (e.g., peer pressure, shyness). Most of the 650 articles run from 1 to 5 pages in length, but those on major subjects, such as preventive medicine, are longer. Illustrations, an outstanding feature, appear on almost every double-page spread and include charts, drawings, and color photographs. The readable text makes the set useful for upper elementary through high school levels.

The last volume contains two indexes (one general, the other thematic), a glossary of medical terms, a list of organizations, first-aid instructions, brief biographies of important figures, and landmarks in medical history. The high cost of the set is its principal drawback. Recommended for all levels. [R: ARBA 92; BL, 1 May 91]

1988 Matthews, John R. **Eating Disorders**. New York: Facts on File, 1991. 168p. $21.95. ISBN 0-8160-1911-8. LC 90-40323.

As are other volumes in the Library in a Book series, this one is intended as a starting point for researching a topic. It covers bulimia, anorexia, obesity, and other eating conditions that are especially prevalent among teenagers.

The volume begins with an exposition of the origins and symptoms of eating disorders and then provides the latest information on treatment. It also examines the legal issues involved and supplies an extensive bibliography of articles, books, government publications, pamphlets, brochures, and audio-visual materials. Recommended for high schools. [R: ARBA 92; RBB, 1 May 91]

1989 **Mayo Clinic Family Health Book**. David E. Larson and others, eds. New York: William Morrow, 1990. 1278p. $54.45. ISBN 0-688-09907-6. LC 90-6065.

Designed to "help you better understand your body and your mind and to help you become a more active partner in your health care," this clearly written work provides current, authoritative medical information. The guide is divided into five sections: life cycles, the world around us, keeping fit, diseases and disorders, and modern medical care. The text is supported by sidebar articles, an abundance of drawings, and an index. [R: LJ, Dec 90; WLB, Jan 91]

E +
1990 **The New Child Health Encyclopedia: The Complete Guide for Parents**. By Boston Children's Hospital. Frederick H. Lovejoy, ed. New York: Delacorte Press/Dell, 1987. 740p. $39.95; $19.95pa. ISBN 0-385-29541-3; 0-385-29597-9pa. LC 87-6809.

Parents and professionals responsible for the care of children will welcome this excellent encyclopedia, which is based on the experience and knowledge of the Boston Children's Hospital staff members. The book is arranged in four sections. "Keeping Children Healthy" surveys growth and development; "Finding Health Care for Children" treats the child's hospitalization and visits to the doctor's office; "Emergencies" explains preparations that should be made for possible emergencies; and "Diseases and Symptoms" covers some 300 health concerns, giving signs and symptoms, diagnosis, cause, treatment, and prevention. [R: ARBA 89; LJ, 15 Nov 87]

1991 Nordquist, Joan, comp. **AIDS: Political, Social, International Aspects**. Santa Cruz, Calif.: Reference and Research Services, 1988. 72p. $15.00pa. ISBN 0-937855-19-7.

This pamphlet, part of the Contemporary Social Issues series, lists over 700 publications arranged in 14 sections. Each covers some aspect of AIDS (e.g., minorities, women, children, drugs). Within sections, books, pamphlets, and documents are in one list, with articles in another. Separate chapters cite bibliographies, periodicals, and other works. Most items indexed were published in 1987, but a few appeared in 1986 and 1988. There are no annotations or indexes. [R: ARBA 89]

1992 **The Oxford Companion to Medicine**. John Walton and others, eds. New York: Oxford University Press, 1986. 2v. $125.00/set. ISBN 0-19-261191-7. LC 85-29846.

An authoritative and comprehensive encyclopedia of medicine, this set treats the theory and practice of the profession. Entries vary from short definitions to long surveys. Such topics as medical fields (e.g., psychiatry, forensics), doctor-patient relationships, and ethical practices (e.g., medical experimentation) all receive extensive coverage.

Over 1,000 biographical articles focus on physicians who have achieved distinction or gained recognition outside the field of medicine (e.g., Arthur Conan Doyle, Anton Chekhov). Noted fictitious doctors, such as Dr. Watson, colleague of Sherlock Holmes, also receive attention. Some 5,000 short entries define medical terms, diseases, and drugs. Appendixes identify abbreviations used for medical titles and specializations.

Many Americans appear among the 150 distinguished contributors; nonetheless, the set has a British bias. It is the only work that provides encyclopedic coverage of the field; therefore, it is recommended for high school libraries. [R: ARBA 87; SBF, Sept 87; WLB, Feb 87]

1993 Rothenberg, Mikel A., and Charles F. Chapman. **Dictionary of Medical Terms for the Non-medical Person**. 2d ed. Hauppauge, N.Y.: Barron's Educational Series, 1989. 490p. $8.95pa. ISBN 0-8120-4098-8. LC 88-26266.

A revision of *Medical Dictionary for the Non-Professional* (Barron's Educational Series, 1984), this work defines medical terms and procedures in "plain English." Each main entry (in boldface capital letters) provides part of speech, definition, example of usage, and plural form (if unusual), but does not indicate pronunciation. *See* and *see also* references are frequently used. Each italicized word in the definition is defined in its own main entry. Illustrations are limited to a few diagrams and tables. This is an excellent work for high schools. [R: ARBA 90]

E+
1994 Smallwood, Carol, comp. **Health Resource Builder: Free and Inexpensive Materials for Librarians and Teachers**. Jefferson, N.C.: McFarland, 1988. 251p. $15.95pa. ISBN 0-89950-359-4. LC 88-42639.

This guide identifies organizations that publish free and inexpensive material on physical problems, mental health, and safety. Alphabetically arranged entries for over 200 subjects (e.g., diseases, child safety belts) give the organization's name, address, and telephone number, and a brief description of the type of material it supplies. The work does not cite titles of specific publications.

A separate section classifies the organizations by type of material provided (e.g., audiovisual, pamphlet, indexes). Appendixes list such state and regional offices as Medicare, with address and telephone number; provide a "National Health Observances Calendar"; and identify federal offices that have a hotline or a telecommunication device for the deaf. Indexed. Recommended for all levels. [R: ARBA 89; BL, 1 Jan 89; VOYA, Feb 89]

1995 **The Surgeon General's Report on Nutrition and Health**. New York: Warren, 1989. 128p. $6.95pa. ISBN 0-446-39061-5.

This condensed version of the Surgeon General's report contains a wealth of material that is useful for reports. It begins with a general message from the Surgeon General, followed by a "Summary and Recommendations" section about specific health threats: coronary heart disease; high blood pressure; cancer; diabetes; obesity; skeletal, dental, kidney, and gastrointestinal diseases; infections and immunity; anemia; neurological disorders; behavior; material and child nutrition; aging; alcohol and drug/nutrient interaction; and dietary fads and frauds. The remainder of the volume includes a section on implications for public health policy and 74 pages of 7-day meal plans (e.g., low fat, low sodium) and recipes.

The complete report, published by the Government Printing Office in 1988, is available in reprint form as *The Surgeon General's Report on Nutrition and Health* (Prima Publications, 1988). *The Surgeon General's Report...: Summary & Recommendations* (Government Printing Office, 1988) is also available and could be more useful to high school students than the full report. [R: LJ, 15 May 90]

1996   Thorpy, Michael J., and Jan Yager. **The Encyclopedia of Sleep and Sleep Disorders**. New York: Facts on File, 1990. 298p. $45.00. ISBN 0-8160-1870-7. LC 89-71520.

The first single-volume reference work devoted exclusively to sleep and sleep disorders, this authoritative work, written in clear, nontechnical language, is designed for laypersons and health professionals. Beginning with two general essays on the history of sleep research, the main part of the book is composed of over 800 alphabetically arranged entries that describe technical, common, and slang sleep terminology and that incorporate current information on treatment alternatives.

Many entries include bibliographies that cite professional literature as well as popular magazines, newspapers, and books. Organizations that supply information on sleep disorders, sleep centers and laboratories, and national and international classification of sleep disorders are all listed in the appendix. [R: BL, 1 Jan 91; SLJ, May 91]

E +
1997   **The World Book Health & Medical Annual**. Edited by the staff of *World Book*. Chicago: World Book. annual. $21.95. ISSN 0890-4480.

The first part of this work, a supplement to *World Book Encyclopedia*, covers a number of topics of current interest (e.g., lyme disease, skin cancer, foot care, weight control). The second half focuses on new developments in the health and medical fields. All articles are signed, and many include bibliographies. Terms that may not be understood by the intended audience are defined.

Similar to all *World Book* publications, this one is profusely illustrated. The index to each volume includes the contents of earlier annuals. Written for the same age levels as *World Book*, this work is recommended for junior and senior high schools. [R: ARBA 90; BL, 15 Sept 89]

1998   **The World Book-Rush-Presbyterian-St. Luke's Medical Center Encyclopedia: Your Guide to Good Health**. Chicago: World Book, 1991. 1072p. $39.95. ISBN 0-7166-3236-5. LC 90-71232.

Based on two earlier publications, *World Book Medical Encyclopedia* (1988), and *The World Book Illustrated Home Medical Dictionary* (1980), this excellent work contains some 4,500 concise articles and 1,200 illustrations. The writing is clear and easy to understand, and cross-references and a comprehensive index provide access. Four especially notable appendixes cover the diagnosis of symptoms, health maintenance, nutrition and exercise, and growing older.

The work was developed by the faculty of Rush Medical College in conjunction with the Rush Presbyterian-St. Luke's Medical Center of Chicago, the American Red Cross, and the National Safety Council. Highly recommended for high schools. [R: ARBA 92; LJ, 1 Apr 91]

MENTAL HEALTH

E +
1999   Bernstein, Joanne E., and Masha Kabakow Rudman. **Books to Help Children Cope with Separation and Loss: An Annotated Bibliography. Volume 3**. New Providence, N.J.: R. R. Bowker, 1989. 532p. $44.95. ISBN 0-8352-2510-0. LC 88-7591.

This selective bibliography of books for children (ages 3 to 16) who have experienced loss or separation is a continuation of the 2d edition by Bernstein (R. R. Bowker, 1983). The current list of over 600 fiction and nonfiction titles is divided into 3 parts. Part 1 contains essays that offer insights into the latest research and theories about the effects of separation and loss on the behavior and development of children. It also supplies the principles and practices of bibliotherapy and suggestions for applying them, and interviews with noted writers of children's books on the theme.

Part 2 contains bibliographic citations grouped under 19 headings (e.g., new school, new neighborhood, losing a friend, working parents). For each title the listing includes full bibliographic data, interest and reading level, annotations that describe the book's plot and theme, and an evaluation of its literary and therapeutic strength and weakness. Part 3, designed for adults who wish further guidance and study, is a bibliography of additional references. The appendix includes a directory of support organizations, followed by five indexes: author, title, subject, interest level, and reading level. Highly recommended for all levels. [R: ARBA 90; BL, 15 Apr 89; LJ, 1 Apr 89; VOYA, Aug 89; WLB, Feb 89]

2000   Bruno, Frank J. **The Family Mental Health Encyclopedia**. New York: John Wiley, 1989. 422p. $24.95. ISBN 0-471-63573-1. LC 88-33968.

This volume consists of articles on mental health written in clear, concise language for the layperson. Entries include terms and concepts (e.g., anxiety, stress, addiction), drugs, persons in the field (e.g., Carl Jung), important schools of thought, and movements. Over 700 alphabetically arranged subject entries and 130 name entries range from brief identifications to short articles. When specialized terms are used within an entry, they are italicized and defined at the point of use. Cross-references are generously used. Suggested for high school level. [R: ARBA 90; BL, 1 Sept 89; LJ, 1 Sept 89; SBF, Jan 90]

2001   Cassell, Carol, and Pamela M. Wilson. **Sexuality Education: A Resource Book**. Hamden, Conn.: Garland, 1989. 446p. (Garland Reference Library of Social Science, v.416). $60.00. ISBN 0-8240-7899-3. LC 88-16994.

This work, which describes ways to plan and implement sexuality education, addresses roles, relationships, emotions, and communication. Thirty-eight specialists have contributed clear, nontechnical essays that are arranged in four sections: sexuality education in the family, sexuality education in the schools, sexuality education programs in the community, and model programs. Each section contains essays on specific aspects of the subject. An annotated bibliography classified by type of material and audience, a directory of audiovisual distributors, and an index conclude the volume. [R: ARBA 90; BL, 1 Sept 89; LJ, 15 June 89; VOYA, Dec 89]

2002   Doctor, Donald M., and Ada P. Kahn. **The Encyclopedia of Phobias, Fears, and Anxieties**. New York: Facts on File, 1989. 487p. $45.00. ISBN 0-8160-1798-0. LC 88-31057.

High school teachers and students will find this source beneficial in health classes or any course that studies psychology. Alphabetically arranged entries describe over 2,000 fears, anxieties, and phobias; suggest ways to treat each; and provide brief biographies of noted professionals in the field. Specific phobias are listed under their common and medical names, with the most complete information under the common name. A bibliography of over 2,500 entries and a brief index conclude the volume. [R: ARBA 90; BL, 15 Oct 89; BR, May/June 90]

E +
2003   Spence, Annette. **Stress and Mental Health**. New York: Facts on File, 1988. 110p. $18.95. ISBN 0-8160-1668-2. LC 87-20092.

This volume in the Encyclopedia of Good Health focuses on stress management and introduces the pandemic hazards of the modern world, placing special emphasis on the concerns of today's teenagers. A clear and easy-to-read text, excellent pictures and drawings, and the generous use of cross-references make this a useful guide for students age 10 and up. A glossary of important terms, a bibliography, a list of contact agencies with addresses, and an index complete the volume. [R: ARBA 90; BL, Aug 89; BR, Sept/Oct 89]

2004   Statt, David A. **The Concise Dictionary of Psychology**. 2d ed. New York: Routledge, Chapman & Hall, 1990. 136p. $9.95pa. ISBN 0-415-02662-8. LC 89-10063.

Entries for 1,300 of the most commonly used psychological terms from all schools of the field (e.g., Freudian, behavioral, humanistic, Gestalt) are succinctly defined in this slim volume. The work also covers notable persons in the field. A few illustrations and figures enhance the text. A good purchase for high school libraries. [R: ARBA 91; BL, Aug 90]

2005   Stratton, Peter, and Nicky Hayes. **A Student's Dictionary of Psychology**. London: Edward Arnold; distr., New York: Routledge, Chapman & Hall, 1988. 216p. $49.50; $13.95pa. ISBN 0-7131-6500-6; 0-7131-6501-4pa.

This British work has a few variations in spelling but provides easily understood definitions of basic terms and concepts in psychology. The focus is on definitions only, with no information provided on pronunciation and usage and no biographical entries. This work is not scholarly, but it is accurate and affordable. Those libraries that require more in-depth coverage may wish to consider *The Encyclopedic Dictionary of Psychology* (MIT Press, 1983), or *Encyclopedia of Psychology* (John Wiley, 1984). [R: ARBA 90; BL, 15 Jan 90]

SELF-HELP

See also **Handicapped**.

E+
2006 **The American Medical Association Handbook of First Aid and Emergency Care**. Stanley M. Zydlo, Jr. and J. A. Hill, eds. New York: Random House, 1990. 352p. $8.95pa. ISBN 0-679-72959-3.

Although intended for home use, this first aid and emergency manual deserves a place on the reference shelf of all school library media centers. A general introduction to procedures is followed by an alphabetical section that has entries on diseases and injuries, giving background information, symptoms, a list of what to do, immediate action to take, and continual care. This edition has a new section on the Heimlich maneuver and sports injuries. [R: LJ, Mar 90]

2007 Butler, Kurt, and Lynn Rayner. **The New Handbook of Health and Preventive Medicine**. Buffalo, N.Y.: Prometheus Books, 1990. 450p. $16.95pa. ISBN 0-87975-581-4. LC 90-32513.

This handbook generally offers sound advice to anyone who wants to stay healthy. Designed for the general public, it contains data on health problems and preventive medicine, with major sections devoted to good health habits, common diseases, dietary needs, nutritional value of foods, prescription drugs, and vaccines. As is true of all books that attempt to provide the latest data available, the information has already been superseded by more recent findings. [R: ARBA 91; LJ, July 90]

2008 Cooper, Martin J. **First Aid for Kids: An Emergency Guidebook for Parents**. Deerfield Beach, Fla.: Health Communications, 1991. 58p. $5.95pa. ISBN 1-55874-093-7.

This small guidebook for emergency care is almost a cross between a book and a card file. Written by a paramedic and based on current information, it is intended as a guide for parents and other laypeople who lack formal medical training. It starts with an alphabetical list of emergencies, such as bites, bleeding, and broken bones. Unexpected topics include frostbite and lost children. Under these topics, discussions are brief and to the point, focusing on treatment, although some include a description of the condition or a list of things not to do. The layout, with clear typography and simple instructions, is easy to follow; the instructions are easy to understand. This book should be valuable for parents, babysitters, and other caretakers.

2009 **The Doctors Book of Home Remedies: Thousands of Tips and Techniques....** By the editors of *Prevention Magazine* Health Book. Emmaus, Pa.: Rodale Press, 1990. 676p. $26.95. ISBN 0-87857-873-0. LC 89-38656.

This thorough and well-organized book contains some 2,400 self-help techniques on 138 health conditions and ailments, from acne to yeast infections. Over 500 qualified experts, including doctors and other professionals (e.g., dermatologists, pharmacologists, cosmetologists) give clear, helpful, and scientifically sound advice. Highly recommended for secondary schools. [R: ARBA 91; LJ, 1 Nov 90]

2010 Pinckney, Cathey, and Edward R. Pinckney. **Do-It-Yourself Medical Testing: 240 Test You Can Perform at Home**. 3d ed. New York: Facts on File, 1989. 368p. $24.95; $14.95pa. ISBN 0-8160-1928-2; 0-8160-2085-Xpa.

Tests described in this work range from taking blood pressure and body temperature to more specialized tests that indicate mental ability or personality. Environmental tests, such as those for indoor and outdoor pollution, asbestos, and radon, also are outlined. Information about the tests includes supplies, an explanation of procedure, what different results signify, and what is normal and what is cause for concern. One chapter discusses tests that may be available in the future. [R: ARBA 90; LJ, 1 June 89]

2011 Rees, Alan M., and Catherine Hoffman. **The Consumer Health Information Source Book**. 3d ed. Phoenix, Ariz.: Oryx Press, 1990. 210p. $39.50pa. ISBN 0-89774-408-X. LC 89-16362.

This excellent guide is arranged in three parts. The introductory chapter surveys health information. Part 2 lists clearinghouses, information centers, hotlines, toll-free numbers, and health organizations, all with access data and explanations of their services. Part 3, the largest, covers materials: basic texts, reference books, health magazines, newsletters, and pamphlets. This section also provides descriptive evaluations of 750 books on such subjects as specific diseases, preventive medicine, and general health. Author, title, and subject indexes give access to the book. [R: ARBA 91; BL, 1 May 90]

E +
2012   Spence, Annette. **Exercise**. New York: Facts on File, 1988. 110p. $18.95. ISBN 0-8160-1671-2. LC 87-20207.

Created specifically for teenagers, this volume of the Encyclopedia of Good Health provides coverage of the different methods and regimens for achieving physical fitness through exercise. Written in an interesting, easy-to-read style, the small work includes excellent pictures, drawings, and charts. A glossary, a list of contact agencies with addresses, and an index complete the work. Recommended for ages 10 and up. [R: ARBA 90; BL, Aug 89; BR, Sept/Oct 89]

E +
2013   Thompson, Trisha. **Maintaining Good Health**. New York: Facts on File, 1989. 115p. $18.95. ISBN 0-8160-1667-4. LC 87-22142.

This volume of the Encyclopedia of Good Health addresses overall health care and the importance of establishing good health and hygiene habits at an early age. Organized in a head-to-toe format, it covers basic healthcare concerns for the entire body. Written for ages 10 and up, the small volume is supported by color and black-and-white illustrations, a glossary of health terms, and an index. [R: ARBA 90; BL, Aug 89; BR, Sept/Oct 89]

□ ═══════════════ # Horticulture ═══════════════ □

2014   Beckett, Kenneth A., with the Royal Horticultural Society. **The RHS Encyclopedia of House Plants Including Greenhouse Plants**. Topsfield, Mass.: Salem House; distr., New York: HarperCollins, 1987. 491p. $34.95. ISBN 0-88162-285-0. LC 87-4546.

This beautiful volume contains well-written descriptions of over 3,500 plant species and hybrids in nearly 800 genera. Over 1,000 superb color photographs illustrate this comprehensive source. The text also covers the history of house plants, cultivation, propagation, pests and disease, and bonsai. A glossary of 250 clearly explained terms completes the volume. [R: ARBA 89; BL, 15 Nov 87; LJ, 1 Mar 88; LJ, 15 Apr 88]

2015   Coughlin, Roberta M. **The Gardener's Companion: A Book of Lists and Lore**. New York: HarperCollins, 1991. 496p. $30.00; $14.95pa. ISBN 0-06-271531-3; 0-06-273069-Xpa. LC 89-45643.

The Gardener's Companion, which includes a treasury of gardening information, is filled with a mixture of lists, tips, and lore, covering everything from trees and shrubs to roses and houseplants. One chapter treats special gardens and lists plants found in colonial gardens, seventeenth-century English gardens, and even gardens that flourished in biblical times. Another focuses on flowers that attract birds, bees, and butterflies. This book for all seasons is supported by line drawings, a bibliography, and an index. Recommended for high schools. [R: RBB, 1 May 91]

2016   Creasy, Rosalind. **The Gardener's Handbook of Edible Plants**. San Francisco: Sierra Club Books; distr., New York: Random House, 1986. 420p. $25.00; $12.95pa. ISBN 0-87156-758-X; 0-87156-759-8pa. LC 86-42518.

Adapted from the author's highly praised work, *The Complete Book of Edible Landscaping* (Sierra Club Books, 1982), this handbook covers a variety of vegetables, herbs, fruit and nut trees, shrubs, and vines. Creasy describes each plant, illustrates it with a drawing, and suggests how to grow or buy it and how to use it. A section on planting and maintaining the edible landscape offers advice on soil preparation, starting and caring for plants, and diseases and pests. A glossary and an annotated bibliography conclude the volume. [R: ARBA 87; BL, 15 Oct 86]

2017   Herwig, Rob. **The New Good Housekeeping Encyclopedia of House Plants**. rev. ed. New York: Hearst Books, 1990. 204p. $22.45. ISBN 0-688-09433-3. LC 89-84718.

This encyclopedia, a revision of a 1985 work, contains an alphabetical list of 350 house plants, giving for each the derivation of its genus name, popular names, various species (some as many as 35), description, and suggestions about care (e.g., watering, feeding, humidity, light) and propagation. Over 700 color pictures illustrate the text. Indexed by common and scientific names. This is an excellent guide for the novice and a useful tool for the experienced gardener. Librarians holding the earlier edition, however, need not replace it. [R: BL, 15 Sept 90]

2018 Larousse Gardens and Gardening. New York: Facts on File, 1990. 624p. $35.00. ISBN 0-8160-2242-9. LC 89-45612.

This translation of a 1988 French work is a comprehensive source for novice and expert gardeners. It offers detailed information on all aspects of the subject: greenhouses, soil structure, irrigation, propagation, diseases, pruning, planting, the history of gardening, and design (ranging from flower to rock gardens).

An encyclopedic section, covering at least half the volume, treats trees, shrubs, flowers, vegetables, and ground cover. One chapter provides alphabetical coverage of ornamental shrubs, including information on cultivating each plant. Another section deals with great botanists and garden designers, horticulturists, botanical gardeners, and others in the field. More than 1,000 full-color photographs illustrate the work, and an index by common and scientific name is included. Recommended for high schools. [R: ARBA 91; LJ, 15 May 90; RBB, 15 Sept 90]

2019 Prentice-Hall Pocket Encyclopedia: House Plants. Scarborough, Ont.: Prentice-Hall Canada, 1989. 240p. $12.95pa. ISBN 0-13-711219-X.

This inexpensive guide contains descriptions of 119 leaf/flowering plants, 22 cacti, and 7 bulbous plants. Chapters deal with plant and container selection, arrangement and location, and care. The plant section, arranged alphabetically by Latin name, includes plant requirements (light, humidity, temperature, and moisture), level of difficulty in growing them, and other information about their care. Small color photographs of plants and black-and-white drawings of pests illustrate the volume, which also includes charts of common problems. Indexed by common and Latin names. [R: ARBA 90]

2020 Smith, Miranda, and Anna Carr. Rodale's Garden Insect, Disease & Weed Identification Guide. Emmaus, Pa.: Rodale Press, 1988. 328p. $21.95; $15.95pa. ISBN 0-87857-578-0; 0-87857-759-9pa.

This guide covers over 200 common insects, plant diseases, and weeds. The first section focuses on insects, providing keys (one for the larval and one for the adult stage) that refer the reader to the alphabetical section, arranged by common name. Entries, accompanied by black-and-white illustrations, give range, description, life cycle, feeding habits, and host plants, with information on prevention and control. Color photographs in the back of the volume depict the 50 worst pests and the damage each can cause.

Entries for diseases, categorized by the cause of the problem (e.g., fungus, virus) and arranged alphabetically by common name, provide information similar to that given for insects. Weeds are grouped according to life cycle (annual, biennial, perennial, and woody perennial) and then arranged alphabetically by common name. The extensive coverage of this guide makes it a basic source for horticulture collections. [R: ARBA 89; BL, 15 May 89]

Mathematics

BIBLIOGRAPHIES

E

2021 Roberts, Patricia L. Counting Books Are More Than Numbers: An Annotated Action Bibliography. Hamden, Conn.: Library Professional Publications/Shoe String Press, 1990. 270p. $32.50. ISBN 0-208-02216-3. LC 89-19936.

This bibliography focuses on picture books that introduce children, preschool through second grade, to the concepts and skills of mathematics. The 350 annotated titles each contain bibliographic information; grade level; and a section called "Features," which identifies specific skills and concepts taught or reinforced by the book.

The volume is divided into four chapters: ABC and 1-2-3 books; rhymes (e.g., counting, singing); collections of related objects and stories, arranged by subject; and collections of unrelated objects, arranged by number of items counted. The appendix lists some of the titles by the skill taught (e.g., the concepts of infinity, ordinals). Teachers will find this a useful bibliography. [R: ARBA 91; BL, 15 Mar 90]

2022   Schaaf, William L. **The High School Mathematics Library**. 8th ed. Reston, Va.: National Council of Teachers of Mathematics, 1987. 83p. $7.80pa. ISBN 0-87353-238-4. LC 87-1651.

The 8th edition of this work, which first appeared in 1960 and has been revised every 3 to 5 years since then, is a bibliography of some 1,100 mathematics titles useful on high school and junior college levels. Entries for each title, most published since 1980, include author/editor, title, publisher, year, and paging. For some titles there are brief annotations, and about 300 are starred as suggestions for first purchase. All are arranged under 19 categories: philosophy, history, biography, recreational mathematics, and specific mathematical areas (e.g., algebra, geometry, computer science). Special sections list professional books for teachers, reference materials, and periodicals. [R: ARBA 88]

DICTIONARIES AND ENCYCLOPEDIAS

E+
2023   Bendick, Jeanne. **Mathematics Illustrated Dictionary: Facts, Figures, and People**. rev. ed. New York: Franklin Watts, 1989. 247p. ISBN 0-531-10664-0. LC 89-8977.

The revised edition of this dictionary, which first appeared in 1965, provides succinct explanations of mathematical principles and concepts, and definitions of terms for students in grades 6 through 12. Basic computer terms have been added to this edition, which also has brief biographical sketches of famous mathematicians. Bendick's dictionary is similar to *The Facts on File Dictionary of Mathematics*, but most libraries will need both. Recommended for all levels. [R: ARBA 91; BL, 15 Mar 90; BR, May/June 90]

2024   Downing, Douglas. **Dictionary of Mathematics Terms**. Hauppauge, N.Y.: Barron's Educational Series, 1987. 241p. $8.95pa. ISBN 0-8120-2641-1. LC 87-12565.

Six hundred terms, formulas, and theorems are covered by this softcover volume, which is designed to meet the needs of high school and college students. Areas include algebra, geometry, analytic geometry, trigonometry, probability, statistics, logic, computer math, and calculus. The alphabetically arranged definitions are supplemented by a section on symbols; a list of selected entries arranged into 12 subject categories; and an appendix of tables of logarithms, trigonometric functions, and frequently used distributions. This is a valuable quick-reference source. [R: ARBA 88]

2025   **The Facts on File Dictionary of Mathematics**. rev. ed. Carol Gibson, ed. New York: Facts on File, 1988. 235p. $24.95; $12.95pa. ISBN 0-8160-1867-7; 0-8160-2365-4pa. LC 88-045704.

This basic work contains clear, concise, nontechnical definitions of mathematical terms and a few terms selected from related fields, such as cartography and economics. The intended reader is identified as "anyone who uses mathematics in every day life," but high school students should find it a good quick-reference source. [R: ARBA 89]

2026   James, Glenn, and Robert James. **Mathematics Dictionary**. 4th ed. New York: Van Nostrand Reinhold, 1976. 509p. $32.50. ISBN 0-442-24091-0. LC 76-233.

A mainstay of most mathematical reference collections, this work defines more than 8,000 terms. It also includes tables, formulas, mathematical symbols, and biographical sketches of famous mathematicians. Recommended for high schools.

2027   Karush, William. **Webster's New World Dictionary of Mathematics**. New York: Webster's New World; distr., Englewood Cliffs, N.J.: Prentice-Hall, 1989. 317p. $11.95pa. ISBN 0-13-192667-5. LC 89-5759.

Definitions for 1,422 terms from all the various subfields of mathematics comprise this volume. Most entries are brief, but more complex concepts receive lengthy explanations, followed by bibliographies. Diagrams, tables, equations, and graphs are used throughout the text. Appendixes include a bibliography, tables of mathematical symbols, and trigonometric functions. This work, designed for high school and college students, is comparable to *Facts on File Dictionary of Mathematics*, which is shorter and slightly less technical than *Webster's*.

E+
2028   West, Beverly Henderson, and others. **Prentice-Hall Encyclopedia of Mathematics**. Englewood Cliffs, N.J.: Prentice-Hall, 1982. 683p. $39.50. ISBN 0-13-696013-8. LC 82-5352.

Intended for students from grade 6 upward, this work contains 80 articles arranged alphabetically, algebra to zero. Clearly written essays provide histories, explanations, formulas, and definitions of terms, supported by annotated bibliographies. Seven hundred photographs, drawings, and diagrams illustrate the text. Appendixes contain tables of measures, cubes, roots, and logarithms, and general and biographical indexes give access to the text. This outstanding work is highly recommended for middle and high school libraries. [R: SLJ, Mar 83; WLB, Feb 83]

HANDBOOKS

■ *The Biographical Dictionary of Scientists*. *See* entry 2130.

2029   Burington, Richard S. **Handbook of Mathematical Tables & Formulas**. 5th ed. New York: McGraw-Hill, 1972. $38.68. ISBN 0-07-009015-7. LC 78-39634.

A standard source designed for students and professionals in mathematics and other fields, this work is also useful at the high school level. The first part includes important formulas and theorems of algebra, trigonometry, analytical geometry, calculus, and vector analysis. Tables in the second part cover logarithms; trigometric, exponential, and hyperbolic functions; powers, roots, areas, and so forth; statistics; interest, constants, and conversion factors; and four-place tables. A glossary, an index of numeric tables, and a subject index complete the volume. Other standard handbooks include *CRC Standard Mathematical Tables & Formulas* by William H. Beyer (CRC Press, 1991) and *CRC Standard Mathematical Tables*, edited by William H. Beyer (CRC Press, 1984).

■ *Reading the Numbers*. *See* entry 211.

ACTIVITIES

E+
2030   Paige, Donald L., and others. **The Elementary Math Teacher's Handbook: Activities for Teaching Elementary School Mathematics**. 2d ed. New York: Macmillan, 1982. 394p. $29.95pa. ISBN 0-02-390330-9.

Games and other activities for use in grades 1 through 8 focus on numeration, algorithms, measurement, and geometry. A bibliography of books for teachers and students and articles from *Arithmetic Teacher* are suggested for each topic.

E+
2031   **The World Book of Math Power: Math Skills Builder & Everyday Math**. By the editors of *World Book*. Chicago: World Book, 1990. 2v. Write for price information. ISBN 0-7166-3224-1. LC 90-70044.

This two-volume work is designed for home use by elementary-age children and their parents, but middle school and high school students will also find it useful. The first volume acts as a review of basic mathematical concepts, arranged progressively by level of difficulty. Practical math applications are presentcd in the second volume, ranging from math in the kitchen and workshop to finance. It also contains games, puzzles, symbols, formulas, and tables.

Natural Resource Sciences

CONSERVATION

See also **Earth Sciences**.
See also **Zoology** for endangered wildlife.
See **Geography** for national parks.

2032 **The Conservation Atlas of Tropical Forests: Asia and the Pacific**. N. Mark Collins and others, eds. New York: Simon & Schuster, 1991. 256p. $95.00. ISBN 0-13-179227-X. LC 90-675139.
Introductory chapters summarize government policies and conditions in areas, such as the timber trade and agriculture, that impact the Pacific region's tropical forests. The main body of the work provides surveys and maps of the situation in each of the 18 countries that surround the Pacific, describing the forests, efforts to manage them, rates and causes of deforestation, and wildlife in the areas. A table and color maps for each area depict existing and proposed conservation efforts and land use. Each chapter is illustrated by color photographs and supported by bibliographies of items cited. Indexed by subjects, places, organizations, plants, and animal species. [R: ARBA 92; WLB, Jan 91]

■ *The Greenpeace Book of Dolphins*. *See* entry 2268.

2033 Kreissman, Bern, with Barbara Lekisch. **California: An Environmental Atlas & Guide**. Davis, Calif.: Bear Klaw Press, 1991. 255p. $19.95pa. ISBN 0-9627489-9-4. LC 90-083315. (926 Plum Lane, Davis, CA 95616).
Eighty-one black-and-white maps identify California's significant wildlife refuges, habitats, parks, research areas, and government agencies charged with protecting the environment. Each two-page spread includes a map on the left page and explanations and keys to content on the right. Directories of environmental agencies and private organizations, a bibliography, and an index conclude the volume. The atlas is an important acquisition for California libraries and a useful one for others interested in California's well-developed conservation effort. [R: ARBA 92; WLB, June 91]

2034 **The Last Rain Forests: A World Conservation Atlas**. Mark Collins, ed. New York: Oxford University Press, 1990. 200p. $29.95. ISBN 0-19-520836-6. LC 90-22685.
The tragic destruction of rainforests has prompted the publication of several books on the subject. This work, one of the most beautiful and informative, contains photographs, diagrams, drawings, maps, and a well-written text that explains the problems that confront natives and wildlife. The first five chapters define several types of rainforests, give their locations, and explain how they function and benefit the environment.
The second half of the book treats rainforests in Central and South America, Africa, and Asia in articles that range from 2 to 20 pages and are illustrated by maps that show physical features. The last chapter describes measures underway to reverse or arrest this disastrous trend. Recommended for high schools. [R: SLJ, May 91]

ENERGY

2035 **Dictionary of Energy**. 2d ed. Malcolm Slesser, ed. New York: Nichols/GP Publishing, 1988. 300p. $49.50. ISBN 0-89397-320-3. LC 88-12563.
The intended audience for this work, first published in 1982, consists of students, laypersons, and subject specialists. The 2,350 entries, usually a paragraph in length, are profusely illustrated by line drawings and tables. Although the book was compiled in Great Britain, American terms are included and cross-referenced with their British equivalents. This work is recommended for high schools, but those holding the original edition will not find enough new information to warrant purchase of the revision. [R: ARBA 90; RBB, 1 June 89]

2036 Kruschke, Earl R., and Byron M. Jackson. **Nuclear Energy Policy: A Reference Handbook**. Santa Barbara, Calif.: ABC-Clio, 1990. 246p. $37.00. ISBN 0-87436-238-5. LC 89-18132.

This survey of the history and development of foreign and domestic nuclear energy policy is part of the Contemporary World Issues series. The authors have attempted to present a judicious description of pro and con positions. Chapters include a chronology; biographies of individuals on both sides of the issue; excerpts from important documents, treaties, and speeches; and a directory of organizations. An annotated bibliography of print and nonprint materials, a glossary, and an index conclude the volume. This useful introduction to an important public issue is recommended for high schools. [R: ARBA 92; BL, 15 Nov 90; BR, Nov/Dec 90]

2037   **Oil and Gas Dictionary**. Paul Stevens, ed. New York: Nichols/GP Publishing, 1988. 270p. $78.50. ISBN 0-89397-325-4. LC 88-19626.

Many of the 1,980 entries contained in this dictionary, designed for students, laypersons, and subject specialsits, exceed two pages. The work also includes a 24-page chronology of significant events in the oil and gas industry and 33 pages of statistical data. Entries are illustrated by an abundance of line drawings and tables. [R: ARBA 90; RBB, 1 June 89]

ENVIRONMENT

Atlases

See also **Earth Sciences**.

2038   Burger, Julian. **The Gaia Atlas of First Peoples**. New York: Doubleday, 1990. 191p. $15.95. ISBN 0-385-26653-7.

This unique work focuses on the indigenous peoples of the world, with emphasis on those whose cultures are being threatened by modern society. Major "first peoples" are identified and listed geographically, with their population; lifestyle; and crises created by depletion of forests, mining, military action, or other causes that confront them. The text includes poignant quotations from people facing the loss of their way of life. Lists of organizations working to preserve their traditions and a bibliography conclude the volume. Recommended for high schools. [R: SLJ, May 91]

E +
2039   Middleton, Nick. **Atlas of Environmental Issues**. New York: Facts on File, 1989. 63p. $16.95. ISBN 0-8160-2023-X. LC 88-16239.

This atlas supports the premise that children should be taught about environmental concerns; it is directed toward elementary and junior high school students. It treats specific issues, such as acid rain and alternative energy, in readable, double-page spreads. Some articles cover general topics, such as the impact of modernization and industrialization on the environment. The Chernobyl nuclear accident and other events illustrate the essays. Colorful pictures and maps are used throughout the volume. [R: ARBA 90; RBB, 1 Nov 89]

2040   **Rand McNally Children's Atlas of the Environment**. Skokie, Ill.: Rand McNally, 1991. 79p. $14.95. ISBN 0-528-83438-X. LC 91-9395.

An abused environment is a sorry legacy to bequeath. For the younger generation to continue the fight to restore the Earth, they need to understand the issues involved. *Rand McNally Children's Atlas of the Environment* is a wonderful tool to foster that understanding. Colorful maps, illustrations, and photographs help to enlighten as well as to brighten the pages.

The book is divided into three sections. The first looks at the Earth as a balanced system. The topics covered are the effect of the Sun; our changing topography, water, air, vegetation, and population; and how we use the land. The next section looks at the same basic areas and the damages we have inflicted. The final section deals with specific geographical areas — recognition of the problems and how they are being dealt with on a global level. The material is well written, providing enough information to cover the topic without overwhelming the intended audience. Italicized words within the text are defined in the glossary. The second and third sections include "How can we help?" windows. These are not simple things a child can do as a school project; rather, they deal with the topic on a complete scale.

The drawbacks of this book are few. The subject index could be strengthened, and the index to major places on maps is rather confusing. Other than that, this is a fine atlas, fun to look at and filled with information.

2041 **World Wildlife Fund Atlas of the Environment**. Geoffrey Lean and others, eds. New York: Prentice Hall Press, 1990. 192p. $29.95; $19.95pa. ISBN 0-13-050469-6; 0-13-050436-Xpa. LC 90-35903.

Each of the 42 chapters of this atlas covers a specific topic related to the environment. Text, tables, and thematic maps in color explain the interaction of humans with the world's land and resources. Among the subjects covered are acid rain, nuclear energy, animal migration, forests, food production and consumption, agrochemicals, wildlife trade, and fisheries. The text gives background, explains current practices, and projects future results (unless changes are made). This atlas, produced by the World Wildlife Fund, will help students understand the life-and-death significance of environmental issues. [R: WLB, Mar 91]

Bibliographies

E +
2042 **Environmental Resource Directory. September 1990**. Toronto: Public Focus, 1990. 180p. $50.00 looseleaf w/binder.

This bibliography will help primary and secondary teachers find materials for classroom purposes. Organized by subject and then format (e.g., pamphlets, books, kits, magazines), each entry gives approximate level of usefulness, bibliographic and order information, and other relevant facts. The work, of course, emphasizes Canadian publications, but many of the materials will interest teachers and students in the Great Lakes area and in other northern regions of the United States. [R: ARBA 91]

Dictionaries

2043 Allaby, Michael. **Dictionary of the Environment**. 3d ed. New York: New York University Press; distr., New York: Columbia University Press, 1989. 423p. $75.00. ISBN 0-8147-0591-X. LC 88-19184.

This dictionary defines technical terms specific to the study of the environment and terms from science in general, making it a useful reference tool for the high school collection. Written in nontechnical language, the entries also cite relevant government agencies, voluntary organizations, important regulations, and significant environmental disasters (for which Allaby provides a table of dates, locations, and details). There are numerous cross-references. [R: ARBA 90; BL, 15 Sept 90; SBF, Sept/Oct 89]

Directories

2044 Jessup, Deborah Hitchcock. **Guide to State Environmental Programs**. 2d ed. Washington, D.C.: BNA Books, 1990. 700p. $48.00pa. ISBN 0-87179-655-4. LC 90-33867.

A new edition of *Guide to Environmental Programs*, this work is current through December 1989. Entries for environmental programs, arranged alphabetically by state, describe the program and give contact person, address, telephone number, organizational structure, and priorities. Also supplied are the address and telephone number of the Emergency Response Commission for hazardous spills and the governing body for utility activities. Appendixes provide addresses for the Environmental Protection Agency, the Army Corps of Engineers, state and local agencies, and states that have decentralized programs. [R: ARBA 91]

2045 Seredich, John, ed. **Your Resource Guide to Environmental Organizations**. Irvine, Calif.: Smiling Dolphin Press, 1991. 514p. $15.95pa. ISBN 1-879072-00-9. LC 90-091949. (4 Segura, Irvine, CA 92715).

Descriptions of 150 national and international nonprofit environmental organizations comprise this directory. A two- to four-page entry for each gives its purpose, programs, accomplishments, publications, and membership benefits. Addresses and telephone numbers of federal and state agencies are also included. [R: ARBA 92; LJ, 15 June 91]

Handbooks

2046 Altman, Roberta. **The Complete Book of Home Environmental Hazards**. New York: Facts on File, 1990. 290p. $24.95; $12.95pa. ISBN 0-8160-2095-7; 0-8160-2419-7pa. LC 89-39982.

The three sections of this work are "Environmental Hazards Inside the House" (the largest part), "Environmental Hazards Outside the House," and "Buying a Environmentally Sound House." The volume includes the latest information on radon, asbestos, lead, water, pesticides, formaldehyde, nuclear power and weapons plants, and hazardous waste sites. Each section describes the problem, effects on people, regulations, testing, and solutions. Maps locate hazardous waste and nuclear power plant sites. Each chapter concludes with a state-by-state list of government agencies and consumer groups to contact for further information. [R: ARBA 92; BL, 1 Sept 90; LJ, 1 June 90]

2047 **The Atmosphere Crisis: The Greenhouse Effect and Ozone Depletion**. Eleanor Goldstein and others, eds. Boca Raton, Fla.: Social Issues Resources Series, 1989. $85.00 looseleaf. $16.00/annual update. ISBN 0-89777-841-3. ISSN 1043-5972. (P.O. Box 2348, Boca Raton, FL 33427-2348).

High school libraries that need current materials on environmental problems will find this looseleaf service an excellent source. One hundred reprints of articles, one to three pages long and drawn from government documents, professional journals, and naitonal print media that appeared between 1981 and 1989, report worldwide events and opinions. The update adds 20 articles each year. Recommended for high schools. [R: BL, 1 Nov 89; BR, Nov/Dec 89; SLJ, May 90; VOYA, Apr 90]

2048 Corbitt, Robert A. **Standard Handbook of Environmental Engineering**. New York: McGraw-Hill, 1990. 1v. (various paging). $89.50. ISBN 0-07-013158-9. LC 89-12400.

Designed for laypersons, this volume addresses a variety of environmental topics: water use, including quality, wastewater disposal, conservation, and waterborne diseases; air quality; stormwater management; solid waste; and hazardous waste. The information is advanced but clearly written in nontechnical language. The work also cites additional sources. [R: ARBA 91]

2049 **The Earth Report: The Essential Guide to Global Ecological Issues**. Edward Goldsmith and Nicholas Hildyard, eds. Los Angeles, Calif.: Price Stern Sloan, 1988. 240p. $19.95; $12.95pa. ISBN 0-89596-673-0; 0-89596-678-1pa. LC 87-21451.

This is an excellent source for students and teachers concerned about our world's environment, from *accepted daily intake* to *zero population growth*. Part 1 consists of a number of essays by recognized authorities on major ecological issues, explaining the problems and what can be done about them. Part 2 contains some 400 shorter encyclopedia-like articles, arranged alphabetically, on other environmental topics. Generous use is made of internal and end-of-entry cross-references, charts, and graphs. This work, a storehouse of information despite its small size, is highly recommended for high schools. [R: ARBA 89; SLJ, June 89; VOYA, Feb 89]

2050 **Environmental Trends**. By Council on Environmental Quality. Washington, D.C.: Government Printing Office, 1989. 152p. $17.00. S/N 041-011-0084-0.

This reference tool depicts the American environment in colorful, graphic form. Statistics and projects cover minerals, energy, water, climate, air quality, land resources, wetlands, wildlife, park population, transportation, and environmental risks and hazards. Some statistical tables span a century or more. Numerous maps, charts, and other material support the text. [R: LJ, 15 May 91]

2051 **Fighting Toxics: A Manual for Protecting Your Family, Community, and Workplace**. Gary Cohen and John O'Connor, eds. Washington, D.C.: Island Press, 1990. 349p. $31.95; $19.95pa. ISBN 1-55963-013-2; 1-55963-012-4pa.

This manual, sponsored by the National Toxics Campaign Fund, stresses the need to prevent pollution rather than clean up what has already occurred. "Turning the Toxic Tide," the first section, introduces the concept of citizen involvement in regulating and monitoring industrial toxics. "Toxics and the Law" summarizes statutes and covers individual rights and ways to campaign for legislation. "The Ultimate Solution" treats pollution prevention. A resource section concludes the volume. Suggested for secondary level. [R: SBF, Oct 90]

2052 **In Praise of Nature**. Stephanie Mills, ed. Washington, D.C.: Island Press, 1990. 288p. $22.95; $14.95pa. ISBN 1-55963-035-3; 1-55963-034-5pa. LC 90-33875.

Reviews of some 100 books with an environmental message comprise this volume. The reviews are divided into five sections: "Earth," "Air," "Fire," "Water," and "Spirit." Some of the works included are from well-known authors (e.g., Rachel Carson, Aldo Leopold, George Orwell), while others are lesser known. Most of the reviews conclude with a passage quoted from the book. Next, over 100 books are briefly annotated. This is an excellent source for high school science and social studies classes. [R: LJ, 1 Nov 90]

2053   Miller, E. Willard, and Ruby M. Miller. **Environmental Hazards: Air Pollution: A Reference Handbook**. Santa Barbara, Calif.: ABC-Clio, 1989. 250p. $39.50. ISBN 0-87436-528-7. LC 88-39233.
This outstanding work provides objective treatment of the serious effects of air pollution on our planet, discussing historical, natural, and human causes of the hazards. Special features include a summary of federal regulations, a directory of organizations involved in air pollution problems, and a bibliography of primary and secondary source information. The comprehensive index refers to subject information in the bibliography and the text. [R: ARBA 90]

2054   Miller, E. Willard, and Ruby M. Miller. **Environmental Hazards: Radioactive Materials and Wastes: A Reference Handbook**. Santa Barbara, Calif.: ABC-Clio, 1990. 298p. $37.00. ISBN 0-87436-234-2. LC 90-34159.
The use of radioactive materials by our society has both positive and negative consequences. Radiation is used in medicine for diagnosis and treatment, and nuclear power is a less-expensive source of energy. But the dangers of atomic weapons, fear of another Chernobyl, and the safe handling and disposal of radioactive waste all present problems.
This work offers a comprehensive and unbiased treatment of the nature of radiation: its natural and manmade sources, emergency planning and preparedness, effects on health, exposure standards, a history of nuclear development, disposal, and international control of radioactive waste. The volume also contains an extensive bibliography that includes a list of audiovisual materials. [R: ARBA 91; BL, 15 Sept 90; LJ, 15 Apr 90; SLJ, May 91]

2055   Steger, Will, and J. Bowermaster. **Saving the Earth: A Citizen's Guide to Environmental Action**. New York: Alfred A. Knopf/Random House, 1990. 352p. $24.95. ISBN 0-394-58431-7. LC 89-43366.
Each chapter in this excellent work, which is a beginning text on ecology, covers a different environmental issue. Solutions to reverse harmful trends are offered, followed by suggested readings and lists of interest groups from whom additional information can be obtained. Reproducible, copyright-free illustrations, maps, charts, diagrams, and black-and-white photographs are appended. Indexed. Highly recommended for middle and high schools. [R: BL, 1 May 90; BR, Nov/Dec 90; LJ, 15 Apr 90]

2056   **World Resources, 1990-1991**. By the World Resources Institute and the International Institute for Environment and Development Staff. New York: Oxford University Press, 1990. 384p. $29.95; $17.95pa. ISBN 0-19-506228-0; 0-19-506229-9pa.
The 24 chapters of this work, the third in a continuing series on natural resources, cover such global topics as human settlement, food and agriculture, oceans and coasts, human population and health, and energy. Within each topic, current data and trends are presented in graphs and tables arranged by country. This particular volume emphasizes Asia. [R: RBB, 15 Sept 90; SBF, May/June 89; SBF, Nov/Dec 90]

Yearbooks

2057   **The Earth Care Annual**. Russell Wild, ed. Emmaus, Pa.: Rodale Press with National Wildlife Federation; distr., New York: St. Martin's Press. annual. $17.95pa.
In this work, reprints of articles from American periodicals (e.g., *Wall Street Journal*, *Organic Gardening*, *Christian Science Monitor*) focus on solutions to environmental problems. The arrangement is by broad subject, such as acid rain and wildlife. Appendixes describe the proper disposal of hazardous household waste and provide a directory of national environmental groups. This is a useful source for any high school library, especially one that has a limited periodical collection. [R: BL, 15 Mar 90; LJ, 1 Mar 90; LJ, 15 Sept 90; SBF, Oct 90]

NATURAL HISTORY

See **Birds** in **Zoology** for **Birding**.

2058   Allaby, Michael. **The Oxford Dictionary of Natural History**. New York: Oxford University Press, c1985, 1986. 688p. $45.00. ISBN 0-19-217720-6. LC 85-13758.
Intended for students and amateur naturalists, this dictionary defines over 12,000 terms, with emphasis on the scientific names of plants and animals worldwide. It also includes terms from botany; zoology; and related areas such as ecology, statistics, earth sciences, atmospheric sciences, biochemistry, and genetics. Cross-references connect common and scientific names.

This work provides broader coverage than the *Cambridge Illustrated Dictionary of Natural History* but lacks illustrations. It is suitable for advanced high school students. [R: ARBA 87; RBB, 15 Oct 86]

2059 Attenborough, David, and others. **The Atlas of the Living World**. Boston: Houghton Mifflin, 1989. 220p. $39.95. ISBN 0-395-49481-8. LC 89-675210.
    Highly recommended for middle and high school levels, this profusely illustrated volume examines the physical, biological, and environmental processes that shape the Earth and its future. In five major sections, two-page essays cover specific topics such as tropical rain forests, acid rain, and the origins of life. Beautiful photographs, black-and-white drawings, charts, maps, diagrams, and other illustrations enhance the book.
    One section, entitled "A Catalog of Life," has special reference value because it contains diagrams that depict the plant, animal, and vertebrate kingdoms and lists threatened animals and plants. A subject index also gives access to illustrations and maps. In general, the volume has greater value as a resource for student reports than as a reference tool. [R: BL, 1 Jan 90; LJ, 15 Mar 90; WLB, Dec 89]

2060 Benyus, Janine M. **The Field Guide to Wildlife Habitats of the Eastern United States**. New York: Simon & Schuster, 1989. 336p. $24.95; $14.95pa. ISBN 0-671-68203-2; 0-671-65908-1pa. LC 88-37243.

2061 Benyus, Janine M. **The Field Guide to Wildlife Habitats of the Western United States**. New York: Simon & Schuster, 1989. 336p. $24.95; $14.95pa. ISBN 0-671-68204-0; 0-671-65909-Xpa. LC 89-5975.
    These popularly written field guides explain the natural history of woodland and waterway habitats in the eastern and western United States. The text profiles wildlife habitats, such as salt marshes, lakes and ponds, grassy fields, and oak-hickory forests. For the west, it describes rocky coasts, mountain meadows, and redwood forests.
    Each habitat includes a two-page illustration of selected plants and animals; a chart of wildlife refuges, national parks, and similar locations; a exposition of how animals have adapted to the environment; tables of characteristic plants; charts that give nesting and feeding areas for many species; and other information useful to the beginning naturalist.
    Other features include "Resources for the Curious," which lists nature organizations and further readings on natural history. Detailed indexes and glossaries of common and scientific names of plants and animals conclude each volume. Recommended for junior and senior high school levels. [R: ARBA 91]

2062 Benyus, Janine M. **Northwoods Wildlife: A Watcher's Guide to Habitats**. Minocqua, Wis.: NorthWord Press, 1989. 453p. $19.95pa. ISBN 1-55971-003-9. LC 85-13758.
    This guidebook to flora and fauna of the northwoods that border Lake Superior and Lake Michigan addresses 18 habitats, such as woodland ponds and sedge meadows. Each section describes how the habitat originated, how it has changed over time, and the animals it has attracted.
    Other features include a chapter on the best locations for wildlife watching during certain times of the year (e.g., breeding, migration, nest building, hibernation); a wildlife-events calendar; lists of volunteer and educational opportunities, seminars, and preservation groups; and a selective bibliography for further reading. Indexed. Recommended for middle and high schools, especially those located in Minnesota, Wisconsin, Michigan, and other states in the region. [R: ARBA 90]

2063 Durrell, Gerald, and Lee Durrell. **The Amateur Naturalist**. New York: Alfred A. Knopf, 1983. 320p. $29.95. ISBN 0-394-53390-9. LC 83-47940.
    This guide to observing nature is designed for young adults. The lavishly illustrated work describes 17 nature walks in the woods, along the shore, in marshlands, and even in one's own backyard. Projects, techniques, and equipment are carefully explained. Indexed. Recommended for middle and high school collections. [R: BL, 1 Dec 83]

2064 Lincoln, R. J., and G. A. Boxshall. **The Cambridge Illustrated Dictionary of Natural History**. New York: Cambridge University Press, 1987. 413p. $27.95. ISBN 0-521-30551-9. LC 87-8018.
    Cambridge successfully addresses the needs of a nonscholarly audience for the meaning of terminology related to "the rich diversity of living organisms and their habitats." The clear and concise definitions of technical terms in natural history, illustrated by 700 line drawings, are appropriate for advanced high school students. This work is more selective in its coverage of terminology than *The*

Oxford Dictionary of Natural History, but it contains illustrations, which the *Oxford Dictionary* does not. [R: ARBA 88; BL, 1 Mar 88; WLB, Nov 87]

2065 The Official World Wildlife Fund Guide to Endangered Species of North America. David W. Lowe, ed. Washington, D.C.: Beacham, 1990. 2v. $195.00/set. ISBN 0-933833-17-2.

This work focuses on 500 plants and animals the federal government has defined as endangered or threatened. Volume 1 covers plants and mammals; volume 2 deals with birds, fish, insects, and other species.

Two-page entries contain a location map; black-and-white photographs; a table of basic data (e.g., habitat, food, reproduction, status of the species); an essay on the species' behavior, current distribution, and steps being taken for its preservation; a brief bibliography; and directory information for the appropriate endangered-species office. Each volume contains a glossary, color photographs, and an index. Due to its science fair potential, this set is recommended for secondary school libraries. [R: BL, 15 May 90; VOYA, Aug 90; WLB, Sept 90]

E+
2066 World Nature Encyclopedia. Milwaukee, Wis.: Raintree, 1989. 24v. plus paperbound cumulative index. $485.00/set. ISBN 0-8172-3325-3.

Originally published in Italy in 1985, this beautiful collection of monographs on natural history covers the entire world, with equal treatment given to all regions. The editors, ignoring political boundaries, divided areas biogeographically, with the result that some countries receive coverage in more than one volume.

Volumes entitled *The Mediterranean*, *Mountains of Europe*, *Southeast Asia*, and so forth, can be used independently of each other. Information focuses on the interrelationship of people, plants, and climate in each region. Each work begins with a survey of the region, followed by chapters on specific areas, plants, and animals. "A Guide to Areas of Natural Interest" that describes the special features of national and state parks and reserves is included in each volume, along with a glossary and an index. Over 1,300 beautiful, large color photographs and 700 drawings, charts, and maps support the volume. A separate cumulative index covers the set.

Similar sets include *The Living Earth* (Grolier, 1975), which is much shorter and grouped by biomes rather than geographical regions, and *Grzimek's Animal Life Encyclopedia*. The latter work contains more information on animals but does not cover their interrelationship with people and geography. Recommended for grades 6 and up. [R: BL, 15 May 89; LJ, 15 May 89; SLJ, May 89]

2067 Zim, Herbert S., and Lester Ingle. Seashores: A Guide to Animals and Plants along the Beaches. rev. ed. Racine, Wis.: Western Publishing, 1989. 160p. price not reported. ISBN 0-307-24496-2. LC 61-8318.

This is a welcome revision of a popular 1955 guide to seashores. Scientific and common names have been updated, but most illustrations remain the same. The guide provides an excellent introduction to seashore life and can be used to identify the most common invertebrates and plants. Its size, of course, prohibits comprehensive coverage. Western also publishes several regional guides, such as *Seashore Animals of the Southeast*. [R: ARBA 91]

□ _____ **Pets** _____ □

GENERAL

See also **Mythology and Folklore**.

E
2068   Chrystie, Frances N. **Pets: A Complete Handbook on the Care, Understanding and Appreciation of All Kinds of Animal Pets**. 3d ed. Boston: Little, Brown, 1974. 269p. $16.95. ISBN 0-316-14051-1. LC 73-21819.
   This standard of many years is suitable for elementary school students, its intended audience. For common pets, such as dogs, cats, fishes, birds, horses, and a few small wild animals, the work gives advice on care and handling, diseases, and basic first aid. [R: ARBA 75]

E+
2069   Felder, Deborah G. **The Kids' World Almanac of Animals and Pets**. New York: World Almanac/St. Martin's Press, 1989. 288p. $14.95; $6.95pa. ISBN 0-88687-556-0; 0-88687-555-2pa.
   This entertaining book contains interesting and useful facts about all animals, but emphasizes farm and domestic species. It includes evolutionary and taxonomic information, myths and lore, historical facts, habits, breeds, diet, and basic care. Dogs, cats, and horses receive the most attention, but the author does not neglect wild animals around the world. Suggested for reference and circulating collections in elementary and middle school media centers.

E+
2070   Fox, Michael. **The New Animal Doctor's Answer Book**. rev. ed. New York: Newmarket Press, c1984, 1989. 320p. $14.95pa. ISBN 1-55704-035-4. LC 84-6973.
   Questions collected from the author's practice as a veterinarian and columnist for *McCall's* magazine are answered with sound and sympathetic advice. Many of the inquiries focus on common health problems of animals, but some indicate unusual concerns. Fox also discusses the physical needs of pets and provides insights into the psychology of animal behavior. The volume covers birds, cats, dogs, fishes, gerbils, guinea pigs, and some less common pets. Recommended for elementary and middle schools.

E+
2071   Losito, Linda, and others. **Pets and Farm Animals**. New York: Facts on File, 1989. 96p. $17.95. ISBN 0-8160-1969-X.
   This book, a volume in the highly recommended Encyclopedia of the Animal World, gives students in grades 4 through 9 fresh appreciation of familiar animals—dogs, cats, horses, rats, hamsters, goldfish, cattle, pigs, reindeer, ducks, and geese. Its text is enlivened by over 200 full-color illustrations. [R: RBB, July 90; SLJ, May 90]

E
2072   Simons, Seymour. **Pets in a Jar: Collecting and Caring for Small Wild Animals**. New York: Puffin Books, 1985. 95p. $5.95pa. ISBN 0-14-049186-4. LC 74-14905.
   Children in grades 4 through 6 will enjoy this handy guide, which explains how to care for small creatures such as ants, worms, crickets, tadpoles, and other pets often kept in jars. Brief information on each concerns their needs, anatomy, breeding, and other basic information, along with warnings about overcollecting.
   Insect Pets by Carla Stevens (Greenwillow, 1978) is a similar work, also recommended for elementary level. *Our Small Native Animals* by Robert Snedigar (Dover, 1963) tells how to house skunks, turtles, chipmunks, toads, and a wide variety of snakes, lizards, and small mammals.

AQUARIUMS

2073   Axelrod, Herbert R., and others. **Dr. Axelrod's Mini-Atlas of Freshwater Aquarium Fishes**. Neptune, N.J.: T. F. H. Publications, 1987. 992p. $29.95. ISBN 0-86622-385-1.

The introduction provides an extensive list of symbols to assist the aquarium owner—how to identify the sex of fish; their feeding, habits, and reproduction; and aquarium lighting, temperature, pH of the water, and so forth. The work's outstanding feature is the 1,800-plus beautiful full-color photographs of fish. Each caption gives the fish's scientific name and symbols already identified in the introduction.

"Aquarium Maintenance, Plants, and Fish Breeding," a 250-page section, explains how to set up and maintain an aquarium. Color illustrations show fish diseases, plants, and breeding and birthing phases. Separate indexes cover the aquarium management section and the section on fish. This is a basic work on the topic.

The 3d edition of *Dr. Axelrod's Atlas of Freshwater Aquarium Fishes* (T. F. H. Publications, 1989), a more advanced work, includes over 4,500 color photographs. [R: ARBA 89; BL, 1 Dec 87]

2074 Burgess, Warren E., and others. **Dr. Burgess's Atlas of Marine Aquarium Fishes**. Neptune City, N.J.: T. F. H. Publications, 1988. 736p. $69.95. ISBN 0-86622-896-9.

This pictorial handbook on saltwater fish identification is profusely illustrated with over 4,000 photographs and 560 color plates. The work also includes a guide to maintaining marine fish, a systematic list of the families of fishes of the world, lists of scientific and common names and their equivalents, and a conversion table of weights and measures. Useful for reference and circulation, it will serve as a worthy companion to *Dr. Axelrod's Atlas of Freshwater Aquarium Fishes* (T. F. H. Publications, 1989), and, no doubt, will become a standard. [R: ARBA 90; BR, Mar/Apr 89; RBB, 15 Jan 89]

2075 McInerny, Derek, and Geoffry Gerard. **All about Tropical Fish**. 4th ed. New York: Facts on File, 1989. 480p. $29.95. ISBN 0-8160-2168-6. LC 88-84026.

The first 12 chapters of this guide (last revised in 1966) describe how to set up and care for an aquarium. The remaining chapters focus on popular species, such as neon tetras, mollies, catfish, and swordtails, and exotic species, such as angel fish and Siamese fighting fish. For each fish, the work describes physical features, color, identification of males and females, personality, tank requirements, breeding, and raising of young. Illustrations are numerous but *Dr. Axelrod's Mini-Atlas of Freshwater Aquarium Fishes* is better illustrated and provides more detailed information. *All about Tropical Fish*, is a commendable, if not outstanding, book; it deserves consideration. [R: ARBA 90; BL, 1 Mar 90; BR, May/June 90]

CAGE BIRDS

2076 Vriends, Matthew M. **Simon & Schuster's Guide to Pet Birds**. New York: Simon & Schuster, 1985. 11.95pa. ISBN 0-671-50696-X. LC 84-1331.

Vriends' guide describes 206 kinds of birds; makes suggestions on choosing one as a pet; and discusses their care, diet and nutrition, housing needs, and diseases. Data on each bird includes classification, characteristics, habitat and distribution in the wild, and behavior patterns, plus other information such as color, whether they sing or talk, food preferences, and whether they should be housed singly or in pairs. The text is illustrated with excellent photographs.

CATS

E+
2077 Kelsey-Wood, Dennis. **The Atlas of Cats of the World: Domesticated and Wild**. Neptune City, N.J.: T. F. H. Publications, 1989. 384p. $59.95. ISBN 0-86622-666-4.

This encyclopedic work about cats covers their natural history, psychology, nutritional needs, care, and breeding. Also included are 31 wild cats of the world, with such things as classification, nomenclature, distribution, size, and strength. The easy-to-read, informative text is arranged by subject and is supported by some 350 beautiful photographs, most of which are of superior quality. A bibliography and index complete the volume. [R: ARBA 91; BL, 1 Feb 90; LJ, Dec 89]

2078 Pugnetti, Gino. **Simon & Schuster's Guide to Cats**. New York: Simon & Schuster, 1983. 255p. $23.95; $10.95pa. ISBN 0-671-49167-9; 0-671-49170-9pa. LC 83-12634.

Pugnetti devotes a large part of this book to general information on cats—their history, treatment in literature and art, personality traits, psychology, social and family life, and care. The remaining sections describe 40 breeds, giving their origins, physical characteristics, environmental needs, special care, strengths and weaknesses, and other useful information. Color-coded symbols indicate adaptability to a leash, how vocal, whether a good mouser, and similar characteristics. Each breed is illustrated with one or more color photographs. A glossary explains terms. [R: ARBA 85; BL, 1 Feb 84]

E +
2079 Stephens, Gloria. **Legacy of the Cat**. San Francisco, Calif.: Chronicle Books, 1990. 136p. $29.95; $14.95pa. ISBN 0-87701-728-X; 0-87701-695-Xpa. LC 89-70862.

From Abyssinian to Turkish Van, this work profiles 37 breeds of domesticated cats, providing information on their origins, breeding, temperament, showing, and judging. A two-page spread for each breed includes outline drawings of the head and body and beautiful, full-color action photographs. The text also suggests which cats are best suited to apartment living and gives tips on cat care and reproduction. Recommended for reference and browsing. [R: ARBA 91; BL, 15 Dec 90; SLJ, Dec 90]

E +
2080 Taylor, David, with Daphne Negus. **The Ultimate Cat Book**. New York: Simon & Schuster, 1989. 192p. $29.95. ISBN 0-671-68649-6. LC 89-6097.

This guide to 100 varieties of domesticated cats covers basic subjects, such as behavior, origins, grooming, health, first aid, and diet, and gives tips on showing cats, reproduction, and other subjects. Each breed, divided into two alphabetical sections (longhair and shorthair), is concisely described and illustrated by 750 superb full-color photographs. Extensive diagrams, charts, and tables provide information on birthing, maternal behavior, and kitten development. Taylor is a British veterinarian, and Negus is an editor of *Cat World International* magazine. A circulating copy is recommended along with one for reference. [R: ARBA 91; LJ, Dec 89]

DOGS

2081 **The Complete Dog Book**. 17th ed. By the staff of the American Kennel Club. New York: Howell Book House, 1985. 768p. $22.95. ISBN 0-87605-463-7. LC 85-4296.

The official American Kennel Club guide, this work describes standards for 129 breeds, arranged by dog groups: sporting, hounds, working, terriers, and nonsporting. Standards include general appearance, head, neck and chest, legs and feet, tail, coat, movement, weight, and height at shoulders, with statements about disqualifying deviations. Entries provide a brief history of each breed. A large section offers advice on dog care and first aid. [R: BL, 15 June 85]

2082 **The *Reader's Digest* Illustrated Book of Dogs**. Pleasantville, N.Y.: Reader's Digest Books, 1989. 334p. $24.95. ISBN 0-89577-340-6.

This highly recommended book for students in grades 7 through 12 includes a general history of dogs, clues to identifying different breeds, and 2-page descriptions of 145 breeds. For each one the work gives origin, countries where it is registered, nicknames, characteristics (e.g., temperament, general suitability), and appearance. Each breed is illustrated by a full-color photograph. Charts provide information on requirements such as exercise, grooming, and feeding. [R: BL, 1 Jan 90; BR, Mar/Apr 90]

E +
2083 White, Kay. **Pet Owner's Guide to Dogs**. New York: Howell Book House, 1986. 160p. $12.95. ISBN 0-87605-769-5. LC 86-27325.

The first part of this owner's guide addresses the human/dog relationship, the responsibility of pet ownership, and points to consider in buying a dog. The second section treats 58 breeds, providing a color photograph and description of each that details size, color, growing requirements, average life span, health problems, positive and negative characteristics, and related breeds. The last section covers care from puppyhood to mature dog. Indexed. Recommended for all levels. [R: ARBA 88]

2084 Wilcox, Bonnie, and Chris Walkowicz. **Atlas of Dog Breeds of the World**. Neptune City, N.J.: T. F. H. Publications, 1989. 912p. $100.00. ISBN 0-86622-899-3.

This excellent compilation provides the history and evolution of some 400 breeds of dogs recognized by the American Kennel Club, as well as many that are not. For all breeds, there are lengthy descriptions that include personality, size, coat type, and breed origin. Large color photographs of adult dogs and puppies, sometimes several for a breed, illustrate the volume. Both browsers and those seeking information about a specific breed will find this an outstanding source. [R: ARBA 91; BL, 15 Sept 89; WLB, Sept 89]

SNAKES

■ *The Completely Illustrated Atlas of Reptiles and Amphibians for the Terrarium*. *See* entry 2277.

2085 Mattison, Chris. **A-Z of Snake Keeping**. New York: Sterling Publishing, 1991. 143p. $24.95. ISBN 0-8069-8246-2. LC 90-10178.

As the title suggests, topics are arranged alphabetically, encyclopedia style. An entry for a snake species (e.g., *Constrictor constrictor*, listed with the Boas) gives its characteristics and distribution as well as information for keeping the snake. In addition to listings for selective snake species, the reader will find topics on snake cages, diseases, egg-laying, feeding, humidity, incubating eggs, and selective breeding. The book is richly illustrated with photographs, most in color. It concludes with a selective list of magazines and journals from Europe, North America, Australasia, and Africa that can assist the snake keeper. Also included are indexes of snakes by their Latin and common names. The book is very attractive, and the information provided is valuable to readers from middle school through high school. [R: ARBA 92]

Physics

■ *The Biographical Dictionary of Scientists*. *See* entry 2130.

2086 Boorse, Henry A., and others. **The Atomic Scientists: A Biographical History**. New York: John Wiley, 1989. 472p. $27.95. ISBN 0-471-50455-6.

This work consists of profiles of individuals who contributed to the history of atomic theory from about 100 B.C. to the present. These well-researched and readable essays survey the history of this important field. Highly recommended for high school libraries. [R: SBF, Jan/Feb 90]

■ *CRC Handbook of Chemistry and Physics*. *See* entry 1852.

2087 **Encyclopedia of Physics**. 3d ed. Robert Besancon, ed. New York: Van Nostrand Reinhold, 1985. 1278p. $51.95pa. ISBN 0-442-00522-9.

This outstanding work is designed for readers on three levels. Articles on the main divisions of physics are intended for readers with little background on the subject; those on the subdivisions of physics are aimed at readers with a background in the field; and those on very specific topics are geared to advanced readers who have a sound physics background. This authoritative work includes some 350 signed articles, most with bibliographies. Cross-references and an index provide access.

Encyclopedia of Physics, edited by Rita G. Lerner and George L. Triggs (Addison-Wesley, 1981), another useful work, serves as a ready-reference for students and nonscientists.

2088 **The Facts on File Dictionary of Physics**. rev. ed. John Daintith, ed. New York: Facts on File, 1988. 235p. $24.95; $12.95pa. ISBN 0-8160-1868-5; 0-8160-2366-2pa. LC 88-045703.

This readable dictionary clearly and concisely defines the most important and commonly used terms (almost 2,000) in all fields of physical science, including solid-state and quantum physics. Fifty line drawings illustrate complex physical concepts. This dictionary is an excellent choice for high school libraries. [R: ARBA 89; SBF, May/June 89; BR, May/June 89]

E +
2089 Lampton, Christopher. **Super-Conductors**. Hillside, N.J.: Enslow, 1989. 95p. $14.95. ISBN 0-89490-203-2. LC 88-31562.

Designed for young readers from upper elementary school through high school, this work explains the concept of superconductors in easy-to-understand language. The text is supported by an excellent glossary, black-and-white photographs and drawings, a bibliography for further reading, and an index. [R: BL, 1 Dec 89]

2090 **McGraw-Hill Encyclopedia of Physics**. Sybil P. Parker, ed. New York: McGraw-Hill, 1983. 1343p. $82.50. ISBN 0-07-045253-9. LC 82-21721.

Much of the text is reprinted from *McGraw-Hill Encyclopedia of Science and Technology*, but many articles were written especially for this large volume. Articles, varying in length from a few lines to long essays, tend to be descriptive and easily understandable by the general reader; some, however, require a degree of scientific background. Some 1,000 black-and-white illustrations—drawings, tables, and charts—support the text. [R: ARBA 84; BL, 15 Feb 84; SBF, Mar/Apr 84; WLB, June 83]

Science in General

BIBLIOGRAPHIES

E +

2091 **The Best Science Books and AV Materials for Children: An Annotated List of Science and Mathematics Books, Films, Filmstrips, and Videocassettes**. Susan M. O'Connell and others, eds. Washington, D.C.: American Association for the Advancement of Science, 1988. 335p. $20.00. ISBN 0-87168-316-4. LC 88-10575.

This work includes all materials recommended for children from kindergarten through junior high school in *Science Books & Films* between 1982 and 1988. Science experts prepared the original evaluations. The entries for over 800 books and more than 400 films, videos, and filmstrips in this compilation include complete bibliographic and order information, appropriate grade level, and a concise annotation. This book is recommended as long as the period covered by the list is taken into account.

This work was formerly titled *AAAS Science Book List* and directed toward junior and senior high school level. It is still available, but it should be used with great caution since many of the books it lists will be dated. [R: ARBA 89]

E +

2092 **Educators Guide to Free Science Materials**. Randolph, Wis.: Educators Progress Service. annual. $26.25.

This annual describes some 1,700 films, filmstrips, slides, audio and video tapes, and printed matter in the life and physical sciences. An annotation indicates the scope, purpose, and utility of each. Most items are free, but some are available only on loan. Recommended for all levels.

E +

2093 Kennedy, DayAnn M., and others. **Science & Technology in Fact and Fiction: A Guide to Children's Books**. New Providence, N.J.: R. R. Bowker, 1990. 319p. $35.00. ISBN 0-8352-2708-1. LC 89-27374.

2094 Kennedy, DayAnn M., and others. **Science & Technology in Fact and Fiction: A Guide to Young Adult Books**. New Providence, N.J.: R. R. Bowker, 1990. 363p. $35.00. ISBN 0-8352-2701-3. LC 90-32121.

These new guides provide selection information about fiction and nonfiction books for children and young adults on space, aeronautics, computers, robots, and a wide range of other scientific and technical topics. *Children's Books* focuses on recommended books for preschool through age 12; *Young Adult Books* recommends titles for grades 7 through 12. The authors, in consultation with teachers and librarians, chose titles from resources reviewed in standard review media, such as *Appraisal, Children's Literature Association Quarterly*, and *School Library Journal*. Choices are based on literary quality, scientific accuracy, clarity in writing style, appropriateness of topic and illustrations, coordination of text and illustrations, and scope of material.

For each recommended work, the entry gives a summary, evaluation, reading level, and order information. These volumes offer sound advice in selecting books on scientific topics for young people. [R: ARBA 91; RBB, 1 Apr 90; RBB, 15 Oct 90; WLB, June 90]

E +
2095   **The Museum of Science and Industry Basic List of Children's Science Books**. By Bernice Richter and Dwane Wenzel. Chicago: American Library Association. annual. $11.95.

Since 1973, the Museum of Science and Industry in Chicago has held an annual Children's Science Book Fair, featuring the best trade books published that year for children K-12. The initial work consists of books featured in the Fair during its first 12 years, 1973-1984. Since that time, the list has been updated by annual supplements.

All lists, identical in format and criteria, arrange books by broad subject (e.g., animals, astronomy, aviation/space). Citations give full bibliographic data, grade level as suggested by the publisher, a rating of the book's quality and appropriateness, an annotation of around 50 words, and references to reviews in major evaluation tools. Additional sections cite sourcebooks for adults, a directory of publishers, science magazines for children, review journals, science education journals, and author/title indexes.

E +
2096   Schroeder, Eileen E., comp. **Science Education**. Phoenix, Ariz.: Oryx Press, 1986. 103p. (Oryx Science Bibliographies, v.6). $18.75pa. ISBN 0-89774-277-3. LC 86-42578.

Science Education lists and annotates journal articles about teaching science, elementary grades through high school. The 337 entries examine a variety of issues (e.g., teacher education, teaching methodologies, sex-related differences in science achievement) and are arranged in chapters according to the educational level served, special interests, and specific subjects. Most entries cite articles published between 1980 and 1985. Noncritical annotations are appended to key essays. Indexed by author. [R: ARBA 87]

2097   **Science and Technology Annual Reference Review**. H. Robert Malinowksy, ed. Phoenix, Ariz.: Oryx Press. annual. $55.00. ISSN 1041-2557.

STARR, the acronym by which this work is known, provides an annual review of the best science and technology books. The series has grown from 602 titles covered in the first annual in 1989 to some 800 in the 1991 edition. Each entry provides standard bibliographic data and a signed evaluation by a librarian—special, college, public, or school, depending on the level of the work.

Entries are arranged alphabetically by broad subject, subdivided into specific topics and then by type of source (e.g., handbooks, manuals, dictionaries). The critical reviews, 200-500 words, are indexed by title, author/editor, subject, and type of library. High schools may wish to consider the STARR series. [R: ARBA 90; BL, 1 June 89]

■ *Science Books & Films*. *See* entry 8.

E +
2098   **Science for Children: Resources for Teachers**. By the National Science Research Center. Washington, D.C.: National Academy Press, 1988. 176p. $9.95pa. ISBN 0-309-03934-7. LC 88-25445.

This guide, based on the premise that children learn best through observation and experimentation, provides access to a large collection of science materials. The three sections cover core materials for the science curriculum; activity books, resources for teachers, and magazines; and sources for further information, including museums, professional societies, and suppliers. Entries provide a full citation, the grade level, the price, and a descriptive annotation that often includes evaluative remarks. Indexed. Science teachers for grades K-8 will find this a helpful resource, but they must be alert to dated information. [R: ARBA 90; LJ, 15 Mar 89]

CHRONOLOGIES

2099   Asimov, Isaac. **Asimov's Chronology of Science and Discovery**. New York: Harper & Row, 1989. 768p. $29.95. ISBN 0-06-015612-0. LC 89-45024.

There are other excellent chronologies, but this one is unique. A special section places the scientific achievement within the context of concurrent social, political and social events; it supplements brief descriptions of each year's landmark scientific developments. Both positive and negative results of the contributions or discoveries are presented. A quick-reference timetable of over 4,000 years of discovery and an excellent index further enhance this easy-to-use, reliable book. Recommended for secondary schools. [R: BL, 15 Feb 90]

2100   Hellemans, Alexander, and Bryan Bunch. **The Timetables of Science: A Chronology of the Most Important People and Events in the History of Science**. updated ed. New York: Simon & Schuster, 1991. 672p. $19.95pa. ISBN 0-671-73328-1.

The Timetables of Science begins in 2,400,000 B.C. ("Hominids in Africa manufacture stone tools") and ends with events in late May 1988, with 10,000 significant scientific developments, events, and famous scientists in between.

The book is divided into nine major time periods, determined by events important to the evolution of science. Each section is prefaced by a geographical, political, and cultural survey of the era. Entries vary from very brief to some 80 words. About 100 essays scattered throughout the volume focus on special topics (e.g., classic volcanoes). Indexed by name and subject. This is an excellent reference work for high schools.

2101   **The History of Science and Technology: A Narrative Chronology**. New York: Facts on File, 1988. 2v. $160.00/set. ISBN 0-87196-477-5. LC 88-26052.

High school mathematics and science teachers who assign research projects on scientists and their discoveries will want this work for their students. The set surveys scientific development from prehistoric times to 1900 in volume 1, and from 1900 to 1970 in volume 2.

Within each volume, the chronological narrative is divided into segments from centuries to decades and then by specific branches of science. The set recounts all noteworthy discoveries, inventions, developments, milestones, theories, and breakthroughs. Despite some vocabulary problems due to the use of undefined technical terms, this is a useful, if not essential, set for advanced high school students. [R: ARBA 90; BR, Sept/Oct 89]

DICTIONARIES AND ENCYCLOPEDIAS

2102   **Album of Science**. I. B. Cohen, ed. New York: Scribner's, 1978-1989. 5v. $375.00/set. ISBN 0-684-19074-5.

This five-volume set contains a vast collection of pictures that show what society believed to be scientific facts at various times in Western history. Chapter introductions, summaries of major discoveries, sketches of influential scientists, and informative captions accompanying the pictures constitute the only text.

Volumes are chronologically arranged, beginning with *Antiquity and the Middle Ages*, and progressing to *Physical Science in the Twentieth Century*. The types of illustrations move from reproductions of engravings, woodcuts, drawings, and paintings in early science to black-and-white photographs in modern times. Each volume includes an annotated bibliography of suggested readings and an index. The set is designed for college students, but high schools may want to consider it for science and social studies classes. [R: ARBA 90; BR, Jan/Feb 90]

2103   Barnhart, Robert K., with Sol Steinmetz. **Hammond Barnhart Dictionary of Science**. Maplewood, N.J.: Hammond, 1986. 740p. $24.95. ISBN 0-8437-1689-4. LC 86-045735.

This work bridges the gap between overly simplified and highly technical general science dictionaries; therefore, it is well suited to high school use. Alphabetically arranged entries for over 16,000 terms drawn from the physical and biological sciences were selected by prominent scientists and scholars who collaborated with the staffs of the Hammond Company and Barnhart Books. For each term, the entry gives the pronunciation, part of speech, field of study in which it is used, definition, an illustrative sentence to help clarify meaning, the word's origin, and *see also* references to related terms.

With its clear definitions that range from basic to erudite terminology, this outstanding work is highly recommended. It is not as comprehensive as *McGraw-Hill Dictionary of Scientific and Technical Terms*, but it provides more information about each term. [R: ARBA 87; BL, 1 Mar 87; WLB, Mar 87]

E
2104   Brown, Robert, and Brian Jones. **Exploring Space**. Milwaukee, Wis.: Gareth Stevens, 1990. 64p. $12.95. ISBN 0-8368-0029-X. LC 89-11278.

E
2105   Harrison, Virginia, and Steve Pollock. **The World of Animals**. Milwaukee, Wis.: Gareth Stevens, 1990. 64p. $12.95. ISBN 0-8368-0028-1. LC 89-11357.

E
2106   Jones, Brian. **Space Exploration**. Milwaukee, Wis.: Gareth Stevens, 1990. 64p. $12.95. ISBN 0-8368-0004-4.

E
2107   Pollock, Steve. **Animal Life**. Milwaukee, Wis.: Gareth Stevens, 1990. 64p. $12.95. ISBN 0-8368-0003-6. LC 89-11367.
These four volumes are a part of two reference series: My First Reference Library (*Exploring Space* and *The World of Animals*), designed for children in grades 2 and 3; and Gareth Stevens Information Library (*Animal Life* and *Space Exploration*) for children in grades 4 through 6. Other volumes will be released through 1993. Each volume includes 25-30 2-page articles; more than 80 color photographs, drawings, and sketches; a glossary; and an index. Information boxes of unusual or special facts accompany most articles.
Libraries need not hold both series. The Gareth Stevens Information Library is preferable, since My First Reference Library is a scaled-down version of much of the same information. [R: BL, 1 June 90; SLJ, Sept 90]

2108   Ecker, Ronald L. **Dictionary of Science and Creationism**. Buffalo, N.Y.: Prometheus Books, 1990. 263p. $32.95. ISBN 0-87975-549-0. LC 89-63832.
This dictionary presents the pro-evolution position in the creationist-evolutionist controversy. Concise, nontechnical articles provide an "overview of all scientific areas that relate to evolutionary theory." Each entry presents the scientific position and the author's understanding of the creationist interpretation, often referring to works in the extensive bibliography. Not only does the dictionary define terms used by each side but it also cites court cases, such as the Scopes trial, Edwards vs. Aguillard, and McLean vs. Arkansas. Teachers, administrators, and school board members will welcome this volume. [R: ARBA 91; BL, 1 May 90]

2109   **The Encyclopedic Dictionary of Science**. Candida Hunt and Monica Byles, eds. New York: Facts on File, 1988. 256p. $35.00. ISBN 0-8160-2021-3. LC 88-16396.
Written by a team of experts, this comprehensive dictionary of 7,000 entries covers physics, chemistry, environmental sciences, biology, and medicine; it also includes 850 brief biographies of important scientists. *Van Nostrand's Scientific Encyclopedia* has more entries, but the *Dictionary* has other features, such as 50 pages of colorful illustrations. High school students familiar with scientific concepts will appreciate this erudite reference tool. [R: ARBA 89; BR, May 89; SBF, May/June 89]

2110   **McGraw-Hill CD-ROM Science and Technology Reference Set**. New York: McGraw-Hill, 1987. 1 CD-ROM disc, 1 floppy disk, manual. System requirements: IBM-PC, XT, AT, or compatable; 640K RAM; DOS 2.0 or higher; CD-ROM player. $300.00.
This highly recommended electronic set provides access to over 7,000 articles in the *McGraw-Hill Concise Encyclopedia of Science and Technology* and to the 98,599 terms and 115,000 definitions in the *McGraw-Hill Dictionary of Scientific and Technical Terms*. The system, which is easy to install and use, permits the user to search by key word or phrase, browse, read, print, or copy entries to other files. The dictionary can be accessed at any time to define words found in the text. Recommended for high schools requiring broad coverage of information on engineering technology and life, physical, and earth sciences.

2111   **McGraw-Hill Concise Encyclopedia of Science & Technology**. 2d ed. Sybil P. Parker, ed. New York: McGraw-Hill, 1989. 2222p. $110.00. ISBN 0-07-045512-0. LC 88-33275.
The *Concise* (but heavy) single-volume abridgment of the 20-volume *McGraw-Hill Encyclopedia of Science and Technology* is designed for libraries and individuals that do not require or are unable to afford, the full set. It contains 7,000 entries (400 more than the first edition) that cover most areas of the physical and biological sciences, engineering, and technology.
For the most part, explanatory paragraphs, a feature of the full set, have been cut and definitions condensed. Nonetheless, rewritten articles preserve the essence of the original. A number of tables and illustrations have been retained, and new appendixes provide excellent bibliographies for over 130 topics, information about scientific online databases, and much more.

Van Nostrand's Scientific Encyclopedia, the closest competitor of the *Concise*, provides greater depth in its coverage, but there are enough differences between the two to warrant having both in most high schools. Highly recommended. [R: ARBA 90; BR, Sept/Oct 89; LJ, Aug 89; WLB, Sept 89]

2112 **McGraw-Hill Dictionary of Scientific and Technical Terms**. 4th ed. Sybil P. Parker, ed. New York: McGraw-Hill, 1989. 2088p. $95.00. ISBN 0-07-045270-9. LC 88-13490.
Reflecting the growth of scientific knowledge, this edition adds 7,600 new terms to those treated in the 3d edition (1984), bringing the total to 100,000, with 117,500 definitions. Each entry provides pronunciation (new to this edition), a concise definition, and a tag that indicates its subject field. Well-illustrated, with at least one picture per page, the dictionary contains extensive appendixes, such as the International System of Units, the periodic table, mathematical tables, tables of signs and symbols for various fields, schematic symbols, and historical chronologies. Recommended for high schools. [R: ARBA 90; BL, 1 June 89; SBF, Sept/Oct 89; WLB, Feb 89]

2113 **McGraw-Hill Encyclopedia of Science and Technology**. 6th ed. New York: McGraw-Hill, 1987. 20v. $1,600.00/set. ISBN 0-07-079292-5. LC 86-27422.
Last revised in 15 volumes in 1982, this comprehensive encyclopedia has added five volumes to its present edition. Articles added number 400; 500 have been deleted and 1,600 revised, bringing the total to 7,700. Areas that received major revision include computers, nuclear engineering, psychology, tele-communication, and genetics, but all 28 main subject fields reflect extensive updating. Easy-to-understand and readable entries contain numerous cross-references. The set is profusely illustrated by 900 new and 2,000 revised illustrations, bringing the total to some 15,000.
Signed articles by well-known scientists, many of whom are Nobel prize winners, are written in pyramid style, beginning with a definition and expanding from basic to detailed information. The last volume is arranged in four parts: the contributors, scientific tables and style notations, a topical index, and an extensive analytical index.
The *McGraw-Hill Yearbook of Science & Technology* updates the set. The 7th edition has been announced for April 1992. High school libraries unable to afford the full set should hold the *McGraw-Hill Concise Encyclopedia of Science & Technology*. [R: ARBA 88; BL, 15 Sept 87; LJ, Aug 87; WLB, Sept 87]

E +
2114 **The New Book of Popular Science**. Danbury, Conn.: Grolier, 1990. 6v. $199.50/set. ISBN 0-7172-1216-5. LC 89-23494.
This set, recommended for school libraries that serve students from upper elementary through high school levels, covers major topics in all fields of science. This edition (the eighth revision) reflects the major breakthroughs, discoveries, and developments of the last several years (e.g., AIDS, drug abuse, earthquakes, endangered species, smoking and health, waste disposal). Complex concepts and difficult theories are thoroughly explained in a readable style and attractive format.
The areas covered by each volume are indicated on the spine: astronomy, space science, computers, and mathematics; earth sciences, energy, and environmental sciences; physical sciences and biology; plant and animal life; mammals and human sciences; and technology. Several illustrations on each page – photographs (both black-and-white and color) and artists' renderings – all ably illustrate the text. Clear diagrams accompany the description of many complex concepts. Selected readings support each section, and an index of 8,200 entries provides access to specific topics.
Science materials in this set are available in other sources, such as *World Book Encyclopedia*, but its practical organization and attractive format make it a desirable purchase for school libraries. [R: ARBA 92]

2115 Schnelder, Herman, and L. Schnelder. **The Harper Dictionary of Science in Everyday Language**. New York: Harper & Row, 1988. 352p. $25.00. ISBN 0-06-015950-2.
The dictionary defines the most commonly used scientific words and phrases in language a layperson can understand. Cross-references to broader definitions are used throughout the well-illustrated volume. A good choice for secondary schools. [R: SBF, Sept/Oct 89]

2116 Uvarov, E. B., and Alan Isaacs. **The Facts on File Dictionary of Science**. 6th ed. New York: Facts on File, 1986. 468p. $24.95. ISBN 0-8160-1386-1. LC 85-27425.
Continuing the tradition of excellence established by previous editions published under the title *Penguin Dictionary of Science*, this work focuses on the basic vocabulary of physics, chemistry, mathematics, astronomy, biochemistry, biophysics, and molecular biology. The almost 7,000 clear and

concise entries vary from 50 to 200 words. Appendixes cover such topics as conversion factors, the solar system, elements, constants, differential coefficients, and electromagnetic radiation. This praiseworthy dictionary is recommended for senior high school level. [R: ARBA 87; BL, 15 Jan 87; BR, Mar/Apr 87; SBF, Jan 87]

2117 **Van Nostrand's Scientific Encyclopedia**. 7th ed. Douglas M. Considine, ed. New York: Van Nostrand Reinhold, 1989. 2v. $195.00/set. ISBN 0-442-21750-1. LC 88-10601.

This standard encyclopedia and its closest competitor, *McGraw-Hill Concise Encyclopedia of Science & Technology*, are highly recommended for high school libraries. The 7th edition reflects significant changes in many scientific disciplines since the last revision (1982). Some of the fields that have been extensively updated are genetics, astronomy, telecommunications, computers, robotics, and high-energy physics.

The new edition (in two easy-to-handle volumes, instead of its former unwieldly, single volume) contains 4,000,000 words, 500 tabular summaries, almost 3,000 illustrations, and a detailed index of over 100 pages. A concise summary introduces each entry, which then expands into a detailed essay. The extensive coverage of this set makes it a first choice for high school libraries. Those who must choose between *McGraw-Hill Concise* and this work should select *Van Nostrand's*, due to its greater depth of coverage. [R: ARBA 90; SBF, May/June 89]

E +
2118 **The World of Science**. New York: Facts on File, 1984-1987. 25v. $15.95/v.; $319.00/set. ISBN 0-8160-1563-5.

The titles in this series, designed for children ages 8 to 12, provide basic scientific concepts and theories for specific topical areas. Each volume includes some 130 photographs, illustrations, and diagrams; a two-page glossary; and an index. Recommended as beginning level reference works for elementary and middle schools.

The titles in the series are *Astronomy, The Beginning of Life, Birds, Cold-Blooded Animals, Communications and Transports, Computers: An Introduction, Disease and Medicine, Great Discoveries and Inventions, How Does It Work? How Everyday Things Work, Insects and Their Relatives, The Invisible World, Mathematics, Plants, Projects, Seas and Oceans, Through the Microscope, Warm-Blooded Animals, Weather and Its Work, Working with Computers, The World before Man, The World Beneath Us*, and *The World Today*. [R: ARBA 86; BL, 15 Mar 87; BR, May/June 86]

HANDBOOKS AND YEARBOOKS

2119 Emiliani, Cesare. **The Scientific Companion: Exploring the Physical World with Facts, Figures, and Formulas**. New York: John Wiley, 1988. 287p. $14.95pa. ISBN 0-471-62484-5.

This highly recommended work provides a broad survey of science and is an excellent reference work for science teachers and their students. The 12 chapters cover basic physics and chemistry, the Sun, stars, galaxies, the solar system, plants, geology, and more. Written in an informal style, the text includes information on the latest developments, historical notes, and boxed definitions of terms. An abundance of tables deals with such topics as characteristics of planets, constants of nature, conversion factors, chemical elements, and isotopes. Numerous diagrams and illustrations enhance the text. Indexed. For high school level. [R: ARBA 89; SBF, Jan/Feb 89]

2120 **The Facts on File Scientific Yearbook**. Margaret DiCanio, ed. New York: Facts on File. annual. $29.95. ISSN 0883-0800. LC 85-642413.

This series of yearbooks, which began in 1985, reviews the previous year's scientific accomplishments. Covering a wide variety of topics, each annual offers easy-to-understand articles on key achievements and developments. The 1991 yearbook consists of articles on 29 subject areas grouped into 3 sections: life science, earth and space science, and physical science and mathematics. The appendix lists winners of major scientific awards and prizes for the year. For high school level. [R: ARBA 92; BR, Jan 90; SBF, Feb 89]

2121 **Isaac Asimov's Book of Science and Nature Quotations**. Isaac Asimov and Jason A. Shulman, eds. New York: Weidenfeld & Nicolson, 1988. 360p. $19.95. ISBN 1-555-84111-2. LC 87-22489.

This compendium of science and nature quotations is arranged by scientific disciplines (e.g., aeronautics) and more general areas (e.g., errors, facts, the origin of life). Quotations, from the eleventh century B.C. to the present, are arranged chronologically in each category either by the birthdate of the person quoted or the date of the quotation. The work does not give published sources but identifies persons cited by profession and dates. Although not an essential purchase, it adds interest to the science reference collection. [R: ARBA 90]

2122 **McGraw-Hill Yearbook of Science & Technology**. Compiled by the staff of the McGraw-Hill Encyclopedia of Science & Technology. New York: McGraw-Hill. annual. $80.00. ISSN 0076-2016. LC 62-12028.

Designed as a supplement to the *McGraw-Hill Encyclopedia of Science & Technology*, this yearbook reviews the past year's scientific and technical achievements. Alphabetically arranged articles cover virtually all fields of the natural and physical sciences. Since the entries treat recent developments only, users must rely on the main set for historical information. A detailed index and extensive black-and-white photographs, diagrams, and charts enhance the annual's utility. Recommended for high schools. [R: ARBA 91]

2123 Roberts, Royston R. **Serendipidy: Accidental Discoveries in Science**. New York: John Wiley, 1989. 270p. $12.95pa. ISBN 0-471-60203-5.

High school students writing papers and teachers who wish to enliven their lectures will find this excellent volume useful. It contains diverse stories of accidental discoveries in medicine, chemical elements, astronomy, and technologies. Among them are teflon, DNA, antibodies, and safety glass. The well-written articles are supported by black-and-white photographs and drawings. Highly recommended. [R: BR, Jan/Feb 90]

E +
2124 **Science Year: A Review of Science and Technology**. Robert O. Zeleny, ed. Chicago: World Book. annual. $29.95. ISSN 0080-7621. LC 65-21776.

This annual science supplement to *World Book Encyclopedia* focuses on topics of interest to students from elementary through high school levels. The main part of the 1990 yearbook consists of 14 detailed, signed articles on significant topics in science (e.g., giant mammals, an archaeological excavation, garbage disposal). The short, alphabetically arranged articles that follow focus on developments in scientific fields, from agriculture to zoology. Other sections have scientific topics from a consumer viewpoint, biographies of prominent scientists, science awards of the year, and a necrology. Recommended for middle and high schools. [R: ARBA 90; BL, 15 Sept 89; BR, May 90]

E +
2125 Williams, Brian, and Brenda Williams. **The Random House Book of 1001 Wonders of Science**. New York: Random House, 1989. 160p. $11.99. ISBN 0-679-80081-8. LC 89-3954.

This excellent work is organized into nine sections: atoms, the elements, electricity, light and sound, energy and motion, space and time, the Earth, inventions, and transportation. Each section, in turn, is divided into specific topics. Information, presented in question-and-answer format, is concise and comprehensive. Each page includes several illustrations, photographs, and diagrams. Indexed by subject. Recommended for ages 7 to 12, but useful for junior high level as well. [R: SBF, Nov/Dec 90]

2126 **Yearbook of Science and the Future**. David Calhoun, ed. Chicago: Encyclopaedia Britannica. annual. $32.95. ISSN 0096-3291. LC 69-12349.

This yearbook consists of feature articles that survey many areas and brief essays that summarize activities in specific fields. The 1991 volume describes remote sensing devices used by archaeologists, recent space explorations, and the physics of roller coasters. Other articles treat mollusks, the principles of physical science, and activities of the Space Telescope Institute.

Beautiful illustrations are frequently used. All articles are signed and supported by bibliographies for further reading. The subject index is a three-year cumulation. This authoritative and attractive source is recommended for the advanced high school level. [R: ARBA 91]

INDEXES

2127 **General Science Index**. Bronx, N.Y.: H. W. Wilson, 1978- . monthly (except June and Dec.) with quarterly and annual cumulations. sold on service basis. Available May 1984 to date online, CD-ROM, and tape. CD-ROM $1,295.00/yr.

Designed to meet the needs of public, high school, and undergraduate libraries, this is a subject index to 109 English-language periodicals. Plain-language subject headings provide students and others unfamiliar with scientific terminology easy access to articles of interest. There is some overlap with *Readers' Guide to Periodical Literature* its model, but this is an important reference source for high school libraries.

RESOURCE MATERIAL

2128 **SIRS Science**. Boca Raton, Fla.: Social Issues Resources Series. annual. 5v. $80.00/v. 42x microfiche included. also available on CD-ROM.
SIRS Science is a series of five annual volumes that provide relevant, current information on major scientific topics. Each volume contains 70 reprints of articles from newspapers, magazines, government publications, and journals, all chronologically arranged. The set addresses earth, physical, life, medical, and applied science. An index in each volume gives access to the entire set. New books are published in October. [R: BR, Mar/Apr 86]

BIOGRAPHY

2129 **American Men and Women of Science: A Biographical Directory of Today's Leaders in Physical, Biological and Related Sciences**. 18th ed. New providence, N.J.: R. R. Bowker, 1992. 8v. $750.00/set. ISBN 0-8352-3074-2. LC 06-7326.
AMWS, published since 1906, currently contains 125,000 entries, giving basic biographical data and career highlights for engineers and scientists in the physical, biological, and related sciences. Inclusion is based on criteria of education/achievement, publication, or position. Indexed by discipline.
AMWS is available online through Dialog, File 236, and through ORBIT Search Service as File AMWS. It can also be obtained as part of SciTech Reference Plus, a CD-ROM service.

2130 **The Biographical Dictionary of Scientists**. David Abbott, gen. ed. New York: Peter Bedrick Books; distr., New York: HarperCollins, 1984-1986. 6v. $28.00/v.
The six volumes in this series focus on astronomers, biologists, chemists, physicists, mathematicians, and engineers and inventors who have made significant contributions to their respective fields. The 180 sketches of 1 or 2 pages in each volume are designed for high school students and college undergraduates. The narratives emphasize the scientists' historical importance, with a brief survey of their lives and careers. Most entries include a photograph or portrait. Supportive features include cross-references, a glossary of terms, and a name/subject index in each volume. [R: ARBA 86; BL, 1 June 85; LJ, 15 Mar 85; SBF, May/June 85; SBF, Sept/Oct 85]

E+
2131 **A Biographical Encyclopedia of Scientists**. John Daintith and others. New York: Facts on File, 1981. 2v. $125.00/set. ISBN 0-87196-396-5. LC 80-23529.
Students from upper elementary level through high school will find these readable sketches useful. The work profiles 1,966 scientists from all time periods who have made important contributions to scientific development. The alphabetically arranged entries, one to two pages in length, are supported by separate subject and name indexes. A chronology of scientific discoveries and publications from 590 B.C. to A.D. 1981 concludes the volume. [R: ARBA 82]

2132 **Concise Dictionary of Scientific Biography**. By the American Council of Learned Societies. James F. Maurer, ed. New York: Scribner's, 1981. 773p. $95.00. ISBN 0-684-16650-X. LC 81-5629.
A 1-volume abridgment of the renowned 16-volume *Dictionary of Scientific Biography* (Scribner's, 1970-1978), this work contains "essential facts" about the 5,000 people covered in the parent set. Like the *Dictionary of American Biography*, it emphasizes contributions. The abridgment is international in scope, covering scientists from ancient times through those who died prior to 1972. This is an excellent source for high school libraries. [R: ARBA 82]

ACTIVITIES

See also **Activities** in specific fields of science.

2133   Bochinski, Julianne Blair. **The Complete Handbook of Science Fair Projects**. New York: John Wiley, 1991. 206p. $24.95; $12.95pa. ISBN 0-471-52729-7; 0-471-52728-9pa. LC 90-42661.

This book of science fair projects covers the basics of designing and presenting experiments and the criteria used in judging them. A separate section describes 50 award winners that range from simple to very complex. Black-and-white photographs and drawings illustrate some projects. The appendix lists science supply companies. Recommended for junior and senior high schools. [R: SLJ, July 91]

E+
2134   Fredericks, Anthony D., and Isaac Asimov. **The Complete Science Fair Handbook, Grades 4-8**. Glenview, Ill.: Scott, Foresman, 1989. 64p. $8.95pa. ISBN 0-673-38800-X.

This guide urges the improvement of science fair experiments. It is intended primarily for teachers in charge of student projects, but students will find it useful as well. The book focuses on the investigation of problems rather than demonstrations; one section, however, covers scheduling, with time tables for 6- and 12-week projects. Recommended. [R: SBF, May/June 90]

E+
2135   **More Science in Action**. Laura Buller and Ron Taylor, eds. North Bellmore, N.Y.: Marshall Cavendish, 1990. 6v. $89.95/set. ISBN 1-85435-307-1. LC 90-2064.

Each volume in this series of science experiments, designed for children from fifth grade through junior high school, is divided into easy projects and more difficult projects. Each of the 20-plus experiments in every volume is preceded by an introduction that explains the scientific principles involved and lists required materials. The step-by-step instructions are supported by colorful illustrations. Each volume includes a section on safety, and experiments requiring adult supervision are so labeled.

The table of contents lists projects by name or scientific principle. Each volume concludes with a glossary of terms and an index. [R: BL, 15 Mar 91; WLB, Feb 91]

E+
2136   Pilger, Mary Ann. **Science Experiments Index for Young People**. Englewood, Colo.: Libraries Unlimited, 1988. 239p. (Libraries Unlimited Data Book). $35.00. ISBN 0-87287-671-3. LC 88-13870.

E+
2137   Pilger, Mary Ann. **Science Experiments Index for Young People. Update 91**. Englewood, Colo.: Libraries Unlimited, 1991. 150p. (Libraries Unlimited Data Book). $19.50. ISBN 0-87287-858-9.

These indexes cite science project information for elementary and junior high school levels, published from the late 1950s through 1989. Projects, arranged alphabetically by subject, are listed with brief descriptions and a code number referring to the appropriate title in the "Books Indexed" section. More extensive than most in its class, such as *Science Fair Project Index*, the basic volume includes almost 700 books, and the *Update* adds 272 books for a total of 7,509 experiments and activities.

Some of the early titles in the basic volume are out of print; nonetheless, the work is a valuable source for suggesting and explaining science projects. Both volumes are recommended.

The indexes are also available on computer disks: Apple for AppleWorks, Mac for Microsoft Works, and IBM-ASCII comma delimited files. [R: ARBA 89; BL, 1 June 89; SLJ, May 89; WLB, Mar 89]

2138   Rainis, Kenneth S. **Projects for Young Scientists**. New York: Franklin Watts, 1989. 142p. $12.90. ISBN 0-531-10789-2. LC 89-5662.

This work is filled with unusual science projects that focus on bacteria, fungi, and other microorganisms; animals; plants; and the ecology. Thorough explanations are accompanied by black-and-white photographs and drawings, reading lists, and material sources with addresses. An index and questions complete the book. [R: BR, Jan/Feb 90]

E+
2139   **Science Experiments on File: Experiments, Demonstrations, and Projects for School and Home**. New York: Facts on File, 1989. 1v. (various paging). $145.00 looseleaf w/binder. ISBN 0-8160-1888-X. LC 88-3883.

Another Facts on File looseleaf work with pages intended for reproduction, this volume includes 84 inexpensive, innovative experiments in earth science, biology, physical science/chemistry, and physics. The activities are designed for students in grades 6 through 12, but most are for high school students. Experiments were selected from winners and finalists in the Presidential Award for Excellence in Science and Mathematics Teaching Contest.

The instructions for each experiment specify the time and materials needed, safety precautions, procedures, and analysis. Appendixes provide additional information about the experiments: recommended grade level, time constraints, number of participants, and amount of supervision required. [R: ARBA 90; BL, June 89; BR, Sept/Oct 89; SBF, Mar 90; WLB, Apr 89]

E+

2140 **Science Fair Project Index 1981-1984**. Cynthia Bishop and Deborah Crowe, eds. Metuchen, N.J.: Scarecrow, 1986. 686p. $47.50. ISBN 0-8108-1892-2. LC 86-6571.

Earlier editions include *Science Fair Project Index, 1960-1972* (Scarecrow, 1975) and *Science Fair Project Index, 1973-1980* (Scarecrow, 1983). The latest supplement indexes projects and experiments in 135 books and 5 magazines published from 1981 to 1984 and designed for students in grades 5 through 12. The alphabetical arrangement permits access by topic, material or equipment employed, or principle demonstrated. Entries refer to sources listed in a separate section and give appropriate grade level. This is a very useful index for any school in which students compete in science fairs. [R: ARBA 87; SBF, Jan 87; SLJ, May 87; VOYA, Feb 87]

Technology in General

BIBLIOGRAPHIES

See **Science** for sources dealing with both science and technology.

2141 Herring, Susan Davis. **From the Titanic to the Challenger: An Annotated Bibliography on Technological Failures of the Twentieth Century**. Hamden, Conn.: Garland, 1989. 459p. (Garland Reference Library of the Humanities, v.881). $62.00. ISBN 0-8240-3043-5. LC 89-33544.

This unique work focuses on technological failures. The bibliography is arranged by general headings, such as automobiles and chemical plants, and then chronologically, with books preceding articles. Materials listed include encyclopedias, monographs, popular magazines, professional journals, newspapers, and government documents. Some incidents appear under more than one subject. Indexing is by cause of failure, author, and title. Recommended for high schools. [R: ARBA 90; LJ, 15 Sept 89; WLB, Nov 89]

■ *Science & Technology in Fact and Fiction: A Guide to Children's Books*. *See* entry 2093.

DICTIONARIES, ENCYCLOPEDIAS, AND HANDBOOKS

2142 Cone, Robert J. **Key to High-Tech: A User-Friendly Guide to the New Technology**. Rochester, N.Y.: Galcon Press, 1987. 153p. $10.95pa. ISBN 0-943075-17-3. LC 87-81270. (P.O. Box 17835, Rochester, NY 14621).

This book is a general guide to new technologies. The first section includes essays on 17 major topics (e.g., artificial intelligence, fiber optics, robots, supercomputers), 3 to 5 pages in length, which describe the technology, its background, and applications. Section 2 analyzes binary numbers and digital signals; section 3 provides shorter treatment of 12 additional topics (e.g., holographs, communication satellites) that contribute to the technologies introduced in the first section. Subject indexing is provided. Since the work omits engineering details and more advanced information, it is suitable for high school students with budding interests in the subjects covered. [R: BL, 1 Oct 88]

2143   Du Vall, Nell. **Domestic Technology: A Chronology of Developments**. Boston: G. K. Hall, 1988. 535p. $40.00. ISBN 0-8161-8913-7. LC 88-21110.

In order to describe life in earlier times, Du Vall first determined "what tools and techniques were available ... and how they might have been used." Drawing on a number of books, journal articles, and newspaper sources, she has compiled narratives and chronologies that describe the introduction of vairous items of everyday use, beginning with fire around 500,000 B.C. and progressing through advances in computer technology in 1987. The book emphasizes the English-speaking world, and about half of the events/discoveries cited occurred after 1860.

The narrative portion is organized by topic: good origins and production, food preservation and processing, cooking, clothing, cleaning, waste and waste disposal, heating and housing, lighting, tools, health, and children. Each topic, broken down into subtopics, is followed by a chronology of the events covered. A master chronology integrates all chapter chronologies.

This fascinating book is flawed by the lack of adequate indexing; nonetheless, it is recommended for secondary schools. [R: BL, 15 Jan 89]

2144   **An Encyclopaedia of the History of Technology**. Ian McNeil, ed. New York: Routledge, Chapman & Hall, 1990. 1062p. $79.95. ISBN 0-415-01306-2. LC 89-10473.

Twenty-two chapters designed for nonspecialists focus on the creation and application of practical devices from the Stone Age to the present. Topics emphasized are agriculture, architecture, communications, transportation, construction materials, engineering, ports, and shipping. The narrative format does not lend itself to quick-reference use, but the liberal use of subheadings and an index give access to specific information. The British emphasis does not detract from this work's excellent coverage of the history of technology. [R: ARBA 91]

E +

2145   **Growing Up with Science: The Illustrated Encyclopedia of Inventions**. rev. ed. Michael Dempsey, ed. Westport, Conn.: Stuttman, 1987. 26v. $181.48. ISBN 0-87475-841-6. LC 82-63047.

Growing Up with Science, a well-written and attractively designed set, presents a wide range of articles designed to introduce young readers in grades 3 through 9 to the wonders of science, technology, and invention. Entries, ranging from one to three pages, cover topics related to astronomy, medicine, aviation, engineering, biology, physics, electronics, military science, chemistry, agriculture, manufacturing, and other areas. Lavishly illustrated articles (drawings and well-chosen photographs, almost all in color) provide historical background; explain terminology; and carefully explain each invention, advancement, and scientific phenomenon. *See also* entries refer the reader to related articles.

Volumes 1-22 include alphabetically arranged articles, atomic bomb to zoom lens; volume 23 covers inventions; volume 24 focuses on famous scientists; and the last two volumes contain a glossary, simple scientific experiments, and a comprehensive index. The set is a first choice for elementary and middle school levels. High schools requiring an introductory set may also wish to consider it.

2146   **How It Is Made Series**. New York: Facts on File. 14v. 32p./v. $12.95/v; $135.00/set. ISBN 0-8160-2416-9.

E +

2147   **How Bridges Are Made**. By Jeremy Kingston. New York: Facts on File, 1985. ISBN 0-8160-0040-9.

E +

2148   **How Cars Are Made**. By John Taylor. New York: Facts on File, 1987. ISBN 0-8160-1689-5.

E +

2149   **How Electricity Is Made**. By C. W. Boltz. New York: Facts on File, 1985. ISBN 0-8160-0039-5.

E +

2150   **How Glass Is Made**. By Alan J. Paterson. New York: Facts on File, 1985. ISBN 0-8160-0038-7.

E +

2151   **How Jet Engines Are Made**. By Julian Moxon. New York: Facts on File, 1985. ISBN 0-8160-0037-9.

E+
2152   **How Lasers Are Made**. By P. M. M. French and John Taylor. New York: Facts on File, 1987. ISBN 0-8160-1690-9.

E+
2153   **How Oil Rigs Are Made**. By Michael Lynch. New York: Facts on File, 1985. ISBN 0-8160-0041-7.

E+
2154   **How Paper Is Made**. By Lesley Perrins. New York: Facts on File, 1985. ISBN 0-8160-0036-0.

E+
2155   **How Roads Are Made**. By Owen Williams. New York: Facts on File, 1989. ISBN 0-8160-2141-8.

E+
2156   **How Ships Are Made**. By David A. Thomas. New York: Facts on File, 1989. ISBN 0-8160-2040-X.

E+
2157   **How Skyscrapers Are Made**. By Michael Duncan. New York: Facts on File, 1989. ISBN 0-8160-1692-5.
    The volumes in this series, written in easy-to-understand language for students in grades 4 through 7, offers a wealth of information about how things are constructed and how they work. Each well-designed work is illustrated by some 50 diagrams, drawings, and illustrations, more than half in color. Each oversized volume contains a glossary, a chronology, career information, and other supplementary material.
    Others in the series include *How Maps Are Made*, *How Movies Are Made*, and *How Newspapers Are Made*. [R: BL, 15 June 85; LJ, 1 Nov 85; SLJ, Feb 86]

2158   Jackson, Donald C. **Great American Bridges and Dams**. Washington, D.C.: Preservation Press, 1988. 357p. (Great American Places Series). $16.95pa. ISBN 0-89133-129-8. LC 87-22309.
    Older bridges and dams of technological and historical significance are described in this unusual volume, published by the National Trust for Historical Preservation. The introduction presents a historical survey of each engineering feat (e.g., "Bridges: Spanning the Nation"; "Dams: Controlling a Precious Resource"). The text groups bridges and dams into six geographical regions, which, in turn, are arranged alphabetically by state and site. Basic information is highlighted in the outside margin: name, location, engineer, construction company, year completed, and description of structure. Indexed. Appropriate for secondary schools. [R: ARBA 89; LJ, 1 June 88]

E+
2159   Macaulay, David. **The Way Things Work**. Boston: Houghton Mifflin, 1988. 400p. $29.95. ISBN 0-395-42857-2. LC 88-11270.
    The Way Things Work, a delightful reference tool of proven worth in science projects and assignments, combines brief, clear text with humorous, yet exact, drawings to demonstrate how machines work, from the simple to the complex. All fields are included, "from levers to lasers, cars to computers." Like all Macaulay books, this one is spiced with whimsy, making it a joy to read. Highly recommended for all levels. [R: SLJ, Dec 88; VOYA, Apr 89; WLB, Jan 91]

■ *McGraw-Hill Concise Encyclopedia of Science & Technology*. See entry 2111.

E
2160   Wilkins, Mary-Jane. **Everyday Things and How They Work**. New York: Franklin Watts, 1991. 40p. $11.40. ISBN 0-531-19109-5. LC 90-12999.
    Arranged in a question-and-answer format, this work provides explanations of how things work, often accompanied by other facts about the topic and activities to try (e.g., making a camera, making a flicker book). This well-illustrated, informative book answers such questions as "How does a vacuum bottle work?" and "How do refrigerators keep food cold?" Recommended for elementary level. [R: SBF, May 91]

BIOGRAPHY

2161 Aaseng, Nathan. **Twentieth-Century Inventors**. New York: Facts on File, 1991. 132p. (American Profiles Series, 2). $16.95. ISBN 0-8160-2485-5. LC 90-46547.

Invention is currently one of the most popular topics in the K-12 curriculum. *Twentieth-Century Inventors* will lead students in middle and high school to inventors whose names are not well known, but whose works have dramatically changed the way twentieth-century citizens live. The only inventors in this volume likely to be familiar to students are Orville and Wilbur Wright. Other inventors and inventions include Leo Baekeland (plastic), Vladimir Zworykin (television), Chester Carlson (xerography), and Wilson Greatbatch (the implantable pacemaker). Aaseng provides a solid background profile of each inventor. Of particular value is the emphasis on the perseverance, tenacity, and task commitment of these men. Students will leave these profiles with the notion that success comes through hard work and sacrifice. Most of the products created by these inventors are highly technical, yet Aaseng's handling of scientific information can be understood by most lay readers.

If there is any fault to be found with this work, it is that no women or minority inventors are represented. *Black Scientists* and *Women Scientists*, two forthcoming companion volumes should remedy this. *Twentieth-Century Inventors* is an excellent resource book.

■ *The Biographical Dictionary of Scientists*. See entry 2130.

AUTOMOTIVE

See **Transportation** for **Aeronautics**.

2162 Black, Perry O. **Diesel Engine Manual**. 4th ed. New York: Theodore Audel/Macmillan, 1983. $22.50. ISBN 0-672-23371-1. LC 82-20635.

The theory and operation of diesel engines is explained in question-and-answer format. Although the manual has not been revised in some time, it continues to be a sound basic source for the subject.

2163 **Chilton's Auto Repair Manual, 1987-1991**. Radnor, Pa.: Chilton Books. annual. $26.95.

The best known of the auto repair manuals, Chilton's annuals cover all models of the last five years currently available in the United States and Canada. Major systems and components (e.g., electrical, fuel and cooling, emission control) are described and illustrated. The detailed troubleshooting and repair instructions are supported by photographs, diagrams, and schematics. Indexed by subject.

Chilton publishes a Total Car Care series that includes a wide range of repair guides for all makes of cars, trucks, vans, and motorcycles, and for specific systems and maintenance operations such as air conditioning, automatic transmissions, brakes, steering, and suspension. There are also manuals for earlier cars of specific manufacturers, such as *Chevrolet Repair Manual, 1980-1987* and model-specific repair manuals, such as *Camaro, 1982-1988*. Spanish-language editions are available for some titles.

2164 Chudy, Harry T. **The Complete Guide to Automotive Refinishing**. 2d ed. Englewood Cliffs, N.J.: Prentice-Hall, 1988. 496p. $46.00. ISBN 0-13-159807-4.

This manual, designed for teachers and advanced students, provides detailed coverage of automotive refinishing.

2165 Crouse, William H., and Donald L. Anglin. **Automotive Engines**. 7th ed. New York: McGraw-Hill, 1987. 432p. $27.95. ISBN 0-07-014957-7. LC 79-26142.

A text/reference intended for use in automotive shop classes, this work explains engine parts, electrical systems, emission control devices, and other topics related to automobiles. Many high school libraries will require this volume.

2166 Toboldt, William K., and others. **Automotive Encyclopedia**. rev. ed. South Holland, Ill.: Goodheart-Willcox, 1989. 816p. $33.20. ISBN 0-87006-691-9. LC 89-11244.

Automotive Encyclopedia, a clearly written text/reference, provides extensive coverage of auto mechanics, repair, and body refinishing. Topics concerning engine fundamentals, principles of electrical systems and emission control devices, and other appropriate areas are arranged under specific headings. Each section is illustrated with drawings, photographs, and diagrams and concludes with review quesitons. In addition, the volume includes a dictionary section that defines terms and gives mechanical/tuneup specifications for cars manufactured during the past 20 years. Indexed. This work is more extensive than *Automotive Engines*; both are recommended.

BICYCLES

2167 Bicycling Magazine's Complete Guide to Bicycle Maintenance and Repair. By the editors of *Bicycling Magazine.* Emmaus, Pa.: Rodale Press, 1990. $24.95; $16.95pa. ISBN 0-87857-895-1; 0-87857-896-Xpa. LC 90-8057.

2168 Van der Plas, Rob. **The Bicycle Repair Book: Maintaining and Repairing the Modern Bicycle.** rev. ed. Mill Valley, Calif.: Bicycle Books, 1990. 140p. $8.95pa. ISBN 0-933201-11-7. LC 84-50673.

Bicycling Magazine's guide is an excellent, comprehensive manual that covers all repairs from flat tires to complex overhauls. The clear text is supplemented by well-labeled drawings and photographs. *The Bicycle Repair Book* is also a good repair manual; it contains well-written explanations of all aspects of repair. Both works are recommended for middle and high school level.

BUILDING AND FIX-IT

2169 Concise Encyclopedia of Building & Construction Materials. Fred Moavenzadeh, ed. Oxford, England: Pergamon Press; distr., Cambridge, Mass.: MIT Press, 1990. 682p. $175.00. ISBN 0-262-13248-6. LC 89-8517.

This work reprints all articles on building materials published in the 1986 8-volume *Encyclopedia of Material Science and Engineering* by the same publisher, which costs about $2,000. The *Concise Encyclopedia* is one of a series of works on materials in a specific area mined from the parent set, with only limited revision or condensation. High school libraries that require a reference tool on the subject area will welcome this work. [R: ARBA 91]

2170 The Encyclopedia of Wood: A Tree-by-Tree Guide to the World's Most Versatile Resource. Aidan Walker, ed. New York: Facts on File, 1989. 192p. $29.95. ISBN 0-8160-2159-7. LC 89-33439.

This work contains a wealth of information on the world's most valuable and useful woods — their properties, distribution, availability, historical applications, and special uses. The introductory chapters provide background information on wood and the lumber industry. Other chapters view wood from the craftsperson's perspective; explain how trees grow and how growth affects grain and texture; address types of forests and humanity's effects on them; and describe the industry, from cutting and logging to milling and finishing.

The main body consists of an alphabetical list of 150 of the world's most popular woods, giving appearance, characteristics, and uses. Most have distribution maps and color photographs of the finished wood. A chart provides information on density, workability, and other data of interest to the craftsperson. The book concludes with a glossary and index by subject, common name, and scientific name. Highly recommended for secondary schools with shop programs; useful in all types of libraries. [R: ARBA 90; BL, 15 Jan 90]

2171 Feirer, John L. **Carpentry and Building Construction.** New York: Macmillan, 1986. $50.00. ISBN 0-02-537360-9. LC 80-67018.

Feirer's basic textbook/reference for high schools and vocational schools covers all aspects of carpentry and construction, from tools and foundations to exterior and interior finishing. There are useful tables and other special features, including study questions.

2172 The Homeowner's Complete Manual of Repair and Improvement. Allan D. Bragdon, ed. New York: Arco/Prentice Hall Press, c1983, 1984. 576p. $19.95; $14.95pa. ISBN 0-668-05737-8; 0-668-05749-1pa. LC 82-18184.

This excellent house repair and maintenance guide provides a practical approach to the topic. Information is arranged under six sections: interior repairs and decorating; windows, doors, security, and insulation; furniture care and refinishing; electrical fixtures, wiring, and appliances; plumbing and heating; and exterior maintenance and improvement. Clear instructions are supported by photographs, drawings, and numerous charts. Recommended for middle and high school level.

Two other good home repair manuals are *Complete Do-It-Yourself Manual* by the editors of *Reader's Digest* (Random House, 1981) and *Home Repair Handbook* by the editors of *Sunset Magazine and Book* (Sunset Publishing, 1985).

2173 Jackson, Albert, and D. Day. **"Popular Mechanics" Home How-To.** New York: William Morrow, 1989. 512p. $29.95. ISBN 0-688-08512-1. LC 88-17760.

This well-organized and well-designed guide to home maintenance and improvement addresses a wide variety of problems encountered around the house. Its many drawings, charts, and other illustrations enhance the clear explanations. Cross-references are used throughout this excellent work. Recommended for secondary schools. [R: BL, 15 May 89; LJ, 15 May 89]

2174 McMullan, Randall. **Dictionary of Building**. New York: Nichols/GP Publishing, 1988. 262p. $59.50. ISBN 0-89397-319-X. LC 88-12598.

Intended for students, laypersons, and subject experts, this dictionary defines 5,470 terms used in construction. Although compiled in Great Britain, the work includes and cross-references American and British terms. The use of line drawings and tables is extensive. Most entries are brief, but all are adequate, making this a worthwhile selection for high schools requiring a dictionary for the field. [R: ARBA 89; BL, 1 June 89]

ELECTRICITY

See also **Computers and Electronics**.

E

2175 Markle, Sandra. **Power Up: Experiments, Puzzles, and Games Exploring Electricity**. New York: Atheneum, 1989. 40p. $13.95. ISBN 0-689-31442-6. LC 88-7772.

This book of experiments with electricity, designed for mid-level elementary school students, covers paths, circuits, and current flow; conduction and insulation; series and parallel circuits; and fuses and switches. The clearly described experiments, which emphasize safety, require ordinary materials, such as foil, D-cells, flashlights, and orthodontic rubber bands. Projects show students how to build their own circuits and test for conductivity. Excellent black-and-white photographs and other illustrations enhance the work's effectiveness. Recommended. [R: BL, 1 Oct 89; SBF, May/June 90]

2176 Matt, Stephen R. **Electricity and Basic Electronics**. South Holland, Ill.: Goodheart-Willcox, 1989. $23.40. ISBN 0-87006-680-3. LC 87-30964.

A textbook for beginning students, this work can serve as a reference source for middle and high school students as well. Chapters not only cover the basic principles and applications of electricity and electronics but also suggest projects/activities and study questions. Numerous charts, diagrams, drawings, tables, and photographs support the text. Appendixes contain a glossary, formulas, and standard abbreviations. Indexed. [R: BL, 15 Apr 89]

METAL WORK

2177 Althouse, Andrew D., and others. **Modern Welding**. rev. ed. South Holland, Ill.: Goodheart-Willcox, 1988. 736p. $29.00. ISBN 0-87006-668-4.

Welding fundamentals and related topics (e.g., metallurgy, properties of metal, safety procedures) are well presented in this textbook/reference, which is directed toward high school and vocational students. This work is an excellent choice for libraries supporting vocational programs.

2178 Oberg, Eric, and others. **Machinery's Handbook: A Reference Book for the Mechanical Engineer, Designer, Manufacturing Engineer, Draftsman, Toolmaker, and Machinist**. 23d ed. New York: Industrial Press, 1988. 2511p. $55.00. ISBN 0-8311-1200-X.

A standard handbook, frequently revised, this work contains mathematical principles, formulas, tables, signs and symbols, and standards. It also has information on welding, milling, gearing, and many other topics related to machine shop work. The handbook also includes extensive drawings and other illustrative materials. High schools with shop courses will require this volume.

Machine Shop Practice by K. H. Moltrecht (2d ed. Industrial Press, 1981) covers the operation of basic machine tools and related topics. *Tools of Our Trade* by the staff of *American Machinist Magazine* (McGraw-Hill, 1982), another basic work, is also recommended.

Transportation

□ _____ □

GENERAL WORKS

E
2179   Irving, Jan, and Robin Currie. **Full Speed Ahead: Stories and Activities for Children on Transportation**. Englewood, Colo.: Libraries Unlimited, 1988. 244p. $22.50pa. ISBN 0-87287-653-5. LC 88-29540.
This guide focuses on a wide range of activities related to things that go. The story of transportation, which concerns the movement of both animals and humans, is told by some 125 picture books and demonstrated by games, songs, crafts, skits, and other activities. Indexing is alphabetical by skills (e.g., following directions, word recognition, rhythm) and topics. Recommended for preschool through grade 3.

2180   Schumacher, Rose, and others. **World Communication and Transportation Data: A Compendium of Current Information for All Countries of the World, 1989**. Santa Barbara, Calif.: ABC-Clio, 1989. 99p. $29.95. ISBN 0-87436-548-1.
This work provides statistical information on the transportation and communication infrastructure of 172 countries and territories. Alphabetically arranged by official names in English, each entry contains information on roads, vehicles, and railroads; ports and cargo loadings; merchant fleet size and tonnage; airfields and airline passenger miles; and radio, television, newspapers, and telephones. Compiled from the publisher's Kaleidoscope: Current World Data database, the plan is to update the publication every other year. This volume is a convenient compilation of comparative data. Recommended for high school level and above. [R: ARBA 91; BR, May 90; WLB, Feb 90]

AUTOMOBILES AND MOTORCYCLES

See also **Consumer Education**.

2181   Congdon, Kirby. **Motorcycle Books: A Critical Survey and Checklist**. Metuchen, N.J.: Scarecrow, 1987. 135p. $20.00. ISBN 0-8108-1985-6. LC 87-1641.
Some 120 annotated book titles and over 500 catalogs and handbooks make up this bibliography. The books include biographies, children's books, history, racing, reference, and travel guides. Each entry provides complete bibliographic data and a lengthy annotation, but most catalog citations are not annotated. There is no index. [R: ARBA 88; BL, 1 Jan 88; VOYA, Aug 88]

2182   **50 Years of American Automobiles 1939-1989**. Lincolnwood, Ill.: Publications International, 1989. 720p. $49.95. ISBN 0-88176-592-9.
Although unacknowledged, the automobile editors of _Consumer Guide_ compiled this work. It surveys the American automobile over the last 50 years. The first half provides histories and descriptions of the makes and models of 40 major and several minor car makers (e.g., American Bantam, Crosley, Muntz, Tucker, Willys), all illustrated by about 200 good photographs. The text includes engineering, sales trends, and marketing for each make. The second half contains tables of year-by-year specifications for each series—weight, price, production, engine displacement, bores and strokes, and power. [R: ARBA 90; BL, 1 Nov 89]

2183   Flammang, James W. **Standard Catalog of American Cars 1976-1986**. 2d ed. Iola, Wis.: Krause Publications, 1989. 484p. $19.95. ISBN 0-87341-133-1. LC 88-081627.
A companion to _Standard Catalog of American Cars, 1905-1942_ by Beverly Kimes and _Standard Catalog of American Cars, 1946-1975_ (2d ed. Krause Publications, 1987), this volume covers all American automobile manufacturers for the period, including minor ones such as Stutz and Checker. Entries provide a photograph of the automobile; a narrative description; vehicle identification numbers and locations; data on engine, chassis, transmission, and so forth; a list of available options; and cost when new. A historical section provides statistical data (number of models produced) and highlights of the period.

Appendixes list automobile museums, collector car clubs, Indy pace cars, and (new to the series) a current price guide (by condition) for models through the early 1980s. Since a number of collectible cars were produced during the period, this is a valuable source for car buffs. [R: ARBA 91; BL, Aug 90]

2184 Gillis, Jack. **The Used Car Book**. 1991 ed. New York: HarperPerennial/HarperCollins, 1990. 159p. $9.95pa. ISBN 0-06-273070-3. ISSN 0895-3899.

In the introduction to this latest edition of a popular work, Gillis states that the intent is to help get the reader "started in the right direction and help separate the 'peaches' from the 'lemons.'" He has organized the work in three sections, the first of which is titled "Finding Them, Checking Them Out and Getting the Best Price." Here he covers such things as understanding classified advertisements, odometer fraud, checklists for going over the cars, and questions to ask the owner. The second section, "Keeping Them Going," deals with matters of insurance, safety, maintenance, and complaints. Interspersed throughout are sidebars on all sorts of interesting and helpful topics (e.g., how to remove a sparkplug, theft protection). These sections take up about half the book. The other half, "How They Rate," has a few recommendations of models to choose or avoid, but most of it is a set of tables. The arrangement is alphabetical by make and model for the years 1981-1990 (or the years the model was actually produced). Each table has 15 items, including crash test results, miles per gallon, theft ratings, complaints summary, weight, wheelbase, and price range.

2185 Kimes, Beverly Rae. **Standard Catalog of American Cars, 1805-1942**. 2d ed. Iola, Wis.: Krause Publications, 1989. 1568p. $39.95pa. ISBN 0-87341-111-0. LC 85-050390.

This volume, a revision of a 1985 work, treats many obscure American manufacturers and models. Entries vary from a brief statement to more than 20 pages and cover over 5,000 makes of cars. For each the text gives a short history, a detailed description, basic specifications, factory price, and estimated current value.

Special features include a geographical index; a list of alternative power sources, such as electricity and steam; and a list of cyclecars and highwheelers. The volume is packed with information, but the text is printed in small, hard-to-read type. The only illustrations are black-and-white photographs, many of poor quality. [R: ARBA 90]

2186 Langworth, Richard M., and Chris Poole. **Great American Automobiles of the 50s**. New York: Beekman House/Crown, 1989. 320p. $29.95. ISBN 0-517-67556-0. LC 88-63609.

Automobiles of a favorite era in auto history, from Kaiser's Virginian, the Manhattan, and the Dragon to the classic Chevrolets, Fords, and Chryslers are all here. Thirty-two makes and models include development, two to five color illustrations, a brief technical description, and production figures. An interesting work, recommended for high schools. [R: ARBA 90]

AVIATION AND SPACE FLIGHT

See also **Military Science**.

2187 **The Air and Space Catalog: The Complete Sourcebook to Everything in the Universe**. By the editors of *The Map Catalog*. New York: Vintage/Random House, 1990. $16.95pa. ISBN 0-679-72038-3. LC 89-40133.

The Air and Space Catalog is an attractive sourcebook for astronomy, weather, aviation, and space flight. It contains directory information for observatories, planetariums, societies and clubs, private meteorology companies, aviation libraries, and museums. It also provides company names and addresses for purchasing telescopes, maps, weather equipment, model airplanes, flight simulators, hot-air balloons, books, and audiovisual materials. High school libraries may want two copies, one for circulation and one for reference. [R: BL, 15 Mar 90; LJ, Dec 89; SLJ, May 90]

2188 **Astronauts and Cosmonauts: Biographical and Statistical Data**. Washington, D.C.: Government Printing Office, 1989. 447p. $13.00pa. S/N 052-070-06065-4.

All United States astronauts and most Soviet cosmonauts, as of June 30, 1989, are included in this congressional committee print. Single-page biographies of the 215 people launched into space during 121 missions contain personal data, education, military record and rank, and spaceflight responsibilities. A black-and-white photograph accompanies each sketch. Comparative data on the astronauts and cosmonauts, a list of crew members for each flight, and a chronology of all space events are included.

This work, compiled by the staff of the Congressional Research Service, Library of Congress, is distributed through the depository system. Copies may be obtained through the U.S. House of Representatives Committee on Science, Space, and Technology. [R: BL, 15 June 90]

2189   Bond, Peter. **Heroes in Space: From Gagarin to Challenger**. Cambridge, Mass.: Basil Blackwell, 1987. 467p. $29.95. ISBN 0-631-15349-7. LC 86-31004.
Over the 25 years between the flight of *Vostok I* in April 1961 and the *Challenger* disaster in January 1986, 116 manned space flights occurred. This book profiles the almost 200 astronauts and cosmonauts involved in those missions, relating their experiences during the flights and providing insights into their personalities. These well-documented and readable accounts are supported by illustrations. Recommended for secondary schools. [R: ARBA 89; LJ, 1 Mar 88]

E+
2190   Boyne, Walter, Jr. **The Smithsonian Book of Flight for Young People**. New York: Atheneum, 1988. 128p. $16.95; $10.95pa. ISBN 0-689-31422-1; 0-689-71212-Xpa.
Almost 100 photographs and other illustrations show the impact of flight on everyday life, war, and commerce. A readable text covers people and events related to aviation in this century, ending with the *Voyager* flight in 1986. Indexed. [R: BL, 15 Mar 89; SLJ, Apr 89; VOYA, Apr 89]

E
2191   Brown, Robert, and Brian Jones. **Exploring Space**. Milwaukee, Wis.: Gareth Stevens, 1990. 64p. $12.95. ISBN 0-8368-0029-X. LC 87-11278.

E
2192   Jones, Brian. **Space Exploration**. Milwaukee, Wis.: Gareth Stevens, 1990. 64p. $12.95. ISBN 0-8368-0004-4. LC 89-11359.
Exploring Space is a part of the My First Library series, for grades 2 and 3, while *Space Exploration* belongs to the slightly more advanced Gareth Stevens Information Library series, for grades 4 through 6. Each of the parallel volumes contains some 25 2-page articles, which have several useful and attractive illustrations in color. Unusual and special information is scattered throughout the text in boxes. The narrative through 1989 is brief but accurate. Since much of the information is repeated in the two books, most libraries should select only one. [R: BL, 1 June 90]

2193   **The Cambridge Encyclopedia of Space**. Michael Rycroft, ed. New York: Cambridge University Press, 1990. 386p. $65.00. ISBN 0-521-36426-4. LC 90-2444.
This oversized pictorial history of space, which may be more appropriate for browsing than reference, is a translation and revision of *Espace: Le Grand Atlas de l'Espace* (Encyclopaedia Universalis, 1989). Its four sections include "From Dream to Reality," a brief history of rockets and rocketry; "Going into Space," an overview of rocket launchings and information on space centers in several world locations; "Exploring the Universe," brief descriptions of unmanned space probes of the United States and the Soviet Union; and "Living in Space," a survey of manned flights, space research, and space law. The outstanding illustrations and the text, charts, and tables provide a good summary of the topic. Indexed. [R: ARBA 92; BL, 1 Mar 91; LJ, 15 Feb 91]

2194   Cassutt, Michael. **Who's Who in Space: The First 25 Years**. Boston: G. K. Hall, 1987. 311p. $40.00. ISBN 0-8161-8801-7. LC 86-26988.
This biographical volume, divided into three sections, focuses on space travelers and others who underwent rigorous training programs from 1961 through 1986. The first section deals with 250 Americans, including NASA astronauts, civilian shuttle specialists, test pilots, and engineers. Section 2 covers Soviet space travelers, and section 3 addresses those from other nations, 58 persons in all. Entries provide personal data, educational background, and career histories, accompanied by photographs. Recommended for middle and high schools. [R: ARBA 88; BL, 15 June 87; SLJ, May 88; WLB, Sept 87]

2195   Christy, Joe. **1001 Flying Facts and Firsts**. Blue Ridge Summit, Pa.: TAB Books, 1988. 220p. $24.95pa. ISBN 0-8306-9228-5.
The first 87 pages of this handbook are a chronology of significant events in aviation, from 400 B.C. (the use of kites by Koreans and Chinese to send messages on the battlefield) to August 25, 1987 (the appearance of the automated machine to dispense airline tickets). "Record Flights" lists superlatives, such as the longest distance flown by certain types of aircraft. Significant U.S. military

and civilian aircraft are arranged by the year each plane entered service. Other sections include U.S. manned space flights; a list of major aircraft companies; and American Aces, recipients of the U.S. Medal of Honor. The amount of information is impressive, but the caveat is the lack of an index.

2196   Curtis, Anthony. **Space Almanac: Facts, Figures, Names, Dates, Places....** Woodsboro, Md.: Arcsoft, 1989. 955p. $19.95pa. ISBN 0-86668-065-9. LC 89-6593.
    This compendium of space information – history, exploration, and future developments – is highly recommended for secondary schools. Eight sections (e.g., space shuttles, rockets, astronauts and cosmonauts) provide essays and chronologies, all supported by charts, maps, tables, and photographs. Astronomical data is presented for the Moon, Sun, comets, asteroids, solar system, galaxies, pulsars, quasars, and black holes. The work also includes space news from countries around the world. This is an excellent compilation of facts about the universe. [R: ARBA 90; BL, 15 Dec 89; LJ, Oct 89]

2197   Garrison, Paul. **The Illustrated Encyclopedia of General Aviation.** 2d ed. Blue Ridge Summit, Pa.: TAB Books, 1990. 462p. $34.95; $24.95pa. ISBN 0-8306-8316-X; 0-8306-3316-2pa. LC 89-29160.
    Originally published in 1979 as *Illustrated Encyclopedia/Dictionary of General Aviation*, this work includes definitions of terms and phrases, acronyms, abbreviations, individual planes, and manufacturers. Also included are addresses of national and international organizations, codes used on airplanes to identify country of origin, Morse code, conversion tables, aviation publications, and international airshows. More than 400 charts, tables, and black-and-white photographs illustrate the volume.
    Large libraries will require *Jane's Aerospace Dictionary* (3d ed. Jane's Information Group, 1988), a larger and more technical work, but Garrison's book will probably meet the needs of most high schools requiring this type of material. [R: ARBA 91; RBB, 15 June 90]

2198   Gatland, Kenneth. **The Illustrated Encyclopedia of Space Technology.** 2d ed. New York: Salamander Books/Crown, 1990. 306p. $29.95. ISBN 0-517-57427-6. LC 89-3375.
    This comprehensive work, which updates a 1981 publication, covers space theories and travel of the twentieth century and probes planned for the future. Seventeen chapters treat areas such as man in space, the space pioneers, probes to the planets, and spaceships to Mars. The heavily illustrated text (color photographs, drawings, and diagrams) and appendixes that provide a glossary, a chronology, and an index enhance this attractive work.
    The text will challenge the advanced high school student, but even students in lower grades can learn from the numerous illustrations and their captions. Due to its narrative format, the work could be placed in the circulating collection. [R: BL, 1 Sept 90; BR, Sept/Oct 90]

2199   **Jane's All the World's Aircraft.** Alexandria, Va.: Jane's Information Group. annual. $185.00. LC 10-8268.
    The standard reference work of its kind, this annual provides illustrations, descriptions, and specifications for the civil and military aircraft of various countries of the world. The arrangement is by type of craft (e.g., airplanes, helicopters, sailplanes, hang gliders, airships, balloons, military missiles, spacecraft) and then alphabetically by manufacturer. Indexing by type of craft, manufacturer, and model name includes the current volume and the previous 10 annuals. [R: ARBA 90]

2200   Lightbody, Andy, and Joe Poyer. **The Illustrated History of Helicopters.** Lincolnwood, Ill.: Publications International, 1990. 192p. $24.95. ISBN 0-88176-652-6. LC 89-63617.
    The extensive introduction chronicles the evolution of helicopters and explains their technology and weapon systems. The main body of the work treats over 30 military helicopters worldwide, providing a profile, statistics, and colorful photographs and action shots of each. This excellent treatment of the topic cannot compare with *Jane's All the World's Aircraft*, but the work is reasonably priced and will meet most needs in secondary schools. [R: ARBA 91; BL, 1 Sept 90]

2201   **Magill's Survey of Science: Space Exploration Series.** Frank N. Magill, ed. Pasadena, Calif.: Salem Press, 1989. 5v. $425.00/set. ISBN 0-89356-600-4. LC 88-38267.
    The cost of this set prohibits its selection by most school libraries, but it is a useful reference work, covering space exploration and the fundamentals of astronomy. Articles, averaging six pages each, describe all spacecraft and missions, as well as such things as planets, comets, black holes, the cosmic microwave background, and space programs of other nations. The essays survey current knowledge on the subject, address famous individuals associated with the topic, and include a bibliography. [R: ARBA 90; RBB, 1 Oct 89]

2202   The National Air and Space Museum. 2d ed. C. D. B. Bryan, ed. New York: Harry Abrams, 1988. 504p. $65.00. ISBN 0-8109-1380-1.

This update of the 1979 edition presents a marvelous recreation of a visit to the National Air and Space Museum. It includes photographs of the museum's exhibits – "Early Flight," "Golden Age of Flight," "Jet Aviation," "Looking at the Earth," and "Stars" – providing a survey of aerospace history. Foldouts and other illustrative matter support the text. Highly recommended for secondary level. [R: BL, 15 Dec 88; LJ, 15 Feb 89]

2203   Reithmaier, Larry. The Aviation/Space Dictionary. 7th ed. Blue Ridge Summit, Pa.: Aero/ TAB Books, 1990. 461p. $32.95. ISBN 0-8306-8092-6. LC 89-17948.

The original edition of this work was based heavily on glossaries issued by NASA, the FAA, and the military. The new edition (last revised in 1980) increases the number of entries by more than 1,000 and updates many of the 7,000 terms to reflect changes in the last decade. The terminology covers all areas of air traffic control, meteorology, space flight, and aviation. Sixteen appendixes summarize inventions and new developments in military aircraft and aerodynamic concepts. Problems include poor proofreading and unclear photographs. [R: ARBA 91]

2204   Richardson, Doug. Combat Arms: Modern Spyplanes. New York: Prentice Hall Press, 1990. 78p. $14.95. ISBN 0-13-589854-4. LC 90-52990.

Two-page entries for each of 30 aircraft describe the plane, provide technical data (e.g., weight, range, armament), give historical background, and assess operational status and capability. Colorful photographs or paintings accompany each entry. For middle and high school levels.

Similar works by Bill Gunston are *Combat Arms: Modern Attach Aircraft* (Prentice Hall Press, 1989) and *Combat Arms: Modern Helicopters* (Prentice Hall Press, 1990). [R: ARBA 91]

E+
2205   Spangenburg, Ray, and Diane Moser. Exploring the Reaches of the Solar System. New York: Facts on File, 1990. 128p. $22.95. ISBN 0-8160-1850-2. LC 89-37711.

E+
2206   Spangenburg, Ray, and Diane Moser. Living and Working in Space. New York: Facts on File, 1990. 136p. $22.95. ISBN 0-8160-1849-9.

E+
2207   Spangenburg, Ray, and Diane Moser. Opening the Space Frontier. New York: Facts on File, 1989. 136p. $22.95. ISBN 0-8160-1848-0.

E+
2208   Spangenburg, Ray, and Diane Moser. Space People from A-Z. New York: Facts on File, 1990. 100p. $22.95. ISBN 0-8160-1851-0. LC 89-23313.

The Space Exploration series provides an excellent introduction to space travel and a historical survey of recent developments. *Exploring the Reaches of the Solar System* projects the future of man's exploration of other planets in the solar system, the Sun, comets and asteroids, and interstellar space. *Living and Working in Space* focuses on ways in which humans have established themselves in space and covers the history, function, and application of satellites. A chapter is devoted to the Strategic Defense Initiative ("Star Wars").

Opening the Space Frontier recounts the early history of space exploration, from the Congreve rocket of the early nineteenth century through the Apollo moon landings in the late 1960s and early 1970. *Space People from A-Z*, a "who's who" of outer space, profiles researchers, testers, astronomers, writers, astronauts, and cosmonauts, covering everyone of importance in the history of space exploration.

Each volume includes a glossary, a bibliography of suggested readings, line drawings, charts, black-and-white photographs, and an index. These readable, attractive, and informative books are designed for students from upper elementary grades through junior high school. [R: ARBA 91; BR, May 90; BR, Nov/Dec 90; RBB, 15 Apr 90; SLJ, Apr 90; SLJ, Dec 90; VOYA, Apr 90; VOYA, June 90]

2209   Walker, Ormiston. Experimenting with Air and Flight. New York: Franklin Watts, 1989. 76p. $12.40. ISBN 0-531-10670-5. LC 88-38063.

Walker explains the principles of aerodynamics in language understandable to students in grades 7 through 12, and applies them to the structure of birds, airplanes, helicopters, blimps, hot-air balloons, rockets, hovercraft, and kites. He then describes experiments that require little equipment and gives warnings about even the least possible dangers. This slim volume is especially useful for the junior high school level. [R: BL, 15 May 89; BR, Jan/Feb 90; SLJ, July 89]

RAILROADS AND URBAN SYSTEMS

2210 Hubbard, Freeman. **Encyclopedia of North American Railroading: 150 Years of Railroading in the United States and Canada**. New York: McGraw-Hill, 1982. 377p. $72.40. ISBN 0-07-030828-4. LC 81-1997.

Abundantly illustrated articles, ranging from a few lines to six pages, provide general encyclopedic information on railroading in the United States and Canada. Among the topics covered are the historical development of railroads, builders and financiers, railroad lines, events, equipment, and "firsts." Alphabetically arranged articles are supported by cross-referencing and indexing. Appropriate for middle and high schools. [R: ARBA 82]

2211 **Jane's Urban Transport Systems 1990**. 9th ed. Chris Bushell, ed. Alexandria, Va.: Jane's Information Group, 1990. 616p. $185.00pa. ISBN 0-7106-0902-7.

This annual provides the most extensive coverage available on urban public transportation systems worldwide. An alphabetical section gives information about mass transit (e.g., heavy and light rail, buses, trollies, ferries) in 406 major cities. For each system are included a narrative description, statistics (e.g., passengers carried, operating mileage, routes, equipment, fares and finances, ongoing developments), photographs, and some maps. A separate section arranges manufacturers under 11 major headings, giving key personnel, products, current contracts, and recent activities. A directory of consultants and indexing by system and manufacturer conclude the volume. [R: ARBA 91]

2212 Marshall, John. **The Guinness Railway Book**. Enfield, Eng.: Guinness Books; distr., New York: Sterling Publishing, 1989. 200p. $14.95pa. ISBN 0-85112-359-7.

An expansion and update of *Rail Facts and Feats* (1974) and *Rail: The Records* (Borgo Press, 1989), this work provides a wide range of historical and current data on the world's railroads. "World" is an exaggeration, however, since the emphasis is on Great Britain, North America, Europe, and Australia. Although superlatives are not a requirement for inclusion, as with some Guinness publications, "firsts," "longest," "oldest," and other bests do receive a great deal of attention. The broad-topic arrangement makes this work more suitable for browsing than quick reference, but it contains a good index and much useful data, enhanced by numerous photographs, maps, and tables. [R: ARBA 91]

2213 **Rand McNally Handy Railroad Atlas of the United States**. Chicago: Rand McNally, 1988. 64p. $14.95pa. ISBN 0-528-21001-7.

A concise, easy-to-use atlas of U.S. railroads, this work is arranged alphabetically by state (including Alaska and Hawaii), with supplementary maps for major metropolitan areas–New York, Boston, Chicago, San Francisco, and Los Angeles. Maps show rail lines, junction points, and major cities on the lines for common carrier railroads. Tourist railroads, private industrial lines, and urban rapid-transit systems are not shown.

Also included are an alphabetical list of operating companies, mileage charts, a state-by-state directory of companies, a rail map of Canada that shows major trunk lines, and a list of nonrailroad companies operating 1,000 or more private freight cars. Issued since 1928, this atlas is periodically revised. The instability of today's railroad industry, however, makes the accuracy of the information undependable. [R: ARBA 90]

SHIPS

2214 Holland, F. Ross, Jr. **Great American Lighthouses**. Washington, D.C.: Preservation Press, 1989. 346p. $16.95pa. ISBN 0-89133-153-0. LC 89-8825.

Lighthouses around the nation are the subject of this volume, which is intended as a guidebook. The introduction provides historical data and a discussion of lighthouse preservation efforts. The main body of the work, arranged by region and then by state, includes the name of the lighthouse, its closest access point, construction data, reconstruction date (if applicable), height, a brief history, and current ownership. A separate section addresses losses through neglect, storms, and vandalism. Clear photographs and line drawings illustrate the volume. A bibliography, a directory of information agencies, and an index conclude the volume. [R: ARBA 91; BL, 1 Dec 89]

2215 **The Oxford Companion to Ships & the Sea.** Peter Kemp, ed. New York: Oxford University Press, 1976. 971p. $45.00. ISBN 0-19-211553-7.

This authoritative work includes entries "ranging from the ships and men who first opened up the world with their voyages into the unknown, through the struggles of nations as they developed and recognized that power and prosperity depended on the exercise of sea power." Some 3,700 brief narratives, alphabetically arranged, cover persons (including those who wrote about the sea or painted sea scenes), places, ship names, nautical terms, battles, sea lore, and many other topics. Appendixes list military ranks, the international code of flag signals in color, rules of the road, buoyage, and units of measure. Numerous photographs and line drawings illustrate this excellent work. Recommended for high schools. [R: ARBA 78]

Zoology

ATLASES

See also **Biology**, **Natural Resource Sciences**, and **Pets.**

E
2216 **Rand McNally Children's Atlas of World Wildlife.** Skokie, Ill.: Rand McNally, 1990. 93p. $14.95. ISBN 0-528-83409-6. LC 90-52621.

This volume, arranged by continent and subdivided by region or environmental habitat, provides geographical information about selected wildlife. Each section begins with a color relief map and includes several paragraphs describing the climate, vegetation, and terrain. Full-color photographs and drawings depict animals, many of which risk extinction. Information about each includes diet, daily life, and dangers they face.

The atlas associates the location and survival of each species with the available food supply and the impact that social and environmental factors have on it. Indexed by animal and major places on the maps. The page layout is attractive, and the text is large and easy to read. Recommended for elementary level. [R: BL, 1 Feb 91; SLJ, May 91]

DICTIONARIES AND ENCYCLOPEDIAS

■ *Chambers Biology Dictionary.* See entry 1820.

2217 **The Encyclopedia of Aquatic Life.** Keith Banister and Andrew Campbell, eds. New York: Facts on File, 1985. 349p. $45.00. ISBN 0-8160-1257-1. LC 85-10245.

This colorful work in the Encyclopedia of Animals series treats fish, aquatic invertebrates, and sea mammals, explaining their habitats, physical characteristics, diets, and lives. The volume is extensively illustrated with over 300 underwater photographs, drawings, paintings, and other art work. Students from middle school up should find this book attractive and readable. [R: ARBA 86; BL, 1 Feb 86; LJ, 1 Mar 86; WLB, Feb 86]

E
2218 Harrison, Virginia, and Steve Pollock. **The World of Animals**. Milwaukee, Wis.: Gareth Stevens, 1990. 64p. $12.95. ISBN 0-8368-0028-1. LC 89-11357.

E
2219 Pollock, Steve. **Animal Life**. Milwaukee, Wis.: Gareth Stevens, 1990. 64p. $12.95. ISBN 0-8368-0003-6. LC 89-11267.

These two books belong to companion series covering scientific, technical, and cultural topics. *The World of Animals* is in My First Reference Library series, designed as an introduction to reference books for children in grades 2 and 3. *Animal Life*, in the Gareth Stevens Information Library series, has the same focus but is designed for children in grades 4 through 6. Books in both series are scheduled for release over a three-year period.

Volumes in each series have the same page layout and illustrations, but those in the Information Library have some additional text. Each book contains about 80 attractive photographs and drawings, most in color, and is informative and written in text appropriate for the level. The alphabetically arranged topics are supported by interesting boxed information. Some schools may not want to purchase both series, but they are recommended.

2220 **The Marshall Cavendish International Wildlife Encyclopedia**. rev. ed. Maurice Burton and Robert Burton, eds. North Bellmore, N.Y.: Marshall Cavendish, 1990. 25v. $449.95/set. ISBN 0-86307-734-X. LC 88-5375.

This set, which emphasizes animal behavior and ecology, is a revised and expanded version of a 1980 work. It covers the world's fish, birds, reptiles, and mammals, as well as lower orders such as crustaceans and insects. Domestic animals are addressed by groups (e.g., dogs, cats) and by breed (e.g., Great Dane, Siamese).

The arrangement is alphabetical, aardvark to zebra fish. Some 1,000 readable articles, 2 to 3 pages in length, provide a brief description of the animal or group; details about its biology, feeding, reproduction, appearance, and special features; and a brief tabular list of scientific terminology, with 2 or 3 levels of classification. An abundance of outstanding full-page (and smaller) pictures in color and thematic maps illustrate the volume. Subject and systemic indexes give access to the text.

In comparison to *Grzimek's Animal Life Encyclopedia*, this set places less emphasis on taxonomy and anatomy and more on ecology and wildlife preservation. It is an excellent choice for junior and senior high schools. [R: SLJ, May 91]

2221 Milner, Richard. **The Encyclopedia of Evolution: Humanity's Search for Its Origins**. New York: Facts on File, 1990. 481p. $45.00. ISBN 0-8160-1472-8. LC 90-3344.

"Where did we come from?" This reference work, which focuses on this enduring and debated topic, contains more than 500 entries covering all aspects of scholarly and popular thought. Essays explain theories and controversial ideas, ranging from the science-versus-Bible dispute to the beliefs of today's "scientific" creationists and religious fundamentalists. Articles also treat the impact of these ideas on society and include brief biographies of persons who have played significant roles in the controversy throughout history. Recommended for high school libraries. [R: ARBA 92; BL, 1 Jan 91; LJ, Dec 90]

2222 **The Official World Wildlife Fund Guide to Endangered Species of North America**. David W. Lowe, ed. Washington, D.C.: Beacham, 1990. 2v. $195.00. ISBN 0-933833-17-2. LC 89-29757.

Plant and animal species that the U.S. Congress has declared "endangered" or "threatened" constitute the focus of this set. Articles are supported by a map showing primary habitats, short bibliographies, and a contact organization for further information. Black-and-white illustrations and a separate section of color plates in each volume handsomely depict about one-fifth of the species. Each volume opens with a "Ready Reference Index," and a full index and geographical list of all species conclude the set. Recommended for high schools. [R: BL, 15 May 90; SLJ, May 91; VOYA, Aug 90]

2223 **The Oxford Companion to Animal Behavior**. David McFarland, ed. New York: Oxford University Press, 1982. 657p. $49.95; $19.95pa. ISBN 0-19-866120-7; 0-19-281990-9pa. LC 82-80431.

Long, well-written articles intended for nonspecialists treat all aspects of animal behavior and related disciplines, such as physiology, genetics, and psychology. The alphabetically arranged articles are supported by illustrations, maps, and cross-references, but there is no index. Appropriate for advanced high school students.

2224 **Oxford Illustrated Encyclopedia. Volume 2: The Natural World**. Harry Judge and others, eds. New York: Oxford University Press, 1985. 384p. $45.00. ISBN 0-19-869134-3. LC 85-4876.

The volumes of this multivolume set, each on a broad area of knowledge, can stand alone. Consisting of alphabetically arranged concise entries, this work covers the natural world, including all areas of botany and zoology, and fossils. The color and black-and-white illustrations are excellent. The volume also includes maps, tables, diagrams, and an index.

Other volumes in the set are *The Physical World*; *World History from the Earliest Times to 1800*; *World History from 1800 to the Present Day*; and *The Arts*. [R: ARBA 86; BL, 15 June 86; LJ, 1 Mar 86; SLJ, Dec 85]

2225 Predators and Predation: The Struggle for Life in the Animal World. Pierre Pfeffer, ed. New York: Facts on File, 1989. 419p. $40.00. ISBN 0-8160-1618-6. LC 88-3880.

This work, originally published in France under the title *Qui Mange Qui* ("Who Eats Who"), explains how 441 predators (vertebrates and invertebrates) are a part of the natural food chain and live by feeding off each other. A typical entry gives the predator's common and scientific names, taxonomic classification, physical description, habitat, life cycle, mating and progeny, typical prey, and animals that prey on it. Highly recommended for high schools. [R: ARBA 90]

FIELD GUIDES AND HANDBOOKS

2226 Animal Anatomy on File. By the Diagram Group. New York: Facts on File, 1990. 1v. (various paging). $145.00 looseleaf w/binder. ISBN 0-8160-2244-5. LC 89-29772.

This set, a companion to *The Life Sciences on File Collection*, is an excellent source for secondary school biology classes. It offers almost 1,000 illustrations of some 50 species, arranged according to major families of the animal kingdom (e.g., mammals, birds, reptiles and amphibians). Several plates for each species depict external forms, skeleton, and major muscles/organs. As in other On File collections, all of the charts and diagrams are reproducible. A table of contents and an index provide excellent access to the volume. Appropriate for secondary schools. [R: ARBA 91; RBB, Jan/Feb 91; SLJ, Nov 90]

E+
2227 Brodie, Edmund D., Jr. Venomous Animals: 300 Animals in Full Color. New York: Golden Press/Western Publishing, 1989. 160p. $9.95pa. ISBN 0-307-24074-6. LC 89-50058.

Venomous Animals, the latest of the Golden guides, begins with an essay on venom, its delivery and effects, danger to humans, antivenins, and venom research. The 15 sections that follow are arranged by group—spiders, scorpions, insects, fishes, reptiles, and mammals—with general summaries and discussions of the poisonous members of each group.

The clearly written text avoids technical terminology. Numerous color illustrations by John D. Dawson, a distinguished wildlife artist, are a special feature. Recommended for upper elementary grades through high school. [R: ARBA 90]

2228 Miller, George Oxford. A Field Guide to Wildlife in Texas and the Southwest. Austin, Tex.: Texas Monthly Press, 1988. 260p. (Texas Monthly Field Guides). $21.95; $14.95pa. ISBN 0-87719-126-3; 0-87719-072-0pa. LC 88-20054.

This readable and entertaining volume, not a guide or identification book in the true sense, is a compilation of information about a few animals. There are articles about extinct, endangered, and threatened southwestern animals, and appeals for the conservation of those that remain.

The main section, on birds, mammals, reptiles, and invertebrates, provides 45 essays on specific species and families, containing well-written descriptions, tales, and the author's comments about his own scientific investigations. Recommended for secondary school collections in the southwestern area of the United States. [R: ARBA 90]

BIRDS

E+
2229 Bailey, Jill, and Steve Parker. Birds: The Plant- and Seed-Eaters. New York: Facts on File, 1989. 96p. ISBN 0-8160-1964-9. LC 88-33326.

E+
2230 Bramwell, Martyn. Birds: The Aerial Hunters. New York: Facts on File, 1989. 96p. $17.95. ISBN 0-8160-1963-0. LC 88-33319.

E+
2231   Kerrod, Robin. **Birds: The Waterbirds**. New York: Facts on File, 1989. 96p. $17.95. ISBN 0-8160-1962-2. LC 88-33318.

Each of these volumes, produced for the Encyclopedia of the Animal World series, offers a readable style and 200 photographs and other illustrations. Designed for students in grades 4 through 9, the set draws upon the latest field research and observations. Almost half of each book is devoted to illustrative materials.

Aerial Hunters covers hawks, owls, woodpeckers, and flightless birds. *The Plant- and Seed-Eaters* treats songbirds (e.g., larks, swallows, mockingbirds, warblers, starlings). *Water Birds*, those that are at home in the air and in the water, includes loons, geese, pelicans, swans, storks, and gulls.

Other volumes in this series, endorsed by the National Wildlife Federation, cover mammals, insects and spiders, fish, and pets. The series is highly recommended. [R: ARBA 90; BL, July 89; BR, Nov/Dec 89; SLJ, May 90; WLB, Jan 90]

E+
2232   Buckley, Virginia. **State Birds**. New York: E. P. Dutton, 1986. 63p. $16.95; $5.95pa. ISBN 0-525-67177-3; 0-525-67314-8pa. LC 86-2209.

Arthur and Alan Singer, the artists who produced the 1982 U.S. Postal Service stamp block of the birds and flowers of the 50 states, have painted the 27 birds designated as official state symbols for this work. Buckley describes each bird and indicates which states have selected it as its symbol. This colorful and interesting volume is an excellent choice for all levels of school libraries. [R: ARBA 88; BR, Mar/Apr 87; SLJ, Nov 86]

2233   Clark, William S. **A Field Guide to Hawks of North America**. Boston: Houghton Mifflin, 1987. 198p. (Peterson Field Guide Series, 35). $19.95; $13.95pa. ISBN 0-395-36001-3; 0-395-44112-9pa. LC 87-4528.

While most Peterson Field Guides cover several hundred species, this one focuses on the hawk and its relatives, 39 birds in all. Each account includes a description, similar species, flight patterns, status and distribution, behavior, unusual plumage, and more. The birds, arranged in phylogenetic sequence, are illustrated by color plates and black-and-white photographs. Some species are illustrated in regional variant, male, female, and immature stages. This well-organized guide is highly recommended. [R: ARBA 89; LJ, 15 Apr 88]

2234   Dunne, Pete, and others. **Hawks in Flight: The Flight Identification of North American Migrant Raptors**. Boston: Houghton Mifflin, 1988. 254p. $9.95pa. ISBN 0-395-51022-8. LC 87-18929.

This work covers 23 of the most common North American raptors (e.g., falcons, kites, eagles, vultures, ospreys). It identifies them by general body shape when flying (not by specific field marks, which can be seen only through binoculars), the way they move (rhythm and cadence), the places where they are likely to be seen, and when to look for them. Each species, grouped by shared traits of behavior and appearance, is illustrated by pen-and-ink drawings and black-and-white photographs. Recommended for high schools. [R: ARBA 90]

E+
2235   **The Encyclopedia of Birds**. Christopher Perrins and Alex L. A. Middleton, eds. New York: Facts on File, 1985. 445p. $45.00. ISBN 0-8160-1150-8. LC 84-26024.

This outstanding work, written by some 90 subject experts, covers 180 families of birds worldwide. For each family, information includes distribution patterns, characteristics, habitat, diet and feeding habits, size, color, calls, and nesting behavior. The text also includes articles on mating rituals, social organization, and other topics, all illustrated by over 400 beautiful color photographs of birds in flight. Highly recommended for grades 5 and up. [R: ARBA 86; BL, Aug 85; LJ, Sept 85; WLB, Oct 85]

E+
2236   **Familiar Birds of North America: Eastern Region**. Ann H. Whitman, ed. New York: Alfred A. Knopf/Random House, 1986. 192p. $6.95pa. ISBN 0-394-74839-5. LC 86-045588.

E+
2237   **Familiar Birds of North America: Western Region**. Ann H. Whitman, ed. New York: Alfred A. Knopf/Random House, 1986. 192p. $5.95pa. ISBN 0-394-74842-5. LC 86-045589.

Each of these pocket guides contains an introductory essay on birdwatching and describes 80 birds, giving general information, identification, voice, habitat, range, and a range map, with a color photograph on the facing page. Despite the lack of complete coverage of birds for the regions, each manual provides a good introduction to the field. Recommended for all levels. [R: ARBA 88; VOYA, Aug 87]

E +
2238 Farrand, John, Jr. **Western Birds**. New York: McGraw-Hill, 1988. 480p. (Audubon Handbook). $13.95pa. ISBN 0-07-019977-9. LC 87-3425.

Written especially for the amateur birdwatcher, this guide includes all birds seen regularly in the western region of the United States and southwestern Canada. It employs a system of identification that requires the novice to learn to recognize major groups by general appearance, size, behavior, and habitat. Recognizing plumage and voice comes as a second step.

Descriptions are arranged in taxonomic order, each entry giving the common and scientific name, size, habitat, field marks, range, and a small color photograph of the bird. Indexed by common and scientific names. Recommended for all levels. [R: ARBA 90]

2239 Fuller, Errol. **Extinct Birds**. New York: Facts on File, 1988. 256p. $40.00. ISBN 0-8160-1833-2. LC 87-9073.

This work describes well-known extinct birds (e.g., dodo, moa, passenger pigeon), obscure species (e.g., New Zealand takahe), and some hypothetical and mysterious birds (e.g., yellow-fronted bowerbird). Some 200 illustrations, 55 in full color, illustrate the volume, which includes an extensive bibliography. Indexed. [R: SBF, Jan/Feb 89]

2240 Hosking, Eric, and others. **Eric Hosking's Birds of Prey of the World**. New York: Viking Penguin, 1988. 176p. $19.95. ISBN 0-8289-0653-X.

This excellent book contains good photographs, both black-and-white and color, and a readable, up-to-date text. Most of the pictures of hawks, eagles, falcons, and vultures, taken by professional wildlife photographers, show the birds in their natural habitats. The text explains the classification of birds, their unusual behaviors, and their ecology. Conservation and the sport of falconry are also covered. Recommended for middle and high school levels. [R: BL, 1 Sept 88; SBF, Jan/Feb 89]

2241 Jones, John Oliver. **Where the Birds Are: A Guide to All 50 States and Canada**. New York: William Morrow, 1990. 400p. $24.95; $15.95pa. ISBN 0-688-09609-3; 0-688-05178-2pa. LC 89-49399.

The first part of this work, arranged by state and province, lists birding hotlines and bird clubs, describes important birding areas, and gives addresses and telephone numbers for wildlife refuges and government agencies. The second part provides data on birds to be found in each area, giving seasonal status and other useful information. This is not an identification guide, but is intended as an aid to persons interested in birding in a specific location. [R: ARBA 91; BL, 15 May 90; LJ, July 90]

E +
2242 **The Macmillan Illustrated Encyclopedia of Birds: A Visual Who's Who in the World of Birds**. Philip Whitfield, ed. New York: Collier Books/Macmillan, 1988. 224p. $19.95pa. ISBN 0-02-044462-1.

This handsome volume, featuring hundreds of beautiful full-color paintings and descriptions of more than 600 kinds of birds, has been drawn from *The Macmillan Illustrated Animal Encyclopedia* (1984), now out of print. Entries for each bird, arranged by family, provide its common and scientific name, physiology and size, conservation status, range and habitat, and breeding habits. Recommended for all levels.

2243 Peterson, Roger Tory. **A Field Guide to the Birds: A Completely New Guide to All the Birds of Eastern and Central North America**. 4th ed. Boston: Houghton Mifflin, 1980. 384p. $17.95; $13.95pa. ISBN 0-395-26621-1; 0-395-26619-Xpa.

E +
2244 Peterson, Roger Tory. **A Field Guide to Western Birds: A Completely New Guide to Field Marks of All Species Found in North America West of the 100th Meridian....** 3d ed. Boston: Houghton Mifflin, 1990. 432p. $22.95; $15.95pa. ISBN 0-395-51749-4; 0-395-51424-Xpa. LC 89-31517.

Text and paintings have been completely redone for these editions, flagship books in the Peterson Field Guide series. Bird species are arranged in a modified taxonomic sequence, with some groups (unrelated, but similar in appearance) presented together. Entries emphasize identifying characteristics but cover voice, range, habitat, and similar species. Detailed illustrations show major age, sex, and seasonal differences. Range maps for all species are located in separate sections. Highly recommended for all levels. [R: ARBA 91]

E+
2245   Robbins, Chandler, and others. **Birds of North America: A Guide to Field Identification**. Racine, Wis.: Golden Books/Western Publishing, 1983. 360p. (Golden Field Guide Series). $10.95; $7.95pa. ISBN 0-307-37002-X; 0-307-33656-5pa. LC 83-60422.

More than 2,000 birds that represent 700 species of land and water birds of North America are presented in this comprehensive, inexpensive guide. Land and water birds are divided and then sub-divided by family. For each are given popular and scientific name, a brief description, range, habitat, and verbal description of their songs or calls. Full-color illustrations depict the birds. This excellent guide to field identification is recommended for all levels. [R: BL, 1 Jan 84]

E+
2246   Weidensaul, Scott. **A Kid's First Book of Birdwatching**. Philadelphia: Running Press, 1990. 64p. $14.95 (book and audiocassette). ISBN 0-89471-826-6.

This field guide and accompanying audiocassette, which are useful for grades 3 and up, give an excellent introduction to birdwatching. The field guide contains an introduction, followed by a one-page narrative for each bird, arranged by broad categories: waterfowl, hawks, gamebirds, thrushes, finches, and sparrows. For each bird (e.g., downy woodpeckers, red-tailed hawks, mallard ducks, yellow warblers, red-winged blackbirds) the guide includes a beautiful photograph; a distribution map; and notes on plumage, size, behavior, habitat, call, food preference, nest type, and egg color.

Appendixes offer lists for further reading, a short quiz, and an index. The audiocassette, which gives each bird's description and call, follows the book's arrangement. The field guide and cassette can be used together or independently. Highly recommended. [R: WLB, Nov 90]

See **Fossils and Prehistoric Life** in **Earth Sciences**
for **Dinosaurs**.

FISHES

See **Pets** for aquarium fish.

2247   Filisky, Michael. **Peterson First Guide to Fishes of North America**. Boston: Houghton Mifflin, 1989. 128p. $4.95pa. ISBN 0-395-50219-5. LC 88-32887.

Another of the easy-to-use Peterson field guides, this volume treats the common fishes of North America, both freshwater and marine species. Illustrations in color show field markings, and the introduction for each fish describes its shape and anatomy. The guide also indicates distribution. [R: ARBA 91; BL, 1 June 89]

E
2248   Kaufman, Les, and the Staff of the New England Aquarium. **Do Fish Get Thirsty? Questions Answered by the New England Aquarium**. New York: New England Aquarium/Franklin Watts, 1991. 40p. $13.95. ISBN 0-531-15214-6. LC 90-46871.

Written in a question-and-answer format, this slim volume addresses questions frequently asked at the New England Aquarium: "Are fish good parents?" "Are there really any sea monsters?" "Can a fish live out of water?" Answers also concern whales, aquaculture, evolution, and extinction. Each page includes colorful photographs and diagrams. A glossary, bibliography, and index conclude the work. [R: SBF, May 91]

E+
2249   Losito, Linda, and others. **Fish**. New York: Facts on File, 1989. 96p. $17.95. ISBN 0-8160-1966-5.

This small volume in the Encyclopedia of the Animal World series covers the entire fish family, including freshwater and marine species. Students in grades 4 through 9, for whom it is intended, will find articles on seahorses, mudskippers, tuna, mackerel, salmon, skates, lizard fish, eels, sharks, and many others. More than 200 illustrations support the highly readable text. The books in this series, which are endorsed by the National Wildlife Federation, also include volumes about mammals, birds, insects and spiders, reptiles and amphibians, and pets. [R: BL, July 89; BR, Nov/Dec 89; SLJ, May 90; WLB, Jan 90]

INSECTS AND SPIDERS

E
2250   Forey, Pamela, and Cecilia Fitzsimons. **An Instant Guide to Butterflies.** New York: Bonanza/Outlet Books, 1987. $3.98. ISBN 0-517-61801-X.

The color-coded pages of this work assist in making quick identification of butterflies. Also pictured are the caterpillar that produced the butterfly, males and females (often quite different), a distribution map, and habitat.

"Instant" guides published by Bonanza include *An Instant Guide to Reptiles and Amphibians* by the same authors (1987), which features a skull and crossbones on pages depicting poisonous snakes. Other guides cover birds, animals, and insects.

E+
2251   Losito, Linda, and others. **Insects and Spiders.** New York: Facts on File, 1989. 96p. $17.95. ISBN 0-8160-1967-3.

Insects and Spiders, a volume in the Encyclopedia of the Animal World series, is endorsed by the National Wildlife Federation. This highly recommended book explores the fascinating world of these creatures and surveys the great diversity of form and behavior among butterflies, bees, scorpions, earwigs, grasshoppers, centipedes, stick insects, and beetles. Other volumes in this series deal with birds, mammals, invertebrates, fish, and pets. [R: BL, July 89; BR, Nov/Dec 89; SLJ, May 90; WLB, Jan 90]

2252   Mitchell, Robert T., and Herbert S. Zim. **Butterflies and Moths: A Guide to the More Common American Species.** rev. ed. Racine, Wis.: Golden Press/Western Publishing, 1987. 160p. $3.95pa. ISBN 0-307-24052-5. LC 64-24907.

This compact guide focuses on the most "common, widespread, important and unusual butterflies and moths"—diurnal, swallowtails, sulfurs, and whites. The introduction surveys the life history of butterflies and moths and their importance in gardening. Succinct descriptions and vivid illustrations are strong features of this small volume, which also cites organizations that promote the conservation and knowledge of butterflies. Indexed by scientific name. [R: ARBA 89]

E+
2253   Nardi, James B. **Close Encounters with Insects and Spiders.** Ames, Iowa: Iowa State University Press, 1988. 185p. $16.95. ISBN 0-8138-1978-4.

Close Encounters will appeal to students of all ages and teachers who wish to encourage them to observe nature. It is organized according to the habitats in which insects and spiders are commonly found (e.g., "Beneath Our Feet"). The text suggests ways to observe them and provides scientifically accurate information on their behavior and anatomical specifications, supported by over 130 detailed drawings. Recommended for all levels.

INVERTEBRATES

E+
2254   Douglass, Jackie Leatherbury. **Peterson First Guide to Shells of North America.** Boston: Houghton Mifflin, 1989. 128p. $4.95pa. ISBN 0-395-48297-6. LC 88-32884.

A basic guide, this small book provides colorful illustrations designed to aid the novice in identifying the most common shells. Markings are indicated with arrows. An introduction describes shells and mollusks and gives information on distribution and commercial uses. An excellent beginning guide, recommended for all levels. [R: ARBA 91; BL, 1 June 90]

E+
2255   Losito, Linda, and others. **Simple Animals.** New York: Facts on File, 1989. 96p. $17.95. ISBN 0-8160-1968-1.

This book, a volume in the Encyclopedia of the Animal World series, is designed to help students in grades 4 through 9 understand the behavior and ecology of simple invertebrates such as sponges, jellyfish, barnacles, woodlice, snails, slugs, clams, crabs, and octopi. Over 200 full-color illustrations support the very readable text.

Other volumes in this series, which is endorsed by the National Wildlife Federation, are concerned with mammals, insects and spiders, fish, birds, and pets. [R: BL, July 89; BR, Nov/Dec 89; SLJ, May 90; WLB, Jan 90]

2256   Wye, Kenneth R. **The Simon & Schuster Pocket Guide to Shells of the World**. New York: Simon & Schuster, 1990. 192p. $11.95. ISBN 0-671-68263-6.

This excellent guide, a convenient size for a pocket or field pack, covers over 700 of the world's most interesting shells. Beautiful full-color photographs are accompanied by descriptions that give scientific and common names, physical characteristics, distribution and frequency found, and related facts. Other features include a glossary and a world map that shows shell locations. Indexed. [R: ARBA 91]

MAMMALS

E+
2257   Bramwell, Martyn, and Steve Parker. **Mammals: The Small Plant-Eaters**. New York: Facts on File, 1988. 96p. $17.95. ISBN 0-8160-1958-4. LC 88-16934.

E+
2258   Kerrod, Robin. **Primates, Insect Eaters and Baleen Whales**. New York: Facts on File, 1988. 96p. $17.95. ISBN 0-8160-1961-4. LC 88-16931.

E+
2259   O'Toole, Christopher, and John Stidworthy. **Mammals: The Hunters**. New York: Facts on File, 1988. 96p. $17.95. ISBN 0-8160-1959-2. LC 88-16933.

E+
2260   Stidworthy, John. **Mammals: The Large Plant-Eaters**. New York: Facts on File, 1988, 96p. $17.95. ISBN 0-8160-1960-6. LC 88-16935.

These volumes about different kinds of mammals are part of the Encyclopedia of the Animal World series, which is highly recommended for grades 4 through 9. Offering children an understanding of animal behavior and ecology, the books provide a paragraph about each animal in its environment, basic facts about it, and a map showing its habitat. Each highly readable and attractive volume contains 200 full-color illustrations.

Small Plant-Eaters covers herbivores, including exotic animals, such as marmots, koalas, and porcupines, as well as more common ones, such as squirrels, hamsters, and gerbils. *Large Plant-Eaters* treats animals that live and feed in grassland ecosystems (e.g., gazelles, tapirs, kangaroos, buffaloes). *The Hunters*, the predators of the animal kingdom, range from leopards and tigers to whales and dolphins. *Primates, Insect Eaters and Baleen Whales* includes those animals that depend mainly on insects for food (e.g., aardvarks, anteaters, bats, bandicoots).

Other volumes in this series are *Birds: Aerial Hunters, Pets and Farm Animals, Simple Animals, Insects and Spiders, Reptiles and Amphibians, Birds: The Plant- and Seed-Eaters*, and *Birds: The Waterbirds*. The entire set, which is endorsed by the National Wildlife Federation, can be purchased for $170.00. [R: ARBA 90; BR, Nov/Dec 90; SLJ, May 90; SBF, Sept/Oct 89; SBF, Nov/Dec 89; WLB, Jan 90]

E+
2261   Dow, Lesley. **Alligators and Crocodiles**. New York: Facts on File, 1990. 72p. $17.95. ISBN 0-8160-2273-9.

2262   Hatherly, Janelle, and Delia Nicholls. **Dolphins and Porpoises**. New York: Facts on File, 1990. 72p. $17.95. ISBN 0-8160-2272-0.

2263   Coupe, Sheena. **Sharks**. New York: Facts on File, 1990. 72p. $17.95. ISBN 0-8160-2270-4.

2264   Dow, Lesley. **Whales**. New York: Facts on File, 1990. 72p. $17.95. ISBN 0-8160-2271-2.

Each of the oversized volumes in the Great Creatures of the World series contains brief chapters that average four pages each and cover topics such as how the creature evolved, the variety of species, habitat, diet, and reproduction. Color photographs, charts, and maps comprise at least half of each page. Each book concludes with a one-page glossary, a list of scientific names for the species, and an index.

These beautifully illustrated volumes provide a clear picture of the world's most fascinating creatures. The series is recommended for elementary and middle school levels. Additional volumes are forthcoming. [R: BL, 1 Apr 90; SLJ, July 90]

2265 Encyclopedia of Animals: Mammals. Edwin Gould and George McKay, eds. New York: Gallery Books/W. H. Smith, 1990. 240p. $24.98. ISBN 0-8317-2788-8.

This work covers mammals, their classification, how they evolved, their habits and behaviors, particular species, and those now endangered. Photographs, color drawings, and distribution maps all illustrate the volume. Indexed by Latin and common name. Better coverage is provided by the more expensive *Encyclopedia of Mammals*, but this work is worth its cost. Recommended for secondary schools. [R: LJ, 15 Nov 90]

E +
2266 The Encyclopedia of Mammals. David Macdonald, ed. New York: Facts on File, 1984. 895p. $65.00. ISBN 0-87196-871-1. LC 84-1631.

This beautiful book contains some 700 articles by 180 experts, arranged in 8 categories (e.g., carnivores, sea mammals). Animals covered range from the mouse to the elephant and grizzly bear. Articles, varying in length from 2 to 16 pages, cover physical features, habitat, and range. The 1,150 color plates and 72 color illustrations are an outstanding feature of this award-winning book. It is a first choice for school libraries. [R: ARBA 85; BL, 1 Jan 85; BL, 15 May 85; LJ, Jan 85]

2267 Evans, Peter. The Natural History of Whales and Dolphins. New York: Facts on File, 1987. 224p. $24.95. ISBN 0-8160-1732-8. LC 86-24037.

Detailed information on cetaceans is provided by this volume—evolution, classification, distribution, feeding habits, social organization and behavior, and relationship between them and man. Over 100 black-and-white and full-color illustrations, an extensive bibliography, and an index support this excellent work. Recommended for advanced high school students. [R: LJ, 1 Feb 88; VOYA, Oct 88]

E +
2268 The Greenpeace Book of Dolphins. John May, ed. New York: Sterling Publishing, 1990. 160p. $29.95. ISBN 0-8069-7484-2. LC 90-38836.

The first half of this lavishly illustrated, oversized book describes the various dolphin species and their biology and behavior. The second part covers threats to dolphins from fishing, hunting, pollution, and other forms of environmental disruption by humans. The text, written by Greenpeace activists, also treats controversial topics such as the military use of dolphins and aquarium captivity. The book concludes with a glossary, a short bibliography, a list of laws and regulations concerning cetaceans, and an index. Recommended for grade 6 and up.

2269 Grzimek's Encyclopedia of Mammals. 2d ed. Wolf Keienburg, ed. New York: McGraw-Hill, 1990. 5v. $500.00/set. ISBN 0-07-909508-9. LC 89-12542.

This beautifully illustrated set is based on *Grzimek's Life Encyclopedia* (1972-1975) but appears to be entirely new. Volume 1 treats mammals in terms of body structure and functions, behavior, ecology, endangerment, and so forth, and also covers marsupials, bats, flying lemurs, and egg-laying mammals (e.g., the platypus). Volume 2 addresses tree shrews, primates, anteaters, and armadillos; volume 3 covers rodentia and carnivora; volume 4 continues the treatment of carnivores and includes whales, dolphins, aardvarks, elephants, horses, and rhinoceroses; and volume 5 covers pigs, hippopotamuses, camels, deer, giraffes, and cattle.

Arranged by order, suborder, and subclass, the introductory sections (on tinted paper) for each classification provide information on external and skeletal features that distinguish that category of mammals from others and contain maps that show geographical distribution. The extensive information that follows usually includes pictorial family trees that show ancestral species. Summary charts provide comparative data on genera and species (e.g., size, distinguishing features, reproduction and gestation period, number of young per birth, birth weight, life span, food, enemies, habitat). Detailed information about the behavior of animals in their native environments, genetics, and evolution is included.

Exquisite color photographs are an outstanding feature of the set. Many cover a full page or even a two-page spread, and almost every page of text displays smaller color pictures.

The lack of adequate access to the information is the only real criticism of the set. Each volume includes a table of contents and an index, but there is no comprehensive index for all volumes. Nonetheless, this excellent work is a worthwhile addition to any library able to afford it. [R: ARBA 91; BL, 15 Mar 90; SBF, Sept/Oct 90]

2270   Wrigley, Robert E. **Mammals in North America**. New York: Hyperion/Sterling Publishing, c1986, 1990. 360p. $19.95. ISBN 0-920534-33-3.

This attractive volume, originally published in Canada, covers mammals of North America, including Mexico and Central America. One hundred fifteen species arranged by the biome in which they live (e.g., oceans, tundra, grasslands, desert) are described.

Each section opens with a survey of the environment, followed by illustrations of the animals in their natural habitats by Canadian wildlife artist Dwayne Harty. Entries contain several paragraphs about each animal, including such data as common and scientific names, family and order, specific characteristics (e.g., length, weight, color), distribution and status, reproduction and longevity, and food. Stories about each animal describe behavior as observed by Wrigley, curator of mammals at a science museum in Manitoba. Outline maps illustrate the animal's range.

A checklist of North American mammals, arranged by order, family, and species, indicates geographic distribution and status (e.g., whether endangered). A bibliography is provided, but there is no index, an unfortunate omission that requires the reader to rely on the table of contents for access.

This reasonably priced work does not provide the depth offered by the five-volume *Grzimek's Encyclopedia of Mammals*, but it contains an abundance of reliable information useful at the secondary level. [R: BL, 15 Dec 90; LJ, Aug 90]

E+
2271   Zim, Herbert S., and Donald F. Hoffmeister. **Mammals: A Guide to Familiar American Species**. rev. ed. Racine, Wis.: Golden Press/Western Publishing, 1987. 160p. $3.95pa. ISBN 0-307-24058-4. LC 61-8320.

This small volume, one of the familiar Golden guides, focuses on American mammals. The introduction tells how to observe and photograph mammals and gives information on species, range, and numbers. The description of each mammal (e.g., size, color, habits), usually a page in length, is accompanied by a color drawing and a small range map. Indexed. Due to the book's small size, it is more useful as a pocket guide than as a reference tool, but its information is reliable. [R: ARBA 89]

REPTILES AND AMPHIBIANS

2272   Alderton, David. **Turtles and Tortoises of the World**. New York: Facts on File, 1988. 192p. $24.95. ISBN 0-8160-1733-6.

This excellent worldwide review of turtles and tortoises begins with an introductory exposition of the relationship of these creatures to man, including their role in myths and literature. The chapters that follow examine various aspects of their lives, behavior, evolution, anatomy, reproduction, distribution, diversity, classification, adaptability, and conservation. More than 100 illustrations and photographs, including 60 in full color, illustrate the volume. Recommended for high schools. [R: BR, June 89]

2273   Capula, Massimo. **Simon & Schuster's Guide to Reptiles and Amphibians of the World**. New York: Simon & Schuster, 1989. 256p. $22.95; $10.95pa. ISBN 0-671-69136-8; 0-671-69098-1pa. LC 89-21671.

This work treats only 202 species of the more than 10,000 taxa of amphibians and reptiles. Entries for 80 amphibian and 122 reptile species, in brief half-page entries, include scientific and common names, classification, identification, habitat and biology, and a beautiful color photograph on the facing page. Margin symbols indicate each species' behavior and biological characteristics.

Critics have complained about this work's organization (separation of tables from explanations) and coverage of only a small number of species, but it provides an excellent and inexpensive introduction to the subject. Appropriate for middle and high school levels. [R: ARBA 91; SBF, Sept/Oct 90]

2274   Ernst, Carl H., and Roger W. Barbour. **Turtles of the World**. Washington, D.C.: Smithsonian Institution Press, 1989. 313p. $45.00. ISBN 0-87474-414-8. LC 88-29727.

This outstanding work is a manual for the identification and natural history of 257 turtles found throughout the world. Chapters cover each of the 12 turtle families. Every one opens with a summary of current and past distribution and fossil records, followed by a technical description of the family, a summary of subfamilies and genera, a distribution map, a dichotomous key to genera (e.g., anatomy, taxonomy, karyotypes), and data on habitat and natural history.

Color and black-and-white photographs accompany the entries, depicting 56 species. A lengthy bibliography, a glossary, and an index complete the volume. This is a more extensive work than *Turtles and Tortoises of the World*. Highly recommended for high schools. [R: ARBA 90]

2275 Mattison, Chris. **Lizards of the World**. New York: Facts on File, 1989. 192p. $24.95. ISBN 0-8160-1900-2. LC 89-1237.

Written for the general reader, this volume provides a short survey of the evolution of lizards, followed by a section explaining how they adapted to their environment. Successive chapters address their feeding habits, reproduction, distribution, habitat, defense mechanisms, function, and color.

The work is written in a readable, nontechnical style and is profusely illustrated by 50 color and 50 black-and-white photographs, line drawings, and charts. Indexed by common and scientific name. For high school level. [R: ARBA 90]

2276 Mehrtens, John M. **Living Snakes of the World in Color**. New York: Sterling Publishing, 1987. 480p. $50.00. ISBN 0-8069-6460-X. LC 87-9932.

The 540 color photographs of 454 subspecies of snakes provide a good sampling of the more than 3,000 species worldwide. Arranged in three categories—primitive snakes, colubrid snakes (nonpoisonous), and venomous snakes—they are then divided into familiar species, such as vipers, pythons, and rattlesnakes.

Entries provide the common and genus-species names, general habitat and geographical range, and one or two paragraphs on the snake's natural history. At least one photograph accompanies each entry. A small glossary and indexing by common name/subject and by genus/species conclude the volume, which is recommended for secondary schools. [R: ARBA 88; BL, 1 Dec 87; LJ, Dec 87]

2277 Obst, Fritz Jurgen, and others. **The Completely Illustrated Atlas of Reptiles and Amphibians for the Terrarium**. Neptune City, N.J.: T. F. H. Publications, 1988. 830p. $100.00. ISBN 0-86622-958-2.

In readable language, this work provides succinct commentaries in an encyclopedic format for those interested in the maintenance of reptiles and amphibians in terraria and for others with a general interest in these creatures. From abdominal cavity to Zygapis, there are entries for reptiles, terrarium plants, parasites, and hundreds of genera. Entries are illustrated by line drawings and over 1,500 beautiful color photographs. Highly recommended for high schools, which may be deterred by its cost. [R: ARBA 90; BL, 15 June 89; BR, Mar/Apr 89]

2278 Ross, Charles, and others. **Crocodiles and Alligators**. New York: Facts on File, 1989. 240p. $35.00. ISBN 0-8160-2174-0. LC 89-30416.

The natural history of these reptiles; their treatment in mythology, art, religion, and literature; and their place in the living world comprise this excellent work. The text is interspersed with boxed information, tables, and charts; over 200 paintings and photographs depict the animals from birth to death. The volume offers full treatment of all 22 species of crocodilians that have survived from prehistoric times. Highly recommended for grades 8 through 12. [R: BR, May/June 90]

E+
2279 Stidworthy, John. **Reptiles and Amphibians**. New York: Facts on File, 1989. 96p. $17.95. ISBN 0-8160-1965-7. LC 88-33317.

More than half of this excellent volume is devoted to full-color illustrations. The text introduces young people in grades 4 through 9 to the fascinating world of amphibians and reptiles. A broad range of species is covered, including chameleons, pythons, tortoises, newts, geckos, vipers, crocodiles, and iguanas. This book is a volume in the Encyclopedia of the Animal World series; other volumes are included under birds, mammals, insects and spiders, invertebrates, and pets. [R: ARBA 90; BL, July 89; BR, Nov/Dec 89; SLJ, May 90; WLB, Jan 90]

2280 Tyning, Thomas F. **A Guide to Amphibians and Reptiles**. Boston: Little, Brown, 1990. 400p. $19.95; $11.95pa. ISBN 0-316-81719-8; 0-316-81713-9pa. LC 89-28444.

This engaging book includes the natural history of 32 species of U.S. amphibians and reptiles, plus interesting anecdotal narratives about them. Part 1 deals with frogs and salamanders; part 2 covers snakes, alligators, turtles, and lizards. Each account provides information on such things as recognition, sex, breeding, eggs and young, ecology, behavior, and feeding. A range map, a quick-reference chart on the life cycle, and excellent black-and-white illustrations are also included with every account.

The species selected are those most familiar to amateur naturalists. The work, written in a lively style, is recommended for high school level. [R: ARBA 91]

Author/Title Index

Reference is to entry number.

A to z of investing, 302
A to zoo: subject access to children's picture bks, 3d ed, 1170
Aaseng, Nathan, 2161
Abbott, David, 2130
Abbreviations dict, 7th ed, 167
Abingdon dict of living religions, 1741
Abortion, 996
Abraham Lincoln ency, 723
Abrahamson, R. F., 98
Abrahamson, Richard F., 97
Abrams, A. Jay, 612
Abrams, Irwin, 945
Abrams, Margaret Ann, 612
Abramson, Glenda, 496
Abreau, Maria Isabel, 1621
Abridged Dewey decimal classification & relative index, 12th ed, 837
Abridged readers' gd to per lit, 227
Academic Amer ency, 194
Academic freedom, 786
Access Amer: atlas & gd to the natl parks for visitors with disabilities, 613
Access to art: a museum dir for blind ..., 1349
Achtemeier, Paul J., 1765
Achtert, Walter S., 1283
Activities almanac, 890
Adams, Helen R., 872
Adams, James T., 727
Adams, Michael, 1044
Adamson, Lynda G., 634
Administering the school lib media center, 3d ed, 875
Adventuring with bks: a bklist for pre-K-6, 9th ed, 71
Africa, rev ed, 1024
Africa, 1025
African states & rulers, 1027
Aging Amer: trends & projections, 1938
AIDS & women: sourcebk, 1977
AIDS, 1983
AIDS: plague or panic?, 1978
AIDS: political, social, interl aspects, 1991
Air & space cat: complete sourcebk to everything in the universe, 2187
Air wars & aircraft, 913
AIT cat of instructional materials, 428
ALA filing rules, 828
ALA glossary of lib & info science, 820
ALA rules for filing catalog cards, 2d ed, 829
Album of Amer hist, rev ed, 727
Album of Amer hist, supp, 1968-1982, 728
Album of sci, 2102

Alcohol/drug abuse dict & ency, 1952
Alderton, David, 2272
Alexander, Claudia B., 1126
Alexander, Pat, 1768
Alfred Glossbrenner's master gd to free sftwr for IBMs ..., 1869
Ali, Sheikh R., 991
All about tropical fish, 4th ed, 2075
All ears: how to use & choose recorded music for children, 36
All new official cheerleader's hndbk, 1083
All the best contests for kids, 173
Allaby, Michael, 2043, 2058
Allardice, Pamela, 1689
Allen, James, 460
Alligators & crocodiles, 2261
Almanac of Amer politics, 935
Almanac of Amer women in the 20th century, 1123
Almanac of famous people, 4th ed, 239
Almanac of the Amer people, 1105
Almanac of US seapower 1989, 911
Alphabet bks as a key to language patterns, 1164
Alpine wildflowers of the Rocky Mountains, 1829
Alternative press pub of children's bks, 11
Althouse, Andrew D., 2177
Altman, Roberta, 2046
Altmann, Susan, 465
Alves, Michael J., 415
Amateur magician's hndbk, 4th ed, 741
Amateur naturalist, 2063
America as story, 697
American art dir, 1346
American authors, 1600-1900, 1588
American bk of days, 780
American bk pub record, 54
American bk pub record cum, 55
American capitols, 582
American educator's ency, rev ed, 359
American heritage children's dict, 1399
American heritage first dict, 1398
American heritage illus hist of the US, 710
American heritage Larousse Spanish dict, 1491
American heritage picture dict, 1404
American heritage student's dict, 1400
American hist for children & young adults, 698
American homeless, 999
American Indian lits, 1586
American Indian ref bks, 507
American Jewish yr bk 1990, 494
American leaders, 1789-1991, 946
American medical assn ency of medicine, 1979

American medical assn hndbk of first aid & emergency care, 2006
American men & women of sci, 18th ed, 2129
American photographers, 1371
American political dict, 8th ed, 931
American political leaders ..., 948
American presidency, 1776-1990, 986
American presidents, 979
American ref bks annual, 132
American reformers, 255
American sign language, 621
American songwriters, 1639
American Univ & colleges, 13th ed, 394
American women in sport, 1887-1987, 1052
American women writers, 1589
American writers, 1595
American writers for children since 1960, 1172
America's architectural roots, 1363
America's ethnic heritage series, 458
America's national battlefield parks, 736
Ammer, Christine, 302
Amnesty International report, 813
Anatomy of wonder: critical gd to sci fict, 3d ed, 1544
Andersen, Yvonne, 1331
Anderson, Bernhard W., 1759
Anderson, Carol L., 905
Anderson, James, 1659
Anderson, Pauline H., 904
Anderson, Vicki, 1149
Andre Previn's gd to the orchestra, 1655
Andrew, Geoff, 1332
Andrews, John F., 1610
Andrews, Robert, 1716
Angelo, Joseph A., Jr., 1802
Anglin, Donald L, 2165
Animal anatomy on file, 2226
Animal life, 2107
Animal life, 2219
Anniversaries & holidays, 4th ed, 778
Anthony, Susan C, 143
Anzovin, Steven, 988
Apartheid, 1026
Appel, Marsha C., 212-14
Appraisal: children's sci bks, 45
Appropriate word, 1453
Apseloff, Marilyn Fain, 1150
Arad, Yitzhak, 669
Arbuthnot, May Hill, 1145
Archambault, Ariane, 1419, 1481
Architects make zigzags, 1366
Ardley, Neil, 1627
Argent, Jeanne, 1305
Argyle, Christopher, 663
Arnold, Denis, 1633
Arnold, Peter, 743
Aronson, Marc, 655
Art of children's picture bks, 1148
Artist's hndbk of materials & techniques, 5th ed, 1352
Artist's market: where & how to sell your artwork, 1347
ArtsAmerica fine art film & video source bk, 1987, 1350
Ashley dict, 1477
Asimov, Isaac, 1797, 2099, 2121, 2134
Asimov's chronology of sci & discovery, 2099
Assassinations & executions, 1865-1986, 930
Astronauts & cosmonauts: bio & statistical data, 2188

Astronomy from a-z, 1807
At the pirate academy, 889
Athearn, Robert G., 710
Atkinson, Frank, 286
Atlas of Amer hist, 2d ed, 699
Atlas of Amer hist, 701
Atlas of Amer Indian affairs, 510
Atlas of ancient Amer, 233
Atlas of cats of the world, 2077
Atlas of Central Amer & the Caribbean, 534
Atlas of China, 535
Atlas of classical hist, 625
Atlas of Columbus & the great discoveries, 630
Atlas of deep-sky splendors, 4th ed, 1800
Atlas of dog breeds of the world, 2084
Atlas of Eastern Europe, 1032
Atlas of economic issues, 295
Atlas of environmental issues, 2039
Atlas of human evolution, 2d ed, 230
Atlas of medieval Europe, 650
Atlas of modern Jewish hist, 499
Atlas of natural wonders, 603
Atlas of Southeast Asia, 1029
Atlas of the Amer Indians, 513
Atlas of the crusades, 626
Atlas of the Jewish world, 497
Atlas of the living world, 2059
Atlas of the Middle East, 1043
Atlas of the N Amer Indians, 513
Atlas of the natural world, 1883
Atlas of the People's Republic of China, 536
Atlas of the US, 537
Atlas of world issues, 1016
Atmosphere crisis: greenhouse effect & ozone depletion, 2047
Atomic scientists: bio hist, 2086
At-risk youth, 388
Attenborough, David, 2059
Audouze, Jean, 1798
Audubon society field gd to N Amer fossils, 1905
Audubon society field gd to N Amer rocks & minerals, 1906
Audubon society field gd to N Amer wildflowers, western region, 1835
Audubon society filed gd to N Amer wildflowers, eastern region, 1834
Augarde, Tony, 773
Austin, Erik W., 934
Austin, Mary C., 482
Author a month (for nickels), 1236
Author a month (for pennies), 1237
Authors & artists for young adults, 1173
Authors of bks for young people, 3d ed, 1197
Automobile bk, 1992, 349
Automotive ency, rev ed, 2166
Automotive engines, 7th ed, 2165
AV equipment & materials, 430
AV market place, 12
Aversa, Elizabeth S., 859-60
Aviation/space dict, 7th ed, 2203
Award-winning bks for children & young adults, 1199
Axelrod, Herbert R., 2073
Aylesworth, Thomas G., 1066
A-z of opera, 1658
A-z of snake keeping, 2085

Back stage hndbk for permorming arts, 1786
Background notes on the courntries of the world, 1010
Bacon, Josephine, 539
Baechler, Lea, 1593
Bahat, Dan, 1740
Baigel, Matthew, 1337
Bailey, Jill, 2229
Bailey, William G. 117, 807
Bair, Frank A., 1894
Baker, Daniel B., 939
Baker ency of the Bible, 1758
Baker's bio dict of musicians, 8th ed, 1637
Balanchine, George, 1793
Baldauf, Gretchen S., 321
Baldick, Chris, 1498
Baldrige, Letitia, 517
Ballard, Robert D., 1884
Ballplayers: baseball's ultimate biographical ref, 1067
Bancroft-Hunt, Norma, 503
Band music gd, 8th ed, 1648
Banham, Martin, 1779
Banister, Keith, 2217
Banja, Judith, 1189
Barbour, Roger W., 2274
Barkin, Carol, 1278-9
Barnes & Noble bk of quotations, rev ed, 1717
Barnhart, Clarence L., 1389, 1394, 1413-5
Barnhart dict of etymology, 1435
Barnhart, Robert K., 1389, 1394, 1435, 2103
Barone, Michael, 935
Barron, Neil, 1544, 1546-7
Barron, Pamela Patrick, 853
Barron's 300 best buys in college educ, 396
Barron's finance & investment hndbk, 3d ed, 294
Barron's jr fact finder, 190
Barron's profiles of Amer colleges, 16th ed, 413
Barron's profiles of Amer colleges: descriptions of the
    colleges, 17th ed, 395
Barron's student's concise ency, 187
Barstow, Barbara, 72
Bartlett, John, 1718
Barzun, Jacques, 1465
Basch, Rebecca A., 398
Baseball card price gd, 750
Baseball ency, 8th ed, rev ed, 1068
Baseballistics, 1075
Basic classical & operatic recordings collection on
    compact disc for libs, 1654
Basic classical & operatic recordings collections for
    libs, 1653
Basic collection of children's bks in Spanish, 83
Basic docs on human rights, 3d ed, 814
Basic Japanese-English dict, 1486
Basic media skills through games, 2d ed, 891
Baskin, Barbara H., 73
Bast, Carol J., 1059
Basta, Nicholas, 327
Battle chronicles of the Civil War, 711
Battle of bks, 1232
Battles & battlescenes of World War Two, 659
Bauer, Caroline Feller, 775, 1223
Beacham, Walton, 1497, 1524
Beacham's gd to lit for young adults, 1207
Beale, Paul, 1424
Beard, Charles, A., 976
Beck, Emily Morrison, 1718
Beck, Warren A., 700

Becker, Marion R., 1934
Beckett, Kenneth, A., 2014
Beckson, Karl, 1499
Bede, Jean-Albert, 1502
Bedurftig, Friedemann, 680
Beeching, Cyril Leslie, 1433
Beetz, Kirk, 1207
Beginner's dict of Amer English usage, 1380
Beginning French bilingual dict, 1482
Behind the covers, (v1, v2), 1191, 1192
Behr, Sheila, 518
Bell, Irene Wood, 891
Bell, James B., 525
Bell, Robert E., 1690-1
Belliston, Larry, 348
Ben-Asher, Naomi, 495
Bendick, Jeanne, 2023
Bendiner, Elmer, 1980
Bendiner, Jessica, 1980
Benet's reader's ency of Amer lit, 1579
Bennett, H., 1850
Benton, Michael, 1896
Benyus, Janine M., 2060-2
Bercuson, David J., 678
Berger, Gilda, 1950
Berger, Melvin, 1950
Bergstrom, Craig, 173
Bergstrom, Joan M., 173
Bernstein, Joanne E., 1999
Bernstein, Theodore M., 1260
Berry, John N., III, 53
Berry, Margaret, 892
Besancon, Robert, 2087
Best bks for children: preschool-grade 6, 4th ed, 82
Best bks for junior high readers, 1151
Best: high/low bks for reluctant readers, 93
Best in children's bks, 1979-84, 75
Best music for young bands, 1649
Best of Children's Choices, 1163
Best plays, 1787
Best ref bks, 1986-90, 134
Best science bks & av materials for children, 2091
Best videos for children & young adults, 25
Better Homes & Gardens new cook bk, 10th ed, 1914
Better Homes & Gardens new jr cook bk, rev ed, 1915
Beyond picture bks: a gd to first readers, 72
BFI companion to the western, 1310
Biagini, Mary K., 95, 887
Bianco, David, 1676
Biard, J. D., 1479
Bicycle repair bk, rev ed, 2168
Bicycling magazine's complete gd to bicycle
    maintenance & repair, 2167
Bierhorst, John, 1706
Bigotry, 998
Bill of Rights & landmark cases, 801
Billboard bk of number one hits, rev ed, 1677
Biographical bks, 1950-80, 240
Biographical dict of Amer educators, 393
Biographical dict of Amer journalism, 1256
Biographical dict of Hispanic lit in the US, 1590
Biographical dict of medicine, 1980
Biographical dict of scientists, 2130
Biographical dict of the Confederacy, 733
Biographical dict of women artists in Europe & Amer,
    1357
Biographical dir of the Amer congress, 1774-1989, 961

Biographical ency of scientists, 2131
Biographies of Amer women, 1122
Biography index, cum index, 241
Biracree, Nancy, 1105, 1963
Biracree, Tom, 1105, 1963
Birds of N Amer: gd to field identification, 2245
Birds: the aerial hunters, 2230
Birds: the plant- and seed-eaters, 2229
Birds: the waterbirds, 2231
Birnbaum, Max, 397
Birnes, William J., 1876
Birthday book, 1189
Bishop, Cynthia, 2140
Bishop, Peter, 1744
Bisk, Nathan M., 758
Black adolescence, 466
Black Amer in congress, 1870-1989, 962
Black Amer info dir, 1990-91, 467
Black Amer women in lit, 1577
Black Amer women novelists, 1578
Black authors & illustrators of children's bks, 1193
Black experience in children's bks, 1989, 468
Black, Henry Campbell, 791
Black, Jim N., 1257
Black leaders of the nineteenth century, 469
Black music bio, 1640
Black olympic medalists, 1100
Black, Perry O., 2162
Black resource gd, 1990-91 ed, 470
Black Union soldiers in the Civil War, 721
Black writers, 1515
Blackburn, G. Meredith, III, 1214-7
Blackburn, Lorraine A., 1215-6
Blackmore, Stephen, 1825
Blacks in Amer film & TV, 1311
Black's law dict, 6th ed, 791
Black's medical dict, 36th ed, 1981
Blackwell companion to Jewish culture, 496
Blake, Robert, 270-1, 646
Blandford, Percy W., 765
Blassingame, Wyatt, 977
Blemenson, John J., 1364
Blenz-Clucas, Beth, 29
Block, Deborah Perlmutter, 328-9
Blocksma, Mary, 211
Blom, Eric, 1628
Bloom, Ken, 1776
Blum, Laurie, 414
Boarding school gd, 374
Bochinski, Julianne Blair, 2133
Body atlas, 1971
Bogle, Donald, 1311
Bogue, Donald J., 1106
Bolles, Richard Nelson, 330
Boltz, C. W., 2149
Bond, Christopher E., 315
Bond, Peter, 2189
Bond, Robert E, 315
Bonnet, Robert L., 1847-8, 1881
Book bait: detailed notes on adult bks popular with young adults, 4th ed, 101
Book links, 46
Book of a thousand plays, 1788
Book of card games, 743
Book of goddesses & heroines, rev ed, 1703
Book of Irish names, 530
Book of legal anecdotes, 800

Book of saints, 6th ed, 1774
Book of the states, 990
Book report, 1
Book rev digest, 215
Book rev index, 216
Book talk gd, for use with readers age 4-8, 1211
BookBrain grades 1-3, 1152
BookBrain grades 4-6, version 3.0, 1153
BookBrain grades 7-12, version 2.0, 1154
Bookfinder 4: when kids need bks, 1158
Booklist, 2
Bookpeople: a first album, 1238
Bookpeople: a second album, 1239
Books for Catholic elem schools, 1737
Books for children to read alone, 1167
Books for religious educ in Catholic secondary schools, 1738
Books for the gifted child (v1, v2), 73, 74
Books for the teen age, 96
Books for you: a bklist for sr high students, 10th ed, 97
Books in print, 56
Books in print suppl, 58
Books in Spanish for children & young adults, 1978, 88
Books in Spanish for children & young adults, 1983, 87
Books in Spanish for children & young adults, 1985, 86
Books in Spanish for children & young adults, 1987, 85
Books in Spanish for children & young adults, 1989, 84
Books kids will sit still for, 1227
Books of the Bible, 1759
Books out-of-print 1984-88, 60
Books: their care & repair, 826
Books to help children cope with separation & loss, vol 3, 1999
Books to read aloud with children thru age 8, 1224
Books without bias, 2d ed, 504
BookWhiz, 1156
BookWhiz for teens, 1157
BookWhiz, Jr., 1155
Boorse, Henry A., 2086
Border clip art for lib, 907
Bordman, Gerald, 1777-8
Borg, Edward, 1318
Bornstein, Harry, 620
Borton, Terry, 208
Bosco, Dominick, 1916
Bosmajian, Haig A., 786-90
Botany: 49 more science projects, 1848
Botany: 49 science fair projects, 1847
Botermans, Jack, 737
Boughton, Simon, 275
Bowden, Henry W., 1770
Bowermaster, J., 2055
Bowker annual lib & bk trade almanac, 821
Bowker's complete video dir, 1990, 17
Boxshall, G. A., 2064
Boy scouts of Amer. fieldbook, 3d ed, 766
Boyce, Charles, 1301, 1604
Boyer, P. S., 1134
Boyer, Richard, 1107
Boyne, Walter, Jr., 2190
Brace, C. Loring, 230

Bradbury, Phil, 907
Brady, Holly, 105
Bragdon, Allan D., 2172
Bragonier, Reginald, Jr., 1418
Braille bk rev, 41
Brainard, Beth, 518
Brainstorms & blueprints, 903
Bramwell, Martyn, 2230, 2257
Brandon, S.G. F., 1742
Branyan-Broadbent, Brenda, 426
Brawer, Moshe, 1043
Breen, Karen, 242
Breen, Walter, 751
Brewer's dict of phrase & fable, 14th ed, 1500
Brewton, John E., 1213
Brewton, Sara W., 1213
Briggs, Katharine M., 1692
Bristow, M. J., 1684
Britannica world data, 1989, 207
British authors before 1800, 1599
British authors of the nineteenth century, 1600
British writers, 1602
Britt, Stan, 1666
Broadway: ency gd, 1776
Broadway on records, 1673
Brockman, C. Frank, 1840
Broderick, Dorothy M., 9
Brodie, Edmund D., Jr., 2227
Brody, Jane, 1917
Bronson, Fred, 1677
Brooks, Tim, 1266
Brown, Ashley, 674, 1662
Brown, Julie, 594
Brown, Peter Lancaster, 1808
Brown, Raymond E., 1760
Brown, Robert, 2191
Brown, Robert, 594, 2104
Brownlie, Ian, 814
Brownstone, David M., 337, 458, 600, 639, 649,
    735, 1967
BRS/search service, 181
Bruno, Frank J., 2000
Brush up your Shakespeare!, 1606
Brush, Warren D., 1842
Brussell, Eugene E., 1735
Bryan, C. D. B., 2202
Bryson, Bill, 1464
Buckley, Virginia, 2232
Bud's easy term paper kit, 8th ed, 1273
Buhle, Mari Jo., 937
Built in the USA: Amer buildings from airports to
    zoos, 1365
Bulfinch's mythology, 1686
Buller, Laure, 2135
Bulletin of the Center for Children's Bks, 47
Bullock, Alan, 166
Bully pulpit, 978
Bunch, Bryan, 2100
Burbank, Richard, 1626
Burck, Deborah M., 175
Burger, Julian, 2038
Burgess, Warren E., 2074
Burington, Richard S., 2029
Burne, Jerome, 635
Burnie, David, 1841
Burroughs, Lea, 1351
Burton, Maurice, 2220

Burton, Robert, 2220
Buscombe, Edward, 1310
Bushell, Chris, 2211
Business One-Irwin bus & investment almanac, 292
Butcher, Miriam H., 940
Butler, Kurt, 2007
Butterflies & moths, rev ed, 2252
Butterworth, Rod R., 617-8
Buttlar, Lois J., 356
Buying bks, 874
Buying gd issue, 350
Byles, Monica, 2109
Byrne, Deborah J., 830

C. A. Cutter's three-figure author table, 831
C. A. Cutter's two-figure author table, 832
Cadet gray: your gd to military schools, 404
Cahn, Victor L., 1605
Calasibetta, Charlotte Mankey, 1293
Caldecott Medal bks: 1938-57, 1203
Calhoun, David, 2126
California: environmental atlas & gd, 2033
Calligraphers' dict, 1249
Callison, Daniel, 873
Calories & carbohydrates, 9th ed, 1927
Cambridge atlas of astronomy, 2d ed, 1798
Cambridge bio dict, 256
Cambridge ency, 188
Cambridge ency of earth sciences, 1885
Cambridge ency of India, Pakistan ..., 1028
Cambridge ency of language, 1378
Cambridge ency of space, 2193
Cambridge gd to lit in English, 1501
Cambridge gd to world theatre, 1779
Cambridge hist ency of Great Britain & Ireland, 688
Cambridge hist of Latin Amer, 683
Cambridge hndbk of Amer lit, 1580
Cambridge illus dict of British heritage, 689
Cambridge illus dict of natural hist, 2064
Cambridge world gazetteer, 590
Camp, Wesley D., 1719
Campbell, Andrew, 2217
Campbell, William Giles, 1274
Canadian almanac & dir, 144
Canadian bks for children, 1144
Canadian bks for young people, 4th ed, 76
Canadian per index, 217
Canadian world almanac & bk of facts 1991, 145
Canby, Courtlandt, 640
Canned Art: clip art for the Macintosh, 1871
Capital punishment, 997
Caplan, Lawrence H., 1373
Capula, Massimo, 2273
Career discover ency, 331
Career index: selective bibliog for elem schools, 321
Career opportunities in advertising & public relations,
    332
Career opportunities in art, 333
Career opportunities in sports, 334
Cargas, Harry James, 658
Carlisle, Richard, 232
Cardozo, Arlene Rossen, 1773
Carpenter, Allen, 573-5
Carpenter, Charles A., 1539
Carpenter, Humphrey, 1168
Carpentry & building construction, 2171
Carr, Anna, 2020

Carroll, Frances Laverne, 1159
Carruth, Gorton, 704-5, 1047
Carter, B., 97
Carter, Betty, 98
Case, Brian, 1666
Case studies in managing school lib media centers, 873
Cass, James, 397
Cassell, Carol, 2001
Cassell's Latin dict, 1487
Cassidy, Daniel J., 415, 441
Cassidy, Frederic, G., 1427
Cassutt, Michael, 2194
Castillo, Carlos, 1492
Castle, Lance, 1188
Castleman, Harry, 1267
Cat in the hat beginner bk dict, 1402
Cat in the hat beginner bk dict in French & English, 1480
Cat in the hat beginner dict in Spanish & English, 1494
Catalog of fine art reproductions, 1335
Catalog of free-loan video/16mm films and teaching materials, 18
Cataloging correctly for kids, rev ed, 834
Cataloging with copy, 2d ed, 846
Catalogue of reproductions of paintings, 1860-1979, 11th ed, 1336
Catalogue of the world's most popular coins, 12th ed, 759
Catholic fact bk, 1751
Catsberg, C. M. E., 1918
Cattermole, Peter, 1814
Cavendish, Richard, 1701
CD-ROM collection builder's toolkit, 106
Celebrations, 775
Censorship & selection, 851
Cerny, John, 529
Chafetz, Morris, 1956
Chambers biology dict, 1820
Chan, Lois Mai, 835
Chandler, David G., 659
Chang, Sam H., 1448
Chapman, Charles F., 1993
Chapman, Mike, 1104
Chapman, Peter M., 1456
Chapman, Robert, 1432
Chapman, Robert L., 1428
Characters in 20th century lit, 1506
Characters in 20th-century lit, 1536
Charton, Barbara, 1911
Chartrand, Mark R., 1809
Charts on file, 146
Chase's annual events, 776
Cheatham, Annie, 363
Chelsea House series on Indians of N Amer, 505
Chemistry: periodic table, 1849
Chemist's ready ref hndbk, 1857
Chesterman, Charles W., 1906
Chevalier, Tracy, 1196
Chicago manual of style, 13th ed, 1275
Chicano Lit, 1591
Child & youth actors, 1325
Child abuse & neglect: info & ref gd, 1944
Childcraft dict, 1401
Childcraft: the how & why lib, 196
Children & bks, 7th ed, 1145
Children's authors & illustrators, 4th ed, 1174
Children's bk rev index, 218

Children's bk rev index: master cum, 1965-84, 219
Children's bks in print 61
Children's bks of the yr, 77
Children's Britannica, 1991 ed, 197
Children's cat, 16th ed, 66
Children's counting-out rhymes ..., 738
Children's lit: a gd to criticisms, 1147
Children's lit awards & winners, 2d ed, 1200
Children's lit in the elementary school, 4th ed, 1142
Children's lit review, 1175
Children's lit: theory, research & teaching, 1146
Children's mag gd, 220
Children's media market place, 3d ed, 13
Children's writing & publishing center, 1262
Chilton's auto repair manual, 1987-91, 2163
Chilvers, Ian, 1344
Chinese-Amer heritage, 458
Choices: a core collection for young reluctant readers V 2, 90
Choosing bks for children, rev ed, 1160
Christy, Joe, 2195
Chronicle of Amer, 706
Chronicle of the first world war, V 1: 1914-16, 663
Chronicle of the world, 635
Chronicle of the yr, 1989, 147
Chronological atlas of World War Two, 667
Chronology of western architecture, 1370
Chrystie, Frances N., 2068
Chudy, Harry T., 2164
Cianciolo, Patricia J., 78
Ciardi, John, 1436
Cinema sequels & remakes, 1903-87, 1334
Civil War, 729
Civil War battlefield gd, 712
Clark, Gilbert A., 375
Clark, Jerome, 925
Clark, Judith Freeman, 1123, 1943
Clark, Robin E., 1943
Clark, William S., 2233
Clarke, Donald, 1663
Classical ballet techniques, 1796
Classical Greek & Roman drama, 1613
Clay, James, 577
Clayman, Charles, 1979
Clifford, Mike, 1675
Cline, Ruth K. J., 1964
Close encounters with insects & spiders, 2253
Cloyd, Iris, 479
Clubb, Jerome M., 934
CM: A reviewing jl of Canadian material for young people, 3
Coe, Michael, 233
Coffin, Tristram Potter, 1708
Coghlan, Ronan, 530
Cohen, Daniel, 1693
Cohen, Gary, 2051
Cohen, Hennig, 1708
Cohen I. B., 2102
Cohen, Mark N., 319
Cohen, Norman S., 979
Cohen, Richard M., 1073, 1078
Coin atlas, 753
Coin collection as a hobby, 756
Coin world alamanac, 6th ed, 752
Colangelo, Nicholas, 424
Colby, Vineta, 1520, 1529-30
Cole, Sylvia, 169

Coleman, J. Gordon, 823
Collcutt, Martin, 1036
Collection analysis in the school lib, 853
Collection program in schools, 858
Collector's gd to comic bks, 755
College admissions data hndbk, 398
College admissions index of majors & sports, 416
College blue book, 22d ed, 399
College board achievement tests, rev ed, 451
College board gd to high schools, 364
College board gd to jobs & career planning, 339
College cost bk, 1991, 11th ed, 417
College cost explorer, 402
College explorer, 400
College hndbk, 403
College majors: a complete gd, 420
College names of the games, 1057
College planner, 401
Collier's ency: with bibliog & index, 198
Collin, P. H., 1380
Collingwood, G. H., 1842
Collins COBUILD English language dict, 1381
Collins dict of Canadian hist, 678
Collins, Mark, 2034
Collins, N. Mark, 2032
Collins Spanish-English, English-Spanish dict, 2d ed, 1493
Colonial & nineteenth century, 1567
Color atlas of galaxies, 1801
Columbia dict of modern European lit, 2d ed, 1502
Columbia ency of nutrition, 1937
Columbia Granger's gd to poetry anthologies, 1565
Columbia Granger's index to poetry, 9th ed, 1560
Comaromi, John P., 836-7
Combat arms: moder spyplanes, 2204
Commager, Henry S., 730
Commire, Anne, 1195
Community, tech, & jr college statistical yrbk, 376
Como prepararse para el exam del equivalencia de escuela superior en espanol, 456
Companion to Chinese hist, 679
Companion to Russian hist, 684
Comparative gd to Amer colleges, 397
Complete "lite" foods calorie, fat cholesterol, & sodium counter, 1936
Complete baseball record bk, 1069
Complete bk of herbs, spices & condiments, 1933
Complete bk of home environmental hazards, 2046
Complete bk of needlecrafts, 1304
Complete bk of quotations for the Bible, 1766
Complete bk of US presidents, 2d ed, 982
Complete bk of vitamins & monerals, 1919
Complete car cost gd, 1990 ed, 351
Complete dict of furniture, 1303
Complete dir of large print bks & serials, 63
Complete dir to prime time network TV shows, 4th ed, 1266
Complete dog bk, 17th ed, 2081
Complete film dict, 1317
Complete gd to automotive refinishing, 2d ed, 2164
Complete gd to vitamins, minerals & supplements, 1924
Complete golfer, 1088
Complete hndbk of personal computer communication, 3d ed, 1872
Complete hndbk of sci fair projects, 2133
Complete sci fair hndbk, grades 4-8, 2134

Complete step-by-step gd to home sewing, 1305
Completely illus atlas of reptiles & amphibians for the terrarium, 2277
Composers since 1900, 1642
Composers since 1900, first supp, 1643
Comprehensive signed English dict, 620
Compton, Rae, 1306
Compton's ency & fact index, 199
Compton's multimedia ency, 200
CompuServe, 182
Computer glossary: complete illus desk ref, 5th ed, 1864
Computer tutor 1.0, 868
Computer virus protection hndbk, 1873
Computers & the school lib, 861
Computers: 49 science fair projects, 1881
Computing teacher, 103
Concise AACR2, 1988 revision, 839
Concise Baker's bio dict of musicians, 1647
Concise chemical & technical dict, 4th ed, 1850
Concise Columbia dict of quotations, 1716
Concise Columbia ency, 2d ed, 189
Concise dict of acronyms & initialisms, 168
Concise dict of Amer bio, 4th ed, 257
Concise dict of Amer hist, 715
Concise dict of Amer lit bio, 1592
Concise dict of chemistry, 1851
Concise dict of classical mythology, 1699
Concise dict of confusables, 1471
Concise dict of Indian tribes of N Amer, 508
Concise dict of psychology, 2d ed, 2004
Concise dict of scientific bio, 2132
Concise dict of slang & unconventional English, 1424
Concise ency of Australia, 2d ed, 1030
Concise ency of building & construction materials, 2169
Concise ency of interior design, 2d ed, 1302
Concise ency of Islam, 1746
Concise ency of special educ, 432
Concise Oxford companion to Amer lit, 1584
Concise Oxford companion to Amer theatre, 1778
Concise Oxford companion to English lit, 1598
Concise Oxford dict of ballet, 1794
Concise Oxford dict of literary terms, 1498
Concise Oxford dict of proverbs, 1720
Concise Oxford French dict, 2d ed, 1479
Condition of educ: statistical report, 380
Condon, Robert J., 1053
Cone, Robert J., 2142
Conetta, Carl, 951
Congdon, Kirby, 2181
Congress & its members, 3d ed, 969
Congress & the nations, 1985-88, 964
Congress A to Z, 963
Congressional district atlas, 965
Congressional Quarterly's gd to congress 4th ed, 966
Congressional Quarterly's gd to the presidency, 980
Congressional Quarterly's gd to US Supreme Court, 2d ed, 798
Congressional Quarterly's politics in Amer, 1992, 936
Conn, Peter, 1581
Connor, Billie M., 1540
Conservation atlas of tropical forests: Asia & the pacific, 2032
Conservation treatment procedures, 2d ed, 827
Considine, Douglas M., 1922, 2117
Consumer gd computer buying gd, 1870

Consumer health info source bk, 3d ed, 2011
Consumer info cat, 352
Contemporary Amer bus leaders, 314
Contemporary atlas of the US, 548
Contemporary authors, 1516
Contemporary authors new revision series, 1517
Contemporary dramatists, 4th ed, 1541
Contemporary heroes & heroines, 252
Contemporary literary criticism, 1531
Contemporary musicians, 1638
Contemporary novelists, 4th ed, 1518
Contemporary photographers, 2d ed, 1372
Contemporary poets, 4th ed, 1561
Contemporary theater, film, & TV, 1791
Contempory artists, 3d ed, 1355
Contests for students, 174
Continuum dict of women's bio, rev ed, 1132
Conway, McKinley, 1895
Cook, Chris, 641, 656, 938
Cooking a to z, 1920
Cooper, Martin J., 2008
Coppa, Frank J., 682
Corbeil, Jean-Claude, 1419-20, 1476, 1481
Corbin, John, 862
Corbitt, Robert A., 2048
Cordasco, Francesco, 461
Core list of bks & jls in educ, 357
Costume of the western world, 1300
Cotterell, Arthur, 1694
Coughlin, Roberta M., 2015
Counting bks are more than numbers, 2021
Country study series, 1011
County & city data bk, 11th ed, 1108
Coupe, Sheena, 2263
Couper, Alistair, 1913
Courage children's illustrated world atlas, 538
Cover story index, 1960-89, 221
Covington, Michael, 1858
Covington, Timothy R., 1970
CQ almanac, 967
CQ researcher, 994
CQ's gd to current Amer govt, 968
Craig, Robert D., 1695
Crawford, Elizabeth D., 1185
CRC hndbk of chemistry & physics, 1987-88, 1852
Creasy, Rosalind, 2016
Creative ideas for lib media center facilities, 906
Cribb, Joe, 753
Crim, Keith, 1741
Crime & mystery: 100 best bks, 1550
Crime dict, rev ed, 805
Crippen, Cynthia, 655
Criscoe, Betty L., 1199
Crocker, Mark, 1971
Crocodiles & alligators, 2278
Crouse, William H., 2165
Crowe, Deborah, 2140
Crystal, David, 188, 1378
Cullum, Carolyn N., 1225
Cultural atlas of Japan, 1036
Cultural atlas of Russia & the Soviet Union, 1034
Cultural atlases for young people series, 627
Cummings, David, 1628
Cummings, Paul, 1356
Cummins, Blaire, 90
Cummins, Julie, 90
Cunningham, Homer F., 981

Current bio, 245
Current bio cum index, 1940-90, 246
Current bio yrbk, 244
Current issues (Arlington), 995
Current issues: child abuse, 1945
Current issues resource gd, 1008
Current leaders of nations, 947
Current news on file, 148
Curriculum review, 4
Currie, Robin, 2179
Curtis, Anthony, 2196
Cutlip, Glen W., 893
Cutter-Sanborn three-figure author table, 833
Cyclopedia of literary characters II, 1503
Cyclopedia of world authors II, 1534

Daintith, John, 1853, 2088, 2131
Dance hndbk, 1795
Danuloff, Craig, 1859
Darnay, Arsen J., 312
Darnton, Michael, 1744
Dartford, Mark, 674
Davidson, Roger H., 969
Davis, Barbara Kerr, 1575
Davis, Gary A., 424
Davis, H. W. C., 264
Davis, William E., 433
Day by day: the fifties, 653
Day by day: the forties, 652
Day by day: the seventies, 655
Day by day: the sixties, 654
Day, D., 2173
Day, John A., 1891
Day, Serenna F., 1169
Days of the week, 783
De Lange, Nicholas, 497
De Sola, Ralph, 167, 805
Dean, John A., 1855, 1857
Death & dying in children's & young people's lit, 1949
Deedy, John, 1751
Definitive Kobbe's opera bk, rev ed, 1565
DeFord, Miriam, 636
DeGregorio, William A., 982
Dejevcsky, Nikolai, 1034
Dejnozka, Edward L., 359
Delamar, Gloria T., 738, 1678
Delderfield, Eric R., 690
Dellar, Fred, 1665
DeLoach, Charles, 1608
DelVecchio, Valentine, 404
Dempsey, Michael, 193, 2145
DeRouche, Edward F., 377
Deutsch, Babette, 1562
Developing & maintaining video collections in
    libs, 881
DeVries, Mary A., 293, 308
Dewey decimal classification & relative index, 20th
    ed, 826
Dewey decimal classification, 20th ed, 843
Dewey, Melvil, 836
Dewey, Patrick R., 739, 863
Dial-a-fax dir, 3d ed, 1868
DIALOG, 183
DiCanio, Margaret, 1965, 2120
Dickinson's Amer hist fiction, 5th ed, 693
Dicks, Brian, 538
Dickson baseball dict, 1071

Dickson, Paul, 578, 707, 1071, 1425
Dictionary for bus & finance, rev ed, 310
Dictionary of Afro-Amer slavery, 713
Dictionary of Amer art, 1337
Dictionary of Amer bio, 258
Dictionary of Amer bio comprehensive index, 259
Dictionary of Amer hist, rev ed, 714
Dictionary of Amer idioms, 2d ed, 1426
Dictionary of Amer immigration history, 461
Dictionary of Amer lit characters, 1582
Dictionary of Amer negro bio, 471
Dictionary of Amer regional English, vol 1, 1427
Dictionary of Amer religious bio, 1770
Dictionary of Asian Amer hist, 480
Dictionary of astronomical names, 1806
Dictionary of building, 2174
Dictionary of bus terms, 307
Dictionary of Canadian bio, 260
Dictionary of Canadian bio, index 261
Dictionary of classical mythology, 1698
Dictionary of classical mythology: symbols,
    attributes, & assns, 1698
Dictionary of comparative religions, 1742
Dictionary of computer terms, 2d ed, 1858
Dictionary of computing, 3d ed, 1860
Dictionary of comtemporary Amer artists, 5th
    ed, 1356
Dictionary of concepts in hist, 647
Dictionary of confusable words, 1473
Dictionary of costumes, 1296
Dictionary of cultural literacy, 171
Dictionary of days, 777
Dictionary of energy, 2d ed, 2035
Dictionary of eponyms, 3d ed, 1433
Dictionary of fictional characters, rev ed, 1505
Dictionary of finance & investment terms, 3d ed, 303
Dictionary of foreign phrases & abbreviations, 3d
    ed, 1442
Dictionary of furniture, 1301
Dictionary of gods & goddesses, devils & demons,
    1700
Dictionary of hist docs, 642
Dictionary of hist terms, 2d ed, 641
Dictionary of imaginary places, 1509
Dictionary of Irish Mythology, 1696
Dictionary of lib & educ tech, 3d ed, 427
Dictionary of literary bio series, 1519
Dictionary of literary pseudonyms, 4th ed, 286
Dictionary of literary quotations, 1511
Dictionary of mathematics terms, 2024
Dictionary of medical terms for the non-medical
    person, 2d ed, 1993
Dictionary of mental handicap, 437
Dictionary of Mexican Amer hist, 486
Dictionary of military quotations, 919
Dictionary of modern English usage, 2d ed, 1466
Dictionary of modern French lit, 1616
Dictionary of modern Italian hist, 682
Dictionary of modern war, 917
Dictionary of natl bio, 262
Dictionary of natl bio, 1912-21, 264
Dictionary of natl bio, 1922-30, 265
Dictionary of natl bio, 1931-40, 266
Dictionary of natl bio, 1941-50, 267
Dictionary of natl bio, 1951-60, 268
Dictionary of natl bio, 1961-70, 269
Dictionary of natl bio, 1971-80, 270

Dictionary of natl bio, 1981-85, 271
Dictionary of natl bio: sup Jan 1901-Dec 1911, 263
Dictionary of occupational titles, 4th ed, 335
Dictionary of Polynesian mythology, 1695
Dictionary of pseudonyms & their origins, 289
Dictionary of quotations from the Bible, 1767
Dictionary of religion & philosophy, 1747
Dictionary of Russian lit since 1917, 1625
Dictionary of Scandinavian lit, 1623
Dictionary of sci & creationism, 2108
Dictionary of SDI, 922
Dictionary of superstitions, 928
Dictionary of surnames, 532
Dictionary of the environment, 3d ed, 2043
Dictionary of the second world war, 675
Dictionary of the Vietnam war, 660
Dictionary of 20th century hist, 639
Dictionary of war quotations, 924
Dictionary of world politics, 929
Dictionnaire Francais, 1478
Diesel engine manual, 4th ed, 2162
Digest of educ statistics, 378
Digest of sftwr reviews: educ, 108
Diller, Daniel D., 686
Dinosaur data bk, 1897
Dinosaur ency, 1896
Directories of financial aids for minorities, 1989-90,
    422
Directory for exceptional children, 12th ed, 434
Directory of Amer youth orgs, 1990-91, 176
Directory of automated lib systems, 2d ed, 862
Directory of Central Amer classroom resources K-12,
    2d ed, 1042
Directory of college facilities & servs for people with
    disabilities, 3d ed, 435
Directory of financial aids for minorities, 1989-90,
    422
Directory of financial aids for women, 1991-92, 423
Directory of online databases & CD-ROM resources
    for high schools, 870
Directory of school mediation & conflict resolution
    programs, 363
Directory of student sci training progs for high ability
    precollege students, 1991 ed, 365
Discoveries: fiction for elem school readers, 79
Discoveries: fiction for intermediate school yrs, 80
Discoveries: fiction for young teens, 81
Distant planets, 1819
Dixon, Dougal, 1901
Dizik, A. Allen, 1302
Do fish get thirsty? questions answered by the New
    England aquarium, 2248
Doane, Gilbert Harry, 525
Doctor, Donald M., 2002
Doctors bk of home remedies, 2009
Doctors' vitamin & mineral ency, 1925
Documents of Amer hist, 10th ed, 730
Dodge, Meredith D., 687
Dogs, cats & horses, 1165
Do-it-yourself medical testing, 3d ed, 2010
Dolbow, Sandra W., 1616
Doll, Carol A., 853, 1226
Dollinger, Malin, 1982
Dolphins & porpoises, 2262
Domestic tech, 2143
Donelson, Kenneth L., 1140
Dorgan, Charity Anne, 324

Dority, G. Kim, 134
Dorsey dict of Amer govt & politics, 932
Doubleday atlas of the USA, 539
Doubleday bk of famous Amer, 272
Doubleday children's atlas, 540
Doubleday children's ency, 201
Doubleday picture atlas, 541
Doubleday Roget's thesaurus in dict form, rev
     ed, 1451
Douglas, Auriel, 1434
Douglas, J. D., 1761
Douglass, Jackie Leatherbury, 2254
Douglas-Young, John, 1862
Dow, Lesley, 2261, 2264
Downes, John, 294, 303
Downing, Douglas, 1858, 2024
Downs, Robert B., 273
Dr. Axelrod's mini-atlas of freshwater aquarium
     fishes, 2073
Dr. Burgess's atlas of marine aquarium fishes, 2074
Drabble, Margaret, 1597-8
Drama dict, 1780
Drew, Bernard A., 1324
Dreyer, Sharon Spredemann, 1158
Driver, Harold, E., 231
Drost, Jerome, 1495
Drug abuse a-z, 1950
Drug-alert dict & resource gd, 1959
Drury, Nevill, 1940
Drury, Susan, 1940
Du Vall, Nell, 2143
Duft, Joseph F., 1829
Duncan, Michael, 2157
Duncan, Phil, 936
Dunford, Penny, 1357
Dunkling, Leslie, 531, 777
Dunlap, Leslie W., 989
Dunnahoo, Terry, 748
Dunne, Lavon J., 1921
Dunne, Pete, 2234
Dupre, Jean-Paul, 190
Dupuy, R. Ernest, 912
Dupuy, Trevor N., 912
Durrell, Gerald, 2063
Durrell, Lee, 2063
Dvorak, Thomas L., 1649
Dyal, Carole, 827
Dye, David, 1325
Dykeman, Peter A., 1830
Dynes, Wayne R., 1969

Eaglen, Audrey, 874
Eaker, Sherry, 1786
Eakle, Arlene, 529
Earth bk: world atlas, 542
Earth care annual, 2057
Earth report: essential gd to global ecological issues,
     2049
Earth science on file, 1889
Earth's natural forces, 1890
East & Southeast Asia material culture in N Amer, 481
East, Timothy, 1118
Eastern wildflowers: photographic celebration ...,
     1832
Eastman, P. D., 1494
Eastman, Philip D., 1402, 1480
Easton, Robert, 1368

Easy reading, 2d ed, 94
Eating disorders, 1988
Ebony pictorial hist of Black Amers, 472
Ecker, Ronald L., 2108
Eden, Cooper, 1176
Edgerton, William, 1502
Editor & pub market gd, 311
Editorials on file, 1258
Educating the gifted: a sourcebk, 425
Education: A gd to ref & info sources, 356
Education index, 389
Educational film & video locator ..., 4th ed, 19
Educational gd to the natl park system, 610
Educational media & tech yrbk, 426
Educator's desk ref, 381
Educators gd to free AV materials, 20
Educators gd to free films, 21
Educators gd to free filmstrips & slides, 22
Educators gd to free guidance materials, 322
Educators gd to free materials, 125
Educators gd to free science materials, 2092
Educators gd to free social studies materials, 993
Educators gd to free teaching aids, 124
Educators' hndbk to interactive videodiscs, 2d
     ed, 431
Edwards, Paul, 1714
Eerdmans Bible dict, 1762
Eggenberger, David I., 278
Ehrlich, Eugene, 1047, 1443, 1449
Ekhaml, Leticia T., 118
Electricity & basic electronics, 2176
Electromap world atlas, version 1.1, 569
Electronic learning, 104
Elementary math teacher's hndbk, 2d ed, 2030
Elementary school lib collection, 17th ed, 67
Elementary teachers gd to free curricular materials,
     126
Elements of style, 3d ed, 1285
El-Hi textbks & serials in print, 64
Elias, Stephen R., 796
Elias, Thomas S., 1830
Elliot, Charles, 295
Elliot, Jeffrey M., 991
Ellis, Peter Berresford, 1696
Ellrod, J. G., 1312
Elman, Robert, 767
Elsbree, John J., 427
Elwell, Walter A., 1758
Elwood, Ann, 149
Embree, Ainslie T., 677
Emergency librarian, 48
Emiliani, Cesare, 2119
Emily Post on business etiquette, 298
Emily Post on invitations & letters, 521
Emily Post's etiquette, 14th ed, 522
Employee rights hndbk, 803
Emrich, Duncan, 1707
Enciclopedia hispanica, 202
Encyclopaedia of the hist of tech, 2144
Encyclopedia Americana, 203
Encyclopedia Brown's third record bk ..., 771
Encyclopedia Macintosh, 1859
Encyclopedia of adolescence, 1966
Encyclopedia of alcoholism, 2d ed, 1956
Encyclopedia of alternative health care, 1942
Encyclopedia of Amer bus hist & bio, auto industry,
     1896-1920, 304

Encyclopedia of Amer bus hist & bio, auto industry, 1920-80, 305
Encyclopedia of Amer bus hist & bio, iron & steel, nineteenth century, 306
Encyclopedia of Amer comics, 1545
Encyclopedia of Amer crime, 810
Encyclopedia of Amer facts & dates, 8th ed, 704
Encyclopedia of Amer intelligence & espionage, 953
Encyclopedia of Amer religions, 3d ed, 1748
Encyclopedia of Amer war films, 1318
Encyclopedia of Amer wrestling, 1104
Encyclopedia of animals: mammals, 2265
Encyclopedia of aquatic life, 2217
Encyclopedia of Asian hist, 677
Encyclopedia of assassinations, 648
Encyclopedia of assns, 1991, 175
Encyclopedia of biothics, 1821
Encyclopedia of birds, 2235
Encyclopedia of Black Amer, 473
Encyclopedia of blindness & visual impairment, 624
Encyclopedia of British women writers, 1601
Encyclopedia of careers & vocational guidance, 8th ed, 336
Encyclopedia of censorship, 848
Encyclopedia of child abuse, 1943
Encyclopedia of colonial & revolutionary Amer, 716
Encyclopedia of crime & justice, 806
Encyclopedia of death, 1946
Encyclopedia of drug abuse, 2d ed, 1951
Encyclopedia of educl research, 5th ed, 360
Encyclopedia of electronics, 2d ed, 1863
Encyclopedia of evolution, 2221
Encyclopedia of fairies, 1692
Encyclopedia of franchises & franchising, 316
Encyclopedia of hist places, 640
Encyclopedia of Hollywood, 1322
Encyclopedia of homosexuality, 1969
Encyclopedia of Japan, 1038
Encyclopedia of jazz, 1667
Encyclopedia of jazz in the seventies, 1669
Encyclopedia of jazz in the sixties, 1668
Encyclopedia of Jewish hist, 498
Encyclopedia of Judaism, 1743
Encyclopedia of magic & magicians, 742
Encyclopedia of mammals, 2266
Encyclopedia of marriage, divorce & the family, 1965
Encyclopedia of military hist, 2d ed, 912
Encyclopedia of minerals, 2d ed, 1910
Encyclopedia of monsters, 1704
Encyclopedia of N Amer railroading, 2210
Encyclopedia of Native Amer tribes, 514
Encyclopedia of natural medicine, 1941
Encyclopedia of New England, 576
Encyclopedia of occultism & parapsychology, 3d ed, 926
Encyclopedia of philosophy, 1714
Encyclopedia of phobias, fears, & anxieties, 2002
Encyclopedia of physics, 3d ed, 2087
Encyclopedia of police science, 807
Encyclopedia of pop, rock & soul, rev ed, 1664
Encyclopedia of rock, 1674
Encyclopedia of S culture, 579
Encyclopedia of S hist, 717
Encyclopedia of school admin & supervision, 361
Encyclopedia of sculpture techniques, 1342
Encyclopedia of sleep & sleep disorders, 1996
Encyclopedia of special educ, 436

Encyclopedia of suicide, 1947
Encyclopedia of super villains, 1556
Encyclopedia of superheroes, 1555
Encyclopedia of terrorism & political violence, 955
Encyclopedia of textiles, 3d ed, 1309
Encyclopedia of the Amer left, 937
Encyclopedia of the Central West, 573
Encyclopedia of the Far West, 574
Encyclopedia of the First World, 1013
Encyclopedia of the Holocaust, 661
Encyclopedia of the Midwest, 575
Encyclopedia of the NCAA basketball tournament, 1082
Encyclopedia of the second world war, 668
Encyclopedia of the Third Reich, 680
Encyclopedia of the Third World, 4th ed, 1014
Encyclopedia of the world's air forces, 921
Encyclopedia of twentieth-century journalists, 1261
Encyclopedia of witches & witchcraft, 927
Encyclopedia of wood, 2170
Encyclopedia of world bio, 20th century suppl 279
Encyclopedia of world crime, 808
Encyclopedia of world faiths, 1744
Encyclopedia of world hist, 643
Encyclopedia of world lit of the 20th century, 2d ed, 1504
Encyclopedic dict of sci, 2109
Encyclopedic hndbk of culte in Amer, 1754
Eng'lish lan'guage & o'ri-en-ta'tion pro'grams in the US, 9th ed, 1382
English novel explication: supp IV, 1603
English-Russian, Russian-English dict, 1488
Enser, A. G. S., 662, 1326
Environmental hazards: air pollution, 2053
Environmental hazards: radioactive materials & wastes, 2054
Environmental resource dir. Sept. 1990, 2042
Environmental trends, 2050
Epler, Doris, 864
Epstein, Andrea, 6
Equipment dir of AV, computer & video products, 429
ERIC database, 390
Eric Hosking's birds of prey of the world, 2240
Erickson, Hal, 1268
Erickson, Judith B., 176
Ernst, Carl H., 2274
Espy, Willard R., 1444
Essay & general lit index, 222
Estell, Doug, 99
Estes, Glenn E., 1172
Etiquette: Charlotte Ford's gd to modern manners, 519
ETS test collection cat (v2, v3, v4), 446-8
Europe Today, rev ed, 1033
European authors, 1000-1900, 1520
European writers, 1521
Evans, Glen, 1947, 1951
Evans, Graham, 929
Evans, Ivor H., 1500
Evans, Peter, 2267
Everhart, Nancy, 908
Everyday Amer English dict, 1383
Everyday things & how they work, 2160
Everyone's gd to cancer therapy, 1982
Everyone's UN, 10th ed, 952
Everything baseball, 1072

Ewen, David, 1639, 1641-3, 1646
Exceptional child educ abstract, 391
Exciting, funny, scary, short, different & sad
    bks ..., 1159
Exercise, 2012
Experimenting with air & flight, 2209
Exploring our living planet, 1884
Exploring our world series, 584
Exploring space, 2104
Exploring space, 2191
Exploring the reaches of the solar system, 2205
Exploring the world, 594
Exploring your world, 580
Extinct birds, 2239
Extra cash for kids, 348
Extraordinary Black Amer from colonial to
    contemporary times, 465
Extraterrestrial ency, rev ed, 1802
Eyeopeners!, 1233

Fabiano, Emily, 357
Fabulous Facts about the fifty states, rev ed, 586
Faces of Amer, (I, II), 731-2
Facts & dates of Amer sports, 1047
Facts about the presidents, 5th ed, 985
Facts about the states, 581
Facts on file children's atlas, 543
Facts on file dict of archaeology, rev ed, 234
Facts on file dict of astronomy, 2d ed, 1803
Facts on file dict of biology, rev ed, 1822
Facts on file dict of botany, 1825
Facts on file dict of chemistry, rev ed, 1853
Facts on file dict of design & designers, 1289
Facts on file dict of educ, 362
Facts on file dict of first names, 531
Facts on file dict of marine science, 1911
Facts on file dict of mathematics, rev ed, 2025
Facts on file dict of military science, 920
Facts on file dict of new words, 1390
Facts on file dict of physics, rev ed, 2088
Facts on file dict of proverbs, 1721
Facts on file dict of religions, 1745
Facts on file dict of sci, 6th ed, 2116
Facts on file dict of troublesome words, rev ed, 1464
Facts on file dict of 20th century allusions, 169
Facts on file ency of world mythology & legend, 1702
Facts on file English/chinese visual dict, 1476
Facts on file English/French visual dict, 1481
Facts on file jr visual dict, 1419
Facts on file news digest CD-ROM, 1980-90, 150
Facts on file sci yrbk, 2120
Facts on file student's thesaurus, 1452
Facts on file visual dict, 1420
Facts on file world news digest, 151
Facts on file world political almanac, 938
Facts Plus: an almanac of essential info, 143
Fairchild's dict of fashion, 2d ed, 1293
Falla, P. S., 1489
Familiar birds of N Amer: eastern region, 2236
Familiar birds of N Amer: western region, 2237
Familiar quotations, 15th ed, 1718
Family law dict, 796
Family mental health ency, 2000
Famous first facts, 4th ed, 157
Fantasy lit, 1546
Fantasy lit for children & young adults, 3d ed, 1162
Faragher, John Mack, 716

Farberow, Norman L., 1947
Farmer, David Hugh, 1775
Farrand, John, Jr., 2238
Fast, Timothy, 1118
Fay, John J., 792, 1952
Feather, Leonard G., 1667-9
Federal career dir, 345
Feingold, S. Norma, 346
Feinsilber, M., 170
Feirer, John L., 2171
Felder, Deborah G., 2069
Feldman, David, 152
Feldman, Lynne B., 314
Fenton, Ann D., 1685
Fenton, Erfert, 1871
Fenton, Thomas P., 815
Fergusson, Rosalind, 1721
Ferrar, H., 1479
Ferrell, Robert H., 701
Fiction cat, 12th ed, 68
Fiction sequels for readers 10-16, 1149
Field, Elinor Whitney, 1202-3
Field gd to eastern forests: N Amer, 1843
Field gd to hawks of N Amer, 2233
Field gd to N Amer edible wild plants, 1830
Field gd to prehistoric life, 1898
Field gd to the birds, 4th ed, 2243
Field gd to the U.S. economy, 296
Field gd to western birds, 3d ed, 2244
Field gd to wildlife habitats of the Eastern US, 2060
Field gd to wildlife habitats of the Western US, 2061
Field gd to wildlife in Texas & the southwest, 2228
Field, Shelly, 332, 334
Fifth bk of junior authors & illustrators, 1186
Fifty finest athletes of the 20th century, 1053
50 yrs of Amer automobiles 1939-89, 2182
Fighting toxics: manual for protecting your family ...,
    2051
Filisky, Michael, 2247
Film & video finder, 3d ed, 23
Film hndbk, 1332
Filmed bks & plays, rev ed, 1326
Find that tune: index to rock, folk-rock, disco, & soul,
    (vol 1 & 2), 1679-80
Finding a job in the nonprofit sector, 1991, 347
Fireside companion to the theatre, 1784
First aid for kids: emergency gdbk for parents, 2008
First bk of MS-DOS, 2d ed, 1877
First dict of cultural literacy, 172
First ladies, 6th ed, 974
First thesaurus, 1463
First wholc rchab cat, 612
Fish, 2249
Fisher, David, 1418
Fiske, Edward, 418
Fiske, Edward B., 405
Fiske gd to colleges 1991, 405
Fitton, Robert A., 916
Fitzhenry, Robert I., 1717
Fitzsimons, Cecilia, 2250
Five centuries of Amer costume, 1297
Five kingdoms: illus gd to the phyla of life on Earth,
    2d ed, 1824
Flammang, James W., 2183
Flanagan, John T., 273
Flanders, Carl N., 996, 1983
Flanders, Stephen A., 997, 1948, 1983

Fleming, John, 1292
Fleming, Margaret, 238
Fleming, Steve, 1101
Fletcher, Katy, 1551
Fletcher, Marilyn P, 1548
Fletcher, Steve, 1788
Fletcher-Janzen, Elaine, 432
Flexner, Stuart Berg, 1386
Flintham, Victor, 913
Flodin, Mickey, 618
Floyd, Samuel A., Jr., 1640
Focus on families: ref hndbk, 1964
Focus on physical impairments, 614
Focus on school: a ref hndbk, 383
Focus on teens in trouble, 809
Focus units in literature, 1240
Folbre, Nancy, 296
Folding stories, 1231
Folk & festival costumes of the world, 1298
Folklore of Amer holidays, 2d ed, 1708
Folklore on the Amer land, 1707
Folktale, 1687
Follett, Wilson, 1465
Folsom, Rose, 1249
Foner, Eric, 725
Food hndbk, 1918
Food lover's companion, 1926
Foods & food production ency, 1922
Football register, 1084
Ford, Charlotte, 519
Forey, Pamela, 1831, 2250
Form & style, 8th ed, 1274
Forman, Robert J., 1613
Forthcoming bks, 59
Foss, Christopher F., 914
Fossils for amateurs, 1900
Foster, David William, 1618
Foster, Dennis L., 316-7
Fourth bk of junior authors & illustrators, 1185
Fowler, Henry Watson, 1466
Fox, Levi, 1609
Fox, Michael, 2070
Fradin, Dennis Brindell, 274
Fraley, Ruth A., 905
Franchise opportunities hndbk, 21st ed, 318
Franck, Irene M., 337, 458, 600, 639, 649, 735, 1967
Franklin, Benjamin, 1582
Franklin, Carl, 865
Franklin D. Roosevelt, 718
Fredericks, Anthony D., 2134
Free money for college, 414
Free things for teachers, rev ed, 179
Freed, Melvyn N., 381
Freedman, Alan, 1864
Freedman, Gilliam, 537
Freedom of expression, 787
Freedom of religion, 788
Freedom to publish, 789
Freedom to read, 790
Freeman, July, 1227
Freeman, Morton S., 1437, 1467
Freeman, Sally, 1230
Freeman, William, 1505
Freidel, Frank, 696, 983
French, P. M. M., 2152
Friedman, Jack P., 307
Friesel, Evyatar, 499

From Abenaki to Zuni, 516
From the Titanic to the Challenger, 2141
Froschl, Merle, 382
Frost, Carolyn, 838
Frost, Elizabeth, 978
Fryer, Deborah J., 1560
Full speed ahead: stories & activities for children on transportation, 2179
Fuller, Errol, 2239
Fuller, Muriel, 1183
Funk & Wagnalls standard dict of folklore, mythology & legend, 1697

Gaffney, Maureen, 1984
Gagnon, Andre, 76
Gagnon, Ann, 76
Gaia atlas of first peoples, 2038
Gaia atlas of future worlds, 1002
Gale dir of pubs & broadcast media, 1259
Gallant, Jennifer J., 25
Gallaudet survival gd to signing, 619
Gallo, Donald R., 1177
Gammond, Peter, 1661
Ganz, Arthur, 1499
Ganzl, Kurt, 1672
Ganzl's bk of music theatre, 1672
Garden flower folklore, 1709
Gardener's companion, 2015
Gardener's hndbk of edible plants, 2016
Gareffa, Peter M., 247
Gargan, William, 1679-80
Garland, Henry, 1617
Garland, Mary, 1617
Garraty, John A., 719, 725
Garrett, Agnes, 1173
Garrett, Wilbur, 549
Garrett, Wilbur E., 597, 702
Garrison, Paul, 2197
Garst, Robert E., 1260
Gates, Jean Key, 894
Gatland, Kenneth, 2198
Gaultier, Andre Pascal, 928
Gaustad, Edwin S., 1770
Gay, Kathlyn, 998
Gehring, Wes D., 1333
Gemstones: treasures from the Earth's crust, 1907
General ref bks for adults, 135
General sci index, 2127
Generations past: selected list of sources for Afro-Amer genealogical research, 527
Genreflecting, 3d ed, 1554
Geography for A to Z: picture glossary, 585
Geography: resource bk for secondary schools, 583
George, Jean Craighead, 1923
Gerard, Geoffry, 2075
Gerhardstein, Virginia Brokaw, 693
Gerhardt, Lillian N., 7
Get help: solving the problems in your life, 1953
Gibaldi, Joseph, 1283
Gibilisco, Stan, 1863, 1867
Gibson, Anne, 1118
Gibson, Carol, 2025
Giese, James R., 694-95
Gifis, Steven H., 793
Gilbert, Martin, 500
Gilbert, Sara, 177
Gilbert, Sara D., 1953

Gillespie, John T., 82, 875, 1151, 1208-9
Gillis, Jack, 2184
Glassborrow, Jilly, 537
Glasse, Cyril, 1746
Glikin, Ronda, 1577
Gloag, John, 1303
Global studies: Western Europe, 2d ed, 1035
Global/international issues & problems, 1017
Glorious ABC, 1176
Glossbrenner, Alfred, 1869, 1872
Godwin, Mary Jo, 10
Goetz, Philip W., 199, 206
Goldberg, Lana, 406
Goldberg, Lee, 406
Goldinger, Carolyn, 804
Goldsmith, Edward, 2049
Goldstein, Eleanor, 2047
Goldstein, Howard, 812
Goldstein, Sandra E., 422-3
Gomberg, Karen C., 1228
Good reading: gd for serious readers, 23d ed, 1576
Good words to you, 1436
Goodman, Jordan E, 294, 303
Goodspeed, Jonathan, 104
Gorman, Michael, 839
Gorton, Richard A., 361
Gosling, William, 531
Gouke, Mary Noel, 1968
Goulart, Ron, 1358-9, 1545
Gould, Edwin, 2265
Government ref bks 88/89: a biennial gd to US govt
    pubs, 121
Graham, Joe S., 484
Graham, Otis L. Jr., 718
Granatstein, J. L., 678
Grand allusions, 170
Grant, Michael, 1614
Gray, Randal, 663
Great Amer automobiles of the 50's, 2186
Great Amer bridges & dams, 2158
Great Amer lighthouses, 2214
Great battles of the Civil War, 720
Great Britons: twentieth century lives, 281
Great careers, 2d ed, 325
Great comic bk artists, (vol 1 & 2), 1358-9
Great composers, 1300-1900, 1641
Great composers I, 1644
Great composers II, 1645
Great detective pictures, 1327
Great disasters, 153
Great lives, 275
Great lives: exploration, 595
Great lives from hist: Amer series, 276
Great lives from hist: renaissance to 1900 series, 277
Great lives: human rights, 816
Great lives: sports, 1065
Great Plains Natl instructional TV lib (GPN) cat, 26
Great science fiction pictures, 1328
Great science fiction pictures, II, 1329
Great song thesaurus, 2d ed, 1683
Great stage stars, 1792
Great writers of the English lang, 1535
Greek & Latin authors, 800 B.C.-A.D. 1000, 1614
Green, Carol H., 1135
Green, Jonathan, 848
Greenberg, Milton, 931
Greenburg, Stan, 1098

Greenfield, Edward, 37
Greenfield, Jane, 826
Greenfieldt, John, 1790
Greenlaw, Jean, 425
Greenpeace bk of dolphins, 2268
Greenwood, Barbara O., 1190
Greenwood, Val D., 526
Gregory, K. J., 1890
Gregory, Ruth W., 778
Greisman, Joan, 1463
Griffith, H. Winter, 1924
Grimal, Pierre, 1698-9
Gross, Ernie, 708
Gross, John, 1726
Gross, Steve, 351
Grove, Philip Babcock, 1387
Groves, Don, 1912
Growing older: what young people should know
    about aging, 1939
Growing up with sci: illus ency of inventions, rev
    ed, 2145
Grzimek's ency of mammals, 2d ed, 2269
Guadalupi, Gianni, 1509
Guernsey, Otis L., Jr., 1787
Guggenheim, Martin, 799
Guide bk of US coins, 763
Guide for written collection policy statements, 854
Guide to Amer law, 795
Guide to amphibians & reptiles, 2280
Guide to free computer materials, 111
Guide to natl & state educ services, 1348
Guide to natl park areas: E states, 2d ed, 607
Guide to natl park areas: W states, 2d ed, 608
Guide to photography workshops & schools, 2d
    ed, 1373
Guide to popular US govt pubs, 2d ed, 117
Guide to state environmental programs, 2d ed, 2044
Guide to summer camps and summer schools
    1990/91, 26th ed, 769
Guide to the LBI standards for lib binding, 880
Guide to the natl park areas: eastern states, 2d ed, 607
Guide to the natl park areas: western states, 2d ed, 608
Guide to the use of libs & info sources, 6th ed, 894
Guiley, Rosemary Ellen, 927
Guinagh, Kevin, 1442
Guinness bk of answers, 8th ed, 154
Guinness bk of astronomy, 1804
Guinness bk of records, 155
Guinness bk of sports records, 1054
Guinness bk of stamps, 754
Guinness railway bk, 2212
Gunn, James, 1552
Gutman, Israel, 661
Gymnastics safety manual, 2d ed, 1090

Haase, Ynez D., 700
Haban, Rita D., 523
Hackman, Mary H., 895
Haglund, Elaine J., 779
Haigh, Christopher, 688
Haley, Beverly A., 383
Hall, Donald, 1219
Hall, Susan, 1229
Halleron, Trish, 1986
Halliday, Ian, 1815
Halliwell, Leslie, 1313-4
Halliwell's film gd, 1313

Halliwell's filmgoers & video viewer's companion, 9th ed, 1314
Hamilton, Carolyn, 5
Hamilton, Lillian B., 620
Hamilton, Mary, 1658
Hamlyn ency of golf, 1089
Hammond ambassador world atlas, 545
Hammond Barnhart dict of sci, 2103
Hammond gold medallion world atlas, 544
Hammond large type world atlas, 546
Hammond past worlds: the Times atlas of archaeology, 235
Hamock, Delia A., 1932
Hand, Raymond, Jr., 1449
Handbook for AACR2 1988 revision, 840
Handbook for storytellers, 1223
Handbook of Amer film genres, 1333
Handbook of Amer popular lit, 1549
Handbook of Amer women's hist, 1124
Handbook of contemporary fiction for public libs & school libs, 95
Handbook of denominations in the US, 9th ed, 1753
Handbook of gifted educ, 424
Handbook of Latin Amer lit, 1618
Handbook of mathematical tables & formulas, 5th ed, 2029
Handbook of private schools, 366
Handbook of pseudonyms & personal nicknames, 290
Handbook of Russian lit, 1624
Handbook of US coins, 764
Handbook to lit, 5th ed, 1507
Handville, Elizabeth, 340
Hanks, Kurt, 348
Hanks, Patrick, 532
Hansard-Winkler, G. A., 346
Harbin, E. O., 740
Harbrace college hndbk, 11th ed, 1276
Hardy, Phil, 1674
Harewood, Earl of, 1656-7
Hargrove, Hondon B., 721
Harlem renaissance & beyond: lit bio of 100 Black women writers, 1594
Harmon, Mark K., 749
Harmon, William, 1507
Harmony illus ency of country music, rev ed, 1665
Harmony illus ency of jazz, 1666
Harmony illus ency of rock, 6th ed, 1675
Harper atlas of the Bible, 1763
Harper atlas of world hist, 628
Harper dict of contemporary usage, 2d ed, 1469
Harper dict of foreign terms, 3d ed, 1443
Harper dict of modern thought, 2d ed, 166
Harper dict of sci in everyday language, 2115
Harper's Bible commentary, 1764
Harper's Bible dict, 1765
Harper's dict of opera & operetta, 1659
Harrington, Kevin, 319
Harris, Karen H., 73
Harris, Laurie Lanzen, 1506, 1536
Harris, Marcia L., 779
Harrison, Michael, 1221
Harrison, Virginia, 2105, 2218
Harry & Wally's favorite TV shows, 1267
Harry S. Truman ency, 722
Hart, James D., 1583-4
Hart, Thomas L., 896, 906
Hartman, Donald K., 1495

Hartnoll, Phyllis, 1785
Harvard Ency of amer ethnic groups, 462
Harvard gd to Amer hist, 696
Haseltine, Patricia, 481
Hatch, Jane M., 780
Hatherly, Janelle, 2262
Haubenstock, Susan H., 333
Hauck, Eldon, 582
Hauser, Paula, 74
Havard, C. W. H., 1981
Havlice, Patricia P., 1681
Havlice, Patricia Pate, 1353-4
Hawks in flight, 2234
Hawley's condensed chemical dict, 11th ed, 1854
Hay, Henry, 741
Hay, Peter, 800
Haycock, Ken, 48, 876
Haycraft, Howard, 1182, 1588, 1599-1600
Hayes, Nicky, 2005
Haynes, Collin, 1873
Hayward, Linda, 1403
Hazen, Edith P., 1560
Headlines & deadlines, 4th ed, 1260
Health resource builder: free & inexpensive materials ..., 1994
Hearne, Betsy, 47, 1160
Heat wave: Motown fact bk, 1676
Hede, Agnes Ann, 136
Heffron, Mary J., 815
Hegenberger, John, 755
Heim, Mary Ellen, 1290
Heller, Dawn Hansen, 384
Hellmans, Alexander, 2100
Hellweg, Paul, 1452
Henderson, Lesley, 1558
Hendler, Sheldon Saul, 1925
Hendrickson, Linnea, 1147
Her way: a gd to bio of women for young people, 2d ed, 1133
Herald, Diana Tixier, 1554
Herbert, Victor, 1932
Herbst, Sharon Tyler, 1926
Heritage of music, 1629
Heroes in space: from Gagarin to Challenger, 2189
Herring, Susan Davis, 2141
Herwig, Rob, 2017
Heywood, Vernon H., 1828
Hiatt, Doris, 52
High interest easy reading, 6th ed, 92
High school mathematics lib, 8th ed, 2022
High/low hndbk, 3d ed, 91
Hiker's bible, rev ed, 767
Hildyard, Nicholas, 2049
Hill, A. David, 583
Hill, Donna, 1184
Hill, J. A., 2006
Hillerich, Robert L., 1404
Himelstein, Shmuel, 1752
Hincks, Joseph, 1903
Hinnells, John R., 1745
Hirsch, E. D., Jr., 171-172
Hispanic Amer info dir, 1990-91, 485
Hispanic heritage series, 489-91
Hispanic resource dir, 492
Hispanic writers, 1619
Hispanic-Amer material culture, 484
Historic places of early Amer, 735

Historical almanac of the US senate, 970
Historical atlas of the Amer west, 700
Historical atlas of US, 702
Historical dict of modern Spain, 1700-1988, 686
Historical dict of N Amer archaeology, 236
Historical dict of the 1920s, 724
Historical ency of costumes, 1294
Historical gd to children's theatre, 1783
Historical maps on file, 629
Historical statistics of the US, 1109
Historical tables: 58 BC-AD 1985, 11th ed, 637
History of art, 4th ed, 1339
History of art for young people, 3d ed, 1340
History of sci & tech:, 2101
History of the world series, 1074
Hitchcock, H. Wiley, 1630
Hobson, Burton, 756-7, 759
Hockey gd, 1091
Hockey register, 1092
Hodges, Flavia, 532
Hodges, John C., 1276
Hodgson, Terry, 1780
Hoffman, Catherine, 2011
Hoffman, Herbert H., 1563
Hoffman, Rita L., 1563
Hoffmann, Frank, 849
Hoffmeister, Donald F., 2271
Hogg, Ian, 668
Hole, John W., Jr., 1972
Holidays & anniversaries of the world, 2d ed, 782
Holidays, 781
Holland, David T., 203
Holland, F. Ross, Jr., 2214
Hollander, Zander, 1079
Hollywood greats of the golden yrs, 1312
Holman, C. Hugh, 1507
Holocaust, 2d ed, 658
Holston, Kim R., 1650
Holtze, Sally Holmes, 1186-7
Holzeimer, Diane, 45
Hombs, Mary Ellen, 999
Home bk of quotations, classical & modern, 10th
    ed, 1722
Homeowner's complete manual of repair &
    improvement, 2172
Honour, Hugh, 1292
Hook, J. N., 1453
Hooper, David, 744
Hoover's hndbk: profiles of over 500 major corp, 297
Hopke, William E., 336
Hordeski, Michael F., 1865
Horehead, Albert M., 745
Horn Book gd to children's & young adult bks, 49
Horn Book index, 1924-89, 1169
Horn Book mag, 50
Horn, Jane, 1920
Horner, Catherine Townsend, 1161
Horning, Kathleen T., 11
Horror lit, 1547
Horse stories, 1166
Horsemanship: basics for beginners, 1094
Horsemanship: basics for intermediate riders, 1095
Horsemanship: basics for more advanced riders, 1096
Horton, Carrell P., 478
Hosking, Eric, 2240
Houk, Rose, 1832
Houston, James E., 392

How bridges are made, 2147
How cars are made, 2148
How congress works, 2d ed, 971
How electricity is made, 2149
How glass is made, 2150
How it is made series, 2146
How jet engines are made, 2151
How lasers are made, 2152
How oil rigs are made, 2153
How paper is made, 2154
How proudly they wave: flags of the fifty states, 523
How roads are made, 2155
How ships are made, 2156
How skyscrapers are made, 2157
How to get & get ahead in your first job, 329
How to get into the right college, 418
How to prepare for the Amer college test (ACT), 452
How to prepare for the new high school equivalency
    exam, 7th ed, 455
How to prepare for the PSAT/NMSQT, 7th ed, 453
How to prepare for the SAT, 15th ed, 454
How to run a meeting, 749
How to use the lib, 897
How to win a school election, 748
How to write a good term paper, 1279
How to write a great school report, 1278
How to write a winning resume, 328
Howard, Elizabeth F., 697
Howatson, M. C., 1615
Hoyle's rule of games, 2d ed, 745
Hubbard, Freeman, 2210
Hubbard, Linda S., 1791
Huck, Charlotte S., 1141
Hudson, Robert V., 1247
Huffman, D. M., 1838
Hughes, David, 1816
Hughes, Langston, 474
Hughes, Paul, 783-4
Human anatomy & physiology, 5th ed, 1972
Human body: an overview, 1974
Human body on file, 1973
Human rights: a dir of res, 815
Human rights: a ref bk, 818
Human sexuality, 1975
Hunt, Candida, 2109
Hurd, Michael, 1635
Husband, Janet, 1496
Husband, Jonathan F., 1496
Hutchinson, J. A., 1479
Hutera, Donald, 1795
Hutson, James, H., 972
Hypertext/hypermedia in schools, 865

Ideas in conflict series, 1000
Identification gd to the trees of Canada, 1844
Identifying Amer architecture, rev ed, 1364
Illingworth, Valerie, 1803
Illustrated atlas of Jerusalem, 1740
Illustrated atlas of Jewish civilization, 500
Illustrated bio-bibliog of Black photographers
    1940-88, 1377
Illustrated dict of electronics, 5th ed, 1867
Illustrated dict of knitting, 1306
Illustrated dict of microcomputers, 3d ed, 1865
Illustrated dict of natural health, 1940
Illustrated dict of western lit, 1508
Illustrated ency dict of electronics, 2d ed, 1862

Illustrated ency of general aviation, 2d ed, 2197
Illustrated ency of mankind, 232
Illustrated ency of New Zealand, 1046
Illustrated ency of space tech, 2d ed, 2198
Illustrated ency of world geography, 1012
Illustrated hist of helicopters, 2200
Illustrated reverse dict, 1454
Illustrated who's who in mythology, 1705
Illustration index, 4th ed, 212
Illustration index V: 1977-81, 213
Illustration index, VI: 1982-86, 214
Illustrators of children's bks: 1744-1945, 1178
Illustrators of children's bks: 1946-56, 1179
Illustrators of children's bks: 1957-66, 1180
Illustrators of children's bks: 1967-76, 1181
Images of Blacks in Amer culture, 475
Imaginary people, 1510
Immroth's gd to the Lib of Congress Classification,
    4th ed, 835
In praise of nature, 2052
Inaugural addresses of the presidents of the US, 984
Independent study cat: NUCEA's gd to independent
    study, 4th ed, 367
Index to Amer ref bks annual, 1985-89, 133
Index to AV producers & distrs, 24
Index to children's poetry, 1213
Index to children's songs, 1685
Index to collective bios for young readers, 4th ed, 242
Index to fairy tales, 1949-72, 1711
Index to fairy tales, 1973-77, 1712
Index to fairy tales, 1978-86, 1713
Index to literary criticism for young adults, 1538
Index to majors, 419
Index to poetry for children & young people: 1964-69,
    1214
Index to poetry for children & young people: 1970-75,
    1215
Index to poetry for children & young people: 1976-81,
    1216
Index to poetry for children & young people: 1982-87,
    1217
Index to the Wilson authors series, rev ed, 1522
Index to women of the world from ancient to modern
    times, 1129-30
Index to women of the world from ancient to modern
    times, supp, 1130
Indians of N Amer, 2d ed, 231
Indians of the Great Plains, 503
Information finder, 210
Information please almanac, 156
Information please sports almanac, 1055
Information Power: gdlines for school lib media
    programs, 877
Inge, M. Thomas, 1549
Ingham, John N., 314
Ingle, Lester, 2067
Insects & spiders, 2251
Instant gd to butterflies, 2250
Instructions in school lib media center use, 2d ed, 896
Integrating library skills ..., 898
Intellectual freedom & censorship, 849
Intellectual freedom manual, 3d ed, 850
Interactive fiction & adventure games for
    microcomputers 1988, 739
Interesting people: Black Amer hist makers, 476
International dict of films & filmakers, vol 1 & 2,
    1315-6

International dict of art & artists, 1338
International dict of 20th century bio, 283
International gd to children's theatre & educ theatre,
    1781
International index of recorded poetry, 1563
International relations dict, 4th ed, 954
International scholarship bk, 2d ed, 441
International youth hostel hndbk 1991-92, (v1, v2),
    601, 602
Intner, Sheila S., 841
Into the curriculum: lesson plans for lib media skills,
    899
Introducing bookplots 3, 1210
Introducing children to the arts, 1351
Introduction to cataloging & classification, 8th
    ed, 847
Introduction to ref work, 5th ed, 137
Ireland, Norma O., 1129-30, 1711-3
Irving, Jan, 2179
Isaac Asimov's bk of sci & nature quotations, 2121
Isaac Asimov's lib of the universe, 1797
Isaacs, Alan, 689, 2116
Israel, G., 1798
Israel, Peter, 1445
ISS dir of overseas schools, 1990-91, 10th ed, 442
Iverson, Timothy J., 1944

Jacinto, Beatrice, 1349
Jackson, Albert, 2173
Jackson, Byron M., 2036
Jackson, Donald C., 2158
Jackson, Joan S., 636
Jackson, Julia A., 1907
Jacobs, David S., 1985
Jacobs, Dick, 1682
Jacobs, William Jay, 816
Jacquet, Constance H., 1757
James, E. T., 1134
James, Elizabeth, 1278-9
James, Glenn, 2026
James, J. W., 1134
James, Robert, 2026
Jane Brody's good food gourmet, 1917
Jane's AFV recognition hndbk, 914
Jane's all the world's aircraft, 2199
Jane's urban transport systems 1990, 9th ed, 2211
Janson, Anthony F., 1339-40
Janson, Horst W., 1339-40
Jarnow, Jill, 36
Jarrett, William S., 1048-51
Jason, Philip K., 1564
Jazz hndbk, 1670
Jee, Sharilyn, 944
Jelks, Edward B., 236
Jelks, Juliet C., 236
Jemmings, Gertrude, 240
Jenkins, Christine, 1230
Jenkins, Esther C., 482
Jenkins, William A., 1458-9
Jennings, Terry, 584
Jervis, Simon, 1289
Jessup, Deborah Hitchcock, 2044
Jett-Simpson, Mary, 71
Jewish family celebrations, 1773
Jewish heritage in Amer, 501
Jewish primer, 1752
Jewish student's gd to Amer colleges, 406

Jim Kobak's Kirkus reviews, 51
Job hunting sourcebk, 323
Jobs rated almanac, 338
Johnston, Bernard, 198, 204
Johnston, Mea, 442
Jones, Brian, 2104, 2106, 2191-2
Jones, Delores Blythe, 13, 1200
Jones dict of cable TV terminology, 3d ed, 1269
Jones, Glenn, 1269
Jones, Jeffrey A., 616
Jones, John Oliver, 2241
Jones, R. E., 1144
Jones, Virginia L., 870
Jopling, Norma, 1788
Jordan, Sandra, 1826
Joy of cooking, rev ed, 1934
Judge, Harry, 2224
Judge, Harry, 645, 1888
Junior bk of authors, 2d ed, 1182
Junior ency of Canada, 1031
Junior high school lib cat, 6th ed, 69
Junior Jewish ency, 10th ed, 495
Jupiter, 1818

Kadish, Sanford H., 806
Kahn, Ada P., 2002
Kahn, John Ellison, 1454
Kallevig, Christine P., 1231
Kane, Joseph Nathan, 157, 985
Kanellos, Nicolas, 1590
Kaplan, Dorlene V., 1373
Karkhanis, Sharad, 501
Karolides, Nicholas, J., 614
Karp, Rashelle S., 1212
Karush, William, 2027
Kasack, Wofgang, 1625
Kastenbaum, Beatrice, 1946
Kastenbaum, Robert, 1946
Katz, Bill, 128-29, 898
Katz, Linda Sternberg, 128-9, 1565
Katz, William, 1565
Katz, William A., 137
Katzner, Kenneth, 1379, 1488
Kaufman, Les, 2248
Keating, H. R. F., 1550
Keegan, John, 673
Keen, G. Daniel, 1847-8, 1881
Keene, Raymond, 746
Keienburg, Wolf, 2269
Kelly, J. N. D., 1771
Kelly, Joanne, 1232
Kelsey-Wood, Dennis, 2077
Kemp, Betty, 855
Kemp, Peter, 2215
Kempen-van Dommelen, G. J. M., 1918
Kendall, Alan, 1629
Kennedy, DayAnn M., 2093-4
Kennedy, Frances H., 712
Kepos, Paula, 1532
Kern, Robert W., 687
Kernfeld, Barry, 1671
Kerrod, Robin, 2231, 2258
Key to high-tech: user-friendly gd to the new tech, 2142
Keyguide to info sources on animal rights, 1001
Keyser, Daniel, 450
Kids' cat collection, 353

Kids' complete baseball cat, 1077
Kid's complete gd to money, 354
Kid's first bk of birdwatching, 2246
Kids' world almanac of animals & pets, 2069
Kids' world almanac of baseball, 1066
Kids' world almanac rhyming dict, 1445
Kies, Cosette, 100
Killpatrick, Frances, 1056
Killpatrick, James, 1056
Kilvert, Ian Scott, 1602
Kim, Hyung-Chan, 480
Kimes, Beverly Rae, 2185
Kimmel, S., 89
Kingman, Lee, 1180-1, 1204-6
Kings & queens of England & Great Britain, 690
Kingston, Jeremy, 2147
Kinnell, Susan, 865
Kirkendall, Richard S., 722
Kirkpatrick, D. L., 1518, 1541, 1561
Kirshon, John W., 706
Kister, Kenneth F., 185
Kister's concise gd to best ency, 185
Kittredge, Mary, 1974
Klapthor, Margaret Brown, 974
Klein, Barry T., 506
Klein, Leonard S., 1504
Kliatt young adult paperback bk gd, 52
Kloesel, Christian J. W., 1603
Knitting know-how, 1307
Knowing your trees, rev ed, 1842
Knowlton, Jack, 585
Kobbe's illus opera bk, 1657
Kodansha ency of Japan, 1037
Koegler, Horst, 1794
Koehl, Stuart L., 917
Kohn, George C., 642
Konigsberg, Ira, 1317
Korbin, Beverly, 1233
Korean war almanac, 671
Kramer, Jonathan D., 1652
Krantz, Les, 338, 1371
Kraus, Barbara, 1927
Kreissman, Bern, 2033
Krensky, Stephen, 1398
Kricher, John C., 1843, 1899
Kruschke, Earl R., 2036
Kruse, Janice, 358
Kuipers, Barbara J., 507
Kulkin, Mary-Ellen, 1133
Kunitz, Stanley J., 1182, 1520, 1525-6, 1588, 1599-1600
Kurian, Gerorge Thomas, 795, 1013-4
Kurowski, Jeff, 750
Kyte, Kathy S., 354

La Potin, Armand S., 509
La Terreur, Marc, 259
LaBlanc, Michael L., 1638
Laboratory test hndbk, 2d ed, 1985
Lady laureates, 2d ed, 1136
Lahti, N. E., 1341
Laing, Dave, 1674
Lake, Sara, 958
Lamb, Andrew, 1672
Lambert, David, 1889, 1897-8
Lampton, Christopher, 2089
Land of the South, 577

Lands & people, 1015
Lane, Leonard G., 619
Lang, Jenifer Harvey, 1928
Langer, William L., 643
Lange's hndbk of chemistry, 13th ed, 1855
Langford, Michael, 1376
Langman, Larry, 1270, 1318
Langone, John, 1939
Languages of the world, rev ed, 1379
Langworth, Richard M., 2186
LaPier, Cynthia B., 1874
Lare, Gary, 430
Larousse gardens & gardening, 2018
Larousse gastronomique, 1928
Larsen, Anne, 51
Larson, David E., 1989
LaRue, Robert D., Jr., 1017
Laska, Vera, 664
Lasne, Sophie, 928
Lass, Abraham H., 169
Last rain forests: world conservation atlas, 2034
Latham, Alison, 1634
Lathrop, Ann, 108, 866
Latin Amer lit in the 20th century, 1620
Latin Amer today, rev ed, 1039
Latin Amer writers, 1621
Latrobe, Kathy Howard, 909
Laughlin, Mildred Knight, 909, 1234
Lauriault, Jean, 1844
Laurich, Robert Anthony, 1977
LaVecks, James, 325
Law dict, 3d ed, 793
Lawrence, Robert W., 915
Lawson, Sandra M., 527
Lax, Roger, 1683
Layman, Richard, 1945
Lazarus, John, 1660
Leach, Marie, 1697
Leadership: quotations from the military tradition, 916
Leadership: treasury of great quotations, 1731
Leaf, Hayim, 495
Lean Geoffrey, 2041
Learning & info, 893
Learning AIDS 1989: info resources dir, 2d ed, 1986
LeCompte, Michelle, 323
Lederman, Ellen, 420
Lee, George L, 476
Lee, Joann H., 867
Lee, Mein-ven, 1476
Lee, Sidney, 262
Leemings, David A., 1688
Legacy of the cat, 2079
Legat, Michael, 1508
Legg, L. G. Wickham, 266-7
Legget, Glenn H., 1277
Leininger, Phillip, 1579
Leitch, Barbara A., 508
Lekisch, Barbara, 2033
Lemay, Harold, 1390-1
Lend a hand: the how, where & why of volunteering, 177
Lentz, Harris M., III, 930
Leo, John R., 1566
Leonard Maltin's TV movies & video gd, 1271
Leonard, Robin D., 796
Leonard, Thomas M., 652, 655

Lerner, Richard M., 1966
Lesniak, James G., 1517
Lessiter, Mike, 1057-8
Lester, June, 822
Letitia Baldrige's complete gd to the new manner for the 90's, 517
Levasseur-Regourd, Arny Chantal, 1817
Levert, Suzanne, 272
Levey, Judith S., 1406-7, 1421
Levin, Shirley, 368
Levine, Mark L., 1766
Lewis, Norman, 1468
Lewis, Richard J., 1856
Lewis, Richard J., Sr., 1854
Li, Marjorie H., 483
Li, Peter, 483
Librarian's gd to WordPerfect 5.0, 1874
Librarian's thesaurus, 824
Libraries & info servs today, 822
Library displays, 908
Library displays hndbk, 910
Library jl, 53
Library media center programs for middle schools, 883
Library media skills & the sr high school English program, 895
Library media skills, 2d ed, 901
Library of congress: gd to genealogical & historical research, 528
Library of Congress subject headings, 842
Library puzzles & word games for grades 7-12, 902
Library resources for the blind & physically handicapped, 42
Library space planning, 905
Library talk, 5
Libretto, Ellen V., 91
Life sciences on file collection, 1823
Lightbody, Andy, 2200
Lima, Carolyn W., 1170
Lima, John A., 1170
Limburg, Peter R., 785, 1438
Lincoln, R. J., 2064
Lincoln writing dict for children, 1405
Lindop, Edmund, 801
Lindquist, Carolyn Lloyd, 326
Lindsey, Mary P., 437
Lion ency of the Bible, rev ed, 1768
Lipkin, Midge, 438
Lippy, Charles H., 1772
Lipton, Gladys C., 1482
Listen to the music, 1652
Liston, Linda, 1895
Literary hist of the Amer west, 1585
Literary market place: dir of Amer bk pub industry, 1263
Literary terms: a dict, 3d ed, 1499
Literature for children about Asians & Asian Amer, 482
Literature for today's young adults, 3d ed, 1140
Literature in Amer: illus hist, 1581
Literature-based reading, 1234
Litwak, Leon, 469
Litz, A. Walton, 1593, 1595
Living & working in space, 2206
Living snakes of the world in color, 2276
Living with low vision, 2d ed, 622
Lizards of the world, 2275

Loeb, Catherine R., 1119
Loertscher, David V., 878-9, 882, 1188
Logan, Rayford W., 471
Lomask, Milton, 595
Lomeli, Francisco A., 1591
Loney, Glenn, 1782
Longman hndbk of modern European hist, 1763-1885, 656
Look-it-up bk of presidents, 977
Lopez, Elizabeth I., 1976
Lopez, Nancy, 1088
Lopos, George L., 385
Losito, Linda, 2071, 2249, 2251, 2255
Lovejoy, Frederick H., 1990
Lovejoy's college gd, 19th ed, 407
Low, W. Augustus, 473
Lowe, David W., 2065
Loyn, H. R., 651
Lurker, Manfred, 1700
Luttwak, Edward, 917
Lye, Keith, 193
Lynch, Michael, 2153
Lynch, Richard Chigley, 1673
Lynn, Ruth Nadelman, 1162
Lyons, Janet, 1826

Macaulay, David, 2159
Maccigrosso, Robert, 243
Macdonald, David, 2266
MacFall, Russell P., 1900
MacGregor, Geddes, 1747
MacGregor, Morris J., Jr., 734
Machinery's hndbk, 23d ed, 2178
Macintosh Bible: thousands of basic & advanced tips ..., 3d ed, 1875
MacKay, James, 754
Maclin, Alice, 1384
Macmillan bk of fascinating facts, 149
Macmillan dict for children, rev ed, 1406
Macmillan dict of quotations, 1723
Macmillan first dict, rev ed, 1407
Macmillan gd to correspondence study, 3d ed, 369
Macmillan illus ency of birds, 2242
Macmillan illus ency of dinosaurs & prehistoric animals, 1901
Macmillan illus ency of myths & legends, 1694
Macmillan picture wordbk, 1421
Macmillan small business hndbk, 320
Macmillan world hist factfinder, 644
Macrone, Michael, 1606
Maddex, Diane, 1365-7
Madigan, C. O., 149
Mafia ency, 811
Magazine index, 223
Magazines for children, 2d ed, 130
Magazines for libs, 6th ed, 128
Magazines for young people, 2d ed, 129
Magel, Charles, R., 1001
Magill, Frank N., 276-7, 1503, 1512-4, 1534, 1537, 1542, 1587, 1715, 1724-5, 1886, 2201
Magill's quotations in context. first series, 1724
Magill's quotations in context. second series, 1725
Magill's survey of science, 1886
Magill's survey of science: space exploration series, 2201
Magnusson, Magnus, 256
Mahar, Mary, 370

Mahoney, Bertha E., 1178
Mahoney, Jim, 376
Mainiero, Lina, 1589
Maintaining good health, 2013
Major 20th-century writers, 1523
Make it II, 1290
Make your own animated movies & videotapes, rev ed, 1331
Makkai, Adain, 1426
Makower, Joel, 533
Malinowsky, H. Robert, 2097
Mallon, Bill, 1099
Malotte, Stan, 1470
Maltin, Leonard, 1271
Mammals: gd to familiar Amer species, rev ed, 2271
Mammals in N Amer, 2270
Mammals: the hunters, 2259
Mammals: the large plant-eaters, 2260
Mammals: the small plant-eaters, 2257
Man, myth & magic, 1701
Management of online search serv in schools, 859
Managing school lib media programs, 886
Managing the student yrbk, 1257
Mancall, J. C., 859
Mangrum, Charles T., II, 439
Manguel, Alberto, 1509
Mann, Lester, 436
Manning, Beverly, 1131
Manser, Martin H., 1475
Manual for writers of term papers, theses & dissertations, 5th ed, 1286
Manufacturing USA, 312
Map cat, 2d ed, 533
Maps & compasses, 2d ed, 765
Maps on file, 547
Marantz, Kenneth A., 1148
Marantz, Sylvia S., 1148
MARC manual: understanding & using MARC records, 830
Marching band hndbk, 1650
Margulis, Lynn, 1824
Markham, Roberta H., 1280
Markle, Sandra, 2175
Marks, Claude, 1360-1
Mars, 1814
Marsh, Earle, 1266
Marsh, John H., 1031
Marshall Cavendish ency of health, 1987
Marshall Cavendish illus ency of discovery & exploration, 596
Marshall Cavendish illus ency of plants and earth sciences, 1827
Marshall Cavendish illus ency of World War I, 665
Marshall Cavendish illus ency of World War II, 666
Marshall Cavendish illus hist of popular music, 1662
Marshall Cavendish illus hist of the presidents of the US, 987
Marshall Cavendish intl wildlife ency, rev ed, 2220
Marshall, John, 2212
Marshall, Sam A., 1374
Martin, Judith, 520
Martin, Laura C., 1709
Martin, Linda, 1321
Martinez, Julio A., 1591
Martin-Smith's official 1948-89/90 baseball card cross-gd, 758
Marwick, Christine M., 802

Mason, Francis, 1793
Mass Media: a chronological ency, 1247
Master builders: gd to famous Amer architects, 1367
Masterpieces of world lit, 1537
Masterpieces of world philosophy, 1715
Masterplots: rev category ed, Amer fict series, 1587
Masterplots II: Amer fiction series, 1512
Masterplots II: drama series, 1542
Masterplots II: short story series, 1513
Masters gd to sports camps, 1059
Materials & strategies for the educ of trainable
    mentally retarded learners, 440
Mathematics dict, 4th ed, 2026
Mathematics illus dict: fact, figures, & people, rev
    ed, 2023
Matt, Stephen R., 2176
Matthew, Donald, 650
Matthew, Geoffrey, 552
Matthews, John R., 1988
Matthews, Rupert, 603
Mattison, Chris, 2085, 2275
Mattson, Catherine, 548
Mattson, Mart T., 548
Matuz, Roger, 1531
Mauro, Laurie, 1533
Maxwell, Margaret F., 840
May, Charles E., 1571
May, George S., 304-5
May, John, 2268
Mayer, Ralph, 1352
Mayo clinic family health bk, 1989
Mays, James L., 1764
Mazzeno, Laurence W., 1596
McBride, William G., 92
McCarty, John, 1319
McCaslin, Nellie, 1783
McClelland, D., 1859
McClendon, Frank, 1970
McCormick, Donald, 1551
McCormick, Regina, 583
McCue, Helga P., 1173
McDonald, Margaret R., 1235
McDowell, Patricia, 512
McElmeel, Sharron L., 1236-9
McEvedy, Colin, 644, 703
McFarland, David, 2223
McGee, Harold, 1929
McGinnis, Jo, 238
McGraw-Hill CD-ROM sci & tech ref set, 2110
McGraw-Hill concise ency of sci & tech, 2d ed, 2111
McGraw-Hill dict of earth sciences, 3d ed, 1887
McGraw-Hill dict of sci & tech terms, 4th ed, 2112
McGraw-Hill ency of physics, 2090
McGraw-Hill ency of sci & tech, 6th ed, 2113
McGraw-Hill ency of world bio, 278
McGraw-Hill personal computer programming ency,
    2d ed, 1866
McGraw-Hill yrbk of sci & tech, 2122
McGuiness, Colleen, 964
McInerney, Claire, 1281
McInerny, Derek, 2075
McIntosh, M. E., 425
McKay, George, 2265
McKerns, Joseph, 1256
McLauchlan, Gordon, 1046
McLaughlin, John, 1348
McLeish, Kenneth, 1636

McLeish, Valerie, 1636
McMullan, Randall, 2174
McNeil, Ian, 2144
McPherson, James M., 711
McQuain, Jeffrey, 1475
McRae, Barry, 1670
Meacham, Mary, 1159
Mead, Frank S., 1753
Measures of excellence for sch lib media centers, 879
Measuring & computing, 1879
MECC dataquest: Latin Amer, 1040
Media access & org, 838
Media and methods, 6
Media production & computer activities, 900
Media resource cat, 16
Media review digest, 15
Meeting the needs of people with disabilities, 885
Mehrtens, John M., 2276
Meier, August, 469
Meier, Matt S., 486, 487
Melton, J. Gordon, 1748, 1749, 1754
Melzer, Annabelle Henkin, 1330
Mental measurements yrbk, 449
Mercatante, Anthony, 1702
Merit student ency, 204
Merrill-Oldham, Jan, 880
Merrit, Jeffrey, 653
Meserole, Mike, 1055
Messenger, Charles, 667
Meterology source bk, 1892
Metzger, Linda, 1515
Mexican Amer bios, 1836-1987, 487
Meyer, Linnea, 398
Meyers, Belle, 1307
Microcomputer applications hndbk, 1876
Microcomputer sftwr sources, 116
Middle ages: a concise ency, 651
Middle East, 1044
Middle East today, 1045
Middleton, Alex L. A., 2235
Middleton, Nick, 1016, 2039
Miko, Chris John, 1004
Milkis, Sidney M., 986
Miller, Bertha Mahony, 1202-3
Miller, Diane June, 326
Miller, E. Willard, 2053-4
Miller, George Oxford, 2228
Miller, Joan I., 1282
Miller, Lauri, 1347
Miller, Randall M., 713
Miller, Ruby M., 2053-4
Miller, Stuart W., 168
Mills, John, 1342
Mills, Stephanie, 2052
Milner, Richard, 2221
Milner-Gulland, Robin, 1034
Miner, Margaret, 1729, 1767
Miss Manners' gd for the turn-of-the-millennium, 520
Mitchell, Charity, 1254
Mitchell, James, 192
Mitchell, Joyce Slayton, 339
Mitchell, Robert T., 2252
Mitchell, Sally, 692
Mitzel, Harold E., 360
MLA hndbk for writers of research papers, 1283
Moavenzadeh, Fred, 2169
Mochedlover, Helene G., 1540

Mode of costume, 1299
Model for problem solving & decision making, 887
Modern & contemporary, 1566
Modern Amer usage, 1465
Modern Amer women writers, 1593
Modern dict of geography, 2d ed, 587
Modern drama scholarship & criticism, 1966-80, 1539
Modern fantasy: hundred best novels, 1946-87, 1553
Modern horror film, 1319
Modern welding, rev ed, 2177
Molinari, Joseph A., 1270
Monaghan, Patricia, 1703
Monarchs of Scotland, 691
Monk, Jennifer, 689
Monson, Dianne L., 1145
Montgomery, Ann, 384
Month-by-month atlas of World War II, 670
Monthly cat of US govt pubs, 119
Months of the year, 784
Montreville, Doris de, 1184-5
Moody, Douglas, 371-2
Moon, 1816
Mooney, Louise, 248
Moore, Carolyn E., 1930
Moore, Cory, 615
Moore, David M., 1827
Moore, Patrick, 1804-5
Moore, R. I., 631
Moore, Thurston, 772
Mordden, Ethan, 1784
More bks appeal: keep young teens in the lib, 1228
More junior authors, 1183
More memorable Amer, 1750-1950, 273
More picture bk story hours, 1244
More sci in action, 2135
Morgan, Kathleen O'Leary, 1111
Morley, Sheridan, 1792
Moroney, Sean, 1024
Morris dict of word & phrase origins, 2d ed, 1439
Morris, Jacqueline, 873
Morris, Mary, 1439, 1469
Morris, P. S., 892
Morris, William, 1439, 1469
Morrison, Ian, 1089
Morrissett, C., 1871
Morrow, Carolyn Clark, 827
Moseley, Robert K., 1829
Moser, Diane, 2205-8
Moss, Joy F., 1240
Moss, Joyce, 459, 463, 1041, 1167
Mossman, Jennifer, 287-8, 782
Mote, James, 1072
Mother goose comes first: an annotated gd, 89
Motion picture series & sequels, 1324
Motorcycle bks: critical survey & checklist, 2181
Mott, Lawrie, 1931
Mott-Smith, Geoffrey, 745
Mount Sinai sch of medicine complete bk of nutrition, 1932
Movie characters of leading performers ..., 1320
Moxon, Julian, 2151
Multicultural educ, 386
Mumford, Laura Stempel, 1120
Municipal yr bk, 992
Munro, David, 590
Munroe, May, 1189
Murphy Paul C., 709

Murray, Jocelyn, 1025
Murray, Michael T., 1941
Murry, Velma McBride, 466
Museum of sci & industry basic list of children's sci bks, 2095
Mushrooms & other fungi of the midcontinental US, 1838
Mushrooms of N Amer, 1839
Music: illus ency, 1627
Musicians since 1900, 1646
My first dict, 1408
My first muppet dict, 1409
My first picture dict, 1410
My pictionary, 1411
My second picture dict, 1412
Myers, Allen C., 1762
Myers, Norman, 1002
Mythical & fabulous creatures, 1710
Mythology of N Amer, 1706
Myths, gods, & fantasy, 1689

Nabokov, Peter, 1368
Naden, Corinne, J., 82, 1208-9
Nakamura, Joyce, 1174, 1198
Names of the games, 1058
Nardi, James B., 2253
Nash, Jay Robert, 808
National air & space museum, 2d ed, 2202
National anthems of the world, 7th ed, 1684
National debate topic for high schools, 1251
National dir of storytelling, 1990 ed, 1241
National five-digit ZIP code & PO dir, 178
National Geographic atlas of N Amer, 549
National Geographic atlas of the world, 6th ed, 550
National Geographic index, 1888-1988, 597
National Geographic's gd to the natl parks of the US, 604
National hockey league official gd & record bk, 1093
National wildflower research center's wildflower hndbk, 1833
Nations within a nation, 511
Native Amer architecture, 1368
Native Amer voluntary orgs, 509
Natkiel, Richard, 701
Natural hist of whales & dolphins, 2267
Natural wonders of Amer, 600
Naylor, Colin, 1355, 1372
Nazism resistance & holocaust in World War II, 664
NBC handbk of pronunciation, 4th ed, 1449
NBC news Rand McNally world news atlas, 551
NCEA/Ganley's Catholic schools in Amer, 17th ed, 370
Neagles, James C., 528
Nebenzahl, Kenneth, 630
Neely, Mark E., Jr., 723
Neft, David S., 1073, 1078
Negro almanac: ref work on African Amer, 5th ed., 477
Negus, Daphne, 2080
Neill, George W., 112-3
Neill, Shirley Boes, 112-3
Nelson Canadian atlas, 552
Nelson, Douglas, 654
Nelson, Gail A., 74
Nelson, Michael, 980, 986
Neufeldt, Victoria, 1396
New age ency, 1749

New Amer dict of good English, 1468
New animal doctor's answer bk, rev ed, 2070
New bk of knowledge, 205
New bk of popular sci, 2114
New bks: pubs for sale by the GPO, 120
New Catholic ency, 1750
New child health ency, 1990
New comprehensive Amer rhyming dict, 1447
New cosmopolitan world atlas, 553
New dict of Amer slang, 1428
New ency Britannica, 15th ed, 206
New ency of sci fict, 1552
New everyman dict of music, 6th ed, 1628
New fun ency, 740
New Good Housekeeping ency of house plants, rev ed, 2017
New Grolier electronic ency, 195
New Grolier student ency, 208
New Grove dict of Amer music, 1630
New Grove dict of jazz, 1671
New Grove dict of music & musicians, 6th ed, 1631
New Harvard dict of music, 3d rev ed, 1632
New hndbk of health & preventive medicine, 2007
New illus dinosaur dict, 1904
New intl atlas, 554
New intl dict of quotations, 1729
New Merriam-Webster dict for large print users, 1392
New new word dict, rev ed, 1391
New Oxford companion to music, 1633
New Penguin gd to compact discs & cassettes: yrbk 1989, 37
New pseudonyms & nicknames, 288
New read-aloud hndbk, 1989 ed, 1245
New video ency, 1270
New York pub lib bks of chronologies, 165
New York pub lib desk ref, 158
New York Times atlas of the world, rev ed, 555
New York Times: current event edition, 1003
New York Times index, 224
Newbery & Caldecott awards, 1201
Newbery & Caldecott medal bks: 1956-65, 1204
Newbery & Caldecott medal bks: 1966-75, 1205
Newbery & Caldecott medal bks: 1976-85, 1206
Newbery medal bks: 1922-55, 1202
Newnham, Jeffrey, 929
Newsmakers, 1991 cum, 247
Newsmakers: the people behind today's headlines, 248
Newspaper: a ref bk for teachers & librarians, 377
Nicholls, C. S., 271
Nicholls, Christine S., 270
Nicholls, Delia, 2262
Nicholls, Paul T. 106
Nielson, Niels, 1755
Niemeyer, Suzanne, 1207, 1524
Niering, William A., 1834
Nilsen, A. P., 1140
Nilson, Alleen Pace, 102
Nilson, Lenore, 1163
Nimerscheim, Jack, 1877
1992 what color is your parachute, 330
Nineteenth century Amer poetry, 1564
Nineteenth-century literary crictism, 1533
Nisberg, Jay N., 309
NIV compact dict of the Bible, 1761
Nobel peace prize & the laureates, 1901-87, 945
Nobel prize winners, 280
Nonfiction bks for children, 1226

Nonfiction for young adults, 98
Nonprint cataloging for multimedia collections, 2d ed, 844
Nonprint production ..., 2d ed, 825
Noonan, Eileen, 1737-8
Norback, Craig T., 344
Nordquist, Joan, 1954-5, 1991
North Amer human rights dir, 3d ed, 817
North Amer trees exclusive of Mexico & tropical Florida, 4th ed, 1846
Northwoods wildlife: watcher's gd to habitats, 2062
Norton, Donna E., 1142
Norton/Grove concise ency of music, 1634
Norwich, John Julius, 1345
Notable Amer women, 1607-1950, 1134
Notable Amer women: the modern period, 1135
Notable children's films & videos, filmstrips, & recordings, 1974-86, 27
Novel experiences, 1230
Nowlan, Gwendolyn Wright, 1320, 1334
Nowlan, Robert A., 1320, 1334
NTC's Amer idioms dict, 1431
Nuclear energy policy: ref hndbk, 2036
Number one in the U.S.A, 2d ed, 161
Nutrition, 1935
Nutrition almanac, 3d ed, 1921

Oakley, Ruth, 987
Oberg, Eric, 2178
O'Brien, Nancy Patricia, 357
O'Brien, Robert, 576, 1956
O'Brien, Steven G., 948
Obst, Fritz Jurgen, 2277
Occu-facts: info on 565 careers, 1989-90 ed, 340
Occupational briefs, 341
Occupational outlook hndbk, 1990-91, 342
Oceans: bk of questions & answers, 1912
O'Connell, Susan M., 2091
O'Connor, John, 2051
O'Donnell, Timothy S., 1115
O'Donoghue, Michael, 1908
Off-air videotaping in educ, 1250
Office sourcebk, 293
Official baseball register, 1070
Official congressional dir, 1989-90, 973
Official NBA basketball ency, 1079
Official NBA gd, 1080
Official NBA register, 1081
Official NFL record & fact bk, 1086
Official professional rodeo media gd, 1990, 1101
Official world wildlife fund gd to endangered species of N Amer, 2065, 2222
Ohlers, John F., 393
Oil & gas dict, 2037
Old farmer's almanack, 159
Olderr, Steven, 1171
Olderr's young adult fiction index, 1171
Old-house dict, 1369
Oleszek, Walter J., 969
Olexer, Marycile E., 1218
Oliver, Jane, 540
Olmstead, Nancy C., 1834
Olsen, Kristin Gottschalk, 1942
Olsen, Larry Dean, 768
Olson, James, 660
Olson, James S., 724
Olton, Roy, 954

Olympic games, 1098
Olympic record bk, 1099
On food & cooking: science & lore of the kitchen, 1929
On this day, 779
100 best spare-time bus opportunities today, 319
101 microcomputer projects to do in your lib, 863
101 stories of the great ballets, 1793
1001 flying facts & firsts, 2195
1,001 things everyone should know about Amer hist, 719
O'Neill, Hugh B., 679
O'Neill, Rosanna M., 846
One-parent children, the growing minority, 1968
Onions, C. T., 1607
Online & CD-ROM databases in school libs, 866
Online info serv for secondary school students, 2d ed, 860
Online ref & info retrieval, 2d ed, 869
Online searching, 2d ed, 867
Online searching goes to school, 864
Only the best 1985-89: the cum gd to highest-rated educl sftwr, 112
Only the best: the annual gd to highest-rated educl sftwr, 113
Opening the space frontier, 2207
Opera hndbk, 1660
Opfell, Olga S., 1136-37
Opie, Ione, 1220
Opie, Peter, 1220
Opinions '90, 1004
Opposing viewpoints series, 1005
Opus: America's gd to classical music, 38
Original word game dict, 772
Osborn, Jeanne, 843
Osborn, Susan, 179
Osborne, Harold, 1291, 1343-4
O'Toole, Christopher, 2259
O'Toole, G. J. A., 953
Ottemiller's index to plays in collections, 7th ed, 1540
Our flag, 524
Our natl parks: Amer spectacular wilderness heritage, 605
Our sun & the inner planets, 1817
Our vice-presidents & second ladies, 989
Ousby, Ian, 1501
Outdoor survival skills, 5th ed, 768
Oxbury, Harold, 281
Oxford bk of aphorisms, 1726
Oxford bk of children's verse in Amer, 1219
Oxford companion to Amer lit, 5th ed, 1583
Oxford companion to Amer theatre, 1777
Oxford companion to animal behavior, 2223
Oxford companion to Australian lit, 1611
Oxford companion to Canadian lit, 1612
Oxford companion to chess, 744
Oxford companion to children's lit, 1168
Oxford companion to classical lit, 2d ed, 1615
Oxford companion to English lit 5th ed, 1597
Oxford companion to German lit 2d ed, 1617
Oxford companion to law, 797
Oxford companion to medicine, 1992
Oxford companion to popular music, 1661
Oxford companion to ships & the sea, 2215
Oxford companion to Spanish lit, 1622
Oxford companion to the decorative arts, 1291
Oxford companion to the theatre, 4th ed, 1785

Oxford companion to twentieth century art, 1343
Oxford dict of art, 1344
Oxford dict of modern quotations, 1727
Oxford dict of natural hist, 2058
Oxford dict of nursery rhymes, 1220
Oxford dict of popes, 1771
Oxford dict of quotations, 3d ed, 1728
Oxford dict of saints, 2d ed, 1775
Oxford English dict, 2d ed, 1385
Oxford English-Russian dict, 1489
Oxford first companion to music, 1636
Oxford gd to word games, 773
Oxford illus ency of the arts, 1345
Oxford illus ency, v1: physical world, 1888
Oxford illus ency, v2: the natural world, 2224
Oxford illus ency, v3, v4: world hist ..., 645, 646
Oxford jr companion to music, 2d ed, 1635
Oxford Russian-English dict, 2d ed, 1490
Oxford treasury of children's poems, 1221
Oxford-Duden German dict, 1484
Oxford-Duden pictorial English dict, 1422
Oxford-Duden pictorial French-English dict, 1483
Oxford-Duden pictorial German-English dict, 1485

Paciorek, Michael J., 616
Page, James A., 1100
Pagel, Mary I., 868
Paige, Donald L., 2030
Painless path to proper English usage, 1470
Painter, William M., 1242
Paletta, Lu Ann, 975
Palmer, P., 1076
Palmer, Roger C., 869
Parents' bk of facts: child devel from birth to age five, 1963
Parent's desk ref, 1967
Parish, James R., 1327-9
Parisi, Lynn S., 870, 1017
Parisi, Paul, 880
Parker, Helen M., 268-9
Parker, Steve, 2229, 2257
Parker, Sybil P., 1887, 1892, 2090, 2111-2
Parker, Thomas, 654
Partnow, Elaine, 1125-6
Pasachoff, Jay M., 1810
Paskoff, Paul, 306
Pastine, Maureen, 898
Paterson, Alan J., 2150
Patnode, Darwin, 942
Paton, John, 191, 201
Patrick Moore's a-z of astronomy, 1805
Patterns of poetry: an ency of forms, 1570
Patterson, Anna Grace, 132-3
Patterson's Amer educ, 1990 ed, 371
Patterson's elem educ, 1990 ed, 372
Pauer, Gyula, 1029
Paul, Gregory S., 1902
Paul, T. Otis, 624
Paulson, Annie, 1833
Paxton, John, 595, 684, 1020-1
PC Globe 4.0, 570
PC USA, 571
PCGlobe +, 1018
Peace resource bk, 1988-89, 951
Pearce, E. A., 1893
Pearl, Patricia, 1739
Pearson, Olen R., 1878

Pellant, Chris, 1909
Pellowski, Anne, 1243
Pemberton, J. Michael, 35
Penguin atlas of N Amer hist, 703
Penguin dict of decorative arts, rev ed, 1292
Penguin ency of popular music, 1663
People to know, 253
People's gd to vitamins & minerals from a to zinc, rev ed, 1916
Peoples of the world: Latin Amer, 1041
Peoples of the world: N Amer, 459,
Pepper, Frank S., 1736
Perigee visual dict of signing, 617
Perkins, Barbara, 1579
Perkins, Dorothy, 1038
Perkins, George, 1579
Perrett, Bryan, 668
Perrins, Christopher, 2235
Perrins, Lesley, 2154
Perry, Jane Greverus, 609
Perry, John, 609
Personal computer buying gd, 1878
Pervier, Evelyn, 1094-6
Pesticide alert: gd to pesticides in fruits & vegetables, 1931
Pet owner's gd to dogs, 2083
Peters atlas of the world, 556
Petersen, Carolyn Collins, 1818
Peterson, Carol Sue, 1685
Peterson first gd to clouds & weather, 1891
Peterson first gd to dinosaurs, 1899
Peterson first gd to fishes of N Amer, 2247
Peterson first gd to shells of N Amer, 2254
Peterson first gd to the solar system, 1810
Peterson, Roger Tory, 2243-4
Peterson's college money hndbk, 1991, 8th ed, 421
Peterson's competitive colleges, 1991-92, 10th ed, 408
Peterson's drug & alcohol programs & policies at four-yr colleges, 1957
Peterson's gd to certificate progs at Amer colleges & univs, 385
Peterson's gd to colleges with progs for learning disabled students, 2d ed, 439
Peterson's gd to four-yr colleges, 409
Peterson's gd to two-yr colleges, 410
Peterson's summer opportunities for kids & teenagers, 1991, 8th ed, 770
Pets & farm animals, 2071
Pets: complete hndbk on the care, understanding & appreciation ..., 3d ed, 2068
Pets in a jar: collecting & caring for small wild animals, 2072
Pfaffenberger, Bryan, 1861
Pfeffer, Pierre, 2225
Pheby, John A., 1422
Phillips, Roger, 1839, 1845
Phillips, Steven J., 1369
Phipps, Frank T., 1448
Photographer's bible, 1375
Photographer's market: where & how to sell your photographs, 1374
Phythian, B. A., 1471
Pictorial hist of Black Amers, 5th ed, 474
Pictorial hist of the Holocaust, 669
Picture bks for children, 3d ed, 78
Picture ency for children, 191
Pilger, Mary Ann, 2136-7

Pilla, Marianne Laino, 93
Pinckney, Cathey, 2010
Pinckney, Edward R., 2010
Pinkard, Bruce, 1375
Pitt, Barrie, 670
Pitt, Frances, 670
Pitts, Judy M., 903
Pitts, Michael R., 1264, 1327-9
Pizzorno, Joseph E., 1941
Place-names in classical mythology: Greece, 1691
Places rated almanac, 1107
Plain English: a user's gd, 1472
Plain talk about art, 2d ed, 1341
Planetary exploration series, 1813
Planning school lib media facilities, 904
Plano, Jack C., 931, 954
Platt, Suzy, 1730
Play index, 1983-87, 1790
Plays for children & young adults, 1212
Ploski, Harry A., 477
Pocket dict of signing, 618
Podell, Janet, 988
Podrazik, Walter, J., 1267
Poetry anthologies for children & young people, 1218
Poetry hndbk: a dict of terms, 4th ed, 1562
Police dict & ency, 792
Policies of AV producers & distrs, 2d ed, 35
Political facts on the US since 1789, 934
Political quotations, 939
Pollock, Steve, 2105, 2107, 2218-9
Poole, Chris, 2186
Popular ency of plants, 1828
"Popular Mechanics" home how-to, 2173
Popular per index, 225
Popular song index, third supp, 1681
Popular world fiction, 1900-present, 1524
Population of the US, 1106
Porter-Shirley, Bunny, 1957
Portraits: focusing on bio & autobio in secondary school, 238
Portraits in silicon, 1880
Post, Elizabeth L., 298, 521-2
Post-feminist Hollywood actress, 1321
Power up: experiments, puzzles, & games exploring electricity, 2175
Powers, David Guy, 749
Poyer, Joe, 2200
Prance, Ghillean T., 1836
Predators & predation, 2225
Predatory dinosaurs of the world, 1902
Preminger, Alexander, 1568-9
Prentice-Hall ency of mathematics, 2028
Prentice-Hall hndbk for writers, 1277
Prentice-Hall pocket ency: house plants, 2019
Prentice-Hall pocket ency of creative photography, 1376
Presenting children's authors, 1190
Presidents in Amer hist, rev ed, 976
Presidents' last years, 981
Presidents of the USA, 12th ed, 983
Preston, Richard J., Jr., 1846
Previn, Andre, 1655
Price, Robert L., 611
Prichard, James B., 1763
Prichard, Mari, 1168
Primaryplots: a book talk gd for readers age 4-8, 1211
Primates, insect eaters & baleen whales, 2258

Primm, E. Russell, 331
Princeton ency of poetry & poetics, rev ed, 1568
Princeton hndbk of poetic terms, 1569
Pringle, David, 1510, 1553
Pritchard, James B., 1763
Private schools of the U.S., 373
Pro football bio-bibliography, 1087
Pro football gd, 1085
Professional careers sourcebk, 324
Professional rodeo official hndbk, 1987, 1102
Professional secretary's ency dict, 4th ed,308
Projections of educl statistics to 2001, 379
Projects for young scientists, 2138
Prucha, Francis Paul, 510
Pryce, David, 685
Pseudonyms & nicknames dict, 3d ed, 287
Public relations for school media centers, 909
Publication manual of the Amer psychological assn,
    3d ed, 1284
Publishers, distrs, and wholesalers of the US, 14
Pugnetti, Gino, 2078
Punctuation hndbk, 1282
Purchasing an ency, 3d ed, 186
Pyatt, Sherman E., 1026
Pyle, Marian S., 1949

Queens, empresses, grand duchesses & regents, 1137
Que's computer user's dict, 1861
Quick ref gd to astronomy magazine, 1973-90, 1812
Quick ref gd to National Geographic, 1955-mid 1990,
    598
Quotable Shakespeare: topical dict, 1608
Quotable women, 1800-1981, 1125
Quotable women from Eve to 1799, 1126
Quote sleuth: manual for the tracer of lost quotations,
    1733

Racinet, Albert, 1294
Racing on the Tour de France, 1060
Racism in the US, 463
Radio amateur's hndbk, 15th ed, 1265
Radio soundtracks, 2d ed, 1264
Raeburn, Michael, 1629
Rainis, Kenneth S., 2138
Ramsey, Patricia G., 386
Rand McNally atlas of Earth mysteries, 1881
Rand McNally atlas of world hist, rev ed, 631
Rand McNally children's atlas of the environment,
    2040
Rand McNally children's atlas of the universe, 1799
Rand McNally children's atlas of the US, 557
Rand McNally children's atlas of world hist, 632
Rand McNally children's atlas of world wildlife, 2216
Rand McNally children's world atlas, 558
Rand McNally Goode's world atlas, 18th ed, 559
Rand McNally handy railroad atlas of the US, 2213
Rand McNally photographic world atlas, 560
Rand McNally picture atlas of the world, 561
Rand McNally road atlas: US, Canada, Mexico, 562
Rand McNally world facts & maps, 1019
Randel, Don Michael, 1632
Randolph, Ruth Elizabeth, 1594
Random House bk of horses & horsemanship, 1097
Random House bk of 1001 wonders of sci, 2125
Random House crossword puzzle dict, 774
Random House dict of the English language, 2d
    ed, 1386

Random House ency, 3d ed, 192
Random House hndbk of business terms, 309
Random House Webster's college dict, 1393
Ranson, K. Anne, 194
Rapid gd to hazardous chemicals in the workplace,
    2d ed, 1856
Rating gd to franchises, rev ed, 317
Rating gd to life in Amer small cities, 1113
Rawlinson, Nora, 53
Rawson, Hugh, 1429, 1729, 1767
Rayner, Lynn, 2007
Read all your life: suject gd to fict, 1575
Reader's companion to Amer hist, 725
Reader's Digest Amer's historic places, 606
Reader's Digest atlas of the world, 563
Reader's Digest gd to places of the world, 591
Reader's Digest illus bk of dogs, 2082
Reader's gd for parents of children with mental,
    physical, or emotional disabilities, 3d ed, 615
Readers' gd to abstracts, 228
Readers' gd to per lit, 226
Readers' gd to twentieth-century sci fict, 1548
Reading lists for college-bound students, 99
Reading the numbers: a survival gd, 211
Ready, Barbara C., 367
Recommended ref bks for small & medium-sized libs
    & media centers, 138
Recommended videos for schools, 1990, 31
Recording for the blind, 43
Reed, W. L., 1684
Rees, Alan M., 2011
Rees, Clair, 767
Rees, Nigel, 1440
Reese, Lyn, 1121
Reference bks bulletin, 1989-90, 139
Reference bks for children's collections, 140
Reference ency of the Amer Indian, 5th cd, 506
Reference gd to English, 1384
Reference gd to hist fiction for children & young
    adults, 634
Reference gd to US military hist 1607-1815, 918
Reference readiness: a manual, 4th ed 136
Reference shelf, 1006
Reference sources: a brief gd, 9th ed, 142
Rehabilitation resource manual, 3d ed, 623
Reich, Warren T., 1821
Reichman, Henry, 851
Reilly, John M., 1557
Reinfeld, Fred, 759
Reisser, Marsha J., 1640
Reithmaier, Larry, 2203
Religions of the world, 2d ed, 1755
Religions on file, 1756
Religious bks for children, 1739
Remark, John F., 758
Remarkable children: twenty who made hist, 274
Representing children's bk characters, 1246
Reptiles & amphibians, 2279
Requirements for certification of teachers ..., 387
Research gd to Amer histl bio, 243
Research gd to bio & criticism, 1497
Researcher's gd to Amer genealogy, 2d ed, 526
Resource gd to special educ, 2d ed, 433
Resource reading list, 1990 ..., 512
Resources for educating artistically talented students,
    375
Resources for educl equity, 382

Resources for educl equity, 382
Resources for teaching thinking, 358
Respectfully quoted: dict of quotations, 1730
Responses to 101 questions on the Bible, 1760
Restoration drama, 1543
Revell Bible dict, 1769
Revenge of the creature features movie gd, 1323
Reynolds, Cecil R., 432, 436
Reynolds, Jean E., 205, 1015
RHS ency of house plants including greenhouse
    plants, 2014
Richard Scarry's best word bk ever, 1423
Richardson, Doug, 2204
Richardson, Selma K., 130
Richter, Bernice, 2095
Riddick, Floyd M., 940
Riddick's rules of procedure, 940
Ridpath, Ian, 1811
Riggle, Judith, 72
Right college, 1991, 411
Right minds: sourcebk of Amer conservative thought,
    943
Rights of crime victims, 812
Rights of young people, 2d ed, 799
Riley-Smith, Jonathan, 626
Rinzler, Carol Ann, 1933
Ritter, Harry, 647
Rivera, Feliciano, 486
Rix, Martyn, 1845
Robbins, Chandler, 2245
Robbins, Michael, 160
Roberts, Patricia L., 1164, 2021
Roberts, Philip Davies, 1472
Roberts, Royston R., 2123
Robert's rules of order, 942
Roberts, Willard Lincoln, 1910
Robertson, Allen, 1795
Robinson, Francis, 1028
Rochlis, Eugene, 1766
Rocks & minerals, 1908
Rocks, minerals, & fossils of the world, 1909
Rodale's garden insect, disease & weed identification
    gd, 2020
Rodenas, Paula, 1097
Roebuck, Wendy, 541
Rogers, JoAnn V., 844
Roget's II: the new theasaurus, 1455
Roget's internl theasaurusa, 4th ed, 1456
Rogninski, Jim, 1191-2
Roller, David C., 717
Rollin, Jack, 1103
Rollins, Arline McClarty, 1968
Rollock, Barbara, 1193
Rombauer, Irma, 1934
Room, Adrian, 289, 1806
Roosa, Dean M., 1837
Rosenberg, Betty, 1554
Rosenberg, Kenyon C., 427, 1653-4
Roses, Lorraine Elena, 1594
Ross, Charles, 2278
Ross, Stewart, 691
Ross, Wilma S., 586
Rosser, Claire, 52
Rothenberg, Mikel A., 1993
Rothwell, Kenneth S., 1330
Rounds re-sounding: circular music for voices &
    instruments, 1678

Rourke dinosaur dict, 1903
Rovin, Jeff, 1555-6, 1704
Royle, Trevor, 919
Rubinstein, Chaim T., 1740
Rudin, Claire, 819
Rudman, Masha Kabakow, 1999
Ruffner, James A., 1894
Rules of the game, rev ed, 1061
Runkel, Sylvan T., 1837
Ruoff, A. LaVonne Brown, 1586
Ruppert, James, 1567
Ryan, Bryan, 1523, 1619
Ryan, Elizabeth, 1958
Ryan, Elizabeth A., 1457
Rycroft, Michael, 2192
Ryder, Randall J., 94

Sachare, Alex, 1079
Sachs, Moshe Y., 589
Sack, Steven Mitchell, 803
Sader, Marion, 135
Sadie, Stanley, 1630-1, 1634
Safir, Leonard, 1731-2
Safire, William, 1731-2
Salzman, Jack, 1580
Sander, Daryl, 809
Sardegna, Jill, 624
Sarkissian, Adele, 1194
Sattler, Helen Roney, 1904
Saturn, 1815
Saulnier, Karen L., 620
Savage, Jim, 1082
Savage, Kathleen M., 324
Savageau, David, 1107
Saving the Earth: citizen's gd to environmental action,
    2055
Sax, Irving N., 1854
Saye, Jerry D., 844
Scarne, John, 747
Scarne's ency of games, 747
Scarry, Richard, 1423
Schaaf, William L., 2022
Schaeffer, Mark, 910
Schick, Frank, 488
Schick, Renee, 488
Schiller, Andrew, 1458-9
Schlachter, Gail Ann, 422-3
Schlessinger, Bernard S, 282
Schlessinger, June H, 282, 1212
Schlueter, Jane, 1601
Schlueter, Paul, 1601
Schmalz, Peter, 1649
Schneider, Janet Carney, 1957
Schneider, Terry, 770
Schnelder, Herman, 2115
Schnelder. L., 2115
Scholarship bk: complete gd, 3d ed, 415
Scholarships, fellowships & grants for programs
    abroad, 443
Scholastic sftwr cat, k-12, 1990-91, 109
Scholtz, James C., 881
Schon, Isabel, 83-8, 489-91
School Lib & media center acquisition policies ...,
    2d ed, 855
School lib jl, 7
School lib media annual, 823
School lib media file, (v1), 882

School lib program in the curriculum, 876
School Librarian's sourcebk, 819
School media policy development, 872
School Search gd to private schools for students with
    learning disabilities, 438
Schoor, Gene, 1074
Schorr, Alan, 492
Schroeder, Don, 430
Schroeder, Eileen E., 2096
Schumacher, Rose, 2180
Schwartz, Ed, 431
Schwartz, Karlene V., 1824
Schwarzkopf, LeRoy C., 121
Schweighauser, Charles A., 1807
Science & tech annual ref review, 2097
Science & tech in fact & fiction: gd to children's
    bks, 2093
Science & tech in fact & fiction: gd to young adult
    bks, 2094
Science bks & films, 8
Science educ, 2096
Science experiment index for young people, 2136
Science experiment index for young people. update
    91, 2137
Science experiments on file, 2139
Science fair project index 1981-84, 2140
Science for children: resources for teachers, 2098
Science yr: review of sci & tech, 2124
Scientific companion: exploring the physical world ...,
    2119
Sclater, Neal, 1863
Scott, David L, 607-8
Scott, Foresman advanced dict, 1413
Scott, Foresman beginning dict, 1414
Scott, Foresman beginning thesaurus, 1458
Scott, Foresman intermediate dict, 1415
Scott, Foresman, jr thesaurus, 1459
Scott, Foresman Robert's rules of order, 1990,
    9th ed, 941
Scott, Harold, W., 273
Scott, Kay W., 607-8
Scott specialized cat of US stamps, 1991, 761
Scott standard postage stamp cat, 760
Seale, Doris, 504
Searching for your ancestors, 5th ed, 525
Sears list of subject headings, 14th ed, 845
Seashores: gd to animals & plants along the beaches,
    rev ed, 2067
Seaver, Alice R., 901
Seely, Pauline A., 829
Segal, Marilyn, 1944
Segrave, Kerry, 1321
Selected characteristics of occupations defined in the
    dict of occupational titles, 343
Senior high school cat, 13th ed, 70
Senior, Michael, 1705
Seniorplots: a bk talk gd for us with readers ages
    12-16, 1209
Sequels: annotated gd to novels in series, 2d ed, 1496
Seredich, John, 2045
Serendipidy: accidental discoveries in sci, 2123
Sesame Street dict, 1403
Sessoms, Bob, 740
Sex care: complete gd to safe & healthy sex, 1970
Sexuality educ, 2001
Shaefer, Vincent J., 1891
Shafritz, Jay, 362, 920

Shafritz, Jay M., 932
Shakespeare A to Z, 1604
Shakespeare glossary, 3d ed, 1607
Shakespeare hndbk, 1609
Shakespeare on screen, 1330
Shakespeare the playwright, 1605
Shamir, Ilana, 498, 502
Shapiro, Mitchell, 1272
Sharks, 2263
Sharma, Sue, 1679-80
Sharp, Harold S., 290
Shatzkin, Mike, 1067
Shavit, Shlomo, 502
Shaw, John, 1030
Shaw, Warren, 681, 685
Sheehan, Angela, 1987
Shepard, Leslie, 926
Shields, Nancy E., 1538
Shipps, Anthony W., 1733
Shore, Irma, 1349
Shore, Rima, 283
Short story criticism, 1572
Short story index, 1573
Short story index, 1984-88, 1574
Showers, Victor, 1114
Showman, Richard K., 696
Shrader, Charles R., 918
Shrubs, 1845
Shugar, Gershon J., 1857
Shulman, Jason A., 2121
Shulman, Jeffrey, 1959
Sicherman, Barbara, 1135
Siegel, Barbara, 1322
Siegel, Scott, 1322
Siegman, Gita, 180
Sierra club gd to natural areas of New England, 609
Sifakis, Carl, 648, 810-1
Sifakis, Stewart, 726
Silvey, Anita, 50
Similes dict, 1430
Simon & Schuster pocket bk of chess, 746
Simon & Schuster pocket gd to shells of the world,
    2256
Simon & Schuster's gd to cats, 2078
Simon & Schuster's gd to pet birds, 2076
Simon & Schuster's gd to reptiles & amphibians of the
    world, 2273
Simons, Seymour, 2072
Simple animals, 2255
Simpson, D. P., 1487
Simpson, J. A., 1385, 1720
Simpson, James B., 1734
Simpson's comtemporary quotations, 1734
Since 1776: yr-by-yr timeline of Amer hist, 709
Sinclair, John, 1381
Single-parent family in children's bks, 2d ed, 1161
Singleton, Laurel R., 694-5
Sinofsky, Esther R., 1250
Sirett, Hazel, 817
SIRS critical issues series, 1007
SIRS sci, 2128
Sitarz, Paula Gaj, 1244
Sitter, Clara L., 856
Sixth bk of junior authors & illustrators, 1187
Skapura, Robert, 221
Skit bk: 101 skits for kids, 1235
Skyguide: field gd to amateur astronomers, 1809

Slang! topic-by-topic dict for comtemporary Amer lingoes, 1425
Slapin, Beverly, 504
Slater, Robert, 1880
Slavens, Thomas, 161
Slesser, Malcolm, 2035
Slonimsky, Nicolas, 1637, 1647
Slote, Stanley J., 857
Small, John, 587
Smallwood, Carol, 610, 902, 1008, 1994
Smith, C. Carter, 273
Smith, Candace P., 1171
Smith, Carter, 729
Smith, Colin, 1493
Smith, Curtis C., 1559
Smith, Darren L., 467, 485
Smith, David G., 1885
Smith, Devon Cottrell, 325
Smith, Dorothy B., 1222
Smith, Frederick, 1683
Smith, Gordon, 1893
Smith, Jane B., 823, 883
Smith, Jessie C., 475
Smith, Jessie Carney, 478
Smith, John David, 713
Smith, Lillian H., 1143
Smith, Miranda, 2020
Smith, Myron J., Jr., 1087
Smithsonian bk of flight for young people, 2190
Smolik, Jane, 353
Snodgrass, Mary Ellen, 174
Snyder, Karen, 1931
Sobol, Donald J., 771
Sobol, Lester A., 547
Social issues resources series, 1009
Social security hndbk, 10th ed, 355
Software ency, 110
Software Info! for Apple II computers, 114
Software reviews on file, 107
Soldier-statesmen of the Constitution, 734
Sole, Carlos A., 1621
Solorzano, Lucia, 396
Something about the author: facts & pictures, 1195
Something about the author autobio series, 1194
Sommer, Elyse, 1430
Sommer, Mike, 1430
Soper, Mary Ellen, 824
Soup should be seen, not heard, 518
Source bk of franchise opportunities, 1990-91 ed, 315
Source: gdbk of Amer genealogy, 529
South, Malcolm, 1710
Soviet Union, 3d ed, 686
Space almanac: facts, figures, names ..., 2196
Space exploration, 2192
Space explorations, 2106
Space people from a-z, 2208
Spangenburg, Ray, 2205-8
Spanish-language ref bks: an annot bibliog, 141
Sparhawk, Ruth M., 1052
Speaking for ourselves, 1177
Spears, Richard A., 1383, 1431
Spectrum: your gd to today's music, 39
Speech index, 4th ed, 1253
Speech Index, 4th ed supp, 1966-80, 1254
Speeches of the Amer presidents, 988
Spellenberg, Richard, 1835
Spelling bee speller, 1448

Spence, Annette, 1935, 1960, 1975, 2003, 2012
Spirt, Diana L., 875, 1210
Spokes, Penny, 139
Sports & recreation for the disabled, 616
Sports collector's bible, 4th ed, 762
Sports ency: baseball, 9th ed, 1073
Sports ency: pro basketball, 3d ed, 1078
Sports in Amer, 1062
Sports rules ency, 2d ed, 1064
Sprug, Joseph W., 1713
Sprung, Barbara, 382
Spyfiction: connoisseur's gd, 1551
Stade, George, 1521
Stambler, Irwin, 1664
Stamp collecting as a hobby, 757
Standard cat of Amer cars, 1805-1942, 2d ed, 2185
Standard cat of Amer cars 1976-86, 2d ed, 2183
Standard cataloging for school & public libs, 841
Standard hndbk of environmental engineering, 2048
Standard per dir, 14th ed, 131
Stanley, John, 1323
Star & planet spotting, 1808
Stark, James, 812
State & local govt political dict, 991
State & metropolitan area data bk, 1110
State birds, 2232
State maps on file collection, 564
State rankings, 1991, 1111
State-by-state gd to children's & young adult authors ..., 1188
Statesman's yr-bk, 1021
Statesman's yr-bk histl companion, 1020
Statesman's yr-bk world gazetteer, 4th ed, 592
Statistical abstract of the US, 1112
Statistical hndbk of US Hispanics, 488
Statistical hndbk on women in Amer, 1127
Statistical record of Black Amer, 478
Statler, Susan L., 239
Statt, David A., 2004
Stegemeyer, Anne, 1295
Steger, Will, 2055
Stein, Jess, 192
Steinberg, S. H., 637
Steinmetz, Sol, 1394, 2103
Stephen, Leslie, 262
Stephens, Gloria, 2079
Stephens, Meic, 1511
Stepping into research, 892
Sternberg, Martin L. A., 621
Stevens, Joseph E., 736
Stevens, Mark, 320
Stevens, Paul, 2037
Stevenson, Burton Egbert, 1722
Stevenson, John, 656
Stewart, John, 1027
Stidworthy, John, 2259-60, 2279
Stone, Norman, 633
Stories behind words, 1438
Story behind the word, 1437
Story hours with puppets & other props, 1242
Storytime sourcebk, 1225
Stott, Jon C., 1144
Straight talk about drugs & alcohol, 1958
Strategic defense initiative, 915
Stratton, Peter, 2005
Straughn, Barbara Lovejoy, 407
Straughn, Charles T., II, 407

Streep Peg, 1445
Stress & mental health, 2003
Strichart, Stephen S., 439
Strickland, Charlene, 1165
Stringer, Jenny, 1598
Stripling, Barbara K., 903
Strunk, William, Jr., 1285
Stuart, Paul, 511
Stuart-Clark, Christopher, 1221
Student theasurus, 1457
Student's dict of psychology, 2005
Study abroad, 1992-94, 27th ed, 444
Subak-Sharpe, Genell J., 1932
Subject bibliog index, 122
Subject bibliog no 176: college debate topic, 1252
Subject bibliog of the second world war, 662
Subject gd to bks in print, 57
Subject gd to children's bks in print, 62
Subject index to poetry for children & young people, 1957-75, 1222
Substance abuse & kids: dir of educ, info, prevention ..., 1961
Substance abuse, 1960
Substance abuse I: drug abuse, 1954
Substance abuse II: alcohol abuse, 1955
Substance abuse residential treatment centers for teens, 1962
Sugar, Bert Randolph, 762, 1075
Suicide, 1948
Sullivan, George, 1065
Summer on campus: college experiences for high school students, 368
Summers, Harry G., 671-2
Super-conductors, 2089
Supernatural fiction for teens, 2d ed, 100
Supervision of district level lib media programs, 888
Supreme Court at work, 804
Surgeon general's report on nutrition & health, 1995
Survey of contemporary lit, rev ed, 1514
Sussman, Alan, 799
Sutherland, Zena, 75, 1145
Sutton, Roberta Briggs, 1253
Sweeney, Patricia E., 1122
Sweet, Jeffrey, 1787
Sweetland, Richard, 450
Swenson, Mary, 1042
Swidan, Eleanor, 142
Swisher, C. L., 1234
Swortzell, Lowell, 1781
Syndicated TV: the first 40 yrs, 1947-87, 1268

Taeuber, Cynthia, 1127
Taft, William H., 1261
Taggart, Cynthia Crump, 1649
Talbert, Richard J. A., 625
Talking bks topics, 44
T.A.P.P. sources: natl dir of teenage pregnancy prevention programs, 1976
Taxonomies of the school lib media program, 878
Taylor, Arlene G., 846
Taylor, Bruce, 1282
Taylor, David, 2080
Taylor, J. Golden, 1585
Taylor, James, 681
Taylor, John, 2148, 2152
Taylor, Michael, 921
Taylor, Peter J., 933

Taylor, Ron, 2135
Taylor, Thomas J., 1543
Technology & learning, 105
Teenager's gd to study, travel & adventure abroad, 1989-90, 445
Television network prime-time programming, 1948-88, 1272
10 SATs, 4th ed, 457
10 steps in writing the research paper, 4th ed , 1280
Tenney, Merrill C., 1761
Terras, Victor, 1624
Terry, John V., 310
TESS: the eductl sftwr selector, 115
Tests: a comprehensive ref for assessments in psychology, educ & bus, 3d ed, 450
Thackrah, John Richard, 955
The kid's world almanac rhyming dict, 1445
Theatre world, 1789
Themes & setting in fiction, 1495
Thernstrom, Stephan, 462
Thesaurus of Amer slang, 1432
Thesaurus of ERIC descriptors, 12th ed, 392
They wrote for children too, 1150
Third Barnhart dict of new English, 1394
Third bk of junior authors, 1184
Third Reich almanac, 681
This day in Amer hist, 708
Thomas, Carol H., 435
Thomas, David A., 2156
Thomas, G. Scott, 1113
Thomas, James L., 435, 825
Thomas, Nicholas, 1315-6
Thomas, Rebecca L., 1211
Thomas register ..., 313
Thompson, Ida, 1905
Thompson, Stith, 1687
Thompson, Trisha, 2013
Thorn, John, 1076
Thorndike, E. L., 1413-5
Thorpy, Michael J., 1996
300 most selective colleges, 412
Through the eyes of a child, 3d ed, 1142
Tierney, Helen, 1128
Time lines on file, 638
Time navigator, 657
Timelines, 707
Times atlas & ency of the sea, 1913
Times atlas of the second world war, 673
Times atlas of world hist, 3d ed, 633
Times bks world weather gd, 1893
Timetables of sci: chronology of the most important people & events ..., 2100
Timetables of sports hist: baseball, 1048
Timetables of sports hist: basketball, 1049
Timetables of sports hist: football, 1050
Timetables of sports hist: the Olympic games, 1051
Timms, Howard, 1879
Tinling, Marion, 599, 1138
Tips & other bright ideas for school libns, 884
To make all laws, 1789-1989, 972
Toboldt, William K., 2166
Tootill, Elizabeth, 1822, 1825
Top 10: the best of everything according to numbers, 160
Top professions, 327
Total baseball, 1076
Townsend, Kiliaen V. R., 374

Toye, William, 1612
Tracking the fact, 1281
Trager, Oliver, 1062, 1978
Travel & trade routes series, 649
Treboux, Dominique, 1976
Tree, 1841
Trees of N Amer, 1840
Trelease, Jim, 1245
Troll student ency, 193
Trombley, Stephen, 166
Trosky, Susan, 1516
Truett, Carol, 116
Trust your children, 852
Turabian, Kate L., 1286
Turner, Eugene, 460
Turner, Mary Jane, 958
Turner, Rufus P., 1867
Turtles & tortoises of the world, 2272
Turtles of the world, 2274
12,000 words: a supp to Webster's 3rd, 1388
Twentieth century Amer nicknames, 291
Twentieth century authors, 1525
Twentieth century authors, first supp, 1526
Twentieth century children's writers, 3d ed, 1196
Twentieth century European short story, 1571
Twentieth century music, 1900-1980, 1626
20th century theatre, 1782
Twentieth-century choral music, 2d ed, 1651
Twentieth-century crime & mystery writers, 2d
    ed, 1557
Twentieth-century inventors, 2161
Twentieth-century literary criticism, 1532
Twentieth-century romance & historical writers, 2d
    ed, 1558
Twentieth-century sci fict writers, 2d ed, 1559
Twentieth-century shapers of Amer popular religions,
    1772
Twyman, Robert W., 717
Tyning, Thomas F., 2280

UFO's in the 1980's, 925
Uglow, Jennifer, 1132
Ujifusa, Grant, 935
Ulack, Richard, 1029
Ultimate cat bk, 2080
Understanding Asian Amer, 483
Unger, Leonard, 1595
United States govt manual, 959
United States intelligence, 956
United States today: an atlas of reproducible pages,
    566
Universal almanac, 162
Universe gd to stars & planets, 1811
University of Chicago Spanish dict, 4th ed , 1492
University press bks for public & secondary school
    libs, 65
Unreluctant years: critical approach to children's
    lit, 1143
Unterburger, Amy L., 493
Upton, Dell, 1363
Urdang, Laurence, 291, 1473
Urquhart, Fred, 1505
US atlas, 568
US, Canada, and Mexico road atlas, 565
US govt, 958
US govt bks, 123
US govt pubs for the school lib media center, 118

US hist: a resource bk for secondary schools, (v1, v2),
    694-5
USA geography, 572
Used car bk, 1991 ed, 2184
Using media to make kids feel gd, 1984
Using picture storybks to teach literary devices, 1229
Uvarov, E. B., 2116

Van der Plas, Rob, 2168
Van Doren, Charles, 284
Van Nostrand's sci ency, 7th ed, 2117
Van Orden, Phyllis J., 858
Vandergrift, Kay E., 1146
VanMeter, Vandelia, 698
Variety's video dir plus, 28
Vehrenberg, Hans, 1800
Velleman, Ruth A., 885
Venomous animals: 300 animals in full color, 2227
Vernoff, Edward, 283
Verrall, Catherine, 512
Vertical File & its alternatives, 856
Vertical file index, 127
VGM's careers ency, 2d ed, 344
Victorian Britain, 692
Victorian novel: annotated bibliog, 1596
Vidal-Naquet, Pierre, 628
Video gd for libs, 29
Video rating gd for libs, 30
Video source bk, 32
Vietnam war almanac, 672
Viguers, Ruth Hill, 1179
Vinson, James, 1338, 1561
Vital speeches fo the day, 1255
Vogue/Butterick step-by-step gd to sewing
    techniques, 1308
Voice of youth advocates, 9
Votteler, Thomas, 1572
Vriends, Matthew M., 2076

Waddell, Marie T., 1280
Wade, William, 347
Wakelyn, Jon L., 733
Wakeman, John, 1527-8
Waldhorn, Arthur, 1576
Waldman, Carl, 513-5
Waldman, Harry, 922
Walker, Aidan, 2170
Walker, David M., 797
Walker, Elinor, 101
Walker, Ormiston, 2209
Walker, Peter M. B., 1820
Walking the wetlands: hiker's gd to common
    plants ..., 1826
Walkowicz, Chris, 2084
Walter Breen's complete ency to US & colonial coins,
    751
Walton, John, 1992
Wander, Meghan Robinson, 718
War in peace: Marshal Cavendish illus ency, 674
Ward, Martha E., 1197
Ward, Philip, 1622
Warmenhoven, Henri J., 1035
Warren, Gretchen Ward, 1796
Washington info dir, 960
Washington Post gd to Washington, 2d ed, 611
Wasson, Tyler, 280
Waters, T. A., 742

Watson, Bruce, 956
Watstein, Sarah Barbara, 1977
Way things work, 2159
We shall be heard, 1131
We the people: an atlas of Amer ethnic diversity, 460
Weapons, 923
Wear, Terri A., 1166
Weast, Robert C., 1852
Weather almanace, 6th ed, 1894
Weather hndbk, rev ed, 1895
Weaver, J. R. H., 265
Webb, Denise, 1936
Webber, Elizabeth, 170
Webster's Amer bios, 284
Webster's collegiate thesaurus, 1460
Webster's compact dict of synonyms, 1461
Webster's compact rhyming dict, 1446
Webster's dict of English usage, 1474
Webster's elem dict, 1416
Webster's gd to business correspondence, 299
Webster's instant word gd, 1450
Webster's new bio dict, 285
Webster's new dict of synonyms, 1462
Webster's new geographical dict, rev ed, 593
Webster's new ideal dict, 2d ed, 1395
Webster's new world dict of Amer English, 3d ed, 1396
Webster's new world dict of eponyms, 1434
Webster's new world dict of mathematics, 2027
Webster's new world dict of media & communications, 1248
Webster's new world dict of quotable definitions, 2d ed, 1735
Webster's new world secretarial hndbk, 4th ed, 300
Webster's ninth new collegiate dict, 1397
Webster's school dict, 1417
Webster's secretarial hndbk, 2d ed, 301
Webster's sports dict, 1063
Webster's third new internl dict of the English language, 1387
Webster's word hist, 1441
Weeding lib collection, 3d ed, 857
Weidensaul, Scott, 2246
Weihs, Jean, 841
Weilant, Edward, 1004
Weinberg, Meyer, 463
Weiner, David J., 32
Weiner, E. S. C., 1385
Weiner, Eric, 1077
Weiner, Richard, 1248
Weird! complete bk of halloween words, 785
Wells, John, 770
Wells, John H., 367
Wells, Shirley E., 388
Wenzel, Dwane, 2095
Werner, Craig, 1578
West, Beverly Henderson, 2028
West, Mark, 852
Western birds, 2238
Wetterau, Bruce, 165
Wettstone, Eugene, 1090
Weyd, Donna L., 485
Whalen, Lucille, 818
Whales, 2264
What a piece of work is man! Camp's unfamiliar quotations ..., 1719
What do you call a person from ...?, 578

What happened when: chronology of life & events in Amer, 705
What's what: visual glossery of the physical world, rev ed, 1418
Wheal, Elizabeth-Anne, 675
Wheeler, Marcus, 1490
Where the birds are: gd to all 50 states and Canada, 2241
Where the jobs are, 346
Where to start career planning, 8th ed, 326
Whitaker's almanac, 163
White, E. B., 1285
White, James P., 440
White, Jess R., 1064
White, Kay, 2083
White, Perry J., 1651
Whitehouse, Ruth C., 234
Whiteley, Sandy, 139
Whitfield, Philip, 1882, 2242
Whitman, Alden, 255
Whitman, Ann H., 2236-7
Who was when, 3d ed, 636
Who was who in Native Amer hist, 1900, 515
Who was who in the Civil War, 726
Who wrote that song?, 1682
Whole video cat, 1991-92, K-6, 33
Whole video cat, 1991-92, 7-12, 34
Who's who among Black Amers 1990/91, 6th ed, 479
Who's who among Hispanic Amers, 493
Who's who in Amer 1989-91: jr & sr high version, 249
Who's who in Amer: jr & sr high version, v5-v8, 250
Who's who in Amer 1990-91, 46th ed, 251
Who's who in Amer art 19th ed, 1362
Who's who in Amer politics, 18th ed, 949
Who's who in fashion, 2d ed, 1295
Who's who in space: first 25 yrs, 2194
Who's who of Amer women, 1139
Who's who of Nobel prize winners, 1901-90, 2d ed, 282
Why do dogs have wet noses?, 152
Why do we say ...?, 1440
Whyld, Kenneth, 744
Wicked words, 1429
Wieckert, Jeanne E., 891
Wigoder, Geoffrey, 1743
Wilcox, Bonnie, 2084
Wilcox, Ruth Turner, 1296-9
Wild flowers, 1831
Wild, Russell, 2057
Wild, wild cookbk: gd for young wild-food foragers, 1923
Wilde, William H., 1611
Wildflowers of all seasons, 1836
Wildflowers of the tallgrass prairie, 1837
Wilion, John, 145
Wilkins, Mary-Jane, 2160
Wilkinson, Jean, 1121
William Shakespeare: his world, his work, his influence, 1610
Williams, Brenda, 2125
Williams, Brian, 2125
Williams, E. T., 267-9
Williams, James, 477
Williams, Miller, 1570
Williams, Owen, 2155
Willis, John, 1789
Willis-Thomas, Deborah, 1377

Wilson, George, 459, 463, 1041, 1167
Wilson lib bulletin, 10
Wilson, Mary E., 1246
Wilson, Pamela M., 2001
WILSONDISC: readers' gd abstracts, 229
WILSONLINE info system, 184
Winick, Myron, 1937
Winkel, Lois, 67, 89
Winning edge, 1056
Winning ideas from winning schools, 384
Winston, Michael R., 471
Winter, Georgie, 466
Wintle, Justin, 924
Wiseberg, Laurie S., 817
Wit & wisdom of the 20th century: dict of quotations, 1736
Witherick, Michael, 587
Witt, Elder, 798
Wittels, Harriet, 1463
Wittig, Alice J., 118
Wolfe, Gregory, 943
Wolff, Rick, 1068
Wolfson, Evelyn, 516
Wollin, Jay C., 1900
Women in congress, 1917-1990, 950
Women in the world, 1121
Women into the unknown: sourcebk on women explorers & travelers, 599
Women remembered, 1138
Women's atlas of the US, 1118
Women's issues, 1120
Women's studies, 1980-85, 1119
Women's studies ency, 1128
Wood, Janine, 4
Wood, Michael, 237
Wood, R. Kent, 426
Wood, Robert Muir, 1883
Woolls, Blanche, 886, 888
Words of wisdom, 1732
Words on cassette, 40
Words to rhyme with, 1444
Wordwatcher's gd to good writing & grammar, 2d ed, 1467
Work throughout hist series, 337
Workstations & local area networks for libs, 871
World alamanac of the Soviet Union, 685
World almanac & bk of facts, 164
World almanac bio dict, 254
World almanac gd to good word usage, 1475
World almanac of first ladies, 975
World almanac of US politics, 944
World and its people, 588
World artists, 1950-1980, 1361
World artists, 1980-90, 1362
World at arms: Readers' Digest illus hist of World War II, 676
World atlas of archaeology, 237
World authors, 1950-70, 1527
World authors, 1970-75, 1528
World authors, 1975-80, 1529
World authors, 1980-85, 1530
World bk health & medical annual, 1997
World bk of math power: math skills builder & everyday math, 2031
World bk-Rush-Presbyterian-St. Luke's Medical Center ency, 1998
World bk atlas, rev ed, 566

World bk dict, 1389
World bk ency, 209
World communication & transportation data, 1989, 2180
World cup, 1930-90, 1103
World dir of minorities, 464
World Eagle, 1022
World economic data, 3d ed, 1115
World ency of police forces & penal systems, 795
World factbook, 1023
World facts & figures, 3d ed, 1114
World govt, 933
World nature ency, 2066
World of animals, 2105
World of animals, 2218
World of games, 737
World of myth: anthology, 1688
World of sci, 2118
World of storytelling, rev ed, 1243
World of winners, 180
World painting index, first supp, 1973-1980, 1354
World painting index, 1354
World resources, 1990-91, 2056
World Statistics in brief, 12th ed, 1116
World tables, 1117
World wildlife fund atlas of the environment, 2041
Worldmark ency of the states, 2d ed, 589
Wray, James D., 1801
Wright, David, 543
Wright, Jill 543
Wright, John W., 162
Wright, Kieth C., 871
Wright, Robert K., 734
Wrigley, Robert E., 2270
Writers for young adults: bio master index, 3d ed, 1198
Writer's hndbk, 1287
Writer's market: where & how to sell what you write, 1288
Wurman, Richard Saul, 568
Wye, Kenneth R., 2256
Wynar, Bohdan S., 132, 134, 138, 847

Yaakov, Juliette, 69, 1573-4, 1790
Yager, Jan, 1996
Yarwood, Doreen, 1300, 1370
Yearbook of Amer & Canadian churches, 1757
Yearbook of sci & the future, 2126
Yearbook of the UN, 957
Yeoman, R. S., 763-4
Yeomans, Donald K., 1819
Young chef's nutrition gd & cookbk, 1930
Young, Heartsill, 820
Young, Peter, 665-6
Young Reader's ency of Jewish hist, 502
Young, Sue, 1447
Your reading: a bklist for jr high & middle school students, 8th ed, 102
Your resource gd to environmental org, 2045
Your right to govt info, 2d ed, 802

Zeleny, Robert O., 209, 2124
Zentner, Christian, 680
Zim, Herbert S., 2067, 2252, 2271
Zimmerman, Enid D., 375
Zingher, Gary, 889

Zophy, Angela Howard, 1124
Zuck, Virpi, 1623
Zuiderveld, Sharon, 834
Zydlo, Stanley M., Jr., 2006

Subject Index

Reference is to entry number.

ACCR2, 839-40
Abbreviations, 167-8
Abortion, 996
Achievement tests, 451-7
Acronyms, 168
ACT, 452
Actors & actresses, 1312
Adolescence, 1966
Africa
  area studies, 1024-5, 1027
  hist, 649
  politics, 1026
African Americans
  authors, 1193, 1515, 1577-8, 1594
  films, 1311
  genealogy, 527
  hist, 713, 721
  music, 1640, 1664, 1666-71
  photographers, 1377
  politicians, 962
Aging, 1938-9
AIDS, 1977-8, 1983, 1986, 1991
Air quality, 2047, 2053
Aircraft, 913, 921, 2151, 2187, 2190, 2195, 2197,
  2199-2200, 2202-4
Alcohol abuse, 1952, 1955-8
Alligators, 2261, 2278
Allusions, 169-70
Almanacs, 143-9, 154-64, 211, 2069
Alternative medicine, 1940-2
American art, 1337, 1346, 1356, 1362
American artists, 1337
American college test. *See* ACT
American composers, 1639
American Indians. *See* Native Americans
American lit
  African American authors, 1577-8
  bibliog, 1577-8
  bio, 1580, 1583-5, 1588-95
  characters in, 1582
  criticism, 1592-3, 1595
  dict & ency, 1579, 1583-4
  digests, 1512, 1587
  gds, 1585
  hndbks, 1580
  Hispanic authors, 1590-1
  hist, 1581
  Native American authors, 1586
  plot outlines, 1587
  poetry, 1564, 1566-7
Americanisms, 1424-9
Amphibians, 2273, 2277, 2279-80

Amphibians, 2273, 2277, 2279-80
Amusements, 737, 739-42
Anatomy, human, 1971-4
Anglo-American cataloguing rules, 839-40
Animal rights, 1001
Animals
  behavior, 2069, 2220, 2223
  birds, 2229-46
  classification, 2077, 2118
  fishes, 2217, 2247-9, 2263
  hndbks, 2105, 2107
  illus, 2226
  insects, 2250-3
  invertebrates, 2254-6
  mammals, 2216, 2218-20, 2225, 2257-60, 2262,
    2264-71
  rare & endangered, 2065, 2216, 2222
  reptiles & amphibians, 2261, 2272-80
  spiders, 2251, 2253
  venomous, 2227
Animals, mythical, 1693, 1710
Animation (films), 1331
Anthropology, 230, 232
Antiquities, 233-6, 625, 627, 1613-5
Aphorisms, 1726
Apple computers & software, 1859, 1871, 1875-6
Appliances, household, 2159-60
Aquariums, 2073-5
Aquatic biology, 2217, 2247. *See also* Marine biology
Archaeology, 233-7
Architecture, 1339, 1363-70
Armaments, 911-5, 917-8, 921-3, 2204
Armed forces, 911, 921
Armored vehicles, 914
Arms control & peace, 951
Art
  appreciation, 1350-1
  assns, 1346, 1348
  careers, 333, 337
  dicts & encys, 1341, 1343-5
  dirs, 1346, 1348, 1349
  hndbks, 1351-2
  hist, 1339-40
  mktg, 1347
  museums, 1346, 1349
  reproductions, 1335-6
  See also American art; Architecture; Artists;
    Decorative art; Painters & painting;
    Photography
Artists, 1335-8, 1342-4, 1355-62
Artists' materials, 1352
Asia, 1028-9
  hist, 649, 677

Assassinations, 648, 930
Associations, 175
Astronauts, 2188-9, 2194, 2201, 2208
Astronomers, 2130
Astronomy, 1797-1819, 2118-40, 2194, 2201, 2205
Atlases
  Asia, 1029
  Canada, 552
  Central America, 534
  China, 535-6
  electronic, 569-72
  Europe, 1032-5
  Japan, 1036
  Jerusalem, 1740
  Latin America, 534, 1039
  Middle East, 1043, 1045
  US, 537, 539, 548-9, 557, 562, 565, 568, 571-2
  world, 538, 540-6, 550-1, 553-6, 558-61, 563, 566-7,
    569-70
Atlases, historical
  Bible, 1763
  Crusades, 626
  US, 699-703
  wars, 712, 720-1
  world, 625, 627-33, 650, 1002
Atomic weapons. See Nuclear weapons
Audio tapes, 44, 53
Audiovisual equipment
  dirs, 12, 428-9
  manuals, 430, 881
  reviews, 6, 8
Audiovisual media (general)
  free materials, 18, 20-2
  producers & distrs, 12-3, 24, 35
  production, 825
  reviews, 1, 2, 4-10, 15
  selection of, 25, 881, 1984, 2091
  selection aids. See Computer software; Educational
    games; Films & video; Sound recording;
    Talking books
Australia, 1030
Australian lit, 1501, 1611
Author numbers, 831-3
Authors
  bibliog, 1497
  bio, 1174, 1497, 1502, 1504, 1508, 1515-30, 1534-5,
    1579, 1585, 1588-95, 1599-1602, 1614, 1619
    1621
  indexes, 1174, 1522
  juvenile lit, 1172-4, 1176-98
Authors, American, 1577-8, 1579, 1580, 1583-5,
  1588-91, 1593-5
Authors, Australian, 1501, 1611
Authors, African American, 1515
Authors, British, 1501, 1596-1610
Authors, Canadian, 1612
Authors, French, 1616
Authors, German, 1617
Authors, Irish, 1501
Authors, Latin American, 1618-21
Authors, Russian, 1624-5
Authors, Scandinavian, 1623
Authors, South African, 1501
Authors, Spanish, 1622
Authorship, 1278-80, 1283-8
Automobiles, 304-5, 349, 351, 2148,
  2182-6

Automotive repair, 2162-6
Awards and prizes, 180

Backpacking, 767
Ballet, 1793-6
Bands & band instruments, 1648-50
Bangladesh, 1028
Baseball, 1048, 1066-77
Baseball cards, 750, 758
Basketball, 1049, 1078-82
Battles, 659, 711, 712, 720, 912, 918, 923
Behavior, animal. See Animals, behavior
Bereavement, 1999
Best books, 1575-6. See also Book selection; Reading
  guidance
Bhutan, 1028
Bible studies, 1758-69
Bibliography, trade, 54-63
Bibliog, univ press, 65
Bibliotherapy, 1158, 1161
  children's lit, 1999
  See also Reading Guidance
Bicycles & Bicycling, 2167-8
Bigotry, 998
Bill of Rights-U.S., 801
Bioethics, 1821
Biography
  bibliog, 239-40, 243
  chronology, 636
  indexes, 241-2
  teaching of, 238
  universal, 254, 256, 274-9, 283, 285, 648
Biography (by field & nationality)
  actors & actresses, 1311-2, 1320-2, 1325, 1791-2
  Americans (US), 243-51, 255, 257-9, 272-3, 276,
    284, 731-4
  architects, 1367
  artists, 1337-8, 1343-4, 1355-7, 1360-2
  astronauts, 2188-9, 2194, 2201, 2208
  astronomers, 2130
  authors. See Authors
  biologists, 2130
  blacks, 465, 469-77, 479, 962, 1311, 1577-8
  British, 262-71, 281
  business leaders, 304-6, 314
  Canadians, 260-1
  chemists, 2130
  Civil War leaders, 726, 733
  comic book artist, 1358-9
  computer scientists, 1880
  dancers, 1794
  designers, 1289
  dramatists, 1541
  educators, 393
  explorers, 595-6, 599,
  fashion designers, 1293, 1295
  filmmakers, 1315-6, 1322, 1332
  First ladies-U.S., 974-5
  governors, 946
  journalists, 1256, 1261
  judges, 946
  kings, queens, & rulers, 690-1, 1137
  mathematicians, 2023, 2026, 2130
  medical doctors, 1980, 1992
  movie producers, 1173
  musicians, classical, 1630, 1633-7, 1641-7, 1652

musicians, popular, 1173, 1635-9, 1661-3, 1665-71, 1674-5
Nazis, 680-1
performing artists, 1791-2, 1794
philosophers, 1714
photographers, 1371-2, 1377
physicists, 2130
poets, 1561
politicians & statesmen, 734, 930, 935-6, 946-50, 958, 961, 970
presidents, U.S., 718, 722-3, 976-7, 981-5, 987-8
religious, 1770-2
saints, 1774-5
scientists & engineers, 1980, 2086, 2102, 2129-32
social reformers & pacificists, 255
soldiers, 734
songwriters, 1639
sports figures, 1047, 1052-3, 1065
vice-presidents, U.S., 989
women, 1052, 1122, 1129-30, 1132-6, 1139
writers. *See* Authors
Biologists, 2130
Biology, 1820-4
Birds
   dicts & encys, 2118, 2229-32, 2235, 2240, 2242
   field gds, 2233-4, 2236-8, 2241, 2243-6
Birdwatching, 2233-4, 2236-8, 2241, 2243-6
Black American. *See* African Americans
Black music, 1640
Blind & visually impaired
   art museums, 1349
   braille, 41, 79-81
   large-print bks, 63
   orgs & services, 42
   ref bks, 546, 1392
   talking bks, 43-4, 79-81
Board games, 737
Body, human, 1970-6, 1987, 2001
Book awards, 1199-1206
Book reviews, 1-2, 4-7, 9-10, 46-8, 49-53
   indexes, 215-6, 218-9
   science, 8, 45
Book selection
   aids, historical, 694-5
   aids, juvenile, 66-7, 71-8, 82-9, 1160
   aids, mathematics, 2021-2
   aids, poetry, 1565
   aids, sci, 2091, 2093-5, 2098
   aids, women's studies, 1119
   aids, young adult, 68-70, 95, 1575-6, 1738
   policies, 851, 854-5
   See also Children's lit; Reading guidance
Book trade
Bookbinding & repair, 826-7, 880
Books and reading
   oral reading, 1224, 1227
Books, film versions of, 1326
Booktalks, 821, 1158, 1208, 1210-1
Botany, 1823, 1825-48, 2118, 2224
Braille bks, 41, 79-81
Bridges, 2147, 2158
Bldg & repair, 2169-74
Buildings, 2157
Bulletin boards & displays, 781, 908, 910
Business
   almanacs, 292-3
   bio, 304-6, 314

careers, 332, 337
dicts & encys, 302-310
dirs, 297, 298-301
Butterflies, 2250, 2252

Cage-birds, 2076
Caldecott medal, 1201, 1203-6
Calendars, 776, 778-80, 782-4
Calligraphy, 1249
Camping, *See* Summer camps; Sports camps
Canada
   almanacs, 144-5
   bibliog, 2042
   bio, 260
   birds, 2241
   dirs, 144, 311
   encys, 1031
   hist, 678
   maps, 552
   per indexes, 217
   trees & shrubs, 1844
Canadian lit, 1519, 1612
   juvenile, 3, 76, 1144, 1163, 1190
Cancer, 1982
Capital punishment, 996-7
Card games, 737, 743
Card tricks, 741
Careers
   bibliog, 321-5, 326
   dirs, 345-6
   employment, 329, 340-2, 344, 347
   internships, 324
   job searching, 323, 326, 328, 345-7
   job titles, 335, 343
   planning guidance, 324, 326-7, 330-4, 336-42, 344, 446-8
   self-employment, 348
Caribbean, 703
Carpentry, 2169, 2171, 2174
Cataloging & classification, 828-47
Catholic church, 1750-1, 1771, 1774-5
Catholic schools, 370-2, 1737-8
Cats, 2077-80
Celebrations, 775, 780-1, 783-4, 1773
Censorship, 848-52
Central Amer
   bibliog, 1042
   maps, 534
Certification requirements (educl), 385, 387
Characters in films, 1320
Characters in lit, 1500, 1503, 1505-6, 1510, 1536, 1579, 1582
Cheerleading, 1083
Chemistry
   dicts & encys, 1850-1, 1853-4
   hndbks, 1849, 1852, 1855-7
Chemists, 2130
Chess, 744, 746
Child abuse, 1944-5
Child care, 1963, 1967, 1990, 2008
Children in films, 1325
Children's lit
   activities, 1226, 1230-4, 1236-40, 1246
   authors & illus, 1144, 1150, 1168-9, 1172, 1174-97, 1238-9
   awards & prizes, 1199-1206
   bibliog, 61-2, 1150-1, 1163

Children's lit (*continued*)
  bibliotherapy, 1158, 1999
  booktalks, 1210-1
  Canadian, 1163
  dicts & encys, 1168
  fantasy, 1162
  high/low bks, 90, 93
  hist & criticism, 1143, 1146-68
  indexes, 1169
  juvenile mags, 220
  oral reading, 1224, 1227, 1240, 1245
  picture bks, 1148, 1164, 1170, 1229, 1244
  plays, 1212
  plots & synopses, 1158, 1209-11
  poetry, 1213-22
  reading guidance, 90, 93, 1149, 1152-3, 1155-6,
      1165-7, 1170
  reviews, 1-3,5, 7, 10, 45-8, 50-1, 218-9
  reviews, indexes of, 1175
  selection aids, 66-7, 71-8, 82-9, 1152
  series & sequels, 1149
  Spanish, 83-88
  storytelling, 1223, 1225, 1229, 1241, 1243-4
  study of, 1141-3, 1145-56
  See also Book selection; Reading guidance; Young
      adult lit
Children's mags, 220
Children's poetry
  anthologies, 1218-9, 1221
  indexes, 1213-7
  nursery rhymes, 1220
Children's songs, 1681, 1685
China
  hist, 679
  maps, 535-6
Chinese language dicts, 1476
Choral music, 1651
Christianity, 1753
Chronology
  general, 165
  music, 1626
  science & tech, 2099-2101
  US history, 704-9
  world hist, 635-8, 652-5, 657
  See also Calendars
Cinema, 1310. *See* Films & video (theatrical)
Circulation-charging systems (libs), 862
Civil War (U.S.), 711-2, 720-1, 726, 729, 733
Civilization, ancient, 625, 627
Classical lit, 233-6, 1613-5
Classification (bk), 834-7, 839-41, 843, 846-7
Climate, 1888, 1892-5
Clothing, 1293, 1305, 1308
Clubs & social orgs, 749
Coin collecting, 751-3, 756-7, 759, 763-4
Collecting, 750-64
Collection development (libs), 851, 853-8
College Board Achievement tests, 451, 457
Colleges & univs
  databases, 400-3
  dirs, 376, 394-401, 404-9, 412, 416
  handicapped services , 435, 439
  learning disabled programs, 439
  preparation, 418
  programs abroad, 441-4
  programs & courses, 394-5, 397-403, 407, 409-11,
      413, 416, 419-20

  sports programs, 1056
  student finanacial aid, 402, 413-5, 417-8, 421-3
  See also Correspondence courses; Vocational-
      technical educ
Columbus, Christopher, 630, 716
Comic bks, 755, 1358-9, 1545
Communications, 299, 1247-85, 1287-8, 2118, 2180
Community colleges. *See* Colleges and univs
Compass, 765
Composers, 1630-1, 1633-6, 1641-5, 1652
Computer education
  activities & competitions, 900, 1881
  journals, 103-5
Computer languages, 1866
Computer literacy, 868
Computer programming, 1866, 1877
Computer sftwr
  Apple, 1859
  bibliog, 110, 116
  cat, 109, 114
  CD-ROM, 28, 106, 150, 195, 200, 209-10, 569-72,
      866, 870, 2110
  clip art, 1871
  colleges & univs, 400-2
  desktop publishing, 1262
  free, 111, 1869
  hist, 657
  local area networks (LANS), 871
  maps, 533
  producers & dists, 13-14
  research, 106
  reviews, 1-2, 4-8, 10, 48, 103-5, 107-8
  selection aids, 106, 112-3, 115
  social studies, 1018, 1040
  word processing, 1273, 1874
  work stations, 871
Computers
  bio, 1880
  consumer gds, 1870-1, 1875, 1878
  dicts & encys, 1858-61, 1864-6, 1877, 2118
  hndbks, 1872, 1876, 1879
  maintenance, 1873
Confederate States of Amer, 733
Congressional districts, 936, 965
Conservation of natural resources, 2032-4. *See also*
      Ecology
Constellations, 1797, 1800, 1805-11
Construction, 2169, 2171, 2174
Consumerism
  automobiles, 349, 351
  bibliog, 352
  computers, 1870, 1878
  personal finance, 354
  product evaluations, 350, 354
Contemporary issues, 995
  See Current events & issues
Contests & prizes, 173-4
Cookery
  dicts & encys, 1920, 1926
  foreign, 1928
  hndboks, 1929
  recipes, 1914-5, 1917, 1920, 1928, 1930, 1934
Copyediting, 1260
Copyright, 1250
Correspondence courses, 367, 369
Costume, 1291-1300
Counties, 1108

Countries, data & surveys, 1010-1, 1018-21, 1023, 1028-29, 1032, 1039-41, 1044, 1114-17, 2180
Counting-out rhymes, 738
Crafts, 1290-92
Creationism, 2108
Creatures, mythical, 1710
Crime & criminals, 792, 805-6, 810-2
Criticism, 1147, 1495, 1520-1, 1524, 1531-5, 1537-9, 1542-3, 1566-7, 1571-2, 1592-3, 1595-6, 1602-3
Crocodiles, 2261, 2278
Crossword puzzles, 774
Crusades, 626
Cults, 1754
Cultural literacy, 171-2
Current events & issues, 147-8, 150-1, 551, 967-8, 994-7, 1001, 1009, 1016-7, 1019, 1258, 1886

Dams, 2158
Dance, 1793-6
Database utilities, 181-4
Databases
    atlases, 569-72
    history, 657
Days. See Holidays & special days
Deaf & hearing impaired
    sign language, 617-21
Death & dying, 1946-69
Decorative arts, 1289-92
Design & designers, 1289
Desktop publishing, 1262
Detective & mystery stories
    films, 1327
Diagnosis, medical, 1985, 2010
Dictionaries. See English-language dicts; dicts for other langs
Diesel engines, 2162
Diet, 1927, 1936
Dinosaurs, 1896-7, 1899, 1901-4
Disabled. See Handicapped
Disasters, 153
Divorce, 1965
Dogs, 2081-4
Dolphins, 2262, 2267-8
Drama, 1539, 1541-3, 1613, 1780
Dramatists, 1539, 1541-2
Drug abuse, 1950-4, 1956-2

Earth sciences
    atlases, 1882-3
    dicts & encys, 1012, 1827, 1884-8, 2118
    fossils, 1896-1905, 2224
    hndbks, 1889-90
    meteorology, 1891-2
    mineralogy, 1906-1910
    natural disasters, 1882
    oceanography, 1911-3
Eating disorders, 1988
Ecology
    atlases, 2038-41
    bibliogs, 2052
    dict, 1827, 2049
    natural areas, 609, 1826, 2033, 2060-4, 2067
    See also Human ecology; Natural history
Economics
    dicts & encys, 166
    hndbks, 295-6

Editorials, 994, 1258
Education
    bibliog, 356-8, 386, 2096
    bio, 381, 393
    certification, 385, 387
    colleges, 376, 385, 387, 394-413, 416, 418-20, 435
    databases, 389-90, 392, 400-2
    dicts & encys, 359, 362
    gifted children, 365, 375, 424-5
    indexes, 384-92
    instructional tech, 426-7
    learning handicapped, 391, 432-40
    multicultural, 386
    research, 360, 381
    scholarships, 413-5, 417, 421-2
    schools, 364, 366-74, 388
    statistics, 378-80
    test, 381, 446-57
Educational games
    childrens lit, 1231
    construction, 779
    mathematics, 2030-1
    media skills, 890-1, 900, 902
    tech, 2175
Educational guidance, 383, 388
Educational equity, 382
Educational research, 360, 381
Educational Resources Information Center. See ERIC
Educational tests, 446-57
Educators, 393
Egypt, ancient, 233, 627
Electricity & electronics, 1862-3, 1867, 2149, 2175-6
Emergencies, 2006
Employee rights, 803
Employment, 328, 340-2, 344, 346-7. See also Careers
Encyclopedias, general, 146, 185-91, 194-201, 203-10
Encyclopedias, Spanish, 202
Energy resources, 2035-7
Engineers, 2130
English as a second lang, 1380-4
English lang
    composition, 1273, 1278-80, 1283, 1287
    eponyms, 1433-4
    etymology, 1435-41
    grammar & usage, 1276-7, 1285-6, 1464-75
    idioms, 1426, 1431
    punctuation, 1282, 1286
    regional, 1427
    rhyme, 1444-7
    similes, 1430
    slang, 1424-5, 1428, 1432
    spelling & pronunciation, 1448-50
    synonyms, 1451-63
English-lang dicts
    college & desk, 1390-7
    idioms, 1500
    juvenile, 1398-1417
    large print, 1392
    picture, 1418-23
    unabridged, 1385-9
English lit
    bibliog, 1596
    bio, 1597-1602
    critism, 1596, 1602-3
    dicts & encys, 1597-8
    gds, 1501

English lit (*continued*)
    quotation, 1608
    Shakespeare, 1604-10
Environmental pollution, 2039, 2041, 2047, 2049,
    2052-5, 2057
Environmental sci, 2038-57, 2059
Eponyms, 1433-4
Equestrians & equestrian
    sports, 1094-7
ERIC, 390-2
Espionage, 953, 956
Essays, 222
Ethnic minorities
    architecture, 1363, 1368
    genealogy, 527
    Native Americans, 1586
    scholarships, 422
Etiquette, 517-22,
Etiquette, business, 298, 521
Etymology, 1435-41
Europe
    history, 649
    maps, 1033
Europe, Eastern, 1032
Europe, Western, 1035
European lit, 1502, 1520-1
Evolution, 230, 2108, 2221
Exceptional children, 391, 434, 436-7, 440
Explorers, 594-6, 599
Extinct animals, 2239 *See also* Rare & endangered
    animals
Extraterrestrial life, 1802

Fact books. *See* Almanacs
Fairies, 1492
Fairy tales. *See* Mythology & folklore
Family relationships, 1964-8
Fantasy literature, 1162, 1546, 1553
Fashion, 1293, 1295
Fashion designers, 1293, 1295
FAX, 1868
Federal agencies, 959-60
Federal govt
    careers, 345
Federal judiciary, 959. *See also* Supreme Court, US
Feminism, 1131
Fiction
    bibliog, 68, 1149
    characters, 1503, 1505-6, 1510, 1536, 1582
    criticism, 1495, 1524
    genre, 100, 1162, 1496, 1544, 1546-54, 1557-9
    historical, 634, 693, 697
    plots, 1512, 1587
Fiction writing, 1287
Fictitious places, 1509
Film industry, 1317
Film libs, 19, 26
Filmmakers, 1322, 1332
    actors & actresses, 1315-6
Filmmaking, 1331
Films & video (educational)
    cats., 16-7, 19, 23, 26, 28, 32-4
    dict & ency 1247, 1250
    free, 3, 18, 20-1
    indexes, 32,
    reviews, 1-2, 4-10, 15, 29-31, 48, 53
    selection aids, 25, 27

Films & videos (theatrical)
    bio, 1311-2, 1314, 1320-2, 1325, 1332
    books, versions of, 1326
    cats., 17, 28, 1350
    characters in films, 1320
    dicts & encys, 1310
    filmographies, 1311, 1313, 1315-6, 1318-9, 1323-5,
        1327-30, 1334
    genre, 1318-9, 1323, 1327-9, 1333
    in art, 1350
Filmstrips
    cats., 16
    free, 22
    reviews, 1, 4-5, 15-8
Finance, personal, 292, 294, 302, 354
First aid, 766, 2008
First Amendment rights (U.S.), 786-90, 801
First ladies-U.S., 974-5
First World countries, 1013
Fishes, 2217, 2247-9, 2263
Flags, 523-4
Flavorings, 1933
Flowering plants, 1827
Folklore, 1686
Food
    composition, 1916, 1919, 1921, 1924-5, 1927, 1930,
        1932, 1935-7
    dicts & encys, 1926, 1929
    flavorings & additives, 1933
    preparation, 1918
    production & processing, 1918, 1922, 2143
    See also Cookery
Food industry, 1918, 1922
Food preparation, 1914
Food, wild, 768, 1923
Football, 1050, 1084-7
Foreign langs, 1378, 1476-94
Foreign words & phrases, 1442-3
Forensics, 1251-5
Forest conservation, 2032
Fossils, 2224
Franchises, 315-8
Free materials
    AV, 18
    career, 322
    consumerism, 352
    health care, 1994
    indexes, 127
    instructional aids, 179
    sci, 2092
    social science, 993, 1008
    sftwr, 111, 1869
Freedom of info, 802
French-lang dicts, 1477-83
French lit, 1616
Furniture, 1291-2, 1301, 1303. *See also*
    Interior design

Games, 737, 739-40, 745, 747, 1235. *See also* Board
    games; Educl games; Word games
Games, computer, 739
Gardening, 2015-6, 2018, 2020
Gazetteers, 590-3
GED, 455-6
Gemstones, 1907
Genealogy, 525-9

Geography
  bibliog, 583
  dicts & encys, 573-8, 580, 585, 1012
  exploration, 594-9
  gazetteers, 590-3
  hndbks, 584, 587-8, 600, 603
  indexes, 597-8
  maps, 533-572
  travel gds, 600-11, 613
Geology, 1827, 1885-8
German-lang dicts, 1484-5
German lit, 1617
Germany (Nazi), 680-1
Gifted, 73-4, 365, 375, 424-5
Glass, 2150
Gods & goddesses, 1688, 1690, 1694-5, 1697-1700,
  1703, 1705
Golf, 1088-9
Govt publications
  bibliog, 117-23
Governor, 936, 946
Great Britain. *See* United Kingdom
Greece, ancient, 233, 627, 1614-5
Grief, 1999
Gymnastics, 1090

Halloween, 785
Handicapped
  devices, 612
  hndbks, 614-5
  lib services, 42, 885
  museum services, 1349
  recreation, 616
  travel gds, 613
  See also Blind & visually impaired; Deaf
      & hearing impaired; Learning
      handicapped
Handicrafts. *See* Crafts
Hawks, 2233-4
Hazardous materials, 1856, 2044, 2046, 2048, 2051,
  2054
Heads of state, 947. *See also* Kings, queens,
      & rulers
Health care
  alternative, 1940-2
  AV media, 1984
  careers, 337
  free materials, 1994
  human body, 1970-6, 1987
  medicine, 1977-9, 1981-3, 1985-6, 1988-91, 1993,
      1995-8
  mental health, 1999-2003
  orgs & services, 1994
  self-help, 2006-7, 2009-13
Hearing impaired. *See* Deaf & hearing impaired
Helicopters, 2200
Herbs, 1933
Heroes, 1555-6, 1694, 1697-9, 1701-3
High schools, 364, 367, 373-4, 404
Higher education, 376
High/low bks, 90-4
Highways & roads, 562
Hiking & camping, 766-7
Hispanic Americans
  authors, 1590-1
Hispanic lit, 1618-22

Historic places, 640
  battlefields, 712, 736
  US, 606, 735
  women, 1138
Historical fiction, 634, 693, 697
History
  atlas, 695-703
  bibliog, 693-8
  chronology, 635-8, 643, 650, 652-5, 657, 681-5,
      705-9, 711
  dicts & encys, 639-642, 644-8, 651, 656, 677-80, 682,
      687-9, 692, 704, 710, 713-8, 720-4, 726
  maps, 625-33, 649-50, 683, 712
  sources, 642, 662, 727-30, 733-4
History, ancient, 625-7, 645
History, modern
  chronology, 657
  dict & encys, 639, 646, 656, 724
  wars, 658-76
Hobbies. *See* Aquariums; Birding; Collecting; Crafts;
      Natural history; Radio, amateur
Hockey, 1091-3
Holidays & special days, 775-82, 785
Holocaust, 658, 661, 664, 669
Home-study courses, 369
Homeless, 999
Homosexuality, 1969
Horror films, 1319
Horror lit, 1547
Horsemanship. *See* Equestrians & equestrian sports
Horses, 1094-7
Horticulture, 1825, 2014-20
House repair, 2172-3
Houseplants, 2014, 2017, 2019
Human ecology, 1002, 2038, 2056
Human rights, 813-8

IBM PC computer sftwr, 1869
Illustrators (juvenile bks), 1172, 1174, 1176, 1178-95
India, 1028
Indians of North America, 231. *See* Native Americans
Industrial arts
  automotive, 2162-6
  bldg, 2169-74
  electrical, 2176
  metal work, 2177-8
Initialisms, 168
Insects, 2250-1, 2253
Instructional technology
  AV equipment, 428-30
  computers, 428-9
  dicts, 428-9
  dirs, 428-9
  TV, 428-9
  videodiscs, 428-9, 431
  yrbks, 426
  See also AV media; Computer sftwr; TV,
      instructional
Intercollegiate athletics, 1056
Interior design, 1301-3
International relations, 933, 938, 951-2, 954, 957
Internship, 325
Inventions, 2118, 2145, 2161
Inventors, 2130
Invertebrates, 2225, 2254, 2255-6
Ireland
  hist, 688

Islam, 1746
Italy
    hist, 682

Japan, 1036-8
Japanese lang dicts, 1486
Jazz & black music, 1640, 1664, 1666-71
Jerusalem, 1740
Jewish Americans. See Judaica
Jews. See Judaica
Jobs. See Careers; Self-employment
Journalism, 1248, 1256-61
Journalists, 1256
Judaica
    genealogy, 527
    holocaust, 658, 661, 664, 669
    juvenile lit, 1737-9
    religion, 1743, 1752, 1773
Judaism, 1743, 1752, 1773
Jump rope rhymes, 738
Junior colleges. See Colleges & univs
Juvenile books. See Children's lit
Juvenile justice, 799, 809

Kings, queens, & rulers, 690-2, 1137
Knitting, 1306-7
Korean War, 671

Laboratory safety, 1857
Languages, 1378
    ency, 1379
    See also Foreign langs; specific langs
Large-print bks, 63, 546
Lasers, 2152
Latin America
    area studies, 1040-1
    hist, 683
    lit, 1618-21
    maps, 534, 1039
Latin American lit. See Hispanic lit
Latin lang dict, 1487
Law
    careers, 337
    dicts & encys, 791, 793, 796-7
    popular hndbks, 786-90, 794, 799-800, 802-3,
        809, 812
    research gds, 801
    Supreme Court, 798, 804
Law enforcement. See Police
Learning handicapped, 391, 432,-7
Legends. See Mythology & folklore
Libraries
    classification systems, 862
    local area networks, 871
    online search services, 867, 869
    use of, 890-903
Libraries, school. See School libs
Library science
    dict & encys, 427, 820, 824
    censorship, 848-50, 852
    reference work, 137
    yrbks, 820-3
Life sciences. See Biology
Lighthouses, 2214
Lincoln, Abraham, 723
Literary quotations, 1511
Literary terms, 1498-9, 1507-8, 1579

Literature
    bibliog, 658, 1495, 1497
    bio, 1497, 1500-2, 1504, 1515-23, 1525-30, 1534-5,
        1579. See also Authors
    characters, 1505
    criticism, 1518, 1531-35, 1538
    dict & ency, 1498-1508, 1510, 1579
    digests & surveys, 1513-4, 1537
    drama, 1531-3, 1539, 1541-3
    foreign lit, 1611-25
    genre, 100
    places associated with, 1509
    plot outlines, 1513-4, 1537
    poetry, 1531-3, 1535, 1560-70
    quotations, 1511
    short stories, 1513, 1519, 1531-3, 1571-4
    See Characters in lit
    See also American lit; Children's lit; Fiction;
        Mystery & detective stories; other specific
        lits & literary forms
Lizards, 2276
Local area networks (LANS). See Computer software-
    local area networks
Local govt, 991-2

Machines, 2148, 2151, 2153, 2159-60, 2162-6
Machine-shop practice, 2178
Magazines. See Periodicals
Magic & witchcraft, 927
Magicians, 741-2
Maldives, 1028
Mammals, 2216, 2218-9, 2225, 2257-60, 2262, 2264-7,
    2271
Man, 230-2
Man, prehistoric, 233-5
Manufacturers, 312-3
Map reading, 765
Marine biology, 1911-3
Marketing, 311, 1248, 1347, 1374
Marriage, 1965
Mathematicians, 2130
Mathematics
    activities, 2031
    bibliog, 2021
    bio, 2023, 2026
    dict & ency, 2023-8, 2118
    hndbks, 2029, 2031
    selection aids, 2021-2
    teaching, 2030
Media centers. See School libs
Media skills, 890-903
Media sources
    AV, 1-5, 7-10, 12-3. 15-43, 44, 48, 53, 79-81, 881
    bks, 1-5, 7-11, 13-4, 45-78, 82-3, 89-102
    computer sftwr, 4-5, 7-8, 10, 13, 103-16
    free materials & pamphlets, 124-7
    govt, 117-23, 128
    per, 128-31
Medicine
    bio, 1980
    careers, 337
    dict & encys, 1981, 1992-3
    popular hndbks, 1979, 1982, 1985, 1987, 1989-90,
        1998, 2006-7, 2009-13
    yrbks, 1997
Medieval hist. See Middle Ages
Mental health, 1999-2003

Metal work, 2177-8
Meteorology, 1891-2
Metropolitan areas. *See* Municipalities
Mexican Americans. *See* Hispanic Americans
Microcomputers. *See* Computers
    hist, 703
Middle Ages, 626-7, 645, 650
    lit, 1521
Middle East, 1043-5
Midwest, 575
Military schools, 404
Military science
    armaments, 911, 913-5, 917-8, 921-3, 2204
    armed forces, 911, 913, 918, 921
    careers, 337
    dictionaries, 912, 920
    quotations, 916, 919
Mineralogy, 1888, 1906-10
Minors, legal rights , 799, 809
Monsters, 1323, 1693, 1704, 1710
Moths, 2252
Motion pictures. *See* Films & video
Motorcycles, 2181
Municipalities, 992, 1107-8, 1110, 1113
Mushrooms, 1838-9
Music
    bands, 1648-50
    bio, 1631-32, 1633-47, 1652, 1674-5
    black music, 1640, 1664, 1666-71
    choral, 1651
    country & western, 1665
    dict & ency, 1627-8, 1630-6
    hist, 1629-30
    instruments, 1630-6, 1652, 1655
    jazz, 1640, 1666-71
    opera, 1626, 1646, 1653-4, 1656-60
    orchestral, 1626, 1652-5
    popular, 1626, 1631, 1662-4, 1679-83
    rock, 1664, 1674-5
    songs, 1661, 1672-3, 1676-85
    sound recording, 38-9, 1653-4, 1672-3, 1676-7
Musical instruments, 1630-1, 1633-6, 1652, 1655
Musical theater, 1672-3
Musicians
    country, 1665
    classical, 1630-1, 1634, 1637, 1641-7, 1652
    popular, 1631, 1637-40, 1661-4, 1666-71
    rock, 1664
Mystery & detective stories, 1550-1, 1557
Mythology & folklore, 1686
    collections, 1686, 1688
    comics, 1545
    dict & encys, 1545, 1555-6, 1689, 1692-1705
    Greek & Roman, 1690-1, 1698-99
    indexes, 1711-3
    Irish, 1696
    North American, 1706-9
    Polynesian, 1695
    study of, 1687
    symbols, 1690

Names, geographical, 578, 590-3, 1691
Names, personal, 530-2
National anthems, 1684
National debate topic, 1251-2
National parks, 604-5, 607-8, 610, 613, 736

Native Americans
    architecture, 1368
    culture, 231
    lit, 1586
Natural areas. *See* Ecology
Natural disasters, 153, 1882, 1889-90
Natural hist, 2058-67
Natural phenomena, 600, 603, 606, 1882, 1889-90
Natural resources, 2032, 2035-7
Nautical lore, 2215
Nautical terms, 2215
Navies, 911
Nazis, 680-1
Needlework, 1304
New Age movement, 1749
New England, 576
New Zealand, 1046
Newbery medal, 1201-6
Newspapers. 224, 311, 1259
Nicknames, 286-91, 1057-8
Nobel prizes, 280, 282, 945, 1136
North Amer, 549
Novels, 1496, 1531-3, 1596, 1603
Nuclear power, 2036
Nuclear weapons, 915, 922
Nutrition, 1916-7, 1919, 1921, 1924-5, 1927, 1930,
    1932, 1935, 1937, 1995

Occults, 925-8
Occupational educ. *See* Vocational-technical educ
Occupations. *See* Careers
Oceanography, 1888, 1911-3, 2118
Office practice, 299-301, 308
Oil well drilling rigs, 2153
Olympic Games, 1051, 1098-1100
One-parent families, 1968
Opera, 1626, 1646, 1653-4, 1656-60
Oral reading, 1240-5
Orchestras, 1626, 1630-1, 1634, 1652-5
Organizations, 176
Outdoor life, 765-8

Painters & painting
    cats, 1335-6
    dicts & encys, 1337-8, 1343-5
    indexes, 1353-4
    materials and technique, 1352
Pakistan, 1028
Paleontology, 1896-1905, 1909
Pamphlet files, 856
Pamphlets, 124-7
Paper, 2154
Paperback bks, 9, 48, 52, 100
Paranormal phenomena, 926
Parliamentary practice, 749, 940-2
Parties, 740
Peace. *See* Arms control & peace
Penal systems, 795
Periodicals
    dirs, 13, 1259
    indexes, 13, 131, 183-4, 212-4, 217, 220-1, 223,
        225-9, 2127
    selection aids, 128-30
Pesticides, 1931
Pets, 2068-72
    aquarium, 2073-5
    cage-birds, 2076

Pets (*continued*)
  cats, 2077-80
  dogs, 2081-4
  snakes, 2085
Philosophers, 1714
Philosophy, 166, 1714-5, 1747
Photographers, 1371-2, 1377
Photography, 1248, 1371-7
Physically impaired. *See* Handicapped
Physicists, 2130
Physics, 1852, 2086-90
Picture dicts, 1418-23
Picture-bks for children, 1148, 1164, 1170
Pictures, 212-4
Planets, 1808, 1811, 1813-9
Plants, 1827-8
Plants, edible, 1830, 2016
Plants, endangered, 2065
Plants, flowering, 1709, 1829-37
Plants, nonflowering, 1838-9
Plays, 1539
  anthologies, 1787-8
  indexes, 1212, 1540, 1790
  yrbks, 1787, 1789
  See also Drama; Musical theater; Theater
Plots (novels, drama, etc.)
  fiction, 1512, 1514, 1535, 1537, 1587
  juvenile, 1207-11
  plays, 1514, 1537
  poetry, 1514, 1535
  short stories, 1513, 1537
Poetry
  anthologies, 1565
  bio, 1561
  digests, 1566-7
  hndbks, 1562, 1568-70
  indexes, 1213-7, 1222, 1560, 1563, 1565
  juvenile, 1213-20
  sound recordings, 1563
Poets, 1561, 1564, 1566-9
Poisonous plants, 1830
Police, 742, 795
Political parties, 934
Political science
  bio, 937, 945
  encys, 937, 943
  govt, 933, 1012
  intl relations, 933, 938, 952, 954, 957
  political parties, 933-4, 938
  terms & slogans, 166, 929
  world politics, 929-30, 947, 951
  See also Heads of state; War; World politics
Politicians, 935-6, 946, 948-50, 958, 961-2
Popes, 1771
Population. *See* Statistics
Porpoises, 2262
Post offices-US, 178
Postage stamps. *See* Stamp collecting
Precious stones, 1907
Pregnancy, 1976
Prehistoric animals, 1896-1905
Preliminary scholastic aptitude test. *See* PSAT
Presidents, US, 946, 976-7, 982-5, 987-8
Private schools, 366, 371-4
Proverbs, 1720-1
PSAT, 453
Pseudonyms. *See also* Nicknames

Psychic phenomena, 925-7
Psychology, 166, 2004-5
Psychological tests, 449-50
Public relations, 907-10, 1248
Publishers & publishing
  AV, 12-4, 35
  print, 11, 13-14, 821, 1263, 1287-8
  sftwr, 13-4
Publishing, 1248-9, 1263
  manuscript preparation, 1287
  See also Style manuals
Puppets, 1242

Quotations, 1716-9, 1722-5, 1727-36
  Bible, 1766-7
  lit, 1511
  military sci, 916, 919
  politics, 939
  Presidents-U.S., 978
  Shakespeare, 1608
  sci, 2121
  war, 924
  women, 1125-6

Radio, 1247
Radio, amateur, 1265
Radio broadcasting
  dirs, 1259
  programs, 1264
Railroads, 2210-3
Rain forests, 2034
Rare & endangered animals, 2067, 2216, 2222, 2228
Reading guidance
  children
    booklists, 1149, 1152-3, 1155-6, 1159, 1161,
      1165-7, 1170
    booktalks & synopses, 1158
    high/low lists, 90, 93
    textbooks, 1141-2, 1145
  young adults
    booklists, 95-102, 1149, 1154, 1157, 1165-6,
      1575-6
    booktalks & synopses, 1158
    high/low lists, 91-4
Recreation. *See* Games
Reference bks
  govt, 121
  gds, bibliographical, 134, 138, 140-1
  gds, instructional, 136
  reviews, 2, 10, 132-3, 135, 139, 185
  Spanish, 141
Reference work, 137
Religions
  Bible study, 1758-69
  bibliog, 1737-9
  bio, 1770-2
  Catholicism, 1750-1, 1753
  cults, 1754
  customs, 1756, 1773
  dicts & encys, 1741-2, 1744-5, 1747-8, 1750, 1755
  Islam, 1746
  Judaism, 1743, 1752, 1773
  maps, 1740, 1756, 1763
  New Age movement, 1749
  quotations, 1766-7
  yrbks, 1757
Renaissance, 277, 645, 1521

Report writing, 1273, 1278-81, 1497. *See also* Style
        manuals
Reproduction, animal, 2118
Reproduction, human, 1976
Reptiles, 2272-80
Research, 360, 381, 892-3, 903, 1278-9, 1281, 1283
Review journals
    AV, 1-2, 4-10, 15, 48, 53
    bks, 1-2, 4-10, 45-8, 49-53
    sftwr, 1-2, 4-8, 10, 48, 103-5, 107-8
Rhyme & rhyming, 1444-7
Roads, 2155
Rock music, 1664, 1674-5, 1679-80
Rocky Mountain states, 1829
Rodeo, 1101-2
Romance stories, 1558
Rome, ancient, 233, 627, 1614-5
Roosevelt, Franklin D., 718
Russia, 684-6, 1034. *See also* Union of Soviet Socialist
        Republics
Russian-lang dicts, 1488-90
Russian lit, 1625-25

Saints, 1774-5
SAT, 454, 457
Scandinavian lit, 1623
Scholarships, 413-5, 417, 421-3, 443
School drop-outs, 388
School elections, 748
School libs
    automation, 861-3, 865
    bibliog, 819
    collection development, 851, 853-8, 881, 1737-9
    core collections, 66-7, 69-70
    facilities, 904-6
    handicapped services, 885
    management, 872-6, 878-80, 882-9
    media skills, 890-903
    online search services, 859-60, 864, 866-7, 869-70
    periodicals, professional, 1, 5, 7, 9
    policies, 872
    programs, 876, 878-9, 883, 886-7, 889
    public relations, 907-10
    standards, 877
    yrbks, 823
    See also AV media; Book selection; Cataloguing &
        classification; Reading guidance
School lib media centers. *See* School libraries
Schools, 370-4, 382-4, 388, 404
    admin, 361, 363
    high school, 364
    learning handicapped, 438
    programs abroad, 445
    See also Summer schools; private schools
Science
    activities, 2133-40, 2118, 2209
    bio, 2129-32
    bk reviews, 8, 45
    careers, 337
    chronology, 2099-2101
    dicts & encys, 2103, 2108-17, 2145
    hndbks, 2119, 2123, 2125
    hist, 2102
    indexes, 2127
    instructional aids, 2091-6, 2098
    instructional programs, 365

quotations, 2121
source material, 2102, 2128
yrbks, 2097, 2120, 2122, 2124, 2126
Science fair projects, 1847-8, 1881,
        2133-40
Science fiction, 1548, 1552, 1559
    bibliog, 1544
    films, 1328-9
Scientists, 2129, 2130-2
Sculptors & sculptures, 1337-9, 1342, 1345
Seashells, 2154
Secretary's hndbks, 300-1, 308
Selection tools. *See* AV media; Book selection; Media
        sources; Reading guidance; Review journals
Self-employment, 315-20, 348
Self-help, 2007, 2009-13
Separation & loss. *See* Grief
Serials. *See also* Periodicals
Sewing, 1305-8. *See also* Textiles
Sex education, 1970, 1975
Sexuality, 2001
Shakespeare, 1330, 1604-10
Sharks, 2263
Ships, 2156, 2215
Short stories, 1513, 1519, 1571-4
    films & videos made from, 1326
Sign language, 617-21
Skits, 740
Slang, 1424-5, 1428, 1342
Slavery, 713
Slavic lit, 1624-5
Sleep, 1996
Sleep disorders, 1996
Small business, 315-20
Snakes, 2085
Soccer, 1103
Social reformer, 255
Social security, 355
Social studies
    area studies, 1024-5, 1027-32, 1034-8,
        1040-1
    current events & issues, 994-1009
    curriculum aids, 993, 1042
    data sources, countries, 1010-1, 1013-5, 1023
Songs, 1661, 1672-3, 1676-85
Sound recordings
    free, 20
    music, 38, 39, 1653-4, 1672-3, 1676-7
    reviews, 6-7, 9-10, 37, 48
    spoken-word, 1563
    selection aids, 27, 36
Southern states, 577-9, 717
Southeastern states, 579
Space exploration, 1798, 2191-4, 2198, 2201, 2205-8
Spain
    hist, 687
Spanish-lang dicts, 1491-4
Spanish literature, 1622. *See also* Hispanic lit
Special education, 391, 432-8, 440. *See also* Learning
        handicapped
Speeches, 1253-5
    president-U.S., 984, 988
    women, 1131
Spelling & pronunciation, 1448-50
Spices, 1933
Spiders, 2251, 2253
Spoken-word recordings, 15, 40

Sports
    almanacs, 1054-5
    bio, 1047, 1053, 1065
    camps, 1059
    careers, 334
    chronology, 1047-51
    collectibles, 762
    dicts & ency, 1063
    handicapped, 616
    hndbks, 1060-1, 1064
    individual sports, 1066-1104
    issues, 1062
    mascots & logos, 1057-8
    women, 1052
Sri Lanka, 1028
Stamp collecting, 754, 757, 760-1
Stars, 1797-8, 1800-1, 1805-11
States-US
    capitols, 582
    flags, 523
    hndbks, 581, 586, 589
    maps, 564
    politics & govt, 990-1
    statistics, 1110-11
    symbols, 2232
Statistics
    aging, 1938
    educ, 378-80
    marketing, 311
    production, 312
    US, 1105-13
    women, 1118, 1127
    world, 1114-17
Storytelling, 1223, 1225, 1229, 1241-4
Strategic Defense Initiative, 915, 922
Student financial aid, 415-5, 417, 421-3,
    443
Student yrbk, 1257
Study methods, 383-4
Style manuals, 1273-7, 1283-4, 1286
Subject headings, 828-9, 842, 845
Suicide, 1947-8
Summer camps, 769-70
Summer schools, 365, 368, 769-70
Superconductors, 2089
Superstition, 928
Supreme Court-US, 798, 804, 946
Synonyms, 1451-63

Talking bks, 43-4, 79-81
Teaching, 358, 382, 384
Technology
    activities, 2209
    bibliog, 2141
    dicts & encys, 2118, 2142-3, 2145, 2159-60
    hist, 2141, 2144, 2158
    industrial arts, 2162-77
    inventions, 2145
Telefacsimile. See FAX
Television
    dicts & encys, 1247, 1269-70
    films available, 1271, 1311, 1313, 1327-30,
        1350
    programs, 1266-8, 1272
Television stations, 1259, 1270
Term papers. See Report writing
Terrorism, 955

Tests (manual)
    achievement, 451-7
    educ & business, 446-50
Textbooks, school, 4, 6, 8, 64
Textiles, 1305, 1309
Theater
    bio, 1791-2
    chronology, 1782
    dicts & encys, 1776-80, 1784-5
    hndbks, 1781, 1783, 1786
    yrbks, 1787, 1789
    See also Dance; Drama; Musical theater; Plays
Theater, children, 1781, 1783
Third World countries, 1014
Tortoises, 2272
Transportation, 2179-80
    aircraft, 2187, 2190, 2195, 2197, 2199-2200, 2202-4
    automobiles, 2182-6
    motorcycles, 2181
    railroads & urban systems, 2210-3
    ships, 2214-5
    spacecraft, 2187-9, 2191-4, 2196, 2198, 2201, 2203
Travel gds
    Europe, 601-2
    handicapped, 613
    historic places, 606, 642, 712, 735
    national parks, 604-5, 607-8, 610, 736
    natural areas, 609
    US, 611
Trees & shrubs, 1840-6
Trivia, 771
Tropical fish, 2073-5
Truman, Harry S., 722
Turtles, 2272, 2274

UFOs, 925
Union of Soviet Socialist Republics, 684-86, 1034
United Kingdom
    almanacs, 163
    bio, 262-71, 281
    hist, 688-92
United Nations, 952, 957
Universities. See Colleges & universities
US
    armed forces, 911
    bio, 243-9, 250-53, 284
    geography, 577, 579, 581, 600
    govt. See U.S. govt & politics
    historic places, 606, 735
    maps, 537, 539, 547-9, 557, 564-5, 568, 571-2
    national parks, 736
    religions, 1748, 1753, 1772
    statistics, 1105-13
U.S. Congress, 962-4, 966-73
U.S. government & politics
    bio, 935-6, 943, 946, 948-9, 958
    Congress, 935-6, 944, 950, 958, 961-73
    dicts & encys, 931-2, 943, 953, 956
    federal, 934, 937, 944, 949, 958-60
    local, 944, 949, 99s
    presidency, 974-89
    state, 934-6, 944, 949, 990-1
    women, 950
U.S. history
    atlases, 699-703
    bibliog, 696, 694-5, 698
    bio, 243, 257-9, 272-5, 276, 734

chronology, 704-9
Civil War, 711-2, 720-1, 726, 729, 733
dicts & encys, 710, 714-5, 717-9, 722-4, 725, 953
novels, 693, 697
pictorial works, 727-9
Revolutionary War, 716
slavery, 713
sources, 730-2, 958
Urban transit systems, 2221

Venomous animals, 2211
Vice-presidents-U.S., 989
Video, 429, 1270
    See Television
Videodiscs, 431
Videotapes, 17-20, 23, 25-6, 28-9, 32-4
Vietnam War, 659, 672
Vocational-technical educ, 371-2, 376. *See also*
    Careers
Volunteering, 177, 325

War
    battles, 659, 711-2, 720-1, 912, 918
    films, 1318
    modern, 671-2, 674, 913, 917
    quotations, 924
    terrorism, 955
    See also Military science; Weapons
Washington, D.C., 611
Weapons, 917-8, 923
Weather, 1893-5, 2118
Weddings, 521
Welding, 2177-8
Western states
    atlases, 700
    dicts & encys, 573-4
    fiction, 1585
    films, 1310
Western fiction, 1585
Western films, 1310
Wetland, 1826
Whales, 2264, 2267
Wildflowers, 1829, 1831-7
Wildlife
    conservation, 2220
    endangered, 2065, 2216, 2222, 2228
    field gds, 2228
Witchcraft, 1701
    See Magic & witchcraft
Women. *See also* Feminism
    almanacs, 1123
    artists, 1357
    actresses, 1321
    bio, 1119-20, 1122, 1129-30, 1132-7, 1139
    congressional, 950

encys, 1128
explorers, 599
historical, 1121, 1124
histiric sites, 1138
quotations, 1125-6
scholarships, 423
sports, 1052
statistics, 1118, 1127
writers, 1578, 1589, 1593-4, 1601
Wood, 2170
Word games, 772-3
Word Perfect (word processing), 1874
Words, new, 1388, 1390-1, 1394
World conflict, 658-676
World history. *See* History
World politics
    armed conflicts, 913
    current events, 995, 1002, 1016-7, 1019, 1022
    espionage, 953, 956, 2204
    hndbks, 933, 938, 1020-1
    intelligence, 953, 956
    quotations, 939
    terrorism, 955
    United Nations, 952, 957
World War I, 663, 665
World War II, 658-9, 661-2, 664, 666-70, 673,
    675-6, 680-1

Young adult lit
    activities, 1228, 1232
    authors, 1173, 1177, 1182-9, 1198
    awards & prizes, 1199, 1201-6
    bibliog, 1171
    booktalks, 1208
    core collections, 69-70
    fiction, 1171
    high/low bks, 91-4
    plays, 1212
    plots & synopses, 1207-9
    poetry, 1213-8
    reading guidance, 93-102, 1149, 1151, 1154,
        1157, 1165-6
    reviews, 1-3, 7-10, 45, 48-50, 52
    study of, 1140

ZIP codes-US, 178
Zoology
    birds, 2230-46
    dicts & encys, 1820, 1826, 2220, 2223-5
    fishes, 2217, 2247-9
    hndbks, 2105, 2107, 2226-7
    insects & spiders, 2250-3
    mammals, 2216, 2218-9, 2257-60, 2262, 2264-71
    marine animals, 2217, 2254-6
    reptiles & amphibians, 2272-80